T0135373

Lecture Notes of the Institute for Computer Sciences, Social Informatics and Telecommunications Engineering 439

Editorial Board Members

Ozgur Akan
Middle East Technical University, Ankara, Turkey

Paolo Bellavista
University of Bologna, Bologna, Italy

Jiannong Cao
Hong Kong Polytechnic University, Hong Kong, China

Geoffrey Coulson
Lancaster University, Lancaster, UK

Falko Dressler
University of Erlangen, Erlangen, Germany

Domenico Ferrari
Università Cattolica Piacenza, Piacenza, Italy

Mario Gerla
UCLA, Los Angeles, USA

Hisashi Kobayashi
Princeton University, Princeton, USA

Sergio Palazzo
University of Catania, Catania, Italy

Sartaj Sahni
University of Florida, Gainesville, USA

Xuemin Shen
University of Waterloo, Waterloo, Canada

Mircea Stan
University of Virginia, Charlottesville, USA

Xiaohua Jia
City University of Hong Kong, Kowloon, Hong Kong

Albert Y. Zomaya
University of Sydney, Sydney, Australia

More information about this series at https://link.springer.com/bookseries/8197

Shuo Shi · Ruofei Ma · Weidang Lu (Eds.)

6GN for Future Wireless Networks

4th EAI International Conference, 6GN 2021
Huizhou, China, October 30–31, 2021
Proceedings

Editors
Shuo Shi
Harbin Institute of Technology
Harbin, China

Ruofei Ma
Harbin Institute of Technology
Weihai, China

Weidang Lu
Zhejiang University of Technology
Hangzhou, China

ISSN 1867-8211 ISSN 1867-822X (electronic)
Lecture Notes of the Institute for Computer Sciences, Social Informatics and Telecommunications Engineering
ISBN 978-3-031-04244-7 ISBN 978-3-031-04245-4 (eBook)
https://doi.org/10.1007/978-3-031-04245-4

© ICST Institute for Computer Sciences, Social Informatics and Telecommunications Engineering 2022
This work is subject to copyright. All rights are reserved by the Publisher, whether the whole or part of the material is concerned, specifically the rights of translation, reprinting, reuse of illustrations, recitation, broadcasting, reproduction on microfilms or in any other physical way, and transmission or information storage and retrieval, electronic adaptation, computer software, or by similar or dissimilar methodology now known or hereafter developed.
The use of general descriptive names, registered names, trademarks, service marks, etc. in this publication does not imply, even in the absence of a specific statement, that such names are exempt from the relevant protective laws and regulations and therefore free for general use.
The publisher, the authors and the editors are safe to assume that the advice and information in this book are believed to be true and accurate at the date of publication. Neither the publisher nor the authors or the editors give a warranty, expressed or implied, with respect to the material contained herein or for any errors or omissions that may have been made. The publisher remains neutral with regard to jurisdictional claims in published maps and institutional affiliations.

This Springer imprint is published by the registered company Springer Nature Switzerland AG
The registered company address is: Gewerbestrasse 11, 6330 Cham, Switzerland

Preface

We are delighted to introduce the proceedings of the first edition of the European Alliance for Innovation (EAI) International Conference on 6G for Future Wireless Networks (6GN 2021). This conference brought together researchers, developers, and practitioners around the world who are leveraging and developing communication, networking, and signal processing technologies for smarter and more efficient wireless networks. The theme of 6GN 2021 was "6G Inspired Future Technologies: Smarter and More Efficient Wireless Networks".

The technical program of 6GN 2021 consisted of 68 full papers in oral presentation sessions at the main conference tracks. The conference tracks were as follows: Track 1 – Advanced Communication and Networking Technologies for 5G/6G Networks; Track 2 – Advanced Signal Processing Technologies for 5G/6G Networks; and Track 3 – Educational Changes in The Age of 5G/6G. Aside from the high-quality technical paper presentations, the technical program also featured two keynote speeches given by Victor C. M. Leung from Shenzhen University, China, and Chunguo Li from Southeast University, China.

Coordination with the steering chair, Imrich Chlamtac, was essential for the success of the conference. We sincerely appreciate his constant support and guidance. It was also a great pleasure to work with such an excellent organizing committee team for their hard work in organizing and supporting the conference. In particular, we are grateful to the Technical Program Committee, who completed the peer-review process for the technical papers and helped to put together a high-quality technical program. We are also grateful to Conference Manager Lucia Sladeckova for her support and all the authors who submitted their papers to the 6GN 2021 conference and workshops.

We strongly believe that the 6GN 2021 conference provided a good forum for all researchers, developers, and practitioners to discuss all science and technology aspects that are relevant to future wireless networks. We also expect that the future 6GN conferences will be as successful and stimulating, as indicated by the contributions presented in this volume.

Ruofei Ma
Weidang Lu
Shuo Shi
Xiuhua Li

Organization

Steering Committee

Imrich Chlamtac — University of Trento, Italy

Organizing Committee

General Chair

Xuemai Gu — Harbin Institute of Technology, China

General Co-chairs

Victor C. M. Leung — Shenzhen University, China
Zhong Zheng — International Innovation Institute of HIT, Huizhou, China
Xiaofei Wang — Tianjin University, China

Technical Program Committee Chairs

Ruofei Ma — Harbin Institute of Technology, Weihai, China
Weidang Lu — Zhejiang University of Technology, China
Shuo Shi — Harbin Institute of Technology, China
Xiuhua Li — Chongqing University, China

Sponsorship and Exhibit Chairs

Zhenyu Xu — Huizhou Engineering Vocational College, China
Rui E. — Heilongjiang Polytechnic, China

Local Chair

Hui Li — International Innovation Institute of HIT, Huizhou, China

Workshops Chair

Yao Shi — Huizhou Engineering Vocational College, China

Publicity and Social Media Chair

Guoxing Huang	Zhejiang University of Technology, China

Publications Chair

Liang Ye	Harbin Institute of Technology, China

Web Chair

Wanlong Zhao	Harbin Institute of Technology, Weihai, China

Technical Program Committee

Ruofei Ma	Harbin Institute of Technology, Weihai, China
Weidang Lu	Zhejiang University of Technology, China
Shuo Shi	Harbin Institute of Technology, China
Xiuhua Li	Chongqing University, China
Victor C. M. Leung	Shenzhen University, China
Ning Zhang	University of Windsor, Canada
Chunguo Li	Southeast University, China
Mingqian Liu	Xidian University, China
Lu Jia	China Agricultural University, China
Wei Xiang	La Trobe University, Australia
Shuyi Chen	Harbin Institute of Technology, China
Yiliang Liu	Xi'an Jiaotong University, China
Xiqing Liu	Beijing University of Posts and Telecommunications, China
Chunpeng Liu	Harbin Engineering University, China
Siyue Sun	Shanghai Engineering Center for Microsatellites, China
Guanghua Zhang	Northeast Petroleum University, China
Gongliang Liu	Harbin Institute of Technology, Weihai, China
Lei Ning	Shenzhen Technology University, China
Qiang Liu	National University of Defense Technology, China
Guodong Li	Harbin University of Science and Technology, China

Contents

Advanced Communication and Networking Technologies for 5G/6G Networks

Advanced Communication and Networking Technologies for 5G/6G Networks

Lagrange Relaxation Based Inter-satellite Links Scheduling for Satellite Networks

Ruisong Wang, Weichen Zhu, and Gongliang Liu(✉)

Harbin Institute of Technology, Weihai 264209, Shandong, China
liugl@hit.edu.cn

Abstract. Satellite networks have attracted a lot of attention due to their unique advantages such as wide coverage and high data rate. However, the increasing number of satellites make the design of inter-satellite links become more difficult and further lead to low resource utilization rate. Therefore, this paper aims to design an efficient but low complexity inter-satellite links establishment scheme. The energy consumption optimization problem is first formulated as a mixed integer linear programming. Then, a Lagrange relaxation method is used to decompose the optimization problem into two subproblems, i.e., routing problem and inter-satellite links design problem. The optimal routing scheme can be obtained by solving a min-cost max-flow problem. The inter-satellite links design problem can be solved by using branch and bound method in parallel. The suboptimal solution of original problem can be obtained through solving these subproblems. Finally, the simulation results have be given to verify the effectiveness of proposed algorithm.

Keywords: Lagrange relaxation method · Inter-satellite link · Satellite networks

1 Introduction

In recent years, the satellites have been paid more attention to due to the requirement of high communication rate and communication quality. Especially, the wide coverage of satellites is the main advantage and beneficial to the extension of terrestrial network. Hence, some satellite assisted terrestrial networks have been investigated by many scholars. In [1], the authors considered a satellite based Internet of Things system with the application of non-orthogonal multiple access (NOMA) technique. They provided an efficient resource allocation method for improving the network utility from the view of long-term optimization. In [2], the authors provided the deep Q-learning approach for allocating the

This work was supported in part by the National Natural Science Foundation of China under Grant 61971156, in part by the Shandong Provincial Natural Science Foundation under Grant ZR2019MF035 and Grant ZR2020MF141, in part by Science and Technology Development Program at Weihai under Grant 2019KYCXJJYB06.

© ICST Institute for Computer Sciences, Social Informatics and Telecommunications Engineering 2022
Published by Springer Nature Switzerland AG 2022. All Rights Reserved
S. Shi et al. (Eds.): 6GN 2021, LNICST 439, pp. 3–15, 2022.
https://doi.org/10.1007/978-3-031-04245-4_1

computing and communication resources for satellite-terrestrial networks. The satellite acting as the base station has been used to serve the users in remote areas where users are divided into many cells according to location [3]. Moreover, they given the efficient data offloading method to improve the e energy efficiency. Similarly, the authors in [4] have taken into account the energy efficient problem for cognitive satellite terrestrial networks.

However, the existing work above paid more attention to the case of single satellite. In order to meet the higher communication requirements, the satellite services have tended to be networked. Hence, inter-satellite links are the key point for constructing the satellite networks. Some work has been done for the application of inter-satellite links. In [5], the authors investigated the download time allocation method by using inter-satellite links. With the increasing number of inter-satellite links, the optimal routing of each data flow becomes more difficult. Hence, the estimation method of hop-count for each path was studied in [6]. Moreover, the inter-plane connectivity was analyzed by [7]. Based on the analysis, an inter-satellite links establishment method was given. The authors investigated the inter-satellite links design for the dual-hop satellite network by using graph theory. For more details about the inter-satellite communication, the authors in [9] have provided a survey to conclude them.

Motivated by the existing work above, this paper focused on the inter-satellite links establishment method so as to reduce the energy consumption. The main contributions are concluded as follows.

- The satellite network model was introduced to provide the computing service. The inter-satellite links establishment and routing problems were formulated as a mixed integer linear programming.
- To decrease the computation complexity, a Lagrange relaxation method was used to find the suboptimal solution.
- The simulation results have been provided for showing the validity of the proposed algorithm.

The remainder of this paper was organized as follows. In Sect. 2, the system model and problem formulation were given. Section 3 provided the main solution method of energy minimization problem. Section 4 analyzed the simulation results with different parameters. Finally, a conclusion was given in Sect. 5.

2 System Model and Problem Formulation

2.1 System Model

As described in Fig. 1, this paper takes into account such a satellite network that consists of M general satellites, a ground station, and the edge satellite which refers to the satellite with limited computing capabilities. The ground station is supposed to connect to the cloud service center and hence has infinite computing capabilities. In the beginning, the source satellite generates the computation task with a specific delay requirement. However, due to the lack of computing

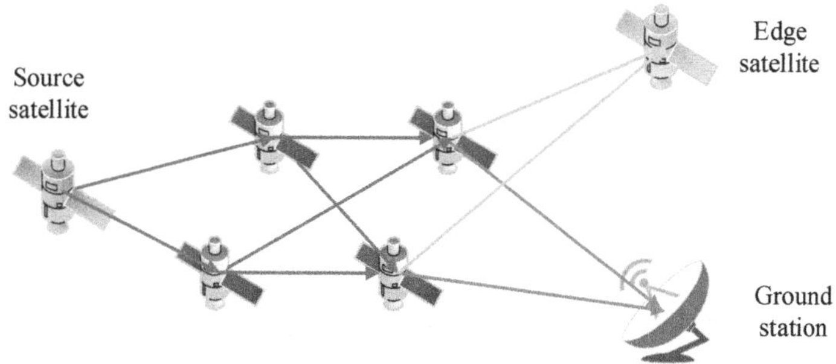

Fig. 1. The satellite network model.

capabilities, the source satellite has to offload the task to the edge satellites or ground station through some relay satellites. For the path from source satellite to the ground station, there are usually a lot of communication cost and storage cost due to the long transmission path. Although the path from source satellite to the edge satellites is short, the costs usually consist of communication cost, storage cost, and computing cost due to the limited computing capabilities. Hence, there is a tradeoff between the two approaches. In addition, due to the limited number of antennas, only some inter-satellite links are feasible even if a satellite is visible to more than one satellite. Hence, it is critical to decide the inter-satellite links in order to ensure that the task can arrive in the specified time with a low cost.

The relative positions between satellites is time varying since the satellites move at high speed in their orbits. Therefore, the inter-satellite links and the satellite-ground links also change dynamically. To deal with the dynamics, the whole time period is divided into N continuous time slots $\mathcal{T} = \{t_1, t_2, \ldots, t_N\}$ of which the duration is τ. The topology of the network is regarded as fixed in each time slot but variational for different time slots.

2.2 Problem Formulation

The main focus of this paper is to minimize the cost of the task transmission with the time constraint. Before giving the optimization problem, the definition of cost is first provided as follows.

$$c^1_{t,i,j} = (p_{t,i,j} + q_{t,i,j})\frac{x_{t,i,j}}{C_{t,i,j}} \tag{1}$$

where $c^1_{t,i,j}$ means the communication cost for the inter-satellite link between the satellite i and satellite j at the time slot t. Specifically, $p_{t,i,j}$ and $q_{t,i,j}$ represent the transmitted power and received power, respectively. $x_{t,i,j}$ and $C_{t,i,j}$ denote the data volume and the transmission rate from satellite i to satellite j at the time slot t, respectively. The transmission rate can be calculated as

$$C_{t,i,j} = B\log(1 + \frac{p_{t,i,j}G^1_i G^2_j L_{t,i,j}}{N_p}) \tag{2}$$

where G_i^1 denotes the transmission antenna gain of satellite i. G_i^2 denotes the receiving antenna gain of satellite j. $L_{t,i,j}$ represents the path loss of inter-satellite link at the time slot t. N_p refers to the noise. The path loss $L_{t,i,j}$ is time varying due to the dynamic change of distance and is expressed as follows.

$$L_{t,i,j} = \left(\frac{v}{4\pi f d_{t,i,j}}\right)^2 \tag{3}$$

where v is the velocity of light, f is the carrier frequency, $d_{t,i,j}$ is the distance between satellite i and satellite j.

Not all data can be transmitted to the destination in one time slot. Hence, the data storage is necessary but also leads to the storage cost which can be expressed as

$$c_{t,i}^2 = \tau b_{t,i} P_i \tag{4}$$

where $b_{t,i}$ is the amount of data stored on the satellite i at the time slot t. P_i is the price of storage.

Due to the limited computing resource, if the task will be transmitted to the edge satellite, then there is a computing cost expressed as

$$c_{t,i}^3 = Q_i \sum_{j=1}^{M} \frac{x_{t,i,j}}{f_i} \tag{5}$$

where f_i is the computing capacities of satellite i and Q_i is the computing price.

Hence, the total cost of task is the summation of the communication cost, storage cost, and computing cost.

$$E = \sum_{t=1}^{N} \sum_{i=1}^{M} \left(\sum_{j=1}^{M} c_{t,i,j}^1 + c_{t,i}^2 + c_{t,i}^3 \right) \tag{6}$$

For each satellite, the input flow should equal the output flow. If the data is not fully transmitted, it should be temporarily cached in itself. Then, we can write it as

$$\sum_{j=1}^{M} x_{t,i,j} + b_{t,i} = \sum_{j=1}^{M} x_{t,j,i} + b_{t-1,i} \tag{7}$$

At the initial moment, the source satellite I create task with the data volume D. To ensure that the task is successfully transmitted, the data volume of task received by destination node J is also D after N time slot. Then, we can obtain the following constraints.

$$\sum_{j=1}^{M} x_{1,I,j} + b_{1,I} = D \tag{8}$$

$$\sum_{t=1}^{N}\sum_{i=1}^{M} x_{t,i,J} = D \tag{9}$$

For each inter-satellite link, the amount of information transmitted can not be more than the link capacity. Then, we can express it as

$$x_{t,i,j} \leq \tau C_{t,i,j} \tag{10}$$

Similar to the Eq. (10), the storage data also can not exceed the satellite's storage capacity, i.e.,

$$b_{t,i} \leq B_i \tag{11}$$

where B_i is the storage capacity of i-th satellite.

Considering the limited number of antennas on the satellite, it is assumed that the satellite or ground station can only communicate with at most U satellites or ground stations within its visual range. In order to express the connection state of communication link, a binary variable $a_{t,i,j}$ is introduced in this model. $a_{t,i,j} = 1$ means that the i-th satellite established the inter-satellite link with the j-th satellite at the time slot t. Based on the definition above, some constraint can be provided.

$$\sum_{i=1}^{M} a_{t,i,j} \leq U \tag{12}$$

$$\sum_{j=1}^{M} a_{t,i,j} \leq U \tag{13}$$

$$a_{t,i,j} = a_{t,j,i} \tag{14}$$

The Eq. (11) and (12) are the constraints of limited number of antennas. The constraint (14) indicates the inter-satellite link is bidirectional.

In addition, the data flow can be transmitted from i-th satellite to j-th satellite only if there exists an inter-satellite link.

$$x_{t,i,j} \leq \tau a_{t,i,j} C_{t,i,j} \tag{15}$$

Finally, the task completion time must not exceed the time requirement.

$$T_{total} \leq T \tag{16}$$

For the constraint (16), we can calculate the number of time slot $N = \frac{T}{\tau}$. Then, the constraint (16) is equivalent to $t \leq N$.

Then, the final optimization problem can be written as

$$\begin{aligned} &\min\ E \\ &s.t.\ (7)-(15) \end{aligned} \tag{17}$$

The main optimization variables are $a_{t,i,j}$ and $a_{t,i,j}$. The optimization problem (17) is the mixed integer linear programming. For obtaining the optimal solution, the exhaustive method is the feasible method but the computational complexity of this method is exponential. Hence, the optimal solution is difficult and impractical. To reduce the complexity, it is necessary to investigate an efficient algorithm.

3 Lagrange Relaxation Based Solving Method

In this section, the Lagrange relaxation based method is applied to deal with the optimization problem (17). It can be seen that the main difficulty is due to the coupling constraint (15). Hence, the optimization problem (17) can be decomposed into two subproblems by relaxing the constraint (15). The relaxed problem is written as

$$\begin{aligned} z(\boldsymbol{\lambda}) = \min\ &E + \sum_{t=1}^{N}\sum_{i=1}^{M}\sum_{j=1}^{M}\lambda_{t,i,j}\left(x_{t,i,j} - \tau a_{t,i,j}C_{t,i,j}\right) \\ s.t.\ &(7)-(9),(10)-(15) \end{aligned} \tag{18}$$

Then, it can be seen that the variables have been separated. Moreover, the relaxed optimization problem (18) is equivalent to the following two subproblems $\mathcal{P}1$ and $\mathcal{P}2$.

$$\begin{aligned} \mathcal{P}1:\min\ &E + \sum_{t=1}^{N}\sum_{i=1}^{M}\sum_{j=1}^{M}\lambda_{t,i,j}x_{t,i,j} \\ s.t.\ &\sum_{j=1}^{M}x_{t,i,j} + b_{t,i} = \sum_{j=1}^{M}x_{t,j,i} + b_{t-1,i} \\ &\sum_{j=1}^{M}x_{1,I,j} + b_{1,I} = D \\ &\sum_{t=1}^{N}\sum_{i=1}^{M}x_{t,i,J} = D \\ &x_{t,i,j} \le \tau C_{t,i,j} \\ &b_{t,i} \le B_i \\ &x_{t,i,j} \ge 0 \end{aligned} \tag{19}$$

$$
\begin{aligned}
\mathcal{P}2: \min \ & \sum_{t=1}^{N}\sum_{i=1}^{M}\sum_{j=1}^{M}\lambda_{t,i,j}\tau a_{t,i,j}C_{t,i,j} \\
s.t. \ & \sum_{i=1}^{M} a_{t,i,j} \le U \\
& \sum_{j=1}^{M} a_{t,i,j} \le U \\
& a_{t,i,j} = a_{t,j,i} \\
& a_{t,i,j} \in \{0,1\}
\end{aligned}
\tag{20}
$$

3.1 Solving Problem $\mathcal{P}1$

There are two options for each task. One is to transmit the task to edge satellite. Because the total data volume is fixed, the computing cost is also fixed. The another is to transmit the task to ground station where the computing cost can be neglected. Hence, regardless of which method the source satellite uses, the computing cost can be regarded as a constant and therefore can be removed for the optimization problem $\mathcal{P}1$. Then, we can rewrite the objective function as

$$
\begin{aligned}
\min \ & \sum_{t=1}^{N}\sum_{i=1}^{M}\sum_{j=1}^{M}\mu_{t,i,j}x_{t,i,j} + \sum_{t=1}^{N}\sum_{i=1}^{M}\rho_{t,i}b_{t,i} \\
s.t. \ & \sum_{j=1}^{M} x_{t,i,j} + b_{t,i} = \sum_{j=1}^{M} x_{t,j,i} + b_{t-1,i} \\
& \sum_{j=1}^{M} x_{1,I,j} + b_{1,I} = D \\
& \sum_{t=1}^{N}\sum_{i=1}^{M} x_{t,i,J} = D \\
& x_{t,i,j} \le \tau C_{t,i,j} \\
& b_{t,i} \le B_i \\
& x_{t,i,j} \ge 0
\end{aligned}
\tag{21}
$$

where $\mu_{t,i,j} = \lambda_{t,i,j} + \frac{p_{t,i,j}+q_{t,i,j}}{C_{t,i,j}}$ and $\rho_{t,i} = \tau P_i$.

It can be seen that the reformulated problem (21) can be regarded as the min-cost max-flow problem. To show it, we first create the time evolution graph $\mathcal{G}$. As shown in Fig. 2, the time evolution graph $\mathcal{G}$ consists of three kinds of edges, i.e., communication edges, storage edges, and virtual edges. According to the problem (21), the cost and capacity of communication edges are $\mu_{t,i,j}$ and $\tau C_{t,i,j}$, respectively. The cost and capacity of storage edges are $\rho_{t,i}$ and B_i,

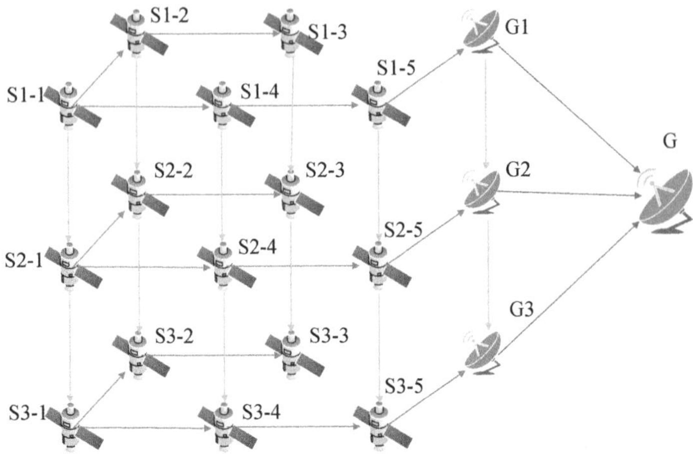

Fig. 2. The time evolution graph of satellite network.

respectively. Because the satellite network is dynamic, the time at which data arrives at its destination may vary. Hence, we add the virtual node to represent the final destination SG and create the virtual edges with the destination at the different time slots. For the virtual edges, the cost is zero and the capacity is infinity. Then, the problem (21) can be though of the min-cost max-flow problem from source satellite to the final destination SG.

3.2 Solving Problem $\mathcal{P}2$

The optimization problem $\mathcal{P}2$ is still an integer programming. But taking notice of that the optimization problem $\mathcal{P}2$ is separable in terms of the time slot, hence the solving complexity can be reduced. Then, the optimization problem $\mathcal{P}2$ can be dealt with by solving the following N subproblems in parallel.

$$\begin{aligned} \min \ & \sum_{i=1}^{M}\sum_{j=1}^{M} \lambda_{t,i,j}\tau a_{t,i,j}C_{t,i,j} \\ s.t. \ & \sum_{i=1}^{M} a_{t,i,j} \leq U \\ & \sum_{j=1}^{M} a_{t,i,j} \leq U \\ & a_{t,i,j} = a_{t,j,i} \\ & a_{t,i,j} \in \{0,1\} \end{aligned} \tag{22}$$

On the one hand, the number of variables is less for each subproblem. On other hand, the optimization subproblem is sparse when U is small. Therefore, the branch and bound method is efficient for solving such a problem.

Algorithm 1. Lagrange relaxation based solving method

1: Initialize maximum number of iterations K_{max}, the lagrangian multipliers $\boldsymbol{\lambda}$, and the convergence threshold ε.
2: Set the edge satellite as the destination.
3: **for** $k = 1 : K_{max}$ **do**
4: Create the time evolution graph $\mathcal{G}$.
5: Solve the min-cost max-flow problem and obtain the optimal solution $\boldsymbol{x}^k$.
6: Solve the N optimization subproblem (22) and obtain the optimal solution $\boldsymbol{a}^k$.
7: Update the lagrangian multipliers $\boldsymbol{\lambda}^k$ according to the equation (24).
8: **if** $\|\boldsymbol{\lambda}^k - \boldsymbol{\lambda}^{k-1}\| < \varepsilon$ **then**
9: Break.
10: **end if**
11: **end for**
12: Update the time evolution graph $\mathcal{G}$ by setting the link capacity as $\tau a_{t,i,j} C_{t,i,j}$.
13: Solve the the min-cost max-flow problem and obtain the new optimal solution $\boldsymbol{x}^*$.
14: Calculate the total cost as E_1.
15: Set the ground station as the destination.
16: Repeat the step 3-13 and calculate the total cost as E_2.
17: **if** $E_1 < E_2$ **then**
18: Select the path from source satellite to the edge satellite.
19: **else**
20: Select the path from source satellite to the ground station.
21: **end if**

3.3 Optimizing Lagrange Multiplier

The optimization problem (17) is rewritten as optimization problem (18) by relaxing the constraint (15). For the fixed lagrangian multipliers, the optimal solution is a lower bound of the optimization problem (17). Then, to get close to the optimal solution, it is necessary to optimize the lagrangian multipliers.

$$\begin{aligned} &\max \ z(\boldsymbol{\lambda}) \\ &s.t. \ \boldsymbol{\lambda} \geq 0 \end{aligned} \tag{23}$$

Then, a subgradient method is applied to find the optimal solution of problem (24). The update rule of lagrangian multipliers is provided as follows.

$$\lambda_{t,i,j}^{k+1} = \left[\lambda_{t,i,j}^k - \phi^k \left(x_{t,i,j}^k - \tau a_{t,i,j}^k C_{t,i,j}\right)\right]_0^+ \tag{24}$$

where $[x]_0^+ = \max\{0, x\}$ and ϕ^k is the step size at the k-th iteration. The step size ϕ^k satisfies the following conditions.

$$\sum_{k=1}^{\infty} \phi^k = \infty, \lim_{k \to \infty} \phi^k = 0 \tag{25}$$

3.4 Solution Reconstruction Method

Although the relaxed solution is close to the optimal solution of problem (17), the relaxed solution may be not feasible. To find an optimized feasible solution, an efficient reconstruction method needs to be investigated. It can be seen that the optimal solution $\boldsymbol{a}$ of problem $\mathcal{P}2$ is always feasible. Hence, we only need to make sure the optimal solution $\boldsymbol{x}$ feasible by keeping the the optimal solution $\boldsymbol{a}$ fixed. Specifically, for the given optimal solution $\boldsymbol{a}$, update the link capacity as $\tau a_{t,i,j} C_{t,i,j}$. Then, solve the the min-cost max-flow problem again and obtain the new optimal solution $\boldsymbol{x}^*$. The whole detailed solution process can be referred to Algorithm 1.

4 Simulation Results

This section provided the simulation results for evaluating the effectiveness of proposed algorithm. By using the Satellite Tool Kit (STK), we created a Walker constellation with the type "Delta". The parameters of seed satellite are listed as follows. The orbit altitude is 14000 km. The inclination is 60°. The right ascension of ascending node is 0°. The true anomaly is 120°. Then, an edge satellite was created with the parameters that the orbit altitude, inclination, right ascension of ascending node, and true anomaly are 3000 km, 45°, 0°, 45°. Other parameters used in this paper are listed in Table 1. Moreover, the random inter-satellite links scheduling are used to compare with the proposed algorithm. The random inter-satellite links scheduling means that the inter-satellite links are built randomly in each time slot under the condition that the constraints are satisfied.

In Fig. 3, the relationship between the length of time slot and the energy consumption has been shown. As we can see, the energy consumption increases with the length of time slot growing. The reason is that the transmission power

Table 1. The parameters in simulation.

Parameters	Value
The convergence threshold	0.001
The Maximum number of iterations	300
The number of satellite	13
The price of storage	10 W/Mbits
The price of computing	1 Mbps
The carrier frequency	20 GHz
The transmitting antenna gain of satellite	27 dBi
The receiving antenna gain of satellite	24 dBi
The receiving antenna gain of ground	25 dBi
The bandwidth	20 MHz

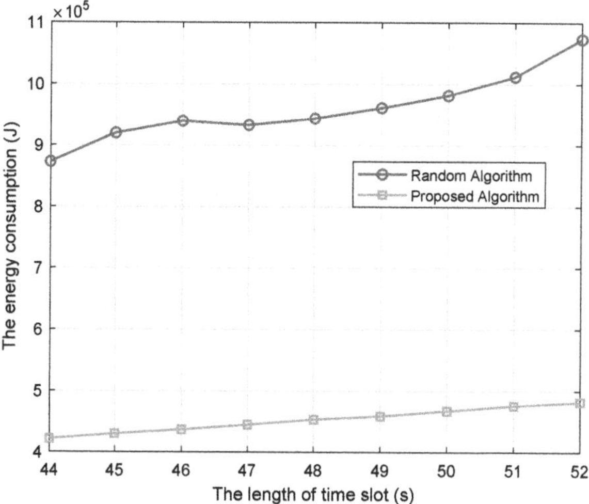

Fig. 3. The energy consumption versus the length of time slot.

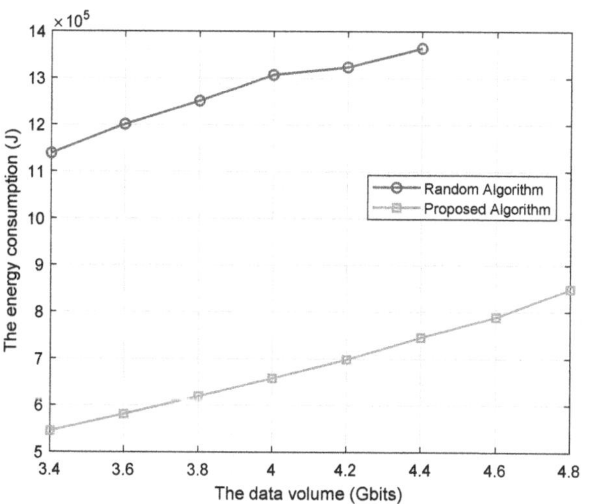

Fig. 4. The energy consumption versus the data volume.

of each satellite is fixed. For some inter-satellite links, the resource is wasted because the link capacity is not fully utilized. In addition, compared with the random algorithm, the energy consumption has been obviously decreased by using our proposed algorithm. Hence, an optimized inter-satellite links scheduling is necessary for improving the network performance.

In Fig. 4, the relationship between energy consumption and data volume is demonstrated. It is obvious that the energy consumption increases with the increasing of the data volume. As we can see, the proposed algorithm is always

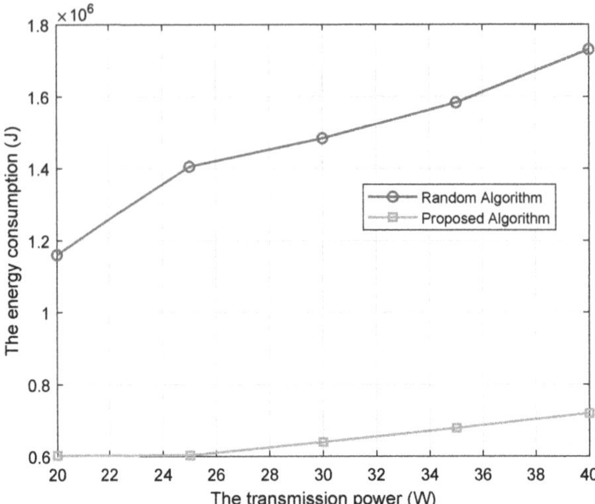

Fig. 5. The energy consumption versus the transmission power.

superior to the random algorithm. For example, the energy consumption is reduced by 108% when the data volume is 3.4 Gbits. Moreover, when the data volume is more than 4.4 Gbits, there is even no feasible path to ensure that the task is successfully transmitted at the required time. Hence, reasonable and efficient inter-satellite link scheduling is crucial to make full use of the resource.

Figure 5 provides the relationship between the transmission power and the energy consumption. For the random algorithm, increased transmission power must lead to the increase of the energy consumption because the length of time slot and number of links are given. For the proposed algorithm, the inter-satellite links are built only if there is data flow through the link. Hence, the energy consumption with the proposed algorithm is always lower than it with the random algorithm. Even though, similar to Fig. 3, the link capacities of some inter-satellite links may be not fully utilized. Moreover, the energy consumption will increases but not by much. Hence, it is unnecessary to improve the transmission power unless there is no feasible paths.

5 Conclusions

This paper proposed the satellite network model aiming to provide the computing services for satellites with some requirements. Once the source satellites generate the computation missions, they can select to offload the missions to edge satellites or ground station. Then, the corresponding optimization problem was formulated as the mixed integer linear programming. To save the energy consumption and allocate resources quickly, a Lagrange relaxation based method was proposed to decide the inter-satellite links design scheme and routing planning. According to the simulation results, the energy consumption was significantly reduced by using the proposed algorithm.

References

1. Jiao, J., Sun, Y., Wu, S., Wang, Y., Zhang, Q.: Network utility maximization resource allocation for NOMA in satellite-based Internet of Things. IEEE Internet Things J. **7**(4), 3230–3242 (2020)
2. Qiu, C., Yao, H., Yu, F., Xu, F., Zhao, C.: Deep Q-learning aided networking, caching, and computing resources allocation in software-defined satellite-terrestrial networks. IEEE Trans. Veh. Technol. **68**(6), 5871–5883 (2019)
3. Ji, Z., Wu, S., Jiang, C., Hu, D., Wang, W.: Energy-efficient data offloading for multi-cell satellite-terrestrial networks. IEEE Commun. Lett. **24**(10), 2265–2269 (2020)
4. Ruan, Y., Lim, Y., Wang, C.X., Zhang, R., Zhang, H.: Energy efficient power allocation for delay constrained cognitive satellite terrestrial networks under interference constraints. IEEE Trans. Wirel. Commun. **18**(10), 4957–4969 (2019)
5. Jia, X., Lv, T., He, F., Huang, H.: Collaborative data downloading by using inter-satellite links in LEO satellite networks. IEEE Trans. Wirel. Commun. **16**(3), 1523–1532 (2017)
6. Chen, Q., Giambene, G., Yang, L., Fan, C., Chen, X.: Analysis of inter-satellite link paths for LEO mega-constellation networks. IEEE Trans. Veh. Technol. **70**(3), 2743–2755 (2021)
7. Leyva-Mayorga, I., Soret, B., Popovski, P.: Inter-plane inter-satellite connectivity in dense LEO constellations. IEEE Trans. Wirel. Commun. **20**(6), 3430–3443 (2021)
8. Zhou, D., Sheng, M., Liu, R., Wang, Y., Li, J.: Channel-aware mission scheduling in broadband data relay satellite networks. IEEE J. Sel. Areas Commun. **36**(5), 1052–1064 (2018)
9. Radhakrishnan, R., Edmonson, W.W., Afghah, F., Rodriguez-Osorio, R.M., Pinto, F., Burleigh, S.C.: Survey of inter-satellite communication for small satellite systems: physical layer to network layer view. IEEE Commun. Surv. Tutor. **18**(4), 2442–2473 (2016)

Research on OLSR Routing Protocol for High-Dynamic and Low-Density UAV Ad-Hoc Network

Shuo Shi[1,2(✉)], Cong Zhou[1], and Zhong Zheng[3]

[1] School of Electronic and Information Engineering, Harbin Institute of Technology, Harbin 150001, Heilongjiang, China
crcss@hit.edu.cn

[2] Peng Cheng Laboratory, Network Communication Research Centre, Shenzhen 518052, Guangdong, China

[3] International Innovation Institute of HIT, Huizhou 516000, Guangdong, China

Abstract. The main content of this paper is to use NS2 simulation to evaluate the performance of the OLSR routing protocol and its performance comparison with routing protocols such as AODV in a motion scenario based on the PPRZM (Paparazzi Mobility) mobile model, and complete a running OLSR The actual measurement of the performance of the UAV self-organizing network of the routing protocol. Based on the above, some suggestions for optimizing the OLSR routing protocol are put forward. This article first analyzes the research status of the UAV self-organizing network, and then explains the main research content of this subject, including the working principle of the OLSR routing protocol, the optimization and implementation of the paparazzi movement model, and the NS2 simulation evaluation of the OLSR routing protocol in the above motion The performance evaluation under the scene and its performance comparison with other routing protocols, and the performance test of an actual UAV self-organizing network OLSR routing protocol. Through the research of the UAV self-organizing network motion scene, the working principle and performance simulation of OLSR, this paper gives the performance comparison of the current mainstream Ad Hoc routing protocol under the UAV self-organizing network, and finally shows the actual UAV Demonstration of running the OLSR routing protocol in a self-organizing network.

Keywords: PPRZM · OLSR · FANETs · High-dynamic

1 Introduction

With the development of technology and society, hardware technology and wireless communication technology have made great progress, which makes the performance of UAV stand-alone improved significantly, such as flight speed, battery capacity and obstacle avoidance. However, its price is declining, which makes it more and more widely used in many fields, such as real-time fire monitoring and management, crop

© ICST Institute for Computer Sciences, Social Informatics and Telecommunications Engineering 2022
Published by Springer Nature Switzerland AG 2022. All Rights Reserved
S. Shi et al. (Eds.): 6GN 2021, LNICST 439, pp. 16–28, 2022.
https://doi.org/10.1007/978-3-031-04245-4_2

pest prevention, target recognition and tracking in complex environment, and temporary communication in earthquake relief, Fig. 1 below shows the schematic diagram of T30 UAV applied in plant protection of DJI.

Fig. 1. DJI T30 plant protection UAV

FANETs (Flying Ad Hoc Networks) are composed of the ground control part and multiple UAV nodes, which together form a wireless self-organizing network. Like the Ad Hoc network, each node is highly equal and has a high degree of autonomy. However, due to the extremely fast moving speed of the UAV node, the topology of the node changes highly, so the requirements for routing are higher. The OLSR routing protocol is classified as a kind of proactive routing in terms of routing search. It has a routing protocol with low delay and good self-adapting performance, and is a routing suitable for mobile ad hoc networks. Although FANETs are also a category of MANET, FANETs have their particular application in sports scenes [1].

The centralized communication structure has a central node, that is, the ground control center of the drone cluster. All nodes communicate and move under the control of the control center, but the drones cannot communicate with each other. All instructions all are issued by the ground control center. This architecture is similar to a wireless network with a central node AP, and all communications between nodes are regulated by the AP. Strictly speaking, this structure is not an ad hoc network in the strict sense, and communication between nodes is not possible. As a result, the application is limited to the movement and communication range of a single UAV, and the types of tasks that can be performed are very narrow. However, this communication structure also has its advantages. Its communication link is stable, the communication between a single UAV and the control center is interrupted, and the communication link will not affect or interfere with the communication between other UAV nodes and ground stations.

The distributed communication structure is based on the centralized communication structure with a communication structure that can also communicate with each other between drones. Under this architecture, the UAV will not be restricted by the fixed restriction of the central control station, and the UAV can communicate with each other and expand the UAV's search range through multi-hop node communication. The information coverage of the UAV self-organizing network is greatly extended. Therefore, the distributed structure of FANETs has the characteristics of wide coverage and flexible coverage search area. It is currently the most suitable communication structure for multi-UAV cluster tasks [2].

The cluster communication structure of FANETs is a communication structure formed by introducing the mutual communication between drones and adding the concept of clustering. All small clusters are composed of drone nodes that are close together, and the entire drone network is a collection of clusters. And each small cluster will generate a central node called the cluster head, and the communication between nodes within the small cluster is carried out through the cluster head. The communication between the small cluster and the small cluster is forwarded through the small cluster. The disadvantage of the cluster communication structure is that in the case of high dynamics, the change rate of small clusters is very high, causing the communication between the cluster head and small cluster members to frequently lose the communication link and continuously create new clusters. The problem of dynamic network and cluster communication structure in the above-mentioned situation has not been solved yet. Therefore, the communication structure of the unmanned aerial vehicle ad hoc network of this subject does not adopt a clustered communication structure.

In summary of the discussion of FANETs communication structure, the communication structure selected in this article is a distributed communication structure. Compared with the ordinary Ad Hoc network, this communication structure has many particularities, which will be discussed below [3].

A single UAV node itself moves fast and can ignore the characteristics of the terrain and all the obstacles that can be surpassed, so it will cause frequent changes in the topology of each UAV network node, and the communication between UAVs must frequently search for routes. Therefore, FANETs The adaptive routing requirements are relatively high. The real-time search task needs to continuously return information to the ground control station, so the end-to-end time delay of the average node of the network is relatively high, so it also puts forward the low delay requirements for the routing of FANETs. Therefore, when communicating between FANETs nodes, the accuracy of the route search and the average end-to-end delay will directly affect the communication quality between the UAV network nodes, which in turn will affect the efficiency of the UAV swarm. And quality has a major adverse effect.

The OLSR routing protocol is a proactive and self-adaptive routing protocol, which is well applied in mobile ad hoc networks, but the application in FANETs is rarely mentioned, so the application performance of OLSR in FANETs is tested. Analysis has certain practical value and reference significance. Based on the search task of the UAV ad hoc network, this paper studies the performance analysis of the application of OLSR in FANETs, and establishes the NS2 simulation scenario PPRZM mobile model. In this motion scenario, the performance of OLSR under various conditions is simulated and evaluated. Finally, based on the simulation results, the applicability and limitations of OLSR in FANETs are discussed, which provides data and theoretical support for the better application of OLSR routing in FANETs [4].

2 Model Establishment

This paper studies the PPRZM mobile model and optimizes the PPRZM model and its implementation in NS2. The PPRZM mobile model, the paparazzi model, is a mobile model proposed by Bouachir O, Abrassart A, and Garcia F at the 2014 International Drone Driving Conference. They demonstrated the PPRZM mobile through experimental simulations in the article report. When the model is used in the UAV cluster self-organizing network, it will be closer to the movement of the UAV cluster network and the communication link. They divided the movement of the drone into five types, namely circling movement, linear movement, scanning movement, elliptical movement and figure-of-eight movement, and gave them different occurrence probabilities. Based on their research, this paper takes into account the task requirements of the area search. In the simulation, the concept of area is introduced. The entire plane is divided into 9 areas, and each area is divided into a random number to represent the area of the task search. The size of the task volume and the distribution of drones between regions are evenly distributed by the size of random numbers. The realization of the motion scene relies on the setdest tool of NS2, and the scene model is introduced by modifying the source code of the setdest tool [4].

2.1 PPRZM Mobile Model

PPRZM is a mobile model based on the movement path of the mobile ad hoc network node. Compared with other mobile ad hoc network models, it simplifies the movement of the drone node into five movement modes. The author in the literature proved through simulation that, compared with the RWP model, when the PPRZM mobile model is used for the simulation of the UAV cluster self-organizing network, the PPRZM model is closer to the real movement trajectory of the mobile node and the communication link. It can also be well reflected. The five nodal trajectories of the PPRZM motion model are given below:

(1) Circling and waiting: The UAV will continue to make a uniform circular motion with the target position as the center of the circle. This is a simulation of the UAV's backhaul after the target is found. Once the UAV finds the target, the UAV will hover in place and wait to return captured information and transmit related videos or pictures.
(2) Waypoint flying in a straight line: The UAV will move straight towards the target position at a constant speed until it reaches the target position. This is a simulation task tracking situation. After the drone captures the target and returns it, it needs to keep track of the target and keep the target's information returning.
(3) Scanning movement: The UAV scans the rectangular area with the starting point and the target point as the diagonal point. This is to simulate the motion state of the UAV when searching for the target. Before the UAV does not capture the target, it needs to perform a relatively comprehensive scan and retrieval of the area in which it is responsible.
(4) "8"-shaped movement: The UAV will use the starting point and the target point as the center points of the two areas to perform a figure-eight cyclic movement. This is the case of simulating the coverage and search of the central area of the UAV. Same as above, the area search of the UAV can also be in the shape of "8".
(5) Ellipse movement: The UAV will take the starting point and the target point as the focus, and perform elliptical trajectory movement. This is the case of a full-area rough search in the simulation task search. When scanning and precise key area search, the drone needs to perform rough detection to find the key detection area [5].

In the PPRZM model, the occurrence probabilities of these five trajectories are different. According to actual experiments, the literature found that the three trajectories of hovering waiting, elliptical motion and scanning motion have the highest probability of occurrence during the movement of the drone. The default probabilities of the five trajectories in the team movement model are circling waiting, elliptical movement, and scanning movement set to 30%, while figure-eight movement and waypoint straight-line flight are set to 5%. However, the probabilities of these five trajectories are not immutable. We can adjust the probabilities of UAV trajectories according to the different characteristics of different services to adapt to the needs of different simulation scenarios.

2.2 Optimization and Realization of PPRZM Mobile Model

When drawing on some other mobile models, in order to better simulate the search task of the drone cluster, we divided the entire plane area into 9 areas, each area is a subset of the search task, and a random number is given to each area. An integer represents the task intensity of the area. The initial area allocation of the UAV will be evenly distributed according to the size of the random number, and the probability of the movement trajectory of the PPRZM model will be realized [6].

The implementation of the PPRZM mobile model is to modify the setdest tool of NS2. Since the setdest tool can only generate nodes with linear random motion, the five trajectories of PPRZM are linearized, and the motion trajectory diagram shown in Fig. 2 is obtained:

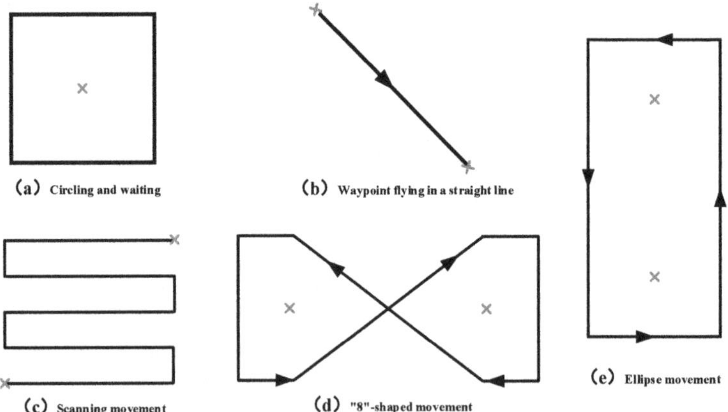

Fig. 2. PPRZM linearized motion trajectory diagram

The realization of this mobile model in this article is achieved by modifying the setdest.h and setdest.cc files of NS2, mainly by adding the realization of several drone flight trajectories (except straight trajectories), and this article reloads the file The RandomDestination() function allows it to move according to the destination position we specify and can evenly distribute the initial position of the drone according to the random number of the divided cell according to the assumption [7].

3 Simulation Test of OLSR in PPRZM Scenario

3.1 Optimization and Realization of PPRZM Mobile Model

The full name of NS2 is the second generation of network simulation simulator, which is an object-oriented, and its driver is realized and carried out using discrete time. NS2 started from the Real Network Simulator project. After years of development and absorbing the achievements of many scientific research institutions and scholars in the world, NS2 has become an excellent network simulation tool.

At present, the mainstream network simulation software includes NS2, NS3, OPNET, etc. Among them, OPNET is a relatively mature commercial simulator, which can build and simulate the network according to different styles of switches and routers, but its expensive charges are comparable to NS2. Compared with open source and free of charge, NS2 is more favored by academia.

NS2 uses two programming languages, C++ and OTcl. Among them, C++ is used to implement specific protocol simulation, because $C++$ can process various information efficiently. Because the OTcl language runs fast and is convenient to repair errors in the program, the network environment parameter settings and specific simulation scenarios are written in the OTcl language.The mutual communication between C++ and OTcl requires a third-party "translation". TclCL is a bridge between these two languages, and it is an encapsulation based on OTcl.

The tree diagrams on the left and right sides represent the hierarchical relationship of objects in C++ and OTcl, respectively, and the dotted line represents that the two can access each other. It can be seen from the figure that the objects in the same level of the two can access each other, and then the information is circulated in the structure through the tree hierarchy [7].

3.2 Simulation Parameter Setting

FANETs are different from other wireless self-organizing networks. Their movement area is the sky. The general flying height is tens of meters, and there is a high vertical height from the ground. Therefore, they are generally not affected by obstructions and belong to line-of-sight propagation. The transmission model we simulated is the Rice fading model, so the channel model in the simulation selects Two Ray Ground.

At present, the mainstream UAV is a rotary-wing UAV. Take the model DJI MATRICE 600 PRO as an example. Its flying altitude is up to 120 m, and its maximum flying speed is 65 km/h under no wind, so we set the node's movement speed range It is 5 m/s–20 m/s. Taking into account the actual situation, in order to accurately model the FANETs task search scene, the motion trajectory of the FANETs node in this paper uses an improved PPRZM model, and the probability of the motion trajectory in the PPRZM model is fine-tuned, and it is assumed that all UAV nodes are in On a unified height. The parameter list is in Table 1 below:

Table 1. NS2 simulation parameter setting

Parameter name	Parameter setting
Simulation software	NS2
Simulation duration	300 s
Mobile model	PPRZM
Propagation model	Two Ray Ground
MAC type IEEE	IEEE 802.11
Topological range	2000 m–2000 m
Number of nodes	20–60
Maximum moving speed	10 m/s–35 m/s
Communication distance	500 m
Packet size	512 Bytes

The simulated motion scene is generated by the Setdest tool of NS2. The Setdest file of NS2 has been modified above to make it a tool file for generating an improved PPRZM motion model. On this basis, you only need to type in the command line: "ns -n 50 -p 0-s 30 -t 300 -x 3000 -y 3000> scene" to generate 50 random nodes in the scene file, the maximum The moving speed is 10 m/s, and it does not stay at the destination, and the range of random movement is 3000 m × 3000 m.

The simulated traffic generator is generated by the Cbrgen tool that comes with NS2. It is a transmission generator that can generate cbr data stream and tcp data stream. Since the UAV self-organizing network is connected in a connectionless manner, it is selected for this topic It is the cbr data stream. Go to the cbrgen.tcl directory, open the terminal, and type the following command on the command line: "ns cbrgen.tcl -type cbr -nn 50 -seed 0 -mc 15> cbr", the cbr file will generate 50 for nodes up to 15 The random cbr data stream of a business link, the specific data stream rate and packet size can be modified twice in the file [7].

4 Simulation Results

The simulation simulates the impact of three parameters on the performance of the routing protocol. They are the number of UAVs, that is, the number of nodes in the network, and the service data volume of UAVs is the cbr rate of the network and the moving speed of the UAV. In order to illustrate the applicability of the OLSR routing protocol to FANETs, a comparative test with the AODV routing protocol was made.

The specific parameters of the set simulation experiment are as follows:

(1) Change the number of nodes in the network: set the number of nodes to 10, 20, 40, 60 and 100 respectively, their cbr speeds are all 1 M/s, and the maximum moving speed of the UAV is 30 m/s.

(2) Change the traffic of the network: set the cbr data stream of the network to 0.5, 2, 5, 10, 15 and 20 M/s respectively, the number of their nodes are all 30, and the maximum moving speed of the drone is 30 m/s.
(3) Change the maximum moving speed of UAV: set the maximum moving speed of nodes to 10, 15, 20, 2, 30 and 35 m/s, cbr speeds are all 2 M/s, and the number of UAV nodes is 30.

The experimental results of changing the number of nodes are shown in Fig. 3, Fig. 4, Fig. 5 and Fig. 6. The comparison diagrams of the packet delivery rate, end-to-end average delay and routing overhead of OLSR and AODV under this condition are respectively given.

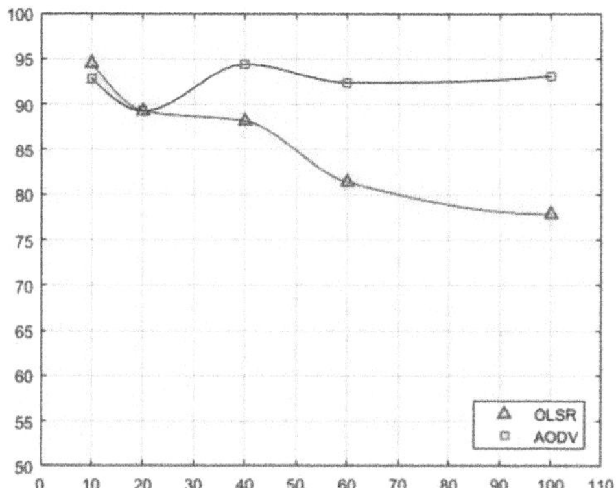

Fig. 3. Comparison of packet delivery rates between OLSR and AODV when the number of nodes increases

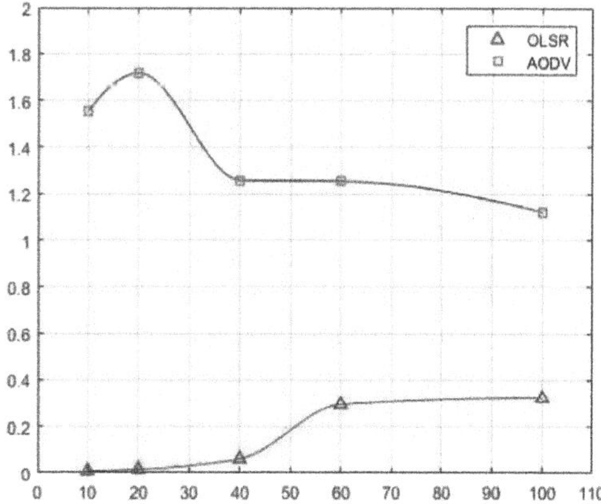

Fig. 4. Comparison of the average delay between OLSR and AODV when the number of nodes increases

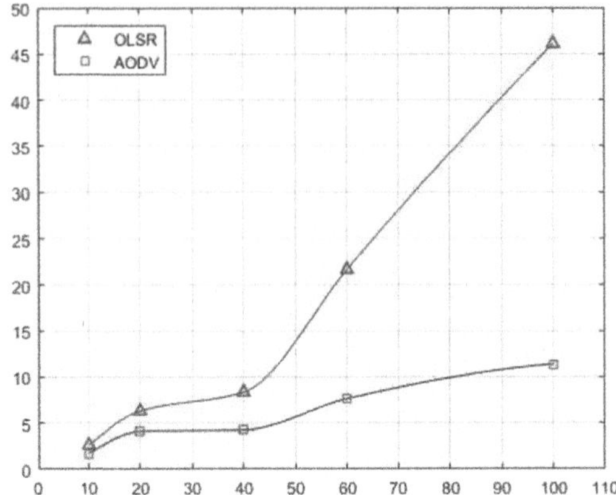

Fig. 5. Comparison of the average delay between OLSR and AODV when the number of nodes increases

From the perspective of packet delivery rate, the efficiency of OLSR gradually decreases with the increase in the number of nodes, and finally stabilizes at about 80%, and the performance of the AODV routing protocol has a larger number of nodes in terms of packet delivery rate, which is in a medium-scale The packet delivery rate under the network is significantly higher than OLSR by about 10%, which is significantly better than the OLSR routing protocol. And in the case of low density, at the beginning of a small network with 10 nodes, the routing cost of OLSR and AODV is similar, but as the number of nodes increases, the routing cost is much higher than that of the AODV protocol. This is because the increase in the number of nodes will cause the control packets sent by the OLSR routing protocol such as HELLO The number of messages and TC packets increased sharply, while the cbr packets remained unchanged, resulting in a sharp increase in routing overhead. From the perspective of average end-to-end delay, the OLSR protocol is far superior to the AODV routing protocol in either low-density scenarios or medium-to-high node density scenarios. This is because OLSR is a proactive routing, and there is no need to find a route during the sending process. AODV is an on-demand routing, so routing needs to be found during the process of sending data, so the performance of OLSR in terms of end-to-end average delay is far better than AODV. The search task of the UAV ad hoc network requires a service with low latency, especially the real-time video transmission service. In the actual UAV test in Chapter 5, the real-time video transmission experiment of the UAV formation will be tested. Because this is a scenario for UAV ad hoc network applications [7] (Fig. 6, Fig. 7, Fig. 8 and Fig. 9).

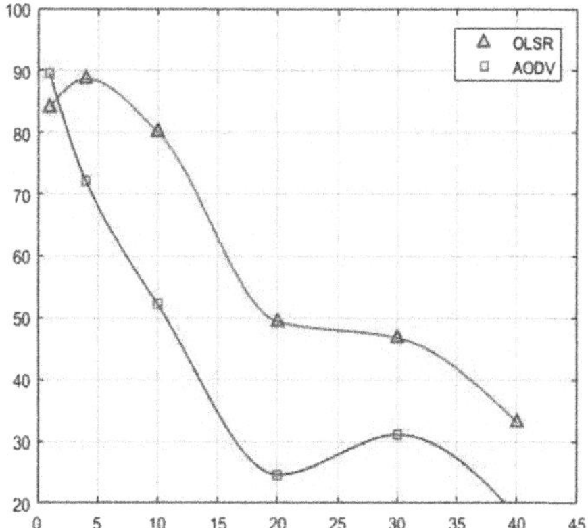

Fig. 6. Comparison of packet delivery rates between OLSR and AODV when the volume of business data increases

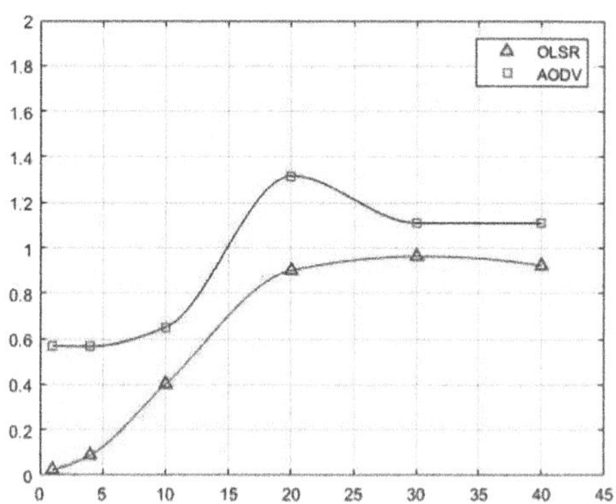

Fig. 7. Comparison of the average delay between OLSR and AODV when the volume of service data increases

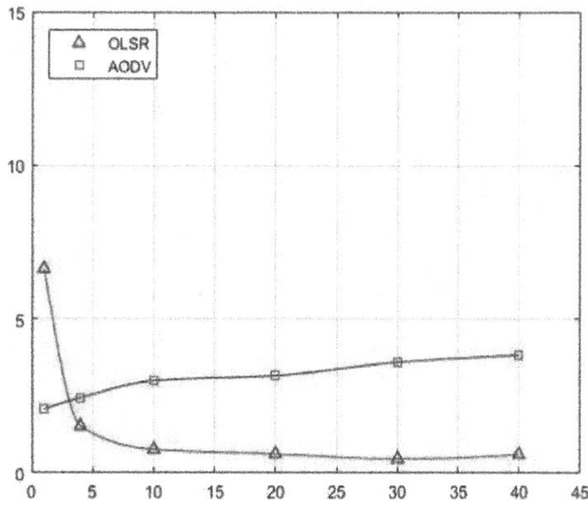

Fig. 8. Comparison of the average delay between OLSR and AODV when the volume of service data increases

The rise in business data has increased the delivery rates of OLSR and AODV, and AODV is slightly higher than the data of OLSR. This is because the rise in business data has increased the possibility of business data collisions, so the correct delivery rate of corresponding data packets has decreased. The increase in business data leads to an increase in the average end-to-end delay of AODV and OLSR. This is because the message packet of the node is transmitted by UDP. The more data, the longer the sending time, and the receiving node must wait for all data to be sent. The sequence numbers of the data packets can be sorted after completion, which leads to the end-to-end average delay side length. For routing overhead, OLSR decreases with the growth of cbr data services. This is because the growth of service data is the original definition of routing overhead compared to the size of control packets. The frequency of OLSR sending control packets is fixed, so the number of control packets Relatively fixed, and the cbr data at this time is increasing, so relatively speaking, the routing overhead of OLSR shows a rapid decline and tends to zero. As for the AODV routing protocol, it is routing on demand, so every time you send data, you need to search for routing and send control packets, so when the business data increases. Its routing overhead is almost unchanged.

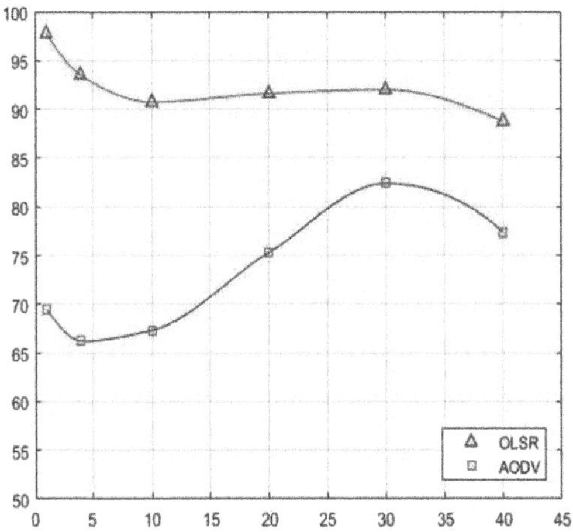

Fig. 9. Comparison of packet delivery rate between OLSR and AODV when the speed increases

It can be seen from Fig. 10 that under a medium-speed and small-scale network structure, a highly dynamic network, when the node's mobile speed is 5 m/s and 30 m/s, the packet delivery rate of OLSR is much higher than that of AODV; From the data reflected in Fig. 11, as expected, the delay of the proactive routing protocol OLSR is much lower than AODV regardless of whether the node is highly dynamic. The average end-to-end delay performance is good, and it is suitable for The routing protocol for the search task of the man-machine ad hoc network; Fig. 12, it can be seen that in terms of routing overhead, the highly dynamic UAV node causes the routing overhead of AODV and OLSR to be almost the same. So on the whole, in the scene of high-speed movement of nodes, the performance of the OLSR routing protocol is better than AODV in terms of routing overhead, packet delivery rate and average end-to-end delay.

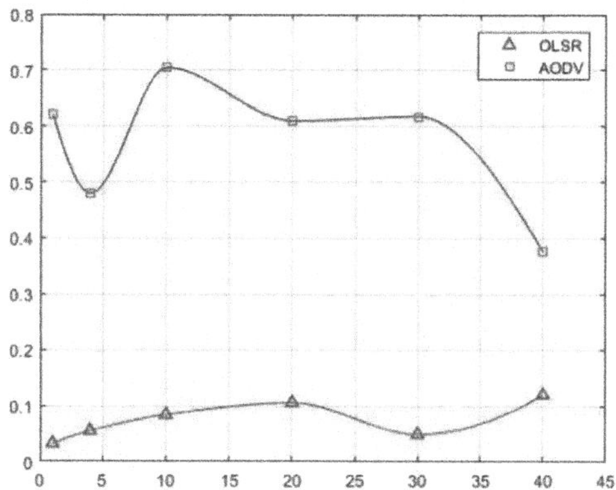

Fig. 10. Comparison of the average delay between OLSR and AODV when the speed increases

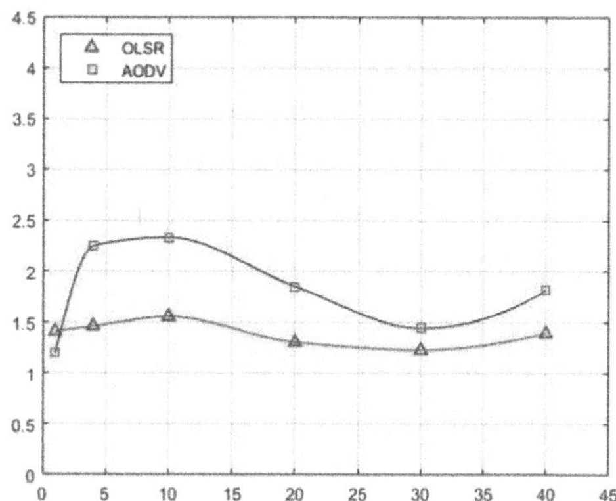

Fig. 11. Comparison of routing overhead between OLSR and AODV when the speed increases

After completing the simulation experiment and data analysis, we come to the following conclusions:

(1) In the PPRZM scenario, the OLSR routing protocol has excellent performance in a low-density, high-dynamic network, that is, a small-scale high-dynamic network, which is significantly better than the AODV protocol, so it can be used in a drone with a small number of nodes. The networking has better applications, and can have better packet delivery rates and delay guarantees in various business data transmission rates, including video transmission and other services.

(2) AODV can be applied to the UAV self-organizing network under the premise of high node density and high network topology change rate, and when the delay requirement is not high, its performance is obviously better than OLSR, but this article The background of the research is the search task of FANETs, so it is generally a small network, and the network delay requirements are high, so in the search task of FANETs, AODV is not well applicable, and the OLSR routing protocol should

be used at this time. Therefore, in the context of this subject, the OLSR routing protocol has good applicability, but it also has its limitations, such as not being suitable for medium and large-scale UAV networks.

References

1. Cao, Y.: Research on the Routing Protocol of UAV Network. Xidian University (2020)
2. Li, C., Yang, Y., Xiao, G., Xie, Y., Tang, X., Zhao, Q.: Research on the routing protocol of node-intensive UAV ad hoc network. Ship Electr. Eng. **41**(03), 93–96+101 (2021)
3. Hu, C.: Research on OLSR Routing Protocol of UAV Ad Hoc Network. Chongqing University of Posts and Telecommunications (2020)
4. Prajapati, S., Patel, N., Patel, R.; Optimizing performance of OLSR protocol using energy based MPR selection in MANET. In: 2015 Fifth International Conference on Communication Systems and Network Technologies, pp. 268–272. IEEE, Gwalior (2015)
5. Chbib, F., Khalil, A., Fahs, W., Chbib, R., Raad, A.: Improvement of OLSR protocol by using basics up MPR and routing table mechanisms. In: 2018 International Arab Conference on Information Technology (ACIT), pp. 1–6. IEEE, Werdanye (2018)
6. Jiaqi, W., Zhi, R., Lei, W., Zijun, Z.: A minimum MPR selection algorithm based on link stability. Small Microcomputer Syst. **41**(11), 2386–2391 (2020)
7. Halim, B., Ahmed, H., Nada, M., Mohammed, S.: Improvement of OLSR protocol using the hello message scheme based on neighbors mobility. J. Comms. **15**(7), 551–557 (2020)

Discussion on the Application of 5G Technologies in Data Link Network of UAV Formation

Yu Zhang(✉), Kai Zhou, and Dongwu Mu

Aviation University of Air Force, Changchun 130022, Jilin, China
Zhangyu1a9z@163.com

Abstract. UAV formation is a research focus currently. Data link network plays a key role in the information exchange in UAV formation, but there are many technical problems to be solved. With the advantages of high speed, low latency and large capacity, 5G communication has been commercialized, and some key technologies of 5G have provided idea inspirations and application feasibilities for data link network of UAV formation. This paper analyzes the characteristics and advantages of key technologies of 5G, such as new network architecture, D2D communication, millimeter wave communication and Massive MIMO, discusses their application methods in data link network of UAV formation, and gives a suggestion on the development of data link network of UAV formation.

Keywords: UAV formation · Data link network · New network architecture · D2D communication · Millimeter wave communication · Massive MIMO

1 Introduction

In recent years, unmanned aerial vehicles (UAVs) have developed rapidly, and UAV formation has become a research focus because of its advantages over a single UAV. UAV data link implements the communication in UAV system. The current UAV system generally takes the mode that one station controls one UAV or that one station controls multiple UAVs, in which the telecontrol data, telemetry data and sensor data are transmitted between the UAV and the ground control station (GCS) through the data link [1]. In the case above, the data link only needs communication between one GCS and one UAV instead of the network communication between UAVs. As UAV formation becomes a developing trend, the traditional data link needs to be extended to data link network to meet the data exchange requirements in a UAV formation. In addition, compared with other wireless networks, data link network of UAV formation is very special, because nodes in this kind of network have strong autonomy, strong mobility, high collaboration requirements, high security requirements and limited energy.

5G technologies are the fifth generation of mobile communication technology [2]. Compared with 4G communication, 5G communication has the advantages of high speed, low latency, low cost, large capacity and energy saving. 5G technologies are

© ICST Institute for Computer Sciences, Social Informatics and Telecommunications Engineering 2022
Published by Springer Nature Switzerland AG 2022. All Rights Reserved
S. Shi et al. (Eds.): 6GN 2021, LNICST 439, pp. 29–37, 2022.
https://doi.org/10.1007/978-3-031-04245-4_3

applicable to three application scenarios: enhanced Mobile BroadBand (eMBB), ultra-Reliable Low-Latency Communication (uRLLC) and massive Machine-Type Communication (mMTC) [3]. 5G communication involves some key technologies, such as new network architecture, D2D communication [4], millimeter wave communication [5], massive MIMO [6] and so on. The *White Paper on 5G UAV Application* released by IMT-2020 (5G) Promotion Group gives the application case of 5G cellular network (on the ground) for industrial and low-altitude UAV formation [7]. However, the given case only considers the industrial UAV formation which has low performance, carries the same payloads and flies below 200 m, while the data link network of military UAV formation is not considered. At present, the data link network of military UAV formation is not supported by the 5G cellular network on the ground. Even so, some key technologies of 5G provide idea inspirations and application feasibilities for data link network of military UAV formation.

In this paper, the technical requirements in data link network of UAV formation and the technical principles of advanced communication technologies are analyzed, the application feasibility of key technologies of 5G is discussed, and the suggest on the develop of the data link network of UAV formation is given. It should be noted that the data link networks discussed below are all aimed at military UAV formation.

2 Enlightenment from New Network Architecture of 5G

2.1 New Network Architecture of 5G

A base station generally consists of three parts: BaseBand processing Unit (BBU), Remote Radio Unit (RRU) and antenna. In 1G and 2G communication, a BBU and corresponding RRU are placed in a same cabinet. In 3G and 4G communication, a BBU and corresponding RRU are separated, and the RRU is placed close to the antenna. In 5G communication, RRUs are closer to the antennas than before, and multiple BBUs are concentrated in the central machine room [8]. In addition, 5G network architecture adopts Network Function Virtualization (NFV) and Software Defined Network (SDN) technology to get more flexibility and better performance. NFV decouples software and hardware. SDN separates the control function and the forwarding function [9]. The new network architecture in 5G communication can not be applied directly to data link network of UAV formation, but the idea of fine function-division is enlightening for data link network of UAV formation.

2.2 A Network Architecture Based on Air Base Station for UAV Formation

Currently, a military UAV often undertakes multiple tasks such as reconnaissance, attacking and communication. As a result, a UAV needs to carry multiple payloads and communication equipments, resulting in a large size of a UAV. This leads to lots of negative impacts on the maneuverability, stealth and endurance of a UAV. In data link network of UAV formation, each UAV is a node. We may assign as few tasks as possible for each node, such as having each node carry a single payload and using team's power to complete all tasks. Figure 1 shows an architecture based on air base station for data link network of UAV formation. In Fig. 1, all nodes are divided into three categories according to their task-division: a reconnaissance cluster (cluster A), an attacking cluster (cluster B) and air base stations (① and ②).

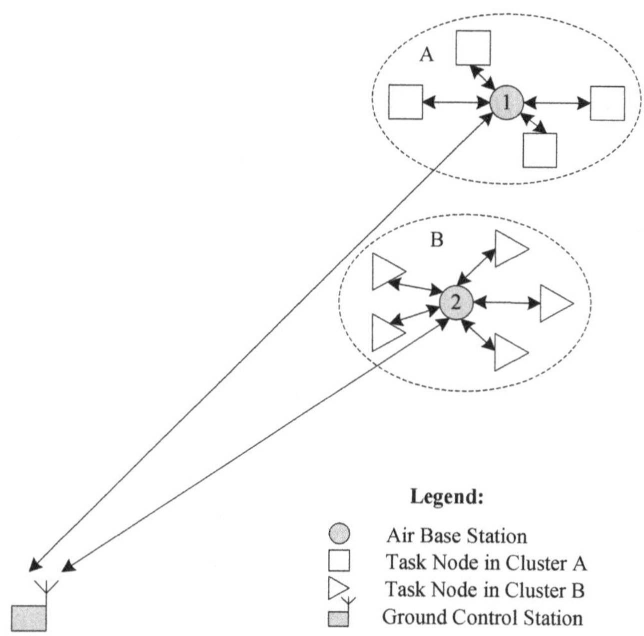

Fig. 1. An architecture based on air base station for data link network of UAV formation

The communication backbone nodes act as air base stations, and they are only responsible for the communication. Air base stations carry equipments for communication, positioning and navigation rather than for reconnaissance or attacking. For an air base station, there are three types of communication objects: a task node (refers to a reconnaissance node or an attacking node), the GCS and another air base station. In addition, air base stations also act as the cluster heads of the reconnaissance cluster and the attacking cluster. That is, the task nodes move following their cluster head to keep the formation. In Fig. 1, the air base station ① is responsible the following tasks: transmitting the telecontrol data from the GCS to task nodes in cluster A; transmitting the telemetry data and sensor data from task nodes in cluster A to the GCS; transmitting formation collaboration data between task nodes in cluster A; transmitting cross-cluster collaboration data between self and air base station ②. The air base station ② is responsible the following tasks: transmitting the telecontrol data from the GCS to task nodes in cluster B; transmitting the telemetry data from task nodes in cluster B to the GCS; transmitting formation collaboration data between task nodes in cluster B; transmitting cross-cluster collaboration data between self and air base station ①.

The network architecture above has the advantages of simplicity and practicality. Because a task node is close to others in a cluster, and only just the collaboration data is required to be exchanged between task nodes in a cluster, that the collaboration data between nodes in a cluster are transmitted through the cluster head is feasible. So there is no direct communication between task nodes. This architecture reduces the computing load and traffic load of task nodes, simplifies formation collaboration process, and the task nodes do not even need satellite positioning and navigation equipment. However, this architecture also has disadvantages, that is, because of the star topology of each cluster, the air base stations are easy to become the key targets and traffic bottlenecks. Once an air base station collapses, the whole cluster collapses. Therefore, it needs to consider backup and redundancy for air base stations.

In some earlier studies, cluster heads in UAV formation have been mentioned, such as in paper [1]. But those cluster heads are essentially powerful UAV leaders, which are tasked with reconnaissance and attacking. The cluster heads in this paper are 5G air base stations, which are communication infrastructures built on UAV platforms. In the future, 5G air base stations will evolve into the air counterpart of the ground mobile cellular network and provide third-party communication service for air customers.

3 Application of D2D Communication

3.1 D2D Communication

D2D communication has attracted lots of attention since the age of 4G communication, and has become one of the key technologies of 5G communication. In its early application, D2D communication is mainly used to solve the problem of overload of base stations in the cellular network. D2D communication refers to direct communication between devices without any base station [10]. D2D communication uses the frequency range of the cellular network, and its communication distance is farther than WIFI and Bluetooth. D2D communication has the characteristics of high spectrum utilization, high speed, low latency and low power consumption [11]. D2D communication not only reduces the load of base station, but also improves the robustness of communication network, which is important for data link network of UAV formation. At present, there is no D2D communication protocol for UAV formation, but there are D2D communication protocols for cars and other ground users. These protocols can be modified for UAV formation.

3.2 Application of D2D Communication in Data Link Network of UAV Formation

Task nodes in a cluster can directly exchange formation collaboration data by D2D communication, and then adjust respective parameters such as the current speed, height, route and so on. Furthermore, with the development of UAV autonomy, task nodes can also exchange more data which can help other task nodes to finish a task. Figure 2 shows an architecture for data link network of UAV formation using D2D communication. In Fig. 2, all nodes are divided into three categories according to their task-division: a reconnaissance cluster (cluster A), an attacking cluster (cluster B) and air base stations (①–⑩).

There are two differences between Fig. 2 and Fig. 1. In Fig. 2, either a single air base station or a group of several air base stations can act as a cluster head. When a group of several air base stations acts as a cluster head, the fine task-division can be determined either in advanced or on the spot according respective traffic load. Air base stations are not only responsible for cross-cluster communication and cluster-GCS communication, but also for relay communication under special circumstances. This can provide routing redundancy for data link network. D2D communication can be used to communicate directly between task nodes in a cluster.

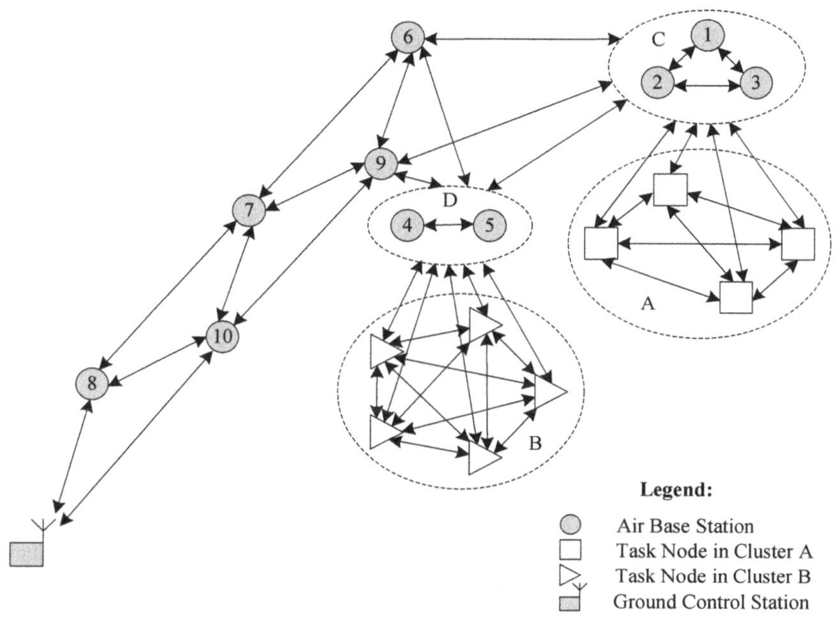

Fig. 2. An architecture for data link network of UAV formation using D2D communication

The network architecture above has the advantages of flexibility and reliability. Since backup and redundancy have been considered for air base stations, the collapse of one air base station will not cause the collapse of the whole cluster. When an air base station collapses, other backup air base stations can continue to complete the communication task, which increases the robustness of the network under bad environment. However, the direct communication between task nodes in a cluster also increases the computation load and traffic load, which makes the formation collaboration process more complex. In addition, each task node needs to carry satellite positioning and navigation equipment for keeping the formation.

4 Application of Millimeter Wave Communication and Massive MIMO

4.1 Millimeter Wave Communication

In 5G communication, due to the requirement of broadband, large-capacity transmission and anti-jamming communication, millimeter wave communication has become a very important technology. However, millimeter wave communication is not a unique technology of 5G. Millimeter wave communication is widely used in radar, guidance, tactical and strategic communication, electronic countermeasure and so on. Millimeter wave is a kind of electromagnetic wave whose frequency is between 30 GHz–300 GHz and whose wavelength is between 1 mm–10 mm. Millimeter wave communication refers to the communication that takes millimeter wave as the medium. Millimeter wave communication has rich spectrum resources, narrow beam and good directivity. In addition, the antennas for millimeter wave communication have smaller volume, lighter weight and lower power consumption than usual antennas [12]. However, millimeter wave communication also has disadvantages. Millimeter wave transmitting in the atmosphere undergoes frequency-selective attenuation, and the rainfall has great influence on the quality of millimeter wave communication. Therefore, most of the application researches on millimeter wave communication focus on several atmosphere window frequencies and several attenuation peak frequencies [13].

4.2 Massive MIMO

Traditional Multiple Input Multiple Output (MIMO) technology generally include two categories: one is spatial multiplexing technology for increasing the channel capacity and spectrum efficiency, by which data for different users are transmitted on respective channels; another is space diversity technology for improving the communication quality in multipath attenuation [14], by which multiple antennas transmit multiple copies of a same data flow. Massive MIMO wireless communication was proposed by Marzetta from Bell Laboratory [15]. The foundation of massive MIMO communication is that, on the multi-user channels, additive white Gaussian noise and small-scale attenuation disappear gradually with the increase of the number of base station antennas. Massive MIMO communication needs to configure an antenna array which consists of dozens or even hundreds of individually controlled antenna elements in base station. 3D beam forming technology can be used to increase the gain of the antenna array. Massive MIMO technology is one of the key technologies of 5G, B5G and 6G communications.

4.3 Application of Millimeter Wave Communication and Massive MIMO in Data Link Network of UAV Formation

Figure 3 shows a data link network of UAV formation using millimeter wave communication and massive MIMO. In Fig. 3, all nodes are divided into two groups: one group consists of the reconnaissance cluster A and the air-base-station cluster C, and the other group consists of the attacking cluster B and the air-base-station cluster D. Communications inside each group (in the ellipses with shadow in Fig. 3) use millimeter wave and massive MIMO antennas, while cross-group communications and group-GCS communications use traditional radio wave and traditional antennas. Because in each group of data link network of UAV formation, the nodes are close to each other and the data traffic is large, such application method in Fig. 3 can make full use of the advantages of millimeter wave communication and massive MIMO.

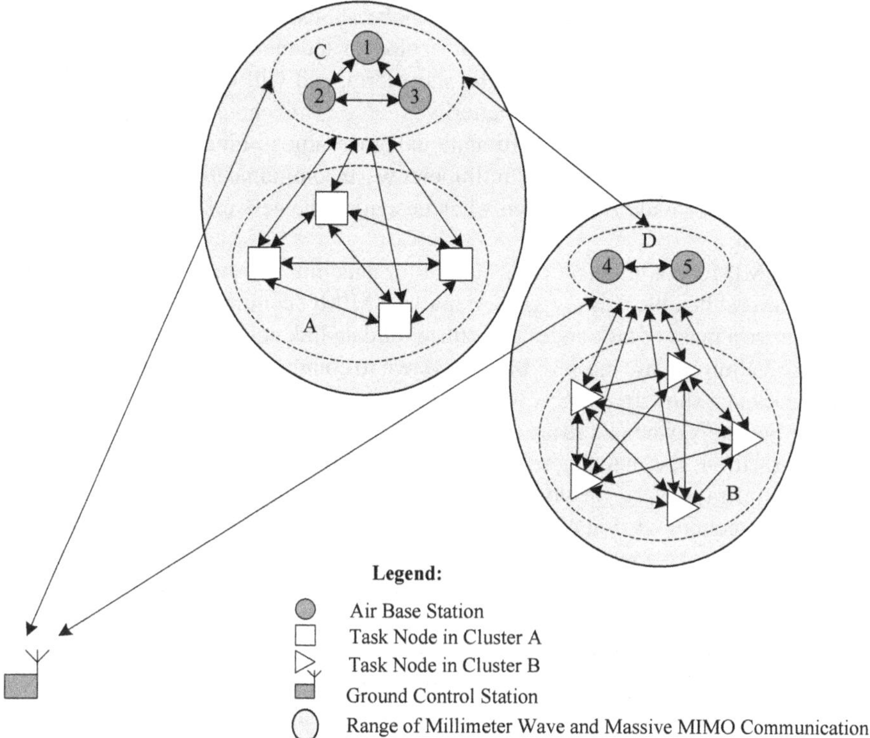

Fig. 3. Data link network of UAV formation using millimeter wave communication and massive MIMO

Millimeter wave communication is a promising technology for data link network of UAV formation. It has the characteristics of large communication capacity, good anti-intercept and anti-jamming performance, and its small antennas are easy to integrate. First of all, the available bandwidth of millimeter wave communication is much wider than the available bandwidth of microwave. The effective bandwidth of millimeter wave communication near several atmosphere windows adds up to more than 100G. Considering the use of channel multiplexing technologies such as SDMA and orthogonal polarization, the channel capacity is even larger. So millimeter wave communication is suitable for transmitting broadband images and videos in data link network of UAV formation. In Fig. 3, each reconnaissance node in cluster A can transmit broadband data to an air base station in cluster C through millimeter wave communication. Secondly, the data link network of UAV formation requires the abilities of anti-intercept and anti-jamming, which the millimeter wave communication is good at. Because the millimeter wave has a short propagation distance in the atmosphere, the millimeter wave signal will become very weak beyond this distance, which increases the difficulty for opponents to intercept or jam. Moreover, the beam is very narrow and the sidelobe is very low in millimeter wave communication, which further reduces the probability of being intercepted and jammed. Thirdly, millimeter wave has strong penetration ability in dust and smoke, and can pass through dust and smoke almost without attenuation. Under the environment of strong scatter caused by explosion and metal chaff, millimeter wave communication will only attenuate in the short term, and will restore communication soon with the diffusion and fall of scattering source. This characteristic is beneficial for UAV formation under highly confrontational environment. Finally, in order to solve the problem of rainfall attenuation of millimeter wave communication, sufficient power attenuation margin should be reserved when designing the network of millimeter wave communication.

Massive MIMO communication is cut out for data link network of UAV formation. There are several flexible ways to applied massive MIMO communication here. Firstly, when there are a mass of task nodes in a cluster of data link network of UAV formation, the air base station can use massive MIMO system to communicate simultaneously with all task nodes in a same frequency, which increases the channel capacity and spectrum efficiency. Secondly, when there are a few of task nodes in a cluster of data link network of UAV formation, the antenna array of massive MIMO system can be divided into several small arrays, each of which can communicate with a task node and use 3D beam forming technology. Finally, massive MIMO communication and millimeter wave communication can be applied in combination. There is a strong requirement of antenna miniaturization for UAV, so it needs to be avoided that the size of antenna array is too big. The size of an antenna element depends on the wavelength of the transmitted electromagnetic wave. The interval between two adjacent antenna elements is usually designed to be half of the wavelength of transmitted electromagnetic wave to avoid interference. It follows that the millimeter wave is cut out for massive MIMO system. Because the wavelength of millimeter wave is very short, the corresponding antenna array can be designed to be a small one. Furthermore, the beam forming gain of antenna array can compensate the atmosphere attenuation of millimeter wave.

5 Conclusions

Many contents of this paper need to be discussed further. The design of data link network with good performance and great practicability is very difficult. Both direct use and indirect reference of all advanced technologies are relatively convenient routes in the design of data link network of UAV formation. It is greatly worthy of our research to apply 5G technologies in UAV formation.

References

1. Cao, K.: Research on Networking Technology of UAV Data Link Network. Xidian University, Xi'an, China (2014)
2. Shafi, M., et al.: 5G: a tutorial overview of standards, trials, challenges, deployment and practice. IEEE J. Sel. Areas Commun. **35**(6), 1201–1221 (2017)
3. ITU-R: IMT vision-framework and overall objectives of the future development of IMT for 2020 and beyond (2015). http://www.itu.int/rec/R-REC-M.2083-0-201509-I/en
4. Fodor, G., et al.: Design aspects of network assisted device-to-device communications. IEEE Commun. Mag. **50**(3), 170–177 (2012)

5. Rappaport, T.S., et al.: Millimeter wave mobile communications for 5G cellular: it will work! IEEE Access **1**, 335–349 (2013)
6. Rusek, F., Persson, D., Lau, B.K., Larsson, E.G., Marzetta, T.L., Tufvesson, F.: Scaling up MIMO: opportunities and challenges with very large arrays. IEEE Signal Process. Mag. **30**(1), 40–60 (2013)
7. IMT-2020: (5G) Promotion Group: White Paper on 5G UAV Application (2018). http://www.imt2020.org.cn/zh/documents/download/102
8. CSDN Blog: 5G Network Architecture (2021). https://blog.csdn.net/k916631305/article/details/107523269. Accessed 22 July 2021
9. IMT-2020: (5G) Promotion Group: White Paper on 5G Network Technology Architecture (2018). http://www.imt2020.org.cn/zh/documents/download/18
10. Zhihong, Q., Xue, W.: Reviews of D2D technology for 5G communication networks. J. Commun. **37**(7), 1–14 (2016)
11. Zhang, Z.: Research on Establishment Mechanism and Resource Reuse for Device- to- Device Communication in 5G Cellular Networks. Southwest Jiaotong University, Chengdu, China (2017)
12. Wu, B.: Research on Key Technologies of Hybrid Precoding for of Millimeter Wave MIMO System. Southeast University, Nanjing, China (2015)
13. Xiaohai, W.: Development and application of millimeter-wave communication. Telecommunications Inform. **10**, 19–21 (2007)
14. Weng, J.: Research on Wideband Millimeter-wave MIMO Antennas. South China University of Technology, Guangzhou, China (2018)
15. Marzetta, T.L.: Non-cooperative cellular wireless with unlimited numbers of base station antennas. IEEE Trans. Wireless Commun. **9**(11), 3590–3600 (2010)

Network Coding-Based Capacity Optimization for Space Dynamic Network

Zhicong Zhong, Ruisong Wang, Ruofei Ma, Wenjing Kang, and Gongliang Liu(✉)

Harbin Institute of Technology, Weihai 264209, Shandong, China
{maruofei,kwjqq,liugl}@hit.edu.cn

Abstract. Network coding (NC) scheme can effectively improve system capacity. Although NC has been widely studied and applied in terrestrial wireless networks, these researches are not suitable for space dynamic networks because of the dynamic topology and limited on-board resources. In order to make better use of on-board resource to improve the system capacity, a capacity optimization scheme is designed for space dynamic network based on network coding and power allocation. Firstly, considering a multicast scenario with single-source and multi-destination in a satellite network, and establishing a system transmission model based on linear network coding and limited power resources for the objective to maximize the multicast rate of the system. Through the analysis of the constraint conditions, the optimization problem is transformed into two subproblems, which are to solve the maximum flow of each destination node and maximize the capacity of the key links. Finally we design a heuristic algorithm to solve these problems. Simulation results demonstrate the effectiveness of the proposed algorithm.

Keywords: Network coding · Multicast · Capacity · Power allocation · Satellite network

1 Introduction

The satellite network bears the important role of extending the ground network and expanding the communication range. Through the satellite network, it can achieve multi-dimensional coverage of air, space, ground and sea, and provide people with more efficient and comprehensive services.

However, the satellite network has the characteristics of dynamic changes in topological structure, long inter-satellite link (ISL) distance, high bit error rate, multi-hop connection, and limited resources on the satellite, which brings challenges to the research and improvement of satellite network transmission performance [1, 2]. Therefore, an efficient and reliable routing strategy is a necessary condition for achieving high-quality communication in satellite networks. In recent years, the emergence of network coding

© ICST Institute for Computer Sciences, Social Informatics and Telecommunications Engineering 2022
Published by Springer Nature Switzerland AG 2022. All Rights Reserved
S. Shi et al. (Eds.): 6GN 2021, LNICST 439, pp. 38–50, 2022.
https://doi.org/10.1007/978-3-031-04245-4_4

(NC) theory, especially the combination of coding perception ideas and network transmission technology [3–5], provides new ideas for the optimization of satellite network routing strategies.

Network coding is considered an extension of the traditional 'store-and-forward' routing technology. Before the advent of network coding, the only task of nodes in the network was to receive and forward data packets to maintain the integrity of the packets. The NC scheme allows the node to encode multiple received data packets into a single encoded packet before forwarding, which can effectively increase the transmission rate of the network [6, 7].

The existing literature on network coding is more focused on the ground wireless network environment research. However, there are big differences in the topological structure, change rules, link characteristics, etc. of the ground network and the satellite network, which leads to the fact that the existing network coding transmission scheme cannot be directly applied to the satellite network environment. In recent years, there have been some researches on the application of network coding in satellite networks. Xu *et al.* [8] introduced the DCAR scheme to the satellite communication network, and conducted a preliminary exploration of the two-layer satellite network using the coding-aware routing algorithm. Tang *et al.* [9] proposed NCMCR protocol, which uses intra-flow network coding to dynamically and coordinately transmit different parts of the same data flow along multiple disjoint paths. Giambene *et al.* [10] studied the combination of network coding and transmission protocol for mobile satellite applications. Godoy *et al.* [11] discussed the application of network coding in two typical satellite network scenarios, namely downlink multi-beam satellite network and multi-source multicast satellite network. However, the above work did not pay attention to the situation of limited power resources. When the total transmission power of a single satellite is limited, how to use network coding to increase the capacity of the satellite network is the focus of our research.

In this paper, we propose a network-coding based multicast capacity optimization scheme for satellite network. Firstly, we consider a multicast scenario with single source and multiple destinations in a satellite network. In this scenario, the source node needs to send the same piece of data to multiple destination nodes, and the destination nodes receive the data at the same rate which is called the multicast rate. This paper aims to maximize the multicast rate when the power resources of satellite nodes are limited. In order to solve this problem, the key links is defined and the problem is transformed into two sub-problems of seeking the maximum flow of each destination node and maximizing the capacity of the key links. Then solve them by utilizing the classic maximum flow algorithm and convex optimization tools. The performance of the proposed scheme is evaluated via simulations. The results demonstrate that the application of network coding in satellite networks is feasible, and the optimization method by combining network coding and power allocation can greatly improve the multicast capacity of satellite networks.

The remainder of the paper is organized as follows. In Sect. 2, we describe the system model and problem formulation. The optimization algorithm is introduced in Sect. 3. The simulation results are analyzed in Sect. 4. Finally, we conclude this paper in Sect. 5.

2 System Model and Problem Statement

2.1 System Model

This paper considers a LEO satellite network consists of M parallel orbital planes and each plane is composed of N satellites. Adjacent satellites in the same orbital plane are connected by intra-plane ISLs, and adjacent satellites in different orbits are connected by inter-plane ISLs, as shown in Fig. 1. In our target environments, a source node s transmits data to the destination node set D through the ISLs. During transmission, the NC scheme is applied to process data packets to improve network capacity. When the transmission starts, the source node divides the original packets into multiple batches containing a fixed number of packets, and then linearly combines the original packets of each batch for transmission. After receiving the coded packets, the intermediate nodes perform a new linear combination of the coded packets to generate new coded packets and then send them out. Finally, the coded packets will not be forwarded after reaching the destination nodes. If the destinations receive a sufficient number of linearly independent packets, they can decode to get the original packets.

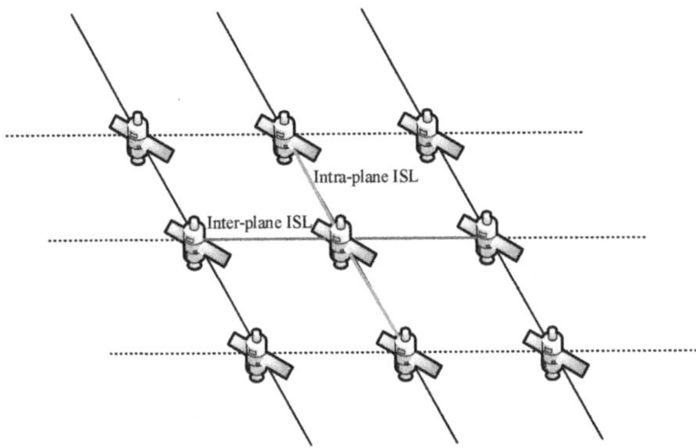

Fig. 1. A LEO satellite network topology

Moreover, we assume that all ISLs have the same bandwidth B and the total transmission power of each satellite P_{total} is the same. If the transmission power allocated to a ISL is $P < P_{total}$, the maximum transmission capacity of the link c can be calculated by Shannon Theory:

$$c = B\log_2(1 + \alpha P) \tag{1}$$

where α is the link quality factor, and we define it as follows:

$$\alpha = \frac{G}{kTBL_f} \tag{2}$$

where G is the total transmission gain containing the transmitting gain and the receiving gain, $k = 1.38 \times 10^{-23}$ J/K is the Boltzmann constant, T is the Equivalent Noise

Temperature, and L_f is the free space transmission loss which is related to link length d and transmission frequency f:

$$L_f = (4\pi df/\mathcal{C})^2 \tag{3}$$

where $\mathcal{C} = 3 \times 10^8$ m/s is the speed of light.

In this paper, it is assumed that each ISL has the same parameters except the link length. Therefore, the link quality factor is determined by the link length d.

The method of time evolution graph is used to depict the dynamic changes of the satellite network in the static graph of discrete time slots. Therefore, in the research process, It is only necessary to study the general model in one time slot and then apply it in each time slot.

In a time slot, the satellite network can be considered as a static topology, and be modeled as a directed graph $\mathcal{G}(\mathcal{V}, \mathcal{E}, C)$, Where $\mathcal{V}$ is the set of satellites, $\mathcal{E} = \{(u, v)|u, v \in \mathcal{V}\}$ is the set of ISLs, and $C = \{c_{u,v}|u, v \in \mathcal{V}\}$ is the set of link capacity. If the ISL can be established between two nodes, there will be two parallel and opposite sides between them. Because the link capacity of the two sides may be different, a bidirectional link cannot be used between two nodes to represent two reverse edges.

2.2 Problem Formulation

Based on the above description of the system model, it can be determined that the problem to be solved in our research is to utilize the linear network coding (LNC) scheme to improve the multicast capacity of the satellite network in a time slot under the condition of limited power. The specific description of the problem is as follows:

$$\text{Maximize} \quad R \tag{4}$$

Subject to:

$$\delta(u, v) = \delta(v, u) = \{0, 1\}, \quad \forall (u, v), (v, u) \in \mathcal{E} \tag{5}$$

$$c_{u,v} = B\log_2(1 + \alpha_{u,v}P_{u,v}) \cdot \delta(u, v) \tag{6}$$

$$\sum_{\{v:(u,v)\in\mathcal{E}\}} P_{u,v} \le P_{total} \tag{7}$$

$$\sum_{\{u:(u,v)\in\mathcal{E}\}} r^d_{u,v} - \sum_{\{w:(v,w)\in\mathcal{E}\}} r^d_{v,w} = \begin{cases} R^d, & v = d, \forall d \in D \\ -R^d, & v = s, \forall d \in D \\ 0, & v = \mathcal{V} - \{s, D\} \end{cases} \tag{8}$$

$$r^d_{u,v} \le r_{u,v}, \forall (u, v) \in \mathcal{E}, \forall d \in D \tag{9}$$

$$R \le R^d, \forall d \in D \tag{10}$$

$$0 \le r_{u,v} \le c_{u,v}, \forall (u, v) \in \mathcal{E} \tag{11}$$

$$0 \le r_{u,v}^{d} \le c_{u,v}, \forall (u, v) \in \mathcal{E} \tag{12}$$

Objective function (4) states that the target of our research is to maximize the multicast capacity of the system. Constraint (4) is the is the constraint of link building between satellite nodes. If the link between node u and node v exists, $\delta(u, v) = \delta(v, u) = 1$, and 0 otherwise. In this paper, we determine whether the link exists by determining the visible relationship between nodes. Constraint (6) is the constraint of link capacity, where B is the link bandwidth, $P_{u,v}$ is the transmission power from node u to node v. Constraint (7) is the constraint of satellite total transmission power, which means that the power of each transmission link of node u is limited by the total power. Constraint (8) is the network flow conservation constraint for each flow between source node s and each destination node. In our hypothetical scenario, the source node only sends packets but does not receive packets, and the destination nodes only receive packets but do not forward packets. Moreover, R^d is the reaching rate of destination node d, which denotes the capacity of each flow from s to each destination d. As shown in constraint (9), $r_{u,v}^{d}$ denotes the flow rate on the link (u,v) for the data delivery from s to the destination node d, and $r_{u,v}$ is the actual flow rate of the coded packets transmitted on link (u,v), which should be no less than $\max\limits_{d \in D} r_{u,v}^{d}$. Constraint (10) combines with objective (4), which means $R = \min\limits_{d \in D} R^d$ and R is the multicast capacity of the system. Constraint (11) and (12) show the constraint of link transmission rate.

The above optimization problem is a nonlinear integer programming problem with many complex variables and constraints, which means that it is difficult to solve. In this paper, we disassembled the optimization problem and transformed it into two less complex problems for solution.

3 Algorithm Design

Firstly, according to the constraint (10), objective (4) can be modeled as the following problem:

$$\begin{aligned} &\max \ \min_{d \in D} R^d \\ &s.t. \ \ (5) - (9), (11) - (12) \end{aligned} \tag{13}$$

It denotes that the optimization goal is to maximize the unicast rate from the source node to each destination node. And then the multicast rate is the minimal unicast rate of the destination nodes. Because with LNC, the coded packets transmitted on each ISL are available to each destination node, the multicast rate is only limited by the one with the minimal unicast rate among the destination nodes. When the capacity of each link in the network is determined, the problem is a typical maximum flow problem which can be solved by using the traditional maximum flow algorithm.

It can be seen from constraints (8), (11) and (12) that the link transmission rate is limited by the link capacity, thus affecting the throughput from the source node to the destination node. Therefore, the key to optimizing the maximum flow of each destination node is to increase the link capacity on the maximum flow path from the source node to each destination node. Among these links, the system capacity is restricted by some links whose link capacity is fully used and the remaining capacity is 0.

As shown in Fig. 2, node *S* has three paths through relay nodes *R1*, *R2* and *R3* to transmit data to node *D*, where the black arcs denote the link capacity, and the blue arcs denote the maximum flow multipath routing. Assuming that the initial link capacity of each link is 10, and in the maximum flow path, the amount of data transmitted by the source node to *R1*, *R2* and *R3* is 10, 5 and 8 respectively. Obviously, the available link capacity from node S to *R2* and *R3* is left and the available link capacity to *R1* is 0. It denotes that in the case of transmitting as much data as possible to the destination node, links (*S*, *R2*) and (*S*, *R3*) still have redundant capacity, while link (*S*, *R1*) may not have enough capacity. If the capacity of the link (*S*, *R1*) is increased, it may be able to transmit more data to the destination node. So the maximum flow from *S* to *D* is limited by the upper limit of the link capacity of (*S*, *R1*). Only by increasing the link capacity of *R1*, it is possible to improve the throughput from *S* to *D*. In this paper, we define these links as *key links*.

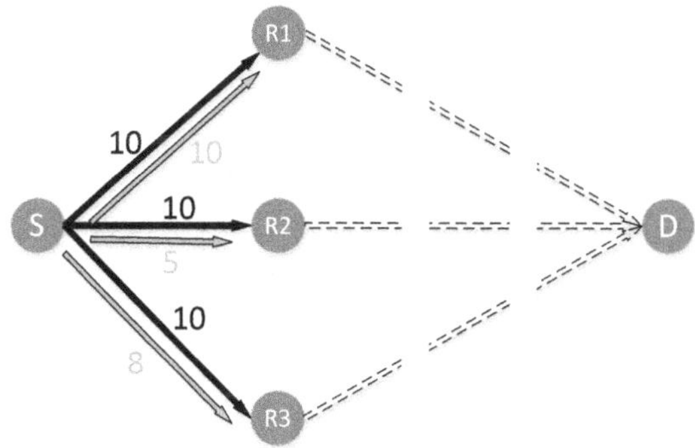

Fig. 2. An example of key links

Let *L* be the set of key links from the source node to the destination nodes. Then the problem can be transformed into:

$$\begin{aligned} \max \sum_{\{v:(u,v)\in L\}} c_{u,v} \\ s.t.\ c_{u,v} = B\log_2(1+\alpha_{u,v}P_{u,v}), \\ \sum_{\{v:(u,v)\in \mathcal{E}\}} P_{u,v} \le P_{total} \end{aligned} \tag{14}$$

It denotes that the power resources of each satellite node should tend to be more allocated to the key links, so that the link capacity of the key links can be improved, and the bottleneck restricting the increase of the system capacity can be broken. Therefore, the problem is transformed into a typical power allocation optimization problem.

For the solution of this problem, it can be specifically divided into 3 cases:

The transmit links of a node are all in the set of key links. It means that there is no remaining power resource for this node, so there is no need to re-allocate it.

There is only 1 key link in the transmit links of a node. It means that the power resources of the other transmission links of the node are excessive. Under the condition that the transmission rate of other links is not lower than the current value, all the remaining power resources are allocated to the key link.

There are more than one key links in the transmission link of a node, and one or more links *have remaining capacity.* Let the maximum transmission rate of key links be $RK_i(i = 1, 2, ..., N)$, where N is the number of the key links. And let the maximum transmission rate of the links which have remaining capacity be $RE_j(j = 1, 2, ..., M)$, where M is the number of the links. The transmission rate of these links in the max-flow multipath routing is $RE_j^{\min}$. Then the remaining power resources are allocated to the key links under the condition that the maximum transmission rate of other links is not lower than $RE_j^{\min}$. We have:

$$\max \sum_{i=1}^{N} RK_i \tag{15}$$

Subject to:

$$RE_j = RE_j^{\min}, \forall j \in \{1, 2, ..., M\} \tag{16}$$

$$\sum_{i=1}^{N} P_i + \sum_{j=1}^{M} P_j \leq P_{total} \tag{17}$$

$$RK_i = B \log_2(1 + \alpha_i P_i), \forall i \in \{1, 2, ..., N\} \tag{18}$$

$$RE_j = B \log_2(1 + \alpha_j P_j), \forall j \in \{1, 2, ..., M\} \tag{19}$$

According to the constraints (16) and (19), we can obtain P_j. Then (14) is simplified to:

$$\max \sum_{i=1}^{N} RK_i \tag{20}$$

Subject to:

$$\sum_{i=1}^{N} P_i \leq P_{total} - \sum_{j=1}^{M} P_j \tag{21}$$

$$RK_i = B \log_2(1 + \alpha_i P_i), \forall i \in \{1, 2, ..., N\} \tag{22}$$

Under the condition that the transmission power of a satellite is limited and the transmission link state is known, the capacity of the key links can be maximized based on the water filling algorithm [12]. The optimal power distribution is as follows:

$$P_i = \max(\mu - \frac{1}{\alpha_i}, 0) \tag{23}$$

where is a constant that is determined by the power and the link quality factor:

$$\mu = \frac{P_{total} - \sum_{j=1}^{M} P_j + \sum_{i=1}^{N} \frac{1}{\alpha_i}}{N} \tag{24}$$

In the specific solution, we solve it by heuristic algorithm. The algorithm steps are as follows:

Algorithm 1: Algorithm for Solving Multicast Capacity based on Network Coding

1: **Input**: ISLs matrix, Inter-satellite distance matrix, source node s, destination nodes set D, link bandwidth B, transmission frequency f, total transmission power P_{total} of a satellite;
2: **Output**: system multicast capacity R;
3: **for** each node $u \in \mathcal{V}$ **do**
4: Obtain the number of transmission links of u, and then Evenly distribute the total transmission power of the node;
5: **end for**
6: According to Equation (6), to obtain the link capacity matrix C;
7: **for** each $d \in D$ **do**
8: $c_{d,v} = 0, \forall v \in \mathcal{V}$;
9: **end for**
10: Use the link capacity matrix as the weight matrix to construct a directed graph G;
11: **for** each $d \in D$ **do**
12: Obtain the capacity of the max-flow R^d and the multipath routing link set E^d from s to d in G by utilizing Edmonds-Karp method;
13: **end for**
14: According to the weight in the link set E^d, calculate the remaining capacity matrix C_Re;
15: Obtain the *key links* set L;
16: According to problem (14), optimize the capacity of key links and update the power allocation scheme of each node;
17: Re-execute steps 6-13 to update R^d;
18: $R = \min_{\forall d \in D} R^d$;

4 Simulation

In this section, we consider a LEO satellite network, which contains three parallel orbital planes with an orbital inclination of 60°, and each orbital plane is distributed with 3 LEO satellites with a height of 1500 km, as shown in Fig. 3.

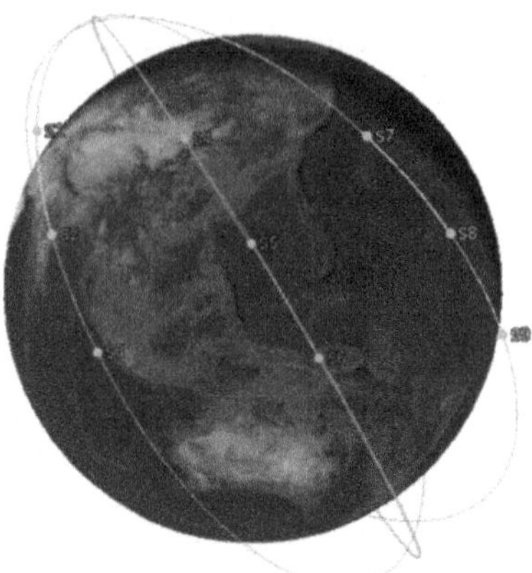

Fig. 3. A LEO satellite network

Through the simulation software STK, the visible relationship and distance between satellites can be analyzed, so as to establish the inter-satellite link building matrix and the inter-satellite distance matrix.

In this simulation experiment, we assume that the bandwidth of all ISLs equal to B, and each satellite node has the same total transmission power P_{total}. In addition, the transmission gain, antenna equivalent noise temperature and transmission frequency of each satellite are all equal, and the free space transmission loss is only determined by the distance between the satellites. The specific simulation parameters are shown in Table 1.

Table 1. Table captions should be placed above the tables.

Parameters	Value
Transmission frequency (f)	10 GHz
Bandwidth of ISLs (B)	100 MHz
Transmission gain (G)	50 dB
Equivalent Noise Temperature (T)	290 K
Total transmission power of a satellite (P_{total})	[50 W, 300 W]

The simulation examines the situation of multicasting data from one source node to two destination nodes. The total transmission power of a single satellite varies from 50 W to 300 W in steps. The source node and the destination node are randomly selected from all nodes with equal probability, and the scene corresponding to each transmission power is simulated for 1000 times and then the average value is taken.

In Fig. 4, other conditions are the same and the network coding scheme is used, and only different power allocation schemes are compared. It can be observed that with the increase of the total transmission power of the satellite, average system multicast capacity is increasing. Under the same total transmission power, the system capacity after power allocation optimization has increased by 7%–13% relative to the one with the average power allocation scheme.

In Fig. 5, other conditions are the same and the same power allocation optimization scheme is adopted, only the impact of the application of network coding on the system's multicast capacity is checked. It can be seen that with the same power, the system multicast capacity with the network coding scheme has increased by about 100% compared to the one with non-network coding scheme.

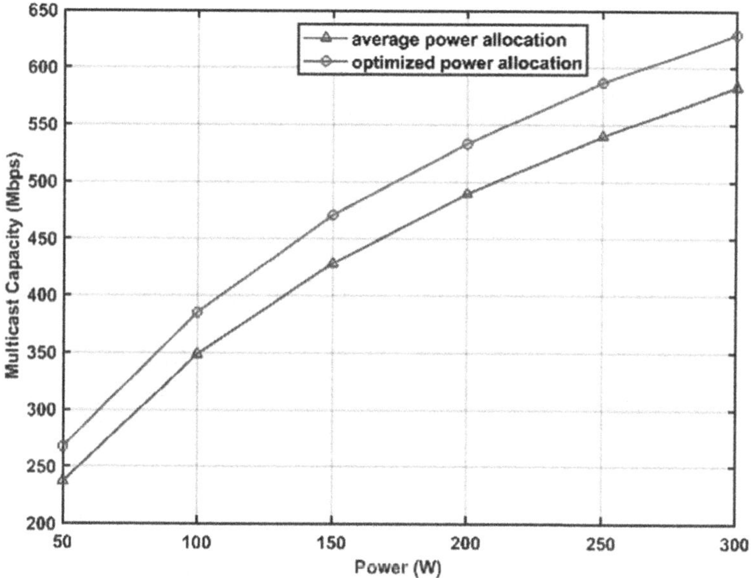

Fig. 4. Performance of optimized power allocation

The above experiments are all based on the situation where one source node multicasts to two destination nodes. In order to explore the influence of the number of destination nodes on the system capacity in the case of single source multicast, we designed a larger satellite Network, including 5 orbital planes, 5 satellites on each orbital plane, a total of 25 LEO satellites. In the simulation, we set the maximum transmission power of a single satellite to 100 W, and other parameters remain unchanged. The source node and destination nodes are randomly selected from all satellite nodes. The number of destination nodes is selected from 2 to 15, and the scenarios corresponding to each number of destination nodes are simulated 1000 times.

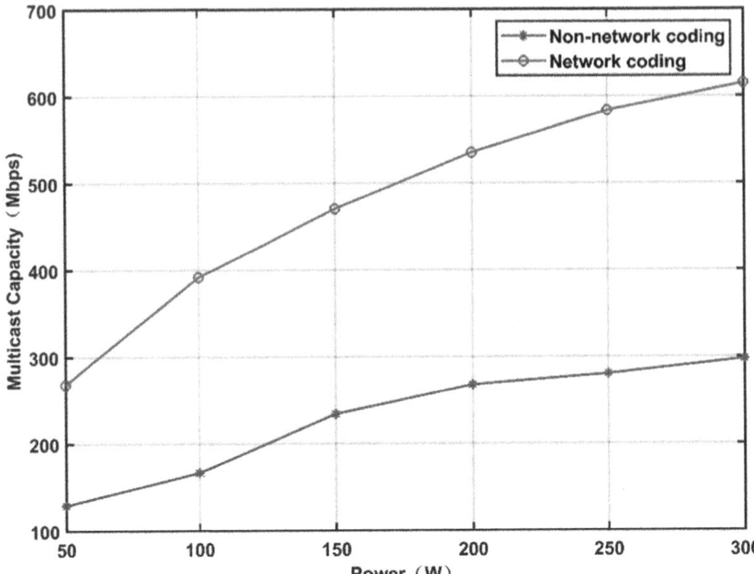

Fig. 5. Performance of network coding

The simulation results are shown in Fig. 6. With the increase in the number of destination nodes, the multicast capacity of the system continues to decrease. Because the destination nodes only receive data and do not relay data, with the increase of destination nodes, the number of relay nodes available in the network decreases, and data forwarding becomes difficult, resulting in a decrease in system capacity. But the network coding scheme has obvious relief to this kind of data congestion. It can be seen from the figure that the network coding scheme has a very obvious improvement in the system multicast capacity compared with the non-network coding scheme. Within a certain range, the more destination nodes, the higher the capacity increase rate of the network coding scheme. It fully proves the significance and practical value of the network coding scheme for the utilization of link resources in the multicast of the satellite network system.

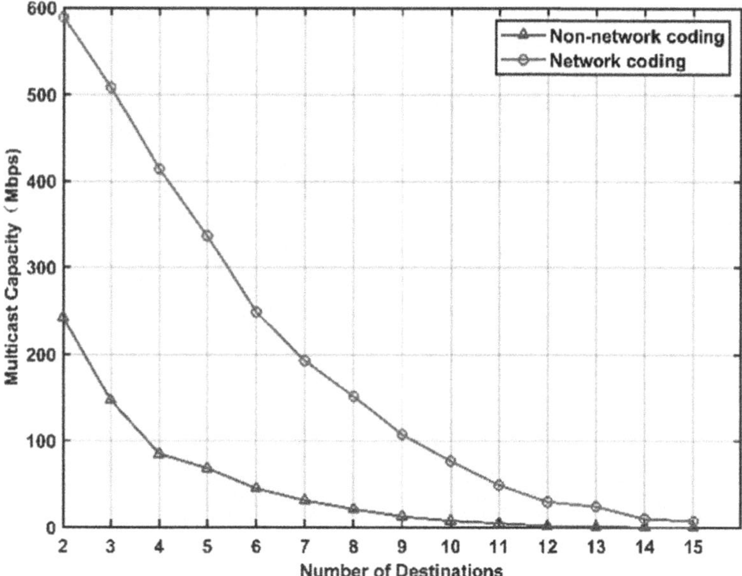

Fig. 6. Performance when the number of destinations is different

5 Conclusion

In this paper, an optimization scheme based on linear network coding and power allocation is proposed to improve the multicast capacity of satellite network. We establish a single-source multicast satellite network model based on linear network coding and power constraints. The key link is defined to solve the power allocation optimization problem, and the multicast capacity based on network coding is obtained by the method of seeking the minimal unicast max-flow. The simulation results show that in the case of limited power resources, the optimization scheme that uses a combination of network coding and power allocation can increase the system multicast capacity by about 100% compared with non-network coding schemes. Moreover, the more the number of multicast destination nodes in a certain range, the greater the improvement of the multicast capacity by the proposed scheme.

Acknowledgement. This work was supported in part by the National Natural Science Foundation of China under Grant 61971156 and Grant 61801144; in part by the Shandong Provincial Natural Science Foundation under Grant ZR2019MF035, Grant ZR2019QF003 and Grant ZR2020MF141; in part by the Scientific Research and Innovation Foundation of HIT under Grant HIT. NSRIF. 2019081; and in part by the National Key Research and Development Program of China under Grant 2020YFB1806703.

References

1. Liu, J., Shi, Y., Fadlullah, Z.M., Kato, N.: Space-air-ground integrated network: a survey. IEEE Commun. Surv. Tutorials **20**(4), 2714–2741 (2018)

2. Yi, X., Sun, Z., Yao, F., Miao, Y.: Satellite constellation of MEO and IGSO network routing with dynamic grouping. Int. J. Satell. Commun. Network. **31**(6), 277–302 (2013)
3. Chen, J., He, K., Yuan, Q., Ruiying, D., Wang, L., Jie, W.: Distributed greedy coding-aware deterministic routing for multi-flow in wireless networks. Comput. Netw. **105**, 194–206 (2016)
4. Mei, Z., Yang, Z.: Active intersession network coding-aware routing. Wireless Netw. **23**(4), 1161–1168 (2017). https://doi.org/10.1007/s11276-016-1221-3
5. Hai, L., Wang, J., Wang, P., Wang, H., Yang, T.: High-throughput network coding aware routing in time-varying multihop networks. IEEE Trans. Veh. Technol. **66**(7), 6299–6309 (2017). https://doi.org/10.1109/TVT.2016.2640313
6. Kafaie, S., Chen, Y., Dobre, O.A., Ahmed, M.H.: Joint inter-flow network coding and opportunistic routing in multi-hop wireless mesh networks: a comprehensive survey. IEEE Commun. Surv. Tutor. **20**(2), 1014–1035 (2018)
7. Ahlswede, R., Cai, N., Li, S.-Y.R., Yeung, R.W.: Network information flow. IEEE Trans. Inf. Theory **46**(4), 1204–1216 (2000)
8. Xu, W.C., Jiang, M., Tang, F.L., Yang, Y.Q.: Network coding-based multi-path routing algorithm in two-layered satellite networks. IET Commun. **12**(1), 2–8 (2018)
9. Tang, F., Zhang, H., Yang, L.: Multipath cooperative routing with efficient acknowledgement for LEO satellite networks. IEEE Trans. Mobile Computing **18**(1), 179–192 (2019)
10. Giambene, G., Luong, D.K., Le, V.A., de Cola, T., Muhammad, M.: Transport layer performance combining multipath and network coding in mobile satellite networks. Int. J. Satell. Commun. Netw. **35**(6), 583–603 (2017)
11. Alegre-Godoy, R., Vazquez-Castro, M.A.: Network coding for system-level throughput improvement in satellite systems. Int. J. Satell. Commun. Network. **35**(6), 551–570 (2017)
12. Yu, W., Rhee, W., Boyd, S., Cioffi, J.M.: Iterative water-filling for Gaussian vector multiple-access channels. IEEE Trans. Inform. Theory **50**(1), 145–152 (2004)

Design and Implementation of Real-Time Video Transmission on Ad Hoc Network

Jian He[1], Shuo Shi[1,2(✉)], Zhong Zheng[3], and Cong Zhou[1]

[1] School of Electronic and Information Engineering, Harbin Institute of Technology, Harbin 150001, Heilongjiang, China
crcss@hit.edu.com

[2] Peng Cheng Laboratory, Network Communication Research Centre, Shenzhen 518052, Guangdong, China

[3] International Innovation Institute of HIT in Huizhou, Huizhou 516000, Guangdong, China

Abstract. Video transmission technology has been widely used in all aspects of life, but the video transmission that we usually see is transmitted on a network with fixed base station support, which is not suitable for earthquakes, fire rescue, and detection without fixed Scenes such as areas covered by base station signals. This article uses Raspberry Pi 3B+ equipped with wireless Ad-Hoc network to realize the function of real-time video transmission, and realizes the push flow control of the central control terminal to the video capture end, which proves the feasibility and practicality of real-time video transmission in the wireless Ad-Hoc network. This article runs the Ubuntu 16.04 system on the Raspberry Pi 3B+, with external physical transmission equipment and cameras, a large number of audio and video related libraries are installed as a dependency of real-time video transmission, and a high-performance SRS streaming media server is deployed on the central control end. Each network node has installed the OLSR routing protocol and carried out related network configuration.

Keywords: Ad-Hoc · Real-time video transmission · SRS streaming server

1 Introduction

In areas that don't have base station, it is more difficult to communicate. Since the end of the 20th century, the development of wireless Ad-Hoc network has solved this demand of people. However, with the improvement of people's quality of life and demand, there is an urgent need for a technology to solve the problem that video cannot be transmitted in areas without base station for signal coverage.

The Ad-Hoc has become a kind of dedicated network with high research value due to its features such as not relying on ground infrastructure, strong node mobility, and nodes in the network that can both forward tasks and actively publish tasks. It is mainly used to provide communication capabilities between nodes in special scenarios such as earthquakes, combat, and detection [1].

© ICST Institute for Computer Sciences, Social Informatics and Telecommunications Engineering 2022
Published by Springer Nature Switzerland AG 2022. All Rights Reserved
S. Shi et al. (Eds.): 6GN 2021, LNICST 439, pp. 51–60, 2022.
https://doi.org/10.1007/978-3-031-04245-4_5

The Ad-Hoc network has the characteristics of high flexibility, low cost, and strong integration. It is one of the key technologies in forest fire prevention, agricultural pest detection, remote identification of objects, and emergency rescue. It is obtained in many neighborhoods and has a high degree of attention and has great advantages when performing tasks such as image acquisition and video transmission. However, at the same time, it is limited by the limited network bandwidth of the Ad-Hoc network and the link is easily interrupted [2]. When the video is transmitted on the Ad-Hoc network, The quality of the video will be affected badly, and the performance degradation will be more obvious when the number of network hops increases [3].

(1) Non-centrality
Each node in the Ad-Hoc network is equal to each other. As long as the relevant network configuration information matches, each node can enter and exit the network by itself. The failure of each node will only change the structure of the network, and will not cause The entire Ad-Hoc network was devastated. Therefore, the wireless mobile Ad-Hoc network does not have a network center.
(2) High dynamic topology
In a mobile wireless Ad-Hoc network, in addition to being free to join and exit the network at any time, each node can move and change its geographic location at will, and each node's signal transmission.
power and received signal gain compensation, channel fading, etc. The factors are unpredictable, which will cause the change in the topology of the Ad-Hoc network to become very rapid and difficult to estimate [4]. Therefore, in the face of rapidly changing Ad-Hoc network topology, it is necessary to design or select a suitable routing protocol to adapt to different scenarios.
(3) Multi-hop data transmission
Because the nodes in the Ad-Hoc network may be out of the communication range of one node due to the low signal transmission power, or the MAC address of the node is blocked by another node for various reasons, this will cause two nodes No direct communication between them. However, each node in the Ad-Hoc network can forward data [5]. Therefore, the node of the wireless mobile Ad-Hoc network can communicate with nodes outside the communication range of its own through the forwarding mechanism of the intermediate node, which means that the Ad-Hoc network has the multi-hop nature of data transmission.
(4) Limitations of nodes
The hardware implementation of the Ad-Hoc network needs to consider many factors. Generally speaking, the mobile terminal of the Ad-Hoc network needs to meet the conditions of portability, which will lead to the limitation of hardware functions [6].When designing a wireless Ad-Hoc network node, it is necessary to comprehensively consider multiple factors, including the weight, volume, endurance, communication range, and information processing speed of the node.
(5) Low security
In the Ad-Hoc network that does not use encryption technology, its nodes can join and exit at will. The information in the wireless Ad-Hoc network communication is

also easy to be intercepted and eavesdropped, thereby leaking the relevant information of the network; similarly, unfamiliar nodes can also easily join the established wireless Ad-Hoc network and disguise it, so Ad-Hoc Poor network security [7].

2 Video Transmission Scheme

2.1 Hardware Scheme

On the premise of ensuring certain performance and considering the convenience of Ad-Hoc network nodes, this article will choose Raspberry Pi 3B+ as the hardware platform to connect the camera and a large network card with higher performance to complete the function of Ad-Hoc network video transmission.

Raspberry Pi is a kind of micro-controller, which is equivalent to a reduced computer. The Raspberry Pi 3B+ is lighter in weight and smaller in size, making it easy to carry, and it can even be equipped with an aircraft to build a flying Ad-Hoc network in the air. At the same time, the performance of Raspberry Pi 3B+ is superior, and the processing speed it provides is sufficient to meet most needs.

The Raspberry Pi 3B+ provides a Micro-USB power interface, an HDMI interface,4 USB2.0 interfaces, 1 RJ45 interface and a camera interface, and the working frequency is 1.4 GHz. In this article, you can choose a USB2.0 camera to connect to the Raspberry Pi 3B+ to collect camera video data; select a signal transmission device to connect to the Raspberry Pi to send and receive data and build a wireless Ad-Hoc network.

Each wireless transmission device has its own address. Enter the address of the transmission device in the browser to enter the configuration interface. Before building a wireless Ad-Hoc network, the frequency of each transmission device must be set in the same frequency band; at the same time, in order to carry a specific routing protocol, the mesh function of the transmission device needs to be turned off. The transmission equipment used in this article works in Ad-Hoc mode by default, so there is no need to perform additional configuration on the network card, only the connection is normal, and the routing protocol suitable for Ad-Hoc networks can be used to complete the networking.

2.2 Software Scheme

The function of real-time video transmission in the Ad-Hoc network designed in this paper is mainly divided into two parts: the video capture terminal and the control terminal.

The video capture terminal needs to call the camera to capture video data, convert the video data into a video stream format and send it to the streaming media server; at the same time, the capture terminal sets aside a port to receive commands from the control terminal and can give a response to the received instructions.

Running the required routing protocol under the Ubuntu system can build a stable and efficient Ad- Hoc network to improve the quality of video transmission in the Ad-Hoc network. The commonly used routing protocols for wireless Ad-Hoc networks include AODV and OLSR [8]. This article uses the olsrd-0.6.8 version of the protocol to build the required wireless Ad-Hoc network. Of course, the "olsrd" protocol version can also be updated or old as needed Version, the different version selection will not substantially affect the function of video transmission. The OLSR routing protocol is a representative of a priori routing protocol in the Ad-Hoc network. Under the rules of OLSR, each network node in the Ad-Hoc network will exchange packet information with its neighboring network nodes in a certain period. So as to realize the awareness of the link state, and then create its own topology. Each node in the network uses this topology to send and receive packet information, and then obtain the topology information of the entire Ad-Hoc network. Each network node can use the topology information of the Ad-Hoc network to calculate according to a certain algorithm The routing table from this node to every other node in the Ad-Hoc network.

The negative impact of the low route discovery and establishment delay is the increase in network overhead. Each node must periodically maintain its own routing information, which will make the entire network use too many resources, especially when the number of nodes in the Ad-Hoc network is increasing, it will produce unbearable network overhead. Therefore, when building a wireless Ad-Hoc network, this article uses only a few Raspberry Pi 3B+ as network nodes, and uses a flat structure to simplify the process of building a Ad-Hoc network, reduce the CPU occupancy rate, and better realize the function of video transmission.

Ordinary servers cannot meet the requirements of this design. In order to achieve video streaming, a streaming media server needs to be built to assist in real-time transmission of multi-hop video in a Ad-Hoc network. Streaming media technology can encode and compress continuous audio and video data and store it on a streaming media server. When the client is watching a media file, it can watch it without downloading the entire multimedia file. When using a streaming media server for video transmission, the basic logic diagram is as shown in the figure Fig. 1.

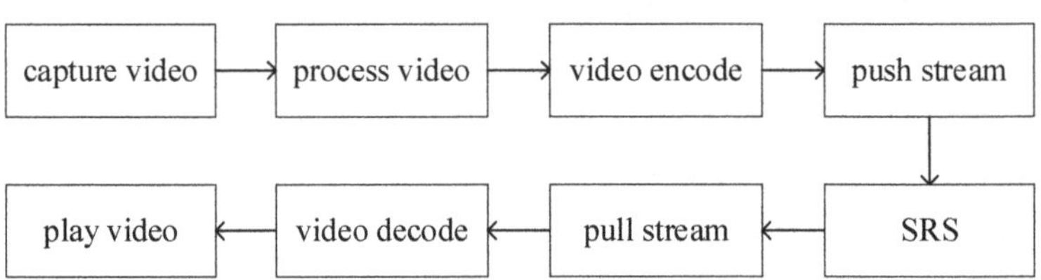

Fig. 1. Server logic diagram

First, the camera video information is collected on the collection side, and then the video is processed (such as adding watermarks, filters, etc.), and then sent to the encoder for video encoding; after the encoding is completed, the stream is pushed, and the real-time video stream is pushed to The streaming media server built. At the central control end, the multimedia stream can be obtained from the streaming media server. At this time, the video stream is encoded, so it needs to be decoded. After decoding, you can obtain the bare video stream that can be played directly. The naked video stream is sent to the player for playback and display, and the function of real-time video transmission can be completed. When the collecting end is pushing the stream, it will first send a request for room creation to the intermediate service server, and then the service server will send a live stream creation request to the streaming server, and the streaming server will send a response to the service server after receiving the request. After that, the service server sends an address for live streaming to the video capture terminal, and the capture terminal pushes the stream to the address according to the live streaming address received in the response, and the entire process of streaming is completed.

The RTMP protocol at the application layer is needed to transmit audio and video streams to improve the quality of audio and video data information transmitted on the network. The RTMP protocol is created on the underlying transport layer protocol.

Generally speaking, the RTMP protocol will establish a connection to the application layer through a handshake based on the establishment of a connection at the TCP protocol layer. On the RTMP-based link, some data used for control will be transmitted, which can be used to transmit actual multimedia data, as well as some other command data for controlling these multimedia data, and so on. When the RTMP protocol is used for data transmission, the transmitted data will be converted into its own format, which is called the message of this protocol, but in fact, when the RTMP protocol transmits these messages, these messages will continue to be divided It is a data block to better realize the splitting of data packets, multiplexing and ensuring the fairness of information. Each data block has a message ID, and each data block has a probability of being a complete message or a part of the message. If the transmitted data block is not a complete message, the data receiving end is also It reads the information in the data block, obtains the data length and message of the data block, and restores the data block belonging to the same ID into a complete message.

3 Realization Process

3.1 Raspberry Pi Platform Construction

Connect a card reader to the Raspberry Pi to install the Ubuntu 16.04 operating system; after installing the operating system, use instructions to update some components of the operating system. In order not to be limited to only transmitting media video files and to increase the function of transmitting real-time video, it is also necessary to configure a camera. Connect the camera to the Raspberry Pi 3B+. When calling the camera, you need to find the folder location where the camera is located. You can use instructions to complete the function of finding the camera. The result may be "/dev/video0".

After the camera is configured, you need to configure the wireless network card. Connect the prepared transmission device to the power adapter to supply power, and use the network cable to connect the Raspberry Pi 3B+ to the transmission device. There is the initial IP address of the network card on the back of the transmission device. Generally, this address does not need to be modified. You can use the ifconfig command in the Raspberry Pi terminal to assign an IP address to each network node. Open the terminal on the Raspberry Pi 3B+ and use the ping command to check whether the wireless transmission device can be pinged (the command is ping 10.10.10.**). If the ping is successful, the wireless transmission device has been successfully connected to the Raspberry Pi.

Next, you need to install a lot of libraries. The installed video library is mainly used to serve "ffmpeg" instructions. The installation video library is mostly installed in the form of a static library, the purpose is to make the compiled file and the static library file link into an executable file, so that the executable file does not depend on the library file afterwards, and enhance the portability of the program. First, you need to install the two required assembly libraries NASM and YASM, and then you can download and install the following libraries: libx264, libx265, libvpx, libfdk-aac, libmp3lame, libopus. Subsequently, these libraries need to be adapted to ffmpeg so that ffmpeg can use these libraries. These libraries are installed using source code.

3.2 Construction of Streaming Media Server

SRS is an excellent streaming media server, open source on git, can be deployed under ubuntu16.04, it is simple and stable, can be used as the source server of RTMP, supports long-term push and pull, and can run on the server During the process of modifying part of the configuration file, functions such as changing the bit rate can be realized without interrupting the service. You need to download the source code of the SRS server. In order to increase the download speed, you can download the relevant code on the code cloud. Next, compile the source code. The third step is to write the SRS streaming media server configuration file as the Fig. 2.

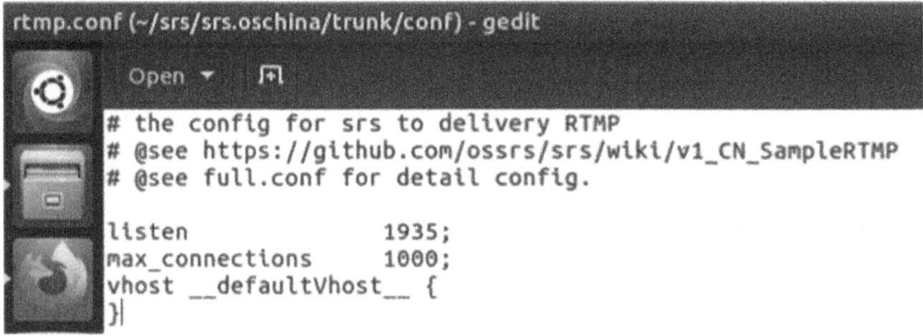

Fig. 2. Configuration file

After configuring the file, you can start the streaming server. After starting the server, you can receive the video stream sent to this port. You can filter through the pipeline or directly query the port to check whether the streaming media server is running.

3.3 Ad-Hoc Network Construction

Connect the prepared big network card to the Raspberry Pi, and then use ifconfig to check whether the connection is successful and query the name of the network card. Since the network card used works in Ad-Hoc mode by default, and all nodes connected to the same network card are in the same network segment, there is no need to perform additional configuration on the network card, just ensure that all communication nodes in the network work at the same frequency Just download. After finding the name of the network card, use the command to assign an IP address of the Ad-Hoc network to the node. After allocating the IP, you need to modify the "olsrd" configuration file; enter the

"/etc./olsrd" directory under the root user, use the command "gedit olsrd.conf" to open the authorized "olsrd.conf" file, and delete it using the library olsrd_txtinfo.so.0.1.Then change the network card that the protocol works to the connected big network card as the Fig. 3.

```
Interface "ens33"
{
    # Interface Mode is used to prevent unnecessary
    # packet forwarding on switched ethernet interfaces
    # valid Modes are "mesh" and "ether"
    # (default is "mesh")

    # Mode "mesh"
}
```

Fig. 3. Set interface

If the subnet masks of different nodes are different, the nodes cannot be connected to the Ad-Hoc network. Use the command to set the subnet mask of each node to 255.0.0.0. When the format of the address is qualified and the subnet mask is the same, you can run "olsrd" under the root user or add "sudo" before the command. The result of the operation is shown in Fig. 4.

```
root@ubuntu: /etc/olsrd
--- 01:59:34.336462 ---------------------------------------------------- LINKS

IP address       hyst      LQ           ETX
10.10.10.88      0.000  1.000/1.000     1.000
10.10.10.26      0.000  1.000/1.000     1.000
10.10.10.44      0.000  1.000/1.000     1.000

--- 01:59:34.336492 ------------------------------------------------ NEIGHBORS

    IP address Hyst     LQ        ETX        SYM    MPR   MPRS  will
10.10.10.88     0.000   1.000/1.000      1.000   YES   NO    NO    3
10.10.10.26     0.000   1.000/1.000      1.000   YES   NO    NO    3
10.10.10.44     0.000   1.000/1.000      1.000   YES   NO    NO    3

--- 01:59:34.336525 --------------------- TWO-HOP NEIGHBORS

IP addr (2-hop)  IP addr (1-hop)  Total cost
10.10.10.88      10.10.10.44      2.000
                 10.10.10.26      2.000
10.10.10.26      10.10.10.44      2.000
                 10.10.10.88      2.000
10.10.10.44      10.10.10.88      2.000
                 10.10.10.26      2.000
```

Fig. 4. Nodes in Ad-Hoc

It can be seen from the figure that there are three nodes in the Ad-Hoc network,10.10.10.88, 10.10.10.26, and 10.10.10.44. Since the geographic distances of the three nodes are in their respective communication ranges, both nodes can pass through one. Communication is performed in a hop mode. In particular, LQ in the figure represents the network state of each node in the network. The closer the value of LQ is to 1, the more stable the node is in the Ad-Hoc network. Each data information in the graph changes dynamically, that is, the state of the entire Ad-Hoc network changes. For example, when a new node joins, the print information of the terminal will be refreshed.

3.4 Real-Time Video Play

When testing the video transmission function under the Ad-Hoc network of the OLSR protocol, the number of Raspberry Pi depends on the number of hops required during the test. In the single-point-to-single- point test, only two Raspberry Pi are needed for networking; when the hop count is greater than 1, more Raspberry Pi are needed for networking. Before playing the video stream transmitted in the Ad-Hoc network, it is necessary to check whether the "FFplay" player functions normally.

After building a Ad-Hoc network and carrying a routing protocol, there are two ways to deploy a streaming media server. One method is to deploy a streaming media server at each node of the video capture terminal. This method can make the central control terminal very convenient. Multi-threaded viewing of videos from multiple video capture terminals has the disadvantage of increasing the CPU occupancy rate of each video capture node and increasing overhead; the other method is to deploy only the streaming media server on the central control terminal, so that it can be passed through The stream key is used to separate the video streams of different nodes, but it will also cause the degradation of the video quality when playing a single video. Deploying the streaming media server on the central control terminal also has obvious advantages. Firstly, it can effectively reduce the resource consumption of the entire network. Secondly, only the configuration of the central node needs to be improved, which makes it easier to manage and control other video capture nodes.

Set the address of the control end to 10.10.10.31, after deploying the SRS server, set the default listening port to 1935, use the push instruction on the video capture node, and change the push target address to rtmp://10.10.10.31:1935/ live/livestream. This instruction is "ffmpeg 128 -f video4linux2 -r 15 -s 720 × 360 -i /dev/video0 -vcodec libx264 -acodec aac -f flv -y rtmp://10.10.10.31/live/livestream". The terminal prints as Fig. 5. This is the instruction in the "ffmpeg" library, where "-r 12" is to set the transmitted frame rate to 12fps, "-s 1280 × 720" is to set the resolution of the transmitted video to 1280 × 720, "-i /dev/video0" is to set the source of the video, you can set the media file or video capture device, here is set to the connected camera, that is, the camera video stream is transmitted, and the last transmitted address is the address of the server.

```
Terminal File Edit View Search Terminal Help
frame=  143 fps= 16 q=26.0 size=    1106kB time=00:00:08.25 bitrate=1097.6kbits/
frame=  151 fps= 16 q=26.0 size=    1222kB time=00:00:08.91 bitrate=1122.9kbits/
frame=  159 fps= 16 q=26.0 size=    1341kB time=00:00:09.58 bitrate=1146.2kbits/
frame=  167 fps= 16 q=26.0 size=    1461kB time=00:00:10.25 bitrate=1167.3kbits/
frame=  175 fps= 16 q=26.0 size=    1583kB time=00:00:10.91 bitrate=1187.5kbits/
frame=  182 fps= 16 q=26.0 size=    1690kB time=00:00:11.50 bitrate=1203.8kbits/
frame=  188 fps= 16 q=26.0 size=    1784kB time=00:00:12.00 bitrate=1217.5kbits/
frame=  194 fps= 16 q=26.0 size=    1876kB time=00:00:12.50 bitrate=1229.0kbits/
frame=  200 fps= 16 q=26.0 size=    1970kB time=00:00:13.00 bitrate=1240.6kbits/
frame=  206 fps= 16 q=26.0 size=    2064kB time=00:00:13.50 bitrate=1252.4kbits/
```

Fig. 5. Pushing stream

In order to reduce the transmission delay, the "-fflags nobuffer" parameter is added when the playback command is executed, that is, the video stream is transmitted in the form of no buffer. Run an order: "ffplay rtmp://10.10.10.31/live/live/livestream". If the video playback window can pop up normally as shown in Fig. 6, it means that the function of real-time video transmission has been successfully implemented.

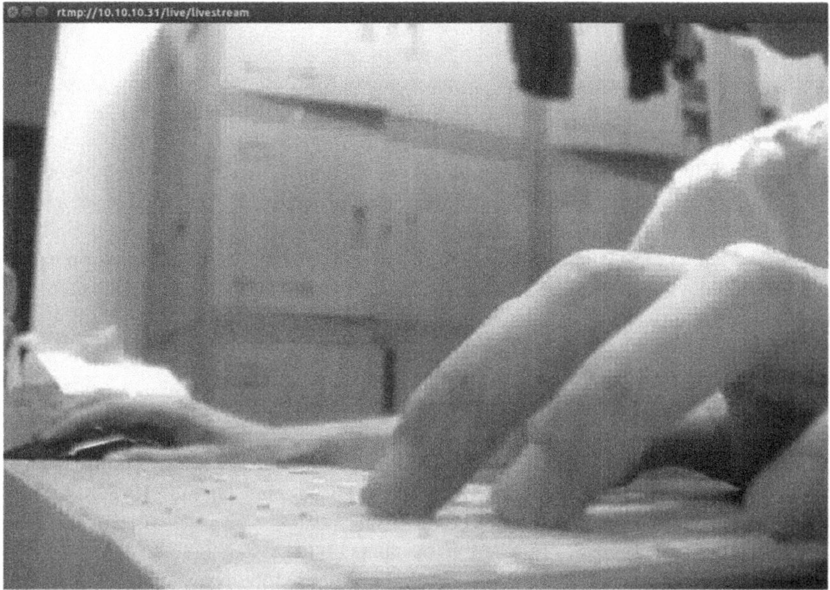

Fig. 6. Pulling stream

4 Conclusions

The focus of this article is to build a wireless Ad-Hoc network to realize the function of real-time video transmission. The overall approach is to use Raspberry Pi 3B+ as the hardware platform, run Ubuntu 16.04 system, build a wireless Ad-Hoc network, carry OLSR routing protocol, install and configure audio and video libraries, use SRS streaming media server, and use RTMP protocol transmission on the application layer for real-time video streaming, the TCP protocol is used on the transmission layer to send control commands. From the analysis of the real-time video transmission quality when the distance between the two nodes is fixed and relatively static, the quality of video transmission can also be improved from the following aspects:

(1) Use a more appropriate routing protocol to achieve higher video frame rate and resolution.
(2) Use physical transmission equipment with higher transmission performance to increase the data transmission rate and effectively improve the quality of video transmission.

(3) Optimize or rewrite the RTMP protocol, or use a streaming media server with higher performance to reduce video delay.

This article has well realized the video transmission function on the Ad-Hoc network, and can improve the transmission performance through cross-layer design in the future.

References

1. Al-Kharasani, N.M., Zukarnain, Z.A., Subramaniam, S.K., Hanapi, Z.M.: An adaptive relay selection scheme for enhancing network stability in VANETs. IEEE Access **8**, 128757–128765 (2020)
2. Rosário, D., Filho, J.A., Rosário, D., Santosy, A., Gerla, M.: A relay placement mechanism based on UAV mobility for satisfactory video transmissions. In: Annual Mediterranean Ad Hoc Networking Workshop, IEEE (2017)
3. Dan, R, Adrian, C., Camelia, A., Adina, A., Benoît, P.: Video content transmission in a public safety system model based on flying Ad-hoc networks. In: International Conference on Automation, Quality and Testing, Robotics, IEEE (2018)
4. Orozco, O.A., Llano Ramirez, G.: OSA: A VANET application focused in energy efficiency. In: 2014 IEEE COLCOM, pp. 1–9 (2014)
5. Rui, C., et al.: Towards a multilyered permission-based access control for extending Android security. Concurr. Comput. Pract. Exp. **30**, e4180 (2018)
6. Oubbati, O.S., Lakas, A., Zhou, F., Güneş, M., Yagoubi, M.B.: A survey on position-based routing protocols for Flying Ad hoc Networks (FANETs). Veh. Commun. **10**, 29–56 (2017)
7. Bujari, A., Palazzi, C.E., Ronzani, D.: A comparison of stateless position-based packet routing algorithms for FANETs. IEEE Trans. Mob. Comput. **17**(11), 2468–2482 (2018)
8. Kang, M.-S., Kum, D.-W., Bae, J.-S., Cho, Y.-Z., Le, A.-N.: Mobility aware hybrid routing protocol for mobile ad hoc network. In: 26th International Conference on Information Networking, pp. 410–414. Bali (2012)

Using Generative Adversarial Networks for Network Intrusion Detection

XuDong Li[1,2], Di Lin[1,2(✉)], Yu Tang[2], Weiwei Wu[2], Zijian Li[2], and Bo Chen[1,2]

[1] Intelligent Terminal Key Laboratory of Sichuan Province, Yibin, China
lindi@uestc.edu.cn

[2] University of Electronic Science and Technology of China, Chengdu, China

Abstract. The network intrusion detection system is an essential guarantee for network security. Most research on network intrusion detection systems focuses on using supervised learning algorithms, which require a large amount of labeled data for training. However, the work of labeling data is complex and cannot exhaustively include all types of network intrusion. Therefore, in this study, we develop a model that only requires normal data in the training phase, and it can distinguish between normal data and abnormal data in the test phase. This model is implemented by using a generative confrontation network. Experimental results show that, on the CIC-IDS-2017 dataset, our model has an accuracy of 97%, which is dramatically higher than the basic autoencoder, which is one of the most widely used algorithms in the network intrusion detection.

Keywords: Generative adversarial network · Network intrusion detection · Network security

1 Introduction

With the increasing complexity of modern networks, the growing popularity of network use, the growing diversification of network attacks, and the rapid development of the Internet, more and more devices are connected to the network, and there are significant challenges to network security. The demand for network intrusion detection systems is therefore increasing. The biggest problem facing the current network intrusion detection system is the lack of awareness of strange events, the lack of detection of unknown risks such as zero-day attacks, and the low detection rate of low-frequency attacks such as worm attacks [1]. If modern network system security still relies on manual detection by administrators, identification and processing are inefficient. So the best solution is to let the machine learn the ability to analyze network data and detect any suspicious or abnormal behavior. Relying on the powerful ability of deep neural networks to extract data features [2] automatically can be achieved.

According to different methods of detecting anomalies, network intrusion detection systems can be divided into signature-based methods and anomaly detection-based methods [1, 3]. Both methods have their own advantages and disadvantages. The

© ICST Institute for Computer Sciences, Social Informatics and Telecommunications Engineering 2022
Published by Springer Nature Switzerland AG 2022. All Rights Reserved
S. Shi et al. (Eds.): 6GN 2021, LNICST 439, pp. 61–68, 2022.
https://doi.org/10.1007/978-3-031-04245-4_6

signature-based method describes the known attacks in detail. It can efficiently and accurately detect various known attacks. However, such methods are not capable of dealing with unknown threats. For example, zero-day attacks cannot be handled. Such attacks often bring more significant harm. The method based on anomaly detection is suitable for responding to unknown threats and can detect unknown or new types of attacks. Anomaly-based network intrusion detection systems can be divided into two categories: network intrusion detection systems based on supervised learning and network intrusion detection systems based on unsupervised learning [4]. Current researches mainly focus on using supervised learning to build intrusion detection systems. Still, the problem is that a large amount of labeled data is needed, and it is almost impossible to obtain a data set that includes all types of attacks because network attack methods are endless. Therefore, this paper uses a generative confrontation network to implement a model that only needs normal data in the training phase. In this process, the model captures the distribution of normal data. In the test phase, the model can distinguish between normal data and abnormal data. To realize the classification task, the data that does not conform to the known distribution is judged as abnormal.

This paper confirms the feasibility of using a Generative Adversarial Network in network intrusion detection. In Sect. 2, the previous research in the field of IDS is discussed. Section 3 first introduces the CIC-IDS-2017 data set used in the experiment. Then the proposed model and corresponding detection framework are presented. In Sect. 4, the evaluation indicators used are explained. Then the performance of the proposed model is evaluated, and the results are discussed. Finally, Sect. 5 discusses the significance and limitations of this study and makes a reasonable outlook for future development.

2 Relate Work

According to different technologies, the current research on network intrusion detection is carried out from the following three directions.

A rule-based approach. This type of method is designed based on the characteristics of known attacks and has sound effects on known attacks but has obvious shortcomings in dealing with unknown threats. A simple rule-based system network intrusion detection system can not meet current industry needs.

Based on traditional machine learning methods. In [5], the author uses a random forest plus XGBoost method to implement a network intrusion detection model and introduces a cost-sensitive function to improve the detection rate of a small sample category. In [6], a 10-fold cross-validation decision tree method was used to study network intrusion detection on a data set containing 22 features (feature selection was made on the NSL-KDD data set). The study in [7] found that random forest performs best in this type of problem. Traditional machine learning algorithms have achieved certain results in network intrusion detection tasks, but they also have limitations. For example, standard machine learning algorithms require manual feature engineering of data to construct sample features.

Based on deep learning methods. Such methods are the best prospects. In response to known attacks, it can make automatic feature selection on a high accuracy rate and low false alarm rate. If the appropriate network architecture design, it also has a role in dealing with unknown threats. For example, in [8], the combined Sparse Auto-Encoder and soft-max model are used to do network intrusion detection. It uses Sparse Auto-Encoder to perform feature learning on the unlabeled data set to obtain the hidden layer encoding. Then take the hidden layer obtained from the previous training step and add soft-max to classify it on the labeled data set to complete the detection. In [9], an asymmetric stacked autoencoder (S-NDAE) plus random forest is used for network intrusion detection. The autoencoder is used for feature extraction, and the random forest is used for classification. In [10], the CNN network is used for network intrusion detection. The detection is completed by increasing the convolution kernel to map the original features to the high-dimensional space to enhance the feature learning ability. In [11], the author uses an improved convolutional neural network to implement a network intrusion detection model. This model uses a cross-layer aggregation network design method, which differs from the traditional convolution-pooling-full connection structure. Experimental results show that this model has achieved good results. In [12], LSTM network architecture is used for network intrusion detection. It uses an autoencoder to extract data features. Using the timing-related characteristics of network data and LSTM network for detection, this method has a specific effect in dealing with unknown threats. GAN network also has specific applications in the field of intrusion detection. For example, in [13], the author used the GAN-PSO-ELM model to conduct network intrusion detection research. It uses GAN to expand the minority samples, uses PSO to optimize the input weight and hidden layer bias of ELM, and finally builds the model. Experiments on the NSL-KDD data set have achieved good results.

3 Model Design

3.1 Dataset

The CIC-IDS-2017 data set used in this paper was published by the Canadian Institute of Cyber Security (CIC). This data set collects 5 days of data, which contains network data under normal conditions and network data under the latest common attacks. It builds an abstract behavior of 25 users based on HTTP, HTTPS, FTP, SSH, and email protocols, which simulates the real-world situation to the greatest extent. It also includes the results of network traffic analysis using CICFlowMeter, which is based on timestamps, source and destination IP, source and destination ports, protocol, and attack marking traffic [14]. Current network intrusion detection research recommends using this data set compared with data sets such as KDD and NSL-KDD.

3.2 Data Processing

Each record of the CIC-IDS-2017 data set contains 78 features, all of which are numerical. The data processing for this includes the following steps:

Step 1: Eliminate data with missing features in the data set.
Step 2: To better convert the data into an image, three all-zero features are added. Each record is composed of 91 features, and the last three features of each record are all 0.

Step 3: Normalize the data to eliminate the influence of extreme data on the model, which helps deep learning model training. The normalization formula is as follows:

$$\mathrm{x} = \frac{x - Min}{Max - Min} \tag{1}$$

3.3 Network Architecture Design

In this section, the proposed GAN model will be described. Its generator and discriminator both use convolutional neural networks.

1) Design discriminator

The structure of the discriminator is shown in Fig. 1. Conv2D, LeakyReLu, and Dropout are one layer, a total of three layers are superimposed, and finally, after the Flatten operation, a Dense output result is connected. In the last layer, we did not use the sigmoid function. The discriminator receives a $9 \times 9 \times 1$ size picture and outputs a score for this picture. The scoring intervals for normal data and abnormal data are different. Use this feature to identify abnormal and normal states in the network.

2) Design generator

The structure of the generator is shown in Fig. 2. The generator receives random noise data and expands it to the same size as the real data for input into the discriminator. The generator also uses the leak-relu activation function, and to get better results, we also added batch normalization. The generator is to help the discriminator to train. The generator is useless when the training is complete.

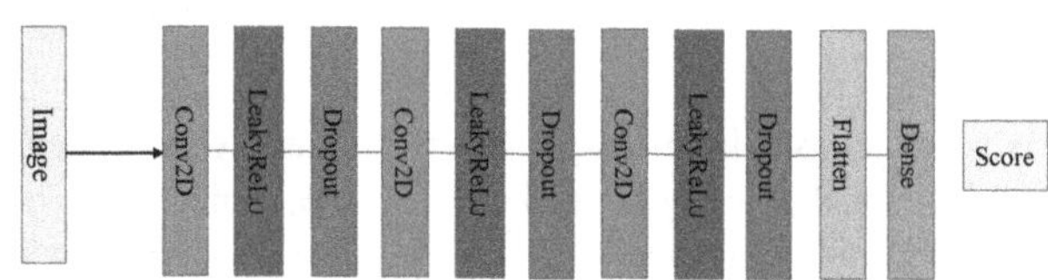

Fig. 1. The discriminator structure of the proposed GAN model

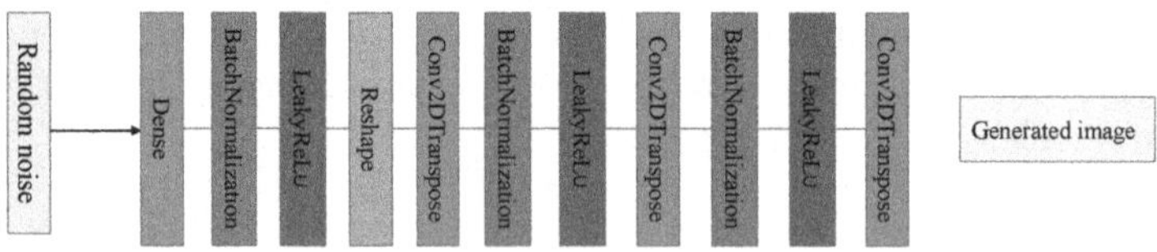

Fig. 2. The generator structure of the proposed GAN model

3.4 Intrusion Detection Framework

The generator's goal in GAN is to generate fake data that is as close to the real data as possible. The purpose of the discriminator is to distinguish whether the input data comes from real data or fake data generated by the generator. After the training process, the discriminator has captured the distribution of real data, the distribution of normal data. Its score for normal data output will stabilize within a range, and its score for abnormal data output that has never been seen will deviate from this range. The study found that the score distribution of the normal data output by the discriminator is similar to the normal distribution. Therefore, the "3σ" principle of a normal distribution is used to determine the division of threshold points in the normal data range. The mean value μ of the data plus or minus three times the standard deviation σ to determine. The threshold division formula is as follows.

$$\text{threshold} = (\mu - 3\sigma, \mu + 3\sigma) \tag{2}$$

The steps of using GAN to detect abnormal data in the network are shown in Fig. 3.

1) To process the original data, the specific steps are as described in Sect. 3.2. After processing, 70% of the normal data is used for training GAN and 30% for testing the model. 100% of abnormal data is used to test the model. It should be noted that the model has never seen 30% of normal data and all abnormal data during the training process.
2) Only use normal data to train GAN. After the training is completed, the generator can generate normal data close to the real, and the discriminator captures normal data distribution.
3) Performance measurement. Take the unused normal data and mix it with the abnormal data. Use the combined data to test the performance of the model.

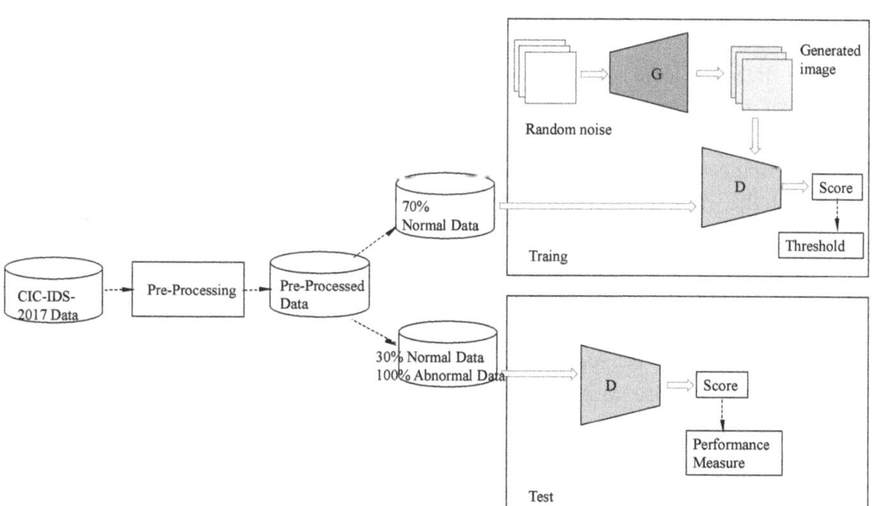

Fig. 3. The framework of the network intrusion detection process using the proposed GAN model includes the training part and the testing part. The threshold division of the training part is carried out according to formula 2.

4 Experiment

4.1 Evaluation Index

There are four evaluation indicators used in this study.

Precision(P): The percentage of intrusions that are correctly judged as intrusions.

$$\text{Precision} = \frac{TP}{TP + FP} \tag{3}$$

Recall(R): judicious invasion percentage of all intrusion traffic.

$$\text{Recall} = \frac{TP}{TP + FN} \tag{4}$$

Accuracy(A): The ratio of the total number of flows that are correctly judged.

$$Accuracy = \frac{TP + TN}{TP + TN + FN + FP} \tag{5}$$

F value: the result of weighted and averaged precision and recall.

$$\text{F} = \frac{2PR}{P + R} \tag{6}$$

Among them, TP is the number of samples of attack behaviors that are correctly classified;

TN is the number of samples of normal behaviors that are correctly classified;
FP is the number of samples of normal behaviors that are misclassified;
FN is the number of examples of misclassified attack behaviors.

4.2 Experimental Results

In the CIC-IDS-2017 data set, the data is divided into normal data and abnormal data (that is, data at the time of the attack). Take 70% of the normal data to train the GAN model. When the training is completed, take the discriminator in the GAN model to achieve the detection task. The visualization of the score obtained by 70% of the normal data through the trained discriminator is shown in Fig. 4. It can be found that it is similar to the normal distribution. Unfortunately, we found that it does not entirely conform to the normal distribution through testing. This is also the reason for the design of the threshold division formula. After that, we take the same amount of abnormal and normal data for experiments, use them to obtain scores through the trained discriminator, and then visualize the results. As shown in Fig. 5, we find that normal data scores and abnormal data scores are gathered in different clusters. This is one of the reasons why our model can work.

The performance of our proposed model was tested on the CIC-IDS-2017 data set and compared with the basic autoencoder. The results are shown in Table 1. According to Table 1, the accuracy of our proposed model is 97.64%, the precision is 99.43%, the recall rate is 95.82%, and the F value is 0.97. All indicators are better than the results obtained by the basic autoencoder. At the same time, these good experimental results also reflect that our proposed model can accurately and comprehensively detect normal data and abnormal data.

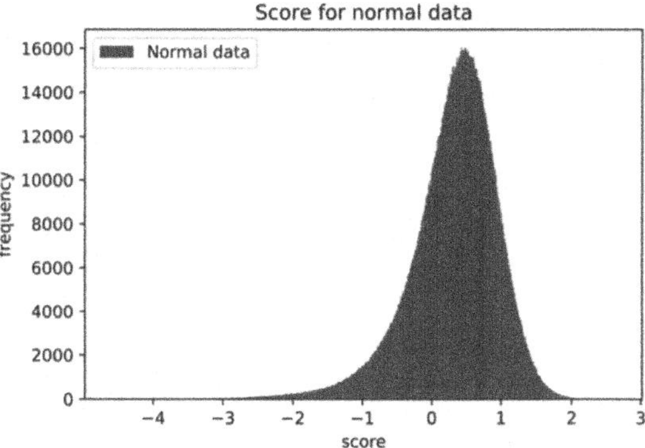

Fig. 4. The normal data used for training is visualized by the score after the trained discriminator

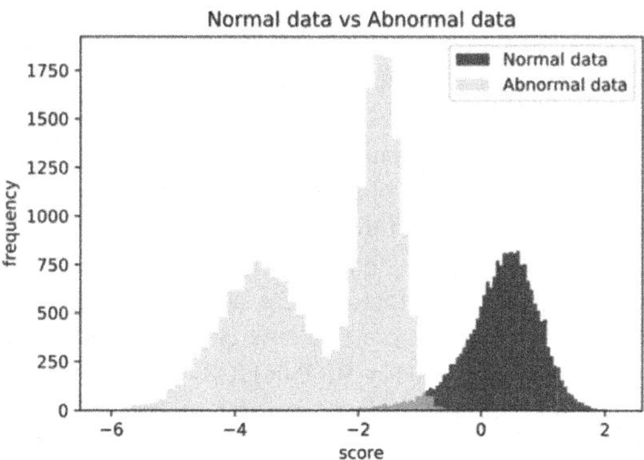

Fig. 5. The normal data and abnormal data used in the test are visualized by the scores of the trained discriminator.

Table 1. Performance comparison between proposed GAN model and basic autoencoder

Model	Accuracy(%)	Precision(%)	Recall(%)	F(%)
GAN discriminator	97.64	99.43	95.82	97.59
Basic autoencoder	84.0	79.39	91.85	85.17

5 Conclusion

In this paper, we propose a Generative Adversarial Network based network intrusion detection algorithm. Specifically, a framework of Generative Adversarial Network is employed to complete intrusion detection and conducts experiments. Experimental results show that this method has a certain degree of stability, and it also outperforms the current methods, e.g., a basic autoencoder. The method proposed in this paper for network intrusion detection can effectively solve the problem of detecting unknown attacks, which is a challenging problem.

Acknowledgment. Partially Funded by Science and Technology Program of Sichuan Province (2021YFG0330), partially funded by Grant SCITLAB-0001 of Intelligent Terminal Key Laboratory of SiChuan Province,and partially Funded by Fundamental Research Funds for the Central Universities (ZYGX2019J076).

References

1. Nassar, M., et al.: Network intrusion detection, literature review and some techniques comparision. In: International Computer Engineering Conference (2019)
2. Lecun, Y., Bengio, Y., Hinton, G.E.: Deep learning. Nature **521**(7553), 436–444 (2015)
3. Vinayakumar, R., et al.: Applying convolutional neural network for network intrusion detection. In: Advances in Computing and Communications, pp. 1222–1228 (2017)
4. Gogoi, P., Borah, B., Bhattacharyya, D.K.: Anomaly detection analysis of intrusion data using supervised & unsupervised approach. J. Converg. Inf. Technol. **5**(1), 95–110 (2010)
5. Chen, Z., Lyu, N.: Network intrusion detection model based on random forest and XGBoost. J. Signal Process. Syst. **36**(7), 1055–1064 (2020)
6. Chae, H.S., Jo, B.O., Choi, S.H., Park, T.K.: Feature selection for intrusion detection using NSL-KDD. In: Recent Advances in Computer Science, pp. 184–187 (2013)
7. Thaseen, S., Kumar, C.A.: An analysis of supervised tree based classiers for intrusionv detection system. In: Pattern Recognition, Informatics and Mobile Engineering (PRIME), 2013 International Conference on, pp. 294–299, IEEE (2013)
8. Javaid, A., et al.: A deep learning approach for network intrusion detection system. In: Proceedings of the 9th EAI International Conference on Bio-inspired Information and Communications Technologies (formerly BIONETICS) (2016)
9. Shone, N., et al.: A deep learning approach to network intrusion detection. IEEE Trans. Emerg. Top. Comput. Intell. **2**(1), 41–50 (2018)
10. Khan, R.U., et al.: An improved convolutional neural network model for intrusion detection in networks. In: 2019 Cybersecurity and Cyberforensics Conference (CCC). IEEE (2019)
11. Yang, H., Wang, F.: Network intrusion detection model based on improved convolutional neural network. J. Comput. Appl. **39**(9), 2604–2610 (2019)
12. Mirza, A.H., Selin, C.: Computer network intrusion detection using sequential LSTM neural networks autoencoders. In: 2018 26th Signal Processing and Communications Applications Conference (SIU). IEEE (2018)
13. Yang, Y., Song, R., Zhou, Z.: Network intrusion detection method based on GAN-PSO-ELM. Comput. Eng. Appl. **56**(12), 66–72 (2020)
14. Sharafaldin, I., Lashkari, A.H., Ghorbani, A.A.: Toward generating a new intrusion detection dataset and intrusion traffic characterization. In: International Conference on Information Systems Security & Privacy (2018)

Perception-Connection Tradeoff for Radar Cooperative Sensing in Multi-hop Vehicular Networks

Mingyi Wang, Ruofei Ma, Wenjing Kang, and Gongliang Liu(✉)

Harbin Institute of Technology, Weihai 264209, Shandong, China
{maruofei,kwjqq,liugl}@hit.edu.cn

Abstract. With radar cooperative sensing, vehicles can not only leverage their own radar to perceive the road condition ahead but also establish a connection with vehicles in front to obtain environment information farther away. In this paper, a radar cooperative sensing scheme based on multi-hop for vehicular networks is proposed for far-reaching perception. Vehicles on the road perform radar sensing while conducting multi-hop communication with front ones to obtain road information outside the LOS range. In order to streamline hardware equipment and deal with the upcoming shortage of spectrum resources, each vehicle is equipped with TD-JRC to realize both radar sensing and communication function within the same frequency band. Besides, we design a resource allocation strategy for this cooperative sensing system, numerical and simulation results show that there is indeed a optimal joint power and time allocation strategy to realize the maximized average RCSCR for a definite vehicle density.

Keywords: V2V · Cooperative sensing · Joint radar-communication · Resource allocation

1 Introduction

In order to achieve high-level autonomous driving, in addition to using the autonomy of the vehicle, the collaborative perception between vehicles is used to share detected obstacles or perception data and expand their perception range, thereby improving their situational awareness ability and driving safety [5].

The realization of collaborative perception requires vehicles on the road to have both radar sensing and data communication capabilities. In the past

This work was supported by the National Natural Science Foundation of China (61971156, 61801144), Shandong Provincial Natural Science Foundation (ZR2019MF035, ZR2019QF003, ZR2020MF141), Scientific Research and Innovation Foundation of HIT (HIT.NSRIF.2019081), Weihai Technology Development and Innoviation Project (2019KYCXJJYB06).

© ICST Institute for Computer Sciences, Social Informatics and Telecommunications Engineering 2022
Published by Springer Nature Switzerland AG 2022. All Rights Reserved
S. Shi et al. (Eds.): 6GN 2021, LNICST 439, pp. 69–82, 2022.
https://doi.org/10.1007/978-3-031-04245-4_7

research on vehicle network, radar sensing and communication modules used separately designed hardware devices, occupying an isolated section of spectrum resources respectively. With the exponential growth of wireless devices and data traffic, the spectrum becomes more and more scarce, and the limited spectrum resources will affect the radar's sensing and data communication performance in the near future.

At the same time, the development of signal process technology as well as hardware design ability make radar and communications are developing in the direction of joint design. Benefiting from the high similarity of radar and communication function in respect of transceiver design, antenna structure and working bandwidth, it is glad to see the joint design of these two systems is available [12]. Therefore, by using unified hardware equipment and spectrum resources, spectrum reuse can be used to alleviate the limitations caused by the shortage of spectrum resources, which is also known as joint radar communication (JRC) technology. The specific implementation of JRC has a time, frequency, beam sharing scheme [8], joint wave design [11], etc.

For autopilot, achieving far-reaching perception through the connection between adjacent vehicles can not only achieve better safety and decision-making capacity than the autonomy of a vehicle but also improve traffic throughput and fuel economy through global route optimization and cooperative driving [4].

To realize this vision, it is necessary to have both strong radar sensing capability and communication connection capability. In the power-constrained JRC system, the tradeoff of Radar perception and communication ability is essential. Increasing radar perception ability will inevitably reduce communication performance and vice versa. A reasonable resource allocation strategy can maximize the range of vehicle cooperative perception and provide a sufficient decision-making basis for safe and reliable autonomous driving.

In order to cope with this challenge, in this paper, we studied how the joint time and power distribution strategy of the time-division joint radar-communication (TD-JRC) system affects the radar cooperative sensing range under different vehicle densities.

Numerical and simulation results show that there is indeed an optimal time and power allocation strategy to maximize the radar cooperative sensing range by leveraging a priori vehicle density information.

2 System Model

2.1 Network Module

In Fig. 1, vehicles with perceptive ability distribute on two lanes with opposite directions of travel. Each vehicle in two lanes has the same dynamic characteristics as well as sensor configurations. Therefore, throughout this paper we focus on one of the road lanes for research conciseness.

Assuming the number of vehicles per unit distance follows the one-dimensional Poisson Process with density ρ as Poisson distribution provides a

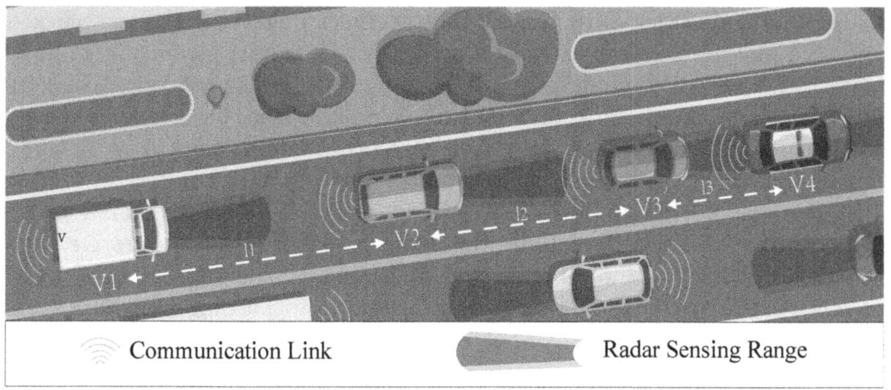

Fig. 1. Radar cooperative sensing in multi-hop vehicular network

practical model for the arrival process of vehicles. Since the number of vehicles follows the Poisson distribution, the distance between two adjacent vehicles can be obtained according to the exponential distribution [7] and the Probability Density Function (PDF) of adjacent vehicles interval l is

$$f_L(l) = \rho e^{-\rho l} \tag{1}$$

For safety requirements, the vehicles interval have to satisfy one preset minimum distance d_{min}, and the distance between a pair of adjacent vehicles is distributed randomly from the minimum distance to infinity, such that using truncated Gaussian probability density function to describe the vehicle interval will make the research results more in line with the actual situation. The revised PDF of vehicles interval from l_{min} to infinity is given as

$$\tilde{f}_L(l) = \frac{\rho e^{-\rho l}}{\int_{l_{min}}^{+\infty} \rho e^{-\rho l} dl} = \frac{\rho e^{-\rho l}}{e^{-l_{min}\rho}} \tag{2}$$

and the corresponding cumulative distribution function (CDF) is

$$\tilde{F}_L(L < l) = 1 - \int_l^{\infty} \tilde{f}_L(l) dl \tag{3}$$

Each vehicle implemented a set of TD-JRC systems at the front and rear to perform radar and communication functions, which sharing the identical Millimeter-wave frequency band, and the conversion between two functions carry out in a time-division manner.

Due to the attenuation characteristics of millimeter waves, assuming vehicles can only establish a connection directly with their neighbor nodes in line-of-sight (LOS) channel, i.e., adjacent ones in front of or behind it, by vehicle-to-vehicle (V2V) link. For nodes out of sight, vehicles establish links via multi-hop by treating nodes within the LOS range as relay nodes. e.g., in Fig. 1, $V2$ has the capability of connecting with $V1$ or $V3$ in a direct link. Nevertheless, blocked by $V3$, $V2$ can not connect with it unless $V3$ acts as a relay node.

With the help of communication links and multi-hop transmission, vehicles can obtain road information far beyond their perceptual coverage. In-vehicle intelligence will benefit from the richer perceptual information to make more accurate and timely decisions.

In this paper, we propose the radar cooperative sensing covered range (RCSCR) of one vehicle to measure the performance of radar cooperative sensing, which is defined as the sum of received forward sensing information covered range perceived by the JRC system implemented in forwarding vehicles and its own.

Besides, we design a joint distribution strategy of power and time for radar sensing and communication function, the objective of such strategy is to maximize average RCSCR for vehicles in the research road with vehicle density ρ.

For the TD-JRC we used, the first part of a frame is used to realize the radar sensing mode while the second part is used to realize the communication mode. The total power of the JRC system is P_s, Limited by the hardware structure, the power distribution between radar and communication are independent of each other.

First, the TD-JRC system works in radar mode and continuously perceives road information ahead, and then, the system work converts to communication mode, receiving perceive information from adjacent vehicles in direct communication and outrange ones in multi-hop.

It is worth noting that the sensing information is transmitted at most one hop within one frame. Considering the time validity of the information and reducing the communication burden of the system, the sensing information that fails to be transmitted will not be retransmitted. In other words, for frame duration T, the information transmitted through N hops from the source node to destination node will elapse a duration of NT. Considering the moving speed of vehicles and transmission hop number, both of which are usually a small value, this transmission delay can be sufficiently short to be thought of as insignificant, so it is reasonable to treat the information transmitted through multi-hop as realtime.

2.2 Radar Model

To achieve better radar cooperative sensing performance, one needs to fully understand the capabilities and characteristics of vehicle-mounted radars. In most application scenarios, the maximum detection range is an essential tactical and technical indicator of radar, and the detection range of the radar is a statistical concept as there is randomness noise in the radar system. The radar equation [9] reflects the relationship of parameters related to the detection range, which is given as

$$R_{max} = \left[\frac{P_t G_t G_r \lambda^2 \sigma}{(4\pi)^3 k T_s F B_n D(m)} \right]^{1/4} \tag{4}$$

where σ represents radar cross-section (RCS), which is not the physical area of the target but reflects the ability of the target to reflect signal power, P_t denotes radar transmit power, G_t is transmit gain, G_r indicates receive gain, F is noise coefficient, B_s represents the system bandwidth for both radar and communication function, $\lambda = c/f_s$ is the carrier wavelength with c and f_s being the speed of light and carrier frequency, respectively, k is Boltzmann constant, T_s indicates the system noise temperature, $D(m)$ is Radar detection factor according to pulse accumulation number $m = \lfloor \tau f_r \rfloor = \lfloor \frac{\tau}{T_r} \rfloor$, which is the number of radar pulses in a time frame.

Where τ is the duration of radar mode within on frame, f_r and T_r represents radar pulse frequency and cycle, respectively.

In order to expand the detection range of the radar, with most instances, accumulation operations can be performed between pulses to improve the signal-to-noise ratio (SNR) of signal output, if m equal-amplitude coherent signals are coherently accumulated, ideally, the accumulated signal-to-noise ratio will be improved by m times. At this time, the value of detect factor D will decrease. Therefore, the maximum radar sensing range is related to the number of pulse accumulation m.

In actual traffic conditions, the characteristics of vehicles are not only constant RCS, but are usually modeled as random RCS models. Swerling II is a typical RCS model which can be used to characterize target fluctuations [6].

According to [2], the detect probability P_d for Swerling II is

$$\begin{aligned} P_d &= 1 - \frac{1}{(m-1)!} \int_0^{V_T/(1+s)} r^{m-1} e^r \, dr \\ &= 1 - P_\gamma \left(\frac{V_T}{s+1}, m \right) \end{aligned} \tag{5}$$

in which s indicates the SNR at the input of the detector, which can be thought as detect factor, essentially. $P_\gamma(x, y) = \int_0^{x\sqrt{y}+1} e^{-t} t^y / (y!) dt$ is incomplete gamma function and the detection threshold V_T can be expressed by the inverse function of the incomplete gamma function as

$$V_T = P_\gamma^{-1} (1 - P_{fa}, m) \tag{6}$$

So the detect factor of m cumulative pulses is derived as

$$D(m) = \frac{P_\gamma^{-1} (1 - P_{fa}, m)}{P_\gamma^{-1} (1 - P_d, m)} - 1 \tag{7}$$

where P_{fa} denotes radar false alarm probability that the system can tolerate.

It can be concluded from the above analysis that the maximum sensing range of the radar can be calculated based on the preset detection and false alarm probability under the premise that the relevant parameters are already available.

2.3 Connection Analysis

Vehicle connectivity is the crucial foundation of vehicular cooperative sensing, and only when vehicles are connected through V2V link, the perception data can be shared successfully.

In this section, the connection probability of a pair of adjacent vehicles under Rayleigh fading is discussed and the closed-form is provided.

Consider a pair of communication nodes, when the received SNR exceeds a certain threshold Φ, it is reasonable to assume the signal can be decoded correctly at receiver [10] and this pair of nodes can be thought of as connected.

Let Pr_c denotes the connect probability of two consecutive vehicles, i.e., the probability of received SNR at V_n sent by V_{n-1} exceed the threshold Φ. In what follows, the Pr_c at a distance d is derived.

The average SNR at distance d can be computed by

$$\overline{\gamma}_c(d) = \frac{G_t G_r \beta P_c}{d^2 P_{cn}} \tag{8}$$

By considering Rayleigh fading as the small-scale fading model, the connection analysis will be more realistic, and the received SNR under Rayleigh fading can be estimated according to the exponential distribution with a mean of average SNR. The PDF of received SNR at a distance d is given as

$$f_\Gamma(\gamma_c(d)) = \frac{1}{\overline{\gamma}_c(d)} e^{-\frac{\gamma_c(d)}{\overline{\gamma}_c(d)}} \tag{9}$$

The corresponding CDF of (12) is given as

$$\begin{aligned} F(\Gamma_c(d) < \gamma_c(d)) &= 1 - e^{-\frac{\gamma_c(d)}{\overline{\gamma}_c(d)}} \\ &= 1 - e^{-\frac{d^2 P_{cn} \gamma_c(d)}{G\beta P_c}} \end{aligned} \tag{10}$$

in which $\Gamma_c(d)$ is the random variable of the receiver SNR in communication process with a distance d.

Therefore, the successful connection probability is expressed as

$$\begin{aligned} Pr_c(d) &= Pr[\Gamma_c(d) > \Phi] \\ &= 1 - Pr[\Gamma_c(d) < \Phi] \\ &= e^{-\frac{d^2 P_{cn} \Phi}{G\beta P_c}} \end{aligned} \tag{11}$$

Constraint by the safe distance d_{min} of vehicle interval, The expectation of successful communication probability within the entire road with vehicle distribution $\tilde{f}_L(l) = \frac{\rho e^{-\rho l}}{e^{-l_{min}\rho}}$ is given as

$$\begin{aligned} Pr_{con} &= \mathbb{E}[Pr_c(L)] \\ &= \int_{d_{min}}^{+\infty} Pr_c(x) \tilde{f}_L(x) dx \\ &= \frac{\rho}{e^{-l_{min}\rho}} \int_{d_{min}}^{+\infty} e^{-(\frac{d^2 P_{cn} \Phi}{G\beta P_c} + \rho x)} \end{aligned} \tag{12}$$

the closed-form of (12) is shown at the top of this page due to space constraint.

It is worth noting that Pr_{con} is the connective probability only suit for one hop, when there are N hops between source and destination node, the end-to-end connective ability is $Pr_N = pr_{con}^N$ as the interval distance of any pair of adjacent vehicles is independent.

$$
\begin{aligned}
Pr_{con} &= \int_0^{+\infty} Pr_c(x)f(x)dx - \int_0^{d_{min}} Pr_c(x)f(x)dx \\
&= \frac{\rho}{e^{-l_{min}\rho}} \left\{ \frac{e^{\frac{\beta G P_c \rho^2}{4\Phi P_{cn}}} \sqrt{\pi} Erfc(\frac{\rho}{2\sqrt{\frac{\Phi P_n}{\beta G P_c}}})}{2\sqrt{\frac{\Phi P_n}{\beta G P_c}}} \right. \\
&\left. - \frac{e^{\frac{\beta G P_c \rho^2}{4\Phi P_{cn}}} \sqrt{P_c G \beta \pi}[-Erf(\frac{\sqrt{\beta G P_c}\rho}{2\Phi P_{cn}})] + Erf(\frac{2d_{min}\Phi P_{cn} + \beta G P_c \rho}{2\sqrt{\beta G \Phi P_{cn} P_c}})]}{2\sqrt{\Phi P_n}} \right\}
\end{aligned}
\tag{13}
$$

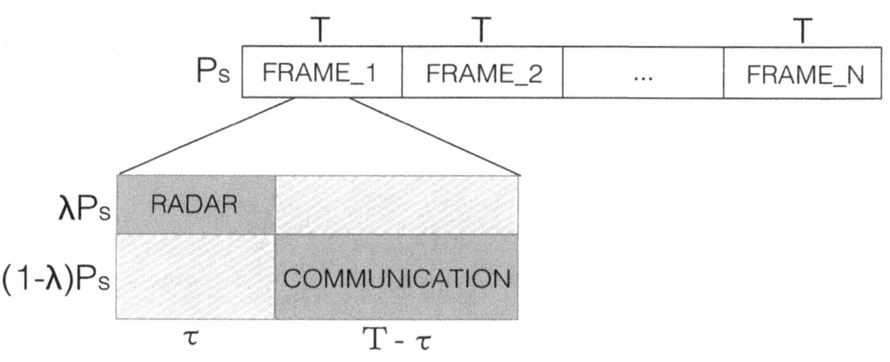

Fig. 2. Joint time and power allocation strategy

3 Perception-Connection Tradeoff

For the proposed radar cooperative sensing scheme, our objective is to maximize the average RCSCR by adjusting the power distribution coefficient $\lambda \in [0, 1]$ and radar sensing duration $\tau \in (0, T]$, with T being the total duration of one frame. The resource allocation strategy is shown in Fig. 2. Under this allocation strategy, the TD-JRC system work in radar mode with power $P_r = \lambda P_s$ within the duration τ, in remainder of one frame, the system work in communication mode with power $P_c = (1 - \lambda)P_s$.

It should be highlighted that the resource allocation scheme we proposed is not for any specific JRC hardware, but for the entire vehicle.

As described in Sect. 2.1, two same JRC hardwares are equipped at the front and rear of the vehicle, performing forward perception-connection and backward perception-connection, respectively. In the proposed cooperative sensing scheme, the JRC at the front of a vehicle is responsible for perceiving road information and receiving the perception information acquired from the adjacent vehicle in front, at the same time, the task of the other one JRC at the rear of the vehicle is to send the combination perception information of the received and its own to the adjacent rear vehicle.

From the above analysis, most of the power allocated to JRC equipped at the front is used for radar perceptive and most of the power allocated to JRC equipped at the rear is used for communication with adjacent one, therefor the radar power consuming at rear and communication power consuming at the front are small enough to be ignored.

To further improve cooperative sensing ability, in the remainder of this section, we will derive how the joint power and time allocation strategy influence the average RCSCR.

Let $\Xi(l)$ be the actual perception range for a vehicle with a distance of l from the car in front. When the vehicle interval is less than the maximum perception range of the radar R_{max}, the actual perception range is equal to vehicle interval due to being blocked by vehicle ahead [1], correspondingly, when there is no vehicle block, the actual perception range is R_{max}, i.e., $\Xi(l) = Min(R_{max}, l)$.

The expectation of radar actual perception range is given as

$$\begin{aligned}\mathbb{E}(\Xi(L)) &= \tilde{F}_L(L > R_{max})R_{max} + \int_{R_{min}}^{R_{max}} \tilde{f}_L(l)ldl \\ &= e^{-\rho R_{max}}R_{max} + \frac{e^{-\rho R_{min}}(1+\rho R_{min}) - e^{-\rho R_{max}}(1+\rho R_{max})}{\rho}\end{aligned} \quad (14)$$

It is unrealistic for the vehicle to connect to all the nodes in front, and the number of vehicles involved in one cooperative process is related to channel capacity and radar data generation data. Let η denotes the volume of data generated per second from radar. The involved vehicle number N for a cooperative process is given as

$$N = \frac{(T-\tau)C}{\eta\tau} \quad (15)$$

with C being the ergodic channel capacity [3], which is given as

$$C = B_s \int_{d_{min}}^{\infty} \tilde{f}_L(l)log(1+\overline{\gamma}_c(d)) \quad (16)$$

The main objective of the radar cooperative sensing scheme we proposed is to maximize the average RCSCR, which is derived as follows.

$$\begin{aligned}\mathbb{E}(RCSCR) = \mathbb{E}(&\Xi(L_1) + \Xi(L_2)Pr_c(L_1) + \Xi(L_3)Pr_c(L_2)Pr_c(L_1) \\ &+ \cdots + \Xi(L_{N+1})Pr_c(L_N)Pr_c(L_{N-1})\cdots Pr_c(L_1))\end{aligned} \quad (17)$$

As the vehicle interval between different pair of vehicles is independently identically distribution (iid), (17) can be organized as

$$\begin{aligned}\mathbb{E}(RCSCR) &= \mathbb{E}(\Xi(L)) + \mathbb{E}(\Xi(L))\mathbb{E}(Pr_c(L)) + \mathbb{E}(\Xi(L))\mathbb{E}(Pr_c(L)) \\ &\quad \mathbb{E}(Pr_c(L)) + \cdots + \mathbb{E}(\Xi(L_N))\underbrace{\mathbb{E}(Pr_c(L))\mathbb{E}(Pr_c(L))\cdots\mathbb{E}(Pr_c(L))}_{N} \\ &= \mathbb{E}(\Xi(L))(1 + \mathbb{E}(Pr_c(L)) + \mathbb{E}^2(Pr_c(L)) + \cdots + \mathbb{E}^N(Pr_c(L))) \\ &= \mathbb{E}(\Xi(L))\frac{1-\mathbb{E}^N(Pr_c(L))}{1-\mathbb{E}(Pr_c(L))} \\ &= \mathbb{E}(\Xi(L))\frac{1-Pr_{con}^N}{1-Pr_{con}}\end{aligned} \tag{18}$$

It can be seen from (18) that the more time and power allocated to radar, the much more sensing range it will have, and at the same time, power and time allocated to communication mode will be reduced, resulting in connection probability decrease. In other words, the improvement of radar sensing capability is achieved by sacrificing communication efficiency and vice versa.

In order to maximize the average objective function, it is necessary to configure the time and power allocation factors reasonably according to the vehicle density, so as to achieve a tradeoff between the radar function and the communication function.

4 Numerical Results and Simulations

In this section, numerical and simulation results will be presented to verify the proposed cooperative sensing scheme and the relationship between system performance and resource allocation strategy. Unless otherwise specified, we set $\Delta T = 4$ ms as time duration for one frame, total power of radar and communication functions is set to $P = 500$ mw, as the TD-JRC is implemented, both communication and radar function work at $f_s = 77$ GHz with $B_s = 200$ MHz, the generation rate of radar sensing data is set as $\eta = 10$ Mbits/s, for driving safety, the minimum distance between vehicles under extreme situation is set as $l_{min} = 10$ m. Other parameters are set as $k = 1.38 \times 10^{-23}$ J/K, $T_s = 293$ K, $G = G_t G_r = 30$ db, $\beta = 0.5$, $\sigma = 1\text{m}^2$, $F = 0.4$, $p_d = 0.99$, $P_{fa} = 0.01$, $T_r = 100$ µs. The communication channel considers both large-scale path loss and small-scale Rayleigh fading, and the radar sensing channel is considered to conform to the large-scale fading model.

In the beginning, numerical results and Monte Carlo simulation results are provided to verify the theoretical analysis drawn in the previous sections, and for each power allocation factor λ, 2000 times Monte-Carlo calculation are conducted. Figure 3 illustrates the relation between power allocation factor and average RCSCR with the fixed $\tau = 2$ ms and $\rho = 13 \times 10^{-3}$. The cures show that the numerical results and Monte Carlo simulation results are matched to each other, which verifies the correctness of the derivation process. The curves

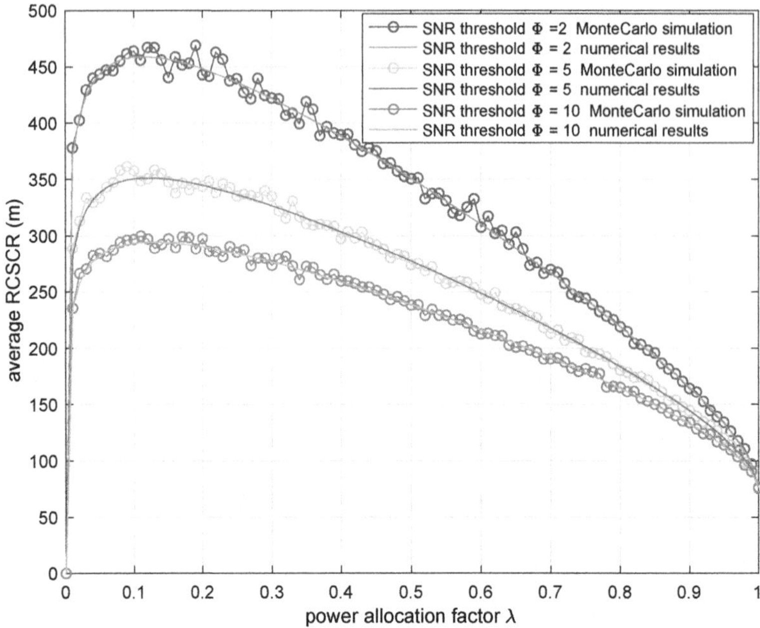

Fig. 3. Relation between average RCSCR and power allocation factor λ with $\tau = 2$ ms, $\rho = 13 \times 10^{-3}$

with different SNR have similar trends, and as Φ decreases, the maximum average RCSCR, i.e., the highest point of each curve, will increase.

Figure 4 illustrates how the allocation strategy of time and power influence the average RCSCR in the form of three-dimensional (3D) graph with vehicle density $\rho = 1 \times 10^{-3}$, 3×10^{-3}, 8×10^{-3} and 25×10^{-3}, respectively. It is obviously seen from results that the vehicle density will greatly affect the power and time allocation scheme. Specifically, when vehicle density is 1×10^{-3}, a relatively low-density state for vehicles on the road, either time or power resource is allocated to radar mode to a large extent. In contrast, when vehicle density is 30×10^{-3}, a relatively high-density state for vehicles on the road, either time or power resource is allocated to communication function to a large extent. When the vehicle density is 3×10^{-3} or 8×10^{-3}, the allocation of resources is relatively balanced, and there is no apparent trend. This is because when vehicles are in a low-density state, the distance between adjacent vehicles is very large. The establishment of a link connection requires a lot of resources and the probability of success is low. The performance gain brought by the exchange of sensor information is very minimal. In this state, the resources of the system are mainly allocated to the radar function to enhance vehicle's own perception ability. When the vehicle is in a high-density state, correspondingly, vehicle's own perception ability is blocked by the preceding vehicle and will not continue to increase with the increase of power and perception time. Therefore, allocating more time and power resources to the communication function will greatly increase the performance of cooperative perception.

Note that regardless of the vehicle density, there is a definite power allocation strategy to maximize average RCSCR under a given vehicle density.

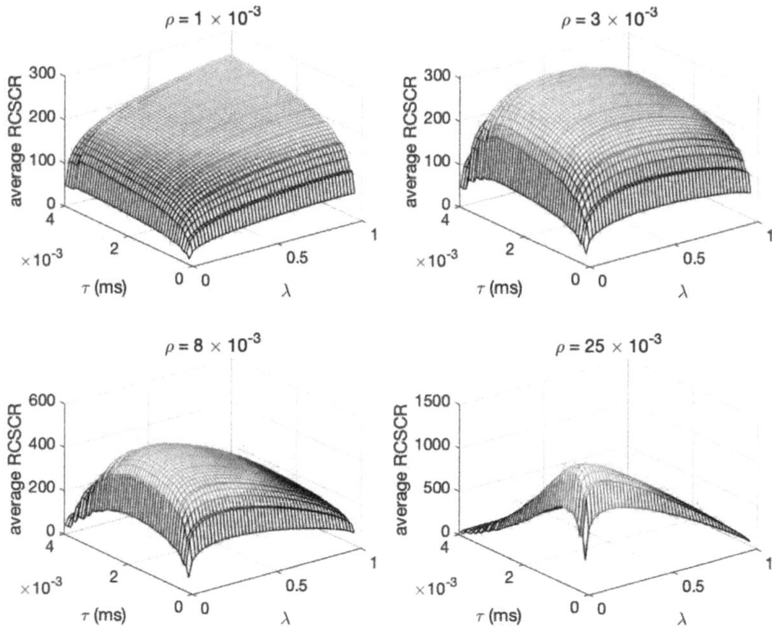

Fig. 4. Relation between average RCSCR and radar sensing time τ as well as power allocation factor λ with $\rho = 1 \times 10^{-3}, 3 \times 10^{-3}, 8 \times 10^{-3}, 25 \times 10^{-3}$, respectively

Figure 5 illustrates the change of the optimal power distribution factor with the vehicle density. It can be seen that in the case of $\tau = 0.2$ ms, 0.5 ms and 2.1 ms, as the vehicle density increases, the power distribution factor gradually decreases. That is, the power allocated to the radar function decreases and the power allocated to the communication function increases, which is consistent with the previous analysis. When $\tau = 3.7$ ms, the optimal power allocation factor will no longer change with the vehicle density but always be 1. In other words, all of the power is allocated to the radar to enhance vehicle's own perception ability. This is because when $\tau = 3.7$ ms, most of the time is allocated to the radar function, and the throughput of the time left for the communication function is not enough to support one-hop communication transmission, that is to say, at this time, the system completely relies on its own radar to realize perception.

Figure 6 illustrates the achievable perception range gain g_p with the proposed radar cooperative sensing scheme under different vehicle density ρ. The benchmark for comparison is the relatively smaller of average vehicle interval $\overline{L} = 1/\rho$

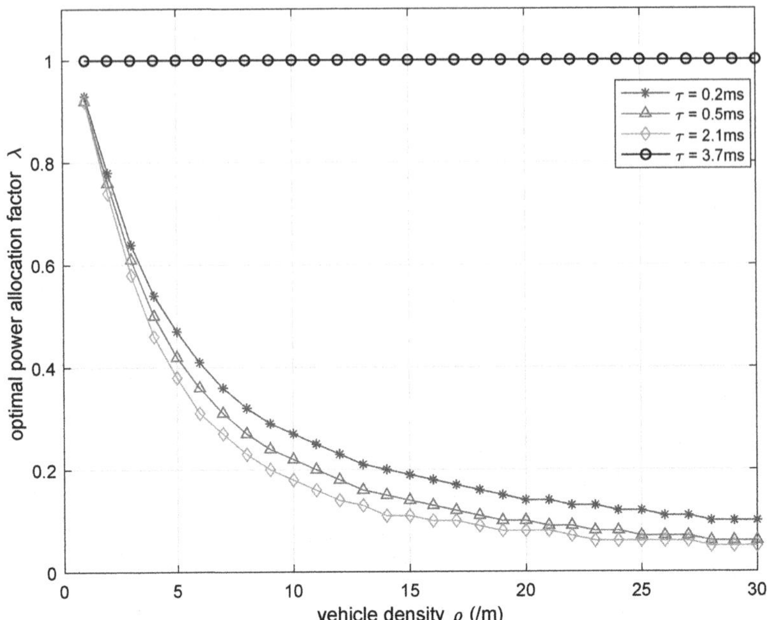

Fig. 5. Relation between vehicle density ρ and the most optimal power allocation factor λ with $t = 0.2, 0.5, 2.1, 3.7$, respectively

and the maximize radar detection range R_{max}, i.e.,

$$g_p = \frac{RCSCR}{min\{\overline{L}, R_{max}\}} \tag{19}$$

For a certain ρ, g_p increases with the decrease of SNR threshold Φ. With lower Φ, vehicles are more likely to establish connections with adjacent vehicles and share perception data. We observe in our simulation that When the vehicle density ρ is greater than 5×10^{-3}, our proposed resource allocation strategy begins to play a significant role, and as the density of vehicles increases, the effect of perception gain become more and more prominent.

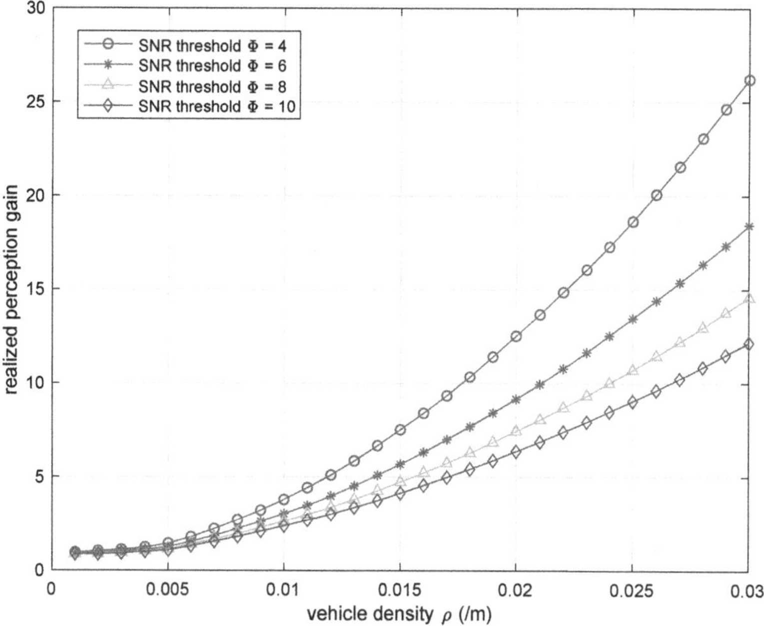

Fig. 6. The relation between realized perception gain and vehicle density ρ

5 Conclusion

This paper has proposed a novel JRC-based radar cooperative sensing scheme for the vehicular network by multi-hop. Through this scheme, vehicles can obtain perceptual information far beyond the range of their own perceptual ability covered. In addition, we focused on analyzing the impact of joint time and power allocation strategy on the performance of the average RCSCR. Numerical and simulation results have proved that for a specific vehicle density ρ, there is a definite joint time and power allocation strategy that maximizes average RCSCR.

References

1. Jia, B., Wei, Z., Liu, B., Feng, Z.: Performance analysis for the coexistence of radar and communication in VANETs. In: 2019 IEEE/CIC International Conference on Communications in China (ICCC), pp. 979–983 (2019)
2. DiFranco, J.R.B.: Radar detection. The Institution of Engineering and Technology (2004)
3. Ozgur, E.: Asymptotic ergodic capacity of multidimensional vector-sensor array MIMO channels. IEEE Trans. Wireless Commun. **7**(9), 3297–3300 (2008)
4. Eskandarian Azim, W., Chaoxian, S.C.: Research advances and challenges of autonomous and connected ground vehicles. IEEE Trans. Intel. Transp. Syst. **22**(2), 683–711 (2021)

5. Kim, S.-W., et al.: Multivehicle cooperative driving using cooperative perception: design and experimental validation. IEEE Trans. Intel. Transp. Syst. **16**(2), 663–680 (2015)
6. Lewinski, D.: Nonstationary probabilistic target and clutter scattering models. IEEE Trans. Antennas Propag. **31**(3), 490–498 (1983)
7. Papoulis, A.: Random Variables and Stochastic Processes. McGraw Hill (1994)
8. Quan, S., Qian, W., Guq, J., Zhang, V.: Radar-communication integration: an overview. In: The 7th IEEE/International Conference on Advanced Infocomm Technology, pp. 98–103 (2014)
9. Richards, M.A., Scheer, J., Holm, W.A., Melvin, W.L.: Principles of modern radar. Citeseer (2010)
10. Abuelenin, S.M., Elaraby, S.: A generalized framework for connectivity analysis in vehicle-to-vehicle communications. IEEE Trans. Intel. Transp. Syst. 1–5 (2021). https://doi.org/10.1109/TITS.2021.3052846
11. Chen, X., Feng, Z., Wei, Z., Zhang, P., Yuan, X.: Code-division OFDM joint communication and sensing system for 6G machine-type communication. IEEE Internet of Things J. **8**, 1 (2021)
12. Feng, Z., Fang, Z., Wei, Z., Chen, X., Quan, Z., Ji, D.: Joint radar and communication: a survey. Chin. Commun. **17**(1), 1–27 (2020)

Unmanned Aerial Underwater Vehicle (UAUV) in the Ocean Sensor Network

Qihang Cao and Gongliang Liu(✉)

Harbin Institute of Technology, Weihai 264209, China
liugl@hit.edu.cn

Abstract. Human exploration of the ocean has never stopped. A large number of sensors are placed in the ocean to establish ocean sensor networks to obtain more information about the marine environment, crustal dynamic changes and so on. With the development of science and technology, autonomous underwater vehicle (AUV) emerges as the times require. As an underwater sensor acquisition system, it has been widely used in ocean sensor networks. Due to the complex and changeable marine environment, the AUV can not travel accurately, resulting in a lot of resources waste of time and energy, even the loss of AUV, so the information can not be timely and effective collected. In this paper, the Unmanned Aerial Underwater Vehicle (UAUV) is introduced into the ocean sensor network, and the advantages and disadvantages of the UAUV in the ocean sensor network are compared objectively from multiple dimensions. Through the ergodic search algorithm, the optimal water entry point for the UAUV to complete the task in the shortest time and the minimum power consumption is found, and the performance of the underwater vehicle's cross domain mode and underwater mode ocean sensor data acquisition task is compared and analyzed. The results show that compared with the traditional underwater mode, the cross domain mode saves 74.7% of the time and 24.34% of the energy consumption, which proves the feasibility, stability and High efficiency of introducing the air submersible into the ocean sensor network.

Keywords: Ocean sensor network · AUV · Unmanned aerial underwater vehicle · Ergodic search algorithm

1 Introduction

Ocean sensor network is more and more attention from scholars in recent years, with the development of The Times, the progress of science and technology, the potential of human exploration of the unknown sea have been digging, a large amount of mature machinery type sensor is arranged in the ocean environment information collection, the

This work was supported in part by the National Natural Science Foundation of China under Grant 61971156, in part by the Shandong Provincial Natural Science Foundation under Grant ZR2019MF035 and Grant ZR2020MF141, in part by Science and Technology Development Program at Weihai under Grant 2019KYCXJJYB06.

© ICST Institute for Computer Sciences, Social Informatics and Telecommunications Engineering 2022
Published by Springer Nature Switzerland AG 2022. All Rights Reserved
S. Shi et al. (Eds.): 6GN 2021, LNICST 439, pp. 83–96, 2022.
https://doi.org/10.1007/978-3-031-04245-4_8

earth's crust, Marine species, Marine dynamic change information of military intelligence, etc. It provides necessary data support for the further research of Marine science, and also provides reliable support for the exploration of the unknown world in the future. Over a wide area of ocean, mechanical sensors can be distributed in a variety of ways. Luo et al. [1] summarized three kinds of sensor network topologies, namely two-dimensional static underwater sensor network, three-dimensional static underwater sensor network and three-dimensional underwater sensor network with AUV. Among them, the data exchange process of each sensor network cannot be separated from wireless communication. Due to different media, the environment of wireless communication is relatively complex in sea water than on land, and accompanied by a series of experimental problems, material problems and energy problems, its development speed is relatively slow, the communication rate is low, and the transmission distance is close. At present, there are three kinds of underwater wireless communication commonly used, namely underwater electromagnetic wave communication, underwater optical communication and underwater acoustic communication. Electromagnetic wave in seawater has weak penetration and extremely serious attenuation [2], so it cannot be used as an effective way of long-distance communication in seawater environment [3]. For optical communication, due to the high available bandwidth of optical communication [4], it can reach a high speed transmission of about 100 m. Research data shows that LED-based visible light communication can establish a communication link as long as 500 m in pure water. However, compared with the vast ocean area on Earth, the communication distance of 500 m is far from enough to meet the communication needs of ocean sensor. Therefore, in the ocean communication system, the communication mode with acoustic wave [5] as the carrier appears. Its transmission distance can vary from several hundred meters to several thousand meters, and it is the only widely used and the most mature underwater remote communication mode at present. Even so, regardless of the energy, for underwater acoustic communication of several thousand meters, it is still unable to effectively transmit the sensor data from tens or even hundreds of kilometers away from the coast to the coastal server. Therefore, AUVs is introduced into the third topology above, that is, a three-dimensional underwater sensor network with AUVs is introduced to solve the problem of sensor information collection and data exchange between nodes. As the carrier of data information of sensor nodes, the AUVs shuttles between sensor nodes and is responsible for collecting a large amount of information and sending it back to the shore server.

At present, the researches of the AUV has made great progress, as well as there has been a mature AUV data acquisition system, which can the sensor at the bottom of the sea and the coast between reciprocating transmission more information. AUV is widely sought after in ocean sensor networks due to its advantages of flexibility, reliability, low cost and labor saving. In order to improve the collection efficiency of water column data, Luo et al. [6] designed an AUV data collection system based on wireless grid network, the AUV data acquisition system is composed of multiple AUVs, were completed in a set of grid data collection work, and then focus on the main AUV for data fusion, due to the method of wireless mesh networks for AUVs provides a relatively reliable communication environment, at a lower cost greatly improve the efficiency of the data acquisition of underwater robot. Lee and Yu [7] designed an AUV with single propeller motion to collect water column data in shallow water. AUV using deformable buoyancy system provides steering function, by reducing the number of propeller, improve the utilization efficiency of the energy of the AUV, which battery life for 9 h, can perform 15 times data acquisition tasks. Huang et al. [8] put forward a realization method based on clustering matrix (ACMC) of AUV auxiliary data collection scheme. By improving K-means algorithm, a two-stage AUV trajectory optimization mechanism based on greedy algorithm is introduced. AUV reduces the time delay and energy consumption of data collection of cluster nodes by about 4 times compared with the original scheme, reduces the energy consumption of nodes by more than 30%, and greatly improves the network life. In order to balance the energy consumption and prolong the service life of sensor networks, Yan et al. [9] expressed the energy optimization problem as minimizing the sum of the side lengths of a specific graph, and proposed a topology optimization scheme and local routing decision algorithm for sensor deployment based on minimum weighted grid graph. At the same time, a path planning strategy based on dynamic value was designed for AUV, making the performance of the whole ocean sensor network has been improved.

In addition, except a lot of work on improving the performance of AUVs data collection and reducing energy consumption, many studies also involve the underwater positioning of AUVs, the collaborative work of AUVs groups, AUVs path planning and other directions, so that AUVs can complete underwater work more efficiently as collecting information from sensors. Miller et al. [10] obtained the information from the seafloor profile by acoustic method, formed a series of seafloor acoustic images to estimate the speed and position of the AUV, and completed the underwater positioning of the AUV. Simulation results show that the algorithm is effective and good estimation quality is obtained. Ferri et al. [11], under the leadership of collaborative autonomy and data fusion of the AUV colony, developed a track management module integrated into the independent software of the AUV to realize information sharing and improve the overall performance of the AUV colony through data-driven collaboration among the AUVs, the average packet transfer rate between AUVs increased to around 50%. Willners et al. [12] proposed a method of using autonomous surface ships (ASVs) as AUV communication and navigation AIDS (CNA). A combination of search tree-based priority expansion and random sampling based exploration was used to locate CNA in strategic locations. At the same time, in order to reduce the position error and uncertainty of the AUV and realize the precise positioning of the AUV, the strategic path point and the best ranging information transmission time of the CNA were sought. Lim et al. [13] proposed 12 algorithms based on particle swarm intelligence (PSI) and applied them to the performance evaluation of AUV optimal path planning problem under underwater obstacles and non-uniform flow environment. The algorithm considers the physical limitations and practicability of AUV, meanwhile the advantages and disadvantages of each algorithm are analyzed comprehensively, and the most appropriate optimization method is selected from a variety of methods.

In the process of the gradual development of the AUV, the ocean sensor network based on the AUV has also made great progress. However, there are many unavoidable physical limitations in the underwater motion of AUV, such as very slow motion speed, poor flexibility, unable to position itself accurately, single communication mode and high energy consumption, which make it still have a great space for development. To solve the inevitable series of problems, a new approach is on the way. In recent years, the unmanned aerial underwater vehicle (UAUV), which combines AUV with UAV, appears in people's vision and gets rapid development. Its high speed flight and underwater movement as well as the ability to work across the field can solve more problems for the ocean sensor network.

Related concepts of UAUV appeared early, but due to the limitations of energy, materials, power and other aspects, the development of UAUV was relatively slow in the early stage. However, with the gradual conquer of related technical problems, the emergence of UAV has once again aroused the extensive interest of many marine and underwater researchers, meanwhile officially entered the human stage.

As early as 2014, Yao et al. [14] introduced a kind of flying and diving submarine "flying fish", which is an early UAUV. By simulating the morphological characteristics of biological flying fish and the variable density method of waterfowl, "flying fish" realized the trans medium conversion of air and water, and finally verified the feasibility of this method through experiments. Weisler et al. [15] described the concept of fixed wing UAUV and developed a fixed wing UAUV to verify its feasibility and analyze its performance. The UAUV adopts the structure of single motor and single propeller, and uses passive inflow and drainage wings to achieve cross domain function. The UAUV combines the advantages of the aircraft's speed and long range, as well as the durability, diving ability and stealth ability of the submersible, this allowed it to avoids a series of shortcomings of the underwater robot, and makes a qualitative breakthrough in the efficiency of underwater related work on the physical level. In the actual test, the UAUV can complete 12 full cycle cross domain tasks at a time. Maia et al. [16] successfully completed the design and implementation of a full working multi rotor UAUV. The dynamic model of an eight-rotor quadcopter was established by Newton Euler method. The results show that the UAUV has achieved good results in both media and can realize seamless transition between the two media. Lu et al. [17, 18] proposed a new solution, which solved the problem of poor durability of the existing UAUV. The scheme combines the design ideas of fixed wing UAV, multi rotor and underwater glider(UG), and adds a new light aerodynamic buoyancy control system. The experiment shows that the UAUV is very suitable for moving in different media and can achieve long-distance endurance in the air or water. Based on the concept of the quadcopter, Kasno et al. [19] constructed a long-distance amphibious UAUV, which can hover in the air at 200 cm height and dive depth in water about 20 cm, which proves the feasibility and effectiveness of the four axis UAV cross motion. In addition, the UAUV is simulated and tested, and its good withstand voltage performance is verified. Wang et al. [20] designed a hybrid aerial aquatic vehicle based on underwater obstacles crossing background to collect water column data. When underwater obstacles are encountered, it can switch to flight mode to cross obstacles and turn on GPS for real-time navigation. At present, the UAUV has been developed and tested. The test results show that the UAUV can sail in shallow water environment, and verify its maneuverability of underwater takeoff and underwater glide.

UAUV, with its multiple advantages of high-speed in the air, accurate positioning, low energy consumption per 100 km, underwater diving, stability, concealment, and cross media avoidance of obstacles and dangers, can improve the data acquisition efficiency of large ocean sensor networks by an order of magnitude. The main research work of this paper is as follows.

1) Scene construction. Firstly, the ideal ocean environment is simulated, the ocean sensor scene is established, and the sensor position and communication distance are set. Then the UAUV is constructed, its initial position and flag state are set, and its related physical parameters are set.
2) Performance comparison of UAUV and AUV. According to the above scene, the time consumption and energy consumption of UAUV data acquisition efficiency under underwater motion and cross-domain motion are compared. It will be proved that the performance of UAUV is much better than AUV, indicating the necessity of introducing UAUV into ocean sensor networks. At the same time, the maneuverability data of UAV underwater movement and cross-domain movement are presented intuitively, so as to guide the further research and development of UAUV.
3) Performance analysis. Through the ergodic search algorithm, the effectiveness and reliability of the UAUV in the ocean sensor network are verified in terms of time and energy consumption. It will be proved that UAUV can effectively improve the overall stability of ocean sensor networks, save a lot of time cost and energy consumption.

2 Scenario Model

UAUV has the ability of high-speed air operations, can reach many large ocean sensor nodes in a short time, and complete a large number of data acquisition work in time. This paper studies a ideal ocean sensor network scenario, and selects an ocean environment with seamounts as the background. The topography of the sea floor is complex. There are many mountains. The top of the mountain is higher than the sea level. The specific scene is shown in Fig. 1. At the same time, sensors are arranged in the key areas of the ocean to collect marine environmental data. Each sensor has a certain communication range. When the UAUV enters the range, it broadcasts the search signal and establishes a connection with the sensor to collect the sensor data. In this scenario, the scale of sensor network is large, and the distance between each two groups of sensors is far. The data information collected in the ocean is collected by the UAUV and sent to the coastal server regularly. For UAUV, in addition to the superiority of air and underwater, it has dual communication system carrying underwater acoustic communication and electromagnetic communication simultaneously. When operating in the air, UAUV can interact with the cloud server or transmit data information to the shore server through electromagnetic wave communication, meanwhile obtain real-time positioning information through the global navigation system, and correct the accumulated underwater positioning error. The data acquisition process of UAUV in underwater sensor network can be divided into two ways: cross domain flight path acquisition of sensor data and full underwater path acquisition of sensor data.

Fig. 1. UAUV data acquisition in ocean sensor networks.

In view of this situation, this paper thinks that the problems to be solved are as follows: In the ideal environment, the best water entry point of UAUV in the cross domain mode is found by traversal search algorithm, and the advantages and disadvantages of cross domain flight path and all underwater path in ocean sensor network data acquisition are compared, which shows that UAUV has high acquisition efficiency and energy saving effect, as well as highlights the necessity and innovation of introducing UAUV.

For this problem, the main parameters to be compared between the two paths are the time required to collect underwater sensor information and the energy consumed to complete a task. This is an ideal model, which does not consider too many complex factors, such as wind speed, water flow, water temperature, air temperature (the consumption and damage of temperature to battery), underwater obstacles, energy consumption of UAUV in and out of the ocean, etc. It is assumed that wind speed and water flow have no effect on UAUV speed, water temperature and air temperature are normal, there is no bad environment in ideal environment, and there is no obstacle in UAUV path planning.

In order to simplify the complexity of the problem, a single sensor is selected as the target point of UAUV data acquisition. As shown in Fig. 2, a two-dimensional ocean plane model from UAUV to single sensor is constructed. Set the UAUV at sea level, and set the starting position of the UAUV coordinate (x_U, h_U) as the origin, set the speed in the air as v_{Air}, and the flight power in the air as P_{Air}. Assuming that P_{Air} does not change with v_{Air}. the flight speed v_{Air} should meet the requirements

$$0 \leq v_{Air} \leq v_{Air}^{\max}, \tag{1}$$

at the same time, the velocity of UAUV in underwater is set as v_{water}, and the power of UAUV in underwater is set as P_{water}. Assuming that P_{water} does not change with the magnitude of v_{water}, the velocity of UAUV in underwater should meet the requirements

$$0 \leq v_{water} \leq v_{water}^{\max}, \tag{2}$$

the communication system of UAUV is a dual communication system, which includes underwater acoustic communication with communication distance r and wireless electromagnetic wave communication with line of sight. The UAUV can choose any communication mode according to its own environment. When the UAUV is underwater, it can use underwater acoustic communication, while in the air, it can use wireless electromagnetic wave communication.

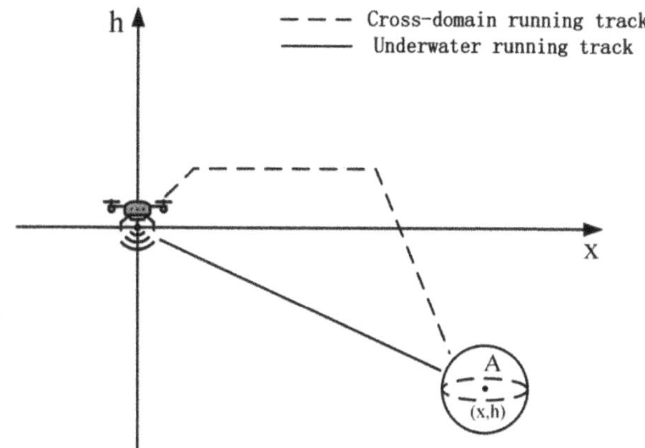

Fig. 2. UAUV with a two-dimensional plane model of a single sensor.

In the study of this problem, the energy of the UAV is not considered, and the total energy of the UAV is expressed as C, C should meet the requirements

$$C \to \infty. \tag{3}$$

In this paper, the coordinate of a sensor node A is (x, h), and the underwater acoustic communication distance of the sensor is the same as r. This paper objectively compares the two modes of cross-domain and underwater motion, and intuitively gives the speed, power and more intuitive data. It is assumed that the R value is fixed and the influence of the underwater channel environment on the communication distance is not considered.

In order to analyze the velocity model of the UAUV in more detail, the air acceleration a_{Air} and the underwater acceleration a_{water} of the UAUV are considered in the model, and it is assumed that the values of a_{Air} and a_{water} are fixed. Due to the acceleration and deceleration process of the UAUV in motion, the relationship between the time t_{water} required for the UAUV to complete a task in the underwater diving mode and the path distance $(l_{water} - r)$ required for the UAUV's current position to move to the vicinity of sensor A can be expressed as

$$t_{water} = \begin{cases} \frac{l_{water}-r}{v_{water}^{\max}} + \frac{v_{water}^{\max}}{a_{water}}, & l_{water} \geq \frac{(v_{water}^{\max})^2}{a_{water}} \\ \sqrt{\frac{2 \cdot (l_{water}-r)}{a_{water}}}, & 0 \leq l_{water} < \frac{(v_{water}^{\max})^2}{a_{water}} \end{cases} \tag{4}$$

where, l_{water} is the Euclidean distance between UAUV and sensor node A, which is expressed as

$$l_{water} = \sqrt{(x - x_U)^2 + (h - h_U)^2}, \tag{5}$$

similarly, the relationship between the time t_{Air} required for UAUV to move in the air and the path distance required for UAUV to move into the location of water entry point x_{Air} can be expressed as

$$t_{Air} = \begin{cases} \frac{l_{Air}}{v_{Air}^{\max}} + \frac{v_{Air}^{\max}}{a_{Air}}, & l_{Air} \geq \frac{(v_{Air}^{\max})^2}{a_{Air}} \\ \sqrt{\frac{2 \cdot l_{Air}}{a_{Air}}}, & 0 \leq l_{Air} < \frac{(v_{Air}^{\max})^2}{a_{Air}} \end{cases}, \tag{6}$$

however, sensor A is installed underwater. the UAUV needs to be converted from air mode to underwater mode on the water surface after flying in the air, therefore t_{Air} cannot be directly expressed as the time t_{cross} needed to travel from UAUV to sensor A. Assuming that the velocity of UAUV from the air to the water is 0, the UAUV mode conversion time and the flight altitude in the air are ignored, and the diving time t_{water} of UAUV is considered on the basis of t_{Air}. Therefore, the cross-domain motion t_{cross} time can be expressed as the sum of t_{Air} and t_{water}, t_{cross} can be expressed as

$$t_{cross} = \begin{cases} \left. \begin{array}{l} \frac{l_1}{v_{Air}^{\max}} + \frac{v_{Air}^{\max}}{a_{Air}}, l_1 \geq \frac{(v_{Air}^{\max})^2}{a_{Air}} \\ \sqrt{\frac{2 \cdot l_1}{a_{Air}}}, 0 \leq l_1 < \frac{(v_{Air}^{\max})^2}{a_{Air}} \end{array} \right\} t_{Air} \\ \left. \begin{array}{l} \frac{l_2 - r}{v_{water}^{\max}} + \frac{v_{water}^{\max}}{a_{water}}, l_2 \geq \frac{(v_{water}^{\max})^2}{a_{water}} \\ \sqrt{\frac{2 \cdot (l_2 - r)}{a_{water}}}, 0 \leq l_2 < \frac{(v_{water}^{\max})^2}{a_{water}} \end{array} \right\} t_{water} \end{cases}, \tag{7}$$

where, l_1 is the flying distance in the air during the UAUV's cross-domain movement, and l_2 is the distance from the sea surface to the vicinity of sensor A during the UAUV's cross-domain movement. The sum of the two represents the total distance l_{cross} of the UAV from air and underwater cross-domain movement to the vicinity of sensor A, i.e.

$$l_{cross} = l_1 + l_2. \tag{8}$$

The whole process of UAUV moving from the starting point to sensor a and then collecting data can be regarded as completing a task, the total energy consumption W_{cross} can be expressed as

$$W_{cross} = P_1 \cdot t_1 + P_2 \cdot t_2 + \cdots, \tag{9}$$

that is, the sum of the product of the power corresponding to the UAUV motion mode and its motion time.

3 Analog Simulation

Through the establishment of the corresponding model of the problem, the system variable planning, and according to the results of the objective analysis of UAUV. The data acquisition method of UAUV underwater motion mode is simple and refined, while the data acquisition method of cross domain mode is relatively complex. In this paper, the best entry point of UAUV is searched by traversal, so as to choose the most effective path and save time and energy as much as possible.

According to the objective data of UAUV given by Wang et al. [20], we may reasonably assume the specific performance parameters of UAUV in this scenario, as shown in Table 1.

Table 1. Performance parameters of UAUV in simulation test.

Parameter	Meaning and value
v_{Air}^{max}	The maximum speed of the UAUV in the air is 20 m/s
a_{Air}	The maximum acceleration of the UAUV in the air is 5 m/s^2
p_{Air}	The operating power of the UAUV in the air is 180 W
v_{water}^{max}	The maximum speed of the UAUV in the sea is 5 m/s
a_{water}	The maximum acceleration of the UAUV in the sea is 1 m/s^2
P_{water}	The operating power of the UAUV is 60 W when submerged in the sea
r	The maximum distance of UAUV and sensor underwater acoustic communication is 1000 m

In the simulation test, given the specific location coordinates $(10^5, 10^3)$ of sensor A, the unit is m, that is, sensor A is placed 1 km under the sea, 100 km horizontally from the starting point of UAUV.

According to the model, the algorithm idea was determined, and the time and power consumption needed to complete the data collection of UAUV underwater motion mode were obtained. The traversal method was used to search the optimal entry point of UAUV cross-domain motion mode, and the shortest time and minimum power consumption to complete the task were calculated respectively.

Algorithm 1: Search algorithm for the best water entry point based on traversal
1: Calculate the time and power consumption of underwater mode
2: Cycle
3: for L1 = 0:5:10^6
4: Calculate and record the minimum time t_{cross} and power consumption W_{cross} of cross domain mode
5: Compare the minimum update time t_{cross} and power consumption W_{cross}
6: Record the best water entry point L1 for the shortest time and minimum power consumption respectively
7: end for
8: Until the end of the loop, traverse the optimal results

4 Performance Analysis

In order to verify the advantages of the UAUV described in this paper, the following results are obtained through simulation. Firstly, the data acquisition time of two motion modes is analyzed. It can be seen that in the underwater navigation mode, the time t_{water} for UAUV to collect data from the initial point to the sensor A is 19806 s, while in the cross domain mode, the time t_{cross} for UAV to complete data collection is only 5002.65 s. From Fig. 3, we can see the relationship between the two modes. Compared with the traditional AUV, the time of the cross domain mode UAUV saves nearly 74.7%. According to the simulation results, the water entry point L1 is the water surface at 9.974 $\times$ 10^4 m from the starting point of UAUV, which is the coordinate point (9.974 $\times$ 10^4, 0), with the shortest time as the leading factor.

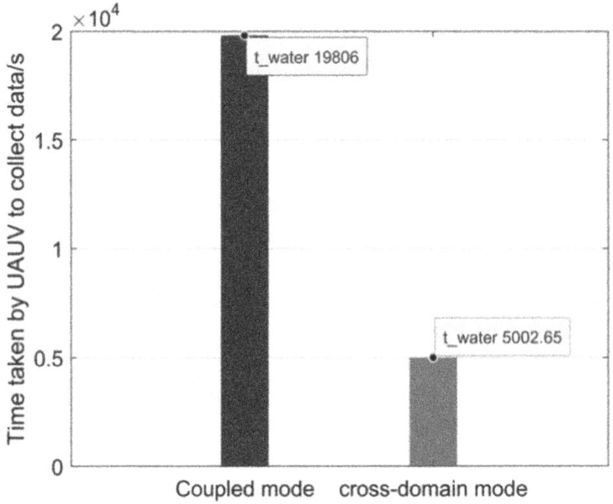

Fig. 3. Comparison of data acquisition time for different motion modes of UAUV.

From the analysis of energy consumption dimension, we can see that the energy consumption W_{water} of UAUV in underwater navigation mode is 330.1 Wh. In cross domain mode, the optimal water entry point L1 with the shortest time as the dominant search is (9.974 $\times$ 10^4, 0), and the energy consumption W_{cross} is 249.744 Wh. We can see from Fig. 4.

Among them, the energy consumption of cross domain UAUV is 24.34% lower than that of traditional AUV. However, with the shortest time as the dominant factor, its energy consumption is not the minimum. The minimum energy consumption W_{cross} of L1 coordinate (9.8865 $\times$ 10^4, 0) is 249.155 Wh, which is 24.52% lower than that of traditional AUV. The results show that the energy consumption based on the shortest time is basically the same as that based on the minimum energy consumption, but it is proved that the energy consumption of UAUV completing the task in the shortest time is not the minimum energy consumption.

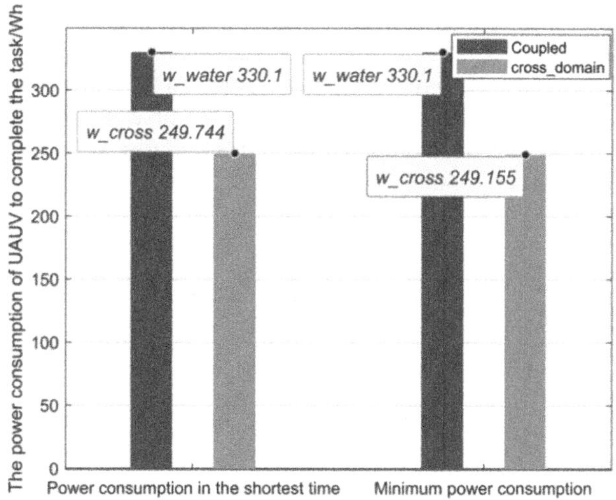

Fig. 4. Comparison of energy consumption for data acquisition in different motion modes of UAUV.

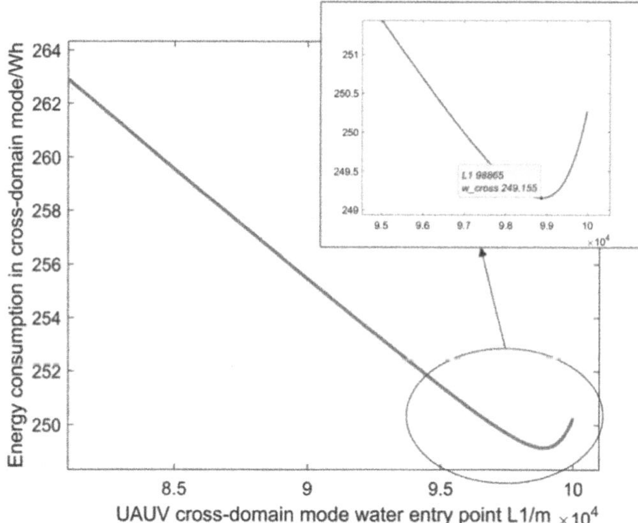

Fig. 5. Relationship between UAUV water entry point L1 and energy consumption.

Taking the water entry point L1 of UAUV cross-domain model as the analysis variable, it can be seen from Fig. 5 that when L1 is less than 9.8×10^4 m, the relationship between the water entry point and the energy consumption is approximately linear, that is, the energy required by UAUV to complete the task gradually decreases with the distance from the water entry point, while L1 increased from 9.8865×10^4 m to the horizontal distance of sensor A 10×10^4 m, the energy consumption shows a rapid upward trend. This indicates that the longer the flight time of UAUV in the air, the less energy is needed to complete the data acquisition task. At the same time, it also reflects the advantages of the UAUV in the air flight, and the necessity of introducing the UAUV into the ocean sensor network to replace the traditional AUV. The relationship between the time of UAUV entering the water point L1 and the time required to complete the task is shown in Fig. 6, and the trend is similar to that in Fig. 5, when L1 is greater than 9.974×10^4 m, the time consumption began to rise.

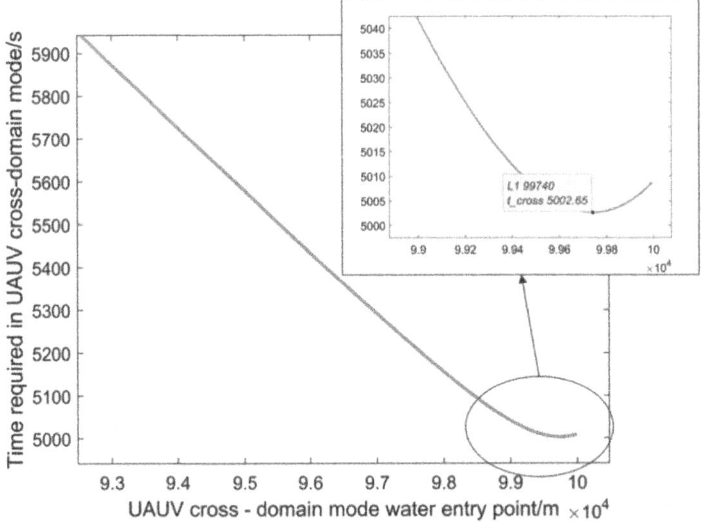

Fig. 6. Relationship between UAUV water entry point L1 and time.

5 Conclusion

This paper introduces the current situation of underwater robot in ocean sensor network and the development of UAUV, analyzes the advantages of UAUV, and proposes to introduce UAUV into ocean sensor network. Firstly, this paper makes a direct comparison between UAUV and traditional AUV in terms of speed and energy consumption. Through traversal search, find the best water entry point. The experimental results show that the running time of UAUV is 74.7% lower than that of AUV, and the energy consumption was reduced by 24.52%. At the same time, the influence of different water entry points on the time and energy consumption when the UAUV cross-domain motion collects sensor data is also shown. The simulation results show that the performance advantages of the UAUV, as well as the real-time performance and energy cost of data acquisition in the ocean sensor network are very good. The simulation results aim to provide intuitive data for further understanding of UAUV, show the advantages of UAUV in collecting ocean sensor data, and provide data support for guiding the next research and development of UAUV. UAUV not only shows advantages in the ocean sensor network, but also can carry servers, etc. Therefore, UAUV also can provide powerful data processing capacity and communication relay capacity for the ocean communication network.

References

1. Luo, J., Chen, Y., Wu, M., Yang, Y.: A survey of routing protocols for underwater wireless sensor networks. IEEE Commun. Surv. Tutor. **23**(1), 137–160, Firstquarter (2021). https://doi.org/10.1109/COMST.2020.3048190
2. Benson, B., et al.: Design of a low-cost, underwater acoustic modem for short-range sensor networks. In: Oceans'10 IEEE Sydney, 2010, pp. 1–9. https://doi.org/10.1109/OCEANSSYD.2010.5603816
3. Akyildiz, I.F., Pompili, D., Melodia, T.: State-of-the-art in protocol research for underwater acoustic sensor networks. In: Proc. 1st ACM Int. Workshop Underwater Netw. (WUWNet), vol. 11, no. 4, Nov. 2006, pp. 7–16
4. Khalighi, M.-A., Gabriel, C., Hamza, T., Bourennane, S., Léon, P., Rigaud, V.: Underwater wireless optical communication; recent advances and remaining challenges. In: Roc. 16th Int. Conf. Transparent Opt. Netw., Graz, Austria, pp. 2–5, 2014
5. Jiang, S.: On securing underwater acoustic networks: a survey. IEEE Commun. Surv. Tutor. **21**(1), 729–752, 1st Quart. (2019)
6. Luo, Z., Liu, Y., Xiang, X.: Design of an AUV system based on wireless mesh network for data collection in the water column. In: 2018 IEEE/OES Autonomous Underwater Vehicle Workshop (AUV), pp. 1–5, 2018.https://doi.org/10.1109/AUV.2018.8729728
7. Lee, M., Yu, S.: Single thruster AUV for collecting water column data in shallow water using buoyancy system. In: 2018 IEEE/OES Autonomous Underwater Vehicle Workshop (AUV), pp. 1–4, 2018. https://doi.org/10.1109/AUV.2018.8729733
8. Huang, M., Zhang, K., Zeng, Z., Wang, T., Liu, Y.: An AUV-assisted data gathering scheme based on clustering and matrix completion for smart ocean. IEEE Internet Things J. **7**(10), 9904–9918 (2020). https://doi.org/10.1109/JIOT.2020.2988035
9. Yan, J., Yang, X., Luo, X., Chen, C.: Energy-efficient data collection over AUV-assisted underwater acoustic sensor network. IEEE Syst. J. **12**(4), 3519–3530 (2018). https://doi.org/10.1109/JSYST.2017.2789283
10. Miller, A., Miller, B., Miller, G.: AUV position estimation via acoustic seabed profile measurements. In: IEEE/OES Autonomous Underwater Vehicle Workshop (AUV), pp. 1–5, 2018. https://doi.org/10.1109/AUV.2018.8729708
11. Ferri, G., Stinco, P., De Magistris, G., Tesei, A., LePage, K.D.: Cooperative autonomy and data fusion for underwater surveillance with networked AUVs. In: IEEE International Conference on Robotics and Automation (ICRA), pp. 871–877, 2020. https://doi.org/10.1109/ICRA40945.2020.9197367
12. Willners, J.S., Toohey, L., Petillot, Y.: Sampling-based path planning for cooperative autonomous maritime vehicles to reduce uncertainty in range-only localization. IEEE Robot. Autom. Lett. **4**(4), 3987–3994 (2019). https://doi.org/10.1109/LRA.2019.2926947
13. Lim, H.S., Fan, S., Chin, C.K.H., Chai, S.: Performance evaluation of particle swarm intelligence based optimization techniques in a novel AUV path planner. In: IEEE/OES Autonomous Underwater Vehicle Workshop (AUV), pp. 1–7, 2018. https://doi.org/10.1109/AUV.2018.8729773
14. Yao, G., Liang, J., Wang, T., Yang, X., Liu, M., Zhang, Y.: Submersible unmanned flying boat: design and experiment. In: 2014 IEEE International Conference on Robotics and Biomimetics (ROBIO 2014), pp. 1308–1313, 2014. https://doi.org/10.1109/ROBIO.2014.7090514
15. Weisler, W., Stewart, W., Anderson, M.B., Peters, K.J., Gopalarathnam, A., Bryant, M.: Testing and characterization of a fixed wing cross-domain unmanned vehicle operating in aerial and underwater environments. IEEE J. Oceanic Eng. **43**(4), 969–982 (2018). https://doi.org/10.1109/JOE.2017.2742798

16. Maia, M.M., Mercado, D.A., Diez, F.J.: Design and implementation of multirotor aerial-underwater vehicles with experimental results. In: 2017 IEEE/RSJ International Conference on Intelligent Robots and Systems (IROS), pp. 961–966, 2017. https://doi.org/10.1109/IROS.2017.8202261
17. Lu, D., Xiong, C., Zeng, Z., Lian, L.: A multimodal aerial underwater vehicle with extended endurance and capabilities. In: 2019 International Conference on Robotics and Automation (ICRA), pp. 4674–4680, 2019. https://doi.org/10.1109/ICRA.2019.8793985
18. Lu, D., Xiong, C., Zeng, Z., Lian, L.: Adaptive dynamic surface control for a hybrid aerial underwater vehicle with parametric dynamics and uncertainties. IEEE J. Oceanic Eng. **45**(3), 740–758 (2020). https://doi.org/10.1109/JOE.2019.2903742
19. Kasno, M., et al.: Performances analysis of underwater Remotely Amphibian Vehicle (RAV). In: 2016 IEEE International Conference on Underwater System Technology: Theory and Applications (USYS), pp. 212–217, 2016. https://doi.org/10.1109/USYS.2016.7893906
20. Wang, J., Yang, Y., Wu, J., Zeng, Z., Lu, D., Lian, L. Hybrid aerial-aquatic vehicle for large scale high spatial resolution marine observation. In: OCEANS 2019 – Marseille, pp. 1–7, 2019. https://doi.org/10.1109/OCEANSE.2019.8867402

Difficulty-and-Beauty Network Evaluation with Interval Number Eigenvector Method

Penghong Yang[1], Yu Zhang[1,2](✉), Hong Peng[1], Guoxing Huang[1], Weidang Lu[1], and Yuan Gao[3,4]

[1] College of Information Engineering, Zhejiang University of Technology, Hangzhou 310023, China
yzhang@zjut.edu.cn
[2] National Mobile Communications Research Laboratory, Southeast University, Nanjing 210096, China
[3] Academy of Military Science of PLA, Beijing 100091, China
[4] Tsinghua University, Beijing 100084, China

Abstract. In consideration of the complexity and difficulty of network evaluation, we propose a "difficulty & beauty" network evaluation framework based on the interval number eigenvector method. In the proposed framework, we adopt the interval number eigenvector method to calculate the weight of each indicator, while its score is obtained from the network test results or expert recommendations. The weighted product and weighted sum methods are used for the aggregation of quantitative indicators and qualitative indicators to obtain the final score of the network. Finally, the feasibility and effectiveness of the proposed framework is verified by numerical experiments.

Keywords: Network evaluation · Difficulty & beauty · Interval number eigenvector method

1 Introduction

With the development of network information technology, the importance of evaluation for network information systems keeps increasing [1]. In order to assess the performance of network information systems more precisely, it is urgent to establish scientific and reasonable network evaluation frameworks.

For different network information systems, the corresponding evaluation methods are different, which are usually combination of weight calculation methods and indicator aggregation methods. There are mainly two weight calculation schemes, namely analytic hierarchy process (AHP) and information entropy method. AHP was first proposed by T. L. Saaty as a multi-criteria decision-making method combining qualitative and quantitative evaluation [2]. Then Lee proposed an improved AHP to evaluate the

© ICST Institute for Computer Sciences, Social Informatics and Telecommunications Engineering 2022
Published by Springer Nature Switzerland AG 2022. All Rights Reserved
S. Shi et al. (Eds.): 6GN 2021, LNICST 439, pp. 97–106, 2022.
https://doi.org/10.1007/978-3-031-04245-4_9

operational potential of the Army's network information system [3]. Manik Chandra Das and others adopted an improved model of AHP, i.e., fuzzy analytic hierarchy process, to evaluate the network system of Indian scientific research institutions [4, 5]. AHP usually uses ordinary numbers to express the judgment, but in practice, there may be some uncertainty for the judgement. In order to handle this issue, interval numbers should be applied to define the elements in the judgment matrix and calculate the weights more objectively. On the other hand, in information theory, information entropy [6] is usually used to describe the uncertainty of random variables. Wang in [7] analyzed the relevant factors affecting the combat effectiveness of the C^4ISR system, and used the method of combining Shannon information entropy and graph theory to put forward a new idea for the C^4ISR system combat effectiveness evaluation. However, if the value of indicator changes very little or suddenly becomes larger or smaller, information entropy method will have some limitations. As for indicator aggregation, the authors in the literature [8, 9] proposed to the arrogate the lower-level indicators to the upper-level indicators by means of weighted sums, ignoring the decisive influence of individual lower-level indicators. Hence it cannot faithfully reflect the actual situation of the object to be evaluated.

In this paper, we propose a novel "difficulty & beauty"-based network evaluation method using interval number eigenvector scheme. Firstly, due to the aforementioned advantages of using interval numbers and information entropy method, the weight of each indicator is calculated by the interval number eigenvector method. Then the score of the quantitative indicator and the qualitative indicator are obtained through the test results of the network or the score from the experts on the network performance. Furthermore, the final score of the network is calculated by the aggregation method combining the weighted product and the weighted sum, wherein for the lower-level indicators that have decisive influence, the weighted product method is applied. Finally, the overall evaluation of the network performance is taken as the average of the final score which is an interval number.

2 "Difficulty & Beauty" Network Evaluation System

We first introduce the "difficulty & beauty" network evaluation system considered in this paper, which is divided into four layers from top to bottom, including 2 first-level indicators and 8 s-level indicators. Under the second-level indicators, a total of 56 appropriate indicator parameters are selected to form the third-level indicators. The specific affiliation is shown in Fig. 1 and Fig. 2 below.

We now briefly introduce one of the third-level indicators, i.e., "Processing" (B3) as an example. Its lower-level indicators are as follows. "Processing error rate" indicates the ratio between the amount of error information and the total amount of information processed; "Access node physical looping ratio" indicates the ratio of the number of physically looped nodes to the total number of access physical nodes; "Access node dual homing rate" indicates the ratio of the number of returned dual homing nodes to

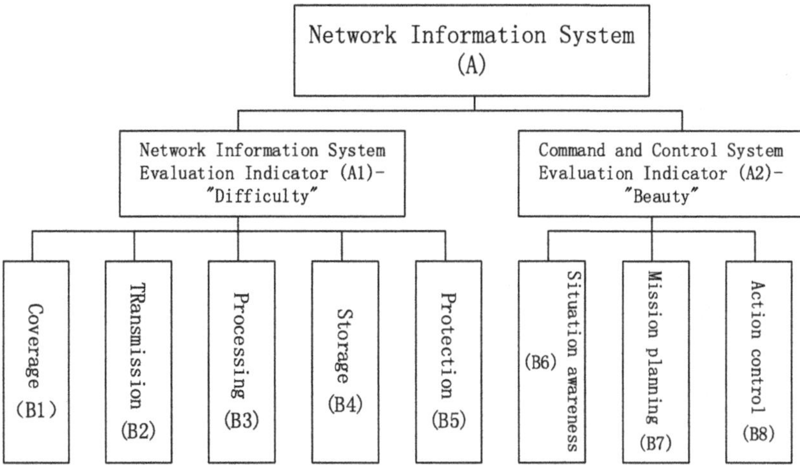

Fig. 1. "Difficulty & beauty" network evaluation system (First and Second levels)

the total number of access nodes; "Processing delay" indicates the time interval between the first bit of a data packet entering the router and the last bit output from the router; "Processing delay jitter" indicates the change of delay.

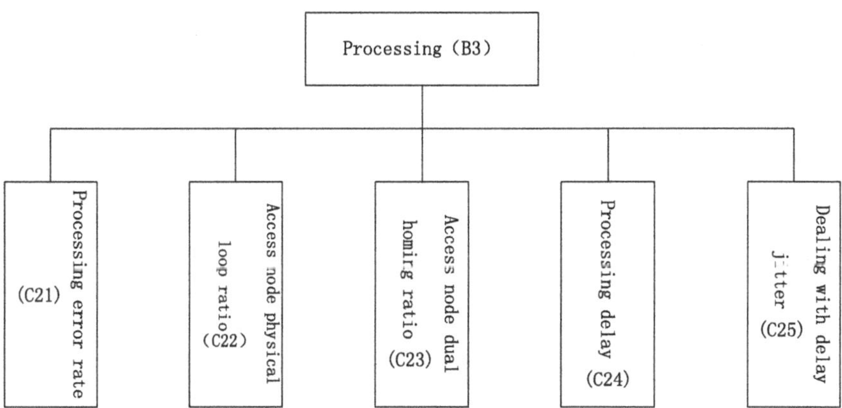

Fig. 2. Third-level indicators under the "Processing" indicator

3 Network Evaluation Based on Interval Number Eigenvector Method

3.1 Overview of the Evaluation Process

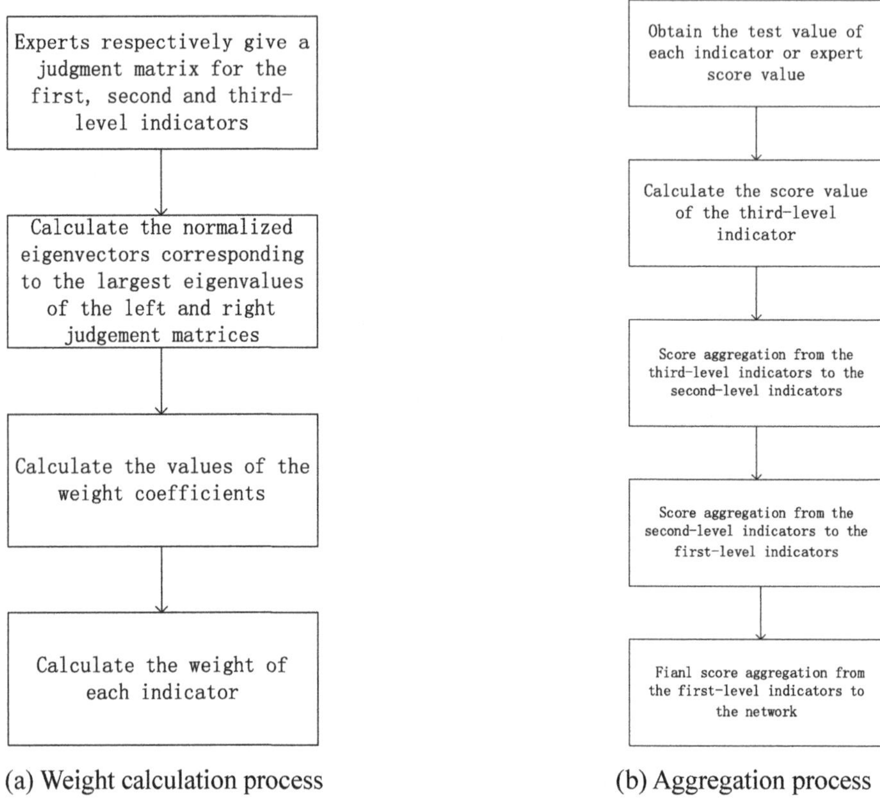

Fig. 3. Flow chart of the evaluation process

The calculation process of the weight of each indicator and the calculation of the final score of the network performance are shown in the above Fig. 3 (a) and (b) respectively.

The weight calculation in Fig. 3(a) is mainly divided into 4 steps. First, the experts give an interval number judgment matrix for the third-level, the second-level indicators and the first-level indicators based on their professional experience. Second, the left and right judgment matrices are processed separately by calculating the normalized eigenvector corresponding to the largest eigenvalue. Then, the value of the weight coefficient is calculated. Finally, the weight of each indicator of the third-level, second-level and first-level is calculated by the data obtained by the above calculations.

Figure 3(b) depicts the score aggregation from lower-level indicators to the upper-level indicators.

3.2 Interval Number Calculation Rules

Due to the introduction of the concept of fuzzy mathematics in the process of the proposed network evaluation method, the weight and the score of an indicator are not given as specific numbers, but in the form of interval numbers. We firstly define an interval number $\hat{x}_i = (x_i^l, x_i^r)$, where the superscript l and r respectively represent the lower and upper bound of interval number. The calculation rules used in this paper are as follows [10]:

Definition 1: Addition rule of two interval numbers:

$$\hat{x}_i + \hat{x}_j = (x_i^l, x_i^r) + (x_j^l, x_j^r) = (x_i^l + x_j^l, x_i^r + x_j^r) \tag{1}$$

Definition 2: Multiplication rule of two interval numbers:

$$\begin{gathered}\hat{x}_{i,j} = \left(x_i^l, x_i^r\right)\left(x_j^l, x_j^r\right) = \\ \left(\min\left\{x_i^l x_j^l, x_i^l x_j^r, x_i^r x_j^l, x_i^r x_j^r\right\}, \max\left\{x_i^l x_j^l, x_i^l x_j^r, x_i^r x_j^l, x_i^r x_j^r\right\}\right)\end{gathered} \tag{2}$$

Definition 3: Power operation rule of two interval numbers:

$$\begin{aligned}\hat{x}_i^{\hat{x}_j} &= \left(x_i^l, x_i^r\right)^{\left(x_j^l, x_j^r\right)} \\ &= \left(\min\left\{\left(x_i^l\right)^{x_j^l}, \left(x_i^l\right)^{x_j^r}, \left(x_i^r\right)^{x_j^l}, \left(x_i^r\right)^{x_j^r}\right\}, \max\left\{\left(x_i^l\right)^{x_j^l}, \left(x_i^l\right)^{x_j^r}, \left(x_i^r\right)^{x_j^l}, \left(x_i^r\right)^{x_j^r}\right\}\right)\end{aligned} \tag{3}$$

3.3 Weight Calculation Process

In the evaluation process, whether the indicator weight is reasonable will directly affect the accuracy of the evaluation result. In this following, the process of calculating the weight using the interval number eigenvector method are specifically introduced [11].

(1) Experts give judgment matrix $\mathbf{A} = (\widetilde{\mathbf{a}}_{ij})_{n\times n} = [\mathbf{A}^-, \mathbf{A}^+]$ based on their own experience, where $\widetilde{\mathbf{a}}_{ij} = (a_{ij}^-, a_{ij}^+)$, $\mathbf{A}^- = \left(a_{ij}^-\right)_{n\times n}$, $\mathbf{A}^+ = \left(a_{ij}^+\right)_{n\times n}$, and a_{ij} represents the importance of the i-th indicator compared with the j-th indicator.

(2) Calculate the normalized eigenvectors $\mathbf{x}_i^-$ and $\mathbf{x}_i^+$ corresponding to the largest eigenvalues of the matrices $\mathbf{A}^-$ and $\mathbf{A}^+$:

$$\mathbf{x}_i^- = \frac{1}{\sum_{j=1}^{n} \mathbf{b}_j^-} \boldsymbol{b}_j^-, \tag{4}$$

$$\mathbf{x}_i^+ = \frac{1}{\sum_{j=1}^{n} \mathbf{b}_j^+} \mathbf{b}_j^+, \tag{5}$$

where $\mathbf{b}_j^- = (b_1^-, b_2^-, \cdots, b_n^-)^T$ and $\mathbf{b}_j^+ = (b_1^+, b_2^+, \cdots, b_n^+)^T$ are the eigenvector corresponding to the largest eigenvalue of matrix $\mathbf{A}^-$ and $\mathbf{A}^+$,respectively.

(3) Calculate the weight coefficient values for $\mathbf{A}^- = \left(a_{ij}^-\right)_{n\times n}$, $\mathbf{A}^+ = \left(a_{ij}^+\right)_{n\times n}$, which is given by

$$k = \sqrt{\sum_{j=1}^{n} \frac{1}{\sum_{i=1}^{n} a_{ij}^+}}, \tag{6}$$

$$m = \sqrt{\sum_{j=1}^{n} \frac{1}{\sum_{i=1}^{n} a_{ij}^-}}, \tag{7}$$

(4) Calculate the weight of each indicator, i.e., $\widetilde{\delta}_i = \left(\delta_i^-, \delta_i^+\right) = \left(k\mathbf{x}_i^-, m\mathbf{x}_i^+\right)$, where δ_i^- and δ_i^+ respectively represent the lower and upper bound set of weights.

3.4 Calculation of the Score for Each Indicator

In this section, we will introduce the method to obtain the score of each third-level indicator. The indicator is classified into qualitative indicator and quantitative indicator.

(1) The score of a qualitative indicator is based on the expert's rating on the actual performance of the network which is mapped into an interval number. Among them, 'excellent' rating corresponds to the interval (0.85, 1), 'good' rating corresponds to the interval (0.75, 0.85), 'qualified' rating corresponds to the interval (0.6, 0.75), and 'unqualified' rating corresponds to the interval (0, 0.6).
(2) The score of a quantitative indicator is based on the test results of the network performance, and the calculation method is as follows. Consider a quantitative indicator evaluation standard, i.e., 'excellent' mapping to the interval (c, d), 'good' (b, c), 'qualified' (a, b), 'unqualified' (0, a). Let the test result of an indicator be an interval number (x^-, x^+), then the corresponding score $\left(y\left(x^-\right), y\left(x^+\right)\right)$ is obtained by the formula given by

$$y(x) = \begin{cases} \frac{0.6}{a} \cdot x, 0 \leq x < a \\ \frac{0.15}{b-a} \cdot (x-a) + 0.6, a \leq x < b \\ \frac{0.1}{c-b} \cdot (x-b) + 0.75, b \leq x < c \\ \frac{0.15}{d-c} \cdot (x-c) + 0.85, c \leq x \leq d \end{cases}, \tag{8}$$

wherein the score interval for 'excellent', 'good', 'qualified', 'unqualified' are consistent with that of qualitative indicators as given in (1).

3.5 The Aggregation Process

In this section, we will introduce how to aggregate the scores of the lower-level indicators to obtain the scores of the upper-level indicators according the corresponding weights, while qualitative indicators and quantitative indicators adopt different aggregation methods.

The third-level indicators under the quantitative indicators are aggregated by the weighted product method to obtain the scores of the corresponding second-level indicators. On the other hand, the third-level indicators under the qualitative indicators are aggregated by the weighted sum method to obtain the scores of the corresponding second-level indicators.

The weighted product aggregation method [12] is given by

$$\hat{x}_i = \prod_{j=1}^{m} \left(\hat{x}_{ij}\right)^{\hat{\delta}_{ij}}, \tag{9}$$

where $\hat{x}_i$ is the score of the i-th indicator, $\hat{x}_{ij}$ represents the score of the j-th indicator under the i-th indicator, and $\hat{\delta}_{ij}$ is the weight of the j-th indicator under the i-th indicator. Note that $\hat{\delta}_{ij}$ needs to meet the normalization condition $\sum_{j=1}^{m} \hat{\delta}_{ij} = [1, 1]$.

The weighted sum aggregation method [12] is given by

$$\hat{x}_i = \sum_{j=1}^{m} \hat{x}_{ij}\hat{\delta}_{ij}. \tag{10}$$

4 Numerical Results

In the simulation, we consider a communication network consisting of multiple cellular networks and a core network. Then we conduct simulation tests on this network, and calculate the weight and score for each indicator. The specific calculation process of weight follows Sect. 3.3, and the specific calculation process of score can be found in Sect. 3.4.

According to the test results, we select some indicators to illustrate their influence on the overall score of the network.

Figure 4 plots final score of the network versus the score of "Task completion benefit" (C55). Indicator C55 represents the weighted sum of the percentage of completed tasks of different levels to the total number of task goals. Since C55 is a third-level indicator under "Action control" (B8) which is a qualitative indicator, it is aggregated upward with other indicators in the same level by the weighted sum method. Note that the weight of C55 is relatively small. As shown in the figure, when its score is 0, the score of the network is high, which means that it has little effect on the score of the entire network. Considering the final score of the network under different scores of C5, it can be observed from Fig. 4 that when the score of C5 is high, the score of the network is high.

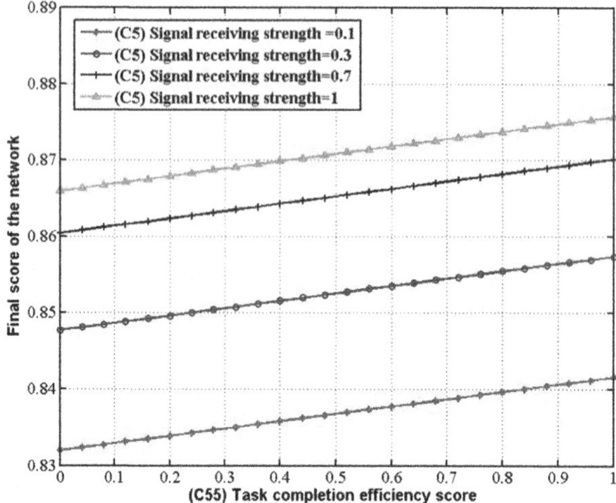

Fig. 4. Overall network score versus the score of "Task completion efficiency" (C55)

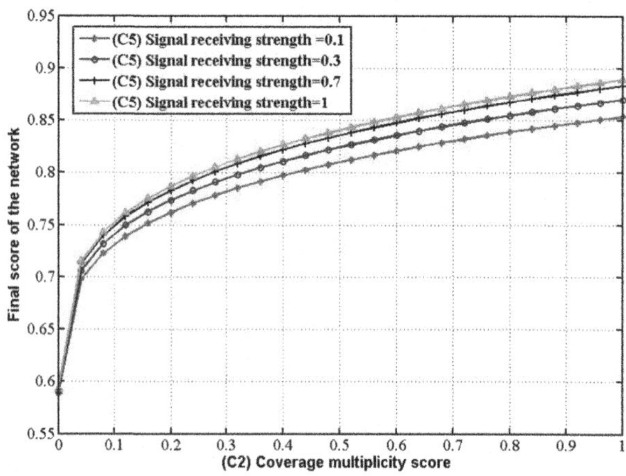

Fig. 5. Overall network score versus the score of "Coverage multiplicity" (C2)

Figure 5 plots final score of the network versus the score of "Coverage multiplicity" (C2). Indicator C2 means the degree of redundancy of coverage in a certain area. If this area is within the coverage of *K* nodes, then its coverage multiplicity is *K*. Since C2 is a third-level indicator under "Coverage" (B1) which is a quantitative indicator, it is aggregated upward with other indicators in the same level by the weighted product method. Note that the weight of C2 is relatively large. As shown in the figure, when its score is 0, the score of the network is low, which means that it has a greater impact on the score of the entire network. Considering the final score of the network under different scores of C5, it can be observed from Fig. 4 that when the score of C5 is high, the score of the network is high.

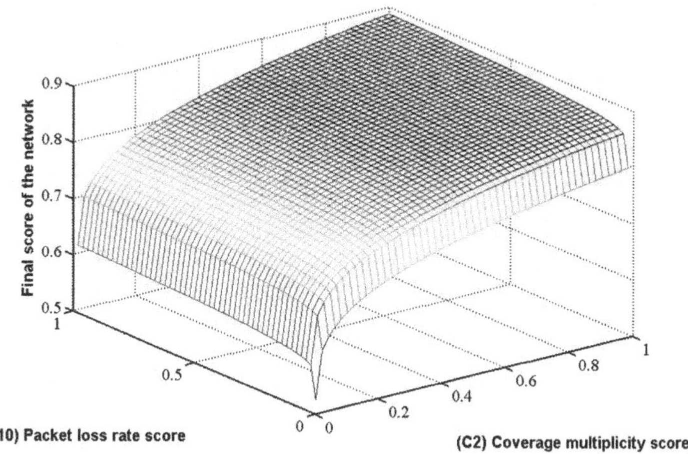

Fig. 6. Overall network score versus the score of "Coverage multiplicity" (C2) and "Packet loss rate" (C10)

"Packet loss rate" (C10) indicator represents the percentage of packets that cannot be forwarded by the network device due to lack of resources in the router under a stable load state, i.e., the ratio of the lost data packets to the total number of transmitted data packets. It can be seen from Fig. 6 that "Coverage multiplicity" has a greater impact on the score of the network than the "Packet loss rate". When the score of the two indicators both change from 0 to 1, the final score of the network changes greatly with "Coverage multiplicity", because the weight of "Coverage multiplicity" is larger than that of "Packet loss rate", which means the corresponding impact to the network rating is more notable.

5 Conclusion

In this paper, we have proposed a "difficult & beautiful" network evaluation framework based on the interval number eigenvector method. In this framework, the judgement matrix is given from the recommendation of experts, and the weight of each indicator can be obtained through the processing and calculation of the judgement matrix. The scores of third-level indicators are obtained through the results of network test or advice of experts, and the scores of second-level indicators and first-level indicators are obtained by aggregation of the weights and scores of the lower-level indicators. For qualitative indicators and quantitative indicators, the weighted sum and weighted product methods are used for aggregation, respectively. The final score of the network is obtained through the level-by-level aggregation. Experimental results show that the proposed framework can evaluate multi-indicator networks appropriately and objectively.

Acknowledgement. This work was supported partially by Zhejiang Provincial Natural Science Foundation of China under Grant LY21F010008 and the National Natural Science Foundation of China (No. 62171412, No. 61871348), and by the open research fund of National Mobile Communications Research Laboratory, Southeast University (No. 2020D10).

References

1. Yang, Y.-H., Li, J.-H., Ding, W., Wang, G.-Q.: Integrated evaluation method for multicriteria index based on nonlinear polymerization. Modern Def. Technol. **41**(03), 81–87 (2013)
2. Saaty, T.L.: How to make a decision: the analytic hierarchy process. Eur. J. Oper. Res. **48**(1), 9–26 (1990)
3. Lee, Y.W., Ahn, B.H.: Static valuation of combat force potential by the analytic hierarchy process. IEEE Trans. Eng. Manag. **38**(3), 237–243 (1991)
4. Das, M.C., Sarkar, B., Ray, S.: A framework to measure relative performance of indian technical institutions using integrated fuzzy AHP and COPRAS methodology. Socioecon. Plann. Sci. **46**(2), 230–241 (2012)
5. Duan, L.-X., Liu, Y., Liu, S.-D., Tang, M.-H.: Safety evaluation of reciprocating compressor unit based on IEM – fuzzy analysis theory. Ind. Safe Environ. Protect. **45**(7), 31–35+39 (2019)
6. Guo, S., Fu, D.-X.: Analysis of the optical imaging system based on information entropy. Software Guide **18**(01), 48–50 (2019)
7. Wang, J.-F., Wu, W.-J., Li, H.-X., Xiong, P.: Evaluation of US Army C^4ISR system effectiveness based on Shannon information entropy. Electronics Opt. Control **13**(2), 24–29 (2006)
8. Hu, W.-G., Hou, G.-J., Zhou, Y.-Q.: Performance evaluation in multi-sensors co-detection based on fuzzy comprehensive evaluation. J Telemetry Tracking Command **31**(4), 36–39 (2010)
9. Wei, B.-H., et al.: Antijamming capability evaluation of radar based on fuzzy synthetic using variable weight. Modern Radar **32**(9), 15–18 (2010)
10. Guo, H., Xu, H.-J., Liu, L.: Measurement of combat effectiveness of early-warning aircraft based on interval number. Syst. Eng. Elect. **32**(5), 1007–1010 (2010)
11. Song, Z.-L.: Method of selecting main defense directions based on IEM. Ordnance Ind. Autom. **28**(4), 18–20 (2009)
12. Liu, Y., Zhao, C.-N., Wang, X.-S., Wang, G.-Y., Feng, D.-J.: Evaluation approach for antiadiation weapon's effectiveness. Acta Armamentar II **32**(03), 321–326 (2011)

Joint Power Control and Resource Allocation Game Algorithm Based on Non-cooperative D2D

Jingqiu Ren[1], Liguang Du[1], Lin Zhang[1], Piao Chen[1], Guanghua Zhang[1](✉), and Weidang Lu[2]

[1] Northeast Petroleum University, Daqing 163318, China
dqzgh@nepu.edu.cn
[2] Zhejiang University of Technology, Hangzhou 310014, China

Abstract. With the continuous development of modern mobile communication technology. D2D (device to device) communication technology, as a research hotspot of a new generation of communication technology. It has become an urgent problem to be solved in D2D communication in terms of solving its spectrum utilization, improving communication quality, improving system fairness, and reducing system delay. This paper studies the interference generated by multiple pairs of D2D users in the network spectrum resources of multiple pairs of cellular users. In order to reduce the interference when reusing resources, this paper establishes a non-cooperative game theory. The cost factor is introduced to determine the utility function. Through the power control of D2D communication link and the resource allocation algorithm, the optimal response function of D2D users participating in the game is obtained. This paper analyzes the equilibrium in the game, determines the existence and uniqueness of the Nash equilibrium, and proves that the strategy of the model can reach a stable state. This paper proves the effectiveness of the algorithm through experimental simulations. Compared with other algorithms, the D2D joint power control and resource allocation algorithm based on non-cooperative game in this paper has higher fairness and lower system delay on the premise of ensuring communication quality.

Keywords: D2D · Game theory · Power control · Resource allocation

1 Introduction

At present, D2D communication is one of the key technologies of 5G communication technology, and it will also be the key technology of next generation communication technology in the future [1]. At present, the main challenge of D2D communication is how to correctly allocate the reusable channel resources, transmit power and reduce the interference between D2D users and cellular users. Therefore, how to reduce interference and improve system resource utilization has become a research hotspot. Game theory is a method of using a mathematical model to resolve actual conflicts of interest [2]. In recent years, it is used to solve the interference problem in mobile communication.

© ICST Institute for Computer Sciences, Social Informatics and Telecommunications Engineering 2022
Published by Springer Nature Switzerland AG 2022. All Rights Reserved
S. Shi et al. (Eds.): 6GN 2021, LNICST 439, pp. 107–119, 2022.
https://doi.org/10.1007/978-3-031-04245-4_10

Game theory is different from other optimization decision theories. The participants in the game theory have conflicts of interest; Each participant should choose the decision to maximize their own interests; The decision-making of each participant will interact with each other; Every participant can carry out rational and logical thinking [3].

Game theory can be divided into cooperative games and non-cooperative games [4]. The cooperative game emphasizes the collective optimal decision-making; Non-cooperative games emphasize the individual optimal decision-making. In non-cooperative games, according to the order of actions of participants it can be divided into static games and dynamic games. The game model is mainly composed of the following three basic elements [5]:

Players: The decision-making body of the game, who will choose their own strategies according to their own interests.

Strategy: The action plan that each participant can choose to adopt during the game. Remember that the strategy i chosen by the participant is $s_i \in S_i$, where S_i is the set of strategies i that participants can choose, known as strategic space. The vector composed of the strategies $s = \{s_1, s_2, \cdots, s_N\}$ selected by the N participants is called the strategy combination.

Preference and utility function: The utility function reflects the participant's preference for the possible output of the game. The output of the game is directly determined by the behavior of the participants, thus establishing a certain relationship between the behavior space and the output space [6]. In the game process, participants choose actions according to their own preferences, that is, participants always choose actions that can increase their utility function.

Non-cooperative game includes repeated game, potential game and so on [7]. Repeated game is that participants choose strategies based on the knowledge of the game. In the potential game model, each participant only chooses the strategy with the greatest interests according to the current situation. This paper chooses potential game model, because it has good mathematical characteristics and can easy to converge to Nash equilibrium point.

In recent years, many scholars have proposed power allocation and resource allocation schemes for D2D communication. In reference [8], for pure game and mixed game, an iterative distributed power allocation method based on SINR (Signal to Interference Noise Ratio) is proposed to improve the performance of D2D users and cellular users. Reference [9] uses the idea of game theory, a relay selection algorithm is proposed, by analyzing the location information and transmission capacity of relay nodes, the system throughput is effectively improved and the coverage is expanded. In reference [10], a mode selection method based on predetermined SINR threshold is proposed. Combining with mode selection and power control methods to meet the minimum power required by users and improve the overall performance of the communication system. In reference [11], D2D communication system is modeled as a Stackelberg model, based on this, a joint scheduling and resource allocation algorithm is proposed to manage interference and optimize network throughput. In reference [12], the power allocation problem is modeled as a reverse iterative combinatorial auction game, using a joint radio resource and power allocation scheme to improve the performance of the uplink system. In reference [13], studied the problem of joint resource allocation and power control, using the characteristics of fractional planning to improve the solution of energy efficiency optimization problems. But the common point of the appeal scheme is that it has high complexity and only needs sub-optimal solution.

The interference in "many-to-many" D2D communication is more complicated. Most of studies focus on power control unilaterally. Facing the complex relationship of "many-to-many" communication. It is necessary to consider the problem of resource division of cellular users. Therefore, this paper considers the resource allocation and power control algorithm to further solve the complex problem of "many-to-many" multiplexing.

On the basis of the above mentioned documents, this paper presents the following conclusions. Considering the characteristics of D2D communication, a game algorithm of joint power control and resource allocation based on non-cooperative D2D is proposed. In view of the power control problems in D2D networks, establishing a potential game model, at the same time, the users of the reused cellular resources act as the players. According to the interference between systems. Using a cost factor combined with channel gain. Using the best strategy to co-ordinate the transmit power of each D2D terminal, so that the system can better achieve Nash equilibrium. In order to improve the fairness of the system and reduce the interference of the system.

2 System Model and Problem Analysis

2.1 System Model

This paper uses multi-user single-cell uplink power control, there is a BS (Base Station), multiple cellular user equipment CUE (Cell User Equipment), and multiple D2D user equipment DUE (Device User Equipment) in the cell. Among them, DT (Device Transmitter) represents the D2D device transmitter, DR (Device Receiver) represents the D2D device receiver, DUE communicates directly by multiplexing the spectrum resources of CUE, that is, a "many-to-many" multi-D2D device multiplexing multi-cellular user resources model is given. As shown in Fig. 1. It can be seen from the figure that there is no communication interference between each CUE, the BS is interfered by the DT, and the DR is interfered by the CUE and other DTs that reuse the same frequency band resources at this time.

CUE_j represents the j-th CUE, $D2D_i$ represents the i-th pair of D2D users, DR_i represents the receiving end and DT_i represents the transmitting end. When the i-th pair of D2D multiplexes the n-th channel, the SINR is:

$$SINR_i^n = \frac{p_i^n g_{i,i}}{p_j^n g_{j,i} + \sum\limits_{k=1,\, k \neq i}^{K} p_k^n g_{k,i} + N_0} \quad (1)$$

where p_i^n represents the transmission power of the i-th pair of D2D users, p_j^n represents the transmission power of the j-th CUE, p_k^n represents the transmit power of the k-th D2D users multiplexing the n-th channel, $g_{i,i}$ represents the channel gain from the transmitting end to the receiving end of the i-th pair of D2D, $g_{j,i}$ represents the interference channel

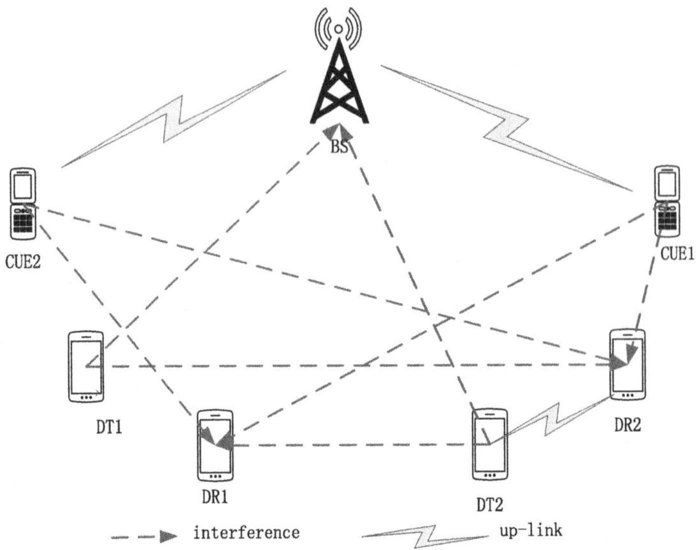

Fig. 1. Uplink D2D communication system model

gain from CUE_j to DR_i, $g_{k,i}$ represents the interference channel gain from DT_k to DR_i, N_0 represents the noise power, $p_j^n g_{j,i}$ represents the CUE interference received when the n-th channel is reused by $D2D_i$, Then the interference of other D2D users can be expressed as $\sum_{k=1,k\neq i}^{K} p_k^n g_{k,j}$.

Therefore, when the i-th pair of D2D users multiplexing the n-th channel, the data rate is expressed as:

$$R_i^n = \log_2\left(1 + SINR_i^n\right) \tag{2}$$

The SINR of the j-th CUE at the base station is as follows:

$$SINR_j^n = \frac{p_j^n g_{j,B}}{\sum_{i=1}^{K} p_i^n g_{i,j} + N_0} \tag{3}$$

where $g_{j,B}$ represents the channel gain from CUE_j to the BS, $g_{i,j}$ represents the gain of the interference channel from DT_i to the BS of the n-th channel of D2D multiplexing, $\sum_{i=1}^{K} p_i^n g_{i,j}$ represents all the interference caused by the DUE in the n-th channel of multiplexing.

Therefore, the data rate of the j-th cellular user at the base station is:

$$R_j^n = \log_2\left(1 + SINR_j^n\right) \tag{4}$$

2.2 Problem Analysis

This paper mainly analyzes the power control problem in the "many-to-many" D2D communication. In this paper, the transmission data rate is the optimization objective, and the mathematical expression of optimization problem can be expressed as follows:

$$\max_{p_i^n, p_j^m} \sum_{i \in N} \sum_{j \in M} \left\{ R_j^m \left(p_i^n, p_j^m \right) + R_i^n \left(p_j^m, p_i^n \right) \right\} \tag{5}$$

$$s.t. \quad 0 \le p_i^n \le p_n^{\max}, \forall i \in N \tag{6}$$

$$SINR_i^n \ge SINR_n^{th}, \forall i \in N \tag{7}$$

$$0 \le p_j^m \le p_m^{\max} \tag{8}$$

$$SINR_j^m \ge SINR_m^{th} \tag{9}$$

$p_n^{\max}$ represents the maximum transmission power of D2D users, $p_m^{\max}$ represents the maximum transmission power of a cellular user. The above formulas (6) and (8) ensure that the transmission power of D2D users and cellular users in the communication system is within the maximum transmission power, $SINR_n^{th}$ represents the minimum SINR threshold required to guarantee the QoS (Quality of Service) of D2D users in the communication system, $SINR_m^{th}$ represents the minimum SINR threshold required to guarantee the QoS of cellular users in the communication system. The above formulas (7) and (9) ensure the communication quality between D2D users and cellular users in the communication system.

Formula (1) is brought into formula (7), which can be deduced as

$$p_j^m \le \frac{p_i^n g_{i,i}}{SINR_n^{th} g_{i,i}} - \frac{N_0 + \sum\limits_{k \in M, k \ne j} p_k^m g_{k,i}}{g_{i,i}} = p_m^{\max 1} \tag{10}$$

According to the above formula (8), it can be concluded that

$$0 \le p_j^m \le p_m^{\max\_th} \tag{11}$$

Among, $p_m^{\max\_th} = \min\left\{ p_m^{\max\_1}, p_m^{\max} \right\}$.

Similarly, substituting (3) in the above formula into (9), we can deduce that

$$p_i^n \le \frac{p_j^m g_{j,B}}{SINR_m^{th} g_{i,j}} - \frac{N_0 + \sum\limits_{k \in N, k \ne i} p_k^n g_{k,j}}{g_{i,j}} = p_i^{n\_\max} \tag{12}$$

It can be seen from the above formula (6)

$$0 \le p_i^n \le p_i^{\max\_th}, \forall i \in N \tag{13}$$

Among, $p_i^{\max\_th} = \min\left\{ p_n^{\max}, p_i^{d\_\max} \right\}$.

3 Joint Power Control and Resource Allocation Game Algorithm Based on Non-cooperative D2D

After the above analysis, D2D communication will increase system interference by reusing frequency resources. In order to solve the above problems, this paper models the resource allocation problem of the D2D system in the uplink as a game theory model. Proposed joint resource allocation and power control algorithm (PRAG), Through resource allocation and power control, the interference between users is coordinated to ensure the good communication performance of each link.

3.1 Utility Function for D2D Users

Based on the game theory model, CUE and DUE can form a pair of trading relationships, as a seller, CUE has channel spectrum resources, DUE as a buyer reuses channel spectrum resources [12]. The reuse process can be expressed as: Multiple CUEs allocate channel resources in advance. At this time, multiple DUEs must select the CUE channel resources that need to be multiplexed. However, how to reuse cue resources requires dues to play games at their own cost. Finally, through the game, DUE obtains the required channel resources and realizes the communication requirements, at the same time, the PRAG algorithm can also better control the interference of D2D users to cellular users, thereby increasing the communication rate of the communication system.

The utility function of D2D users include two parts: income function and cost function. The mathematical formula can be expressed as:

$$U_i\left(p_i^n\right) = B\log_2\left(1 + SINR_i^n\right) - \lambda p_i^n \tag{14}$$

λ represents the power cost factor of D2D users, so the optimization problem required for the utility function is: By matching the transmission power of suitable D2D users and selecting and reusing suitable cellular user channel resources, to make the utility function reach the optimal:

$$\max U_i\left(p_i^n\right) \tag{15}$$

$$s.t.\quad p_{\min} \le p_i^n \le p_{\max} \tag{16}$$

$p_{\min}$ represents the minimum transmit power of D2D user to transmitter, $p_{\max}$ represents the maximum transmit power of D2D user to transmitter, by introducing Eq. (1) into Eq. (14), we get the following result:

$$U_i\left(p_i^n\right) = B\log_2\left(1 + \frac{p_i^n g_{i,i}}{p_j^n g_{j,i} + \sum\limits_{k=1,k\neq i}^{K} p_k^n g_{k,i} + N_0}\right) - \lambda p_i^n \tag{17}$$

Carrying out the p_i^n first-order partial derivative on the above utility function (17), we can get:

$$\frac{\partial U_i\left(p_i^n\right)}{\partial p_i^n} = \frac{B}{\ln 2}\frac{g_{i,i}}{N_0 + p_j^n g_{j,i} + p_i^n g_{i,i}} - \lambda \tag{18}$$

If the first-order partial derivative is 0, we can get:

$$p_i^n = \frac{B}{\lambda \ln 2} - \frac{N_0 + p_j^n g_{j,i}}{g_{i,i}} \tag{19}$$

It can be seen from the above formula that the utility function of D2D users has extreme values. Therefore, to calculate the p_i^n second-order partial derivative of (17), the following formula can be obtained:

$$\frac{\partial^2 U_i\left(p_i^n\right)}{\partial \left(p_i^n\right)^2} = -\frac{B}{\ln 2}\left(\frac{g_{i,i}}{N_0 + p_j^n g_{j,i} + p_i^n g_{i,i}}\right)^2 < 0 \tag{20}$$

Therefore, it can be seen from the above (20) that the utility function of D2D users can have a maximum value. If it is the maximum $p_i^n \in \left[p_{\min}, p_{\max}\right]$, p_i^n is the maximum point of utility function; On the contrary $p_i^n \notin \left[p_{\min}, p_{\max}\right]$, then $p_{\min}$ or $p_{\max}$ is the maximum point of the utility function. According to the derivation of the above formula. It can prove that the Nash equilibrium solution exists and it is unique.

In summary, D2D users reuse all the resources of cellular users, so it can choose the reuse object which can make its utility function maximum, at the same time, it will also determine the transmission power of the D2D user's transmitter.

3.2 Steps of Power Allocation Algorithm

The proposed algorithm not only ensures the maximum throughput of the system, but also takes into account the communication quality of the system. This paper adopts the optimal response strategy design algorithm flow in a decision-making environment. In each iteration, the randomly selected DUE will choose the power allocation scheme with its maximum utility function value. After several iterations, the system will converge to Nash equilibrium. The optimization model of the DUE in the game model is as follows:

$$\min \quad -U_i(s_i, s_{-i}) \tag{21}$$

$$s.t. \quad -p_r^{i,n} \le 0 \tag{22}$$

$$\sum_{r=1}^{RB} p_r^{i,n} - p_{\max}^n = 0 \tag{23}$$

The ultimate purpose of the above optimization model is to maximize utility functions, and the variables p of the optimization problem are finite sets of real numbers, which are convex sets. According to the above formula (20), the utility function is a concave function, so $-u$ is convex, this optimization problem can be transformed into a convex optimization problem. Because the local solution of the convex optimization problem must be the global solution, Therefore, the solution of the optimization model in this paper is a non-empty convex solution set, so there is an optimal solution.

When solving constrained optimization problems, the constrained optimization problem is transformed into unconstrained optimization problem by using penalty function of constraint condition, the main methods are internal penalty function method and Lagrange multiplier method. When solving convex optimization problems, KKT condition is used to solve the problem, The KKT condition is the necessary and sufficient condition for the optimal solution of convex optimization. Therefore, the optimization problem in this paper can be solved by using KKT of the Lagrange condition.

First construct the Lagrange function:

$$L\left(p_r^{i,n}\right) = -u_i(s_i, s_{-i}) - \lambda p_r^{i,n} - \nu\left(\sum_{r=1}^{RB} p_r^{i,n} - p_{\max}^n\right) \tag{24}$$

The corresponding KKT conditions are as follows:

$$\sum_{r=1}^{RB} p_r^{i,n} - p_{\max}^n = 0 \tag{25}$$

$$\lambda p_r^{i,n} = 0 \tag{26}$$

$$\frac{\partial\left(L\left(p_r^{i,n}\right)\right)}{\partial p_r^{i,n}} = -b\sum_{j=1}^{M} g_{ij,r}^{nm} - b\sum_{j=1,j\neq i}^{N} g_{ij,r}^{nn} + \frac{g_{ii,r}^{nn}}{1 + p_r^{i,n} g_{ii,r}^{nn}} - \lambda + \nu = 0 \tag{27}$$

To sum up, the calculation results are as follows:

$$p_r^{*i,n} = \max\left(\frac{1}{ab - \nu} - \frac{1}{g_{ii,r}^{nn}}, 0\right) \tag{28}$$

$a = \sum_{j=1}^{M} g_{ij,r}^{nm} + \sum_{j=1,j\neq i}^{N} g_{ij,r}^{nn}$, ν constraints for equality, it can be obtained by (25) of the above formula.

The flow chart of power allocation algorithm is shown in the figure below. Firstly, specify an initial value for the transmit power of the D2D terminal. Each iteration randomly selects a user, at the same time, calculate the optimal power distribution plan under this condition. When the number of iterations is more than the preset maximum number of iterations, the calculation is stopped. The condition at this time is that the Nash equilibrium has been reached, other D2D user terminals can no longer obtain better benefits by changing their own strategies (Fig. 2).

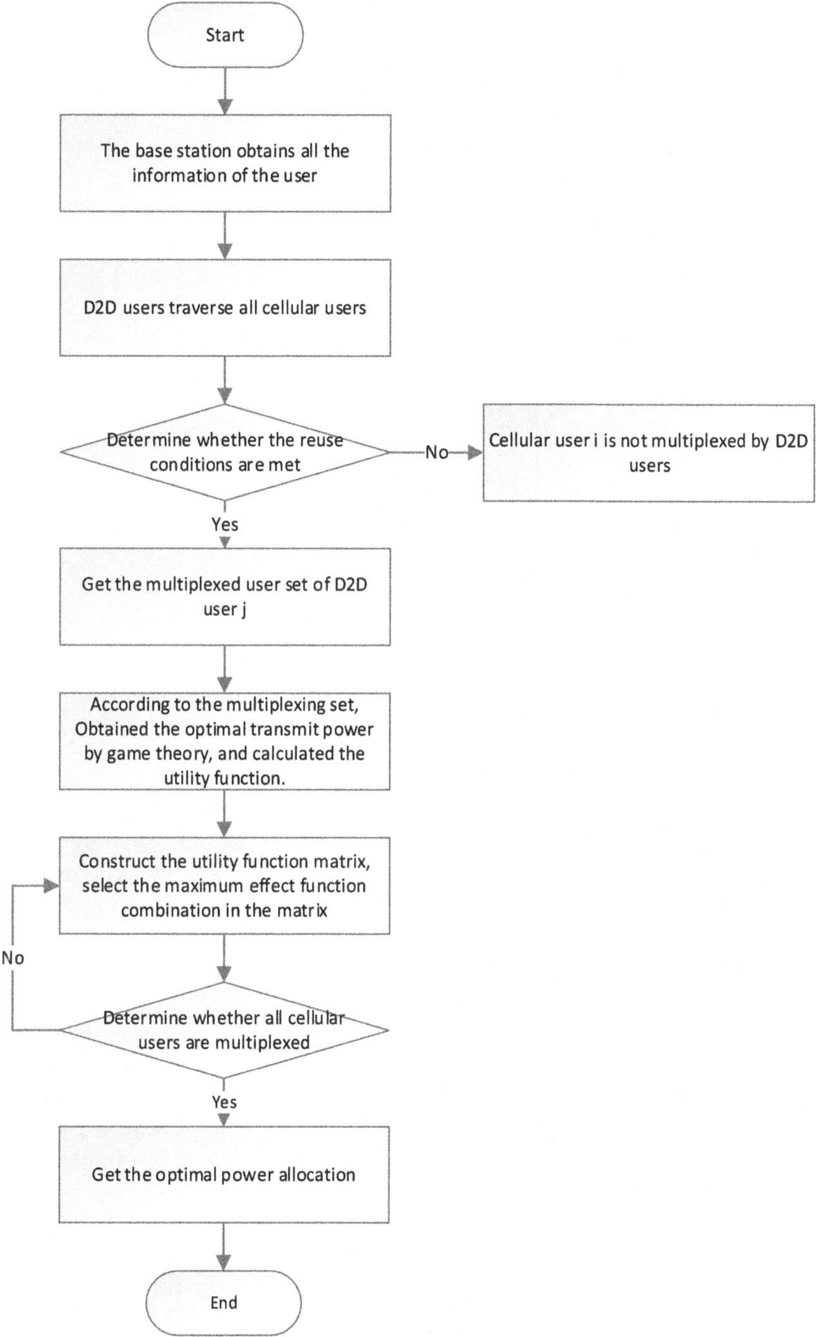

Fig. 2. Flow chart of power control algorithm.

4 Simulation Results and Analysis

This paper assumes that the environment is a single cell environment, cellular users and D2D users are randomly distributed in the cell. The receiver of D2D user is distributed in a 50 m radius circle with the transmitter of D2D user as the center. The cell radius is 500 m. The simulation parameters are shown in Table 1.

Table 1. Values of simulation parameters

Parameter	Numerical value
Cell radius	500 m
System bandwidth	10 MHz
Number of cellular terminals	20
Number of D2D users	20
Path loss between terminals	$148 + 40 \times \log 10(d[km])$
Path loss between terminal and BS	$128.1 + 37.6 \times \log 10(d[km])$
Maximum distance between D2D user pairs	50 m
User maximum transmit power	24 dBm
Noise power spectral density	−174 dBm/Hz
Cellular scheduling algorithm	Polling algorithm
Number of resource blocks	50

In this paper, Matlab is used to simulate and analyze the communication performance, an approximate value is obtained by taking the average value through multiple static simulation analysis. Firstly, setting up an initial network environment. According to the corresponding power control algorithm, resources are allocated for D2D users. Then the throughput of the communication system is calculated by transmitting power, SINR, channel path loss and other parameters.

1. The influence of D2D communication distance of different algorithms on system communication quality
   This paper simulates and compares three algorithms, Power and Resource Allocation Game algorithm (PRAG), Joint power control and resource allocation game algorithm based on non-cooperative D2D (NC-PRAG) and Random algorithm (RA). As shown in Fig. 3 below, comparative analysis of the changes in the utility function of different algorithms when the communication distance changes. It can be seen from the figure that when the communication distance increases, the utility function decreases, The closer the distance, the better the communication effect. By analyzing the three algorithms. The communication quality of RA is the lowest, followed by PRAG, and the algorithm NC-PRAG proposed in this paper is better. It can be seen that when D2D users change with distance, the communication effect will decrease, but the communication quality can be improved by reasonable power control and resource allocation.

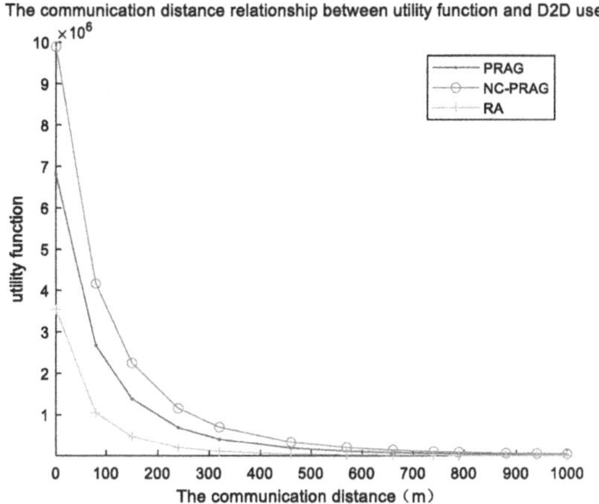

Fig. 3. Variation curve of communication quality with D2D communication distance

2. The influence of D2D communication distance of different algorithms on transmission power
   As shown in Fig. 4 below, analyzed and compared the transmission power of different algorithms with the change of communication distance. It can be seen from the figure that with the increase of communication distance, the transmission power of the system will also increase. Through simulation comparison, the transmission power of the RA algorithm increases faster. When the PRAG algorithm is introduced, the increase of transmission power decreases obviously. The NC-PRAG algorithm proposed in this paper further reduces the transmission power and saves the waste of transmission resources. Therefore, the algorithm proposed in this paper can reduce the waste of resources and improve the utilization of the system on the premise of ensuring the quality of communication.

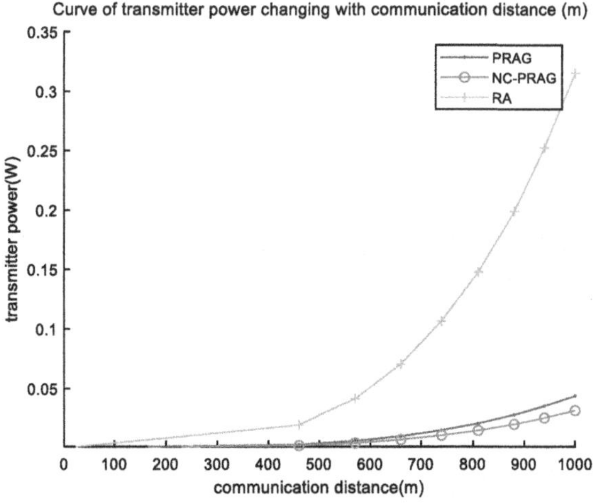

Fig. 4. Transmission power variation curve with communication distance

3. The influence of different algorithms on system delay.
As shown in Fig. 5 below, the simulation analyzes the system delay changes under three different algorithms. It can be analyzed from the figure below that compared to the RA algorithm, both the PRAG algorithm and the NC-PRAG algorithm significantly reduce the system delay. The system delay is increased by 1.25 times and 1.38 times respectively. It improves the transmission rate of communication system better, compared with the PRAG algorithm, the NC-PRAG algorithm is also improved by 1.1 times. The system delay is reduced accordingly. The simulation results show that NC-PRAG algorithm can better reduce system delay and increase transmission rate.

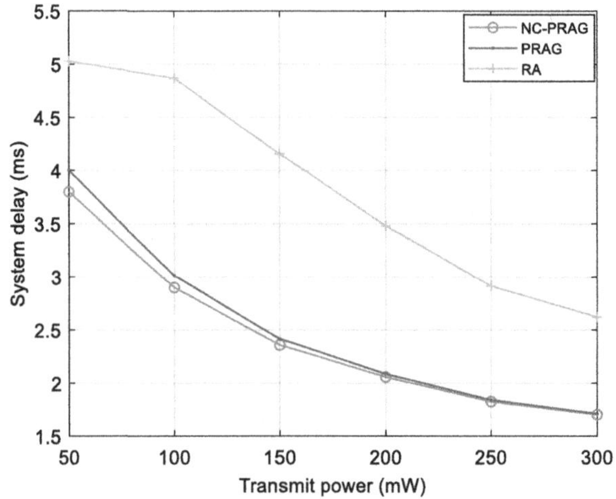

Fig. 5. System delay variation curve

5 Conclusion

With the development of modern wireless communication technology, D2D communication technology has become a research hotspot of a new generation of communication technology. It has become an urgent problem to be solved in D2D communication in terms of solving its spectrum utilization, improving communication quality, improving system fairness, and reducing system delay. This paper proposes a non-cooperative D2D joint power control and resource allocation game algorithm based on the above problems. The "many to many" D2D communication system is designed, Firstly, this paper improves the utility function of the algorithm, which is the product of the throughput and the terminal usage time of the communication system, and optimizes the utility function. Secondly, combined with D2D power control and resource allocation problems, a potential game model is established, and the theory proves that the Nash equilibrium point of this method exists and is unique. The simulation results show that, introduced the algorithm into the D2D communication system. On the basis of ensuring the communication quality, it greatly improves the throughput and fairness of the system, and reduces the system delay. Through system simulation, compared with the random algorithm, the transmission power of the system is reduced by 87.5%, and compared with the joint power control and resource allocation algorithm by 33.4%; Compared with the random algorithm, the throughput of the system is increased by 4.6 times, and compared with the joint power control and resource allocation algorithm by 1.91 times; The system delay is also reduced by 1.38 times and 1.1 times. Therefore, the non-cooperative D2D joint power control and resource allocation algorithm proposed in this paper is obviously better than the comparison algorithm.

References

1. Zhao, S., Feng, Y., Yu, G.: D2D communication channel allocation and resource optimization in 5G network based on game theory. Comput. Commun. **169**, 26–32 (2021)
2. Mohammed, V., Sreenivasa, P.M., Ravishankar, T., et al.: Energy efficient resource allocation for device-to-device communication through noncooperative game theory. Int. J. Commun. Syst. **33**(5), e4279 (2020)
3. Hao, X., Gong, Q., Hou, S., Liu, B.: Joint channel allocation and power control optimal algorithm based on Non-cooperative game in wireless sensor networks. Wireless Pers. Commun. **78**(2), 1047–1061 (2014)
4. Adiwal, M., Singh, N..P.: RAT selection for a low battery mobile device for future 5G networks. Int. J. Commun. Syst. **32**(13), e4055.1-e4055.17 (2019)
5. Shrivastava, T., Pandey, S., Mishra, P. K., Verma, S.: A non-cooperative game theoretic approach for resource allocation in D2D communication. In: Chiplunkar, N.N., Fukao, T. (eds.) Advances in Artificial Intelligence and Data Engineering. Advances in Intelligent Systems and Computing, vol. 1133, pp. 1323–1334. Springer, Singapore (2021). https://doi.org/10.1007/978-981-15-3514-7_99
6. Sun, Y., Miao, M., Wang, Z., Liu, Z.: Resource allocation based on hierarchical game for D2D underlaying communication cellular networks. Wireless Pers. Commun. **117**(2), 281–291 (2021)
7. Najeh, S., Bouallegue, A.: Game theory for SINR based power control in device-to-device communications. Phys. Commun. **34**, 135–143 (2019)
8. Zhang, S., Peng, Y.: D2D communication relay selection algorithm based on game theory. Procedia Comput. Sci. **166**, 563–569 (2020)
9. Sn, A., Ab, B.: Distributed vs centralized game theory-based mode selection and power control for D2D communications - ScienceDirect. Phys. Commun. **38**(C), 100962 (2020)
10. Wang, F., Son, L.Y., Han, Z., et al.: Joint scheduling and resource allocation for device-to-device underlay communication. In: Wireless Communications and Networking Conference (WCNC), Shanghai, China, pp. 134–139. IEEE (2013)
11. Wang, F., Xu, C., Song, L.Y., et al.: Energy efficient radio resource and power allocation for device-to-device communication underlaying cellular networks. In: International Conference on Wireless Communications and Signal Processing (WCSP), Huangshan, China, pp. 1–6. IEEE (2012)
12. Jiang, Y., Liu, Q., Zheng, F., et al.: Energy-efficient joint resource allocation and power control for D2D communications. IEEE Trans. Veh. Technol. **65**(5), 6119–6127 (2016)
13. Zhou, Z., Dong, M., Ota, K., et al.: Game-theoretic approach to energy-efficient resource allocation in device-to-device underlay communications. IET Commun. **9**(3), 375–385 (2015)

A Channel Estimation Scheme of Short Packets in Frequency Selective Channels

Chenguang He, Jianhui Zhang(✉), Yu Wang, and Shouming Wei

Communications Research Center, Harbin Institute of Technology, Harbin, China
{hechenguang,weishouming}@hit.edu.cn, {20s105128, 20s105137}@stu.hit.edu.cn

Abstract. In order to meet the needs of low delay in the IoT (Internet of Things) technology, short packets communication have recently attracted the attention of many researchers. In our scenario, the interference of multiple users cannot be ignored. Therefore, in order to overcome multi-user interference without affecting the efficiency of short packets transmission, we propose an efficient short packets receiving process for fast moving vehicles under a frequency-selective fading channel. During transmission, the obtained data are used to assist channel estimation. This method can also solve the problem of channel estimation quality degradation caused by a small number of pilots. Under the condition of high SNR, the performance of this scheme is improved significantly, which is close to perfect channel knowledge. Under the condition of low SNR, since the influence of the bit error rate of soft decision cannot be ignored, we adopt the scheme to eliminate multipath interference, which can effectively improve the estimation performance.

Keywords: Multipath channels · Channel estimation · Short packets · Virtual pilots

1 Introduction

With the rapid development of 5G and the gradual miniaturization and intelligence of devices, there will be more intelligent devices connected to the network in the future. Growing number of device connections promotes the development of IoT technology. In the field of IoT, MTC (Machine-Type Communications) is a hot research topic recently. The length of data sent by MTC is short and not fixed. The key requirement of MTC is to achieve low delay and high reliability [1]. According to its characteristics and requirements, a direct method is to directly use short packets for transmission.

Short packets communication is different from most wireless communication systems. In order to achieve Shannon capacity, the physical layer design of most current wireless communication systems relies on long codes. Due to the small size of the packets, the error probability of short packets during reception cannot be ignored [2–5]. In the future, short packets communication will be applied to a wider range of scenarios. For example, in urban scenarios, high-speed vehicle sensors communicate with roadside units or base stations to inform drivers of road information.

© ICST Institute for Computer Sciences, Social Informatics and Telecommunications Engineering 2022
Published by Springer Nature Switzerland AG 2022. All Rights Reserved
S. Shi et al. (Eds.): 6GN 2021, LNICST 439, pp. 120–129, 2022.
https://doi.org/10.1007/978-3-031-04245-4_11

In this article, we focus on two things. First is the access of a large number of devices will cause interference to the reception of target devices. One solution is to introduce interference training cycles [6], which are smaller than information cycles when systems are typically designed to carry long packets. When the packets are short, the training cycle must be kept small, which will cause a serious decline in the quality of channel estimation. Moreover, fewer pilots will reduce the quality of channel estimation [7]. Therefore, we use the data acquired during transmission as virtual pilots to optimize the performance of the receiver, and we combine the virtual pilots and traditional pilots for channel estimation. On the one hand, this method can avoid the loss of transmission rate caused by interference training cycle, on the other hand, it can assist with less pilot for accurate channel estimation.

The second is the design of receiver for transmitting short packets under high speed background.

In this situation, the stability of vehicle transmission link and the quality of transmission data are greatly reduced [8, 9]. We propose an estimation method of frequency selective channel based on short packets. Since the low bit error rate of this method has a great influence on the soft decision of virtual pilot, a multipath interference cancellation method is used to improve the detection ability.

The rest of the article is organized as follows. In the second section, we describe the system model and establish the transceiver relationship. In the third section, we propose a joint channel estimation method based on virtual pilot and traditional pilot. In the fourth section, we compare the proposed methods and improve the receiving performance under low SNR. The fifth section ends this article.

2 System Model

As shown in Fig. 1, we consider the uplink communication of high-speed moving vehicles in the urban background, such as the collection of vehicle information via wireless sensor network, the reporting of vehicle quality, and whether the driver's driving state conforms to traffic rules. Assuming that the sensor of the target vehicle has an antenna, the received

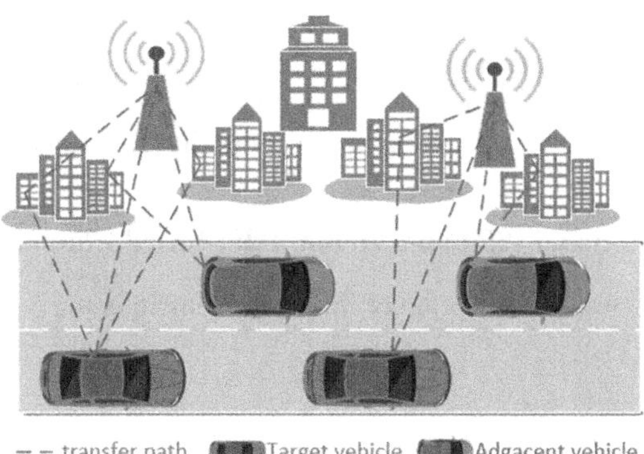

Fig. 1. Information transmission of target vehicle and interference of adjacent vehicle

signal contains not only the required information, but also the interference from the sensor of the adjacent vehicles. There are I interference sources in the communication process.

Assume that the total number of data transmission is N, N_d is the number of data transmission, N_P is the number of traditional pilot, and N_f is the FFT points for OFDM transformation. The received data can be expressed as

$$\boldsymbol{y}_r = \partial_t \boldsymbol{D}_{r,t} \boldsymbol{x}_t + \sum_{i=1}^{I} \partial_i \boldsymbol{D}_{r,i} \boldsymbol{x}_i + \boldsymbol{n}_r \tag{1}$$

where $y_r = \left[y_0^{(r)}, \cdots, y_{N-1}^{(r)}\right]^T$ is N observed values received, $x_t = \left[x_0^{(t)}, \cdots, x_{N-1}^{(t)}\right]^T$ is the signal emitted by the target vehicle, $\boldsymbol{D}_{r,t} \in \mathbb{C}^{\mathrm{N\times N}}$ is the data transmission matrix of the target vehicle, $\boldsymbol{D}_{r,i} \in \mathbb{C}^{\mathrm{N\times N}}$, $\mathrm{i} \in (1, 2, \cdots \mathrm{I})$ is the data transmission matrix of the i-th interfering vehicle, $\boldsymbol{n}_r = \left[n_0^{(r)}, \cdots, n_{N-1}^{(r)}\right]^T$ is the noise, ∂_t is the antenna transmitting power of the target vehicle, and $\partial_i, i \in (1, 2, \cdots I)$ is the transmitting power of the i-th interfering vehicle. And

$$\boldsymbol{D}_{r,t} = \boldsymbol{Q}_{r,t} \boldsymbol{H}_{r,t} \boldsymbol{P}_{r,t} \tag{2}$$

where $\boldsymbol{Q}_{r,t} \in \mathbb{C}^{N\times N_f}$ is the FFT transformation matrix of N_f points, $\boldsymbol{P}_{r,t} \in \mathbb{C}^{N_f\times N}$ is the IFFT transformation matrix of N_f points, $\boldsymbol{Q}_{r,t}\boldsymbol{P}_{r,t} = \boldsymbol{I}_N$, and $\boldsymbol{H}_{r,t} \in \mathbb{C}^{N_f\times N_f}$ is the channel gain matrix.

3 Joint Channel Estimation Using Virtual Pilot and Traditional Pilot

In this section, we use traditional pilot and virtual pilot to conduct channel estimation to improve the quality of estimation. The workflow of the whole system is shown in Fig. 2: firstly, channel estimation is performed using traditional pilot for the obtained signal. The estimated results are judged by LLR (log likelihood ratio), and then decode. Secondly, the decoded data is used for interference reduction operation, and then the appropriate virtual pilot and traditional pilot are selected for channel estimation. Thirdly, the data is decoded by the re-estimated channel, and the above iterative process is repeated until the conditions are met for output. The selection of virtual pilot is to select a small number of reliable data symbols from all available data symbols for channel estimation.

3.1 The Joint Traditional Pilot and Virtual Pilot Based Channel Estimation

The traditional pilot observation value of the target vehicle is

$$\boldsymbol{y}_p = \partial_t \boldsymbol{D}_{r,t} \boldsymbol{p}_t + \mathbf{n}_r \tag{3}$$

where $\boldsymbol{p}_t = \left[p_0^{(t)}, \cdots, p_{N_p-1}^{(t)}\right]^T$ is the pilot sent by the target vehicle, $\boldsymbol{y}_p = \left[y_0^{(r)}, \cdots, y_{N_p}^{(r)}\right]^T$ is the pilot receiving value.

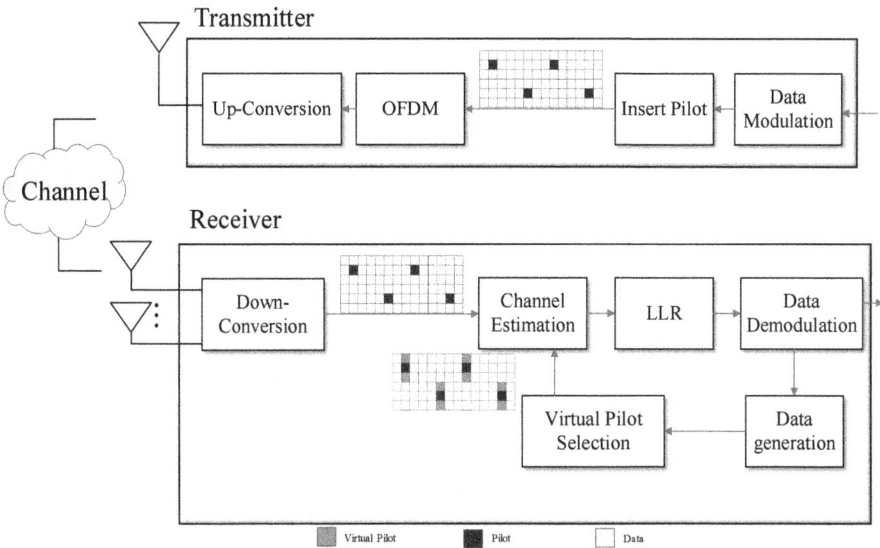

Fig. 2. Channel estimation scheme using virtual pilot signals

With the increase of N_P, the quality of channel estimation increases gradually, and the estimated channel vector converges to perfect channel knowledge. Because the short packets contain fewer pilots, the channel estimation quality will degrade. In order to improve the quality of channel estimation without increasing pilot overhead, we use virtual pilot to re-estimate the channel. When the number of virtual pilots selected is N_s, the received value can be expressed as

$$\boldsymbol{y}_s = \partial_t \boldsymbol{D}_{r,t} \boldsymbol{s}_t + \sum_{i=1}^{I} \partial_i \boldsymbol{D}_{r,i} \boldsymbol{s}_i + \boldsymbol{v}_r \tag{4}$$

where $\boldsymbol{s}_t = \left[s_0^{(t)}, \cdots, s_{N_s-1}^{(t)}\right]^T$ is N_s virtual pilots selected from the data symbols sent by the target vehicle, $\boldsymbol{s}_i = \left[s_0^{(i)}, \cdots, s_{N_s-1}^{(i)}\right]^T$, $i \in (1, 2, \cdots I)$ is the i-th interfering vehicle data symbols, $\boldsymbol{y}_s = \left[y_0^{(r)}, \cdots, y_{N_s-1}^{(r)}\right]^T$ is the observed value of the received data, and $\boldsymbol{v}_r$ is the noise.

The traditional pilot observation vector $\boldsymbol{y}_p$ is superimposed with the virtual pilot vector $\boldsymbol{y}_s$ to obtain the compound observation vector $\boldsymbol{y}_c$.

$$\boldsymbol{y}_c = \begin{bmatrix} \boldsymbol{y}_p \\ \boldsymbol{y}_s \end{bmatrix} = \partial_t \boldsymbol{D}_{r,t} \begin{bmatrix} \boldsymbol{p}_t \\ \boldsymbol{s}_t \end{bmatrix} + \sum_{i=1}^{I} \partial_i \boldsymbol{D}_{r,i} \begin{bmatrix} \boldsymbol{0} \\ \boldsymbol{s}_i \end{bmatrix} + \begin{bmatrix} n_r \\ \boldsymbol{v}_r \end{bmatrix} \tag{5}$$

Note that the second item in Eq. (5) is not the signal from the transmitting antenna but the interference. Since the estimation of channels using this interference-corrupted observation vector is undesirable, using newly updated soft information of data symbols, we cancel the interferences

$$\tilde{\boldsymbol{y}}_c = \begin{bmatrix} \tilde{\boldsymbol{y}}_p \\ \tilde{\boldsymbol{y}}_s \end{bmatrix} = \begin{bmatrix} \boldsymbol{y}_p \\ \boldsymbol{y}_s \end{bmatrix} - \sum_{i=1}^{I} \partial_i \hat{\boldsymbol{D}}_{r,i} \begin{bmatrix} \boldsymbol{0} \\ \bar{\boldsymbol{s}}_i \end{bmatrix} \tag{6}$$

where the estimate of the interstream interference $\partial_i \hat{\boldsymbol{D}}_{r,i} \bar{\boldsymbol{s}}_i$ is constructed from the soft estimate of the data symbols $\bar{\boldsymbol{s}}_i \triangleq \left[\bar{s}_0^{(i)}, \cdots, \bar{s}_{N_s-1}^{(i)}\right]^T$ and the channel estimate $\hat{\boldsymbol{D}}_{r,i}$ obtained from the previous iteration. Where

$$\bar{s}_j^{(i)} = E\left[s_j^{(i)}\right] = \sum_{\theta \in \Theta} \theta \prod_{k-1}^{Q} \frac{1}{2}\left(1 + c_{j,k}^{(i)} \tanh\left(\frac{1}{2} L\left(c_{j,k}^{(i)}\right)\right)\right) \tag{7}$$

where Θ is a constellation set, $c_{j,k}^{(i)}$ is the k-th coded bit, Q is the number of bits mapped to a data symbol $s_j^{(i)}$ in 2Q-ary QAM (quadrature amplitude modulation) constellations, and $L\left(c_{j,k}^{(i)}\right)$ is the LLR of the k-th coded bit mapped from a data symbol $s_j^{(i)}$, we have

$$\bar{\lambda}_j^{(i)} = E\left[\left|s_j^{(i)}\right|^2\right] = \sum_{\theta \in \Theta} |\theta|^2 \prod_{k=1}^{Q} \frac{1}{2}\left(1 + c_{j,k}^{(i)} \tanh\left(\frac{1}{2} L\left(c_{j,k}^{(i)}\right)\right)\right) \tag{8}$$

We use $\boldsymbol{y}_c$, $\boldsymbol{p}_t$ and $\boldsymbol{s}_t$ for LS channel estimation:

$$\hat{\boldsymbol{h}}_{LS} = \begin{bmatrix} \boldsymbol{p}_t \\ \boldsymbol{s}_t \end{bmatrix}^{-1} \tilde{\boldsymbol{y}}_c \tag{9}$$

where $\hat{\boldsymbol{h}}_{LS} \in \mathbb{C}^{(N_p+N_s)\times 1}$ is the estimated value of the LS channel parameters. Hence, the MMSE(Minimum Mean Squared Error) channel estimation matrix is

$$\hat{\boldsymbol{D}}_{r,t}(l,k) = \boldsymbol{W}_{mmse}^T \hat{\boldsymbol{h}}_{LS}, \, l, k \in (1, 2, \cdots N) \tag{10}$$

where $\boldsymbol{W}_{mmse} \in \mathbb{C}^{(N_p+N_s)\times 1}$ is the weight vector which can be expressed as:

$$\boldsymbol{W}_{mmse} = \boldsymbol{R}_{\hat{h}_{LS}, D_{r,t}(l,k)} \boldsymbol{R}_{\hat{h}_{LS}, \hat{h}_{LS}}^{-1} \tag{11}$$

with $\boldsymbol{R}_{\hat{h}_{LS}, \hat{h}_{LS}} \in \mathbb{C}^{(N_p+N_s)\times(N_p+N_s)}$ denoting the correlation matrix of the LS channel estimates and $\boldsymbol{R}_{\hat{h}_{LS}, D_{r,t}(l,k)} \in \mathbb{C}^{(N_p+N_s)\times 1}$ the correlation vector between the LS channel estimates and one element of transmission matrix $D_{r,t}$.

3.2 Selection Method of Virtual Pilot

The quality and quantity of virtual pilot will directly affect the quality of channel estimation. The best way to select virtual pilot is to compare the performance of all virtual pilot signals and traditional pilot signal combination, and then compare the smallest

MSE(mean square error) to get the best combination as the virtual pilot symbol. This method has a large amount of calculation, so we adopt a simple method: we only use a single symbol to analyze the MSE, and then choose a virtual pilot symbol. This method is not optimal because it does not consider the correlation between the virtual pilot symbols, however, the computational complexity is much less than the method which use all possible symbol combinations. Our method can effectively improve the quality of channel re-estimation. The n-th data symbol is used as the virtual pilot, and its MSE metric $\varepsilon(n)$ is expressed as

$$\varepsilon(n) = E\left\| \boldsymbol{h}_{r,t} - \hat{\boldsymbol{h}}_{r,t} \right\|^2 \tag{12}$$

where $\hat{\boldsymbol{h}}_{r,t} = diag(\hat{\boldsymbol{D}}_{r,t})$, $\boldsymbol{h}_{r,t} = diag(\boldsymbol{D}_{r,t})$. We consider the case that the traditional pilot interval is very large, so the correlation between pilots is very weak. In the case of high SNR, we can get [10]:

$$\tilde{\varepsilon}(n) = \frac{1}{1 - \frac{\left|\bar{s}_n^{(i)}\right|^2}{\sum_{i=1}^{I} \partial_i \lambda_n^{(i)} + \lambda_n^{(t)} + 1}} + \frac{1}{1 - \left\| R_{h_p, h_{s,n}} \right\|^2} \tag{13}$$

where $R_{\boldsymbol{h}_p, h_{s,n}}$ is the correlation function between the channel parameter vector $\boldsymbol{h}_p = \left[h_0^{(t)}, \cdots h_{N_p-1}^{(t)}\right]^T \in \mathbb{C}^{N_p \times 1}$ of traditional pilot and the channel parameter $h_{n,s}$ of the n-th virtual pilot. According to Eq. (13), $\tilde{\varepsilon}(n)$ depends on the reliability of soft decisions and the correlation (of channel gains) between the virtual pilot and the traditional pilot.

4 Simulations

Our pilot distribution mode adopts the diamond-shaped pilot pattern, and each resource block has 12 subcarriers with a sub-carrier interval of 15 kHz [12, 13]. There are 14 data symbols in a time slot, and various modulation methods (4QAM, 16QAM) are used. The channel is modeled as an Extended Vehicular A (EVA) channel model with the vehicle speed set at 80–200 km/h and the doppler mode introduced as the Jakes model. We set the sampling rate to 400 kHz, and there will be frequency selective fading in this channel mode.

Figure 3 show the distribution of traditional pilot, data and virtual pilot frequency when the number of virtual pilot is 16. Figure 3(a) shows the distribution of small interference from adjacent vehicles. The quality of soft decision has a great influence on the selection of virtual pilot. Meanwhile, the correlation (of channel gains) between the virtual and the traditional pilot also affects the choice of virtual pilots, most of which are located around the traditional pilot. When the interference is large, the virtual pilot frequency distribution is shown in Fig. 3(b). The correlation (of channel gains) between the virtual pilot and the traditional pilot have a significant effect on the choice of the pilot, and virtual pilots are distributed around the traditional pilot. It is well known that the signal distributed around the traditional pilot is of better quality at recovery. In this paper, the performance of the virtual pilot selected by random selection and the virtual pilot selected by this method will be compared.

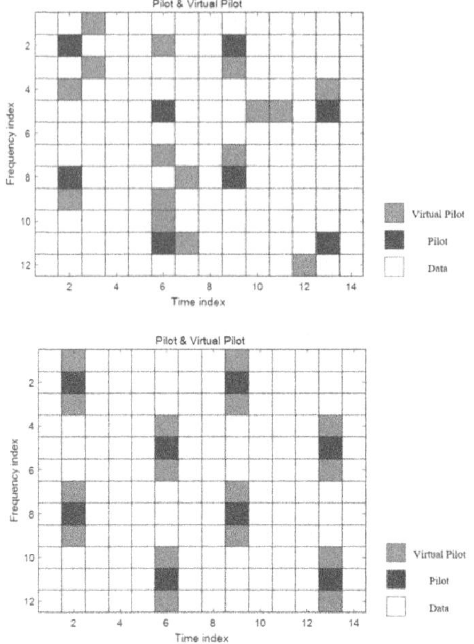

(a) Interference is small (b) Interference is large

Fig. 3. Virtual pilot distribution under different vehicle interference

Figure 4 shows the performance of different channel estimation algorithms at high SNR (15–30). We set the number of virtual pilots to 16 and interfering vehicles to 4. It can be seen that the LS method is the worst for channel estimation. Compared with flat slow fading channel, LS estimation has worse performance than MMSE in selective

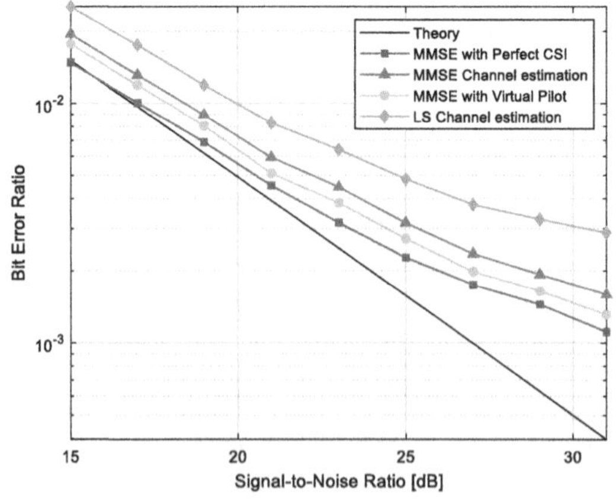

Fig. 4. BER performance of receiver techniques at high SNR

fading channel. It can be seen from Fig. 4 that under the condition of high SNR, the proposed method can obtain a gain of about 2dB, and the channel estimation performance is gradually approaching the perfect channel knowledge.

In the case of a low SNR (5–15), the simulation results are shown in Fig. 5(a). Due to the inevitable influence of error code in soft judgment, it has a negative impact on re-estimation, which is more serious under low SNR. As can be seen from Fig. 5(a), our proposed method only has a gain of 0.2dB to 0.5dB.

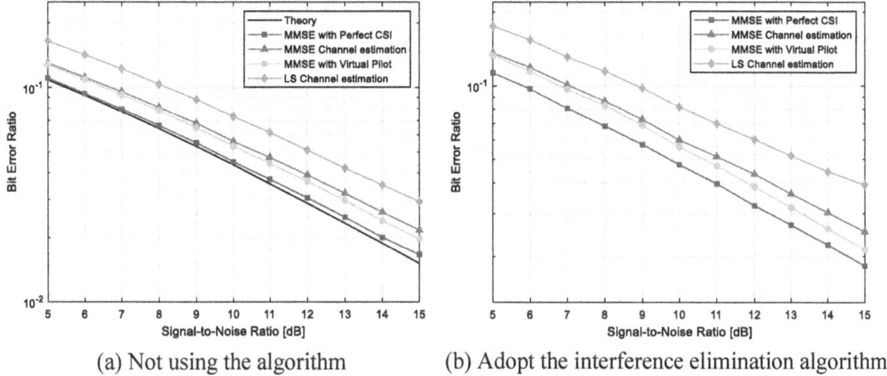

(a) Not using the algorithm (b) Adopt the interference elimination algorithm

Fig. 5. BER performance of receiver techniques at low SNR

In order to get a better gain effect, this paper adopts a cyclic iteration method to eliminate multipath interference to improve the detection performance under low SNR. Similar as suggested in [11], we can Improve detection performance by

$$\boldsymbol{y}_r^{(i+1)} = \boldsymbol{y}_r - (\hat{\boldsymbol{D}}_{r,t} - diag(\hat{\boldsymbol{D}}_{r,t}))\hat{\boldsymbol{x}}_t^{(i)} \tag{14}$$

Where $\hat{\boldsymbol{x}}_t^{(i)}$ represents the signal estimate updated in the i-th iteration, $\boldsymbol{y}_r^{(i+1)}$ is the value of interference elimination obtained in the $i+1$ iteration. $\hat{\boldsymbol{D}}_{r,t} - diag(\hat{\boldsymbol{D}}_{r,t})$ represents all the off-diagonal elements of $\hat{\boldsymbol{D}}_{r,t}$. As shown in Fig. 5(b), the performance of the algorithm to eliminate multipath interference is better than that of the above situation, and its performance is improved by about 1dB.

Figure 6 shows the comparison between the method of randomly selecting the virtual pilot and the method of selecting the virtual pilot using Eq. (13). The simulation results show that the random selection method can't achieve better results in channel re-estimation because of the low quality of soft decision.

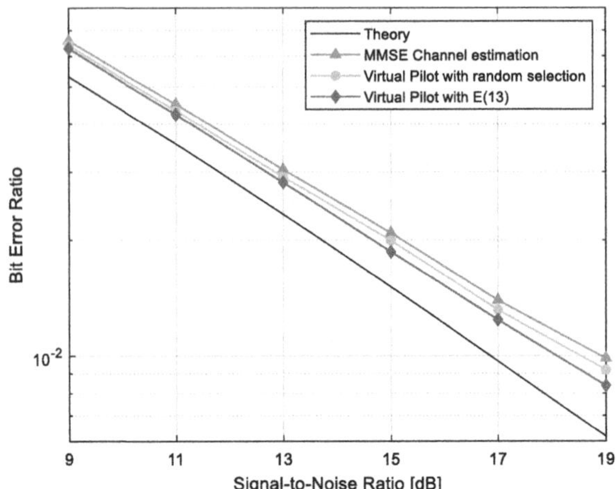

Fig. 6. Comparison of the method of Eq. (13) and the method of random selection

5 Conclusion

In this paper, we analyze the receiving mechanism of short packets transmission under high speed and frequency selective fading channel, and effectively solve the decline of channel estimation quality caused by insufficient interference training period and less pilot number of short packets. The influence of bit error rate cannot be ignored in the proposed method. Because the transmission performance of the proposed method is not improved significantly at low SNR, our algorithm to eliminate the influence of multipath can improve the bit error rate performance.

Acknowledgments. This paper is supported by the National Key R&D Program of China (No.2020YFE0205800).

References

1. Johansson, N., Wang, Y.P.E., Eriksson, E., Hessler, M.: Radio accessfor ultra-reliable and low-latency 5G communications, In: Proc. IEEE Int. Conf. Commun. (ICC), Jun. 2015, pp. 1184–1189
2. Polyanskiy, Y., Poor, H.V., Verdu, S.: Channel coding rate in the finite blocklength regime. IEEE Trans. Inf. Theory **56**(5), 2307–2359 (2010). https://doi.org/10.1109/TIT.2010.2043769. May
3. Polyanskiy, Y., Poor, H.V., Verd, S.: Dispersion of the Gilbert-Elliott channel. IEEE Trans. Inf. Theory **57**(4), 1829–1848 (2011). Apr.
4. Ozcan, G., Gursoy, M.: Throughput of cognitive radio systems with finite blocklength codes. IEEE J. Sel. Areas Commun. **31**(11), 2541–2554 (2013). Nov.
5. Yang, W., Durisi, G., Koch, T., Polyanskiy, Y.: Quasi-static multiple antenna fading channels at finite blocklength. IEEE Trans. Inf. Theory **60**(7), 4232–4265 (2014). Jul.

6. Jindal, N., Andrews, J.G., Weber, S.: Multi-antenna communication in ad hoc networks: achieving MIMO gains with SIMO transmission. IEEE Trans. Commun. **59**(2), 529–540 (2011). https://doi.org/10.1109/TCOMM.2010.120710.090793. Feb.
7. Lee, B., Park, S., Love, D.J., Ji, H., Shim, B.: Packet structure and receiver design for low latency wireless communications with ultra-short packets. IEEE Trans. Commun. **66**(2), 796–807 (2018). https://doi.org/10.1109/TCOMM.2017.2755012. Feb.
8. He, C., Qu, G., Ye, L., Wei, S.: A two-level communication routing algorithm based on vehicle attribute information for vehicular ad hoc network, Wireless Communications and Mobile Computing (2021) https://doi.org/10.1155/2021/6692741
9. Wu, Y., Qiao, D., Qian, H.: Efficient bandwidth allocation for URLLC in frequency-selective fading channels, in Proc. GLOBECOM 2020 - 2020 IEEE Global Communications Conference, 2020, pp. 1–6
10. Park, S., Shim, B., Choi, J.W.: Iterative channel estimation using virtual pilot signals for MIMO-OFDM systems, IEEE Trans. Signal Process. **63**(12), 3032–3045 (2015). (June15) https://doi.org/10.1109/TSP.2015.2416684
11. Nissel, R., Rupp, M., Marsalek, R.: FBMC-OQAM in doubly-selective channels: A new perspective on MMSE equalization, in Proc. 2017 IEEE 18th International Workshop on Signal Processing Advances in Wireless Communications (SPAWC), Sapporo, Japan, Jul. 2017, pp. 1–5
12. NR; Physical channels and modulation (Release 16), 3GPP TS 38.211 V16.5.0(2021–03)
13. NR; Physical layer measurements (Release 16), 3GPP TS 38.215 V16.4.0(2020–12)
14. Jiang, J.-C., Wang, H.-M.: Massive random access with sporadic short packets: Joint active user detection and channel estimation via sequential message passing, IEEE Trans. Wireless Commun. https://doi.org/10.1109/TWC.2021.3060451
15. Shi, J., Wesel, R.D.: A study on universal codes with finite block lengths. IEEE Trans. Inf. Theory **53**(9), 3066–3074 (2007). https://doi.org/10.1109/TIT.2007.903156. Sept.

Cross-Layer Joint Scheduling for D2D Communication in Cellular Systems

Bi Xixi[1], Qin Zhiliang[2], and Ma Ruofei[1,2(✉)]

[1] Harbin Institute of Technology, Weihai 264209, Shandong, China
2213715472@qq.com, maruofei@hit.edu.cn
[2] Beiyang Electric Group Co. Ltd., Weihai, Shandong, China
qinzhiliang@beiyang.com

Abstract. The introduction of device-to-device (D2D) communications into cellular system can improve spectrum efficiency and reduce traffic load of the core network, but it can also increase the scheduling complexing at the base station (BS). Hence designing an efficient scheduling algorithm has become a hot topic for developing D2D communications in cellular systems. But most existing work on the scheduling algorithm commonly assume that all the channel state information (CSI) are known at the BS, i.e., the BS can obtain all the CSI that it needs to perform scheduling, but the scheduling algorithms designed based on the assumptions usually corresponds to a very high overhead on channel measurement when they are implement into actual systems. With this background, a cross-layer joint scheduling scheme that can jointly perform power coordination, channel allocation for D2D capable users by taking into account both the transmission rate criteria of physical layer and the transmission delay criteria of link layer under the condition that the CSI are partly known at the BS are proposed, also the supported D2D mode for D2D-capable users in the cellular system is only the reuse direct D2D mode. Meanwhile, according to the channel probability and statistical characteristics for the interference channels, the end-to-end transmission delay estimation method for the reuse direct D2D mode is presented. Simulation results validate the effectiveness of the joint scheduling scheme and the increase of the system performance brought in the reuse direct D2D mode, in addition, the influence of the major system parameters of the performance on the joint scheduling scheme are also analyzed.

Keywords: Device-to-device (D2D) communication · Channel state information · Queue theory · Transmission delay · Joint scheduling

This work was supported partially by National Natural Science Foundation of China (Grant No. 61801144, 61971156), Shandong Provincial Natural Science Foundation, China (Grant No. ZR2019QF003, ZR2019MF035), and the Fundamental Research Funds for the Central Universities, China (Grant No. HIT.NSRIF.2019081).

© ICST Institute for Computer Sciences, Social Informatics and Telecommunications Engineering 2022
Published by Springer Nature Switzerland AG 2022. All Rights Reserved
S. Shi et al. (Eds.): 6GN 2021, LNICST 439, pp. 130–144, 2022.
https://doi.org/10.1007/978-3-031-04245-4_12

1 Introduction

Device-to-Device (D2D) communication is a promising technique for allowing two proximity user equipment to communicate directly [1]. And it can be classified into two categories according to the frequency band which can work, one is licensed-band D2D and the other is unlicensed-band D2D [2]. For the reason that the interference produced by the licensed-band D2D is easily controlled by the BS, hence the most existing works commonly focus on the licensed-band D2D [3]. But meanwhile, there are existing problem on the resource scheduling of the whole system. Hence designing an efficient resource scheduling scheme is very important.

There are three aspects that the scheduling scheme needs to concern, i.e., mode selection, resource allocation and power coordination. Especially, the earlier scheduling schemes mainly focus on the resource allocation or power coordination for the reuse direct D2D mode, and particularly, scheduling schemes on resource allocation are more based on graph theory [4–7]. For the scheduling scheme on mode selection and channel allocation, [8, 9] complete the channel allocation during the mode selection under the fully loaded cellular network and relatively lightly loaded cellular network based on the three D2D mode, i.e., cellular mode, direct D2D mode and relay D2D mode, especially when the cellular network is fully loaded, i.e., the cellular network only considers the reuse D2D mode, the thought that letting the integer programming transform linear programming is proposed under the condition that the relay is considered or not. In addition, there are existing mode selection and resource allocation which apply the D2D communication to the vehicular communication based on the cellular mode, dedicated mode and reused mode [10], and more special in the paper, the mode selection among the cellular mode and dedicated mode is selected based on the distance between the vehicular to vehicular. And the scheduling schemes based on the reinforcement learning and graph theory on mode selection and resource allocation also exist [11, 12]. For the resource allocation and power coordination, in [13], the paper transforms the constraint into feasible region, and derive the optimal power allocation that the D2D users reuse the cellular users and then using the Hungarian algorithm to solve the final problem. In [14], the paper also first delimits the feasible region, and then deduces the optimal power allocation that single D2D users reuse the cellular user, and then using the KM algorithm to solve the multi-pair D2D users to reuse the spectrum resources of the cellular users. For the jointly considering the mode selection, resource allocation and power coordination, in [15], the optimal power allocation of the reuse direct D2D mode and reuse relay D2D mode is derived first, and then the paper compares the transmission rate of the above two modes under the optimal power allocation, and then based on the results, the optimal working mode is determined and the Hungarian algorithm is finally adopted to derive the final results. Integrating the above papers, the core work is power allocation, and when finish the power allocation, the final results can be derived by adopting some casual algorithm.

But the above algorithms possess two limitations. One is that the scheduling algorithms mainly assume that the BS can acquire the perfect channel state information (CSI) of the channel that the BS needs, but lacking the consideration of the partly-known CSI of the channel and the other is that the most algorithms only consider the criteria on the physical layer and lacking the consideration of the criteria on the link layer. Thus it is important to propose a joint scheduling scheme which jointly considers the criteria on physical layer and link layer under the condition that the CSI is partly-known. Accordingly, in this paper, scheduling algorithms that can jointly perform power coordination, channel allocation for the D2D users which can only work on the reuse direct D2D mode by taking into account both the transmission rate criteria of the physical layer and the transmission delay criteria of the link layer are proposed, and the end-to-end transmission delay estimation schemes for the reuse direct D2D mode are also presented when only the statistical characteristics for the interference channel are known.

The rest of the paper is organized as followed. In Sect. 2, the considered system model is displayed. Section 3 is the problem formulation, and delay estimation, optimization objective solving are also introduced in the Sect. 3. Section 4 is the performance evaluation, Sect. 5 concludes the paper.

2 System Model

As illustrated in Fig. 1. The considered system model is a single-cell system scenario, and M cellular user equipments (CUEs), K pairs of D2D user equipments (DUEs) coexist in the cell. $\{C_1, C_2, ..., C_m, ..., C_M\}$ denote the M CUEs, $\{S_1, S_2, ..., S_k, ..., S_K\}$ and $\{D_1, D_2, ..., D_k, ..., D_K\}$ denote the source and destination DUE of the K pairs of DUEs. For emphasizing the effect on introducing D2D communications, the system model is assumed as a fully loaded system model where DUEs can only access the system via the channel reuse, moreover, the DUEs can only work on the reuse direct D2D mode and each CUE's channel can only be reused by one D2D pair. DUE must reuse the uplink channel of the selected CUE.

Owing to the CSI of the channel between CUE-DUE which needs much signal overhead to acquire, thus BS can't acquire the perfect CSI of the channel between CUE-DUE and only masters the pass loss based on the distance, thus the channel gain in the system is build by two situations. The channel gain between transmit a and receive b except for the CUE-DUE is expressed as followed:

$$g_{a,b} = k_0 \zeta^f_{a,b} \zeta^s_{a,b} l^{-\alpha}_{a,b} \tag{1}$$

where k_0 and α denote the path loss constant and path loss exponent, $\zeta^f_{a,b}$ and $\zeta^s_{a,b}$ denote the fast and slow fading components. And the channel gain of the CUE-DUE is expressed as:

$$h_{C_m,D_k} = k_0 \beta_{C_m,D_k} l^{-\alpha}_{C_m,D_k} \tag{2}$$

where β_{C_m,D_k} denotes channel fading component and l_{C_m,D_k} denotes the distance between CUE-DUE.

3 Problem Formulation

The purpose of the paper is to maximize the transmission rate of the system while guaranteeing the delay constraint of the DUEs and QoS of the DUEs and CUEs under the condition that the CSI are partly known by the BS. For the reason that the BS can

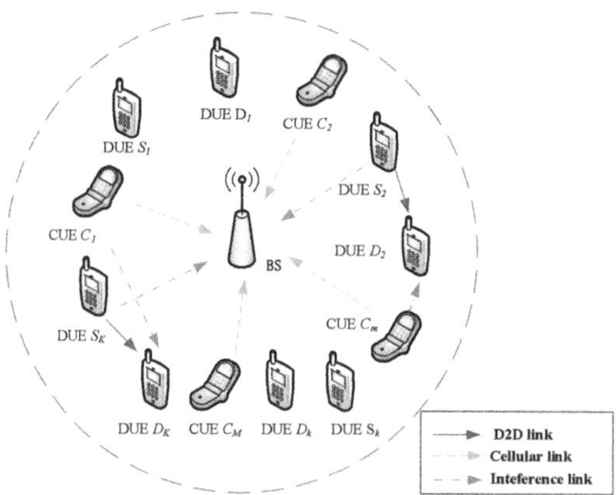

Fig. 1. System model

not master the perfect CSI of the interference channel CUE-DUE, thus the minimum SINR requirement of the DUE can't be guaranteed, hence in this paper, we refer related literature to use the statistical characteristics for the interference channels to guarantee the QoS of the interference channel CUE-DUE, i.e., the probability of the actual SINR of DUE which lower than SINR requirement lower than a given threshold:

$$\Pr\left\{\frac{p_{k,m}^{(D)} g_{S_k,D_k}}{\sigma^2 + p_{k,m}^{(C1)} h_{C_m,D_k}} < \xi_{\min}\right\} \le \psi \tag{3}$$

where $p_{k,m}^{(D)}$ and $p_{k,m}^{(C1)}$ denotes the transmit power of DUE and reused CUE, g_{S_k,D_k} denotes the channel gain of DUE, σ^2 and $\xi_{\min}$ denote the noise power and minimum requirement of SINR, and ψ denotes the maximal outage overflow probability of the system.

For the reason that BS can't master the perfect CSI of the interference channel CUE-DUE, hence the transmit outage is inevitable, so we also refer the related literature to use the indicator function Φ to denote the outage event of the DUE. When Φ equals to 1, which denotes the received SINR lower than the given SINR requirement and the receiver of the DUE can't demodulate the signal from the transmit, otherwise, the receiver of the DUE can modulate the signal from the transmit, thus the transmit rate can be denoted as:

$$r_{k,m}^{D} = \mathbb{E}\left\{\left[B_0 \log_2\left(1 + \frac{p_{k,m}^{(D)} g_{S_k,D_k}}{\sigma^2 + p_{k,m}^{(C1)} h_{C_m,D_k}}\right)\right] | \Phi = 0\right\} \tag{4}$$

where B_0 denotes the bandwidth of the channel.

According to the related literature, above equitation can also denoted as followed:

$$r_{k,m}^{D} = \int_0^l B_0 \log_2\left(1 + \frac{p_{k,m}^{(D)} g_{S_k,D_k}}{\sigma^2 + \beta_{C_m,D_k} p_{k,m}^{(C1)} H_{C_m,D_k}}\right) \frac{f(\beta_{C_m,D_k})}{F(l)} d\beta_{C_m,D_k} \tag{5}$$

where l denotes the critical value of β_{C_m,D_k} and equals to $\frac{p_{k,m}^{(D)} g_{S_k,D_k} - \xi_{\min}\sigma^2}{p_{k,m}^{(C1)} \xi_{\min} H_{C_m,D_k}}$, H_{C_m,D_k} equals to $k_0 l_{C_m,D_k}^{-\alpha}$, $f(\cdot)$ and $F(\cdot)$ denote the probability density function and cumulative distribution function when the channel obey Rayleigh fading, and the value can be denoted as:

$$f(\beta_{C_m,D_k}) = \begin{cases} \lambda e^{-\lambda \beta_{C_m,D_k}} & \beta_{C_m,D_k} > 0 \\ 0 & \beta_{C_m,D_k} \leq 0 \end{cases} \tag{6}$$

$$F(\beta_{C_m,D_k}) = \begin{cases} 1 - \lambda e^{-\lambda \beta_{C_m,D_k}} & \beta_{C_m,D_k} \geq 0 \\ 0 & \beta_{C_m,D_k} < 0 \end{cases} \tag{7}$$

where λ denotes the mean value of β_{C_m,D_k}, and assumed that it equates to 1.

When CUE is not reused by DUE, the rate of the CUE can be denoted as:

$$r_m^{(C)} = B_0 \log_2\left(1 + \frac{p_m^{(C)} g_{C_m,B}}{\sigma^2}\right) \tag{8}$$

where $p_m^{(C)}$ and $g_{C_m,B}$ denote the transmit power of CUE when the CUE is not reused by the DUE and the channel gain between CUE and BS.

When the CUE is reused by the DUE, the rate of the CUE can be denoted as:

$$r_{k,m}^{(C1)} = B_0 \log_2\left(1 + \frac{p_{k,m}^{(C1)} g_{C_m,B}}{p_{k,m}^{(D)} g_{S_k,B} + \sigma^2}\right) \tag{9}$$

where $g_{S_k,B}$ denotes the channel gain between DUE and BS.

Hence the joint scheduling algorithm can be mathematically modelled as:

$$(\mathbf{p}^*, \mathbf{x}^*) = \arg\max_{\mathbf{p},\mathbf{x}} \left\{ \sum_{k=1}^{K} \sum_{m=1}^{M} x_{k,m}^{(1)} \left(r_{k,m}^{(C1)} + r_{k,m}^{(D)} \right) + \sum_{m=1}^{M} \left(1 - \sum_{k=1}^{K} x_{k,m}^{(1)} \right) r_m^{(C)} \right\} \tag{10}$$

$$subject\ to: x_{k,m}^{(1)} \in \{0, 1\}, \forall k, m \tag{11}$$

$$\sum_{k=1}^{K} x_{k,m}^{(1)} \leq 1, \forall m \tag{12}$$

$$\sum_{m=1}^{M} x_{k,m}^{(1)} \leq 1, \forall k \tag{13}$$

$$\sum_{m=1}^{M} x_{k,m}^{(1)} u_{k,m} \leq u_{\max}, \forall k \tag{14}$$

$$\sum_{m=1}^{M} x_{k,m}^{(1)} p_{k,m}^{(D)} \leq P_{max}^{D}, \forall k \tag{15}$$

$$\sum_{k=1}^{K} x_{k,m}^{(1)} p_{k,m}^{(C1)} + \left(1 - \sum_{k=1}^{K} x_{k,m}^{(1)}\right) p_m^{(C)} \le P_{\max}^{C}, \forall m \tag{16}$$

$$\sum_{m=1}^{M} x_{k,m}^{(1)} \Pr\left\{ \frac{p_{k,m}^{(D)} g_{S_k,D_k}}{\sigma^2 + p_{k,m}^{(C1)} h_{C_m,D_k}} < \xi_{\min} \right\} \le \sum_{m=1}^{M} x_{k,m}^{(1)} \psi, \forall k \tag{17}$$

$$\sum_{k=1}^{K} x_{k,m}^{(1)} \frac{p_{k,m}^{(C1)} g_{C_m,B}}{p_{k,m}^{(D)} g_{S_k,B} + \sigma^2} + \left(1 - \sum_{k=1}^{K} x_{k,m}^{(1)}\right) \times \frac{p_m^{(C)} g_{C_m,B}}{\sigma^2} \ge \xi_{\min}, \forall m \tag{18}$$

where $x_{k,m}^{(1)}$ denotes the channel select factor, and when the k-th DUE reuse the channel of the m-th CUE, $x_{k,m}^{(1)} = 1$, otherwise, $x_{k,m}^{(1)} = 0$. $u_{k,m}$ and $u_{\max}$ denotes the delay of the channel of DUE and delay requirement. P_{max}^{D} and $P_{\max}^{C}$ denote the maximal transmit power of the DUE and CUE. (12) and (13) restrict that a DUE can most be reused by one DUE. (14) is the delay requirement constraint. (15) and (16) are the transmit power constraint. (17) and (18) are the QoS constraint of DUE and CUE.

In order to solve the above optimization problem, the first thing is to derive the delay of the reuse direct D2D communications based on the channel probability and statistical characteristics for the interference channels.

3.1 Delay Estimation

D2D link can be treated as a queue server, and it can be denoted by a queuing model, as illustrated in Fig. 2. DUE S_k and D_k denote the source and destination DUE. $A_{k,t}$ and $Q_{k,t}$ denote the number of new arrival packet and queue packets at source DUE at t-th time slot, $U_{k,t}$ denotes the number of the transmitted packets.

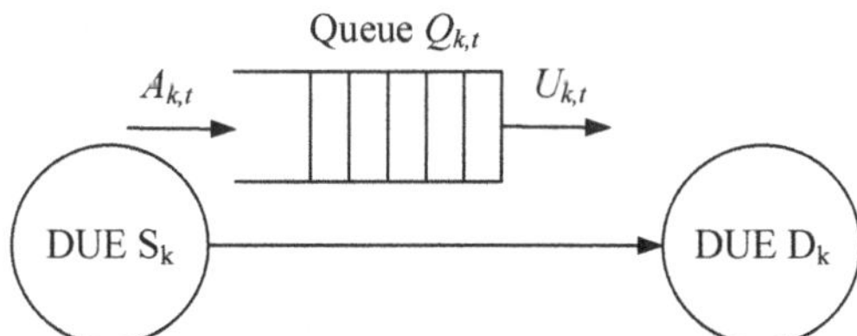

Fig. 2. Queuing model of D2D link

For better depicting the model, the time axis is divided into time slots with length of ΔT. Assuming that packet arrival process is stationary and follows passion distribution, and the arrive rate is λ_k, then the probability of j packets arriving at the source DUE at t-th time slot is depicted as:

$$p(A_{k,t} = j) = \frac{(\lambda_k \Delta T)^j}{j!} e^{-\lambda_k \Delta T}, j \in (0, 1, 2, \cdots) \tag{19}$$

Assuming that the transmitted packets always happen before the new arrival packets at every slot, then the relationship between $Q_{k,t}$ and $Q_{k,t-1}$ can be described as followed:

$$Q_{k,t} = \min\left[B, \max\left(0, Q_{k,t-1} - U_{k,t}\right) + A_{k,t}\right] \tag{20}$$

where B denotes the buffer size, i.e., the number that the source DUE can store at most.

For the reason that the BS can not master the perfect CSI of the interference link CUE-DUE, hence the transmitted rate $U_{k,t}$ is uncertain. Under the condition, the probability of transmitting n packets at t-th time slot can be obtained based on the statistical characteristics of the interference channels, and the process of the solving is presented as followed:

$$\begin{aligned}
\Pr\{U_{k,t} = n\} &= \Pr\left\{\left\lceil \frac{\Delta Tr_{k,m}^{(D)}}{L} \right\rceil = n\right\} \\
&= \Pr\left\{\frac{nL}{\Delta T} \le B_0 \log_2\left(1 + \frac{p_{k,m}^{(D)} g_{S_k,D_k}}{\sigma^2 + p_{k,m}^{(C1)} k_0 \beta_{C_m,D_k} l_{C_m,D_k}^{-\alpha}}\right) < \frac{(n+1)L}{\Delta T}\right\} \\
&= \Pr\left\{2^{nL(\Delta TB0)^{-1}} - 1 \le \frac{p_{k,m}^{(D)} g_{S_k,D_k}}{\sigma^2 + p_{k,m}^{(C1)} k_0 \beta_{C_m,D_k} l_{C_m,D_k}^{-\alpha}} < 2^{(n+1)L(\Delta TB0)^{-1}} - 1\right\}
\end{aligned} \tag{21}$$

where L denotes the number of data bits in a packet.

Further simplify (21), the above equitation can be depicted as:

$$\begin{aligned}
\Pr\{U_{k,t} = n\} &= \Pr\left\{\beta_{C_m,D_k} \le \frac{a-(c-1)\sigma^2}{(c-1)b}\right\} - \Pr\left\{\beta_{C_m,D_k} < \frac{a-(d-1)\sigma^2}{(d-1)b}\right\} \\
&= \Pr\{\beta_{C_m,D_k} \le e_1\} - \Pr\{\beta_{C_m,D_k} < f_1\}
\end{aligned} \tag{22}$$

where $a = p_{k,m}^{(D)} g_{S_k,D_k}$, $b = p_{k,m}^{(C1)} k_0 l_{C_m,D_k}^{-\alpha}$, $c = 2^{nL(\Delta TB_0)^{-1}}$ and $d = 2^{(n+1)L(\Delta TB_0)^{-1}}$, $e_1 = \frac{a-(c-1)\sigma^2}{(c-1)b}$, $f_1 = \frac{a-(d-1)\sigma^2}{(d-1)b}$.

and then (22) can be further depicted as:

$$\Pr\{U_{k,t} = n\} = \begin{cases} 0 & e_1 \le 0, f_1 < 0 \\ 1 - e^{-e_1} & e_1 > 0, f_1 \le 0 \\ e^{-f_1} - e^{-e_1} & e_1 > 0, f_1 > 0 \end{cases} \tag{23}$$

According to the expression of $A_{k,t}$ and $U_{k,t}$, the value are not related to the time, hence the following will let the A_k and U_k express the number of new arrival packets and transmitted packets at arbitrarily slot.

Based on the relationship between the number of buffers at two slots, the queue state transition probability matrix can be depicted as:

$$P(Q_{k,t} = \theta_k | Q_{k,t-1} = \varphi_k)$$

$$= \begin{cases} \Pr\{A_k = \theta_k\} & \varphi_k = 0, 0 \le \theta_k \le B - 1 \\ \sum_{j=B}^{\infty} \Pr\{A_k = j\} & \varphi_k = 0, \theta_k = B \\ \sum_{n=\varphi_k}^{\infty} \Pr\{A_k = 0\} \Pr\{U_k = n\} & 1 \le \varphi_k \le B, \theta_k = 0 \\ \sum_{n=\varphi_k}^{\infty} \Pr\{A_k = \theta_k\} \Pr\{U_k = n\} & \\ + \sum_{n=\varphi_k-\theta_k}^{\varphi_k-1} \Pr\{A_k = \theta_k + n - \varphi_k\} \Pr\{U_k = n\} & 1 \le \varphi_k \le B, 1 \le \theta_k \le \varphi_k, \theta_k \ne B \\ \sum_{n=\varphi_k}^{\infty} \Pr\{A_k = \theta_k\} \Pr\{U_k = n\} & \\ + \sum_{n=0}^{\varphi_k-1} \Pr\{A_k = \theta_k + n - \varphi_k\} \Pr\{U_k = n\} & 1 \le \varphi_k \le B - 1, \varphi_k < \theta_k \le B - 1 \\ \sum_{j=B}^{\infty} \sum_{n=\varphi_k}^{\infty} \Pr\{A_k = j\} \Pr\{U_k = n\} & \\ + \sum_{n=0}^{\varphi_k-1} \left(\Pr\{U_k = n\} \sum_{j=B+n-\varphi_k}^{\infty} \Pr\{A_k = j\} \right) & 1 \le \varphi_k \le B, \theta_k = B \end{cases} \tag{24}$$

And the packet queuing state transition can be depicted by a Finite state Markov Chain (FSMC), then the stationary probability vector $\Omega_{k,m}$ can be denoted by:

$$\begin{cases} \Omega_{k,m} = \Omega_{k,m} P \\ \sum_{i=0}^{B} \Omega_{k,m}^{i} = 1 \end{cases} \tag{25}$$

where $\Omega_{k,m}^{i}$ denotes the stationary probability of the i packets stored in the source of the DUE. The average packet queue length $\overline{Q_{k,m}}$ can be obtained by:

$$\overline{Q_{k,m}} = \sum_{i=0}^{B} \left(i \times \Omega_{k,m}^{i} \right) \tag{26}$$

Let $u_{k,m}$ denote the delay of the D2D link, and it can be denoted as followed based on the Littles law:

$$u_{k,m} = \overline{Q_{k,m}} / \left(\left(1 - \phi_{k,m} \right) \times E[A_{k,t}] \right) \tag{27}$$

where $E[A_{k,t}] = \lambda_k \Delta T$ denotes average number of the packets arriving at the source DUE at a slot and $\phi_{k,m}$ denotes the packet loss rate. And $\phi_{k,m}$ can be obtained by:

$$\phi_{k,m} = D_{k,m} / (E[A_k]) \tag{28}$$

where $D_{k,m}$ denotes the loss number caused by the limited length of the buffer at source DUE, and A_k denotes the stationary distribution of $A_{k,t}$. The calculation of the $D_{k,m}$ can be obtained by:

$$\begin{aligned} D_{k,m} = & \sum_{m=1}^{B} \Omega_{k,m}^{m} \sum_{n=0}^{m-1} \Pr\{U_k = n\} \sum_{j=B+n-m}^{\infty} (m+j-n-B) \Pr\{A_k = j\} \\ & + \sum_{m=1}^{B} \Omega_{k,m}^{m} \sum_{n=m}^{\infty} \Pr\{U_k = n\} \sum_{j=B}^{\infty} (j-B) \Pr\{A_k = j\} \\ & + \Omega_{k,m}^{0} \sum_{j=B}^{\infty} (j-B) \Pr\{A_k = j\} \end{aligned} \tag{29}$$

Based on the derivation process, the end-to-end delay can be obtained.

3.2 Optimization Objective Solving

From (10), we can know that the optimization objective is not the linear function and the optimization problem contains the integer variable, hence the optimization problem belongs to the MINLP. For the MINLP, it is difficult to derive the final resolution. Hence we will divide the original problem into two problem to solve, that are power allocation and channel allocation, but the first thing to do first is to control the DUEs to access the network, i.e., access control.

Access Control The accessing control based on the delay requirement, power constraint requirement and QoS requirement will be presented as followed. Only when the DUE satisfy the above three requirements, the DUE can access the network, otherwise, the DUE can't access the network.

When the k-th DUE can reuse the m-th CUE to access the network, the DUE must satisfies the following equations:

$$u_{k,m} \leq u_{\max} \tag{30}$$

$$p_{k,m}^{(D)} \leq P_{max}^{D}, p_{k,m}^{(C1)} \leq P_{\max}^{C} \tag{31}$$

$$\frac{p_{k,m}^{(C1)} g_{C_m,B}}{p_{k,m}^{(D)} g_{S_k,B} + \sigma^2} \geq \xi_{\min} \tag{32}$$

$$\Pr\left\{ \frac{p_{k,m}^{(D)} g_{S_k,D_k}}{\sigma^2 + p_{k,m}^{(C1)} h_{C_m,D_k}} < \xi_{\min} \right\} \leq \psi \tag{33}$$

when the constraints don't consider the delay constraint, i.e., don't consider the (30), whether the k-th DUE can reuse the channel of m-th CUE to work on the reuse direct D2D communications can judge by the distance of CUE-DUE. And only when the real distance of CUE-DUE exceeds the shortest distance, DUE can reuse the channel of the CUE to work on the reuse direct D2D communications. Moreover when the distance

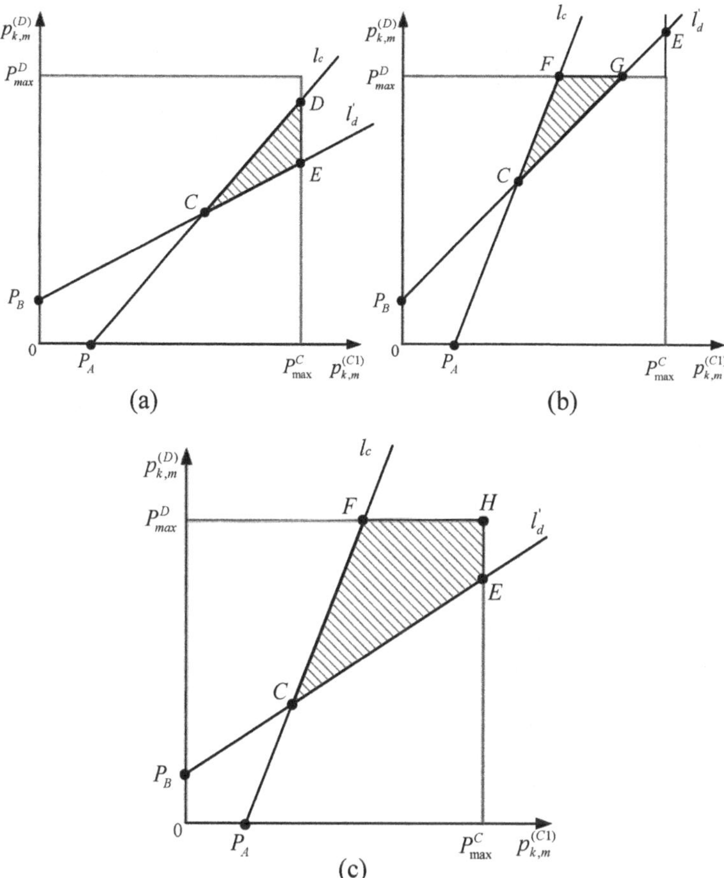

Fig. 3. Three kinds of feasible access regions which don't consider delay constraint

satisfy the distance requirements, there are multiple transmit power pairs $(p_{k,m}^{(D)}, p_{k,m}^{(C1)})$ which can satisfy the (31)-(33) and they can construct three kinds of the feasible access areas, as illustrated in Fig. 3. Three kinds of feasible access regions which don't consider delay constraint where *lc* denotes that the (32) takes the equation, and l_d' denotes that the (33) takes the equation.

Assuming that the set of the CUE which satisfies the requirement of distance is CS, if the CS is null, the DUE can't work on the reuse direct D2D communications, otherwise, the delay requirement of the DUE which reuses the CUE in the set need to verify in addition. According to the literature [13, 14], we verified the minimum delay in the feasible access region are D and F. Hence if the D or F satisfy the delay requirement, the DUE can reuse the channel of the CUE to work on the reuse direct D2D communications, otherwise, delete the CUE from the CS, and then justify the CS whether is null, if the CS is null, the DUE can't work on the reuse direct D2D communications, otherwise, D2D can work on the reuse direct D2D communications.

Power Allocation and Channel Allocation The following will allocate the power for the DUEs which can access the network and reused CUEs to maximize the sum rate of them, i.e., $y = r_{k,m}^{(C1)} + r_{k,m}^{(D)}$ and the optimization problem can be described as:

$$\left(p_{k,m}^{(C1)^*}, p_{k,m}^{(D)^*}\right) = \underset{\left(p_{k,m}^{(C1)}, p_{k,m}^{(D)}\right)}{\arg\max}\ y \tag{34}$$

subject to: (30)–(33).

When the optimization problem doesn't consider the delay requirement, the heuristic solution of the optimization is:

(1) In Fig. 3 (a), the optimal allocation point is D and E;
(2) In Fig. 3 (b), the optimal allocation point is F and G;
(3) In Fig. 3 (c), the optimal allocation point is F, H and E.

D and F must satisfy the delay requirement, but the E, G and H may not satisfy delay requirement, hence in this paper, we let the D and F to be the power allocation point, but it is also a heuristic solution and may not an optimal solution. The power of D and F are $(P_{\max}^{C}, \frac{P_{\max}^{C} g_{Cm,B} - \xi_{\min}\sigma^2}{\xi_{\min} g_{S_k,B}})$ and $(\frac{(P_{max}^{D} g_{Sk,B} + \sigma^2)\xi_{\min}}{g_{Cm,B}}, P_{max}^{D})$.

When finishing the power allocation, the original optimization problem can be denoted as followed:

$$\left(\boldsymbol{x}^*\right) = \arg\max_{\boldsymbol{x}} \left\{ \sum_{k=1}^{K} \sum_{m=1}^{M} x_{k,m}^{(1)} \left(r_{k,m}^{(C1)} + r_{k,m}^{(D)} - r_{m}^{(C)} \right) \right. \tag{35}$$

subject to: (11)-(13).

And the resolution can be solved by related software.

4 Performance Evaluation

The simulation scenario is a single cell with radius 500m. CUE and DUE randomly distribute with the center of BS, and the destination D2D randomly distributes with the center of source DUE. The major parameters are listed in Table 1.

Table 1. Major parameters used in performance evaluation

Parameters	Value
Cell radius	500 m
Path loss exponent (α)	4
Pass loss constant (k_0)	10^{-2}

(continued)

Table 1. (*continued*)

Parameters	Value
Noise power spectral density	−174 dBm/Hz
Channel bandwidth	0.9 MHz
Maximal transmit power of CUE $P_{\max}^{C}$	24 dBm
Maximal transmit power of DUE P_{max}^{D}	21 dBm
Minimum SNR/SINR $\xi_{\min}$	10 dB
Number of data bits in a packet L	1024
Duration of a time slot ΔT	1 ms
Fast fading	Exponential distribution with unit mean
Slow fading	Log-normal distribution with standard deviation of 8 dB

The following will validate the effective of the algorithm, the promotion of the system performance and the influence on the performance of methods by some major parameters in the system.

Based on the proposed algorithm, the first step is the evaluation of system transmit performance promotion of introducing the reuse direct D2D mode, as illustrated in Fig. 4. In the simulation, the parameter set as: $M = 10$, $\psi = 0.2$, $\lambda = 7000$, $B = 30$ and $u_{\max} = 4$. From Fig. 4, we can see that comparing to the situations without considering the reuse direct D2D mode, considering the reuse direct D2D mode can better promote the system performance, moreover the promotion of the performance increases with the D2D pairs. The results also validate the effective of the algorithm and the importance of considering the reuse direct D2D mode.

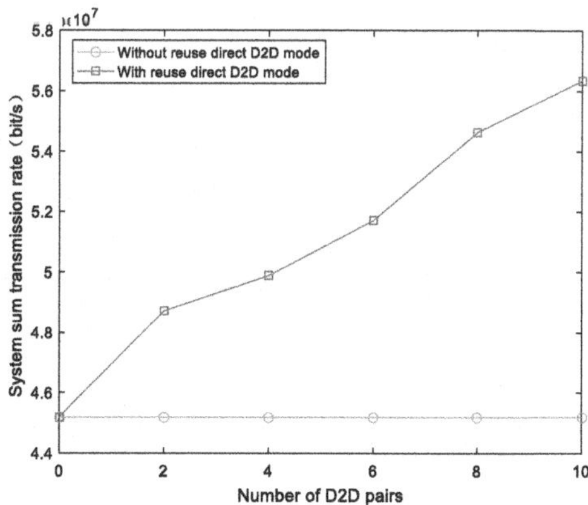

Fig. 4. System sum transmission rate versus number of D2D pairs

The major characteristic of the paper is considering the transmission delay, thus the influence on the delay by the major parameters is evaluated as followed. Randomly generating a pair of DUE and CUE, observing the influence on the delay by the major parameters. The parameters of the channel generate randomly with fixed distribution and the position of the CUE and DUE generate randomly, hence the change of the delay is wide. In order to observe the influence by the parameters better and provide the reference for the latter, we only retain the relatively small delay results, as illustrated in Fig. 5. The parameters set as: $p_{k,m}^{(D)} = 21$ dBm and $p_{k,m}^{(C1)} = 24$ dBm. From the figure, we can see that when the buffer fixes, the delay will increase with the packets arrival rate, because the increasing of the packets arrival rates will lead to the increasing of average packet queue length and loss rate, hence the delay will increase. In addition, the delay will also increase with the buffer size, that is because increasing of the buffer size will lead to the increasing of the average packet queue length.

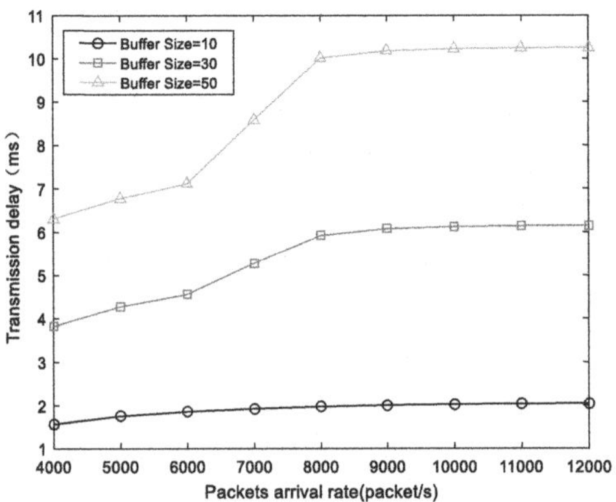

Fig. 5. Transmission delay versus packets arrival rate and buffer size

Above simulation evaluates the delay performance, the following will evaluate the influence by major parameters in the system on the performance of the system, as illustrated in Fig. 6. The parameters in the simulations set as: $M = 10$, $K = 5$, $\psi = 0.2$ and $u_{\max} = 4$. From the results we can see that when the buffer is 30 and 50, the rate of the system is more easily influenced by the packets arrival rate and decreasing with the packets arrival rate. The reason is that the delay will change more obvious with the larger buffer, and the number of the DUE satisfied the delay constraint will decrease, hence the sum rate of the system will decrease.

The following will evaluate the influence by maximal outage overflow probability and delay requirement on the system sum transmission rate. The simulation results illustrate in Fig. 7. And the parameters set as: $M = 15$, $K = 10$, $\lambda = 7000$ and $B = 30$. From the figure, we can see that the system sum transmission rate will increase with the maximal outage overflow probability and delay requirement. The reason is that the number satisfied the access constraint will increase no matter the increasing of the maximal outage overflow probability and delay requirement.

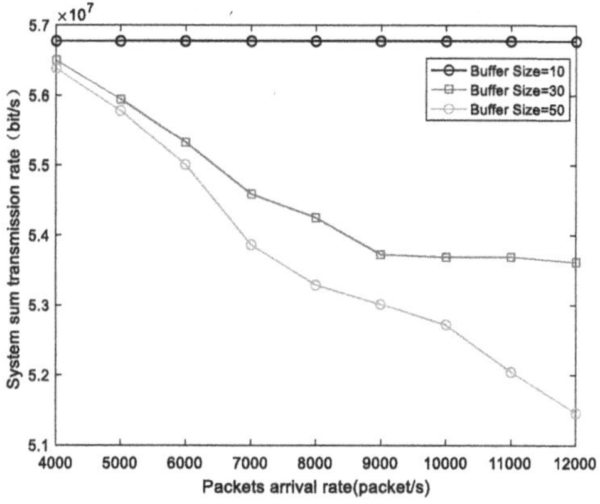

Fig. 6. System sum transmission rate versus packets arrival rate and buffer size

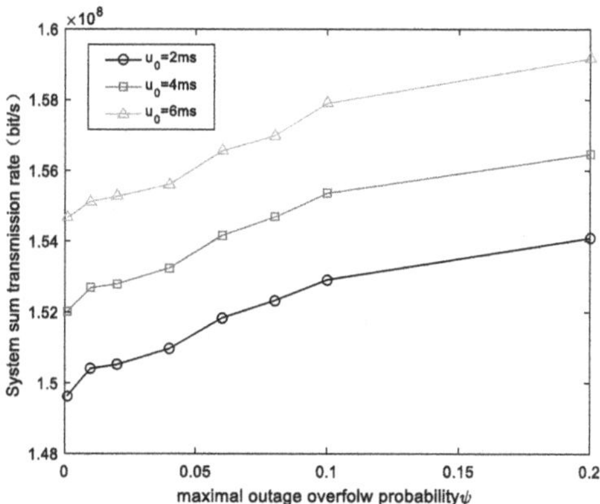

Fig. 7. System sum transmission rate versus maximal outage overflow probability and delay requirement

5 Conclusions

In this paper, we consider the CSI are partly known at the BS and propose a cross-layer joint scheduling scheme that can jointly perform power coordination, channel allocation for D2D capable users by taking into account both the transmission rate criteria of physical layer and the transmission delay criteria of link layer, and meanwhile, the delay estimation method of the reuse direct D2D mode is given. At last, the effectiveness of the joint scheduling scheme and the increase of the system performance brought in the reuse direct D2D mode are validated, in addition, the simulations also analyze the influence of the major system parameters on the performance on the joint scheduling scheme.

References

1. Sakr, A.H., et al.: Cognitive spectrum access in device-to-device-enabled cellular networks. IEEE Commun. Mag. **53**(7), 126–133 (2015)
2. Mach, P., Becvar, Z., Vanek T.: In-band device-to-device communication in OFDMA cellular networks: a survey and challenges. IEEE Communications Surveys & Tutorials **17**(4), 1885–1922 (2015)
3. Liu, J., Kato, N., Ma, J., Kadowaki, N.: Device-to-device communication in LTE-advanced networks: a survey. IEEE Communications Surveys & Tutorials **17**(4), 1923–1940 (2015)
4. Cai, X., Zheng, J., Zhang, Y.: A graph-coloring based resource allocation algorithm for D2D communication in cellular networks. In: 2015 IEEE International Conference on Communications (ICC), pp. 5429–5434 (2015)
5. Mondal, Neogi, A., Chaporkar, P., Karandikar, A.: Bipartite graph based proportional fair resource allocation for D2D communication. In: 2017 IEEE Wireless Communications and Networking Conference (WCNC), pp. 1–6 (2017)
6. Hoang, T.D., Le, L.B., Le-Ngoc, T.: Resource allocation for D2D communication underlaid cellular networks using graph-based approach. IEEE Transactions on Wireless Communications **15**(10), 7099–7113 (2016)
7. Zhang, R., et al.: Interference Graph-Based Resource Allocation (InGRA) for D2D communications underlaying cellular networks. IEEE Trans. Veh. Technol. **64**(8), 3844–3850 (2015)
8. Chen, C., Sung, C., Chen, H.: Capacity maximization based on optimal mode selection in multi-mode and multi-pair D2D communications. IEEE Trans. Veh. Technol. **68**(7), 6524–6534 (2019)
9. Chen, C., Sung, C., Chen, H.: Optimal mode selection algorithms in multiple pair device-to-device communications. IEEE Wirel. Commun. **25**(4), 82–87 (2018)
10. Jiang, L., Yang, X., Fan, C., Li, B., Zhao, C.: Joint mode selection and resource allocation in D2D-enabled vehicular network. In: 2020 International Conference on Wireless Communications and Signal Processing (WCSP), pp. 755–760 (2020)
11. Zhang, T., Zhu, K., Wang, J.: Energy-efficient mode selection and resource allocation for D2D-enabled heterogeneous networks: a deep reinforcement learning approach. IEEE Transactions on Wireless Communications **20**(2), 1175–1187 (2021)
12. Jeon, H.-B., Koo, B.-H., Park, S.-H., Park, J., Chae, C.-B.: Graph-theory-based resource allocation and mode selection in D2D communication systems: the role of full-duplex. IEEE Wireless Communications Letters **10**(2), 236–240 (2021)
13. Guo, C., Liang, L., Li, G.Y.: Resource allocation for vehicular communications with low latency and high reliability. IEEE Transactions on Wireless Communications **18**(8), 3887–3902 (2019)
14. Feng, et al.: Device-to-device communications underlaying cellular networks. IEEE Transactions on Communications **61**(8), 3541–3551 (2013)
15. Hoang, T.D., Le, L.B., Le-Ngoc, T.: Joint mode selection and resource allocation for relay-based D2D communications. IEEE Communications Letters **21**(2), 398–401 (2017)

Cross-Layer Joint Scheduling Scheme for Relay-Involved D2D Communications in Cellular Systems

Kaixuan Wang[1], Zhiliang Qin[2], Xixi Bi[1], and Ruofei Ma[1](✉)

[1] Department of Communication Engineering, Harbin Institute of Technology, Weihai, Weihai, China
maruofei@hit.edu.cn

[2] Technology R&D Center, Weihai Beiyang Electric Group Co. Ltd., Weihai, China
qinzhiliang@beiyang.com

Abstract. In order to further improve the system performance under device-to-device(D2D) communication, considering the reuse of D2D mode is a very promising way. However, involving the reuse mode will make the design of scheduling scheme at the base station (BS) side even more challenging. This work focuses on the design of a scheduling scheme involving multiplexing relay D2D mode for the base station which jointly considers the user's requirements of service quality and delay comprehensively, and proposes a cross-layer joint scheduling algorithm aiming at maximizing the transmission rate of the whole system. We formulate such a scheduling issue into a mathematical optimization problem, and then we decompose the problem into three sub-problems according to power allocation, channel allocation and mode selection, and solve them respectively. The simulation results verify the importance of considering the multiplexing relay D2D mode and the influence of some main parameter Settings on the delay and transmission rate of the system, which provides a reference value for improving the transmission rate of the system by changing the parameter of the system.

Keywords: Device to device (D2D) communication · Channel state information · Transmission delay

1 Introduction

With the improvement of living standards, more and more advanced wireless network applications, such as smart home, unmanned, augmented reality, began to appear in the field of vision of people, to meet the needs of people's life convenient [1], but at the same time, the emergence of these new wireless network applications also brings great

This work was supported partially by National Natural Science Foundation of China (Grant No. 61801144), Shandong Provincial Natural Science Foundation, Chna (Gra-nt No. ZR2019QF003), and the Fundamental Research Funds for the Central Univer-sities, China (Grant No. HIT.NSRIF.2019081).

© ICST Institute for Computer Sciences, Social Informatics and Telecommunications Engineering 2022
Published by Springer Nature Switzerland AG 2022. All Rights Reserved
S. Shi et al. (Eds.): 6GN 2021, LNICST 439, pp. 145–159, 2022.
https://doi.org/10.1007/978-3-031-04245-4_13

challenge to the communication network, resulting in the boost of data traffic and the scarcity of frequency resources. At the same time, the time delay and data transmission rate requirements are also increasingly high.

D2D communication allows devices that are close to each other to directly transmit data [2], which can reduce transmission delay and improve data transmission rate. The introduction of D2D technology can not only relieve the pressure of the base station to transmit the internal data of the cellular network, reduce the end-to-end transmission delay, but also reduce the power loss of the equipment and extend the working time of the communication equipment [3]. Therefore, it is significant to study the introduction of D2D communication in the cellular network. But at the same time, it will also bring another problem, that is, the whole system resource scheduling problem.

Since this paper mainly considers the scheduling g algorithm of the base station, the following will analyze the state of art of D2D. According to the functions realized by the algorithm, it can be generally divided into two categories: one is the base station scheduling algorithm which only considers mode selection, resource allocation or power control; The other is the joint scheduling algorithm of base station.

However, the early base station scheduling algorithms are mostly focused on the first type of resource allocation and power control scheduling algorithms and are mostly used to reuse direct D2D mode. Among them, most scheduling algorithms on resource allocation are based on graph theory [4, 5]. For the power control algorithm, in order to reduce the interference caused by reuse, the commonly used schemes including: limiting the transmitted power of D2D users to reduce the interference [6]; Power regulator is set to increase the transmitting power of cellular users to reduce the interference from D2D users [7]. Under the condition of ensuring the communication quality between cellular users and D2D users, the joint power allocation of D2D users and cellular users based on optimization theory is proposed [8]. However, the above scheduling algorithms only consider a single aspect. [9] considers using the size between the actual distance and the threshold to select the working mode of D2D users, but the premise of its application is multiple base stations and D2D users have mobility. [10] proposed a selection scheme based on the traffic load mode, and verified that the method would improve the packet rate of the system and the performance of end-to-end transmission delay, and the optimization objective was the total packet loss rate of the system. However, no matter it only considers mode selection, resource allocation or power control, it is only expanded for one aspect of the scheduling problem, and it has constraints for the system scheduling that introduces D2D communication in the cellular network, so a more comprehensive consideration should be conducted for the joint scheduling algorithm.

In this paper, we propose a cross-layer joint scheduling algorithm for maximizing the transmission rate of the whole system under the condition that the channel state information is partially known and the user's service quality and delay requirements are considered comprehensively. In this paper, the transmission delay of D2D users is calculated under the two modes of multiplexing direct D2D and multiplexing relay, and mode selection is needed for D2D users. Finally, the proposed algorithm is evaluated by simulation.

The remainder of this paper is organized as follows. Section 2 introduce the system model. In Sect. 3, in order to maximize the transmission rate of the whole system under the condition of satisfying the user's requirements of service quality and delay, the mathematical modeling is carried out. The optimization objective is solved by power allocation, channel allocation and mode selection in Sect. 4. Simulation results are provided in Sect. 5. Finally, the paper is concluded in Sect. 6.

2 System Model

When the communication distance is too large, the quality of communication link is poor, D2D communication is prone to interrupt. Therefore, this paper considers the combination of reusing direct D2D mode and reusing relay D2D mode to ensure the effective and reliable transmission of information. Aiming at the above two working modes, a cross-layer joint scheduling algorithm is proposed to maximize the transmission rate of the whole system under the condition that the channel state information is partially known and the user's service quality and delay requirements are considered comprehensively.

2.1 System Hypothesis

The system model considered in this paper is shown in Fig. 1. There are M cellular users and K pairs of D2D users, respectively denoted as $\{C_1, C_2, ..., C_m, ..., C_M\}$, $\{S_1, S_2, ..., S_k, ..., S_K\}$, $\{D_1, D_2, ..., D_k, ..., D_K\}$, The latter two terms respectively correspond to the sender and receiver of the D2D user, and it is assumed that the base station has allocated a channel with the same bandwidth and orthogonal to each other for each cellular user, and a fully loaded cellular network is considered. In the system model, D2D users have two working modes, that is, reusing direct D2D mode and reusing relay D2D mode. When the user works in reuse direct D2D mode, it is provided that the D2D user can only reusing one channel of the cellular user, and it is assumed that only the uplink channel of the cellular user can be reused. When working in the reuse relay D2D mode, assume that each pair of D2D users is surrounded by N alternative relay users which support their work in the reusable relay D2D mode, and it is assumed that the D2D sender and the relay node, the relay node and the D2D receiver can reuse the same cellular user's channel, and only the uplink-channel can be reused. The communication between the two hop links should be completed in two time slots. In this system, the channel of a cellular user can only be reused by a pair of D2D users at most.

The communication mode in which D2D users work depends on the final scheduling results of the base station. It is assumed that the base station only grasps part of the channel state information between the cellular user and the D2D receiver (CUE-DUE) and the cellular user and the relay node (CUE-RUE), i.e. the path loss based on distance. However, for other related channels, the base station grasps their perfect channel state information.

2.2 Channel Model

According to the channel state information collected by the base station, channels in the system model can be divided into two categories. One is the channel where the base station has perfect channel state information. The new channel belonging to this type are the channel from the relay node to the base station (RUE-BS), the channel from the D2D sender to the relay node (DUE-DUE), and the channel from the relay node to the D2D receiver (RUE-DUE). The channel gains are respectively $g_{R_{k,n},B}$, $g_{S_k,R_{k,n}}$ and $g_{R_{k,n},D_k}$, respectively. The other is the channel where the base station only holds partial channel state information. The new channel belonging to this type is Cellular User to Relay Interference Channel (CUE-RUE). For the channel base station, only the path loss based on distance is mastered, $H_{C_m,R_{k,n}} = k_0 l^{-\alpha}_{C_m,R_{k,n}}$. Its channel gain is expressed as:

$$h_{C_m,R_{k,n}} = k_0 \beta_{C_m,R_{k,n}} l^{-\alpha}_{C_m,R_{k,n}} \tag{1}$$

where $\beta_{C_m,R_{k,n}}$ is the channel fading component, and $l_{C_m,R_{k,n}}$ represents the distance between the sending node and the receiving node.

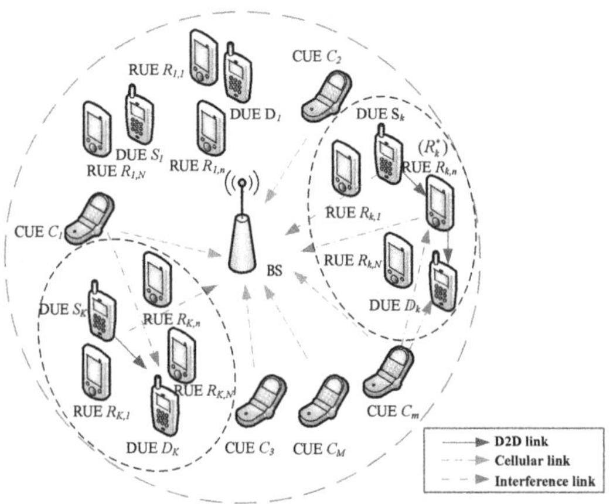

Fig. 1. A system model with relays

3 Problem Formulation

3.1 Transmission Model

When the D2D user works in the reusing relay D2D mode, it is stipulated that the communication process of the D2D user should be completed in two time slots. In the first slot, data is transmitted from the sending node to the relay node, and in the second slot, data is transmitted from the relay node to the receiving node. However, before data transmission, it is necessary to select the optimal relay R_k^* from N alternative relay nodes to assist D2D users in data transmission.

Then, after the selection of the relay nodes is completed, the QoS requirements of D2D users and cellular users should be guaranteed in the first place if the k-pair D2D users want to reuse the channel of cellular user C_m and work in the relay mode. Since the base station does not know the accurate channel gain from the cellular user to the relay node and the interference channel of the D2D user's receiver, the QoS requirement of the D2D user under the two-hop link at this time requires the channel probability statistics characteristics to ensure that the transmission interrupt probability of the D2D user will not exceed a certain value.

Based on the characteristics of channel probability and statistics, the probability that the actual SNR of the D2D user receiving terminal is set to be less than the requirement of the SNR of the link does not exceed a given threshold:

$$\Pr\left\{\frac{p_{k,m}^{(D)}g_{S_k,D_k}}{\sigma^2+p_{k,m}^{(C1)}h_{C_m,D_k}}<\xi_{\min}\right\}\leq\psi \tag{2}$$

where, $p_{k,m}^{(D)}$ is the kth pair of D2D users reuse the transmitting power of the cellular user channel when it is working, $p_{k,m}^{(C1)}$ denotes the transmitted power of cellular user C_m when it is reused by the kth pair of D2D users, σ^2 indicates noise power, $\xi_{\min}$ represents the requirements of minimum signal-to-noise ratio (SNR)/signal-to-noise ratio (SNR),and ψ is the system sets the maximum interrupt overflow probability acceptable to D2D users.

At the same time, when the base station does not know the accurate channel gain information from the cellular user to the D2D receiver, the transmission interruption phenomenon is inevitable in the communication process of the D2D user. Indicator function is used to represent the transmission interrupt event of the D2D receiver [11], i.e. when the actual SNR of the D2D receiver is less than the SNR required by the system, the D2D receiver cannot demodulate the signal sent by the starting terminal. In this case, the indicator function $\Phi=1$; Otherwise, the indicator function is 0, indicating that the D2D receiver can demodulate the signal sent by the starting terminal. When $\Phi=0$, the D2D receiver can demodulate the signal sent by the transmitting end, and the transmission rate of the D2D user in this case can be expressed as

$$r_{k,m}^{D}=B_0\log_2\left(1+\frac{p_{k,m}^{(D)}g_{S_k,D_k}}{\sigma^2+p_{k,m}^{(C1)}h_{C_m,D_k}}\right) \tag{3}$$

where, B_0 is the channel bandwidth.

On the contrary, when $\Phi=1$, the D2D receiver cannot demodulate the signal sent by the sending terminal, and the transmission rate of the D2D user is 0. In summary, considering the transmission rate of D2D users in the two cases, the transmission rate of D2D users can be expressed as

$$r_{k,m}^{D}=\mathbb{E}\left\{\left[B_0\log_2\left(1+\frac{\mathrm{p}_{\mathrm{k,m}}^{(\mathrm{D})}\mathrm{g}_{\mathrm{S_k,D_k}}}{\sigma^2+\mathrm{p}_{\mathrm{k,m}}^{(\mathrm{C1})}\mathrm{h}_{\mathrm{C_m,D_k}}}\right)\right]|\Phi=0\right\} \tag{4}$$

where $\mathbb{E}\{\cdot\}$ is the conditional expectations.

According to reference [12], Eq. (4) can be expressed as

$$r_{k,m}^{D}=\int_0^l B_0\log_2\left(1+\frac{p_{k,m}^{(D)}g_{S_k,D_k}}{\sigma^2+\beta_{C_m,D_k}p_{k,m}^{(C1)}H_{C_m,D_k}}\right)\frac{f(\beta_{C_m,D_k})}{F(l)}d\beta_{C_m,D_k} \tag{5}$$

where l denotes the critical value of β_{C_m,D_k}, $l = \frac{p_{k,m}^{(D)} g_{S_k,D_k} - \xi_{\min}\sigma^2}{p_{k,m}^{(C1)} \xi_{\min} H_{C_m,D_k}}$.

Above discussion guarantees for D2D users and QoS requirements are completed. Next, there are delay requirements for D2D users. Assuming that the end-to-end transmission delay of D2D user k reusing cellular user C_m channel is $u_{k,m}$, the delay shall meet the requirements:

$$u_{k,m} \leq u_{\max} \tag{6}$$

where, $u_{\max}$ denotes the requirements of D2D end-to-end transmission delay.

The optimization objective in this paper is to maximize the overall system transmission rate. When no D2D user reuses the channel of the cellular user, the transmission rate of the cellular user is expressed as

$$r_m^{(C)} = B_0 \log_2\left(1 + \frac{p_m^{(C)} g_{C_m,B}}{\sigma^2}\right) \tag{7}$$

where $p_m^{(C)}$ is the transmitted power of cellular users.

When the cellular user's uplink channel is reused by the kth D2D pair in direct D2D mode, the transmission rate of the cellular user's uplink channel can be expressed as

$$r_{k,m}^{(C1)} = B_0 \log_2\left(1 + \frac{p_{k,m}^{(C1)} g_{C_m,B}}{p_{k,m}^{(D)} g_{S_k,B} + \sigma^2}\right) \tag{8}$$

When the cellular user's uplink channel is reused by the kth D2D pair in relay-assisted D2D mode, the transmission rate of the cellular user's uplink channel in the first and second transmission time slots corresponding to the two-hop relay-assisted D2D transmission can be expressed respectively as

$$\begin{cases} r_{(k,m)}^{(C21)} B_0 \log_2\left(1 + \frac{p_{k,m}^{(CR1)} g_{C_m,B}}{p_{k,m}^{(R1)} g_{S_k,B} + \sigma^2}\right) \\ r_{(k,m)}^{(C22)} B_0 \log_2\left(1 + \frac{p_{k,m}^{(CR2)} g_{C_m,B}}{p_{k,m}^{(R2)} g_{R_k^*,B} + \sigma^2}\right) \end{cases} \tag{9}$$

where $p_{k,m}^{(CR1)}$ is the transmit power of the cellular user in the first time slot; $p_{k,m}^{(R1)}$ is the transmit power of the transmitter of D2D users in reused relay mode; $p_{k,m}^{(CR2)}$ is the transmitting power of the cellular user in the second time slot; $p_{k,m}^{(R2)}$ is transmit power of the relay node.

Then the transmission rate of the cellular user in a scheduling time slot of the base station is expressed as

$$r_{k,m}^{(C2)} = \frac{1}{2}\left(r_{k,m}^{(C21)} + r_{k,m}^{(C22)}\right) \tag{10}$$

In the first time slot, the transmission rate from the D2D sender to the relay node is expressed as

$$r_{k,m}^{(R1)} = \mathbb{E}\left\{\left[\mathrm{B}_0 \log_2\left(1 + \frac{\mathrm{p}_{\mathrm{k,m}}^{(\mathrm{R1})} \mathrm{g}_{\mathrm{S_k},\mathrm{R_k^*}}}{\sigma^2 + \mathrm{p}_{\mathrm{k,m}}^{(\mathrm{CR1})} \mathrm{h}_{\mathrm{C_m},\mathrm{R_k^*}}}\right)\right] | \Phi = 0\right\} \tag{11}$$

In the second slot, the transmission rate from the relay node to the receiver is expressed as

$$r_{k,m}^{(R2)} = \mathbb{E}\left\{\left[\mathrm{B}_0 \log_2\left(1 + \frac{\mathrm{p}_{\mathrm{k,m}}^{(\mathrm{R2})} \mathrm{g}_{\mathrm{R}_\mathrm{k}^*,\mathrm{D}_\mathrm{k}}}{\sigma^2 + \mathrm{p}_{\mathrm{k,m}}^{(\mathrm{CR2})} \mathrm{h}_{\mathrm{C}_\mathrm{m},\mathrm{D}_\mathrm{k}}}\right)\right] | \Phi = 0\right\} \tag{12}$$

Then the transmission rate of a D2D user in a scheduled time slot of the base station is expressed as

$$r_{k,m}^{(R)} = \frac{1}{2}\min\left\{r_{k,m}^{(R1)}, r_{k,m}^{(R2)}\right\} \tag{13}$$

3.2 Transmission Delay Estimation

The packet queuing state transition can be described and solved by using a finite state Markov chain (FSMC) to obtain the stable probability of packet queuing state and then the average queue length. Suppose $\Omega_{k,m}^i$ is the source node, and there is a stability probability of packet caching, and $\Omega_{k,m}$ is a stability probability vector composed of $\Omega_{k,m}^i$, then the stability probability vector can be expressed as $\Omega_{k,m}$

$$\begin{cases} \Omega_{k,m} = \Omega_{k,m} P \\ \sum_{i=0}^{B} \Omega_{k,m}^i = 1 \end{cases} \tag{14}$$

Then, the average length of the packet queue of the source node can be expressed as

$$\overline{Q_{k,m}} = \sum_{i=0}^{B} \left(i \times \Omega_{k,m}^i\right) \tag{15}$$

If $u_{k,m}$ represents the end-to-end transmission delay, it can be obtained by the following formula according to Little's rule

$$u_{k,m} = \overline{Q_{k,m}} / \left(\left(1 - \phi_{k,m}\right) \times E[A_{k,t}]\right) \tag{16}$$

where $E[A_{k,t}]$ represents the average number of packets arriving at the sending node in a time slot, where $E[A_{k,t}] = \lambda_k \Delta T$; $\phi_{k,m}$ represents the packet drop rate.

The formula for calculating packet loss rate is as follows

$$\phi_{k,m} = D_{k,m} / (E[A_k]) \tag{17}$$

where $D_{k,m}$ represents the number of packets lost by the source node due to the limited cache capacity; A_k is a stable distribution of $A_{k,t}$ and $E[A_k] = E[A_{k,t}]$.

Where $D_{k,m}$ can be obtained by the following formula

$$D_{k,m} = \sum_{m=1}^{B} \Omega_{k,m}^{m} \sum_{n=0}^{m-1} \Pr\{U_k = n\} \sum_{j=B+n-m}^{\infty} (m + j - n - B) \Pr\{A_k = j\}$$
$$+ \sum_{m=1}^{B} \Omega_{k,m}^{m} \sum_{n=m}^{\infty} \Pr\{U_k = n\} \sum_{j=B}^{\infty} (j - B) \Pr\{A_k = j\} \quad (18)$$
$$+\Omega_{k,m}^{0} \sum_{j=B}^{\infty} (j - B) \Pr\{A_k = j\}$$

When a D2D user works in the reuse of relay D2D mode, it is equivalent to two hop links. The first hop link is the link from the D2D sender to the relay node, and the second hop link is the link from the relay node to the D2D receiver. Assuming that the transmission delay of the link from the D2D sender to the relay node is $u_{k,m}^{R1}$, and the transmission delay of the link from the relay node to the D2D receiver is $u_{k,m}^{R2}$, then the total end-to-end transmission delay is expressed as:

$$u_{k,m}^{R} = u_{k,m}^{R1} + u_{k,m}^{R2} \quad (19)$$

For the second hop link, that is, the link from the relay node to the D2D receiver, the packet arrival process of the relay node in the t slot is no longer subject to the Poisson arrival process, but is related to the number of packets $Q_{k,t-1}$ at the D2D sender at the end of the $t-1$ slot of the a hop link and the number of packets transmitted by the a hop link in the t slot $U_{k,t}$. When $Q_{k,t-1} \leq \mathrm{U_{k,t}}$, the number of packets arriving at the relay node in time slot t is $Q_{k,t-1}$, otherwise $U_{k,t}$. Assuming that the number of relay nodes arriving in time slot t is j, then when $j = 0$, its arrival probability is

$$p(A_{r,t} = 0) = \Omega_{k,m}^{0} + (1 - \Omega_{k,m}^{0}) \Pr\{U_{k,t} = 0\} \quad (20)$$

when $1 \leq j \leq B$, its arrival probability is

$$\Pr\{U_{k,t} \geq j\} + (1 - \sum_{i=0}^{j} \Omega_{k,m}^{i}) \Pr\{U_{k,t} = j\}$$
$$= \left\{1 - \sum_{n=0}^{j-1} \Pr\{U_{k,t} = n\}\right\} \Omega_{k,m}^{j} + (1 - \sum_{i=0}^{j} \Omega_{k,m}^{i}) \Pr\{U_{k,t} = j\} \quad (21)$$

Another difference is that during the delay measurement of the second hop link, if the average length of the packet queue of the relay node is already $\overline{Q_{k,m}^{R}}$, then the delay calculation formula of the second hop link is

$$u_{k,m}^{R2} = \overline{Q_{k,m}^{R}} / \left(\left(1 - \phi_{k,m}^{R}\right) \times E[A_{r,t}] \right) \quad (22)$$

where, $\phi_{k,m}^{R}$ represents the packet loss rate of the relay node; $E[A_{r,t}]$ represents the average number of packets arriving at a relay node in a slot.

Where, $E[A_{r,t}]$ calculation formula should be obtained by the following formula

$$E[A_{r,t}] = \sum_{j=0}^{B} \left[j \times p(A_{r,t} = j) \right] \quad (23)$$

3.3 Joint Scheduling Problem Formulation

The goal of the scheduling algorithm in this paper is to maximize the transmission rate of the whole system while ensuring the QoS requirements of D2D users, cellular users and the delay requirements of D2D users. Then the mathematical expression can be expressed as follows:

$$\begin{aligned}(\boldsymbol{p}^*, \boldsymbol{x}^*) = \arg\max_{p,x} \Bigg\{ & \sum_{k=1}^{K}\sum_{m=1}^{M} x_{k,m}^{(1)}\left(r_{k,m}^{(C1)} + r_{k,m}^{(D)}\right) \\ & + \sum_{k=1}^{K}\sum_{m=1}^{M} x_{k,m}^{(2)}\left(r_{k,m}^{(C2)} + r_{k,m}^{(R)}\right) + \sum_{m=1}^{M}\left(1 - \sum_{k=1}^{K} x_{k,m}^{(1)} - \sum_{k=1}^{K} x_{k,m}^{(2)}\right) r_m^{(C)} \Bigg\}\end{aligned} \tag{24}$$

$$subject\ to: x_{k,m}^{(1)}, x_{k,m}^{(2)} \in \{0, 1\}, \forall k, m \tag{25}$$

$$\sum_{k=1}^{K} (x_{k,m}^{(1)} + x_{k,m}^{(2)}) \le 1, \forall m \tag{26}$$

$$\sum_{m=1}^{M} (x_{k,m}^{(1)} + x_{k,m}^{(2)}) \le 1, \forall k \tag{27}$$

$$\sum_{m=1}^{M} (x_{k,m}^{(1)} u_{k,m} + x_{k,m}^{(2)} u_{k,m}^{R}) \le u_{\max}, \forall k \tag{28}$$

$$\sum_{m=1}^{M} x_{k,m}^{(1)} p_{k,m}^{(D)} + \sum_{m=1}^{M} x_{k,m}^{(2)} \max(p_{k,m}^{(R1)}, p_{k,m}^{(R2)}) \le P_{max}^{D}, \forall k \tag{29}$$

$$\begin{aligned}& \sum_{k=1}^{K} x_{k,m}^{(1)} p_{k,m}^{(C1)} + \sum_{k=1}^{K} x_{k,m}^{(2)} \max(p_{k,m}^{(CR1)}, p_{k,m}^{(CR2)}) \\ & + \left(1 - \sum_{k=1}^{K} x_{k,m}^{(1)} - \sum_{k=1}^{K} x_{k,m}^{(2)}\right) p_m^{(C)} \le P_{\max}^{C}, \forall m\end{aligned} \tag{30}$$

$$\begin{aligned}& \sum_{m=1}^{M} x_{k,m}^{(2)} \max\left\{ \Pr\left\{ \frac{p_{k,m}^{(R1)} g_{S_k,R_k^*}}{\sigma^2 + p_{k,m}^{(CR1)} h_{C_m,R_k^*}} < \xi_{\min} \right\}, \Pr\left\{ \frac{p_{k,m}^{(R2)} g_{R_k^*,D_k}}{\sigma^2 + p_{k,m}^{(CR2)} h_{C_m,D_k}} < \xi_{\min} \right\} \right\} \\ & + \sum_{m=1}^{M} x_{k,m}^{(1)} \Pr\left\{ \frac{p_{k,m}^{(D)} g_{S_k,D_k}}{\sigma^2 + p_{k,m}^{(C1)} h_{C_m,D_k}} < \xi_{\min} \right\} \le \sum_{m=1}^{M} x_{k,m}^{(2)} \psi + \sum_{m=1}^{M} x_{k,m}^{(1)} \psi, \forall k\end{aligned} \tag{31}$$

$$\begin{aligned}& \sum_{k=1}^{K} x_{k,m}^{(1)} \frac{p_{k,m}^{(C1)} g_{C_m,B}}{p_{k,m}^{(D)} g_{S_k,B} + \sigma^2} + \sum_{k=1}^{K} x_{k,m}^{(2)} \min\left(\frac{p_{k,m}^{(CR1)} g_{C_m,B}}{p_{k,m}^{(R1)} g_{S_k,B} + \sigma^2}, \frac{p_{k,m}^{(CR2)} g_{C_m,B}}{p_{k,m}^{(R2)} g_{R_k^*,B} + \sigma^2}\right) \\ & + \left(1 - \sum_{k=1}^{K} x_{k,m}^{(1)} - \sum_{k=1}^{K} x_{k,m}^{(2)}\right) \times \frac{p_m^{(C)} g_{C_m,B}}{\sigma^2} \ge \xi_{\min}, \forall m\end{aligned} \tag{32}$$

where $x_{k,m}^{(1)}$,$x_{k,m}^{(2)}$ respectively denote mode selectors and channel selectors for reuse of direct D2D modes and reuse of relay D2D modes. When the kth pair of D2D users works in reusing direct D2D mode and reusing the mth cellular user channel, $x_{k,m}^{(1)} = 1$, otherwise $x_{k,m}^{(1)} = 0$. When the kth pair of D2D users works in reusing relay D2D mode and reusing the mth cellular user channel, $x_{k,m}^{(2)} = 1$, otherwise $x_{k,m}^{(2)} = 1$.

where, $u_{k,m}^{R}$ denotes the end-to-end transmission delay for the kth D2D user when working in the reusing relay D2D mode and the MTH cellular user is reused by it.

Formula (25) indicates that the value of mode selection and channel selection factor is 0 or 1; Formula (26) indicates that the D2D user can only choose one of the direct D2D mode or the relay mode and that the channel of a cellular user can only be reused by a pair of D2D users. Formula (27) indicates that D2D users can only choose one of the two working modes to work and a pair of D2D users can only reuse the channel of one cellular user at most. Formula (28) indicates that the end-to-end transmission delay of D2D users under two working modes cannot exceed the delay requirements; Formula (29) indicates that the transmitted power of D2D sender in the reusing direct D2D mode and the transmitted power of D2D sender and relay node in the reusing relay mode shall not exceed the power constraint of D2D user. Formula (30) indicates that the transmitting power of the cell user reused in the direct D2D mode, the transmitting power of the cell user reused in the relay D2D mode at two time slots and the transmitting power of the cell user without D2D user reusing shall not exceed the power constraint of the cell user. Formulas (31) to (32) represent the QoS guarantee for the relevant transmission link.

4 Joint Scheduling Scheme Design

4.1 D2D User Access Control

This section will determine whether a D2D user can access the network in a reused relay D2D mode. To determine whether a D2D user can access the network in a reused relay D2D mode, it is necessary to determine whether there is a cellular user in the network that can be reused. The judgment condition of reusing relay D2D mode is that there are power pairs $(p_{k,m}^{(CR1)}, p_{k,m}^{(R1)})$ and $(p_{k,m}^{(CR2)}, p_{k,m}^{(R2)})$ in the first and second time slots, so that they meet the formula (33) ~ (37), namely delay requirements, power constraint requirements and user's QoS requirements:

$$u_{k,m}^{R} \leq u_{\max} \tag{33}$$

$$\max(p_{k,m}^{(R1)}, p_{k,m}^{(R2)}) \leq P_{max}^{D} \tag{34}$$

$$\max(p_{k,m}^{(CR1)}, p_{k,m}^{(CR2)}) \leq P_{\max}^{C} \tag{35}$$

$$\max\left\{\Pr\left\{\frac{p_{k,m}^{(R1)} g_{S_k,R_k^*}}{\sigma^2 + p_{k,m}^{(CR1)} h_{C_m,R_k^*}} < \xi_{\min}\right\}, \Pr\left\{\frac{p_{k,m}^{(R2)} g_{R_k^*,D_k}}{\sigma^2 + p_{k,m}^{(CR2)} h_{C_m,D_k}} < \xi_{\min}\right\}\right\} \leq \psi \tag{36}$$

$$\min\left(\frac{p_{k,m}^{(CR1)} g_{C_m,B}}{p_{k,m}^{(R1)} g_{S_k,B} + \sigma^2}, \frac{p_{k,m}^{(CR2)} g_{C_m,B}}{p_{k,m}^{(R2)} g_{R_k^*,B} + \sigma^2}\right) \geq \xi_{\min} \tag{37}$$

The first is based on distance judgment, and the second is based on time delay judgment. If the two power pairs $(p_{k,m}^{(CR1)}, p_{k,m}^{(R1)})$ and $(p_{k,m}^{(CR2)}, p_{k,m}^{(R2)})$ meet the time delay requirements, then at least the power pairs $(p_{k,m}^{(CR1)}, p_{k,m}^{(R1)})$ and $(p_{k,m}^{(CR2)}, p_{k,m}^{(R2)})$ in the first and second time slots are guaranteed, so that the whole link can meet the time delay requirements when reusing the cellular user channel. Otherwise, it means that the link cannot reusing the cellular user channel at this time in the multiplexing relay D2D mode.

4.2 Resource Allocation and Mode Selection Design

(1) Power allocation

This section will mainly complete the power allocation of D2D users in the reused relay D2D mode and the cell users that are reused.

For users working in reused relay D2D mode, it is hoped that the optimal transmission power pairs $(p_{k,m}^{(CR1)}, p_{k,m}^{(R1)})$ and $(p_{k,m}^{(CR2)}, p_{k,m}^{(R2)})$ can be found in the two links for D2D users and their reused cellular users. Reuse the D2D communication relay mode needs to be done in two time slots, that is the first time slot for sending node to relay node communication, and the second time slot for the relay node to the receiving node communication. Therefore, for the power allocation in the multiplex relay mode, the power can be allocated to each hop link separately. The only factor that needs to be considered is whether the power allocation result meets the time delay requirement. The answer is yes, because the power allocation result of each link is the value brought in when judging whether the D2D user can access the network in the multiplexed relay D2D mode.

(2) Channel allocation and mode selection

After power allocation, mode selection and channel allocation are required. Based on the results of power allocation, the original optimization problems (24) ~ (32) can be simplified into the following expressions:

$$(\boldsymbol{x}^*) = \arg\max_{x}\left\{\sum_{k=1}^{K}\sum_{m=1}^{M} x_{k,m}^{(1)}\left(r_{k,m}^{(C1)} + r_{k,m}^{(D)} - r_m^{(C)}\right) + \sum_{k=1}^{K}\sum_{m=1}^{M} x_{k,m}^{(2)}\left(r_{k,m}^{(C2)} + r_{k,m}^{(R)} - r_m^{(C)}\right)\right\} \tag{38}$$

subject to: (25) ~ (27).

Where, $r_{k,m}^{(C1)} + r_{k,m}^{(D)} - r_m^{(C)}$ and $r_{k,m}^{(C2)} + r_{k,m}^{(R)} - r_m^{(C)}$ are a constant based on the obtained power allocation $\boldsymbol{p}^*$, so the above optimization problem can be converted into a 0–1 integer optimization problem for $x_{k,m}^{(1)}$ and $x_{k,m}^{(2)}$.

Then the base station can schedule the resources of the whole system according to the scheduling algorithm mentioned above.

5 Performance Evaluation

In this section, a cell with a radius of 500 m centered on the base station is considered. The positions of the transmitting terminal of cellular users and D2D users are randomly distributed centered on the base station, while the receiving terminal of D2D users is randomly distributed centered on the sending terminal of D2D users. There are alternative relay users around each pair of D2D users, and the position of the candidate relay user is in a circle enclosed by the D2D sender as the center and the distance of the D2D user pair as a radius. The main parameters are shown in Table 1.

We jointly consider the multiplexed direct D2D mode and multiplexed relay D2D mode, hoping to make up for the impact of the multiplexed direct D2D mode on the transmission performance of the system, which is easily affected by the communication distance and communication link. Therefore, the comparison of the change of the total transmission rate of the system with the number of D2D is simulated in the case that only the multiplexed direct D2D mode is considered and the two D2D modes. The results are shown in Fig. 2.

Table 1. The main parameters in the simulation are set.

Parameter Settings	The numerical
Radius of neighborhood	500 m
Path loss index α	4
Path loss constant k_0	10^{-2}
Noise power spectral density	174 dBm/Hz
Channel bandwidth	0.9 MHz
Maximum transmitting power for cellular users $P_{\max}^C$	24 dBm
The maximum transmitting power of the D2D user P_{max}^D	21 dBm
User minimum SNR requirement $\xi_{\min}$	10 dB
The number of bits contained in a packet L	1024
Time slot width ΔT	1 ms
Multipath fading	An exponential distribution with a mean of 1
Shadow fading	The standard deviation is 8 dB log normal distribution

The parameters involved in simulation are set as follows: the number of cellular users $M = 10$, the number of relay nodes $N = 10$, the maximum interrupt overflow probability $\psi = 0.2$, the packet arrival rate $\lambda = 7000$ packet/s, the maximum cache capacity of nodes $B = 30$, and the delay requirement $u_{\max} = 4$ ms. When the number of D2D users is certain, the total transmission rate corresponding to the two working modes of multiplexing direct D2D mode and multiplexing relay D2D mode is indeed higher than the system transmission rate corresponding to the multiplexing direct D2D mode. It indicates that it is meaningful to consider the multiplexing relay D2D mode in this section. At the same time, it can be seen that the system transmission rate corresponding to the two working modes involved in this section increases as the number of D2D user pairs increases. The simulation results also demonstrate the effectiveness of the proposed scheduling algorithm.

It can be seen that the delay varies with the main parameters, and the simulation results only retain a relatively small delay, as shown in Fig. 3, where the transmission power of the transmitter and relay node of the D2D user is $p_{k,m}^{(R1)} = p_{k,m}^{(R2)} = 21$ dBm, and the transmitting power of the cellular user in the first time slot and the second time slot is $p_{k,m}^{(CR1)} = p_{k,m}^{(CR2)} = 24$ dBm. The conclusion can be drawn from the figure, when nodes cache capacity must be biggest, the increase of packet arrival rate will affect the transmission delay, delay will increase with the increase of packet arrival rate (diagram node, at a maximum capacity of 10 data is also increasing, only increases not much), and design in this experiment three nodes under the maximum cache capacity, when the packet arrival rate must be. The latency increases as the maximum cache capacity of the node increases.

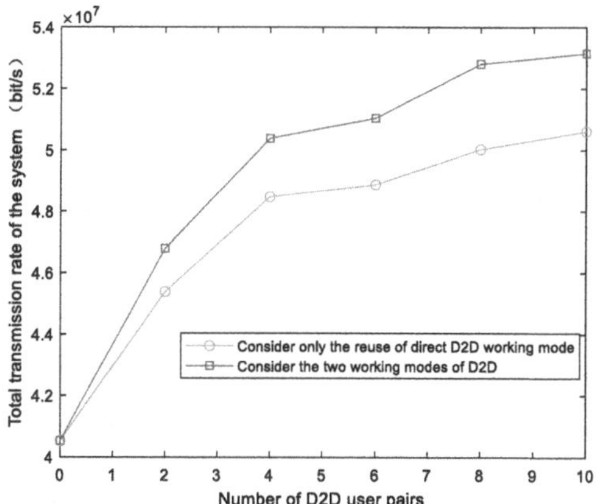

Fig. 2. The total transmission rate of the system varies with the number of D2D user pairs

Finally, this section will evaluate the influence of the maximum probability of outage overflow and different settings of delay requirements on the total transmission rate of the system. The simulation results are shown in Fig. 4. The parameters set in the simulation are the number of cellular users $M = 20$, the number of D2D user pairs $K = 10$, the number of relay nodes $N = 10$, packet arrival rate $\lambda = 7000$ Packets /s, and the maximum cache capacity of nodes $B = 50$.

The following conclusions can be drawn, overall increase maximum interrupt overflow probability can improve the transmission rate of the system, secondly, with the increase of delay for the system transmission rate also increases, the reason is that when the delay requirement increases, the increase in the number of D2D users will meet the requirements of delay, lead to more optional D2D users can select the power allocation model and channel allocation, so the total transfer rate will go up.

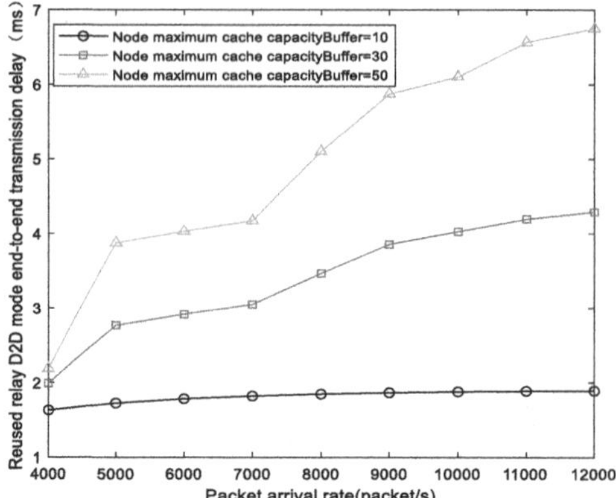

Fig. 3. Delay performance in multiplexed relay D2D mode varies with node maximum cache capacity and packet arrival rate Settings

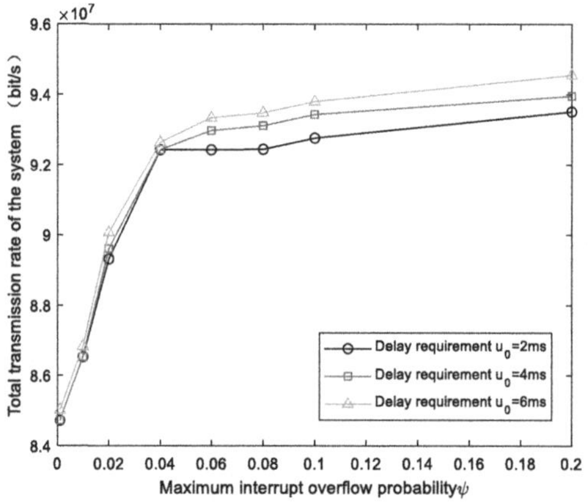

Fig. 4. The change curve of the system transmission rate with the maximum interrupt overflow probability under different delay requirements

6 Conclusion

This paper mainly focuses on the base station scheduling algorithm design problems faced after the introduction of D2D communication technology in the cellular network. Completed the time delay estimation problem of multiplexing direct D2D mode and multiplexing relay D2D mode in the case of the channel state information part, and the cross-layer joint scheduling problem of base stations for the transmission rate of the entire system. The specific research content and results are as follows:

First, a system model that comprehensively considers the two D2D working modes is constructed, and then the work in the multiplexing relay D2D is introduced in detail. The calculation of the transmission rate of the mode users and their multiplexed cellular users, and then the mathematical modeling is carried out for the purpose of maximizing the transmission rate of the entire system while meeting the service quality and delay requirements, and then the multiplexing relay is given. The calculation method of the end-to-end transmission delay in the D2D mode, and finally the optimization goal is solved through power allocation, channel allocation and mode selection. After that, it was verified through simulation that the importance of considering the D2D mode of multiplexing relays and the impact of some main parameter settings in the system on the delay and system transmission rate. It is hoped that these parameter settings will affect the transmission rate.

References

1. Qian, Z., Tian, C., Wang, X.: The key technology and development of intelligent and connected transportation system. J. Electron. Inf. Technol. **42**(1), 2–19 (2020)
2. Sakr, A., et al.: Cognitive Spectrum access in device-to-device-enabled cellular networks. IEEE Commun. Mag. **53**(7), 126–133 (2015)
3. Fodor, G., et al.: Design aspects of network assisted device-to-device communications. IEEE Commun. Mag. **50**(3), 170–177 (2012)
4. Cai, X., Zheng, J., Zhang, Y.: A Graph-coloring Based Resource Allocation Algorithm for D2D Communication in Cellular Networks. 2015 IEEE International Conference on Communications (ICC) 5429–5434 (2015)
5. Mondal, I., Neogi, A., Chaporkar, P., Karandikar, A.: Bipartite Graph Based Proportional Fair Resource Allocation for D2D Communication. 2017 IEEE Wireless Communications and Networking Conference (WCNC), 1–6 (2017)
6. Doppler, K., Rinne, M., Wijing, C., Ribeiro, C.B., Hugl, K.: Device-to-device communication as an underlay to LTE-advanced networks. IEEE Communications Magazine **47**(12), 42–49 (2009)
7. Anis, P., Koivunen, V., Ribeiro, C., Korhonen, J., Doppler, K., Hugl, K.: Interference-Aware Resource Allocation for Device-to-Device Radio Underlaying Cellular Networks. IEEE 69th Vehicular Technology Conference (VTC Spring 2009), 1–5 (2009)
8. Yu, C.H., Doppler, K., Ribeiro, C.B., Tirkkonen, O.: Resource sharing optimization for device-to-device communication underlaying cellular networks. IEEE Trans. Wireless Commun. **10**(8), 2752–2763 (2011)
9. Omır, A., Hasna, M.O.: A distance based mode selection scheme for D2D enabled networks with mobility. IEEE Trans. Wireless Commun. **17**(99), 4326–4340 (2018)
10. Kim, et al.: Adaptive mode selection in D2D communications considering the bursty traffic model. IEEE Communications Letters **20**(4), 712–715 (2016)
11. Kang, X., et al.: Optimal power allocation strategies for fading cognitive radio channels with primary user outage constraint. IEEE J. Sel. Areas Commun. **29**(2), 374–383 (2011)
12. Papoulis, A., Pillai, S.: Probability, Random Variables, and Stochastic Processes. 4th ed. New York, NY: Mc Graw-Hill (2002)

Power Allocation Algorithm Based on Machine Learning for Device-to-Device Communication in Cellular Network

He Ma[1], Zhiliang Qin[2], and Ruofei Ma[1(✉)]

[1] Harbin Institute of Technology, Weihai 264209, Shandong, China
maruofei@hit.edu.cn
[2] Beiyang Electric Group Co. Ltd., Weihai, Shandong, China
qinzhiliang@beiyang.com

Abstract. With the development of the Internet, more and more mobile user equipment access to the cellular network, so the shortage of wireless spectrum resources has become increasingly prominent. Device-to-device (D2D) communication, as a key technology to solve this problem, can greatly improve the spectrum utilization rate and reduce the load of the base station. However, in the communication process of cellular users, D2D users occupying the same channel will bring complicated electromagnetic interference to them. This paper will establish a single-cell system model in which cellular users and D2D users coexist, and apply the method of power allocation to solve the problem of interference in the communication system. Then, we propose power allocation algorithm based on Q learning. Finally, the performance of the power allocation algorithm based on Q learning is analyzed and evaluated through the results of simulation experiments to verify the superiority of the algorithm over the performance of traditional power allocation algorithm.

Keywords: Device-to-device (D2D) communication · Power allocation · Q learning

1 Introduction

Device-to-device (D2D) communication technology which has been included into the development framework of a new generation of mobile communication system by the 3rd Generation Partnership Project is one of the key technologies of 5G. K. Doppler et al. put forward the concept of D2D communication in 2009 [1]. D2D communication is a technology that supports the direct communication between two terminal equipment. Because the distance between transmitting user and receiving user is relatively close, they

This work was supported partially by National Natural Science Foundation of China (Grant No. 61801144, 61971156), Shandong Provincial Natural Science Foundation, China (Grant No. ZR2019QF003, ZR2019MF035), and the Fundamental Research Funds for the Central Universities, China (Grant No. HIT.NSRIF.2019081).

© ICST Institute for Computer Sciences, Social Informatics and Telecommunications Engineering 2022
Published by Springer Nature Switzerland AG 2022. All Rights Reserved
S. Shi et al. (Eds.): 6GN 2021, LNICST 439, pp. 160–171, 2022.
https://doi.org/10.1007/978-3-031-04245-4_14

no longer need to relay through base station (BS) to carry out information exchange [2]. The main features of D2D communication are to save resources, improve transmission efficiency, and reduce interference [3]. When D2D users and cellular users choose to use the same spectrum resources, the spectrum utilization efficiency can be improved. But at the same time, the access of D2D users also brings complex electromagnetic interference to cellular users. Therefore, effective control of interference and reasonable allocation of resources become extremely important in D2D communication [4].

With the rapid development of computer technology, artificial intelligence and machine learning are becoming more and more closely related to our daily lives [5]. As one of research areas of artificial intelligence, machine learning technology in the robot technology, virtual personal assistant, computer games, pattern recognition, natural language processing and online transportation network has been widely applied [6]. Nowadays, the research based on machine learning has made great progress in the field of communication, which provides solutions for the management of wireless resources of D2D communication.

In [7], a Capacity Oriented Resource ALlocation (CORAL) algorithm for resource allocation in D2D communication underlaying mobile cellular network is proposed. The CORAL algorithm assumes that a D2D user can occupy the communication resources of multiple cellular links. At the same time, a Capacity-Oriented REstricted (CORE) region of the D2D user is introduced to determine the candidate cellular user set for the D2D user. And the CORAL algorithm is superior to the traditional random allocation algorithm in terms of system capacity and rate loss of all cellular users. In [8], the authors study several power allocation schemes for D2D communication, including a fixed power scheme, a fixed SNR target scheme, an (LTE) open loop fraction power control scheme, and a close loop power control scheme. In [9], an enhanced single-leader-multiple-followers Stackelberg game model is presented to investigate distributed power control strategies.

In addition, the problem of resource allocation for D2D communication is also connected with the current popular machine learning, and more solutions are obtained. These resource allocation algorithms in [10–12] all consider applying Q learning algorithm to solve the problem of resource allocation. Moreover, CART Decision Tree algorithm is also applied to research problem in [12].

In this paper, we consider the situation of D2D user multiplexing uplink of cellular user to communicate in a single-cell cellular network. The goal is to improve the performance of the communication system through resource allocation without affecting the QoS of the cellular users, and ultimately maximize the throughput of the entire system. At the same time, the machine learning method is applied to the research of resource allocation for D2D communication.

The rest of this paper is as follows. In Sect. 2, we establish a system model and formulate the problem. Section 3 briefly introduces Q learning, then we propose the power allocation algorithm based on Q learning for D2D communication. Section 4 provides the simulation results and performance analysis. Finally, we conclude in Sect. 5.

2 System Model and Problem Formulation

2.1 System Model

In this paper, we study a single-cell model as shown in Fig. 1. There is a base station (BS) fixed in the center of the cell. In its coverage area, cellular user equipment (CUE) and D2D user equipment (DUE) are randomly and evenly distributed. The number of CUE is M, denoted as $C = \{C_1, C_2, \cdots, C_M\}$. The number of DUE is N, denoted as $D = \{D_1, D_2, \cdots, D_N\}$. A D2D transmitter (DUE Tx) and a D2D receiver (DUE Rx) together make up a D2D, and they can communicate directly. It is assumed that there are a total of K orthogonal spectrum resource blocks (RB), denoted as $B = \{B_1, B_2, \cdots, B_K\}$. This paper considers the scenario of D2D user multiplexing uplink of cellular user.

In order to facilitate the discussion of future problem, we assume that only one cellular user can communicate on each resource block in the cell, and the number of cellular users is equal to the number of the resource blocks. Each D2D user can occupy only one spectrum resource block, and each resource block can be occupied by at most one D2D user. The communication of the mobile user equipment with the same communication mode is independent of each other and does not interfere with each other. It is worth noting that the transmitting power of the cellular users keeps constant throughout the communication process during the study. As this paper studies the power allocation of D2D communication, the spectrum allocation of cellular users and D2D users is fixed, that is to say, the base station will randomly allocate spectrum resource blocks to user equipment before D2D communication, and the spectrum will always be fixed during the communication process.

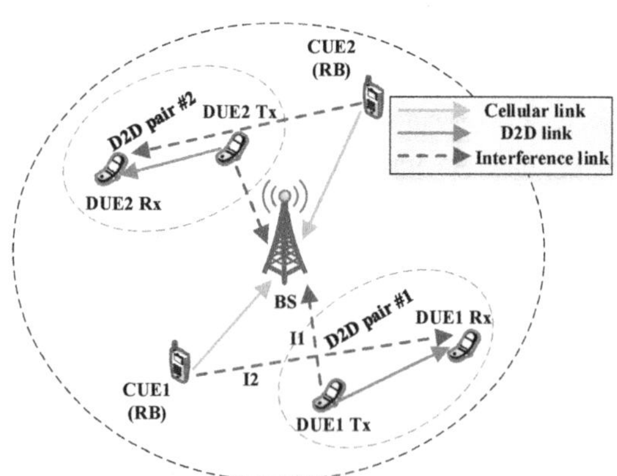

Fig. 1. System model

Due to the randomness of the location of D2D users and the communication between cellular users and base station, D2D users multiplexing the uplink resources of cellular users for communication will cause interference. According to the above definitions and assumptions of the system model, there are two main kinds of interference in the system: I_1 is the interference received by BS from DUE Tx; I_2 is the interference received by DUE Rx from CUE occupying the same resource block.

The next step is to set BS to represent the base station, C_i represents CUE i in the cell and D_j represents DUE j. Then we can analyze the channel gain between C_i and D_j, as well as between user equipment and BS.

For CUE and BS, we consider free space path loss model, and then the channel gain of C_i and BS is calculated according to the following equation:

$$G_{BS,C_i} = 10^{-PL_{BS,C_i}/10} \tag{1}$$

where PL_{BS,C_i} is the path loss between BS and C_i.

In this paper, a simple single-slope path loss model is used to calculate the channel gain between two mobile user equipment. Therefore, the channel gain between C_i and D_j is defined as:

$$G_{C_iD_j} = k \cdot d_{C_iD_j}^{-\mu} \tag{2}$$

where $d_{C_iD_j}$ is the distance between C_i and D_j, k represents gain index and μ represents path loss index.

The channel gain of D2D link can be defined as:

$$G_{D_jD_j} = k \cdot d_{D_jD_j}^{-\mu} \tag{3}$$

where $d_{D_jD_j}$ is the distance between the transmitter and receiver of D2D user.

2.2 Problem Formulation

We consider the condition that the resource blocks of the system have been well allocated. The goal of the problem of power allocation is to use the corresponding power allocation algorithm to assign the optimal transmitting power to each D2D user in the system, so as to reduce the influence of the interference existing in the above system on the communication of user equipment and maximize the throughput of the system.

Signal-to-interference-noise ratio (SINR) is an important index to measure the communication quality of link. The *SINR* of D2D user D_j, which occupies the resource block Br can be defined as:

$$SINR_{D_j}^r = \frac{p_{D_j}^r \cdot G_{D_jD_j}^r}{\sigma^2 + p_{C_i}^r \cdot G_{C_iD_j}^r} \tag{4}$$

where $p_{C_i}^r$ and $p_{D_j}^r$ are respectively the transmitting power of cellular user C_i and D2D user D_j, σ^2 is the noise power, and $p_{C_i}^r \cdot G_{C_iD_j}^r$ is the interference received by D_j from C_i, which shares the same resource block.

Similarly, the *SINR* of cellular user C_i occupying resource block Br can be defined as:

$$SINR_{C_i}^r = \frac{p_{C_i}^r \cdot G_{BS,C_i}^r}{\sigma^2 + p_{D_j}^r \cdot G_{C_iD_j}^r} \tag{5}$$

where $p^r_{D_j} \cdot G^r_{C_iD_j}$ is the interference received by C_i from D_j, which shares the same resource block.

When the resource block is not occupied by the D2D user, the cellular user occupying this resource block will not be disturbed by the D2D user. At this time, the *SINR* of the cellular user can be defined as:

$$SINR^r_{C_i} = \frac{p^r_{C_i} \cdot G^r_{BS,C_i}}{\sigma^2} \tag{6}$$

We can use Shannon equation to calculate the throughput of cellular users and D2D users to obtain the total throughput of the whole system:

$$R_D = \sum_{j=1}^{N} W \cdot \log_2(1 + SINR^r_{D_j}) \tag{7}$$

$$R_C = \sum_{i=1}^{M} W \cdot \log_2(1 + SINR^r_{C_i}) \tag{8}$$

$$R = R_D + R_C = \sum_{j=1}^{N} W \cdot \log_2(1 + SINR^r_{D_j}) + \sum_{i=1}^{M} W \cdot \log_2(1 + SINR^r_{C_i}) \tag{9}$$

where R_D and R_C are the throughput of D2D users and cellular users respectively, W is the bandwidth of the system and R is the throughput of the whole system.

Therefore, the goal of maximizing the throughput of the system:

$$\begin{gathered} \max_{p^r_{D_j}}\{R\} \\ s.t.\quad SINR^r_{C_i} \geq \tau_0 \\ p_{\min} \leq p^r_{D_j} \leq p_{\max}, \forall j, r \end{gathered} \tag{10}$$

where τ_0 is the minimum *SINR* of the cellular user when it can work normally. Therefore, the constraint condition to achieve the goal of maximizing throughput is that the *SINR* of each cellular user should be higher than the threshold value. At the same time, the transmitting power of each D2D user should be kept within the allowable range.

3 Algorithm Description

3.1 Q Learning

Q learning algorithm is a model-independent reinforcement learning algorithm proposed by Watkins [13] in 1989. The algorithm does not need to know the environment model, and at the same time, it updates the policy in the continuous learning process, and finally obtains an optimal policy to solve the problem.

The value function in Q learning is defined by Q function:

$$Q_t(s, a) = E_\pi[\sum_{i=1}^{\infty} \gamma^{i-1} r_{t+i} | S_t = s, A_t = a] \tag{11}$$

where $Q_t(s, a)$ represents the expectation of the gain from taking action a when the state is s, and γ represents the discount factor.

Therefore, it can be seen that the main idea of Q learning algorithm is to build state s and action a into a two-dimensional table to store the value of Q function, that is, the Q value table. As shown in Table 1, the rows in the Q table represent the state, and the columns represent the action to be selected, and the corresponding values of $Q_t(s, a)$ between them mean the feedback given by the environment when the action a is executed under the state s.

Table 1. Q table

Q table	a_1	a_2	...	a_N
s_1	$Q(s_1, a_1)$	$Q(s_1, a_2)$	...	$Q(s_1, a_N)$
s_2	$Q(s_2, a_1)$	$Q(s_2, a_2)$	...	$Q(s_2, a_N)$
...	...	...	...	...
s_M	$Q(s_M, a_1)$	$Q(s_M, a_2)$	...	$Q(s_M, a_N)$

The Basic Process of Q Learning

1. A Q table is firstly created, and it can be used to store values of $Q(s, a)$. Then initialize all values of $Q(s, a)$ to 0.
2. This paper adopts $\varepsilon - greedy$ policy to choose action. When the random probability is less than ε, the action will be chosen randomly; otherwise, the current action with the highest Q value will be chosen. This algorithm can be defined by the equation:

$$A = \begin{cases} \text{Random action } a \in A,\ p < \varepsilon \\ \arg\max\limits_{a} Q(s, a), \qquad \text{others} \end{cases} \tag{12}$$

   where p is the random probability in the process of iteration.
3. The action that has been chosen is adopted.
4. The return function value is calculated through the feedback given by the environment.
5. According to the return function and Eq. (13), it can update Q table.

$$Q_{t+1}^r(s, a) = Q_t^r(s, a) + \alpha[r_{t+1} + \gamma \max_{a'} Q_t^r(s', a') - Q_t^r(s, a)] \tag{13}$$

   where $Q_t^r(s, a)$ represents the value of Q function on the resource block Br during the t-th iteration; $\alpha \in (0, 1]$ represents learning rate, which determines the degree to which the return function value affects the update of Q value in the iteration process. When the learning rate is small enough and the learning process can access all the combinations of states and actions for many times, the update and iteration are carried out according to Eq. (13), and finally Q function will converge to the optimal value Q^*. The γ is the discount factor with a value between 0 and 1, which is used to determine the relative proportion of delayed return and current return. The larger the value of γ, the more attention is paid to long term returns. Since the final result of Q learning is Q^*, the optimal policy obtained by learning is to select the optimal action a under the state s to make Q value reach maximum.

6. The iterative process from step 2 to step 5 is repeated until the Q value converges.

3.2 Definition of Basic Components

This section solves the power allocation problem of D2D communication in the cellular network based on the Q learning algorithm. For the system model which we are considering, different user equipment occupies different resource block, so there is no interference with user equipment. Therefore, the problem of throughput optimization for each resource block in the whole system can be regarded as an independent Q learning problem. Firstly, the D2D user equipment, system throughput, and transmitting power of D2D user are related to the components of reinforcement learning, and then they are introduced one by one.

Agent. It is the performer of the action. Each D2D user is an agent in the communication system.

State. According to the related theory of reinforcement learning, it can be known that the agent will have an influence on the environment after executing the action, which makes the environment change its state after receiving the action. And in the subsequent learning process, we can get the optimal policy finally by changing actions and states to explore and adjust policy, so that we can know what actions should be taken under state s. However, in the transition process of different states, the time required for the Q value to converge to the optimal value becomes longer. Therefore, the following power allocation algorithm based on Q learning will adopt the single-state Q learning algorithm, that is, the state has no practical significance, which not only simplifies the Q table, but also shortens the convergence time of Q learning.

Action. The action performed by the agent is defined as the transmitting power of D2D user, denoted as $p \in \{p_1, p_2, \cdots, p_L\}$. There are L powers that D2D transmitter can choose.

Return Function. We can define the throughput of resource block Br as:

$$r = \begin{cases} W \cdot \log_2(1 + SINR^r_{C_i}) + W \cdot \log_2(1 + SINR^r_{D_j}), & SINR^r_{C_i} \geq \tau_0 \\ -1, & \text{others} \end{cases} \tag{14}$$

According to Eq. (14), if the $SINR$ of the cellular user occupying the resource block Br is greater than the minimum threshold τ_0, the value of return function is the sum of the throughput of all mobile user equipment occupying this resource block. Otherwise, the return function is equal to -1, which is regarded as punishment.

3.3 Steps of the Algorithm

1. Firstly, we should input K orthogonal spectrum resource blocks, M cellular users, N D2D users and L powers that can be chosen.
2. For the j-th D2D user to create and initialize the Q table, there is only a one-dimensional table to create.
3. The resource block Br that has been allocated for the D2D user is chosen. Firstly according to $\varepsilon - greedy$ policy, the agent chooses the action a and adopt the action a, that is, transmitting power is allocated to D2D user through policy. Then calculate the return function and update the Q table on the basis of the Eq. (14). Finally, this process is repeated until the Q table converges, and the corresponding optimal action in the Q table is obtained, that is, D2D user obtains the optimal transmitting power.

4 Simulation Results

This section analyzes the performance of the power allocation algorithm based on machine learning on the basis of the above system model and algorithm description. The simulation experiment is carried out on the Python3 simulation platform. In the simulation process, this paper considers a single-cell scene with a coverage radius of 500 m. D2D users share the uplink resources with cellular users, and different user equipment is distributed randomly and evenly in the cell. The number of resource blocks in the system is equal to the number of cellular users. The simulation parameters are shown in Table 2.

Table 2. Simulation parameters

Parameter	Value
Number of D2D user	1–100
Cell radius	500 m
Transmitting power of cellular user	24 dBm
Selectable powers set of D2D user	{1, 6.5, 12, 17.5, 23} dBm
Noise power density (σ^2)	−134 dBm/Hz
Gain index (k)	1
Path loss index (μ)	4
Channel gain model of cellular user	$128 + 37.6\lg(d(\text{km}))$ dB
Minimum SINR of cellular user (τ_0)	3 dB
Distance between D2D user	50 m
Bandwidth of RB (W)	180 kHz
Learning rate (α)	0.5
Discount factor (γ)	0.9
Initial value of ε	0.9

As shown in Fig. 2, a single-cell scene with a radius of 500 m is drawn. Orange represents the base station, which is located in the center of the cell; blue represents the cellular user equipment, red represents the D2D transmitting user equipment, and green represents the receiving user equipment which is 50 m away from the transmitting user.

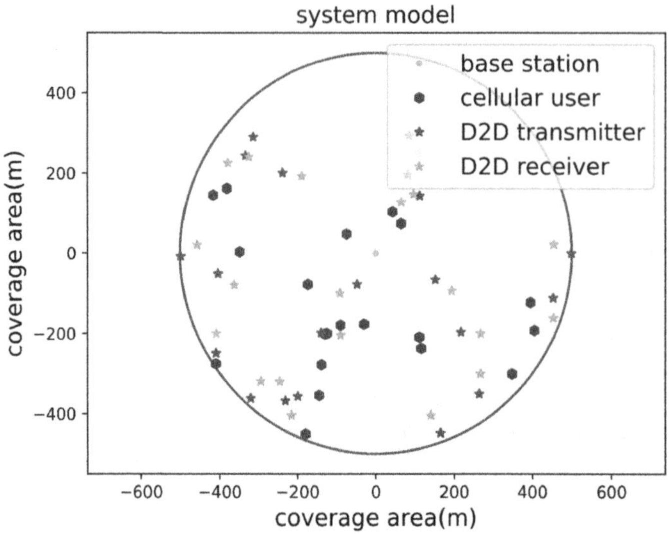

Fig. 2. System model for simulation. (Color figure online)

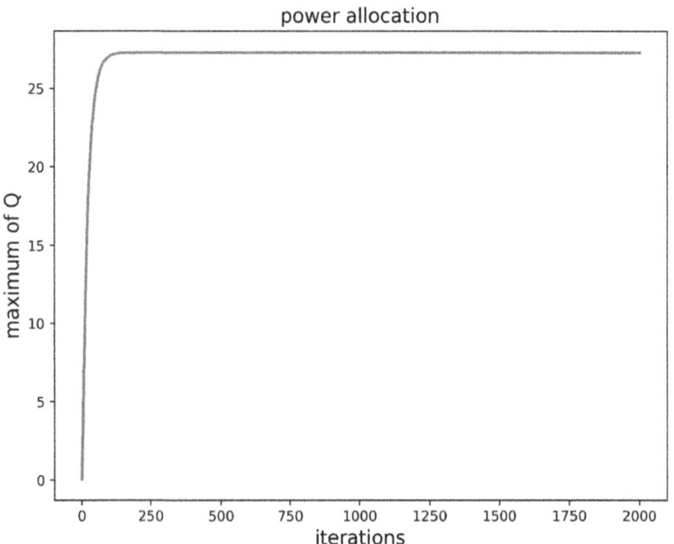

Fig. 3. Convergence of power allocation algorithm

Figure 3 shows the convergence of Q value of the power allocation algorithm based on Q learning on the same resource block. During the simulation, since this paper sets that a cellular user can be multiplexed by at most one D2D user for uplink resources, $M = 1$ and $N = 1$ are set to evaluate the convergence of the algorithm. The abscissa represents the number of iterations and the ordinate represents the maximum value of Q for each iteration. Therefore, the simulation result shows that the value of Q will eventually converge to the optimal value, and D2D user can obtain the optimal transmitting power.

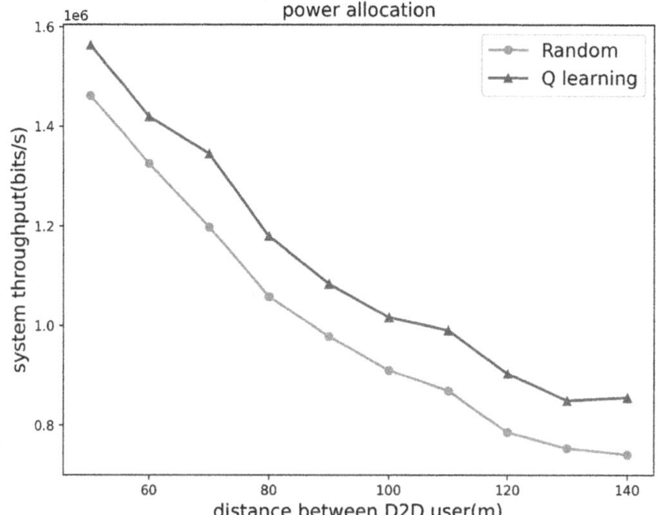

Fig. 4. Performance comparison of different power allocation algorithms

Figure 4 shows the variation of system throughput on a resource block. The abscissa represents the distance between D2D user and the ordinate represents the throughput of system. As the distance between D2D user increases, the system throughput of the two algorithms decreases gradually. The performance of the algorithm in the paper is better.

Figure 5 shows that the total throughput of the system increases significantly with the increase of number of D2D users, that is to say, the access of D2D users in the system improves the performance of the system. The performance of the power allocation algorithm based on Q learning in this paper is better than the random power allocation algorithm.

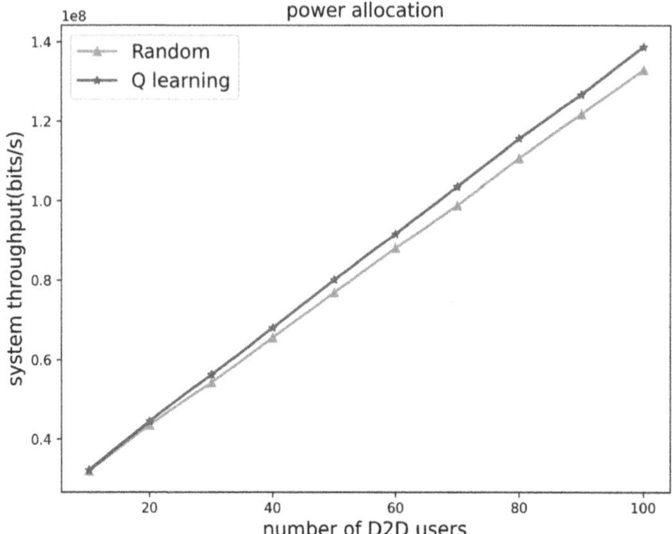

Fig. 5. Variation of system throughput with number of D2D users

5 Conclusion

The power allocation method of D2D communication in cellular system is studied in this paper. On the basis of studying and researching on the theory of D2D communication and machine learning, a power allocation algorithm for D2D communication based on Q learning is proposed. Based on the consideration of the SINR of cellular users, the algorithm aims at maximizing the system throughput. Each D2D user, as an agent, uses the $\varepsilon - greedy$ policy to select the transmitting power as the next action to be executed in the iteration process. Then the conditional throughput on the corresponding resource block is calculated, that is, the return function value, and then the Q table is updated. In the iteration, the agent will find the optimal selection policy and get the optimal action under the optimal policy. According to the simulation results, it can be observed that the power allocation algorithm based on Q learning is superior to the traditional random power allocation algorithm.

References

1. Doppler, K., et al.: Device-to-device communication as an underlay to LTE-advanced networks. IEEE Commun. Mag. **47**(12), 42–49 (2009)
2. Adnan, M.H., Zukarnain, Z.A.: Device-to-device communication in 5G environment: issues, solutions, and challenges. Symmetry **12**(11), 1762 (2020)
3. Su, L., et al.: The research of key technologies in the fifth-generation mobile communication system. In: International Industrial Informatics & Computer Engineering Conference, pp. 483–487 (2015)
4. Asadi, A., Wang, Q., Mancuso, V.: A survey on device-to-device communication in cellular networks. Commun. Surv. Tutor. **16**(4), 1801–1819 (2014)

5. Mjolsness, E., et al.: Machine learning for science: state of the art and future prospects. Science **293**(5537), 2051–2055 (2001)
6. Ray, S.: A quick review of machine learning algorithms. In: 2019 International Conference on Machine Learning, Big Data, Cloud and Parallel Computing (COMITCon), pp. 35–39
7. Cai, X., et al.: A capacity oriented resource allocation algorithm for device-to-device communication in mobile cellular networks. In: IEEE International Conference on Communications, pp. 2233–2238 (2014)
8. Xing, H., Hakola, S.: The investigation of power control schemes for a device-to-device communication integrated into ofdma cellular system. In: IEEE International Symposium on Personal Indoor & Mobile Radio Communications, pp. 1775–1780 (2010)
9. Sun, C., et al.: Distributed power control for device-to-device network using stackelberg game. In: 2014 IEEE Wireless Communications and Networking Conference (WCNC), pp. 1344–1249 (2014)
10. Luo, Y., Shi, Z., Zhou, X., Liu, Q., Yi, Q.: Dynamic resource allocations based on q-learning for d2d communication in cellular networks. In: 2014 11th International Computer Conference on Wavelet Active Media Technology and Information Processing (ICCWAMTIP) IEEE, pp. 19–21 (2014)
11. Nie, S., Fan, Z., Zhao, M., Gu, X., Zhang, L.: Q-learning based power control algorithm for D2D communication. In: 2016 IEEE 27th Annual International Symposium on Personal, Indoor, and Mobile Radio Communications (PIMRC) IEEE, pp. 1–6 (2016)
12. Fan, Z., et al.: D2D power control based on supervised and unsupervised learning. In: 2017 3rd IEEE International Conference on Computer and Communications (ICCC), pp. 558–563 (2017)
13. Watkins, C., Dayan, P.: Q-learning. Mach. Learn. **8**(3–4), 279–292 (1999)

Design and Application of a Desktop CNC Lathe Control System

E. Rui(✉)

Heilongjiang Polytechnic, Heilongjiang, China
e_rui123@163.com

Abstract. With the acceleration of the development process of various industries, the demand for high-end CNC lathes in the manufacturing industry is increasing, and the development of CNC lathes has great potential to create new opportunities while facing challenges. Desktop CNC lathes reduce cost and volume to a certain extent, this paper puts forward the joint dual STM32 and FPGA embedded numerical control system, re-divide the processing mode, design the corresponding hardware and software system, after laboratory verification, the experiment proves that the embedded CNC system can meet the general CNC processing needs.

Keywords: CNC machine tools · Embedded development · STM32 · FPGA

1 Introduction

CNC lathe is the product of the combination of modern electronic information industry and manufacturing industry, taking numerical control technology as the core system and keeping up with the pace of world electrical integration is an important goal of lathe development at present. The world machine tool manufacturing industry has entered the era of mechatronics development with electronic digital manufacturing technology as the core, that is, using digital information control system to support technology development, and CNC lathe is one of the main representative achievements of its technology development.

As far as the social economy itself is concerned, manufacturing industry is an important foundation to support it to carry out a series of activities efficiently, and the production and processing technology and equipment quality involved will have an impact on the national economy to a certain extent. When China's manufacturing industry is aware of the rapid development of foreign manufacturing industry, it should keep up with its pace of development, innovate and reform CNC machine tools, and promote the improvement of the technical level of the whole manufacturing industry in society.

With the continuous enhancement of China's comprehensive development strength, the manufacturing industry has ushered in new opportunities. In recent years, CNC lathes in China have been continuously innovated and widely used in aerospace, shipping and other fields. CNC lathe has become the core equipment of China's modern manufacturing

© ICST Institute for Computer Sciences, Social Informatics and Telecommunications Engineering 2022
Published by Springer Nature Switzerland AG 2022. All Rights Reserved
S. Shi et al. (Eds.): 6GN 2021, LNICST 439, pp. 172–181, 2022.
https://doi.org/10.1007/978-3-031-04245-4_15

industry, with the continuous development of China's economy, the demand for CNC lathe in the domestic market has increased, how to improve the overall quality of machine tools and meet the urgent needs of the future market, so as to boost the economy more effectively, is an important direction of the CNC lathe industry. After realizing the present situation and future trend of domestic CNC lathes, relevant manufacturing units can effectively promote the progress of the machine tool manufacturing industry and help improve the production quality and efficiency of their machine tool products, which is one of the important ways to improve the severe situation that the use of machine tools is in short supply. For the whole society, Exhibition, the national economy can also get substantial progress because of the innovation of modern CNC lathe.

The system completes the work by FPGA and touch screen instead of PLC, and uses STM32F4 to drive the touch screen to complete human-computer interaction, greatly improving the task completion efficiency of CNC lathes, reducing overhead and meeting the needs of automated processing.

2 CNC Lathe Overview

CNC lathe is the abbreviation of digital information control lathe, and it is an automatic machine tool with internal electronic information as the core program control system. Compared with ordinary lathes, this type of machine tool is intelligent and efficient, the central control system can scientifically and orderly handle the operation of specific control instruction codes or other specified operating procedures, and can actually compile them into codes according to the actual operation conditions, thus controlling the machine and machining parts. Under the control of digital information, the machine tool can accurately control the dimensional accuracy and geometric accuracy of parts, and process them into the required shapes. As the machine tool for parts processing, CNC machine tools have a complex system, which is usually composed of digital control system, servo system, quality inspection system and other related auxiliary systems, each system operates in coordination and cooperates in an orderly manner to complete parts processing with good quality and quantity.

3 Hardware System Design for CNC Machine Design of Desktop CNC Lathe Control System Based on Dual STM32 + FPGA

According to the new requirements of desktop CNC lathe for cost and volume, an embedded CNC system based on dual STM32 and FPGA is designed. The machining mode of NC system is subdivided, and the task of NC system is divided into two parts according to the client-server design mode. According to the task requirements of the two parts, the corresponding hardware system is designed, and the specific software functions are researched and realized on the corresponding hardware platform. Finally, turning experiments are carried out on two different desktop lathes, which verify the shortcomings of the modified CNC system in terms of function, precision and stability, experiments show that the embedded CNC system can meet the general needs of CNC machining.

3.1 CNC Lathe Control System Mode Classification

The boundary of traditional NC system mode is fuzzy, which easily confuses beginners. The analysis of the functions and implementation modes of these modes can be summarized into two modes: manual processing and automatic processing.

Reasonable functional classification helps to clarify the task content and lower the threshold of use. In the specific implementation, the two modes have overlapping implementation modes, and some hardware and software can be shared. According to the client-server design pattern (C/S), the control system of CNC lathe is divided into two parts: client and server. Client mainly completes human-computer interaction, and server mainly completes parameter modification, action execution and core functions of CNC system, and G code execution. The two parts mainly realize that the server receives and executes the client instructions and returns the execution results through the self-defined asymmetric communication protocol, so as to cooperatively realize the two processing modes.

3.2 Hardware Design

Hardware is the foundation of numerical control system, and the hardware design should meet the requirements of numerical control system in data processing capability, multi-axis linkage synchronization, storage capability and anti-electromagnetic interference. Due to the limited space, the specific circuit schematic diagram is not expanded here, and only the hardware part of the numerical control system is analyzed and designed from the demand point of view.

The main task of the client part is man-machine interaction, and the screen display and virtual buttons are the main equipment of man-machine interaction. In order to reduce the workload and improve the development efficiency, many embedded designs use serial port screen to realize human-computer interaction [4, 11, 12], but the design is limited and the serial port screen is oriented to general industrial application scenarios, which cannot meet the high real-time requirements such as coordinate display. Therefore, the STM32F429+ touch screen is used to develop the human-computer interaction in the client hardware design. At the same time, make full use of the rich peripherals of STM32, and add USB and SD interfaces for external G code input such as U disk, keyboard and SD card; Use Flash to realize in-board storage of g code; Add 32MB SDRAM to expand STM32F429 memory, and use it as display memory at the same time; Expand the handwheel interface for external electronic handwheel; Ethernet and RS485 interfaces are reserved to increase system openness and function expandability.

Because the server undertakes most tasks in automatic machining, the server hardware needs to meet the requirements of real-time, synchronization and stability of CNC system. The STM32F767, which has a main frequency of up to 216 MHz and supports floating-point operation, is adopted to meet the real-time requirement of numerical control system. EP4CE15F484 is adopted to synchronously send the motion instructions of each axis to the motor driver. Add SDRAM to expand memory and increase the maximum number of G code lines to avoid system crash; Master-slave communication between STM32 and FPGA using FMC; Because FPGA is directly connected with actuators and sensors, optical coupling isolation is added to avoid external signal interference.

Although the tasks of client and server are completed by two MCU, considering the size and installation, the two parts are integrated in the same PCB circuit, sharing necessary modules such as power supply, clock, emergency stop and indicator light. The overall hardware architecture of the NC system is shown in Fig. 1:

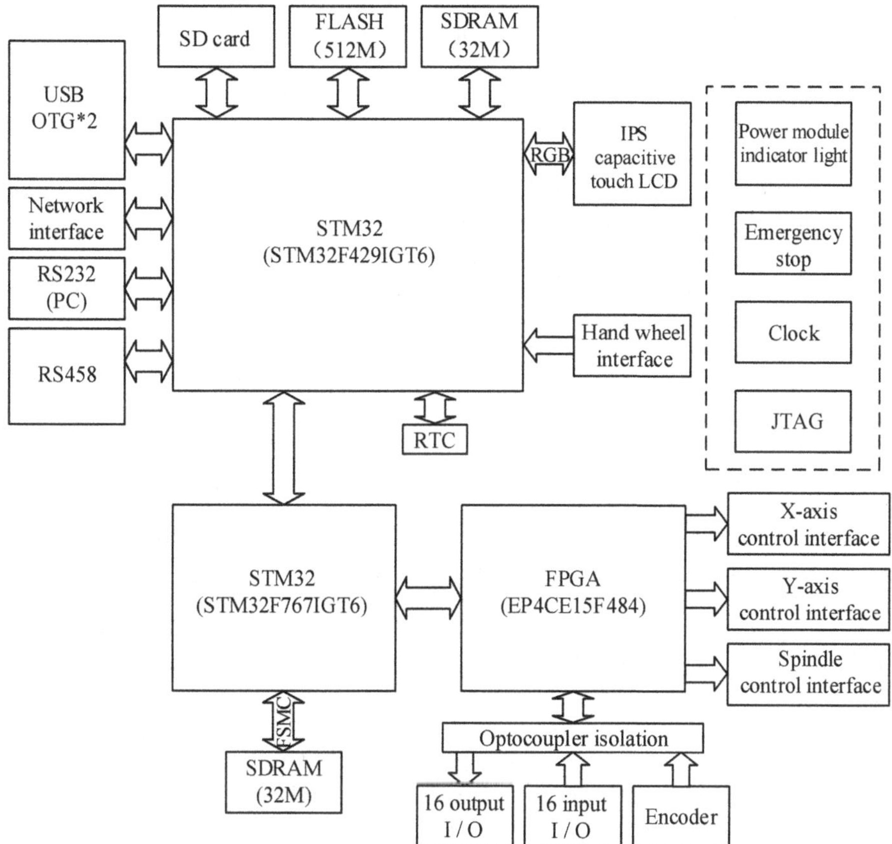

Fig. 1. Embedded CNC system hardware architecture

3.3 Software Design

Software design mainly analyzes and designs client functions and server tasks. Limited to space, and there are many documents [13–16] Decoding, cutter compensation and interpolation are introduced, and all sub-function modules are not described in detail here.

EmWin is a graphic software library developed for embedded platform. The emWin control can be used to complete interface editing like building blocks, and then the LTDC controller of STM32 drives the display screen to realize interface display. EmWin supports touch screen, periodically detects touch interaction, obtains click position coordinates in screen coordinate system, judges whether the control is operated by comparing click position with interface control position, and writes response function in control callback function to realize virtual button function. By coding different button controls, the virtual key input of standard G code or other types of data can be completed by writing the corresponding codes into memory in the button control callback function. Traditional CNC lathes support the use of electronic handwheels, Compared with buttons, electronic handwheels can realize flexible micro-feeding, and control the motor feeding speed according to the shaking speed, which provides great convenience for tool setting and other operations. FatFs is a file system module designed for embedded systems, FatFs can read and write data according to sector information, protect necessary data, and provide generic operation for different storage media. 4 Mbps serial communication is used between client and server to meet the real-time response of big data instructions. There are many types of results returned by the server, and the serial port receives interrupt analysis.

It may cause the client system to have large time jitter, so it is necessary to temporarily store the results with high real-time requirements (such as coordinates) in FIFO buffer, and then analyze the results after other tasks are completed. Touch detection, screen display and result analysis are macroscopically parallel tasks, so the embedded operating system μ C/OS-iii is used for task scheduling, which is the same as the previous one. EmWin and FatFs can also use the semaphore and other shared resource protection mechanisms provided by the operating system for resource protection.

Due to the limited size of server memory, decoding, interpolation and other modules need to be executed in parallel to reduce the demand for buffer, which brings problems of task scheduling and shared resource management. With the development of hardware, the size of on-chip RAM of MCU increases, and RAM can be expanded to increase system memory, so many parallel tasks can be converted to serial execution, thus simplifying design, reducing system coupling and increasing system robustness.

Because the server passively responds to the client's instructions, when the server is idle, it should constantly inquire whether there are instructions delivered through data communication, and call and execute service tasks such as parameter modification, action execution and G code execution through function pointers according to the contents of the instructions. Parameter modification task not only provides necessary parameter modification for automatic machining such as tool setting data, but also can modify motor parameters (maximum speed, acceleration, etc.) and machine tool parameters (maximum stroke, front/rear tool rest, thread pitch, etc.) to improve the flexibility of NC system. The order in which the action instructions are sent will inevitably destroy the synchronization of linkage, so the action execution task only needs to consider the uniaxial action at the same time, that is, the corresponding manual processing mode.

G code tasks include decoding, cutting compensation, speed planning, G code interpretation and other subtasks [16]. Text files read into the system through FatFs are stored in character arrays, if you look for instructions when interpreting g code, you can't meet the real-time requirements of processing speed. Therefore, decoding needs to extract and check the instruction and its data from the character array in advance. Tool length compensation means that when the tool length can't cut the workpiece due to tool change and wear, it can compensate for this missing part without re-setting the tool, saving time; Speed control mainly refers to acceleration and deceleration control, and there is also speed preview control for continuous tiny line segments [17], The trajectories described in G code all start from zero speed and end at zero speed. According to Newton's law, there must be acceleration and deceleration processes, for stepping motors, the machining accuracy is not high under the starting frequency, so acceleration and deceleration can be ignored. Frequent start-stop affects the machining efficiency, and speed preview control introduces switching speed to avoid motor start-stop. G code interpretation converts G code into specific instructions to drive actuator movement. For simple actuators, such as coolant, lighting, etc., only need to control FPGA to generate corresponding high and low levels; For a single complex actuator, such as DC brushless motor, control FPGA to generate corresponding enable, direction level signal and speed pulse signal sequence to send to DC brushless driver; For the linkage of multiple complex actuators, the displacement of each axis is decomposed by point-by-point comparison interpolation, and then the FPGA is controlled to generate corresponding direction level signals and pulse sequences containing displacement speed information, which are sent to the stepper motor driver.

Emergency stop is used for the emergency stop of machine tools in critical situations, if the emergency stop only powers off the main circuit, there is a possibility that the motor will continue to move after the emergency stop is reset, so the emergency stop signal needs to be provided to the numerical control system at the same time to control the motor to stop, for the large inertia part of the spindle, if necessary, reverse the electromagnetic torque properly or increase the mechanical locking device. To sum up, the reference model of the server part is shown in Fig. 2.

This determines the asymmetry of communication protocols. Clients need to call the services provided by the server according to the server protocol, Because of the uncertainty of G code data, if the server receives data in an indefinite way, the time jitter is large, in order to realize fixed-length reception, clients need to send an instruction to tell the server the length of G code first, and then send the corresponding length of G code in the next instruction.

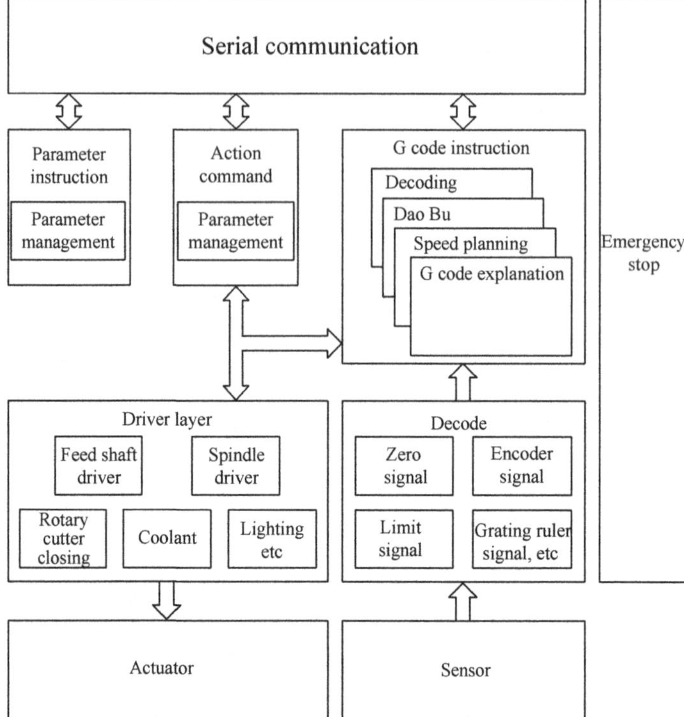

Fig. 2. Server reference model of CNC system

4 Experimental Verification

In order to verify and modify the embedded numerical control system, two machine tools were used respectively, one of which was Nanjing Yima ET 100-ZT NC assembly and adjustment training lathe, and the cutting experiment was completed after selecting the motor and cutting tools; Second, self-designed machine tools. Turning experiments were carried out using the part drawing as shown in Fig. 3.

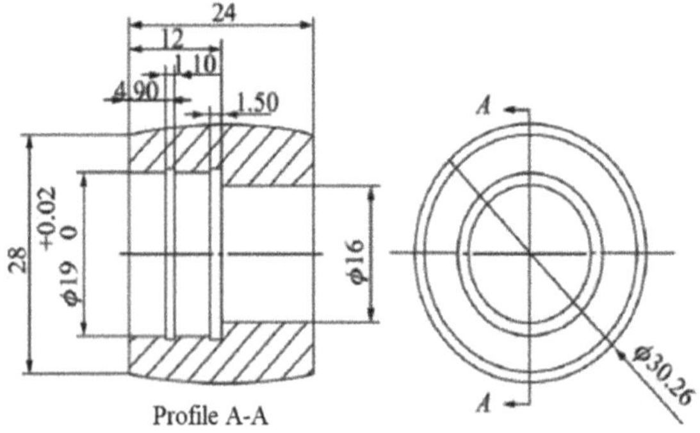

Fig. 3. Drawing of parts to be processed

Fig. 4. ET100-ZT machining parts drawing

Fig. 5. Self-designed machine tool machining parts drawing

Table 1. Experimental data for machined part 1

Machine	ET100-ZT	Self-designed machine
Workpiece length	23.985/24	23.991/24
Left end face circle	9.991/10	27.864/28
Right end face circle	9.979/10	29.198/28
Large inner hole	–	18.891/19
Small inner hole	–	16.099/16

Table 2. Experimental data for machined part 2

Machine	ET100-ZT	Self-designed machine
Workpiece length	23.979/24	23.990/24
Left end face circle	9.989/10	27.866/28
Right end face circle	9.981/10	29.199/28
Large inner hole	–	18.892/19
Small inner hole	–	16.098/16

The machining results are shown in Fig. 4 and Fig. 5, and the machining parts data are shown in Tables 1 and 2.

The x-axis stiffness of the self-designed machine tool is poor, which leads to the relatively poor dimensional accuracy of parts in the x-axis direction and the machining surface quality is not as good as ET100-ZT.

5 Conclusion

The traditional CNC system uses PLC to complete most of the input and output signal processing, such as CNC panel compilation, limit signal acquisition and spindle tool change control, etc. This system uses FPGA and touch screen to replace PLC to complete related work, and uses STM32F4 to drive the touch screen to complete human-computer interaction. Use STM32F7 to interpret and execute operator instructions. Reduce the cost of PLC, CNC panel, PC and other parts, and integrate all the hardware in the A4 size PCB board to meet the volume requirements of desktop machine tools. Experiments prove that the embedded CNC system meets the general automated processing requirements and meets the cost and volume requirements of the desktop CNC lathe.

However, due to many choices in the design stage, this CNC system must have many shortcomings: The use of an MCU based on the Cortex-M core sacrifices some human-computer interaction functions, such as trajectory display and simulation processing; at the same time, electronic handwheel pulses are collected on the client side. There must be a problem that the motor execution lags behind the handwheel by one collection cycle, which may bring safety hazards and will be improved in the subsequent design.

References

1. Huang, Z., Zhao, K.: Design of 5-axis CNC machine tool based on MACH3. Mach. Manuf. Self Dynamic **2**, 11–14 (2018)
2. Zhou, D.: Development of SOFT-type CNC Numerical Control System Control Software. Zhejiang UniversityStudies, Hangzhou (2004)
3. Ian, H., et al.: Open CNC system of micro lathe based on USB busSystematic research and design. Mach. Tool Hydraulics. **48**(1), 51–56, 78 (2020)
4. Song, K., et al. Embedded data of micro lathe based on STM32+FPGA control system research and design. Manuf. Technol. Mach. Tool. (3), 67–73, 77 (2019)

5. Zhao, M.: Design and implementation of CNC system based on embedded Linux. Micro. Appl. **35**(9), 12–13, 25 (2019)
6. Li, G.: Design of embedded CNC system based on ARM and FPGA. Autom. Technol. Appl. **37**(10), 129–135 (2018)
7. Qu, J.: Research and Development of Embedded CNC System Based on ARM and Linux. Nanjing University of Aeronautics and Astronautics, South Beijing (2013)
8. Jiang, X.: Research on real-time realization of embedded CNC system based on Xenomai. Electronic Test (16), 68–69, 102 (2019)
9. Du, X., et al.: Windows real-time improvement based on resource reallocation made. Microelectronics and Computer. **29**(5): 95–98,103 (2012)
10. Huang, J., et al.: Optimized design of desktop CNC lathe structure. China Section Technical Papers **11**(10), 1143–1146 (2016)
11. Xie, O., Li, H., Li, Y.: The communication between ARM and touch screen in the embedded CNC system of internal grinder Letter realization. Precis. Manuf. Autom. **3**, 42–44 (2008)
12. Hu, Z., Rao, G., Li, X.: The design and development of the dual-axis control system of the CNC slicing machine. Computer Meas. Control **22**(5), 1461–1463 (2014)
13. Hong, S., Xu, J., Wu, S.: Design of G code interpretation module of embedded numerical control system and realization. Mech. Des. Manuf. **11**, 37–39 (2012)
14. Kang, J.: Research on C-Function Tool Radius Compensation Technology of CNC Machine Tool. Hefei Workers Industry University, Hefei (2009)
15. Hua, M., Cao, J.: Algorithm for realizing economical CNC system C tool offset creation and cancellation research. Modern Manuf. Eng. (2), 37–39, 21 (2007)
16. Yan, Y., Zhang, F.: Numerical Control Technology. Tsinghua University Press, Beijing (2012)
17. Zhu, C.: Forward Planning Algorithm for Path And Speed of CNC System For High-Speed Machining of Continuous Micro-Line Segments Research. Zhejiang University, Hangzhou (2018)

Video Stereo Grid Construction Method for Accurate Forest Fire Location

Jichang Cao[1,2(✉)], Yichao Cao[3], Qing Guo[1], Liang Ye[1], and Jialing Zhen[1]

[1] School of Electronic and Information Engineering,
Harbin Institute of Technology, Harbin 150001, Heilongjiang, China
caojichang@126.com

[2] Science and Technology and Industrialization Development Center of Ministry of Housing and Urban-Rural Development, Beijing 100835, China

[3] School of Automation, Southeast University, Nanjing 210096, Jiangsu, China

Abstract. Accurate forest fire location during the initial stages is vital for suppressing forest fires. However, in some mountainous areas, accurate automatic fire location is still a challenging task. There is a lack of a good association mechanism between video space and external geographic information. In this paper, we propose a method to measure the fire location and accurately map it to the stereo space coding, which uses the feedback parameters (yaw angle, pitch angle, geographic location and altitude where the camera installed) and digital elevation model. The position of the fire point from the image coordinate system is obtained by computer vision method, and then transform it to the camera coordinate system and the world coordinate system by coordinate transformation. And we establish the mapping from longitude, latitude and height coordinates into stereo grid code to achieve the construction of video stereo grid space. The proposed method has also been deployed and verified in actual forest video monitoring system.

Keywords: Forest fire location · Video stereo space · Grid space

1 Introduction

1.1 Video Based Forest Fire Detection

Forest fire spreads in a large area in the forest area, and causes a lot of losses to the forest ecosystem. They are one of the most frequent, devastating, and difficult natural disasters in the world. They are the greatest threat to the security of forest resources. China is an ecologically fragile country and a country prone to forest fires. The task of forest fire prevention is the primary task of national forest resource protection, and it is related to the safety of people's lives and property and forest resources.

Forest loss is the most direct loss caused by forest fires. At the same time, forest fires will damage the ecological environment and cause the loss of assets in the disaster area. In order to suppress forest fires, the government needs to invest a lot of manpower, material and financial resources, and the rescue process will also cause serious loss of

© ICST Institute for Computer Sciences, Social Informatics and Telecommunications Engineering 2022
Published by Springer Nature Switzerland AG 2022. All Rights Reserved
S. Shi et al. (Eds.): 6GN 2021, LNICST 439, pp. 182–191, 2022.
https://doi.org/10.1007/978-3-031-04245-4_16

people's lives and property. Therefore, early detection of forest fires and timely and efficient rescue measures are of great significance for protecting forest resources and reducing loss of life and property.

In recent years, with the development of video technology and computer vision technology, video-based forest fire video surveillance systems have provided new approaches and methods for forest fire detection [1]. Forest fire video monitoring technology is a non-contact forest fire monitoring technology using computer vision. The traditional forest fire detection technology uses sensor equipment distributed in the forest area to monitor. But the deployment and maintenance costs are generally high. In recent years, computer hardware and image processing technology have begun to make great progress, and forest fire video surveillance systems have begun to occupy a more important position in forest fire detection with its unique advantages [2].

Front-end monitoring equipment used for forest fire prevention usually includes monitoring cameras, lenses, drive motors, network equipment, etc. The digital camera devices with parameter feedback can obtain the camera's pitch, yaw, spatial position, and lens parameters in real time. By analyzing input images and these important parameters, accurate fire positioning could be achieved.

1.2 Video Geographic Data Association

The research on the integration of video data and geographic information began in 1970. Andrew Lippman [3] proposed the integration of video and geographic information for the first time and completed a set of interactive video geographic information systems. With the continuous development of positioning technology, data storage technology, data computing technology and other technologies, video and geographic data are more and more closely related, and many excellent research results have been obtained.

Geographic Information System (GIS) has been developed since the 1960s and is used to obtain, store, operate, analyze, manage and display all types of geographic data [4]. The video geographic information system is designed to combine geographic information and video to dynamically generate hyper-video that can be navigated through geographic content [5]. A large number of videos are organized and used by integrating with geographic information and using GIS research methods to form a variety of organizations and expressions. The integration of video and geographic data can be divided into real-time association and later through external data association from the different organizational association methods.

Kim et al. [6] proposed to use sensors to collect metadata while collecting videos, and store them in the database in real time to associate with the video frames, and proposed a feasible technical framework for this method. Lewis et al. [7] through in-depth research on the integration of video and geographic information, proposed a flexible and versatile and easy to expand spatial video data model ViewPoint, which can be applied to 2D and 3D GIS analysis and visualization [7]. Ying Lu et al. [8] built a new type of R-tree index to store the field of view (FOV), location and other information of the video, thereby improving the efficiency of video query and retrieval based on geographic information and meeting real application requirements. The current video geographic data organization and expression methods are mostly associated and organized with video as an independent object and geographic information, without in-depth exploration of the video space; and the organization based on video semantics is also a relatively shallow way of in-video events or The organization of moving targets does not carry out spatial modeling and data organization and management of the entire video space. Therefore, when the video is associated with geographic data, it is necessary to choose an appropriate method to fully organize and express the video space, and the data structure of the multi-level grid has the characteristics of multi-scale, which can adapt to the needs of multiple applications.

In addition to expressing geographic data by latitude and longitude, there are many methods of data modeling expression to supplement geographic information. Among them, the earth subdivision grid has the characteristics of multi-scale and flexible expression, and has been widely used in many geographic data modeling application scenarios. The earth subdivision grid is a way of simulating the earth sphere by continuously subdividing and fitting the earth sphere with a grid. According to the different generation methods, the geospatial grid division model can be divided into: division based on latitude and longitude and division of physical elements [9–11]. Since latitude and longitude is currently the most commonly used method for describing geographic data coordinates, the following will mainly introduce the division method based on latitude and longitude.

The division based on latitude and longitude has two forms of equal division and equiangular division according to the different ways of equal division, both of which are based on latitude and longitude. The equal area method is to consider the area of the grid unit and divide the earth space into equal areas. The division method is more complicated. Literature [12] proposes a projection method to project the earth onto a plane and then back to a spherical surface to obtain a grid of latitude and longitude divided by equal areas. The equiangular method means that the latitude and longitude of the unit grid differ by integer multiples, and the different levels are recursively divided. For three-dimensional video space, the grid structure can provide a feasible and convenient method for modeling and expression. The earth division grid based on latitude and longitude is well integrated with the existing theoretical systems and is easy to expand the model. The stereo data model can express the video space at multiple scales and fully reflect the geographic attributes of the video space. On the basis of three-dimensional grid coding, based on the needs of video applications, the extended grid model expression can fully meet the needs of video space modeling.

2 Proposed Method

2.1 Latitude and Longitude Location Method

In this paper, we propose a forest fire location method based on computer vision method and digital elevation model. The key idea is to calculate the position of the fire point from the image coordinate system by computer vision algorithm, and then transform it to the camera coordinate system and the world coordinate system by coordinate transformation. After the fire point is detected from the frame, the sight from monitoring pan-tilt-zoom camera to the fire point is generated firstly. After the introduction of digital elevation model, we can obtain the surface height information within the monitoring range. Then, we calculate the corresponding intersection of the line of sight on the elevation model. Finally, we can get the 3D spatial position code from the longitude and latitude information of the intersection. The overall flow chart of proposed method is shown in Fig. 1.

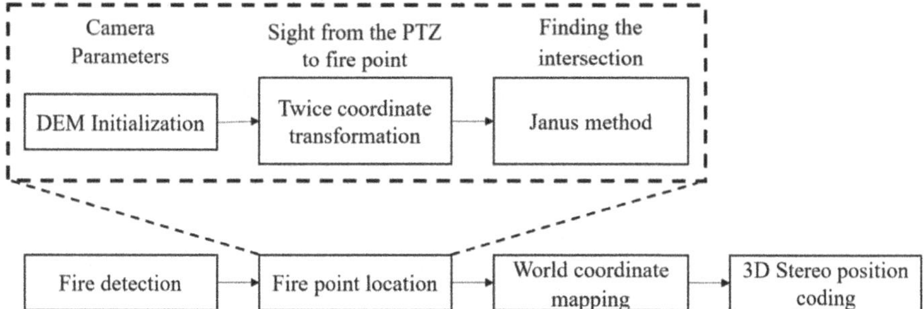

Fig. 1. Schematic flow diagram of the 3D stereo fire position coding from video frames.

As can be seen from Fig. 1, the first step of forest fire location is to detect the early forest fire from continuous frames. In this stage, we use deep learning algorithm to recognize the sequence image and locate the fire source point. Usually, the target detection algorithm will detect a rough target box. We adopt the method in [13] to detect the abnormal smoke target and accurately locate the fire pixel. In Fig. 2, the green box marks the smoke area of the forest fire, and the red dot marks the source area of the fire.

Fig. 2. Forest fire detection and fire smoke source pixel prediction. (Color figure online)

Images are composed of pixels, and pixel coordinates are the position of pixels in the image. To determine the coordinates of the pixels, we must first determine the image coordinate system. Common coordinate systems include image coordinate system, camera coordinate system, world coordinate system, etc.

In order to further locate the fire point in the world coordinates, we need to carry out coordinate transformation for fire source pixel. As shown in the Fig. 3, the image coordinate system takes the image center as the origin, where the pixels $M\ (x, y)$ represent the coordinates of point M in the image coordinate system, and W and H represent the width and height of the image. Camera model is an important part of visual positioning model, which is based on camera coordinate system, whose origin is located in the center of light of camera imaging lens. Camera coordinate system origin O_c is defined as the center of light of the camera lens, X_c and Y_c axis are parallel to the x- and y-axis of the image coordinate axis respectively, oO_c is the optical axis of the camera. The world coordinate system can be converted to the camera coordinate system by rigid body transformation. As shown in the figure, after the fire pixels are located by the fire source estimation algorithm, the world coordinates can be located in the following way.

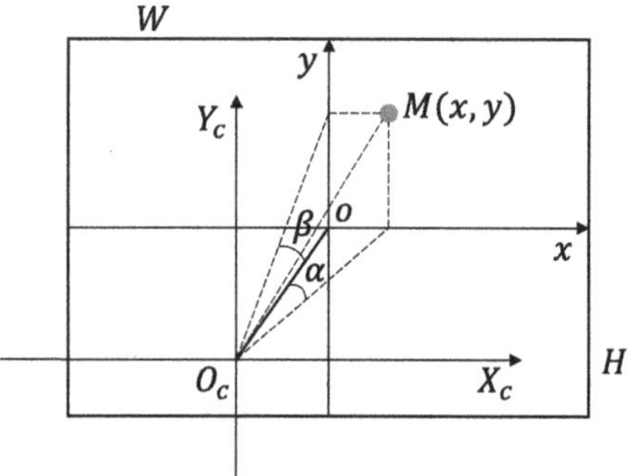

Fig. 3. Schematic diagram for the camera coordinate system.

In this paper, the digital terrain data is based on digital elevation model (DEM), which is a kind of solid terrain model that uses a group of ordered numerical array to represent the ground elevation. It is the digital simulation of the ground terrain (digital expression of the terrain surface shape) through the limited terrain elevation data. Usually in a certain area, dense terrain model points (X, Y, Z) are used to express the ground shape, which is widely used in terrain analysis and becomes an important part of spatial data infrastructure. The digital elevation model reflects the terrain changes in the monitoring area.

This study takes the map data and attribute data of Laoshan area in Nanjing as an example. The map data includes administrative division map and topographic map, and the attribute data includes forest farm name, forest class number and small class number. Figure 4 shows the DEM data visualization of Laoshan area in Nanjing. The red region in the picture indicates the place with higher altitude, and the green region indicates the place with lower altitude.

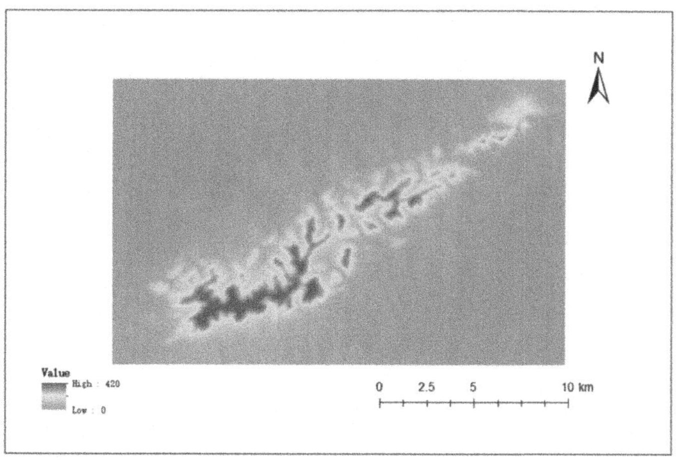

Fig. 4. Visualization of digital elevation model in Laoshan area of Nanjin. (Color figure online)

It is a challenging task to accurately locate the fire point in the world coordinate system from the pixel coordinate system. Not only we need to determine the direction of the fire, but also need to determine the distance from the fire to the camera. Fortunately, we can use the height, direction and angle information of PTZ camera, combined with DEM data to achieve this goal.

Janus method is a commonly used visibility analysis algorithm of grid digital elevation model. Its basic idea is to divide the line of sight into $step = int(max\Delta/m)$ parts by using the maximum movement of the coordinates between the observation point and the target point量 $max\Delta$ and the resolution m of the digital elevation model, and calculate the elevation difference between the terrain elevation value of the dividing point and the corresponding line of sight point ΔL: if $\Delta L > 0$, then two-point intervisibility, and make the next judgment; Otherwise, there is no intervisibility between the two points. In the following content, we describe in detail how to locate the forest fire location.

Firstly, the DEM Data of the monitoring area is initialized, and the longitude and latitude coordinates $P(lng, lat)$ and altitude h_c of the camera are located. The pitch angle Ψ and yaw angle Θ of the camera at the current moment is obtained by the feedback information of the digital PTZ camera; Fig. 5 shows a top view of fire location equipment. In this study, the monitoring PTZ camera will be manually calibrated to ensure the horizontal installation, and the position information (longitude and latitude) of forest fire monitoring point is measured. The front-end image processing equipment has the authority to control the PTZ camera, and can obtain the camera angle at any time.

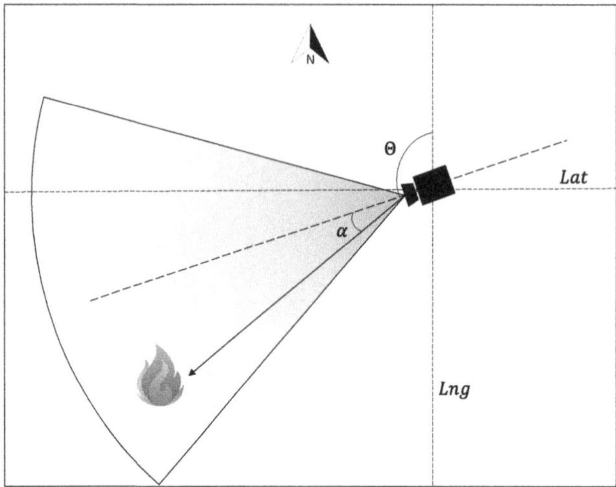

Fig. 5. Top view for the fire location process.

Secondly, computer vision algorithms can process video images in real time and detect forest fire targets in the images. We use the FFENet method [13] to accurately locate the fire pixels in the video. Based on the detection results of the forest fire recognition algorithm and the lens magnification and other parameters, the horizontal angle α and vertical angle β of the fire point relative to the camera's optical axis in the image coordinate system can be calculated. In Fig. 3, O_c is the origin of the camera coordinate system, o is the origin of the image coordinate system, and the image size is $W \times H$. For a surveillance camera with a horizontal field of view of Q_W and a vertical field of view of Q_{H}. If a fire is detected at $M(x, y)$ in the image, the two angles corresponding to the fire can be calculated by the following formula.

$$\begin{bmatrix} \alpha \\ \beta \end{bmatrix} = \begin{bmatrix} 2Q_W/W & 0 \\ 0 & 2Q_H/H \end{bmatrix} \begin{bmatrix} x \\ y \end{bmatrix} \tag{1}$$

Obtain the horizontal angle α and vertical angle β between the line of sight l from the camera to the fire point and the central axis of the camera from the image coordinate system. Because the pitch and yaw angles of the camera can be directly controlled by the digital gimbal, the pitch and yaw angles can be directly mapped to the angle offset of the digital gimbal. In this way, the direction of the fire point relative to the monitoring camera can be obtained.

Finally, we need to calculate the distance between the fire point and the monitoring camera. The line of sight is generated by increasing the offset on the existing yaw and pitch angle according to the geographic location and spatial height of the PTZ. Janus algorithm is used to calculate the intersection coordinates of line of sight l on the digital elevation model, that is, the position of fire point (the position of $\Delta L \to 0$ in Fig. 6).

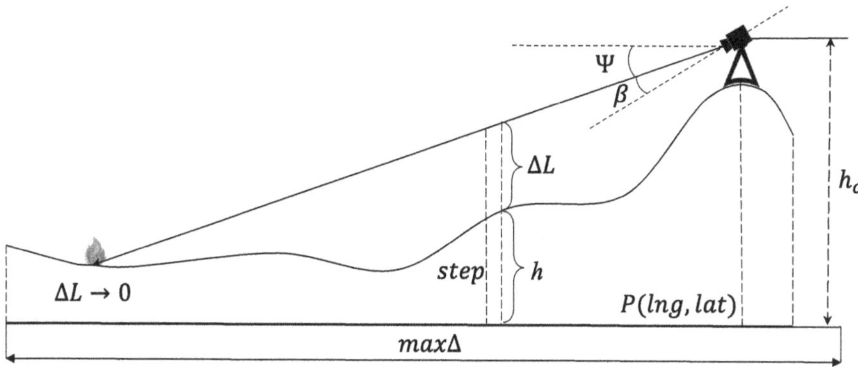

Fig. 6. Cross-sectional profile of the fire point location process.

2.2 Video Stereo Grid Construction Method

The algorithm needs some prior knowledge to complete the construction of the mapping relationship. It mainly needs to determine two parameters, one is the scale of the world coordinate system and the real distance, and the other is the real direction of the world coordinate system, which is defined as the angle between the X axis of the world coordinate system and the north direction. Scale relation needs to know the real distance of a line segment in the video scene, and direction information needs to know the orientation of the video scene in the real 3D world. Therefore, it is necessary to know the true longitude and latitude coordinates of at least two ground pixels in order to solve the two required parameters.

Firstly, the longitude and latitude coordinates of two pixels on the ground in three-dimensional space are assumed to be known. The world coordinate system is a uniform Cartesian three-dimensional coordinate system. The origin of the world coordinate system can be set as one of the two known points. Given the longitude and latitude coordinates of two points, the azimuth of one point relative to another can be calculated by the inverse solution method of geodetic theme And the real distance between two points. Azimuth is the angle from the north of a point to the target line. In this algorithm, it is the angle from the north of the origin of the world coordinate system to the line between two points.

Because the world coordinate system is not necessarily the right-handed system, we can infer whether the Y axis is 90° counterclockwise of the X axis through the camera imaging model. The judgment method is to project the unit world coordinates of the X and Y axes of the two points into the pixel coordinates $P_1 = (u_1, v_1)$, $P_2 = (u_2, v_2)$, and form the vector $\overrightarrow{P_0P_1}$ and $\overrightarrow{P_0P_2}$ with the origin pixel coordinates $P_0 = (u_0, v_0)$. Because the pixel coordinate system is not a right-handed system, the cross product value of the two vectors could be used to judge. If the cross product value is less than zero, the X axis is 90° counterclockwise of the Y axis, otherwise it is not.

At the same time, the angle between the two points and the x-axis in the world coordinate is calculated. Through the relationship between azimuth and XY axis, the angle degree between X axis and due north direction can be calculated. We set a counter clockwise direction from X to due north. When the Y axis is 90° clockwise of the X axis, $degree = \varphi - \theta$, When the y-axis is 90° counter clockwise to the x-axis, then $degree = \varphi + \theta$. Even if there is only one known longitude and latitude point, the North vector and a known distance can be marked on the video image. It can also calculate the world coordinates of the points on the image, so as to get the required parameters.

When the degree and scale parameters are obtained, the mapping relationship can be established. Because the angle between the x-axis of the world coordinate system and the true north direction and the scale relationship with the real world are known, the projection and the direction angle of the point on the plane of the world coordinate system can be calculated.

$$\begin{cases} \theta = \arccos\left(\frac{x}{\sqrt{x^2+y^2}}\right) \\ \varphi = degree + flag * \theta (flag = -1 \; if \; xy \; is \; right-handed \; system \; else \; 1) \\ d = \sqrt{x^2+y^2} * scale \\ H = z * scale \end{cases} \tag{2}$$

After the latitude and longitude coordinates of a point are obtained, the azimuth between the point and the origin of the world coordinate system can be calculated according to the latitude and longitude of this point. According to the two parameters of *degree* and *scale*, the X and Y coordinates of this point in the world coordinate system can be obtained. The Z coordinate can be obtained by dividing the height by *scale* directly.

$$\begin{cases} \theta = flag * (degree - \varphi)(flag = -1 \; if \; xy \; is \; right-handed \; system \; else \; 1) \\ x = cos\theta * d / scale \\ y = sin\theta * d / scale \\ z = H / scale \end{cases} \tag{3}$$

The above method establishes the mapping from longitude and latitude to the world coordinate system. The following will introduce how to transform the longitude, latitude and height coordinates into stereo grid code, so as to achieve the construction of three-dimensional grid space. Given that the latitude and longitude coordinates of a certain position are (Lng, Lat, H), the formulas for calculating the N-level stereo grid position code is are follows:

$$CodeLng_n = \begin{cases} \left\lfloor \frac{Lng+256}{2^{9-n}} \right\rfloor_2 0 \le n \le 9 \\ CodeLng_9\left(\frac{64}{2^{15-n}}\right) + \left\lfloor (Lng + 256 - CodeLng_9)\frac{60}{2^{15-n}} \right\rfloor_2 10 \le n \le 15 \\ CodeLng_{15}\left(\frac{64}{2^{21-n}}\right) + \left\lfloor (Lng + 256 - CodeLng_{15})\frac{60}{2^{21-n}} \right\rfloor_2 16 \le n \le 32 \end{cases} \tag{4}$$

$$CodeLat_n = \begin{cases} \left\lfloor \frac{Lat+256}{2^{9-n}} \right\rfloor_2 0 \le n \le 9 \\ CodeLat_9\left(\frac{64}{2^{15-n}}\right) + \left\lfloor (Lat + 256 - CodeLat_9)\frac{60}{2^{15-n}} \right\rfloor_2 10 \le n \le 15 \\ CodeLat_{15}\left(\frac{64}{2^{21-n}}\right) + \left\lfloor (Lat + 256 - CodeLat_{15})\frac{60}{2^{21-n}} \right\rfloor_2 16 \le n \le 32 \end{cases} \tag{5}$$

$$CodeH_n = \left\lfloor H \times \frac{2^n}{512 \times 11130} \right\rfloor_2 0 \leq n \leq 32 \tag{6}$$

Based on the above formulas, the latitude longitude and height can be converted into stereo space coding, so as to form the mapping path from pixel coordinates to stereo space coding, and construct the spatial geometric model of video stereo grid.

3 Conclusion

In this paper, we propose a video stereo location method for early forest fire. Specifically, the proposed approach can be summarized as two parts: a) computer vision based method is used to locate initial forest fire pixel in image coordinate system, and then transform it to the camera coordinate system and the world coordinate system by coordinate transformation; b) we establish the mapping from longitude, latitude and height coordinates into stereo grid code to achieve the construction of spatial geometric model of video stereo grid. The application in the project confirmed the effectiveness of our proposed method.

References

1. Li, X., Chen, Z., Wu, Q.M.J., Liu, C.: 3D parallel fully convolutional networks for real-time video wildfire smoke detection. IEEE Trans. Circuits Syst. Video Technol. **30**(1), 89–103 (2020). https://doi.org/10.1109/TCSVT.2018.2889193
2. Yuan, F., Zhang, L., Xia, X., Wan, B., Huang, Q., Li, X.: Deep smoke segmentation. Neurocomputing **357**, 248–260 (2019). https://doi.org/10.1016/j.neucom.2019.05.011
3. Lippman, A.: Movie-maps: an application of the optical videodisc to computer graphics. ACM SIGGRAPH Comput. Graph. **14**(3), 32–42 (1980). https://doi.org/10.1145/965105.807465
4. Goodchild, M.F.: Geographical information science. Int. J. Geogr. Inf. Syst. **6**(1), 31–45 (1997)
5. Navarrete, T., Blat, J.: VideoGIS: segmenting and indexing video based on geographic information (2011)
6. Kim, S.H., Arslan Ay, S., Zimmermann, R.: Design and implementation of geo-tagged video search framework. J. Vis. Commun. Image Represent. **21**(8), 773–786 (2010)
7. Lewis, P., Fotheringham, S., Winstanley, A.: Spatial video and GISUJ. Int. J. Geogr. Inf. Sci. **25**(5), 697–716 (2011)
8. Lu, Y., Shahabi, C., Kim, S.H.: An efficient index structure for large-scale geotagged video databases. In: The 22nd ACM SIGSPATIAL International Conference. ACM (2014)
9. Goodchild, M.F., Shiren, Y.: A hierarchical spatial data structure for global geographic information systems. In: CVGIP: Graphical Models and Image Processing, vol. 54, No. 1, pp. 31–44 (1992)
10. Goodchild, M.F.: Discrete global grids: retrospect and prospect. Geogr. Geo-Inf. Sci. **28**(1), 1–6 (2012)
11. Goodchild, M.F.: Geographical grid models for environmental monitoring and analysis across the globe (panel session) (1994)
12. Tobler, W., Chen, Z.: A quadtree for global information storage. Geogr. Anal. **18**(4), 360–371 (1986)
13. Cao, Y., et al.: EFFNet: enhanced feature foreground network for video smoke source prediction and detection. IEEE Trans. Circuits Syst. Video Technol. (2021)

Research on Training Pilots of Agriculture and Forestry Protection Drone by MR Technology

Zhenyu Xu(✉), YeTong Wu, and JunHong Zhong

Huizhou Engineering Vocational College, Huizhou, China
hitusa@126.com

Abstract. With the rapid development of China's agricultural modernization, horticultural plant pest control and agricultural and forestry protection need to realize spraying through ground remote control or navigation flight control. However, whether UAV sprays toxic and harmful drugs or powders are not suitable for students' practical teaching, resulting in students' difficulty in understanding, lack of practical operation experience and unsatisfactory teaching effect. In order to solve the problems of lack of training equipment, relative lack of curriculum resources and single teaching means in the teaching of UAV application technology specialty, this paper studies the application of mixed reality technology (MR) in the teaching of UAV application technology specialty, and takes the teaching of UAV agricultural and forestry protection as the carrier to solve the pain points in teaching, Improve the application of information-based teaching ability in majors, and explore new ways to improve the quality of talent training. Create a new teaching and training experience with unprecedented authenticity, interest, security and convenience, significantly improve the effect and reduce the teaching cost.

Keywords: Aided-Teaching MR · UAV agriculture forestry protection · Pilots training

1 Introduction

China is a large agricultural country. With the rapid development of social economy, China's agricultural construction technology is becoming more and more advanced. In recent years, a variety of polluting and toxic agricultural products continue to enter the market, which has seriously affected people's life safety and social stability and development. In order to meet the requirements of social development, green and environmental protection planting technology should be used for agricultural production to provide people with safe and assured crops.

At present, an important trend of agricultural development is ecological agriculture, which is to give consideration to environmental protection in agricultural production, do not damage the environment, and realize the high yield of agricultural production on this basis. In order to meet people's requirements for crop products and ensure the ecology,

© ICST Institute for Computer Sciences, Social Informatics and Telecommunications Engineering 2022
Published by Springer Nature Switzerland AG 2022. All Rights Reserved
S. Shi et al. (Eds.): 6GN 2021, LNICST 439, pp. 192–203, 2022.
https://doi.org/10.1007/978-3-031-04245-4_17

efficiency, safety, high quality and high yield of agricultural production, it is necessary to change the traditional agricultural production mode, use advanced scientific production technology and methods, use advanced management concepts to guide agricultural production and promote the development of agricultural production.

China's pesticide machinery research is relatively backward, the operation efficiency is low, the pesticide utilization rate is not high, there is a lack of efficient multi-functional pesticide machinery, the product quality of pesticide machinery is unstable, the overall performance is poor, the atomization quality is poor, and the drip phenomenon is serious. According to statistics, the highest effective utilization rate of pesticides in China is less than 30%, but the loss is as high as 60–70%. The efficiency of pesticides is low, which is harmful to the quality and safety of agricultural products, ecological environment and personal safety. Therefore, it is imperative to improve the spraying effect, operation quality and effective utilization rate of pesticides [1].

UAV is an unmanned aircraft operated by radio remote control equipment and self-contained program control device. As a new high-tech industry, it initially had a huge market demand in the military field. In recent years, with the development and progress of technology, the application of UAV has gradually extended from the military field to the civil field, and the application scope has been continuously widened. It is becoming more and more mature in the industries of consumption, plant protection, electric power, security, surveying and mapping and so on. UAV application is playing a more and more important role in national economy and social production and life [2].

In 2020, the civil UAV industry will continue to develop rapidly, with an output value of 60 billion yuan and an average annual growth rate of more than 40%. According to the prediction of the Ministry of human resources and social security, by 2025, considering the development law after the improvement of industrial maturity, the civil UAV industry will gradually mature from high-speed growth. According to the average annual growth rate of 25%, the output value of civil UAV will reach 180 billion yuan by 2025. Under the market demand of the UAV industry, the UAV driver profession came into being. The birth of a new profession made the UAV operation more professional, legal and standardized, and provided professional skills support for the rapid development of the industry [3].

As a new plant protection machine, agricultural and forestry protection UAV has the advantages of high operation efficiency, fast speed and less drift. In recent years, the development of plant protection UAVs has been strongly supported by the state and the government. Enterprises and scientific research institutes studying plant protection UAVs are gradually increasing. The developed plant protection UAVs are more and more accepted by the majority of farmers. At present, agricultural UAVs have occupied an important position in the field of aviation plant protection equipment.

Unmanned aerial vehicle (UAV) agricultural and forestry protection "– plant protection UAV spray operation as one of the main contents of the course is the working skill that must be mastered by UAV application technology students. However, the chemicals and powders sprayed by UAV are toxic and harmful to human body. Because students are not skilled in UAV operation, they are prone to poisoning accidents, so they are not suitable for students' practical training and teaching. It leads to students' difficulty in understanding, lack of practical operation experience and unsatisfactory teaching effect.

In order to enable students to experience the effect of real plant protection UAV spraying, intuitively understand the concept of droplet density and deposit volume, accurately evaluate the spray performance of UAV, and grasp the operational standard of plant protection UAV under the influence of ground effect. Huizhou engineering Career Academy has proposed a new digital system under the background of 3D simulation, multi-media and virtual reality technology. The main structure of the system is a teaching system based on mixed reality technology (MR), which involves the flight control, disassembly and maintenance, spraying diagnosis and other practical operations of plant protection UAV. Through the learning of mixed reality technology (MR) teaching system, students can accurately master the actual control technology of plant protection UAV, find and correct their errors in the flight control process of plant protection UAV, ensure the rationality of chemical spraying and the accuracy of control, and improve learning efficiency. Achieve the working ability that can be slowly obtained in five or six years of practice in a short time to meet the demand for technical talents in the plant protection UAV industry [4].

2 Mixed Reality Technology

Mixed reality technology is the latest technology of magic leap. It was first introduced by Intel at the 2016 idf16 developer conference in San Francisco. The virtual scene it creates can enter real life. For example, seeing a scene in the eye through a device can measure the scale and orientation of objects in real life, Its biggest feature is that the virtual world and the real world can interact [5].

At present, the main application fields of mixed reality technology include: medical treatment, military, aviation and games. However, the research and practice of mixed reality technology in the field of education are relatively few. Foreign educators Mullen, Baker and Brooks first proposed to develop virtual teaching products, software and environment based on mixed reality technology to assist teachers' teaching practice. Through the application of mixed reality technology, teachers can build education and teaching environments such as virtual classroom and virtual laboratory, develop new education and teaching methods such as virtual lesson preparation, virtual teaching and virtual examination, promote learner centered personalized learning and promote the transformation of teaching mode [6].

In foreign countries, mixed reality technology has some application attempts in the field of education. For example, pointmedia in Norway brought Microsoft's mixed reality technology hololens to the classroom to show cosmic galaxies and teach stem courses to help students understand the solar system. Canberra grammar school in Australia uses "3D periodic table application" to help students remember the boring chemical periodic table. It can not only learn the periodic table in the air, but also interact with a single element, combine multiple elements and see the effect after reaction. In addition, mixed reality technology is applied in biology, architecture, music and other disciplines.

At present, domestic higher vocational colleges have not carried out the teaching application research of mixed reality technology in UAV agricultural and forestry protection industry, but virtual reality technology has been applied in higher vocational colleges. With the maturity of virtual reality technology, people begin to realize the application value of Virtual Reality Laboratory in the field of education. In addition to assisting scientific research in Colleges and universities, it also has many advantages in experimental teaching, such as high utilization rate, easy maintenance and so on. In recent years, many domestic universities have established some virtual laboratories according to their own scientific research and teaching needs. There are four kinds of Virtual Reality Laboratory and desktop Augmented Reality Laboratory in China: Virtual Reality Laboratory and Virtual Reality Laboratory.

According to the research status at home and abroad, mixed reality technology has broad application prospects in the field of education and training, especially in the training of practical technical skills in vocational colleges, it can give full play to its advantages of high interactive, immersive and experiential learning [7].

3 Related Educational Theories

3.1 Experiential Learning

Experiential learning refers to recognizing knowledge or things through practice and experience, or enabling learners to fully participate in the learning process, so that learners can truly become the protagonist of the classroom. Traditional learning is external to students, but experiential learning, like any other experience in life, is internal and the income of personal participation in body, emotion and knowledge. Because of the whole-hearted participation, the learning efficiency, knowledge un-derstanding and knowledge memory durability are greatly improved. The efficiency of experiential learning method is 3–5 times that of traditional learning method. Therefore, this immersive mixed reality holographic teaching mode can effectively improve students' understanding of UAV agricultural and forestry protection related knowledge points and mastery of control skills [8]. Experiential learning.

Experiential learning refers to recognizing knowledge or things through practice and experience, or enabling learners to fully participate in the learning process, so that learners can truly become the protagonist of the classroom. Traditional learning is external to students, but experiential learning, like any other experience in life, is internal and the income of personal participation in body, emotion and knowledge. Because of the whole-hearted participation, the learning efficiency, knowledge understanding and knowledge memory durability are greatly improved. The efficiency of experiential learning method is 3–5 times that of traditional learning method. Therefore, this immersive mixed reality holographic teaching mode can effectively improve students' understanding of UAV agricultural and forestry protection related knowledge points and mastery of control skills [8].

3.2 Constructivist Theory

The The constructivist teaching model is summarized as follows: taking students as the center, teachers play the role of organizer, mentor and promoter in the whole teaching process, make use of learning environment elements such as situation, cooperation and conversation, give full play to students' initiative, enthusiasm and initiative, and finally achieve the purpose of enabling students to effectively realize the construction of current knowledge. Mixed reality technology has the characteristics of virtual reality combination, real-time interaction and three-dimensional registration, which can improve the efficiency of students' meaning construction of knowledge and skills. The holographic teaching of MR technology follows the learning theory of constructivism, and the learning activities are reflective and innovative, so as to realize the reflection on the work content, working environment and personal actions in the vocational field, so as to promote the innovation of vocational learning. Through information means, we should transform the complex work reality into learners' controllable learning situation, learning content and communication mode, and provide technical support for learners' knowledge construction in the process of action. MR technology holographic teaching also provides a new way for career learning and career development, changes the traditional way of career learning, systematically designs the learning tasks of cross career and multi learning places supported by information technology, and realizes the transformation from cognitivism to contextualism [9].

3.3 Holographic Technology Improves Learning Efficiency

Holography is complete information. With the continuous progress of holographic technology, its advantages are constantly highlighted and more widely used. Educational experts believe that the rational and effective integration of holography with education can change the way of intelligent learning, make learners change from learning from teachers to learning from resources, and make classroom teaching more vivid and active; At the same time, it also provides a more convenient and advanced equipment environment for smart classrooms and smart laboratories. Among them, mixed reality technology is the most effective technical means to build a holographic teaching system. By introducing real scene information into the virtual environment, an interactive feedback information loop is set up between the virtual world, the real world and users, so as to enhance the realism of user experience [10].

4 Construction of UAV Agricultural Forestry Protection Teaching Using MR Technology Project in Huizhou Engineering Vocatio-Nal College

Huizhou Engineering Vocational College is a municipal public higher vocational college approved to be established in 2017, formerly known as Huizhou agricultural school established in 1950 and Huizhou Industrial Science and technology school established in 1973. The college has nearly 60 years of school running history of secondary vocational education and has a rigorous and high-level teaching staff, including 99 associate professors and more than 100 doctors and masters. One won the title of national excellent educator, one won the title of national model teacher and famous teacher of "special support plan" in Guangdong Province, 10 won the title of chief teacher in Huizhou, 20 won the title of excellent teacher in Huizhou, and 10 won the title of rookie in Huizhou education. In recent years, the teachers of the college have undertaken and participated in more than 30 provincial and municipal scientific research topics, published more than

50 academic monographs, published more than 2000 papers in academic journals at home and abroad, including nearly 300 papers in core journals at home and abroad, and ranked among the top universities of the same kind in the province [11].

Huizhou Engineering Vocational College has good hardware facilities and advanced teaching and management facilities such as intelligent manufacturing, Haier Smart Home Internet of things training base, electronic integration, automatic control, industrial robot production training center, Ruijie network, new energy vehicle training base, cold chain logistics center and professional basic laboratories. During the 14th Five Year Plan period, the college focused on building and transforming the virtual reality experiment and training room into a productive and service-oriented base, integrating the functions of teaching, training, vocational skill appraisal and technology R & D.

The spraying agent of UAV is toxic and harmful to human body. Improper operation of student machine is easy to lead to poisoning accidents. It is not suitable for students' practical training and teaching, resulting in difficulties in students' understanding, lack of practical operation experience and unsatisfactory teaching effect. In order to solve the problems of insufficient training equipment, relative lack of curriculum resources and single teaching means in the current UAV agricultural and forestry protection teaching, Huizhou engineering vocational college studies the application of mixed reality technology (MR) in UAV professional teaching, and takes the teaching of UAV agricultural and forestry protection as the carrier to solve the pain points in teaching, Improve the application of information-based teaching ability in majors, and explore new ways to improve the quality of talent training.

At present, in order to solve the problem of insufficient teaching and training equipment, many domestic colleges and universities have built VR training rooms to make the equipment structure, principle and maintenance process into virtual threedimensional animation. Students can use VR technology to conduct virtual operation of setting actions. Users can watch virtual images without the support of real equipment by wearing intelligent glasses. However, VR is a pure virtual digital picture, and its learning resources are relatively scarce. There is a large gap between virtual operation and real operation, so it is difficult to achieve the ideal learning effect. MR is a combination of digital reality and virtual digital picture, which belongs to the combination of virtual and reality, that is, Mr can let users see the reality that can not be seen by naked eyes through a camera. The new MR technology will be put into richer carriers. Relevant research work considers helmets, mirrors and transparent equipment as new carriers [12].

VR technology makes it more difficult for users to see the real world than Mr technology; In terms of delay, the current mainstream VR equipment only needs to limit the delay to less than 20 ms to obtain acceptable effect, but MR needs to reduce the delay to less than 10ms at least; In terms of interaction with the real world, VR only needs to know the user's own state to interact with the virtual world, while Mr also needs to know all kinds of information of the surrounding real world in order to make the virtual digital object interact with the real world dynamically. At present, mixed reality (MR) has not formed a unified technical standard, and major technology giants are still exploring. Compared with the "low threshold" of VR hardware equipment, the cost of MR head display equipment is higher, which also hinders the large-scale application in schools.

In the professional teaching of UAV related to agricultural and forestry protection, mixed reality technology is more suitable for the practical operation of UAV equipment cognition, disassembly and maintenance, flight control and spraying, especially for the demonstration of pesticide and powder spraying control, and the study of performance evaluation such as droplet density and deposition of UAV. On the premise of ensuring the safety of students, Quickly master the specifications, steps and results of spraying operation of plant protection UAV, so as to obtain intuitive onsite feedback that cannot be felt in the traditional teaching environment and deepen understanding and memory. At present, there is little research on the application of MR technology to the field of modern agriculture, and the same is true in the teaching of UAV agricultural and forestry protection. The construction is very urgent.

Mixed reality technology (MR) is a further development of virtual reality technology. By introducing real scene information into the virtual environment, it sets up an interactive feedback information loop between the virtual world, the real world and users, so as to enhance the realism of user experience. The application of mixed reality technology in the cultivation of UAV agricultural and forestry protection talents is more unique and forward-looking. The scientific fields involved mainly include mixed reality technology (MR), holographic technology, UAV application technology, horticultural plant pest control technology, Computer Science (flash, 3D Max), pedagogy, etc. When the traditional teaching methods and means are difficult to meet the teaching needs, the combination of virtual and reality displayed in the form of mixed reality will improve students' interest in learning, make them more clearly observe the composition, structure, flight control and spraying of agricultural and forestry protection UAV equipment, and improve learning efficiency, Reform the teaching methods and means of UAV agricultural and forestry protection.

Huizhou Engineering Vocational College combines the training objectives of the course with MR technology, formulates teaching standards, constructs teaching resources and teaching platform, and creates a complete and fine three-dimensional model of agriculture and forestry growth and case characteristics in UAV agricultural and forestry protection; Divide knowledge points according to the requirements of knowledge objectives and ability objectives in the curriculum system; In the process of teaching implementation, Mr technology is used to display and demonstrate the knowledge points in a virtual environment, so that students can simply, intuitively and conveniently learn the agricultural basic knowledge of UAV plant protection, diseases and pests, safety, maintenance, flight operation, function and maintenance of mainstream plant protection UAVs, Be able to study the working process of UAV spraying in an all-round way in MR environment, and reflect and improve teaching.

5 Construction Significance

The introduction of mixed reality technology (MR) into the training of UAV agricultural and forestry protection courses has changed the traditional laboratory training mode, broken through the time and space constraints of the learning process, helped to assist the development of teaching activities and improve the training effect. The development of the system integrates "theory, demonstration, training and feedback" and integrates "teaching, learning and doing", which can effectively cultivate the comprehensive application ability of users. At the same time, using virtual training instead of physical training teaching can solve the problems of equipment cost and difficult observation, which is of great value and significance to reduce cost and improve efficiency [13].

5.1 Theoretical Significant

In the application research of UAV holographic teaching of agricultural and forestry protection course based on mixed reality technology, there is no relevant case in the research literature at home and abroad, which is novel. Subsequently, according to the growth process of crops, the high incidence period of diseases and pests and the picture characteristics of different diseases and pests, image samples can be collected respectively to make a virtual resource database. Through the storage and application of horticultural plant pest control and UAV agricultural and forestry protection knowledge and expert experience, simulate the thinking of experts through artificial intelligence methods, analyze faults, and obtain expert level diagnosis and maintenance level. Based on the history of UAV operation and analysis of UAV in agriculture and forestry protection industry, it provides the common solutions for UAV operation in agriculture and forestry protection industry. According to the current data information of UAV and the expert experience knowledge given by artificial intelligence, the management of agricultural remote visual diagnosis, control, early warning and treatment can be realized. So as to assist field technicians to make correct judgments on water, fertilizer, temperature, humidity, organic matter, diseases and pests in the plant growth stage, which can improve the efficiency and accuracy of UAV agricultural and forestry protection, and has certain theoretical research value in teaching application [14].

5.2 Practical Significant

First, through the research of this subject, the principles, strategies and implementation ways of applying mixed reality technology to UAV agricultural and forestry protection course are summarized. Under the framework of talent training program, the teaching mode, teaching methods and means are reformed and innovated, which will effectively stimulate students' learning interest and improve students' professional skills, It has strong practical significance for students' personal growth and social needs.

Second, break the restrictions of space and time, save cost and improve teaching effect. Due to the limitations of UAV training courses related to agricultural and forestry protection, such as equipment, site, funds and safety, many experiments cannot be carried out. The use of mixed reality technology can completely break the restrictions of time and space. Students can do all kinds of experiments without leaving home. They can gain the same experience as real experiments without risk. On the premise of ensuring the teaching effect, the cost is greatly saved.

5.3 Popularizing Significant

In The research results of this subject will play a good reference and reference role for other majors to apply mixed reality technology and reform teaching mode. The correct way to implement vocational education is that in the vocational work situation, learners master knowledge and skills by participating in the professional activities of the community of practice. Therefore, the informatization of vocational education must also enable learners to subjectively construct their work intention, knowledge and skills in a real or virtual work environment, and put forward informatization solutions for work tasks, so that learners can cultivate professional ethics and professional identity while acquiring and mastering knowledge of the work process. Learners need real typical work tasks and work processes, complex action space, a certain degree of freedom and action authority. Therefore, the informationization of vocational education must be based on the characteristics and laws of vocational education, and use information technology to provide learners with a medium of interaction and exchange learning in different working situations.

To sum up, this study aims at promoting the organic connection of UAV education chain, talent chain, industrial chain and innovation chain, takes improving talent training quality as the core, closely focuses on the theme of professional construction and curriculum reform, focuses on student competition activities, research project application, scientific research achievement transformation, social and technical services, makes systematic planning, overall promotion and key breakthroughs, Realize the purpose of "professional guidance, peer assistance, exchange and discussion and common development" of the studio. Strive to form a UAV application technology teaching and research teacher team integrating "learning, production, research, training and training" after about three years of cultivation and construction, and give full play to the demonstration, guidance and radiation driving role of the studio in talent training innovation, professional construction optimization, curriculum reform practice, scientific research project application, achievement transformation and promotion, social and technical services, etc., Enhance the adaptability of UAV professional construction to industrial development, and further enhance the contribution of UAV professional personnel training to the economic and social development of the whole province and even the Great Bay area of Zhuhai, Hong Kong and Macao.

6 The Following Key Issues

Huizhou Engineering Vocational College is steadily promoting information-based teaching, including virtual reality (VR), augmented reality (AR), mixed reality (MR) and other projects. At present, the construction of UAV application technology training room has been completed and MR equipment has been purchased. MR equipment includes binocular Mr holographic smart glasses, binocular ar smart glasses, holographic teacher teaching platform Mr live, holographic courseware creation platform Mr studio, holographic enterprise school student interaction platform Mr world, etc. The basic holographic projection equipment, network equipment and basic supporting equipment of the training room shall be jointly constructed by the school enterprise cooperation unit and the school.

With the implementation of the project, the college will establish a virtual simulation training room for UAV agricultural and forestry protection, develop UAV agricultural and forestry protection holographic resources and resource management platform, meet the practical training of students majoring in UAV application technology, improve teaching quality, improve students' interest in learning, and help the great leap forward development of the college. Huizhou Engineering Vocational College will solve the following key problems in the next step:

(1) Taking UAV spraying operation as the carrier, this paper explores the application of mixed reality in UAV agriculture, forestry, plant protection and prevention industry Taking the three-dimensional agricultural and forestry model resources with rich growth and case characteristics in the course of UAV agricultural and forestry protection as the spraying operation object of UAV, this paper explores the implementation ways and main contents of applying mixed reality technology to the relevant courses of UAV agricultural and forestry protection industry. This paper summarizes the organic integration strategies and evaluation methods of mixed reality technology and higher vocational courses, so as to provide reference for other majors to carry out the curriculum teaching mode reform based on mixed reality technology.

(2) Relying on the holographic teaching mode, realize the work process oriented learning
Work process orientation is realized in the application of mixed reality (MR) holographic teaching. Information technology and modern agricultural production mode put forward higher requirements for the key professional ability of agricultural technicians, which can only be obtained in the process of work. Mixed reality (MR) holographic teaching can promote this "vocational learning in the process of work". Take learners as the center, help learners understand learning objects, follow the principles of work process orientation and action orientation, and cultivate students' professional action ability, including professional ability, method ability, social ability and personal ability. Mixed reality (MR) holographic teaching can also promote learners' joint participation, help learners complete comprehensive work tasks in specific work areas, work environments and working conditions, and integrate learning into the work process.

(3) Relying on holographic teaching platform to improve teaching effect
A complete holographic teaching platform based on mixed reality technology is studied and developed, and applied to the teaching practice of UAV agricultural and forestry protection course. Under the holographic teaching mode, establish a complete and fine three-dimensional model of agricultural and forestry growth and case characteristics, and build a learning system from the agricultural basic knowledge, diseases and pests, safety and maintenance of UAV plant protection to the flight operation, function use and maintenance of mainstream plant protection UAVs, so as to realize the integration, dynamic and realistic expression of knowledge, The interaction of students' classroom participation has been increased to 100%, the average skill level has been improved by more than 80%, and the teaching effect has been significantly improved compared with the traditional model; According to the talent training goal of UAV application technology specialty, students can skillfully master the practical skills related to UAV agricultural and forestry protection course through mixed reality technology.

7 Conclusion

Based on the course of UAV agricultural and forestry protection, this paper studies and uses mixed reality technology to solve the pain points of traditional teaching mode, in order to improve the training quality of UAV application technology professionals. It is proposed to construct a new teaching mode of UAV agricultural and forestry protection by means of mixed reality technology, which better fills the gap in the application of agricultural and forestry mixed reality technology in domestic vocational colleges. It is expected to greatly improve the teaching effect and better cultivate students' practical operation skills. The core content of the teaching mode is: student-centered, teachers use the holographic teaching mode to immerse students in learning the professional course content, and focus on solving the problems existing in the current UAV agricultural and forestry protection course, such as the lack of training equipment, the teaching mode does not adapt to industrial development, the operation capacity is prone to poisoning and other safety accidents.

From the perspective of systematicness, professionalism and practicality, combined with relevant educational theories, this paper explores the application of mixed reality technology in UAV agricultural and forestry protection course, and explores the construction strategy, main content and implementation way of the application of mixed reality technology in a specific course. So as to effectively improve the training quality of students majoring in UAV application technology, and provide reference for other majors to carry out the curriculum teaching mode reform based on mixed reality technology.

Acknowledgment. The work was sponsored by the Rural Revitalization Strategy Foundation of Guangdong China (No. 2021sc01052002).

References

1. Bu, X.: Analysis of the status quo and industrial development of UAV agricultural plant protection. New Agriculture **14**, 85–86 (2021)
2. Zhang, Z.: Plant protection drones become the "new favorite" in the field. Xing'an Daily, (003) (20 July 2021)
3. Ying, J., Yang, Y., Lin, Z., Ying, Y., Zhou, N., Wang, H.: Several thoughts on the promotion of plant protection UAV flying defense technology in Xianju county. Bulletin of Agricultural Science and Technology **07**, 8–11 (2021)
4. Ma, C., Yuan, Y., Xu, Y., Tan, L., Yuan, Y.: CFD-based flow field numerical simulation and cooling characteristics analysis of agricultural plant protection drones. J. Shaanxi Univ. Sci. Technol. **39**(04), 136–141 +181 (2021)
5. Chen, S., et al.: Influence of lateral wind on droplet drift of plane fan nozzle of aerial plant protection UAV. J. South China Agric. Univ. **42**(04), 89–98 (2021)
6. Lu, X.: Dongying city, cultivate rural craftsmen and help rural revitalization. Shandong Human Resources and Social Security **07**, 48–49 (2021)
7. Zhang, J.: The unified defense rule starts to defend Xiaozhan rice. China Agric. Mater. **26**, 15 (2021)
8. Sun, J., Kang, Z.: "Flying prevention" of rice diseases and insect pests is imperative. Ningbo Daily (A06) (13 July 2021)

9. Yao, Y.: The role of agricultural plant protection drones on the development of modern agriculture. New Agric. **13**, 61–62 (2021)
10. Sun, Z., Lan, Y.: Development status and promotion of Heilongjiang plant protection drones. China Collective Economy **22**, 161–162 (2021)
11. Zhang, S.: Plant protection drones to prevent and control crop diseases and insect pests. Agricultural Development and Equipment **06**, 139–140 (2021)
12. Lei, J.: Analysis of the advantages and disadvantages of plant protection UAVs in practical applications. Agricultural Staff **12**, 81–82 (2021)
13. Wei, S.: Research on the application of plant protection drones in the control of rice diseases, pests and weeds. Nongjia Staff **12**, 85–86 (2021)
14. Song, B., Dong, Y.: Xiuzhou District promotes the large-scale application of plant protection drones. Quality and Supervision of Agricultural Machinery **06**, 10 (2021)

Resource Optimization of Power Line Communication Network Based on Monte Carlo Method

Peiru Chen[1], Zhixiong Chen[1(✉)], Leixin Zhi[1], and Lixia Zhang[2]

[1] School of Electrical and Electronic Engineering, North China Electric Power University, Baoding 071003, Hebei, China
zxchen@ncepu.edu.cn

[2] Information and Communication Branch of State Grid Shanxi Electric Power Company, Taiyuan 030021, Shanxi, China

Abstract. The power system communication network uses power lines as a medium, which is an important means to ensure the safe, stable, and economic operation of the power grid. In order to improve the throughput of the power line communication (PLC) network and realize the optimization of network resources, a method based on the machine learning algorithm, namely the Monte Carlo method, is proposed to optimize the media access control (MAC) layer protocol of the PLC. Firstly, based on the lognormal fading and impulse noise in the physical layer of the PLC channel, and the IEEE 1901 CSMA backoff mechanism in the MAC layer, the main factors leading to packet loss are analyzed. Secondly, the throughput calculation model based on the above packet loss factors is established. Finally, according to the idea of Monte Carlo algorithm, the MAC layer contention window selection algorithm is established based on the principle of maximum throughput. And compared with the original algorithm standard simulation results, the effectiveness of the method is verified. The results show that the contention window value obtained based on the proposed algorithm can achieve higher system throughput, and has certain practical reference value in the corresponding PLC network scenario.

Keywords: Power line communication · IEEE 1901 · Resource optimization · Monte Carlo

1 Introduction

The widespread use of power line communication (PLC) networks and distribution lines makes PLC become an excellent choice for industrial command and control and facility automation systems [1].

The problem of power line energy consumption has always been a hot research topic. Reference [2] proposed a household energy management system, which can actually record household energy consumption and optimize energy consumption. [3] proposed

© ICST Institute for Computer Sciences, Social Informatics and Telecommunications Engineering 2022
Published by Springer Nature Switzerland AG 2022. All Rights Reserved
S. Shi et al. (Eds.): 6GN 2021, LNICST 439, pp. 204–214, 2022.
https://doi.org/10.1007/978-3-031-04245-4_18

a program to design a PLC system. For parameter optimization, it is committed to finding the best compromise between maximizing bit rate, minimizing bit error rate, and minimizing signal power. [4] proposed an optimal content placement algorithm to reduce the backhaul energy consumption of each size and content.

For resource allocation and routing optimization, there are also many literatures using machine learning algorithms to conduct research. Literature [5] uses orthogonal frequency division multiple access technology to achieve cross-layer optimization of PLC systems, and it is better for multi-objective resource allocation. For other multi-user algorithms, [6] proposed an ant colony algorithm that can optimize PLC routing. Among them, the shortest path and the optimal path are found through route optimization. This is the optimization of network resources by optimizing routing. [7] proposed a customized opportunistic routing, and fully investigated its feasibility in PLC access network. This opportunistic routing can reduce the transmission delay of the packets without reducing the reliability of the transmission. [8] proposed a solution based on the greedy method, which can effectively improve the system performance. [9] described a framework, that is, the control and communication network of an interactive power electronic network that jointly optimizes network control. This framework includes two coupling blocks to ensure the best performance of the power network within its stability range and to optimize the flow of information in the communication network.

Self-organizing protocols and scheduling methods can also optimize the resources of the PLC network to a certain extent, [10] based on the problem of deploying the PLC network on the medium voltage network. In a multi-objective optimization method, the cost of enabling access points is minimized and the reliability of the PLC network path is maximized, and it also considers the network resilience and capacity constraints. [11] proposed a channel self-organization protocol in which two domains are allowed to cooperate to achieve dynamic sharing and the transmission capacity optimization. And each system will detect interference from its neighbors and organize its resources to maximize channel utilization. [12] proposed an application of a scheduling method to allocate the available channel set to PLC units better and more equitably. The advantage of this kind of scheduling is reflected in the improvement of algorithm convergence.

The above research does not involve the improvement of the PLC protocol. [13] proposed an adaptive MAC protocol, which improves the system throughput by adjusting the data transmission rate and contention window (CW) size according to the station transmission delay and channel conditions. However, it did not point out the CW value corresponding to the best throughput, and the specific analysis of the best CW value corresponding to the physical layer (PHY) parameters and different numbers of stations were not mentioned.

In this paper, we propose a power line MAC layer protocol optimization algorithm based on Monte Carlo method. The main contributions of this paper are as follows. Firstly, we analyze the main factors that cause packet loss based on the fading and noise of the power line PHY and the IEEE 1901 CSMA backoff mechanism of the MAC layer. Secondly, we establish a system throughput calculation model based on the packet loss factors. Finally, according to the Monte Carlo algorithm, the CW selection algorithm is established based on the principle of maximum throughput. Compared with the original algorithm standard, the effectiveness of the method is verified through the simulation results.

2 System Model

We consider the MAC layer and PHY in the single-hop power line. For the MAC layer, we consider the IEEE 1901 CSMA protocol for characterization, as for PHY, we consider lognormal fading and impulse noise in the channel.

2.1 IEEE 1901 MAC Layer

The implementation of the CSMA/CA backoff algorithm in the IEEE 1901 standard uses the following three counters: backoff procedure counter (BPC): BPC indicates the number of backoff stages; backoff counter (BC): BC indicates the random backoff time; deferral counter (DC): DC is used to evaluate the busyness of the current channel, moreover, it also makes the station react to the high load in the network without the collision.

The following describes the specific usage of these three counters through the working mechanism: After the station firstly undergoes initialization, BC is randomly selected in $\{0, \ldots, \mathrm{CW}_0 - 1\}$, where CW_0 is the value of the CW corresponding to the 0th backoff stage. DC_i and CW_i corresponding to the backoff stage i are shown in [14].

The station detects the channel every time it goes through a time slot. When the station detects that the channel is idle, BC is reduced by one, and when the channel is detected to be busy, BC and DC are reduced by one respectively. If the station detects that the channel is busy and DC is equal to 0 and the value of BC has not decreased to 0, the station enters the next backoff phase, BPC is increased by one (or re-enters the last backoff phase, if it is already in this phase), BC is revalued without trying to transmit, and DC is revalued at the same time. If BC of the station is reduced to 0, the station attempts to send the packet. If the transmission is successful, the station is initialized, and if the transmission fails, the station enters the next backoff stage.

2.2 IEEE 1901 PHY Layer

We assume a single-hop transmission model and consider log-normal fading and impulse noise in the channel. We assume that S is the source node and D is the destination node. Then the signal received at D can be expressed as:

$$y_{\mathrm{D}} = \sqrt{P_{\mathrm{S}}} H_{\mathrm{SD}} x_{\mathrm{S}} + \mathrm{n} \tag{1}$$

In the formula: P_{S} is the transmission power, and x_{S} is the transmission signal, which satisfies $\mathrm{E}\left[(x_{\mathrm{S}})^2\right] = 1$. H_{SD} represents the influence of log-normal fading in the channel when the signal experience the transmission. And $H_{\mathrm{SD}} = h_{\mathrm{SD}}/(d_{\mathrm{SD}})^{\alpha}$, where h_{SD} is the log-normal fading coefficient, and d_{SD} is the distance between the source node and the destination node,α is the path attenuation factor, n is the noise model modeled by

Bernoulli Gaussian model [15], which consists two parts, namely background noise and impulse noise. Its probability density function form can be expressed as:

$$f(n) = p_0 N(0, N_G) + p_1 N(0, N_G + N_I) \tag{2}$$

where p_0 represents the probability of background noise, and p_1 represents the probability that background noise and impulse noise are coexisted. N_G and N_I represent the power of background noise and impulse noise, respectively, and $N(0, N_G)$ and $N(0, N_G + N_I)$ represent the normal distribution, we set $k = N_G/N_I$.

2.3 Characterize Throughput Based on PHY-MAC Layer

Based on the MAC layer model, if two or more packets are sent at the same time, the packets will be collided, causing the failure of transmission. As for PHY, if the signal-to-noise ratio (SNR) is less than the threshold, the transmission will be interrupted, which will also cause the failure of transmission. These two transmission failure situations will affect the performance of the system, especially the factors of fading parameter in PHY and the value of CW in MAC layer.

The Packet Loss of Physical Layer. Based on the modeling in Sect. 2.2, the outage probability of the channel can be characterized as:

$$P_{\text{out}} = \text{P}_\text{r}\left[\frac{P_S h_{SD}^2}{d_{SD}^{2\alpha} N_v} < b\right] = \int_0^b \sum_{v=0}^{1} \frac{p_v}{\sqrt{2\pi}\sigma_{N_v} x} \exp\left[-\frac{\left(\ln x - \mu_{N_v}\right)^2}{2\sigma_{N_v}^2}\right] dx \tag{3}$$

where b is the threshold, N_v is the noise power, μ_{N_v}, σ_{N_v} respectively represent the mean and variance of the variable $\ln h_{SD}$ under the corresponding noise environment. Let h_{SD} $LN(\mu, \sigma^2)$, according to the conversion properties of log-normal variables, then $[\sigma_{N_0}]^2 = [\sigma_{N_1}]^2 = 4\sigma^2$, $\mu_{N_0} = 2\mu + \ln\frac{P_S}{d_{SD}^{2\alpha} N_G}$, $\mu_{N_1} = 2\mu + \ln\frac{P_S}{d_{SD}^{2\alpha}(N_G + N_I)}$. In order to avoid the influence of channel fading on the average power of the signal, let $\text{E}\left[h_{SD}^2\right] = \exp\left(2\mu + 2\sigma^2\right) = 1$, that is $\mu = -\sigma^2$.

The Packet Loss of MAC Layer. Based on the collision probability model defined in [16]:

$$\text{p} = 1 - (1 - \tau)^{N-1} \tag{4}$$

It can be seen that when multiple stations send packet at the same time, it will cause packet loss, while considering PHY, the overall packet loss probability p can be characterized as [17]:

$$\text{p} = 1 - (1 - \tau)^{N-1}(1 - P_{\text{out}}) \tag{5}$$

The system throughput based on PHY-MAC. The system throughput S_{th} is characterized as:

$$\text{S}_{\text{th}} = \frac{\text{p}_\text{s} D}{\text{p}_\text{s} T_\text{s} + \text{p}_\text{c} T_\text{c} + \text{p}_\text{e} T_\text{e} + \text{p}_\text{o} T_\text{o}} \tag{6}$$

where p_s, p_c, p_o, and p_e respectively represent the probability that the packet is successfully sent, the transmission fails due to collision, the transmission fails due to interruption, and the channel is sensed to be idle. The corresponding multiplication is the corresponding time consumed.D represents packet transmission duration. The four parts of the denominator are all reflected in the Monte Carlo simulation in the next section.

3 Realize System Performance Optimization Based on Monte Carlo Algorithm

Based on the Monte Carlo method, the CW value corresponding to the optimal throughput can be obtained, which can provide a certain reference value for the selection of the backoff window value under the condition of the certain PHY channel parameter and the certain number of stations.

The Monte Carlo method is a type of machine learning algorithm. In this Monte Carlo method, we set the size of the cycle period to 10^6. The meaning of this value is the number of successfully transmitted packets. In each round of the loop, we let a certain number of stations experience the backoff of CSMA, and we set the initial value of the minimum backoff window to 4, and each station performs the independent backoff process. In this process, if the backoff CW of X stations are reduced to 0, these stations will be sent. And if X is greater than one, these packets will be collided. If the transmission fails, the number of failures will be counted.

If X is equal to one, the station will be transmitted in the channel, but due to the possible poor channel conditions, the transmitted packet is affected by lognormal fading and noise. For $X = 1$ in each cycle, we generate a random number that obeys lognormal fading under the certain variance and generate the noise concerning Bernoulli-Gaussian process. According to these two parameters and the transmission power, the SNR expression is constructed, and it will be compared with the threshold, if the SNR is lower than the threshold, the channel will be interrupted, and the packet transmission fails, otherwise, the packet will be transmitted successfully. And the *Success* and *Fail* will be counted according to the success or failure of the transmission.

After 10^6 packets are successfully transmitted, the throughput of the system is calculated and the CW value is recorded, then the value of the CW is doubled, the process on the right side of the diagram is repeated again. If the throughput corresponding to CW value is lower than the previous value, the experiment is terminated, and the corresponding CW value and the throughput are recorded. The basis for this is that with the increase of the CW value, the throughput can only have the two trends: 1. Keep decreasing (when the number of stations is small); 2. First increase and then decrease (the number of stations is slightly larger).

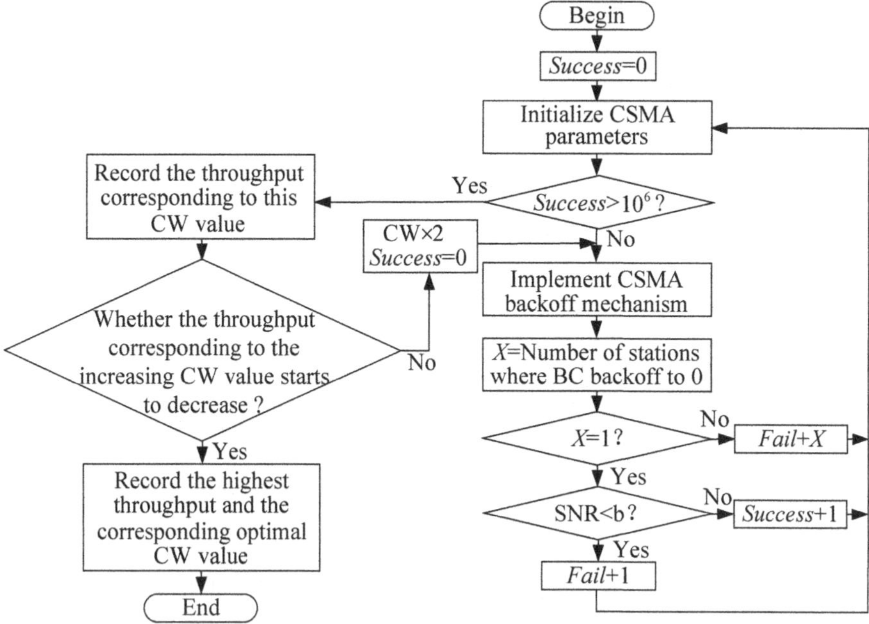

Fig. 1. Flow chart of finding the optimal CW based on Monte Carlo algorithm

Based on this experiment, the CW value corresponding to the highest throughput under the certain number of stations can be obtained, because for the certain number of sending stations, a lower or higher CW value may cause performance degradation, that is, there is always exist the most suitable CW value. The specific Monte Carlo algorithm flow chart is shown in Fig. 1. Based on the theoretical framework, the normalized throughput S_{th} is expressed as:

$$S_{th} = \frac{Success}{Success + Fail} \tag{7}$$

where *Success* represents the number of successfully transmitted packets, and *Fail* represents the number of the lost packets.

4 Simulation and Result Analysis

We use the Monte Carlo algorithm to conduct multiple experiments on the events in which packets are sent under the corresponding number of stations. When the number of successfully transmitted packets reaches to 10^6, the experiment stops. The number of successfully transmitted packets and the number of lost packets are used to calculate the normalized throughput corresponding the PHY channel environment and the MAC layer parameter configuration. And the initial CW value is set to 4, DC is set to [0 1 3 15]. Without loss of generality, the transmission power and distance are both normalized in the simulation. And if there is no special instructions, the parameter settings are shown in Table 1.

Table 1. Simulation parameters

Parameter	Time(us)
T_e	35.84
T_o	2602.64
T_c	2920.64
T_s	2542.64
Frame duration D	2050

Figure 2 shows the throughput performance curve under different initial CW values and N. It can be seen from the curve that as the number of stations N increases, the corresponding throughput first increases and then decreases. Therefore, for different N, there is an optimal window value corresponding to the maximum throughput. We select the number of stations to participate in the Monte Carlo simulation. In addition to collecting the results of the algorithm described in the Sect. 3, we also separately simulate the throughput under the adjacent CW to verify the effectiveness of the algorithm. It can be seen from the graph that the Monte Carlo algorithm can indeed help to find the best window value and the corresponding maximum throughput, and as the window value increases (from 4 to 8), the more stations there are, the faster the throughput will increase. However, as the window value continues to increase, the throughput will decrease first when the number of stations is small, indicating that in order to ensure the better system performance, when the number of stations is larger, it is suitable to use the larger window value.

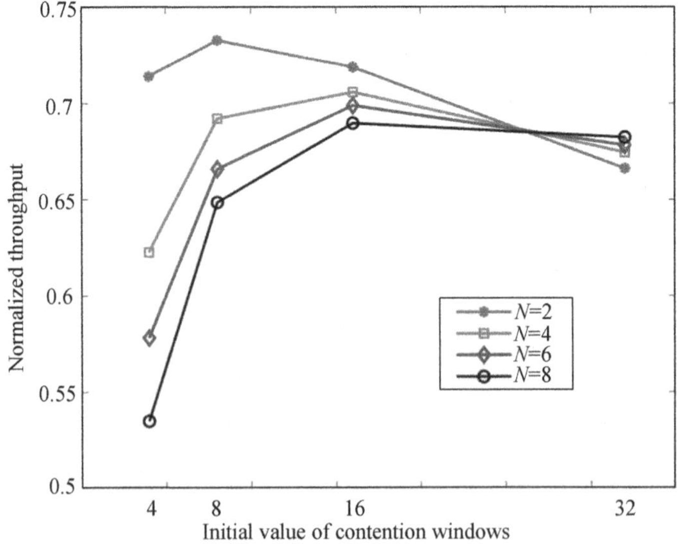

Fig. 2. Numerical results of throughput with different numbers of stations N and CW, $\sigma = 1$ dB, $p_1 = 0.1$, $k = 0.02$, $P_S = 1$ W, SNR = 10 dB

Figure 3 shows the initial value of the CW corresponding to the extreme point of throughput under the number of stations N from 1 to 15. It can be seen that as the number of stations N increases, the corresponding optimal CW increases. This is because, as N increases, the larger CW value can lead to the lower packet loss probability, so the corresponding throughput can be improved. Because in the algorithm, we increase CW by a multiple of two, the fewer the number of stations, the more obvious the change in the CW value of the corresponding best system performance. The result in the figure is not only the result of the number of stations, but also the result of the combined effect of the CSMA backoff mechanism and the PHY parameters.

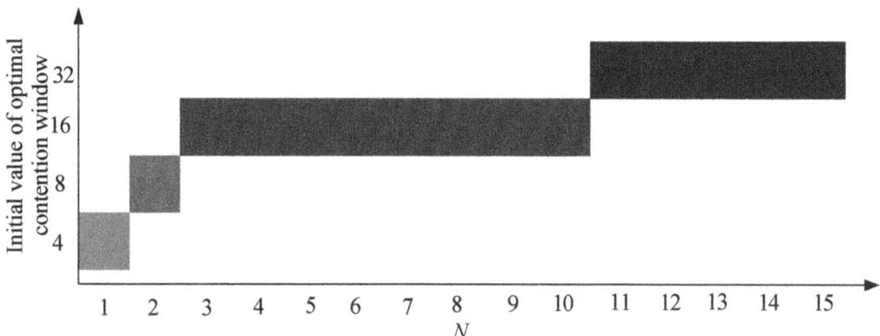

Fig. 3. The CW value corresponding to the maximum throughput under different number of stations, $\sigma = 1$ dB, $p_1 = 0.1$, $k = 0.02$, $P_S = 1$ W, SNR = 10 dB

Figure 4 shows the performance results based on the IEEE 1901 CSMA protocol standard and the curve comparison chart of the throughput corresponding to the optimal CW value under different fading coefficients obtained based on the Monte Carlo algorithm. As shown in the figure, the CW value found by the Monte Carlo algorithm is actually the optimal solution, and its performance is better than that of the calculation in the IEEE 1901 standard. And the smaller the channel fading coefficient is, the more obvious this advantage is. This is because when the channel fading coefficient is smaller, the SNR is larger at this time, so the outage probability of system is smaller, resulting in a smaller system packet loss probability and the higher throughput. Therefore, if the channel fading become severe, the system performance will has the negative impact, but even so, the Monte Carlo algorithm is still better than the original standard performance. To a certain extent, this algorithm can not only improve the system performance, but also in the face of unpredictable and inevitable fading in the channel, the system performance will not be affected too much.

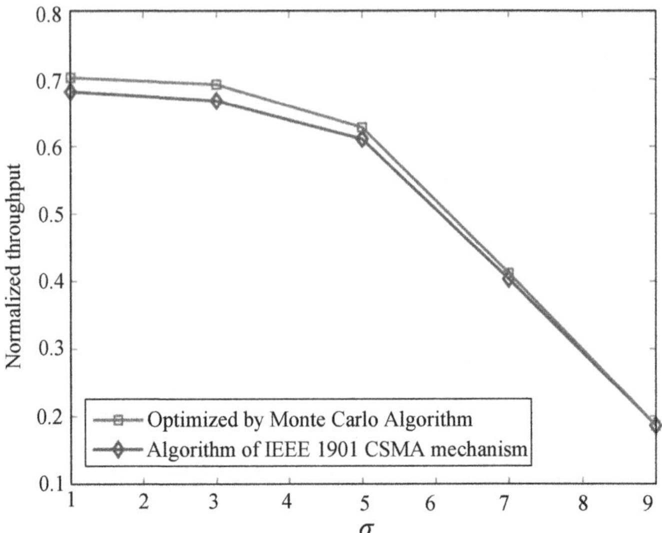

Fig. 4. Throughput of two algorithms under different channel fading coefficients, $N = 5, p_1 = 0.1$

Figure 5 shows the performance results based on the IEEE 1901 CSMA protocol standard and the throughput corresponding to the optimal CW value under different impulse noise occurrence probabilities based on the Monte Carlo algorithm. It can be seen that the Monte Carlo algorithm finds the performance of obtained CW value is obviously better than the performance corresponding to CW = [8 16 32 64] in the IEEE 1901 protocol standard. Regardless of the probability of impulse noise, the performance

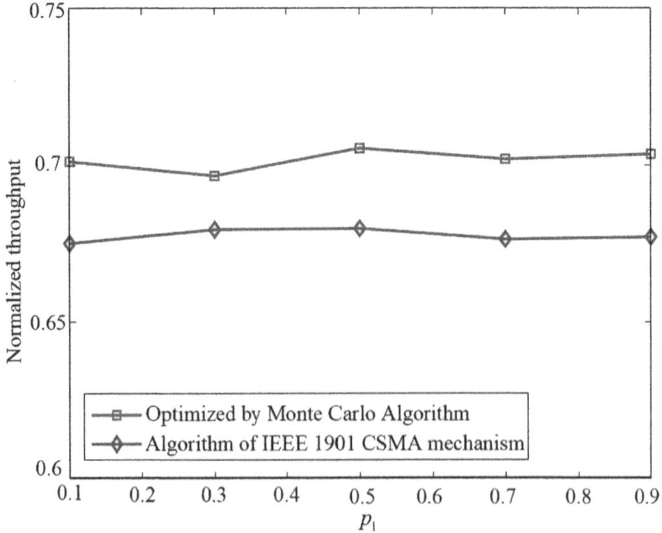

Fig. 5. Throughput of two algorithms under different impulse noise probabilities, $N = 5$, $\sigma = 1$ dB, $k = 0.02$, $P_S = 1$ W, SNR = 10 dB

of these two algorithms does not change significantly. This is because under a certain SNR, even if the probability of impulse noise is changed, the noise power is actually not affected so much, and the impact on SNR is not obvious. Therefore, compared with fading, noise has an not obvious impact on system performance.

5 Conclusion

This paper uses Monte Carlo algorithm to optimize the performance of the power line system. Considering the lognormal fading in the channel, impulse noise and the backoff mechanism in the MAC layer, the corresponding PHY-MAC throughput performance is analyzed. Furthermore, how to obtain the CW value under the optimal performance through the Monte Carlo algorithm is studied. The results show that based on the Monte Carlo optimization algorithm, the optimal CW value under the corresponding number of stations can be obtained, and for the low-fading environment, the degree of optimization is particularly obvious, thereby optimizing the network resources of the PLC.

Acknowledgements. This paper was funded by the Science and Technology Project of State Grid Shanxi Electric Power Company (contract number: SGSXXT00JFJS2100106).

References

1. Bumiller, G., Lampe, L., Hrasnica, H.: Power line communication networks for large-scale control and automation systems. IEEE Commun. Mag. **48**(4), 106–113 (2010)
2. Son, Y.S., et al.: Home energy management system based on power line communication. IEEE Trans. Consum. Electron. **56**(3), 1380–1386 (2010)
3. Carcangiu, S., Fanni, A., Montisci, A.: Optimization of a power line communication system to manage electric vehicle charging stations in a smart grid. Energies **12**(9), 1767 (2019)
4. Qian, Y., et al.: Cache-enabled power line communication networks: caching node selection and backhaul energy optimization. IEEE Trans. Green Commun. Netw. **4**(2), 606–615 (2020)
5. Xu, Z., Zhai, M., Lu, J.: Crosslayer optimization of user scheduling and resource allocation in power-line communication systems. IEEE Trans. Power Delivery **26**(3), 1449–1458 (2011)
6. Sun, W., et al.: On route design with ant colony optimization algorithm for power line communication network. In: 2020 IEEE International Conference on Advances in Electrical Engineering and Computer Applications (AEECA), pp. 799–802. IEEE (2020)
7. Yoon, S.G., et al.: Opportunistic routing for smart grid with power line communication access networks. IEEE Trans. Smart Grid **5**(1), 303–311 (2013)
8. Vo, T.N., et al.: Achievable throughput optimization in OFDM systems in the presence of interference and its application to power line networks. IEEE Trans. Commun. **62**(5), 1704–1715 (2014)
9. Mazumder, S.K., Acharya, K., Tahir, M.: Joint optimization of control performance and network resource utilization in homogeneous power networks. IEEE Trans. Industr. Electron. **56**(5), 1736–1745 (2009)
10. Canale, S., et al.: Optimal planning and routing in medium voltage powerline communications networks. IEEE Trans. Smart Grid **4**(2), 711–719 (2012)
11. Lehnert, R.: A channel self-organizing protocol supporting for coexistence of access and in-home PLC systems. In: ISPLC2010, pp. 291–296. IEEE (2010)

12. Haidine, A., Lehnert, R.: Improvement of bandwidth assignment in broadband PLC access networks by means of dispatching method. In: 2009 IEEE International Symposium on Power Line Communications and Its Applications, pp. 107–112. IEEE (2009)
13. Liu, K.H., et al.: Throughput improvement for power line communication by adaptive MAC protocol. In: 2012 IEEE International Power Engineering and Optimization Conference Melaka, Malaysia, pp. 135–140. IEEE (2012)
14. Vlachou, C., et al.: How CSMA/CA with deferral affects performance and dynamics in power-line communications. IEEE/ACM Trans. Netw. **25**(1), 250–263 (2016)
15. Dubey, A., Mallik, R.K., Schober, R.: Performance analysis of a multi-hop power line communication system over log-normal fading in presence of impulsive noise. IET Commun. **9**(1), 1–9 (2015)
16. Vlachou, C., et al.: Analysis and enhancement of CSMA/CA with deferral in power-line communications. IEEE J. Sel. Areas Commun. **34**(7), 1978–1991 (2016)
17. Xiang, Z., et al.: A cross-layer analysis for symbiotic network using CSMA/CN protocol. IEEE Internet Things J. **8**(7), 5697–5709 (2020)

Design and Research of Forest Farm Fire Drone Monitoring System Based on Deep Learning

Shaoxiong Zheng[1,2], Weixing Wang[1,3(✉)], and Zeqian Liu[1]

[1] College of Electronic Engineering, South China Agricultural University, Guangzhou 510642, China
173403997@qq.com
[2] Guangdong Eco-engineering Polytechnic, Guangzhou 510520, China
[3] Guangdong Engineering Research Center for Monitoring Agricultural Information, Guangzhou 510642, China

Abstract. In this work, we present a forest fire monitoring system using drones and deep learning. The proposed technique aims to solve the problems of traditional forest fire monitoring techniques, such as blind spots, poor real-time performance, expensive operational costs, and large resource consumption. We use image processing techniques to determine if the frame re-turned by the drone contains fire. This process is accomplished in real time and the resultant information is used to decide if any rescue operation is needed. The method proposed in this work has simple operations, high operating efficiency, and low operating costs. In addition, the proposed technique provides digital ability to monitor the forest fires in real-time effectively. Thus, it can assist in avoiding disasters and greatly reduce labor costs and other costs for forest fire disaster prevention and suppression.

Keywords: Deep learning algorithm · Drone · Forest farm · Fire insurance

1 Introduction

With the rapid development of society, people have put forward new requirements for the ecological environment. Fire hazard, as one of the eight natural disasters, has the characteristics of fast spreading, difficult to control, and strong destructiveness. Therefore, after fire hazard, it often severely damages the ecological environment and threatens the safety of property and life.

At present, the existing forest fire monitoring methods include artificial patrol, observation tower and satellite remote sensing, etc., each of which has its own advantages and disadvantages. Artificial patrolling can go deep into the forest to check the blind areas that are difficult to observe. It has strong mobility and can selectively select key patrolling routes, but the efficiency is low, the field of view is narrow, and it is greatly affected by the topography and landform; The observation tower has a wide field of view and can observe a large area of forest with the help of telescopes and other equipment. However, in the densely wooded areas, there are blind areas of vision and poor mobility

© ICST Institute for Computer Sciences, Social Informatics and Telecommunications Engineering 2022
Published by Springer Nature Switzerland AG 2022. All Rights Reserved
S. Shi et al. (Eds.): 6GN 2021, LNICST 439, pp. 215–229, 2022.
https://doi.org/10.1007/978-3-031-04245-4_19

and the observation range depends on the position of the observation tower; Satellite remote sensing has the broadest detection area, can accurately locate, and conduct all-weather observations, but the cost is high and can only be identified when a large fire area is formed. As a product of the rapid development of science and technology, drone technology has the advantages of fast flying speed, easy control and strong real-time performance. Therefore, it play an important role in promoting and has been widely applied in forest fire prevention and detection, fire behavior and rescue monitoring of forest fire prevention.

The proposed deep learning-based forest fire monitoring system comprises a drone and a remote monitoring system terminal. The proposed forest fire disaster monitoring introduces the drone platform in the forest fire prevention system, which has the capability to provide early warnings on the basis of video fire detection technology [1]. The work flow of the forest fire monitoring system based on deep learning and drone technology consists of multiple steps. First, the drone is equipped with a high-definition camera and performs the flight operation according to the preset patrol route to ensure that it covers the entire area under observation in such a way that there are no blind spots [2]. And the drone's position is determined by GPS in real time [3]. Second, the drone transmits the collected video and image information to the ground remote monitoring software in real time [4]. Third, this monitoring system makes use of forest fire deep learning algorithm to analyze and determine whether there is a fire disaster. When a fire incident occurs, the system triggers the alarm [5], and the user observes the dynamic information of the forest fire on the monitored host computer interface in real time [6]. This information is dispatched to the relevant person to take fire preventive measures [7]. Figure 1 presents the flowchart of the proposed system.

2 Overall System Design

2.1 System Hardware Design

1) **UAV system design**

   The UAV forest fire monitoring system comprises a GPS module, an image acquisition and transmission module, a communication module, and a flight control module [8]. These UAV components accomplish various tasks, such as the UAV flight control, autonomous landing, GPS based positioning, image acquisition and transmission [9].

   In this work, we select CUIM600 drone for the implementation of forest fire monitoring system. This drone adopts a modular design similar to M100, which is convenient to use and easy to install. The CUIM600 drone is also equipped with an efficient power system, integrated with dustproof, autonomous cooling in addition to other functionalities. The drone has the capability to carry items up to 6.0 kg and flies for 30 min with no load attached. In addition, the drone has a maximum flight speed of 18 m/s (ignoring wind conditions). The professional-level A3 flight control system and the sine drive technology application for intelligent ESCs also assist significantly in improving the reliability of flight performance [10]. In order to suppress the impact of the drone flight on the image captured during the drone flight, the proposed system uses the DJI Zenz Z3 gimbal camera. This is a three-axis

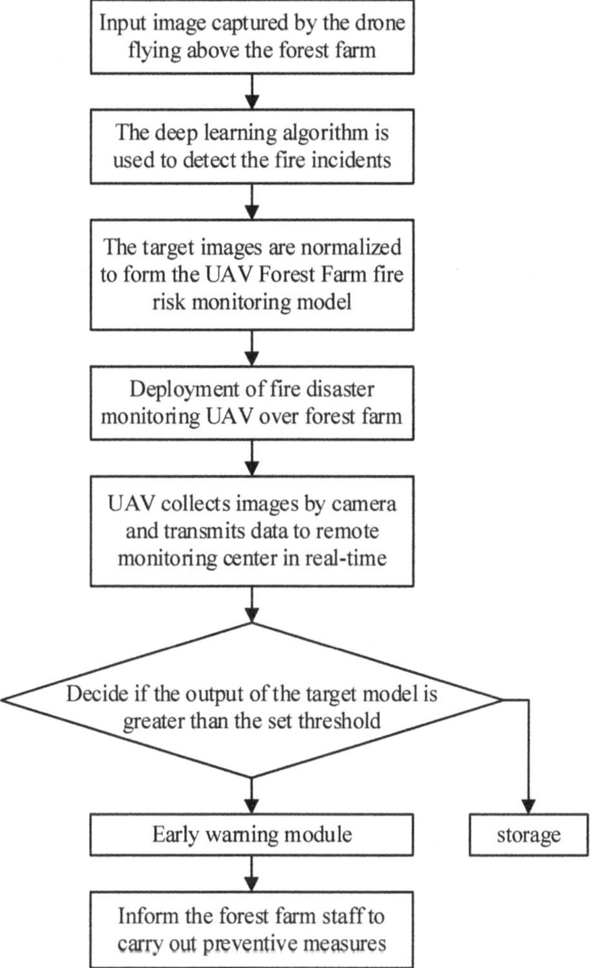

Fig. 1. The flowchart of the proposed deep learning-based forest fire monitoring system.

stabilizing gimbal camera. This camera has the ability to efficiently compensate for the jitters caused during the image acquisition process [11], when the drone moves forward, backward or when the flight altitude changes, thus, ensuring the good quality of the acquired images. Moreover, the cam-era also supports 3.5× optical zoom and 2× digital zoom, and also supports 4K Ultra HD video recording at 30 fps.

2) **Design of remote terminal monitoring system**
The remote monitoring system is used for receiving, processing and storing the data acquired by the drone. In addition, the ground center also provides the functionalities of deep learning-based fire detection and alarm triggering [12]. The staff have the ability to observe the acquired forest images in real-time on the ground monitoring terminal. When a fire incident occurs, the ground center provides real-time

dynamic information. The ground center's hardware equipment includes a PC and a communication module for receiving image information and other data, such as drone location, etc. [13].

3) **Hardware aspects of image acquisition**
The signal obtained from the video source is transmitted to the image acquisition card through the video interface. The signal first undergoes A/D conversion, and is then decoded by a digital decoder. The resultant is then compressed into a digital video, and is transmitted to the PC [14]. The frame grabber collects the image frames continuously from the input video, and transfers the data to the PC before acquiring the next image frame [15]. Therefore, the key to achieve real-time acquisition is highly dependent on the time taken to process each frame. If the time required to process a frame exceeds the interval between two adjacent frames, the image data is lost, i.e., the phenomenon of frame loss occurs. The video acquisition and compression operations of the image acquisition card are implemented together [16].

2.2 System Software Design

The software part of this system consists of unmanned aerial vehicle control system, data processing and communication system, and remote upper computer management system. This setup is presented in Fig. 2.

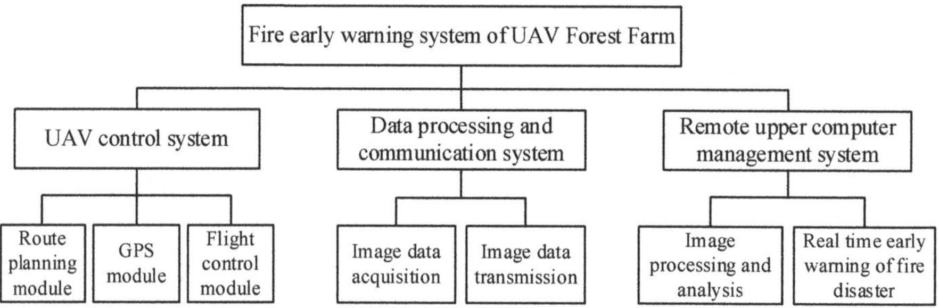

Fig. 2. System software composition design.

1) **UAV control system**
The drone control system is used to control the drone flight and flight information feedback from the drone, including information from route planning module, GPS module, and flight control module [17].

2) **Data processing and communication system**
The data processing and communication system is used to transmit the data and process the received forest images. In addition, this software is also responsible for managing the acquired data, including fault information, information regarding fire incidents and disasters, drone flight status information, and user login information. The data processing flowchart is presented in Fig. 3.

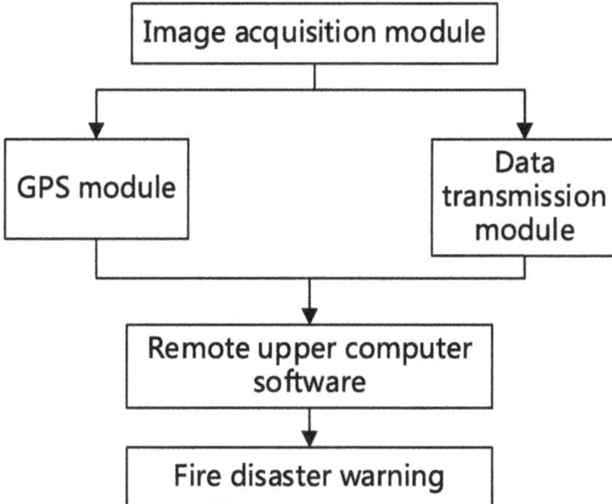

Fig. 3. The data processing flowchart of the process executed by data processing software

The communications in the proposed system enables the system to send and receive the data. This data includes various information acquired by different modules of forest fire monitoring system. This mainly includes the data interaction between the drone and the remote monitoring system. The parameters are transmitted back to the ground monitoring terminal in real time. The ground terminal realizes the control of the drone flight [18]. The entire process of data interaction between different modules is presented in Fig. 4.

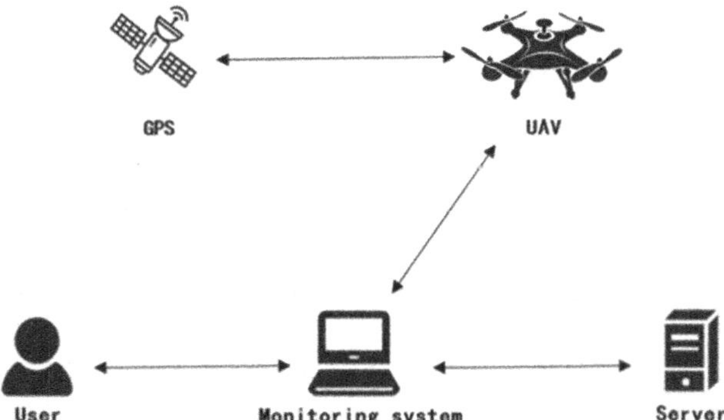

Fig. 4. The interaction between different modules of the proposed forest fire monitoring system

The communications of the drone are written using the serial port function. Every time serial communications are performed, the listening thread is opened. After monitoring is completed, the listening thread is closed. It is noticeable that if the listening thread is not closed, the next monitoring session is not executed successfully. The overall logic is to initialize the serial port for Init Port, set the open serial port and baud rate. After confirming that the serial port is opened, setup Packet Config initializes the data transmission format, frame header, frame tail, frame length, and storage byte position. When it is ensured that the listening thread has been opened, then data ready is set to TRUE. The data can only be read after confirmation. After reading the data, data ready is set to FALSE, otherwise the thread no longer works. In case that the serial port is no longer working, the port needs to be closed by using ClosePort, otherwise another serial port can-not be opened [19].

3. **Remote upper computer management system**
   The remote host computer monitoring management system has functions of image processing on one hand, and the fire danger disaster warning function of host computer software on the other. The function of image transmission and processing is to collect the aerial images of the forest captured using the PTZ camera mounted on the drone. Then, by using the image transmission system, it transmits the video in real time to the PC on the ground terminal of forest fire monitoring system. In addition, this system is also responsible to detect forest fire in the imagery data using the deep learning algorithm. The function of video capturing and transmission depends on the PTZ camera, image capturing card TC-4000 SD and image transmission system [20]. The image captured by the camera mounted on drone is transmitted to the mobile terminal of the drone remote control using image transmission system. The image is then transmitted to the image acquisition card through HDMI, and then transferred to the ground monitoring system via USB PC [21]. The image transmission and processing flow is presented in Fig. 5 and Fig. 6.

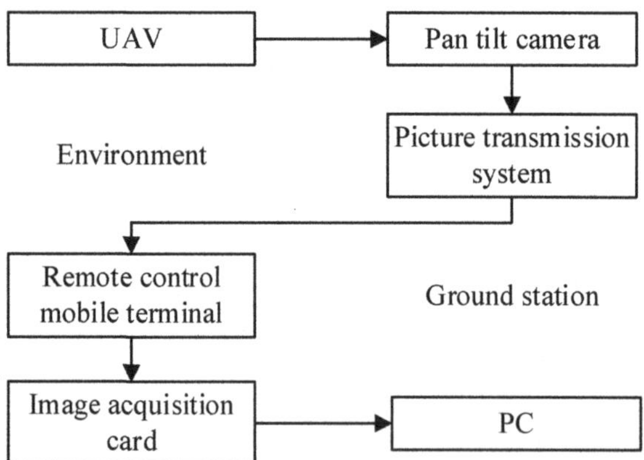

Fig. 5. The flowchart of data acquisition and transmission.

The proposed forest fire monitoring system uses DJI's Lightbridge2 image transmission system. The Lightbridge2 image transmission system supports a variety of interface outputs, such as USB, mini-HDMI and 3G-SDI. In addition, it also supports up to 1080 p/60 fps full HD output.

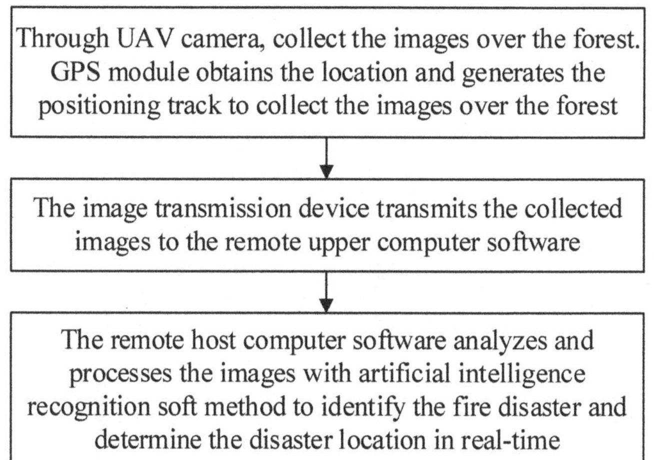

Fig. 6. The data acquisition and transmission flowchart.

The Lightbridge2 video transmission system uses wireless link dynamic adaptation technology to compensate the effects of distance, electromagnetic radiations in environment and picture quality. It automatically selects the best channel, and switches the transmission channels in case of channel disruptions. In addition, it also adjusts the video bandwidth, when necessary to ensure smooth video and effectively reduces the picture defects and interruptions. Using the deep learning algorithm, the image delay is further reduced to 50 ms when the maximum transmission distance is 5 km. The Lightbridge2 image transmission system combines high-speed processors and deep learning algorithms to make the wireless transmission of images more stable and reliable.

The modules of the remote upper computer management system include basic information module of the forest farm, image processing and early warning module, and manual data processing module. The basic information module introduces the list of state-owned forest farms in Guangdong province and the corresponding prefecture-level forestry bureau links. On this interface, it is convenient for forest staff to find the relevant forest farm information. According to the forestry bureau's portal website links, it is possible to find the local forestry bureau that belongs to a particular forest farm, and its keeps the staff abreast of the local forestry bureau's developments.

Similarly, it also has a map interface of various forest farms, which provides the geographical location of its own forest site, such as its own city and latitude and longitude, etc. This is helpful in the process of drone deployment for forest fire danger monitoring system.

On the basis of image processing module, we detect the fire incidents in the forest. In case of fire disaster detection, the system displays the geographic location and promptly alerts the forest farm staff. The signal is displayed in red for disaster warning and green for normal conditions. The fire warning interface of the monitoring system is shown in Fig. 7.

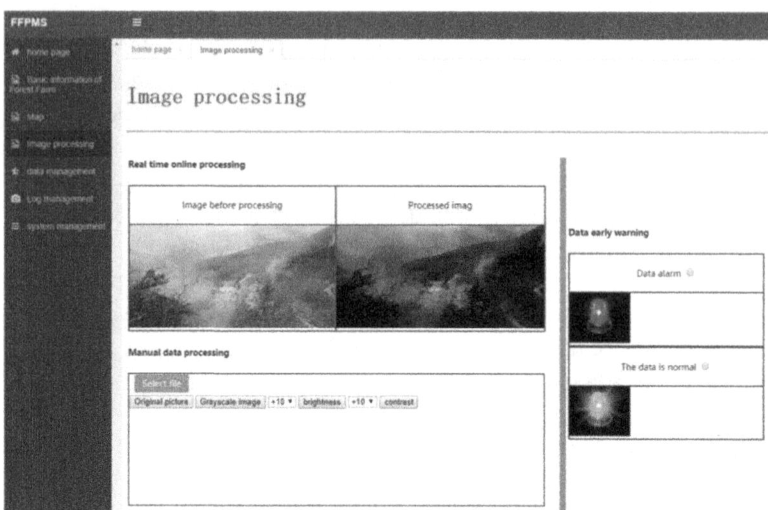

Fig. 7. The fire disaster warning interface for the proposed system.

When it is necessary to manually process the images, we perform image processing by using the manual processing interface. In addition, there is a picture management interface that is used to store pictures of forest fire prevention, and displays the pictures from the picture library according to the user's needs. It also provides the forest staff with a view of historical image data. This is presented in Fig. 8.

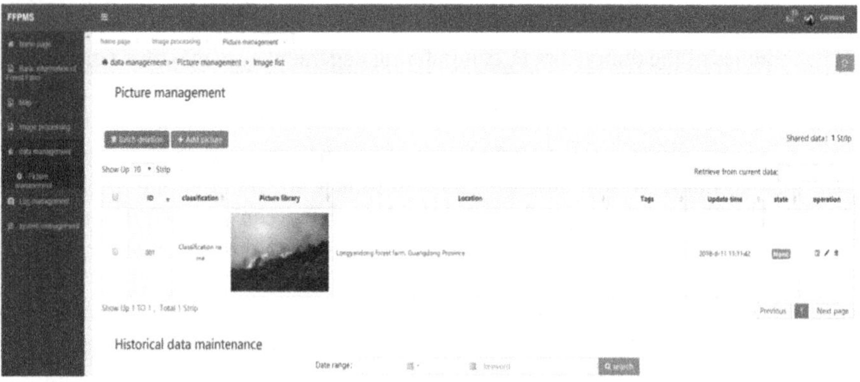

Fig. 8. The picture management interface of the proposed system.

In addition, in the log management interface, historical background data processing records are stored, and historical management operations are backed up.

3 Design of Fire Insurance Monitoring Algorithm

The design of the forest fire monitoring algorithm uses digital pattern processing and digital image processing techniques, such as image segmentation, feature extraction, image classification and recognition, etc. to accomplish the digital, automated, unmanned real-time monitoring and early warning [22].

The workflow of the forest fire monitoring algorithm is discussed below.

1) UAV equipped with visible high-definition camera is used to capture images which are transmitted to the PC on the ground monitoring system terminal via image acquisition card.
2) The ground monitoring system terminal receives the images transmitted by the drone and reads the video frame.

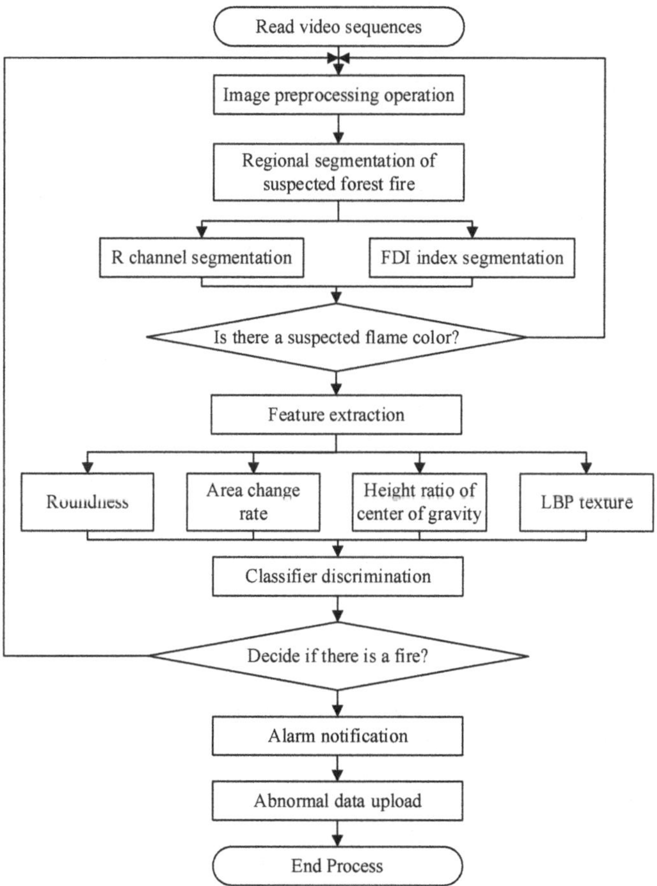

Fig. 9. The algorithm flowchart for the proposed forest fire monitoring system.

3) The acquired image may be corrupted due to interference such as noise. This interference is not conducive to forest fire monitoring and identification at later stages. Therefore, we perform image preprocessing.
4) Use the flame segmentation method based on the combination of FDI index and R channel to extract the suspected flame area.
5) Extract the dynamic and static features of the suspected forest fire color area, including circularity features, area change rate, gravity center height ratio features, and LBP texture features.
6) The extracted feature vector is subject to the trained classifier for classification and recognition to determine if a fire incident has occurred.
7) In case of fire incident, trigger the alarm device to raise an alarm and notify the relevant personnel to prepare for firefighting, otherwise continue to perform cyclic monitoring.

Figure 9 presents a flowchart of forest fire monitoring algorithm design.

4 Simulation Results and Analysis

The UAV system uses STM32 development board, integrated embedded Hash memory and RAM for program and data storage. It adopts SDK secondary development to achieve custom control and function expansion. The proposed remote monitoring system is configured with six-core Intel Core (TM) i7-8700K CPU@3.7gGHz, 16 GB RAM, and Windows 10 operating system. The algorithm is developed using OpenCV library and C++.

4.1 System Hardware Function Test

The hardware function test of the forest fire and disaster monitoring system based on deep learning and drone technology is accomplished by repeated debugging of each hardware function and long-term running test of the entire system. The purpose is to test whether the drone system works normally and whether the entire system runs successfully for a long time, etc.

4.2 System Software Function Test

Deep learning-based software tests of drone forest fire disaster monitoring system include reliability and real-time testing of the proposed system. In addition, we perform testing on various functions, such as user login test, abnormal alarm test, historical abnormal traceability test, and equipment fault prompt function, etc.

The method used for testing reliability and real-time test of the forest fire disaster monitoring algorithm is to log multiple segments of video with flames and interference videos (such as the video of car lights or people, objects, etc. that have a high similarity index with flames). The algorithm performs detection and identification on these videos and analyzes whether the accuracy rate, false alarm rate, and execution time of statistical monitoring meets the monitoring requirements [23]. Similarly, the method for testing the user login function is to test the correct and incorrect user names and passwords multiple times to ensure that the system logs in normally. In order to ensure that alarm is triggered accordingly, we test if wrong fire detection leads to triggering the alarm. In order to ensure the historical data correctness, we test if the user can query the impact of historical abnormal events and related information through software. The method used for equipment fault prompt function test is to deliberately modify normal operations of the system's equipment and check whether the equipment fault prompt occurs.

4.3 System Communication Function Test

The test of the communications of the forest fire disaster monitoring system based on the drone is tested on the basis of data interaction between the devices at different distances. The functional test results are presented in Table 1.

Table 1. The communication function testing for the proposed forest fire monitoring system

Communication distance	200 m	800 m	1400 m	2000 m	2600 m
Communication between UAV and remote server	Normal	Normal	Normal	Normal	Normal
Communication between UAV and remote controller	Normal	Normal	Normal	Normal	Normal
Image transmission	Normal	Normal	Normal	Normal	Normal

4.4 Comparison of the Results of Algorithms

4.4.1 Data Processing Speed

We consider a video of length 4 min and 19 s. There are 29 images per second, a total of 7511 images. The size of each frame is 960×540. We calculate the time consumed by the algorithms to complete the relevant processes. The processing speed and delay rate of the corresponding algorithms are calculated and presented in Table 2.

When the algorithm directly processes the video, it lowers the processing speed. In order to achieve real-time data processing, video frame capturing method needs to reduce the number of frames in preprocessing. When the flight speed of UAV is constant, the change of the scene information recorded by the video is limited. When the video frame is set to 5 frames per second, the inter frame difference method and background subtraction method are used to speed up the process. The processing speed of division and deep learning algorithm meets the requirements of real-time data processing. The deep learning algorithm meets the requirements of processing speed and accuracy under similar conditions.

Table 2. The completion time, processing speed and delay rate of each algorithm processing the original data.

Processing method	Processing speed	Completion time	Delay rate
Original video	29 frames/s	4 min 19 s	0%
Deep Learning algorithm	5.83 frames/s	21 min 28 s	80%
Inter frame difference method	7.12 frames/s	17 min 35 s	75.45%
Background subtraction	6.84 frames/s	18 min 18 s	76.41%
Vibe algorithm	0.85 frames/s	2 h 27 min 17 s	97.1%

4.4.2 Accuracy of Data Processing

In this experiment, different algorithms are used to process drone imagery, and the results are compared with the deep learning algorithm. The results show that the modified algorithm has advantages over other algorithms. The results of different algorithms are presented in Fig. 10 and Table 3.

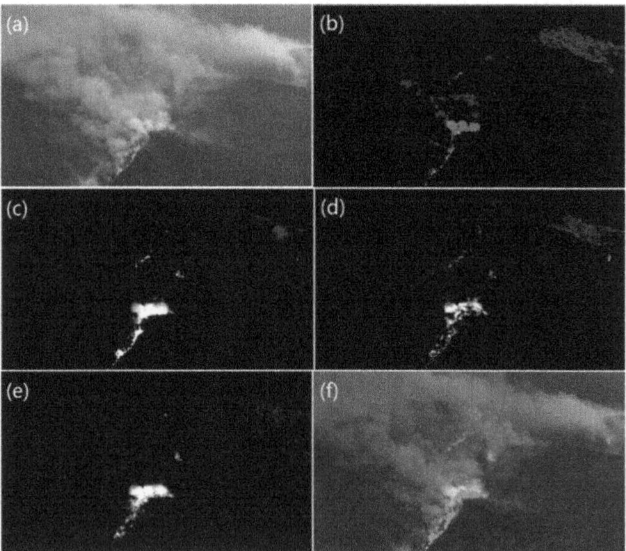

Fig. 10. The comparison among identification results of different pyrotechnic identification methods. (a) original picture; (b) deep learning algorithm; (c) inter-frame difference method; (d) background subtraction; (e) vibe algorithm; (f) manual statistics.

As presented in Fig. 10 and Table 3, the deep learning algorithm is compared with inter frame difference method, background subtraction method and Vibe algorithm. The deep learning algorithm has superior results. In Table 3, we pre-sent manual statistics which show that more accurate experimental results are obtained by manually marking the pyro-technic area.

Table 3. The comparison between identification results of different pyrotechnic identification methods.

	Deep learning algorithm	Inter frame difference method	Background subtraction	Vibe algorithm	Manual statistics
Pixel number of pyrotechnic areas	327	183	214	216	406
Number of similar pixels	2125	117	309	437	0
Miscalculation of pixel number	2386	6185	1051	3419	0
The pixel number of the result is determined	2909	6583	2336	4424	406
Relative accuracy	81%	45%	53%	53%	1
Judging accuracy	11%	3%	9%	5%	1

In this experiment, the result of the deep learning algorithm is closer to the result of manual statistics. This proves that the deep learning algorithm is better than other methods in terms of recognition accuracy. When combined with the experimental results of removing suspected fire areas, the algorithm processes the statistical results of relative decision ac-curacy and decision accuracy rate is further improved.

In addition, through the comparison of processing results of the general recognition algorithm and the deep learning algorithm, we observe inter frame difference. The method is not suitable for UAV video detection and is easily affected by the environment and motion conditions, which makes the recognition results poor. The recognition accuracy is almost 0. The comparison between the results of background subtraction and deep learning algorithm makes evident that the processing results of background subtraction method vary greatly when UAV is moving and hovering.

5 Conclusion

In this work, we propose a deep learning and drone technology-based forest fire monitoring system. Through detailed testing of the system, we ensure that the communication between various modules of the proposed system is flawless. The distance of the UAV image transmission is up to 5 km. The actual measurement range has a good transmission effect within 2 km. This transmission distance meets the requirements of forest inspection. In this experiment, different algorithms are used to process drone imagery, and the results are compared with the deep learning algorithm. The relative ac-curacy of deep learning algorithm is 81%, and the results show that the modified algorithm has advantages over other algorithms, which meets the reliability and real-time performance of forest farm fire disaster monitoring. The other functions of the system are tested and all of them function normally.

Acknowledgements. Thanks to Guangdong Academy of Forestry Sciences for providing image acquisition support for our UAV and we also thank Guangdong longyandong forest farm for providing site support for the research.

References

1. Belgiu, M., Drăguţ, L.: Random forest in remote sensing: a review of applications and future directions. ISPRS J. Photogramm. Remote. Sens. **114**, 24–31 (2016). https://doi.org/10.1016/j.isprsjprs.2016.01.011
2. Horning, N.: Remotely piloted aircraft system applications in conservation and ecology. Remote Sens. Ecol. Conserv. **4**, 5–6 (2018)
3. Chu, T., Guo, X., Takeda, K.: Remote sensing approach to detect post-fire vegetation regrowth in Siberian boreal larch forest. Ecol. Ind. **62**, 32–46 (2016)
4. Fernandez-Carrillo, A., McCaw, L., Tanase, M.A.: Estimating prescribed fire impacts and post-fire tree survival in eucalyptus forests of Western Australia with L-band SAR data. Remote Sens. Environ. **224**, 133–144 (2019). https://doi.org/10.1016/j.rse.2019.02.005
5. Collins, L., Griffioen, P., Newell, G., Mellor, A.: The utility of random forests for wildfire severity mapping. Remote Sens. Environ. **216**, 374–384 (2018)
6. Biasi, R., Brunori, E., Ferrara, C., Salvati, L.: Assessing impacts of climate change on phenology and quality traits of Vitis vinifera L.: the contribution of local knowledge. Plants **8**, 121 (2019)
7. Jiménez López, J., Mulero-Pázmány, M.: Drones for conservation in protected areas: present and future. Drones **3**, 10 (2019)
8. Bendig, J., et al.: Combining UAV-based plant height from crop surface models, visible, and near infrared vegetation indices for biomass monitoring in barley. Int. J. Appl. Earth Obs. Geoinf. **39**, 79–87 (2015). https://doi.org/10.1016/j.jag.2015.02.012
9. Fabra, F., Zamora, W., Masanet, J., Calafate, C.T., Cano, J.-C., Manzoni, P.: Automatic system supporting multicopter swarms with manual guidance. Comput. Electr. Eng. **74**, 413–428 (2019). https://doi.org/10.1016/j.compeleceng.2019.01.026
10. Wang, N., Su, S.-F., Han, M., Chen, W.-H.: Backpropagating constraints-based trajectory tracking control of a quadrotor with constrained actuator dynamics and complex unknowns. IEEE Trans. Syst. Man Cybern.: Syst. **49**, 1322–1337 (2018)
11. Muhammad, K., Ahmad, J., Baik, S.W.: Early fire detection using convolutional neural networks during surveillance for effective disaster management. Neurocomputing **288**, 30–42 (2018)
12. Ullah, A., Ahmad, J., Muhammad, K., Sajjad, M., Baik, S.W.: Action recognition in video sequences using deep bi-directional LSTM with CNN features. IEEE Access **6**, 1155–1166 (2017)
13. Amos, C., Petropoulos, G.P., Ferentinos, K.P.: Determining the use of Sentinel-2A MSI for wildfire burning and severity detection. Int. J. Remote Sens. **40**, 905–930 (2019)
14. Tran, B.N., Tanase, M.A., Bennett, L.T., Aponte, C.: Evaluation of spectral indices for assessing fire severity in Australian temperate forests. Remote Sens. **10**, 1680 (2018)
15. Vega Isuhuaylas, L.A., Hirata, Y., Ventura Santos, L.C., Serrudo Torobeo, N.: Natural forest mapping in the Andes (Peru): a comparison of the performance of machine-learning algorithms. Remote Sens. **10**, 782 (2018). https://doi.org/10.3390/rs10050782
16. Carvajal-Ramírez, F., Marques da Silva, J.R., Agüera-Vega, F., Martínez-Carricondo, P., Serrano, J., Moral, F.J.: Evaluation of fire severity indices based on pre-and post-fire multispectral imagery sensed from UAV. Remote Sens. **11**, 993 (2019)

17. Fernández-Guisuraga, J.M., Sanz-Ablanedo, E., Suárez-Seoane, S., Calvo, L.: Using unmanned aerial vehicles in postfire vegetation survey campaigns through large and heterogeneous areas: opportunities and challenges. Sensors **18**, 586 (2018)
18. Al-Sa'd, M.F., Al-Ali, A., Mohamed, A., Khattab, T., Erbad, A.: RF-based drone detection and identification using deep learning approaches: An initiative towards a large open source drone database. Future Gen. Comput. Syst. **100**, 86–97 (2019). https://doi.org/10.1016/j.future.2019.05.007.
19. Kellenberger, B., Marcos, D., Tuia, D.: Detecting mammals in UAV images: best practices to address a substantially imbalanced dataset with deep learning. Remote Sens. Environ. **216**, 139–153 (2018). https://doi.org/10.1016/j.rse.2018.06.028
20. Marcos, E., et al.: Evaluation of composite burn index and land surface temperature for assessing soil burn severity in Mediterranean fire-prone pine ecosystems. Forests **9**, 494 (2018). https://doi.org/10.3390/f9080494
21. McKenna, P., Erskine, P.D., Lechner, A.M., Phinn, S.: Measuring fire severity using UAV imagery in semi-arid central Queensland, Australia. Int. J. Remote Sens. **38**, 4244–4264 (2017)
22. Brunori, E., Maesano, M., Moresi, F.V., Matteucci, G., Biasi, R., Mugnozza, G.S.: The hidden land conservation benefits of olive-based (Olea europaea L.) landscapes: an agroforestry investigation in the southern Mediterranean (Calabria region, Italy). Land Degrad. Dev. **31**, 801–815 (2020). https://doi.org/10.1002/ldr.3484
23. Zharikova, M., Sherstjuk, V.: Forest firefighting monitoring system based on UAV team and remote sensing. In: Automated Systems in the Aviation and Aerospace Industries, pp. 220–241. IGI Global (2019)

Research on the Construction of Forestry Protection Drone Project-Take the Construction of Forest Fire Monitoring Project of Huizhou Engineering Vocational College as an Example

Zhenyu Xu(✉), Li Xinlu, and XiuLian Lin

Huizhou Engineering Vocational College, Huizhou, China
hitusa@126.com

Abstract. With the development of electronic communication technology, high technology has been continuously applied to agricultural and forestry plant protection monitoring. Including digital, infrared and laser camera monitoring technology, image recognition and processing technology, remote sensing mapping technology, UAV technology, wireless communication technology, etc. The research on agriculture, forestry protection drone in China started late. In addition to manual patrol, satellite remote sensing and other methods also play a major role. Taking the construction of UAV forest fire monitoring project of Huizhou Engineering Vocational College as an example, this paper puts forward the method of establishing open space cooperative network by combining wireless sensor network and UAV to monitor forest fire.

Keywords: FANET · Agricultural and forestry protection · Forest fire monitoring · WSN

1 Introduction

At about 2 p.m. on April 3, 2021, a mountain fire broke out on the south side of Jinbang tunnel in Huizhou City. After all efforts to put out the fire, the open fire was put out at 2 a.m. on the 4th, and there were no casualties. According to preliminary estimation, the fire area reached about 460 mu, which is the largest fire in Honghua Lake scenic spot since its establishment (Fig. 1).

Recently, there have been many mountain fires in Huizhou. Only in the first half of 2021, Huizhou forest public security organ established 27 forest fire related cases, including 24 criminal cases and 3 administrative cases; 20 cases were solved, including 17 criminal cases, 3 administrative cases and 18 criminal suspects (Fig. 2).

Forest is the basis for the sustained, rapid and healthy development of the whole national economy, and plays an irreplaceable role in national economic construction and sustainable development. As a frequent natural disaster, forest fire has caused serious losses and harm to ecosystem, forest resources and human life and property.

© ICST Institute for Computer Sciences, Social Informatics and Telecommunications Engineering 2022
Published by Springer Nature Switzerland AG 2022. All Rights Reserved
S. Shi et al. (Eds.): 6GN 2021, LNICST 439, pp. 230–244, 2022.
https://doi.org/10.1007/978-3-031-04245-4_20

Fig. 1. Traditional forest fire extinguishing scene

Fig. 2. Deep forest fire

Therefore, the importance of forest fire prevention is not mentioned but compared, which needs to be paid unremitting attention as a regular and important work. At present, although China's forest fire prevention work has made some progress, it is still at a low level on the whole. It is urgent to explore advanced fire monitoring and identification means and establish a scientific forest fire monitoring and fighting system [1, 2].

2 Forest Fire Prevention Monitoring Technology

Forest fire prevention technology is divided into fire prediction technology, fire monitoring technology and fire prevention communication technology. At present, there are several ways of forest fire monitoring technology used at home and abroad [3–5]:

(1) GPS and GIS technology: GPS technology has been applied in forest fire protection for the longest time and the earliest. It has unique advantages in clarifying the location and scope of fire and estimating disaster losses. It has greatly improved the efficiency of fire prevention and has therefore been recognized by the forestry department. The application of GPS technology first records the key points into GPS according to the characteristics of the walking route of disaster relief personnel in

the process (affected by fire, generally not straight line), and then GPS can quickly and accurately provide the most suitable route for rescue personnel according to its positioning function. At the same time, due to the possibility of re ignition of the fire, the GPS receiver quickly provides the fire location for the staff. Subsequently, due to the emergence of "3S" technology, the combination of GPS and GIS technology is more efficient and can predict the change and trend of fire on the display screen. It can also realize the function of automatic fire extinguishing by connecting with the fire extinguisher, which reflects its unique advantages. In foreign countries, in the early days, the Canadian bureau used the infrared rays emitted by satellites to detect the surface of the monitoring area. The data analysis was used as the basis for judgment. When the monitored infrared wavelength was up to 4.0 microns, the general temperature would be between 120 and 180 degrees Celsius, which indicated that there was a great possibility that a fire had occurred. Based on GIS and wireless communication technology The web browser monitoring system combined with inertial navigation system and thermal infrared sensor can establish an effective model for forest fire prediction, which can find the fire in time and even predict the spread direction.

(2) Remote sensing technology: remote sensing technology is committed to the embryonic stage of fire. Because this technology is very effective in predicting fire and can classify combustibles, it is of great significance to carry out forest fire protection. It is now known that there is a lack of information on the classification of combustibles in the forest all over the world, because the future development direction of this technology is committed to the division of combustibles in the forest, using different resolutions to draw combustibles in the forest in an all-round and multi-scale way, so as to provide more standardized standards for forestry information reform. In terms of disaster monitoring, China has specially launched radar and optical satellites to help the monitoring work. "Environment No. 1" is a monitoring system integrating multiple measurement methods. Its advantage is that it can monitor the region in a wide range and all-weather, and the abnormal conditions can be displayed on the remote sensing image at the first time. German researchers have developed the fire watch forest fire intelligent alarm system, which is the basis provided by digital camera technology and can observe the monitoring area from a long distance. Firstly, the smoke in forest fire is discriminated by specially written software, and then the forest fire can be located by using GIS technology and digital PTZ. Realize digital fire discrimination and positioning.

(3) Collaborative monitoring system of remote sensing technology and Internet of things technology: take "3S" technology as the support to solve the problems of independence and data sharing of monitoring methods. Take Internet of things technology as the framework, establish a two-in-one forest fire monitoring system by means of remote sensing data interpretation and sensor thermal infrared detection method, It provides a new way for the timeliness and accuracy of forest fire monitoring information. Some European and American countries led by the United States are relatively mature in satellite remote sensing technology, which can be used to monitor forest fire. At the beginning of the 21st century, ESA carried an AATSR (Advanced extended orbit scanning radiometer) on the satellite. The equipment can

accurately measure the surface temperature, and also provide guarantee for early detection and later positioning of forest fires.

(4) UAV application: UAV only has flight control mode and navigation and positioning system. It has a wide variety. Fixed wing and multi rotor UAVs are mainly used in forestry. In the 1980s, the D-4 fixed wing UAV of Northwest University of technology tried to explore geology and draw maps, creating the application of UAV from military to civilian. In 2013, Z5 unmanned helicopter participated in the navigation mission in Daxinganling forest area and achieved success, which is the first application in forestry. Russia has already successfully developed a set of television system, which is a complete closed-circuit television system composed of electronic observation equipment installed at a high place in the area (such as a lookout) and the display screen of the terminal. Through technical processing, the observer can clearly grasp the panoramic image between the device radius of 15 km on the terminal equipment, and can get whether there is any abnormality through technical support. At the end of the 20th century, in the United States, with the support of the government, relevant departments installed fire mapper (an Airborne Multispectral radiometer) on aircraft. This is a fire plotter, which can also pass through the smoke at an altitude of 1500 ft to detect the smoke produced by forest fire.

(5) WSN (Wireless Sensor Network) technology: in the United States, as a pioneer in introducing WSN technology into forest fire monitoring, a monitoring system called firebug was developed. TinyOS operating system combines the hardware with multiple sensor nodes and GPS locator to monitor the fire. The nodes communicate with the remote server through the base station. The forestry department can understand the realtime situation in the forest as long as it accesses the terminal equipment. This monitoring system has also been applied in the United States.

In fact, there are several monitoring methods adopted in China, including artificial ground Patrol: Forestry personnel continuously patrol in the forest area; Lookout Patrol: it is placed high in the monitoring area and can cover the forest observation within a large radius; Aviation Patrol: low altitude flight can cover a larger area, find dangerous situations in time, and make the changes of monitoring environment clearer. However, these are not the best forest fire prevention monitoring methods because of the problems of untimely discovery or high investment cost.

In general, the domestic research in this field still has great limitations, and it is only a preliminary exploration. For forest monitoring, we can continue to make in-depth exploration on the basis of the research of these excellent researchers.

3 Construction of UAV Forest Fire Monitoring Project of Huizhou Engineering Vocational College

Huizhou Engineering Vocational College is a modern, public vocational college with high standard and high starting point approved by the people's Government of Guangdong Province in 2017. It is located in Huizhou, the central city of Guangdong, Hong Kong, Macao and the Pearl River Delta. It is adjacent to Shenzhen, Hong Kong,

Guangzhou and Dongguan, Shanwei in the East and Heyuan and Shaoguan in the north. It has convenient transportation and prominent regional advantages. Its predecessor was Huizhou agricultural school established in 1950 and Huizhou Industrial Science and technology school established in 1973. The college has nearly 60 years of school running history of secondary vocational education and has a rigorous and high-level teaching staff, including 99 professors and associate professors and more than 100 doctoral and graduate students.

Huizhou Engineering Vocational College strongly supports the reform and development of information-based teaching. Based on the principle of "student-oriented, teacher model, integration and innovation", and the school orientation of cultivating compound technical and skilled talents integrating knowledge and practice, Huizhou Engineering Vocational College has created a "five in one" education mode of base, enrollment, teaching, scientific research and employment, and practiced the "three education" reform through in-depth cooperation between schools and enterprises, The college cooperates and shares high-quality resources, pays attention to cultivating students' professional ability and comprehensive quality, integrates the cultivation of professional ethics, professional spirit and innovation and entrepreneurship ability into the curriculum system, and forms a distinctive technical talent training system integrating industry and education and integrating knowledge and practice, which provides a good foundation and Implementation platform for the research of education and teaching reform in various fields.

Huizhou Engineering Vocational College has been serving the development of local economy and industry, studying UAV agriculture, forestry and plant protection technology and wireless ad hoc network technology, and applying them to the innovative forest fire early warning mode urgently needed in Huizhou, strengthening response measures and building a perfect forest fire early warning response system.

Wireless sensor networks (WSN) integrates sensor technology and wireless communication technology. It is a self-organizing and distributed wireless network. It is composed of a large number of wireless sensor nodes and base stations. It forms an intelligent network system through wireless self-organizing communication, which can monitor the environment of the sensor network, data fusion processing, target tracking and positioning. Typical wireless sensor networks include distributed sensor nodes, sink nodes or base stations, background task processing centers, etc. Sensor nodes are randomly deployed in the monitoring area to collect data from the target or integrate and forward data with other nodes. The sink node is responsible for summarizing the monitoring data in its responsible area, and its communication and data processing functions are better than those of the sensor monitoring node. The gateway or base station is responsible for monitoring external networks such as area aware data summary, communication protocol conversion, task release and connection server. Users can view the sensing node data of the monitoring area through tools such as PC or app and make corresponding processing.

WSN has become a research hotspot of information technology because of its convenient deployment, automatic data acquisition, low power consumption, low cost and can be applied to harsh environment. With the decline of computer cost and the reduction of microprocessor size, WSN has become more and more powerful. Its application in forestry has changed the traditional forestry resource management mode, broken the limitations of traditional data acquisition methods, and promoted the implementation of intelligent forestry system in China.

The forest fire early warning system based on wireless sensor network is divided into three parts: data acquisition subsystem, control center subsystem and emergency response subsystem. The data acquisition subsystem mainly uses wireless sensor networks to collect the temperature, humidity, smoke, flame and other data of the target forest area, combined with positioning and other information, and transmits it to the monitoring server of the forestry department in real time to help it determine the fire emergency plan and quickly detect potential fire risks. The control center subsystem is responsible for processing various information collected by the nodes and displaying it in real time, determining the fire location and predicting the fire spread direction, etc. all information is placed in the monitoring server of the forestry department. In the emergency response subsystem, the forestry bureau is responsible for formulating corresponding emergency fire-fighting measures according to the forest fire monitoring data monitored in real time, and notifying the firefighters of the forest farm to accurately command the fire-fighting.

In the research on the application of wireless sensor networks to forest fire monitoring, some deploy sensor nodes in forest areas through WSN technology. When the temperature and smoke concentration exceed the threshold, the wireless sensor network system green orbs transmits data information to the base station in a wireless multi hop manner, and sends alarm signals to the ground through Beidou satellite, and relevant personnel make emergency treatment; Some wireless sensor network monitoring nodes use ZigBee technology combined with various sensors to realize real-time early warning of forest fire. The gateway will transmit the collected data to the host computer through GPRS, and the corresponding personnel will analyze and process it. In view of the shortcomings of ZigBee technology in forest wireless sensor networks, such as short communication distance and constrained by natural environment, a wireless sensor network based on Lora technology is designed to realize the software and hardware of sink nodes and acquisition nodes, and a forest data monitoring cloud platform is constructed to realize the visual presentation, early warning and supervision of pc-web terminal and app mobile terminal.

To sum up, the current wireless sensor network scheme for the data acquisition subsystem of forest fire early warning is mainly divided into two ways: ZigBee ad hoc communication technology and Lora low-power long-distance communication technology. The scheme of combining the above two technologies for forest fire early warning has not been found in the relevant literature research, the specific node deployment and network coverage connectivity are not clearly planned and studied.

As a mobile air information carrier, UAV (unmanned aerial vehicle) became mature in the 1970s. It plays a key role in military operations, such as intelligence collection, important area control, surveillance and so on. Since the 1990s, satellite geographic positioning technology and communication technology have opened up a new road for unmanned reconnaissance aircraft, making UAVs gradually move from military field to civil field.

With the development of mobile Internet, more and more devices are connected to the mobile network, and new services and applications emerge in endlessly. The explosive growth of mobile data demand promotes the development of communication technology. In 2019, "5g" (5th generation mobile communication) was successfully applied, gradually realizing the goals of "interconnection" and "convergence" of all things, and becoming an important engine of economic growth and social development. Facing the upgrading and iteration of business applications, the focus of communication network will gradually shift to scalability, security, mobility and flexibility, and take distributed storage computing, centralized management optimization and intelligent decision scheduling as the main objectives to meet the future business needs.

Due to the increasing number of mobile communication, Internet of things and other access network users, the substantial growth of data consumption and the complexity of information sources, the network will show the trend of multi network coexistence and multi-source heterogeneity in the future. Facing the increasingly complex information environment and the increasing types of data, UAV can quickly and accurately capture information to the air platform and expand the network dimension to get rid of the constraints of the environment on information transmission and collection. However, in the face of long-time, large-scale and strong interference tasks, the shortcomings of UAV, such as short endurance time, limited flight radius and excessive dependence on communication resources, seriously affect the task completion. In contrast, UAV group has distributed self-organization structure and flexible group mode. Through networking for perceptual interaction, information transmission and cooperative work, it can prolong the endurance time and reduce the overall flight resistance; Realize wide field of vision investigation and high-precision positioning.

Because of its advantages of low flight cost, diverse functions and strong flexibility, UAV often acts as an air base station or flight relay to complete communication tasks such as detection network, blind area coverage, link recovery and information collection in the air. When the UAV group performs tasks in an overall form, it can greatly improve the mission success rate and overall hit rate, and achieve the purpose of "blinding" with high stability and high coverage. In the process of UAV performing various communication tasks, interference is an important factor affecting the quality of network communication. Facing the complex and changeable communication environment, real-time and effective interference management measures are a powerful guarantee for the UAV cluster to successfully complete the communication task. In addition, the signal energy interaction between UAV group and ground network can greatly improve the communication efficiency, prolong the network life, fully tap the potential of information and energy, and provide more possibilities for the establishment and switching of communication links between air network and ground network.

When UAV actually performs tasks, it not only needs to face the errors caused by network equipment, channel conditions and other factors in the real environment, but also needs to consider the compatibility of software, hardware and environment, such as the docking of flight decision and flight control command, the constraints of transmission requirements and channel conditions, the difficulty of algorithm and the limitation of processing ability, etc. Therefore, in order to improve the fault tolerance and robustness of the system, it is essential to establish a demonstration platform based on networking and intelligent flight control. It will provide auxiliary means such as planning and evaluation for UAV to ensure the safety of actual operation.

At present, UAV has penetrated into all aspects of life, changed the way people obtain and transmit information, and has become an indispensable technical means in various fields in the future, such as VR live broadcast, security deployment and control, high-altitude patrol inspection, emergency communication, information collection and other applications. UAV can also be used as an edge server to interact with cloud or other aircraft to bring convenience to life [6]. However, due to the limitation of endurance capacity, UAV can not maintain long-term air operation. In order to make up for the energy shortage, expand the application scenarios of UAV, give full play to the synergy of UAV and achieve the goal of "freedom of take-off and landing", the construction of UAV airport and vehicle portable Airport is the only way for UAV industrialization (Fig. 3).

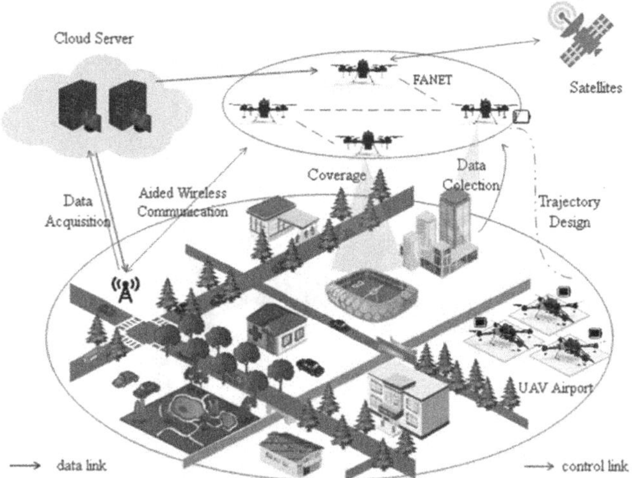

Fig. 3. UAV application scenario

UAV intelligent technology and its radiated peripheral applications seem to have become the mainstream technology and application direction in the future. Our University attaches great importance to the development of UAV field and the construction of UAV specialty. After early investment and construction, we have preliminarily planned a training room with a certain scale and an industrial college jointly built with companies in the industry, forming the prototype of industry university research chain. Through further increasing investment, integrating advantages and refining direction, we will face the high-tech, high-tech and scientific research in the UAV field in the future Intelligent technology and application, it is planned to build a UAV technology and Application Research Center for our university and our city [7].

With the advent of the Internet of things and the era of big data, the development of information technology is changing with each passing day. The whole human society is making great strides towards globalization, modernization and intelligence. More and more services are based on the reliable access to effective information. The demand for information in social development exceeds that in any previous period. Due to its high flexibility, strong deploy ability and other advantages, UAV has unique advantages in the fields of information collection and regional blind filling. It was first proposed by Britain in the 1920s and mainly serves military operations. With the continuous development of UAV technology, civil UAV has developed rapidly in various countries. There are more than 130 development units and 15000 civil UAVs in China, and the types of civil UAVs are gradually enriched, including fixed wing UAV, rotor UAV, etc. To a large extent, the above achievements are the result of the gradual penetration of military UAV technologies such as high altitude, high speed and large load into civil use. There are two types of civil UAV development units in China: one is subordinate units of military industry group and scientific research institutes; Second, more and more private enterprises are involved in the development of UAVs. For example, Dajiang company has reached the world leading level in the development of consumer UAVs. The UAVs developed by Dajiang company are shown in Fig. 4.

Fig. 4. Dajiang Jingwei M100 UAV

The representatives of foreign civil UAV companies are 3D robotics of the United States and parrot of France. Both of them have realized various functions such as aerial photography, video recording, mapping and 3D modeling on UAVs, and have the ability to provide high-tech solutions in the field of urban UAVs. The UAVs produced by 3D robotics and parrot of France are shown in Fig. 5.

Fig. 5. UAVs of 3D robotics and parrot

Compared with foreign countries, domestic civil UAVs have also begun to emerge in recent years. At present, the two fields of agriculture, forestry and plant protection and power and energy inspection have shown an urgent demand trend, and have a considerable market scale prospect. In recent years, civilian UAVs have developed rapidly. Some scholars have carried out UAVs equipped with communication equipment to assist in 5g network blind patch, UAV intelligent path planning, stable and reliable networking of large-scale UAVs, information and energy interaction between UAV network and ground sensor network, and UAVs provide computing unloading services as edge computing servers, This series of research on UAV anti-jamming technology has attracted the most attention, as shown in Fig. 6.

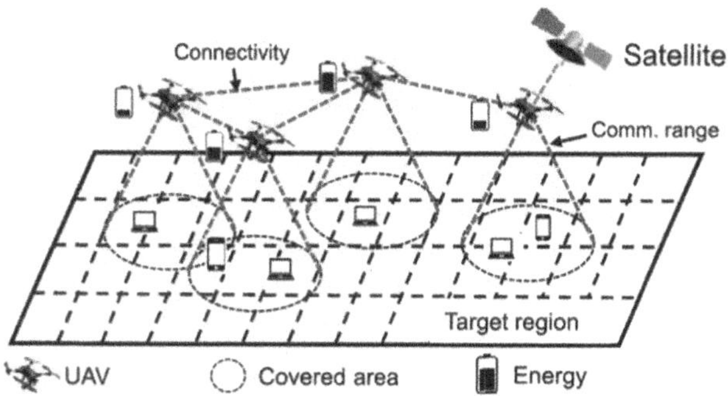

Fig. 6. UAV information acquisition

However, the limitations of limited communication distance, low battery capacity and less payload of civil UAV still exist. When performing large-scale, all-weather tasks, due to the need for frequent charging, the task execution efficiency is low and the repetition rate is high. Countries also cooperate with universities and enterprises to carry out innovative research on the shortcomings of civil UAVs. It is generally believed in the industry that based on the existing capabilities, civil UAVs will develop towards synergy and intelligence in the future. Collaboration means that dozens or even hundreds of UAVs perform tasks at the same time. UAVs share information through networking technology to avoid repeated work. They are uniformly scheduled by the ground control platform to improve task execution efficiency. At the same time, due to the large number of UAVs performing tasks, the design of efficient routing protocol can ensure that the temporary offline of a single UAV will not affect the whole UAV network, so as to improve the robustness of the system. The schematic diagram of multi UAV networking using routing protocol is shown in Fig. 7.

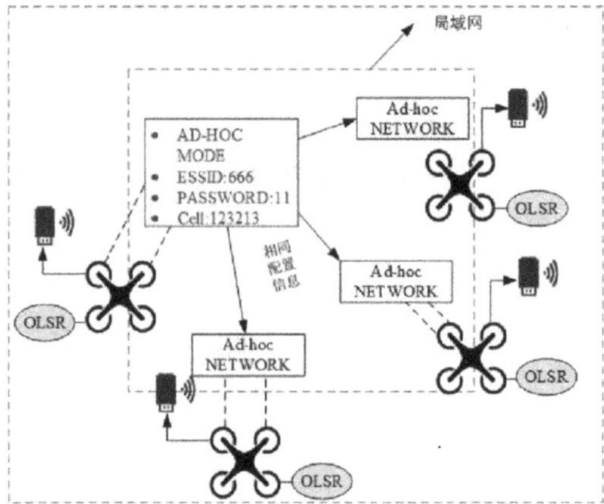

Fig. 7. Multi UAV networking using routing protocol

At the same time, the industry is also designing UAV airports that can automatically charge UAVs, which are mainly divided into fixed and vehicle mounted. The wide application of UAV airports can greatly improve the endurance ability of UAVs when performing tasks and reduce the burden of UAV data processing and transmission. The schematic diagram of UAV airports is shown in Fig. 8.

Fig. 8. Fixed and vehicle mounted UAV Airport

Intelligence means that UAVs can complete tasks independently and efficiently. At present, the control of civil UAV is mainly completed by "flying hand". However, the cultivation of professional "flying hand" requires a lot of time and resources. Combined with the deep learning and reinforcement learning technology in artificial intelligence, the development of UAV intelligent path planning, target recognition, information collection, regional monitoring and other functions is in full swing. Intelligent UAV can liberate the labor force. It can be predicted that the future civil UAV will become an important part of the intelligent society and will play a more important role in all walks of life.

The traditional network construction includes four stages: node startup and pre-allocation, neighbor node discovery and exchange, broadcasting and stable synchronization. The network topology is single and simple, generally star or ring structure. The network composed of UAV group and ground station usually has the characteristics of multi-dimensional, high dynamic and fast entry and departure. In the face of complex environment and task requirements, the traditional networking technology can not meet the requirements of delay, throughput and security. Therefore, it is necessary to adopt reliable random access and stable routing mechanism on the basis of traditional networking theory to ensure the stability of control and data link. Aiming at the topology change of high dynamic and multi-dimensional UAV cluster, this paper studies the networking technology with the characteristics of fast addressing, self-healing, high reliability and low overhead, realizes the high-speed and dynamic entry and departure of each node, and establishes a stable and reliable air link for the transmission and interaction of control information and data information.

Integrate and improve the networking technology based on node information and link state to form a distributed and hybrid networking theory to meet the needs of different business scenarios. At the same time, although the reliable networking theory has laid the foundation for the implementation of various tasks, the specific technical implementation is still a difficult problem to be solved. The implementation of the protocol needs to customize appropriate physical transmission boards, standardize and unify various development interfaces, protocol simulation and embedded implementation.

4 Construction Objectives

Based on the future development plan of China's forest fire prevention monitoring network, do a good job in customizing diversified and personalized solutions for different regions and industries, and meet the intelligent trend of air cooperation network in an all-round and multi-level manner. Improve the popularity of UAV forest fire prevention monitoring system, expand the application scope of intelligent air ground collaborative Internet of things communication, make the research results with leading performance facilitate the development of industry and agriculture, and activate the driving force of rapid industrial growth. The ultimate goal is to improve the architecture of the open space (A2G) collaborative network nationwide, formulate the forest fire prevention monitoring industry standard of the open space collaborative network, enable the open space collaborative network communication system, shape a new generation of network communication form, give full play to the advantages of the open space collaborative network, cover the shortcomings of the existing forest fire prevention monitoring network system, and break the network performance bottleneck, Comprehensively improve the overall performance.

(1) Solve the key technical problems of the unmanned unit network, such as energy consumption, mobile routing, road planning and other topics, give play to the advantages of our university's platform and talents, form a series of peak achievements in scientific research, master the core technology of the unmanned unit network, and enable Huizhou to form a large leading advantage in this field in the medium and long term.

(2) Form specific application cases, construct Huizhou open space collaborative network forest fire prevention monitoring industrial chain, and create demonstration application groups in some application directions where open space collaborative networking has great advantages. In the fields of urban patrol inspection, information collection, emergency communication, agriculture, forestry and plant protection, through coordination and cooperation with Huizhou Municipal government and municipal enterprises, incubate practical projects for open space collaborative networking applications, deeply tap technical potential, continuously optimize integration, and do a good job in the combination of industry, University and research. On this basis, realize the deeper integration of air space collaborative networking technology and socio-economic development, actively promote industrial development, and form an air space collaborative network monitoring related industrial chain with greater economic benefits and greater contributions to society.
(3) In the UAV application technology major of Huizhou Vocational College of engineering, we will set up characteristic courses related to air ground cooperative network, strengthen talent training, and build a research team related to air ground cooperative network, so as to conduct long-term and stable research and form technology accumulation and project pre research experience. While serving the local economy of Huizhou, promote the improvement of employment rate and talent reserve.

5 The Following Key Issues

In the process of forest fire monitoring by air ground cooperative network combined with sensor network and UAV, Huizhou Engineering Vocational College will solve the following key problems in the next step:

(1) Research on information energy interaction in cluster collaboration.

In the actual application scenario of wood fire monitoring, the air UAV network and ground sensor network are energy limited networks. Whether the node energy can be saved as much as possible has a great impact on the life cycle of the whole network. Generally, node silence is a good way to save energy. In the studied scenario, the information energy transmission mode of clustering cooperation is adopted. The sub nodes in the cluster (UAV or ground sensor) summarize the information to be transmitted at the main node. The air and ground networks only communicate between the main nodes, while other sub nodes are silent. Considering the energy level of system nodes, the information transmission scale between heterogeneous networks, the energy collection requirements of ground network and the path design requirements of UAV network, appropriate clustering cooperation mode is adopted to achieve the required system performance indicators.

(2) Research on path planning of UAV.

Due to the limited energy of aircraft, it is very important to design an appropriate flight path to realize the information transmission between air and ground networks and the energy collection required by ground networks. On the basis of the research on the information energy interaction of clustering cooperation, considering the constraints required to realize the system requirements, such as throughput constraints, energy efficiency constraints, UAV network link constraints, additional mission constraints, etc., the joint trajectory optimization problem is established and the optimal path of UAV is designed.

(3) Research on optimal resource allocation scheme.

In the process of communication and energy interaction, the wireless energy transmission of UAV to ground nodes will inevitably lead to the decline of wireless communication performance. Therefore, it is necessary to study the optimal resource allocation in this process. By studying this problem, we can further understand the relationship between UAV network coverage, transmission success rate and energy collection efficiency. Make a trade-off between wireless communication performance and energy collection efficiency, solve the problem of reasonably allocating the time ratio between energy transmission and data transmission within the time limit, and plan the transmission power of sensor nodes and UAV under the condition of limited energy, so as to meet the required performance index requirements.

6 Conclusion

During the construction of UAV agriculture, forestry and plant protection project of Huizhou Vocational College of engineering, it is oriented to the cutting-edge technology of open space collaborative network, which provides effective support for improving the core technical ability of forest fire prevention monitoring in Huizhou, mainly including open space collaborative blinding and management, open space collaborative efficient networking and stable routing mechanism.

Air ground cooperative blind patch and management is a typical application of UAV assisted wireless sensor networks, including air ground network topology modeling, inter air ground channel state modeling, blind area detection and effective coverage, UAV autonomous path planning, relay node deployment strategy, interference perception and management, etc. It involves information transmission system of air ground cooperative ad hoc network, 5g / b5g cooperation and auxiliary communication, UAV path planning, MAC layer access control, computing unloading under the background of Internet of things, etc.

Efficient networking and stable routing mechanism is an important guarantee for the effective operation of air ground cooperative network, including the design of stable low collision access protocol, the optimization of routing protocol driven by task, network self-healing and reconstruction under the condition of network topology change, and the stability research of large-scale high dynamic network. The theoretical research content is in NS2, MATLAB, Actual verification on Python and other simulation platforms.

References

1. Na, S.: The current situation and countermeasures of forest fire prevention in my country. South. Agric. (15) (2019)
2. Yanhui, W.: Discussion on forest fire prevention countermeasures in nature reserves. New Agric. **14**, 51 (2021)

3. Li, H., Song, G., Wu, P.: Status and prospects of foreign forest fire prevention communication technology. Chinese Forestry (19), 50–51 (2008)
4. Xuemei, Y.: Analysis on the status quo and trend discussion of forest fire prevention technology at home and abroad. Agric. Technol. **36**(006), 173 (2016)
5. Cui, X., Liu, Y.: Research on UAV in forest fire monitoring. Sci. Technol. Innovation (007), 128–130 (2014)
6. Li, H.: The application and prospect of UAV system in forest fire prevention. Rural Sci. Technol. **251**(11), 70+72 (2020)
7. Jiao, Z.: Research on Forest Fire Fighting UAV System. Xi'an University of Technology (2019)

Safety Helmet Wearing Behavior Detection Under Low Visibility Based on Deep Learning

Min Lin[1](✉), Haiying Wu[2], and Hongtao Zhang[1]

[1] Institute of Surveying, Mapping and Remote Sensing Information, Guangdong Polytechnic of Industry and Commerce, Guangzhou 510510, China
407252699@qq.com

[2] College of Economics and Trade, Guangdong Polytechnic of Industry and Commerce, Guangzhou 510510, China

Abstract. This paper analyzes the intelligent identification technology, intelligent early warning system and intelligent control method of engineering construction safety risk, constructs the engineering construction safety intelligent management system from three aspects of "knowledge", "police" and "control", and puts forward the construction scheme of construction safety intelligent management platform, which provides reference for the construction of intelligent construction site.

Keywords: BIM · Construction safety · Intelligent identification · Intelligent early warning · Intelligent control

1 Introduction

1.1 Preface

The emergence of BIM and the rapid development of big data, artificial intelligence, cloud computing, Internet of Things, 5G and other emerging information technologies have brought vitality and vitality to the intelligent management of engineering construction safety.

At present, many scholars at home and abroad have studied the engineering safety warning and management. For example, Gaba et al. (2018) improved the monitoring and early warning of construction site based on RFID. Kumar et al. (2018) proposed an automated framework to create a dynamic site layout model, using a combination of BIM technology, AI algorithm and genetic algorithm to develop an optimization that takes into account the actual driving path of site personnel and equipment. Yu Jianxin et al. (2020) constructed online health.

The health monitoring system can carry out long-term online real-time monitoring during the construction period and operation period of the cross tunnel to ensure the construction safety. The linkage of intelligent identification, intelligent early warning and intelligent control of construction safety risks is the key to realize more intelligent construction safety management. This paper analyzes the linkage of "recognition", "police" and "control" of construction safety risks.

© ICST Institute for Computer Sciences, Social Informatics and Telecommunications Engineering 2022
Published by Springer Nature Switzerland AG 2022. All Rights Reserved
S. Shi et al. (Eds.): 6GN 2021, LNICST 439, pp. 245–251, 2022.
https://doi.org/10.1007/978-3-031-04245-4_21

2 Intelligent Identification of Construction Safety Risks

2.1 The Important Reasons Leading to Construction Safety Accidents

One of the important reasons leading to construction safety accidents is that the data collection and transmission of construction safety risk are not timely, and the risk identification is not intelligent enough. It is very important to form the corresponding security intelligent identification technology with the support of emerging information technology and the uniqueness of specific engineering activities. 2.1 Security identification technology based on the Internet of Things.

The security identification based on the Internet of Things is to collect and transmit engineering safety related data automatically in real time through the integrated application of various sensors and network facilities (wired or wireless), and carry out real-time analysis and discrimination of safety risks by combining data analysis methods and early warning mechanisms [1].

This technology involves many kinds of sensors, such as temperature, humidity, pressure, gas body, light, sound, stress, strain, displacement, position, identity identification and other sensors, often used in geological environment, deep foundation pit, main structure, edge hole, dangerous gas monitoring. However, due to the complexity of the engineering environment and the large number of RFID tags identified by personnel, materials and equipment, the intelligent perception technology needs to solve the power supply, electromagnetic shielding, huge amount of communication data and other problems of the sensor [2]. Data transmission and transmission are susceptible to the impact of the field environment, resulting in great fluctuations in its accuracy.

2.2 Security Identification Technology Based on Machine Vision

Machine vision based security identification technology is to use image or video analysis methods or technologies to quickly and automatically process engineering safety-related images or videos and extract safety elements, and then to identify security risks. This kind of technology depends on the project site video acquisition equipment and image processing technology. Often used in worker behavior, dangerous areas, material safety testing, etc. However, this kind of technology is greatly affected by the field light, line of sight, dynamic, etc., and is also limited by the performance of algorithm and computing equipment.

2.3 Mobile Terminal Based Security Identification Technology

The security identification technology based on mobile terminal is to obtain engineering safety related data by manual means, identify and report the hidden security problems existing in the project, and then carry out the comprehensive identification of security risks. This kind of technology benefits from mobile terminal equipment and WeChat or small program [3]. Through scanning QR code on the spot, the information transmission and processing of real data are often used for on-site inspection and identification of potential safety hazards or wind risk factors. This kind of technology is applicable to a wide range of applications, but limited by manual detection and reporting of relevant data, resulting in a narrow or incomplete data coverage.

3 Intelligent Early Warning of Construction Safety Risks

3.1 Through Intelligent Identification Technology, the Collected Data Is Linked to the BIM Database

The monitoring results will be transferred to the BIM database. Through the BIM model, the actual situation data of the construction site will be compared and analyzed with plans and standards, so as to realize the data patrol and dynamic and visual monitoring and early warning. The early warning system can divide the wind risk level into three levels through the deviation range between the actual value and the planned standard value, and issue the corresponding alarm. warning.

Common modules of the system include, Smart monitoring modules:

(1) Through the sensor to the construction process of real-time monitoring, especially the important parts and key working procedure, to collect data, such as stress, strain and displacement, the timely transmission to BIM database, when monitoring data than risk alert limit, the system will automatically alarm and to lead the project processing.
(2) Intelligent video monitoring module: through on-site monitoring, the abnormal behavior of on-site workers and material conditions can be monitored and controlled and warned in real time throughout the day. If abnormal conditions such as workers not wearing safety helmets and smoking appear in the monitoring picture, the system can send an alarm and provide useful information the fastest.
(3) Dangerous area warning module: the system will be based on the operation personnel and risk.

    The relative distance of the risk area, and compare with the BIM model, calculate and determine its safety state, and timely remind the staff to keep enough safety distance.
(4) Tower crane collision module: using on the tower crane hook sensors and cameras, wind speed, height of the tower crane real-time acquisition, rotation Angle and the stress condition data, and analyses the transmission of data to the early warning system, for tower crane anomalies or illegal operation and so on to realize remote monitoring, remote alarm, ensure the safety work of special equipment and specifications [4].
(5) Labor personnel management module: labor workers' real-name management is realized through the one-card, and attendance, positioning and work efficiency are managed through biometric identification, intelligent access control, intelligent safety helmet and other technologies.
(6) Intelligent inspection module: scan the QR code of the building components through the mobile APP, enter the page of the security management platform, fill in the relevant inspection capacity, and realize digital archival and acceptance. If the safety data does not meet the requirements, the problem can be collected and sent to the terminal of the relevant responsible person in time for further processing and problem status tracking. Only when the construction conditions meet the acceptance conditions in the safety list can the process acceptance or the next step of construction be carried out.

4 Intelligent Control of Construction Safety Risks

The selection of benchmarking system for vocational education informatization is mainly to establish guiding standards for the construction of vocational education informatization under the support of specific concepts [5]. From the perspective of selection, one needs to consider the measurement capability of the standard, and the other needs to consider the realistic environment of evaluation. Specifically, the selection principles of the following three aspects should be included.

4.1 Establish a Dynamic Database of Construction Safety Risks

Collect the historical data of similar completed construction safety accidents, causes and countermeasures.

4.2 Integrity and Dispersion

According to the accident cause theory, the static database of engineering construction safety risks is established through the SQL Server database platform. Then the crawler information through the network technology, the real-time data gathering new large risk accident cases on the network, and the risk source, risk factors, cause and the risk of policy risks, such as data classification, tagging, digital expression in time, or via the users to the growing use of safety risk library, updated indirectly improve the security risks of case data, or by artificial means entry security risks, to implement the intelligent of the library information storage, call, form engineering construction safety risk dynamic database. The intelligent management of the risk dynamic database can self-learn, self-update and self-advance, and constantly meet the needs of users for different risk management scenarios.

4.3 Establish the Auxiliary Decision-Making Management System for Engineering Construction Safety

Based on the visual dynamic simulation technology of BIM, the construction safety auxiliary decision-making management system can be established, which can simulate the engineering construction technology, process and construction plan, so as to find the hidden danger in the construction in advance, optimize the construction plan and on-site management measures, and reduce the incidence of safety accidents.

Based on the BIM 3D model, the corresponding finite element software is developed.

Interface, plus material attributes, boundary conditions and load conditions, can real-time monitor the safety state of personnel and mechanical substances in the construction of the project, simulate the stress and strain state of the engineering structure in the construction, effectively prepare safety management measures, real-time maintenance and correction of safety emergency management plan. BIM technology can be used for dangerous partial projects or complex heterosexual structure installation.

Virtual visualization construction is carried out to verify the rationality of the construction scheme and the safety and reliability of the construction technology, and assist the managers to make safety management decisions. For example, before entering the site for installation, the identification of the high support mold, the simulation of lifting, rigging or scaffold lapping, testing and optimizing the scheme.

4.4 Establish the Emergency Management System for Engineering Construction Safety Accidents

Construction safety intelligent management platform stores all kinds of engineering safety accident cases and events, as well as the emergency management personnel, materials and emergency plans of each project. If there is a construction safety warning or safety accidents, emergency management system module according to the scene of the early warning system for information, as well as the construction site of multi-source data capture or a description of the safety accident, get the keywords, automatically matching case has been stored in the library of all kinds of risk and the corresponding risk plan, assist manager to group decision-making and daily disaster drills and training, so as to enhance safety emergency management efficiency.

In addition, when a safety accident occurs, BIM model, together with sensors and visual monitoring system, can provide rescuers with complete information of abnormal areas and status information of engineering equipment, assist managers to make the best disposal plan and rescue route, etc., and improve the effectiveness of emergency management.

5 Construction of BIM Based Construction Safety Intelligent Management Platform

Taking the dynamic database of engineering construction safety risk as the content of the platform, constructing the intelligent management platform of engineering construction safety based on BIM is the inevitable way to realize the joint management of engineering construction safety risk "recognition", "police" and "control". The platform consists of five layers: perception layer, transmission layer, data layer, algorithm layer and functional application layer, as shown in Fig. 1.

(1) Perception layer by sensors, video collection equipment or devices such as mobile terminal end, automatic collection and identification of the whole project construction safety risk According to the perception of the whole project running status and intelligent construction safety risk identification, and through the cable and wireless communications networks, to implement the data layer and two-way interactive transmission [6].
(2) Transmission layer: 5G can adapt to the special scenarioization request of the construction industry, build the scale networking of the construction site, and meet the requirements of the data transmission of various business scenes of the construction industry, such as the complex construction environment and large personnel mobility, so as to realize intelligent identification, positioning, tracking, monitoring and management.

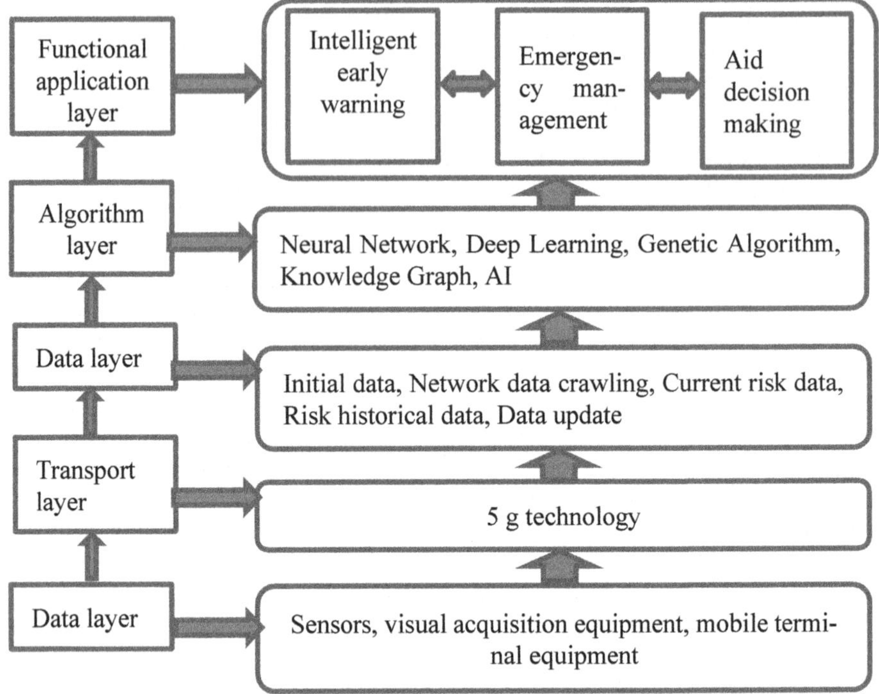

Fig. 1. Construction safety intelligent management platform architecture

(3) Data layer: including three data sources: initial data of BIM model, updated data of risk database and real-time data collected by intelligent identification system. The data layer can use database platform such as SQL Server database platform to realize data storage and retrieval.
(4) Algorithm layer: the algorithm layer is the core of the construction safety intelligent management platform. It is necessary to construct the intelligent management model of construction safety through the theories of neural network, deep learning, genetic algorithm, knowledge graph spectrum, AI, etc., and realize the risk discrimination, intelligent early warning and intelligent management of construction safety through the constant updating and iteration of data in the data layer.
(5) Functional application layer: Functional application layer mainly includes intelligent early warning and intelligent control. Intelligent early warning based on the intelligent discrimination of security risk automatic alarm, including intelligent sensor monitoring module, intelligent video monitoring module, dangerous area early warning module, tower crane anti-collision module, labor management module, intelligent patrol module, etc. Intelligent management and control system includes auxiliary decision module, emergency management module and so on.

6 Conclusion

Based on BIM technology, the automatic identification of engineering construction safety risk factors, intelligent early warning of safety accidents, efficient decision-making of safety emergency rescue management, and the establishment of a scientific and perfect engineering construction safety intelligent management system is a scientific and modern solution to the problem of frequent safety accidents. Smart compared with traditional safety management, safety management with the aid of BIM to visualization of dynamic simulation, real-time monitoring of the Internet of things, the depth of the large data analysis and auxiliary decision-making of artificial intelligence, real time control of the construction site can be realized Conditions, the dynamic analysis of safety risk factors, predict the safety trend, accurate formulate safety protection measures, effectively implement the safety management measures.

Foundation Project. The special fund for science and technology innovation strategy of Guangdong Province in 2021 (project number: **pdjh2021b0744**);2019 general university scientific research project of Guangdong Provincial Department of education "Research on helmet wearing behavior based on deep learning under low visibility **2019gktscx021**"; Refe2020 key scientific research project of colleges and universities of Guangdong Provincial Department of Education - **2020zdzx2095**;2021 school level entrusted special project of Guangdong Polytechnic of Industry & Commerce (GDPIC)-**2021-zx-18**;2022 basic and applied basic research project of Guangzhou basic research plan (general project) "Research on bonding mechanism of seawater and sand concrete based on thread characteristics of BFRP reinforcement-**1714**".

References

1. Xu Liqiang, F., Mingqin, W.C.: Research on the application of BIM technology in assembly building safety management. Building Econ. **42**(04), 53–56 (2021)
2. Leng, L.: Construction site management based on BIM. Build. Sci. **37**(03), 157 (2021)
3. Yang, J.: Analysis on construction safety management strategy of assembly building. Indus. Build. **51**(02), 230
4. Wang, J., Wang, J., Wang, J., Wang, J., Wang, J., Wang, J., Wang, J
5. Wu, Y.: Application of BIM technology in construction of new high speed railway across business line. Railway Standard Design 1–6 (2021) https://doi.org/10.13238/j.issn.1004-2954.202009240004
6. Gai Tongtong, Y., Dehu, S.B.: Yang Shujuan. Build. Sci. **36**(06), 119–126 (2020). (in Chinese)

Advanced Signal Processing Technologies for 5G/6G Networks

FAST-Det: Feature Aligned SSD Towards Remote Sensing Detector

Yutong Niu[1(✉)], Ao Li[1], Jie Li[2], and Yangwei Wang[2]

[1] School of Computer Science and Technology, Harbin University of Science and Technology, Harbin, China
yutong_niu@126.com

[2] Shandong Provincial Innovation and Practice Base for Postdoctors, Weihaizhenyu Intelligence Technology Co., Ltd., Weihai, China

Abstract. Object detection based on large-scale, high-resolution visible light Remote sensing images are widely used in military such as reconnaissance and civilian such as marine resource management. It is also an important task for the application of computer vision in remote sensing images. With the development of deep learning, more and more object detectors use deep network as the backbone, and accurate detection results and indicators can be obtained on conventional images. However, compared with conventional images, remote sensing images have more object numbers and object sizes, and the object distribution is also denser, which makes detection more difficult. At present, there are two types of object detectors: single-stage and two-stage. The single-stage detector directly obtains the detection result based on the feature map and pays more attention to the detection speed, while the two-stage detector generates the region of interest (RoI) by using feature map. More attention is paid to the accuracy of the test results when the test results are obtained through RoIs. This paper proposes a bilateral filtering refining method based on a single-stage detector, which refines the results obtained by a single-stage detector and approaches the performance of a two-stage detector without losing too much detection speed. Experiments conducted on the public large-scale visible light remote sensing dataset DOTA have proved the effectiveness of this method.

Keywords: Deep learning · Object detection · Bilateral filtering

1 Introduction

Now remote sensing technology is in a relatively mature state. Remote sensing images are widely used in military such as reconnaissance and civilian such as marine resource management. At present, the object detection applied to remote sensing images is mainly realized by deep neural network, which is composed of backbone and head. Backbone is usually a convolutional neural network, which uses a convolution operator to extract features from the input image step by step to generate a feature map for object detection;

© ICST Institute for Computer Sciences, Social Informatics and Telecommunications Engineering 2022
Published by Springer Nature Switzerland AG 2022. All Rights Reserved
S. Shi et al. (Eds.): 6GN 2021, LNICST 439, pp. 255–263, 2022.
https://doi.org/10.1007/978-3-031-04245-4_22

the head of detector will perform object category and location detection on the feature [1].

Ross Girshick proposed a design idea of a classifier regression for object detection tasks in RCNN [2], and implemented end-to-end multi-task learning in Faster RCNN [3]. Common object detectors still maintain this design idea. Under the multi-task training of classification and regression, feature maps suitable for two tasks can be obtained together. It can be found by using the heat map to visualize the feature map that the features suitable for the classification task do not completely overlap with the features suitable for the regression task, and there is a deviation in the center point of the feature distribution. The reason is that the classification task has the invariance of translation and scale and pays more attention to the extraction of the difference information between the classes; the regression task is more sensitive to the location and scale information of the object and pays more attention to the extraction of the boundary information of the object. This causes the classification and regression feature centers to shift. This feature shift makes the anchor center with a higher classification score not necessarily close to the object geometric center. The offset of the classification regression feature center and the offset of the anchor center and the object geometric center increase the difficulty of regression from the anchor to the prediction bounding box and have a certain impact on the detection results [4, 5].

Compared with conventional images, remote sensing images have more objects, more object sizes, and denser distribution. This makes conventional object detectors unable to obtain accurate detection results on remote sensing images. Compared with the horizontal bounding box, the rotating bounding box is more suitable for object detection tasks with dense object distribution. In this work we present a feature-aligned rotating SSD detector, which can effectively adapt to remote sensing images. Specifically, the FPN structure is used to generate multi-size feature maps for detection. The larger feature map is more suitable for setting small anchors to detect small targets. On the contrary, a large anchor should be set for a smaller feature map to adapt to a large target, because it has a larger receptive field. In the first stage, the object is roughly detected to obtain a prediction bounding box. Compared with the anchor center, prediction bounding box center should be closer to the actual geometric center of the object. Therefore, the bilateral filter is used to calculate the central feature estimation of the prediction bounding box, integrate it into the original feature point position, generate a new feature pyramid, and complete the feature alignment. Using the aligned feature pyramid to perform the second classification regression can get a better detection effect. Through experiments on the DOTA dataset and calculation of indicators, the effectiveness of this model is verified.

2 Related Work

2.1 One-Stage and Two-Stage Object Detector

The object detection network based on deep learning can be divided into two categories according to the detection process. One is a single-stage detector that uses feature maps to detect directly. The other is a two-stage detector that relies on the region of interest. Faster RCNN [3], as a classic two-stage end-to-end object detector, can fully reflect the characteristics of the two-stage object detector. The detection process of this type of detector is carried out in two steps. The first stage is to obtain anchors according to the feature map of the picture in the Region Proposal Network (RPN) and get the region of interest (RoI). The second step is to pool the RoIs to the same size and perform the second detection. The two-stage object detector only classifies foreground and background in the first stage, and the focus is on calculating RoIs. The RoIs has undergone a regression, and its center point is closer to the object geometric center than the anchors, which helps to improve the accuracy of the second classification regression. In the second stage, the RoIs is fine-grained classification and further regression, and more accurate detection results are obtained. The two-stage detector requires RPN for anchor screening and RoIs generation, which requires more detection time. Most of the remote sensing images have a large size, so it is necessary to use a sliding window method for stepwise detection and then merge the results, so using a two-stage detector for remote sensing image detection will consume more time.

The single-stage detector directly performs classification and regression on the characteristics of the picture. The entire detection process only needs one step, and it focuses more on the speed of detection, and is more suitable for the distribution detection method based on sliding windows. SSD [6], as a representative of single-stage object detector, generates anchors of several sizes for each feature point in the feature map calculated by backbone. And directly perform fine-grained classification and bounding box regression on each anchor at one time. Finally, post-processing is performed by non-maximum suppression NMS to suppress redundant bounding boxes. Because there is no RPN subnetwork, the detection speed is greatly improved, and it can better adapt to the sliding window method in high resolution image object detection.

2.2 Multi-scale Features Object Detector

Large object sizes and more small objects are the main challenges for object detection in visible light remote sensing images. The object detector used for remote sensing images should have the ability to detect objects of different sizes at the same time. Multi-scale feature maps are used in SSD for detection [6]. Large-size feature maps are more suitable for detecting small objects due to their smaller receptive fields. Therefore, several small-size anchors with aspect ratios are generated in the large feature maps. The small feature map is at the high level of the network and has a larger receptive field, which is suitable for detecting large objects. Therefore, several large-size anchors with aspect ratios are generated in the small feature map. SSD performs NMS on the object bounding boxes generated by these anchors in the post-processing stage to remove redundant bounding boxes. Single-stage and multi-scale features make SSD has fast detection speed and accurate detection results.

However, in order to prevent the low-level features from affecting the performance of the detector, the SSD adds a convolutional layer to the high-level of the backbone to generate a multi-size feature map, and only uses the high-level information. The information in the underlying feature map is particularly important in small objects detection.

In order to make rational use of multiple size feature maps, RetinaNet [7] adds the feature pyramid network FPN [8] on the SSD model. FPN will up-sample the high-level features, expand the size and add it to the bottom-level feature map, which makes each layer of the generated feature pyramid have relatively complete feature information. The detection of large and small objects can be considered at the same time, which improves the recall rate of the detector.

3 The Proposed Method

3.1 Multi-scale and Rotation

In order to make the single-stage object detector SSD more suitable for remote sensing images, we choose ResNet as the backbone of the detector. Because ResNet uses the residual block as the basic structure of the network, the shortcut connection in the residual block can play the role of identity mapping, thereby effectively preventing the degradation caused by the deepening of the network layer. Further improve the feature extraction ability of the input image. And add FPN structure between backbone and head, FPN and ResNet are connected horizontally to calculate feature pyramid. In the feature extraction stage, two paths are formed. ResNet calculates various scale feature maps from low to high, and FPN up samples high-level features from high to low, and adds them to low-level feature maps step by step to perform high-level feature information. Supplement. The feature pyramid calculated in this part maintains the feature information of various sizes from low to high, and the bottom-level information is also supplemented by the high-level information. Small-sized high-level feature maps are suitable for setting large-sized anchors, because they have greater feelings, and are more suitable for detecting large-sized objects. On the contrary, the receptive field of the underlying feature map is smaller and suitable for detecting small objects, and a smaller size anchor should be set.

In the case of dense object distribution, the horizontal bounding box will introduce other object information, which makes the bounding boxes affect each other, which is not conducive to the performance of the detector. In the remote sensing image of airport, harbor and parking lot scenes, there are a large number of objects, and the objects are very dense and the directions are changeable. At the same time, there are also long objects like bridges in remote sensing images. These reasons make it difficult for object detectors that use horizontal bounding boxes to achieve actual detection results.

Further, we add a rotation vector to the traditional 4-dimensional regression vector (center point $[x, y]$ bounding box width w and height h). It also stipulates that the edge with an acute angle to the *x–axis* is defined as the height of the bounding box, the other side is the width of the bounding box.

3.2 Feature Alignment and Bilateral Filter

The object detector based on deep learning uses a multi-task method to train the network. In the training phase, the classification sub-network for object classification and the regression sub-network for object bounding box prediction are trained at the same time. The multi-task training method enables the trained feature extraction network to extract features suitable for two tasks synergistically. However, after using the heat map to visualize the feature map, it can be found that the features suitable for the classification task do not completely overlap with the features suitable for the regression task, and there is a deviation in the center point of the feature distribution. The reason is that the classification task has the invariance of translation and scale, and the category judgment will not change due to different sizes and positions. The feature maps trained by the classification task pay more attention to the extraction of the difference information between the classes. However, the feature map trained on the regression task should have the location feature of the object. The difference of focus makes the classification regression feature center biased. In other words, the classification feature is offset from the geometric center of the object. In actual applications, in order to prevent the disappearance of the gradient of the deep neural network, the idea of migration learning is often used when training the classifier, and the ImageNet classification task is used to pre-train the backbone to enhance its feature extraction ability. This also makes the feature map more biased towards the classification task, which makes it difficult to return to the bounding box.

The single-stage object detector represented by SSD will generate anchors of several sizes at each point in the feature map and use the anchors directly to calculate classification confidence and bounding box prediction. Since the center of the classification feature may not be at the geometric center of the object, the anchor center with high confidence may not be closer to the geometric center of the object. The resulting feature shift phenomenon.

The two-stage detector first adjusts the anchor to the proposal through the RPN, and then determines the region of feature map corresponding to the proposal, which is called the region of interest RoI, and then uses the pooled RoI for fine-grained classification and more accurate bounding box prediction. The movement from the center of the anchor to the center of the RoIs alleviates the feature shift to a certain extent. Inspired by this approach, we propose a method for feature alignment of a single-stage object detector. First, use bilinear interpolation to linearly estimate the feature value of center point. In addition, a nonlinear bilateral filter is used for nonlinear reconstruction, and the reconstructed features are spliced with the original features for secondary detection. The structure of FastDet is shown in Fig. 1. The bilateral filter is composed of a distance filter and a difference filter. The distance filter formula is shown in (1), and the difference filter is shown in (2).

$$
\begin{aligned}
r_{d_{lt}} &= \frac{\frac{1}{d_{lt}}}{\frac{1}{d_{lt}}+\frac{1}{d_{rt}}+\frac{1}{d_{lb}}+\frac{1}{d_{rb}}} \quad r_{d_{rt}} = \frac{\frac{1}{d_{rt}}}{\frac{1}{d_{lt}}+\frac{1}{d_{rt}}+\frac{1}{d_{lb}}+\frac{1}{d_{rb}}} \\
r_{d_{lb}} &= \frac{\frac{1}{d_{lb}}}{\frac{1}{d_{lt}}+\frac{1}{d_{rt}}+\frac{1}{d_{lb}}+\frac{1}{d_{rb}}} \quad r_{d_{rb}} = \frac{\frac{1}{d_{rb}}}{\frac{1}{d_{lt}}+\frac{1}{d_{rt}}+\frac{1}{d_{lb}}+\frac{1}{d_{rb}}}
\end{aligned}
\tag{1}
$$

where, *lt*, *rt*, *lb*, *rb* are neighbor pixels of the center point. $d_\bullet$ indicates the distance from the point to *lt*, *rt*, *lb*, *rb*.

$$
\begin{aligned}
r_{v_{lt}} &= \frac{\frac{1}{\Delta v_{lt}}}{\frac{1}{\Delta v_{lt}}+\frac{1}{\Delta v_{rt}}+\frac{1}{\Delta v_{lb}}+\frac{1}{\Delta v_{rb}}} \quad r_{v_{rt}} = \frac{\frac{1}{\Delta v_{rt}}}{\frac{1}{\Delta v_{lt}}+\frac{1}{\Delta v_{rt}}+\frac{1}{\Delta v_{lb}}+\frac{1}{\Delta v_{rb}}} \\
r_{v_{lb}} &= \frac{\frac{1}{\Delta v_{lb}}}{\frac{1}{\Delta v_{lt}}+\frac{1}{\Delta v_{rt}}+\frac{1}{\Delta v_{lb}}+\frac{1}{\Delta v_{rb}}} \quad r_{v_{rb}} = \frac{\frac{1}{\Delta v_{rb}}}{\frac{1}{\Delta v_{lt}}+\frac{1}{\Delta v_{rt}}+\frac{1}{\Delta v_{lb}}+\frac{1}{\Delta v_{rb}}}
\end{aligned}
\tag{2}
$$

where, *lt*, *rt*, *lb*, *rb* are neighbor pixels of the center point. $\Delta v_{\bullet}$ represents the difference between the point interpolation feature value and *lt*, *rt*, *lb*, *rb* feature value.

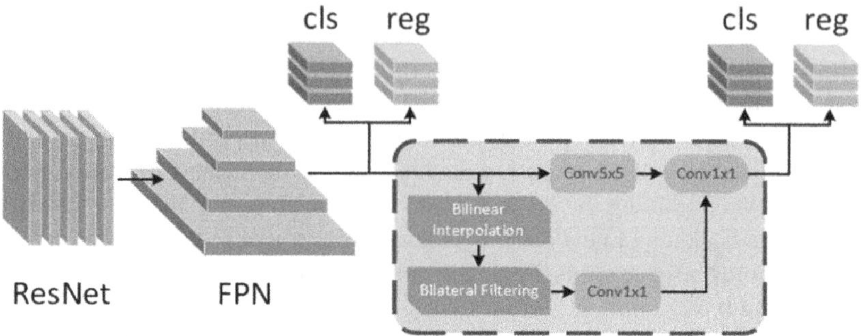

Fig. 1. The structure of FastDet

4 Experiments

4.1 Dataset

The experimental dataset uses Large-scale Aerial Images dataset DOTA [9]. The DOTA dataset contains 2806 aerial images, 15 categories, and a total of 188282 objects. Among them, 1/2 is divided into training set, 1/6 is divided into validation set, and 1/3 is divided into test set (unpublished label). The bounding box labeling method is different from the traditional parallel bounding box labeling method on opposite sides. DOTA uses a quadrilateral of any shape and direction determined by 4 points to label the object. The 15 categories included in DOTA cover common objects of different sizes, as well as objects with different aspect ratios (such as bridges and airplanes). And used the HRSC2016 [10] dataset. This dataset contains ship class and background class. The size ranges from 300 to 1500. The training set contains 436 images, the validation set contains 181 images, and the test set contains 444 images.

4.2 Process and Results

In this paper, we use six baseline methods and our proposed FastDet to conduct experiments on the DOTA dataset. The Baseline method uses R-FCN [11], Faster RCNN with rotating bounding box [3], PIoU [12], ICN [13], RADet [14], O2-DNet [15]. Use the DOTA dataset to test and calculate indicators. The following Table 1 gives a summary of the baseline model and this work presented model experimental results.

The category abbreviations in the table are as follows: BD stands for baseball diamond, GTF stands for ground track field, SV stands for small vehicle, LV stands for large vehicle, TC stands for tennis court, BC stands for basketball court, ST stands for storage tank, SBF stands for soccer ball field, RA It stands for roundabout, SP stands

Table 1. The AP of the baseline model and the model proposed in this work on DOTA

	R-FCN	FR-R	PIoU	ICN	RADet	O^2-DNet	FastDet
Plane	39.57	79.42	80.9	81.4	79.45	89.31	**89.56**
BD	46.13	77.13	69.7	74.3	76.99	82.14	**82.89**
Bridge	3.03	17.7	24.1	47.7	48.05	47.33	**52.79**
GTF	38.46	64.05	60.2	**70.3**	65.83	61.21	63.96
SV	9.1	35.3	38.3	64.9	65.46	71.32	**77.55**
LV	3.66	38.02	64.4	67.8	74.40	74.03	**80.76**
Ship	7.45	37.16	64.8	70.0	68.86	78.62	**86.53**
TC	41.97	89.41	**90.9**	90.8	89.70	90.76	89.56
BC	50.43	69.64	77.2	79.1	78.14	82.23	**85.43**
ST	66.98	59.28	70.4	78.2	74.97	81.36	**83.83**
SBF	40.34	50.3	46.5	53.6	49.92	**60.93**	58.29
RA	51.28	52.91	37.1	62.9	**64.63**	60.17	58.36
Harbor	11.14	47.89	57.1	67.0	66.14	58.21	**66.56**
SP	35.59	47.4	61.9	64.2	**71.58**	66.98	66.61
HC	17.45	46.3	64.0	50.2	**62.16**	61.03	61.87
Avg	30.84	54.13	60.5	68.2	69.09	71.04	**73.64**

for swimming pool, HC stands for helicopter, and Avg stands for the average indicator (AP) of all categories.

In order to get more comprehensive experimental results, we have carried out additional experiments on the HRSC2016 dataset. We choose three baseline models and our proposed FastDet for experiments, R2CNN [16], RRPN [17] and RoI-Transformer [18]. The following Table 2 gives a summary of the baseline model and this work presented model experimental results. The table shows backbone, speed and mAP (using VOC2007 and VOC2012 two calculation methods).

Table 2. AP and speed of the baseline model and FastDet on HRSC2016

Method	Backbone	mAP (VOC2007)	mAP (VOC2012)	Speed
R^2CNN	ResNet101	73.07	79.73	5 fps
RRPN	ResNet101	79.08	85.64	1.5 fps
RoI-Transformer	ResNet101	86.20	–	6 fps
FastDet	ResNet50	**87.60**	89.29	**19 fps**
FastDet	ResNet101	87.52	**89.40**	16 fps

4.3 Result Analysis

We used six baseline models and the model proposed in this paper to conduct experiments on DOTA. According to the experimental results, we can find that the performance of FastDet is significantly better than other baseline networks. The mAP is 138.7% higher than R-FCN. Most types of AP in the DOTA dataset are higher than other models. Especially on densely distributed objects, such as LV and Ship, the AP of FastDet can reach 80.76 and 86.53 respectively.

We also used three baseline models and the model proposed in this paper for supplementary experiments. For the model FastDet proposed in this paper, we used two backbones for experiments. When using the VOC2007 performance calculation method, FastDet with ResNet50 achieved the best results, which mAP is 87.60. When using the VOC2012 performance calculation method, FastDet with ResNet101 achieved the best results, which mAP was 89.40. Therefore, the model proposed in this paper has good performance in a variety of datasets. We also conducted related experiments on the speed of the detector. When using ResNet50 as the backbone, it can detect 19 images per second, which is much higher than the other three models. When using ResNet101 as the backbone, it can detect 16 images per second, which is the fastest model in using this backbone.

5 Conclusion

This paper present a feature-aligned rotating SSD detector FastDet, which uses the FPN structure to generate multi-size feature maps for detecting objects of different sizes. And the refining module is used to refine the detection results of the first stage. The refining module uses a non-linear bilateral filter to estimate the feature value of the center of the prediction bounding box and splice it to the original feature value position to make the feature more complete. Use the refined feature pyramid for the second detection to make the detection more accurate. Through experiments on the FastDet and baseline models on the DOTA and HRSC2016 dataset, it can be proved that our proposed network has higher detection performance.

Acknowledgment. This work was supported in part by the National Natural Science Foundation of China under Grant 62071157, Natural Science Foundation of Heilongjiang Province under Grant YQ2019F011 and Postdoctoral Foundation of Heilongjiang Province under Grant LBH-Q19112.

References

1. Zou, Z., Shi, Z., Guo, Y., et al.: Object detection in 20 years: a survey. arXiv preprint arXiv: 1905.05055 (2019)
2. Girshick, R., Donahue, J., Darrell, T., et al.: Rich feature hierarchies for accurate object detection and semantic segmentation. In: Proceedings of the IEEE Conference on Computer Vision and Pattern Recognition, pp. 580–587 (2014)
3. Ren, S., He, K., Girshick, R., et al.: Faster R-CNN: towards real-time object detection with region proposal networks. arXiv preprint arXiv:1506.01497 (2015)

4. Liu, L., Ouyang, W., Wang, X., et al.: Deep learning for generic object detection: a survey. Int. J. Comput. Vis. **128**(2), 261–318 (2020)
5. Yang, X., Liu, Q., Yan, J., et al.: R3Det: refined single-stage detector with feature refinement for rotating object. arXiv preprint arXiv:1908.05612 (2019)
6. Liu, W., et al.: SSD: single shot MultiBox detector. In: Leibe, B., Matas, J., Sebe, N., Welling, M. (eds.) ECCV 2016. LNCS, vol. 9905, pp. 21–37. Springer, Cham (2016). https://doi.org/10.1007/978-3-319-46448-0_2
7. Lin, T.Y., Goyal, P., Girshick, R., et al.: Focal loss for dense object detection. In: Proceedings of the IEEE International Conference on Computer Vision, pp. 2980–2988 (2017)
8. Lin, T.Y., Dollár, P., Girshick, R., et al.: Feature pyramid networks for object detection. In: Proceedings of the IEEE Conference on Computer Vision and Pattern Recognition, pp. 2117–2125 (2017)
9. Xia, G.S., Bai, X., Ding, J., et al.: DOTA: a large-scale dataset for object detection in aerial images. In: Proceedings of the IEEE Conference on Computer Vision and Pattern Recognition, pp. 3974–3983 (2018)
10. Liu, Z., Yuan, L., Weng, L., et al.: A high resolution optical satellite image dataset for ship recognition and some new baselines. In: International Conference on Pattern Recognition Applications and Methods, vol. 2, pp. 324–331. SCITEPRESS (2017)
11. Dai, J., Li, Y., He, K., et al.: R-FCN: object detection via region-based fully convolutional networks. arXiv preprint arXiv:1605.06409 (2016)
12. Chen, Z., et al.: PIoU loss: towards accurate oriented object detection in complex environments. In: Vedaldi, A., Bischof, H., Brox, T., Frahm, J.-M. (eds.) ECCV 2020. LNCS, vol. 12350, pp. 195–211. Springer, Cham (2020). https://doi.org/10.1007/978-3-030-58558-7_12
13. Azimi, S.M., Vig, E., Bahmanyar, R., Körner, M., Reinartz, P.: Towards multi-class object detection in unconstrained remote sensing imagery. In: Jawahar, C.V., Li, H., Mori, G., Schindler, K. (eds.) ACCV 2018. LNCS, vol. 11363, pp. 150–165. Springer, Cham (2019). https://doi.org/10.1007/978-3-030-20893-6_10
14. Li, Y., Huang, Q., Pei, X., et al.: RADet: refine feature pyramid network and multi-layer attention network for arbitrary-oriented object detection of remote sensing images. Remote Sens. **12**(3), 389 (2020)
15. Wei, H., Zhang, Y., Chang, Z., et al.: Oriented objects as pairs of middle lines. ISPRS J. Photogram. Remote Sens. **169**, 268–279 (2020)
16. Jiang, Y., Zhu, X., Wang, X., et al.: R2CNN: rotational region CNN for orientation robust scene text detection. arXiv preprint arXiv:1706.09579 (2017)
17. Ma, J., Shao, W., Ye, H., et al.: Arbitrary-oriented scene text detection via rotation proposals. IEEE Trans. Multimed. **20**(11), 3111–3122 (2018)
18. Ding, J., Xue, N., Long, Y., et al.: Learning RoI transformer for oriented object detection in aerial images. In: Proceedings of the IEEE/CVF Conference on Computer Vision and Pattern Recognition, pp. 2849–2858 (2019)

Facial Expression Recognition Based on Multi-feature Fusion

Zhuang Miao, Jingyu Li(✉), and Kezheng Lin

School of Computer Science and Technology, Harbin University of Science and Technology, Harbin, China
920948105@qq.com

Abstract. In order to solve the problems of insufficient facial expression feature extraction and large parameter amount in some convolutional neural networks, a facial expression recognition algorithm based on multi-feature fusion is proposed. This method first modifies the residual block in the ResNet network, reduces the amount of network parameters and uses pre-activation to reduce the error rate. After that, the features extracted by the improved ResNet network are fused with the features extracted by the VGG network after the cut layer, and the network model P-ResNet-VGG is obtained. The loss function uses the cross entropy loss function. This model has been extensively tested on the FER2013 and JAFFE datasets. The experimental results show that this model has improved accuracy on the expression data set than other models, and it has a significant effect on the FER2013 and JAFFE data sets.

Keywords: Deep learning · Convolutional neural network · Facial expression recognition · Feature fusion

1 Introduction

Nowadays, there are many ways that humans express their emotions, but the most direct way is to judge them by their facial expressions. Guess the other person's mental activities and emotions based on their facial expressions. Facial expression recognition is one of the hot spots in the direction of computer vision. Its application field is also very extensive. Including man-machine interaction, safe driving, intelligent monitoring, assisted driving, case detection, etc.

Early facial expression recognition research is based on hand-made features [1]. In the ImageNet large-scale visual recognition competition [2], the success of the AlexNet [3] network model has made deep learning widely used in the field of computer vision. Facial expression recognition (FER) challenge [4] proposed the use of deep learning in the early days. The best performance in the 2013 FER Challenge was the deep convolutional neural network [5], and the manual feature model only ranked fourth [6]. In 2017, Tang Chuan Gao et al. [7] used deep learning to win the championship in the field of facial expression recognition. Later, the convolutional neural network has achieved good

© ICST Institute for Computer Sciences, Social Informatics and Telecommunications Engineering 2022
Published by Springer Nature Switzerland AG 2022. All Rights Reserved
S. Shi et al. (Eds.): 6GN 2021, LNICST 439, pp. 264–275, 2022.
https://doi.org/10.1007/978-3-031-04245-4_23

results in the field of facial expression recognition, but with the deepening of research, problems have also been discovered.

The network based on the attention model proposed by Chu et al. [8] achieved an accuracy of 97.45% on the CK+ data set. Lu et al. [9] designed a 7-layer CNN to perform expression recognition on CK+ and only achieved an accuracy of 81.5%. It can be inferred that too few network layers, single network model extraction features, etc. are the reasons for the lower recognition rate. Later, researchers try to combine multiple feature fusion [10–12] or multiple network models [13–15] for expression recognition In order to achieve a higher accuracy rate.

Therefore, this paper proposes a network model based on multi-feature fusion. First, the residual block in the ResNet network is improved, the number of network layers is modified, and the pre-activation method is introduced. After that, the network is combined with the modified VGG network to obtain a P-ResNet-VGG (Pre-activated residual network and Visual Geometry Group) dual-channel network structure. The fused network structure extracts more feature information and can improve The recognition rate of the sample reduces the time cost of the model training in the expression recognition training process.

2 Deep Learning Model

2.1 VGG Network Model

The VGG network uses a continuous 3×3 convolution kernel instead of a larger convolution kernel. For a given receptive field, it is better to use multiple small convolution kernels. Non-linear operations can be achieved through the activation function, which can train more Good network structure, and the cost will not increase. The activation function selects the R-ReLU function, which can make up for the shortcomings of the RelU function. Its function is.

$$RRelu(x) = \begin{cases} x, & x > 0 \\ ax, & x < 0 \end{cases} \tag{1}$$

The advantage of using R-ReLU compared to ReLU is that the negative values in the ReLU function are all zero. If a large gradient flows through the RelU neuron to update the gradient, this neuron will lose activation of some data, and the gradient will change. 0 leads to neuron death. The a in the RReLU function is a value randomly selected from a given uniform distribution range, and it will be fixed during the test. Solved the problem that the ReLU function may cause neuron death.

2.2 ResNet Network Model

The ResNet network adds the concept of residuals to the convolutional neural network. After several layers of convolutional layers, shortcut connections are used. This allows you to return to the previous shallow network when the increase in depth causes the accuracy of the model to decrease. This will find the optimal number of network layers during the training process, and will not cause the model to be worse due to the complexity of the network settings.

The residual network is composed of multiple residual blocks, and the residual blocks need to be fitted to the residual mapping $f(\boldsymbol{x}) - \boldsymbol{x}$ related to the identity mapping. The residual mapping is easier to optimize in practice, and the residual block is shown in Fig. 1. The residual unit formula can be expressed as

$$\begin{cases} y_l = h(x_l) + F(x_l, W_l) \\ x_{l+1} = f(y_l) \end{cases} \tag{2}$$

Among them, x_l and x_{l+1} respectively represent the input and output of the l residual unit. F is the residual function, $h(x_l) = x_l$ is the identity mapping, and f is the RRelu activation function. Based on formula (2), the learning characteristics from shallow l to deep L can be obtained as

$$x_L = x_l + \sum_{i=l}^{L-1} F(x_i, W_i) \tag{3}$$

Using the chain rule, the gradient of the reverse process can be obtained

$$\frac{\partial loss}{\partial x_l} = \frac{\partial loss}{\partial x_L} \cdot \frac{\partial x_L}{\partial x_l} = \frac{\partial loss}{\partial x_L} \cdot \left(1 + \frac{\partial}{\partial x_L} \sum_{i=l}^{L-1} F(x_i, W_i)\right) \tag{4}$$

Among them, $\frac{\partial loss}{\partial x_L}$ represents the gradient of the loss function to L, and 1 can ensure that the gradient will not disappear, so that the residual network training will be easier.

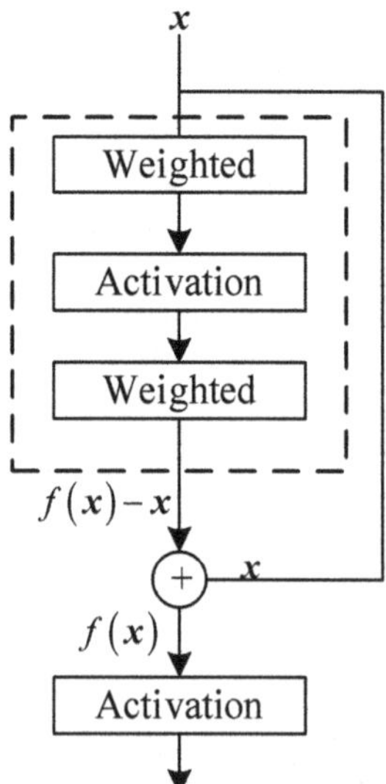

Fig. 1. Residual block

3 P-ResNet-VGG Network Structure

3.1 Improved ResNet Network

In order to extract richer facial features in the image and improve the accuracy of facial expression recognition, the residual block in the ResNet network is improved. The improvement to the network is to change the residual block to a three-layer convolutional layer, and one convolution kernel before and after is a 1×1 convolutional layer. The size of the convolution kernel of the middle convolutional layer has not changed, thus adding a convolution Operation, and the amount of network parameters is greatly reduced.

On this basis, in order to prevent the gradient from disappearing, alleviate the occurrence of overfitting, and enhance the nonlinear expression ability of the network, the RRelu activation function is added after each convolution. As shown in Fig. 2.

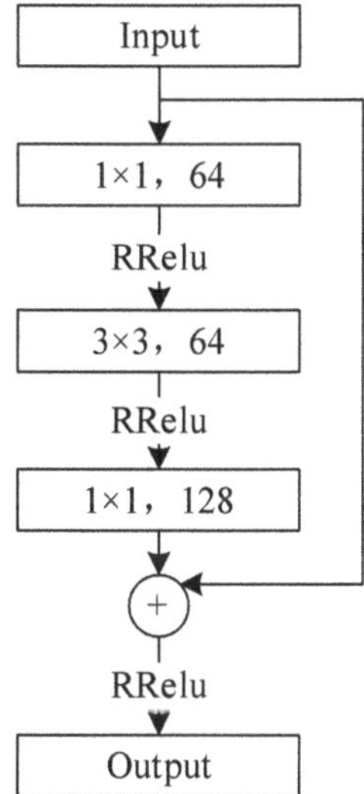

Fig. 2. Modified residual block

At the same time, the BN layer is also used for batch normalization, which can make the training of deeper neural networks easier, speed up the convergence of the network model, and improve the accuracy of the trained model. After the BN layer and the activation layer are mentioned before the convolutional layer, pre-activation can be achieved. The modified P-ResNet network will be faster than the original ResNet network in training speed, and the error will be reduced, which is more helpful for deeper networks, such as As shown in Fig. 3

Then the modified residual block is added to the original network, the input is the original picture, and the feature map is generated after multiple residual block processing, and then passed to the subsequent fully connected layer for classification processing.

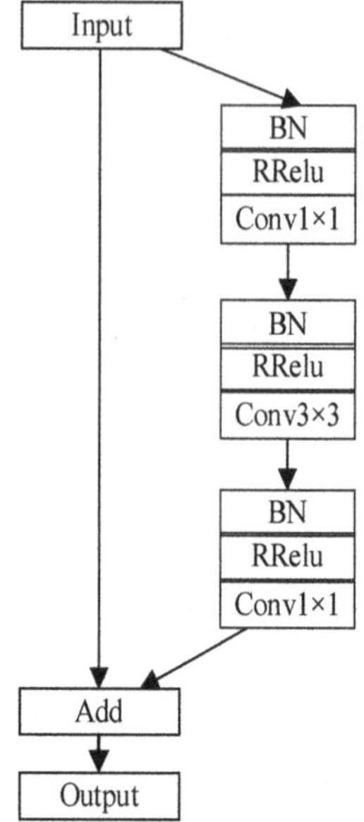

Fig. 3. Preactivation flow chart

3.2 Loss Function

The loss value of the prediction result can be obtained by bringing the feature vector and label value mentioned by the neural network into the loss function. And through the back propagation of the loss value to optimize the gradient, the commonly used multi-class loss function is the cross entropy loss function

$$L_1 = -\sum_{i=1}^{N} y^{(i)} log\ \hat{y}^{(i)} + \left(1 - y^{(i)}\right) log\left(1 - \hat{y}^{(i)}\right) \tag{5}$$

Among them, N represents the total number of samples, $y^{(i)}$ represents the output value of the i sample forward propagation, $\hat{y}^{(i)}$ represents the probability that i samples are positive samples, and L_1 represents the total loss value.

3.3 Overall Network Structure

An increase in network depth means a larger amount of parameters, longer training time, and more difficult optimization. Therefore, the overall network structure is to cut the number of VGG19 layers, and then merge with the P-ResNet network. Then the shallow information and the deep information are combined and input to the next convolutional layer, so that the extracted feature information can be more complete. Such a network structure can better obtain image features that are conducive to classification without increasing the training time. Compared with the features extracted from a single channel, the fused features are easier to match the real tags, and the recognition effect is better.

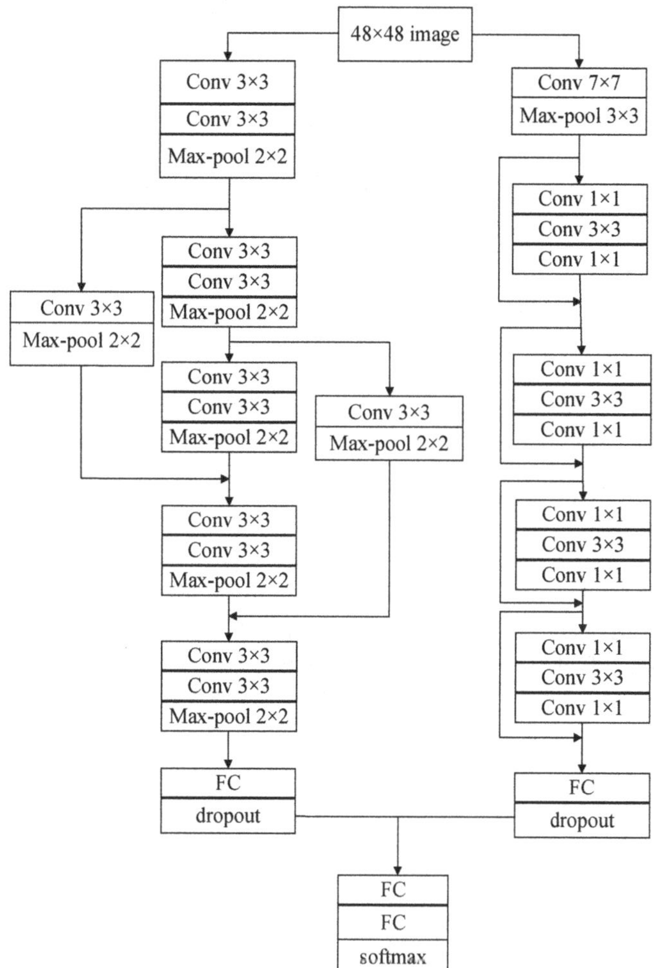

Fig. 4. Overall network structure

The 3 × 3 convolution kernel is the smallest size that can capture the eight-neighborhood information of a pixel. The limited receptive field of two 3 × 3 stacked volume base layers is 5 × 5; the receptive field of three 3 × 3 stacked volume base layers is 7 × 7, so large-size convolution can be replaced by stacking of small-size convolutional layers Layer, and the size of the field remains the same. Therefore, three 3 × 3 filters can be regarded as a decomposition of a 7 × 7 filter. The middle layer has a nonlinear decomposition and plays a role of implicit regularization. Multiple 3 × 3 volume base layers are more non-linear than a large-size filter volume base layer, making the decision function more critical. The network structure diagram after adding feature fusion is shown in Fig. 4. The input layer is a 48 × 48 single-channel picture with pixels. The VGG network is used as the basic structure on the left. The size of the convolution kernel is 3 × 3, and 0 padding is added to the periphery to ensure that the size of the feature map obtained by the convolution kernel remains unchanged., And then pass the maximum pooling layer to reduce the feature map size to half. There are five such convolutional layers in total. The channel numbers of the five convolution kernels are 64, 128, 256, 512, 512, and there are two branches. Used as a feature fusion, the size is adjusted by the convolutional pooling layer for fusion. After the two channels pass through the fully connected layer, they become feature vectors and then fused together. In order to prevent overfitting, a dropout layer is introduced. Then it is passed to the following fully connected layer and softmax layer for classification prediction, and the prediction result is obtained. In order to introduce non-linear operations to obtain better results, the R-Relu function is selected as the activation function. The overall network structure is shown in Fig. 4.

Among them, stochastic gradient descent (SGD) is used for optimization. The objective function is the average of the loss function of each sample in the data set. The goal of stochastic gradient descent is used to minimize the loss function. The loss function selects the cross-entropy loss function, because the gradient of the last layer of weight is no longer related to the derivative of the activation function, but is only proportional to the difference between the output value and the true value. The convergence is faster at this time. Backpropagation is continuous multiplication, so the update of the entire weight matrix will be accelerated. Secondly, the derivation of multi-class cross entropy loss is simpler, and the loss is only related to the probability of the correct class. Let $f_i(\boldsymbol{x})$ be the loss function of the training data sample with index i, n is the number of training data samples, $\boldsymbol{x}$ is the model parameter vector, and the objective function is

$$f(\boldsymbol{x}) = \frac{1}{n}\sum_{i=1}^{n} f_i(\boldsymbol{x}) \tag{6}$$

The derivative of the objective function at $\boldsymbol{x}$ is

$$\nabla f(\boldsymbol{x}) = \frac{1}{n}\sum_{i=1}^{n} \nabla f_i(\boldsymbol{x}) \tag{7}$$

In each iteration of stochastic gradient descent, a sample index $i \in \{1, \ldots, \text{n}\}$ is randomly sampled uniformly, and gradient $\nabla f_i(\boldsymbol{x})$ is calculated to iterate $\boldsymbol{x}$, the formula is as shown in (8)

$$\boldsymbol{x} = \boldsymbol{x} - \eta \nabla f_i(\boldsymbol{x}) \tag{8}$$

Among them, η is the learning rate, and the computational cost of each iteration is reduced from O(n) for gradient descent to a constant O(1). And stochastic gradient $\nabla f_i(\boldsymbol{x})$ is an unbiased estimate of gradient $\nabla f(\boldsymbol{x})$, as shown in formula (9), which means that on average, stochastic gradient descent is a good estimate of gradient.

$$E_i \nabla f_i(\boldsymbol{x}) = \frac{1}{n}\sum_{i=1}^{n} \nabla f_i(\boldsymbol{x}) = \nabla f(\boldsymbol{x}) \tag{9}$$

3.4 Algorithm Design

The steps of the P-ResNet-VGG network algorithm are shown in Algorithm 1:

Algorithm 1: P-ResNet-VGG algorithm

Input: facial expression image $\boldsymbol{X}$
Output: the extracted feature vector $\boldsymbol{D}$
(1)Perform data processing on the input facial expression image to generate the data format required by the neural network $\boldsymbol{x}$ 。
(2)Construct P-ResNet-VGG network model, input data $\{\boldsymbol{x}_i\}$, Use formula $\boldsymbol{a}_i = f(\boldsymbol{e}) = f(\boldsymbol{w} \cdot \boldsymbol{x}_i + \boldsymbol{b})$ Calculate the feature vector of the convolutional layer, $\boldsymbol{w}$ Represents the weight matrix of the convolutional layer, $\boldsymbol{b}$ Is the offset, $f(\cdot)$ Represents the activation function. Then through the pooling layer, the feature vector size is reduced to half of the original two. After multiple convolutional pooling operations, the two networks each obtain a one-dimensional feature vector $\boldsymbol{D}_1$ and $\boldsymbol{D}_2$, Combining $\boldsymbol{D}_1$ and $\boldsymbol{D}_2$ to obtain $\boldsymbol{D}$, the class prediction is obtained through the fully connected layer and the softmax layer.
(3)Use the cross-entropy loss function to compare the result obtained in step 2 with the real label to calculate the total loss, and then use the stochastic gradient descent algorithm to update the weights $\boldsymbol{w}$ 。
(4)After multiple iterations of step2 and step3, until the loss value stabilizes, save the model with the highest accuracy, and then input the test image into the trained network to obtain a new feature vector, The $\boldsymbol{D}$ is classified and predicted by the Softmax method, and the prediction result is its predicted label.

---

4 Experiments

4.1 Experimental Environment and Data Preprocessing

The experiment in this paper uses two data sets, FER2013 and JAFFE, for training and testing, both of which are implemented on the GPU version of the Pytorch deep learning framework.

Before the experiment, the size of the pictures in the two data sets was unified to 48 × 48. In order to prevent over-fitting, the pictures were enhanced by data, and the pictures were mirrored horizontally and rotated slightly.

4.2 Data Set

The FER2013 dataset is one of the most commonly used public facial expression datasets, with a total of 35888 unique facial expression images, including faces of various poses, light intensity and different proportions. The images are all 48 × 48 pixel grayscale images, as shown in Fig. 5. Each image in the data set is labeled for each of the seven categories: 0 anger, 1 disgust, 2 fear, 3 happiness, 4 sadness, 5 surprise, and 6 neutral.

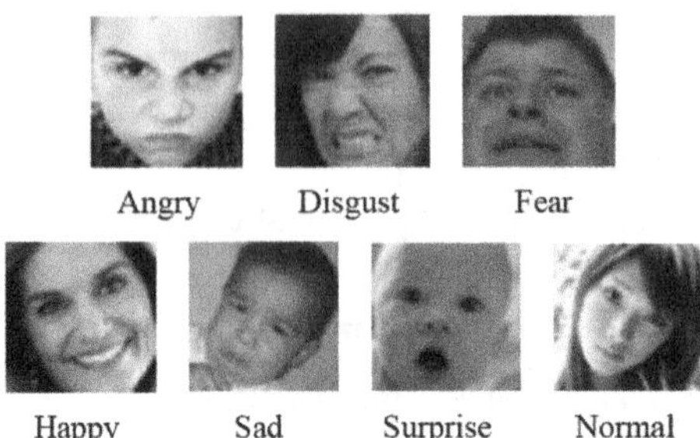

Fig. 5. Examples of seven expressions in the FER2013 dataset

The JAFFE dataset consists of 213 pictures composed of facial expressions of ten Japanese women, each with 7 facial expressions (Angry, Disgust, Fear, Happy, Sad, Surprise and Normal). Figure 6 is a sample drawn from the JAFFE database.

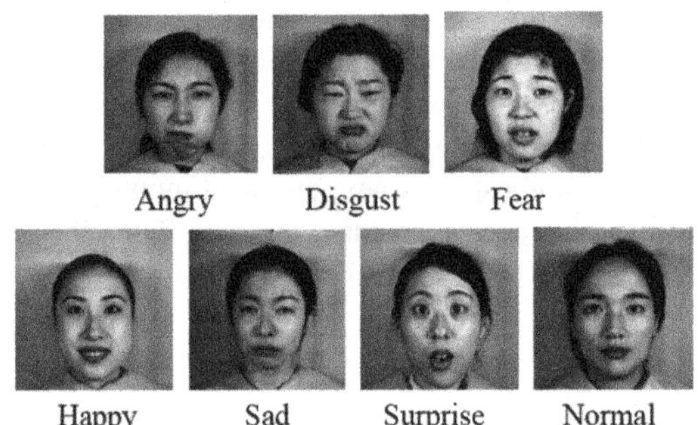

Fig. 6. Example of seven expressions in Jaffe dataset

4.3 Experiment and Result Analysis

For the FER2013 data set, 28,000 sheets are selected as the training set and 3,500 sheets as the test set. During the network training process, the epoch is set to 200, the batch size is 128, and the learning rate is set to 0.01. The learning rate of the first 50 iterations remains unchanged. When the number of iterations exceeds 50, the learning rate begins to decay, once every 5 rounds. The learning rate becomes 0.9 times the original.

In order to prevent over-fitting, the JAFFE data set adopts a cross-validation method. The data set is divided into 5 parts. Each time 4 parts are used as the training set and 1 part is used as the test set. Each network is trained for 30 epochs. The model with the lowest test loss value is used as the final training model. In the experiment, two models,

P-ResNet and P-ResNet-VGG, were used for experiments on the FER2013 and JAFFE datasets. Tables 1 and 2 show the results of the model on the two data sets.

Table 1. Accuracy of P-ResNet on two data sets %

Emotion	FER2013	JAFFE
Angry	71.27	95.31
Disgust	69.43	97.01
Fear	71.53	97.66
Happy	75.71	98.48
Sad	74.51	98.41
Surprise	72.38	96.83
Normal	72.45	97.10
Average	72.47	97.25

Table 2. Accuracy of P-ResNet-VGG on two data sets %

Emotion	FER2013	JAFFE
Angry	73.25	97.66
Disgust	70.63	98.51
Fear	72.47	99.22
Happy	77.38	100.00
Sad	75.42	99.21
Surprise	74.61	98.41
Normal	71.91	98.55
Average	73.67	98.79

As shown in Table 3, the accuracy of several models in the experiment is compared with the overall accuracy of facial expression recognition of other models.

On the JAFFE data set, the P-ResNet-VGG model has a higher accuracy rate, Table 4 shows the comparison of the accuracy of several models on the JAFFE data set. In the comparison experiment, the method of Zhang et al. [19] is a stacked hybrid autoencoder based on deep learning. The method of Kommineni et al. [20] uses a hybrid feature extraction technique. Kola et al. [21] used a local binary pattern based on adaptive windows for facial expression recognition. The comparison experiment has a more detailed accuracy rate comparison, which can intuitively indicate that the model in this paper is relatively stable and has a higher accuracy rate.

It can be seen from the experimental results that the P-ResNet-VGG model is better than several other models. Improved accuracy on both data sets. When the data set is

Table 3. Comparison of accuracy rates with other models on the FER2013 dataset %

Model	Accuracy
Ref. [16]	70.86
Ref. [17]	71.80
Ref. [18]	71.91
P-ResNet	72.47
P-ResNet-VGG	73.67

Table 4. Comparison of accuracy rates of several models on Jaffe dataset %

Model	Accuracy
Ref. [19]	96.70
Ref. [20]	98.14
Ref. [21]	92.81
P-ResNet	97.25
P-ResNet-VGG	98.79

large, the effect of the parallel network model fusion is better and more accurate. In addition, the features after deep and shallow layer fusion are more complete, and the recognition rate is higher; fewer network layers are used for training, which makes up for the slow model training problem of the CNN network due to the large network of training data. Requires advanced problems, so while reducing training time, a higher recognition rate is obtained.

5 Conclusion

The method based on parallel network feature fusion combines the advantages of the two network structures of VGG and ResNet. On the one hand, it takes full advantage of the fast training speed and fewer parameters of the ResNet network to improve network training efficiency; on the other hand, the fusion of different networks and the fusion of deep and shallow features of the network itself can have a certain recognition rate for expressions in big data. Improved, and at the same time, compared with other deep network training time has been effectively reduced. From the experimental results, it can be seen that the P-ResNet-VGG model has certain advantages compared with the compared models. It plays a role in training time and accuracy, and the effect of increasing the amount of data is more obvious. In terms of feature extraction, the use of better and more accurate methods to distinguish the gaps between different expressions will be the next step in research work to further reduce training time and improve recognition accuracy.

References

1. Logie, R.H., Baddeley, A.D., Woodhead, M.M.: Face recognition, pose and ecological validity. Appl. Cogn. Psychol. **1**(1), 53–69 (2015)
2. Krizhevsky, A., Sutskever, I., Hinton, G.E.: ImageNet classification with deep convolutional neural networks. In: Proceedings of Advances in Neural Information Processing Systems, New York, pp. 1097–1105 (2012)
3. Russakovsky, O., Deng, J., Su, H., et al.: ImageNet large scale visual recognition challenge. Int. J. Comput. Vis. **115**(3), 211–252 (2015)
4. Goodfellow, I.J., Erhan, D., Carrier, P.L., et al.: Challenges in representation learning: a report on three machine learning contests. Neural Netw. **64**, 59–63 (2015)
5. Xu, M.Y., Tang, Z.M., Yao, Y.Z., et al.: Deep learning for person reidentification using support vector machines. Adv. Multimed. **2017**, 11–18 (2017)
6. Wang, Y., Su, W.J., Liu, H.L.: Facial expression recognition based on linear discriminant locality preserving analysis algorithm. J. Inf. Comput. Sci. **9**(11), 4281–4289 (2013)
7. Tang, C., Zheng, W., Yan, J., et al.: View-independent facial action unit detection. In: Proceedings of the 12th IEEE International Conference on Automatic Face and Gesture Recognition, Los Alamitos, CA, USA, pp. 878–882 (2017)
8. Chu, J., Tang, W., Zhang, S.: Facial expression recognition algorithm based on attention model. Laser Optoelectron. Prog. **57**(12), 121015 (2020)
9. Lu, G., He, J., Yan, J.: A convolutional neural network for facial expression recognition. J. Nanjing Univ. **36**(1), 16–22 (2016)
10. Li, X., Niu, H.: Facial expression recognition based on feature fusion based on VGG-NET. Comput. Eng. Sci. **42**(03), 500–509 (2020)
11. Li, M., Li, X., Wang, X., et al.: Real-time face expression recognition based on multi-scale kernel feature convolutional neural network. J. Comput. Appl. **39**(09), 2568–2574 (2019)
12. Mishra, G., Vishwakarma, V.P., Aggarwal, A.: Face recognition using linear sparse approximation with multi-modal feature fusion. J. Discrete Math. Sci. Crypt. **22**(2), 161–175 (2019)
13. Wang, H.: Enhanced forest microexpression recognition based on optical flow direction histogram and deep multiview network. Math. Probl. Eng. **2020**(8), 1–11 (2020)
14. Li, D., Zhao, X., Yuan, G., et al.: Robustness comparison between the capsule network and the convolutional network for facial expression recognition. Appl. Intell. **51**(4), 2269–2278 (2020)
15. Zhang, T., Zheng, W., Cui, Z., et al.: A deep neural network-driven feature learning method for multi-view facial expression recognition. IEEE Trans. Multimed. **18**(12), 2528–2536 (2016)
16. Guo, Y.N., Tao, D.P., Yu, J.: Deep neural networks with relativity learning for facial expression recognition. In: Proceedings of the 2016 IEEE International Conference on Multimedia and Expo Workshop, Washington, pp. 166–170 (2016)
17. Zhou, S., Liang, Y., Wan, J., Li, S.Z.: Facial expression recognition based on multi-scale CNNs. In: You, Z., et al. (eds.) CCBR 2016. LNCS, vol. 9967, pp. 503–510. Springer, Cham (2016). https://doi.org/10.1007/978-3-319-46654-5_55
18. Hua, W., Dai, F., Huang, L., et al.: HERO: human emotions recognition for realizing intelligent Internet of Things. IEEE Access **7**, 1 (2019)
19. Zhang, Z.Y., Wang, R.Q., Wei, M.M.: Stack hybrid self-encoder facial expression recognition method. Comput. Eng. Appl. **55**(13), 140–144 (2019)
20. Kommineni, J., Mandala, S., Sunar, M.S., et al.: Accurate computing of facial expression recognition using a hybrid feature extraction technique. J. Supercomput. **77**(11), 1–26 (2020)
21. Kola, D.G.R., Samayamantula, S.K.: A novel approach for facial expression recognition using local binary pattern with adaptive window. Multimed. Tools Appl. **80**(12), 1–20 (2020)

LSTM-Based MACD Strategy Parameter Restructuring

Huan Deng[1,2(✉)], Jiali Liu[2], Yu Tang[2], Di Lin[1,2], and Bo Chen[1,2]

[1] Intelligent Terminal Key Laboratory of Sichuan Province, Yibin, China
[2] University of Electronic Science and Technology of China, Chengdu, China
201922090528@std.uestc.edu.cn, lindi@uestc.edu.cn

Abstract. Moving average convergence divergence (MACD) strategy has been applied in much research in financial area. Studies has demonstrated the excellent performance of the MACD strategy in quantitative investment. However, traditional parameter set (12, 26, 9) performs differently in various regions and market environments. Hence, we propose a LSTM-based method to optimize MACD strategy parameters. The proposed method offers the ability to predict advanced MACD strategy parameters in any time interval. We use all stocks from China A-Shares over the period of 2015–2020 as experiment data. We find that after applying different MACD parameter sets produced by our model, balance outperforms than the non-optimized parameter set. Our model provides an easy-to-use investment tool that discovers potential positive returns.

Keywords: MACD · Parameters optimization · LSTM · China A-Shares

1 Introduction

With the advent of the era of big data and the development of artificial intelligence, machine learning methods have become an advanced means of solving problems. Therefore, the financial field has set its sights on the field of machine learning to realize the commercialization of big data and artificial intelligence in financial markets and institutions, such as quantitative trading and other applications.

The MACD strategy is a commonly used and effective technical analysis method in the financial market. It uses the convergence and divergence of the long- and short-term exponential moving averages of the closing price to determine the timing of buying and selling. Prior experience has used fixed parameters (12, 26, 9) for a long time. However, the market is volatile, and the efficiency levels of the excess returns obtained by using the MACD strategy in different regions are different [1]. Therefore, we consider dynamically adjusting parameters to adapt to different market environments in order to obtain greater economic benefits [2]. Marques et al. [3] used genetic algorithms and fuzzy logic to test

© ICST Institute for Computer Sciences, Social Informatics and Telecommunications Engineering 2022
Published by Springer Nature Switzerland AG 2022. All Rights Reserved
S. Shi et al. (Eds.): 6GN 2021, LNICST 439, pp. 276–284, 2022.
https://doi.org/10.1007/978-3-031-04245-4_24

the MACD strategy and improved the MACD parameters, proving the potential benefits of adjusting the MACD parameters.

We proposes a neural network based on LSTM to optimize and restructuring the parameters of the MACD strategy to make it more adapted for different market environments. The experimental results prove the advantages of using neural network method and the possibility of bringing more benefits.

The rest of this paper is structured as follows. In Sect. 2 we review the related work. Section 3 introduces the proposed method. Then, in Sect. 4 we present and analyze the experimental results. Section 5 concludes.

2 Related Work

Moving average convergence divergence (MACD) is a trading indicator for stock price technical analysis created by Gerald Appel in the 1970s. By revealing the strength, direction, momentum and continuous direction changes of the stock price trend, it guides investors to buy or sell for returns. The formula is as follows [2,4,5]:

$$EMA_{Nt} = EMA_{Nt-1} * \frac{N-1}{N+1} + \frac{2 * Close_t}{N+1} \tag{1}$$

$$EMA_{Mt} = EMA_{Mt-1} * \frac{M-1}{M+1} + \frac{2 * Close_t}{M+1} \tag{2}$$

$$DIF_t = EMA_{Nt} - EMA_{Mt} \tag{3}$$

$$DEA_{Pt} = DEA_{Pt-1} * \frac{P-1}{P+1} + \frac{2 * DIF_t}{P+1} \tag{4}$$

$$MACD_t = 2(DIF_t - DEA_{Pt}) \tag{5}$$

where $Close_t$ is the closing price of t_{th} time. By drawing MACD and signal curves, triggering buy and sell signals are revealed.

The optimization methods of MACD parameters can be divided into two categories, model-based methods and data-driven methods. The model-based method finds the optimal parameter sets through existing mathematical methods. Marques et al. [3] used genetic algorithms to establish an optimal window value based on the MACD model, and fuzzy logic to indicate the best time to buy and sell, which can generate higher profits. It revealed the potential returns of adjusting MACD parameters. Based on the Nikkei 225 futures market, Kang [6] evaluated the potential positive returns brought by changes in MACD parameters through the establishment of traditional MACD models, comparative models and optimized models. The data-driven method selects and analyzes a large amount of data through machine learning methods to find the potential relation between the optimal parameters and the data. Yang [5] used SVM and RVM methods to optimize trading signals in MACD, and added indicators such as market activity, volatility, and deviation. Javan et al. [7] established a SeroFAM network based on the MACD model, and added its predicted value to the MACD signal to reduce the lagged effect of MACD.

Predicting methods based on time series are of great significance in various knowledge fields. In the financial field, more and more scholars have begun to use time series analysis methods. Yu et al. [8] used BP network and fuzzy logic to predict the value of TAIEX (Taiwan Stock Exchange Capitalization Weighted Stock Index) price series. Sidra et al. [9] used CNN to build a regression model and predict the future index value based on the NIFTY50 of the National Stock Exchange (NSE) of India. Inspired by the above work, we propose a neural network based on LSTM, which optimizes the parameters of the MACD strategy from time series stock data.

3 Method

The network structure constructed in this paper mainly includes LSTM and two fully connected layers. The input stock data is preprocessed and then input to the LSTM. After Dropout, the hidden layer output h_t is obtained. The predicted values of the MACD strategy parameters are calculated through the two-layer full connection as the final result (see Fig. 1).

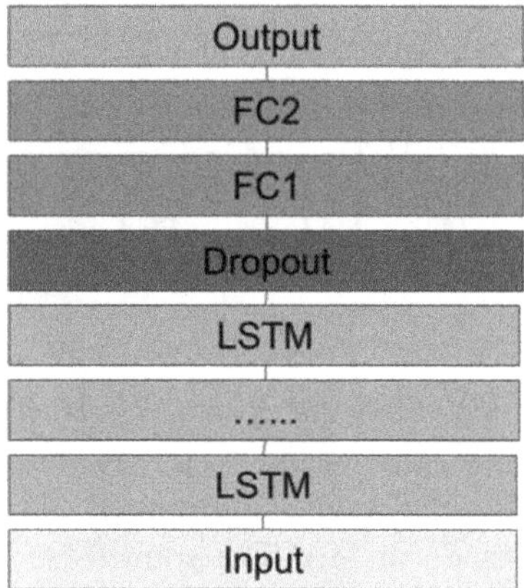

Fig. 1. The overall structure of the network.

3.1 Network

Recurrent Neural Network. RNN is a common artificial neural network, which specializes in processing sequence problems. Sequence usually refers to a piece of text or audio. For this paper, it refers to stock data in a certain time window. A simple feed-forward neural network usually contains an input layer, a hidden layer and an output layer. RNN has more loops on the hidden layer based on it. The output of the hidden layer at the t_{th} time and the input of the next time are calculated as the input of the hidden layer together, so as to realize the preservation of information. But RNN has a hidden short-term memory problem, which is caused by the nature of back propagation. In order to solve this problem, LSTM is introduced.

Long Short-Term Memory. The core of LSTM is the cell state c_t, which carries relevant information (memory). Similar to the hidden state h_t, but it will not be passed to the next layer of the network. In addition, three new gate components are added to the hidden layer, the forget gate f_t, the input gate i_t and the output gate o_t [10]. The formula is as follows:

$$f_t = \sigma(U_f x_t + W_f h_{t-1}) \tag{6}$$

$$i_t = \sigma(U_i x_t + W_i h_{t-1}) \tag{7}$$

$$o_t = \sigma(U_o x_t + W_o h_{t-1}) \tag{8}$$

$$\hat{c}_t = tanh(U_c x_t + W_c h_{t-1}) \tag{9}$$

$$c_t = f_t \odot c_{t-1} + i_t \odot \hat{c}_t \tag{10}$$

$$h_t = o_t \odot tanh(c_t) \tag{11}$$

Different gates determine whether information needs to be saved or forgotten, and selective control of memory is achieved through the superposition of multiple gated units, thereby solving the problem of short-term memory.

3.2 Data Preparation

The source of the data in this article comes from Sina Finance and Tonghuashun Finance. It contains all the stocks of China A-shares, that is, common stocks issued by companies registered in China and listed in the country for a variety of investors to subscribe and trade in RMB. A total of about 3800 stocks and data over the period of 2015–2020. In units of days, it contains data such as opening and closing prices.

At the same time, we used vn.py, a Python-based open source quantitative trading system development framework. It integrates a variety of trading interfaces, and provides a simple and easy-to-use API for specific strategy algorithms and function development. Based on the MACD strategy, through the Enumeration method, with the annualized rate of return as an indicator, the optimal parameters of the corresponding MACD strategy under each time window are calculated as our training data.

There are missing data values in the acquired data, and we performed padding operations on them. In addition, the characteristics of stock data may also affect the training of the model (see Fig. 2). The price per share of different stocks varies greatly. The price of some stocks may be a few yuan, while others may be in the hundreds or even thousands. In order to avoid problems such as potential gradient explosion caused by too large numerical differences, and at the same time maintain the data distribution, we used the z-score standardization method to map them to the same interval. The formula is as follows:

$$z = \frac{x - \mu}{\delta} \tag{12}$$

where μ is the population mean, and δ is the population standard deviation.

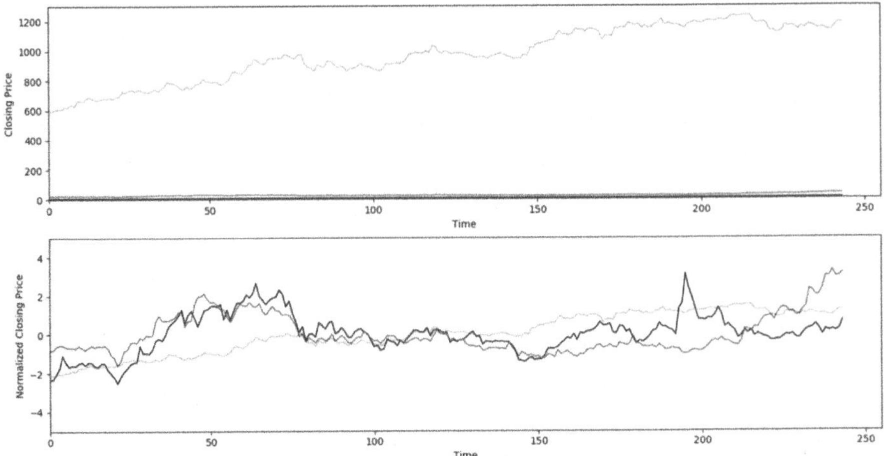

Fig. 2. Original and normalized data after applying z-score.

The z-score standardization method is suitable for situations where the maximum and minimum values of features are unknown, or there are outliers that exceed the value range. After using the z-score method, the model losses converges steadily and promptly during the training. While improving the accuracy of the model, the gradient explosion problem is avoided.

4 Results

4.1 Experiments

We use 200 stocks of all stocks for testing, and the rest for model training. Training data includes stock code, date, opening price, highest price of the day, lowest price of the day, closing price, volume and amount values. There is also the optimal parameter value of the MACD corresponding to each stock under the time window, which is given by Enumeration method and backtesting. When calculating the optimal parameter value, the parameter value ranges between (2, 31). We used a two-layer LSTM network with 1024 units in each layer. In the end, the hidden layer output is mapped to 3 dimensions through the fully connected layer. In the training process, we used the K-fold method for validation to evaluate the training effect of the model, where $K = 10$. In addition to Dropout, we also use the Early Stopping method to control the suspension time of model training, in order to obtain a model with relatively good generalization performance, while reducing training costs. Exponential decay is used to control the learning rate. At first, a larger learning rate is used to obtain a better solution, and then the learning rate is gradually reduced to control the stability of the model in the later stage of training. We use the Xavier initializer method to effectively initialize the network to ensure the training effect. RMSE and MAE are used as the evaluation methods of MACD optimal parameter prediction performance.

RMSE (Root Mean Square Error) reflects the degree of dispersion between the actual value and the predicted value. The formula is as follows:

$$RMSE = \sqrt{\frac{1}{m}\sum_{i=1}^{m}(y_i - \hat{y_i})^2} \tag{13}$$

MAE (Mean Average Error) is the average of the absolute value between the actual value and the predicted value, which can avoid the errors from canceling each other out, thereby accurately reflecting the size of the actual prediction error. The formula is as follows:

$$MAE = \frac{1}{m}\sum_{i=1}^{m}|y_i - \hat{y_i}| \tag{14}$$

where y_i is the actual value, and $\hat{y_i}$ is the predicted value. We use MSE as the loss function and Adam as the optimizer.

Table 1 shows the RMSE and MAE of the prediction of MACD parameters, using linear regression, GRU and LSTM. Where fast, slow and signal are the three parameters of the MACD strategy. It can be seen that LSTM achieves the lowest RMSE and MAE among the three methods, especially on MAE. GRU is slightly inferior to LSTM method. The linear regression method performs the worst, which proves that the neural network method has more advantages than the traditional linear method.

Table 1. RMSE and MAE of MACD parameters prediction with 3 methods

	RMSE			MAE		
	Fast	Slow	Signal	Fast	Slow	Signal
LR	7.91	4.75	6.99	7.17	4.14	6.2
GRU	7.41	4.19	6.47	6.33	3.24	5.34
LSTM	**7.19**	**3.93**	**6.29**	**5.78**	**2.71**	**4.93**

Figure 3 shows the balance, drawdown, daily profit & loss (PnL) and its distribution. The daily PnL begins to produce large deviations and fluctuations in November 2017, but the overall balance is positive. From the distribution of daily PnL, we can see a more detailed profit and loss value. For more than 400 days, it remained near the zero line, the maximum profit is close to 1000 and the maximum loss is close to 750. The population is normally distributed. Figure 4 shows the balance of trades using MACD parameters (12, 26, 9) and (2, 20, 20). Where parameter set (2, 20, 20) are the optimal value predicted by our model. During 2015–2018, we set an initial capital of 10,000 yuan. In 752 trading days, in comparison, the latter's closing funds are much higher than those of the default MACD parameter settings (12, 26, 9), and the overall balance is better than the former. This proves that dynamic adjustment of MACD strategy parameters can adapt to different market environments and obtain greater economic efficiency.

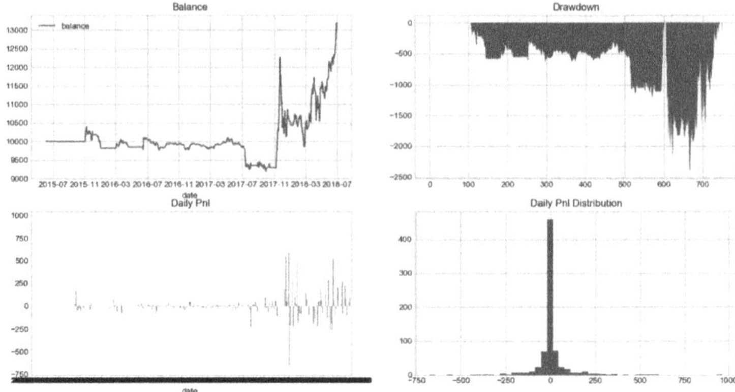

Fig. 3. Balance, drawdown and PnL.

4.2 System

We have built a prototype system to provide investors with a simple and easy-to-use investment tool. We built the back-end part of the prototype system based on the Django framework, and then integrated the algorithm module into the system. The back-end part provides user management and back-testing modules, and the algorithm provides asset allocation recommendation functions. The front end uses Javascript and Vue framework. The database storage uses MySQL, Redis and MongoDB databases and related technologies. Workflow is shown in Fig. 5.

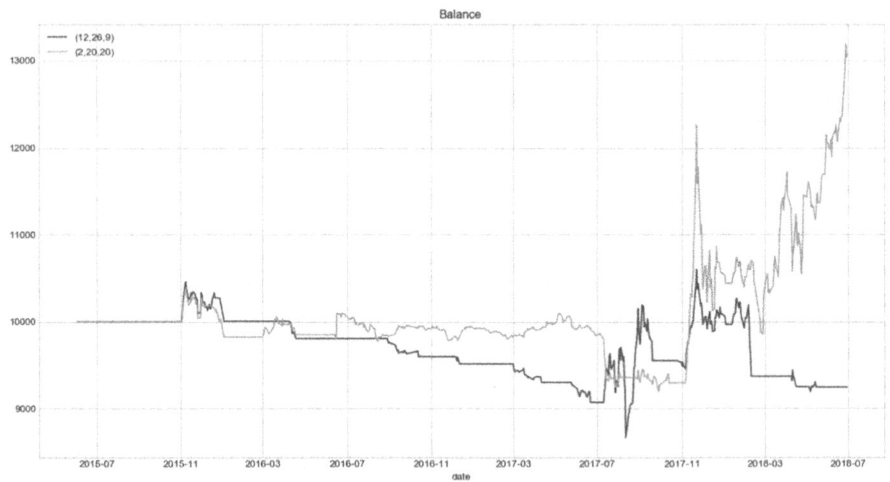

Fig. 4. Balance with different MACD parameter sets.

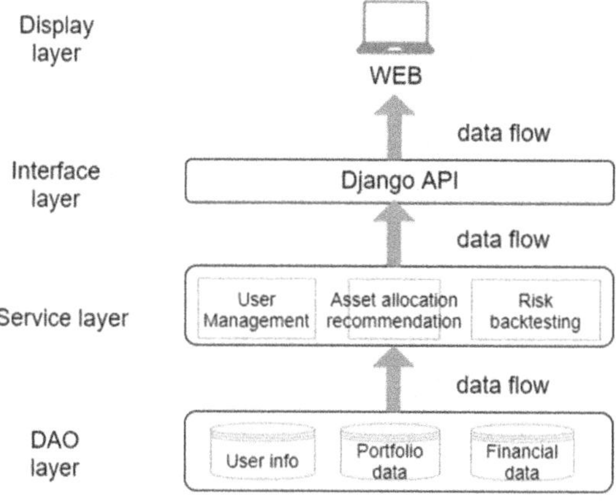

Fig. 5. System workflow.

We use the form of risk questionnaires to evaluate investors' risk-bearing ability to facilitate rating, and then according to the MACD strategy, we recommend a set of appropriate asset allocation based on the user's investment principal.

5 Conclusion

In this work we contribute to MACD strategy parameters restructuring by building a deep learning method using LSTM network. We investigate in MACD strategy and devise a new way of optimizing the gains of trades using MACD strategy. It is clear that balance improves after applying deep learning architectures to capture the information between statistics. LSTM network predicts the advancing MACD parameters, which could be used between any time periods, providing an easy-to-use investment instrument. Overall, this yields a new perspective to operate traditional MACD strategy, makes it more adapted to different market environments while brings more possibilities of potential returns. Future work will mainly focus on mining deeper stock statistics, constructing more effective features and denoising. At the same time trying more new neural network methods.

Acknowledgement. Partially Funded by Science and Technology Program of Sichuan Province (2021YFG0330), partially funded by Grant SCITLAB-0001 of Intelligent Terminal Key Laboratory of SiChuan Province and partially Funded by Fundamental Research Funds for the Central Universities (ZYGX2019J076).

References

1. Anghel, G.D.I.: Stock market efficiency and the MACD. Evidence from countries around the world. Proc. Econ. Finan. **32**, 1414–1431 (2015). Emerging Markets Queries in Finance and Business 2014, EMQFB 2014, 24–25 October 2014, Bucharest, Romania (2014)
2. Wu, M., Diao, X.: Technical analysis of three stock oscillators testing MACD, RSI and KDJ rules in SH SZ stock markets. In: 2015 4th International Conference on Computer Science and Network Technology (ICCSNT), vol. 01, pp. 320–323 (2015)
3. Marques, F.C.R., Gomes, R.M., de Almeida, P.E.M., Borges, H.E., Souza, S.R.: Maximisation of investment profits: an approach to MACD based on genetic algorithms and fuzzy logic. In: IEEE Congress on Evolutionary Computation, pp. 1–7 (2010)
4. Chen, Y.-M., Chung, T.-Y., Lai, M.-Y., Hsu, C.-H.: MACD-based motion detection approach in heterogeneous networks. EURASIP J. Wirel. Commun. Netw. **2008**, 1–14 (2008)
5. Yang, Y.: Predicting stock price trend by optimizing MACD model. J. Guangxi Acad. Sci. **33**(6) (2017)
6. Kang, B.-K.: Improving MACD technical analysis by optimizing parameters and modifying trading rules: evidence from the Japanese Nikkei 225 futures market. J. Risk Financ. Manag. **14**(1), 37 (2021)
7. Tan, J., Zhou, W.J., Quek, C.: Trading model: self reorganizing fuzzy associative machine - forecasted MACD-histogram (SeroFAM-fMACDH). In: 2015 International Joint Conference on Neural Networks (IJCNN), pp. 1–8 (2015)
8. Chen, C.-C., Kuo, Y.-C., Huang, C.-H., Chen, A.-P.: Applying market profile theory to forecast Taiwan index futures market. Expert Syst. Appl. **41**(10), 4617–4624 (2014)
9. Mehtab, S., Sen, J.: Stock price prediction using convolutional neural networks on a multivariate timeseries (2020)
10. Hochreiter, S., Schmidhuber, J.: Long short-term memory. Neural Comput. **9**(8), 1735–1780 (1997)

Multiview Subspace Clustering for Multi-kernel Low-Redundancy Representation Learning

Zhuo Wang[1(✉)], Ao Li[1], Jie Li[2], and Yangwei Wang[2]

[1] School of Computer Science and Technology, Harbin University of Science and Technology, Harbin, China
wz1997sapphire@163.com

[2] Shandong Provincial Innovation and Practice Base for Postdoctors, Weihaizhenyu Intelligence Technology Co., Ltd., Weihai, China

Abstract. The purpose of the multiview subspace clustering algorithm is to construct a consensus subspace representation matrix by looking for complementary information among multiple views. However, most of the existing algorithms only learn the common information shared between multiple views and ignore the different information among multiple views, which will also have a positive impact on the clustering effect. To solve this problem, we integrate the subspace representation matrix of all views, introduce tensor analysis, and learn to obtain the low-rank tensor subspace representation matrix to capture the high-order correlation between multiple views. Comprehensive experiments have been conducted on three data sets, and the experimental results show that the proposed algorithm is much better than the comparison algorithms in recent literature, and the superiority of the proposed algorithm is verified.

Keywords: Multiview subspace clustering · Multi-kernel · Low-redundancy representation

1 Introduction

In real life, with the development of advanced technology, an object can often be fully described by multiple views. For example, using different languages to describe the same thing; shoot the same object from different angles. These views can be various measurements, such as real-time images, text records in different languages, etc. Each of these views generates a description of the same object, and different views typically describe the same and different information about the object. Learning better representations by analyzing all views is a challenging problem [1].

Considering that a single view is not enough to describe the information of data, subspace clustering has been extended to the case of multiple views. Different from the single-view subspace clustering method, Xu [2] proposed that the multiview learning method should fully use the principles of consensus and complementarity to ensure success. In order to realize the consensus principle, a classical strategy is to obtain a

© ICST Institute for Computer Sciences, Social Informatics and Telecommunications Engineering 2022
Published by Springer Nature Switzerland AG 2022. All Rights Reserved
S. Shi et al. (Eds.): 6GN 2021, LNICST 439, pp. 285–294, 2022.
https://doi.org/10.1007/978-3-031-04245-4_25

potential subspace that can be shared by multiple views through subspace learning [3]. At the same time, some scholars proposed many algorithms to explore the complementary information between different views, and achieved good performance. Gao [4] proposed a algorithm, which performed subspace clustering on each view of the data and used a common class indicator matrix to ensure the consistency of the data. Although the effect of this algorithm is better than that of single-view clustering, it does not restrict the self-representation coefficient of the data. It cannot well explore the internal structure of the data. Zhang [5] presented a method to learn the potential representation based on the features of multiple views and generate a common subspace representation to explore the potential complementary information among multiple views. Inspired by Sparse Subspace Clustering (SSC) [6] and Low-Rank Representation (LRR) [7], Zhang [8] proposed a algorithm, which extended LRR-based subspace clustering to multiview learning using rank-constrained subspace tensors of different modal expansion. It is a good way to explore complementary information from multiple sources, and greatly improve the subspace clustering.

Although the above multiview subspace clustering method has good performance, it still has some limitations. These clustering methods only use the linear subspace of the data in the original feature space, which is not enough to capture the complex correlation between actual data. In this regard, Abavisani [9] proposed a multi-mode extension method based on SSC and LRR subspace clustering algorithms, and used kernel learning to make the multimodal subspace clustering method nonlinear. Li [10] proposed to capture higher-order, nonlinear relationships between different views by introducing the Hilbert Schmidt Independent Standard (HSIC).

The above multiview subspace clustering method is proved to be effective in many scenarios. However, most of the above models use the original data and corresponding kernel matrix as the model's input, and both the original data and corresponding kernel matrix contain a lot of redundant information, which will affect the clustering effect. To solve this problem, we present a multiview subspace clustering method with multi-kernel and low redundancy representation learning. Raw data through learning method to get the corresponding kernel matrix, at the same time to avoid a single-kernel method is heavily dependent on the choice of kernel function problems, we select multiple kernel function to map, respectively mapped to the corresponding high-dimensional reproducing kernel Hilbert space. Then, the kernel matrix is removed by feature decomposition, and the low redundancy data self representation matrix is obtained, and then the subspace representation matrix is constructed on each view, and then the subspace representation matrix of each view is collected to construct the tensor to capture the consistency and difference information between different graphs, to obtain better clustering results. The contributions are summarized as follows.

(1) The low redundant data representation is used to replace the original data as the model input, thus reducing the influence of the redundant information in the original data on the clustering effect.
(2) Feature decomposition into multiview subspace clustering algorithm provides low redundancy data representation. At the same time, the multiview subspace clustering algorithm leads the eigendecomposition to produce the low redundancy data representation, which is more suitable for clustering.

(3) Integrate the subspace representation matrix of all views to construct a tensor to explore the high-order correlation among multiple views and obtain a better clustering effect.

2 Related Work

This paper mainly explores the multiview subspace clustering method for multi-kernel low-redundant representation learning. The following will introduce some basic related work and analysis involved in this method.

2.1 Subspace Clustering

Given a dataset $\mathbf{X} \in \mathbb{R}^{d \times n}$ of n data from k class clusters. The general formula of subspace clustering algorithm can be expressed as:

$$\min_{\mathbf{Z}} \ \mathcal{L}(\mathbf{X}, \mathbf{XZ}) + \lambda\Omega(\mathbf{Z}) \quad \text{s.t.} \ \mathbf{Z} \in \mathbb{R}^{n \times n} \tag{1}$$

where $\mathcal{L}(\cdot)$ and $\Omega(\cdot)$ represent the regularization terms. Considering the noise contained in the original data, an error matrix $\mathbf{E}$ was adopted, and the least square regression was proposed to express the target formula:

$$\begin{aligned} &\min_{\mathbf{Z}} \ \|\mathbf{E}\|_F + \lambda\|\mathbf{Z}\|_F \\ &\text{s.t.} \ \mathbf{X} = \mathbf{XZ} + \mathbf{E}, \ \ \text{diag}(\mathbf{Z}) = \mathbf{0} \end{aligned} \tag{2}$$

2.2 Multiview Subspace Clustering

Given data containing V views, where $\mathbf{X}_v \in \mathbb{R}^{d_v \times n}$ represents the original data, d_v means the characteristic dimension of the v view, n represents the number of samples of the original data, and $\mathbf{Z}_v$ is the subspace representation matrix of the v view. The multiview subspace clustering algorithm can be expressed as:

$$\min_{\{\mathbf{Z}_v\}_{i=1}^{V}, \mathbf{Z}} \ \mathcal{L}(\{\mathbf{X}_v, \ \mathbf{X}_v\mathbf{Z}_v\}_{v=1}^{V}) + \lambda\Omega(\{\mathbf{Z}_v\}_{v=1}^{V}, \mathbf{Z}) \tag{3}$$

We extend the least square regression algorithm in (2) to the framework that follows the multiview subspace clustering algorithm in (3), and get the objective function of the least square regression algorithm on multiview subspace clustering as follows:

$$\begin{aligned} &\min_{\mathbf{Z}_v, \beta} \ \lambda\sum_{v=1}^{V}\|\mathbf{Z}_v\|_F^2 + \sum_{v=1}^{V}\beta_v\|\mathbf{X}_v - \mathbf{X}_v\mathbf{Z}_v\|_F^2 \\ &\text{s.t.} \ \text{diag}(\mathbf{Z}_v) = \mathbf{0} \end{aligned} \tag{4}$$

where λ represented the trade-off parameter, and β_v represents the weight coefficients of different views.

3 Model

3.1 Objective

We first define several kernel mappings $\{ \phi_s(\cdot)\}_{s=1}^{S}$. For the v - th view, the kernel matrix is calculated as follows:

$$\mathbf{K}_s^{(v)}(i,j) = \phi_s\left(\mathbf{x}_i^{(v)}\right)^{\mathrm{T}}\phi_s\left(\mathbf{x}_j^{(v)}\right) \tag{5}$$

where $i, j \in \{1, 2, \cdots, n\}$ represents the instance index, $x_i^{(v)}$ represents the i - th column vector of the v - th view, $\mathbf{K}_s^{(v)}$ represents the s - th kernel matrix of the i - th view. According to $m = S{*}\mathrm{V}$, it can be seen that when there are V views and S kings of kernel mappings, there will be m corresponding kernel matrices. The set of its kernel matrix is $\{ \mathbf{K}_q\}_{q=1}^{m}$.

Literature [11] pointed out that the redundant information contained in the original data could not be removed by simple kernel learning. Thus, we use the eigendecomposition method to obtain the low redundancy data representation, i.e.

$$\begin{aligned} &\underset{\mathbf{U}_q}{\arg\max} \quad \mathrm{Tr}(\mathbf{UKU}^{\mathrm{T}}) \\ &\text{s.t.} \ \ \mathbf{U} \in \mathbb{R}^{\mathrm{c}\times\mathrm{n}} \end{aligned} \tag{6}$$

We use the low redundancy data obtained in (6) to represent, i.e. $\{\mathbf{U}_q\}_{q=1}^{m}$, replace the input of Eq. (4), i.e. $\{\mathbf{X}_q\}_{q=1}^{m}$. By integrating these two processes into one framework, we can get:

$$\begin{aligned} &\min_{\{\mathbf{U}_q\}_{q=1}^m,\, \mathbf{Z}_q,\, \beta,\, \gamma} \lambda\sum_{q=1}^{m}\|\mathbf{Z}_q\|_F^2 + \sum_{q=1}^{m}\beta_q\|\mathbf{U}_q - \mathbf{U}_q\mathbf{Z}_q\|_F^2 - \sum_{q=1}^{m}\gamma_q\mathrm{Tr}(\mathbf{U}_q\mathbf{K}_q\mathbf{U}_q^{\mathrm{T}}) \\ &\text{s.t.} \ \ \mathrm{diag}(\mathbf{Z}_q) = \mathbf{0} \end{aligned} \tag{7}$$

where γ_q represents the weight coefficients of different views.

Meanwhile, we propose to use the tensor kernel norm to capture the higher-order correlation between different views. We construct a low-rank tensor subspace representation matrix $\mathcal{Z}$ of order three by integrating all subspace representation matrix $\mathbf{Z}_q$, and obtain the primary objective function of our model:

$$\begin{aligned} &\min_{\{\mathbf{U}_q\}_{q=1}^m,\, \{\mathbf{Z}_q\}_{q=1}^m,\, \mathcal{Z},\, \beta,\, \gamma} \lambda\|\mathcal{Z}\|_{\circledast} + \sum_{q=1}^{m}\beta_q\|\mathbf{U}_q - \mathbf{U}_q\mathbf{Z}_q\|_F^2 - \sum_{q=1}^{m}\gamma_q\mathrm{Tr}\left(\mathbf{U}_q\mathrm{K}_q\mathbf{U}_q^{\mathrm{T}}\right) \\ &\text{s.t.} \ \ \mathcal{Z} \in \mathbb{R}^{\mathrm{n}\times\mathrm{n}\times\mathrm{q}},\ \mathbf{Z}_{\mathrm{q}} \in \mathbb{R}^{\mathrm{n}\times\mathrm{n}},\ \mathbf{U}_{\mathrm{q}}\mathbf{U}_{\mathrm{q}}^{\mathrm{T}} = \mathbf{I},\ \mathbf{U}_{\mathrm{q}} \in \mathbb{R}^{\mathrm{c}\times\mathrm{n}} \\ &\qquad \beta^{\frac{1}{2}\mathrm{T}}\mathbf{1} = 1,\ \beta \in \mathbb{R}_+^{\mathrm{m}},\ \gamma^{\mathrm{T}}\gamma = 1,\ \gamma \in \mathbb{R}_+^{\mathrm{m}} \end{aligned} \tag{8}$$

3.2 Optimization

An alternate optimization strategy is adopted to minimize the solution of each variable iteratively under the condition that other variables remain unchanged.

Due to the high correlation between variables $\mathcal{Z}$ and $\mathbf{Z}_q$, it is tough to solve Eq. (8). We introduce auxiliary variable $\mathcal{Q}$ to make the variables separable, so optimization the Eq. (8) becomes:

$$\begin{aligned}\min_{\{\mathbf{U}_q\}_{q=1}^m,\ \{\mathbf{Z}_q\}_{q=1}^m,\ \mathcal{Q},\ \mathcal{Z},\ \beta,\ \gamma} \quad & \lambda\|\mathcal{Q}\|_{\circledast} + \|\mathcal{Q}-\mathcal{Z}\|_F^2 + \sum_{q=1}^{m}\beta_q\left\|\mathbf{U}_q-\mathbf{U}_q\mathbf{Z}_q\right\|_F^2 \\ & - \sum_{q=1}^{m}\mathrm{Tr}\left(\mathbf{U}_q\mathbf{K}_q\mathbf{U}_q^{\mathrm{T}}\right) \\ \text{s.t.} \quad & \mathcal{Q}=\mathcal{Z}\end{aligned} \tag{9}$$

$\mathcal{Z}$-subproblem: It's clear that each of these subspaces represents the matrix $\{\mathbf{z}_q\}_{q=1}^m$ that is independent, so fixed $\{\mathbf{Z}_t\}_{t=1,t\neq q}^m$, $\mathcal{Z}$, $\mathcal{Q}$, $\{\mathbf{U}_q\}_{q=1}^m$, β and γ. The optimization Eq. (9) becomes:

$$\begin{aligned}\min_{\mathbf{Z}_q} \quad & \left\|\mathbf{Z}_q-\mathbf{Q}_q\right\|_F^2 + \beta_q\left\|\mathbf{U}_q-\mathbf{U}_q\mathbf{Z}_q\right\|_F^2 \\ \text{s.t.} \quad & \mathbf{Z}_q\in\mathbb{R}^{\mathrm{n}\times\mathrm{n}}\end{aligned} \tag{10}$$

The Eq. (11) is optimized by using the formula $\mathbf{Z}_q-\mathbf{Q}_q=\mathbf{Z}_q'$:

$$\begin{aligned}\min_{\mathbf{Z}_q'} \quad & \left\|\mathbf{Z}_q'\right\|_F^2 + \beta_q\left\|\mathbf{U}_q-\mathbf{U}_q\mathbf{Q}_q-\mathbf{U}_q\mathbf{Z}_q'\right\|_F^2 \\ \text{s.t.} \quad & \mathrm{diag}(\mathbf{Z}_q')=0\end{aligned} \tag{11}$$

The Eq. (11) is optimized by using the formula $\mathbf{U}_q'=\mathbf{U}_q-\mathbf{U}_q\mathbf{Q}_q$:

$$\min_{\mathbf{Z}_q'} \left\|\mathbf{Z}_q'\right\|_F^2 + \beta_q\left\|\mathbf{U}_q'-\mathbf{U}_q\mathbf{Z}_q'\right\|_F^2 \tag{12}$$

Since the diagonal of $\mathbf{Z}_q'$ is forced to be 0, we remove the i - th column of $\mathbf{U}_q'=\{\mathrm{u}_q^{'(i)}\}_{i=1}^n\in\mathbb{R}^{\mathrm{c}\times\mathrm{n}}$ to get $\mathbf{F}_q^{(i)}=\{\mathrm{u}_q^{'(1)},\ldots,\mathrm{u}_q^{'(i-1)},\mathrm{u}_q^{'(i+1)},\ldots,\mathrm{u}_q^{'(n)}\}\in\mathbb{R}^{\mathrm{c}\times\mathrm{n}}$, and optimize each column of $\mathbf{Z}_q'$ to get:

$$\begin{aligned}\min_{\mathbf{z}_q^{'(i)}} \quad & \left\|\mathbf{z}_q^{'(i)}\right\|_F^2 + \beta_q\left\|\mathrm{u}_q^{'(i)}-\mathbf{F}_q^{(i)}\mathbf{z}_q^{'(i)}\right\|_F^2 \\ \text{s.t.} \quad & \mathbf{z}_q^{'(i)}\in\mathbb{R}^{\mathrm{n}-1}\end{aligned} \tag{13}$$

Then optimization $\mathbf{Z}_q^{'(i)*}-$ is:

$$\begin{aligned}& \mathrm{z}_q^{'(i)*}=(\mathbf{E}_q^{(i)})^{-1}\beta_q\mathbf{u}_q^{'(i)}\mathbf{F}_q^{(i)\mathrm{T}} \\ \text{s.t.} \quad & \mathbf{E}_q^{(i)}=\mathbf{I}+\beta_q\mathbf{F}_q^{(i)\mathrm{T}}\mathbf{F}_q^{(i)}\end{aligned} \tag{14}$$

$\mathcal{Q}$-subproblem: fixed $\mathcal{Z}$, $\mathbf{Z}_q$, $\{\mathbf{U}_q\}_{q=1}^m$, β and γ. Optimization Eq. (9) becomes:

$$\begin{aligned} &\min_{\mathcal{Q}} \ \lambda\|\mathcal{Q}\|_{\circledast} + \|\mathcal{Q} - \mathcal{Z}\|_F^2 \\ &\text{s.t. } \ \mathcal{Q} \in \mathbb{R}^{n \times n \times q} \end{aligned} \tag{15}$$

According to the tensor kernel norm minimization algorithm based on T-SVD in reference [12], it can be solved.

U-subproblem: Because the data with low redundancy means that $\{\mathbf{U}_q\}_{q=1}^m$ is independent of each other, fixed $\{\mathbf{U}_t\}_{t=1,t\neq q}^m$, $\mathcal{Z}$, $\mathcal{Q}$, $\{\mathbf{Z}_q\}_{q=1}^m$, β and γ. The optimization Eq. (9) becomes:

$$\min_{\mathbf{U}_q} \ \beta_q\left\|\mathbf{U}_q - \mathbf{U}_q\mathbf{Z}_q\right\|_F^2 - \gamma_q \mathrm{Tr}(\mathbf{U}_q\mathbf{K}_q\mathbf{U}_q^{\mathrm{T}}) \tag{16}$$

Equation (16) can be translated into:

$$\begin{aligned} &\max_{\mathbf{U}_q} \ \mathrm{Tr}(\mathbf{U}_q\mathbf{N}_q\mathbf{U}_q^{\mathrm{T}}) \\ &\text{s.t. } \ \mathrm{N}_q = 2\beta_q\mathbf{Z}_q^{\mathrm{T}} - \beta_q\mathbf{Z}_q\mathbf{Z}_q^{\mathrm{T}} + \gamma_q\mathbf{K}_q \end{aligned} \tag{17}$$

Equation (17) can be efficiently solved by eigendecomposition.

β-subproblem: fixed $\mathcal{Z}$, $\mathcal{Q}$, $\{\mathbf{Z}_q\}_{q=1}^m$, $\{\mathbf{U}_q\}_{q=1}^m$ and γ. Optimization Eq. (9) becomes:

$$\begin{aligned} &\min_{\beta} \ \beta^{\mathrm{T}} v \\ &\text{s.t. } \ v_q = \left\|\mathbf{U}_q - \mathbf{U}_q\mathbf{Z}_q\right\|_F^2 \end{aligned} \tag{18}$$

According to the Cauchy-Schwartz inequality, we optimize the Eq. (18) as:

$$\beta_q^* = 1/\left(v_q \sum_{t=1}^m \frac{1}{v_t}\right)^2 \tag{19}$$

γ-subproblem: fixed $\mathcal{Z}$, $\mathcal{Q}$, $\{\mathbf{Z}_q\}_{q=1}^m$, $\{\mathbf{U}_q\}_{q=1}^m$ and β. Optimization Eq. (9) becomes:

$$\begin{aligned} &\max_{\gamma} \ \gamma^{\mathrm{T}} v \\ &\text{s.t. } \ v_q = \mathrm{Tr}(\mathbf{U}_q\mathbf{K}_q\mathbf{U}_q^{\mathrm{T}}) \end{aligned} \tag{20}$$

According to the Cauchy-Schwartz inequality, we optimize the Eq. (20) as:

$$\gamma_q^* = v_q/\left(\sum_{t=1}^m v_t^2\right)^{\frac{1}{2}} \tag{21}$$

To sum up, we summarize the solving steps of the objective function of the proposed model in Algorithm 1.

Using the low-rank tensor subspace representation matrix $\mathcal{Z}$, $\mathbf{J} = \frac{1}{m}\sum_{q=1}^{m}\left(\left|\mathcal{Z}^{(q)} + \mathcal{Z}^{(q)T}\right|\right)$ is used to calculate the fusion subspace representation matrix $\mathbf{J}$ ($\mathcal{Z}^{(q)}$ represents the q slice of $\mathcal{Z}$ along the angle of view), and then using the fusion subspace representation matrix, $\mathbf{T} = \frac{1}{2}(\mathbf{J} + \mathbf{J}^{T})$ is used to calculate the affinity subspace representation matrix $\mathbf{T}$, which is sent into the spectral clustering algorithm to calculate the clustering results.

Algorithm 1

Input: the original data $\{\mathbf{X}_v\}_{v=1}^{V}$, dimensions represented by low redundancy data c and parameter λ.

Output: the low-rank tensor subspace representation matrix $\mathcal{Z}$.

1. Generate the kernel matrices $\{\mathbf{K}_q\}_{q=1}^{m}$ from $\{\mathbf{X}_v\}_{v=1}^{V}$.
2. Initialize $\mathcal{Q}$, $\{\mathbf{U}_q\}_{q=1}^{m}$, β and γ.
3. **while** $(obj^{t-1} - obj^{t}) / obj^{t} \leq \sigma$ **do**
4. Update $\mathbf{Z}_q^{'}$ with Eq. (14).
5. According to formula $\mathbf{Z}_q = \mathbf{Z}_q^{'} + \mathbf{Q}_q$, get the $\mathbf{Z}_q$.
6. Structure tensor $\mathcal{Z} = \phi(\mathbf{Z}_1, \mathbf{Z}_2, \ldots, \mathbf{Z}_q)$.
7. Update $\mathcal{Q}$ with Eq. (15).
8. Update $\{\mathbf{U}_q\}_{q=1}^{m}$ with Eq. (17).
9. Update β with Eq. (19).
10. Update γ with Eq. (21).
11. $t = t + 1$.
12. Calculate objective value obj^{t} with Eq. (10).
13. **end while**

---

4 Experiment

4.1 Dataset

The following three data sets are used to evaluate the effectiveness and superiority.

BBC-Sport It consisting of 737 files from the BBC-Sport website, corresponding to sports news in five subject areas. There are two different views.

ORL It consists of 400 facial images of 40 people of different genders, in which each person has 10 facial images taken from different angles. There are three different views.

UCI-Digits It consists of 2,000 digital images corresponding to 10 categories. Fourier coefficient, pixel average and morphological features are extracted to represent these digital images. There are three different views.

4.2 Comparison of Experimental Settings and Experimental Results

In the experiment, in order to prove the effectiveness of the presented method, this paper will compare the above three data sets with three advanced multiview subspace clustering methods. These three methods are: Latent multi-view subspace clustering (LMSC) in [5], Multimodal sparse and low-rank subspace clustering (MSSC) in literature [9], and Multiview subspace clustering via co-training robust data representation (CoMSC) in [11].

We run each method on each dataset ten times, and take the mean value of the experimental results the 10 times as the result of the clustering evaluation index. For the clustering results, we used three measurement methods of ACC, NMI and purity to evaluate the clustering results. For these indicators, the higher the value, the better the clustering effect.

Table 1. ACC, NMI and Purity comparison of different clustering algorithms on the three public datasets.

	Method	ACC	NMI	Purity
BBC-Sport	LMSC	0.891 ± 0.02	0.796 ± 0.03	0.891 ± 0.02
	MSSC	0.971 ± 0.00	0.898 ± 0.00	0.971 ± 0.00
	CoMSC	0.956 ± 0.02	0.876 ± 0.02	0.956 ± 0.02
	Ours	**0.979 ± 0.02**	**0.933 ± 0.04**	**0.979 ± 0.02**
ORL	LMSC	0.809 ± 0.04	0.909 ± 0.02	0.840 ± 0.03
	MSSC	0.835 ± 0.00	**0.930 ± 0.00**	0.865 ± 0.00
	CoMSC	0.805 ± 0.02	0.903 ± 0.01	0.833 ± 0.01
	Ours	**0.844 ± 0.02**	0.922 ± 0.01	**0.870 ± 0.01**
UCI-Digits	LMSC	0.862 ± 0.03	0.784 ± 0.03	0.862 ± 0.03
	MSSC	0.924 ± 0.00	0.859 ± 0.00	0.924 ± 0.00
	CoMSC	0.903 ± 0.02	0.837 ± 0.03	0.903 ± 0.02
	Ours	**0.986 ± 0.01**	**0.967 ± 0.01**	**0.986 ± 0.01**

The experimental results of the three indexes are shown in Table 1. It can be seen from the experimental results that the method presented in this paper is better than other methods in almost all three indexes. In the there datasets of BBC-Sport, ORL and UCI-Digits, in the ACC index and Purity index, the performance of the presented method was roughly the same as that of the MSSC method in the BBC-Sport and ORL datasets, 6.2% on UCI-Digits; In terms of NMI index, the presented method is slightly lower than the MSSC method only in the ORL dataset and superior to the comparison method in all other datasets.

4.3 Parameter Selection and Convergence Verification

For the method of comparison, we adjusted all the parameters for optimal performance. For our approach, Gaussian kernel mapping, polynomial kernel mapping, linear kernel mapping, symbolic polynomial kernel mapping and inverse polynomial kernel mapping are applied to obtain the kernel matrix corresponding to the original data. We will set the value range of dimension c represented by low redundancy data as $\{k, 2k, \ldots, 20k\}$ and parameter λ as 2.^$\{-10, -8, \ldots, 10\}$, and select the parameter combination with the optimal clustering performance to conducting experiment.

To verify the convergence of the proposed method, the target value of the algorithm is used as the convergence criterion for each iteration. In this paper, the convergence curves of the BBC-Sport dataset at λ=2^0 and c = $20k$ are given, as shown in Fig. 1. The method in this paper converges between 8 and 10 iterations with stable convergence performance.

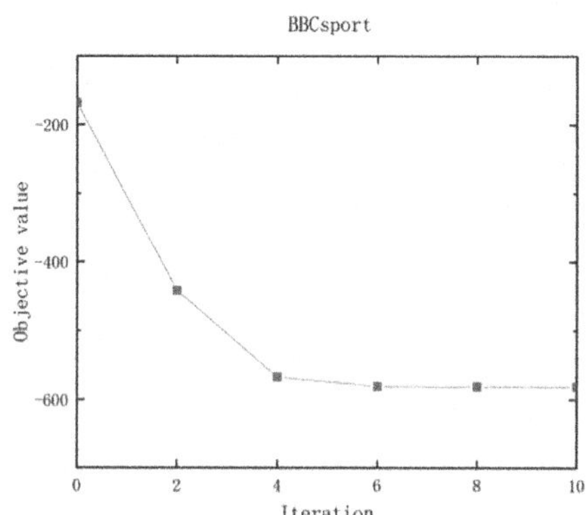

Fig. 1. Convergence validation on and BBC-Sport.

5 Conclusion

In this paper, we propose a multiview subspace clustering method for multi-kernel and low redundancy representation learning. This method uses multi-kernel learning to capture the more complex correlation information between actual data. It uses the feature decomposition method to remove the redundant information in the data to obtain the low redundant data representation. To explore the complementarity information among multiple views and the difference information among multiple views, the subspace representation matrix of each view is reorganized into tensor form, and the high-order correlation among multiple views is explored by using tensor low-rank constraint. The proposed multiview clustering model is compared with some classical multiview subspace clustering methods on three public datasets, and the convergence and parameters of the model are analyzed. Experimental results show that the effectiveness of the proposed model are superior to other methods.

Acknowledgement. This work was supported in part by the National Natural Science Foundation of China under Grant 62071157, Natural Science Foundation of Heilongjiang Province under Grant YQ2019F011 and Postdoctoral Foundation of Heilongjiang Province under Grant LBH-Q19112.

References

1. Zhao, J., Xie, X., Xu, X., et al.: Multi-view learning overview: recent progress and new challenges. Inf. Fusion **38**, 43–54 (2017)
2. Xu, C., Tao, D., Xu, C.: A survey on multi-view learning. arXiv preprint arXiv:1304.5634 (2013)
3. Chaudhuri, K., Kakade, S.M., Livescu, K., et al.: Multi-view clustering via canonical correlation analysis. In: Proceedings of the 26th Annual International Conference on Machine Learning, pp. 129–136 (2009)
4. Gao, H., Nie, F., Li, X., et al.: Multi-view subspace clustering. In: Proceedings of the IEEE International Conference on Computer Vision, pp. 4238–4246 (2015)
5. Zhang, C., Hu, Q., Fu, H., et al.: Latent multi-view subspace clustering. In: Proceedings of the IEEE Conference on Computer Vision and Pattern Recognition, pp. 4279–4287 (2017)
6. Elhamifar, E., Vidal, R.: Sparse subspace clustering: algorithm, theory, and applications. IEEE Trans. Pattern Anal. Mach. Intell. **35**(11), 2765–2781 (2013)
7. Liu, G., Lin, Z., Yan, S., et al.: Robust recovery of subspace structures by low-rank representation. IEEE Trans. Pattern Anal. Mach. Intell. **35**(1), 171–184 (2012)
8. Zhang, C., Fu, H., Liu, S., et al.: Low-rank tensor constrained multiview subspace clustering. In: Proceedings of the IEEE International Conference on Computer Vision, pp. 1582–1590 (2015)
9. Abavisani, M., Patel, V.M.: Multimodal sparse and low-rank subspace clustering. Inf. Fusion **39**, 168–177 (2018)
10. Li, R., Zhang, C., Hu, Q., et al.: Flexible multi-view representation learning for subspace clustering. In: IJCAI, pp. 2916–2922 (2019)
11. Liu, J., Liu, X., Yang, Y., et al.: Multiview subspace clustering via co-training robust data representation. IEEE Trans. Neural Netw. Learn. Syst. **PP**, 1–13 (2021)
12. Kilmer, M.E., Braman, K., Hao, N., et al.: Third-order tensors as operators on matrices: a theoretical and computational framework with applications in imaging. SIAM J. Matrix Anal. Appl. **34**(1), 148–172 (2013)

Research on Engineering Project Process and Method that Applied Talents Should Master Under Intelligent Manufacturing Technology

Wanpeng Tang(✉)

Guangzhou City Polytechnic, Guangzhou, China
46186518@qq.com

Abstract. With the application of 5G network technology and the popularization and improvement of information technology, many applications of industrial Internet of Things have been born corresponding to industrial technology. Almost every industrial field has its corresponding industrial APP, constantly approaching the direction of "Internet of Everything". Engineering projects include a large number of intelligent manufacturing, artificial intelligence, industrial robots, automation project transformation, in this field, there is a special group of talents, that is, many higher vocational colleges and application-oriented undergraduate universities training engineering application-oriented talents. They are the core participants of the industrial Internet of Things and intelligent manufacturing industry, and they need to master the research methods and project process of engineering projects in the era of information and intelligence.

Keywords: Intelligent manufacturing · Engineering project · Application-oriented talents · Industrial robot · Artificial intelligence (AI)

With the popularization and improvement of information technology, 2G and 3G networks have developed to 4G and 5G networks. With the application of 5G network technology, many applications of industrial Internet of Things have been born. Almost every field has its corresponding industrial APP, constantly approaching the direction of "Internet of Everything". In this field, there is a special group, that is, the engineering applied talents trained by higher vocational colleges and applied undergraduate colleges. They are core players in the industrial Internet of Things and intelligent manufacturing industry. The theoretical knowledge of such talents is not solid enough. Meanwhile, the growth of engineering application-oriented talents needs time to settle. They cannot systematically master the engineering application project process and lack in-depth understanding of the engineering project operation method. Application-oriented talents need to master the process of engineering projects and research methods of intelligent manufacturing projects.

© ICST Institute for Computer Sciences, Social Informatics and Telecommunications Engineering 2022
Published by Springer Nature Switzerland AG 2022. All Rights Reserved
S. Shi et al. (Eds.): 6GN 2021, LNICST 439, pp. 295–307, 2022.
https://doi.org/10.1007/978-3-031-04245-4_26

1 Intelligent Manufacturing Engineering and Industrial Robots

1.1 Artificial Intelligence in Intelligent Manufacturing

In the dictionary, intelligence means "the ability to learn and solve problems"; Artificial intelligence is the ability to solve new problems, act rationally and act like people. It is the basic principle of intelligence research. It is the use of intelligent robots to simulate the thinking process of people, and it is the study of how to use intelligent equipment to complete the work that depends on human intelligence. Artificial intelligence is a strategic project for many countries. With the emergence of 5G signals, new mobile terminal technologies, big data, and IOT sensing technologies, a number of new smart needs and applications have been born, such as smart home, smart driving, smart city, smart economy, smart manufacturing, and smart medical care. At the same time, some new industries were born, such as human-machine hybrid enhancement, big data intelligence, autonomous intelligence, cross-media intelligence and so on [1] (Figs. 1 and 2).

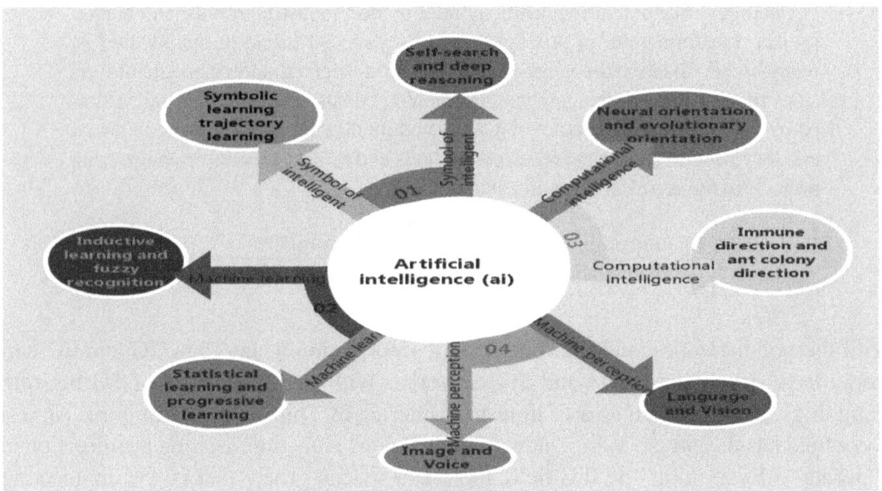

Fig. 1. Artificial-intelligence

Artificial intelligence changes the course of The Times. Carl Benedikt Frey and Michael Osborne of Oxford University found that "47% of American jobs could be replaced by machines". Job automation and artificial intelligence "have a creative destruction impact" that will lead to huge reductions in the cost of employment and the loss of many jobs. The McKinsey GlobalInstitute concludes that "AI is driving social transformation that is 10 times faster, 300 times larger, and almost 3,000 times greater than the industrial revolution". In 2019, the scale of China's AI industry reached 34.43 billion yuan [2].

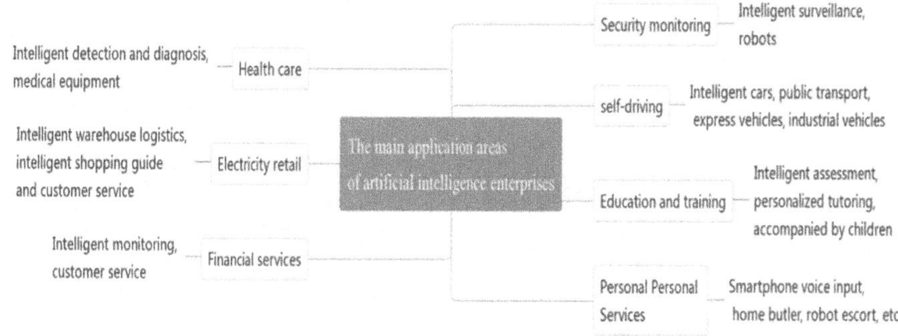

Fig. 2. The main application areas of artificial-intelligence

1.2 Industrial Robots in Intelligent Manufacturing

1.2.1 Advantages of Industrial Robots

The era of intelligent manufacturing is coming, and the robot industry is about to explode. In 1920, in "Rosum the Universal Robot," Chapik described "a robot named Robert who looks like a man and acts like a man" (Czech for forced labor). Since then, the word "robot" and the Chinese word for "robot" have become popular. "Automation with human appearance or functioning like human".

With the use of robots, intelligent manufacturing in automated factories eliminate simple and repetitive processes. The blowout of industrial robots will be applied in every process and every production line of "Made in China". The application of industrial robots reflects the upgrading of China's manufacturing industry. The use of industrial robots in factories can save labor costs, reduce personnel safety accidents, product specifications, improve production efficiency, etc. (Fig. 3).

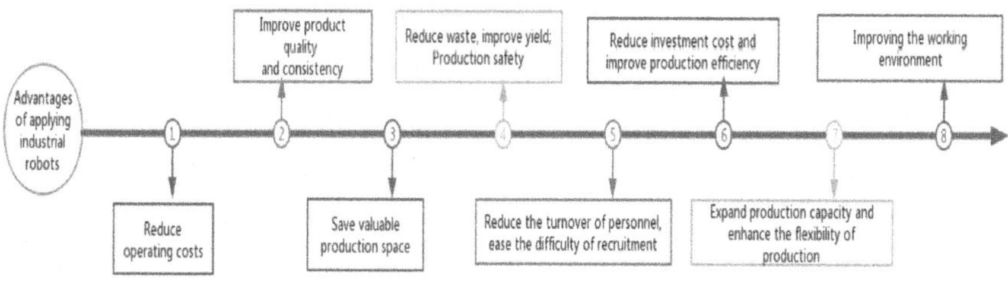

Fig. 3. Advantages of applying industrial robots

Generally, when a factory invests in an automated production line, the payback cycle is set to be 2–3.5 years. Currently, most local governments have a proper proportion of incentives for the purchase of industrial robots, which greatly speeds up the payback cycle [3] (Fig. 4).

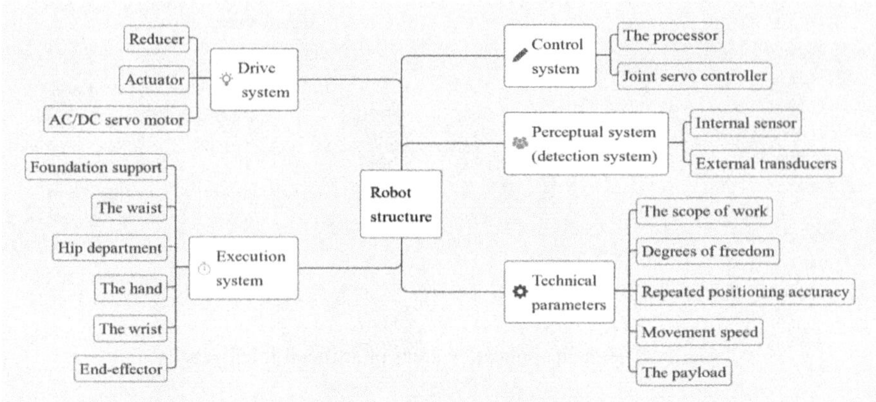

Fig. 4. Robot structure

1.2.2 Positions of Industrial Robots

Industrial robots are widely used in palletizing, painting, welding, handling and assembly. At present, the education structure of the personnel engaged in this position is: about 45% in technical secondary schools, 45% in junior colleges and higher vocational colleges, and 10% are undergraduate postgraduates.

Jobs	The specific work
The project manager	Based on industrial robot system technology, according to the manufacturing process of products, propose automation solutions and organize the implementation
System integration development engineer	Be able to complete the design and upgrade of robot workstation and automation line
Technical support engineer before and after sales	Can be engaged in industrial robot related mechanical and electrical equipment installation, programming, debugging, maintenance, operation and management work
Installation, commissioning and maintenance engineer	Knowledge of industrial robot principle, operation, teaching programming, reproduction and debugging

1.2.3 Development Status and Trend of Industrial Robot Enterprises

	Reducer	Servo system	Robot body equipment in the middle stream	Upstream component control equipment	Downstream system integration
Domestic listed company	Shanghai electromechanical, Qinchuan Machinery Development	Shanghai step, Huichuan Technology, Central China CNC, INVT	Xinsong Robotics, Bosch Holdings, Tianqi shares, Avea shares, Jasic robotics, Central China CNC, Huachangda, Superstar Technology, SCIYON Automation	Shinmatsu robot, Shanghai step, Cixing shares	Xinsong Robotics Co., Ltd., Bosch Co., Ltd., Tianqi Co., Ltd., Avea Co., Ltd., Jasic Technology Co., Ltd., Ruiling Co., Ltd., Huazhong CNC Co., Ltd., Huachanda Co., Ltd., Xingxing Technology Co., Ltd., Cixing Co., Ltd., Keyuan Co., Ltd.
Domestic non-listed companies	Green Harmonic, Nantong Zhenkang, Zhejiang Hengfengtai	Guangzhou CNC, Nanjing Eston	Anwei Eft, Guangzhou CNC, Nanjing Eston, Shanghai triowin, Dongguan Qizhi, Suzhou platinum automation	Guangzhou CNC, Nanjing Eston, Shenzhen googo	Anhui Efort, Guangzhou CNC, Nanjing Eston, Huaheng Welding Co., Ltd., Juyi Automation, Suzhou Platinum Electric, Huaheng welding

(*continued*)

(*continued*)

	Reducer	Servo system	Robot body equipment in the middle stream	Upstream component control equipment	Downstream system integration
The foreign company	Harmonic, Nabtesco, Sumitomo	Luntz, Bosch Rexroth, fanuc, yaskawa, Panasonic, Mitsubishi, Sanyo, B&R, Siemens	ABB, Fanuc, Yaskawa, KUKA. Panasonic, Kawasaki, Nachi, COOMAU, Aidepu	ABB, Fanuc, yaskawa, KUKA, Panasonic, Nachi, Mitsubishi, B&R	ABB, Fanuc Yaskawa, KUKA

2 Process of Intelligent Manufacturing and Industrial Robot Engineering Application Projects

2.1 Intelligent Manufacturing and Industrial Robot is a Comprehensive System Engineering

The most important characteristic of the system is the integrity of the system. Engineering project system also has the characteristics of openness (accessibility), fragility (a poor system is invaded and may face collapse) and robustness(the system may lose its original function in the face of input error, interference and invasion). The project team should have a correct understanding of this [4] (Fig. 5).

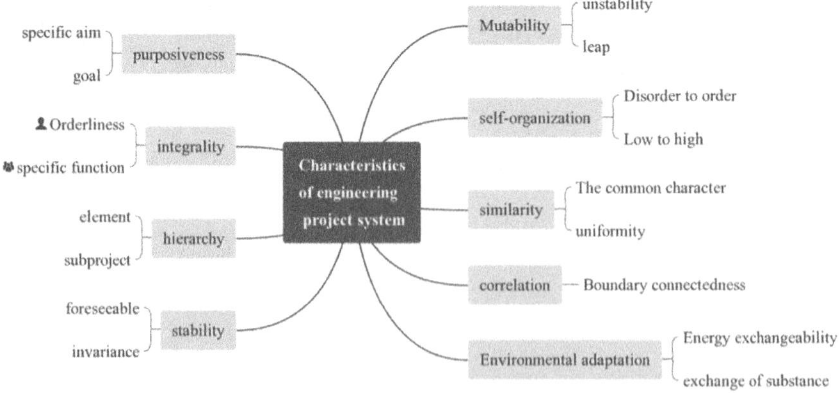

Fig. 5. Characteristics of engineering project system

2.2 Current Characteristics of Intelligent Manufacturing

Since the 1990s, technological innovation and the popularization of the Internet have been prominent features of the global economy and society. Each country in cyberspace, mobile Internet, intelligent manufacturing, cloud computing, industrial Internet, big data, information security and other comprehensive competition, intelligent manufacturing industry has become the strategic point of the core competitiveness of each country. Application-oriented talents of intelligent manufacturing should master the various processes of organizational structure, management process, production skills and production tools in the production process. At the same time, it is urgently needed that these personnel know all-round technology and management, and can know the application-oriented talent team from project initiation to project completion. Application-oriented talents have a comprehensive grasp of the five process groups that need project management, namely "Plan -- Do -- Check -- Act". The loop is linked by results, which form the basis for the next step.

Intelligent manufacturing engineering projects have large investment, long construction cycle and high risk, which are more difficult and complex than general technical projects. In engineering acceptance, engineering projects need to be modified and maintained constantly with the change of external factors. At the same time, intelligent manufacturing engineering projects use a certain number of years, the upgrade will be upgraded, the elimination will be eliminated, with the new system to replace the old system is certain. Engineering application-oriented talents need to understand the process of engineering projects at each stage, which is called the life cycle of intelligent manufacturing engineering projects. The life cycle of intelligent manufacturing engineering includes the following figure (Fig. 6):

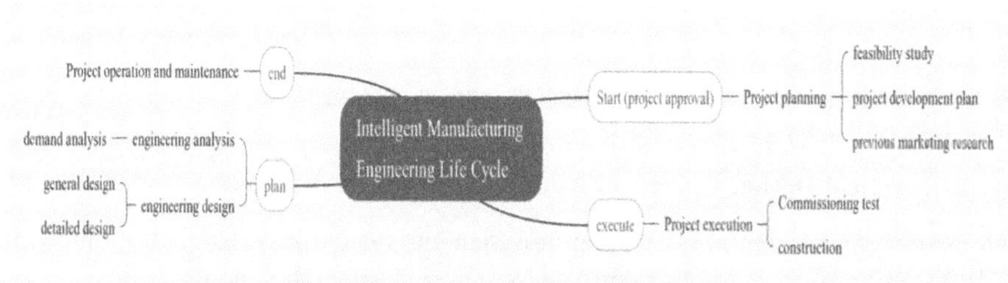

Fig. 6. Intelligent manufacturing engineering life cycle

2.3 Overall Process of Intelligent Manufacturing

The whole process of intelligent manufacturing is divided into four stages, namely, project approval, development, operation and maintenance, and extinction. Design methods include: structured approach (dividing the project life cycle into planning, analysis, system design, implementation, maintenance, etc.) and prototyping approach (clarifying the functional requirements of the system and determining the system boundary) [5] (Figs. 7, 8 and 9).

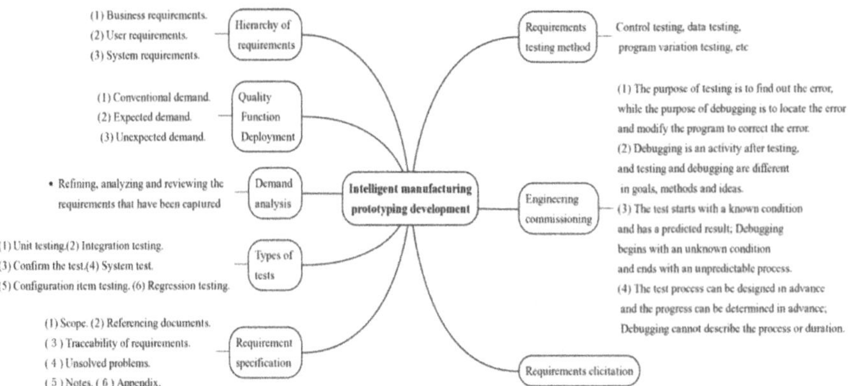

Fig. 7. Intelligent manufacturing prototyping development

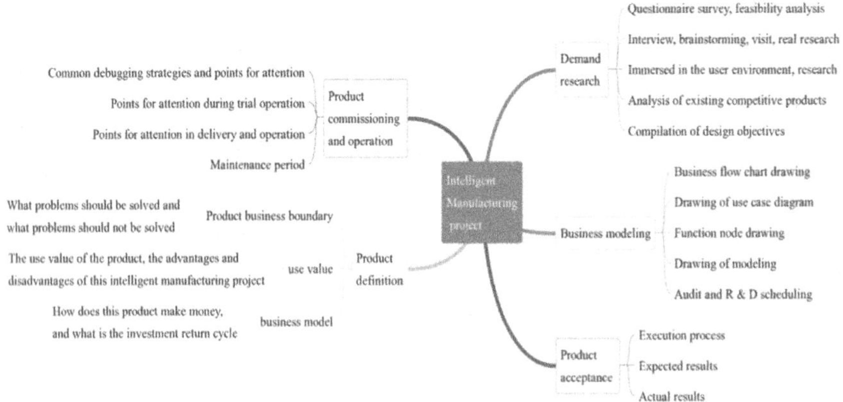

Fig. 8. Intelligent manufacturing project

2.4 Theoretical Design Process of Automatic Production Line

Automation engineering projects often use Siemens system knowledge, the following S7-1200 design as an example: control system design principles and processes.

Any control system system design, first of all need to do a comprehensive understanding of the object, and on a deep analysis of the technological process, equipment, etc., to seriously study the function of the system requirements to achieve and, the performance indexes of the control scheme is determined, so as to guarantee the quality of products, improve product yield, saving energy and reducing consumption, improve production efficiency and improve the management level of purpose [6].

(1) Design principles

In general, the following principles should be followed.

A. Stable operation, safe and reliable

The design of the control system can be in the external disturbance, system parameters in a certain range of long-term stable operation, in the whole production

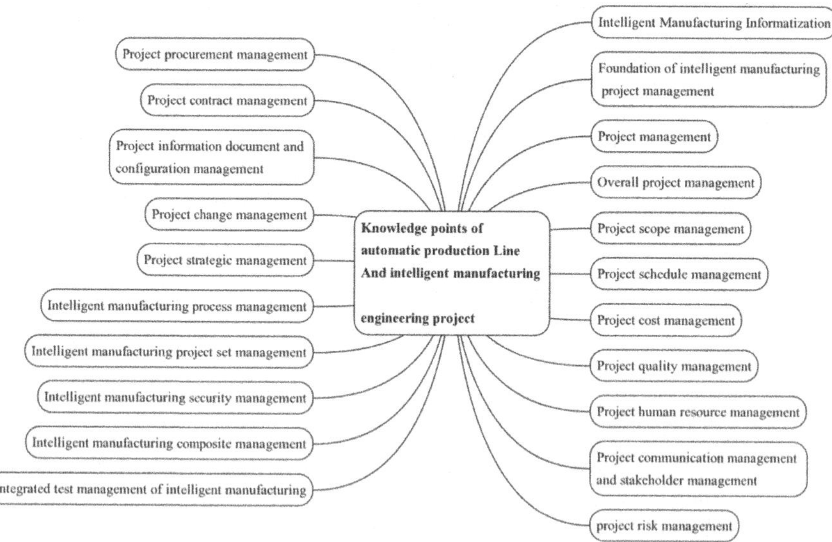

Fig. 9. Knowledge points of automatic production Line And engineering project

process, to ensure the safety of people and equipment, is the most basic requirements of the control system. Therefore, the device selection, system design and software programming must be considered comprehensively. For example, in the hardware and software design, not only under normal conditions, to ensure that the system can run reliably, but also to ensure that under abnormal conditions (system power down, misoperation, parameters out of limit, etc.), can work correctly and reliably.

B. Meet the requirements

Satisfying control requirements is an important principle in designing control system. Designers should go deep into the site before the design, understand the collection of site data, production process, access to information related to the system at home and abroad, maintain close cooperation with the site engineering management personnel, technical personnel, operators and consult the specific site conditions, joint research and design.

C. Economical and practical, easy to expand

Under the premise of improving product quality, output and work efficiency, the design should be optimized to ensure that the benefits of the project can be continuously expanded and the project cost can be effectively reduced at the same time.

In order to meet the control system can continue to improve and improve, in the design of automatic control system to consider the future upgrade, in the choice of PLC models and expansion modules, leave a certain margin.

(2) Design process and design content

- Complete the design and determine the control scheme according to the production process and analysis control requirements.
- Select input and output devices.
- Select the PLC model.

- Assign input and output of PLC and draw external hardware wiring diagram of PLC.
- Write programs and debug them.
- Design control cabinet and install wiring diagram.
- Compile design specification and operation specification.

(3) Design steps

A. Technology analysis

After receiving the design task, first understand the site conditions, working characteristics, technological process, working process and control requirements of the controlled object, coordinate the reasonable division of the system, design the conversion conditions between the control processes, and draw the flow chart or function diagram [7].

B. Choose the right PLC model

The selection of models is mainly considered as follows: the selection of functions (to meet the needs of system functions), the determination of I/O points (to have a certain amount of reserve) and the estimation of memory.

C. Assign I/O points and draw a hardware wiring diagram

D. The program design

According to the production process requirements, draw the flow chart or function diagram, and then design the program for debugging and modification, until the control requirements.

E. Control cabinet design and site construction

F. Control system overall debugging

G. Compile technical documents

3 General Research and Method of Engineering Technology

3.1 Basic Process of Engineering Technology Research

A. Application research: under the guidance of basic research theory, the research on technical basis and technical principle is carried out in order to obtain new products, new processes, new materials and new methods, with the focus on solving theoretical and feasibility problems in engineering design of technology application.

B. Technological development: using new materials, establishing new devices, designing new processes, producing new products and providing new services. The development results are samples, prototypes, device prototypes and technical documents [8].

C. Engineering design: to produce the final product as the object, solve all the process and technical problems from the prototype to the actual production, to meet all the needs of formal production.

D. Engineering construction: for the actual production operation to establish hardware workshop, production lines, equipment, auxiliary facilities and software organizational structure, technical standards, production plans, personnel allocation, etc.

E. Production operation: it is necessary to timely discover and solve various technical and non-technical problems in the production process in accordance with the continuity or dispersion characteristics of product production to ensure the normal operation of production.
F. Technical service: it is a new requirement for engineering and technical personnel under the condition of market economy. It is of great significance for producers to improve product quality, improve product performance and develop new products.

3.2 Main Stages of Engineering Technology Research

A. Technical planning stage: demand establishment, development prediction, purpose setting and consequence assessment.
B. Technology invention stage: it is the basic idea for the technology creator to solve the problem.
C. Technical design stage: it should be creative ideas obtained by the specific price of the vision.
D. Development and implementation stage: after the evaluation of the technical design scheme, the technological creation enters the development, experiment and technical appraisal of the physical and chemical form.

3.3 Invention and Creation Methods of Engineering Technology Research

A. The general process of engineering technological invention

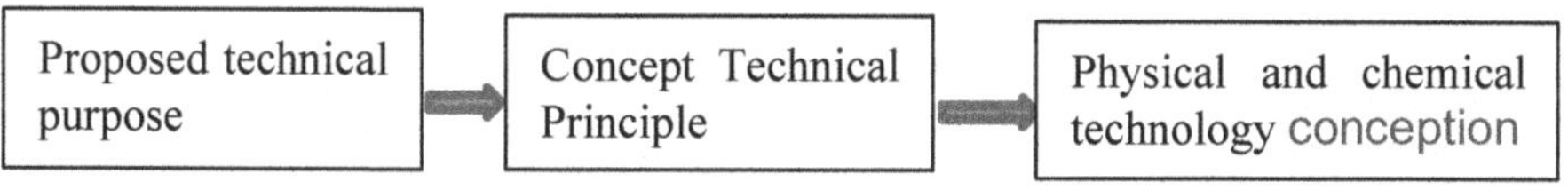

It is pointed out that the purpose of technological research is the root of invention, and whether the purpose is appropriate or not directly affects the success or failure of subsequent invention. The principles of architecture technology are central to technological invention. The formation of technical principles depends on the engineering and technical personnel's existing natural scientific knowledge and original technical practice experience and is proposed through the inventor's innovative thinking. The conception of physical-chemical technology is the technical entity (such as sample and prototype) that is transformed into the physical form through the way of technical practice.

Common types of technical rationale ideas (Fig. 10).

3.4 Design Experiment Method of Engineering Technology Research

A. Design method of engineering technology

Experience design period: an engineering product is designed by craftsmen based on the experience and knowledge accumulated in long-term production practice without complex theoretical calculation.

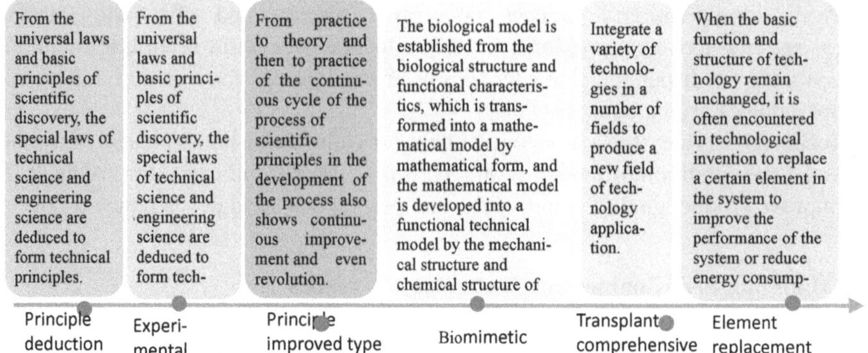

Fig. 10. Common types of technical rationale ideas

B. The concurrent design period of experience and theory: technical design is in the parallel state of experience plus theory.
C. The period of modern design: after the Second World War, the integrated development of science and technology gave birth to a new period of modern design, and the use of mathematical language and models greatly improved the scientific nature of design.

General methods of engineering technology design:

(1) Form design method, from the existing technical means, technical information to find solutions to the problem.
(2) System design method, the use of the concept and principle of the system, elements and the relationship between elements, design an optimal program.
(3) Function value analysis and design method, considering the function of the object in the design, so as to optimize the function and economic effect.
(4) Probability design method, the use of mathematical statistics to deal with the design data containing uncertain factors, can make the designed products to meet the given reliability indicators.
(5) Optimal design method: based on the mathematical optimization theory, select the design variable values to obtain the best design scheme.

Basic procedure of engineering test:

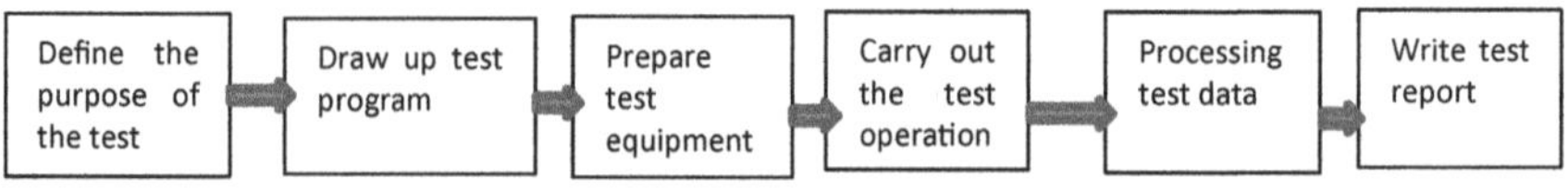

4 Conclusion

In this paper, from the artificial intelligence in intelligent manufacturing, industrial robots in intelligent manufacturing, classification, development status and the current development of industrial robot companies, through the actual application example of automation project, the project process of intelligent manufacturing engineering project is studied, and finally the project process of intelligent manufacturing is proposed. The general research method and process of engineering project are put forward. It provides a useful exploration for application-oriented engineering and technical personnel to participate in project operation and management.

References

1. https://www.docin.com/p-233007020.html
2. Cover article of economist: revolution of artificial intelligence. http://www.fliport-pco.com/xinwen/1525005
3. The development history of robots. https://max.book118.com/html/2019/0419/6043120210002023.shtm
4. Li, X.H., Guo, Y.C., Song, T.: Forward kinematics analysis and Simulation of 6-DOF Industrial robot arm. J. Anhui Univ. Sci. Technol. (Nat. Sci.) (6), 33-2 (2013). https://kns.cnki.net/kcms/detail/detail.aspx?dbcode=CJFD&dbname=CJFD2013&filename=HLGB201302010&uniplatform=NZKPT&v=jsB4OIvplDyJn_Qv8lnptk4xZDMHYxK5I2c9IF9lsbPbZX9ypMi9E7nUDKL5Kb5s. (in Chinese)
5. Information system project manager course, 3rd edn. https://www.renrendoc.com/paper/126254229.html
6. Siemens PLC application system design example Technology. https://max.book118.com/html/2016/0708/47651681.shtm
7. Jiao, Z.: Greenhouse PLC control system design. Electronic world (2014). (in Chinese)
8. Main methods of Engineering Technology Research. https://max.book118.com/html/2018/0529/169385125.shtm

Image Defogging Algorithm Based on Inception Mechanism

Jiahao Geng, Zhuang Miao, and Kezheng Lin(✉)

School of Computer Science and Technology, Harbin University of Science and Technology, Harbin, China
540228873@qq.com, link@hrbust.edu.cn

Abstract. In order to solve the problem that the existing defogging algorithms can't differentiate according to the characteristics of different regions of the fogged image, an Image Defogging Algorithm Based on Inception Mechanism is proposed(I-defog algorithm). The attention mechanism is added to the algorithm to adaptively assign weights to the features of different regions; It is more accurate and effective to use the module with perception mechanism to predict the global value. The predicted value, transmittance and foggy image are input into the atmospheric scattering model to get the defogging image, and the defogging image is input into the Markov discriminant (PatchGAN) to judge whether it is true or not. The results show that the algorithm achieves good defogging effect on both indoor and outdoor images, and improves the brightness and saturation of defogging images.

Keywords: Pattern recognition · Image defogging · Deep learning · Attention mechanism · PatchGAN

1 Introduction

The long-term rapid development of China's economy has accelerated industrialization and urbanization, and the frequency of haze weather across the country has increased significantly. In this low visibility haze environment, due to the influence of suspended water droplets and aerosols in the atmosphere, the saturation and contrast of images obtained by outdoor shooting equipment have decreased, and many important details have been lost, It is not conducive to the feature extraction of subsequent equipment, and increases the difficulty of image processing, which makes it difficult for various security measures such as monitoring system and target detection system to play a normal role. Therefore, the study of image defogging algorithm has great research significance, practical value, and great application prospects [1, 2]. How to effectively restore degraded image in fuzzy environment to clear image has become more and more important [3–5].

Traditional defogging algorithms can be divided into classical image enhancement algorithms [6]. The first kind of classical algorithms, such as histogram equalization [7, 8], Retinex algorithm [9, 10], wavelet transform [11], and so on. Although it was

© ICST Institute for Computer Sciences, Social Informatics and Telecommunications Engineering 2022
Published by Springer Nature Switzerland AG 2022. All Rights Reserved
S. Shi et al. (Eds.): 6GN 2021, LNICST 439, pp. 308–321, 2022.
https://doi.org/10.1007/978-3-031-04245-4_27

proposed earlier and implemented simply, it did not consider the real cause of fog generation. The second kind of image defogging algorithm based on image restoration is to estimate the physical quantities in the atmospheric scattering model by using prior knowledge, and then inverse and restore the defogging image, such as dark channel prior defogging algorithm (DCP) [12], nonlocal prior defogging algorithm [13], variational model defogging algorithm [14], image defogging algorithm including sky region [15], The methods of defogging in elliptic model [16], adaptive fog attenuation algorithm [17], color attenuation model (CAP) [18]. Due to the prior knowledge can not adapt to all the fog scenes, the image defogging algorithm based on prior has poor robustness.

Image defogging algorithm based on deep learning can obtain atmospheric light value, medium transmittance and other information related to image haze through convolution neural network, which has good robustness. For example, dehazenet (dehaze) proposed by Cai uses convolution neural network to directly estimate the transmittance and atmospheric light value of foggy image, so as to obtain foggy image [19, 20]; AOD net proposed by Li et al. Is an end-to-end defogging algorithm [21]; Zhang et al. Proposed a defogging network based on pyramid dense connection and u-net [22]; A domain adaptation paradigm proposed by Shao et al. Can make up the gap between synthetic domain and real domain [23].

This Algorithm Based on Inception Mechanism. In the algorithm, the attention mechanism can adaptively assign weights to the features of different regions of the image, which makes the algorithm more focused on the feature information related to the haze. The larger the haze is, the larger the weight will be, and the smaller the haze is, the smaller the weight will be; The intrusion mechanism can obtain more receptive fields, and reduce the computational complexity of the algorithm.

2 Related Work

2.1 Atmospheric Model

Atmospheric model is usually used to simulate the degradation process of foggy image. Because of its versatility, it is used in the research of image algorithm. The atmospheric model is shown in formula (1).

$$I(x) = J(x)t(x) + A(1 - t(x)) \tag{1}$$

In the formula: $I(x)$ is the observed value of foggy image at x, $J(x)$ is the observed value of the clear image at x, $t(x)$ used to represent the attenuation of light reaching the camera lens, From formula (1), we can know that as long as the atmospheric light value and perspective of foggy image are known, the foggy image can be restored to non foggy image, so the algorithm needs to correctly estimate the medium perspective and atmospheric light value. However, the accuracy of estimating the medium transmittance and atmospheric light value is uncertain, which will have a great impact on the defogging effect. The algorithm proposed in this paper adopts the mechanism of perception and attention, which can effectively improve the accuracy of the prediction of medium perspective and atmospheric light value.

2.2 Network Attention Mechanism

The traditional deep learning defogging network model can process the pixel features of each channel and each region equally. The corresponding weights of different regions with different haze should be different. In addition, each channel should also have different weight information, which should have different weights, It will waste resources on a large amount of useless information In order to make the algorithm adaptive weight allocation according to the characteristics of different regions, attention mechanism is added to the algorithm. The design of attention mechanism module is shown in Fig. 1.

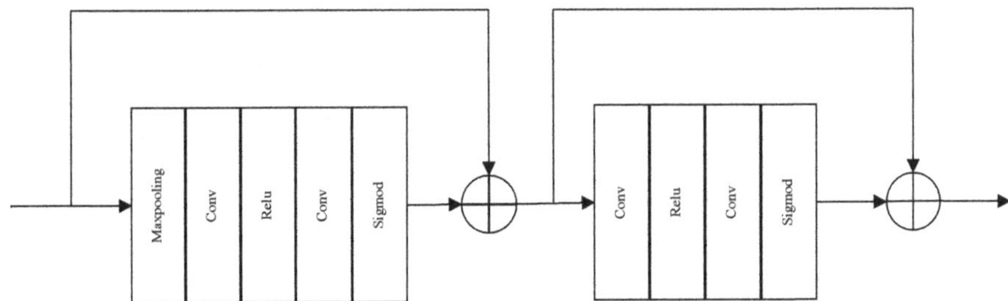

Fig. 1. Attention module

In the attention mechanism module, firstly, the channel spatial information is transformed into channel descriptors by maximizing pooling, as shown in formula (2).

$$g_C = Z_{mp}(F_C) = \frac{1}{H \times W} \sum_{i=1}^{H} \sum_{j=1}^{W} X_C(i,j) \tag{2}$$

In the formula: $X_C(i,j)$ is the value of the image C channel at position (i,j), Z_{mp} is the maximum pooling function, The convolution kernel with the same size as the image is used to maximize pooling, convert the size of feature graph from $C \times H \times W$ to $C \times 1 \times 1$, Then, the feature map is input into the two-layer convolution layer, as well as the Relu activation function and Sigmod activation function, as shown in formula (3).

$$A_C = \sigma(\mathrm{Conv}(\omega(\mathrm{Conv}(g_C)))) \tag{3}$$

In the formula: ω is the Relu function, σ is the Sigmod function, Conv is the convolution function, A_C is the weight of the output, Finally, the corresponding F_C and A_C are multiplied, as shown in formula (4).

$$F_C^* = A_C F_C \tag{4}$$

F_C^* is output to the next stage, which is different from the first stage. In this stage, there is no pooling layer, and F_C^* is directly input into the two-layer convolution layer, as well as the Relu activation function and Sigmod activation function, as shown in formula (5).

$$A_p = \sigma\left(\mathrm{Conv}\left(\omega\left(\mathrm{Conv}\left(F_C^*\right)\right)\right)\right) \tag{5}$$

In the formula: ω is the relu function, σ is the Sigmod function, Conv is the convolution function, and A_p is the weight of the output. Finally, the output of the attention module is obtained by multiplying the corresponding F_C^* and A_p, as shown in formula (6).

$$F_p^* = A_p F_C^* \tag{6}$$

2.3 Perception Mechanism

Concept convolution neural network is proposed by googlenet. It has gone through four versions. Concept 1 uses 1 * 1, 3 * 3, 5 * 5 convolution kernels to extract features of different scales. At the same time, it also adds maximum pooling. In order to reduce the number of network parameters, reduce the difficulty of operation, and accelerate the convergence speed, In addition to batch normalization, two 3 * 3 convolution kernels are used to replace the original 5 * 5 convolution kernels. On the basis of concept 2, concept 3 proposes a parallel convolution structure, which makes convolution and pooling run in parallel, and then combines them to reduce the dimension without causing the loss of information extraction. On the basis of concept 3, concept 4 adds a residual network (RESNET), which achieves good results and improves the training speed. The concept module used in this article is shown in Fig. 2.

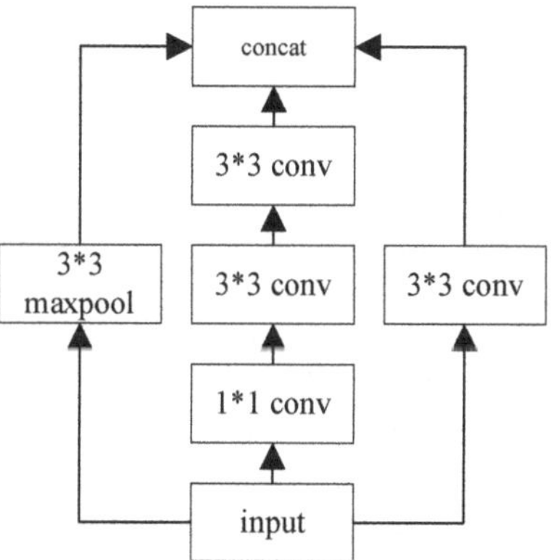

Fig. 2. Introduction mechanism

3 Method of This Paper

The foggy image is input into the defogging network to predict the value. The predicted value of atmospheric light, the medium transmittance and the foggy image. The foggy image is input into the Markov discriminator to judge whether it is true or not. The overall framework of algorithmic network is shown in Fig. 3.

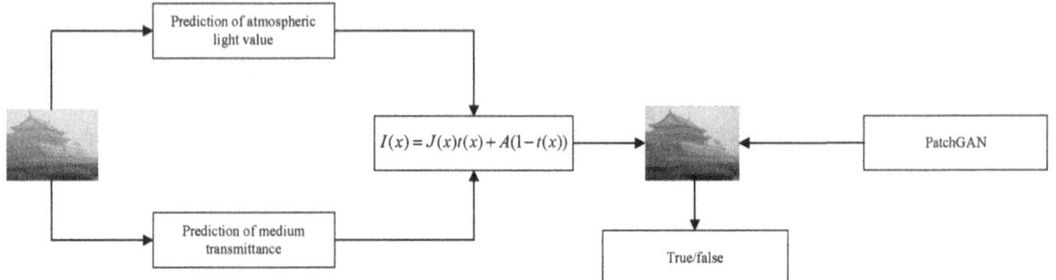

Fig. 3. Network framework

3.1 Prediction of Medium Transmittance

In addition, the attention mechanism can make use of the features with different weights to complement each other instead of focusing only on the local features. The media perspective estimation network based on attention mechanism used in this algorithm is shown in Fig. 4.

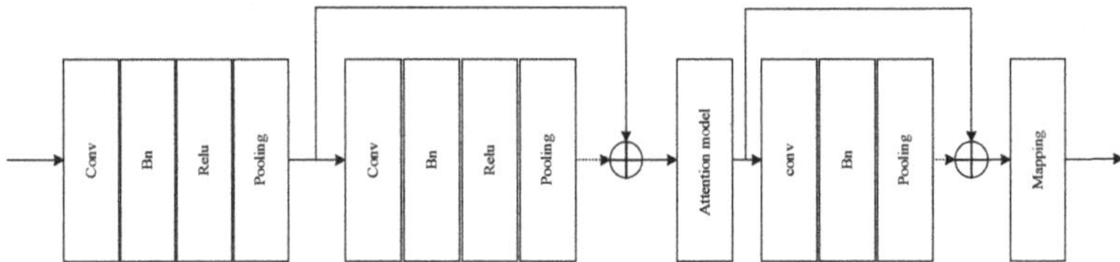

Fig. 4. Predictive transmission network

In order to obtain the haze, edge, texture and other information of different regions of the image for the subsequent use of deep network, the shallow network in the prediction transmittance module is used for feature extraction. Convolution layer and batch processing layer (BN layer) are used. In BN layer, the size of batch size can not be too large or too small. If the size of batch size is too small, the convergence speed of the model will be too slow, Appropriately increasing the batch size can increase the generalization ability and convergence speed of the model, but too large may lead to gradient disappearance or gradient explosion of the model. In this paper, the size of batch size is 64, and the relu activation layer and pooling layer are used to process the image, as shown in formula (7).

$$F_{\mathrm{s}} = H_{\mathrm{SF}}(I) \tag{7}$$

In the formula: I is the input foggy image, H_{SF} is the feature extraction function, F_s and is the output of shallow feature extraction. The F_s is input to the following residual module and attention module, and the F_s is down sampled. The residual module adds residual connection on the basis of feature extraction module. Residual connection can reduce the consumption of computing resources in the training of defogging network,

The subsequent attention mechanism module can automatically assign weights to the extracted features, so that the network module can focus more on processing the relevant feature information related to the medium transmittance, as shown in formula (8).

$$F_{\mathrm{d}} = H_{\mathrm{AM}}\{H_{\mathrm{RN,d}}\{\cdots\{H_{\mathrm{RN,1}}(F_{\mathrm{s}})\}\cdots\}\} \tag{8}$$

In the formula: $H_{\mathrm{RN,d}}$ represents the d residual convolution network function, H_{AM} represents the attention module function, and F_{d} represents the overall output of the function. In order to reconstruct the transmittance map, the deconvolution neural network is used for up sampling, as shown in formula (9).

$$F_{\mathrm{b}} = H_{\mathrm{DRN,b}}\{\cdots H_{\mathrm{DRN,2}}\{\{H_{\mathrm{DRN,1}}(F_{\mathrm{d}})\}\}\} \tag{9}$$

In the formula: $H_{DRN,b}$ represents the b residual convolution network, and F_b represents the overall output of the function. Finally, input F_b to the next layer of convolutional neural network, through the mapping layer, we can get the medium transmittance map, as shown in formula (10).

$$t = H_{\mathrm{MAP}}(F_{\mathrm{b}}) \tag{10}$$

3.2 Prediction of Atmospheric Light Value

To improve the convergence speed of the network and reduce the computational complexity in the network design of atmospheric light value prediction, we do not use the method of down sampling and up sampling, which is used to predict the medium perspective. Instead, we use the network based on the perception module to continuously down sampling. From the graph to the point, the final 1 * 1 result is the predicted atmospheric light value. The advantage of using the perception mechanism is that it can obtain more receptive fields, extract more global related information, and predict atmospheric light value more accurately, without the problem of taking the local optimal value as the global t value. At the same time, the perception module can speed up the network. The network with perception module is used to predict the atmospheric light value. The image processing process is shown in Fig. 5.

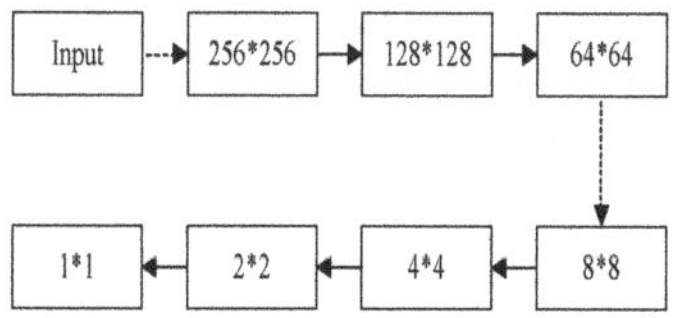

Fig. 5. Image processing process

3.3 Discriminator Network

In this paper, Markov discriminant (patchgan) is used to judge the true and false images after defogging. Different from the traditional discriminant model, in patchgan, the input is no longer a random high-frequency variable, but an image. When the image is input into patchgan, the discriminant will first segment the image into a n * n matrix (patch) to distinguish all patches, Finally, true or false is output according to the average value of all patch discrimination results of an image.

3.4 Algorithm Description

The first part is the mean square error loss function, as shown in formula (11).

$$L_{\mathrm{MSE}} = \frac{1}{N}\sum_{x=1}^{N} \|Y(x) - I(x)\|_2 \tag{11}$$

In the formula: $Y(x)$ represents the image before defogging, $I(x)$ represents the image after defogging, and N represents the total number of images contained in the training set. The second part is the discriminant loss function, as shown in formula (12).

$$L_{\mathrm{GAN}}(G, D) = E_{x,y}[\log_{10}^{D(x,y)}] + E_{x,y}[\log_{10}^{(1-D(x,G(x,z)))}] \tag{12}$$

In the formula: $E_{x,y}[\log_{10}^{D(x,y)}]$ is the probability to judge the original fog free image as true, $E_{x,y}[\log_{10}^{(1-D(x,G(x,z)))}]$ is the probability to judge the defogging image as false。

The expression of total loss function is shown in formula (13).

$$L = \partial L_{\mathrm{MSE}} + \beta L_{\mathrm{GAN}} \tag{13}$$

In the formula: ∂, β is the coefficient of the mean square error loss function and the discriminator error loss function respectively, and the default is 0.5.

This paper proposes a defogging algorithm, the specific process is shown in Algorithm 1.

algorithm 1 I-defog algorithm

input: Foggy image

output: Defogging image

(1) Input foggy imageI;

(2) Use formula (7) to extract shallow features and get feature map F_s ;

(3) Firstly, F_s is downsampled by residual network to get , and attention mechanism is used to allocate weight $F_d = H_{AM}\left(F_s + \mathcal{F}\left(F_s, W_l\right)\right)$, H_{AM} is the whole function of attention mechanism, $\mathcal{F}\left(F_s, W_l\right)$ is the residual;;

(4) Then the deconvolution residual network is used for up sampling to get F_b, $F_b = F_d + \mathcal{F}\left(F_d, W_l\right)$;

(5) The transmittance map is obtained by using the mapping function, $t = H_{MAP}\left(F_b\right)$;

(6) Using Inception module, the atmospheric light value of foggy image is predicted $A = F_{Inc,n}\left(\ldots F_{Inc,1}\left(I\right)\right)$;

(7) The defogging image J can be obtained,

$$J(x) = \frac{I(x) - A(1 - t(x))}{t(x)};$$

(8) Using PantchGAN to judge whether it is true or false;

(9) Further training the network, repeat (1) to (8) until the network loss is optimal, and the training is completed;

(10) Save the optimal model.

4 Experiments

4.1 Experimental Environment Configuration and Data Set

Hardware configuration: interi7-9700k processor (CPU), NVIDIA gtx-2060ti graphics card (GPU); The operating system is Ubuntu 20.04, and the model is built and trained under the deep learning framework pytorch.

The training data used in this paper is the reside data set, and the images in the data set are indoor foggy images, a total of 13900, which are synthesized from 1390 images in the existing indoor depth data set nyu2, each image is synthesized into 10 foggy blurred images. In addition, sots data set and HSTs data set will be used to verify algorithm.

4.2 Evaluating Indicator

PSNR first calculates the mean square error of two images. The smaller the mean square error is, the larger the PSNR value is, which indicates that the similarity of two images is greater, as shown in formula (14).

$$PSNR = 20 \log_{10}\left(\frac{MAX_I}{\sqrt{MSE}}\right) \tag{14}$$

In the formula: MAX_I is the maximum value of pixel color, MSE is the mean square error of fogged image and non fogged image.

Different from PSNR, the more similar the image is and the smaller the image distortion is, as shown in formula (15).

$$SSIM(x, y) = \frac{(2\mu_x\mu_y + c_1)(2\sigma_{xy} + c_2)}{\left(\mu_x^2 + \mu_y^2 + c_1\right)\left(\sigma_x^2 + \sigma_y^2 + c_2\right)} \tag{15}$$

In the formula: μ_x represents the average of x, μ_y represents the average of y, σ_x^2 represents the variance of x,σ_y^2 represents the variance of y, σ_{xy} is the covariance of x and y, c_1 and c_2 are two constants.

4.3 Algorithm Validation

In this paper, RESIDE data set is used as training set, SOTS data set and HSTS data set are used as test set to verify the effectiveness of the algorithm. SOTS data set is composed of foggy images generated from indoor images, while HSTS data set is composed of foggy images generated from outdoor images.

The comparison results of some test sets between the algorithm in this paper and other algorithms, the comparison results of PSNR and SSIM in some sots datasets are shown in Fig. 6 and Fig. 7, and the comparison results of PSNR and SSIM in some HSTS datasets are shown in Fig. 8 and Fig. 9. It can be seen from Fig. 6, Fig. 7, Fig. 8 and Fig. 9 that when processing indoor foggy images, the algorithm in this paper performs well in both PSNR value and SSIM value, which is improved compared with cap algorithm, DCP algorithm and mscnn algorithm. The images before and after defogging with slightly lower evaluation index are analyzed, It is found that these images contain a large number of sky regions, which has an impact on the estimation of atmospheric light value, resulting in a slightly lower image evaluation index after defogging. The PSNR and SSIM values of cap algorithm and DCP algorithm decrease greatly when they deal with some outdoor images which are difficult to defog, and the defog effect is poor. Although the algorithm in this paper and dehaze algorithm decrease a little, the decrease is relatively stable.

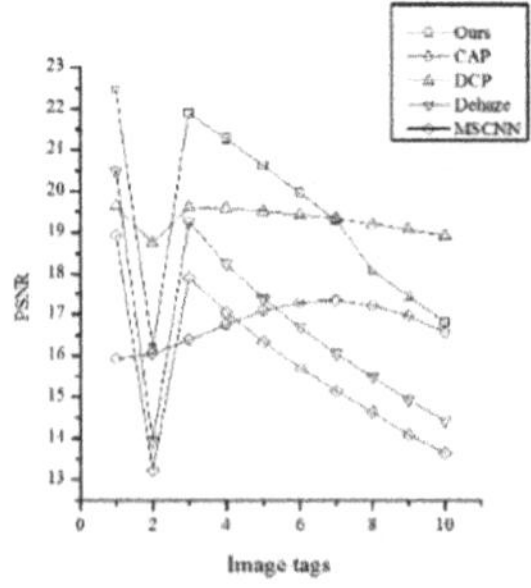

Fig. 6. Comparison of indoor PSNR

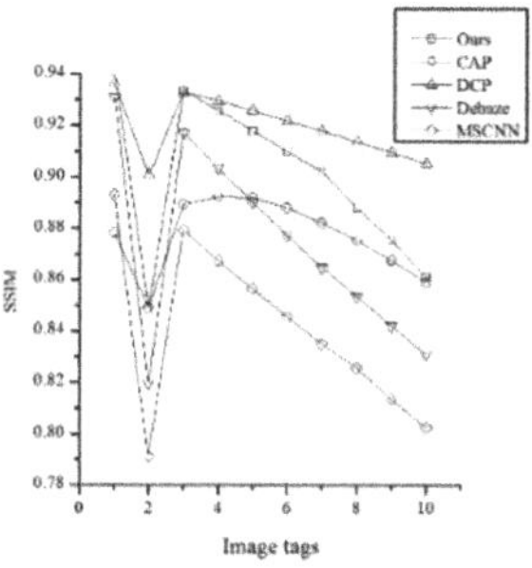

Fig. 7. Comparison of indoor SSIM

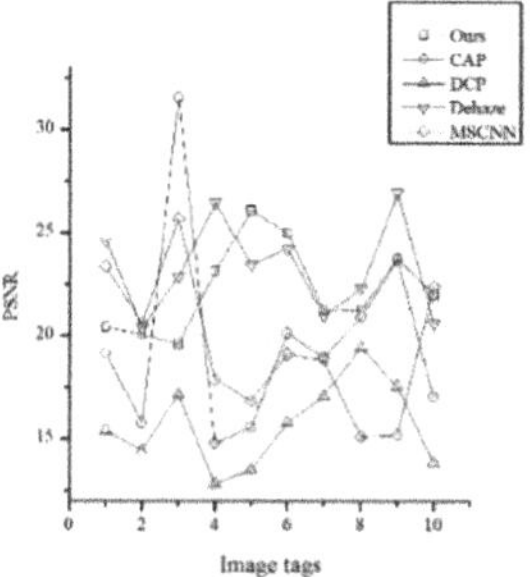

Fig. 8. Comparison of outdoor PSNR

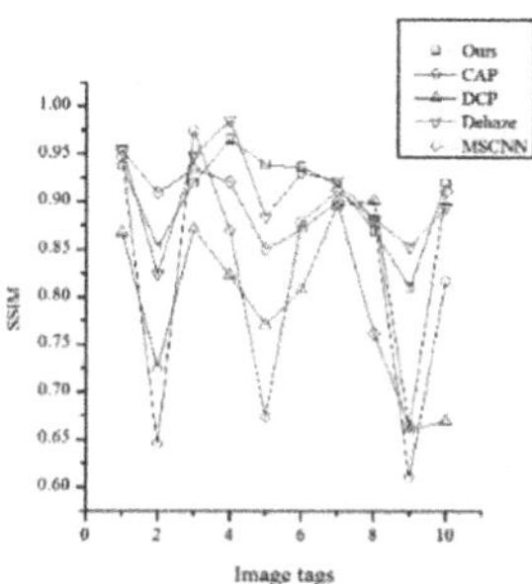

Fig. 9. Comparison of outdoor SSIM

The average comparison results of the algorithm in this paper and other algorithms in all test sets, In Table 1 and Table 2. SSIM is 0.024, 0.0059, 0.0008 and 0.0695 higher than cap, DCP, dehaze and MSCNN, and PSNR is 0.48 lower than dehaze, but 1.9, 1.89 and 3.74 higher than cap, DCP and MSCNN, respectively. On HSTs dataset, SSIM is 0.1079, 0.0843, 0.0052 and 0.0306 higher than cap, DCP, dehaze and MSCNN, respectively, and PSNR is 4.12, 6.37 and 2.75 higher than cap, DCP and MSCNN.

Table 1. SOTS dataset comparison results

Method	Evaluating indicator	
	SSIM	PSNR
CAP	0.8624	19.96
DCP	0.8505	19.97
Dehaze	0.8656	22.34
MSCNN	0.8169	18.12
Ours	0.8964	21.77

Table 2. HSTS dataset comparison results

Method	Evaluating indicator	
	SSIM	PSNR
CAP	0.7859	18.24
DCP	0.8095	15.99
Dehaze	0.8886	22.94
MSCNN	0.8632	19.61
Ours	0.8978	22.42

The visual comparison results of some outdoor scene images with fog in this algorithm and other comparison algorithms are shown in Fig. 10. It can be seen from Fig. 10 that the overall color of the image processed by cap algorithm is dark, and the sky part of the image is slightly distorted; DCP algorithm has serious distortion in sky area and character edge due to incomplete defogging. The values of four outdoor scene images are compared with other algorithms in this paper. The Fig. 11 and Fig. 12 show that the algorithm in this paper is relatively stable in terms of defogging performance. It performs well in PSNR and SSIM of four outdoor scene images, and some images have a large downward trend in DCP algorithm and MSCNN algorithm.

The values of four outdoor scene images are compared with other algorithms in this paper. The Fig. 11 and Fig. 12 show that the algorithm in this paper is relatively stable in terms of defogging performance. It performs well in PSNR and SSIM of four outdoor scene images, and some images have a large downward trend in DCP algorithm and MSCNN algorithm.

Fig. 10. Comparison of algorithms in outdoor (a) origin image (b) CAP results (c) DCP results (d) Dehaze results (e) MSCNN results (f) our results

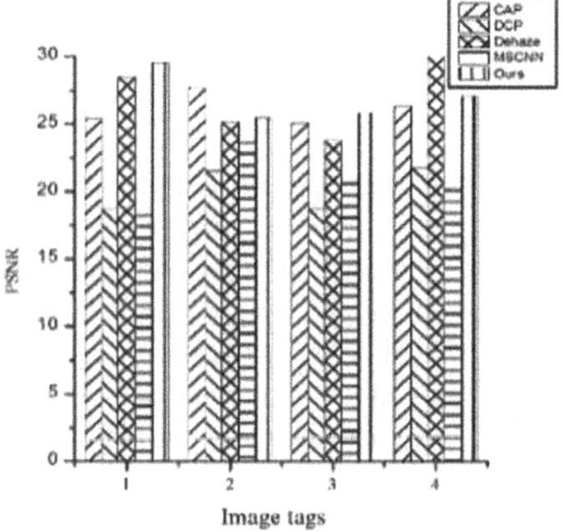

Fig. 11. Comparison of PSNR

4.4 Run Time Comparison

The average running time of this algorithm compared with cap algorithm, DCP algorithm, dehaze algorithm and MSCNN algorithm is shown in Table 3. The average processing time is 0.93 s. Compared with the comparison algorithm, the time is controlled within 1s, which has higher running efficiency.

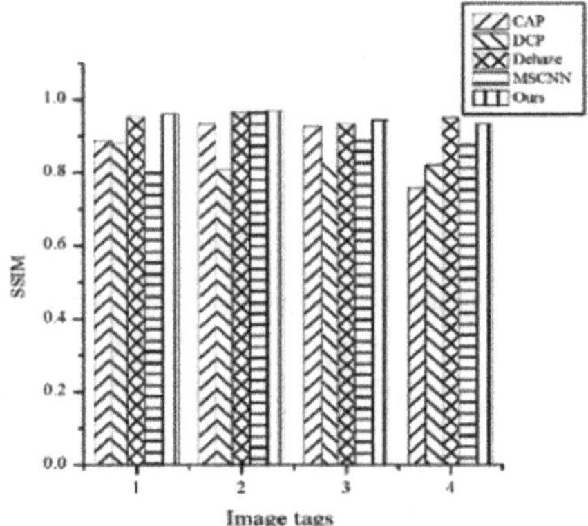

Fig. 12. Comparison of SSIM

Table 3. Comparison of average running time of different algorithms

Method	CAP	DCP	Dehaze	MSCNN	Ours
Time/s	1.43	10.11	1.77	1.71	0.97

5 Conclusions

This Algorithm Based on Inception Mechanism. On the one hand, it solves the problem that the traditional image defogging algorithm can not carry out differential processing according to different haze characteristics. On the other hand, the algorithm can make use of the features with different weights to complement each other instead of only focusing on the local features, makes better use of the global related information, makes the results more accurate. The results show that can achieves good defogging effect in both indoor and outdoor data sets, and improves the brightness and saturation of the image while effectively defogging.

References

1. Shu, Q.L., Wu, C.S., Zhong, Q.X., et al.: Alternating minimization algorithm for hybrid regularized variational image dehazing. Optik – Int. J. Light Electron Opt. **185**, 943–956 (2019)
2. Pu, H.F., Huang, Z.Y.: Review of image defogging algorithms. Softw. Eng. **24**(05), 2–6 (2021)
3. Tufail, Z., Khurshid, K., Salman, A., et al.: Improved dark channel prior for image defogging using RGB and YcbCr color space. IEEE Access **6**(1), 32576–32587 (2018)
4. Zhang, W.D., Dong, L.L., Pan, X.P., et al.: Single image defogging based on multi-channel convolutional MSRCR. IEEE Access **7**(1), 72492–72504 (2019)
5. Zhang, D.Y., Ju, M.Y., Qian, W.: Research status and Prospect of image defogging algorithm. J. Nanjing Univ. Posts Telecommun. (Nat. Sci. Ed.) **40**(05), 101–111 (2020)
6. Nolim, U.A.: Single image dehazing using adaptive dynamic stochastic resonance and wavelet-based fusion. Optik - Int. J. Light Electron Opt. **195**, 163111 (2019)

7. Gonzalez, R.C., Woods, R.E.: Digital image processing. Prentice Hall Int. **28**(4), 484–486 (2008)
8. Kim, T.K., Paik, J.K., Kang, B.S.: Contrast enhancement system using spatially adaptive histogram equalization with temporal filtering. IEEE Trans. Consum. Electron. **44**(1), 82–87 (1998)
9. Shi, R.X., Gao, B.L., Qiao, Y.J.: Improved Retinex low illumination image enhancement algorithm based on fusion strategy. Comput. Meas. Control **29**(04), 159–164 (2021)
10. Ou, J.M., Hu, X., Yang, J.X.: Low light image enhancement algorithm based on improved Retinex net. Pattern Recogn. Artif. Intell. **34**(01), 77–86 (2021)
11. Zhang, Z.H., Lu, J.G.: Fog image enhancement based on wavelet transform and improved Retniex. Comput. Appl. Softw. **38**(01), 227–231 (2021)
12. Li, Y.M., Zhang, X.J., Xie, B.W.: Improved dark channel prior image defogging algorithm based on brightness model fusion. Progr. Laser Optoelectron. **57**(22), 67–73 (2020)
13. He, K., Sun, J., Tang, X.: Single image haze removal using dark channel prior. IEEE Trans. Pattern Anal. Mach. Intell. **33**(12), 2341–2353 (2010)
14. Berman, D., Avidan, S.: Non-local image dehazing. In: Proceedings of the IEEE Conference on Computer Vision and Pattern Recognition, pp. 1674–1682 (2016)
15. Guo, T., Li, N., Sun, L., et al.: A defogging method including sky region image. Progr. Laser Optoelectron. 1–14 [2021–06–16].http://kns.cnki.net/kcms/detail/31.1690.TN.20210409.0934.038.html
16. Jiao, Z., Fan, Z., Qian, L.: Research on fog removal based on RGB color space ellipsoid model. Progr. Laser Optoelectron. 1–15 [2021–06–16]. http://kns.cnki.net/kcms/detail/31.1690.TN.20210517.1011.002.html
17. Yan, Y., Zhang, J.: Image defogging algorithm based on fog concentration distribution and adaptive attenuation. Progr. Laser Optoelectron. 1–14 [2021-06-16]. http://kns.cnki.net/kcms/detail/31.1690.TN.20210301.1016.018.html
18. Liu, Y., Shang, J.X., Pan, L., et al.: A unified variational model for single image dehazing. IEEE Access **7**, 15722–15736 (2019)
19. Cai, B., Xu, X., Jia, K., et al.: Dehaze-net: an end-to-end system for single image haze removal. IEEE Trans. Image Process. **25**(11), 5187–5198 (2016)
20. Ren, W., Liu, S., Zhang, H., Pan, J., Cao, X., Yang, M.-H.: Single image dehazing via multi-scale convolutional neural networks. In: Leibe, B., Matas, J., Sebe, N., Welling, M. (eds.) ECCV 2016. LNCS, vol. 9906, pp. 154–169. Springer, Cham (2016). https://doi.org/10.1007/978-3-319-46475-6_10
21. Li, B.Y., Peng, X.L., Wang, Z.Y., et al.: AOD-Net: all-in-all dehazing network. In: IEEE International Conference on Computer Vision, pp. 4770–4778 (2017)
22. Zhang, H., Patel, V.M.: Densely connected pyramid dehazing network. In: 2018 IEEE/CVF Conference on Computer Vision and Pattern Recognition, Salt Lake City, UT, pp. 3194–3203 (2018)
23. Shao, Y., Li, L., Ren, W., et al.: Domain adaptation for image dehazing. In: 2020 IEEE/CVF Conference on Computer Vision and Pattern Recognition (CVPR), Seattle, WA, pp. 2805–2814 (2020)

Compressed Sensing Joint Image Reconstruction Based on Multiple Measurement Vectors

Juntao Sun, Guoxing Huang(✉), Weidang Lu, Yu Zhang, and Hong Peng

College of Information Engineering, Zhejiang University of Technology, Hangzhou 310023, China
hgx05745@zjut.edu.cn

Abstract. In order to improve the quality of the reconstructed image for compressed sensing, a novel compressed sensing joint image reconstruction method based on multiple measurement vectors is put forward in this paper. Firstly, the original image is processed under the multiple measurement vectors (MWV) mode and random measured by two compressive imaging cameras, in vertical direction and horizontal direction, separately. Secondly, the vertical sampling image and horizontal sampling image are reconstructed with the multiple measurement vectors. Finally, the mean image is used to capture the correlation between these two similar images, and the original image is reconstructed. The experiment result showed that the visual effect and peak signal to noise ratio (PSNR) of the joint reconstructed image by this method is much better than the independent reconstructed images. So, it is an effective compressed sensing joint image reconstruction method.

Keywords: Compressed sensing · Image reconstruction · Joint reconstruction · Single measurement vector (SMV) · Multiple measurement vectors (MMV)

1 Introduction

Over the past few years, there have been increased interests in the study of compressed sensing—a new framework for simultaneous sampling and compression of signals [1]. Compressed sensing exploits the sparsity of an unknown signal to recover the signal from much fewer linear measurements than required by the Nyquist-Shannon sampling [2]. The fact that compressed sensing requires very few measurements makes it very useful to reduce sensing cost in a variety of applications.

Signal reconstruction algorithm is the key to compressed sensing theory. Presently, various reconstruction algorithms have been proposed, such as the orthogonal matching pursuit (OMP) algorithm [3], the basis pursuit (BP) algorithm [4], the hybrid simulated annealing thresholding algorithm [5], and the orthogonal super greedy algorithm 错误!未找到引用源。. However, all these reconstruction algorithms for compressed sensing are based on the sparsity of original signal, which can be described as the internal signal correlation. In order to make full use of the correlation between different image signals,

© ICST Institute for Computer Sciences, Social Informatics and Telecommunications Engineering 2022
Published by Springer Nature Switzerland AG 2022. All Rights Reserved
S. Shi et al. (Eds.): 6GN 2021, LNICST 439, pp. 322–332, 2022.
https://doi.org/10.1007/978-3-031-04245-4_28

some researchers have investigated the multi-view correlation and presented the relevant reconstruction methods. However, these methods either require estimating the relative camera positions or do not perform the reconstructions simultaneously. To date, how to improve the accuracy of reconstruction image via using the correlation between different image signals remains a critical problem [6].

In this paper, we assume that the original image is processed under the multiple measurement vectors (MWV) mode and random measured by two compressive imaging cameras, in vertical direction and horizontal direction, separately. The correlation between these two different sampling direction images is captured by the mean of these two visual similar images. In this way, the original image is joint reconstructed and the accuracy is improved. Firstly, each column and each row of the original image signal is individual treated as one-dimensional signal, and then linear measured via MWV framework separately [7]. Secondly, all one-dimensional signals are recovered and composed of two sampling direction reconstruction images. Finally, the original image is joint reconstructed by the mean of these two images.

2 The Basic Principle of Compressed Sensing

Compressed sensing, also known as compressed sampling or sparse sampling, is a technique for finding sparse solutions to underdetermined linear systems. Compressed sensing is applied in electronic engineering, especially signal processing, to obtain and reconstruct sparse or compressible signals. This method takes advantage of the sparse nature of the signal and is able to reconstruct the entire desired signal from fewer measurements than Nyquist's theory. The basic idea of compressed sensing is that any sparse or compressible signal can be projected from high dimension space into low dimensional space via linear measurement processing [8]. And then the original signal can be reconstructed by solving an optimization problem. Premise condition of compressed sensing is that the signal is sparse or compressible [9], but the actual signal usually can't meet this condition. To solve this problem [10], the orthogonal transformation processing can be performed [11]. For such signals without sparse properties, the processing process of compressed sensing is shown in Fig. 1 below:

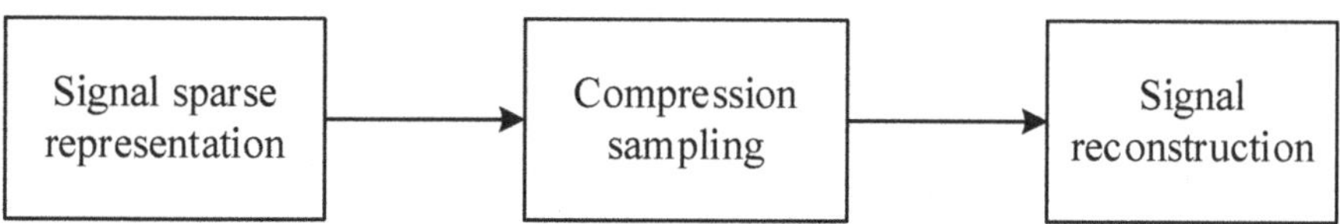

Fig. 1. The processing of compressed sensing

Compressed sensing, also known as compressed sampling, looks more intuitive. Compressed sensing is a signal sampling technology, it through some means, to achieve "compression sampling", to be precise, in the sampling process to complete the data compression process. Compressed sensing is to solve the problem of how to restore the signal perfectly under the condition of under-sampling. The classical signal processing system is built on the basis of classical linear algebra and statistics, so the number of equations is less than the number of unknowns to deal with this kind of under-sampled reconstruction problem. According to the theory of classical signal processing, this kind of problem has infinitely many solutions (can't uniquely and definitively recover the target image perfectly). We call this kind of problem an ill-posed problem, and Compressed Sensing is used to solve ill-posed inverse problems.

Consider a real-valued, finite-length, one-dimensional, discrete-time signal x, with the length of N. The signal x can be expressed as (1):

$$x = \sum_{i=1}^{N} \psi_i \alpha_i = \Psi \alpha, \tag{1}$$

where $\Psi = \{\psi_i\}_{i=1}^{N}$ is an orthogonal base matrix of $N \times N$ and α is a coefficient vector of $N \times 1$. If there are only $K < < N$ non-zero coefficients in vector α, the signal x can be seen as a sparse signal in the Ψ domain and the sparse degree is K.

Compressed sensing samples signal by directly acquiring a compressed signal representation without going through the intermediate stage of acquiring N samples. Consider a general linear measurement process that computes $M < N$ inner products between x a collection of vectors $\Phi = \{\varphi_j\}_{j=1}^{M}$, the measurement process can be expressed as (2):

$$y = \Phi x = \Phi \Psi \alpha, \tag{2}$$

where y is a measurement vector of $M \times 1$, and Φ is a measurement matrix of $M \times N$.

A necessary and sufficient condition for measurement matrix Φ to reconstruct the length-N signal x from $M < N$ measurements is that Φ must satisfy restricted isometry property (RIP) criterion [12]. The RIP criterion requires the matrix $\Theta = \Phi\Psi$ must satisfy the expression (3):

$$1 - \varepsilon \leq \frac{||\Theta\alpha||_2}{||\alpha||_2} \leq 1 + \varepsilon, \tag{3}$$

where $\varepsilon \in (0, 1)$ is a constant. The equivalent condition of RIP criterion is that measurement matrix Φ is incoherent with the basis Ψ.

Since $M < N$, the Eq. (2) appears ill-conditioned. However, α is a K sparse vector which means that there is only K non-zero coefficients, and then the problem can be solved provided $M \geq K$. The most direct way to reconstruct α is by solving optimization problem under l_0 norm:

$$\widehat{\alpha} = \arg\min ||\alpha||_0 \quad s.t. \;\; y = \Phi\Psi\alpha, \tag{4}$$

where $||\alpha||_0$ is the l_0 norm of vector α, i.e. the number of its non-zero coefficients. Finally, the signal x can be reconstructed by (1). The schematic diagram of compressed sensing is shown in Fig. 2.

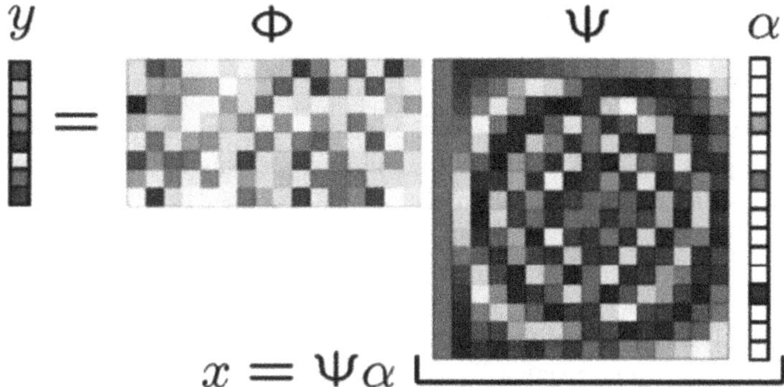

Fig. 2. The schematic diagram of compressed sensing

3 Compressive Imaging Based on Multiple Measurement Vectors

3.1 Random Measurement in Vertical and Horizontal Direction

According to the theory of compressed sensing introduced in the last section, any natural image signal X of $N \times P$ can be orthogonal transformed as (5), and the transposed matrix X^T of $P \times N$ can be also orthogonal transformed as (6):

$$X = \Psi_H S, \tag{5}$$

$$X^T = \Psi_L D, \tag{6}$$

where Ψ_H is an orthogonal base matrix of $N \times N$ and S is a sparse coefficient matrix of $N \times P$; Ψ_L is an orthogonal base matrix of $P \times P$ and D is a sparse coefficient matrix of $P \times N$.

In previous research of compressive imaging, most scholars will convert the two-dimensional image signal into one-dimensional signal when process image signal. For example, all columns of an image of $N \times P$ are linked end-to-end to compose a column vector of $N \cdot P \times 1$, which means that a long one-dimensional signal is processed under the single measurement vector (SMV) mode. But in this way, the scale of the measurement matrix would be very big, which will significantly increase the amount of calculation and storage space, and lead to a very long processing time.

In order to reduce the scale of the measurement matrix and improve the accuracy of reconstruction, each column of the image signal can be individual treated as one-dimensional signal of $N \times 1$. And P measurement vectors of $M \times 1$ can be obtained by the same measurement matrix, which means that the two-dimensional image signal is processed under the multiple measurement vectors (MWV) mode [13].

We assume that the original image X of $N \times P$ is processed under MWV mode and random measured by two compressive imaging cameras, in vertical and horizontal direction separately. In vertical direction, each column of the image signal is individual treated as one-dimensional signal of $N \times 1$, and then random liner measured by a random matrix Φ_H of $M \times N$. This linear measurement process can be described as (7):

$$y_i = \Phi_H X_i = \Phi_H \Psi_H S_i \quad (i = 1, 2 \cdots P), \tag{7}$$

where $y_i \quad (i = 1, 2 \cdots P)$ is observation vector of $M \times 1$, $X_i \quad (i = 1, 2 \cdots P)$ is the i column vector of original image signal X, and $S_i \quad (i = 1, 2 \cdots P)$ is the i column vector of sparse coefficient matrix S.

In horizontal direction, each row of the image signal is individual treated as one-dimensional signal of $1 \times P$, and then random liner measured by a random matrix Φ_L of $M \times P$. This linear measurement process can be described as (8):

$$z_j = \Phi_L X_j^T = \Phi_L \Psi_L D_j \quad (j = 1, 2 \cdots N), \tag{8}$$

where $z_j \quad (j = 1, 2 \cdots N)$ is observation vector of $M \times 1$, $X_j^T \quad (j = 1, 2 \cdots N)$ is the j row vector of original image signal X, and $D_i \quad (j = 1, 2 \cdots N)$ is the j column vector of sparse coefficient matrix D.

3.2 Image Joint Reconstruction

To reconstruct the original image X of $N \times P$ with the measurement vectors $y_i \quad (i = 1, 2 \cdots P)$ and $z_j \quad (j = 1, 2 \cdots N)$ [14], the most direct way is by solving two optimization problems under l_0 norm as (8) and (9) separately:

$$\widehat{S}_i = \arg\min ||S_i||_0 \quad s.t. \quad y_i = \Phi_H \Psi_H S_i \quad (i = 1, 2 \cdots P), \tag{9}$$

$$\widehat{D}_j = \arg\min ||D_j||_0 \quad s.t. \quad z_j = \Phi_L \Psi_L D_j \quad (j = 1, 2 \cdots N), \tag{10}$$

where $||S_i||_0$ is the l_0 norm of vector S_i, i.e. the number of its non-zero coefficients; $||D_j||_0$ is the l_0 norm of vector D_j, i.e. the number of its non-zero coefficients. Signal reconstruction algorithm of compressed sensing, such as orthogonal matching pursuit (OMP) algorithm and basis pursuit (BP) algorithm, can be used to solve (9) and (10). So, we can get $\widehat{S} = \left\{\widehat{S}_i\right\}_{i=1}^{P}$ and $\widehat{D} = \left\{\widehat{D}_j\right\}_{j=1}^{N}$.

Here we can get two image-by-image reconstruction images as $\widehat{X}_H = \Psi_H \widehat{S}$ and $\widehat{X}_L = (\Psi_L \widehat{D})^T$. Reconstruction images $\widehat{X}_H$ and $\widehat{X}_L$ would be the same in the case of exact reconstruction. But the error would be introduced in actual measurement and calculation, which would lead to certain differences between $\widehat{X}_H$ and $\widehat{X}_L$. In order to improve the quality of the reconstruction image, we advocate the mean of these two-view image signals to capture the correlation between them. So, the joint reconstruction image is calculated as (11):

$$\widehat{X} = (\Psi_H \widehat{S} + \widehat{D}^T \Psi_L^T)/2, \tag{11}$$

3.3 Process of This Method

The specific steps of multi-view compressive imaging based on multiple measurement vectors can be concluded as follows:

Step 1: Initialization. It is assumed that the size of the original image signal X is $N \times P$, where N is the number of the rows of the figure and P is the number of lines of the figure. Measurement matrix Φ_H is a random matrix with the size of $M \times N$; and Measurement matrix Φ_L is a random matrix with the size of $M \times P$.

Step 2: Linear measurement. The original image is random measured by two compressive imaging cameras, in vertical and horizontal direction separately. In vertical direction, each column of the image signal X is individual treated as one-dimensional signal of $N \times 1$, and then linear measured by (7). In horizontal direction, each row of the image signal X is individual treated as one-dimensional signal of $1 \times P$, and then linear measured by (8).

Step 3: One-dimensional signal reconstruction. Sparse signal $\widehat{S}_i \quad (i = 1, 2 \cdots P)$ and $\widehat{D}_j \quad (j = 1, 2 \cdots N)$ can be recovered by solving the optimization problems in (9) and (10). In this paper, the classical greed iterative algorithm, i.e. orthogonal matching pursuit algorithm (OMP) [15], is used to solve these optimization problems. Then the sparse coefficient matrixes can be calculated as $\widehat{S} = \left\{\widehat{S}_i\right\}_{i=1}^{P}$ and $\widehat{D} = \left\{\widehat{D}_j\right\}_{j=1}^{N}$.

Step 4: Joint image reconstruction. Two image-by-image reconstruction images can be reconstructed as $\widehat{X}_H = \Psi_H S$ and $\widehat{X}_L = (\Psi_L D)^T$, and the final reconstructed image signal can be calculated as (11).

4 The Simulation Experiment Results

In order to verify the compressed sensing joint image reconstruction method presented in this paper, simulation experiments are carried out to four standard test images with the size of 256×256. These tests imaged are image "Lenna", "Cameraman", "Fruits" and "Peppers". In the experiments, the image signal is sparse represented with wavelet base matrix [16–18]; the measurement matrix is Gaussian random matrix; the vertical sampling rate and horizontal sampling rate are the same. Considering the fast calculation and high accuracy of OMP algorithm in compressed sensing signal reconstruction, the com parison experiments were conducted with single measurement vector OMP (SMV-OMP) algorithm in, multiple measurement vectors OMP (MMV-OMP) algorithm in [19], and the method in this paper. Classic compressed sensing problems can be summarized as: with a known single observation vector to solve the unknown single observation vector, namely the SMV problem. In the actual application of a variety of scenarios, however, there are multiple measurement vector valued known conditions, the sparse vector to recover at the same time, different from the SMV model said it to multiple measurements (MMV) model, that is, multiple sparse vector at the same time refactoring (recovery K sparse matrix x) at the same time, the vector matrix form. Multiple measurement vector model in terms of a single measurement vector model, can further use the signal and the signal correlation in between, with the same multiple of sparse vector for recovery at the same time, can improve the reconstruction accuracy. The simulation experimental conditions are as follows: Windows 7 SP1, Intel(R) Core (TM) i5-3210M CPU @ 2.50 GHz, 3.88 GB memory, and the tool is MATLAB R2012b.

The original image, simulation experiment results of SMV-OMP algorithm, MMV-OMP algorithm and the method in this paper are illustrated in Fig. 3, 4, 5 and 6 [20]. From these simulation experiment results it can be seen that the accuracy and visual effect of the joint reconstruction images by this method are much better than the reconstruction results by the other two algorithms. Form the reconstruction results of image "Lenna", "Cameraman", "Fruits" and "Peppers" we can see that the image acuity and visual effect of the proposed joint reconstructed image is much better than that of the SMV-OMP reconstructed image and MMV-OMP reconstructed image, which verify the effectiveness of the proposed method.

In order to quantitatively evaluate the performance of these algorithms, peak signal to noise ratio (PSNR) is used as evaluation index of the image reconstruction algorithm. Peak signal-to-noise ratio (PSNR) [21], an objective criterion for image evaluation, has been applied in many scenarios. It is local, PSNR is the abbreviation of Peak Signal to Noise Ratio. Peak means peak in Chinese. PSNR is generally used for an engineering project between the maximum signal and the background noise. Usually after image compression, usually the output image will be different from the original image in some way. In order to measure the image quality after processing, we usually refer to the PSNR value to measure whether a process is satisfactory or not. The PSNR shows the difference degree between the reconstructed image and the original image, and it can be calculated as (12):

$$PSNR \triangleq 10\log_{10}\left[\frac{255\times 255}{\frac{1}{N\times P}\sum_{i=1}^{N}\sum_{j=1}^{P}|X(i,j)-\widehat{X}(i,j)|^2}\right], \tag{12}$$

where $N \times P$ is the size of original image signal X, and $\widehat{X}$ is the reconstruction image.

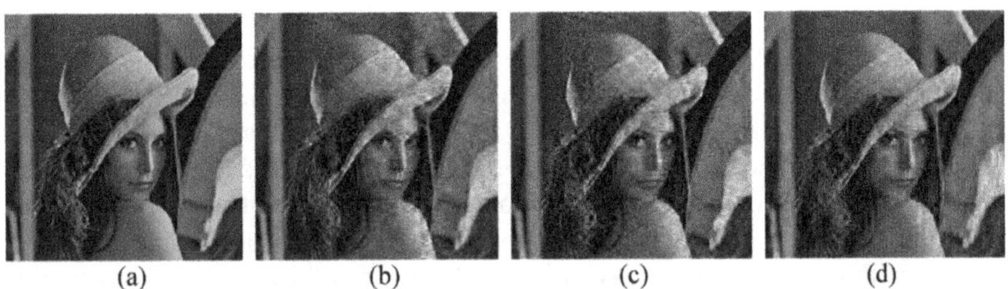

(a) (b) (c) (d)

Fig. 3. Reconstruction results of image Lena, sampling rate is 40%. (a) Original image; (b) SMV-OMP reconstructed image; (c) MMV-OMP reconstructed image; (d) Joint reconstructed image

Table 1 shows PSNR of the simulation experiment results with the sampling rate of 0.3, 0.4 and 0.5. From Table 1, it can be seen that, the reconstructions quality of all algorithms is improved with the increase of sampling rate. And we can conclude that under the same simulation conditions, the joint reconstruction images in this method provide higher PSNR than the images reconstructed by SMV-OMP algorithm and MMV-OMP algorithm.

Fig. 4. Reconstruction results of image Cameraman, sampling rate is 40%. (a) Original image; (b) SMV-OMP reconstructed image; (c) MMV-OMP reconstructed image; (d) Joint reconstructed image

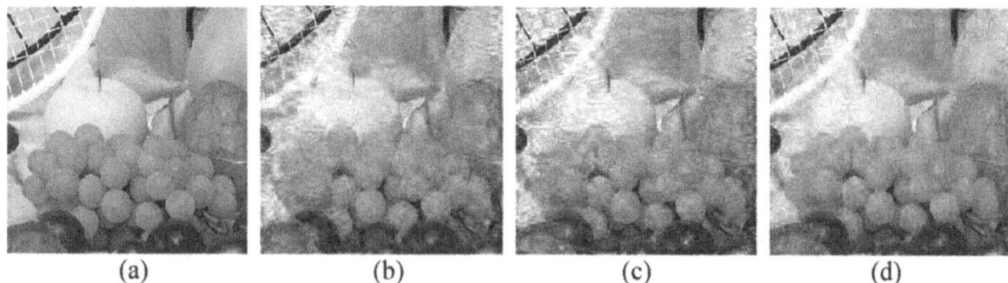

Fig. 5. Reconstruction results of image Fruits, sampling rate is 40%. (a) Original image; (b) SMV-OMP reconstructed image; (c) MMV-OMP reconstructed image; (d) Joint reconstructed image

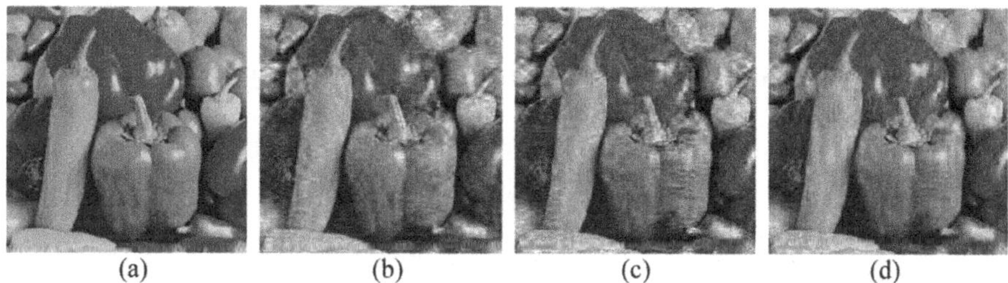

Fig. 6. Reconstruction results of image Peppers, sampling rate is 40%. (a) Original image; (b) SMV-OMP reconstructed image; (c) MMV-OMP reconstructed image; (d) Joint reconstructed image

Table 1. The PSNR of simulation results (dB).

Test images	Sampling rate = 30%			Sampling rate = 40%			Sampling rate = 50%		
	SMV OMP	MMV OMP	Joint result	SMV OMP	MMV OMP	Joint result	SMV OMP	MMV OMP	Joint result
Lena	18.94	21.51	**22.32**	23.56	24.28	**25.41**	26.46	27.19	**27.49**
Cameraman	14.79	19.82	**21.78**	21.74	22.10	**24.47**	24.01	24.44	**27.07**
Fruits	15.54	20.72	**22.94**	22.11	22.96	**25.55**	24.74	25.40	**28.06**
Peppers	15.86	20.04	**22.20**	22.16	22.83	**25.04**	25.21	25.32	**27.55**

For the range of sampling rate is large, the experiment also can verify the robustness of the method. Figure 7 shows the PSNR comparison chart of image Lena, under the condition of different sampling rate. From Fig. 5 it can be seen that the PSNR of the joint reconstruction images in this method provide higher PSNR than the images reconstructed by the other two algorithms, under the same sampling rate. And the performance of this method dose not appears large fluctuations. It maintains a good stability with the change of sampling rate. So it is an effective compressive imaging method [22, 23].

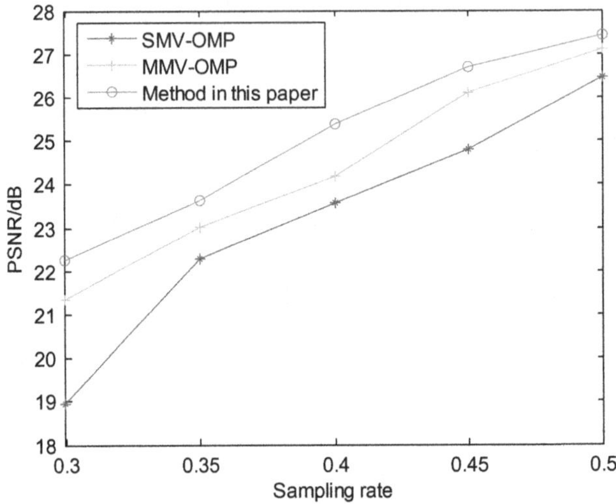

Fig. 7. The PSNR contrast diagram of image Lena under different sampling rate

5 Conclusions

A novel compressed sensing joint image reconstruction method based on multiple measurement vectors is put forward in this paper. We assume that the original image is processed under the multiple measurement vectors (MWV) mode and random measured by two compressive imaging cameras, in vertical direction and horizontal direction, separately. After these two different sampling direction images are reconstructed, the mean image is used to capture the correlation between them and the original image is joint reconstructed. The experiment results showed that the accuracy and visual effect of the joint reconstruction images by this method are much better than the reconstruction results by SMV-OMP algorithm and MMV-OMP algorithm. And the performance of this method dose not appears large fluctuations with the change of sampling rate. So, it is an effective compressed sensing joint image reconstruction method.

References

1. Donoho, D.L.: Compressed sensing. IEEE Trans. Inf. Theory **52**(4), 1289–1306 (2006)
2. Baraniuk, R.: Compressive sensing. IEEE Sig. Process. Mag. **24**(4), 118–124 (July 2007)
3. Zhou, Y., Zeng, F.-Z., Gu, Y.-C.: A gradient descent sparse adaptive matching pursuit algorithm based on compressive sensing. In: 2016 International Conference on Machine Learning and Cybernetics (ICMLC), vol. 1, pp. 464–469 (2016)
4. Khajehnejad, M.A., Xu, W., Avestimehr, A.S., Hassibi, B.: Improving the thresholds of sparse recovery: an analysis of a two-step reweighted basis pursuit algorithm. IEEE Trans. Inf. Theory **61**(9), 5116–5128 (2015)
5. Xu, F.M., Wang, S.H.: A hybrid simulated annealing thresholding algorithm for compressed sensing. Sig. Process. **93**(6), 1577–1585 (June 2013)
6. Fei, X., Li, L., Cao, H., Miao, J., Yu, R.: View's dependency and low-rank background-guided compressed sensing for multi-view image joint reconstruction. IET Image Process. **13**(12), 2294–2303 (2019)
7. Qiao, H., Pal, P.: Guaranteed localization of more sources than sensors with finite snapshots in multiple measurement vector models using difference co-arrays. IEEE Trans. Sig. Process. **67**(22), 5715–5729 (2019)
8. Wang, J., Kwon, S., Li, P., Shim, B.: Recovery of sparse signals via generalized orthogonal matching pursuit: a new analysis. IEEE Trans. Sig. Process. **64**(4), 1076–1089 (2016)
9. Amel, R., Feuer, A.: Adaptive identification and recovery of jointly sparse vectors. IEEE Trans. Sig. Process. **62**(2), 354–362 (2014)
10. Wen, J., Yu, W.: Exact sparse signal recovery via orthogonal matching pursuit with prior information. In: ICASSP 2019 - 2019 IEEE International Conference on Acoustics, Speech and Signal Processing (ICASSP), Brighton, United Kingdom, pp. 5003–5007 (2019)
11. Shousen, C., Quanzhu, J., Qiang, X.: Image super-resolution reconstruction based on compressed sensing. In: 2017 4th International Conference on Information Science and Control Engineering (ICISCE), Changsha, pp. 368–374 (2017)
12. Tillmann, A.M., Pfetsch, M.E.: The computational complexity of the restricted isometry property, the nullspace property, and related concepts in compressed sensing. IEEE Trans. Inf. Theory **60**(2), 1248–1259 (2014)
13. Xuan, V.N., Hartmann, K., Weihs, W., Loffeld, O.: Modified orthogonal matching pursuit for multiple measurement vector with joint sparsity in super-resolution compressed sensing. In: 2017 51st Asilomar Conference on Signals, Systems, and Computers, Pacific Grove, CA, pp. 840–844 (2017)
14. Zhu, J., Wang, J., Zhu, Q.: Compressively sensed multi-view image reconstruction using joint optimization modeling. In: 2018 IEEE Visual Communications and Image Processing (VCIP), Taichung, Taiwan, pp. 1–4 (2018)
15. Zhuang, S., Zhao, W., Wang, R., Wang, Q., Huang, S.: New measurement algorithm for supraharmonics based on multiple measurement vectors model and orthogonal matching pursuit. IEEE Trans. Instrum. Meas. **68**(6), 1671–1679 (2019)
16. Anselmi, N., Salucci, M., Oliveri, G., Massa, A.: Wavelet-based compressive imaging of sparse targets. IEEE Trans. Antennas Propag. **63**(11), 4889–4900 (2015)
17. Cao, Y., Chen, M., Xu, B.: Theory and application of natural-based wavelet method. J. Harbin Inst. Technol. (New Ser.) **26**(06), 86–90 (2019)
18. Liu, Y., Ji, Y., Chen, K., Qi, X.: Support Vector Regression for Bus Travel Time Prediction Using Wavelet Transform. J. Harbin Inst. Technol. (New Ser.) **26**(03), 26–34 (2019)
19. Picariello, F., Tudosa, I., Balestrieri, E., Rapuano, S., Vito, L.D.: RF emitters localization from compressed measurements exploiting MMV-OMP algorithm. In: 2020 IEEE 7th International Workshop on Metrology for AeroSpace (MetroAeroSpace), Pisa, Italy, pp. 582–587 (2020)

20. Zhao, C., Zhu, H., Cui, S., Qi, B.: Multiple endmember hyperspectral sparse unmixing based on improved OMP algorithm. J. Harbin Inst. Technol. **22**(05), 97–104 (2015)
21. Kulkarni, A., Mohsenin, T.: Low overhead architectures for OMP compressive sensing reconstruction algorithm. IEEE Trans. Circuits Syst. I: Regul. Pap. **64**(6), 1468–1480 (2017)
22. Lagunas, E., Sharma, S.K., Chatzinotas, S., Ottersten, B.: Compressive sensing based target counting and localization exploiting joint sparsity. In: 2016 IEEE International Conference on Acoustics, Speech and Signal Processing (ICASSP), pp. 3231–3235 (2016)
23. Bernal, E.A., Li, Q.: Tensorial compressive sensing of jointly sparse matrices with applications to color imaging. In: 2017 IEEE International Conference on Image Processing (ICIP), pp. 2781–2785 (2017)

3D Point Cloud Classification Based on Convolutional Neural Network

Jianrui Lu[1], Wenjing Kang[1], Ruofei Ma[1], and Zhiliang Qin[2(✉)]

[1] Department of Communication Engineering, Harbin Institute of Technology Weihai, Weihai, China
{kwjqq,maruofei}@hit.edu.cn

[2] Technology R&D Center, Weihai Beiyang Electric Group Co. Ltd, Weihai, China
qinzhiliang@beiyang.com

Abstract. With the development of science and technology, the requirements for 3D point cloud classification are increasing. Methods that can directly process point cloud has the advantages of small calculation amount and high real-time performance. Hence, we proposed a novel convolutional neural network(CNN) method to directly extract features from point cloud for 3D object classification. We firstly train a pre-training model with ModelNet40 dataset. Then, we freeze the first five layers of our CNN model and adjust the learning rate to fine tune our CNN model. Finally, we evaluate our methods by ModelNet40 and the classification accuracy of our model can achieve 87.8% which is better than other traditional approaches. We also design some experiments to research the effect of T-Net proposed by Charles R. Qi et al. on 3D object classification. In the end, we find that T-Net has little effect on classification task and it is not necessary to apply in our CNN.

Keywords: 3D object classification · Convolution neural network · Point cloud processing

1 Introduction

In recent years, convolutional neural networks (CNN) has achieved great progress in computer vision. Areas like recognition, classification, detection and segmentation [1–4] has made lots of achievements, especially in two-dimensional (2D). In the field of 2D images, there are already many mature algorithms to complete various signal processing tasks such as recognition and detection. With the development of autonomous driving [5–7] and augmented reality (AR) [8–10], more and more attention were paid on three-dimensional (3D) based convolution and the demand of three-dimensional (3D) point cloud understanding is

This work was supported partially by National Natural Science Foundation of China (Grant No. 61801144, 61971156), Shandong Provincial Natural Science Foundation, China (Grant No. ZR2019QF003, ZR2019MF035), and the Fundamental Research Funds for the Central Universities, China (Grant No. HIT.NSRIF.2019081).

© ICST Institute for Computer Sciences, Social Informatics and Telecommunications Engineering 2022
Published by Springer Nature Switzerland AG 2022. All Rights Reserved
S. Shi et al. (Eds.): 6GN 2021, LNICST 439, pp. 333–344, 2022.
https://doi.org/10.1007/978-3-031-04245-4_29

increasing, especially 3D point cloud classification. Hence, we proposed a novel CNN model to complete 3D point cloud classification task. In general, there are three approaches to process 3D point cloud data. The first method is based on 3D convolution which is a main way to convert 3D point cloud to a regular grid and then directly apply 3D convolution to complete various tasks [13–15]. The second method is based on projection. The first step is to project 3D point cloud to 2D views such as bird-eye-view [16,17]. The second step is to extract features from those 2D views. The third method is based on point which directly process the 3D point cloud. The first and second methods mentioned above usually can achieve good performance, but the amount of calculation is too large and the training time is too long, which make those two method is not suitable for some tasks need high real-time. Hence, in order to have a best performance and high real-time, our proposed CNN model is based on the third method.

For point-based method, the most classic method is PointNet [13] proposed by Charles R. Qi, Hao Su, et al. PointNet can directly consumes point clouds so that it is highly efficient. Besides, the authors of PointNet proposed a mini-network which called T-Net to achieve transformation invariance and batch normality, which is helpful to improve the performance of 3D point cloud segmentation. With reference to the network structure of PointNet, we proposed a novel CNN model. There are totally seven convolution blocks in our model and each block contains one convolution layer and a Batch Normalization layer. ReLU function is selected to be a activation function after every convolution block. The complete network structure will be introduced in detail in the third section.

In our experiment, we firstly train our model (called pre-training model) with ModelNet40 dataset and then adjust the learning rate to fine tune our pre-training model. Fine tuning is a common approach to improve the performance of classification system. According to different size of the target dataset and the similarity between the source dataset and the target dataset, there are different methods to fine tune the model to better fit our training data. How to fine tune a model in different cases will be introduced in detail in Sect. 3. For our model, we freeze the first five layers of our extractor and adjust the learning rate to better train our model. In the end, the classification accuracy of our model can achieve 87.8%, which is better than traditional 3D point cloud classification methods.

In addition, to research the effect of T-Net in 3D point cloud classification, we add two T-Net in our proposed CNN. One is after the first convolution block to adjusts the view of 3D object and achieve transformation invariance. The other one is after the third convolution block to batch normalize data for speeding up the training processing. However, we find that T-Net has little effect on classification task but increase the training time. Hence, in the final version, we do not apply T-Net in our CNN model.

All in all, the contributions of our paper are as follow: 1) we proposed a novel CNN model for 3D object classification task and achieve a high accuracy which is better than other traditional classification methods. 2) we apply T-Net in our CNN model and find that T-Net has little effect on classification task which mean you can replace T-Net to decrease your training time.

2 Related Works

3D Point Cloud Processing: Point cloud is a collection of points sampled from the surface of a 3D object. 3D point cloud is usually used to represent data whose latitude is lower than the latitude of the background space such as curved surfaces in the space. In general, a 3D point cloud is denoted as $P = \{p_i | i = 1, 2, ..., n\}$, where each point p_i is a vector that contains the (x, y, z) coordinates and possibly some other features, e.g., colors, intensity.

Traditional convolution operations are order-dependent and depended on spatially-local correlation. Hence, CNN is effective for data, such as images, that is order and has spatially-local correlation. In recent years, lots of CNNs have been proposed to complete kinds of 2D object tasks and have achieved good performance, e.g., Xception [11], VGG-19 [12]. However, the data represented in point cloud form is unordered and irregular. It is mean that the traditional convolution operations are not suitable for extracting directly features from point cloud. We need to find other approaches to deal with point cloud. At present, methods for point cloud processing mainly are as follow:

- 3D convolution-based method
- projection-based method
- point-based method

3D convolution-based method is one of the main approach to process point cloud. In this method, point cloud data are firstly rasterize into regular grids (called voxels). This operation is called as voxelization. Then, 3D convolution is applied on those regular grids to complete various tasks, e.g., classification, segmentation [13–15].

Projection-based method is based on 2D convolution to extract features from 2D views projected by 3D point cloud. The bird-eye-view projection [16,17] and the spherical projection [18,19] are often used in point cloud processing. Besides, 3D point cloud can be processed with multi-view representation [20,21]. Hang Su et al. proposed a multi-view convolutional neural network (MVCNN) [20] to combine the same 3D shape images from different perspectives to extract 3D shape description operators and used a new structure called view-pooling layer to complete effectively recognition task.

In point-based method, 3D point cloud is directly processed. The most classic method is PointNet [13] proposed by Charles R. Qi, Hao Su, et al. Unlike the two methods mentioned above, PointNet provides a unified architecture to directly consumes point clouds so that the original data can avoid unnecessarily voluminous and some problems. Besides, due to directly processing 3D point cloud, PointNet is highly efficient. Nowadays, PointNet is widely applied in all kinds of applications ranging from 3D object classification, segmentation, to semantic parsing.

PointNet: According to Charles R. Qi et al., inputs of PointNet are unordered point sets. The jth point cloud is represented as $P_j = \{p_i | i = 1, 2, ..., n\}$, where each point p_i is a vector that only contains the (x, y, z) coordinates. For the point cloud classification task, points are multiplied by a transformation matrix predicted by a mini-network (T-Net in Fig. 1). Two T-Nets are used in PointNet, the first T-Net is used to achieve transformation invariance and the second T-Net is used to batch normal data. Besides, PointNet uses multi MLP to extract the global feature of point cloud and at the last layer, one MLP is used to output k scores for all the k candidate classes. The detailed network architecture is shown in Fig. 2.

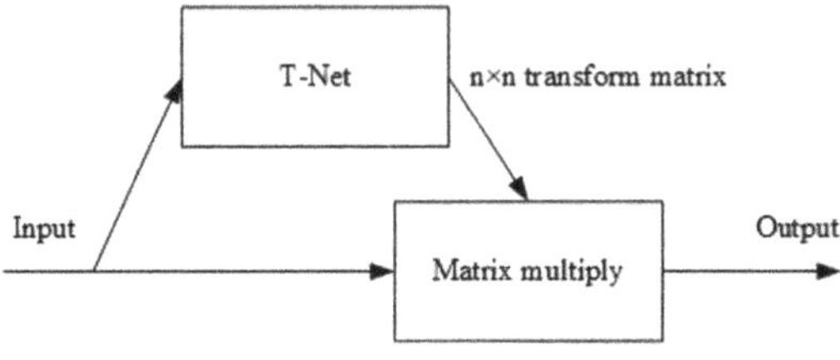

Fig. 1. T-Net

3 Methodology

Our Model: PointNet, first applied input and feature transformations to the input points, has been successfully used in different applications to achieve better performance [13].

With reference to PointNet, we proposed a novel CNN for 3D object classification task. For our model, a point cloud, including lots of points, is given as input. A point cloud is denoted as $P_j = \{p_i | i = 1, 2, \cdots, n\} (j = 1, 2, \cdots, m)$, where p_i means the ith point of the jth point cloud and it is a vector that only contains the (x, y, z) coordinates. m and n mean the number of point clouds and the number of points contained by each point cloud, respectively. Besides, each point cloud data has a label $y_j \in \{1, 2, \cdots, c\}$ where c is the number of classes. We firstly randomly rotated and jittered the data to finish data augmentation. Then, we used a CNN ($ConvNet$) to extract the global feature of inputs and then used a classifier f to predict the label of input point cloud. Formally, we have $y_j = f(ConvNet(P_j))$. At the end, our model will output a $(1 \times c)$ vector $O_j = \{o_1, o_2, \cdots, o_c\}$ which contains the probability that the jth point cloud data belongs to each category. The whole system structure and the neural network training process is shown in Fig. 3.

Our proposed ConvNet mention above has the similar structure as the PointNet [13]. There are seven convolutional blocks and each convolutional block consists of one convolution(Conv) layer with convolution filters and a batch normalization (BN) layer. BN layer is used to speed up our learning processing. After Conv layer and BN layer, The Rectified Linear Units (ReLu) function is used to achieve non-linearity.

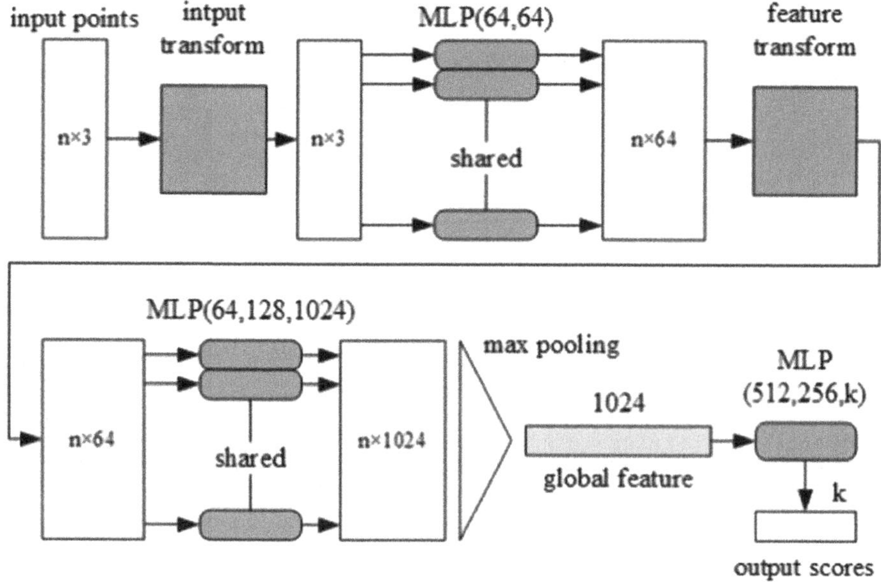

Fig. 2. PointNet

After all Conv layers, max-pooling is performed and the output of max-pooling layer is reshape with size of (,1024). In the end, we used dropout layers (the probability is set to 0.3) to decrease the possibility of over-fitting and fully connected (FC) layers followed by a softmax function to get the score of each 3D object class and classify the point cloud data. The whole architecture of our proposed ConvNet is described in Table 1.

Fine Tuning: In general, when we have a model, we do not simply use this model just as a feature extractor. Adjusting the model to better fit our training data is necessary. For model adjusting, fine tuning is a excellent approach to fit the training data for better performance and this is also the most commonly used. According to different characteristics of our training data, there are different situations of fine tuning. We can denote the data set of source domain as D_S and the data set of target domain as D_T. Our network can be divided into two parts, the first part is a feature extraction denoted as E and the second part is a classifier denoted as C. When our D_T is small but has a high similarity to the D_S used by the pre-trained model, we can only retrain the classifier C. Because of the small size of D_T, there is a risk of over-fitting during retraining E. However, due to the similarity between D_T and D_S is high, both the local feature and global feature are relatively similar. What mean is that the original feature extractor E can do well in D_T and we just need to retrain the C to suit our task. When the D_T is small and it is very different from the D_S, fine tuning is not suitable. In this case, a better solution is generally to extract features from

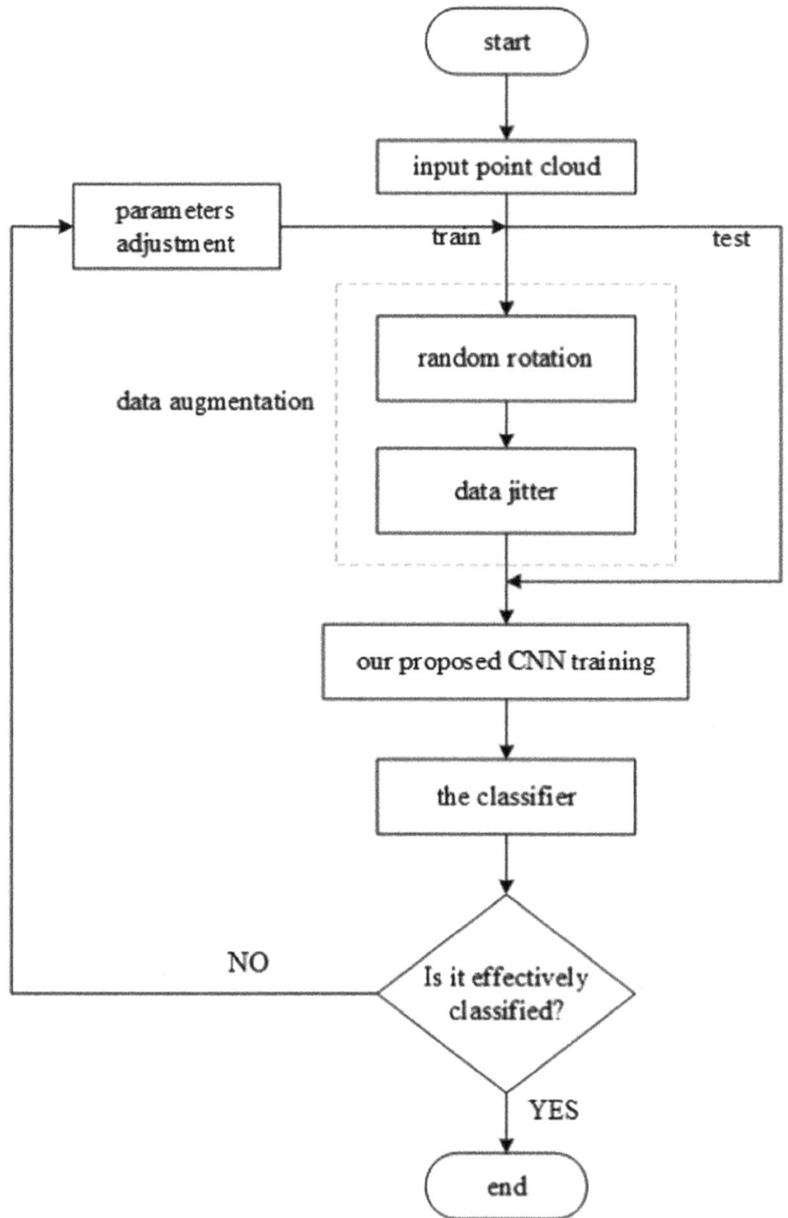

Fig. 3. System structure diagram

a certain layer of E and then train a support vector machines (SVM) classifier. When the D_T is large but it is very different from the D_S, fine tuning is also not suitable. However, due to the large size of the D_T, we can train a model from

Table 1. CNN architecture

Layer	Output shape	Parameter
Input layer	(,2048,3)	0
Conv1-64,BN,ReLU	(,2048,64)	512
Conv1-64,BN,ReLU	(,2048,64)	4416
Conv1-64,BN,ReLU	(,2048,64)	4416
Conv1-128,BN,ReLU	(,2048,128)	8832
Conv1-256,BN,ReLU	(,2048,256)	34048
Conv1-512,BN,ReLU	(,2048,512)	133632
Conv1-1024,BN,ReLU	(,2048,1024)	529408
Max Pooling layer	(,1,1024,1)	0
reshape layer	(,1024)	0
Dropout layer	(,512)	0
FC layer	(,256)	131328
Batch Normalization layer	(,256)	1024
Dropout layer	(,256)	0
FC layer	(,Number of Classes)	10280

scratch or train all layers of E and C. When the D_T is large and has a high similarity to the D_S, we do not have to worry about over-fitting, so it is better to fine tune the entire network structure.

In our experiment, we firstly used ModelNet40 (a dataset contained 12311 CAD models from 40 object categories) [22] to train our CNN model. Then we also used ModelNet40 to fine tune our model. For feature extractor E, we froze the first five layers which only extract some basic local features and updated the later layers of our CNN structure. This is because the features obtained in the first few layers of the network are more basic such as edge and corner feature, which are easily applied to all tasks. Hence it is not necessary to retrain the first few layers. Beisdes, the higher the network layer number, the closer the connection with the data set global information and those global features are closely related to the original data.

4 Experiment and Results

Experiment Settings: ModelNet40 is used in our experiment to evaluate our proposed CNN. There are totally 12311 CAD models from 40 man-made object categories [22]. The dataset is split into two groups: 9843 samples for training and 2468 for testing. For this experiment, Processor used is Intel Core i5-10400F, Graphics card in this system is NVIDIA GeForce GTX 1660 Ti. The software used in this experiment is as follows: python with the version of 3.7.6, keras 2.2.4 and tensorflow 1.14.0 with GPU. For the pre-training process, the learning rate is set to 0.0003 and the batch size is set to 16.

Result: In our experiment, we train and fine tune our CNN model from 10 epoch to 200 epoch, the training accuracy and the validation accuracy is shown in Fig. 4. As shown in Fig. 4, no matter training accuracy and validation accuracy are increasing with number of epoch going up. While the number of epoch is up to 75, the two accuracy curves start to converge. In the end, our model can achieve a best performance on validation set (87.8%) and the number of epoch is 177. Figure 5 shows the training and validation loss. We can know from Fig. 5 that training loss and validation loss were decreased to below 0.2 when the training epoch is up to 60. This performance is shown us our method is effective. As shown in Table 2, we compare our proposed CNN model to some traditional methods based on 3D-convolution or projection. It is seen from Table 2 that our system has a better performance compared with other methods and the accuracy of our proposed CNN model can achieve 87.8%. Our model obtains an

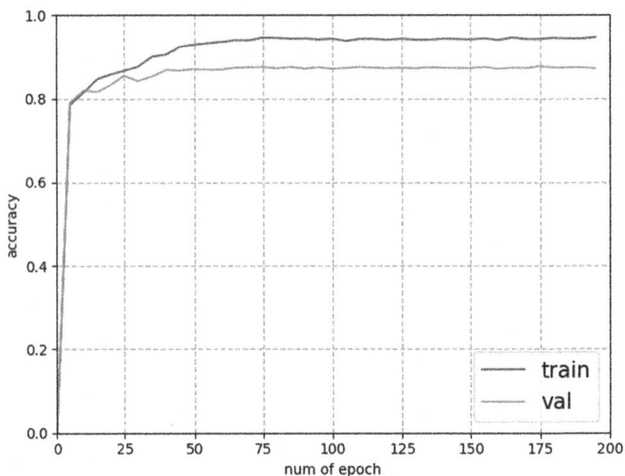

Fig. 4. Training and Validation accuracy

Table 2. The overall compare of performance on ModelNet40

Model	Average accuracy
3D-GAN [23]	83.3%
VoxNet [24]	83%
3DShapeNets [26]	77%
Primitive-GAN [25]	86.4%
Xu and Todorovic proposed [27]	81.26%
ECC [28]	83.2%
Ours	**87.8%**

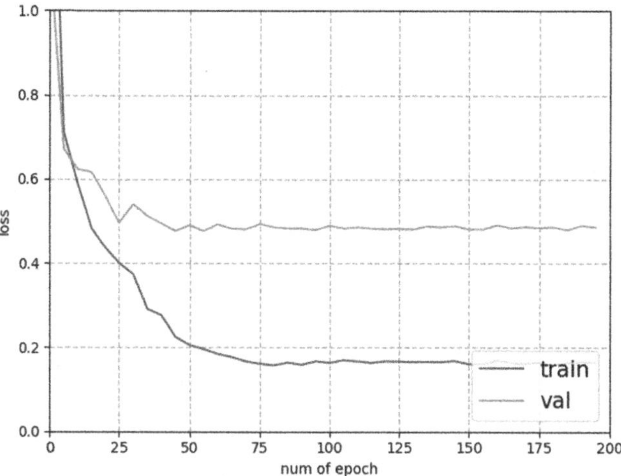

Fig. 5. Training and Validation loss

improvement of 4.5%, 4.8%, 10.8%, 1.4%, 6.54% and 4.6% to other methods, respectively. In addition, we want to research if the T-Net, proposed by Charles R. Qi et al., will improve the performance of our classification system. Hence, we apply two T-Net blocks in our CNN model. The first T-Net block is used after the first Conv block to eliminate the viewing angle of the 3D object and achieve transformation invariance. The second T-Net block is used after the third Conv block to finish batch normalizing. The comparison between system using T-Net and not using T-Net is shown in Fig. 6 and the training time of each epoch is shown in Table 3.

Table 3. The training time of different system

System using T-Net	System not using T-Net
140 s/epoch	70 s/epoch

From Fig. 6, we can see that the accuracy curve of the system using T-Net is similar to the accuracy curve of the system not using T-Net, which mean that T-Net has little effect on our CNN model for classification task. However, it takes 140 s per epoch to train the model if T-Net is used in the system, which is 50% more time than a system that does not use T-Net. Hence, T-Net is not a good choose for our system to complete the 3D object classification task.

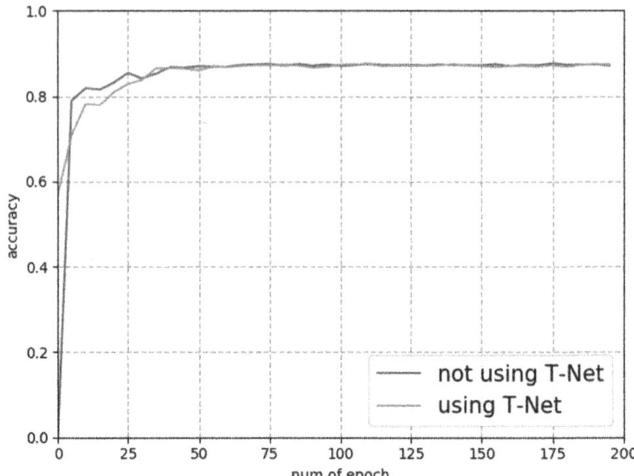

Fig. 6. Validation accuracy of the system not using T-Net and using T-Net

5 Conclusion

In this work, we propose a novel convolutional neural network that directly consumes point cloud. Our network was firstly trained on ModelNet40 and then using the same dataset to fine tune the model. Via some appropriate training, our model achieved a better accuracy (87.8%) than other traditional approaches. As shown in the result of our experiments, the proposed CNN model could be applied in other 3D object tasks such as 3D object segmentation.

References

1. Girshick, R., Donahue, J., Darrell, T., Malik, J.: Rich feature hierarchies for accurate object detection and semantic segmentation. In: 2014 IEEE Conference on Computer Vision and Pattern Recognition, pp. 580–587 (2014). https://doi.org/10.1109/CVPR.2014.81
2. Ren, S., He, K., Girshick, R., Sun, J.: Faster R-CNN: towards real-time object detection with region proposal networks. IEEE Trans. Pattern Anal. Mach. Intell. **39**(6), 1137–1149 (2017). https://doi.org/10.1109/TPAMI.2016.2577031
3. Long, J., Shelhamer, E., Darrell, T.: Fully convolutional networks for semantic segmentation. In: CVPR, January 2015
4. Malbog, M.A.: MASK R-CNN for pedestrian crosswalk detection and instance segmentation. In: 2019 IEEE 6th International Conference on Engineering Technologies and Applied Sciences (ICETAS), pp. 1–5 (2019). https://doi.org/10.1109/ICETAS48360.2019.9117217
5. Behley, J., et al.: SemanticKITTI: a dataset for semantic scene understanding of LiDAR sequences. In: Proceedings of the IEEE/CVF International Conference on Computer Vision (ICCV) (2019)

6. Caesar, H., et al.: nuScenes: a multimodal dataset for autonomous driving. In: Proceedings of the IEEE/CVF Conference on Computer Vision and Pattern Recognition, pp. 11621–11631 (2020)
7. Yue, X., Wu, B., Seshia, S.A., Keutzer, K., Sangiovanni-Vincentelli, A.L.: A LiDAR point cloud generator: from a virtual world to autonomous driving. In: Proceedings of the 2018 ACM on International Conference on Multimedia Retrieval, pp. 458–464 (2018)
8. SketchUp: 3D modeling online free 3D warehouse models (2021). https://3dwarehouse.sketchup.com
9. Wu, Z., et al.: 3D ShapeNets: a deep representation for volumetric shapes. In: Proceedings of the IEEE Conference on Computer Vision and Pattern Recognition (CVPR), June 2015
10. Shi, B., Bai, S., Zhou, Z., Bai, X.: DeepPano: deep panoramic representation for 3-D shape recognition. IEEE Sig. Process. Lett. **22**(12), 2339–2343 (2015)
11. Chollet, F.: Xception: deep learning with depthwise separable convolutions. In: 2017 IEEE Conference on Computer Vision and Pattern Recognition (CVPR), Honolulu, HI, pp. 1800–1807 (2017)
12. Simonyan, K., Zisserman, A.: Very Deep Convolutional Networks for Large-Scale Image Recognition. arXiv e-prints arXiv:1409.1556, September 2014
13. Qi, C.R., Su, H., Mo, K., Guibas, L.J.: PointNet: deep learning on point sets for 3D classification and segmentation. In: Proceedings of the IEEE Conference on Computer Vision and Pattern Recognition, pp. 652–660 (2017)
14. Li, Y., Bu, R., Sun, M., Wu, W., Di, X., Chen, B.: PointCNN: convolution on x-transformed points. In: Advances in Neural Information Processing Systems, pp. 820–830 (2018)
15. He, K., Gkioxari, G., Dollar, P., Girshick, R.: Mask R-CNN. arXiv preprint arXiv:1703.06870 (2017)
16. Yang, B., Luo, W., Urtasun, R.: PIXOR: real-time 3D object detection from point clouds. In: Proceedings of the IEEE Conference on Computer Vision and Pattern Recognition, pp. 7652–7660 (2018)
17. Lang, A.H., Vora, S., Caesar, H., Zhou, L., Yang, J., Beijbom, O.: Pointpillars: fast encoders for object detection from point clouds. In: Proceedings of the IEEE/CVF Conference on Computer Vision and Pattern Recognition, pp. 12697–12705 (2019)
18. Wu, B., Zhou, X., Zhao, S., Yue, X., Keutzer, K.: SqueezeSegV2: improved model structure and unsupervised domain adaptation for road-object segmentation from a lidar point cloud. In: ICRA (2019)
19. Xu, C., et al.: SqueezeSegV3: spatially-adaptive convolution for efficient point-cloud segmentation. In: Vedaldi, A., Bischof, H., Brox, T., Frahm, J.-M. (eds.) ECCV 2020. LNCS, vol. 12373, pp. 1–19. Springer, Cham (2020). https://doi.org/10.1007/978-3-030-58604-1_1
20. Su, H., Maji, S., Kalogerakis, E., Learned-Miller, E.: Multi-view convolutional neural networks for 3D shape recognition. In: 2015 IEEE International Conference on Computer Vision (ICCV), pp. 945–953 (2015). https://doi.org/10.1109/ICCV.2015.114
21. Liang, Q., Wang, Y., Nie, W., Li, Q.: MVCLN: multi-view convolutional LSTM network for cross-media 3D shape recognition. IEEE Access **8**, 139792–139802 (2020). https://doi.org/10.1109/ACCESS.2020.3012692
22. Wu, Z., et al.: 3D ShapeNets: a deep representation for volumetric shapes. In: Proceedings of the IEEE Conference on Computer Vision and Pattern Recognition, pp. 1912–1920 (2015)

23. Wu, J., Zhang, C., Xue, T., Freeman, W.T., Tenenbaum, J.B.: Learning a probabilistic latent space of object shapes via 3D generative-adversarial modeling. In: NIPS (2016)
24. Maturana, D., Scherer, S.: VoxNet: a 3D Convolutional Neural Network for real-time object recognition. In: 2015 IEEE/RSJ International Conference on Intelligent Robots and Systems (IROS), pp. 922–928 (2015). https://doi.org/10.1109/IROS.2015.7353481
25. Khan, S.H., Guo, Y., Hayat, M., Barnes, N.: Unsupervised primitive discovery for improved 3D generative modeling. In: 2019 IEEE/CVF Conference on Computer Vision and Pattern Recognition (CVPR), pp. 9731–9740 (2019). https://doi.org/10.1109/CVPR.2019.00997
26. Zhirong, W., et al.: 3D ShapeNets: a deep representation for volumetric shapes. In: 2015 IEEE Conference on Computer Vision and Pattern Recognition (CVPR), pp. 1912–1920 (2015). https://doi.org/10.1109/CVPR.2015.7298801
27. Xu, X., Todorovic, S.: Beam Search for Learning a Deep Convolutional Neural Network of 3D Shapes. arXiv e-prints arXiv:1612.04774 (2016)
28. Simonovsky, M., Komodakis, N.: Dynamic edge-conditioned filters in convolutional neural networks on graphs (2017). https://arxiv.org/abs/1704.02901

Adaptive Feature Selection Based on Low-Rank Representation

Ying Wang[1(✉)], Lijun Fu[1], Hongwei Zhao[2], Qiang Fu[2], Guangyao Zhai[2], and Yutong Niu[1]

[1] School of Computer Science and Technology, Harbin University of Science and Technology, Harbin, China
747456619@qq.com

[2] Shandong Provincial Innovation and Practice Base for Postdoctors, Shandong Baimeng Information Technology Co. Ltd., Weihai, China

Abstract. In the existing feature selection methods, the ways of construct the similarity matrix is: the first way to construct is give fixed value to two data, and the second is to calculate the distance between the two data and use it as the similarity. However, the above-mentioned method of constructing a similarity matrix is usually unreliable because the original data is often affected by noise. In the article, an adaptive feature selection method based on low-rank representation was proposed. In the method, we would dynamically construct a similarity matrix with local adaptive capabilities based on the feature projection matrix learned by the method. This construction way can reduce the influence of noise on the similarity matrix. To verify the validity of the method, we test our method on different public data sets.

Keywords: Adaptive · Feature selection · Low-rank

1 Introduction

With the advent of the information age, how to accurately classify a large amount of high-dimensional information has become an urgent problem for today's research. Feature selection is to extract features that have a greater impact on data classification from high-dimensional data. The more representative supervised feature selection methods are Relief-F [1] method proposed by K. Kira and L. A. Rendell. I. Kononenko extended the Relief-F method two years later [2]. In 2010, F. Nie et al. proposed the adaptive feature selection method [3]. In the same year, O. D. Richard et al. proposed a method for scoring feature relevance [4]. In 2012, S. Xiang et al. proposed the discriminative least squares regression method [5], which increased the discriminativeness of features by increasing the distance between different classes. In recent years, the representative semi-supervised feature selection methods include the method via spline regression method [6] proposed by Y. Han et al. and the method via rescaled linear regression method proposed by X. Chen et al. [7]. In the unsupervised feature selection method,

© ICST Institute for Computer Sciences, Social Informatics and Telecommunications Engineering 2022
Published by Springer Nature Switzerland AG 2022. All Rights Reserved
S. Shi et al. (Eds.): 6GN 2021, LNICST 439, pp. 345–353, 2022.
https://doi.org/10.1007/978-3-031-04245-4_30

because there is no label information available, the feature correlation is obtained by calculating the feature similarity. The more representative methods are Laplacian Score [8], RSFS [9] and SOGFS [10].

Among the proposed feature selection methods, the construction of similarity matrix is mostly constructed once and then the similarity matrix is unchanged. This construction method is easy to ignore the class structure, which leads to inaccurate results. Most unsupervised feature selection methods construct the similarity matrix by calculating the similarity of the original data, but because the original data is usually susceptible to noise, the way would learn the wrong feature structure.

Because the existing feature selection methods have the above problems, we proposed a feature selection method based on low-rank representation. Our method used iterative learning to obtain the similarity matrix and feature projection matrix. When constructing the similarity matrix, the low-rank representation is used as a constraint to measure the similarity of features. Using this constraint condition can solve the influence of noise on the learning feature projection matrix, so that it performs better in classification and recognition tasks. To verify the validity of the method, we test our method on several public data sets, and the experimental results are good. The main results of our paper are as follows:

1. We proposed a feature selection method based on low-rank representation. The method used low-rank representation constraints as a similarity measure. Using this similarity measure can make our feature selection method more dynamic and adaptability.
2. In our objective function, we also impose non-negative constraints on the low-rank representation coefficient, to the coefficient could dynamically and adaptively.
3. In terms of solving the objective function, we use a Lagrangian multiplier algorithm to solve the proposed method.
4. We have verified the validity of the method of our method on multiple public data sets.

The structure of the article is as follows: The second part is a review of current feature selection methods. The third part proposes our objective function and solution strategy. The fourth part describes our experimental results and analyzes the experimental results. The fifth part is a summary of this article.

2 Related Work

2.1 Low Rank Representation

Because low-rank representation can eliminate the influence of noise on sample data, low-rank representation has been applied in many fields since it was proposed, such as subspace learning, image processing and so on. The low-rank representation model is as follows:

$$\begin{aligned} &\|Z\|_* + \lambda\|E\|_{2,1} \\ &s.t.\ X = XZ + E \end{aligned} \tag{1}$$

In the LRR, $\|\bullet\|_*$ is the nuclear norm and $\|\bullet\|_{2.1}$ is the l_{21} norm. We assume $X = [X_1, X_2, \ldots, X_k]$ is a matrix composed of raw data from k categories, Z is a self-representation matrix, E is a noise matrix, and λ is a balance parameter. LRR not only learn the subspace of the data in noisy environment, but also discover the potential structure.

2.2 Linear Discriminant Analysis

The Linear Discriminant Analysis (LDA) method is widely used because it can find a more discriminative feature subspace, which has the more discriminative subspace. In this method, we let $X \in R^{d \times n}$ is a data set composed of n objects. The data set contains a total of c categories. The method can be expressed as:

$$\max_{W^T W=1} Tr(W^T S_w W)^{-1}(W^T S_b W) \tag{2}$$

Among them, S_w is the inter-class scatter matrix, and S_b is the intra-class scatter matrix.

$$S_w = \sum_{i=1}^{c} \sum_{x_i \in y_l} (x_i - \mu_l)(x_i - \mu_l)^T \tag{3}$$

$$S_b = \sum_{i=1}^{c} (\mu_l - \mu)(\mu_l - \mu)^T \tag{4}$$

In the S_w and S_b, μ is the global eigenvector, and μ_l is the lth eigenvector. In the method, $Tr(\bullet)$ represents the trace and W is the projection matrix. The LDA method can find a more discriminative feature subspace.

3 Our Proposed Method

In this part, we will propose an adaptive feature selection method based on low-rank representation and analyze the proposed method from the details. In order to solve our proposed method, we will adopt a numerical strategy.

3.1 The Composition of Our Approach

As previously introduced, in the traditional methods based on the LDA framework, most methods use label information to obtain the feature subspace with the more discriminative subspace. These method of constructing feature subspace can be understood as giving different sample data the same similar weight value. It is unrealistic to adopt this construction method because of the influence of some practical factors, because in real life, even data from the same category may be different due to the influence of some factors. For example, in real life, human face images may be affected by different angles and different lighting.

Therefore we proposed an adaptive feature selection method based on low-rank representation. In the method, we used the self-representation coefficient calculated based on the original data as the weight coefficient to measure the similarity of the samples. The objective function is:

$$\begin{aligned} &\min_{W,Z,E} \|Z\|_* + \lambda\|E\|_{2,1} + \tfrac{1}{2}\sum_{ij} Z_{ij}\left\|W^T(X_i - X_j)\right\|_2 + \lambda\|W\|_{2,1} \\ &s.t.\ \ X = XZ + E, Z_{ij} > 0,\ W^T W = I_W \end{aligned} \tag{5}$$

In the Eq. (5), $X \in R^{d\times n}$ is a data set composed of n objects from c categories, $W \in d \times m$ is a projection matrix, Z is a self-representation matrix, and E is a noise matrix. In our objective function, the influence of noise on the data can be eliminated. $\left\|W^T(X_i - X_j)\right\|_2$ represents the distance between the samples after projected into the feature subspace. As shown in the objective function, we use Z_{ij} to constrain the structural similarity of samples X_i and X_j. At the same time, we impose non-negative constraints on Z to ensure the non-negativity of feature projection distance. If the similarity between the two samples Z_{ij} is smaller, and vice versa Z_{ij} is larger. In addition, so as to reduce the influence of redundant data on feature projection, we impose orthogonal constraints $W^T W = I_W$ on the projection matrix, I_W is the unit matrix of $W \times W$.

3.2 Optimization

In this part, we adopt a numerical strategy to solve the objective function we proposed. Because the objective function minimization problem of all variables is a non-concave problem, we use the inexact ALM algorithm to get an approximate solution. Moreover, so as to better solve the minimization problem, we have introduced auxiliary variables G and J.

$$\begin{aligned} &\min_{W,Z,E,J,G} \|J\|_* + \lambda\|E\|_{2,1} + \tfrac{1}{2}\textstyle\sum_{ij} G_{ij}\left\|W^T(X_i - X_j)\right\|_2 + \lambda\|W\|_{2,1} \\ &s.t.\ \ X = XZ + E, G_{ij} > 0,\ W^T W = I_W, Z = J, Z = G \end{aligned} \tag{6}$$

The augmented Lagrangian form of Eq. (6) is as follows:

$$\begin{aligned} \mathcal{L}(Z, W, M, J, G) = {} & \|J\|_* + \lambda_1\|E\|_{2,1} + \tfrac{1}{2}\textstyle\sum_{ij} G_{ij}\left\|W^T(X_i - X_j)\right\|_2 \\ & + \lambda_2\|W\|_{2,1} + Tr(Y_1(X - XZ - E)) + Tr(Y_2(Z - G)) \\ & + Tr(Y_3(W^T W - I_W)) + Tr(Y_4(Z - J)) + \\ & \tfrac{\mu}{2}(\|X - XZ - E\|_F^2 + \|Z - G\|_F^2 + \|Z - J\|_F^2) \\ & s.t.\ \ G_{ij} > 0 \end{aligned} \tag{7}$$

Among them, Y_1, Y_2, Y_3 are Lagrange multipliers.

In the ALM method, the minimization problem can be solved iteratively by fixing variables that have nothing to do with the solving variables. In order to solve our objective function, we first fixed G, so Eq. (6) can be transformed into:

$$\begin{aligned} &\min_{G} \left\|Z^{k+1} - G + \frac{Y_2^k}{\mu}\right\|_F^2 + \sum_{ij} G_{ij}\left\|W^T(x_i - x_j)\right\|_2^2 \\ &\qquad s.t.\ G_{ij} \geq 0 \end{aligned} \tag{8}$$

In order to look more clear, Eq. (8) can be rewritten as:

$$\begin{gathered}\min_{G}\left\|Z^{k}+1-G+\frac{Y_{2}^{k}}{\mu}\right\|_{F}^{2}+\sum_{ij}\left(R^{k}\otimes G_{ij}\right)\\ \text{s.t. } G_{ij}\geq 0\end{gathered}\tag{9}$$

Because each variable in formula (9) is non-negative and can be calculated independently, the minimization problem of formula (9) is a weighted norm minimization problem. This kind of problem can be mentioned in the literature [11] to solve.

In order to solve J, we eliminate variables unrelated to J, we can get

$$\min_{J}\frac{1}{\mu}\|J\|_{*}+\frac{1}{2}\left\|J-\left(Z^{k}+Y_{4}^{k}/\mu\right)\right\|_{F}^{2}\tag{10}$$

Equation (10) is a rank minimization problem, which could be obtained through the singular value method in [8].

In order to solve W, we delete variables irrelevant to W, then we can get:

$$\min_{W}\frac{1}{2}\sum_{ij}G_{ij}\left\|W^{T}(x_{i}-x_{j})\right\|_{2}^{2}+\lambda\|W\|_{2,1}+Tr\left(Y_{3}\left(W^{T}W-I\right)\right)\tag{11}$$

Because $\|W\|_{2,1}$ in Eq. (11) is equivalent to $\sum_{l=1}^{d}\sqrt{W^{l}(W^{l})^{T}}$, Eq. (11) can be rewritten as:

$$\min_{W}\frac{1}{2}\sum_{ij}G_{ij}\left\|W^{T}(x_{i}-x_{j})\right\|_{2}^{2}+\lambda\sum_{l=1}^{d}\sqrt{W^{l}(W^{l})^{T}}+Tr\left(Y_{3}\left(W^{T}W-I\right)\right)\tag{12}$$

Calculating the partial derivative of W in Eq. (11), we get

$$\frac{\partial\mathcal{L}(W)}{\partial W}=\sum_{i,j-1}^{n}s_{ij}\frac{\partial\left\|W^{T}(x_{i}-x_{j})\right\|_{2}^{2}}{\partial W}+2\lambda QW+WY_{3}\tag{13}$$

Among them, each element in the similarity matrix is:

$$s_{ij}=\frac{1}{G_{ij}\left\|W^{T}(x_{i}-x_{j})\right\|_{2}^{2}}\tag{14}$$

In Eq. (13), Q is a diagonal matrix:

$$q_{ll}=\frac{1}{W^{l}(W^{l})^{T}}\tag{15}$$

When we solve W, Eq. (13) can be transformed into:

$$\min_{W^{T}W}=I\left[Tr\left(W^{T}XL_{S}X^{T}W\right)+\lambda Tr\left(W^{T}QW\right)\right]\tag{16}$$

Therefore, solving W can be obtained by solving the m smallest eigenvectors of $XL_{S}X^{T}+\lambda Q$.

Because, G and J are auxiliary variables, and there are constraints $Z = J, Z = G$ on it, because after solving G and J, the objective function of Z about can be obtained by fixing the remaining variables:

$$\min_{Z} Tr(Y_1(X - XZ - E)) + Tr(Y_2(Z - G)) + Tr(Y_4(Z - J)) + \frac{\mu}{2}(\|X - XZ - E\|_F^2 + \|Z - G\|_F^2 + \|Z - J\|_F^2) \tag{17}$$

Equation (17) is a second-order convex minimization problem. We only need to set the derivative of to zero to solve it.

Finally, we omit the irrelevant variables to E obtain the objective function of the noise matrix:

$$\min_{E} \frac{\lambda_1}{\mu}\|E\|_{2,1} + \frac{1}{2}\|E - (X - XZ + Y_1/\mu)\|_F^2 \tag{18}$$

By setting $\Psi = X - XZ + Y_1/\mu$, the minimization problem of the above formula could be solved through the method mentioned in [9].

Algorithm: feature subspace learning scheme

Input: training set $X, Z = J = G = 0, E\ Y_1 = Y_2 = Y_3 = Y_4 = 0$,

$\mu = 0.6$, $\mu_{\max} = 10^{10}$, $\rho = 1.1$

Output: W,

While not convergence **do**

1. Update G^{k+1} using (9)

2. Update J^{k+1} using (10)

3. Update W^{k+1} using (16)

4. Update Z^{k+1} using (17)

5. Update E^{k+1} using (18)

6 Update the Y_1^{k+1}, $Y_2^{k+1}, Y_3^{k+1}, Y_4^{k+1}$ and μ;

end while

---

4 Experimental Results and Analysis

To prove the effectiveness of the method, we compared the proposed method with the existing concentrated feature subspace learning methods. The comparison methods include PCA, LDA, NPE, and LSDA.

In order to verify the effectiveness of the method, this paper uses three data sets to evaluate the adaptive feature selection model based on low-rank representation. The data sets are described as follows:

AR. AR dataset contains 3000 images of 120 targets, and each target has 26 images from different angles and illuminations. A sample picture of the data set is shown in Fig. 1(a). In the experiment, we chose 13 photos for each subject as the training set.

COIL20. The COIL20 data set contains a total of 20 objects. The camera takes pictures of each object every 5°. The data set contains a total of 1440 photos. A sample picture of the data set is shown in Fig. 1(b). When selecting training samples, the quantity of training samples for every object is 10.

USPS. The USPS dataset contains 9289 images in 10 categories. The sample image of the data set is shown in Fig. 1(c). In order to save data storage space and calculation time, the images in the data set are cropped to 16×16 pixels.

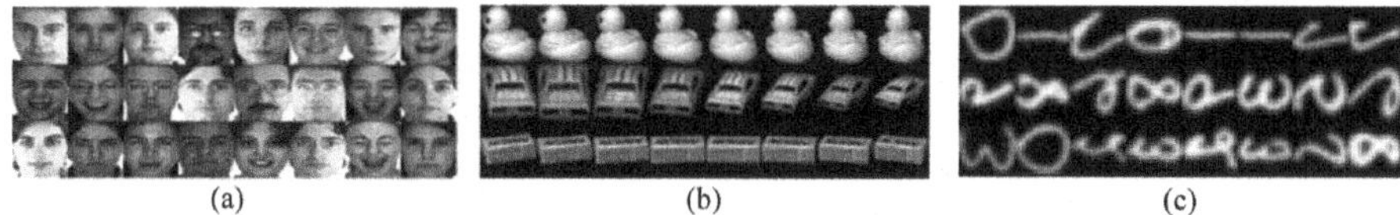

(a) (b) (c)

Fig. 1. (a) is sample images of AR, (b) is sample images of COIL20, (c) is sample images of USPS.

Next, we compared the ACC of the proposed method with the comparison method on the k-nearest neighbor (KNN) classifier. In our lab, the K value is set to 1. Our comparison experiment was carried out for each comparison method five times and then the standard deviation of five times was calculated. The experimental results are shown in Table 1.

According to the results, we can know that compared with the comparison, the proposed method performs better under the same conditions. Our method can find the structure of the data so as to perform label prediction on unknown label data.

Table 1. The experimental results

Methods	COIL20	AR	USPS
PCA	85.41 ± 0.32	79.12 ± 0.97	78.35 ± 1.78
LDA	84.28 ± 0.74	83.28 ± 1.46	72.53 ± 0.74
NPE	85.54 ± 1.72	81.83 ± 1.69	62.32 ± 2.21
LSDA	83.32 ± 1.63	74.27 ± 0.52	56.18 ± 2.17
Ours	92.43 ± 1.2	85.49 ± 2.21	85.32 ± 0.38

5 Conclusion

This paper proposed an adaptive feature selection method based on low-rank representation for classification. In this method, we used low-rank representation as a measure of sample similarity, and used low-rank representation as a constraint to increase the adaptability of projection space. To solve the function, we used the ALM method to solve each variable in the function. In order to verify the effectiveness of the method, we compared the performance of our proposed method with comparison on different data sets. The results show that our method performs better.

Acknowledgment. This work was supported in part by the National Natural Science Foundation of China under Grant 62071157, Natural Science Foundation of Heilongjiang Province under Grant YQ2019F011 and Postdoctoral Foundation of Heilongjiang Province under Grant LBH-Q19112.

References

1. Kira, K., Rendell, L.A.: A practical approach to feature selection. In: Proceedings of the 9th International Workshop Machine Learning, pp. 249–256 (1992)
2. Kononenko, I.: Estimating attributes: analysis and extensions of RELIEF. In: Bergadano, F., De Raedt, L. (eds.) ECML 1994. LNCS, vol. 784, pp. 171–182. Springer, Heidelberg (1994). https://doi.org/10.1007/3-540-57868-4_57
3. Nie, F., Huang, H., Cai, X., Ding, C.H.: Efficient and robust feature selection via joint $\ell 2$, 1-norms minimization. In: Proceedings of Advances in Neural Information Processing System, pp. 1813–1821 (2010)
4. Richard, O.D., Hart, P.E., Stork, D.G.: Pattern Classification. Wiley, Hoboken (2010)
5. Xiang, S., Nie, F., Meng, G., Pan, C., Zhang, C.: Discriminative least squares regression for multiclass classification and feature selection. IEEE Trans. Neural Netw. Learn. Syst. **23**(11), 1738–1754 (2012)
6. Han, Y., Yang, Y., Yan, Y., Ma, Z., Sebe, N., Zhou, X.: Semisupervised feature selection via spline regression for video semantic recognition. IEEE Trans. Neural Netw. Learn. Syst. **26**(2), 252–264 (2015)
7. Chen, X., Yuan, G., Nie, F., Huang, J.Z.: Semi-supervised feature selection via rescaled linear regression. In: Proceedings of the 26th International Joint Conference on Artificial Intelligence (IJCAI), pp. 1525–1531 (2017)

8. Candès, E.J., Li, X., Ma, Y., et al.: Robust principal component analysis? J. ACM (JACM) **58**(3), 11–49 (2011). https://doi.org/10.1145/1970392.1970395
9. Yang, J., Yin, W., Zhang, Y., et al.: A fast algorithm for edge-preserving variational multichannel image restoration. SIAM J. Imaging Sci. **2**(2), 569–592 (2009). https://doi.org/10.1137/080730421
10. Wen, Z., Yin, W.: A feasible method for optimization with orthogonality constraints. Math. Program. **142**(1–2), 397–434 (2012). https://doi.org/10.1007/s10107-012-0584-1
11. Yang, J., Zhang, Y.: Alternating direction algorithms for ell_1-problems in compressive sensing. SIAM J. Sci. Comput. **33**(1), 250–278 (2011)

Multiview Learning via Non-negative Matrix Factorization for Clustering Applications

Jiajia Chen[1(✉)], Ao Li[1], Jie Li[2], and Yangwei Wang[2]

[1] School of Computer Science and Technology, Harbin University of Science and Technology, Harbin, China
544953065@qq.com

[2] Shandong Provincial Innovation and Practice Base for Postdoctors, Weihaizhenyu Intelligence Technology Co., Ltd., Weihai, China

Abstract. Multiview clustering is to more fully use the information between views to guide the division of data points, and multiview data is often accompanied by high-dimensionality. Since non-negative matrix factorization can effectively extract features while reducing dimensionality, this paper proposed a multi-view learning method based on non-negative matrix factorization. Compared with other NMF-based multiview learning methods, the proposed method has the following advantages: 1) graph regularization is added to traditional NMF to explore potential popular structures, so that the learned similarity graph contains more potential information. 2) A common graph learning strategy is designed to integrate hidden information from different views. 3) Put the NMF-based similarity graph learning and common graph learning strategies into a unified framework, and optimize the similarity graph and common graph at the same time, so that the two promote each other. Experiments on three public datasets show that the proposed method is more robust than the existing methods.

Keywords: Non-negative matrix factorization · Multiview clustering · Similarity learning · Spectral clustering

1 Introduction

Due to the rapid development of multimedia technology, in practical applications, more and more data show high-dimensional and unlabeled. Therefore, how to deal with this kind of data effectively has become the current research hotspot, and dimensionality reduction and clustering also highlight the application value they contain. The main purpose of dimension reduction is to explore a low dimensional structure hidden in high dimensional space, which will contain useful information in high dimensional space as much as possible [1]. The purpose of clustering is to divide samples into different clusters according to the similarity of data [2–6]. Therefore, how to combine the two sufficiently to obtain a clustering model with high robustness is a challenge.

© ICST Institute for Computer Sciences, Social Informatics and Telecommunications Engineering 2022
Published by Springer Nature Switzerland AG 2022. All Rights Reserved
S. Shi et al. (Eds.): 6GN 2021, LNICST 439, pp. 354–361, 2022.
https://doi.org/10.1007/978-3-031-04245-4_31

In recent years, non negative matrix factorization (NMF) has become an effective dimension reduction method for multi view clustering. For example, Zong [7] et al. proposed a NMF based clustering framework to solve the problem of clustering unmapped data in multiple views. In order to understand the influence of the orthogonality of the vectors in the division matrix and the representation matrix, a new NMF model with co-orthogonality constraint was proposed by Liang et al. [8]. Similarly, Liang et al. [9] proposed a semi supervised multi view clustering method to solve the impact of dimensionality reduction on label data categories. In addition, Zhou et al. [10] proposed a grid sparsity based multi popular regularized multi NMF method for multi view clustering to capture the shared cluster structure among different views.

Although the above methods have achieved good performance, they adopt a two-step strategy for the information within and between views, and do not consider the possibility of mutual guidance between the two. The influence of noise on model learning is not considered. Our proposed a multiview learning strategy based on non-negative matrix factorization. This method can not only use the representation ability of non-negative matrix to retain the effective information between views, but also use a graph regularization constraint to learn the similarity relationship within views. To sum up, this paper has the following advantages:

(1) A non-negative matrix graph learning mechanism is constructed to explore the hidden lines in the view, which makes the common graph more robust.
(2) A joint optimization framework is designed, in which the similarity graph learning and common graph learning based on non-negative matrix are put into a unified framework for joint optimization. In the iterative process, hidden information can be transmitted among variables to increase the accuracy of clustering model.
(3) A numerical method is developed to obtain the optimal solution for each variable.

2 Related Work

2.1 Nonnegative Matrix Factorization

Given an original data $X \in R^{n\times d}$, where m is the sample dimension and n is the number of samples. The purpose of nonnegative matrix factorization is to find two nonnegative matrices $U \in R^{m\times r}$ and $P \in R^{n\times r}$, which can be as close as possible to the original data X, where $r < d$. The objective function of NMF can be expressed as follows:

$$\begin{aligned} &\min \left\| X - UP^T \right\|^2 \\ &s.t. U \geq 0, P \geq 0 \end{aligned} \tag{1}$$

where U is the base matrix and P is the coefficient matrix. In order to optimize formula (1), an iterative multiplication updating method is proposed as follows:

$$U_{ij} \leftarrow \mathbb{U}\frac{(XP)_{ij}}{\left(UP^T P\right)_{ij}} \tag{2}$$

$$P_{ij} \leftarrow \mathbb{P}\frac{\left(X^T U\right)_{ij}}{\left(PU^T U\right)_{ij}} \tag{3}$$

2.2 Similarity Graph Learning

Inspired by locality preserving projection method, Nie et al. [11] proposed an adaptive nearest neighbor graph learning method. Suppose that s_{ij} represents the probability similarity of two samples x_i and x_j, then the probability of similarity between two samples can be defined by the following formula:

$$\min_{s_i} \sum_{j=1}^{n} \left(\frac{1}{2} \|x_i - x_j\|_2^2 s_{ij} + \gamma s_{ij}^2 \right) \tag{4}$$

where $\|\cdot\|_2^2$ is the l_2-norm and γ is the trade-off parameter. By defining the graph Laplacian matrix $L = W - \left(S + S^T/2\right)$, formula (4) can be rewritten as follows:

$$\begin{aligned} &\min_{s} \ \mathrm{Tr}\left(XLX^T\right) + \gamma \|s\|_F^2 \\ &s.t. \ \ \mathbf{S1} = 1, 0 \le s \le 1. \end{aligned} \tag{5}$$

where W is a diagonal matrix satisfying $W_{ii} = 0.5\left(\sum S_{i*} + \sum S_{*i}\right)$. By optimizing formula (5), a similarity graph S can be adaptively learned from the data to represent the similarity relationship between samples.

3 Our Proposed

3.1 Similarity Graph Learning Based on Non-negative Matrix

The traditional graph construction process is independent of NMF. In the process of matrix decomposition, graph S is fixed. In order to overcome this problem, this paper integrates the non-negative matrix factorization process into the graph construction, so that the graph construction is based on the matrix factorization, rather than two independent processes. Given a set of multi view data $X = \left\{X^1 X^2, \ldots, X^v, v = 1, \ldots, m\right\}$ and v denote the number of views, the multi view graph learning objective function based on non-negative matrix is as follows:

$$\begin{aligned} &\min_{U,P,S} \sum_{v=1}^{m} \left\|X^v - U^v (P^v)^T\right\|_F^2 + \alpha Tr\left(P^v L^v (P^v)^T\right) + \beta \|s^v\|_F^2 \\ &s.t. \ \ \mathrm{U} \ge 0, \mathrm{P} \ge 0, 0 \le \mathrm{S} \le 1, \ \ \mathbf{S1} = 1 \end{aligned} \tag{6}$$

where α and β are trade-off parameters, $\|\cdot\|_F$ is Frobinus norm and $Tr(\cdot)$ is trace. By optimizing the above formula, the coefficient matrix P and the similarity graph S will transfer hidden information to each other in the iterative process, so that the coefficient matrix and the similarity graph of the next view contain more hidden cues.

3.2 Objective Function

This paper designs a common graph learning strategy, so that the learned common graph can fuse the effective information from different views, and use the common graph in the subsequent clustering process to increase the accuracy of the model. In order to get better consistency information between views, the above models are put into a unified framework to increase the robustness of the model. The specific formula is as follows:

$$\min_{U,P,S,G} \sum_{v=1}^{m} \left\| X^v - U^v (P^v)^T \right\|_F^2 + \alpha Tr\left(P^v L^v (P^v)^T \right) + \beta \| s^v \|_F^2 + \| C - S^v \|_F^2$$
$$s.t.\ \mathrm{U} \geq 0, \mathrm{P} \geq 0, 0 \leq \mathrm{S} \leq 1,\ \mathbf{S1} = 1 \tag{7}$$

From formula (7), we can see that common graph C contains consistency clues and latent clues from various views. In the joint framework, the representation matrix P and the similarity graph S can be alternately optimized to obtain high quality common graph.

3.3 Optimization Strategy of Objective Function

It can be seen from Eq. (7) that all variables are coupled in the objective function. Therefore, in order to achieve the optimal value of each variable, this paper uses an alternative optimization strategy to solve the objective function.

Through some algebraic formulas, formula (7) is rewritten as:

$$\min_{U,P,S,G} \sum_{v=1}^{m} \left\| X^v - U^v (P^v)^T \right\|_F^2 + \alpha Tr\left(P^v L^v (P^v)^T \right) + \beta \| S^v \|_F^2 + \| C - S^v \|_F^2$$
$$= tr\left(XX^T \right) - 2tr(XPU^T) + tr\left(UP^T PU^T \right) + \alpha tr\left(P^v L^v (P^v)^T \right) + \beta \| S^v \|_F^2 + \| C - S^v \|_F^2 \tag{8}$$

Using Eq. (8), the objective function is divided into the following sub optimization problems.

Update U^v: Fix other variables and update U^v with formula (9):

$$\min_{U^v} tr\left(UP^T PU^T \right) - 2tr(XPU^T) \tag{9}$$

By derivation of the above formula, we can get the following formula:

$$\left[2UP^T P - 2XP \right]_{ij} U_{ij} = 0 \tag{10}$$

According to formula (10), the update rule of U^v is as follows:

$$U_{ij} = U_{ij} \frac{[XP]_{ij}}{\left[UP^T P \right]_{ij}} \tag{11}$$

Update P^v: Fix other variables and update P^v with formula (12):

$$\min_{P^v} tr\left(UP^T PU^T \right) - 2tr(XPU^T) + \alpha tr\left(P^v L^v (P^v)^T \right) \tag{12}$$

By deriving the above formula, we can get the following formula:

$$\left[-X^T U + PU^T U + \alpha LP \right]_{ij} P_{ij} = 0 \tag{13}$$

Since $L = D - S$, according to formula (12), the update rule of P^v is as follows:

$$P_{ij} = P_{ij} \frac{\left[X^T U + \alpha SP\right]_{ij}}{\left[PU^T U + \alpha DP\right]_{ij}} \tag{14}$$

Update S^v: To fix other variables, S^v can be updated with the following formula:

$$\begin{aligned} &\min_{s_i} \sum_{j=1}^{n} \left(\tfrac{\beta}{2} \left\| p_i - p_j \right\|^2 s_{ij} + \gamma s_{ij}^2 + \left(c_{ij} - s_{ij} \right) \right) \\ &s.t.\ \ \mathrm{s}_i^T \mathbf{1} = 1,\ 0 \le \mathrm{s_{ij}} \le 1 \end{aligned} \tag{15}$$

Define $f_{ij} = \left\| p_i - p_j \right\|^2 - \frac{4}{\beta} c_{ij}$ and $f_i \in R^{n \times 1}$, then formula (15) can be rewritten as:

$$\min_{s_i^T \mathbf{1} = 1, 0 \le \mathrm{s_{ij}} \le 1} \left\| s_i + \frac{\beta}{4\gamma} f_i \right\|_2^2 \tag{16}$$

By removing the constraints of the above equation, the Lagrangian form of Eq. (16) is given as follows:

$$\begin{aligned} \mathcal{L}(s_i, \eta, \xi) = &\left\| s_i + \tfrac{\beta}{4\gamma} f_i \right\|_2^2 \\ &- \eta \left(s_i^T \mathbf{1} - 1 \right) - \xi_i^T s_i \end{aligned} \tag{17}$$

where η and $\xi \in R^{n \times 1}$ are Lagrange multipliers. Under the KTT condition, the solution is obtained by the following formula:

$$\begin{cases} s_{ik} = \dfrac{\eta}{2} - \dfrac{\beta f_{ik}}{4\gamma_i} > 0 \\ s_{i,k+1} = \dfrac{\eta}{2} - \dfrac{\beta f_{i,k+1}}{4\gamma_i} \le 0 \\ s_i^T \mathbf{1} = \sum_{j=1}^{k} \left(\dfrac{\eta}{2} - \dfrac{\beta f_{ij}}{4\gamma_i} \right) = 1 \end{cases} \Rightarrow \begin{cases} s_{ij} = \dfrac{f_{i,k+1} - f_{ij}}{k f_{i,k+1} - \sum_{r=1}^{k} f_{ir}}, j \le k \\ \gamma_i = \dfrac{\beta}{4} \left(k f_{i,k+1} - \sum_{j=1}^{k} f_{ij} \right) \\ \eta = \dfrac{2}{k} + \dfrac{\beta}{2k\gamma_i} \sum_{j=1}^{k} f_{ij} \end{cases} \tag{18}$$

Update C: To fix other variables, C can be updated with the following formula:

$$\min_{C} \sum_{v=1}^{m} \left\| C - S^v \right\|_F^2 \tag{19}$$

The optimal solution can be obtained by solving each row of matrix C:

$$\min_{c_i^T \mathbf{1} = 1, c_{ij} > 0} \sum_{v=1}^{m} \left\| c_i - s_i^v \right\|_F^2 \tag{20}$$

Formula (19) can be solved by an iterative algorithm, which was proposed in reference [12].

4 Experiments

4.1 Datasets

COIL20 dataset: COIL20 is a collection of grayscale images, including 20 objects shot from different angles. The images of the objects are taken every 5 degrees. There are 72 images of each object, 1440 images in total. According to the shooting angle, this article divides it into four different viewing angle data: V1[0°–85°], V2[90°–175°], V3[180°–265°], V4[270°–360°].

UCI dataset: This data set contains 10 digital handwritten images from 0, 1, 2,..., 9. Each number has 200 samples, and the entire data set has a total of 2000 samples. This paper selects 500 samples from them, and extracts three different features from each sample as three different perspectives. The first perspective extracts 216-dimensional profile-related features, the second perspective extracts 76-dimensional Fourier coefficients, and the third perspective extracts a 6-dimensional morphological feature.

YALE dataset: Yale collected facial images from 15 different people. Each of these people has 11 photos with different light, pose and expression, for a total of 165 images. This paper will extract three features of gray intensity (Gray), local binary pattern (LBP) and Gabor for each sample in the data set as three different perspective data.

4.2 Experimental Results and Analysis

In the experiment, in order to fully prove the effectiveness of the proposed method, this paper will compare with four advanced methods on the above three datasets. The four methods are: the classical k-nearest neighbor graph construction method via Gaussian distance kernel (GCG), rbust graph learning from noisy data (RGC) in reference [13], parameter-free auto-weighted multiple graph learning(AMGL) [14], and Multi-Graph Fusion for multi-view Spectral Clustering(GFSC) in reference [15].

In the experiment, the missing value rate is used to generate noise data. The rate of missing values changed from 0.1 to 0.5, and the interval step was 0.1. It can be seen from Table 1, 2 and 3 that with the increasing noise intensity, the ACC index of this method is basically higher than other comparison methods. Only in UCI dataset, when the noise intensity is 0.4 and 0.5, our method is lower than GFSC method, but it can be seen that our method is still above the average baseline, which proves the robustness of our proposed model.

Table 1. Accurate results of clustering on UCI dataset.

Missing rate	GFSC	AMGL	RGC	GCG	Ours
0.1	60.16	72.92	41.16	37.65	65.13
0.2	57.26	70.38	35.6	42.31	63.35
0.3	59.60	57.59	36.72	32.45	60.23
0.4	59.30	55.84	30.27	28.64	55.98
0.5	54.52	48.74	20.15	25.56	32.91

Table 2. Accurate results of clustering on YALE dataset.

Missing rate	GFSC	AMGL	RGC	GCG	Ours
0.1	48.78	56.84	51.91	54.79	65.26
0.2	41.12	55.73	58.74	56.26	63.98
0.3	30.20	59.75	45.06	52.16	60.05
0.4	24.65	58.62	43.20	52.91	59.19
0.5	19.38	55.04	24.86	46.42	58.94

Table 3. Accurate results of clustering on COIL20 dataset.

Missing rate	GFSC	AMGL	RGC	GCG	Ours
0.1	65.47	57.25	77.58	66.84	81.12
0.2	60.58	60.51	79.13	65.04	80.24
0.3	55.42	70.52	74.35	66.46	77.56
0.4	50.19	70.28	71.65	63.14	73.48
0.5	42.01	63.14	23.31	54.82	67.26

5 Conclusions

Aiming at the negative influence of noise on model learning, our proposed a multiview learning strategy via non-negative matrix factorization. This method combines non negative matrix factorization with graph learning model, so that they can transfer hidden information to each other and better explore the potential structure of data. In addition, a common graph learning strategy is proposed to fuse the effective information from different views, and a joint strategy is proposed to make the variables promote each other in the iterative process and increase the robustness of the model. Experimental results on three open datasets show that the proposed method is superior to the existing excellent multi view learning methods.

Acknowledgment. This work was supported in part by the National Natural Science Foundation of China under Grant 62071157, Natural Science Foundation of Heilongjiang Province under Grant YQ2019F011 and Postdoctoral Foundation of Heilongjiang Province under Grant LBH-Q19112.

References

1. Yi, Y., Wang, J., Zhou, W., et al.: Non-Negative Matrix Factorization with Locality Constrained Adaptive Graph. IEEE Trans. Circuits Syst. Video Technol. 1 (2019)
2. Wang, Q., Dou, Y., Liu, X., Lv, Q., Li, S.: Multi-view clustering with extreme learning machine. Neurocomputing **214**, 483–494 (2016)

3. Zhang, C., Hu, Q., Fu, H., Zhu, P., Cao, X.: Latent multi-view subspace clustering. In: Computer Vision and Pattern Recognition, pp. 4333–4341 (2017)
4. Li, B., et al.: Multi-view multi-instance learning based on joint sparse representation and multi-view dictionary learning. IEEE Trans. Pattern Anal. Mach. Intell. **39**, 2554–2560 (2017)
5. Jing, X., Wu, F., Dong, X., Shan, S., Chen, S.: Semi-supervised multi-view correlation feature learning with application to webpage classification. In: Proceedings of the Thirty-First AAAI Conference on Artificial Intelligence, pp. 1374–1381 (2017)
6. Wu, J., Lin, Z., Zha, H.: Essential tensor learning for multi-view spectral clustering. IEEE Trans. Image Process. **28**, 5910–5922 (2019)
7. Zong, L., Zhang, X., Liu, X.: Multi-view clustering on unmapped data via constrained non-negative matrix factorization. Neural Netw. **108**, 155–171 (2018)
8. Liang, N., Yang, Z., Li, Z., et al.: Multi-view clustering by non-negative matrix factorization with co-orthogonal constraints. Knowl.-Based Syst. **194**, 105582 (2020)
9. Liang, N., Yang, Z., Li, Z., et al.: Semi-supervised multi-view clustering with graph-regularized partially shared non-negative matrix factorization. Knowl.-Based Syst. **190**, 105185 (2020)
10. Zhou, L., Du, G., Lü, K., et al.: A network-based sparse and multi-manifold regularized multiple non-negative matrix factorization for multi-view clustering. Expert Syst. Appl. **174**, 114783 (2021)
11. Nie, F., Wang, X., Huang, H.: Clustering and projected clustering with adaptive neighbors. In: ACM SIGKDD International Conference on Knowledge Discovery and Data Mining, pp. 977–986 (2014)
12. Duchi, J.C., Shalevshwartz, S., Singer, Y., Chandra, T.D.: Efficient projections onto the l1-ball for learning in high dimensions. In: International Conference on Machine Learning, pp. 272–279 (2008)
13. Kang, Z., Pan, H., Hoi, S.C.H., Xu, Z.: Robust graph learning from noisy data. IEEE Trans. Cybern. 1–11 (2019)
14. Nie, F., Li, J., Li, X.: Parameter-free auto-weighted multiple graph learning: a framework for multiview clustering and semi-supervised classification. In: International Joint Conference on Artificial Intelligence, pp. 1881–1887 (2016)
15. Kang, Z., et al.: Multi-graph fusion for multi-view spectral clustering. Knowl. Based Syst. **189**, 102–105 (2020)

Target Detecting and Target Tracking Based on YOLO and Deep SORT Algorithm

Jialing Zhen[1], Liang Ye[1,2(✉)], and Zhe Li[3]

[1] Department of Information and Communication Engineering, Harbin Institute of Technology, Harbin 150080, China
yeliang@hit.edu.cn

[2] Health and Wellness Measurement Research Group, OPEM Unit, University of Oulu, 90014 Oulu, Finland

[3] China Academy of Launch Vehicle Technology, Beijing 100076, China

Abstract. The realization of the 5G/6G network can ensure high-speed data transmission, which makes it possible to realize high-speed data transmission in the monitoring video system. With the technical support of 5G/6G, the peak transmission rate can reach 10G bit/s, which solves the problems of video blur and low transmission rate in the monitoring system, and provides faster and higher resolution monitoring pictures and data, and provides a good condition for surveillance video target tracking based on 5G/6G network. In this context, based on the surveillance video in the 5G/6G network, this paper implements a two-stage processing algorithm to complete the tracking task, which solves the problem of target loss and occlusion. In the first stage, we use the Yolo V5s algorithm to detect the target and transfer the detection data to the Deep SORT algorithm in the second stage as the input of Kalman Filter, Then, the deep convolution network is used to extract the features of the detection frame, and then compared with the previously saved features to determine whether it is the same target. Due to the combination of appearance information, the algorithm can continuously track the occluded objects; The algorithm can achieve the real-time effect on the processing of surveillance video and has practical value in the future 5G/6G video surveillance network.

Keywords: Target detecting · Target tracking · Deep convolutional neural network · Kalman filter

1 Introduction

At present, in the field of target tracking, tracking algorithms are mainly divided into two categories, Generative Algorithm and Discriminant Algorithm. The generative algorithm is to first establish the target model or extract the target features [1], and then search for similar features in subsequent frames to track. In recent years, the relevant representative algorithms include Kalman Filter [2], Mean Shift, ASMS, and so on [3], Discriminant Algorithm [4] means that the target model and background information are taken into

© ICST Institute for Computer Sciences, Social Informatics and Telecommunications Engineering 2022
Published by Springer Nature Switzerland AG 2022. All Rights Reserved
S. Shi et al. (Eds.): 6GN 2021, LNICST 439, pp. 362–369, 2022.
https://doi.org/10.1007/978-3-031-04245-4_32

account at the same time. The current frame takes the target area as the positive sample and the background area as the negative sample. The machine learning method [5] trains the classifier. In recent years, the related representative algorithms include TLD, SVM, and so on [6].

2 Target Detecting Based on YOLO V5s

The YOLO network is mainly composed of three main parts [7]:

- Backbone: a convolutional neural network that aggregates different fine-grained images and forms image features
- Neck: A series of network layers that mix and combine image features and transmit image features to the prediction layer
- Head: The image features are predicted to generate boundary boxes and prediction categories (Fig. 1)

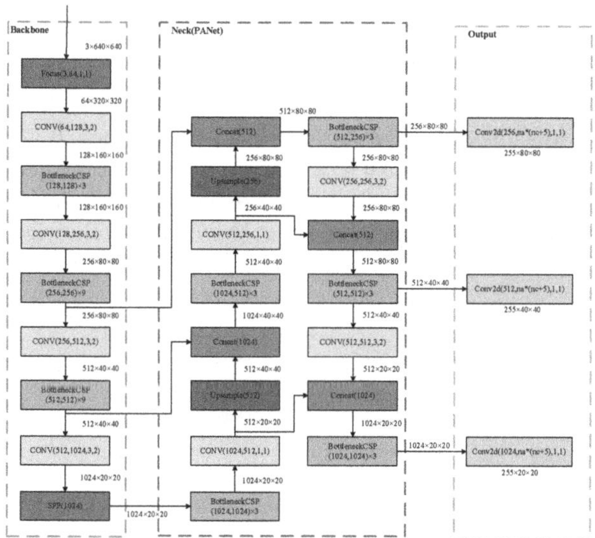

Fig. 1. The overall model

2.1 Focus

Yolov5 first uses the input of 3 × 640 × 640, and the function of the Focus layer is to copy four copies of it. Then, the four images are cut into four 3 × 320 × 320 slices through slicing operation, and then concat is used to connect the four slices in-depth, and the output is 12 × 320 × 320. After that, the output of 32 × 320 × 320 is generated through the convolution layer with the convolution kernel of 32. Finally, the output is input to the next convolution layer through Batch Normalization and Leaky ReLU. The selection of activation functions is crucial for deep learning networks. YOLO V5s uses Leaky ReLU and Sigmoid activation functions as shown below, the middle/hidden layer uses Leaky ReLU activation functions, and the final detection layer uses Sigmoid shaped activation functions (Fig. 2).

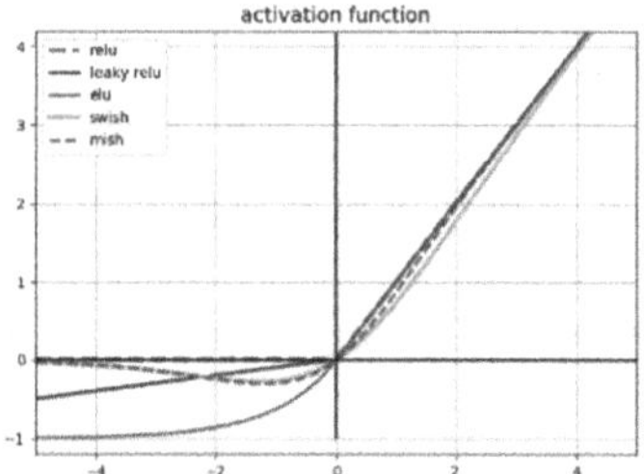

Fig. 2. The activation function

2.2 CSP

YOLO uses CSP Darknet as Backbone to extract rich information features from input images. The CSP structure of YOLO V5s is divided into two parts, Bottleneck and CSP. While bottleneck is a classic residual structure: firstly, 1×1 convolution layer (Conv + Batch Normalization + Leaky ReLU) then 3×3 convolution layer, and finally, the residual structure is added to the initial input, as shown in the following Fig. 3.

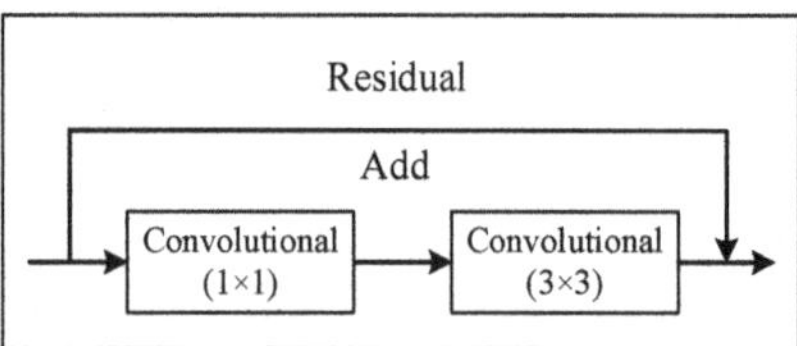

Fig. 3. Residual structure

2.3 SPP

SPP is the Spatial Pyramid Layer. It outputs the input feature graph of $512 \times 20 \times 20$ through the convolution layer of 1x1and then subsamples the three parallel convolution cores. For different branches, the padding sizes are different. In this way, the size of each pooled result is the same, and then the splicing results are added to the initial features. Finally, the 512 convolution kernel is used to restore the feature map to the size of $512 \times 20 \times 20$, as shown in the schematic diagram below (Fig. 4):

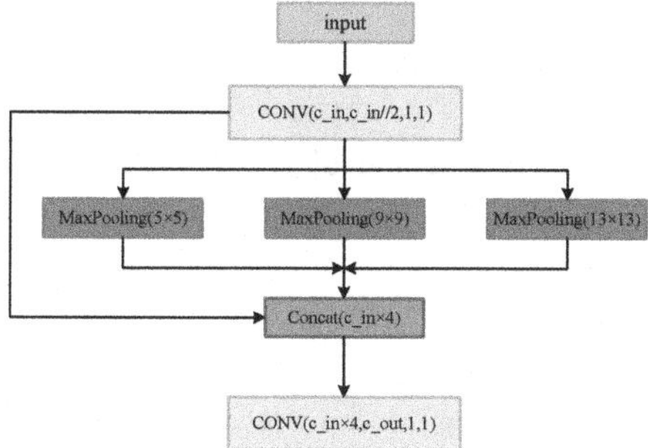

Fig. 4. SPP structure

3 Target Tracking Based on Deep SORT Algorithm

3.1 Motion Information

First introduced motion feature extraction part, the following eight states are described for a detection box.

- Test box center abscissa
- Longitudinal coordinates of the center of detection
- Detection frame size
- Aspect ratio
- Variable speed of the abscissa of the center of the detection box
- Variable speed of longitudinal coordinates at the center of the detection
- Variable speed of the size of the detection box
- Change speed of aspect ratio

Based on the above, use an 8-dimensional state vector to describe the change of the detection box.

$$\mathbf{x} = [u, v, s, r, \dot{u}, \dot{v}, \dot{s}, \dot{r}]^T \tag{1}$$

The Kalman Filter here is a linear uniformity model [8], using a Mahalanobis distance to measure the distance between the predicted Karman filtering state and the newly obtained measurement value (Detection box), as shown below:

$$d^{(1)}(i,j) = \left(\mathbf{d}_j - \mathbf{y}_i\right)^{\mathrm{T}}\mathbf{S}_i^{-1}\left(\mathbf{d}_j - \mathbf{y}_i\right) \tag{2}$$

In the above formula, (y_i, S_i) represents the projection of the i -th track (Kalman Filter distribution) on the measurement space, y_i is the average, and S_i is the covariance, and is predicted by Kalman Filter. To perform distance measurements, must go to the same spatial distribution to do. The Mahalanobis distance calculates the uncertainty between state estimates by measuring the standard deviation and detection frame between the tracking position means of the Kalman Filter, $d^1(i,j)$ is the Mahalanobis distance between i-th track and the j-th detection, here two symbolic meaning are:

i: Tracking serial number
j: The serial number of the detection box

Using the 95% confidence interval calculated by the inverted square distribution as the threshold.

3.2 Appearance Information

Deep convolution network to extract the appearance characteristics of the detected target, detect and track each frame, performing a target appearance feature extraction and saving [9]. When each frame is performed later, it is necessary to perform the similarity calculation of the appearance characteristics of the current frame, the motion characteristics and appearance features will be combined as a total discrimination basis. The structure of deep neural network is shown in the following figure (Table 1):

Table 1. Network structure

Name	Patch Size	Stride	Output Size
Conv 1	3×3	1	$32 \times 128 \times 64$
Conv 2	3×3	1	$32 \times 128 \times 64$
Max pool 3	3×3	2	$32 \times 64 \times 32$
Residual 4	3×3	1	$32 \times 64 \times 32$
Residual 5	3×3	1	$32 \times 64 \times 32$
Residual 6	3×3	2	$64 \times 32 \times 16$
Residual 7	3×3	1	$64 \times 32 \times 16$
Residual 8	3×3	2	$128 \times 16 \times 8$
Residual 9	3×3	1	$128 \times 16 \times 8$
Dense 10			128
Batch and l_2 normalization			128

The network has 2,800, 864 parameters. Training the depth convolutional neural network to extract the characteristic information of the target, and trained the model on the Re-ID data set, the data set contains 1100,000 images of 1261 people, very suitable for the target tracking. On the NVIDIA GTX1050M graphics card, input 30 Bounding Box, extraction features approximately use 30 ms, and the training iterative loss value of the network is as follows (Fig. 5):

The last output of the network is a 128-dimensional vector, considering the task target tracking under 5G/6G monitoring video, the requirements for tracking algorithms are mainly pedestrian tracking, so the input size is set to 128×64 rectangle. Here are three definitions:

Initialization: If a detection is not associated with the previously recorded Track, then starting from this detection, initializing a new goal.

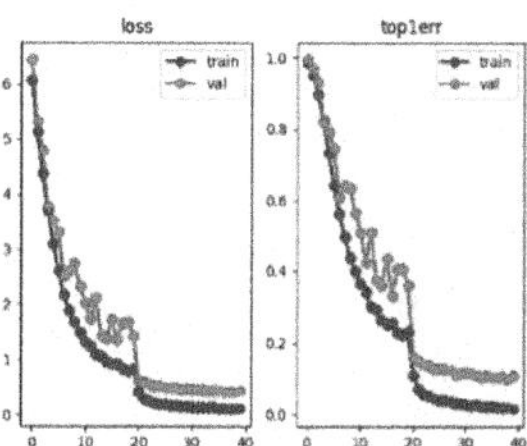

Fig. 5. Iterative loss value

Freshmen: After a goal is initialized, and in the first three frames are normal capture and association, then the object produces a new track, otherwise it will be deleted.
Disappearing: If the maximum save time is exceeded, if it is not associated, then this object leaves the video screen, the information of the object (the appearance features and behavior features of the record) will be deleted.

Use residual network to extract appearance features. The network accepts the target as input in the detection box, returns the vector of 128 dimensions, for each detection box (numbered j) inner object d_j, its 128 dimension of the vector is set to r_j, the vector of r_j is 1, $\|r_j\| = 1$. A matrix is created for each target$k$, which is used to store the appearance feature (128 dimensional vector) of the target in different frames, indicated by R_k, the expression is as follows [10], the meaning of k is the target k, That is, the serial number of Object-in-track, i is tracking sequence number [11].

$$R_k = \left\{r_k^{(i)}\right\}_{k=1}^{(L_k)} \tag{3}$$

The L_k size is up to 100, which can only store the target appearance characteristics in 100 frames before the current time of the target k. At some point, you get the appearance characteristics of the detection box (numbered j), remember to r_j. The minimum cosine distance $d^{(2)}(i,j)$ is then solved by the appearance characteristics of all known R_k matrices and the appearance characteristics of the obtained detection frame (numbered j).

$$d^{(2)}(i,j) = \min\left\{1 - \mathbf{r}_j^{\mathrm{T}}\mathbf{r}_k^{(i)} \middle| \mathbf{r}_k^{(i)} \in \mathcal{R}_i\right\} \tag{4}$$

4 Verification

With the high-definition monitoring video recorded by the camera, use the algorithm to identify and track. The effect is as shown in the figure below, it can be seen that the algorithm can again identify the target again, and give the same ID, to continue tracking.

The first case: monitoring video objectives are short-lived due to interaction (Fig. 6)

Fig. 6. Interaction.

The second case: surveillance video objectives have marginalized or even briefly left monitoring (Fig. 7)

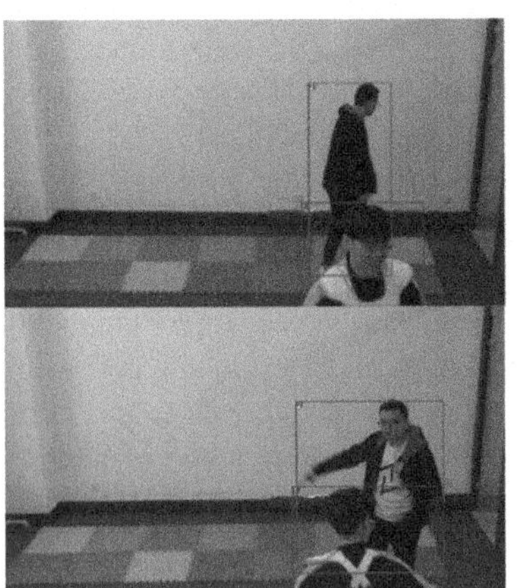
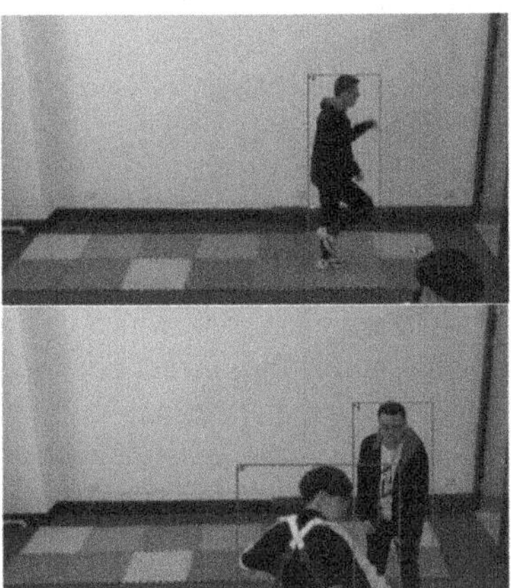

Fig. 7. Marginalized.

Acknowledgment. This work was supported by the National Natural Science Foundation of China (41861134010), the Basic scientific research project of Heilongjiang Province (KJCXZD201704), the Key Laboratory of Police Wireless Digital Communication, Ministry of Public Security (2018JYWXTX01), and partly by the Harbin research found for technological innovation (2013RFQXJ104) national education and the science program during the twelfth five-year plan (FCB150518). The authors would like to thank all the people who participated in the project.

References

1. Wang, Z.D., Zheng, L., Liu, Y.X., et al.: Towards real-time multi-object tracking. In: 16th European Conference on Computer Vision, pp. 107–122. Springer, Heidelberg (2020)
2. Kuanhung, S., Chingte, C., Lin, J., et al.: Real-time object detection with reduced region proposal network via multi-feature concatenation. IEEE Trans. Neural Networks Learn. Syst. **31**(6), 2164–2173 (2020)
3. Luo, W.H., Xing, J.L., Milan, A., et al.: Multiple object tracking: a literature review. Artif. Intell. **293,** 103448 (2020)
4. Kalman, R.E.: A new approach to linear filtering and prediction problems. J. Basic Eng. **82**(1), 35–45 (1960); Zhang, J.W.: Gradient descent based optimization algorithms for deep learning models training [EB/OL]. [2019–03–21]. https://www.researchgate.net/publication/331670579
5. Chen, L., Ai, H.Z., Zhuang, Z.Z., et al.: Real-time multiple people tracking with deeply learned candidate selection and person re-identification. In: IEEE International Conference on Multimedia & Expo (ICME), pp. 1–6. IEEE, New York (2018)
6. Redmon, J.,Farhadi, A.: Yolov3: An incremental improvement [E B/O L]. [2 0 1 8 - 0 4 - 0 8]
7. Fu, Z.Y., Naqvi, S.M., Chambers, J.A.: Collaborative detector fusion of data-driven PHD filter for online multiple human tracking. In: Proceedings of the 21st International Conference on Information Fusion, pp. 1976–1981. IEEE, New York (2018)
8. Ren, S.Q., He, K.M., Girshick, R., et al.: Faster R-CNN: towards real- time object detection with region proposal networks. IEEE Trans. Pattern Anal. Mach. Intell. **39**(6), 1137–1149 (2017)
9. Bewley, A., Ge, Z.Y., Ott, L., et al.: Simple online and real time tracking. In: 2016 IEEE International Conference on Image Processing, pp. 3464–3468. IEEE, New York (2016)
10. Wojke, N., Bewley, A., Paulus, D.: Simple online and real time tracking with a deep association metric. In: 2017 IEEE International Conference on Image Processing, pp. 3645–3649. IEEE, New York (2017)
11. Cipolla, R., Gal, Y., Kendall, A.: Multi-task learning using uncertainty to weigh losses for scene geometry and semantics. In: 2018 IEEE/CVF Conference on Computer Vision and Pattern Recognition (CVPR), pp. 7482–7491. IEEE, New York (2018)

Multi-feature Fusion Network Acts on Facial Expression Recognition

Jingyu Li[1](✉), Weiyue Cheng[2], Jiahao Geng[1], and Kezheng Lin[1]

[1] School of Computer Science and Technology, Harbin University of Science and Technology, Harbin, China
920948105@qq.com

[2] Heilongjiang College of Business and Technology, Harbin, China

Abstract. In order to solve the problem of single-channel convolutional neural network feature loss in the process of facial expression recognition, a facial expression recognition algorithm based on multi-feature fusion network is proposed. The algorithm uses the dual-channel convolutional neural network model DCNN-FER (Dual-channel Convolutional Neural Network Model for Facial Expression Recognition). The pre-processed face image is input to channel one to obtain global features, and the face image that has been processed by Local Binary Patterns (LBP) is input to channel two to obtain local texture features. At the same time, it is used in part of the convolutional layer. The Convolutional Block Attention Module (CBAM) enhances the network's focus on the useful information of the image and suppresses useless features. Finally, new features are formed by weighted fusion and sent to the softmax layer for classification. This algorithm not only considers the extraction of overall facial features, but also enriches local texture features. Compared with other methods on the FER2013 and CK + facial expression data sets, the method in this paper shows good robustness.

Keywords: Facial expression recognition · CNN · Feature fusion · LBP

1 Introduction

Facial expression is an important way of communication between people. It is the significant information to understand the emotional state of a specific target. Even the smallest change on a person's face may be a different emotion signal. Ekman et al. divided expressions into six basic forms for the first time [1]. Facial expression recognition has gradually become a research hotspot in the field of computer vision. It has shown a wide range of application prospects in communication engineering, medical and health, safe driving [2], and social sentiment analysis.

Traditional feature extraction algorithms mainly include PCA [3] (Principal Component Analysis), SIFT (Scale-Invariant Feature Transformation), LBP [4, 5] (Local Binary Patterns), Gabor wavelet transform [6, 7] as well as the HOG(Histogram Of Gradient) [8], the classification algorithms mainly include SVM (Support Vector Machine),

© ICST Institute for Computer Sciences, Social Informatics and Telecommunications Engineering 2022
Published by Springer Nature Switzerland AG 2022. All Rights Reserved
S. Shi et al. (Eds.): 6GN 2021, LNICST 439, pp. 370–382, 2022.
https://doi.org/10.1007/978-3-031-04245-4_33

k-Nearest Neighbor [9] and so on. However, traditional facial expression recognition methods are susceptible to image noise and human interference factors, resulting in poor recognition accuracy.

Deep learning methods have shined in the field of image recognition, and DNN (Deep Neural Networks) have been applied to facial expression recognition and achieved good results [10]. CNN (Convolutional Neural Network) [11] is a machine learning model under deep supervised learning, and CNN convolutional layer uses multiple filters to extract image features, weight sharing compresses the number of parameters, and uses backpropagation to optimize parameters, which has achieved good results in facial expression recognition [12, 13]. Literature [14] added a network attention model to CNN, and automatically determined the area of interest by adjusting the channel and spatial weight, focusing on useful information, and suppressing useless information.

Studies have found that when a single-channel neural network is used to extract facial features, it may lead to insufficient focus on facial features and loss of part of effective information. ZENG et al. embedded manual facial features into a CNN and proposed a new Loss algorithm to obtain a higher recognition rate [15]. Wang et al. used CNN and SIFT to extract facial features respectively, and used SVM to realize expression classification after fusion of the two, and achieved good results [16]. Literature [17] combines the depth features extracted from CNN with the SIFT features of the image to form new features for expression classification. Rikhtegar et al. used genetic algorithm combined with CNN to extract image features, and finally used SVM to replace the last layer of CNN to complete the task of facial expression classification [18]. Gao Jingwen et al. used a three-channel convolutional neural network to focus on the face, eye, and mouth regions of the human face, and then extracted features [19]. Finally, the fusion technology based on the decision-making layer was used to fuse the features of the three channels for expression discrimination. Obtain the overall optimal recognition rate. Therefore, in the process of facial expression recognition, different algorithms or different levels of feature fusion can obtain more complex features, which to a certain extent become a significant means to solve feature loss, so this paper proposes an algorithm based on dual-channel convolutional neural network, The method of fusing global features and local texture features is used to obtain complex features.

2 Related Work

2.1 Convolutional Neural Network

CNN as a network structure of weight sharing, has stronger ability to extract image features, mainly composed of convolutional layer and pooling layer. The main structure in the convolutional layer is the filter, also known as the convolution kernel. The size of the filter is called the receptive field. The receptive field determines the size of the sliding window. The sliding window is used to extract the complex features of the image, and the activation function is used to process the complex features and output the features. The calculation process is shown in Formula (1).

$$X_j^L = f(\sum_{i \in M_j} X_i^{L-1} \cdot K_{ij}^L + b_j^L) \tag{1}$$

among them, L is the current layer; $X_j{}^L$ represents the j-th feature area of the current layer; $X_i{}^{L-1}$represents the i-th feature area of the previous layer; K represents the convolution kernel of the two regions.

2.2 Convolutional Block Attention Module

CBAM can improve the neural network's focus on useful information. In the two dimensions of feature space and channel, it can enhance valuable features, suppress useless features, and greatly improve the feature extraction ability of the network. As shown in Fig. 1, the feature map F passes through the 1-dimensional channel attention module M_c and the 2-dimensional spatial attention module M_s to obtain the final output feature map.

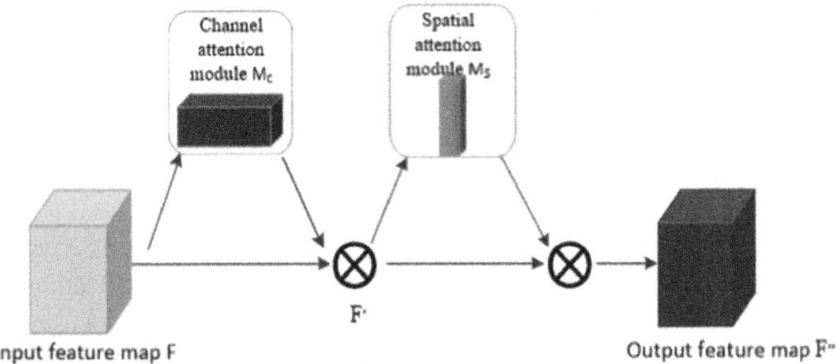

Fig. 1. CBAM structure diagram

In order to aggregate the feature information of the feature map on each channel, the average pooling and maximum pooling operations are used to generate two different channel context descriptors, then the two descriptors Don't send it into a multi-layer perceptron network (MLP) with a hidden layer, and finally combine the output feature weight parameters by element-by-element summation.

The spatial attention module first applies the average pooling and maximum pooling operations to the feature map to generate two two-dimensional feature maps, which respectively represent the average fusion feature and the maximum fusion feature on each channel. Then the attention weights in these two dimensions are sent to the convolutional layer to finally get the attention weights in the spatial dimension.

3 DCNN-FER Method

3.1 Method Structure

The DCNN-FER model has two feature extraction channels, including the HE-CNN channel for extracting global features and the LBP-CNN channel for extracting local features. In the HE-CNN channel, the original image is sent to the improved ResNet18 network to extract global features after the histogram equalization process. In the LBP-CNN channel, the original image is processed by LBP to obtain the LBP feature map, and then the LBP feature is sent Extract local features into a specific CNN, and then combine the global features and local features after dimensionality reduction. The fused new features are sent to the softmax layer to complete the classification task. The DCNN-FER algorithm flow diagram is shown in Fig. 2.

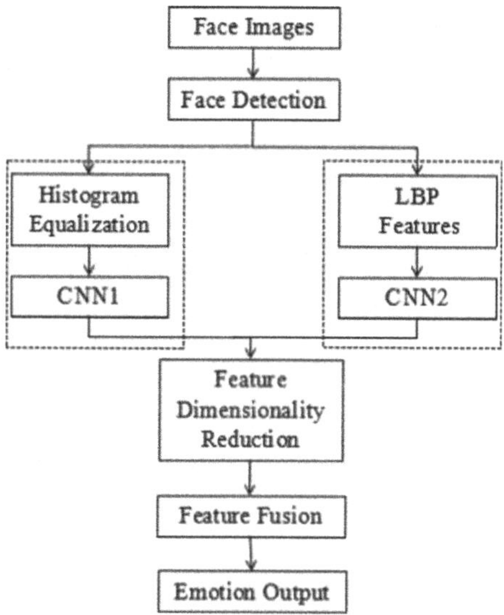

Fig. 2. Schematic diagram of DCNN-FER algorithm flow

The input layer of the HE-CNN channel is a grayscale image with pixels of 64px × 64px. In order to enhance the contrast of the image, the original image is histogram equalized. The gray levels of the original images of the FER2013 and CK + data sets are distributed in a relatively narrow interval. In order to better obtain the global features of the image, the channel uses the deep convolutional neural network ResNet18 for feature extraction. The residual unit is added to the ResNet network through the short-circuit mechanism to form residual learning, which solves the degradation problem of the deep network. As shown in Fig. 3(a), the original residual block consists of two convolutional layers and two BN layers, and each module has a fast input and output connection. In this paper, the original residual block structure is improved. As shown in Fig. 3(b), the two BN layers in the original structure are removed, and ReLU is added after the second convolutional layer to improve the residual The non-linear expression ability of the unit avoids the destruction of image space information by the BN layer. In order to enhance the performance of the residual network and reduce the burden of network training, a cross-layer integration strategy is proposed. As shown in Fig. 3(c), the output feature map of each residual unit is combined through shortcut connections. The network structure changes from global residuals to local residuals, and at the same time avoids over-fitting in model training and the disappearance of gradients in back propagation.

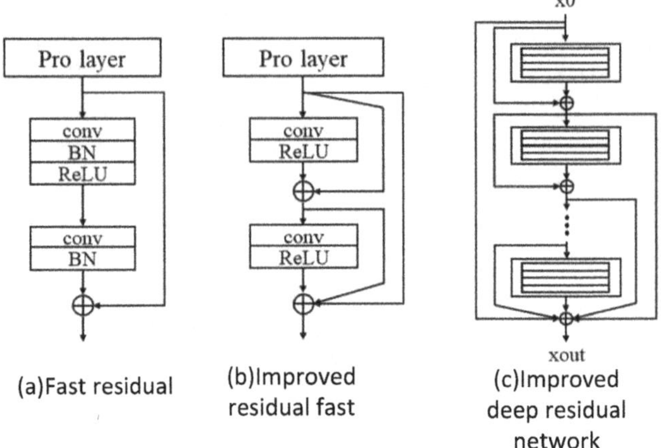

Fig. 3. Improved residual structure

The output of the network can be defined as:

$$X_{out} = \sum_{l=0}^{N} X_l = X_0 + X_1 + \cdots + X_N \tag{2}$$

among them, X_0 represents the gradual feature of the low-resolution image extracted by the feature extraction network. X_l is the output of the l-th residual unit. There are a total of N residual units, The parameters of each layer of the HE-CNN channel are shown in Table 1.

Table 1. Parameters of each layer of the HE-CNN channel network

Convolutional layer	Output size	Convolution Kernel
Conv1	32 × 32 × 64	7 × 7, 64, stride 2
Conv2_x	16 × 16 × 64	$\begin{bmatrix} 3 \times 3, 64 \\ 3 \times 3, 64 \end{bmatrix} \times 2$
Conv3_x	8 × 8 × 128	$\begin{bmatrix} 3 \times 3, 128 \\ 3 \times 3, 128 \end{bmatrix} \times 2$
Conv4_x	4 × 4 × 256	$\begin{bmatrix} 3 \times 3, 256 \\ 3 \times 3, 256 \end{bmatrix} \times 2$
Conv5_x	2 × 2 × 512	$\begin{bmatrix} 3 \times 3, 512 \\ 3 \times 3, 512 \end{bmatrix} \times 2$
Fc1	1000	–
Fc2	6	–

According to the requirements of facial expression classification tasks, the ResNet18 network is finally connected to a fully connected layer with 6 nodes, and Softmax classification is adopted. The network attention mechanism is added to the first and last layers of the improved ResNet18 network to focus on effective features, suppress useless features, and effectively enhance the feature extraction capabilities of the network.

In the LBP-CNN channel, the original image of the data set must first be processed by the LBP algorithm. LBP is less sensitive to image gray changes and can better extract the image The local texture feature eliminates the influence of noise such as lighting. The LBP operator compares the neighboring pixels of the center pixel with the center pixel. The pixel larger than the center point is 1, and the pixel smaller than the center point is 0, so the 8-bit binary code is The LBP value of the center pixel is used to reflect the texture information of the area. The LBP operation is shown in Formula (3) and Formula (4).

$$LBP(g_c) = \sum_{i=0}^{p-1} s(g_i - g_c)2^i \tag{3}$$

$$s(x) = \begin{cases} 1, x > 0 \\ 0, else \end{cases} \tag{4}$$

among them, $s(x)$ represents the sign function, g_c represents the pixel value of the central pixel, g_i represents the pixel value of the surrounding adjacent pixels, p represents the number of adjacent pixels.

The generated LBP feature map is sent to the convolutional neural network. The LBP-CNN channel network structure is shown in Fig. 4. After the LBP feature map passes through the convolution operation, it passes through CBAM processing is sent to the pooling layer. The first layer of convolutional layer uses a filter with 32 channels and a size of 5 × 5; the second layer uses a filter with 64 channels and a size of 3 × 3; the third layer uses 128 channels and a size of 3 × 3; The fourth layer uses a filter with a channel of 256 and a size of 3 × 3; the feature map is sent to a fully connected layer with 500 nodes through the flattening layer, and finally it is sent to the feature fusion network. The parameters of each layer of the LBP-CNN channel network are shown in Table 2.

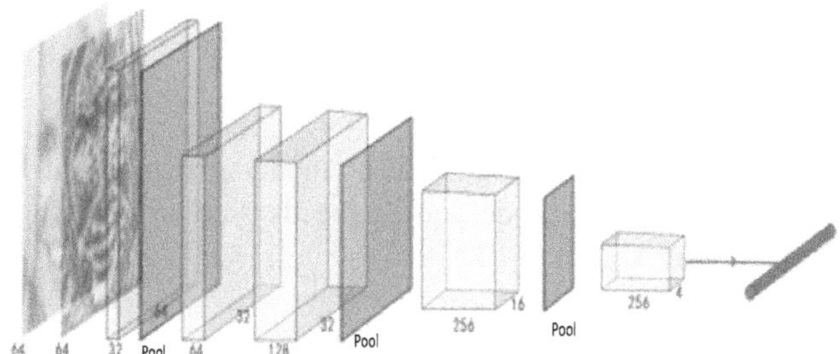

Fig. 4. LBP-CNN feature extraction process diagram

Table 2. Parameters of each layer of the HE-CNN channel network

Network layer	Input size	Convolution kernel	Output size
Conv1	64 × 64 × 1	5 × 5 × 32	64 × 64 × 32
Pool1	64 × 64 × 32	2 × 2 × 32	32 × 32 × 32
Conv2_1	32 × 32 × 32	3 × 3 × 64	32 × 32 × 64
Conv2_2	32 × 32 × 64	3 × 3 × 128	32 × 32 × 128
Pool2	32 × 32 × 128	2 × 2 × 128	16 × 16 × 128
Conv3	16 × 16 × 128	3 × 3 × 256	8 × 8 × 256
Pool3	8 × 8 × 256	2 × 2 × 256	4 × 4 × 256
Fc1	–	–	500
Fc2	–	–	6

3.2 Feature Fusion

After the original picture extracts the global feature and local texture feature feature through the dual-channel network, it is sent to the feature fusion layer, and finally the expression category is output. In order to adjust the proportion of the two channel features, the feature fusion layer adopts a weighted fusion method and sets the weight coefficient k to adjust the weight of the two channel features.

$$F_Z = k \cdot f_H + (1 - k) \cdot f_L \tag{5}$$

in the Formula (5), F_z represents the feature after fusion, f_{H} represents the features extracted by the HE-CNN channel, f_{L} represents the features extracted by the LBP-CNN channel. When the value of k is set to 0, it means that there is only the LBP-CNN channel, and when the value of k is set to 1, it means that there is only the HE-CNN channel. Choosing an appropriate value of k is the key to feature fusion. After a lot of experiments, select the most appropriate value of k through accuracy.

As shown in Fig. 5, the recognition rate of the model changes with the change of the value of k. The recognition rate reaches the highest when k is 0.6, and the recognition effect is the best.

3.3 Description of Algorithm Steps

According to the above-mentioned DCNN-FER model structure and feature fusion method, the training process of the model and the specific steps of expression recognition are described in Algorithm 1.

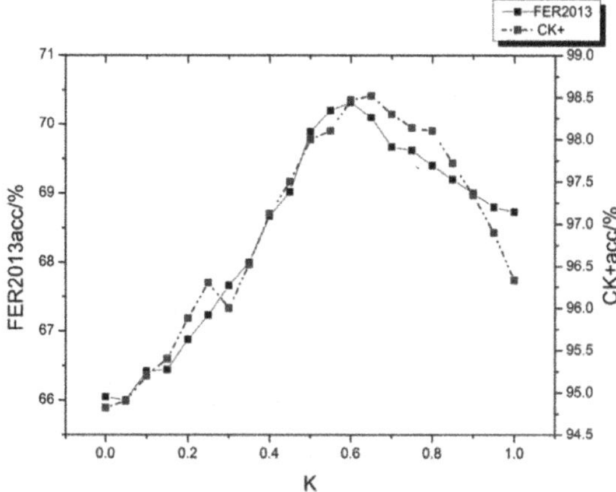

Fig. 5. Accuracy rate of accuracy rate under different k values

---

Algorithm 1: DCNN-FER algorithm

Input: The face samples in the data set are unified into 48×48 grayscale images.

Output: Emoticon category.

(1) Batch input image data {x1, x2,...} for histogram equalization.

(2) Use $LBP(g_c) = \sum_{i=0}^{p-1} s(g_i - g_c)2^i$ to find the LBP feature map of the image.

(3) The image processed by the histogram equalization is put into the ResNet18 convolutional neural network, and the 6-dimensional feature vector $f_H = \{s_1, s_2, ..., s_6\}$ is obtained after convolution operation $X_j^L = f(\sum_{i \in M_j} X_i^{L-1} \cdot K_{ij}^L + b_j^L)$, pooling operation and feature dimensionality reduction.

(4) The LBP feature is subjected to a five-layer convolution operation $X_j^L = f(\sum_{i \in M_j} X_i^{L-1} \cdot K_{ij}^L + b_j^L)$ and a three-layer maximum pooling operation, and a feature vector $f_L = \{t_1, t_2, ..., t_6\}$ with a dimension of 6 is obtained after feature dimensionality reduction.

(5) f_H and f_L are weighted and fused using formula $F_Z = k \cdot f_H + (1-k) \cdot f_L$, and the new feature after fusion is F_Z .Send it to the softmax layer for classification.

---

4 Experiments

4.1 Facial Expression Data Set

This article conducts experimental verification on two public data sets of FER2013 and CK+.

The FER2013 data set [20] has 35886 face grayscale images with a fixed size of 48px × 48px. Among them, there are 28708 images in the training set, and 3589 images in the test set and verification set. They are divided into 6 categories, corresponding to labels 0–6. For the convenience of research, this article will remove the original data set. Neutral pictures and experiment with other 6 types of pictures.

The CK + data set [21] is the extended Cohn-Kanada facial expression database (The Extend Cohn-Kanade Data, CK+), which contains a diverse group of Asian and European races covering male and female genders. It was collected and published by the University of Pittsburgh in 2010. The data set collected 593 frontal face images of 123 experimenters, including 8 expressions. This article only studies the first 6 basic expressions. 80% of the pictures in the data set are classified as the training set, and the remaining pictures are the test set.

Figure 6 is a partial sample of each expression in the FER2013 and CK + datasets.

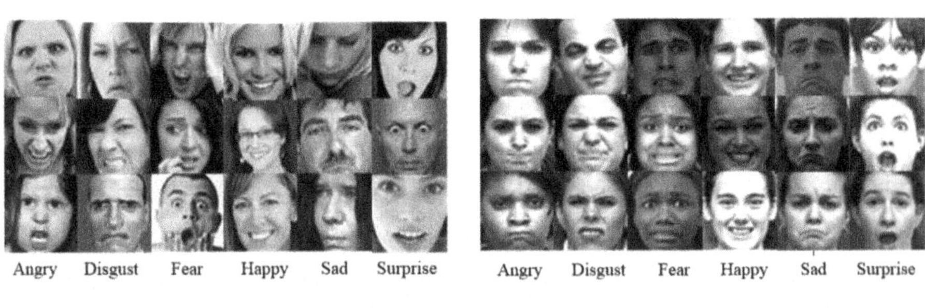

(a) Part of the image of the FER2013 (b) Part of the image of the CK+

Fig. 6. Examples of FER2013 and CK + dataset images

4.2 Algorithm Validity Verification

Use the DCNN-FER model to train on the FER2013 and CK + datasets and verify its effectiveness. In order to expand the data set on the basis of the original sample, the original image is randomly zoomed, translated, flipped, and rotated to increase the model training data. The number of data sets after data enhancement becomes 9 times the original, which greatly increases the amount of model training and reduces the risk of overfitting.

The experiment uses Tensorflow as the basic experimental framework, Python3.7 as the programming language. The learning rate is in the form of dynamic changes, and the initial value is set to le−4, with the increase of epochs Gradually decay to (le−4)/epoches. In order to prevent over-fitting, Dorpout regularization is used in the fully connected layer, some neurons are randomly discarded, the initial value of the Dropout regularization parameter is set to 0.5, and L2 regularization is added, and the regularization coefficient is 0.01. Figure 10 shows the accuracy and loss curves of the DCNN-FER model on the two data sets.

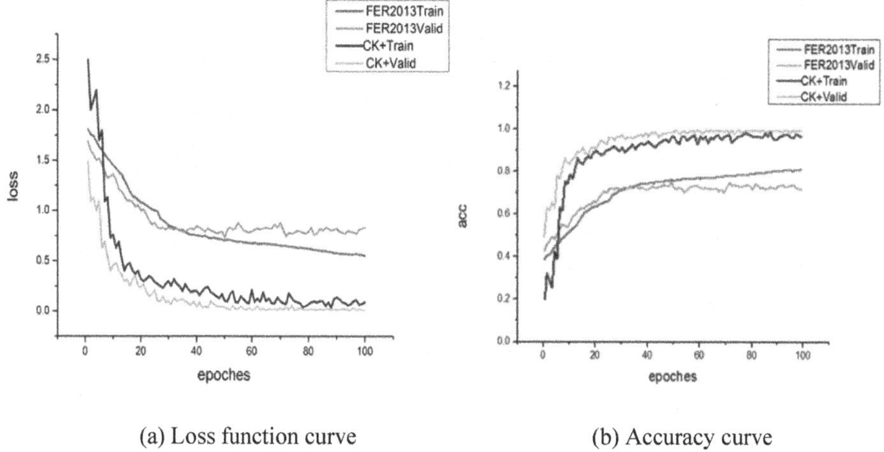

(a) Loss function curve (b) Accuracy curve

Fig. 7. Training process curve diagram

It can be seen from Fig. 7 that as the iteration period (epoches) increases, the loss of the model on the two datasets gradually decreases, and the accuracy (acc) gradually increases. The accuracy rate of the FER2013 verification set finally stabilized at about 70.49%, and the accuracy rate of the CK + verification set finally stabilized at about 98.31%, achieving the expected results.

Figure 8 is a comparison of the accuracy of DCNN-FER and HE-CNN and LBP-CNN with only a single channel on different expressions. It can be seen from the figure that the DCNN-FER model is on two data sets compared to a single channel neural

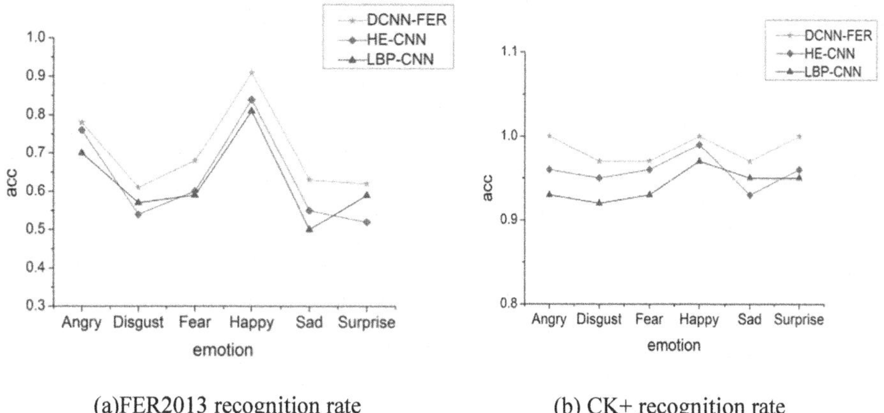

(a)FER2013 recognition rate (b) CK+ recognition rate

Fig. 8. Comparison of recognition rates under different models

network. Both achieve the desired effect. Although the recognition rate of individual models is low, the overall recognition rate is better than the other two models.

The confusion matrix of the DCNN-FER model on the FER2013 and CK + data sets is shown in Fig. 9.

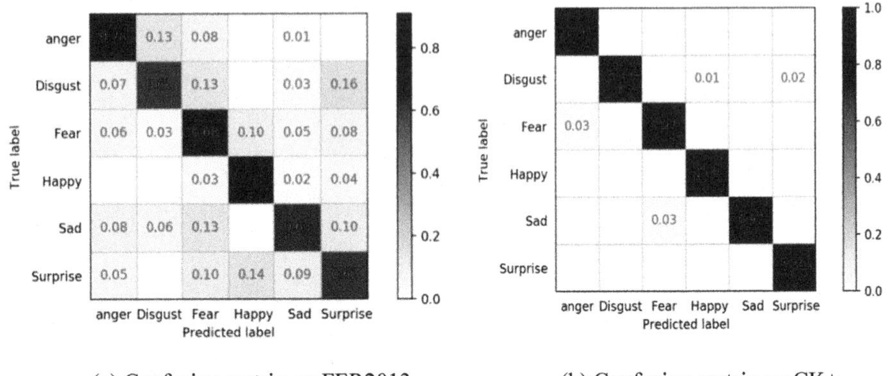

(a) Confusion matrix on FER2013 (b) Confusion matrix on CK+

Fig. 9. Confusion matrix of DCNN-FER under different data sets

From Fig. 9(a), it can be seen that the model has a higher recognition rate for angry and happy on the FER2013 data set, reaching 78% and 91%, respectively. The recognition results for disgust, fear, sadness and surprise are not good, because the number of these expressions in the data set is relatively small, and the similarity between the expressions is high, which is more likely to cause classification errors. In addition, the FER2013 data set itself There are also label errors, and some images are still occluded, resulting in low classification accuracy. From the matrix in Fig. 9(b), the model has a recognition rate of 100% for happy, surprised and angry expressions on the CK + dataset. Due to the similarity of expressions, the recognition of disgust and fear is The rate is relatively low, but it also reached 97%.

Table 3 and Table 4 are the accuracy comparisons of different methods on the FER2013 and CK + data sets, respectively. The data shows that the accuracy rate of DCNN-FER on FER2013 reached 70.47%, which is 4 to 5% points higher than other models. It also showed a good recognition effect on CK+, and the accuracy rate was increased to 98.48%, which was 2 to 3% points higher than other models. Compared with DNN and FER-Net [25], although the method in this paper costs more time Many, but our method shows great advantages in recognition accuracy. Therefore, the feasibility of the algorithm in facial expression recognition is verified.

Table 3. Comparison of recognition rates of different methods on the FER2013 (%)

Method	Accuracy
Ref. [12]	65.03
DNN [13]	66.4
Ref. [15]	61.86
FER-Net [22]	69.72
DCNN-FER	70.49

Table 4. Comparison of the recognition rate of different methods on the CK + (%)

Method	Accuracy
DNN [13]	93.2
Ref. [15]	97.35
Ref. [17]	94.82
Ref. [23]	95.79
DCNN-FER	98.31

5 Conclusions

Aiming at the problem of single-channel neural network feature loss in the process of facial expression recognition, a facial expression recognition algorithm based on feature fusion network is proposed. Through the feature fusion method, this algorithm overcomes the problem of partial effective feature loss of single-channel neural network on the one hand, that is, fully extracts global features, and effectively retains local effective features. The two complement each other, complement each other, and improve expression Accuracy of recognition. This paper also uses the network attention model to automatically focus the feature area of interest in the network, suppress useless information. The next step of research will continue to improve the network model to include more detailed local features, make full use of the features of the facial features and global features to further improve the accuracy.

References

1. Ekman, P., Friesen, W.V.: Constants across cultures in the face and emotion. J. Pers. Soc. Psychol. **17**(2), 124 (1971)
2. Lutao, G.: Research on Driver State Analysis Method Based on Facial Expression. University of Electronic Science and Technology of China (2019)
3. Wold, S., Esbensen, K., Geladi, P.: Principal component analysis. Chemom. Intell. Lab. Syst. **2**(1–3), 37–52 (1987)
4. Jia, Q., Gao, X., Guo, H., et al.: Multi-layer sparse representation for weighted LBP-patches based facial expression recognition. Sensors **15**(3), 6719–6739 (2015)

5. Shan, C., Gong, S., Mcowan, P.W.: Facial expression recognition based on local binary patterns: a comprehensive study. Image Vis. Comput. **27**(6), 803–816 (2009)
6. Zhou, J., Zhang, S., Mei, H., et al.: A method of facial expression recognition based on Gabor and NMF. Patt. Recognit. Image Anal. **26**(1), 119–124 (2016)
7. Gu, W., Xiang, C., Venkatesh, Y.V., et al.: Facial expression recognition using radial encoding of local Gabor features and classifier synthesis. Patt. Recogn. **45**(1), 80–91 (2012)
8. Wang, X., Jin, C., Liu, W., et al.: Feature fusion of HOG and WLD for facial expression recognition. In: IEEE/SICE International Symposium on System Integration. IEEE (2014)
9. Liu, P., Zhou, J.T., Tsang, I.W.H., et al.: Feature disentangling machine-a novel approach of feature selection and disentangling in facial expression analysis. In: European Conference on Computer Vision, pp. 151–166. Springer, Cham (2014). https://doi.org/10.1007/978-3-319-10593-2_11
10. Fulan, Q., Jianhong, L., Shu, Z., et al.: Rating recommendation based on deep hybrid model. J. Nanjing Univ. Aeronaut. Astronaut. **51**(5), 592–598 (2019)
11. Krizhevsky, A., Sutskever, I., Hinton, G.E.: Imagenet classification with deep convolutional neural networks. Adv. Neural. Inf. Process. Syst. **25**, 1097–1105 (2012)
12. Lopes, A.T., de Aguiar, E., De Souza, A.F., et al.: Facial expression recognition with convolutional neural networks: coping with few data and the training sample order. Pattern Recogn. **61**(12), 610–628 (2017)
13. Pons, G., Masip, D.: Supervised committee of convolutional neural networks in automated facial expression analysis. IEEE Trans. Affect. Comput. **9**(3), 343–350 (2017)
14. Woo, S., Park, J., Lee, J.-Y., Kweon, I.S.: CBAM: Convolutional Block Attention Module. In: Ferrari, V., Hebert, M., Sminchisescu, C., Weiss, Y. (eds.) ECCV 2018. LNCS, vol. 11211, pp. 3–19. Springer, Cham (2018). https://doi.org/10.1007/978-3-030-01234-2_1
15. Zeng, G., Zhou, J., Jia, X., et al.: Hand-Crafted feature guided deep learning for facial expression recognition. In: Proceedings of 2018 13th IEEE International Conference on Automatic Face&Gesture Recognition (FG 2018), Xi'an, pp. 423–430. IEEE (2018)
16. Sun, X., Lv, M.: Facial expression recognition based on a hybrid model combining deep and shallow features. Cogn. Comput. **11**(4), 587–597 (2019)
17. Wang, F., Lv, J., Ying, G., et al.: Facial expression recognition from image based on hybrid features understanding. J. Vis. Commun. Image Represent. **59**(1), 84–88 (2019)
18. Rikhtegar, A., Pooyan, M., Manzuri-Shalmani, M.T.: Genetic algorithm-optimised structure of convolutional neural network for face recognition applications. IET Comput. Vis. **10**(6), 559–566 (2016)
19. Jingwen, G.A.O., Yongxiang, C.A.I.: TP-FER: Three-channel facial expression recognition method based on optimized convolutional neural network. Appl. Res. Comput. **38**(07), 2213–2219 (2021)
20. Goodfellow, I.J., Erhan, D., Carrier, P., et al.: Challenges in representation learning: a report on three machine learning contests. In: Proceedings of International Conference on Neural Information Processing, pp. 117–124. Springer, Heidelberg (2013). https://doi.org/10.1007/978-3-642-42051-1_16
21. Lucey, P., Cohn, J.F., Kanade, T.J., et al.: The extended Cohn-Kanade dataset (CK+) a complete dataset for action unit and emotion-specified expression. In: Proceedings of 2010 IEEE Computer Society Conference on Computer Vision and Pattern Recognition, San Francisco, pp. 94–101. IEEE (2010)
22. Ma, H., Celik, T.: FER-Net: facial expression recognition using densely connected convolutional network. Electron. Lett. **55**(4), 184–186 (2019)
23. Zeng, N., Zhang, H., Song, B., et al.: Facial expression recognition via learning deep sparse autoencoders. Neurocomputing **273**, 643–649 (2018)

Facial Expression Recognition with Small Samples Under Convolutional Neural Network

Cheng Weiyue[1], Jiahao Geng[2], and Kezheng Lin[2(✉)]

[1] Heilongjiang College of Business and Technology, Harbin, China
cheng_weiyue@sina.cn

[2] School of Computer Science and Technology, Harbin University of Science and Technology, Harbin, China
link@hrbust.edu.cn

Abstract. In order to further improve the accuracy of facial expression recognition in small samples, a small sample expression recognition method based on deep learning and fusion of different models is proposed. In this method, a single CNN model is first compared, and the relatively appropriate convolutional neural network (CNN) is selected by preserving probability of different nodes in the dropout layer. Then, the scale-invariant feature transformation (SIFT) algorithm is used to extract features. The purpose of extracting features with SIFT is to improve the performance of small data. And then, in order to reduce the error, avoid over fitting, all the model to carry on the summary, all the model of the weighted Average CNN-SIFT-AVG (Convolutional Neural Network and Scale Invariant Feature Transformation business) model. Finally, only a few sample data are used to train the model. The model has been tested on FER2013, CK+ and JAFFE datasets. Experimental results show that this model can greatly improve the accuracy of small sample facial expression recognition, and has produced excellent results in FER2013, CK+ and JAFFE dataset, with a maximum improvement of about 6% compared with other facial expression recognition methods.

Keywords: Facial expression recognition · CNN · SIFT · Small sample

1 Introduction

Facial expression recognition has always been a challenging research topic and has been widely used in detecting mental disorders and human-computer interaction [1]. It could help create more intelligent robots capable of recognizing human emotions. Many real-life applications, such as fatigue driving detection and interactive game development, also benefit from the technology. At present, various feature extraction and machine learning algorithms are used in the field of facial expression recognition. After the success of ILSVRC [2] and AlexNet [3] deep convolutional neural network model, deep learning has begun to be widely used in the field of computer vision. The challenge of facial expression recognition [4] may be one of the earliest works that put forward the deep learning method for facial expression recognition. After that, the system with the

© ICST Institute for Computer Sciences, Social Informatics and Telecommunications Engineering 2022
Published by Springer Nature Switzerland AG 2022. All Rights Reserved
S. Shi et al. (Eds.): 6GN 2021, LNICST 439, pp. 383–396, 2022.
https://doi.org/10.1007/978-3-031-04245-4_34

highest score in the FER challenge in 2013 is the deep convolutional neural network [5], while the best model of manual features only ranks fourth [6].With a few exceptions [7, 8], most recent studies on facial expression recognition are based on deep learning [9–14].Recent research [15] proposes to train convolutional neural network cascade to improve performance. Others [16] combine deep features with handmade features in dynamic video expression recognition.

In most cases, the training of the CNN depend on a large amount of data, however, the facial expression recognition, the data set is limited while the scale invariant feature transform [17] and other traditional local feature extraction method of accurate results than CNN, but they don't need a lot of data sets can be obtained as a result, therefore, put forward the deep learning under the fusion of different characteristics of facial expression recognition method of small sample first carries on the comparison to a single CNN model, screening of relatively suitable CNN, then SIFT local feature extracting, finally summary and all model, get a CNN-SIFT-AVG model. This method was evaluated on FER2013, CK+ and JAFFE data sets respectively.

2 Related Work

2.1 CNN

(1) Convolutional layer
Characteristics of the input data are extracted, and its interior contains multiple convolution kernels, composed of convolution kernels of each element corresponding to a weight coefficient and a bias term each neuron in the convolution layer from the previous layer close to the location of multiple neurons connected area, the size of the area depends on the size of the convolution kernels convolution kernels at work, will regularly sweep input characteristics, within the receptive field of input characteristics do matrix elements multiplication summation and superposition deviation value, calculated as shown in formula (1):

$$Z^{l+1}(i,j) = [Z^l \otimes w^i](i,j) + b = \sum_{k=1}^{K_l}\sum_{x=1}^{f}\sum_{y=1}^{f}[Z_k^l(s_0 i + x, s_0 j + y)w_k^{i+1}(x,y)] + b$$
$$(i,j) \in \{0, 1, \ldots L_{l+1}\} L_{l+1} = \frac{L_l + 2p - f}{s_0} + 1 \qquad (1)$$

The summation part of the equation is equivalent to solving for a cross correlation. b for the deviation value, Z^l and Z^{l+1} represent the convolution input and output of the $l+1$ layer, also known as the feature graph. L_{l+1} is the size of Z^{l+1}. It is assumed that the feature graph has the same length and width. Z(i, j) corresponds to the pixel of the feature graph, K is the number of channels of the feature graph, f, s_0 and p are the parameters of the convolutional layer, Corresponding to the size of convolution kernel, stride and padding layers.

(2) Dropout regularization method
Dropout layer is by iterating through each layer of the neural network node, and then based on the layer of a neural network is set up the node retention probability p, that

is, the layer of the node has the probability of p is retained, p values range between 0 and 1 by setting the probability of retention of the layer of neural network, the nerve network won't go to a certain node (because the node may have been deleted), so that the weight of each node will not too big, to alleviate neural network fitting standard network as shown in Fig. 1(a), with the comparison of dropout network as shown in Fig. 1(b).

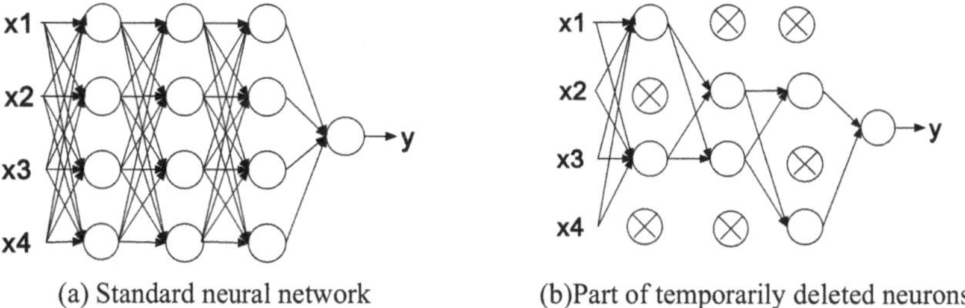

(a) Standard neural network (b)Part of temporarily deleted neurons

Fig. 1. Comparison of standard network and dropout network

In the training model stage, each unit of the training network should add a probability process. Formula (2) without Dropout method was used. When you make a prediction, you're going to pre-multiply each of the parameters of the cell by p.

$$Z_{\mathrm{i}}^{(l+1)} = w_i^{(l+1)} y^l + b_i^{l+1} \text{ and } y_i^{(l+1)} = f(z_i^{l+1}) \text{ and } Z_{\mathrm{i}}^{(l+1)} = w_i^{(l+1)} y^l + b_i^{l+1} \tag{2}$$

The formula for using Dropout network is shown in formula (3).

$$\begin{aligned} &r_j^{(l)} \sim Bernoulli(p) \text{ and } \tilde{y}^{(l)} = r^{(l)} * y^{(l)} \\ &z_i^{(l+1)} = w_i^{(l+1)} \tilde{y}^l + b_i^{(l+1)} \text{ and } y_i^{(l+1)} = f(z_i^{l+1}) \end{aligned} \tag{3}$$

(3) Activation function
The ReLU function is shown in Eq. (4). When $x < 0$, as the training progresses, some of the input will fall into the hard saturation region and the corresponding weight cannot be updated. Therefore, for the hard saturation problem with $x < 0$, Leaky ReLU function is adopted, as shown in Eq. (5).

$$\mathrm{Re}LU(x) = \begin{cases} 0, x < 0 \\ x, x \geq 0 \end{cases} \tag{4}$$

$$Leaky\ \mathrm{Re}LU(x) = \begin{cases} ax, x < 0 \\ x, x \geq 0 \end{cases} \tag{5}$$

The advantage of using Leaky ReLU over ReLU is that it sets all negative values to zero, whereas Leaky ReLU gives all negative values a smaller non-zero value. This can solve the problem of neurons not learning after the ReLU function enters the negative range.

2.2 Local Feature Extraction

SIFT characteristics under the condition of rotating scale zoom brightness can keep invariance, so for each image, the SIFT extracted from face image point positioning key points, key to the adjacent pixels is used to calculate the direction and size of the grid in order to identify the main direction, set up the gradient histogram finally, SIFT descriptor by image segmentation into 4 x4 square to determine for each square of the 16 squares, using a vector to represent the length of 8By merging all the vectors, the eigenvectors with the size of $4 * 4 * 8 = 128$ for each key point are obtained, and the normalization is finally done.

3 Proposed Method

3.1 CNN Network Model Structure

In this paper, a network model of the structure of the input layer is for 48 * 48 pixels gray image is the one of single channel image, so the dimension of the input image by 48 * 48 * 1 convolution filter layer is a 3 * 3, in order to keep the input and output specifications of the size is changeless, added zero padding around the border padding filter processing matrix depth and the depth of the current neural network node matrix is consistent, so it is 1 through a filter and the convolution of the input image can get a 48 characteristic figure, with 32 filter got 32 consecutive feature maps. After the convolution, the pixel position of the input image is then sliding, and the stride length is equal to 1.

Then the convolution result is integrated with the maximum pool, which is a kind of nonlinear down sampling. A 2 * 2 filter is used here for each 2 * 2 region element. At the same time, each time the maximum pooling layer is added, the number of the next convolution kernel will be doubled. So the number of convolution filters is 64,128 and 256, respectively.

After the convolutional layer output, flatten was completed and then input to the entire connection layer, which was composed of 2048 neurons. Dropout layer is introduced after each maximum pooling layer to reduce the risk of network over fitting. Finally, in the last phase of the network, you place a softmax layer with seven outputs.

According to the analysis in the previous section, in order to introduce non-linearity to CNN, Leaky ReLU was used as the activation function, and the function image was shown in Fig. 2 Specific parameters are shown in formula (6).

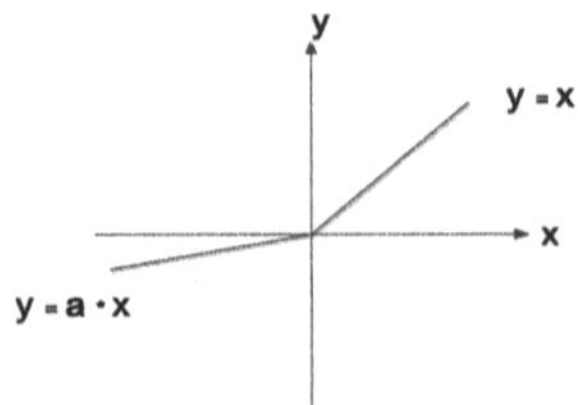

Fig. 2. Leaky ReLU functional image

$$f(x) = \begin{cases} \frac{x}{20}, x < 0 \\ x, x \geq 0 \end{cases} \tag{6}$$

Finally, the loss function is optimized by the method of classification cross entropy and the adaptive gradient optimization method Adam.

In order to achieve better classification performance, multiple CNN models were used to establish three different dropout probability models, namely, dropout1 = 0.25, dropout2 = 0, dropout2 = 0.5c2, dropout1 = 0.1, dropout2 = 0.1, dropout3 = 0.4, dropout1 = 0.1, dropout2 = 0.1, dropout3 = 0.4, dropout1 = 0.1, dropout2 = 0.1, dropout3 = 0.4, dropout1 = 0.1, dropout2 = 0.1 and dropout3 = 0.5c2 at C1, C2 and C3. The dropout probability is 0.5 to increase the diversity of the model. The overall CNN model is shown in Fig. 3.

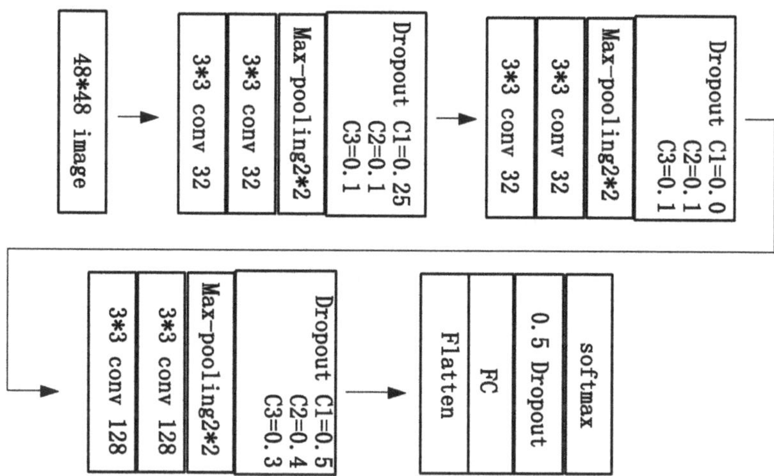

Fig. 3. CNN model adopted

3.2 Different Feature Fusion Models

In order to use the key point descriptor in SIFT in the classification, a fixed size vector is required. For this purpose, k-means is used to group descriptors into clusters. Then by calculating the number of descriptors contained in each cluster to form a bag of key points, the size of the eigenvector obtained is K.

K vector is adopted by the full connection layer of 4096 and the dropout layer. The weight of the fully connected layer is regularized with L2 norm and the value is 0.01. Three different modes S1, S2 and S3 have been tested, and the K values of each model are K1 = 256, K2 = 512 and K3 = 1024, respectively. Finally, it is merged with the C2 schema, as shown in Fig. 4.

In order to improve the accuracy of the model, the average and the CNN-ONLY,CNN-SIFT,CNN-SIFT-AVG outputs are respectively summarized, as shown in Fig. 5, where CNN-ONLY is the weighted average of C1, C2 and C3, as shown in formula (7), CNN-SIFT is the weighted average of S1, S2 and S3, as shown in formula (8). Finally, the weighted average of the six models is added to the CNN-SIFT-AVG model, as shown in formula (9).

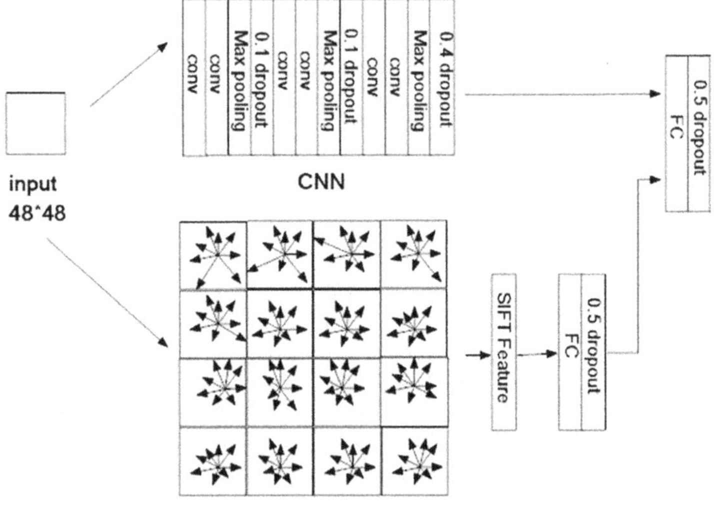

Fig. 4. CNN and SIFT model fusion

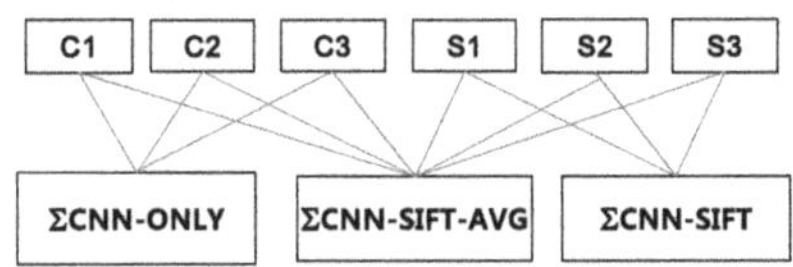

Fig. 5. Aggregating all models into CNN-ONLY, CNN-SIFT and CNN-SIFT-AVG

$$P_1(e|x) = \frac{C(e|x_{C1}) + C(e|x_{C2}) + C(e|x_{C3})}{3} \tag{7}$$

$$P_2(e|x) = \frac{S(e|x_{S1}) + S(e|x_{S2}) + S(e|x_{S3})}{3} \tag{8}$$

$$P_3(e|x) = \frac{C(e|x_{C1}) + C(e|x_{C2}) + C(e|x_{C3}) + S(e|x_{S1}) + S(e|x_{S2}) + S(e|x_{S3})}{6} \tag{9}$$

x_{Ci} represents the input dropout probability under Ci (i = 1, 2, 3) model, and $C(e|x_{\mathrm{Ci}})$ represents the probability to be judged as a certain expression under Ci mode. x_{Si} represents the input in Si mode. As can be seen above, in S1, K = 256, in S2, K = 512, and in S3, K = 1024. $S(e|x_{Si})$ represents the probability of judging an expression in Si mode. $P_1(e|x)$ represents the probability that is determined as a certain expression under the CNN-ONLY model. $P_2(e|x)$ represents the probability of judging as a certain expression in the CNN-SIFT model. $P_3(e|x)$ represents the probability of judging as a certain expression in the CNN-SIFT-AVG model. Because each model has a softmax layer as the last layer, the output is limited to between 0 and 1.

3.3 Algorithm Steps

Based on the previous analysis, this paper takes the model as an example to elaborate the specific operation steps of this method.

Step 1: The size of facial expression images in the training samples and test samples is unified as 48 * 48, and all images are normalized into vectors with zero mean and unit variance.
Step 2: Construct a CNN network model and input training data $\{x_i\}$, respectively using C1, C2 and C3 as dropout probability values p, and the number of nodes in the hidden layer is $y_1, y_2, \ldots, y_i$. During dropout, p* i of the two nodes are set to 0.
Step 3 SIFT feature extraction is carried out for the samples in the database. According to formula (6), each key point descriptor is obtained, and vector $S = \{s_1, s_2, \ldots s_{128}\}$ with size of 128 is obtained. Then k-means algorithm is adopted to divide the cluster into $C = \{C_1, C_2, \ldots, C_j\}$. By calculating the number of descriptors contained in each cluster to form a bag of key points, the size of the feature vector obtained is K.K has three numerical modes of K1, K2 and K3 respectively.
Step 4: merge the three modes obtained in step 3 with the dropout = C2 model of CNN network, and cascade the extracted features to the full connection layer.
Step 5: the model obtained in step 1 is weighted average of the model results obtained in step 4.
Step 6: for the test sample, dropout layer could screen out some neurons, and the vector should be scaled, i.e., multiplied by $1/(1 - p)$. In other parts, steps 1–5 are successively adopted to obtain the corresponding classification and recognition accuracy of facial expressions.

4 Experiments

4.1 Experimental Environment and Data Preprocessing

In order to verify the effectiveness of the proposed method in this paper, three data sets of fer-2013, CK+ and JAFFE were used in the experiment to evaluate the performance of the proposed method. Table 1 shows the quantity distribution of each expression in FER201, CK+ and JAFFE dataset. Before the experiment, the size of the image was unified as 48×48, and all images were normalized into vectors with zero mean and unit variance.

Based on the tensorflow deep learning framework, this paper conducts relevant experiments on the windows10 operating system using Python3.6 programming language. Hardware platform: 7th-generation Intel core i5, Nvidia Geforce GTX 1070Ti GPU, graphics memory 8 GB.

Table 1. Expression quantity distribution of FER201, CK+ and JAFFE dataset

Experimental	FER2013	CK+	JAFFE
Angry	4953	45	30
Disgust	547	59	29
Fear	5121	25	32
Happy	8989	69	31
Normal	6198	0	31
Sad	6077	28	30
Surprise	4002	83	30

4.2 Data Set Introduction

FER2013 image size is 48 * 48 pixels, 7 expressions in the data set are marked with 0–6 Numbers, respectively, angry, disgust, fear, happy, sad, surprise. The data set contains training set and test set, in which the training set contains a total of 28,709 images and the test set contains 3,589 images. Figure 6 shows the sample image CK+ data set of 7 kinds of expressions in FER2013 database, which contains 327 expressions.

Fig. 6. Sample images of 7 expressions in FER2013 database

In order to make the experiment compatible with other experiments and FER2013 data, the contempt expression was deleted, so 309 pictures of the remaining 6 expressions were used to train the model. Figure 7 shows that all the sample networks in CK+ database only trained for 20 cycles to prevent data overfitting.

Fig. 7. Sample images of 7 expressions in CK+ database

JAFFE data set is a basic expression database specially used for expression recognition research by Japanese ATR. The database contains 213 Japanese women's face expression database, including 10 people, each woman has 3 or 4 of each expression, and each person has 7 kinds of expressions (including Angry Normal Disgust, Fear, Happy Sad and Surprise).The JAFFE database is all positive faces, and the original image is adjusted and pruned to make the position of eyes in the database image roughly the same, the face size is basically the same, and the illumination is all positive light source, but the illumination intensity is different. Figure 8 shows the sample in JAFFE database.

Fig. 8. Sample image of seven expressions in the JAFFE database

4.3 Experimental Results and Analysis

For FER2013 dataset, all models have been trained with 28,709 samples. Of these 28,709 were used as training sets and 3,589 as test sets. Each network trains 300 epochs with a batch size of 128.

CK+ data set to use all of the 309 images for training, according to one thousand one hundred percent of cross validation method to every experiment repeat 10 times in order to prevent a fitting, all network training only 20 epoch. FER2013 CK+ and JAFFE expression distribution of the data set as shown in Table 1. JAFFE dataset using cross validation method, the images of the data set can be divided into five copies, each with one of the four as a training set, the remaining one as a test set.

In FER2013 database, in this paper, three models of the highest recognition rate has been a Happy, also known from the analysis of the above data sets, Happy features than other expressions more apparent by the experimental result shows that the integrated model has the significant improvement effect on the individual, CNN-SIFT and CNN-SIFT-AVG model is superior to CNN-ONLY model, especially the CNN-SIFT-AVG model than the other two model to improve the accurate rate of about 1%, and the use of two methods are significantly improves performance. Compared with other advanced models, the accuracy of facial expression recognition in this paper is compared, as shown in Fig. 9. It can be seen that the model in this paper is relatively stable. Although the recognition rate of some expressions is slightly lower, the overall recognition accuracy is slightly higher than that of other models, as shown in Table 2.

In the CK+ data set experiment, it can be found that, with the decrease of the number of expression samples, the performance of CNN-SIFT and CNN-SIFT-AVG is improved compared with the accuracy and performance of CNN-ONLY model, and the performance of CNN-SIFT-AVG model is relatively better. Figure 10(a) shows the confusion matrix of CK+ data set in CNN-SIFT-AVG model. It can be seen from the figure that Angry, Fear and Sad will be slightly confused and lead to errors in the recognition. Compared with other expressions, Happy is easier to be recognized.

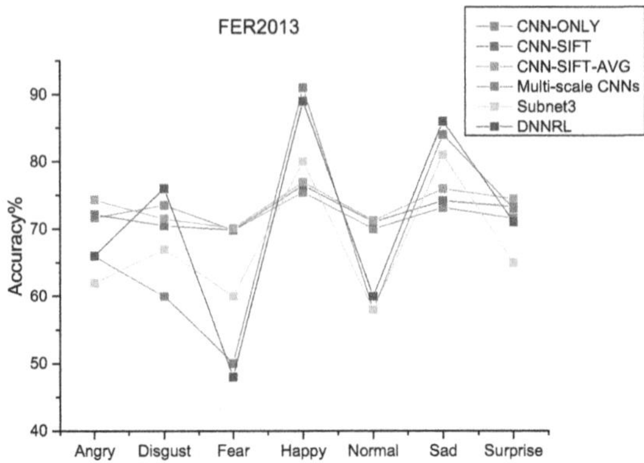

Fig. 9. Comparison diagram about the accuracy on FER2013 (left)

Table 2. Comparison of overall accuracy of FER2013 data set with other methods (%)

Model	Accuracy %
CNN-ONLY	72.17
CNN-SIFT	72.49
CNN-SIFT-AVG	73.51
Multi-scale CNNs [18]	71.80
Subnet3 [19]	62.44
DNNRL [20]	70.86

However, with the reduction of data sets, the advantages of SIFT show obvious effects. Compared with FER2013 database, in CK+ database, the recognition accuracy is greatly improved. Figure 11 shows the comparison of the accuracy of different model recognition under CK+ data set. Table 3 compares the overall accuracy of CK + data set with other methods. It can be seen from the experimental results that the model in this paper is superior to other models, whether it is the recognition accuracy of each expression or the overall recognition rate. The recognition accuracy of this paper is at least 3 percentage points higher than other methods, and the CNN-SIFT-AVG model is relatively better.

In the JAFFE data set, the model in this paper achieved a good accuracy rate, in which the Happy and Sad facial expression recognition achieved the result of no error. Figure 10(b) shows the confusion matrix of JAFFE data set on the CNN-SIFT-AVG model. Each row represents the actual category, and each column corresponds to the probability of the predicted category.

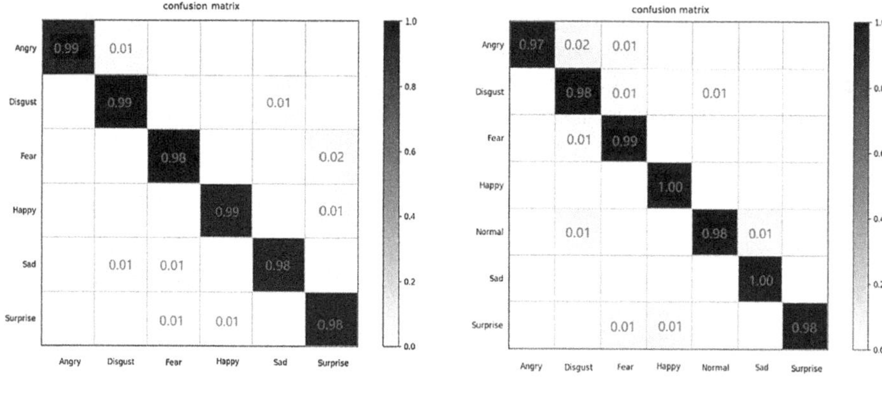

(a) Confusion matrix of CK+ data set **(b)** Confusion matrix of JAFFE data set

Fig. 10. The confusion matrix of CK+ and JAFFE data set on CNN-SIFT-AVG model

Table 3. Comparison of overall recognition accuracy of CK+ data set with other methods (%)

Model	Accuracy %
CNN-ONLY	98.33
CNN-SIFT	98.47
CNN-SIFT-AVG	99.11
Xu Linlin [21]	94.03
CNN	81.67
ZHANG Z [22]	96.30

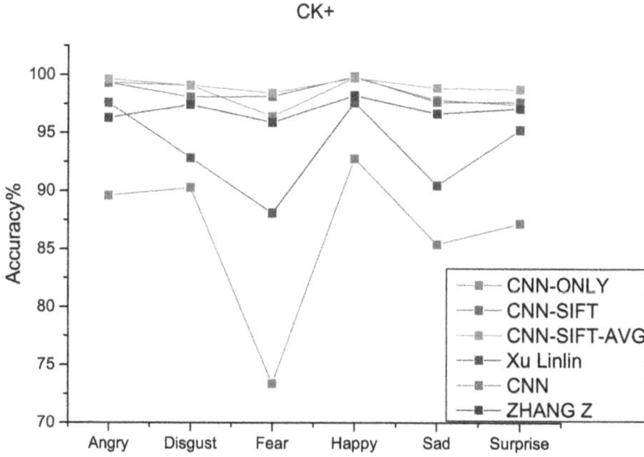

Fig. 11. Comparison of the accuracy of model recognition under CK+ dataset

Figure 12 shows the accuracy comparison of different model recognition in JAFFE data set. Table 4 compares the overall accuracy of JAFFE data set with other methods. The results show that both CNN-SIFT model and CNN-SIFT-AVG model are superior to the existing models. In particular, the recognition rate of CNN-SIFT-AVG model in JAFFE small sample database reaches 98.96%, which is 2 to 6 percentage points higher than other methods.

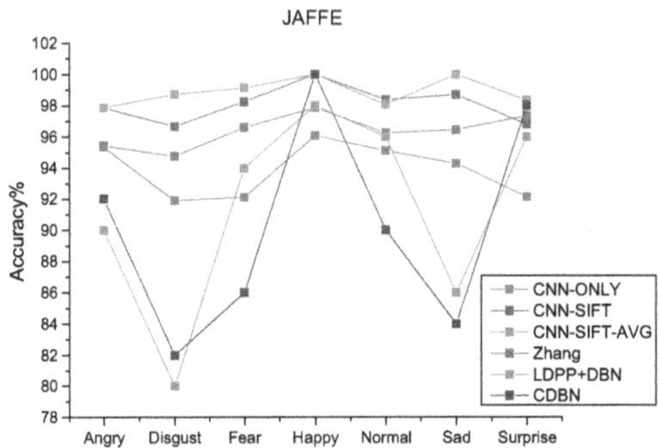

Fig. 12. Comparison of the accuracy of model recognition in JAFFE dataset (right)

Table 4. Comparison of overall recognition accuracy of JAFFE data set with other methods (%)

Model	Accuracy %
CNN-ONLY	93.86
CNN-SIFT	98.76
CNN-SIFT-AVG	98.96
ZHANG Z [22]	96.70
LDPP + DBN [23]	94.28
CDBN [24]	92.85

5 Conclusion

In this paper, an expression recognition method based on deep learning with different feature models is proposed to solve the problem of expression recognition rate in small sample data sets. This paper has shown how SIFT features and convolutional neural networks work together, and this hybrid method combines the advantages of the two methods. On the one hand, it makes full use of the advantages of SIFT that it does not need a large amount of data to extract features and improve the performance of small data. On the other hand, relatively suitable CNN is selected through comparison, and then features of SIFT are extracted and fused to summarize the model, which solves the problem that CNN needs a lot of data training and improves the accuracy of facial expression recognition under small samples. According to the experimental results, the CNN-SIFT-AVG model in this paper has obvious advantages and plays the role of SIFT in small samples to a large extent. The smaller the data is, the more obvious the improvement effect is.

Acknowledgment. This paper was supported in part by National Natural Science Foundation of China (62071157), Natural Science Foundation of Heilongjiang Province of China (No. F2015040), the Technology Research Project of Education Center in Heilongjiang Province (11551087).

References

1. Logie, R.H., Baddeley, A.D., Woodhead, M.M.: Face recognition, pose and ecological validity. Appl. Cogn. Psychol. **1**(1), 53–69 (2015)
2. Krizhevsky, A., Sutskever, I., Hinton, G.E.: ImageNet classification with deep convolutional neural networks. In: In Annual Conference on Neural Information Processing Systems 2012, United states, 3–6 December 2012, pp. 1106–1114. Neural Information Processing Systems Foundation (2012)
3. Russakovsky, O., Deng, J., Su, H., et al.: ImageNet large scale visual recognition challenge. Int. J. Comput. Vision **115**(3), 211–252 (2015)
4. Goodfellow, I.J., Erhan, D., Carrier, P.L., Courville, A., et al.: Challenges in representation learning: a report on three machine learning contests. Neural Netw. **64**, 59–63 (2015)
5. Mengyu, X., Zhenmin, T., Yazhou, Y., et al.: Deep learning for person reidentification using support vector machines. Adv. Multimedia **2017**, 11–18 (2017)
6. Wang, Y., Su, W.J., Liu, H.L.: Facial expression recognition based on linear discriminant locality preserving analysis algorithm. J. Inf. Comput. Sci. **9**(11), 4281–4289 (2013)
7. Owusu, E., Zhang, Y.Z.: An SVM-AdaBoost facial expression recognition system. Appl. Intell.**40**(3), 536–545 (2014)
8. Lekdioui, K., Messoussi, R.: Facial decomposition for expression recognition using texture/shape descriptors and SVM classifier. Sig. Process. Image Commun. **58**, 300–312 (2017)
9. Zhao, X.M., Shi, X.G., Zhang, S.Q.: Facial expression recognition via deep learning. IETE Tech. Rev. **32**(5), 347–355 (2014)
10. Wu, B.F., Lin, C.H.: Adaptive feature mapping for customizing deep learning based facial expression recognition model. IEEE Access **6**, 12451–12461 (2018)
11. Zeng, N.Y., Zhang, H., Song, B., et al.: Facial expression recognition via learning deep sparse autoencoders. Neurocomputing **273**, 643–649 (2018)
12. Zhang, T., Zheng, W.M., Cui, Z., et al.: A deep neural network-driven feature learning method for multi-view facial expression recognition. IEEE Trans. Multimedia **18**(12), 2528–2536 (2018)
13. Sun, X., Pan, T.: Static facial expression recognition system using ROI deep neural networks. Tien Tzu Hsueh Pao/Acta Electronica Sinica **45**(5), 1189–1197 (2017)
14. Yan, G.L., Deng, X.J., Liu, C.: Facial expression recognition model based on deep spatiotemporal convolutional neural networks. J. Central South Univ. (Sci. Technol.) **47**(7), 2311–2319 (2016)
15. Wen, G., Hou, Z., Li, H., et al.: Ensemble of deep neural networks with probability-based fusion for facial expression recognition. Cogn. Comput. **9**(5), 597–610 (2017)

16. Kaya, H., Gürpınar, F., Salah, A.A.: Video-based emotion recognition in the wild using deep transfer learning and score fusion. Image Vision Comput. **65**, 66–75 (2017)
17. Leng, X., Yang, J.H.: Research on improved SIFT algorithm. J. Chem. Pharm. Res. **6**(7), 2589–2595 (2014)
18. Zhou, S., Liang, Y., Wanf, J., et al.: Facial expression recognition based on multi-scale CNNs. In: You, Z., et al. (eds.) CCBR 2016. LNCS, vol. 9967, pp. 503–510. Springer, Cham (2016). https://doi.org/10.1007/978-3-319-46654-5_55
19. Liu, K., et al.: Facial expression recognition with CNN ensemble. In: Proceedings - 2016 International Conference on Cyberworlds, Chongqing, 28–30 September 2016, pp. 163–166. IEEE (2016)
20. Guo, Y., Tao, D., Yu, J.: Deep neural networks with relativity learning for facial expression recognition. In: 2016 IEEE International Conference on Multimedia and Expo Workshop, United states, 11–15 July 2016, pp. 166–170. IEEE (2016)
21. Xu, L.L., Zhang, S.M., Zhao, J.L.: Expression recognition algorithm for constructing parallel convolutional neural network. Chin. J. Image Graph.
22. Zhang, Z., Wang, R, Wei, M., et al.: Stacked hybrid auto-encoder facial expression recognition method. Comput. Eng. Appl. (2019)
23. Lee, H., Yan, L., Pham, P., et al.: Unsupervised feature learning for audio classification using convolutional deep belief networks. In: International Conference on Neural Information Processing Systems, pp. 1096–1104 (2009)

Design of Porcelain Insulator Defect Recognition System Based on UAV Line Inspection Image

Zhaoyu Li[1](✉), Zhong Zheng[1,2], Shuo Shi[1], and E. Rui[3]

[1] School of Electronic and Information Engineering, Harbin Institute of Technology, Harbin 150001, Heilongjiang, China
20S005028@stu.hit.edu.cn

[2] International Innovation Institute of HIT in Huizhou, Huizhou 516000, Guangdong, China

[3] Heilongjiang Polytechnic, Harbin 150001, Heilongjiang, China

Abstract. With the progress of technology and the improvement of equipment quality, the coverage of China's transmission network is expanding rapidly. Large power grids across complex and volatile terrain and dangerous high-voltage transmission lines are also being extended. Therefore, the traditional method of checking the circuit manually is no longer feasible due to its low efficiency, low precision, high risk and high cost. However, unmanned aerial vehicles (uavs) are a perfect way to circumvent these problems by inspecting transmission lines instead of workers. This paper takes the application of unmanned aerial vehicle in power line patrol as the research background, takes the porcelain vase in power transmission as an example, and realizes the image recognition and damage judgment system of the porcelain vase with specific target. Based on the image processing technology of machine learning and MATLAB, the target detection method of YOLO v3, the semantic segmentation method of Deeplab v3+, and the improved damage analysis method of ellipse fitting were respectively used to make the damage judgment and analysis of porcelain vats based on the intelligent image recognition interception, contour extraction and semantic segmentation. In the actual site of 166 porcelain bottles damage detection, damage detection accuracy reached 86.7%. Finally, the identification system of porcelain vase defect is realized.

Keywords: UAV · Image processing · Semantic segmentation

1 Introduction

1.1 Research Status

UAV technology includes image processing, electronic technology, flight technology, and automatic control. In the UAV power inspection circuit, image processing is a necessary step for the system to finally obtain intuitive results [1].

Since 2014, the State Grid Corporation of China has successively convened ten pilot units, established drone inspection bases in Shandong and Wuhan, and established a professional drone training college for power systems in Laiwu City, Shandong Province.

© ICST Institute for Computer Sciences, Social Informatics and Telecommunications Engineering 2022
Published by Springer Nature Switzerland AG 2022. All Rights Reserved
S. Shi et al. (Eds.): 6GN 2021, LNICST 439, pp. 397–408, 2022.
https://doi.org/10.1007/978-3-031-04245-4_35

Provide talents for the development of mechanical and electrical inspections. At the same time, power companies in various regions have established a special drone system and a complete drone inspection business process. At the same time, the State Grid Chongqing Electric Power Company has realized the establishment of a three-dimensional model of the transmission line, and has made phased progress in the visualization of the inspection system. The State Grid Zhejiang Power Transmission and Transformation Company realized the construction of high tower lines in January 2019. Among them, the tower is 380 m high and uses drone traction and unwinding technology. The application of this technology can greatly reduce costs and operational risks., While effectively improving work efficiency. The success of this project is of great significance for UAV power line inspection [2, 3].

At present, according to the latest data released by the State Grid Corporation of China, the efficiency of UAV line inspection is 8 to 10 times that of manual line inspection. In the current power line inspection work, UAV power line inspection is in actual production. The application in life has also reached 1/2. It is not difficult to see that in the near future, UAV power line inspection will become the most important and most widely used inspection method for power grid units [4].

In 2000, an unmanned aerial vehicle for transmission line inspections was developed by scholars at the University of Wales in the United Kingdom. Electric energy can be extracted automatically from the running line, and the distance to the inspection line is very close, so there will be no problem of crossing with other waterways. The design scheme has passed the feasibility verification.

Japan's current research on the application of UAV line inspection systems to transmission lines is relatively mature. The system can already realize automatic fault detection, three-dimensional image monitoring, and automatic detection of lightning flashover points, the inclination of towers, the rust of iron tower materials, and whether cement poles are automatically detected. There are major defects such as cracks.

Australia's GSIRO Research Institute has completed the design of a fully automated line patrol UAV. Due to its advantages such as long endurance, stable flight status, high definition of collected images, and good detection effect, it is currently at the forefront of research on UAV line patrol.

Based on GPS positioning and computer vision analysis, Mejias and others of the Polytechnic University of Madrid, Spain, focused on the design of the navigation system in the process of UAV patrol. They have made innovative progress in UAV navigation and target positioning, and added automatic Obstacle avoidance function, this research has made breakthroughs in improving the accuracy of fault detection and the safety of UAV flight and landing [5].

In general, the research on UAV inspection systems in developed countries has not only completed the hardware part, but most of them have been paying attention to the later image and video processing, and a few have begun to use higher-end Lidar UAV applications [6–8].

1.2 The Research Method and Content of This Article

This article takes porcelain bottles as an example, aiming at the images taken by the UAV during the line inspection process, aiming to realize that the system can automatically and intelligently identify whether the electrical equipment is intact without manual intervention. Thereby reducing the workload of line inspection and manual screening of images in the later stage, which has certain practical value corresponding to the actual production.

Based on the YOLO v3 model and Deeplab v3+ model, this design intelligently recognizes and intercepts the exterior porcelain bottle images taken by the drone, and performs semantic segmentation on the intercepted independent images. Finally, the algorithm is used to determine whether the porcelain bottle is damaged according to the contour of the porcelain bottle. And carried on the simulation test to the above content.

2 Target Detection Part

2.1 YOLO Overview

In recent years, machine learning algorithms have developed rapidly. Among many image processing technologies, machine learning-based image processing technologies are increasingly becoming mainstream. In this design, a target detection technology based on the YOLO (You Only Look Once) algorithm is used.

YOLO is the abbreviation of You Only Look Once proposed by Redmon and Diccala, and is currently and updated to the third generation. The model algorithm is based on the deep neural network, and finally realizes the identification and positioning of the target. Its advantage lies in the extremely high efficiency, so it can be used in projects with high real-time requirements [10–12].

The fast detection speed of YOLO (You Only Look Once) is attributable to its use of regression to analog target detection. In order to achieve end-to-end recognition, YOLO directly predicts the parameters of the box surrounding the target in the original image. Compared with early algorithms such as edge detection algorithm and directional gradient histogram algorithm, it has the advantages of high accuracy and stronger robustness [13].

2.2 The Structure and Algorithm of YOLO

YOLO merges the candidate areas, so the overall structure presents a five-layer structure of first input layer, then 24 convolutional layers, then pooling layer, and finally 2 fully connected layers and output layer, as shown in Fig. 1. By improving R-CNN, YOLO extracts image features by using a convolutional neural network that is more suitable for target detection, and then improves the use of fully connected layers to detect target positions and types, thereby greatly improving the running speed and detection accuracy [14].

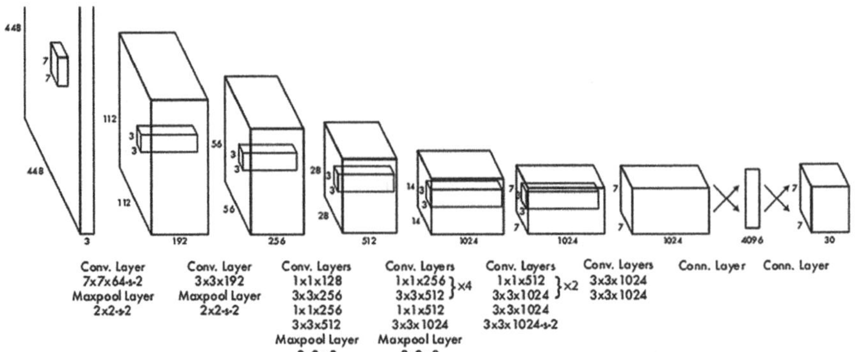

Fig. 1. The structure of the YOLO

As shown in Fig. 1, the leftmost is the input layer of YOLO, as the entrance to the entire network, it is responsible for image preprocessing, which corresponds to the process of generating feature maps in the convolutional neural network. The input layer of YOLO has no requirements for the number of input image pixels. Through the normalization of the original image, proportional cropping, image enhancement and other processing, as well as the decomposition of the RGB (red, yellow and blue) three channels in the color image. Superimposed, the output of YOLO's input layer is an image with a fixed pixel size of 448 * 448 * 3 in each dimension. On the right side of the input layer are 24 convolutional layers. Their function is to convolve the result feature map produced in the previous step. Through a series of convolutions and operations, the feature information in the feature map is refined. This information will be used for subsequent target detection, positioning and classification [14].

2.3 Improvements in YOLO V3

The main idea of the YOLOv3 algorithm is to absorb the advantages of the major algorithms, and to further improve efficiency while maintaining the performance of the previous version. In addition, the YOLO v3 version has made innovative adjustments to the detection of small targets and achieved significant results. Effectiveness. Among them, the most exciting improvement is embodied in the proposal of Darknet-53 backbone network and multi-scale feature detection.

The basic network structure of YOLO v3, which contains many 1 * 1 * 3 * 3 size convolution operations, which are mainly used to extract image features. After each convolution, there is a normalization operation and an activation operation of Leaky RELU. A 1 * 1 layer and a 3 * 3 layer are superimposed together as a frame, and the produced frame is superimposed with the frame of the previous layer to produce a frame difference. Then increase the speed (step size) of the convolution kernel to downsample the image. In addition, YOLO v3 replaces the fully connected layer in the previous version of the neural network with a 1 * 1 * 3 * 3 convolutional layer, and outputs the results in three different sizes of feature layers [15–17].

2.4 YOLO V3 Algorithm Target Detection

Environment Configuration

Darknet is an open source code. After downloading from the official website, install it according to the specific situation of the computer.

Production of Data Set

Use labeling to select the target, and the resulting labeled image is shown in Fig. 2. And use the VOC2007 format as a template to make a data set.

Fig. 2. The production of VOC data set

Model Training

Use the prepared data set to train the YOLOv3 model in Darknet until a certain weight file is output.

Model Test

Use drone aerial images to test the trained data set, and the model test result after training is shown in Fig. 3.

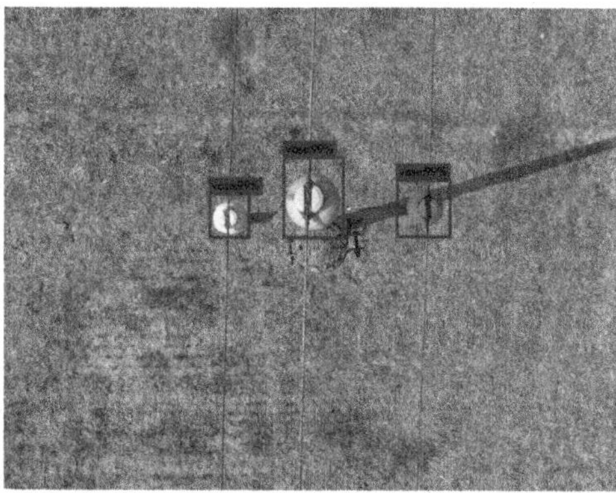

Fig. 3. YOLO v3 model target detection results

3 Semantic Segmentation Module Based on Deeplab Algorithm

3.1 Introduction of the Deeplab Model

DeepLab is a semantic segmentation method with the main idea structure including deep convolutional neural networks (DCNNs) and fully connected conditional random field models (DenseCRFs).

It organically combines the outermost layer of the deep convolutional neural network with the conditional random domain, mainly absorbs the hole convolution algorithm, broadens the receptive field to obtain the image information of the farther area of the edge of the marked object contour, so as to realize the improvement of the neural network. The positioning accuracy is as high as 71.6% in the semantic image segmentation task of the Pascal voc dataset in 2012. And faster running speed can be obtained on GPU [18].

3.2 Optimization History of Deeplab

The Deeplab series has now been updated to the v3+ version, and the entire series shows a trend of continuous optimization. For the Deeplab v2 version, there are two main improvements compared to the previous version. One is that the VGG16 embodied in

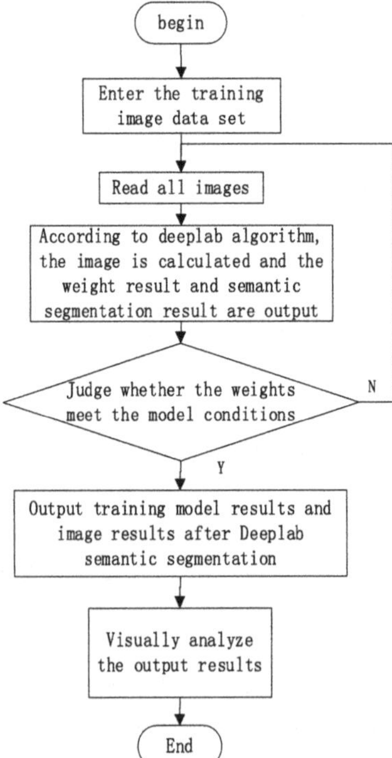

Fig. 4. The semantic segmentation part structure

the base layer is used in the v3+ version. It is ResNet, which obtains more accurate segmentation results than the previous version. The second is to add "porous spatial pyramid pooling", thereby increasing the multi-scale nature of segmentation.

Deeplab v3+ version adds the decoder part on the basis of Deeplab v3 version. Specifically, the entire process of the v3 version is used as an encoder in the v3+ version structure, and a part of it is added as a Deeplab v3+ version of the decoder at the back end. Therefore, the v3+ version presents a new encoder-decoder structure as a whole.The semantic segmentation part is shown in Fig. 4 [25–27].

Next, the semantically segmented data set was made as shown in Fig. 5

Fig. 5. Production of semantically segmented data sets

The Deeplab v3+ version uses dilated convolution to control and adjust the resolution extracted by the decoder, thereby improving the operating efficiency while maintaining the accuracy of the results. The semantic segmentation results of the target contour of the deeplab model is shown as Fig. 6.

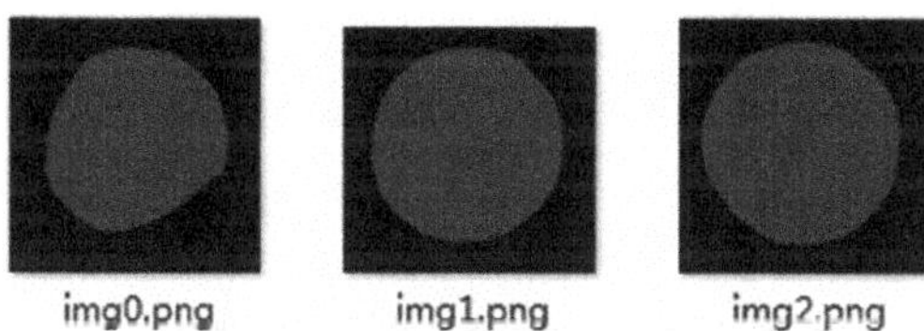

Fig. 6. Semantic segmentation results of the target contour of the deeplab model

4 Ceramic Vase Contour Damage Identification Module

4.1 Edge Detection

Edge detection is to extract the transform discontinuous part from the original image, that is, the image edge. Boundary information is hidden in the edge of an image. Edge detection provides a basis for further image processing and analysis using this information. At the same time, because edge detection can weaken a lot of useless information and noise in the image at the same time can retain the basic object characteristics. It also has the function of reducing workload and improving efficiency [28–30].

4.2 Canny Operator

The Canny operator organically combines the first derivative with the Gaussian function, and adds optimization ideas. The Canny operator advocates three principles: low error rate, high positioning accuracy, and unilateral response. Using the symmetry and variable separability of the two-dimensional Gaussian function effectively improves the accuracy of edge detection [31, 32].

Canny's edge detection operator is relatively complete and robust, with high accuracy of detection results, and can automatically eliminate false edges. But its disadvantage is that the amount of calculation is large and the adaptability is poor, that is, the output picture is not clear [33].

4.3 Fitting the Contours of Porcelain Vases

As shown in Fig. 7, in the image of the porcelain bottle taken by the drone, the image on the left is the image of the complete porcelain bottle, and the image on the right is the image of the damaged porcelain bottle, and their respective contours are shown in Fig. 8. The contour of the porcelain bottle image processed by deeplab is very obvious, so the accuracy of the edge detection operator is not high. In view of the smooth curve fitting in the next step, the design selects the canny operator for edge extraction.

Fig. 7. Image comparison of intact and damaged porcelain bottles

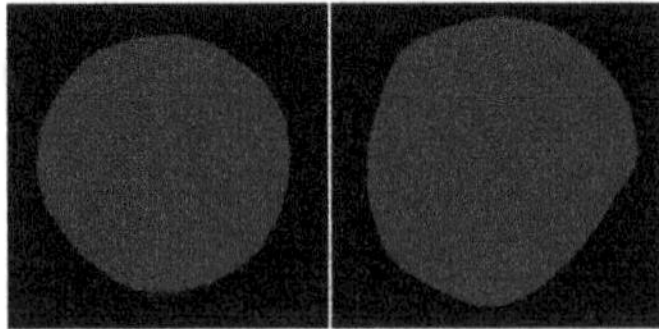

Fig. 8. Comparison of the contours of complete and damaged porcelain bottles

It can be seen that the outline of the upside down image of the complete porcelain bottle is close to a perfect circle, while the upside down image of the damaged porcelain bottle is an irregular figure.

Due to exposure to the wild, the damage of porcelain bottles is mostly out of control. In practice, we found that the damage of the porcelain bottle will appear to be close to an oval after damage as shown in Fig. 9.

Fig. 9. Approximately oval porcelain bottle image after damage

After fitting it to an ordinary ellipse, the result is shown in Fig. 10.

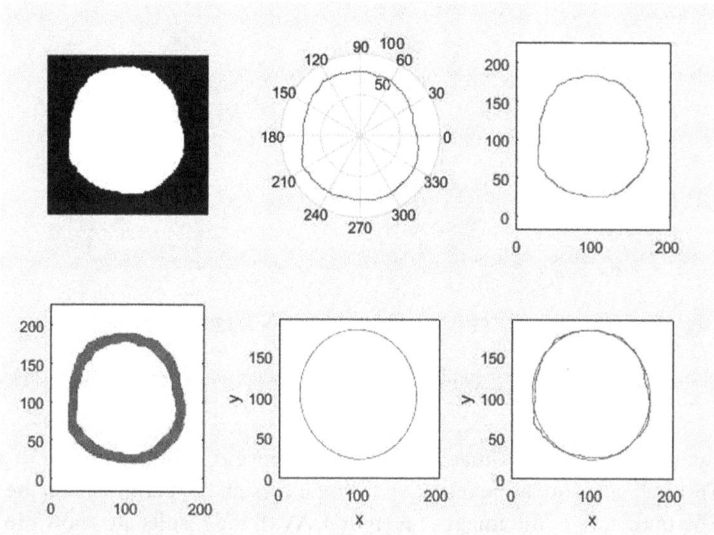

Fig. 10. Ellipse fitting to approximate the contour of an elliptical porcelain bottle after damage

The contour of the damaged porcelain bottle is very similar to the contour after the ordinary ellipse fitting, so ordinary ellipse fitting cannot be used. The method used in this article is to simulate and restore the state before the damage. Assuming that the contour edge before the damage is a standard ellipse, calculate the difference between before and after the damage Error to get a quantified damage index.

The algorithm steps are as follows:

(1) Binarize the output result of the semantic segmentation of the Deeplab v2 model into a grayscale image with only two colors of black and white.
(2) Using the edge detection algorithm, this paper uses the sobel operator for edge extraction to obtain the single-line image of the contour of the porcelain bottle.
(3) Set up the ellipse equation, fit the contour to the ellipse, and find its geometric center.

(4) Declare the identification variables. If the fitted ellipse contour has an intersection with the actual contour, the ellipse contour will be enlarged to 1.01 times the original ellipse until the circumscribed ellipse of the actual contour of the porcelain bottle is approximated.
(5) Use the improved standard deviation algorithm to calculate the fitting error between the contour of the external ellipse and the contour of the original porcelain bottle.
(6) Draw up the threshold through a large amount of data statistics.

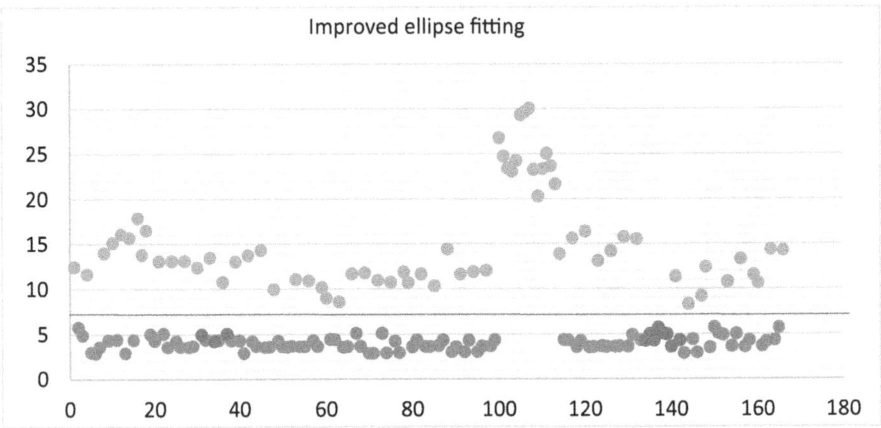

Fig. 11. Experimental results are fitted with improved ellipse

The algorithm can approximate the minimum envelope fitting ellipse of the vase contour. Through subsequent quantitative fitting errors and experiments on the existing data set (166 porcelain bottle images taken by UAVs), the results are shown in Fig. 11. As you can see, the available data are within reasonable bounds.

5 Conclusion

In this paper, a damage detection method based on YOLO_v3 and Deeplab_v3+ machine learning models is designed. Considering the randomness of the shape of damaged porcelain bottles, the existing ellipse fitting algorithm is improved to realize whether the porcelain bottles are damaged. In the experimental data, the experimental accuracy is 100%, and in the actual production, the accuracy is 86.7%. This paper puts forward a solution to the difficult problem of long-distance transmission equipment detection, which is of practical significance to production practice.

References

1. Peng, X., Liu, Z., Mai, X., Luo, Z., Wang, K., Xie, X.: UAV power line safety inspection system and key technologies. Remote Sens. Inf. 51–57 (2015)

2. Yao, W.: Research on UAV Power Line Inspection Technology, Guangdong University of Technology (2019)
3. Alvarez, L.M.: A visual servoing approach for tracking features in urban areas using an autonomous helicopter. In: Proceedings 2006 IEEE International Conference on Robotics and Automation, 2006, pp. 2503–2508 (2006)
4. Chen, Y.: UAV Power Line Detection Based on Image Recognition. Hangzhou Dianzi University (2018)
5. Chang, C.: Special issue on development of autonomous unmanned aerial vehicles. Mechatronics **21**(5) (2011)
6. Fu,Y., Li, Z., Jiang, H.: Research on the development and application of UAV line inspection. Heilongjiang Sci. Technol. Inform. (2014)
7. Lu, J.: Application of image processing technology in UAV power line inspection. Commun. Power Technol. **36**(06), 84–85 (2019)
8. Luo, X.: Research on UAV Power Inspection Route Planning Based on Fish School Algorithm . Nanchang University (2019)
9. Miao, X., Liu, Z., Yan, Q.: Overview of UAV transmission line intelligent inspection technology. J. Fuzhou Univ. (Natl. Sci. Ed.) **48**(02), 198–209 (2020)
10. Redmon, J., Divvala, S., Girshick, R., Farhadi, A.: You only look once: unified, real-time object detection. In: 2016 IEEE Conference on Computer Vision and Pattern Recognition (CVPR), pp. 779–788 (2015)
11. Redmon, J., Ali, F.: YOLO9000: better, faster, stronger. In: 2017 IEEE Conference on Computer Vision and Pattern Recognition (CVPR), pp. 6517–6525 (2017)
12. Lv, H.: Design and implementation of automatic aiming system based on YOLO. In: Sun Yat-sen University, East China Normal University, Singapore International Association for Computer Science and Information Technology, pp. 426–432 (2019)
13. Guo, J., Chen, B., Wang, R., Wang, J., Zhong, L.: Real-time inspection of UAV power line tower inspection images based on YOLO. China Electr. Power **52**(07), 17–23 (2019)
14. Ruan, J.: Design and Implementation of Target Detection Algorithm Based on YOLO. Beijing University of Posts and Telecommunications (2019)
15. Redmon, J., Farhadi, A.: YOLOv3: An Incremental Improvement. ArXiv (2018)
16. Liu, L.: Research on Intelligent Traffic Traffic Statistics Based on YOLO Network. Xi'an University of Science and Technology (2019)
17. Fang, Z.: Research on pedestrian detection technology in road traffic environment based on YOLOv3 . South China University of Technology (2019)
18. Chen, L., Papandreou, G., Kokkinos, I., Murphy, K., Yuille, A.: Semantic image segmentation with deep convolutional nets and fully connected CRFs (2014)
19. Wang, Y., Feng, F.: Road scene semantic segmentation method based on fully connected conditional random field. Comput. Knowl. Technol. **15**(18), 212–214 (2019)
20. Zhang, Q., Zhao, X.: Application of SIFT algorithm in feature extraction of UAV remote sensing images. Henan Water Conserv. South-to-North Water Diversion **48**(11), 63–65 (2019)
21. Chen, L., Papandreou, G., Kokkinos, I., Murphy, K., Yuille, A.: DeepLab: semantic image segmentation with deep convolutional nets, atrous convolution, and fully connected CRFs. IEEE Trans. Pattern Analy. Mach. Intell. **40**(4), 834–848 (2018)
22. Chen, L., Papandreou, G., Schroff, F., Adam, H.: Rethinking Atrous Convolution for Semantic Image Segmentation (2017)
23. Teichmann, M.T., Cipolla, R.: Convolutional CRFs for Semantic Segmentation (2018)
24. Ren, F., He, X., Wei, Z., Lu, Y., Li, M.: Semantic segmentation based on DeepLabV3+ and superpixel optimization. Opt. Precis. Eng. **27**(12), 2722–2729 (2019)
25. Chen, L, Yukun, Z., George, P., Florian, S., Hartwig, A.: Encoder-decoder with atrous separable convolution for semantic image segmentation. In: Proceedings of the European Conference on Computer Vision (ECCV), pp. 801–818 (2018)

26. Zhao, Y., Rao, Y., Dong, S., Zhang, J.: A review of deep learning target detection methods. J. Image Graph. **25**(04), 629–654 (2020)
27. Varghese, A., Gubbi, J., Sharma, H., Balamuralidhar, P.: Power infrastructure monitoring and damage detection using drone captured images. In: 2017 International Joint Conference on Neural Networks (IJCNN), pp. 1681–1687 IEEE (2017)
28. Chen, L., Papandreou, G., Kokkinos, I., Murphy, K., Yuille, A.: DeepLab: semantic image segmentation with deep convolutional nets, atrous, convolution, and fully connected CRFs. IEEE Trans. Pattern Anal. Mach. Intell. **40**(4), 834–848 (2018)
29. Kuang, H., Wu, J.: A review of research on image semantic segmentation technology based on deep learning. Comput. Eng. Appl. **55**(19), 12–21 (2019)
30. Yang, W.: Research on key technologies and methods of image semantic segmentation based on deep learning . Nanjing University of Posts and Telecommunications (2019)
31. Liu, Z., Zhang, Z.: Overview of semantic object segmentation technology. J. Shanghai Univ. (Natl. Sci. Ed.) 477–484 (2007)
32. Zhao, X., et al:. A review of semantic segmentation algorithms based on deep learning . Shanghai Aerosp. **36**(05), 71–82 (2019)
33. Hu, T., Li, W., Qin, X.: Overview of image semantic segmentation methods. Measur. Control Technol. **38**(07), 8–12 (2019)

Research on Digital Curriculum Resources Construction of Modern Agronomic Technology Specialty

JunHong Zhong, XiuLian Lin, and Zhenyu Xu(✉)

Huizhou Engineering Vocational College, Huizhou, China
hitusa@126.com

Abstract. The vigorous development of the planting industry is inseparable from the support of modern agricultural technology and talents.

With the popularization of modern information technology applications and the continuous deepening of teaching reforms, the teaching mode and teaching methods of secondary vocational schools increasingly rely on modern education technology with information technology, network technology and multimedia technology as the core. The article mainly elaborates the existing problems, construction principles, research content, research results, etc. of the construction of digital curriculum resources for modern agronomic technology majors, in order to improve the quality of talent training, and provide reference and reference for brother colleges and universities.

Keywords: Modern agronomic technology · Digitalization · Curriculum resource construction

1 Introduction

The "14th Five-Year Plan" of the education industry emphasizes: "Implement the Education Informatization 2.0 Action Plan, and basically achieve the development goals of "Three Alls, Two Highs, One Big" by 2025, that is, digital campus construction covers all schools and teaching applications cover all teachers, Learning applications cover all students, the level of informatization application and the information literacy of teachers and students have generally improved, and a large platform of "Internet+ Education" has been built to promote the transformation from educational resources to educational resources, from enhancing teachers and students' information technology application capabilities to comprehensively improving their Information literacy changes, from integrated applications to innovative development, and strive to build a new model of talent training under the conditions of "Internet + ", develop a new model of Internet-based education services, and explore a new model of education governance in the information age."

The modern agronomic technology major mainly trains students to develop in the direction of agronomists, fungus gardeners, vegetable gardeners, crop plant protection

© ICST Institute for Computer Sciences, Social Informatics and Telecommunications Engineering 2022
Published by Springer Nature Switzerland AG 2022. All Rights Reserved
S. Shi et al. (Eds.): 6GN 2021, LNICST 439, pp. 409–417, 2022.
https://doi.org/10.1007/978-3-031-04245-4_36

workers, and agricultural product brokers. In the process of reform and opening up, the modern agrotechnical specialty of secondary vocational schools has actively adapted to the needs of reform and economic construction, and has achieved considerable development. It has trained a large number of professional and technical personnel for the planting industry in my country, especially in rural areas. In Guangdong, modern agronomic technology has played a pivotal role in cultivating planting technical talents, especially with the improvement of people's living standards, people's demand for horticultural products continues to increase, and the planting industry is developing rapidly. However, with the continuous advancement of agricultural science and technology and the continuous adjustment of the industrial layout, the current secondary vocational modern agronomy professional teaching has been lagging, especially the lagging of talent training in emerging industries, and the instability of rural scientific and technological teams have severely restricted the entire planting industry. development of. Therefore, the training of modern agronomic technology professionals needs reform, and it is particularly important to innovate training models and training methods.

With the popularization of computers and networks, digitization of information has become a major trend in economic and social development in the world today, and an important indicator of the comprehensive strength, core competitiveness and modernization degree of countries and regions. The profound changes that digital technology has brought to education have brought about a qualitative leap in educational thoughts, concepts, models, methods, and methods. The construction of digital campus in higher vocational colleges is an inevitable choice for the implementation of informatization in our country's education reform, and it plays an important role in promoting teaching reform and informatization in higher vocational colleges [1].

Digital curriculum resources are the core of the construction of digital teaching environment. It is based on digitalization, with subjects and majors as the main line, and courses as the center. It integrates teaching plans, curriculum settings, syllabus and other teaching documents and teachers' handouts, courseware, and reference materials., Multimedia resources and other types of teaching resources, and integrate the integrated resources into the teaching process organically, providing teachers and students with a full range of practical teaching information and teaching reference resource services.

Make full use of modern informatization methods, transform teaching methods, integrate them with modern information technology, improve the current deficiencies in modern agronomic technology training and teaching, realize the optimization and sharing of educational resources, realize technological changes in education, and transform learning methods The purpose of improving teaching quality has become an urgent task. Modern agronomic technology is a major with strong practicality. Due to factors such as limited equipment, it has brought many difficulties to the teaching of this major in schools. Only by using information technology and teaching resources, can we keep up with technological updates without a large increase in the investment of hardware equipment, ensure the training of students' learning skills and operation, and ensure the quality of teaching [2].

2 Principles for the Construction of Digital Curriculum Resources for Modern Agronomic Technology Majors

2.1 Scientific Principle

The construction of the digital curriculum teaching resource database must conform to the learning rules of secondary vocational students and the rules of secondary vocational education, and achieve the purpose of "be able to learn" and "assisted learning". The professional curriculum teaching resource library not only has the top-level design of talent training at the macro level, but also has the curriculum development and resource construction at the micro level [3]. In the construction, the teaching is implemented according to the content, environment and process of the production activities of the enterprise, so that the professional teaching mode is connected with the actual production of the enterprise. There should be teaching resources, curriculum standards, corporate job standards, corporate project cases, and the latest industry information in the resource database to meet the needs of talent training, curriculum learning, and corporate positions.

2.2 Practicality Principle

Digital curriculum resources of modern agronomy technology, integrating four courses of flower cultivation, vegetable cultivation, edible fungus cultivation, and plant disease and insect pest control, and realize the organic integration of information technology and course teaching goals, so that teachers and students can achieve the course in the course of doing, teaching and learning. Harmony and unity can effectively improve the quality of teaching by applying modern educational methods [4].

2.3 Standardization Principle

The construction of the digital teaching resource management platform, such as organizational arrangements, framework structure, etc., needs to be unified with relevant standards, conform to the habits of online learning, and facilitate students to achieve personalized learning. All types of digital teaching resources, from texts to various materials, must be standardized to facilitate upload, download, use and update. The organizational structure should be rigorous, reasonable, and orderly to facilitate accurate and convenient data extraction and safe and controllable platform management. In addition, an intelligent feedback evaluation mechanism should be set up to meet interactivity requirements [5].

2.4 Openness Principle

At present, many digital curriculum resource developers are mainly enterprise software designers, with few teachers, students and other personnel participating, making the resource development software lack of practicality, effectiveness, and system. Therefore, developers are required to develop curriculum resources. Pay attention to content diversity, interactivity, scalability, etc. One is the participation of multiple parties in the development. The teaching resource library is jointly constructed by the government, schools, industry enterprises, and development units. The school teaching team is the main body of the curriculum resource library. The construction of digital resources should start from the perspective of the demand for talents in corporate jobs and introduce standardized professional qualifications and job skills standards to provide skills guarantee for the training of professional talents. The second is the common use of resources. The professional teaching resource bank is a platform for schools, industries, and the government to cooperate in educating people and social services. The construction results must be opened to the outside world in a certain way, and the teaching and learning functions of the resource bank must be fully utilized. The effect of "feeding back".

2.5 Sustainability Principle

Digital curriculum resources allow teachers and students to study any curriculum in a way that suits them at any time and any place. Teachers and students can add new resources and new information to the resource library anytime and anywhere, and open it to the whole society, and can form a lifelong education system, so that the construction of digital curriculum resources can continue to develop.22.

3 The Construction of Digital Course Teaching Resource Database

3.1 Build a Digital Course Learning System

Build a digital course learning support platform for modern agronomic technology integration training room; build a digital courseware resource management system for modern agronomic technology integration training room. At the same time, through the integrated training room high-definition teaching video recording and broadcasting system, it can collect a variety of scene teaching videos, and automatically store the videos in the resource storage system, and integrate with the learning support platform.

The types of teaching resources for digital courses include text, graphics, audio, video, animation, virtual simulation and other materials. The development of digital curriculum teaching resources is mainly based on video and animation. This article mainly introduces the design ideas and development points of curriculum resources.

Practice training is an important part of vocational education teaching activities. The teaching design of digital training courses needs to be integrated into the company's job skill standards, and combined with the common characteristics of teaching practice demonstrations and job skill operations. Text scripts should not be copied directly from the textbooks, and the content of the textbooks should be creatively reconstructed in accordance with professional standards, so as to be as simple and understandable as possible. There are four key steps in the instructional design process of digital training courses:

The first step: clarify the theme and import the content. There are many ways to introduce the teaching design of digital courses of practical training type, such as situation introduction, old knowledge introduction, problem introduction and so on. Different import methods have their own characteristics, but they must be concise and clear, and the import time should not be too long.

The second step: clarify the principle and clarify the requirements. Secondary vocational students have a weak foundation, so they should simply point out the principles before practical training and demonstration. If complex content is involved and cannot be reviewed quickly, the teacher can provide guidance. In addition, it is necessary to clearly explain the requirements of the training, such as the use requirements of materials, equipment operation requirements, and industry vocational skills requirements, so that the teaching process can be seamlessly connected with the production process of the enterprise.

Step 3: Show the production (principle) process. Demonstrating the training operation process is the top priority of the entire digital course, accounting for 60%–70% of the entire duration, and usually includes the training process, operation steps, and training phenomena. The presentation of this link should highlight the principles of clarity and smoothness, student-oriented, simplified complexity, key points, combination of virtual and reality, appropriate scaling, and ease of communication. Try to remove all redundant information that affects effective communication and reduce the cognitive load of learners.

The fourth step: Summarize and expand. The end of the digital course should be a refinement of the entire process, not "top-heavy". If it is imported as a question, the answer to the imported question is clearly given, and the answer is echoed from the beginning to the end. At the end of the digital course, the content should be summarized and expanded in order to enhance the learning effect and form a knowledge system structure [6].

3.2 On the Learning System

Four courses have been uploaded: "Floriculture, Vegetable Cultivation, Edible Fungus Cultivation, Plant Disease and Pest Control, etc.". Among them, specific teaching resources include course introductions, course standards, electronic teaching plans, teaching PPT, related videos, related teaching courseware, exercises and test question banks (including homework/test papers), digital teaching materials, etc. The development of digital courses in vocational education should first extract typical work tasks according to the needs of vocational positions, list the exercise steps of the experiment, require a clear demonstration process, grasp the demonstration time, and use short videos to solve a certain knowledge point or a certain point as efficiently as possible. Teaching link. The presentation of knowledge points or teaching links is modularized, which helps relieve the fatigue of students' attention and strengthen the construction of professional knowledge. The development of digital courses is based on close-ups, clearly highlighting the process of skill action (craft), enhancing the continuity of the picture, and removing irrelevant information. The subtitles of digital courses are presented in the form of "full subtitles+ keyword groups", in which the keyword groups are presented in different colors or fonts, which can attract the physical sensory attention of students, and can also emphasize the key points and key content of the picture to arouse students' psychology Attention to the above, ultimately achieve the optimization of the micro-course design and development and the maximization of learning efficiency. The fine and important skill actions are displayed in the form of animation, which promotes students to better understand the principle of skill and the action process. If individual action screens display various information, they will be presented in the form of "virtual reality", which is convenient for showing the actual operation or realization principle and enhancing the presentation of content [7].

3.3 On the Basis of the Original School-Level High-Quality Courses

Continue to improve and revitalize the digital teaching resources of flower cultivation, vegetable cultivation, edible fungus cultivation, and plant disease and insect pest control. The built teaching resources include course introduction, course standards, electronic teaching plans, teaching PPT, and related videos., Relevant teaching courseware, exercises and test question bank (including homework/test papers), digital teaching materials, etc., and archive these resources and update them continuously.

The construction of the digital curriculum teaching resource management platform must start with the top-level design of talent training. First, industry research, analysis of job positions, extraction of typical tasks, and clarification of the needs of the enterprise; and then clarify the platform's requirements according to the requirements of professional curriculum teaching and the needs of students. The functional framework can not only meet the learning of professional core competence, but also take into account the knowledge expansion and ability improvement. The digital course learning platform mainly includes interactive teaching module, courseware resource management module, online resource playing module, course exchange discussion module, Q&A module, assignment/submission/check module, test question bank, etc. In addition, the curriculum resources have added resources such as the corporate technical personnel curriculum library, the corporate management file library, and the professional standard library.

In vocational education, the curriculum is composed of each project, and the project is the basic component and carrier of the construction of fragmented teaching resources. The teaching resource management platform stores teaching resources in fragments, and teachers can combine and reconstruct the fragmented resources according to the learning needs of students. The construction of the vocational education teaching resource database should strengthen the connection between the curriculum content and the regional industry vocational standards, and break the original linear curriculum system. On the digital course learning platform, teachers create courses, create assignments, and create test questions by adding digital teaching resources. Students choose the courses they need to learn through this platform, watch videos and animations, read text resources, participate in online course discussions and teaching evaluations, complete homework online, and participate in exams.

3.4 Solve the Problem of Sharing High-Quality Teaching Resources

The function of the teaching resource library is to promote the "learning" of students and the "teaching" of teachers. The content of the resource library not only contains the teaching elements of the courses, but also has the elements of industry enterprises. The professional teaching team is the main body of the resource library construction. The main task is to provide necessary professional teaching materials, write digital course scripts, and integrate various teaching resources. To give full play to the importance of school-enterprise cooperation, the construction of the resource database needs to integrate the company's job requirements standards and technical (technical) standards. The development unit is responsible for video shooting and editing, platform construction and debugging, and teaching resource integration. In addition, students are not only users of the resource library, but also participants in construction. In the process of use, they can feed back their opinions on the use of the resource library, upload excellent works, share resources, and further promote the construction of resource banks. By establishing a unified learning support platform and resource management platform, and realizing the seamless connection between the resource management platform and the learning support platform, it is conducive to help teachers sort out resources and teaching ideas, and is conducive to the management, preservation and sharing of excellent resources in the school.

4 Research Results

4.1 The Establishment of a Modern Agronomic Technology Information Teaching Resource Database Has Realized Efficient Teaching

This information-based teaching resource library uses text, pictures, 3D, animation, video and other file formats to refine, simplify, and digitize complex skills teaching content with the help of computer technology, which has high promotion and application value. At present, there are 4 courses of flower cultivation, vegetable cultivation, edible fungus cultivation, and plant disease and insect pest control. There are a total of 120 PPT presentations, 300 pictures, 78 videos, teaching standards, teaching plans, teaching design, 12 sets of question banks, There are 200 classroom tests and 30 cases. The construction of the above resources enables teachers and students to teach anytime and anywhere, especially under the current normal situation of the new crown epidemic, the construction of a teaching resource database breaks the time and space constraints and realizes efficient teaching.

4.2 Through the Construction of a Learning Support Platform, the Network Learning Space Is Connected to Everyone

The network-based access and the use of the learning management platform provide students in the classroom with an environment where they can learn, inquire, submit questions and homework at any time. This makes learning change from a teacher-led and one-way teaching model to student discovery and active learning. It has also changed the traditional teaching that "you can only ask the teacher if you don't understand, and you can only watch it once for demonstration"; cultivate students to learn independently Habits also reduce the intensity of teachers' work.

By opening the online classroom regularly during the self-study period, allowing students to log on to the learning platform, watch videos and courseware, and conduct pre-class and post-class review as required, changing the traditional teaching situation where students can only learn from boring textbooks and text when they leave the workshop, Improve the effect of self-study classes, and promote the actual effect of project-based teaching with students as the main body.

4.3 Build a Resource Management Platform to Achieve High-Quality Resource Class-to-Class Communication

Create a modern model of teaching and learning, improve the reuse rate of teaching resources, set up a high-definition video recording and broadcasting system, and collect videos of teaching, observation, and learning in multiple streams.

At present, each teaching teacher has its own teaching resources, but these resources are in the hands of the teachers. The school does not have a unified resource management platform. Many good teaching cases and teaching resources cannot be promoted. The teaching resources are scattered and each teacher teaches. There is no unified management of resources and their own governance. By establishing a unified learning support platform and resource management platform, and realizing the seamless connection between the resource management platform and the learning support platform, it is conducive to help teachers sort out resources and teaching ideas, and is conducive to the management, preservation and sharing of excellent resources in the school.

4.4 Develop a Digital Course Learning Platform to Facilitate the Cultivation of New-Type Professional Farmers

The open learning platform provides new professional farmers with independent learning conditions, meets the learning needs of different places and different levels, makes teaching resources continue to extend, flexible and convenient, and achieves a win-win situation for economic and social benefits.

5 Conclusion

The construction of digital teaching resources for modern agronomic technology adopts the cooperation method of enterprises and schools, and sorts out the key and difficult points of teaching according to the teaching standards of the courses. This research establishes a teaching resource library for core courses of modern agronomic technology such as edible fungus cultivation, flower cultivation, vegetable cultivation, and plant disease and insect pest control. The results are mainly presented in the form of teaching case videos, PPT courseware and electronic teaching plans of Word documents. Through the network, it can be applied on a computer or mobile terminal. Continuously update and improve the professional resource library of modern agronomic technology, so that it can be displayed in the training room of the professional "integration of science and practice". This digital teaching resource construction project fills the gap in this field in Guangdong Province, lays a foundation for the professional adaptation to the development of social informatization, and also provides basic digital resources for modern agronomic technology professional teaching in vocational colleges in Guangdong Province and even the whole country.

To sum up, this article studies the problem of sharing high-quality teaching resources, solving the problems of re-learning and resource sharing of students inside and outside the school, and solving the problem of distance learning in training new-type professional farmers. Vigorously promote professional construction and teaching reform, promote the pace of informatization construction in the whole school, and realize the sharing of applications and resources from inside to outside the school through inter-school promotion, and promote the construction and application of informatization in brother schools. Realize resource sharing with enterprises and brother schools, so that relevant practitioners can share relevant resources from the Internet, which has greatly promoted the development of the planting industry in Guangdong and even the whole country.

References

1. Zheng, Y.: Construction and research of digital education resource sharing mechanism. Res. New Curriculum (mid day - Single) (3), 29–30 (2015)
2. Li, L.: Research on cloud sharing mode and mechanism of digital education resources in secondary vocational schools. Comput. Knowl. Technol. **14**(11), 4–5 (2018)
3. Yang, W., Zhao, H.: Research and practice of high-quality education resource sharing cloud platform in higher vocational colleges. Digit. Users **23**(24), 149 (2017)
4. Yu, Y.: Research and practice on the construction of digital resource database and sharing mechanism. Sci. Educ. Guide – Electron. Ed. (Middle) **3**, 16 (2017)
5. Zhang, L.: Research on the construction and application of digital teaching resource database in vocational colleges – taking tieling normal college as an example. J. Liaoning Norm. Coll. Soc. Sci. Ed. **3**, 50–58 (2014)
6. Liu, X., Sui, Q., Yao, Y.: Research on the construction of digital resources in higher vocational education. Inf. Commun. **2**, 290–291 (2018)
7. Yang, X.: The important role of digital teaching resources in college teaching. Heilongjiang Sci. **4**, 38–39 (2018)

Multi Point Intelligent Temperature Synchronous Monitoring System Based on 5G Internet of Things Technology

Guoping Zhang(✉)

Guangzhou Huashang Vocational College, Guangzhou, China
695436425@qq.com

Abstract. A temperature monitoring and early warning system based on multi-point intelligent transmission is designed to monitor and early warn the temperature and reduce the risk and probability of fever. Combined with the clinical research data, the key factors and general range of temperature threshold setting were determined, and the system was designed by modules. The system is divided into individual temperature monitoring unit and system monitoring unit, and 2.4 GHz frequency band transmission technology is selected as the data transmission mode. In addition to the temperature of a single monitoring terminal exceeding 38.5 °C as the threshold to trigger the alarm, the temperature of a single monitoring terminal rises too fast and the temperature of several monitoring terminals is abnormal as the warning basis. The system data transmission is stable, and the fever warning is more sensitive, accurate and real. The system design can not only meet the monitoring needs of key units, but also adapt to the monitoring needs of groups.

Keywords: 5G Internet of things · Intelligent body temperature · Body temperature monitoring

1 Introduction

Body temperature refers to the internal temperature of the body, which is an important condition for the body to play its normal functions. It is also of great significance in daily health care, patient monitoring, clinical diagnosis and prevention and control of large-scale infectious diseases [1]. Accurate diagnosis of body temperature is helpful to understand the health status of the body, make a correct judgment of the disease, and facilitate the timely development of treatment. At present, the vast majority of hospitals collect the temperature of clinical patients mainly through manual timing measurement. The medical staff measure the temperature of each patient through the traditional mercury thermometer, record and draw the temperature curve manually, so as to help doctors analyze the patient's condition [2].

© ICST Institute for Computer Sciences, Social Informatics and Telecommunications Engineering 2022
Published by Springer Nature Switzerland AG 2022. All Rights Reserved
S. Shi et al. (Eds.): 6GN 2021, LNICST 439, pp. 418–432, 2022.
https://doi.org/10.1007/978-3-031-04245-4_37

This method not only consumes a lot of manpower, but also can not achieve large-scale measurement, real-time monitoring of the patient's temperature changes, so it can not find abnormalities in time, which may make patients miss the best opportunity for treatment, and frequent contact, for infectious diseases, it is easy to cause infection of medical staff [3]. In order to solve the above shortcomings of traditional medical monitoring, this paper is committed to applying the emerging multi-point intelligent sensor network technology to the medical industry in recent years, and designs and implements a body temperature monitoring system based on 5G Internet of things technology. According to the actual application needs of the system, 5G Internet of things tree structure network is adopted to realize large-scale, fast and accurate monitoring of group body temperature [4]. Timely detection of abnormal body temperature.

This research is based on a multi-point intelligent temperature stick. Through the mobile phone or hospital equipment, the body temperature can be monitored 24 h without interruption, and the high temperature or low temperature alarm function can be set at the same time.

2 Related Work

In reference [5], the design of multi-point temperature monitoring system for injection molding machine based on Lora technology is proposed. In the design of the system, a set of multi-point temperature monitoring system for injection molding machine based on Lora technology is designed. The system mainly controls the barrel temperature, inlet temperature, nozzle temperature, mold temperature and oil temperature. The temperature sensor collects the temperature signal and transmits it to the controller through Lora module, The results show that: the system can realize the accurate monitoring of multi-point temperature, provide accurate data for the temperature control of injection molding machine, which is of great significance to the temperature control of injection molding machine. The system can also be applied to the temperature collection, but the accuracy of the information collected by the sensor in the design of the system has some limitations, which needs further improvement.

Reference [6] proposed the research of ambient temperature compensation algorithm for two-dimensional optical codec link monitoring system. In order to solve the problem that the reflected optical pulse signal changes with temperature in the link monitoring system of two-dimensional optical codec access network, a temperature compensation algorithm is proposed. The interaction process between the retrieval pulse optical signal and two-dimensional optical encoder is analyzed dynamically, and the expressions of temperature drift of the center wavelength of coded fiber grating and the waveform of the reflected optical signal are derived, The dynamic relationship with temperature is given. The experimental system is set up, and the temperature coefficient of coded fiber grating center wavelength is 0.009 32 nm/°C. The system can work normally in –30–80 °C environment through temperature compensation, and realize accurate judgment of fiber link state. This method effectively compensates the temperature monitoring results and has a certain effect.

In reference [7], a wireless monitoring system of blast furnace hearth temperature field based on mesh wireless network is proposed. In order to improve the data transmission reliability and stability of the temperature field monitoring system of blast furnace hearth, and reduce the construction cost and operation and maintenance cost of the temperature field monitoring system, a wireless monitoring system of blast furnace hearth temperature field based on mesh wireless network is proposed. The data acquisition node of the system is installed on the outer wall of blast furnace hearth, and the analog signal of thermocouple is converted into digital signal, The transmission distance of thermocouple analog signal is greatly shortened, and the external interference is reduced. Then the temperature data is transmitted to the monitoring center through the mesh wireless network for analysis and modeling and monitoring of blast furnace hearth state. The mesh wireless data transmission network is based on IEEE802.11, Based on the optimized link state routing protocol, an adaptive routing protocol of dual path backup and an adaptive switching mechanism of active and standby routes are designed. A prototype system is built based on open wrt open source platform, which is installed and tested in a blast furnace of Laiwu Iron and steel plant. It can run stably for a long time and meet the needs of blast furnace hearth temperature field monitoring.

In view of the above problems, this paper designs a new multi-point monitoring system. The system designs a temperature monitoring and early warning system based on multi-point intelligent transmission to realize temperature monitoring and early warning and reduce the risk and probability of heating. Combined with clinical research data, the key factors and general range of temperature threshold setting are determined, and the system is designed by module. The system is divided into single temperature monitoring unit and system monitoring unit, and 2.4 GHz frequency band transmission technology is selected as the data transmission mode. Except that the temperature of a single monitoring terminal exceeds 38.5 °C as the threshold to trigger the alarm, the temperature of a single monitoring terminal rises too fast, and the abnormal temperature of multiple monitoring terminals is used as the basis for early warning. The data transmission of the system is stable, and the fever warning is more sensitive, accurate and real. The system design can not only meet the monitoring needs of key units, but also adapt to the monitoring needs of each group.

3 Methodology

3.1 Hardware Configuration of Multipoint Intelligent Temperature Synchronous Monitoring System

5g communication technology is the latest generation communication technology developed from the previous generation communication technology. At present, the two key technologies are wireless technology and network technology. At present, 5g technology is the focus of R & D worldwide. Different from the previous four generations of communication technologies, 5g technology has a variety of applications. In the future, the full use of 5g technology will greatly promote the development of relevant communication technology applications and drive the application development of some basic industries, such as relevant software chips and devices. In addition, the steady development of the Internet of things in the 5g technology era will lead to new progress in ICT Information Technology.

The smart body temperature sticker is divided into two parts: the battery module and the core module of the Internet of things. The core module is the development of China Mobile nbot technology chip. Multipoint intelligence is an emerging technology, which supports the cellular data connection of low-power devices in Wan. Its devices have the characteristics of long standby time and low power consumption. Through the temperature signal acquisition, the signal is digitized and stored in the nbot chip register [8]. After intelligent calculation, the number is sent to the antenna module, and sent to the relevant receiving equipment through the antenna. Signal interference screen is added to the equipment to avoid external signal interference and increase data accuracy. The multi-point intelligent temperature monitoring system uses the wristband terminal, which is the terminal collection node worn by the tested personnel, to measure the temperature data [9]. The multi-point intelligent temperature monitoring system is composed of coordinator data gathering and uploading and command sending node, routing data relay and forwarding node, and terminal collection node.

The system takes the ward building as the monitoring unit, and sets up a multi-point intelligent temperature monitoring network based on 5G Internet of things technology in each ward building. The clinical patients use the mobile temperature terminal node to measure the temperature [10]. The temperature data is transmitted and gathered through 5G Internet of things network, and finally connected to the computer of nurse station in each building through the serial port of the coordinator, The temperature data will be displayed on the computer connected to facilitate the observation, analysis and processing of temperature data by the nursing staff. Meanwhile, the temperature threshold value shall be set [11]. If the temperature of the wearer of the terminal node of temperature is higher or lower than the temperature threshold, an alarm signal will be sent to facilitate the timely occurrence of the condition. The terminal acquisition part is the lowest level of the whole system, which is mainly responsible for collecting the temperature information parameters of the wrist of the tested personnel [12]. When receiving the request of uploading the temperature data instruction, the measured data is uploaded to the coordinator node through 5G Internet of things network [13]. The terminal acquisition node integrates the temperature measurement part and data receiving and receiving part on the wrist strap terminal worn by the person under test. Although the size of the wrist strap terminal is small, its internal structure is not simple, including microprocessor, temperature sensor, power supply, etc. [14]. The transmission range of 5G Internet of things technology is generally 10–100 m. The upper computer can not only display the patient's temperature measurement data, but also display other data of the patient, but also can save the temperature data, and draw the temperature change curve according to the temperature data. The utilization of upper computer system C++ language is written [15]. Each patient is assigned a terminal acquisition node, and routing nodes are arranged in the appropriate places such as ward and corridor. A coordinator and a P are arranged in the office area of each ward building forms a separate network. The network nodes of the temperature monitoring system based on 5G Internet of things are divided into three types: the block diagram of terminal acquisition node, routing node and co node is shown in the Fig. 1.

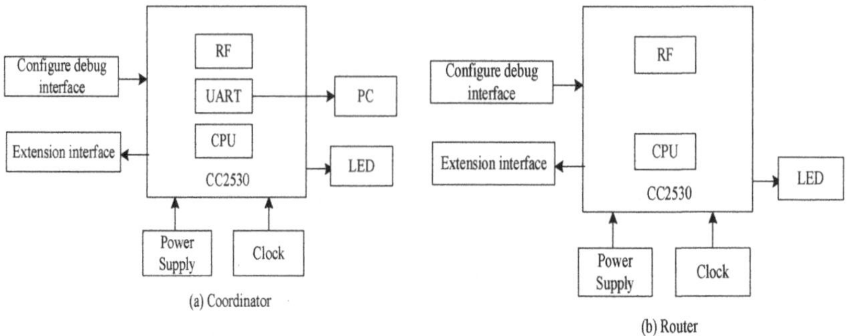

Fig. 1. System coordinator framework

The main function of coordinator node is to start 5G Internet of things multipoint intelligent network, receive data sent by terminal collection node and routing node, realize data aggregation and serial communication with PC in the system, which is simple in hardware structure. The routing node and coordinator node constitute a data transmission network, which is mainly responsible for receiving the data packets sent by the collection node, routing the data packets and sending them to the coordinator Routing nodes do not need to communicate with P °C machine communication, the hardware part can not contain the serial part. The functions of the terminal acquisition node mainly include status indication, data acquisition, body temperature data transmission with routing nodes, and reduce power consumption as much as possible while ensuring the performance. In order to be portable, the terminal acquisition node is required to be miniaturized. In this system, it is designed as a wristband terminal, which requires the hardware design to reduce peripherals as much as possible. Therefore, the acquisition node module does not include the debugging interface. When designing the circuit board, it adopts the button board type, which is connected to the power board. When using, the main control board is removed from the power board, Connect to the power expansion board with debugging interface, download the application program, and then reassemble it to normal use. Considering the working voltage range of 2 v–3.6 v, the system uses 3V button battery power supply, which can ensure the normal operation of the module and reduce the physical volume of the node. The sensor module is divided into analog sensor and digital sensor. The analog sensor converts the changing information into voltage or current output. The amount of data is often very small, and it needs to be processed by amplification circuit and conditioning circuit. In this way, the increase of external circuit will not only increase the physical volume of the node, but also reduce the accuracy of the measurement results. The system adopts the single bus digital temperature sensor TS1 of ist company, the output of the sensor is digital output mode. Only one data line is needed between the sensor and the microprocessor to realize two-way communication. The sensor is fixed on both sides of the lower abdominal trunk of the patient for temperature measurement.

3.2 System Software Function Optimization

In order to achieve high-precision and reliable measurement, the human body basic temperature real-time monitoring system needs to have six functions: data receiving, data filtering, real-time data display, body temperature historical data query, body temperature monitoring node maintenance. As shown in the figure, the PC client completes the above six functions through four modules: real-time monitoring interface, database operation, historical data query and node maintenance.

The real-time monitoring interface completes the setting of serial port parameters, the real-time display of data received by serial port, the display of node information, the control of data storage and the display of multi-channel data waveform. The database operation module includes three functions: querying the historical data table, creating a new data table to store and historical node to continue to store. It is mainly used to determine the location of the data to be stored after starting mysql. If it is a new node, create a new data table in the MySQL database; If it is an existing node, you can query the original data table of the node and continue to store it. Body temperature data query includes three functions: obtaining historical data list, data list display, and data waveform display. It displays the patient's body temperature data in different ways, which is convenient for medical staff to better understand the patient's body temperature change trend. Node maintenance includes node maintenance instruction sending, node maintenance countdown, node status parameter display and node status diagnosis result list display. It is mainly used to detect the node battery power to avoid the impact on the measurement accuracy when the node power is insufficient.

The goal is to establish a temperature monitoring system based on multi-point intelligent transmission, covering the main parameters of the system operation. The temperature monitoring and early warning system includes the determination of temperature alarm threshold, the selection of sensors, the evaluation of human-computer interaction performance, and the design of data transmission system.

In this system, the coordinator is responsible for the establishment of the network, data aggregation and serial communication with the host computer. After the coordinator establishes the network, it will broadcast beacon frames to the adjacent 5G IOT device nodes in the network, and then enter the multi-point intelligent monitoring state. After the routing node and the terminal acquisition node are powered on, they will first send beacon requests to find the network, and then receive the response from the coordinator, send network access requests, and only when they receive the permission response from the coordinator, can they join the network, At the same time, the coordinator adds it to its neighbor list as a child node and assigns it a unique 16 bit short network address.

After the coordinator establishes the network, it is always in the monitoring state, whether there are nodes joining and exiting, whether it receives the instruction information from the serial port, whether it receives the temperature data information uploaded by the terminal collection node or the routing relay node, and makes corresponding processing according to the information type. The terminal collection node is mainly responsible for collecting the body temperature of the wearer, The main function of the software program is to provide initialization of the system acquisition node, temperature acquisition and communication with the parent node. After power on, the initialization operation is carried out first, and then the network is added. The network access process is shown in the Fig. 2.

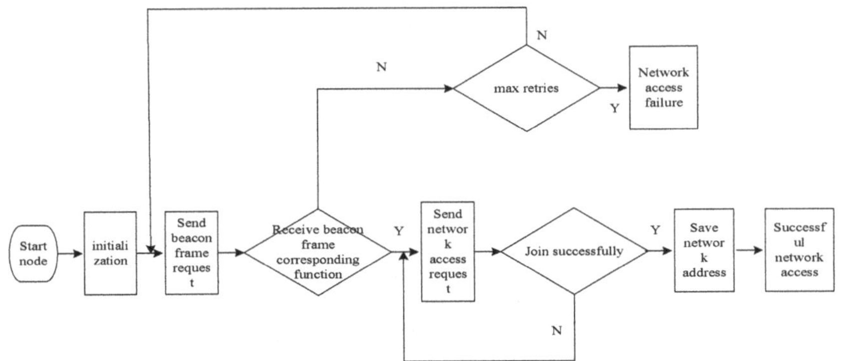

Fig. 2. Information retrieval process of terminal node accessing network

In the aspect of body temperature acquisition, this design provides two methods of body temperature data acquisition, instruction acquisition and timing acquisition. In this system, the timing function is called to set the timing time and the events to occur. When the timing time is up, the events will occur. After entering the network, the terminal acquisition node starts to judge whether it has received the data acquisition instruction from the coordinator, or whether it has reached the timing time. If it has not received the acquisition instruction and has not reached the timing time, the node enters the sleep mode to reduce the power consumption. In the timing mode, the temperature sensor constantly reads the temperature value, and does not send data upward when the body temperature is normal, In this mode, the terminal collection node packs and uploads the temperature data, and the temperature data is finally transmitted to the PC, which can ensure the timely detection and processing of abnormal body temperature.

Temperature data acquisition is mainly by means of temperature sensor. TSI is selected in this design digital temperature sensor, Kalman filter algorithm, takes the optimal estimation x–1, k–1 at k–1 as the criterion, predicts the state variable x (k | x–1) at the time, and at the same time observes the state to get the observation variable / x), then analyzes between prediction and observation, or corrects the prediction by observation, Thus, the optimal state estimation x (k | x) at time e is obtained. Based on the previous state, the current state x (k|k–1) is predicted as follows, where x (k–1 | k–1)) is the initial state of the previous state.

$$x(k|k-1) = Ax(k-1|k-1) + Bu(k) \tag{1}$$

The previous state calculates the covariance P (k | k–1) of the current state prediction, where p (k–1 | x–1) is the covariance of the previous state, as shown in the formula, A2 represents the transpose matrix of A, and Q is the covariance of the system process.

$$P(k|k-1) = AP(k-1|k-1)A^T + Q \tag{2}$$

The optimal estimation of current state is as follows:

$$x(k|k) = x(k|k-1) + kg(k)(z(k) - Hx(k|k-1)) \quad (3)$$

The results show that:

$$kg(k) = P(k|k-1)H^T / \left(HP(k|k-1)H^r + R\right) \quad (4)$$

3.3 The Realization of Intelligent Temperature Synchronous Detection

The flow chart of the improved Kalman filter algorithm based on SVM is shown in the figure. The real-time data is input to the support vector machine classification model, and the model outputs a value. If the value is 1, the input data is basically stable, and the Kalman filter algorithm can be started; If the input value is not equal to 1, the input real-time temperature data will be judged again until the input temperature data is stable and the Kalman filter will be turned on.

The flow chart shows that the original temperature data is processed into four characteristic values and one label sample. The samples are divided into training set and test set. The training model is used to verify the model error by testing set and training set direction. The classification model with minimum training error and minimum test error is selected by adjusting the training parameters of the model. The actual data collected is sent to the classification model, and the input data is normal data/interference signal according to the output result of the model 1/11 (Fig. 3).

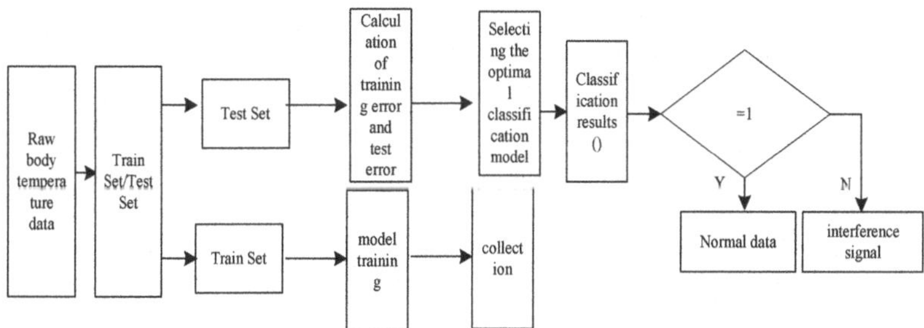

Fig. 3. Implementation process of support vector machine classification filtering algorithm

Because the appearance of interference signal is random, the probability of occurrence is small in the long-term measurement process. In order to improve the recognition accuracy of the classification model for the interference signal, according to the characteristics of the human body basic temperature measurement environment, more samples with the label of 0 containing the interference signal are generated. The expansion of sample data includes two steps: first, analyzing the characteristics of interference signals in historical data; In step 2, the sample is composed of four data. The first three data are normal data continuously measured in historical data. In the fourth data, according to the interference signal characteristics analyzed in step 1, 4000 samples with random interference signal in the temperature range of 250 c–420 c are generated by using random function, and each sample is labeled 0, The table shows the sample data with the label of 0 (Table 1).

Table 1. Extended samples and labels

sample	x1	x2	x3	x4	label
y1	36.50	36.53	36.51	43.5	0
y2	36.50	36.53	36.51	42.5	0
y3	36.50	36.53	36.51	49.5	0
y4	36.50	36.53	36.51	41.5	0
y5	36.50	36.53	36.51	55.5	0
y6	36.50	36.53	36.51	13.5	0
y7	36.50	36.53	36.51	21.5	0
y8	36.50	36.53	36.51	39.5	0
y9	36.50	36.53	36.51	18.5	0
y10	36.50	36.53	36.51	56.5	0

When the node starts up for the first time, it will initialize the system, and then automatically search for 5G Internet of things network signal. When searching the network formed by router or coordinator, it will send the network access request, and receive the reply, it will get an 8-bit ID number assigned by route or coordinator. At this time, it can collect and transmit the relevant data. After the temperature sensor array collects the temperature data, the data is packaged according to the data frame format shown in the table and sent to the routing or Coordinator (according to the network of the node). In practice, patients wearing data collection nodes can move freely, and the nodes will be separated from a subnet. At this time, the node network status is generic app_ NWK state judgment. When the state is devnwk-orphan, execute system reset() system restart, and then automatically join the new network again (Fig. 4).

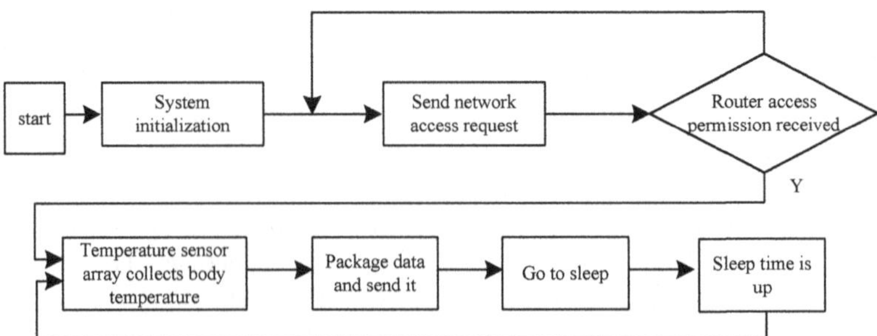

Fig. 4. Temperature data acquisition node control program

Temperature monitoring client software is based on Visual Studio 2010 platform MFC, using C++ high-level programming language development. Microsoft's visual studio 2010, which supports multi language development, is mainly used for the development of Windows platform applications. MFC is a basic class library provided by Microsoft. It provides a large number of windows APIs encapsulated in C++ classes, and also includes an application framework. By using this framework, software developers can simplify a series of routine and tedious work, such as windows AP worker registration, windows AP registration, and so on Generation and management router in this system is mainly responsible for data forwarding, and the control program flow chart is shown in the figure. After the system is initialized, a subnet is set up and a routing table is set up. After receiving the data, judge the data. When the data is a node's network access request, verify the legitimacy of the node, assign an 8-bit network ID and send the network access permission to the node; When the data is forwarded by the node or the upper route, the router will forward the data again or directly send it to the coordinator according to the routing table information, so as to realize the real-time collection and monitoring of body temperature changes, and ensure the operation effect of the system.

4 Results and Discussion

The instrument monitoring was carried out according to the metrological technical specification "calibration specification for medical electronic thermometer" issued by the General Administration of quality supervision, inspection and Quarantine of the people's Republic of China. The monitoring objects are 10 temperature collection terminals and 1 indicator unit of multi-point intelligent continuous temperature monitoring system. The ambient temperature is 250 °C. The relative humidity is 35%. The temperature monitoring methods of critical patients were discussed. Firstly, a multi-point intelligent continuous temperature monitoring system is established; Secondly, the multi-point intelligent continuous temperature monitoring system is used to monitor the body temperature of healthy volunteers, and the feasibility of the system is verified; Thirdly, the multi-point intelligent continuous temperature monitoring system is applied to the temperature monitoring of patients after cardiac surgery and compared with the body core temperature; Finally, on the basis of the previous three parts, the multi-point intelligent continuous temperature monitoring system was applied to the temperature monitoring of critically ill patients. The temperature of the upper orbital temperature measuring point and axillary temperature measured by the multi-point intelligent continuous temperature monitoring system were compared with those measured by the mercury filled glass thermometer. The temperature of patients was measured every 4 h and every 1 h, And the relationship between the 24-h average body temperature and APACHE II score, white blood cell count, neutrophil percentage, procalcitonin and other blood test indexes. The measuring equipment includes: standard thermometer, constant temperature bath, water three-phase point bottle, reading telescope, outside micrometer, steel ruler, etc. The measuring equipment, technical requirements and application are shown in the Table 2.

Table 2. Measuring equipment and technical requirements.

measuring equipment	technical requirement	purpose
Thermostatic bath	The temperature difference between any two points in the working area shall not exceed 0.01 °C, and the temperature fluctuation at constant temperature shall not exceed ± 0.01 °C/min	Provide temperature source
Standard thermometer	Measurement range: (345 –445) °C Graduation value: no more than 0.05 °C	As measurement standard
Reading telescope	—	Read the indication of standard thermometer
Water triple point bottle	—	Zero position of measurement standard
Steel ruler	(0–300) mm	Measure the outer diameter of the temperature probe
Outside micrometer	(0–25)mm	Measuring the insertion depth of temperature probe

The indication error of the temperature monitoring system is calculated according to the formula.

$$\Delta t = E_t - (t_0 + t_{\mathrm{d}} - a_0) \tag{5}$$

Before calibration, the multi-point intelligent continuous temperature monitoring system is checked for measurement range, resolution, appearance and prompt function. The results of all inspection meet the standard requirements.

The calibration results of indication error meet the specification requirements. The calibration results of indication error are shown in the Table 3.

Table 3. Calibration results of the indication error

Calibration temperature point (°C)	Expanded uncertainty (°C)	Indication error of calibrated temperature monitoring system (°C)	freedom
25	0.008	0.01	50
35	0.005	0.00	50
37	0.003	0.00	50

(continued)

Table 3. *(continued)*

Calibration temperature point (°C)	Expanded uncertainty (°C)	Indication error of calibrated temperature monitoring system (°C)	freedom
39	0.005	0.00	50
41	0.001	0.01	50
45	0.010	0.01	50

The mean axillary temperature measured by multi-point intelligent continuous temperature monitoring system was 36.31 ± 0.79 among the 200 measurements in 100 patients °C. The average temperature of the intraorbital temperature measurement point was (36.33 ± 0.80) °C. The mean axillary temperature measured by mercury filled glass thermometer was (36.39 ± 0.78) 0C. The temperature results measured by the three methods are shown in the Tables 4 and 5.

Table 4. Temperature measurement results of three temperature measurement methods

Temperature measuring tool	Temperature measuring part	Mean ± Standard deviation (°C)	Mean ± Standard deviation (°C)	95% confidence interval (°C)
Wireless continuous temperature monitoring system	Intraorbital and supraorbital thermometry	36.39 ± 0.78	35.15,38.10	35.60 – 37.35
Mercury filled glass thermometer	armpit	36.31 ± 0.79	35.10,37.90	35.50 – 37.10
Wireless continuous temperature detection system	armpit	36.33 ± 0.80	35.10,38.00	35.55 – 37.15

Table 5. Pearson correlation analysis of two measurement tools

group	Correlation coefficient (r)	P value
Axillary temperature of thermometer and monitoring temperature of upper orbital thermometer	0.941	0.000
Thermometer axillary temperature and monitoring axillary temperature	0.970	0.000

The paired t-test results of axillary temperature measured by multi-point intelligent continuous body temperature monitoring system and mercury filled glass thermometer showed that the axillary temperature measured by the two methods was at a = 0.05 level, and the difference was not statistically significant (P > 0.05), as shown in the Table 6.

Table 6. Comparison of axillary temperature measured by different methods

group	df	T value	P value	Difference(°C)	95% confidence interval (°C)
Thermometer axillary temperature and monitoring axillary temperature	199	1.519	0.604	– 0.041 ± 0.283	– 0.859 – 0.003

Pearson correlation analysis showed that the axillary temperature measured by the multi-point intelligent continuous temperature monitoring system was highly positively correlated with that measured by the mercury filled glass thermometer (r = 0.970, P < 0.05, the scatter plot had a linear trend, the simple linear regression model was fitted, and the regression equation was listed, Within the 95% consistency limit, the maximum absolute value of the difference between the two is 0.320 c, and the average difference is 0.070 c, indicating that the two have good consistency, as shown in the figure below (Figs. 5 and 6).

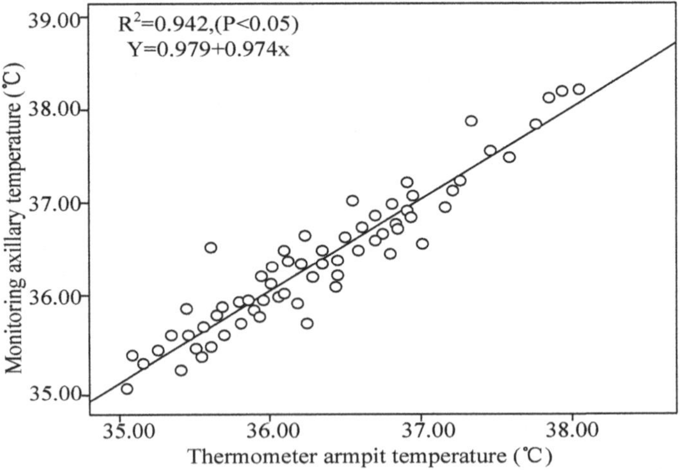

Fig. 5. Scatter analysis of relationship between axillary temperature of thermometer and monitoring axillary temperature.

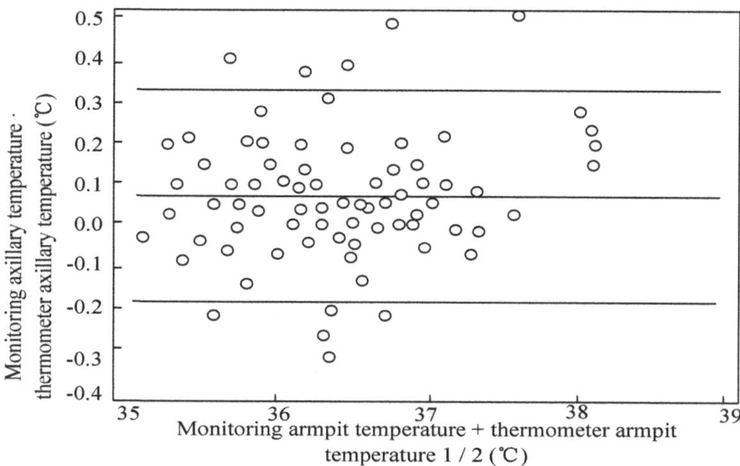

Fig. 6. The dispersion value of thermometer axillary temperature and monitoring axillary temperature.

5 Conclusions

In the current medical practice, real-time monitoring of physiological parameters can effectively obtain the specific physiological conditions of patients, which has positive significance for early detection and treatment of diseases. As an important data in patient monitoring, body temperature has outstanding reference value for specific disease diagnosis and treatment. This paper studies and designs a temperature monitoring system based on multi-point intelligent transmission technology, and makes a specific analysis of the hardware design and software design of the system, which has a prominent guiding role in the practical work.

Acknowledgement. This work was supported grant of No. 2019GKTSCX168 from the Department of Education of Guangdong Province, China.

References

1. Usamentiaga, R., Daniel, G., Perez, J.M.: High-speed temperature monitoring for steel strips using infrared line scanners. IEEE Trans. Ind. Appl. **21**(99), 1 (2020)
2. Tornello, L.D., Scelba, G., Scarcella, G., et al.: Combined rotor-position estimation and temperature monitoring in sensorless, synchronous reluctance motor drives. IEEE Trans. Ind. Appl. **55**(99), 3851–3862 (2019)
3. Llera, M., Tow, K.H., Bergerat, S., et al.: Fiber Bragg grating-based thermometer for drill bit temperature monitoring. Appl. Opt. **58**(22), 5924 (2019)
4. Vita, E.D.D., Zaltieri, M., Tommasi, F.D.D., et al.: Multipoint temperature monitoring of microwave thermal ablation in bones through fiber bragg grating sensor arrays. Sensors **20**(11), 3200 (2020)
5. Li Lilan, L., Wei.: Multi-point temperature monitoring system of injection molding machine based on LoRa. China Synth. Resin Plast. **36**(5), 85–87 (2019)

6. Guo, H.: Research on ambient temperature compensation algorithmfor 2D optical codec link monitoring system. Chin. J. Electron Dev. **43**(1), 1–4 (2020)
7. Liu, C., Ruan, J., Han, K., Han, T.: WMN-based wireless hearth's temperature filed monitoring system of blast furnace. J. Electron. Measur. Instr. **33**(1), 183–190 (2019)
8. Coote, J.M., Torii, R., Desjardins, A.E.: Dynamic characterisation of fibre-optic temperature sensors for physiological monitoring. Sensors **21**(1), 221 (2020)
9. Beccaria, A., Bellone, A., Mirigaldi, A., et al.: Temperature monitoring of tumor hyperthermal treatments with optical fibers: comparison of distributed and quasi-distributed techniques. Optic. Fiber Technol. **60**(11), 102340 (2020)
10. Subahi, A.F., Bouazza, K.E.: An intelligent IoT-based system design for controlling and monitoring greenhouse temperature. IEEE Access, PP(99), 1–1 (2020)
11. Jeong, W., Kim, M., Ha, J.-H., et al.: Accurate, hysteresis-free temperature sensor for health monitoring using a magnetic sensor and pristine polymer. RSC Adv. **9**(14), 7885–7889 (2019)
12. Mai, Y., Li, B., Zhou, G., et al.: Research on temperature sensor using rhodamine6g film coated microstructure optical fiber. IEEE Sens. J. **20**(1), 202–207 (2019)
13. Marques, G., Rui, P.: Non-contact Infrared temperature acquisition system based on internet of things for laboratory activities monitoring. Procedia Comput. Sci. **155**(C), 487–494 (2019)
14. Mariani, S., Sebastian, A., et al.: Compensation for temperature-dependent phase and velocity of guided wave signals in baseline subtraction for structural health monitoring. Struct. Health Monit. **19**(1), 26–47 (2019)
15. Wong, D., Yu, J., Li, Y., et al.: An integrated wearable wireless vital signs biosensor for continuous inpatient monitoring. IEEE Sens. J. PP(99), 1–1 (2019)

FRI Sampling for Ultra-wideband Gaussian Pulses Based on Non-ideal LPF

Linlin Chen, Guoxing Huang(✉), Chenyiming Wen, Weidang Lu, and Yu Zhang

College of Information Engineering, Zhejiang University of Technology, Hangzhou 310023, China
{hgx05745,luweid,yzhang}@zjut.edu.cn

Abstract. In the field of radar signal processing, the ultra-high sampling frequency has always limited the development of radar technology. Finite rate of innovation (FRI) sampling theory can effectively reduce the sampling frequency of radar pulses in recent years. But the existing radar pulses sampling systems based on FRI have not considered the non-ideal effects caused by non-ideal filters in hardware implement, which affects the accuracy of system reconstruction. In this paper, we proposed a FRI sampling scheme for ultra-wideband gaussian pulses based on non-ideal LPF, which can achieve high-precision reconstruction under non-ideal physical component environment. The proposed system has two identical channels based on non-ideal LPF. The two channels samples the ultra-wideband gaussian pulses and the basis signal with a sub-Nyquist sampling frequency after filtered by non-ideal LPF, then we can obatin Fourier coefficients with non-ideal effects. Then we propose a new estimation algorithm to reconstruct the ultra-wideband gaussian pulses, which can eliminate non-ideal effects and improve the reconstruction performance. Finally, simulation results have verified the effectiveness of the proposed scheme.

Keywords: Finite rate of innovation (FRI) · Ultra-wideband Gaussian pulses · Non-ideal LPF

1 Introduction

The ultra-wideband gaussian pulses means ultra-high bandwidth. According to the traditional Nyqiust sampling theorem [1], the sampling rate must be greater than twice the highest frequency of the signal, so that the original signal can be reconstructed without distortion. So sampling an ultra-wideband signal requires a very high sampling frequency, which is difficult to achieve. In order to effectively reduce the sampling frequency of signal and reconstruct the original signal, many experts have carried out a series of research on the sub-Nyquist sampling method [2,3]. Finite rate of innovation (FRI) sampling theory is a feasible solution to reduce the sampling frequency of ultra-wideband gaussian pulses, whose base pulse is known.

© ICST Institute for Computer Sciences, Social Informatics and Telecommunications Engineering 2022
Published by Springer Nature Switzerland AG 2022. All Rights Reserved
S. Shi et al. (Eds.): 6GN 2021, LNICST 439, pp. 433–444, 2022.
https://doi.org/10.1007/978-3-031-04245-4_38

Since finite rate of innovation firstly proposed by Vetterli [4], and many experts have been researching on it. Then the following conclusions are obtained: as long as it is a function that satisfies the fixed constraint conditions, the function of the exponential spline curve, and any function with the rational Fourier transform can be used as the sampling kernel [5]. Therefore, Vetterli and Dragotti proposed tightly supported sampling kernels in the time domain, which are mainly divided into three categories: exponential regenerative kernels, rational number sampling nuclei and polynomial regenerative kernels [6]. The above-mentioned time-domain tightly supported sampling kernels all use the moment of the signal to recover the signal. The aforementioned sampling kernels are often oriented towards a small number of FRI signals [7–9], so their versatility is extremely poor. Therefore, Eldar and Tur designed a sampling structure based on SoS sampling kernel for the sampling and reconstruction of arbitrary shape pulse signals [10].

The above FRI sampling structure is mostly single-channel, in order to further reduce the signal sampling rate. The multi-channel FRI sampling structure came into being. Eldar and Gedalyahu [11] designed a filter bank multi-channel sampling structure suitable for half-period signals (the amplitude changes in each cycle while the delay is unchanged). In this structure, the input signal is first sent to P channels at the same time, the signal is filtered in each channel, and then the discrete sampling value is obtained through low-speed sampling, and then a correction filter is used to filter the discrete sampling value. After the data is passed into the joint sub-empty Harbin Institute of Technology Master's degree thesis-4 to perform calculations, the free parameters of the original signal can be restored [12]. Tur and Gedalyahu [13] designed a parallel multi-channel mixing sampling structure. Its characteristic is to use the known single frequency signal to mix and integrate the input signal under test in each channel, and then obtain the necessary information for reconstruction through subsequent processing. Xiaoyao Wei [14] gradually extended the traditional FRI sampling structure framework to an approximate FRI framework that works with arbitrary sampling cores, and realized the reconstruction of the input signal of the parameterized model.

The estimation algorithm of free parameters is another core research problem in FRI sampling theory. Therefore, Dragotti and Blu et al. [15] made appropriate improvements on the basis of the null filter method and proposed a comprehensive least squares method. Crespo and Erdozain et al. conducted in-depth research on subspace invariance, and proposed a state space method for this purpose [16]. Its reconstruction effect is far superior to the former. According to the idea of parameter optimization, Yonina and Michaeli [17] designed a method to reconstruct the signal by solving an unconstrained optimization problem. This method is applicable to a wide range of conditions, and the reconstruction effect is good. It has low requirements on the sampling core, strong versatility, and complex calculations in the reconstruction process as its main features. Goyal and Tan [18] designed a simple, efficient, and high-precision signal parameter reconstruction method based on statistical ideas, but this method has strict requirements on the type of sampling kernel, and its versatility is poor.

Some of the above FRI sampling systems did not propose specific hardware implementation schemes, and some did not consider the impact of non-ideal effects in hardware implementation. In actual design, LPF is usually used as the sampling kernel function. There is a non-ideal effect between the ideal LPF and the non-ideal LPF, which is bound to have a bad influence on the reconstruction accuracy. So we proposed a new FRI sampling for ultra-wideband gaussian pulses based on non-ideal LPF. In the proposed system, we introduced a sampling channel of the base signal to obtain sampling samples of the base signal containing non-ideal effects. Then through the processing of the algorithm, we can eliminate the non-ideal effects. Finally we can reconstructed signal by these samples.

2 Problem Formulatiom

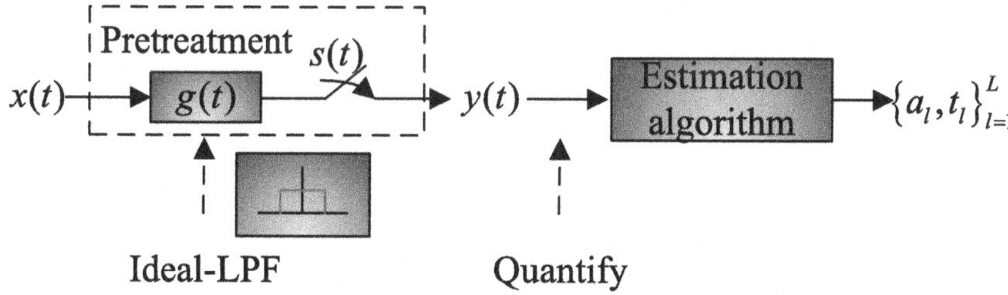

Fig. 1. Classic FRI sampling system

With the classic FRI sampling system, which show in Fig. 1. Taking the basic sinc sampling kernel as an example, we modeled the process of FRI sampling and reconstruction of the ground penetrating radar ultra-wideband gaussian pulses. In a radar system, the superposition of the received echo can be used to express the complete echo signal, and without noise and other interference, the radar echo signal can be expressed as

$$x(t) = \sum_{l=1}^{L} a_l h(t - nT - t_l), \tag{1}$$

where $h(t)$ is a known gaussian pulse waveform, $\{a_l, t_l\}_{l=1}^{L}$ correspond to the amplitude parameter and time delay parameter of the detected pulse respectively and T is radar pulse repetition interval. Then $x(t)$ is filtered by ideal LPF, The signal after filtered can be expressed as

$$y(t) = x(t) * g(t) = \int_{-\infty}^{\infty} x(t)g(t - \tau)d\tau, \tag{2}$$

where $g(t)$ is the frequency response of ideal filter. After sampled with sub-Nyquist sampling frequency, The samples can be expressed as

$$y[n] = y(t)_{t=nT_s}, \tag{3}$$

where T_s is the sampling interval.

According to (3), the samples contain part of the fourier coefficients of the gaussian pulses. After simplification, a typical parameter estimation problem can be obtained. By solving this problem, the amplitude and delay parameters of the pulses can be obtained. However in the hardware implementation process, it will bring non-ideal effects and affect the reconstruction accuracy because the filter cannot achieve the same effect of simulation. In order to eliminate non-ideal effects caused by non-ideal LPF, we proposed a new FRI sampling for ultra-wideband gaussian pulses which is based on non-ideal LPF.

3 FRI Sampling for Ultra-Wideband Gaussian Pulses Based on Non-ideal LPF

3.1 Sampling Framework

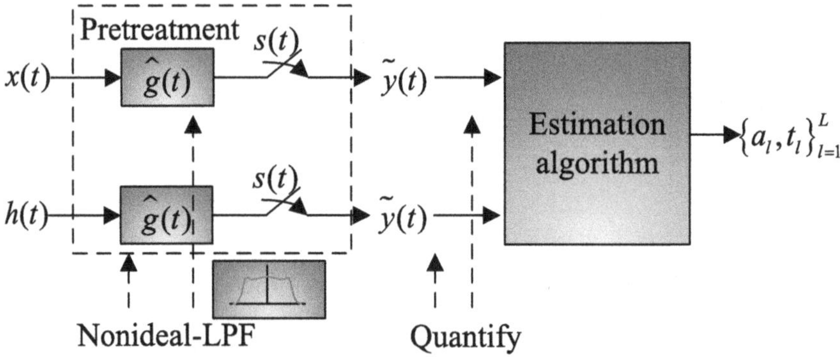

Fig. 2. Proposed FRI sampling system

The proposed FRI sampling framework has been showed in Fig. 2, and it has two parallel channels. In both channels we use a continuous pulses signal to sampling gaussian pulses with a sub-Nyquist sampling frequency, and the continuous pulses signal can be expressed as

$$s(t) = \sum_{n=0}^{\infty} \delta(t - nT_s), \tag{4}$$

where T_s is the sampling interval. Its CTFT can be expressed as

$$S(\Omega) = \Omega_s \sum_{n=0}^{\infty} \delta(\Omega - n\Omega_s). \tag{5}$$

We model $x(t)$ as linear addition of base gaussian pulse, and $x(t)$ can be written as

$$x(t) = \sum_{l=1}^{L} a_l h(t - t_l), \tag{6}$$

where $h(t)$ is a known gaussian pulse waveform, and $h(t)$ can be written as

$$h(t) = \exp(-\frac{t^2}{2\sigma^2}) \tag{7}$$

In the one channel, the gaussian pulses $x(t)$ is sampled by $s(t)$ after filter by non-ideal LPF, whose frequency response can be written as $\widehat{g}(t)$. The signal after sampled can be showed as

$$\widetilde{y}(t) = [x(t) * \widehat{g}(t)] \cdot s(t). \tag{8}$$

For subsequent processing, we need to quantify the sample $\widetilde{y}(t)$, and we can obtain the samples

$$\widetilde{y}[n] = \widetilde{y}(t)_{t=nT_s}(n = 0, 1, \cdots, N-1, N = \frac{T}{T_s}). \tag{9}$$

In the other channel, the base gaussian pulse $h(t)$ is sampled by $s(t)$ after filter by non-ideal LPF, whose frequency response can be written as $\widehat{g}(t)$. The signal after sampled can be showed as

$$\widetilde{h}(t) = [h(t) * \widehat{g}(t)] \cdot s(t). \tag{10}$$

And after quantization, we can obtain the samples

$$\widetilde{h}[n] = \widetilde{h}(t)_{t=nT_s}(n = 0, 1, \cdots, N-1, N = \frac{T}{T_s}). \tag{11}$$

From (9) and (11) we can obatin the samples which contain part of the fourier coefficients of the gaussian pulses. But those samples $\widetilde{y}[n]$ and $\widetilde{h}[n]$ contain non-ideal effects caused by non-ideal LPF, which can lead to low reconstruction accuracy. We design a new estimation algorithm to eliminate non-ideal effects by these samples.

3.2 Estimation Algorithm

The new estimation algorithm can be summarized as Theorem 1, and the proof process is given.

Theorem 1. *Consider a gaussian pulses $x(t)$ in (6), where the base function $h(t)$ is known, and $h(t)$ in (7). Assume that these two pulses are input the proposed system in Fig. 2, then we can obatin that the samples are given by $\widetilde{y}[n]$ and $\widetilde{h}[n]$, respectively. If the sampling frequency satisfies $f_s \geq 2f$, where f is the cutoff frequency of non-ideal LPF. Finally we can estimate the $\{a_l, t_l\}_{l=1}^{L}$ from those samples uniquely under high precision*

Proof. According to (8) and convolution theorem, the CTFT of (8) can be written as

$$\widetilde{Y}(\Omega)=\frac{\Omega_s}{(2\pi)^2}\sum_{n=0}^{\infty}(X(\Omega-n\Omega_s)\widehat{G}(\Omega-n\Omega_s)) \tag{12}$$

It is obvious that $\widetilde{Y}(\Omega)$ is a period signals and the period is $\Omega_s = 2\pi/T_s$. When the sampling frequency satisfies $f_s \geq 2f$, where f is the cutoff frequency of non-ideal LPF, according to the Shannon-Nyquist sampling theorem we can avoid frequency aliasing. and its frequency domain information can use a period to complete, so (12) can be simplified to

$$\widetilde{Y}(\Omega) = \frac{1}{2\pi T_s}X(\Omega)\widehat{G}(\Omega). \tag{13}$$

According to (10) and convolution theorem, the CTFT of (10) can be written as

$$\widetilde{H}(\Omega)=\frac{\Omega_s}{(2\pi)^2}\sum_{n=0}^{\infty}(H(\Omega-n\Omega_s)\widehat{G}(\Omega-n\Omega_s)), \tag{14}$$

and its frequency domain information can use a period to complete, so (14) can be simplified to

$$\widetilde{H}(\Omega) = \frac{1}{2\pi T_s}H(\Omega)\widehat{G}(\Omega). \tag{15}$$

We know the relationship between $x(t)$ and $h(t)$, so we can obtain the frequency relationship between $x(t)$ and $h(t)$ and it can be expressed as

$$X(\Omega) = \sum_{l=1}^{L} a_l H(\Omega)e^{-j\Omega t_l}. \tag{16}$$

Take k samples, equivalent to $\Omega = 2\pi k/T$, we can obatin

$$X(\frac{2\pi k}{T}) = \sum_{l=1}^{L} a_l H(\frac{2\pi k}{T})e^{-j\frac{2\pi k}{T}t_l} \tag{17}$$

By using (13) and (15), we can obtain the samples

$$Y(\Omega) = \frac{\widetilde{Y}(\Omega)}{\widetilde{H}(\Omega)} = \frac{\frac{1}{2\pi T_s}X(\Omega)\widehat{G}(\Omega)}{\frac{1}{2\pi T_s}H(\Omega)\widehat{G}(\Omega)} = \frac{X(\Omega)}{H(\Omega)}, \tag{18}$$

Take k samples and after simplification, the samples can be written as

$$Y[k] = \sum_{l=1}^{L} a_l e^{-jkwt_l} = \sum_{l=1}^{L} a_l e^{-jk\frac{2\pi}{T}t_l}, \tag{19}$$

which does not contain non-ideal effects, and (19) is a typical parameter estimation problem. We can solve this problem by use annihilation filter algorithm or others algorithm.

For better understanding of Theorem 1, we conclude the process in Algorithm 1.

Algorithm 1. Estimation algorithm

Input: Time length T; Number of components L; Bandwidth B; Sampling period T_s; Samples obtained by the proposed system $\tilde{y}[n]$ and $\tilde{h}[n]$, where $n = 0, 1, \cdots, N-1$ and $N = \lfloor T/T_s \rfloor$.

Output: Estimated parameters $\{\hat{a}_l, \hat{t}_l\}_{l=1}^{L}$.

Computer the CTFT of the samples of the one channel $\widetilde{Y}(\Omega) = \frac{1}{2\pi T_s} X(\Omega)\widehat{G}(\Omega)$;
Computer the CTFT of the samples of the other channel $\widetilde{H}(\Omega) = \frac{1}{2\pi T_s} H(\Omega)\widehat{G}(\Omega)$;
Eliminate non-ideal effects by $Y(\Omega) = \frac{\widetilde{Y}(\Omega)}{\widetilde{H}(\Omega)} = \frac{\frac{1}{2\pi T_s} X(\Omega)\widehat{G}(\Omega)}{\frac{1}{2\pi T_s} H(\Omega)\widehat{G}(\Omega)} = \frac{X(\Omega)}{H(\Omega)}$;
for $k = -\lfloor BT \rfloor$ to $\lfloor BT \rfloor$ **do**
    $Y[k] = \tilde{Y}\left(\frac{2\pi}{T}k\right) / \tilde{R}\left(\frac{2\pi}{T}k\right)$;
end for
Estimate $\{\hat{a}_l, \hat{t}_l\}_{l=1}^{L}$ by solving (19) under annihilation filter algorithm [19].
return $\{\hat{a}_l, \hat{t}_l\}_{l=1}^{L}$.

3.3 Anti-noise Methods

Because in the hardware implementation process, noise is inevitable. We propose two methods to improve the noise robustness of the system.

Method 1: Use reconstruction algorithm which has strong noise robustness. ESPRIT and MUSIC algorithms [20,21] has better anti-noise performance than annihilation filter algorithm, when estimating parameters with a noise environment.

Method 2: Increase Properly the sampling frequency which should be greater than two times the filter cutoff frequency, and we can use more samples to estimated parameters.

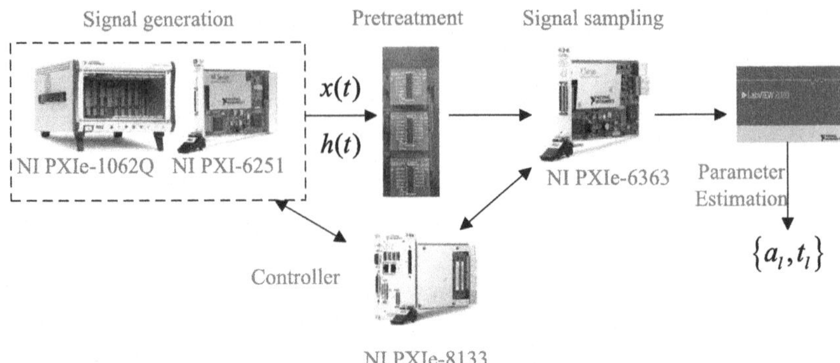

Fig. 3. Specific hardware implementation structure of the proposed FRI sampling system

4 Hardware Prototype

We propose a hardware implementation system based on this method, and the specific structure diagram of this hardware system is shown in the Fig. 3. It can be seen from the Fig. 3 that includes a pretreatment board, which consists of power supply module and filter module. In this system, we use MAX275 as a non-ideal sampling kernel function. MAX275 is a universal active filter produced by MAXIM Corporation in the United States. It contains two independent second-order active filter circuits, which can perform low-pass and band-pass filtering at the same time, and can also realize fourth-order active filtering through cascading. The center frequency/cutoff frequency can reach 300 kHz. MAX275 does not require a clock circuit, so compared with switched capacitor filters, its noise is lower and its dynamic characteristics are better. It can be widely used in various precision test equipment, communication equipment, medical instruments and data acquisition systems. Because the cutoff frequency of the filter can be adjusted by adjusting the size of the resistor. We also proposed an experimental platform based on the PXI instruments, which are used for the signal generation, sampling, and parameter estimation. The functions of these instruments are as follows:

NI PXIe-1062Q: PXI chassis, provide containers for other PXI devices. It has 4 PXI peripheral slots, 1 PXI Express slot with system timing function, and 2 PXI Express hybrid slots that can support PXI and PXI Express peripheral modules.

NI PXI-6251: Data acquisition card, use for signal generation $x(t)$ and $h(t)$ with NI PXIe-1062Q, then output them. This equipment provides low-cost reliability for various applications ranging from laboratory automation, research, design verification/testing to manufacturing testing.

NI PXIe-8133: Controller, control the operation of the entire system, equivalent to a host computer.

NI PXIe-6363: Data acquisition card, use for signal sampling. It has high-throughput PCI Express bus and multi-core optimized drivers and application software to provide high-performance features.

5 Simulation and Hardware Experiments

In order to verify the feasibility and advancement of the proposed system, we designed several experiments to prove it. The parameters in the experiment are set as follows: $x(t)$ is show in (6) and $h(t)$ is show in (7), $t_l = [0.2, 0.4, 0.6, 0.8]$ set as delay parameters, $a_l = [0.9, 0.6, 0.8, 0.5]$ set as amplitude parameters, $t_0 = 0.5$ is the initial delay of the base gaussian pulse, and $\sigma = 0.001$.

Simulation 1: In this simulation without noise, we verify the feasibility of the system and prove that it can reconstruct the unknown parameters of the signal through the samples. We compare the experimental results with the classic FRI sampling system, which show in Fig. 1. The experimental results with ideal-LPF can be show in Fig. 4 and the experimental results with nonideal-LPF can be show in Fig. 5. Figure 4 proved that this method can reconstruct unknown parameters. and it is obvious that with non-ideal LPF the reconstruction results of proposed system is closer to the original parameters than that of classic FRI system.

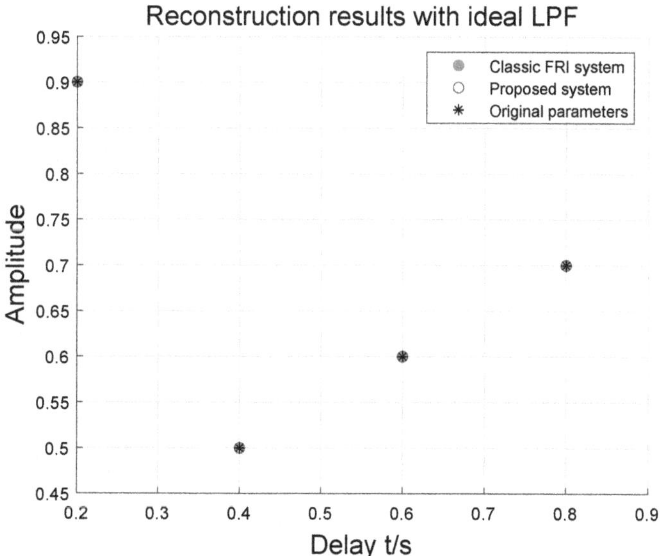

Fig. 4. Simulation results with ideal-LPF under non-noise.

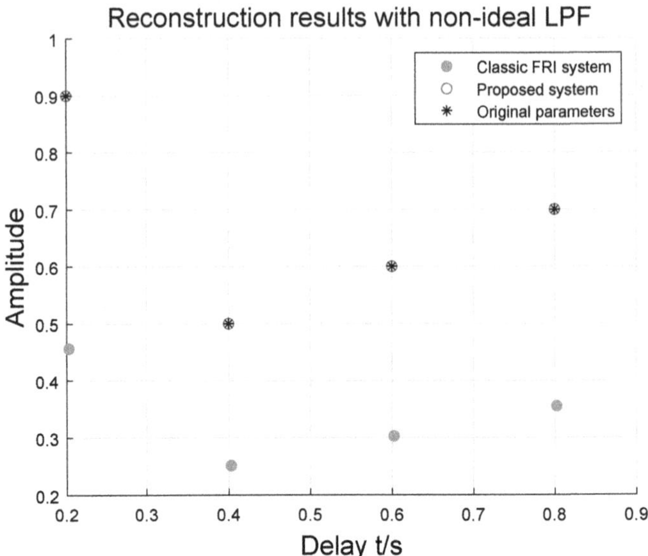

Fig. 5. Simulation results with nonideal-LPF under non-noise.

Simulation 2: In order to verify the strong robustness of the noise of the proposed system, simulation 2 is produced. In this simulation, we use the normalized mean square error (NMSE) to measure the accuracy of reconstruction and compare it with the classic FRI sampling system. Since the error of amplitudes is proportional to the corresponding time delays, we only use the NMSE of time delays to measure the efficiency of the proposed method. In order to obtain more data, annihilation filter algorithm and ESPRIT algorithm are used to estimate the unknown time delays and amplitudes parameters. The simulation results of the NMSE of estimated time delays are show in Fig. 6. From the figure, we can see the NMSE of proposed system always less than the NMSE of classic FRI system. When systems with high SNR 20 dB, the FRI system using de-noising ESPRIT algorithm closes to the proposed system, which used annihilating filter algorithm. When the signal-to-noise ratio of the system reaches 60 dB, the proposed system using annihilation filter algorithm keep it steady in −85 dB. And the proposed system using ESPRIT algorithm has the smallest NMSE.

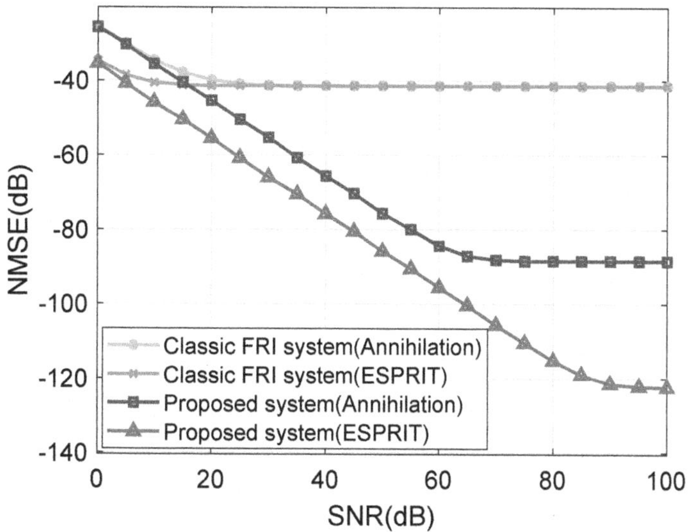

Fig. 6. Simulation results with noise

6 Conclusions

In this paper, we proposed a FRI sampling scheme for ultra-wideband gaussian pulses, which is based on non-ideal LPF and can eliminate the effects of non-ideal physical components and improve the reconstruction results. The proposed scheme is consist of two sampling channels, in which we can obtain a part of Fourier coefficients of both the import signal and the basis signal. Then we proposed a new estimation algorithm to estimate the unknown parameters from the obtained Fourier coefficients. We also design a hardware implementation system and several experiments to verify the feasibility of the proposed system. Simulation results have verified the effectiveness of the proposed scheme.

References

1. Tsimbinos, J., Lever, K.V.: Input Nyquist sampling suffices to identify and compensate nonlinear systems. IEEE Trans. Sig. Process. **46**(10), 2833–2837
2. Kipnis, A., Goldsmith, A.J., Eldar, Y.C., Weissman, T.: Distortion rate function of sub-Nyquist sampled gaussian sources. IEEE Trans. Inf. Theory **62**(1), 401–429
3. Wang, X., Jia, M., Gu, X., Guo, Q.: Sub-Nyquist spectrum sensing based on modulated wideband converter in cognitive radio sensor networks. IEEE Access **6**, 40411–40419
4. Vetterli, M., Marziliano, P., Blu, T.: Sampling signals with finite rate of innovation. IEEE Trans. Sig. Process. **50**(6), 1417–1428
5. Hayuningtyas, P.J., Marziliano, P.: Finite rate of innovation method for DOA estimation of multiple sinusoidal signals with unknown frequency components. In: 2012 9th European Radar Conference, pp. 115–118 (2012)

6. Dragotti, P.L., Vetterli, M., Blu, T.: Sampling moments and reconstructing signals of finite rate of innovation: Shannon meets Strang-Fix. IEEE Trans. Sig. Process. **55**(5), 1741–1757
7. Baechler, G., Freris, N., Quick, R.F., Crochiere, R.E.: Finite rate of innovation based modeling and compression of ECG signals. In: 2013 IEEE International Conference on Acoustics, Speech and Signal Processing, pp. 1252–1256 (2013)
8. Nair, A., Marziliano, P.: P and T wave detection on multichannel ECG using FRI. In: 2014 36th Annual International Conference of the IEEE Engineering in Medicine and Biology Society, pp. 2269–2273 (2014)
9. Nair, A., Marziliano, P.: Fetal heart rate detection using VPW-FRI. In: 2014 IEEE International Conference on Acoustics, Speech and Signal Processing (ICASSP), pp. 4438–4442 (2014)
10. Tur, R., Eldar, Y.C., Friedman, Z.: Innovation rate sampling of pulse streams with application to ultrasound imaging. IEEE Trans. Sig. Process. **59**(4), 1827–1842
11. Gedalyahu, K., Eldar, Y.C.: Time-delay estimation from low-rate samples: a union of subspaces approach. IEEE Trans. Sig. Process. **58**(6), 3017–3031
12. Bajwa, W.U., Gedalyahu, K., Eldar, Y.C.: Identification of parametric underspread linear systems and super-resolution radar. IEEE Trans. Sig. Process. **59**(6), 2548–2561
13. Gedalyahu, K., Tur, R., Eldar, Y.C.: Multichannel sampling of pulse streams at the rate of innovation. IEEE Trans. Sig. Process. **59**(4), 1491–1504
14. Wei, X., Dragotti, P.L.: Universal sampling of signals with finite rate of innovation. In: 2014 IEEE International Conference on Acoustics, Speech and Signal Processing (ICASSP), pp. 1803–1807 (2014)
15. Blu, T., Dragotti, P., Vetterli, M., Marziliano, P., Coulot, L.: Sparse sampling of signal innovations. IEEE Sig. Process. Mag. **25**(2), 31–40 (2008)
16. Erdozain, A., Crespo, P.M.: Reconstruction of aperiodic FRI signals and estimation of the rate of innovation based on the state space method. Sig. Process. **91**(8), 1709–1718 (2011)
17. Michaeli, T., Eldar, Y.C.: Xampling at the rate of innovation. IEEE Trans. Sig. Process. **60**(3), 1121–1133
18. Tan, V.Y.F., Goyal, V.K.: Estimating signals with finite rate of innovation from noisy samples: a stochastic algorithm. IEEE Trans. Sig. Process. **56**(10), 5135–5146
19. Huang, G., Fu, N., Qiao, L., Cao, J., Fan, C.: A simplified FRI sampling system for pulse streams based on constraint random modulation. IEEE Trans. Circ. Syst. II Express Briefs **65**(2), 256–260
20. Wijenayake, C., Antonir, A., Keller, G., Ignjatović, A.: An adaptive denoising algorithm for improving frequency estimation and tracking. IEEE Trans. Circ. Syst. II Express Briefs **67**(1), 172–176
21. Piccinni, G., Torelli, F., Avitabile, G.: Innovative DOA estimation algorithm based on Lyapunov theory. IEEE Trans. Circ. Syst. II Express Briefs **67**(10), 2219–2223

Solving Portfolio Optimization Problems with Particle Filter

Zeming Yang, Guoxing Huang(✉), Yunxian Chen, Weidang Lu, and Yu Zhang

College of Information Engineering, Zhejiang University of Technology, Hangzhou 310023, China
{hgx05745,luweid,yzhang}@zjut.edu.cn

Abstract. In order to improve precision of the solution to the portfolio optimization problem, a optimization scheme based on particle filter is proposed. Portfolio optimization problem is modeled by the Markowitz's portfolio theory, and it is a nonlinear optimization problem with multiple constraints. In this paper, particle filter is considered, to solve portfolio optimization problem. The nonlinear optimization problem is converted to filtering problem of particle filter. Then the nonlinear optimization problem can be solved by particle filter method. To solve portfolio optimization problem, a optimization scheme based on particle is proposed. To improve precision of the solution, crossover and mutation of genetic algorithm is considered in the proposed scheme. Lastly, results of simulation have demonstrated that the proposed optimization scheme outperforms other traditional methods in the precision of the solution of the portfolio optimization problem.

Keywords: Particle filter · Portfolio investment · Nonlinear function · Optimization problem

1 Introduction

Securities investment is a form of investment that obtains dividends, interest and capital gains by buying securities such as stocks, bonds, fund bonds and their derivatives. The goal of securities investment is to obtain returns and reduce risks, which requires the optimal combination of benefits and risks. One of the most important theories of securities investment is the portfolio theory proposed by Harry Markowitz. Portfolio refers to investors take appropriate methods to select multiple securities as investment objects based on the risks and benefits. The goal of the portfolio is to minimize the investment risk under the premise of ensuring the expected return, or to maximize the return of the investment under the premise of controlling the risk. In Markowitz's portfolio theory, the returns are supposed to obey Gaussian distribution, and the portfolio optimization problem is a nonlinear programming problem with multiple constraints.

© ICST Institute for Computer Sciences, Social Informatics and Telecommunications Engineering 2022
Published by Springer Nature Switzerland AG 2022. All Rights Reserved
S. Shi et al. (Eds.): 6GN 2021, LNICST 439, pp. 445–456, 2022.
https://doi.org/10.1007/978-3-031-04245-4_39

However, the real investment seldom follow a Gaussian distribution [1], and subject to multiple constraints. The traditional methods [2,3] use the gradient-based optimization method to solve the multiple-constraints optimization problem, but they are often not very effective. There are many researches take another tack to optimized the portfolio problem, such as apply heuristic algorithms to optimize the portfolio optimization problem. In literature [4–6], the portfolio optimization problem was optimized by genetic algorithm (GA) based methods. GA is an efficient and fast optimization method, but it is prone to trap into local extreme points, and converges prematurely. In literature [7–9], particle swarm optimization (PSO) is considered, to solve the portfolio optimization problem. So that a optimal portfolio strategy can be effective found out. The PSO algorithm is easy to program and converges quickly, and have a good balance in the global search and local search. But still, the performance of local search of PSO is not good enough and lead to a low search accuracy in the optimization. In literature [10,11], simulated annealing (SA) algorithm is considered. SA algorithm is simple but effective, and has good robustness, but has a slow convergence speed. GA, PSO and SA, they have some defects in local search and convergence speed, which will decrease the precision of the optimization. For GA, PSO and SA, they are parametric methods, which performance relies on the parameter settings. A complex parameter settings lead to a complex optimization and a unstable solution.

Particle filter (PF) is a non-parametric method, which is widely deployed in localization [12,13], target tracking [14,15] and navigation [16,17]. Particle filter is a estimation method, to estimate the state of the nonlinear and non-Gaussian systems [18–20]. Particle filter was deployed to solve filtering problem, instead of optimization problem. Therefore, conversion from optimization problem to filtering problem is needed.

In this paper, a optimization scheme is proposed, which is based on particle filter method, to solve the portfolio optimization problem. The portfolio optimization problem is converted to a filtering problem, then particle filter can be deployed in solving the portfolio problem. Crossover and mutation of genetic algorithm is considered in the proposed scheme to improve precision of the solution. To test the performance of the particle filter based optimization scheme, several simulations are formulated.

The content of this paper is organized as follows: Sect. 2 formulates the optimization problem. Section 3 introduces the theory of particle filter. Section 4 proposes the optimization scheme based on particle filter. Section 5 conducts several simulations. Section 6 draws a conclusion to this paper.

2 Problem Formulation

Markowtiz used the mean of the expected return rate to represent the level of the expected return, and used the variance of the return rate to assess the degree of the investment risk. Thereby the mean-variance model of the portfolio investment was established. Investors are normally making choice with uncertain returns and risks. In Markowtiz's portfolio model, mean and variance are used to describe returns and risks. In the mean-variance model, the mean value refers to the expected rate of return of the portfolio. The mean value is the weighted average of the expected rate of return of a single security. The weight is the corresponding investment ratio. The variance refers to the variance of the return rate of the investment portfolio.

Investors make a choice to select portfolio by measuring returns and risks in the investment. Investors might select portfolio by maximizing the expected return based on a certain expected risk, or minimizing the expected risk based on a certain expected return. A basic principle of Markowtiz's portfolio theory is to minimize the risk after investment for a specific expected rate of return R.

$$\min \sum_{i=1}^{n} \sum_{j=1}^{n} \omega_i \omega_j \sigma_{ij}. \tag{1}$$

Subject to

$$\begin{cases} \sum_{i=1}^{n} \omega_i \mu_i = R, \\ \sum_{i=1}^{n} \omega_i = 1, \\ 0 \leq \omega_i \leq 1. \end{cases} \tag{2}$$

Here n represents the number of securities to be selected by investors, ω_i refer to the investment ratio coefficient of the security i, μ_i refer to the expected rate of return of security i. σ_{ij} represents the covariance of the return rate of correct i and the return rate of security j, and R refer to the expected rate of return.

3 Basis Theory of Particle Filter

Particle filter is a state estimation method, which is used to estimate the state of the nonlinear and non-Gaussian systems. Particle filter was used to solve filtering problem, to make a optimal estimation to the state. The optimal estimation to the state is approximated by updating probability density of the state.

Update function of a nonlinear and non-Gaussian system is expressed as follows

$$x_k = f_k(x_{k-1}, w_k), \tag{3}$$

its measurement function is expressed as follows

$$z_k = h_k(x_k, v_k). \tag{4}$$

Here, the update function f_k is a nonlinear function, and w_k is the process noise. The measurement function h_k a nonlinear function, and v_k is the detecting noise. k is a discrete time. The state x_k of the system is estimated according to samples of the solution domain of the measurement function, under noise scenario. Figure 1 is a flowchart of particle filter. The probability density function $p(x_{k-1}|z_{k-1})$ is a prediction of next location of the state, it is approximated

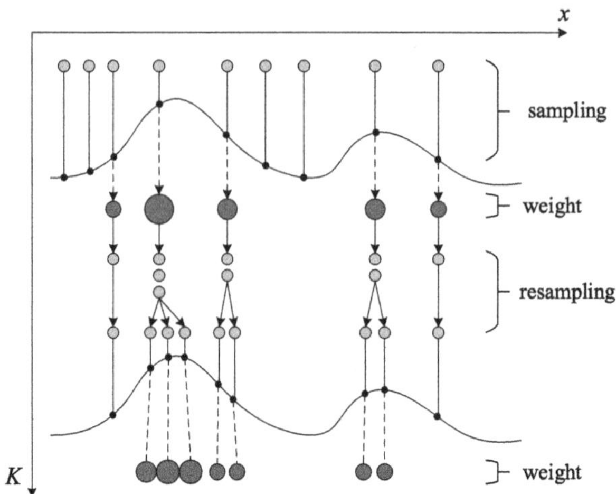

Fig. 1. Flowchart of particle filter

by the particles and their weights. By iteratively updating the probability density function of the state and the weight of particles, the minimum variance estimation of the state can be obtained.

The prediction probability density $p(x_k|x_{k-1})$ of is calculated by the update function f_k of and the update function $p(x_{k-1}|z_{k-1})$, that is

$$p(x_k|z_{k-1}) = \int p(x_k|x_{k-1})p(x_{k-1}|z_{k-1})\,\mathrm{d}x_k. \tag{5}$$

The update function $p(x_{k-1}|z_{k-1})$ is calculated by the measurement function h_k and the prediction probability density, that is

$$p(x_k|z_k) = \frac{p(z_k|x_k)p(x_k|z_{k-1})}{p(z_k|z_{k-1})}. \tag{6}$$

Assumed that the initial probability density $p(x_0)$ is given by priory knowledge, then the filtering problem can be solved. Particle is a Monte Carlo method, which use a lot of particles to approximate the probability density of the state. By the Bayesian theory, the estimated state can be expressed as

$$\hat{x} = \int x_k p(x_k|z_k)\,\mathrm{d}x_k. \tag{7}$$

Analytical solution of the Eq. (7) is limited by the integral calculation.

For particle filter, the update function $p(x_k|z_k)$ is approximated by a lot of samples of the measurement function and their corresponding weight. By the law of large numbers, the approximated update function is denoted as follows

$$\hat{p}(x_k|z_k) = \frac{1}{N}\sum_{m=1}^{M}\delta(x_k - x_k^m) = \sum_{m=1}^{M} w_k^m \delta(x_k - x_k^m), \tag{8}$$

where $\delta(x)$ is Dirichlet function. w_k^m is weight of particle x_k^m, which subject to

$$w_0^m = \frac{1}{M}, \tag{9}$$

$$w_k^m = w_{k-1}^m \frac{p(z_k|x_k^m)p(x_k^m|x_{k-1}^m)}{p(x_k^m|x_{k-1}^m, z_k)}. \tag{10}$$

Then, the state is approximated as follows

$$\hat{x} = \int x_k p(x_k|z_k)\,\mathrm{d}x_k = \sum_{m=1}^{M} w_k^m x_k^m. \tag{11}$$

The state of system is estimated by the update function and the samples of the measurement function, particle filter used a lot of samples particles to update the state, and obtained an optimal estimation.

4 PF Based Optimization Scheme

Particle filter is deployed to estimate state of nonlinear and non-Gaussian systems. Particle filter was designed for solving filtering problem, instead of optimization problem. To solve a optimization problem, conversion from optimization problem to filtering problem is needed.

4.1 Basis Principle of PF Based Optimization Scheme

The portfolio optimization problem is a nonlinear optimization problem with multiple constraints. The nonlinear optimization problem is converted to a estimation problem of the state. Then particle filter can be deployed in solving the portfolio optimization problem.

Consider an objective function as follows

$$\min fitness(x), \tag{12}$$

which subject to

$$a_i \leq x^i \leq b_i, i \in n. \tag{13}$$

here $fitness(.)$ is the fitness function, x^i is the variable, $[a_i, b_i]$ is the domain of the variable x^i.

To converted optimization problem to filtering problem, the optimization is considered as a nonlinear dynamic time-varying system, which the change of the global optimal solution is a nonlinear process. For the dynamic time-varying system, its discrete time is the iterations of the optimization. The state to the system is a solution of the optimization, and the update function is the changes of the solution during the iterations. The measurement function is the fitness function of the optimization. Consequently, the optimization problem is converted to a estimation problem of the state, and the global optimal solution can be obtained when the iteration is accomplished.

Consider an optimization problem, which its fitness function is $fitness(x)$. For particle filter, the state update function is denoted as follows

$$x_k = f_k(x_{k-1}, w_k). \tag{14}$$

The measurement function is expressed as

$$y_k = fitness(x), \tag{15}$$

where x_k is the state, w_k is process noise. The update function $f_k(.)$ is the change of the global optimal solution during the iteration, which is a nonlinear function. The measurement function is $fitness(x)$, which is the same as fitness function of the optimization problem. The solution of the optimization problem continues to approximate the optimal solution during the iteration, and lastly converge on the global optimal solution.

4.2 PF for Optimization

In this paper, a optimization scheme based on particle is proposed for solving portfolio optimization problem, which can improve precision of the solution. The objective function of the portfolio optimization problem is given in Eq. (1) and Eq. (2), which is a nonlinear function with multiple constraints. Flow chart of the optimization scheme based on particle filter is represented in Fig. 2. The following is the specific steps of the process.

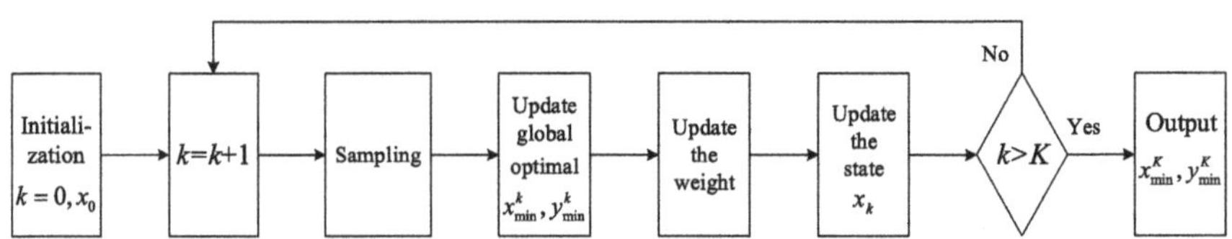

Fig. 2. Schematic of the proposed scheme

step 1: Initialization: The state is initialized as a random sample of the solution domain the measurement function (1), which subject to (2). Amount of particle is M. Maximum iterations is K, and initial iteration is $k = 0$.

step 2: Iteration: The iteration is $k = k + 1$. The solution of portfolio optimization problem is iteratively updated, and converge on global optimal solution when the iteration is accomplished.

step 3: Sampling: Particle $m \in \{1, M\}$ is sampled according to $x_k^m \sim p(x_k^m|z_k)$. Here, a uniform distribution $U(x_k^m - c_k, x_k^m + c_k)$ is used instead of $p(x_k^m|z_k)$. It is a random sampling, a new particle is generated as follows

$$x_k^m = \frac{\Lambda \cdot rand}{a^k} + x_{k-1} - \frac{1}{2} \cdot \frac{\Lambda}{a^k}. \tag{16}$$

here, a is a number slightly larger than 1. Λ is argument domain to the measurement function (1). The sampling region Λ is narrowed with increasing the iteration k.

step 4: Crossover and Mutation: Crossover operation and mutation operation of GA is considered in the proposed scheme to improve precision of the solution,. By introducing crossover operation and mutation operation, variety of particles is enriched, which contribute to avoid local optimal solutions. Details of crossover operation and mutation operation is given as follows

- *Crossover*: The crossover operation is a single-point crossover. Any two particles are choosed to pair. Elements in the same position of the variable of the particles are exchanged, which can generate two new particles.
- *Mutation*: Select a variable from the set of variables and replace it with a new variable within the range of its values.

step 5: Optimal solution : According to the measurement function (1), measurement value y_k^m of particle x_k^m is calculated. Then, the minimum fitness value y_{min}^k among y_k^m can be found, so the corresponding solution x_{min}^k.

step 6: Weights updated: Measurement value y_{k-1} of x_{k-1} is calculated according to the measurement function (1), which will be the observed value. Measurement values y_k^m of the particles x_k^m are compared with the observed value y_{k-1} to update the weights as follows

$$w_k^m = \begin{cases} 0, & y_k^m \leq y_{k-1} \; or \text{ fail to meet the constraints (2)} \\ 1/q_k^m, & \text{otherwise,} \end{cases} \tag{17}$$

where

$$q_k^m = \frac{1}{s\sqrt{2\pi}} exp(-\frac{(y_k^m - y_{k-1})^2}{2\sigma^2}). \tag{18}$$

Measurement values $\{y_k^m\}$ of $x_k^m, m \in \{1, M\}$ are considered to follow normal distribution $N(y_{k-1}, s^2)$, and σ is variance of measurement values $\{y_k^m\}$. Then, the weights of the particles are normalized as follows

$$w_k^m = \frac{w_k^m}{\sum\limits_{m=1}^{M} w_k^m}. \tag{19}$$

step 7: Resampling: As iteration goes on, effective particles might decrease significantly, which lead to the optimization converged prematurely. Number of effective particles is calculated as follows

$$N_{eff} = \frac{1}{\sum\limits_{m=1}^{M} (w_k^m)^2} \tag{20}$$

where threshold $N_{th} = 2M/3$. The resampling is started when $N_{eff} < N_{th}$, and independent resampling [21] is considered.

step 8: State updated: The state x_k is approximated by the particles and their corresponding weights as follows

$$\hat{x} = \sum_{m=1}^{M} w_k^m x_k^m. \tag{21}$$

step 9: If iteration $k \leq K$, go back to step 2 and continue the iteration. When $k > K$, the optimization is accomplished, and return a global optimal solution x_K^{min} and its corresponding fitness value y_K^{min}.

The specific steps of the optimization scheme based on particle filter is organized in Algorithm 1. For the portfolio optimization, the nonlinear optimization problem is converted to the filtering problem of particle filter, and solve by particle filter method.

Algorithm 1

Set: K, M
Initialize state particle x_0
for $(k = 1 : K)$ **do**
  Random sampling $\{x_k^m\}$
  Crossover and Mutation
  Update optimal solution: $[y_{min}^k, index] = min(y_k^m)$, $x_{min}^k = \{x_k^m\}(index)$
  Update the weight of the particle according to the Eqs. $(18, 17, 19)$
  Calculate N_{eff} **according to the Eqs. (20)**
  if $(N_{eff} < 2M/3)$ **then**
    Independent resampling
  end if
  Update the state particle according to Eqs. (21)
end for
Output: The optimal solution: x_K^{min} and y_K^{min}.

5 Simulation Results

To test the performace of the optimization scheme based on particle filter, several simulations are conducted. Outcomes of the proposed optimization scheme are compared with other heuristic algorithm based methods, such as GA based method in [4], PSO based method in [7] and SA based method in [11]. In the mean-variance model, the mean represents the expected return rate of the portfolio, and the variance represents the variance of the expected return rate.

Table 1. The expected return rate and its corresponding covariance of the portfolio which is composed of 3 securities.

Securities	Return rate (%)	Covariance		
		1	2	3
1	5.8	0.004	0.018	0.022
2	8.8	0.018	0.118	0.074
3	7.9	0.022	0.074	0.081

Simulation 1: A portfolio is assumed composed of 3 securities, expected return rate of investment is 6.8%. The expected return rate and its corresponding covariance are shown in Table 1. In the mean-variance model, the expected return rate refers to mean value, and the covariance of the expected return rate refers to the covariance. The goal of the optimization problem in this simulation is to minimize the investment risk under the premise of ensuring the expected return, that is minimize the covariance. We used the proposed PF based scheme to optimize the portfolio optimization problem, and compare with other methods. The minimum investment risk ratio coefficient vector of the portfolio obtained by the proposed PF based scheme is $\omega = [0.60916817456292, 0.19805907398015, 0.19277275145693]$. The global optimal solutions are shown in Table 2. It can be observed from Table 2 that the optimal solution obtained by our proposed PF based scheme is smaller, which means that investment risk of the portfolio of our scheme is smaller.

Table 2. Results of *Simulation 1* obtained by the PF based scheme and other methods.

Methods	The global optimal solution
PF based scheme	0.03764344490657
GA based method in [4]	0.03764370000000
PSO based method in [7]	0.03764370000000
SA based method in [11]	0.037654411009027

Simulation 2: In this simulation, a portfolio is assumed composed of 6 securities, expected return rate of investment is 20.5%. The expected return rate and its corresponding covariance are shown in Table 3. The portfolio in here has more securities, that means the dimensionality of the variable to be optimized increases, which will lead to a more complicated optimization. The goal of the portfolio optimization problem in this simulation is to minimize the investment risk under the premise of ensuring the expected return, that is minimize the covariance. We used the proposed PF based scheme to optimize the portfolio optimization problem, and the minimum investment risk ratio coefficient

Table 3. The expected return rate and its corresponding covariance of the portfolio which is composed of 6 securities.

Securities	Return rate (%)	Covariance					
		1	2	3	4	5	6
1	18.5	0.210	0.210	0.221	−0.216	0.162	−0.215
2	20.3	0.210	0.225	0.239	−0.216	0.168	−0.219
3	22.9	0.210	0.239	0.275	−0.246	0.189	−0.247
4	21.8	−0.216	−0.216	−0.246	0.256	−0.185	0.254
5	16.7	0.162	0.168	0.189	−0.185	0.142	−0.188
6	23.1	−0.215	−0.219	−0.247	0.254	−0.188	0.266

vector of the portfolio obtained by the proposed PF based scheme is $\omega = [0.07459492705459, 0.00000000001454, 0.16811832788656, 0.24520471325523, 0.29758477229673, 0.21449725949235]$. The global optimal solutions obtained by our proposed PF based scheme and other methods are shown in Table 4. According to Table 4, the investment risk of the portfolio optimized by our proposed PF based scheme is smaller than other methods. Although the optimization problem becomes more complicated and the dimension of the variable to be optimized increases, but still our proposed PF based scheme can obtain a higher precision global optimal solution compare with other methods.

Table 4. Results of *Simulation 2* obtained by the PF based scheme and other methods.

Methods	The global optimal solution
PF based scheme	0.00363465183449
GA based method in [4]	0.00363475500000
PSO based method in [7]	0.00363475500000
SA based method in [11]	0.003634848401176

6 Conclusion

In order to improve precision of solution of portfolio optimization problem, and avoid the optimization trap into local optimal solution, a optimization scheme based on particle filter is proposed. Portfolio optimization problem is a nonlinear optimization problem with multiple constraints, and it is converted into the state estimation problem of particle filter. To solve the portfolio optimization problem, a particle filter based optimization scheme is proposed. Crossover operation and mutation operation of genetic algorithm is introduced to improve precision of the solution. Simulation results have demonstrated that the proposed PF based scheme outperforms the GA, PSO and SA based methods. The investment risk optimized by our proposed PF based scheme is smaller than other methods. The PF based optimization scheme provide a more effective and high precision way to optimize the portfolio problem.

References

1. Zhou, R., Palomar, D.P.: Solving high-order portfolios via successive convex approximation algorithms. IEEE Trans. Sign. Process. **69**, 892–904 (2021)
2. Bean, A.J., Singer, A.C.: Portfolio selection via constrained stochastic gradients. In: 2011 IEEE Statistical Signal Processing Workshop (SSP), pp. 37–40 (2011)
3. Hegde, S., Kumar, V., Singh, A.: Risk aware portfolio construction using deep deterministic policy gradients. In: 2018 IEEE Symposium Series on Computational Intelligence (SSCI), pp. 1861–1867 (2018)
4. Chou, Y.H., Kuo, S.Y., Lo, Y.T.: Portfolio optimization based on funds standardization and genetic algorithm. IEEE Access **5**, 21885–21900 (2017)
5. Liao, B.Y., Chen, H.W., Kuo, S.Y., Chou, Y.H.: Portfolio optimization based on novel risk assessment strategy with genetic algorithm. In: 2015 IEEE International Conference on Systems, Man, and Cybernetics, pp. 2861–2866 (2015)
6. Faia, R., Pinto, T., Vale, Z., Corchado, J.M., Soares, J., Lezama, F.: Genetic algorithms for portfolio optimization with weighted sum approach. In: 2018 IEEE Symposium Series on Computational Intelligence (SSCI), pp. 1823–1829 (2018)
7. Erwin, K., Engelbrecht, A.: Improved set-based particle swarm optimization for portfolio optimization. In: 2020 IEEE Symposium Series on Computational Intelligence (SSCI), pp. 1573–1580 (2020)
8. Yin, X., Ni, Q., Zhai, Y.: A novel PSO for portfolio optimization based on heterogeneous multiple population strategy. In: 2015 IEEE Congress on Evolutionary Computation (CEC), pp. 1196–1203 (2015)
9. Sharma, B., Thulasiram, R.K., Thulasiraman, P.: Portfolio management using particle swarm optimization on GPU. In: 2012 IEEE 10th International Symposium on Parallel and Distributed Processing with Applications, pp. 103–110 (2012)
10. Wang, X., He, L., Ji, H.: Modified generalized simulated annealing algorithm used in data driven portfolio management. In: 2016 IEEE Information Technology, Networking, Electronic and Automation Control Conference, pp. 1014–1017 (2016)
11. Sen, T., Saha, S., Ekbal, A., Laha, A.K.: Bi-objective portfolio optimization using archive multi-objective simulated annealing. In: 2014 International Conference on High Performance Computing and Applications (ICHPCA), pp. 1–6 (2014)
12. Pak, J.M., Ahn, C.K., Shmaliy, Y.S., Lim, M.T.: Improving reliability of particle filter-based localization in wireless sensor networks via hybrid particle/FIR filtering. IEEE Trans. Ind. Inform. **11**(5), 1089–1098 (2015)
13. Ullah, I., Shen, Y., Su, X., Esposito, C., Choi, C.: A localization based on unscented kalman filter and particle filter localization algorithms. IEEE Access **8**, 2233–2246 (2020)
14. De Freitas, A., et al.: A box particle filter method for tracking multiple extended objects. IEEE Trans. Aerospace Electron. Syst. **55**(4), 1640–1655 (2019)
15. Zhang, T., Liu, S., Xu, C., Liu, B., Yang, M.H.: Correlation particle filter for visual tracking. IEEE Trans. Image Process. **27**(6), 2676–2687 (2018)
16. Pei, L., Liu, D., Zou, D., Lee Fook Choy, R., Chen, Y., He, Z.: Optimal heading estimation based multidimensional particle filter for pedestrian indoor positioning. IEEE Access **6**, 49705–49720 (2018)

17. Minetto, A., Gurrieri, A., Dovis, F.: A cognitive particle filter for collaborative DGNSS positioning. IEEE Access **8**, 194765–194779 (2020)
18. Amor, N., Kahlaoui, S., Chebbi, S.: Unscented particle filter using student-t distribution with non-gaussian measurement noise. In: 2018 International Conference on Advanced Systems and Electric Technologies (IC_ASET), pp. 34–38 (2018)
19. Song, W., Wang, Z., Wang, J., Alsaadi, F.E., Shan, J.: Particle filtering for nonlinear/non-gaussian systems with energy harvesting sensors subject to randomly occurring sensor saturations. IEEE Trans. Sign. Process. **69**, 15–27 (2021)
20. Psiaki, M.L.: Gaussian mixture nonlinear filtering with resampling for mixand narrowing. IEEE Trans. Sign. Process. **64**(21), 5499–5512 (2016)
21. Lamberti, R., Petetin, Y., Desbouvries, F., Septier, F.: Independent resampling sequential Monte Carlo algorithms. IEEE Trans. Sign. Process. **65**(20), 5318–5333 (2017)

Polynomial Reproducing Kernel Based Image Reconstruction for ECT

Juntao Sun, Guoxing Huang(✉), Qinfeng Li, Weidang Lu, and Yu Zhang

College of Information Engineering, Zhejiang University of Technology, Hangzhou 310023, China
hgx05745@zjut.edu.cn

Abstract. Electrical capacitance tomography (ECT) is one of an electrical tomography technique, which is widely used in industrial process monitoring. It is based on multiphase flow detection and has been widely used in many fields in recent years. It is one of the research hot topics of process tomography. For purpose of improving the accuracy of ECT image reconstruction, a new image reconstruction method for ECT based on polynomial reproducing sampling kernel is put forward in this paper. Firstly, the grayscale of image is a Dirac pulse train, and it can be modeled into a discrete finite rate of innovation (FRI) model. Then, the feature information of polynomial is extracted by FRI sampling. Finally, a new observation equation is constructed by using the feature information. The original image was obtained by solving the L0 norm optimization problem. Simulations have shown that the image accuracy reconstructed by this method are better than existing algorithms.

Keywords: Image reconstruction · Electrical capacitance tomography (ECT) · Polynomial reproducing kernel · L0 norm · Finite rate of innovation (FRI)

1 Introduction

Electrical capacitance tomography (ECT) a new technology applied to multi-phase flow parameter detection [1], which can measure the material distribution of different dielectric constants by measuring the capacitance. ECT has the advantages of fast response, non-intrusion and good security [2]. Image reconstruction technology is the key to capacitance imaging application in industrial practice. Therefore, ECT technology has been developed for many years, and the research results are constantly improved and deepened [3].

The research of image reconstruction is a hot research field in recent years, and the progress is fast, and a variety of image reconstruction algorithms have been proposed [4]. The linear back projection (LBP) algorithm is the most basic and direct algorithm for ECT reconstruction. Its refactoring principle is to superimpose all the electric field lines in the induction area, and obtain the reconstructed image by solving the gray value in reverse [5]. But the image accuracy reconstructed by LBP algorithm is not enough. The image quality is lower than other algorithms when the flow pattern is complex. The

© ICST Institute for Computer Sciences, Social Informatics and Telecommunications Engineering 2022
Published by Springer Nature Switzerland AG 2022. All Rights Reserved
S. Shi et al. (Eds.): 6GN 2021, LNICST 439, pp. 457–469, 2022.
https://doi.org/10.1007/978-3-031-04245-4_40

Landweber algorithm can reconstruct a better image and obtain clearer image edges [6]. But Landweber uses the gradient descent method. Step size parameter problems may lead to local convergence. The quality of the image reconstructed by Tikhonov regularization algorithm has been greatly improved in the measurement center area, and an approximately stable image can be obtained [7]. The Tikhonov regularization algorithm uses the regularization solution as an approximation of the exact solution to solve the ill condition of ECT. Since this algorithm sacrifices a part of pixels in the iteration process, the image quality reconstructed by the algorithm will become worse. The Newton-Raphson algorithm obtains the least squares solution. This algorithm can reduce iteration error [7]. But the imaging speed of the algorithm is slow. The neural network algorithm is suitable for solving complex nonlinear problems [9]. But it needs to use a large number of samples, thus reducing the imaging speed. The singular value decomposition (SVD) algorithm has better reconstruction effect than LBP algorithm [10]. However, it cannot satisfy the clear reconstruction of images in the case of complex flow patterns. The algebraic reconstruction technique (ART) algorithm is better than SVD algorithm [11]. However, due to the influence of noise, the accuracy of SVD imaging needs to be improved. The Kalman filter algorithm estimates the image by iteration [11]. However, the Kalman filter algorithm takes too long because it needs matrix inversion in the iterative solution process.

In this paper, a new ECT image reconstruction method based on polynomial regenerated kernel is proposed. This method has high accuracy and correlation coefficient. First, the grayscale of image is a typical Dirac pulse train, we model the gray vector as a FRI signal. Subsequently, in the FRI sampling framework, we use polynomial reproducing kernel to filter the FRI signal. Feature extraction is carried out by uniform sampling. Finally, we combine the original data with FRI observation information. The extended sensitivity matrix and capacitance vector were reconstructed by zero filling. We rearrange the row vectors of sensitivity matrix and capacitance vector randomly, and we construct a new observation equation. The original image was obtained by solving the L0 norm optimization prob-lem. Experimental results show that this method can improve the accuracy of the image reconstruction.

The arrangement of this article is as follows: Firstly, in Sect. 2, we describe the basic principles of the ECT system. And then, in the Sect. 3, the proposed method of this paper is given. At last, based on some simulation results, we make a brief summary in Sects. 4 and 5.

2 ECT Image Reconstruction Problem

The ECT system consists of sensor array, projection data acquisition system and imaging signal processing computer, as shown in Fig. 1. Sensor systems usually consist of pairs of capacitance plates mounted uniformly on the outer walls of insulated pipes. The data acquisition device can obtain the projection data under different observation angles by measuring the capacitance values between any plate pairs, and then feed the data into the imaging computer.

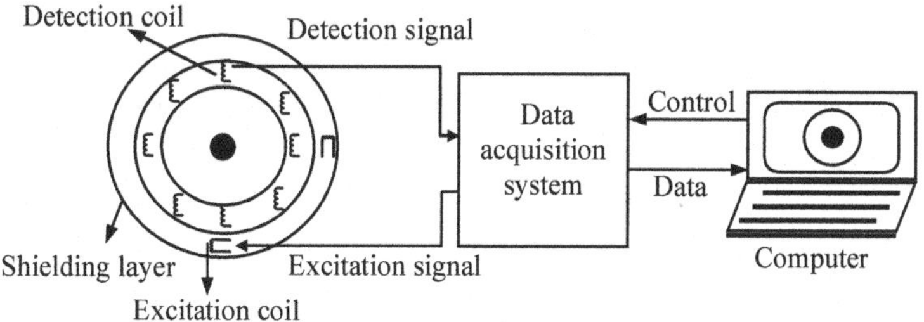

Fig. 1. The ECT system structure

2.1 The Forward Problem of ECT

The forward problem of ECT is to use some numerical analysis method to calculate the capacitance value of each electrode plate in the ECT system under the condition that the distribution of the dielectric constant in the measured area is known. We can use Maxwell's equation to describe the electromagnetic field:

$$\begin{cases} \nabla \times H = J_e + \frac{\partial D}{\partial t} \\ \nabla \times E = -\frac{\partial B}{\partial t} \\ \nabla \cdot B = 0 \\ \nabla \cdot D = \rho, \end{cases} \tag{1}$$

Here H is the magnetic field intensity, J_e is the conduction current density, E is the electric field intensity, B is the magnetic induction intensity and D is the displacement currents.

The measured field of ECT is electrostatic field, and it means that there is no isolated charge in the field. The boundary condition of the sensitive field in ECT is to measure the voltage value of the electrode. The forward problem can be generalized to the first kind of boundary value problem of Laplace equation: $\nabla \cdot (\varepsilon \cdot \nabla\varphi) = 0$. When the electrode i is excited by the electrode, the corresponding boundary conditions can be expressed as:

$$\mathrm{u}(x, y) = \begin{cases} u_0, (x, y) \subseteq \Gamma_i \\ 0, (x, y) \subseteq \Gamma_k + \Gamma_s + \Gamma_g, k = 1, 2, \ldots, 8, k \neq i, \end{cases} \tag{2}$$

where $\mathrm{u}(x, y)$ is electric potential distributions. u_0 is the excitation voltage. Γ_i and Γ_k represent the space position of the excitation and measurement electrode, Γ_s and Γ_g represent the space position of shielding layer and radial electrode.

Suppose i is the excitation electrode, and j is the detection electrode. The capacitance can be expressed as follows:

$$C_{ij} = \frac{Q_{ij}}{U_{ij}} = -\frac{\oint_\Gamma \varepsilon(x.y)\nabla\varphi(x, y) \cdot d\Gamma}{V}, \tag{3}$$

where V is the electrical potential difference between two electrodes, and Γ is the arbitrary closed curve surrounding electrode j, Q_{ij} represents the amount of charge on electrode j.

The sensitivity field is quickly calculated by the potential distribution method. The sensitivity matrix is calculated by calculating the variation of the potential in the measured region when the i and j electrodes are excitation electrodes respectively:

$$S_{ij}(k) = \frac{\triangle\, C_{ij}}{\triangle\, \varepsilon} \approx -\frac{\int_{v} \nabla\varphi_i \cdot \nabla\varphi_j ds}{V^2} \tag{4}$$

3 ECT Image Reconstruction Problem

The inverse problem belongs to the solution of ECT imaging problem. For the reconstruction of ECT image. Firstly, we need to obtain the known capacitance values, and then we get the sensitivity matrix of the sensitive field through simulation. Finally, we calculate the distribution of the dielectric constant of the medium in the measured area. The relationship between the dielectric constant distribution and the capacitance vector can be expressed as follows:

$$C_i = \iint_D S_i(x, y)\varepsilon(x, y)dxdy, \tag{5}$$

where D is the measured area. (5) is a nonlinear relation of integration. Therefore, the above formula requires discretization, linearization and normalization, and it can be rewritten into matrix form:

$$\mathbf{C} = \mathbf{Sg}, \tag{6}$$

where **g** is the normalized gray value vector, **C** is the normalized capacitance vector, m is the number of measured capacitance values, **S** is the normalized sensitivity matrix. and n is the number of pixels. Both m and n are integers.

The solution of (6) is the solution process of ECT inverse problem. And the number of pixels in the reconstruction area is far more than the number of capacitance values obtained, which leads to the unhealthy problem of ECT image reconstruction and the instability of the solution of ECT inverse problem. Therefore, for the sake of enhance the image reconstruction accuracy, an improved ECT image reconstruction algorithm is proposed, which is based on the use of polynomial regenerated kernel.

4 FRI Signal Modeling and Feature Extraction

In this section. What we need to do is feature extraction: Firstly, we model the gray vector as a FRI signal. In the FRI sampling system, the FRI signal is filtered by polynomial reproducing kernel and uniformly sampled. Subsequently, measurements are calculated from the samples to obtain observational feature information. Finally, the original data were combined with FRI observation information. The extended sensitivity matrix and capacitance vector were reconstructed by zero filling. We randomly rearrange the row vectors of sensitivity matrix and capacitance vector. In this way, we construct a new observation equation. The L0 norm optimization problem can be solved, so that the original signal can be recovered [13].

4.1 FRI Signal Modeling

The original image is a grayscale image composed of gray value 0 or 1. Therefore, the original signal cannot be directly sampled. We use a approximate solution to carry out FRI modeling [14]. The grayscale value of the approximate solution is between 0 and 1, which is a Dirac pulse sequence signal. So, we model the approximate solution as a typical (FRI) signal g(x):

$$g(x) = \sum_{l=0}^{L-1} a_l \delta(x - x_l), \tag{7}$$

where $x = 1, 2 \ldots, N$ is the pixel position, $x_l \in \{1, 2, ..., N\}$ is the non-zero gray value pixel position. This signal g(x) is an equally spaced signal, and can be uniformly sampled at the rate $f = \rho = 2L/n$.

4.2 Filtering and Sampling Process

In this paper, we use polynomial reproducing kernel [15]. Polynomial reproducing kernel with the order of $M - 1$ can be written as:

$$\sum_{k \in Z} \mathbf{C}_{m,k} \varphi(x - k) = x^m, m = 0, 1, \ldots, M - 1, M \in Z, \tag{8}$$

where the coefficients $\mathbf{C}_{m,k}$ can be expressed as:

$$\mathbf{C}_{m,k} = \int_{-\infty}^{\infty} x^m \, \tilde{\varphi}(x - k) dx, \; m = 0, 1, \ldots, M - 1; \; k = 1, 2, \ldots, K \tag{9}$$

Now we use this kernel to filter the FRI signal, and then we sample g(x) at the rate $f = \rho$ to extract polynomial feature information. In this way, we can get K sample values y_k. The classic FRI sampling structure is shown in Fig. 2. Filtering and sampling process can be simplified to the following formula:

$$\begin{aligned} y_k &= g(x) * h(x)|_{x=kT} \\ &= < \sum_{l=0}^{l-1} a_l \delta(x - x_l), \varphi(x/T - k)> \\ &= \sum_{l=0}^{L-1} a_l \varphi(x_l/T - k), \end{aligned} \tag{10}$$

where $< \cdot, \cdot >$ is the inner product process, T is the sampling interval. K is the total number of samples, and k = 1, 2…K is the sample label.

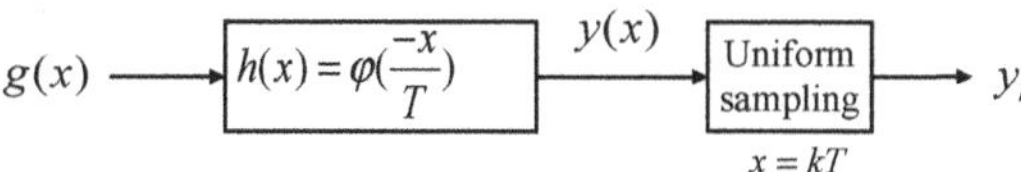

Fig. 2. Classic FRI sampling structure

4.3 Comprehensive Observation Equation

It can be known from the principle of polynomial reproducing kernel, the kernel of order $M-1$ can reproduce $M-1$ order polynomial. Measurement values can be obtained by the following formula:

$$\begin{aligned}\tau_m &= \sum_k \mathbf{C}_{m,k} y_k \\ &= \sum_{l=0}^{L-1} a_l \sum_k c_{m,k}\varphi(x_l/T-k) \\ &= \sum_{l=0}^{L-1} a_l (x_l/T)^m, m = 0, 1\cdots, M-1,\end{aligned} \tag{11}$$

where $a_l \in [0, 1]$. The measured value u_m is expressed as a complete linear combination of all the elements in $\{1, 2, \ldots, N\}$. Assume that $u_m = \tau_m \cdot T^m$, we can rewrite the formula into the form of matrix:

$$\begin{bmatrix} u_0 \\ u_1 \\ \vdots \\ u_{M-1} \end{bmatrix} = \begin{bmatrix} 1 & 1 & \cdots & 1 \\ 1 & 2 & \cdots & N \\ \vdots & \vdots & \cdots & \vdots \\ 1 & 2^{M-1} & \cdots & N^{M-1} \end{bmatrix} \cdot \begin{bmatrix} g_0 \\ g_1 \\ \vdots \\ g_N \end{bmatrix} \tag{12}$$

$$\mathbf{U} = \mathbf{A}\mathbf{g}, \tag{13}$$

where $\mathbf{U} = [u_0, u_1, \ldots, u_{M-1}]^T \in \mathbf{R}^{M\times 1}$ is FRI observation vector, $\mathbf{A} = \{1^m, 2^m, \ldots, N^m\}_{m=0}^{M-1}$ is FRI observation matrix, $\mathbf{g} = [g_1, g_2, \ldots, g_N]^T$ is gray vector.

There was not enough information in the original signal. We have extracted the feature information, So, we can combine the data, namely the two observation equations can be combined to get a new observation equation. The new observation equation after data fusion can be simplified to the following formula:

$$\begin{bmatrix} \mathbf{C} \\ \mathbf{U} \end{bmatrix} = \begin{bmatrix} \mathbf{S} \\ \mathbf{A} \end{bmatrix} \cdot \mathbf{g} \tag{14}$$

$$\boldsymbol{\lambda} = \boldsymbol{\Phi}\mathbf{g}, \tag{15}$$

where $\boldsymbol{\lambda} = [\mathbf{C}; \mathbf{U}]$ is the observation vector after data fusion, and $\boldsymbol{\Phi} = [\mathbf{S}; \mathbf{A}]$ is the Sensitivity matrix after data fusion.

In the ECT system, the number of pixels is much larger than the number of capacitance values obtained, which leads to the unhealthy problem of ECT image reconstruction and the instability of the solution of ECT inverse problem. It results in a low sampling rate, which ultimately reduces reconstruction accuracy. So, in this paper, we add capacitance values into the ECT system, through zero vector expansion method [16]. In this way, the observation equation becomes sparse, therefore, we can simplify the mathematical model of the ECT system:

$$\boldsymbol{\lambda}_{new} = \boldsymbol{\Phi}_{new}\mathbf{g}, \tag{16}$$

where $\boldsymbol{\lambda}_{new}$ is comprehensive observation vector, $\boldsymbol{\Phi}_{new}$ is comprehensive observation matrix.

4.4 Solving L0 Norm Optimization Problem

Signal sparsity can meet reconstruction requirement, but the signal is not sparse enough in the ECT system [17]. Therefore, the input signals need to be converted into sparse signals. The original signal **g** can be transformed as follows [18]:

$$\mathbf{g} = \boldsymbol{\psi}\mathbf{s}, \tag{17}$$

where matrix $\boldsymbol{\psi}$ is sparse basis, the original signal **g** is projected onto the sparse basis to get sparse vector **s**.

After orthogonal transformation, the signal becomes sparse. Because of the sparsity of the signal **s**, the sparse solution **s** is usually obtained by solving the L0 norm optimization problem. In this paper, we use orthogonal matching pursuit (OMP) algorithm [19] to solve this problem [20]:

$$\hat{\mathbf{s}} = \arg\min ||\mathbf{s}||_0 \quad s.t.\ \boldsymbol{\lambda}_{new} = \mathbf{S}_{new}\boldsymbol{\psi}\mathbf{s}, \tag{18}$$

where the L0 norm $||\mathbf{s}||_0$ represents the number of nonzero coefficients in **s**. So, the estimation of the original image signal can be obtained as:

$$\hat{\mathbf{g}} = \boldsymbol{\psi}\hat{\mathbf{s}} \tag{19}$$

4.5 Process of the Method

Step 1: Initialization and normalization. The measured capacitance and the sensitivity matrix need to be normalized. The order of polynomial reproducing kernel is set to M-1.
Step 2: Input signal. The approximate solution $\mathbf{g}v = \left(\mathbf{S}^T \cdot \mathbf{S} + \alpha\mathbf{I}\right) \cdot \mathbf{S}^T\mathbf{C}$ is modeled as a FRI signal g(x) by formula (7).
Step 3: Filtering and sampling. After modeled, the signal *g(x)* is filtered by polynomial reproducing kernel *φ(x)*. Then Equal interval sampling is used to extract sample information by formula (10).

Step 4: Comprehensive observation equation. Combining with formula (6) and formula (13), a FRI observation equation can be obtained by formula (14). A comprehensive observation equation is constructed by formula (16).
Step 5: Sparse solution reconstruction. In order to solve the observation equation, we can represent the signal **g** by orthogonal transformation as shown in (17). Then the L0 norm optimization problem is solved by formula (18) based on OMP algorithm.
Step 6: Image reconstruction. Finally, the ECT image can be estimated and reconstructed as formula (19).

5 Simulation Results

In order to verify the performance of the proposed method in this paper, the simulation model is carried out. The numerical simulation model was established with COMSOL software. The simulation model established is as follows: the pipe is square. The height of the pipe is 0.13 m, and the width of the pipe is 0.06 m. The thickness of the shielding layer is 0.007 m. The thickness of the pipe is 0.015 m. There are 8 measuring electrodes mounted on the four sides of the pipe, i.e. M = 28. The cross section of the area being measured is divided into 20 × 20 pixels, i.e. N = 400. The gray obtained by the Tikhonov regularization algorithm is modeled as a FRI signal. The polynomial sampling kernel is selected. The order of polynomial reproducing sampling kernel is 3. When the excitation voltage is applied to the excitation electrode, the potential isogram of the measured area is shown in the Fig. 3.

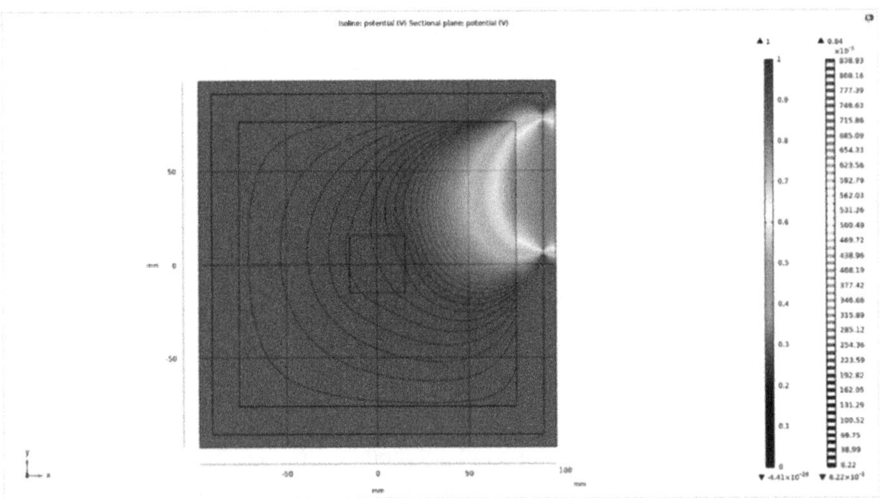

Fig. 3. The potential isogram of the measured area

The reconstructed images of the four flow patterns under different algorithms are shown in Table 1. It can be seen from the reconstruction results that the reconstructed image of the method in this paper is the closest to the original image. In general, the reconstructed image quality of the proposed method is obviously better compared with other traditional algorithms.

Table 1. The reconstruction effects of different algorithms

	(a)	(b)	(c)	(d)
Original image			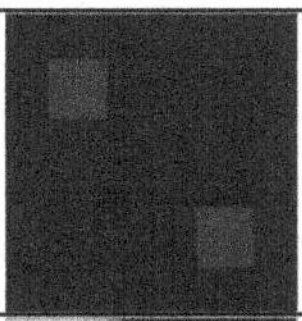	
LBP			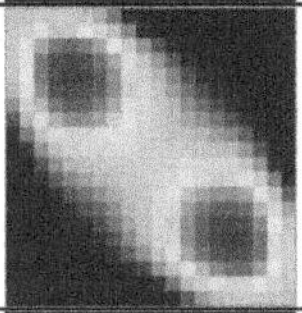	
Landweber		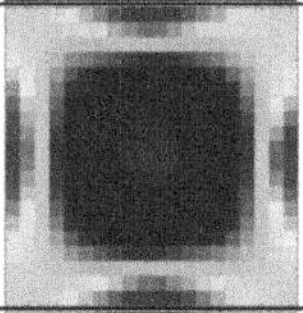	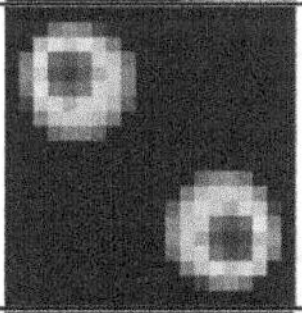	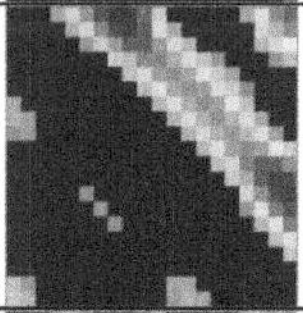
Tikhonov regularization		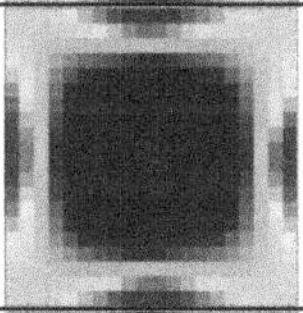		
Kalman			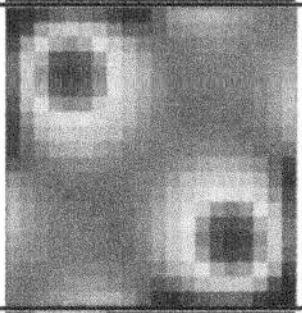	
ART			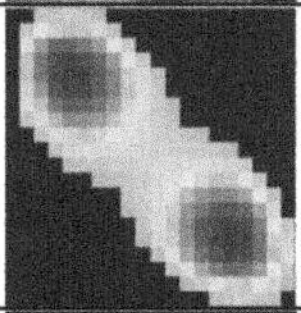	
Method of this paper			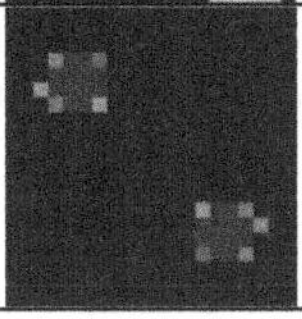	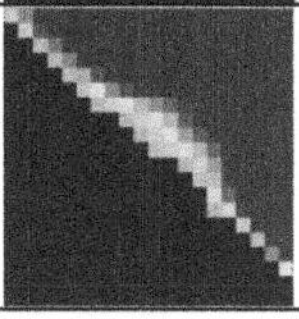

In order to qualitatively analyze the image reconstruction quality of the method in this paper, we choose to use relative error and correlation coefficient as performance indexes. The relative image error is defined as the difference degree. Image quality is inversely proportional to relative image error. The correlation coefficient is defined as the linear correlation. The higher the value, the closer the two images are, and the better the image reconstruction effect is. Tables 2 and 3 is the reconstruction image relative errors and correlation coefficients of different algorithms.

Table 2. Image errors of different algorithms

Algorithms	Flow pattern			
	(a)	*(b)*	*(c)*	*(d)*
LBP	1.2765	0.4214	1.3891	0.3118
Landweber	0.4464	0.4550	0.6476	0.7199
Tikhonov	0.4348	0.4630	0.5925	0.7198
Kalman	0.5175	0.5122	1.1745	0.5906
ART	0.8315	0.6836	0.5170	0.4874
Proposed method	0.3411	0.1742	0.2189	0.2811

Table 3. Correlation coefficients of different algorithms

Algorithms	Flow pattern			
	(a)	*(b)*	*(c)*	*(d)*
LBP	0.5725	0.8968	0.5347	0.9169
Landweber	0.9001	0.8732	0.7739	0.5759
Tikhonov	0.8936	0.8704	0.8020	0.5866
Kalman	0.8909	0.8524	0.7373	0.5959
ART	0.5474	0.9567	0.5170	0.9117
Proposed method	0.9352	0.9765	0.9736	0.9267

It can be seen from Tables 2 and 3 that the reconstructed image error of the method in this paper is much lower than other traditional algorithms, and the correlation coefficient is higher than traditional algorithms. Clearly, the images reconstructed by the proposed method have high quality and high precision. The curves of image relative errors and correlation coefficients of different algorithms are shown in the Figs. 4 and 5:

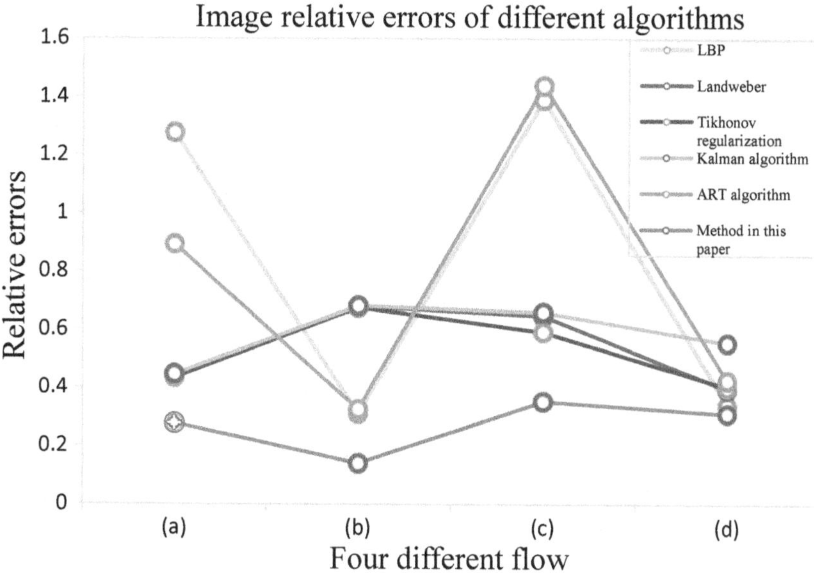

Fig. 4. The curves of image relative errors

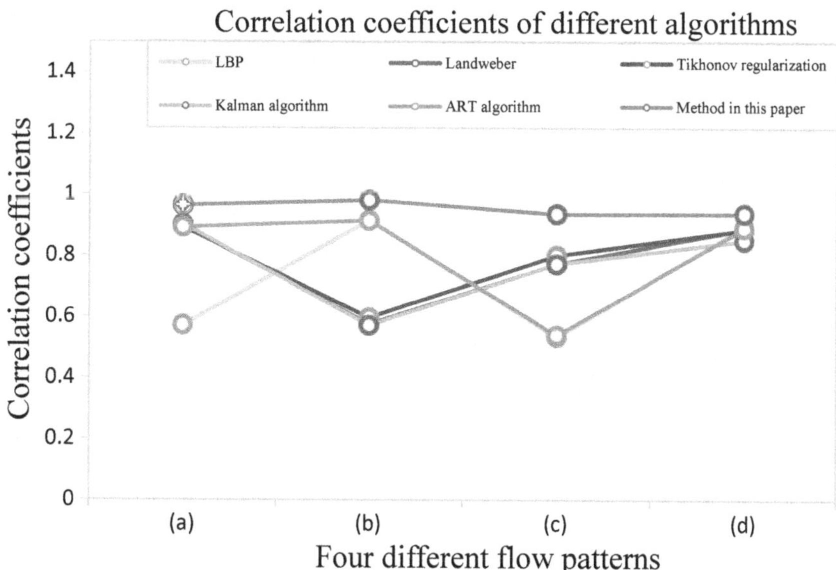

Fig. 5. The curves of correlation coefficients

6 Conclusion

Image reconstruction technology is the key to the application of capacitance imaging in industrial practice. In this paper, an ECT image reconstruction method based on polynomial reproducing is proposed to improve the image reconstruction accuracy. First, the approximate solution is modeled as an FRI signal and aligned for feature extraction. Then, a new observation equation was constructed to solve the L0 norm optimization problem to reconstruct ECT images. Simulation results have shown that compared with other existing methods, the proposed method can reconstruct the image better, and the image quality is closer to the original image. Therefore, the proposed method is effective and has better image reconstruction effect than other existing methods. On the whole, this method has a high precision of image reconstruction and is worth further study.

References

1. Meribout, M., Saied, I.M.: Real-time two-dimensional imaging of solid contaminants in gas pipelines using an electrical capacitance tomography system. IEEE Trans. Industr. Electron. **64**(5), 3989–3996 (2017)
2. Tian, Y., Cao, Z., Hu, D., Gao, X., Xu, L., Yang, W.: A fuzzy pidcontrolled iterative calderon's method for binary distribution in electrical capacitance tomography. IEEE Trans. Instrum. Meas. **70**, 1–11 (2021)
3. Sun, S., et al.: Sensitivity guided image fusion for electrical capacitance tomography. IEEE Trans. Instrum. Meas. **70**, 1–12 (2021)
4. Ji, H., et al.: A new dual-modality ECT/ERT technique based on C4D principle. IEEE Trans. Instrum. Meas. **65**(5), 1042–1050 (2016)
5. Guo, Q., et al.: A novel image reconstruction strategy for ECT: combining two algorithms with a graph cut method. IEEE Trans. Instrum. Meas. **69**(3), 804–814 (2020)
6. Ran, L., Zongliang, G., Ziguan, C., Minghu, W., Xiuchang, Z.: Distributed adaptive compressed video sensing using smoothed projected landweber reconstruction. China Commun. **10**(11), 58–69 (2013)
7. Nguyen, N., Milanfar, P., Golub, G.: A computationally efficient superresolution image reconstruction algorithm. In: IEEE Trans. Image Process. **10**(4), 573–583 (2001)
8. Wang, C., Guo, Q., Wang, H., Cui, Z., Bai, R., Ma, M.: ECT image reconstruction based on alternating direction approximate newton algorithm. IEEE Trans. Instrum. Meas. **69**(7), 4873–4886 (2020)
9. Martin, S., Choi, C.T.M.: A new divide-and-conquer method for 3D electrical impedance tomography. IEEE Trans. Magn. **54**(3), 1–4 (2018)
10. Guo, Q., Zhang, C., Zhang, Y., Liu, H.: An efficient SVD-based method for image denoising. IEEE Trans. Circuits Syst. Video Technol. **26**(5), 868–880 (2016)
11. Yao, Y., Tang, J., Chen, P., Zhang, S., Chen, J.: An improved iterative algorithm for 3-D ionospheric tomography reconstruction. IEEE Trans. Geosci. Remote Sens. **52**(8), 4696–4706 (2014)
12. Deabes, W., Bouazza, K.E.: Efficient image reconstruction algorithm for ect system using local ensemble transform kalman filter. IEEE Access **9**, 12779–12790 (2021)
13. Huang, G., Fu, N., Zhang, J., Qiao, L.: Image reconstruction method of electromagnetic tomography based on finite rate of innovation. In: 2016 IEEE International Instrumentation and Measurement Technology Conference Proceedings, pp. 1–6 (2016)
14. Mulleti, S., Seelamantula, C.S.: Ellipse fitting using the finite rate of innovationsampling-principle. IEEE Trans. Image Process. **25**(3), 1451–1464 (2016)

15. Uriguen, J.A., Blu, T., Dragotti, P.L.: FRI sampling with arbitrary kernels. IEEE Trans. Sig. Process. **61**(21), 5310–5323 (2013)
16. Ye, J., Wang, H., Yang, W.: Image reconstruction for electrical capacitance tomography based on sparse representation. IEEE Trans. Instrum. Meas. **64**(1), 89–102 (2015)
17. Ma, J., Yuan, X., Ping, L.: Turbo compressed sensing with partial DFT sensing matrix. IEEE Sig. Process. Lett. **22**(2), 158–161 (2015)
18. Hsieh, S., Lu, C., Pei, S.: Compressive sensing matrix design for fast encoding and decoding via sparse FFT. IEEE Sig. Process. Lett. **25**(4), 591–595 (2018)
19. Wang, J., Kwon, S., Li, P., Shim, B.: Recovery of sparse signals via generalized orthogonal matching pursuit: a new analysis. IEEE Trans. Sig. Process. **64**(4), 1076–1089 (2016)
20. Park, D.: Improved sufficient condition for performance guarantee in generalized orthogonal matching pursuit. IEEE Sig. Process. Lett. **24**(9), 1308–1312 (2017)

Amplitude Blind Estimation of Co-channel Time-Frequency Overlapped Signals

Mingqian Liu, Zonghui Lu(✉), Qiqi Ren, and Shuo Chen

State Key Laboratory of Integrated Service Networks, Xidian University, Xi'an 710071, Shaanxi, China
mqliu@mail.xidian.edu.cn, 1204102557@qq.com

Abstract. With the rapid development of wireless communication technology, modulation signals are more and more intensive in the same frequency. Based on the background of non-cooperative communication system, the research on blind estimation of time domain parameters of time-frequency overlapped signals is conducted. An amplitude estimation method of time frequency overlapped signal over single channel based on forth order cyclic cumulants is proposed. This method employs the fourth-order cyclic cumulants amplitude spectrum of the overlapped signal to estimate the amplitude at the cycle frequency of the respective signal symbol rate, thereby obtaining the amplitude estimation value of each signal component. Simulation results show that the proposed blind amplitude estimation method can achieve better estimation performance in low SNR conditions. Compared with the existing estimation method, the proposed method has better estimation performance.

Keywords: Amplitude estimation · Co-channel signal · Cyclic cumulants · Cyclic spectrum · Time-frequency overlapped signal

1 Introduction

Cooperative communication mode is the most commonly used communication mode in modern communication systems. That is, the receiver knows some relevant information in advance, such as the senders modulation type, communication system, carrier frequency, coding method, and other parameters such as amplitude, phase, phase, etc. However, in some practical applications, there is also a non-cooperative communication mode. Non-cooperative communication is an unauthorized access communication mode, which needs to be connected to

This work was supported by the National Natural Science Foundation of China under Grant 62071364, in part by the Aeronautical Science Foundation of China under Grant 2020Z073081001, in part by the Fundamental Research Funds for the Central Universities under Grant JB210104, and in part by the 111 Project under Grant B08038.

© ICST Institute for Computer Sciences, Social Informatics and Telecommunications Engineering 2022
Published by Springer Nature Switzerland AG 2022. All Rights Reserved
S. Shi et al. (Eds.): 6GN 2021, LNICST 439, pp. 470–481, 2022.
https://doi.org/10.1007/978-3-031-04245-4_41

the cooperative communication system and does not affect the normal communication of the cooperative communication parties [1,2]. In the non-cooperative communication mode, in order to successfully implement blind demodulation of the received signal, it is necessary to make a comprehensive and accurate estimation of the modulation parameters of the received signal. Therefore, parameter estimation of communication signals is an indispensable key technology in non-cooperative communication.

Signal parameter estimation refers to constructing sample function statistics, then substituting the sample values into the statistics, and using the observed values of the statistics as the estimated values of the corresponding parameters [3]. It is one of the important branches of mathematical statistics and a basic form of statistical inference. The parameter estimation of the time-frequency overlap signal refers to the extraction of parameter information about the signal from the intercepted received signal. The parameter estimation of the modulated signal includes the modulation parameters such as the carrier frequency, symbol rate, amplitude, initial phase and time delay of the received signal. estimate. At present, the research on parameter estimation of single signal is relatively mature, but the research on parameter estimation of time-frequency overlapping signal has some problems that need to be solved urgently.

In the radio communication process, due to the influence of factors such as channel fading and noise interference, the amplitude of the communication signal will change, which will have a greater impact on the estimation of the signal amplitude. For time-frequency overlapping signals, the amplitudes of the signal components cannot be separated when they are superimposed, which further increases the difficulty of amplitude estimation. Traditional signal amplitude estimation is mostly for a single signal, and there are mainly maximum likelihood estimation methods [4], which determine the signal amplitude based on the maximum likelihood estimation value of the sampled samples, but the amount of calculation is relatively large. Fourier spectrum analysis method [5,6], the disadvantage of this method is that there is spectrum leakage, which reduces the accuracy of signal amplitude estimation.

In view of the problem of poor amplitude estimation performance of existing methods when the signal-to-noise ratio is low, a amplitude estimation method of co-channel time-frequency overlapped signal based on the fourth-order cyclic cumulants is proposed. This method employs the fourth-order cyclic cumulants amplitude spectrum of the overlapped signal to estimate the amplitude at the cycle frequency of the respective signal symbol rate, thereby obtaining the amplitude estimation value of each signal component. Simulation results show that the proposed method effectively realizes the co-channel time-frequency overlapped signal amplitude parameter estimation. Moreover, the proposed method has strong anti-noise performance.

2 System Model

The model of time-frequency overlapped signal can be given as [7]

$$x(t) = \sum_{i=1}^{N} s_i(t) + n(t), \tag{1}$$

where $s_i(t) = \sum_{m=1}^{M_i} A_i a_i(m) q(t - mT_{bi} - \tau_i) \exp[j2\pi f_{ci} t + \theta_i]$. These elements A_i, $a_i(m)$, M_i and f_{ci} represent signal amplitude, symbol sequence , symbol number and carrier frequency of every signal component respectively. Also, T_i is a symbol cycle, whose reciprocal is symbol rate f_{ci}; θ_i is initial phase; $q_i(t)$ is pulse shape function. Note that if $q_i(t)$ is rectangular shape, it can be expressed as $q_i(t) = \begin{cases} 1, & |t| \leq \frac{T_i}{2} \\ 0, & others \end{cases}$. If cosine raised, it can be expressed as $q_i(t) = \frac{\sin \pi t/T_i}{\pi t/T_i} \cdot \frac{\cos \alpha \pi t/T_i}{1-4\alpha^2 t^2/{T_i}^2}$, where $\alpha(\alpha = 0.35$ usually) is roll-off factor, τ_i is signal delay, n(t) is the additive Gaussian noise. Signals in this model are independent mutually, and the same to each signal and noise.

Assume that the number of overlapped signal i = 2. We do not consider the noise n(t) for simplification. Thus, the equation can be simplified as

$$\begin{aligned} x(t) &= A(t)e^{j\phi(t)} \\ &= A_1 e^{j(2\pi f_1 t + \varphi_1(t) + \theta_1)} + A_2 e^{j(2\pi f_2 t + \varphi_2(t) + \theta_2)} \\ &= A_1 e^{j\phi_1(t)} + A_2 e^{j\phi_2(t)}, \end{aligned} \tag{2}$$

where $\phi\,(t)$ is the phase function of the received overlapped signal, so that $\phi_1\,(t)$, $\phi_2\,(t)$ represent the 2 components phase function of overlapped signal in receiver respectively. $A(t)$ represents the amplitude function, and A_1, A_2 represent the 2 components amplitude function of overlapped signal. We can note that the vector sum of A_1, A_2 constitutes time-frequency overlapped signals amplitude $A(t)$.

3 Amplitude Estimation Based on Fourth-Order Cyclic Cumulants for Time-Frequency Overlapped Signal

Cyclostationarity is one of the prominent characteristics of digital communication signal. Hence, cyclic cumulant has been an effective tool to analyze digital communication signal. Given the property of cyclic cumulants, the cyclic cumulants of stationary and non-stationary Gaussian (color) noise is zero if its order is greater than 2, so that received signals cyclic cumulants have a good ability to resist noise. This paper proposes an amplitude estimation method about time-frequency overlapped signal by using 4-order cyclic cumulants.

The 4-order cyclic cumulants $C_{42}^{\alpha}\,(\tau_1, \tau_2, \tau_3)$ is defined as

$$\begin{aligned} C_{42}^{\alpha}\,(\tau_1, \tau_2, \tau_3) = M_{4s}^{\alpha}\,(\tau_1, \tau_2, \tau_3) - M_{2s}^{\alpha}\,(\tau_1) \cdot M_{2s}^{\alpha}\,(\tau_3 - \tau_2) \\ - M_{2s}^{\alpha}\,(\tau_2) \cdot M_{2s}^{\alpha}\,(\tau_1 - \tau_3) - M_{2s}^{\alpha}\,(\tau_3) \cdot M_{2s}^{\alpha}\,(\tau_2 - \tau_1)\,. \end{aligned} \tag{3}$$

If $\tau_1 = \tau_2 = \tau_3 = 0$, (3) can be given as

$$C_{42}^{\alpha} \triangleq C_{42}^{\alpha}(0,0,0) = M_{40}^{\alpha}(0,0,0) - 2M_{21}^{\alpha}(0) \cdot M_{21}^{\alpha}(0) - M_{20}^{\alpha}(0) \cdot M_{20}^{\alpha}(0), \quad (4)$$

and rewrite (3) as

$$C_{42}^{\alpha} = \begin{cases} \frac{A^4 C_{\alpha,42}}{T_s} \int_{-\infty}^{+\infty} \prod_{j=1}^{4} (q(t)) e^{-j2\pi\alpha t} dt, \alpha = \pm\frac{d}{T_s}, d \in Z, \\ 0, \qquad others, \end{cases} \quad (5)$$

where $C_{\alpha,42}$ is the 4-order cyclic cumulants value of $s(t)$. if $q(t)$ is raise cosine pulse, $C_{42}^{\alpha}(\tau_1, \tau_2, \tau_3)$ is non-zero in $\alpha = \pm d/T_s, d \in Z$. Besides, its maximum value appears at $\alpha = 0$ and the secondary is at $\alpha = \pm 1/T_s$.

We should notice that cyclic cumulants has another key property: signal selectivity. Considering the following multi-channel model, whose signals and noise are independent mutually. Co-channel signal can be expressed as follows

$$x(t) = s_1(t) + s_2(t) + \cdots + s_M(t) + n(t), \quad (6)$$

and its cyclic cumulants can be expressed as

$$C_{kx}^{\alpha}(\tau) = \sum_{i=1}^{M} C_{ks_i}^{\alpha}(\tau) + C_{kN}^{\alpha}(\tau). \quad (7)$$

For the cyclic cumulants of stationary and non-stationary Gaussian (color) noise is zero when the order of value is greater than 2, the 4-order cyclic cumulants of noise is 0. Hence, (7) can be written as

$$C_{kr}^{\alpha}(\tau) = \sum_{i=1}^{M} C_{kx_i}^{\alpha}(\tau). \quad (8)$$

Combining with the model in this section, the cycle frequency of time-frequency overlapped signal in the co-channel is

$$\alpha = \bigcup_{i=1}^{N} \alpha_i = \bigcup_{i=1}^{N} (k/T_{si}), k = 0, 1. \quad (9)$$

According to the property of cyclic cumulants, we can conclude that the cyclic cumulants has linear properties and the received signal in the single-channel is the linear combination of original signal. An achievement can be made that the cyclic cumulants to the received signal and the sum of every signals cyclic cumulants is the same. This property indicates that cyclic cumulants can reflect the cyclostationarity of every independent signal component and it is suitable for the estimation on time-frequency signal in the co-channel.

For MPSK signals, the expression can be written as

$$s(t) = \sum_{k} A a_k q(t - kT_s) e^{j(2\pi f_c t + \varphi_0)}, \quad (10)$$

where a_k is the symbol sequence of signals in interval $t \in (kT_s - T_s/2, kT_s + T_s/2)$, $a_k \in \{e^{j2\pi(m-1)/M}, m = 1, 2, \ldots, M\}$, and $q(t - nT_s)$ is cosine shaping pulse whose roll-off factor is 0.35. f_c, T_s and φ_0 are carrier frequency, symbol period and initial phase, respectively.

Substitute the expression of MPSK signals into the definition of 4-order cyclic cumulants and MPSK signals 4-order cyclic cumulants can be given as

$$C^{\alpha}_{42-MPSK} = \frac{A^4 C_{\alpha,42}}{T_s} \int_{-\infty}^{+\infty} \prod_{j=1}^{4} (q(t)) e^{-j2\pi\alpha t} dt, \tag{11}$$

where $\mathrm{C}_{\alpha,42}$ is 4-order cumulants value of $s(t)$. For QPSK signals, because $a_k = e^{j(m-1)2\pi/4}, m = 1, 2, \cdots, 4$ and $a_k^2 = \pm j, a_k^4 \equiv 1$, QPSK signals 4-order cumulants is

$$\mathrm{C}_{\alpha,42-\mathrm{QPSK}} = M_{\alpha,42} - 2(M_{\alpha,21})^2 - |M_{\alpha,20}|^2 = -\frac{1}{N}\sum_{k=1}^{N} {a_k}^4 = -1. \tag{12}$$

Further more, the 4-order cyclic cumulants of the signal is

$$C^{\alpha}_{42-QPSK} = -\frac{A^4}{T_s} \int_{-\infty}^{+\infty} \prod_{j=1}^{4} (q(t)) e^{-j2\pi\alpha t} dt. \tag{13}$$

The $|C^{\alpha}_{42}|$ value of QPSK signals is shown in Fig. 1. From Fig. 1, we can see that the maximum value of $|C^{\alpha}_{42}|$ appears at $\alpha = 0$, and the secondary at $\alpha = \pm 1/T_s$. So that we can estimate signals component amplitude based on the value of great discrete spectrum line.

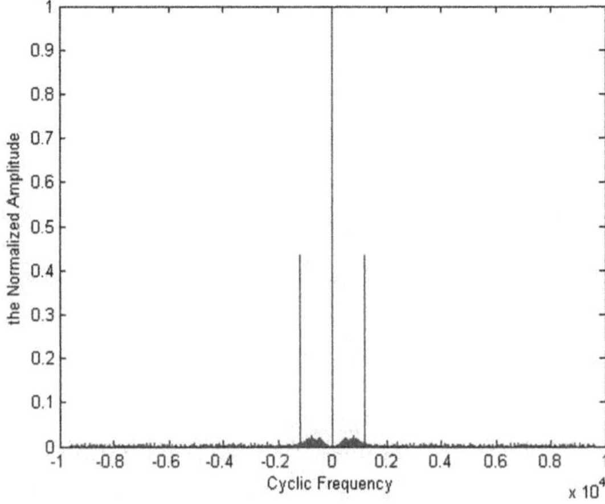

Fig. 1. $|C^{\alpha}_{42}|$ of co-channel two QPSK overlapped signals.

For 8PSK signals, because of $a_k = e^{j(m-1)2\pi/8}, m = 1, 2, \cdots, 8$, whose 4-order cumulants is given as

$$\mathrm{C}_{\alpha,42-8\mathrm{PSK}} = M_{\alpha,42} - 2(M_{\alpha,21})^2 - |M_{\alpha,20}|^2 = -\frac{1}{N}\sum_{k=1}^{N} {a_k}^4 = -1. \quad (14)$$

Hence, the 4-order cyclic cumulants of 8PSK can be expressed as follows:

$$C^{\alpha}_{42-8PSK} = -\frac{A^4}{T_s}\int_{-\infty}^{+\infty}\prod_{j=1}^{4}(q(t))e^{-j2\pi\alpha t}dt. \quad (15)$$

For 16QPSK signals, because of $a_k = e^{j(m-1)2\pi/16}, m = 1, 2, \cdots, 16$, the 4-order cumulants is given as

$$\mathrm{C}_{\alpha,42-16\mathrm{PSK}} = M_{\alpha,42} - 2(M_{\alpha,21})^2 - |M_{\alpha,20}|^2 = -\frac{1}{N}\sum_{k=1}^{N} {a_k}^4 = -1. \quad (16)$$

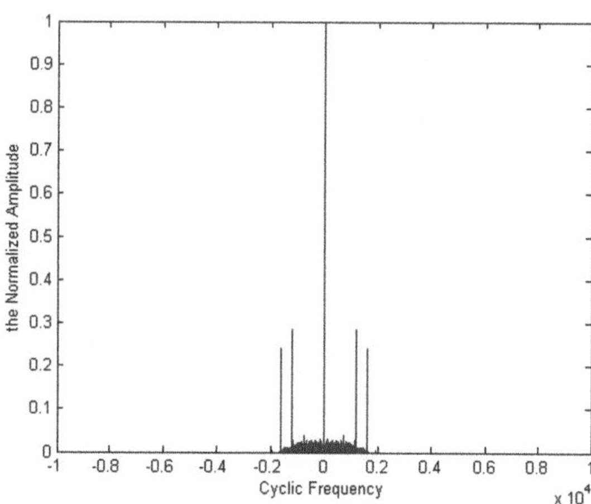

Fig. 2. $|C^{\alpha}_{42}|$ of co-channel QPSK and 16PSK overlapped signals.

From the above analysis, PSK signals, QPSK, 8PSK and 16PSK have the same expression for 4-order cyclic cumulants. More importantly, the value of their cyclic cumulants are non-zero at the cycle frequency $\alpha = \pm k/T_s, k \in Z$, the maximum value at $\alpha = 0$, and the secondary at $\alpha = \pm 1/T_s$. The following figure shows two mixed signals $|C^{\alpha}_{42}|$ value. In Fig. 2, the maximum value of $|C^{\alpha}_{42}|$ appears at $\alpha = 0$, but signals are overlapped and cant be distinguished. Every signal components discrete spectrum line exists in the area where the cycle frequency equals the symbol rate. If $\alpha = \pm 1/T_s$ and roll-off coefficient of raised cosine takes a fixed value, the integral term of 4-order cyclic cumulants

$\int_{-\infty}^{+\infty} \prod_{j=1}^{4} (q(t))e^{-j2\pi \alpha t}dt$ is given by constant number and be expressed by G_i. It is only in this case that the symbol rate of time-frequency overlapped signals component are not equal and do not exist any integer multiple relationship, can we estimate the symbol cycle T_{s_i} by detecting the position of discrete spectrum line. This paper uses raised discrete spectrum line to estimate discrete spectrum line. Specific process is as follows:

Assuming that $u(f)$ is the amplitude spectrum of 4-order cyclic cumulants, where f_0 means the frequency when $|u(f)|$ takes the maximum. Using the ratio of $|u(f_0)|$ and the mean of $|u(f)|$ to express the prominence of f_0. If the ratio is bigger than a certain threshold, there shall be a discrete spectrum line atf_0. Because of frequency resolution, there are many approximate discrete spectrum line of 4-order cyclic cumulants but only one. In order to prevent these discrete spectrum line which has a bad effect when searching the maximum during the next time, we need to set $|u(f)|$ zero in a section $[f_0 - \delta_0, f_0 + \delta_0]$, where $\delta_0 > 0$. If $\alpha_1 = 1/T_1$, $\alpha_2 = -1/T_1$, the first signal components symbol cycle $\hat{T}_1 = \frac{2}{|\alpha_1 - \alpha_2|}$. In the same way, we can estimate symbol cycle of other signals. Substituting these values into the above formula respectively, we can acquire the value of every signals amplitude estimation.

From the above, a amplitude blind estimation of time-frequency overlapped signals based on 4-order cyclic cumulants in co-channel is proposed, and the steps of the proposed method are as follows:

Step 1: Search the value of 4-order cyclic cumulants $\left|C_{r,42}^{\alpha}\right|$ of time-frequency overlapped signals $r(t)$ in single channel, then get the amplitude spectrum of 4-order cyclic cumulants overlapped signals $\alpha - \left|C_{r,42}^{\alpha}\right|$;

Step 2: When the symbol rate of time-frequency overlapped signals component is not equal and does not exist integer multiple relationship, we can estimate the symbol rate of signal component $1/T_{s_i}$, according to discrete spectrum line detection method;

Step 3: In the light of the symbol rate $1/T_{s_i}$, search the value of $C_{x,40}^{1/T_{s_i}}$ in $\alpha - \left|C_{r,42}^{\alpha}\right|$ when $\alpha_i = 1/T_{s_i}$;

Step 4: According to the value of step 2 and step 3, search the amplitude estimation value of every signal component $\hat{A}_i = \sqrt[4]{|C_{42}^{\alpha}| \cdot T_{s_i}/G_i}$.

4 Simulation Results and Discussion

Simulation experiment has been done by using MATLAB to validate the effectiveness of the estimation method in this paper. Time-frequency overlapped signals and additive white gaussian noise are adopted in this experiment. In order to assess the performance of the method in different ways, we take different kinds of signals (QPSK, 8PSK and 16PSK) into simulation experiment, and the coefficient of roll-off is 0.35. It also takes 1000 Monte Carlo tests. The evaluation criteria of amplitude estimation is MSE.

In order to measure the SNRs effects on the performance of amplitude estimation on time-frequency overlapped signals, we can put the arbitrary combination of two in QPSK, 8PSK and 16PSK signals, and the parameter setting is as follows: carrier frequency$f_{c1} = 2.7$ KHz and $f_{c2} = 3.3$ KHz; symbol rate $f_{b_1} = 1.2$ KBaud and $f_{b2} = 1.6$ KBaud; sample rate $f_s = 19.2$ KHz; data length 5000. The simulation result is shown in Fig. 3.

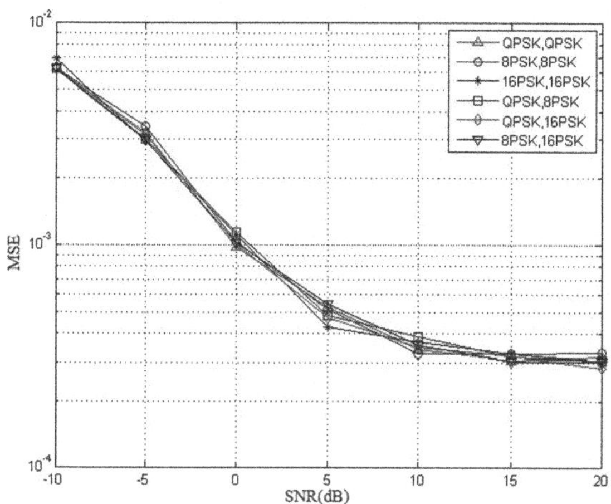

Fig. 3. Amplitude estimation performance of time-frequency overlapped signals with different SNRs.

As can be seen from the Fig. 3, in the case of double overlapping signals, when the SNR is bigger than 0, the method of amplitude estimation can achieve ideal estimation performance, and with the increase of SNR , the estimation performance increase.

In order to test the influence of sample data length to the amplitude estimation of time-frequency overlapped signals, we can put the arbitrary combination of two in QPSK, 8PSK and 16PSK signals, and the SNR is 10 dB. the parameter setting is as follows: carrier frequency $f_{c1} = 2.7$ KHz and $f_{c2} = 3.3$ KHz; symbol rata $f_{b_1} = 1.2$ KBaud and $f_{b2} = 1.6$ KBaud; sample rata $f_s = 19.2$ KHz. the simulation results are as Fig. 4.

From Fig. 4, with the increase of sample data length, the estimated performance increases for the decrease of the amplitude estimation MES from time-frequency overlapped double signals. The reason is that cyclostationarity which is reflected by cyclic cumulants is an asymptotic property, so that the estimation performance of amplitude estimation method can be improved by increasing the data length.

In order to measure the influence of spectrum overlap rate to the performance of amplitude estimation on time-frequency overlapped signals, we can put the arbitrary combination of two in QPSK, 8PSK and 16PSK signals, and the SNR is 10 dB. The parameter setting is as follows: sample rate $f_s = 19.2$ KHz, data length is 5000, carrier frequency combination are $f_{c1} = 1.9$ KHz and $f_{c2} = 3.3$

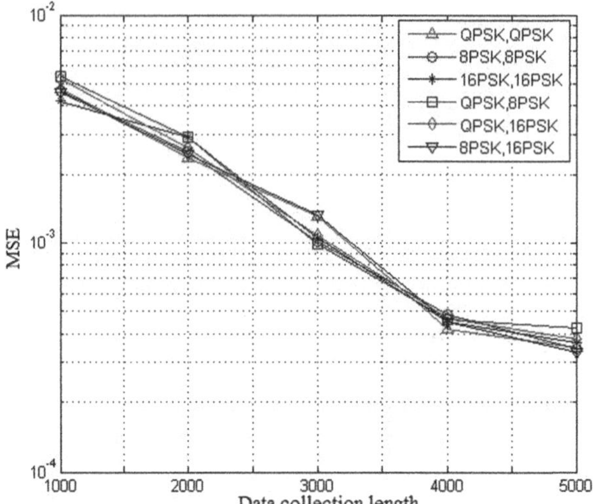

Fig. 4. Amplitude estimation performance of time-frequency overlapped signals with different data length.

KHz; f_{c1} = 2.2 KHz and f_{c2} = 3.3 KHz; f_{c1} = 2.5 KHz and f_{c2} = 3.3; KHz f_{c1} = 3.1 KHz and f_{c2} = 3.3 KHz respectively. Symbol rate f_{b1} = 1200 Baud and f_{b2} = 1600 Baud.The simulation results are shown in Fig. 5.

As can be seen from Fig. 5, spectrum overlap rate has a little influence on amplitude estimation. The reason is that when data length is fitful, if the symbol rate of signal component is different, using cyclic cumulants of signals to estimate amplitude is helpful in distinguishing different signals amplitude information, while its performance will not be affected by other signals.

In order to measure the influence of power ratio to the performance of amplitude estimation on time-frequency overlapped signals. We can put the arbitrary combination of two in QPSK, 8PSK and 16PSK signals, and the SNR is 10 dB. the power ratio of two signals is 1.2. The parameter setting of the two signals is as follows: carrier frequency f_{c1} = 2.7 KHz and f_{c2} = 3.3 KHz; symbol rate f_{b_1} = 1.2 KBaud and f_{b2} = 1.6 KBaud; sample rate f_s = 19.2 KHz ; data length 5000. The simulation results are as Fig. 6.

From Fig. 6, which compares with Fig. 3 whose power ratio is 1.0, the increase of signals component s power ratio can make the estimation performance decrease. When the power ratio of two signals is 1:2 and the SNR is 10 dB, the amplitude estimation method can achieve an ideal performance. As the 4-order cyclic cumulants estimation in face is done with the biquadrate magnitudes of signals, so that the change of signals power can bring a big change to the 4-order cyclic cumulants.

In order to compare the performance of the method in this paper with the existing method, the overlapped signals are two misxed QPSK. In the same simulation environment and the parameter setting, the method in this paper has to compare with the method in [12]. The result is shown in Fig. 7.

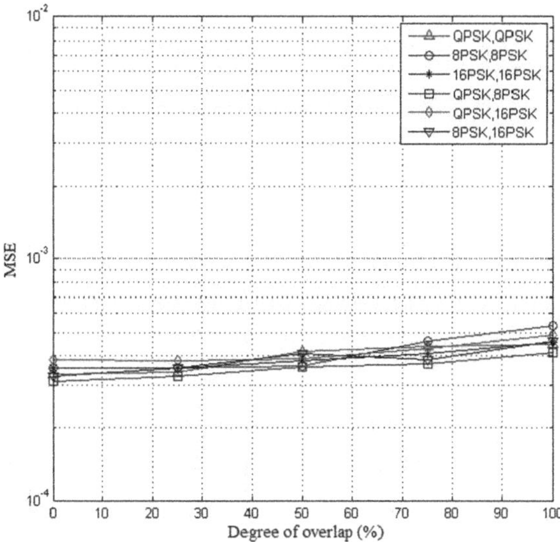

Fig. 5. Amplitude estimation performance of time-frequency overlapped signals with different spectrum overlap rates.

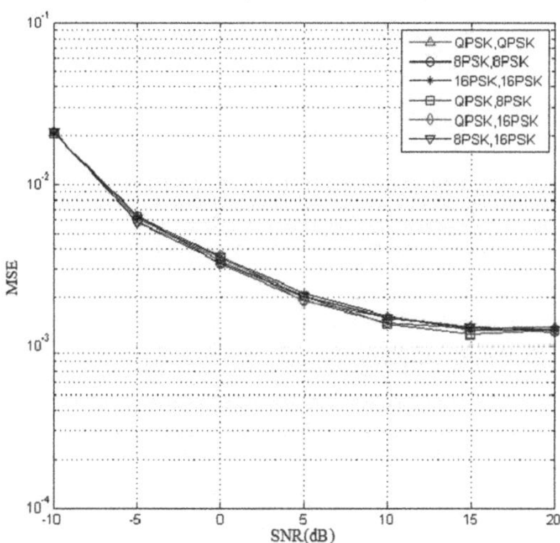

Fig. 6. Amplitude estimation performance of time-frequency overlapped signals when the power ratio is 1.2

As can be seen in Fig. 7, in the same simulation condition, the method in this paper has a better performance than the method which is based on max-min method. In the case of low SNR, the max-min arithmetic does not have an ideal estimation performance. But the method in this paper can be better, due to that cyclic cumulants can suppress noise. The method in [12] needs $4(M+N)-6$ times

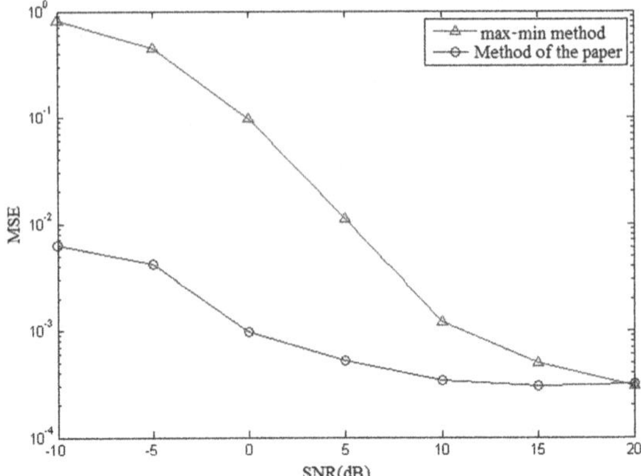

Fig. 7. Amplitude estimation performance comparison with different methods

addition of complex number and 4N multiplication of complex number, where M is window length; in this paper, the times of addition and multiplication of complex are $2N\log_2 N+N$ and $[N\log_2 N+5N$, so that the algorithm complexity in this paper is bigger, but the performance is better than the method in [12], especially in the low SNR condition.

5 Conclusion

In order to to solve the poor performance in amplitude estimation when the SNR is low, this paper introduces an amplitude estimation method based on the 4-order cyclic cumulants for time-frequency overlapped signals in co-channel. Simulation results show that the proposed method has a good anti-noise performance. Moreover, the proposed method has better estimation performance compared with the existing methods.

References

1. Wang, Q., Peng, H., Wang, B.: Co-channel multi-signal detection and signal source number estimation algorithm based on cyclic cumulants. J. Inf. Eng. Univ. **13**(2), 184–188 (2012)
2. Haitao, F.: Analysis of Single-Channel Time-Frequency Overlapping Signal based on Cyclostationarity. University of Electronic Science and Technology (2009)
3. Yang, X., Zhang, Q., Han, Y.: Signal amplitude estimation under undersampling. Commun. J. **20**(Supplement), 318–322 (1999)
4. Collmeyer, A.J., Gupta, S.C.: Estimating the amplitude of a sinusoid from noisy random samples. IEEE Trans. Inf. Theory **6**(4), 488–489 (1970)
5. Huang, X.D., Wang, Z., Huo, G.Q.: New method of estimation of phase, amplitude, and frequency based all phase FFT spectrum analysis. In: Proceedings of 2007 International Symposium on Intelligent Signal Processing and Communication Systems, pp. 284–287. Xiamen, China (2007)

6. Qi, G., Jia, X.: Amplitude estimation of sinusoidal signal based on DFT Phase. J. Dalian Marit. Univ. **27**(3), 71–74 (2001)
7. Jain, V.K., Jr, C.W.L., Davis, D.C.: High-accuracy analog measurements via interpolated FFT. IEEE Trans. IM **28**(2), 113–122 (1979)
8. Wu, J.K., Long, J., Liang, Y.: Estimation of frequency, amplitude and phase of sinusoidal signals. In: IEEE 2004 International Symposium on Industrial Electronics, Palais des Congres Ajaccio, pp. 353–356 (2004)
9. Leopoldo, A., Antonio, N.: True-power measurement in digital communication systems affected by in-channel interference. IEEE Trans. Instrum. Measure. **58**(12), 3985–3994 (2009)
10. Huang, C., Liu, Z., Jiang, W., et al.: Chip time width, carrier frequency and amplitude estimation of spread spectrum direct sequence signal based on cyclic spectral envelope. Electron. J. **30**(9), 1353–1356 (2002)
11. Pan, S., Bai, D., Yi, N., et al.: Estimation of interference signal amplitude in paired carrier multiple access system. Vac. Electron. Technol. **21**(2), 21–24 (2003)
12. Bin, X., Rui, G., Chen, B.: An algorithm for estimating the amplitude of single antenna Co-frequency mixed signal. Telecommun. Technol. **51**(10), 20–23 (2011)
13. Rui, G., Bin, X., Zhang, S.: Amplitude estimation algorithm for single-channel mixed signals. Commun. J. **32**(12), 82–87 (2011)

Initial Phrase Blind Estimation of Co-channel Time-Frequency Overlapped Signals

Mingqian Liu(✉), Zhenju Zhang, and Shuo Chen

State Key Laboratory of Integrated Service Networks, Xidian University, Xi'an 710071, Shaanxi, China
mqliu@mail.xidian.edu.cn

Abstract. In order to successfully implement blind demodulation of the received signal, it is necessary to make a comprehensive and accurate estimation of the parameters of the received signal. Therefore, parameter estimation of communication signals is an indispensable key technology in underlay cognitive networks. This paper focuses on the initial phase estimation method of time-frequency overlapped signals and the initial phrase blind estimation method based on four-order cyclic cumulants is proposed. In this paper, the four-order cyclic cumulants is computed firstly, then the test statistics are constructed by the ratio of four-order cyclic cumulants in specific frequency and specific cycle frequency. Finally, and the initial phrase of signal component are estimated based on the test statistics. Simulation results show that the proposed method achieves initial phrase estimation of time-frequency overlapped signals effectively and the performance is better.

Keywords: Co-channel signal · Cyclic spectrum · Forth-order cyclic cumulants · Initial phrase estimation · Time-frequency overlapped signal

1 Introduction

In communication systems, multiple signals often appear in the same frequency band at the same time, which is the so-called time-frequency overlapped signal, such as co-channel or adjacent channel interference in mobile communication, mutual interference of frequency bands in satellite communication, multiple echoes in radar systems. In the non-cooperative communication mode, in order to successfully implement blind demodulation of the received signal, it is necessary

This work was supported by the National Natural Science Foundation of China under Grant 62071364, in part by the Aeronautical Science Foundation of China under Grant 2020Z073081001, in part by the Fundamental Research Funds for the Central Universities under Grant JB210104, and in part by the 111 Project under Grant B08038.

© ICST Institute for Computer Sciences, Social Informatics and Telecommunications Engineering 2022
Published by Springer Nature Switzerland AG 2022. All Rights Reserved
S. Shi et al. (Eds.): 6GN 2021, LNICST 439, pp. 482–490, 2022.
https://doi.org/10.1007/978-3-031-04245-4_42

to make a comprehensive and accurate estimation of the modulation parameters of the received signal. Therefore, parameter estimation of communication signals is an indispensable key technology in non-cooperative communication.

The parameter estimation of the time-frequency overlap signal refers to the extraction of parameter information about the signal from the intercepted received signal. The parameter estimation of the modulated signal includes the modulation parameters such as the carrier frequency, symbol rate, amplitude, initial phase and time delay of the received signal. Furthermore, the initial phase estimation methods for the signal can be divided into two categories, one is the initial phase estimation based on auxiliary data [1–3], and the other is the blind estimation of the initial phase without auxiliary data. In non-cooperative communication systems, auxiliary data such as pilot frequency and training sequence are all unknown information and cannot be obtained from the received signal. Therefore, the paper mainly studies the blind estimation method of initial phase without auxiliary data.

This paper firstly introduces a initial phase estimation method for time-frequency overlapped signal based on fourth-order cyclic cumulants. Signal method. The method constructs a test statistic based on the ratio of the fourth-order cyclic cumulants, and estimates the initial phase of each signal component based on the phase information of the test statistic. Simulation results show that the method can effectively estimate the initial phase parameters of co-channel time-frequency overlapped signals.

2 System Model

The model of time-frequency overlapped signal can be given as [7]

$$x(t) = \sum_{i-1}^{N} s_i(t) + n(t), \tag{1}$$

where $s_i(t) = \sum_{m=1}^{M_i} A_i a_i(m) q(t - mT_{bi} - \tau_i) \exp[j2\pi f_{ci} t + \theta_i]$. These elements A_i, $a_i(m)$, M_i and f_{ci} represent signal amplitude, symbol sequence, symbol number and carrier frequency of every signal component respectively. Also, T_i is a symbol cycle, whose reciprocal is symbol rate f_{ci}; θ_i is initial phase; $q_i(t)$ is pulse shape function. Note that if $q_i(t)$ is rectangular shape, it can be expressed as $q_i(t) = \begin{cases} 1, & |t| \le \frac{T_i}{2} \\ 0, & others \end{cases}$. If cosine raised, it can be expressed as $q_i(t) = \frac{\sin \pi t/T_i}{\pi t/T_i} \cdot \frac{\cos \alpha \pi t/T_i}{1-4\alpha^2 t^2/{T_i}^2}$, where $\alpha(\alpha = 0.35$ usually) is roll-off factor, τ_i is signal delay, n(t) is the additive Gaussian noise. Signals in the model are independent mutually, and the same to each signal and noise.

3 Initial Phrase Estimation of Time-Frequency Overlapped Signals Based on Fourth-Order Cyclic Cumulants

The definition of 4-order cyclic cumulants $C_{a,40}$ and $C_{a,42}$ is as follows respectively.

$$C_{40}^{\alpha} = \frac{E^2 C_{a,40} e^{j4\varphi_0}}{T_s} \int_{-\infty}^{\infty} p^4\left(t\right) e^{-j2\pi(\alpha-4f_c)t} dt, \tag{2}$$

$$C_{42}^{\alpha} = \frac{E^2 C_{a,42}}{T_s} \int_{-\infty}^{\infty} p^4\left(t\right) e^{-j2\pi\alpha t} dt, \tag{3}$$

where φ_0 is initial phrase, f_c is carrier frequency, and $1/T_s$ is symbol rate.

The commonly used modulation signals in digital communication are BPSK, QPSK, 16QAM and 64QAM, the value of 4-order cumulants are as follows

$$\begin{aligned} &C_{a,40-BPSK} = C_{a,42-BPSK} = -2, \\ &C_{a,40-QPSK} = C_{a,42-QPSK} = -1, \\ &C_{a,40-8PSK} = 0, C_{a,42-8PSK} = -1, \\ &C_{a,40-16QAM} = C_{a,42-16QAM} = -0.68, \\ &C_{a,40-64QAM} = C_{a,42-64QAM} = -0.62. \end{aligned} \tag{4}$$

Hence, the value of the 4-order cyclic cumulants for these signals are

$$C_{40-BPSK}^{\alpha} = -\frac{2E^2 e^{j4\varphi_0}}{T_s} \int_{-\infty}^{+\infty} p^4\left(t\right) e^{j2\pi(\alpha-4f_c)t} dt, \tag{5}$$

$$C_{42-BPSK}^{\alpha} = -\frac{2E^2}{T_s} \int_{-\infty}^{+\infty} p^4\left(t\right) e^{-j2\pi\alpha t} dt, \tag{6}$$

$$C_{40-QPSK}^{\alpha} = -\frac{E^2 e^{j4\varphi_0}}{T_s} \int_{-\infty}^{+\infty} p^4\left(t\right) e^{j2\pi(\alpha-4f_c)t} dt, \tag{7}$$

$$C_{42-QPSK}^{\alpha} = -\frac{E^2}{T_s} \int_{-\infty}^{+\infty} p^4\left(t\right) e^{j2\pi\alpha t} dt, \tag{8}$$

$$C_{40-8PSK}^{\alpha} = 0, C_{42-8PSK}^{\alpha} = -\frac{E^2}{T_s} \int_{-\infty}^{+\infty} p^4\left(t\right) e^{j2\pi\alpha t} dt, \tag{9}$$

$$C_{40-16QAM}^{\alpha} = -\frac{0.68E^2 e^{j4\varphi_0}}{T_s} \int_{-\infty}^{+\infty} p^4\left(t\right) e^{j2\pi(\alpha-4f_c)t} dt, \tag{10}$$

$$C_{42-16QAM}^{\alpha} = -\frac{0.68E^2}{T_s} \int_{-\infty}^{+\infty} p^4\left(t\right) e^{j2\pi\alpha t} dt, \tag{11}$$

$$C_{40-64QAM}^{\alpha} = -\frac{0.62E^2 e^{j4\varphi_0}}{T_s} \int_{-\infty}^{+\infty} p^4\left(t\right) e^{j2\pi(\alpha-4f_c)t} dt, \tag{12}$$

$$C_{42-64QAM}^{\alpha} = -\frac{0.62E^2}{T_s}\int_{-\infty}^{+\infty} p^4(t)\, e^{j2\pi\alpha t} dt. \tag{13}$$

From the above expression of 4-order cyclic cumulants, we can note that C_{40}^{α} includes initial phrase information, but C_{42}^{α} does not. So that we can use the ratio of C_{40}^{α} and C_{42}^{α} to estimate the initial phrase.

From (2), we know that when $\alpha = 4f_c + 1/T_s$ the expression of C_{40}^{α} is

$$C_{40}^{4f_c+1/T_s} = \frac{E^2 C_{a,40} e^{j4\varphi_0}}{T_s}\int_{-\infty}^{\infty} p^4(t)\, e^{-j2\pi t/T_s} dt, \tag{14}$$

and when $\alpha = 1/T_s$ the expression of C_{42}^{α} is given as

$$C_{42}^{1/T_s} = \frac{E^2 C_{a,42}}{T_s}\int_{-\infty}^{\infty} p^4(t)\, e^{-j2\pi t/T_s} dt. \tag{15}$$

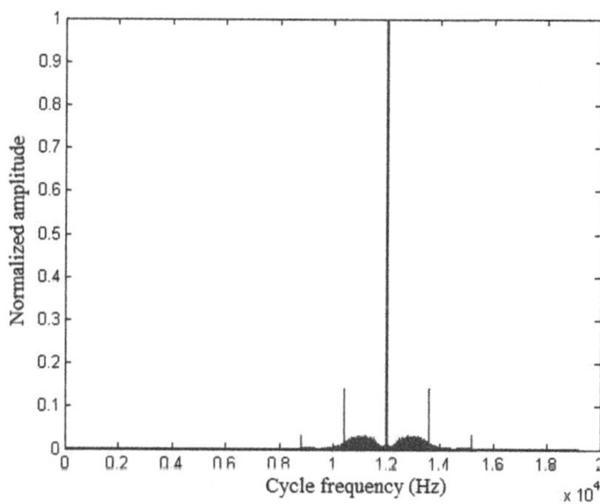

Fig. 1. The 4-order cyclic cumulants C_{40}^{α} of QPSK.

In order to make it more intuitive, the 4-order cyclic cumulants C_{40}^{α} and C_{42}^{α} are shown in Fig. 1 and Fig. 2, respectively. It can see that the value of C_{40}^{α} and C_{42}^{α} is bigger and not zero at $\alpha = 4f_c + 1/T_s$ and at $\alpha = 1/T_s$ respectively. Besides, from Eqs. 14 and 15, it can find it that the integral part of the two expressions are the same, but only Eq. 14 has initial phrase information. Therefore we can estimate the signal components initial phrase by structuring characteristic parameters T. The expression of T is show as

$$T = \frac{C_{40}^{4f_c+1/T_s}}{C_{42}^{1/T_s}} = \frac{\frac{E^2 C_{a,40} e^{j4\varphi_0}}{T_s}\int_{-\infty}^{\infty} p^4(t)\, e^{-j2\pi t/T_s} dt}{\frac{E^2 C_{a,42}}{T_s}\int_{-\infty}^{\infty} p^4(t)\, e^{-j2\pi t/T_s} dt} = \frac{C_{a,40} e^{j4\varphi_0}}{C_{a,42}}. \tag{16}$$

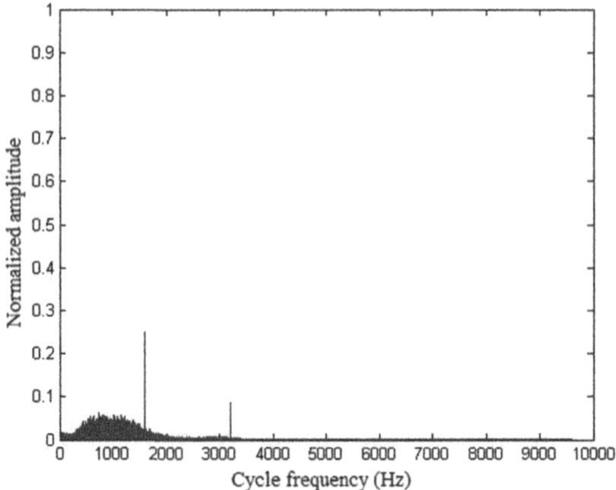

Fig. 2. The 4-order cyclic cumulants C_{42}^{α} of QPSK.

As $C_{a,40}$ of BPSK, QPSK, 16QAM and 64QAM are all real, the initial phrase information is included in parameter T. Thus we can estimate the initial phrase by detecting T, the estimator of initial phrase ϕ_i is as follow.

$$\overset{\wedge}{\phi_i} = \frac{1}{4}\arg(T), \tag{17}$$

where arg() means compute phrase for plural.

From the above, the specific steps of initial phrase estimation method based on 4-order cyclic cumulants are as follows:

Step 1: Computing 4-order cyclic cumulants $C_{x,40}^{\alpha}$ and $C_{x,42}^{\alpha}$ of time-frequency overlapped signals by (3–8) and (3–9), then get the 4-order cyclic cumulants spectrum $\alpha - C_{x,40}^{\alpha}$ and $\alpha - C_{x,42}^{\alpha}$;

Step 2: In light of the known signals carrier frequency f_{c1}, f_{c2} and symbol rate $1/T_{s1}$, $1/T_{s2}$, get the value $C_{x,40}^{4f_{c1}+1/T_{s1}}$ of $\alpha - C_{x,40}^{\alpha}$ at $\alpha = 4f_{c1} + 1/T_{s1}$ and $C_{x,40}^{4f_{c2}+1/T_{s2}}$ at $\alpha = 4f_{c2} + 1/T_{s2}$;

Step 3: According to symbol rate of the known signals $1/T_{s1}$ and $1/T_{s2}$, get the value $C_{x,42}^{1/T_{s1}}$ of $\alpha - C_{x,42}^{\alpha}$ at $\alpha = 1/T_{s1}$ and $C_{x,42}^{1/T_{s2}}$ at $\alpha = 1/T_{s2}$;

Step 4: In line with the value coming from step 2 and step 3, structure characteristic parameters $T_1 = C_{x,40}^{4f_{c1}+1/T_{s1}} / C_{x,42}^{1/T_{s1}}$ and $T_2 = C_{x,40}^{4f_{c2}+1/T_{s2}} / C_{x,42}^{1/T_{s2}}$;

Step 5: Computing phrase angle Φ_1 of characteristic parameters T_1 and Φ_2 of T_2, then get the initial phrase $\varphi_{01} = \Phi_1/4$ and $\varphi_{02} = \Phi_2/4$.

4 Simulation Results and Discussion

The validity of the method in the paper is verified via MATLAB simulate experiment. Time-frequency overlapped signals model is used in the paper, and the noise is white Gaussian noise. For evaluating performance from different sides, the next simulation experiment uses time-frequency overlapped signals whose type are MPSK and MQAM. The signals use raised cosine shaping function whose roll-factor is 0.35. And do Monte Carlo experiments 1000 times, the evaluative criteria of initial phrase is MSE.

In order to test impact of SNR to time-frequency overlapped signals initial phrase estimation, any two random combination from BPSK, QPSK,16QAM and 64QAM. Any two signals parameter setting is as follows: carrier frequency $f_{c1} = 2.7$ KHz and $f_{c2} = 3.3$ KHz, symbol rate $1/T_{s1} = 1.2$ KBaud and $1/T_{s2} = 1.6$ KBaud, sampling frequency $f_s = 19.2$ KHz, data length is 5000. The simulation result is shown in Fig. 3.

As seen from Fig. 3, in the case of two overlapped signals, when input SNR is bigger than 5 dB, the method in the paper can achieve ideal performance. With the increase of SNR, the estimation performance is also improved.

For the purpose of test the impact of data length on time-frequency overlapped signals initial phrase estimation, we should combine any two random signals from BPSK, QPSK, 16QAM, 64QAM (the SNR is 10 dB). Signals parameter setting is as follows: carrier frequency $f_{c1} = 2.7$ KHz and $f_{c2} = 3.3$ KHz; symbol rate $1/T_{s1} = 1.2$ KBaud and $1/T_{s2} = 1.6$ KBaud; sampling frequency $f_s = 19.2$ KHz. The simulation result is shown in Fig. 4.

As can be seen from Fig. 4, the MSE of time-frequency overlapped signals the estimation performance increase with the increase of sampling data length. As the cyclostationarity reflected by cyclic cumulants is an asymptotic behavior, thus we can improve estimated performance by increasing data length.

In order to test the impact of spectrum overlap rate on initial phrase estimation performance for overlap signals, we should use any two random signals from

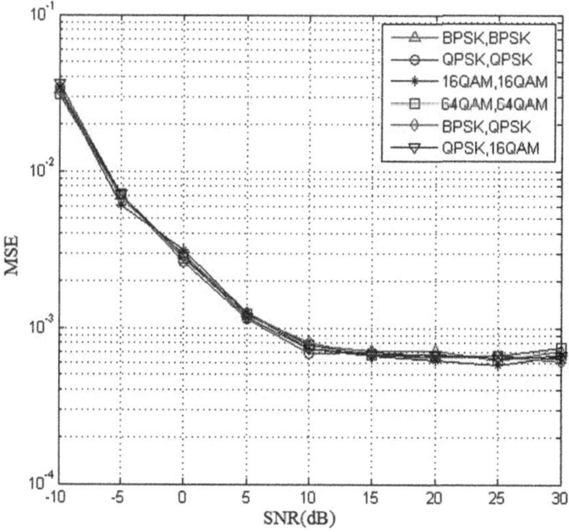

Fig. 3. Initial phrase estimation performance of time-frequency overlapped signals with different SNRs.

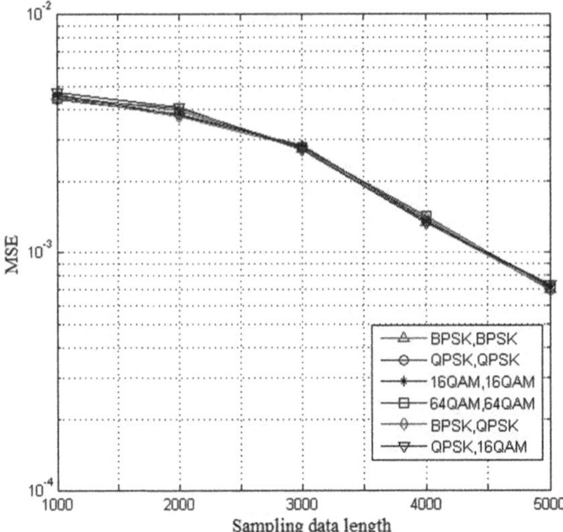

Fig. 4. Initial phrase estimation performance of time-frequency overlapped signals with different data length.

BPSK, QPSK, 16QAM, 64QAM (the SNR is 10 dB). Sampling rate $f_s = 19.2$ KHz, data length 5000, and any two signals performance setting is as follows: the combination of carrier frequency are $f_{c1} = 1.9$ KHz and $f_{c2} = 3.3$ KHz, $f_{c1} = 2.2$ KHz and $f_{c2} = 3.3$ KHz, $f_{c1} = 2.5$ KHz and $f_{c2} = 3.3$ KHz, $f_{c1} = 2.8$ KHz and $f_{c2} = 3.3$ KHz, $f_{c1} = 3.1$ KHz and $f_{c2} = 3.3$ KHz. The spectrum overlap rate of each combination is $0\%, 25\%, 50\%, 75\%$ and 100%, respectively. Symbol rate are $= 1.2$ KBaud and $= 1.6$ KBaud. The simulation result is shown in Fig. 5.

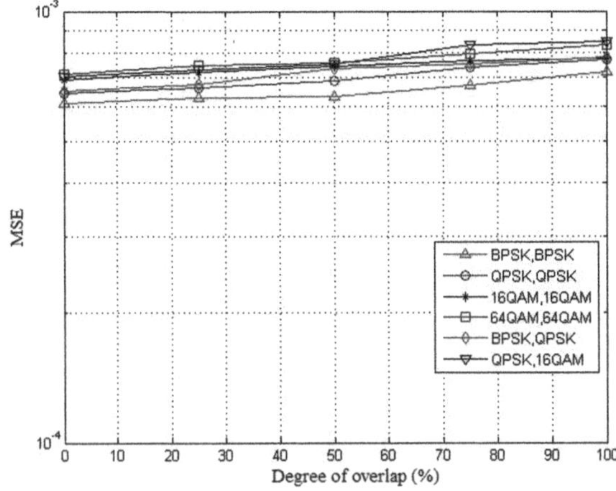

Fig. 5. Initial phrase estimation performance of time-frequency overlapped signals with different spectrum overlapped rates.

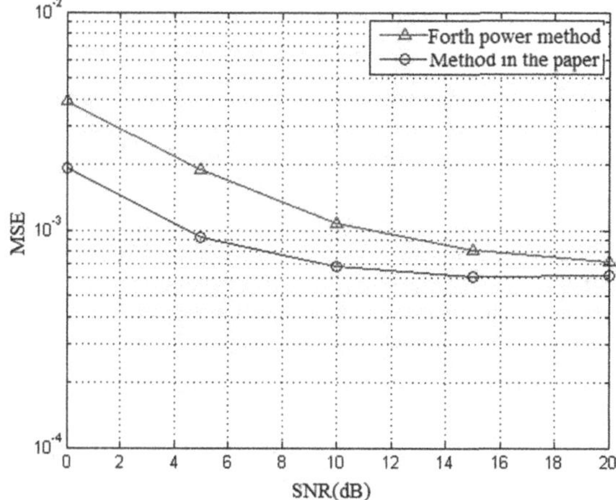

Fig. 6. Initial phrase estimation performance comparison with different methods.

From Fig. 5, we can know that the impact of spectrum overlap rate on initial phrase estimation is small. Because as the increase of spectrum overlap rate, the interval of signal components cyclic cumulants will become smaller. Therefore it can make the signal components be influenced more. As long as the symbol rate of every signal component are different, due the cyclostationarity that we can get the amplitude and phrase information, and decrease the impact of other signal component at the same time.

In order to assess the performance of the method in the paper and the existing method, the overlap signal contains two QPSK. Under the same simulation environment and parameter setting, the method introduced in the paper has to compare with the method in literature [16]. And the result is shown in Fig. 6.

From Fig. 6, it draws that as the increase of SNR, the EMS of initial phase estimation decrease. Under the same simulation condition, the method introduced in the paper is better than the existing method based on biquadrate. The method of biquadrate needs $2(N-1)^2+1$ times addition of complex quantities and $8N\,(N+1)$ times complex multiplication. The method in the paper needs addition of complex quantities and complex multiplication $2N\log_2 N+N$ times and $N\log_2 N+5N$ times and the calculation complexity reflected in complex multiplication. In a word, the calculation complexity in the paper is smaller.

5 Conclusion

In this paper, an initial phrase blind estimation method based on 4-order cyclic cumulants is introduced. The proposed method employs the ratio of 4-order cyclic cumulants by C_{40}^{α} and C_{42}^{α} in carrier frequency and symbol rate of every signal component constructing characteristic parameter, then it adopts the phrase angle information of characteristic parameter to estimate initial phrase. Simulation results show that the proposed method has a better estimation performance compared with the existing methods.

References

1. Shi, F.: Analysis method of spread spectrum signal of LEO satellite. Radio Commun. Technol. **37**(1), 41–43 (2011)
2. He, C., Li, C., Chen, H., Pan, S.: A carrier synchronization algorithm for burst 16APSK signals. Radio Eng. **42**(5), 61–64 (2012)
3. Wang, X., Zuo, J., Chen, Y., Lai, Y.: Direct sequence fast acquisition algorithm based on phase prediction and optimal search. J. Projectile Guidance **28**(3), 233–236 (2008)
4. Tretter, S.A.: Estimating the frequency of a noisy sinusoid by linear regression. IEEE Trans. Inf. Theory **31**(6), 832–835 (1985)
5. Xie, M., Xie, X., Ding, K.: Phase difference correction method for phase and frequency correction in spectrum analysis. J. Vibr. Eng. **12**(4), 454–459 (1999)
6. Qi, G., Jia, X.: High precision estimation method of sine wave frequency and initial phase based on DFT phase. Electron. J. **29**(9), 1164–1167 (2001)
7. Li, J., Wang, Y.: DFT Phase estimation algorithm and analysis of noise sensitive frequency. J. Electron. Inf. **3**(9), 2099–2103 (2009)
8. Rife, D.C., Vincent, G.A.: Use of the discrete Fourier transform in the measurement of frequencies and levels of tones. Bell Syst. Tech. J. **49**(2), 197–228 (1970)
9. Agrez, D.: Improving phase estimation with leakage minimization. In: Proceedings of 2004 Instrumentation and Measurement Technology Conference, Como, Italy, pp. 162–167. IEEE (2004)
10. Liu, X.: Fast and high precision synthetic algorithm for frequency estimation of sine wave. Electron. J. **27**(6), 126–128 (1999)
11. Lu, W., Yang, W., Hong, J., Yu, J.: A new method for frequency and initial phase estimation of sinusoidal signal. Telecommun. Technol. **52**(9), 1459–1464 (2012)
12. Feng, W.: Initial phase estimation of sinusoidal signal in Gaussian white noise. J. Xi'an Univ. Posts Telecommun. **15**(1), 59–61 (2010)
13. Huang, C., Jiang, W., Zhou, Y.: Cyclic spectrum estimation of initial phase of direct sequence spread spectrum signal and initial time of spread spectrum code sequence. Commun. J. **23**(7), 1–7 (2002)
14. Liu, M., Zhang, L., Zhong, Z.: Parameter estimation of direct sequence spread spectrum signal based on spectral correlation. Mil. Autom. **32**(3), 57–59 (2013)
15. Viterbi, A.: Nonlinear estimation of PSK-modulated carrier phase with application to burst digital transmission. IEEE Trans. Inform. Theory **29**(4), 543–551 (1983)
16. Wan, J., Shilong, T., Liao, C., et al.: Theory and Technology of Blind Separation of Communication Mixed Signals. National Defense Industry Press, Beijing (2012)

Educational Changes in the Age of 5G/6G

The Teaching Mode and Evaluation of Computer Course in Higher Vocational Colleges in the Intelligent Era

Jiangtao Geng[1,2], Yong Tang[1(✉)], and Chao Chang[1]

[1] South China Normal University, Guangzhou 510631, Guangdong, China
{johngeng,ytang}@m.scnu.edu.cn

[2] Guangzhou International Economic College, Guangzhou 510540, Guangdong, People's Republic of China

Abstract. The intelligent era brings new opportunities and challenges to the development of higher vocational education, requiring higher vocational colleges to train high-quality compound skilled talents. However, the current higher vocational students have a poor learning foundation and lack the motivation to learn, so it is necessary to reform the training of talents and the traditional classroom teaching mode of higher vocational colleges. Based on the specific teaching practice of the computer "Bilingual C Programming" course on the intelligent cloud platform, this paper explores the unique characteristics of higher vocational teaching under the background of mobile Internet and big data technology, according to different learning conditions and different teaching environments. Combining multiple teaching modes organically, achieving complementary advantages through the use of online and offline mixed teaching, using flipped classroom and PAD (Presentation Assimilation Discussion) class teaching modes, and adopting process evaluation methods to achieve teaching goals of "teaching with improvement, learning with achievement, teaching and learning mutually beneficial". The results of empirical research show that the students who adopt the flipped classroom and the PAD class teaching mode show good learning results and stronger learning motivation.

Keywords: Higher vocational teaching research · Classroom teaching mode · Flipped classroom · PAD (Presentation Assimilation Discussion) class

1 Development and Reform of Higher Vocational Education in Intelligent Era

The "nuclear fusion reactions" of the new generation of information technologies, represented by big data, intelligence, mobile Internet 5G, and cloud computing, have pushed human society into an intelligent era. The new round of scientific and technological revolution not only makes the development of China's higher

© ICST Institute for Computer Sciences, Social Informatics and Telecommunications Engineering 2022
Published by Springer Nature Switzerland AG 2022. All Rights Reserved
S. Shi et al. (Eds.): 6GN 2021, LNICST 439, pp. 493–512, 2022.
https://doi.org/10.1007/978-3-031-04245-4_43

vocational education get unprecedented opportunities but also brings many challenges, which makes the reform of talent training and traditional classroom teaching mode more urgent.

1.1 Opportunities for Development

National Strategies and Policies Indicate the Direction of Higher Vocational Education Reform and Development in the Intelligent Era. To build the first-mover advantage and grasp the initiative of the new round of scientific and technological revolution strategy, the Chinese State Council issued the "Guideline: A New Generation of Artificial Intelligence Development Plan" [1] puts forward: improve the artificial intelligence education system, strengthen the cooperation between industry, university, and research, and meet the demand for high-skilled jobs brought by the development of artificial intelligence in China. This national strategic guideline points out the direction for the talent cultivation of higher vocational education and aims to cultivate high-end and adaptable talents meeting the needs of the intelligent era.

To carry out a comprehensive reform to the vocational education sector, the Chinese State Council published its "National Vocational Education Reform Implementation Plan" [2], strengthened vocational education is a different form of education from its main-stream counterpart but of equal importance and raised the importance of vocational education to the status of "no vocational education modernization, no education modernization". The reform plan requires: to establish series of vocational education national standards, including teaching standards, curriculum standards, and other standards, and vocational colleges and universities to independently formulate talent training programs according to the standards; to promote the reform of "three aspects of education" in the field of vocational education and strive to realize the high integration of vocational skills and professional spirit training. Major construction and curriculum construction are the most important in the development of vocational education, and it is also the key to training talents in vocational education. The introduction of this reform plan points out the direction of reform and provides important and specific guidance for a series of construction activities such as the professional construction and curriculum development, setting, and implementation of vocational education.

Meanwhile, the Chinese State Council published a significant plan "China's Education Modernization 2035 Plan" [3] to drive continued reform in and advancement of China's education sector. And the Ministries of Education and Finance issued a national level development plan "Instructions on implementing the construction plan of high-level higher vocational schools and majors with Chinese characteristics" [4] (Double High-Level Initiative). In the reform development task of vocational education, it is clear that: to promote the integration of information technology and intelligent technology into the whole process of education, teaching, and management, and to integrate the means of big data and artificial intelligence to promote the transformation of school management mode, to meet the demand of "Internet + vocational education", and to promote the co-construction and sharing of digital resources and educational data, and widely apply online and offline mixed teaching, to promote autonomous, ubiquitous, personalized learning. This points out the specific direction for the teaching mode and management service reform of higher vocational education.

The Innovation of Intelligent Technology Provides Technical Support for the Development of Vocational Education. With the wide application of intelligent technology in the field of education, it promotes the intelligent development of vocational education to realize all-round multi-level intelligent development of "learning, teaching, and management", and promotes the intelligent study, teaching, and management, which injects new vitality into the development of vocational education.

(1) *In terms of learning,* the intelligent age makes personalized autonomous and ubiquitous learning a reality. With the breakthrough of artificial neural network technology, big data and cloud computing technology, expert system, natural language understanding, and other technologies, many products such as learning resource systems, intelligent teaching systems, and collaborative learning systems supported by big data and cloud platforms are pushed into the market, students can realize autonomous, personalized and ubiquitous online learning through mobile terminals with seamless access to learning services. At the same time, with the development of big data driven learning analysis technology, students' learning needs, learning behaviors, learning process, and learning results can be quantitatively analyzed, which can provide learners with personalized feedback and provide a great convenience for personalized autonomous learning.

(2) *In terms of teaching,* the educational technology and teaching in the intelligent era are fully integrated, and the rich knowledge construction tools provide abundant teaching resources, teaching methods, and convenient technical conditions for teachers' high-quality teaching. The extensive application of online and offline hybrid teaching methods enables between students, and between teachers and students to communicate, share, cooperate, and question each other in the process of exploration, building a "learning community". In the core link of vocational education, it is possible to break through the time and space limitations of teaching and learning, and build smart classrooms, virtual training scenes, and virtual factories through various information technologies and artificial intelligence technologies such as Virtual Reality (VR), Augmented Reality (AR), online industrial skills, etc. It enables students to learn and train in a more realistic and immersive intelligent experience situation, which helps to fully mobilize students' interest in learning.

(3) *In terms of management of teaching quality,* various intelligent technologies such as data mining and learning analysis are applied in the intelligent era to analyze students' individual learning habits and the distribution of learning situation of the whole class, making the management and evaluation of

education and teaching more standardized, refined, efficient and scientific. Especially in the evaluation of talent training, with the support of intelligent technologies such as big data and deep learning, the intelligent evaluation and evaluation system is used to track the learning situation of students in the whole process, real-time and continuously, and analyze various data such as students' learning performance and activity participation, so as to realize the overall evaluation of students' learning process and objective and accurate result feedback, to promote the overall evaluation of students' learning process. At the same time, the teaching mode, teaching design, and on-the-spot teaching of teachers should be evaluated scientifically, comprehensively, and comprehensively to promote intelligent teaching.

1.2 Challenges to Development

The rise of artificial intelligence makes social production increasingly automated and intelligent, and large-scale "machine replacement" brings a strong impact on the labor market, which brings severe challenges to the development of higher vocational education.

The Development of Higher Vocational Education in the Intelligent Era Must Deepen the Talent Training Mode of Integration of Production and Education. In the intelligence era, the global Internet technology enterprises have shifted their development focus to the field of artificial intelligence. The intelligence of enterprises is becoming more and more obvious. Under the emerging industrial pattern, the demand for talents from the market and enterprises continues to increase, and more attention is paid to the high integration of vocational skills and professional spirit training. However, the talent training in higher vocational colleges is often difficult to keep up with the market demand for talents. To solve these problems and realize the precise and effective supply of talents, only by deepening the school-enterprise cooperation of industry and education integration can we promote the organic connection of education chain, talent chain, industry chain, and innovation chain, and build a new intelligent vocational education ecosystem.

The National Development and Reform Commission and the Ministry of Education issued the "National Pilot Implementation Plan for the Construction of Integration of Industry and Education" [5], which clarified the principles, conditions, and support policies for the construction of an industry-education-integrated enterprise in China, and regarded the construction of an industry-education-integrated enterprise as a modern enterprise system. The important direction is to adopt a combination of policies to guide and encourage enterprises to participate in the reform of integration of production and education and to further open up the supply and demand of the talent training system and the technological innovation chain. But in reality, the school-enterprise cooperation with industry-education integration still faces many challenges in practice.

The Majors Setting and Development of Higher Vocational Colleges Are Facing New Challenges in the Intelligent Era. In the intelligent era, new industries and enterprises are constantly emerging, and a large number of talents are urgently needed in new professional fields. Serving the regional economic and social development is the premise of vocational education majors setting. To connect the economic development and industrial upgrading, higher vocational colleges must do a good job in the forward-looking prediction and planning of majors setting, so as to realize the professional chain docking with the industrial chain. Through the establishment of the dynamic adjustment mechanism of majors, new majors should be added, or obsolete majors should be canceled according to the industrial development trends.

Furthermore, intelligent production has become the main production mode of enterprises, which has a profound impact on the working mode and the skill requirements of talents, and there will be a general phenomenon of professional integration and professional crossover. Therefore, higher vocational colleges should pay attention to the majors' team construction, set up wide adaptive majors, adjust and integrate traditional majors and new majors, face the general purpose jobs, and realize the integration and application of multidisciplinary knowledge, and strengthen the adaptation to career migration of students across positions, deep levels, diversification, systematization and professional quality, to effectively meet the demand of the new job market for high-quality, high-skilled, compound and applicable talents.

The Professional Teaching Content of Higher Vocational Colleges Must Be Updated in the Intelligent Era. The current teaching content of Higher Vocational Education in China is mainly based on the requirements of industry 3.X, namely the automation and information age, for talent training. With the arrival of the intelligent era, China's industry has entered the 4.0 intelligent era. Therefore, higher vocational colleges must take the initiative to reform and develop, respond to the demands of the times with a new attitude, and promote the ecologically sustainable development of higher vocational education, pay more attention to the new knowledge and new skills involving human-computer cooperation, and increase the AI course to learn artificial intelligence knowledge.

1.3 Urgency and Necessity of Reform the Traditional Classroom Teaching Mode

With the advent of the intelligent era, the goals and standards for talent training are increasing day by day, and it is necessary to cultivate compound talents with technical skills. In addition, the popularization of higher education has resulted in the decrease of admission barriers and the quality of students. The increasing "scissors gap" between "entry and graduation" colleges have brought huge challenges to the training of traditional talents in higher vocational colleges, making the reform of traditional classroom teaching mode more urgent and necessary:

(1) *The traditional classroom is teacher-led type.* Teachers give priority to teaching and students passively accept knowledge, which makes students lack the initiative in learning.
(2) *The traditional classroom teaching mode cannot adapt to the requirements* of autonomous ubiquitous learning in intelligent education in the intelligence era. At the same time, it cannot adapt to the popularization of mobile terminals and the fragmented time for learning.
(3) *Higher vocational students have poor admission scores and poor study habits.* After entering the colleges, many vocational students lose the motivation and goal of learning, the absentee rate is high, the phenomenon of playing mobile phones in class and not listening carefully is common, and the time after class is more likely to be wasted.

How to fully mobilize the inner driving force of higher vocational students to study, change the status quo and improve teaching has become a very urgent task. It has also become a more urgent task in the reform of classroom teaching mode that students can make full use of classroom and spare time.

2 Analysis of Current Classroom Teaching Mode and Teaching Reform in Higher Vocational Education

Vocational higher education and general higher education are two different types of education. They have the same important status [2] and follow the basic teaching rules. At present, the following classroom teaching modes are mainly used in higher vocational colleges:

2.1 Lecture Teaching Mode

The lecture teaching mode has dominated world teaching for nearly 400 years and has become synonymous with traditional teaching. The traditional lecture teaching mode is led by teachers, explains concepts, narrates facts, demonstrates principles, and completes the presentation of established content to students through oral language. The lecture teaching method is economical, simple, and large in knowledge capacity, which is conducive to greatly improving the effect and efficiency of classroom teaching, helping students systematically master basic knowledge, forming basic skills, and improving cognitive structure, and is conducive to giving full play to the leading role of teachers [6]. It is the foundation of other teaching modes.

However, the essence of the lecture teaching mode is passive learning. There are fundamental defects of low student participation and initiative, which is not conducive to taking into account individual differences of students, and it is easy to make poor students feel frustrated and gradually lose their motivation to learn. In the intelligent era, especially when higher vocational colleges emphasize practical teaching today, the core defect that the lecture teaching mode is a passive classroom is thoroughly exposed.

2.2 Teaching Mode of Team Learning Based on Discussion

The teaching reform in the last century has tried to break through the traditional lecture teaching mode. The most important achievement is the new teaching mode of team learning based on discussion. This is a creative teaching theory and mode commonly used in many countries in the world. Because of its remarkable effectiveness, many famous foreign universities regard this mode as the second-largest teaching mode after classroom lecture teaching.

Team learning is a teaching activity in which teachers assign learning tasks and control teaching processes, take team cooperation as the basic form, evaluate the criteria with team performance, and mutual assistance and cooperation among peers in classroom interactions to jointly achieve teaching goals [7]. The teaching mode of team learning based on discussion is based on heuristic teaching ideas. Teachers prompt and guide students to think actively and improve their initiative and participation [8], especially in the teaching method of "learning by doing" for vocational students played an extremely important role.

The teaching mode of team learning based on discussion mainly follows the basic process of lecture teaching mode, however, this method, especially the discussion session, it has higher requirements for teachers' subject quality and classroom control, as well as students' learning motivation and investment. More importantly, this mode makes the knowledge learning system not strong enough, not efficient enough, and the effect is not good enough, so it is greatly limited in practical application.

2.3 Case-based Teaching and Problem-Based Learning

The Case-based teaching mode is the process of typifying real situations in real life and forming case libraries, allowing students to complete the learning of the established teaching content through independent research and mutual discussion [9]. PBL (problem-based learning, project-based learning) teaching mode allows students to place themselves in complex and meaningful problem situations by designing authentic project tasks, and solve the problem through independent exploration and cooperation, get the subject knowledge behind the problem [10]. The essence of this kind of teaching mode is opposed to the traditional one-way lecture teaching mode, focusing on students to learn knowledge and develop abilities by completing tasks, doing projects, or solving problems. This kind of teaching method is very suitable for the integrated classroom teaching mode of teaching, learning, and doing under the background of the integration of production and education in higher vocational colleges to highlight the practical ability of students.

Cases, problems projects, and projects in case teaching mode and PBL learning mode are the core advantages of the teaching mode, but they are also the fundamental difficulties. Cases, projects, and tasks emphasize their authenticity and complexity and hope that they can be typical and open, and can systematically cover the knowledge that needs to be learned. This requires high requirements for collecting, compiling, and constructing case libraries, project libraries, and problem libraries, which has become the main obstacle to the promotion and popularization of this kind of teaching mode.

2.4 Flipped Classroom and MOOC

In the past two decades, two major teaching reform modes that have emerged worldwide are flipped classrooms and MOOCs.

The flipped classroom teaching mode requires students to learn new content by watching a class lecture video before arriving at class and then using the in-class time to practice, discuss, and solve problems with peers and teachers, so as to achieve a deep understanding of learning content [11]. This teaching mode inverts teachers' and students' responsibilities in classrooms, the decision-making power of learning is transferred from teachers to students. With the precious time in the classroom, students are required to actively plan their learning process and interact with peers and teachers to acquire knowledge, focus more on active problem-based and project-based learning, making their learning more flexible, active, and more participatory.

Massive open online courses (MOOCs) are a novel and emerging mode of online learning activities for large numbers of participants worldwide. The MOOC has a wide audience and a large number of students, breaking through the time and space limitations of traditional courses, and everyone can participate. MOOC integrates a variety of social network tools and various forms of digital resources. They offer the advantages of online learning and provide content including short video lectures, digital readings, interactive assignments, discussion fora, and quizzes [12]. Student learning, teacher guidance, and Q&A, and assessments are all carried out online. MOOC uses the Internet to build virtual classrooms, creates high-quality courses through famous teachers, and improves the efficiency of knowledge transfer through scale, which is convenient for improving teaching quality, reducing higher education costs, and enhancing education equity. In higher vocational education, the requirements of intelligent vocational education and the introduction and comprehensive application of related products have promoted the reform of vocational teaching education and education and promoted the construction of a learning-oriented society. However, in practice, many factors restrict the development of MOOCs, such as teacher-student interaction, student-student interaction problems in a large-scale environment, high dropout rates, and poor effects of online learning, especially for higher vocational students with poor learning initiative. The inability to solve the problem directly led to the low level of MOOC development worldwide.

2.5 PAD Class

The PAD class (Presentation Assimilation Discussion) is a new teaching mode proposed by Professor Xuexin Zhang of Fudan University. The PAD class allocates half of the class time to the teacher's presentation and the other half to students' discussion, but the key idea is to introduce a psychological individualized assimilation link between lecture and discussion. The presentation and discussion are separated so that students can have one more day in between for self-paced and individualized assimilation, then participate in the discussion after they absorb the lecture content [13]. The PAD class emphasizes the individualized assimilation process, combines the advantages of lecture mode and discussion mode, which not only ensures the efficiency of the transfer of knowledge system, but also gives full play to the initiative of the students, and adapts themselves to the needs of the social and economic development of the intelligent era in terms of personalized learning, creative learning, deep learning and improving learning efficiency. Under the current educational background, combined with various new educational technologies, the mode of online and offline mixed PAD class has achieved outstanding results in higher education, especially higher vocational education.

2.6 Analysis on the Reform of Classroom Teaching Mode

The traditional classroom teaching mode with lecture mode as the core can "produce" professional and skilled personnel in batches to meet the needs of social and economic development in the industrialized era. From the post-industrial era to the intelligent era, personal freedom has greatly increased, and social and economic life and other relationships have never been more complicated. Traditional lecture teaching mode must be reformed to promote individualized development and adapt to the needs of the times.

In the past century, the four classical learning theories, behaviorism, cognitivism, constructivism, and humanism, developed by educational psychology [14], have great theoretical significance for the reform of education and teaching. Among them, the principle of "student-centered" emphasized by humanism and constructivism, the principle of "active learning cooperative learning" emphasized by constructivism and cognitivism, and the principle of "behavioral process" emphasized by both cognitivism and behaviorism have become the theoretical basis of the new classroom teaching reform mode of flipped the classroom and PAD class.

The application of intelligent technology and modern information technology provides strong technical support for the new teaching mode such as flipped classrooms and PAD classes, enabling them to be implemented. In addition, considering the limitations of "student-centered" humanism and constructivism learning theory, in the specific teaching practice, it is necessary to combine a variety of teaching modes organically, according to the different students' situations and the different teaching environments, especially the unique characteristics of higher vocational teaching, and to achieve the teaching goal through the use of online and offline hybrid teaching with complementary advantages.

3 Practice and Exploration of Reform of Classroom Teaching Mode of a Computer Course in Higher Vocational Colleges

3.1 Teaching Goals and Current Situation

Teaching Goals: The "Bilingual C Programming" is the first major core basic course of Software Technology and other majors of Guangzhou International Economic College (GZIEC). Its goal is to enable students in the form of bilingual teaching to master the basic ideas and methods of programming, understand Computational Thinking, and know the current use of computer programming advanced technology. Through a complete education mode of teaching and educating students, who are trained to possess professional quality, craftsmanship spirit, and the ability to adapt to the rapid development of computer technology.

Current Teaching Situation: To improve professional competitive advantages, GZIEC has been implementing bilingual teaching since 2013, and breakthroughs have been made in the internationalization of education [15]. In the practice of bilingual teaching of courses for many years, not only the teaching mode of foreign universities based on team cooperation learning, discussion mode, case-based teaching, and PBL teaching is adopted, but also the bilingual teaching mode of a step-by-step and phased teaching is adopted according to the actual situation of higher vocational students [16]. With the support of big data and intelligent cloud teaching platforms such as SCHOLAT[1] academic social network, Mosoteach[2] Cloud Classes, the PAD class and flipped classroom teaching mode, combined with online and offline mixed teaching, can better solve the serious problems of higher-order cognition and autonomous learning of higher vocational students.

3.2 Analysis of Student Learning

With the popularization of higher education, the cancellation of admission stage of private higher vocational and multiple parallel voluntary reforms in the college entrance examination admission policy, the enrollment performance of students in private vocational colleges have dropped sharply, their learning ability is weak, and there are serious learning problems as follows.

(1) *Weak learning ability and a strong sense of learning frustration.* They have suffered serious setbacks generally in previous studies, lack self-confidence in learning, and are more likely to give up when encountering difficulties, and are prone to inferiority complex.
(2) *The learning goal is not clear.* They have poor self-control, lack of motivation to learn, and lack of initiative.

[1] https://www.scholat.com/.
[2] https://www.mosoteach.cn/.

(3) *The practical ability of higher vocational students is stronger than theoretical learning ability.* Their learning foundation is weak, and they are more willing to conduct practical operations and exploration practices.

3.3 Curriculum Teaching Design Plan

Innovative Application of Bilingual Education Pyramid Theory. (see Fig. 1) In the reform of bilingual teaching, the contents of thought, moral character, and culture are organically integrated into the teaching session of the curriculum, and a complete education mode of "curriculum thinking and political" is constructed to cultivate students with humanistic qualities, craftsmanship, and the concept of the rule of law.

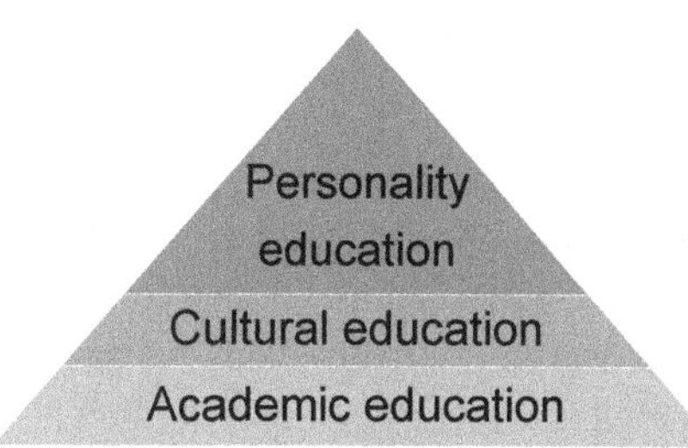

Fig. 1. Bilingual education pyramid.

Distribute Teaching Resources and Organize Teaching Activities. To adapt to the characteristics of individualized and ubiquitous learning of students in the intelligent era, and to meet the needs of extracurricular learning in the flipped classroom and PAD class teaching mode, there are distributed more than 100 micro-class videos and other teaching resources and organized more than 100 teaching activities.

Professional Vocabulary and Mind Maps. To apply and integrate international learning resources [17], and integrate international vocational education certification standards into the training of professional talents, the course is taught following Global Learning and Assessment Development Center (GLAD) international standard for computer professional English vocabulary Professional Vocabulary Quotient Credential (PVQC) [18], and urge students to master the professional keywords through weekly tests vocabulary. At the same time, to enable students to build a complete knowledge system of the course, mind maps of the whole course and each chapter are provided.

Classroom Teaching Mode. The main classroom teaching modes are flipped classrooms and PAD class, while exercise class is based on the discussion mode and the PBL teaching mode of teamwork learning.

Course Teaching Platform. In the early stage of the course, the flipped classroom teaching mode was implemented mainly with the help of the Mosoteach Cloud Classes teaching platform, and then the PAD class teaching mode was implemented with the help of the SCHOLAT course platform.

3.4 Practice of Flipped Classroom Teaching Mode

The application of the flipped classroom mode based on mobile learning in computer teaching in higher vocational colleges is of great significance. This will not only realize the continuous innovation of educational content but also facilitate teachers to demonstrate various new knowledge and skills in the computer field. The learning links after adopting the flipped classroom teaching mode are as follows:

Pre-class: Teachers use the guide plan (learning task list) to guide students to use learning resources to realize ubiquitous autonomous learning. Teachers are the designers and instructors of learning, and students are the main body of self-study, according to the need to repeatedly watch video resources to solve learning difficulties and check their mastery degree through the self-test system.

In Class: The focus of the class is transformed into the innovative mode of knowledge internalization. Teachers use the methods of "problem guidance, project discussion, teamwork, presentation and evaluation" to help students internalize their knowledge and expand their abilities.

Post-class: Students complete programming assignments, improve their programming skills and demonstrate the results of individual or team cooperative learning in exercise sessions.

Using the flipped classroom teaching mode, good results have been achieved in the first half of the semester. But there are also prominent problems:

(1) *The student's pre-class tasks could not be completed on time.* Students in private higher vocational colleges have weaker learning abilities and poor self-learning abilities. At the beginning of college, they were motivated and motivated to study. However, with the increasing difficulty of the curriculum, learning enthusiasm decreased, more than half of the students were unable to complete the pre-class guided learning task list on time, which made the flipped classroom teaching mode impossible to implement as planned, and the teaching effect was greatly reduced.
(2) *Mosoteach Cloud Classes teaching platform has no teaching team cooperation function.* As the leader of the intelligent cloud teaching platform, Mosoteach Cloud Class provides many methods that are conducive to the development of modern teaching modes, but it cannot realize the function of the teaching team, which limits the use of basic courses in higher vocational education.

3.5 Practice of PAD Class Teaching Mode

To solve the problem existing in the flipping classrooms, the PAD class teaching mode and the SCHOLAT course platform are adopted in the later stage and subsequent semesters.

In the teaching philosophy, the PAD class teaching mode advocates teaching first and then learning, while the flipped classroom advocates first learning and then teaching. In this regard, the two teaching modes are completely opposite. When the enthusiasm of higher vocational students is poor and unable to complete the pre-class learning tasks, the advantage of the presentation of lecture teaching mode in the PAD class is extremely prominent. The learning links after adopting the PAD class teaching mode are as follows:

Presentation: The teacher first conducts refined lectures and builds the curriculum knowledge framework through sufficient but not excessive guidance, but intentionally is not detailed, not thorough, and incomplete, leaving room for students thinking after class.

Assimilation: Students are required to think independently, understand personally, and assimilate knowledge. Teachers assign homework, guide, and supervise students to review after class, ensure that students understand the basic content, and prepare for group interaction and discussion.

Discussion: Student groups discuss their own problems, and through this process, solve low-level problems, discover, and condense high-level problems. Then through the teacher to answer questions, they solve high-level problems.

The application of online and offline mixed PAD class teaching mode has solved the problems in the implementation of the flipped classrooms and achieved good results. In addition, the homework adopted in the PAD class teaching mode not only includes the knowledge summary of the learning content, but also the traditional programming exercises and reflective assignment. In addition, the PAD class teaching mode strengthens the process evaluation, does not correct the right or wrong of the usual homework, does not look at the content carefully, and emphasizes unique thinking, and encourages innovation. On the SCHOLAT course platform to support the teaching team, it is easier to realize the process evaluation of teaching.

4 Evaluation and Analysis of Teaching Mode Reform

4.1 Evaluation Method of Course Teaching Mode

With the help of an intelligent cloud platform, we implement the flipped classroom and PAD class teaching mode, and through the application of big data technology, collect, classify, clean and analyze the teaching behavior data of teachers and the learning behavior data of students in the teaching process, realize the evaluation of curriculum and teaching resources, the analysis of the course learning behavior (online use) and learning effect, and improve the quality of teaching. To make up for the lack of a small amount of curriculum data in the initial stage of implementation, we conduct a simple questionnaire survey on the teaching class at the end of each semester. Students answer the questionnaire online through WeChat, and the effective questionnaire reaches 100%.

4.2 Evaluation Results and Analysis

Participation in Teaching Activities and Attendance. From the participation percentage of teaching activities shown in Fig 2, it can be seen that students' participation in various types of learning activities organized by teachers is relatively high, of which attendance (Sign-in activities) percentage averages 98%, participation in self-test activities reaches 83%, and students complete homework on-time percentage for 86%, indicating that flipped classroom and PAD class teaching mode mobilized students' enthusiasm for learning. In particular, the course attendance percentage shown in Fig 3, shows that even the lowest attendance percentage reached 91%, which is extremely difficult for private higher vocational students with a weak foundation, low learning enthusiasm, and lack of motivation to learn.

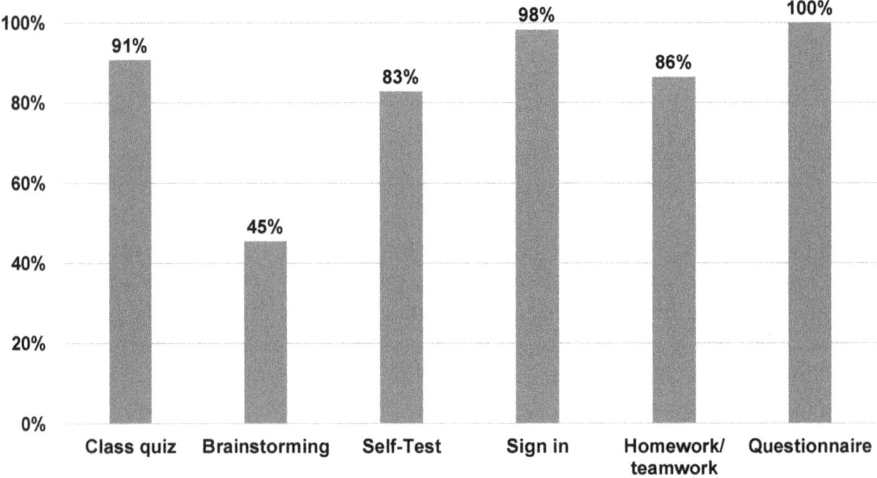

Fig. 2. Teaching activity participation percentage.

Evaluation of the Learning Process of All Students. It can be seen from the way in which all students obtain learning experience points in Fig. 4, that the maximum experience points percentage 62% is online learning, i.e. total experience points of learning online teaching resources for whole students reaches 17,074, considering that students only get 1 experience point for each teaching resource (such as mind map) after class, and learning a teaching video only obtains 2 experience points, so this result shows that students' autonomous and

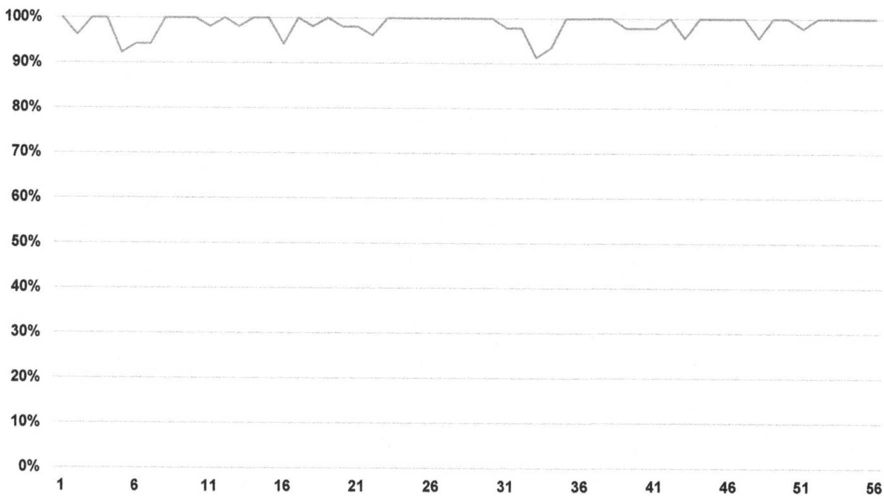

Fig. 3. Teaching activity participation percentage.

ubiquitous learning has achieved remarkable results. In addition, the total experience points obtained by students' attendance, participation in teaching activities, and completion of homework accounted for 38%, indicating that students have a high degree of participation in various teaching links and have formed a habit of active learning.

Analysis of Individual Student Learning. Figure 5 is a radar chart of the analysis of individual student learning.

The data series are defined as follows:

Best: The student with the most experience points among all students.

Excellent: The student with the average experience points of all students whose experience points exceeds 80% of the best student experience points.

Average: The average experience points of all students.

Worst: The student with the least experience points among all students.

From the analysis of the radar chart, the best students perform well in the three process evaluation dimensions of homework/teamwork, self-test, and brainstorming, setting an example for other students. However, the worst students have a large gap in these three process evaluation dimensions, and teachers can conduct targeted attribution analysis based on this to help them solve learning difficulties.

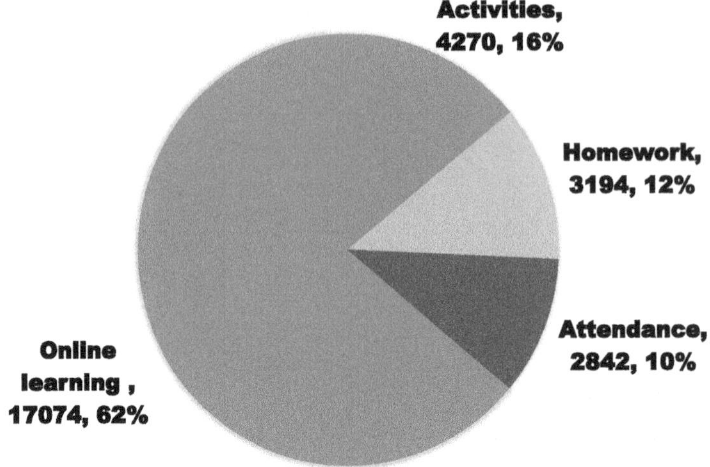

Fig. 4. The way all students obtain learning experience points.

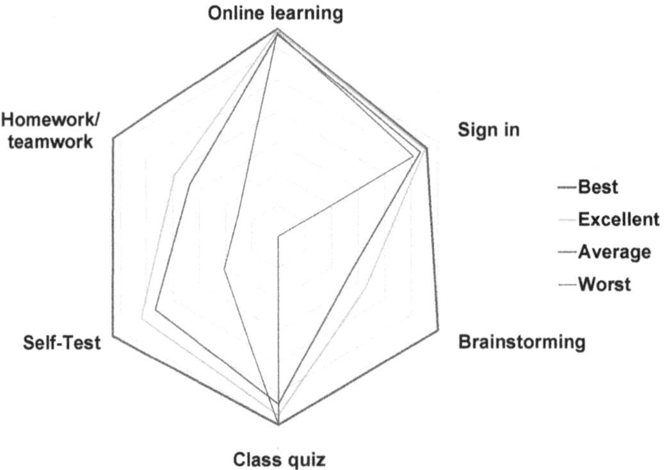

Fig. 5. Evaluation dimensions analysis of individual student learning.

Simple Analysis of Questionnaire Survey Results. From the results of the teaching satisfaction questionnaire in Table 1, the following conclusions can be drawn:

Table 1. Teaching satisfaction survey results.

Teaching satisfaction item	Very satisfied	Satisfied	General	Less satisfied	Very dissatisfied
Flipped classroom	58.7%	32.6%	8.7%	–	–
PAD class	58.5%	37.8%	3.8%	–	–
Evaluate for teacher	70.4%	27.7%	1.9%	–	–
2018 Student self-evaluation	5.7%	26.4%	62.3%	5.7%	–
2019 Student self-evaluation	8.3%	33.3%	41.7%	14.6%	2.1%
2020 Student self-evaluation	3.5%	54.4%	40.4%	1.8%	–

Flipped Classroom Teaching Mode: There are 91.3% (=58.7%-Very satisfied + 32.6%-Satisfied) of students who think this mode is helpful to students' learning, and 58.7% of them think it is very helpful.

PAD Class Teaching Mode: up to 96.3% (=58.5%-Very satisfied + 37.8%-Satisfied) of students think this mode is helpful to students' learning, and 58.5% of them think it is very helpful. This shows that the use of the PAD class teaching mode has mobilized students' learning enthusiasm and has been unanimously recognized by students.

Comprehensive Satisfaction of Teachers' Teaching: The survey shows that up to 98.1% (=70.4%-Very satisfied + 27.7%-Satisfied) of students are satisfied with the teachers' teaching, and there are no students who are dissatisfied with the teachers' teaching, indicating that the teachers' hard work in teaching reform has been recognized by the students.

Self-evaluation of Students' Learning Situation: Based on the self-evaluation of students in the three grades from 2018 to 2020, the satisfaction of students' self-evaluation has increased year by year for three consecutive years from 32.1% (=5.7%-Very satisfied + 26.4%-Satisfied, similarly hereinafter) in 2018 to 41.6% (=8.3% + 33.3%) in 2019, and 57.9% (=3.5% + 54.4%) in 2020, indicating that students' learning initiative, and sense of acquisition have been further enhanced. This result is not easy to achieve, because nearly 60% of the students' admission scores are only about 16 points in the converted 100 point system, and over 80% of students' admission scores of English courses are less than 40 points. This also shows that under the guidance of teachers' reform of teaching mode, students' autonomous learning ability has made significant progress, and meets the learning requirements of the intelligent era. The course teaching has reached the goal of teaching with improvement, learning with achievement, teaching and learning mutually beneficial.

4.3 Summary

The use of the teaching mode reform of PAD class and flipped classroom enables teachers and students to communicate effectively, improves students' enthusiasm for independent learning and ubiquitous learning, not only enhances students' ability to actually program, independent learning, summary, but also improves students' ability to think independently, pioneering and innovative and presentation, effectively improves the classroom teaching effect, promotes the development of students' personal comprehensive quality, and truly realizes the cultivation of knowledge, ability, and quality.

5 Conclusion and Limitation

In response to the need for the cultivation of high-end talents in higher vocational education in the intelligent era, this study analyzes the characteristics of various teaching modes in higher vocational curriculum teaching and discusses combined with various new educational technologies, the teaching mode of online and offline mixed flipped classroom and PAD class. After the implementation of the "Bilingual C Programming" classroom, the results of empirical research show that the students who adopt the flipped classroom and the PAD class teaching mode show good learning results and stronger learning motivation. In particular, it was found that, with the support of intelligent cloud platforms such as the SCHOLAT Network, the emphasis on ability training and teacher-student interaction, combined with online and offline mixed teaching of the PAD class teaching mode, can better adapt to the current level of higher vocational students' poor foundation, lack of self-confidence status, and realize the goal of teaching with improvement, learning with achievement, teaching and learning mutually beneficial.

Nevertheless, this study has the following limitations. On the one hand, this research was only conducted in three classes of three grades of "Software Technology" major, with a small sample size. On the other hand, the scale design and analysis of the questionnaire survey are relatively simplified, and an effective and in-depth analysis of reliability, validity, and correlation has not been implemented. These are the directions for further in-depth study in the future, but the conclusions drawn from the research are general and can provide references for further teaching mode implementation.

Acknowledgments. Our work is supported by the National Natural Science Foundation of China (No. U1811263), University Characteristic Innovation Natural Science Project from the Department of Education of Guangdong Province (No .2021KTSCX341 and No. 2020KTSCX375), and the Teaching Reform Project from Guangzhou International Economic College (No. SWZL202109, and No. SWZL202108).

References

1. P.R. China, The State Council: Guideline: A New Generation of Artificial Intelligence Development Plan. (in Chinese). http://www.gov.cn/zhengce/content/2017-07/20/content_5211996.htm. Accessed 16 Sept 2021
2. P.R. China, The State Council: National Vocational Education Reform Implementation Plan. (in Chinese). http://www.gov.cn/zhengce/content/2019-02/13/content_5365341.htm. Accessed 16 Sept 2021
3. P.R. China, The State Council: China's Education Modernization 2035 Plan. (in Chinese). http://www.gov.cn/xinwen/2019-02/23/content_5367987.htm. Accessed 16 Sept 2021
4. P.R. China, The Ministry of Education: Instructions on implementing the construction plan of high-level higher vocational schools and majors with Chinese characteristics. (in Chinese). http://www.moe.gov.cn/srcsite/A07/moe_737/s3876_qt/201904/t20190402_376471.html. Accessed 16 Sept 2021
5. P.R. China, The National Development and Reform Commission: National Pilot Implementation Plan for the Construction of Integration of Industry and Education. (in Chinese). https://www.ndrc.gov.cn/fzggw/jgsj/shs/sjdt/201904/t20190403_1121563.html?code=&state=123. Accessed 16 Sept 2021
6. Darling-Hammond, L., Bransford, J.: Preparing Teachers for a Changing World: What Teachers Should Learn and Be Able to Do. E-book. Jossey-Bass, San Francisco (2017)
7. Widmann, A., Mulder, R.: The effect of team learning behaviours and team mental models on teacher team performance. Instr. Sci. **48**(1), 1–21 (2020)
8. Brookfield, S., Preskill, S.: The Discussion Book: 50 Great Ways to Get People Talking. E-book. Jossey-Bass, San Francisco (2016)
9. TAWFIK, A.: Do cases teach themselves? a comparison of case library prompts in supporting problem-solving during argumentation. J. Comput. High. Educ. **29**(2), 267–285 (2017)
10. Jensen, K., Stromso I.: Problem-based learning: the emergence of new scripts and roles for teachers to render epistemic practices transparent. Vocations Learn. **12**(3), 343–360 (2019)
11. Lai, L., Lin, T., Yueh, P.: The effectiveness of team-based flipped learning on a vocational high school economics classroom. Interactive Learn. Environ. **28**(1), 130–141 (2020)
12. Pickering, J., Henningsohn, L., Deruiter, M., De Jong, P., Reinders, M.: Twelve tips for integrating massive open online course content into classroom teaching. Med. Teach. **39**(7), 1–6 (2017)
13. Zhang, X.: The PAD Class: New Wisdom of Chinese Education. Science Press, Beijing (2017).(in Chinese)
14. Woolfolk, A.: Educational Psychology: Active Learning Edition, 14th edn. Pearson, Upper Saddle River (2019)
15. Geng, J., Kuang, Z., Yu, Z.: Research on Speeding up the Internationalization of Private High Vocational Education. In: 3rd International Conference on Social Science, Management and Economics (SSME 2017). DEStech Transactions on Social Science Education and Human Science, 600–605, ISBN: 978-1-60595-462-2 pp. DEStech Publications, Pennsylvania (2017). https://doi.org/10.12783/dtssehs/ssme2017/13030

16. Geng, J., Xiong, X., : Consideration on the Bilingual Teaching of Computer Courses in Higher Vocational Colleges. 2nd International Conference on Informatizstion in Education, Management and Business (IEMB 2015). Proceedings of the 2015 Conference on Informatization in Education, Management and Business, pp. 302–306. Atlantis Press, Dordrecht. https://doi.org/10.2991/iemb-15.2015.59, ISBN: 978-94-6252-105-6
17. Dai, J., Nie, L.: The mode of introducing international learning resources into colleges and Universities. High. Educ. Explor. **3**, 5–10 (2019). (in Chinese)
18. Global Learning and Assessment Development Center: Professional Vocabulary Quotient Credential. http://www2.gladworld.net/gladworldtest/EN_PVQC.php. Accessed 16 Sept 2021

The Practical Challenges and Ways Forward for News & Communication in Higher Vocational Education Under the Influence of 5G Technology

Jian Wang(✉) and Liyuan Zhu

Dongguan Polytechnic, Dongguan 523808, Guangdong, China
kingsword520@qq.com

Abstract. As a revolutionary technology, 5G has 6 basic features: high speed, ubiquitous network, low power consumption, low latency, Internet of Everything and reconfiguration of security systems; these together allows a leap from the Traditional Internet and Mobile Internet to an age of Intelligent Internet where all things are connected and always online. 5G has been restructuring the media industry by inducing changes in its four fundamental qualities and properties, i.e., communicators, users, contents and media. The Higher Vocational Education of News & Communication should take a turn and rethink the traditional model of education and teaching practices which had been built on the mode of mass communication; progressive, reformative strategies should be adopted in light of the current realities and past experiences in this field; goals of its training of talents should be repositioned with reference to the demands around media industry in the 5G Era, so as to address important questions such as who are to be cultivated, how this process of cultivation should be done and for whom are we carrying out such a process. Meanwhile, however, educators should note the risks associated with the technology and make it artistic.

Keywords: 5G technology · Higher Vocational Education of News & Communication · Restructure of the media industry · Major reality · Major outlet

1 Research Background and the Research Question

1.1 Influence of Social Change on Vocational Education

As a major builder in higher vocational education school, I know that running a good major is a win-win situation for students, teachers, schools and enterprises. However, it is not easy to do a good job in speciality management. Moreover, vocational education also has its fluidity, which is regulated by the orientation that vocational education serves the regional economic and social development. It is obvious that regional economic and social development is constantly varying at the micro-level, affected by many factors,

© ICST Institute for Computer Sciences, Social Informatics and Telecommunications Engineering 2022
Published by Springer Nature Switzerland AG 2022. All Rights Reserved
S. Shi et al. (Eds.): 6GN 2021, LNICST 439, pp. 513–522, 2022.
https://doi.org/10.1007/978-3-031-04245-4_44

including policy inclination, scientific and technological progress, and industrial structure adjustment. In brief, it is a complex problem for all vocational educators to deal with the fluidity, adjust the practical structure and development direction of vocational education.

Vocational education is accustomed to caters to the demands of enterprises, industries and the higher vocational education of News & Communication (hereinafter referred to as HVENC), which, even experiences more dramatic and complex challenges from the change of News & Communication industry, also called the media industry in this paper, comparing with other fields. It is observed that the media industry has been deeply impacted by revolutionary media technology. Moreover, this influence has been transmitted to higher education, especially the market-oriented higher vocational education. Therefore, the question of how higher vocational education could respond to the drastic technological changes has become essential for every HVENC's builder and researcher. At the same time, it will determine the development space and survival of the major.

1.2 Reshaping of the Media Industry and Its Institutionalization on Communication Practice

For the media industry, the media technology between communicators and users, stipulates the form of produce-distribute-present of content and the format of contact-select-accept of the users. Media technology usually refers to media tools used to create and disseminate cultural content [1]. Marshall McLuhan, a famous Canadian communication scholar, his famous view of the media is the message tells us that media technology not only perceptibly shapes the media industry, constructs the pseudo environment, proposed by Walter Lippmann about 100 years ago, like air, people are in it and often forget its existence, but also constructs our cultural environment, changes our knowledge, consciousness, and our experience of time and space [2–4]. Furthermore, technology determinist in today's world asserts that media technology fundamentally determines, not shape, the media industry. We will not discuss the right or wrong of technological determinism, but we must admit that media technology plays a fundamental role in shaping society's existence, including certain forms of social behavior [5]. In other words, media technology can construct the whole life of social reality and new social-life space which is different from any previous form.

However, not every media technology has the ability to restructure the media industry. Any work on media history tells us that printing, broadcasting, the Internet and social media are the only revolutionary media technologies known to people in history. W. Brian Arthur, a famous technology thinker, considers that technology is autopoietic, which created different forms and practices in media history, and constitute the current media ecology, composed of Newspaper, Magazine, Book, Radio, Television, Portals Website, Social Networking Services, Microblog, Instant Messaging, Short-Form Video etc., that we can perceive, even intervene. Obviously, each media form has disciplined communicators and users through long-term contact and use, then create a unique media Technoculture [6]. Currently, we are concerned about emerging media technologies, but only Blockchain, Big Data, Cloud Computing and 5G are worthy of discussion. In this paper, it must be demonstrated that the 5G technology accelerating the diffusion at present, will lead to a revolution in the media industry. In other words, 5G technology will reconstruct the media industry after printing technology, electronic technology, digital technology and Internet technology to construct a media reality with all-new theoretical logic and practical paradigm. However, it does not imply that other technologies are unimportant, but they are not revolutionary enough compared with 5G.

As a major builder who has received professional education for many years and engaged in higher vocational education for a long time, I have to admit an objective reality: the current HVENC is based on print media, electronic media, digital and network media. However, due to the non- synchronization in communication practice and theoretical norms, the former is in a strong position, while the latter is in a weak position. Whether digital media or network media, it could be defined as unformed and immature media technology and communication form. In addition to the irresistible path dependence brought by the media elite tradition which formed by the long-term practice of print media and electronic media, while the failure of practice does not affect the legitimacy of ideology and the leadership and orthodoxy of culture, HVENC still follows the mature mass communication mode and practices the media tradition, that is one to many, point to surface, as well as mend the curriculum in the name of internet and new media forced by the vigorous development of digital communication. In short, digital and internet media outside, while print and electronic media inside. And the mutual-construction between the traditional media industry and society has reached a steady-state and been a pattern. Thus, the former owns the leading power of how to communicate. On the contrary, digital and network media have incomplete connectivity with the limitation of technology level, although it can trigger some changes of the media industry, it still has not the ability to reconstruct basically.

1.3 Initiative on Vocational Education Design

As a type of education, vocational education and general education are different, but have same aim at cultivating people in common. Vocational education takes employment as the guidance, making people professional and social, that is, to achieve the so-called utilitarian goal of occupation and the humanistic goal of education. Therefore, vocational education should not passively adapt to the guidance, but should actively design the guidance [7]. In other words, vocational education content cannot simply adapt to the development of technology and the requirements of vocational work tasks. However, it must pay more attention to the relationship among work, technology, education and their interaction process, and actively participate in this process [7]. The major builders of HVENC have to consider the question of how 5G will restructure the media industry, adopt what type of action framework will be adopted and what new social occupations and post groups will be created, what requirements would be requested on practitioners' knowledge, skills and attitudes, and what action knowledge structure will be needed. The professional connotation of vocational education, which is the logical starting point of major construction, is determined by these problems of new jobs brought by 5G. Due to the Limitation of the length of this paper, I have no intention to discuss some micro operational issues, such as how to integrate structuring action knowledge and transferring structured knowledge into the curriculum for further design. Instead, I focus on some macro-issues with far-reaching impact, that is, what kind of structural changes will take place in the media industry after the large-scale commercialization of 5G in the future, and how this change affects the response of HVENC to the fundamental question of who are to be cultivated and how this process of cultivation should be done and for whom are we carrying out such a process.

2 5G as a Revolutionary Technology and Reconstruction of Media Industry

2.1 5G as the New Start of the Intelligent Internet

5G is the fifth-generation mobile communication technology. On June 6, 2019, MIIT (Ministry of Industry and Information Technology of the People's Republic China) issued 5G licenses for commercial use, marking that China has officially entered the 5G-era. 5G New Media Industry White Paper pointed out that the media industry will be benefited from the 5G first, and 5G will bring more than 40 billion RMB of market space to China's media industry before 2022. Meanwhile, 5G users in China kept growing rapidly. China accounted for 70% of all 5G connections in 2020 alone, and has been home to the largest number of 5G base stations and 5G users across the globe. GSMA's research has further suggested that at some point after 2025 and quite likely in as early as 2026, the Chinese communications market will experience a structural transformation during which its 5G users may exceed its 4G counterpart in number, making the former the largest user group in the communications market, as demonstrated below (see Fig. 1) [8].

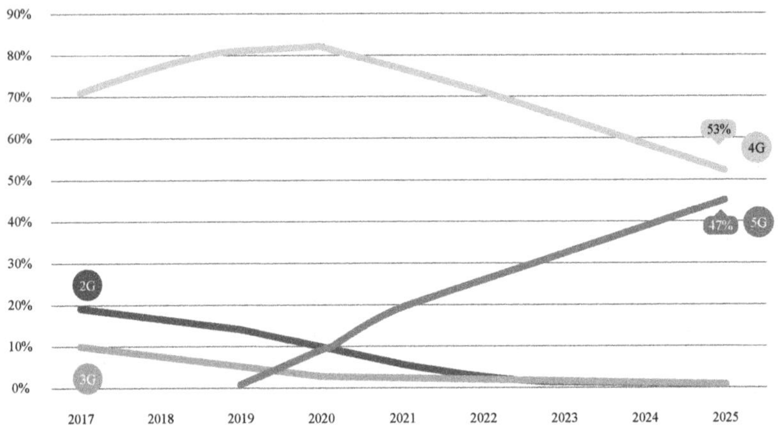

Fig. 1. The mobile economy China 2020

Up to the present, 5G has been a new generation of wireless mobile communication technology with the most revolutionary potential. In addition to providing basic communication services between people, 5G also extends the communication ability to people and machines and becomes the foundation of the Intelligent Internet [9]. W. Brian Arthur believes that all technologies are generated by previous technologies. In other words, technologies are generated from existing technologies or the combination of existing technologies [6]. Timeline of the mobile wireless communication history shows 1G mobile analogue communication, 2G mobile digital communication, 3G mobile intelligent communication, 4G mobile intelligent digital communication, and 5G mobile communication technology which is in the process of innovation and diffusion. Paul Levinson, an American media theorist, proposed the Remedial Medium Theory, the whole process of media evolution can be regarded as remedial measures, that is to say, the new media has a remedial impact on old media. Taking 5G as an example, it has offset all the disadvantages, integrated and improved all technical advantages from 1G to 4G. IMT-2020 (5G) Propulsion Group defines four major technical advantages and key performance indicators of 5G, including continuous wide area coverage, high capacity of the hotspot, low power consumption and large connection, low latency and high level of reliability. ITU released three application contexts of 5G: First, Enhanced Mobile Broadband (eMBB), which is reflected in the ultra-high-speed and capacity of network data transmission, can be widely used in smartphones, tablet computers, 4K/8K video, 3D video and VR/AR; Second, Massive Machine Type Communication (mMTC), that is, large-scale Internet of things, can connect billions or even billions of mobile devices and IoT devices in the future (by 2025, only China's mobile terminal products will reach 10 billion, with more than 8 billion IoT terminals), which can be applied to intelligent meter reading, surveillance cameras, smart home devices, mobile phones, etc. Third, Ultra-Reliable Low-Latency Communications (uRLLC), is a communication technology that supports super response connection, less than 1ms air interface delay, medium and high data speed and high-speed mobile communication, and its applications include internet-connected vehicle, automatic driving and industrial Internet [10].

In a word, the technical features and advantages of 5G can be summarized as follows: high speed, ubiquitous network, low power consumption, low latency, Internet of Everything, and reconfiguration of security systems. These six fundamental features ensure the basic experience of users in the 5G era. Moreover, 5G will make 'communication between people, people and things, things and things' reality with the continuous development of core technology around the three goals. It is not only the inheritance and improvement of 3G technology solving the communication of people to people and 4G technology solving the interaction of people to information, but also a basic communication network with the function of paradigm shift, that is to say, the wide use of 5G will realize the transition from Traditional Internet (PC as the core terminal) and Mobile Internet (smart phone as the core terminal) to Intelligent Internet.

2.2 5G Has Been Restructuring the Media Industry

5G will bring mankind into an era of intelligent Internet that can integrate mobile Internet, intelligent sensing, big data and intelligent learning, and become the foundation of the 7th information revolution and the fundamental guarantee for the completion of the construction. 5G has broken through the limitation of traditional bandwidth, and will fundamentally solve the problem of information transmission with the ability to connect massive terminals and its ultra-low latency. 5G can fully stimulate the potential of intelligent sensing, big data and intelligent learning, and integrate them into a powerful service system, which can not only change the society, but also influence all aspects of human life [9]. Specifically, these revolutionary changes are shown in the following four aspects: First, 5G will enable the link elements in the world to be connected and permanently online theoretically, and maintain the constant existence of basic relationships in the digital world; Second, 5G makes it a reality for the User Experience without speed barrier and traffic barrier; Third, 5G will create more products and applications of daily-life scenes; Fourth, 5G will accelerate the development of artificial intelligence and create a fully-mobile and fully-connected intelligent society [5].

Reconstruction usually refers to the reorganisation of the structure by changing elements' number or relationship and innovating elements' nature or attribute. No matter how the media industry transforms, the most basic elements are still communicators, users or receivers, content or message, and the media, which cannot escape from the underlying framework of human-information-technology.

The communication reality illustrates that 5G is gradually altering the connotation and extension of the four elements, thus triggering a structural change in the media industry. Specifically manifested in four aspects:

First of all, Communicators. 5G further releases the subjectivity of the communicator based on 4G, and due to the low threshold of video expression, being a communicator has become a reality from theory. Moreover, in the 5G era, relying on sensors that are always connected and the technical ability of artificial intelligence to process massive amounts of data, machines will become communicators alongside users, professional media, professional media person and professional communication agencies, participating in the production of future content, which contains unique values.

Secondly, Users. In the framework of human-information-technology, human-information is the core. Human need information to transform the world, and information need human to realize its value, while technology, as an intermediary and means, to a certain degree, can shape the relationship and form of human and information to a certain extent, but its ultimate goal is to become the hidden art, the stars of the arching moon. The absolute technological advantage of 5G will gradually highlight the core position of users in communication. Therefore, understanding human, how to accurately insight and manage users, and how to better connect content with users, services with users, will become the core competitiveness of communicators in the era of 5G.

Thirdly, Contents. What forms of contents would become mainstream in the 5G era? There is little disagreement among scholars and experts: video will replace text as the mainstream of social expression, with short videos drawing attention and setting issues, and medium-length videos having a significant impact on the choices and judgments of social decision-makers [5]. It is a basic judgment, but more importantly, the value and type of content only reflected in the dissemination of Message is not enough in mass communication of the 5G era. It will become an important value dimension and practice guide that content as a relationship to express emotions and assist the communication between subjects, and as a medium to build contexts and create new communication modes,

Lastly, Media. In the era of mass communication, we usually understand the medium as physical media such as radio, television, newspapers and magazines, which is an extension of the physical sense of human body functions. However, social media, emerging and active in the era of Traditional Internet and Mobile Internet, means the transformation from physical media to relational media. In the 5G era, permanent online sensors will create a new virtual reality world, where our physiological, psychological and emotional messages are sensed intelligently and interconnected with the physical world through processors and interfaces. But to gain insight into the secrets of the new world, we must rely on algorithms, which will play a fundamental role in the future of communication. While it is almost useless for the human to transform the world by merely sensing the information of the surface structure and generating fragmented data. Only by using algorithms to reveal and describe the deeper structure of information and data can generate the value belongs to human.

In short, the media industry based on 5G has its radical connectivity and an evolving intelligence that allow it to form a social information system of complexity and fluidity by integrating physical, social, physiological and psychological factors. The mutual-construction between social information system and the individual communication system will be the basic logical starting point for understanding the current media industry. Obviously, the interaction goes far beyond the explanation scope and practice radius of the traditional mass communication model.

3 A Response from HVENC: A New Radical Way of Thinking

3.1 The Current Situation of HVENC

As a developing country, higher vocational education has made an indelible historical contribution to constructing a modern industrial system with a complete range of disciplines. However, with the reform of the education system, vocational education as a type of education has gradually become a loser in education stratification and social stratification, and the cost-benefit gap with general education is widening. Although in 2019, the Chinese government promulgated the National Vocational Education Reform Implementation Plan, which achieved formal equality in political status between vocational education and general education, while substantive equality in a social sense is still a long way off. This means that, although a small number of higher vocational colleges are currently piloting vocational education at the undergraduate level, the vast majority are still at the junior college level.

Thus, HVENC has to face up two uncontrollable primary limitation stems from junior level: firstly, time is limited, that is, to complete the training of qualified professional talents at the junior college level within three years; secondly, the source of the student is limited, that is, the training objects have different types and structures of intelligence from general high school students, and they are usually better at figurative thinking [7]. These two basic limitations set the spatial and temporal boundaries for discussing the major's connotation and construction.

As mentioned above, another powerful force that can be controlled but difficult to control, is the tradition or mode developed by HVENC and usually based on the basic assumption of the mass communication mode. In addition to following the general pedagogy of vocational education, such as work-learning integration and industry-education integration, the practice of vocational education for the mass media industry, including the formulation of talent training objectives, talent training specifications, design of curriculum systems, exploration of training models, should also follow the communication logic and practical paradigm of mass communication, and gradually be institutionalized and patterned into a stable force according to the degree of effectiveness of implementation. While once formed, this force usually has no incentive to change itself, or if it does, it is difficult to make fundamental changes, such as reconfiguration.

The VEHNC, which carries out education and teaching practice according to the talent demand standard of the mass media industry, is usually in a tension between elite talent demand and weak training target. The communication logic and practice paradigm of the traditional mass media industry can be simply summarized as four aspects: specialization and elitism of communicator; content of the communication is message-oriented; the medium of the communication is based on the physical medium; audience (not user) is regarded as the consumer of information [11]. In other words, the traditional mass media industry is centered on the communicator. While newspapers, magazines, radio stations, television stations and portals websites own absolute discourse and elite consciousness and dominate the communication order with users at the bottom. It is difficult for higher vocational education institutions, which are relatively disadvantaged in all aspects of education, to bridge the gap that arises from the tension. As a result, although the traditional higher vocational education of journalism and communication has its own advantages, such as focusing on the training of basic knowledge and basic skills, and often pointing to the improvement of comprehensive ability, it still does not prevail in the education competition and has to remain in a marginal position in the talent supply of the traditional mass media industry.

3.2 Opportunities and Challenges: The Progressive Reform in the 5G Era

The historical experience of China's social revolution and Economic Reform and open up has long proved that radical transformation without considering social cost and social impact usually means upheaval and disruption. The same applied to education, unless there is no historical and traditional burden and to catch the new trend right out of the gate. The Ship of Theseus, a famous question in philosophy, shows that we can complete the paradigm shift in the gradual change of time as long as we carefully design and actively push forward, thus promoting structural change. This is a question of action strategy, which has proven its feasibility, while what opportunities and challenges do the media industry in the 5G era present for HVENC, and what do we need to do to reform tradition and complete renewal is the more crucial question.

There is no doubt that our current students are all real 21st century people who are strictly digital natives. For them, computer games, E-mail, the Internet, mobile phones, and instant messaging are already part of their lives, but familiarity does not necessarily mean understanding. Otherwise, education would be meaningless. As a major builder, we need to design these digital natives, that is, what kind of people do we want to cultivate?

First of all, I would like to answer that even in the new era of 5G, vocational education will not become general education. In other words, it is not in our plan to train students to become leaders in the media industry of the 5G era. Remember, the world is random. I hope they will become actual participants and builders of the communication society in the 5G era and be localized.

Secondly, our students should own a user mindset in the face of technology and learn to cooperate with machines. Technologists have the advantage of mastering a complex terminology system and the technical principles behind it, through which they make a living. However, our students do not necessarily need to master them. They just need to understand the way of thinking behind it, to know what technology to use to analyze the problems and how to interpret the results correctly [12]. Namely, it is enough to be a user who can apply technology. The machine is the concretization of technology. It will become a content producer, possessing the subjectivity of the communicator, especially after having sensors and algorithms. That is to say, the machine will play the role of workmates or competitors. For students, learning to be colleagues with machines will become an essential part of vocational education.

Thirdly, our students should have empathy and communication skills, can consciously understand and insight into others. In the 5G era, the media industry has realized Kant's great prediction that people are the purpose, not the means. User has completely left the right boundary of information consumer and obtained the absolute dominant position. For communicators who will understand users and grasp their needs precisely will become the key to the success of communication in the future. However, it is clear that this type of competency is very generic and challenging to develop, but at least it indicates the work focus and direction for HVENC.

Fourthly, our students should master the language of video, which will replace elitist textual language as the dominant form of social expression in 5G era. Years of teaching practice has proved that our students are not good at using written language to rationally express facts and logic, it is not fun in itself, but their interest is often drawn to the dynamic video. In other words, rather than struggling to improve students' textual skills, it is better to focus on cultivating their video expression skills. It can be an interesting journey to learn more about short video and medium-length video, grasp their use logic and operation rules, and guide the whole learning process.

Finally, being a context constructor, 5G will make context construction, which includes virtual context and augmented context based on VR technology, and it will definitely become the mainstream of value innovation in the future communication [13]. The functional feature of context lies in promoting the interconnection, aggregation, collaboration and value realization among users, producers, products and services, so as to provide a high-quality experience to users in the context and to meet their personalized needs to the greatest extent [5]. Obviously, building contexts through content, social interaction, games, and sharing will become an essential high-level competence for the future communicator.

4 Conclusion

The basic proposition of technological determinists is that technology is autonomous and that technological change leads to social change. Karl Theodor Jaspers, a famous philosopher, believes that technology is a scientific process of human being controlled over nature that aim to shape their own existence, free themselves from want, and give human environment a form in which everything depends on themselves. The appearance of human technology to nature, and how this technological process acts on human beings, forms one of the historical baselines. Through this path, the way humans work, the organization of work and the development of environment has changed themselves [14].

That is to say, while people use technology, they must also follow the logic of technology, but this logic is not always good for people, technology creates exquisite things according to the possibilities of science, it does not redefine human nature, but distorts it by trying to redefine life, moreover, technology contains all the risks that may be unbearable [15]. 5G may be a great technology with revolutionary trans-formative power. As a result, the media industry has undergone structural changes, which in turn leads to the reform of HVENC. Then we major builders must rethink the countermeasures in order to transform our students. In other words, the technology we have invented is forcing us to adapt ourselves to it in the name of human welfare. Obviously, it is not a question I could answer, but we should know that what we think and what we do is not only motivated by the logic of technology or the logic of machine, but also by a return to the core purpose of the logic of human beings, and make technology artistic, that is, creating exquisite life according to the logic of humanity, which expresses only humanity and never more than humanity [15].

Therefore, the reorganisation of the media industry by 5G and the reposition of HVENC could be essentially defined as a question of technology, of how people are educated to become qualified professionals. However, learning lifelong learning, self-reflection, communication, and how to be a member of society with a sound personality would be the most humane-centered and timeless education purposes.

References

1. Lelia, G.: Technoculture, 2nd edn. Allen & Unwin, Sydney (2002)
2. McLuhan, M.: Understanding Media: The Extensions of Man, 2nd edn. Mentor Books, New York (1964)
3. Lippmann, W.: Public Opinion, 2nd edn. Free Press, Florence & Washington (2002)
4. Flew, T.: New Media, 4th edn. Oxford University Press, Oxford (2003)
5. Yu, G., Qu, H.: Introduction to Network New Media, 2nd edn. Posts and Telecommunications Press, Beijing (2021)
6. Arthur, W.B.: The Nature of Technology: What It Is and How It Evolves. Simon & Schuster, New York (2009)
7. Jiang, D.: The Essence of Vocational Education, 2nd edn. Normal University Press, Beijing (2017)
8. GSMA Homepage: The Mobile Economy China 2020. www.gsmaintelligence.com. Accessed 17 Mar 2020
9. Xiang, L.: 5G Era: What is 5G, How 5G Change World, 2nd edn. Renmin University Press, Beijing (2019)
10. The coming of 5G Era. https://www.goldmansachs.com/worldwide/greater-china/insights/5g-era.html. Accessed 11 Apr 2019
11. Yu, G., Qu, H.: Introduction to Network New Media, 2nd edn. China Renmin University Press, Beijing (2019)
12. Li, L.: Introduction to Media Economics. University of Political science and Law Press, Beijing (2017)
13. Scoble, R., Israel, S.: Age of Context. CreateSpace Independent Publishing Platform, New York (2013)
14. Jaspers, K.: The Origin and Goal of History. Routledge, London (2011)
15. Zhao, T.: A World Without Worldview: Political Philosophy and Cultural Philosophy. Guangxi Normal University Press, Guangxi (2005)

Research on Higher Vocational Art Design Education from the Perspective of Key Information Technology Based on Cloud Design

Xiaodan Peng(✉)

Guangdong Nanhua Vocational College of Industry and Commerce, Guangzhou 510507, Guangdong, China
yangyihua0739@163.com

Abstract. With the development and progress of network information technology, the concept of "cloud" has gradually derived, such as being on some new computing service technologies of cloud services, cloud computing, cloud manufacturing. Among them, cloud design is a new type of product and service design born in this technological environment, which integrates cloud computing technology, cloud technology and three-dimensional digital design and manufacturing technology, and integrates these technologies and process clouds into a resource pool. Demand sharing means that companies can perform cloud testing to optimize their own resources, so that they can make full use of their own resources and realize their best economic efficiency. This paper analyzes what is cloud design, and explores the core technology construction of cloud design technology under the background of the current network era. The application of cloud technology promotes the innovation and reform of Higher Vocational Art and design education, and cultivates high-quality art and design talents who can apply new technology to innovative design.

Keywords: Cloud design · Key information technology · Construction path · Art design education

1 Introduction

In the new network era, network design is based on the Internet and information technology as the basis and carrier. It is an important and basic characteristic of the development

X. Peng—This work was supported by Guangdong Province's key platforms and major scientific research projects (Characteristic innovation category) in 2018: Higher vocational art design professional education and teaching and "intangible cultural heritage" skills inheritance collaborative innovation development research (Grant No. 2018GXJK323), and was supported by Guangdong Province Educational Science "Thirteenth Five-Year Plan"-2019 College Philosophy and Social Science Special Research Project: Research on the Inheritance of "Intangible Heritage" and the Collaborative Innovation Development of Higher Vocational Art Education in the Context of Cultural Confidence (Grant No. 2019GXJK253).

© ICST Institute for Computer Sciences, Social Informatics and Telecommunications Engineering 2022
Published by Springer Nature Switzerland AG 2022. All Rights Reserved
S. Shi et al. (Eds.): 6GN 2021, LNICST 439, pp. 523–531, 2022.
https://doi.org/10.1007/978-3-031-04245-4_45

of network design technology based on the "cloud" carrier. It also conforms to the needs of the progress and development of the times. A concentrated expression of a new Internet and information technology. At present, "cloud" terminal technology and network technology have been continuously progressing and developing, and its application in our production and life is increasing [1]. Therefore, from the perspective of the development of the Internet, the advancement and development of computer and cloud design technology provide a strong guarantee for promoting the innovation and application of network information technology. According to the training goals of art design professionals in higher vocational colleges and the corresponding job groups, cloud design technology can be used to define students as designers, building materials suppliers, project managers, cloud design platform developers and other different identities, tailored for accuracy nourish [2]. The application of cloud technology in higher vocational art design education is the inherent trend and demand for the sustainable and healthy development of my country's future design industry.

2 What is Cloud Design

Cloud design is mainly based on cloud computing technology, which integrates the planning technology and planning process in the production and activities of human creations into a resource pool, which can be shared in real time according to the needs of users, that is, users can evaluate the design results through the network [3]. To optimize their own resources, so as to give full play to the best management functions. Common cloud design application platforms and software include: threeWeijia, Design Cloud, Tencent Cloud, etc. In the actual application process of cloud design, it has the following advantages:

(1) Concentrate high-performance software and hardware resources to improve work efficiency;
(2) Realize the collaborative work of project members;
(3) Realize knowledge accumulation and management;
(4) Unified management of data resources, safe and controllable;
(5) Make remote office and project meeting presentation reports convenient and quick;
(6) Reduce software and hardware purchase capital investment and save costs.

3 Key Information Technologies for Cloud Design

Cloud design can be applied to multiple design scenarios and environments, breaking time and space constraints, and transforming design work from pure offline to online and offline integration. The key information technologies of cloud design mainly include cloud technology, cloud computing and three-dimensional digital design, etc. Each technology has different functions and their core technology constructions are also different. It is these technologies with different dimensions and different functions that effectively promote the formation and development of cloud design.

3.1 Cloud Technology

Cloud technology can be regarded as a kind of hosting technology, which realizes the storage, calculation and sharing of data by integrating hardware, software, network and other resources. Its key core technologies are virtualization technology, distributed mass data storage, and mass data. It consists of management technology, cloud computing platform management technology, and programming methods [4].

(1) Virtualization technology
The main meaning of virtualization software technology is that the virtual computers and component devices in the virtual computer system can work normally on other virtual software devices. One of its main goals is that the software can greatly increase the storage capacity of virtual hardware and simplify the virtual software. The re-installation configuration operation process reduces the cost related to the use of other virtual hardware devices in the virtual software device, and can support a wider variety of operating systems at the same time. Through this kind of aggregation technology of underlying virtual hardware, the information isolation between software applications and multiple underlying virtual hardware can be easily realized. In the realization of cloud computing, the basic virtualization concept of computing system is the basic theory of all information services and network application architecture models used to build "cloud".

(2) Distributed massive data storage
Cloud computing has strong computing and data processing capabilities, and is implemented through a large number of servers. Conventional storage methods can not meet the storage of massive data, so on the cloud computing platform, a special distributed data storage method is adopted. To put it simply, it means distributing design data such as dimensions, drawings, drawings, etc. to multiple servers, using redundant methods to decompose and inherit tasks. This not only ensures the reliability of the design data issued, but also can use low-configuration servers to save storage costs [5].

(3) Mass data management technology
The data processed by cloud computing is massive and distributed, which requires a management platform to process and analyze it. The platform not only has powerful computing capabilities, but also requires massive data management capabilities. This technology has good management capabilities for large-scale data uploaded by large-scale design projects, ensuring the integrity and accuracy of the design data.

(4) Cloud computing platform management technology
Traditional computers cannot process big data stored using distributed technology, which affects the data calculation and storage process of some cloud design projects to a certain extent. In order to solve this problem, cloud computing adopts a new type of computing architecture. Under this structure, the cloud computing platform has a huge number of nodes and servers. They need to coordinate with each other, work in a unified and effective manner, and also ensure the reliability of the entire system. This requires the cloud computing platform to be able to perform intelligent management.

(5) Programming method
The cloud computing programming system architecture uses a unique programming system model-map-reduceuc model. This new programming system model is actually a parallel-based programming system model, and the programming ideas are concise and clear. And through this programming method, better task scheduling can be carried out. For users, they only need to customize the Map function and Reduce function. The operation is relatively simple and saves a lot of programming time [6].

3.2 Cloud Computing

From a narrow perspective, cloud computing is a kind of distributed computing, which decomposes a huge data calculation into countless small calculations, and then analyzes and processes them with the help of servers and systems and sends the results back to users. From a broad perspective, cloud computing is not only a network technology, but also a network application concept. With the Internet as the core, fast and secure data computing and storage services are established on the network. The types of technologies involved are distributed. Type resource management technology, parallel programming technology.

(1) Distributed resource management technology
In most cases, the simulation system of the information system will be in a concurrent execution environment of multiple nodes for a long time. If you want to effectively ensure the accuracy of the system's operating state, you must effectively ensure the distributed data between the nodes. Consistency of transmission. In order to solve the consistency problem of cloud computing, many enterprises and researchers in the computer field of our country have put forward various agreements. These agreements are some laws that we need to follow. That is to say, before the birth of traditional cloud computing, the solution to the consistency problem of cloud computing still relied on many agreements, but for large-scale or even super-large-scale distributed network systems, it is impossible to be sure that all departments and subsystems can Using the same network protocol, there is no way to determine the distribution consistency of the network. This problem can be effectively solved. The distributed resource management technology in cloud computing applications has satisfactorily solved the problem [7].
(2) Parallel programming technology
The cloud computing model is a computing model based on parallel and programmable. In this parallel data programming system mode, some key details such as design data concurrent processing, fault tolerance, data distribution, load balancing, etc. are directly processed through abstraction and integrated into a system function library, through this unified function With the interface, users can perform size calculation and design task automation, that is, a system task is automatically divided into multiple independent subsystem tasks, and the massive calculation data of more users can be directly processed in parallel and effectively.

3.3 3D Digital Design

Three-dimensional digital design is built on the basis of graphic design and two-dimensional design, and is the basis of intelligent and networked design platforms, making the design goals more three-dimensional and visual. The core ideas and technologies involved in 3D digital design include standard modular ideas and associated design technologies.

(1) Standard modular thinking
Modularity refers to a period of sharp contradictions between the diversification and change of market demand and the sharp contradiction between product development and technological innovation capabilities, and the modular product development strategy of "changing with changes" and "changing with few changes" [8]. In other words, modularization is actually a standardized high-level form. Module usually refers to a mixture of various components or parts, with independent functions, can be constructed as a series of separately produced and manufactured standardized product units, which are formed by combining different types and forms of interfaces with other units. The products are separable, coordinated, and interchangeable. Modularization technology is based on various modules, and combines the advantages of various universal, serialization and combination integration, and is used to solve the standardized technical form of rapid adaptation to various complex systems. After years of research and statistical analysis, the results show that in the development of a new generation of products, about 40% of the time is reused in the past part design, and about 40% of the time is spent on all the designed parts. Modification, and only about 20% of the time is completely replaced with new parts. Through research and adoption of new technologies such as group technology, standardized management technology, and modular design of main parts elements, it is possible to standardize the production of 90% of the internal structural elements of the main parts, and standardize the production of 60%–70% of the main part elements., The main part elements of this part are produced and modularized. This part of the product standardization, standardization and the use of modular mechanical parts design is an important theoretical basis for the mechanical design of the design company's series of products, and can be widely tailored for mechanical design practitioners to make professional choices. Once these similar parts are re-screened, they include digital production models, drawings, processes, production process codes, tooling, measurement and testing equipment, etc., which are currently achievable, and can directly redesign and manufacture similar parts The total quantity is basically controlled between 10%–20%, which is very likely to greatly shorten the basic design and manufacturing cycle of similar products and the development cycle of product research institutes, and improve the overall production efficiency of products.

(2) Associated design technology
In a broad sense, data association design technology mainly refers to the construction of a fully digital three-dimensional collaborative system design data information processing platform and design environment system based on technical research and design as the main technical research core, solidifying the design and parallel

lean process based on the application of three-dimensional data collaborative system The management operation process realizes various data association transfers based on design model-based 3D collaborative system design and lean process management applications, and improves the operation process of data structure design, the operation process of parallel 3D collaborative design data transfer and distribution, and the data running status. Optimize the operation process of monitoring and process control, the planning and design of various collaborative information processing processes and systems. In a development environment designed in a collaborative manner, the various design features (such as design parameters, geometric structure characteristics, etc.) in the upstream collaborative design development file user must be a design function file that the user can directly pass through the collaborative development (publication) To directly realize the mutual sharing of design information for downstream users of collaborative design development files [9]. And when there may be major changes in the system parameters or system characteristics that are released each time, the downstream system designer can also automatically re-implement the real-time update of the released data [10]. For example, when the structural parameters or structural features of a parallel skeleton design model change, the partial design of the parallel skeleton of all models is considered to be able to update the corresponding partial design of its model directly. The difficulty of the specific implementation of the related skeleton design is mainly reflected in the top-level structural planning and design of the product related skeleton design specifications of the structural boundaries and definitions, which mainly include the product skeleton design model and the structural boundary definition of the product interface, and sort out the various design professions. The actual operation management process, the boundary definition of the top-level product structure and professional organization, and the definition of the boundary of the skeleton design model.

3.4 The Key Information Technology Construction Path of Cloud Design

Cloud design is based on the "cloud" form of design work. It is different from traditional single and flat design software and methods, and tends to be more three-dimensional, informatized, intelligent and technical.The key information technology construction path of cloud design are depicted in Fig. 1.

Path 1: Cloud technology integrates network information technology, resource integration technology, platform management technology and other comprehensive applications of cloud computing mode to form a resource pool, and utilizes virtual technology with the help of distributed resource management technology and parallel programming of cloud computing Calculate, manage and interpret the massive data uploaded and stored in the cloud in the cloud-designed server and system platform.

Path 2: Through the integrated technology and resource pool of cloud technology, reduce the expenditure and complexity of network technology, and realize the construction and listing of cloud design with the help of cloud technology and three-dimensional digital design. In fact, cloud computing and cloud technology are interoperable in terms of data storage, processing and programming. The organic integration of the two provides effective technical support for the development of cloud design.

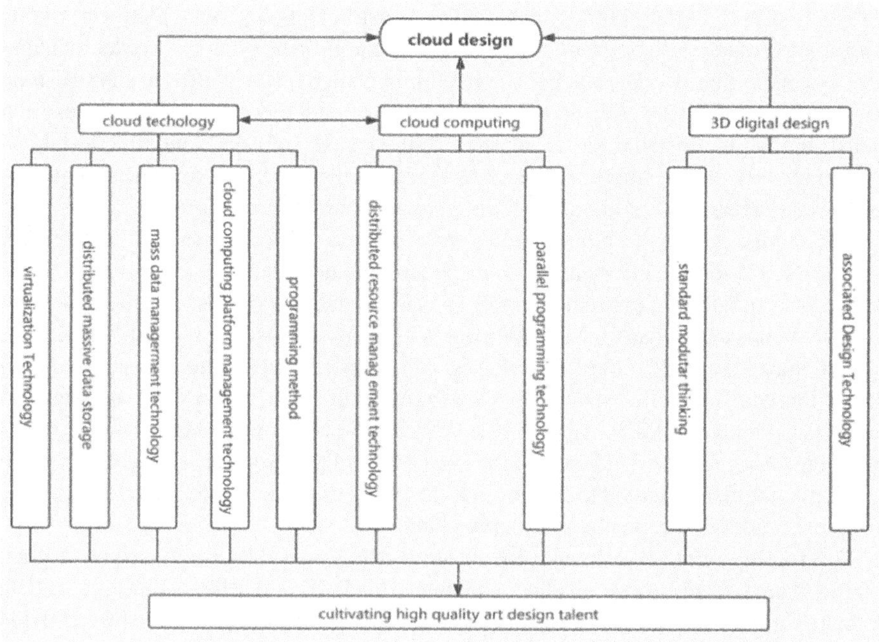

Fig.1. Cloud design key information technology construction roadmap

Path 3: Three-dimensional digital design realizes the three-dimensional design. The product or material to be designed is presented in the form of a combined model. In the whole design process, more attention is paid to the logical relationships such as construction logic and usage logic. And integrate standard modular thinking and associated design concepts into the data processing and storage programming of cloud technology and cloud computing, and promote the concept development and product launch of cloud design from the two perspectives of network technology and design thinking.

4 Higher Vocational Art Design Education Based on the Application of "Cloud Design" Technology

At present, enterprises use cloud design technology to realize information exchange, process control, data intelligent analysis, decision-making assistance and other functions through digital platforms, realize real-time digital collaborative management of supply, production, and sales, and complete digital management, digital manufacturing, digital marketing and digitalization. The all-round upgrade of the supply chain collaboration has established an integrated front-end and back-end system [11]. The formation of a complete data-driven enterprise research and development, design, production, marketing, supply chain management and service system, mainly through the following four links of innovation:

The first is to build a product personalized customization service platform: online confirmation of quotations, production orders and entering the platform's order management system, orders are automatically split and scheduled on the platform, and real-time data interaction with the MES system. After the production is realized, processes such as distribution and installation are automatically arranged. At the same time, establish a customer service bus, import CRM systems, call center 400, etc., to achieve real-time control and precise marketing of each link in the customer service process.

The second is to build a large-scale customization platform database: through the company's full-service information management, create a database of customer information, product design, product technology, and product services in the customization industry to provide support for the company's business analysis and decision-making.

The third is to build a digital workshop that supports large-scale personalized customization: transform and expand cabinets, baking paint, blister workshops and logistics warehouses, integrate MES, APS, SCADA, WMS, SCM systems, and introduce visual management to achieve kitchen Flexible and customized production of cabinet products. Collaborative manufacturing through the network realizes the unified scheduling of remote production capacity and supply chain systems.

The fourth is data asset management: collect business data from various sectors, external data, collect, store, calculate, and unify standards and calibers through the data center to form group data assets, support internal management decision-making, provide external value-added services, and support front-end business Innovation reduces the burden on the back-end system, helps the manufacturing industry drive the continuous improvement of data application capabilities, solves the problems in the use of data in various departments of the enterprise, and drives business innovation and development.

To meet the development and progress of information technology, especially the needs of the development of "cloud design" technology, the education and teaching of art design majors in higher vocational colleges should also be continuously reformed and innovated. Combining the needs of the company's "cloud design" position, "cloud design" should be opened. In accordance with the characteristics of "theoretical learning is not high and the practical ability is strong" in the art and design majors of higher vocational colleges, in the teaching of art design majors in higher vocational colleges, a "integrated course of theory and practice" is offered: theory The course mainly focuses on the cognition of the basic concepts and principles of "cloud design"; the practical course mainly makes full use of the school-enterprise cooperation training practice base, through enterprise practical teaching and the actual position practice of "cloud design", correspondingly to further promote students' The theoretical knowledge of "cloud design" is mastered, so that students' comprehensive ability level can be improved in an all-round way, and high-quality "cloud design" technical skills talents can be cultivated for enterprises.

5 Conclusions

The emergence and establishment of cloud design is conducive to the realization of the informatization of multi-mode design from industrial design and business design to the in-depth development of the Internet, intelligence, and service. It is the only way to achieve the great development of design culture and the prosperity of the art industry. The road Through the construction of key information technology of cloud technology, promote the innovation and reform of higher vocational art design education, and cultivate high-quality art design talents who can apply new technologies for innovative design. Of course, like any new thing, the survival and development of Cloud Design will encounter certain arduous difficulties and twists, but as long as these environments are available, it will definitely be able to reach its glorious apex.

References

1. Hasan, M., Hossain, E.: Distributed resource allocation for relay-aided device-to-device communication: a message passing approach. IEEE Trans. Wirel. Commun. **13**(11), 6326–6341 (2014)
2. Nomikos, N., et al.: A survey on buffer-aided relay selection. IEEE Commun. Surv. Tutor. **18**(2), 1073–1097 (2016)
3. He. X., Xu, J., Chen X., et al.: Cloud computing architecture and key technologies. Mod. Inf. Technol. 112–113 (2017)
4. Dinh, T.Q., Tang, J., La, Q.D., et al.: Offloading in mobile edge computing: task allocation and computational frequency scaling. IEEE Trans. Commun. **65**(8), 3571–3584 (2017)
5. Yang, B.: Research on 3D CAD and Information System Integration Based on Private Cloud Platform, pp. 168–173. Huazhong University of Science and Technology (2018)
6. Lu, J., Lu, C., Wang, P.: Discuss cloud design again. Comput. Simul. 35–37 (2013)
7. Hong, S., Yang, S.: Research on key technologies of cloud computing and cloud computing model based on hadoop. Software Guide 9–11 (2010)
8. Lin, B.: Key technologies of distributed storage in cloud computing environment. Inf. Comput. (Theoret. Ed.) 41–42 (2017)
9. Hui, X., Wu, Z., Liu, Z.: Application evaluation of parametric 3D design software in custom home furnishing industry. Furniture 20–24 (2020)
10. Chen, X., Jiao, L., Li, W., et al.: Efficient multi-user computation offloading formobile-edge cloud computing. IEEE/ACM Trans. Netw. **24**(5), 2795–2808 (2015)
11. Mao, Y., Zhang, J., Letaief, K.B.: Dynamic computation offloading for mobile-edgecomputing with energy harvesting devices. IEEE J. Sel. Areas Commun. **34**(12), 3590–3605 (2016)

AI Application in English Vocational Education Through 6G Revolution

Yujuan Liang[1(✉)] and Jian Zeng[2]

[1] South China College of Business and Trade, Baiyun District, Guangzhou 510550, China
lynn_lyj@163.com

[2] Guangdong Eco-Engineering Polytechnic, Tianhe District, Guangzhou 510520, China

Abstract. The advent of 6G is making AI Application in English vocational education in a more profound yet convenient and user-friendly environment. The use of AI will be blended with the online to offline class to boost English teaching and learning efficiency. AI analysis based on the big learning data will also make it possible for English teachers to deliver more personalized English class by distributing aptitude-oriented materials to accelerate real learning via adaptive learning. The language teaching Model will therefore become more flexible to meet the blended class and the adaptive learning. Even the English assessment will be heavily relying on the AI solution and make it more meaningful compared to the traditional final assessment. The new technology may post challenges as well as opportunities to English teachers. Therefore, embracing the current trend in both technology and vocational education reform as well as keeping the right attitude towards life-long learning will be the only way out for English teachers if they want to keep their place in vocational education.

Keywords: 6G · AI application · English vocational education

1 Technological Background and English Vocational Education Needs

1.1 Technological Background

Before 5G Telecommunication got its releasing license in public, 6G had already undergone numerous theoretical assumptions and practical experiments and tests since 2018 [1]. It will at least take another 10 years to finally bring 6G into commercial use though, its speed, capacity and potential revolution in the network will make it possible for more extensive and intensive AI Application in English teaching in Vocational Education.

What 5G can already do but not yet a satisfactory solution to current commercial needs will be finally solved by 6G. These application cases include faster transmitting speed and more accurate positioning, a result of 6G's wider broadband. A key indicator of the 6G Technology lies in its tremendously fast speed, with its peak speed at 100Gbps-1Tbps, which is 10 to 100 times faster than that of 5G [2]. This stunning speed will reduce

© ICST Institute for Computer Sciences, Social Informatics and Telecommunications Engineering 2022
Published by Springer Nature Switzerland AG 2022. All Rights Reserved
S. Shi et al. (Eds.): 6GN 2021, LNICST 439, pp. 532–545, 2022.
https://doi.org/10.1007/978-3-031-04245-4_46

in-house positioning deviation to as small as 10 cms and 1-m outdoor, 10 times more precise than that of 5G, with which the likelihood of internet disconnection rate will be decreased to somewhere lower than 1ppm. To most ordinary household users, one does not even notice the break between now and the next second, which is of great importance to English learning in vocational education, where massive internet connection and app applications are requested at fast intervals. Below is a table to compare the key performance indicators of 5G and 6G (Table 1).

Table 1. Comparison of key performance indicators of 5G and 6G [3]

Indicators	5G	6G
Speed rate	10 Gbps–20 Gbps at Peak	100 Gbps–1 Tbps at Peak
Time delay	1 ms	0.1 ms
Mobility	>500 km/h	>1000 km/h
Spectral efficiency	100 bps/Hz	200–300 bps/Hz
Position accuracy	10 m outdoors, <1 m indoors	1 m outdoors, 0.1 m indoors

Another highlight of 6G is its possibility to build a digital twin network. Compared with the 5G coverage which is limited to the land as we are experiencing currently, the 6G network will be able to cover the deep sea as well as the outer space. Although it may take another decade to finally implement its air and sea extension, it is certainly a great leap forward in human telecommunication and even human civilization. This change will definitely bring tremendous impact on future education mode. Below is an

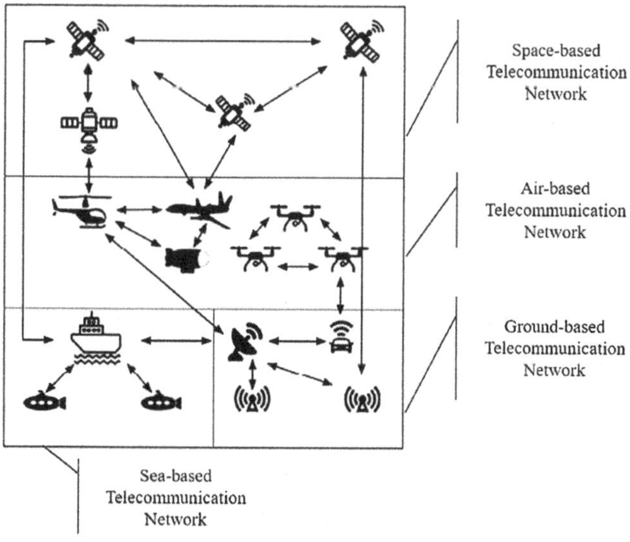

Fig. 1. Space, air, ground and sea telecommunication network [3]

idea of the comprehensive 6G telecommunication system network that will be likely to solve the integration problem of Terrestrial Network (TN) and Non-terrestrial Network (NTN) (Fig. 1).

This data-based network will enable more extensive and intensive use of AI in education and ultimately change the way of English teaching and learning and yield more fruitful results. It is targeted to improve the interaction of 5 components (Student Model, Pedagogical Module, Domain Knowledge, Expert Model and Communication Model) in the intelligent tutoring system beyond 5G limitation [4]. More personalized learning will take place in classrooms, making language learning a more enjoyable and learner-friendly process than ever. This digital twin network will enable learning to be individual-oriented, feedback specific, interaction-sensitive and skill-acquirable under the 6G network.

1.2 English Vocational Education Trend and Limitation with Current 5G Technology

Unlike other school subjects in China, English has been a learning course since one stepped in primary school, not to mention some pre-schools in bigger cities to employ foreign teachers for English enlightenment on toddlers who are still struggling to express themselves in their mother tongue. English is still a compulsory course in post-graduate education. When it comes to non-English majors in the three-year-learning Vocational Program in China, these learners have already been learning the language as a main subject earlier for at least 12 years. Yet this group of learners have achieved a much lower score and consequently lower motivation in English learning compared to their peers who have successfully enrolled in the four-year-learning program in universities. As a result, their English level tends to be lower. Many of them may be rated as the lower-level English learners based on the Cambridge English testing criteria [5, 6].

Therefore, the goal of English Vocational Education in the first place is set to teach no more than necessary, and very often English educators in vocational education have to turn to the more advanced technological inventions to assist teaching in order to retain students' interest in English learning. Moreover, teacher-student relationship in most Chinese classrooms may not be very close due to the deference to teacher power, which may constrain students from enjoying the classroom learning to some extent. However, as most millennial students are born "digital natives" [7], they are by all means supportive to the idea of using an advanced gadget in class. The advent of AI is an important solution.

Since the National Educational Bureau proposed the Action Plan of Educational Informatization 2.0 in 2018, a substantial proportion of capitals have flown into the vocational education industry. According to a vzkoo report [8], China has risen to Top 2 in the world in numbers of AI educational enterprises, and more than 300 billion yuan will be invested to diploma vocational education in the coming two to three years.

With the support of national policy, English teachers in vocational education have been active in applying the already existing AI Technology in course design and teaching. The invention of VR and AR already benefits many other subjects in teaching and learning. For instance, this invention allows students to approach the virtual reality or augmented reality for operational purposes or situational setting. It also helps to dissolve some abstract theories or rules into more visible models or intelligible framework. In terms of English learning, some popular English learning APPs are able to give simultaneous rating or immediate rectification as soon as the learner produces the utterances. 5G technology has already promoted AI application in English learning to the next level. For instance, English teaching in vocational education program has also benefited much from such software as iFly tech for English pronunciation testing, iWrite for English writing practice, Lexile for English reading practice, EI for personalized adaptive English learning program under 5G network [9]. Yet there are still some practical matters that await a more advanced network system to settle, especially in language learning with lower-level English learners.

First, current AI is not able to carry out more complicated human-computer interaction under the existing 5G technology, which is comparatively essential in English learning. One obstacle is its inability to recognize the subtle changes in the voice in more complicated contexts. The device may only search and provide the information that is previously input in it. This leaves some unsolved areas that only engineers alone cannot code. For instance, 5G AI-assisted tools lack the ability to capture subtle human intonation change, facial expressions or even gestures which are commonplace among lower-level English learning group in the course of a natural interaction. Under this circumstance, the feedback from the device may not appear to be very accurate or human-bond. This will further intimidate most of these learners and prevent them from seeking further help from it. The "insensitiveness" of the current 5G AI will leave an impression on these learners that it cannot really understand their needs. "A machine is a machine" may be their final conclusion and this may disinterest the human side to continue using the tool for language learning or improvement, or at least constrain them from getting the most of it.

Second, the adaptive learning system, which is one of the most effective and productive method to assist English learning, has not been in massive use yet under the 5G network. Most of the APPs in use to serve the purpose of adaptive learning are costly and mostly found in private classes in language training centers or enterprises [10], whereas in vocational education classrooms, such APPs are far beyond the reach of a typical above-40-student language learning environment. One reason may lie in the technical aspect as this type of learning may heavily rely on the costly information assessment and massive cloud computing. Without an open and perhaps low-cost virtual network as the 6G technology is trying build, the expensive service may not be affordable to the mass English learners either in diploma vocational schools or other schools of higher education or public organizations.

Third, 5G signal coverage is limited to only station-built areas, which may also restrain the extensive use of the network, let alone AI application. Many backwater areas in China still find the network signal weak and it will take longer for these areas to adopt it in their daily activities, including education. The coverage of the network needs to be further extended. Otherwise, AI application is even beyond the reach of this group of people.

2 Related Work

In the late 20th century, AI application has drawn vast attention of both the public and scientists. AI application in education (AIEd) is a more complex research field which involves collaboration between learning scientists, cognitive and linguistic scientists, and computer scientists, which can be traced back only in the recent decade, where multimodal learning analytics was the focal point [11].

Till now, such a powerful and satisfactory utility is yet to be improved, but it does not stop researchers, scholars and educators on their way to explore the subject from different perspectives and various academic results have been yielded. So far, AIEd research has been done in 40 articles in 16 countries, and only 2 of them covered the topic of foreign language learning in higher education [12].

One of them is focusing the on longer-term effects of technology on students' task and course interest by comparing the AI tool- Chatbot and human. It is found that the human wins over the Chatbot in the long-term effects [13]. This research indicates that unnatural talk with Chatbot under the current technology may not be sustainable. Yet the research is done under the existing 5G network, a more advanced 6G network improvement is not taken into consideration.

Another one is exploring the machine learning approach for the assessment of learning style changes, and proves the effectiveness for assessing the changes of learning styles [14]. But the students tested belong to the higher-level learning group who have much greater motivation of learning and better academic performance in general. It is still unknown whether the same effect can be achieved in lower-level learners in the vocational education program.

Moreover, most of the AIEd research articles were outcomes of collaborative work with two or more authors in multiple disciplines [12], but cross-discipline exploration of the topic was relatively few in quantity, and discussion on 6G-based AIEd in the public vocational program has not been conducted yet. Another frequently-discussed AI-related perspective in China is concerning the ethical aspects of the AI application, suggesting to promote ethical education for every stakeholder in AI research and development, application, and management before responsible conduct with AI [15].

Given the complexity of AIEd research and the sensitiveness of ethical matters of AI application, this article tends to shed some lights on AI application in English vocational education in the prospective 6G telecommunication. By observing the current 5G contribution in China and 6G development trend, this article tends to explore 2 questions in discussion: What can 6G do for future English Vocational education? How can English teachers adapt themselves to the new trend and take actions proactively?

3 6G-Based AI Solution in English Vocational Education

Unlike the 5G technology, 6G is tempting to build a ubiquitous virtual network with the use of satellites and digital data, covering land, outer-space and the deep sea [16]. So is the reform it will bring in English teaching in the coming decade. There are at least four aspects of 6G-based AI Solution to English vocational education.

3.1 Blended Learning and Teaching Methods Under 6G Boost Vocational Education

One important feature of the AI-assisted tools under 6G is their ability to capture human's subtle change in facial expressions or voices, which may be an important indicator of their learning difficulty, especially among lower-English-level students in vocational education program. AI-assisted learning and teaching methods under 6G will give both students and teachers a chance to communicate virtually before their offline classroom meeting and the blended learning and teaching methods will make English vocational classroom learning more efficient. Learner-based flipped class will be widely adopted by English teachers as their focus will shift from traditional lecturing and demonstration to a more meaningful learner-centered guidance of class activities.

On one hand, with the help of AI-assistant as a "walking dictionary" outside the classroom, students will be able to make better use of the fragmented time to undertake the preview or review tasks requested by the language learning target. They get notifications from their assistant, irrespective of the operating system. The broad coverage of 6G network will enable them to assess English learning in tunnels or concealed areas, whenever their learning moment comes. Their preview or review English tasks are just one click away from the web and their AI assistant will be at service. Answers can be found at their fingertip and they will be more likely to turn to their virtual friend for help. More importantly, this friendly tool can interpret the emotion in their faces and facilitate English learning just to meet their personal needs. Students' interest of language learning will be intrigued by AI's non-stop supportive and understanding features.

Blended learning empowers lower-level English learners in vocational education program to get ahead of necessary amount of theory or knowledge thanks to the digital twin network the 6G is building, enabling them to participate in more meaningful exploration of the topic in class just like their intelligent peers in renowned universities. With adequate perception of the task and pre-class preparation, students will be more target-oriented and cooperative in class, pay closer attention to both the teacher's suggestions and other students' opinions and join the discussion with more enthusiasm. They will be more eager to share their opinions or questions with the peers or find out what others think about and how others solve the problem. Class participation rate and learning efficiency will therefore be improved. A well-cycled learning mechanism will be formed among these lower-level English learners.

On the other hand, teachers in vocational education will benefit from their AI helper in that their workload may be partially shared and their sense of accomplishment may be created by their students' improvement in English. They feel more valued and be more dedicated to teaching.

The AI-assisted tools driven by the powerful 6G network are ready to share much workload from the teachers and give them more time to devote themselves to pedagogical improvement and self-development. The teacher may not be involved in students' discussion unless requested, as the AI assistant will act as a counselor and participant to guide them to express their opinions. The smart AI assistant can help to capture students' difficulty in learning and pass it onto their teachers, based on which teachers may be able to focus more on providing personalized guidance to individual students. They can then assign corresponding tasks to individual students and steer the wheel of learning to keep students on the right learning track in class. In the course of teaching, teachers will gain more sense of understanding in their students as well as the sensibility to provide solutions.

The notion of "Learner-centered Education" will not just be a slogan but more an actual description of the teaching and learning phenomenon with the AI-assisted tools under the 6G network. Teachers may find their lower-English-level students in the vocational education program as brilliant or to even outperform their peers who used to take the lead in academic English learning, just in one aspect or another. The blended learning and teaching process in vocational education will boost the learning effect with the application of AI under the 6G network.

3.2 Adaptive Language Learning Materials Build up Student Confidence

Thanks to the big data to keep track of students' learning habits and learning process, the 6G-based AI learning system will be able to provide adaptive English learning materials to individual student based on their aptitude rather than the traditional teaching syllabus and textbooks, and the teachers will also be able to manage a class with more than 40 students with materials of varied levels and provide help accordingly. Students' confidence can be built up more easily with both the teacher and the AI's attentiveness.

For lower-English level learners in the vocational education program, many of them lack interest or confidence in learning the target language just because they have to struggle in many ways in the traditional English class. Their difficulty may range from vocabulary to grammatical sentence structure, from pronunciation to fluent speech, from mother tongue impediment to English thinking logic, even from narrow available handy resource selection to brain-blasting online knowledge exposure.

AI can smartly cater to individual student's conceivable needs in terms of English learning with its capacity to provide adaptive learning materials. With the help of 6G cloud computing, data analysis from blended learning results will provide evidence of students' individual learning strengths and weaknesses and distinguish them according to their aptitude and learning preference respectively. They will get a personalized learning plan that suits their current English levels and learning habits, based on which their teacher may just select the relevant materials for individual students. The adaptive language learning resource will enable students to finish the tasks more easily and gradually their confidence can be built as they are on their own track of learning. Adaptive language material can even combine games and simulated settings to place students in a mimic scenario so that students' engagement in learning will be kept in a longer time span. As a result, the students are more likely to overcome the difficulties when they are given such interesting yet not too demanding learning materials.

The lower English level learners in vocational education program will also feel less stressed in learning and be more likely to accomplish the tasks that are not too far beyond their English levels with the adaptive learning materials. Their confidence of English learning can be enhanced as they achieve their adaptive learning target one by one and their performance can be seen or even encouraged by their teacher. The digital twin network 6G is trying to build will allow students in the vocational education program to emerge in an English environment to acquire what they need in the target language and gain more self-confidence.

3.3 6G-Based AI Application Connects Teachers and Students with Flexibility

Under the 6G network, the 6G-based AI Application Model is proposed to show how AI application can connect teachers and students flexibly. In general, the 6G-based AI application will serve as a mysteries mechanism that undergoes a complicated computing and analysis process, playing a liaison role to-and-fro between the teacher and students, making their connection more frequently and flexibly (Fig. 2).

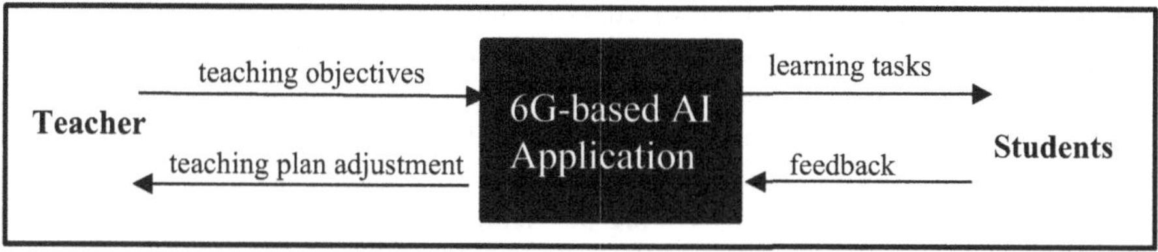

Fig. 2. AI-assisted English teaching and learning model framework

The above English Teaching and Learning Model Framework shows AI's role between the teacher and students in the course of English learning in vocational education. As mentioned earlier, the goal of vocational education is to teach no more than necessary, this Model Framework starts from doing instead of lecturing, followed by explanation or demonstration, and finally gets back to skill practice in varied situations. Therefore, this Model Framework with 6G-based AI application is tailored to vocational English education, where "teaching, learning and doing is done simultaneously" is highlighted and emphasized. Considering the power a teacher exerts on students in traditional

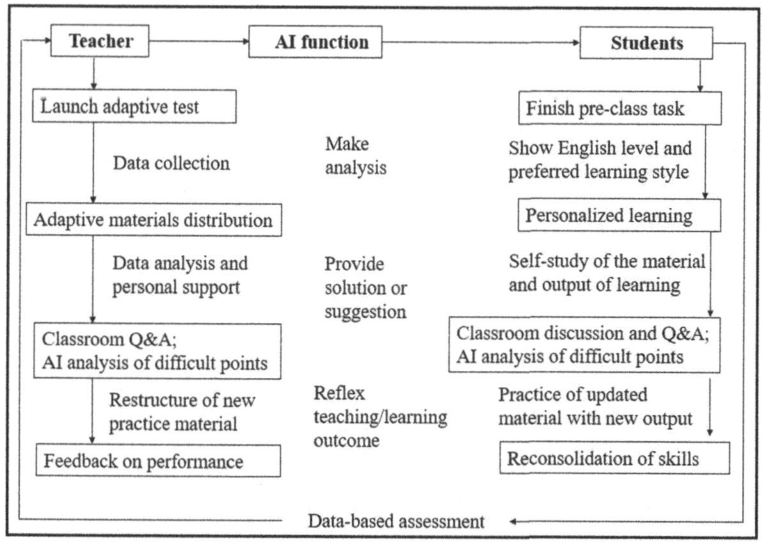

Fig. 3. AI-assisted English teaching and learning model

classrooms, 6G-based AI application can connect the teacher and students more often and flexibly and make English teaching and learning an activity with a mutually trusted medium. Their relationship may be improved as a result.

To understand the Model Framework better, we further extend the following teaching and learning Model to see how AI is applied to lubricate the path of English teaching and learning in vocational education (Fig. 3).

In the above Model, we can see how AI functions as a liaison party between the teacher and the students. The teacher's role is to launch the adaptive test, distribute adaptive materials, hold classroom discussion, make analysis of difficult points, and finally give feedback on students' performance. While on the part of the students, they need to finish pre-class task, then do personalized learning with the adaptive materials, join classroom discussion or watch teacher demonstration of difficult points, and finally have another practice for re-consolidation of skills.

To accelerate the process of teaching and learning as is shown in the Model, the 6G-based AI will perform functions differently in different stages of it, connecting both sides of the English class. When the teacher design and launch the adaptive test, AI first serves as the language reservoir to support the test design; after the students finish the task, it is working as an assistant to make analysis based upon the data. When it comes to the stage of classroom learning, the AI-assisted tools will on one hand distribute adaptive learning material on the part of the teacher, and on the other hand give suggestions or solutions to students who are trying to learn the adaptive materials personally or in groups. Either way, AI is bringing both sides of the English class closer with each other in a more frequent and flexible manner.

The most significant function of AI under 6G is its capacity to capture student emotion such as facial expressions and gestures and respond accordingly. For instance, when the AI assistant spots frowning or hesitations from the students, it will be able to recognize the possible learning difficulty and adjust the difficulty level of the materials. With its tremendously fast computing and analyzing speed, AI will perform as a chatbot to transfer messages between the teacher and each student and ensure more frequent and flexible communication between them. Trust or a sense of intimacy between students and the teacher will be more likely to be built in the process of the frequent communication.

The following two figures further explain AI's roles on both the teacher and the students in English vocational education (Fig. 4).

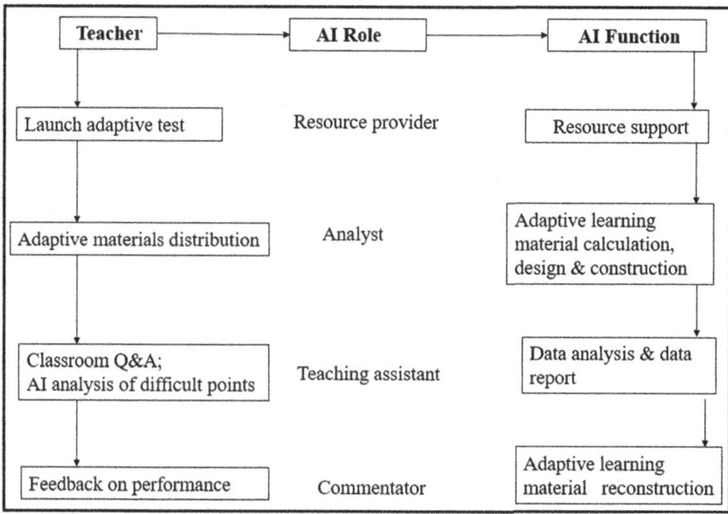

Fig. 4. 6G-based AI English teaching model for teachers

In terms of teacher and AI relationship, we can see from the above chart how AI is serving as a helpful assisting tool to the teacher. It serves as a resource provider at the beginning, including the language resource as well as the virtual environmental resource. It then acts as an analyst to calculate, design and construct adaptive learning materials. In the third stage, it serves as a teaching assistant for data analysis and report, and finally it takes on the role of a commentator based on students' performance and reconstructs adaptive learning materials accordingly. AI's role will be of great help to the teacher in

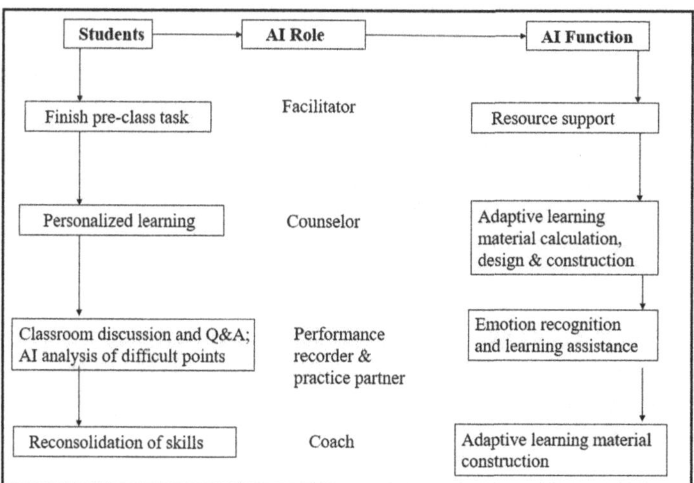

Fig. 5. 6G-based AI English learning model for students

the whole cycle of English vocational teaching procedure. It will help the teachers to form a more correct understanding of their students and thus give their students more caring and support, either online or offline (Fig. 5).

Student-AI intimacy is built on the basis of easy access. Owing to the 6G technology, AI is serving more like a learning partner to the students. In the first step, the AI tool is taking on the role as the facilitator to students so that they can finish the pre-class task on time. This step is especially essential to vocational students as their motivation of learning is comparatively low and a well-designed pre-class task in a simulated setting will be a "bait" to get their attention in the topic. In the second step, AI will put on the role of a counselor, giving students personalized materials for practice based on the result of their aptitude test. Students will be fully engaged in doing the task in a meaningful context created by AI. In the classroom Q&A and discussion section, AI is a performance recorder and practice partner to students. The final step where AI acts as a personal coach is a skill reconsolidation practice for students. A new cycle of English learning will commence. Students are more likely to form trust on their virtual friend, behind which is their English teacher, and be more willing to be approached by their teachers online or offline.

Virtual environmental setting is made throughout the course of English learning where even the lower-English-level students are able to empathize and resonate, and form positive opinion on their teacher. They may be more willing than ever to continue the discussion and exploration of the topic with their teacher outside the classroom with flexible means.

In sum, AI is serving as a smart liaison, bringing closer mental contact and more flexible physical communication between the teacher and the students. Thus, the teacher power is diminished to some extent and the student-teacher relationship may be improved.

3.4 More Justified AI Assessment Based on Individual Progress

With the help of 6G-based data analysis and cloud computing, assessment may no longer be so dependent on final examinations. Everyone will be making progress with the help of AI, and they will just pass the assessment as long as self-improvement is made in English which can meet their learning target and vocational purposes. Without the cruel competition to stand out in their peers, they just need to outperform the old themselves to a particular extent to show progress. Students may even form new perspectives towards English learning instead of just passing CET4 (College English Test Band 4) or CET6 (College English Test Band 6).

Such a new type of assessment based on individual progress rather than standardized test gives individual learners, especially lower-level English learners a chance to just get "fed" with no more than they need, and they will be more likely to get the right "fruit" within one jump. They will get the credits with due efforts. To them, such assessment is more justified and encouraging.

This type of assessment will be in line with the aim of modern vocational education. Students will be encouraged to discover their inner call and their true interest. They can therefore follow their heart to chase for what they need in order to grow into a working person they dream to be with survival English skills in their working field. In the process, students will be self-motivated to learn English. And they are fully aware that their efforts will be paid off, as they can see progress in themselves and the possibility of using the language skills in their future career. They will have a stronger sense of achievement.

On the part of the teacher, they just need to observe and monitor the process with the ongoing learning data the smart online platform provides, and make more personalized evaluation based on students' learning process. Formative evaluation is more likely to be given by the teachers as their students do perform and learn something with AI assistance. Teachers may be bolder in taking a step forward in the English education reform when they get positive feedback from their students. There is no doubt the 6G-based AI solution may bring the best outcome for both sides of English learning in vocational education.

4 Challenges and Opportunities English Teachers Will Be Confronted

Technology is a two-sided sword. Some English teachers may find it a useful tool, while others regard it as a threatening weapon. They may be stunned by its power and alongside the desperate feeling of losing control of the podium they used to be familiar with. Yet there is no way back. The millennial students, the working people from all walks of life, AI developers, the government and even their younger fellow colleagues are pushing the new technology forward, posting a question to all English teachers - Are we ready? Below are some feasible advice for English teachers in vocational education.

4.1 An Open Mind to Embrace Changes in English Vocational Education

Changes are taking place all the time throughout history in all industries. Language change may not be so obvious, but language teaching methods should be adapted alongside with the development of the modern world. Looking back on previous educational reform in China's history, no one can prevent it from moving forward. So, it is important for English teachers to keep an open mind toward the 6G and AI technology, which will take us to the new era of Industrialization 4.0. When English teachers are aware that educational reform will be taking place in middle school English tests, they should also be ready the embrace changes in their students' latter English learning path.

Since AI application is already on its way to release people's burdens in family chores, it can also be a good partner in teachers' career, as long as they keep an open mind to embrace the change. In fact, many students are already getting ahead of their teachers in using some advanced technological inventions. It is particularly essential for English teachers to upgrade themselves when their students are in the vocational education program. These students may be facing an international working environment where English is the universal communication language. They need to be able to understand and give English instructions in their work and make basic English conversations with technical experts from other countries.

Therefore, all English vocational teachers should integrate the existing knowledge and skills with the modern technology and grow with 6G in order to prepare students with their future work.

4.2 The Resolution to Get Familiar with AI- Assisted Tools in the Short Term

While online education becomes a common practice worldwide in the heavily hit areas of the covid-19 pandemic, the sporadic outbreak of the virus even in a well-controlled city in China is still possible. Therefore, the chance to conduct online English teaching with the AI-assisted tools is an important solution, given that the current online teaching with only videos and live broadcast can be boring.

Offline English teaching with the assistance of AI is also a popular choice to improve learning effect as the AI-assisted tools can make the English learning process more interesting and attractive. It can engage learners like a friend and be helpful to teachers at the same time. To get familiar with the AI tools to make online English teaching easier is not just a future plan, but a task on the recent to-do list for teachers.

4.3 Keep up with Society by Cross-disciplinary Learning in the Long Run

Life-long learning is not just a catchphrase for young people, it should be everyone's ultimate goal towards life - to live and learn. Therefore, in the long run, English teachers should be prepared to learn outside their comfort zone and explore more fields of disciplines. When it comes to a new era that knowledge multiplies at a much faster speed, no one can be exempt from learning if he wants to keep up with the society. Think about how we-chat was firstly designed as another online social media like QQ and then became the most popular virtual communication platform in China that now even the senior citizens are using it to update posts of daily activities. 6G is the trend, and AI is also the trend.

With the advantage of getting to know the trend in advance, English teachers should by all means prepare themselves well before 6G comes. Inter-discipline learning will therefore give them a brand-new horizon to explore more than just language teaching. Further progress is expected to be made with cross-disciplinary learning and even interdisciplinary collaboration with other scholars, researchers and scientists.

5 Conclusion and Future Work

6G is going to bring unprecedented changes in all industries, influencing almost everyone both at work or in their daily life. Whether we like it or not, it is going to be part of the future life. For English vocational education where students' English levels vary substantially, 6G-based AI application is perhaps the optimal solution to integrate teacher pedagogical experience and smart technological invention to the upcoming educational reform.

Unfortunately, the current study is carried out from the perspective of future trend. We are not able to collect instantaneous learning data to prove the significance 6G-based AI application will bring to our students. Therefore, we are calling for cross-disciplinary collaboration among educators, learning scientists, cognitive scientists and computer scientists to shape what we hope from 6G and then more empirical studies can be done when 6G becomes a reality in the future.

References

1. China Science Communication. https://baike.baidu.com/item/6G/16839792?fr=aladdin
2. People's Daily. http://paper.people.com.cn/. Accessed 16 Nov 2019
3. Chen, D., Guo, X.: 6G research progress and analysis of key technologies. Shanxi Electr. Technol. **4**, 56–58 (2021)
4. Beck, J., Stern, M., Haugsjaa, E.: Application of AI in education. ACM Mag. Stud. **3**(1), 11–15 (1996)
5. Sevilla-Pavón, A., Martínez-Sáez, A., Gimeno-Sanz, A.: Assessment of competences in designing online preparatory materials for the Cambridge first certificate in English examination. Procedia Soc. Behav. Sci. **34**, 207–211(2012)
6. Ofrim-Stăncună, A.: A multiple intelligences approach 3: Cambridge assessment. Procedia Soc. Behav. Sci. **203**, 90–94 (2015)
7. Chen, J., Jia, Z.: A tentative study on IT-based FL learning modes in the big data era. Technol. Enhanced Foreign Lang. Educ. **8**(176), 3–8 (2017)
8. AI Influence on Education Industry and Analysis on Market Investment Opportunities. https://www.vzkoo.com/doc/7291.html?a=1&keyword, last accessed 2019/12/23
9. Li, C.: The application and research focus of artificial intelligence in foreign language teaching. Chin. J. ICT Educ. **6**, 29–32 (2019)
10. Li, H., Wang, W.: Intelligent adaptive learning model supported by artificial intelligence. Intell. Lead Wisdom Educ. **12**(283), 88–95 (2018)
11. Oviatt, S., Schuller, B., Cohen, R.P., Sonntag, D., Patomianos, G., Krüger, A.: The Handbook of Multimodal-Multisensor Interfaces, vol. 2, 1st edn. Association for Computing Machinery and Morgan & Claypool Publishers, New York (2018)
12. Zhang, K., Aslan, A.B.: AI technologies for education: recent research & future directions. Comput. Educ. Artif. Intell. **2** (2021). https://doi.org/10.1016/j.caeai.2021.100025
13. Fryer, L.K., Ainley, M., Thompson, A., Gibson, A., Sherlock, Z.: Stimulating and sustaining interest in a language course: an experimental comparison of Chatbot and Human task partners. Comput. Hum. Behav. **75**, 461–468 (2017)
14. Wei, Y., Yang, Q., Chen, J., Hu, J.: The exploration of a machine learning approach for the assessment of learning styles changes. Mechatron. Syst. Control (Formerly Control Intell. Syst.) **46**(3), 121–126 (2018)
15. Wu, W., Huang, T., Gong, K.: Ethical principles and governance technology development of AI in China. Engineering **6**(3), 302–309 (2020)
16. CAIST. http://www.caict.ac.cn/kxyj/qwfb/ztbg. Accessed 04 Jun 2020

Research on the Development Path of Information Vocational Education for Intelligent Manufacturing Specialty Under the Background of "5G+ Industrial Internet" Era

Wanpeng Tang and Xiaoman Li(✉)

Guangzhou City Polytechnic, Guangzhou, China
332092426@qq.com

Abstract. With the transformation and upgrading of intelligent manufacturing technology under the background of "5G+ industrial Internet", great changes have taken place in industry, production mode and talent demand. Cultivating intelligent manufacturing high-skilled talents adapted to The Times has become the primary task of higher vocational education. By analyzing the impact of the coming of the era of "5G+ Industrial Internet" on the intelligent manufacturing industry, this paper explores the development path of information vocational education for intelligent manufacturing majors under the background of "5G+ Industrial Internet".

Keywords: 5G era · Industrial Internet · Intelligent manufacturing · Vocational education · Informationized teaching

1 Foreword

"Developing an industrial Internet platform" has been written into the Chinese government work report for four consecutive years. 5G has the traits of high speed, low delay and interconnection of everything, which can make different devices become intelligent and build a bridge between different industries. With the advent of the 5G era, the industrial Internet has gained considerable development. 5G is used to promote the development of manufacturing enterprises toward the direction of "Internet of everything and control of everything". A total of 1,500 5G+ industrial Internet projects are under construction, which will strongly promote the upgrading of traditional manufacturing to networking, technologies and digitalization.

With the development of vocational education to a high level, it is urgent to train all kinds of high-level technical talents. With the arrival of "5G+ Industrial Internet", the transformation of enterprise industrial structure also puts forward new demands for the knowledge, skills and personal qualities of manufacturing talents in different fields. The demand of single operation skilled talents turns to the demand of technical skill

© ICST Institute for Computer Sciences, Social Informatics and Telecommunications Engineering 2022
Published by Springer Nature Switzerland AG 2022. All Rights Reserved
S. Shi et al. (Eds.): 6GN 2021, LNICST 439, pp. 546–553, 2022.
https://doi.org/10.1007/978-3-031-04245-4_47

complex talents. Under the personalized market demand, applied talents need to have the ability of innovative thinking, digitalization and information technology. "5G", "Internet plus", information technology and "artificial intelligence plus" provide important carriers for cultivating interdisciplinary talents. It is necessary to grasp the multi-disciplinary knowledge efficiently and quickly [1].

2 New Development of Intelligent Manufacturing Under the Background of "5G+ Industrial Internet"

With the explosive growth of information, the emergence of new technologies such as industry 4.0, "Internet plus" and "manufacturing" is being transformed into "intelligent manufacturing". Skilled application of 5G technology provides a reliable platform and innovation impetus for the upgrading of China's manufacturing industry. 5G technology is promoting the in-depth development of digital, green and intelligent manufacturing industry.

2.1 Industrial Convergence

The scale of China's manufacturing industry is huge, and it needs the participation of multiple industries no matter it is transformation, renewal or upgrading. In order to adapt to intellectual technology, traditional machines and equipment need to integrate digital twinning, innovative human-computer interaction, 3D printing, intelligent maintenance and other intelligent technologies. Intelligent manufacturing is connected by manufacturing management (MES), supply chain management (SCM), enterprise resource planning (ERP), product life cycle management (PLM), customer relationship management (CRM) and other systems [2]. The advantages of 5G and industrial Internet information technology will be utilized to promote the combination of manufacturing and other industries to form a series of emerging sectors, such as design, research and development, experiment and other departments dedicated to providing R&D services for the manufacturing industry and adapting to the development needs of industrial Internet; And testing, maintenance, component customization, third-party logistics, supply chain management optimization and other industrial sectors that use 5G technology to provide professional services for the development of the manufacturing industry [3]. In order to adapt to the interconnection of all things in the whole society driven by 5G, product innovation in the manufacturing industry can be promoted, and more intelligent and networked products will appear. More and more industries are integrated around intelligent manufacturing through the industrial Internet, and more emerging industries are derived.

2.2 Transformation of Manufacturing Mode

"Industry 4.0" and digital twinning have made it possible for China's intelligent manufacturing to overtake at corners. The simulation process of digital twin technology is completed in the virtual space to map the entity equipment cycle process. By collecting customers' personalized needs and matching the best design, technology and production with the industrial Internet platform, products can be quickly launched and captured in the market. Intelligent manufacturing is transforming from production-oriented to service-oriented, and standardized production is transforming to personalized customization. Vocational education and training should be adjusted in time to the change of manufacturing mode.

2.3 Demand for Intelligent Manufacturing Talents

The accelerated development of information technology has led the human society to the era of industrial Internet. The industrial economic model has been transformed from scale economy emphasizing scale and standardization to flexible economy emphasizing value-added and individualization. The personnel, organizations and posts of enterprises have undergone great changes. First of all, intelligent equipment replaces traditional processing equipment, simple and repetitive front-line operators are replaced by industrial robots, high-end management talents are replaced by big data and some powerful APP and management software, but the design, maintenance and project management talent will be increased. Second, job task complicated, intelligent devices is all sorts of information technology and the integration of machinery and equipment, machinery industry has gradually become smarter, flexibility, networked, motors, globalization, at the same time, the change of production pattern, product specifications and more and more single batch quantity is small, more personalized requirements, higher to the requirement of process, technology and customer service. The industrial transformation and upgrading and the arrival of 5G+ Internet era have a fundamental change in the demand for talents. The employees in the intelligent manufacturing industry must master the digital ability, innovative thinking ability and information technology ability, and can participate in on-site debugging and solve substantive problems with complex technical skills [4].

3 The Dilemma of Information Vocational Education

With the rapid development of "5G+ Industrial Internet", intelligent manufacturing expands from traditional and narrow manufacturing process upgrading to broader process reengineering. Low-end vocational education disconnects the quality of talent supply and industrial development. Industrial hollowing leads to a widening gap between existing labor force technology and high-end industry requirements, and existing talents cannot meet the demand for intelligent manufacturing positions in the industrial Internet era. Vocational education informatization reform is the key to cultivate technical talents suitable for the current labor market demand of manufacturing industry. In essence, there are many difficulties in the development of vocational education informatization, which are embodied in the following aspects:

3.1 Smart Campus is Taking Shape

Smart campus is the extension and expansion of digital campus. As the core content of university informatization construction, smart campus fully integrates scientific research, management, teaching and campus life based on the Internet of Things and the application service system as the carrier [5]. The smart campus aims to create an intelligent, open, convenient and comfortable working, learning and living environment for teachers and students. After more than ten years of construction, in terms of life services, the smart campus has basically achieved complete informatization of consumption and borrowing. However, the construction of course informatization is still an isolated island, which involves property rights and copyright protection, campus network restrictions, the information course platform between universities cannot be shared, and high-quality course resources cannot be fully utilized. The campus platform also lacks the function of online live broadcasting. Its main function is tutoring and teaching, which does not play a leading role in information-based teaching. Offline teaching is still based on PPT teaching, supplemented by other information means. Without a unified course information platform, teachers' online information teaching channels are diversified and data are scattered. Students in the same class install different APPS to attend classes, which is not only inconvenient for school teaching management, but also easy to cause confusion in students' learning.

3.2 The Rate of High-Quality Shared Courses is Low

It is the inherent law of education that informatization drives modernization, and excellent open online courses are powerful measures to promote education informatization [6, 7]. Exquisite online courses show the characteristics of openness and sharing, break the restrictions of traditional course teaching, and establish a knowledge sharing and learning platform for vocational education [8]. To build high-quality online open and exquisite courses, it is necessary to excavate high-quality course content resources and make full use of information means to create high-level teaching materials, teaching videos, animation and other teaching resources. This requires teachers not only have excellent professional knowledge, but also need to be able to skillfully use a variety of information technology as a blessing. Moocs(Massive Open Online Courses) and online shared courses are the most frequently used platforms., for example, super Star learning, Blue 'Moyun' class, Mushroom nail, 'Weizhi' Library, vocational education cloud, rain class. In the special period of epidemic, almost all teachers of online courses will use these platforms to assist teaching. Although there are many high-quality courses, there are few high-quality open courses that can be directly used, and most of them are carried out in the way of live teaching.

3.3 Lack of Training Equipment Management and Simplification of Training Course Information

"The Circular of The State Council on the Implementation Plan of The National Vocational Education Reform" points out that "in principle, the practical teaching hours of vocational colleges account for more than half of the total hours". The implementation of the policy and the cultivation of qualified personnel in urgent need of enterprises need to build and plan the practical construction of higher vocational education, including the construction of practical training equipment and practical training courses. The information management of most training rooms and bases still needs to be improved and strengthened. The existing training rooms are mostly managed in the form of record books, relying on experimentalists to inspect and find problems, or teachers to inform problems, and there is no effective supervision system to ensure the normal operation of the training rooms. The integration of information technology and practical training courses is widely applied in the design of courses. Practical training courses that need to operate machines are usually in the mode of teacher demonstration. Video demonstration is the most commonly used information application of practical training courses, because of the lack of information technology means, students are not interested in learning and lack of enthusiasm.

4 Development Strategies of Informatization of Vocational Education and Teaching for Intelligent Manufacturing Majors

We will develop modern vocational education to ensure that talents in 360 fields gather and shine in the stars. Vocational education is employment-oriented and market-oriented, and our mission is to provide much-needed talents for society. In November 2021, Xi Jinping pointed out that the integration of "5G+ Industrial Internet" will speed up the construction of a digital China, a smart society and China's new industrialization process. We will build a "green campus" based on 5G communication technology and provide an environment for "smart learning". Accelerate the higher and faster development of teaching informatization, so that students can master the multidisciplinary integration knowledge as soon as possible, and prepare knowledge and skills for intelligent manufacturing.

4.1 Increase Investment in and Upgrade of Smart Devices

To cultivate interdisciplinary talents in programming, assembly and adjustment, maintenance and repair of intelligent manufacturing and production, transformation, design and technical service of intelligent production line. Intelligent manufacturing major is mainly composed of four parts of the course: The first part is the basic ability of mechanical and electrical products, mainly around the mechanical ontology in intelligent manufacturing, electrical foundation related courses; The second part is the electromechanical integration module of intelligent equipment, which mainly focuses on the courses of frequency conversion speed regulation, gas and hydraulic drive, electromechanical drive, servo control, PLC control and so on; The third part is the industrial robot system, which focuses on the programming control, visual color intelligent sensing, bus communication and other courses related to the industrial robot application system. The fourth part of the intelligent production line system integration programming, debugging, combined with intelligent sensing, frequency conversion, industrial bus, AGV, RFID technology, pneumatic hydraulic technology, servo, man-machine interface and other integrated programming, debugging, can use the MES management system to issue task orders. There are many intelligent devices involved and the investment is large. Higher vocational colleges should increase the support for the application of intelligent manufacturing equipment by means of special funds and purchase of services. Give play to the role of the market and let enterprises participate in the construction of vocational education informatization. The government establishes the management mechanism of information products and services, and mobilizes social resources to build the training room of intelligent manufacturing [9].

4.2 Promote the Co-construction and Sharing of High-Quality Digital Education Resources

Higher vocational teachers have heavy teaching tasks, but also need to undertake the task of scientific research and teaching reform, and the intelligent manufacturing industry upgrading and upgrading fast, the course reform is also changing with each passing day, it is unrealistic to teach subjects into high-quality digital teaching resources. Building and sharing high-quality resources can reduce the repetitive construction of courses, improve the resource certification standards and trading mechanism of the sharing platform, network the teaching resource database of vocational education majors, and build digital teaching resources of vocational colleges according to regional and industrial characteristics. Industry, enterprises and vocational colleges jointly build digital information resources.

4.3 Information Management of Training Base and Curriculum Information Construction

In the construction of training base information management, the establishment of the base cloud platform, the collection of equipment information data from procurement - use - maintenance - scrap, experimental managers and teachers timely understand the equipment, can effectively ensure the safety and normal operation of the training base. Virtual simulation courses and training bases are constructed to make up for difficult training projects that are costly, invisible and dangerous in practical training. With manufacturing technology "intelligent design, virtual manufacturing, information management, intelligent Internet of Things" four links as the main line, the development of rich virtual simulation experimental teaching resources, the formation of ability training as the core of the teaching system. For example, CAD courses use three-dimensional software such as Solid Works or 'ZW3D(Software developed by a Chinese company)' and related "advanced simulation" function modules to complete typical mechanism modeling, assembly and motion simulation and dynamic analysis from simple to complex. Social training talents make full use of cross-professional cross-training. With the help of intelligent equipment and AR and VR technology, AR and VR courses can also be opened, and "cloud classroom" can be developed in cooperation with enterprises to build a trinity of mixed teaching in the online front-line and next-training room.

4.4 Enhance the Information Literacy of Teachers, Students and Managers

Vocational education focuses on practice and operation. The national policy clearly states that vocational school teachers should have working experience in enterprises in the future, that is, vocational teachers themselves must be able to understand theories and be able to operate. Under the information technology, teachers of vocational education should keep pace with The Times, improve their knowledge of information technology, and improve their application ability of "5G+ Internet" information technology. Teachers should strengthen the communication of teaching ability and enhance the level of information technology in mutual learning with their peers. Students are the main body of learning, with the application of information technology, students should build independent use of existing information technology to consult data, show, discuss, and answer questions. Endow students with new roles and reconstruct the interaction mode between teachers and students. The comprehensive application training of information technology should be strengthened to improve students' professional ability of information technology. Meanwhile, information training should be carried out for school administrators to enhance administrators' awareness of information technology and improve their planning, execution and evaluation abilities [10].

5 Commissioning and Conclusion

This article discusses the transformation and upgrading of intelligent manufacturing technology under the background of "5G+ industrial Internet", the industry, production mode and talent demand have changed greatly, and the primary task of higher vocational education is to cultivate intelligent manufacturing high-skilled talents to adapt to The Times. By analyzing the influence of the coming of "5G+ Industrial Internet" era on intelligent manufacturing industry, the development path of intelligent manufacturing professional information vocational education under the background of "5G+ Industrial Internet" is explored, the predicament of current information vocational education is discussed, and several ideas to solve the difficulties are put forward. Under the background of "5G+ Industrial Internet" intelligent manufacturing technology, information education should increase the investment and upgrade of intelligent equipment, promote the co-construction and sharing of high-quality digital education resources, change the information management of training bases and the information construction of courses, and improve the information literacy of teachers and students and managers.

References

1. Beijing Vocational College of Electronic Science and Technology -- Science and Technology Division. https://www.bpi.edu.cn/kjc/zjyd/202011/t20201117_82542.html
2. Yu, X.H., Liu, M., Jiang, X.H.: Industrial internet architecture 2.0. Comput. Integr. Manuf. Syst. (12), 2983–2996 (2019)
3. Zhang, B.Y., Lin, R.Y.: Development trend and countermeasures of China's manufacturing industry in the "14th Five-Year" period under the background of 5G. Econ. Res. Ref. (10), 21–32 (2020)
4. Cao, H.F., Wang, Q., Bu, H.F.: Application research of low power wide area Internet of Things in college smart campus. Technol. Internet Things 211,11(03), 64–67
5. Huang, R.H., Zhang, J.B., Hu, Y.B.: Smart Campus: a must for the development of digital campus. Open Educ. Res. **18**(04), 12–17 (2012)
6. Wang,H.C.:The Logic of the "Three Steps" of Higher Education Modernization Research on Lifelong Education, 2019 (5) 3–10

7. Chen, X.H., Wu, J.F.: Artificial Intelligence Reshapes the World, pp. 27–35. People's Posts and Telecommunications Press, Beijing (2019)
8. Xu, Y.: Research on Policy Effectivity of Online Open Course Construction in Colleges and Universities. Southwest University, Chongqing (2018)
9. Guidance Opinions of Ministry of Education on Further Promoting the Development of Vocational Education Informationization. www.moe.gov.cn/srcsite/A07/zcs_zhgg/201709/t20170911_314171.html
10. Under the background of artificial intelligence and intelligent manufacturing, mechanical and electrical specialty of higher vocational college is adaptive transformation. www.doc88.com/p-09229297414935.html

Study on Benchmarking System of Vocational Education Under Future Information Technology

Min Lin[1](✉), Zhang Hongtao[1], and Haiying Wu[2]

[1] Institute of Surveying, Mapping and Remote Sensing Information, Guangdong Polytechnic of Industry and Commerce, Guangzhou 510510, China
linmin3000@163.com

[2] College of Economics and Trade, Guangdong Polytechnic of Industry and Commerce, Guangzhou 510510, China

Abstract. Selecting benchmarking system for vocational education informatization, guiding vocational college informatization construction and responding to the demands of the era of "Internet+" are important issues for vocational education informatization construction and also important contents for vocational education development. To that end, the article is given priority to with benchmarking method To thought, to extract the benchmarking standards as the goal, the comprehensive many kinds of research methods, combined with the characteristics of vocational education informationization, established a set of informatization level of business support, information technology, information technology, information management and information technology application performance continuous development ability of five dimensions, depth of coverage, the information technology application of information technology and information technology intensive degree, information technology business synergy degree of 26 observation indexes such as benchmarking system vocational education informatization evaluation standard system, And how to set the observation content of 26 observation indexes is systematically expounded.

Keywords: Vocational education · Informatization · Benchmarking · Evaluation criteria · The content dimension

1 Introduction

1.1 Preface

Informatization is playing a constantly improving role in shaping a more open, more suitable, more people-oriented, more fair and more sustainable education ecology. It is an important content of education development in the new era to comprehensively enhance the level of educational informatization. In the field of vocational education, big data, cloud computing and artificial intelligence have gradually infiltrated into the overall

© ICST Institute for Computer Sciences, Social Informatics and Telecommunications Engineering 2022
Published by Springer Nature Switzerland AG 2022. All Rights Reserved
S. Shi et al. (Eds.): 6GN 2021, LNICST 439, pp. 554–564, 2022.
https://doi.org/10.1007/978-3-031-04245-4_48

layout of vocational education informatization, and a large number of foundations have emerged.

In the application of new technology information, a new generation of information characteristics characterized by system, integrity and openness has been gradually formed. On the basis of summarizing the results of information construction, how to further promote information construction and better serve vocational education has been put on the agenda. Based on this, the Action Plan for Improving Quality and Cultivating Excellence in Vocational Education (2020–2023) points out that "guidance should be given to the vocational school system ". To design the overall solution of school informatization" "to select 300 left and right vocational education informatization benchmarking system". However, what is the benchmark school of vocational education informatization, what are the characteristics of the standard school of vocational education informatization, what dimensions are included in the evaluation criteria, and what are the observation contents etc. need to be further studied.

2 The Connotation of Vocational Education Informatization Benchmarking System and Its Metaphor

2.1 The Connotation of Vocational Education Informatization Benchmarking

With the gradual deepening of information technology [1], the construction of networked, digital, intelligent, personalized and life-long education system has become the development direction of education form supported by information technology. Information technology has promoted the reform of educational concept, educational content, teaching and learning methods Type change, education evaluation reform, education management system, such as a full range of change, formed from concept to practice, from the tool to the elements, from the node to the structure, from the base to the application of comprehensive education form change, as the education main body activity promotion, efficiency improving, innovation improvement, coordination ability and competitiveness improvement, and the "differentiation, personalized learning, fine management, teaching wisdom can service": First, to form some aspects such as research and practice into a fruit [2]. It is necessary to find out the supporting relationship between the performance of vocational education informationization and the development of system and establish an appropriate evaluation index system to ensure the direction of vocational education informationization development, so as to guide vocational colleges to correctly formulate informationization strategies in line with the internal needs of vocational education. Benchmarking system vocational education informatization is in accordance with the specific evaluation standard, will obtain good information in the field of vocational education of colleges and universities, the elements of a full autopsy, forming a series of standards, making it the other vocational school informatization construction reference, to information technology on professional education of the whole party, realize information the overall benefit of vocational education.

2.2 The Metaphor of Vocational Education Informatization Benchmarking System

In fact, the selection of benchmarking system for vocational education informatization is to establish a set of evaluation standards for the development of vocational education informatization, which can be used to guide the corresponding construction of vocational education informatization [3]. According to Braudel's view of time period, a short period refers to an event occurring in a specific time; Intermediate period refers to a structure that is stable in relation to each other over time; Long time is a measure of centuries, a structure that evolves slowly over long periods of time. Obviously, the influence of informationization is applicable to the analysis of thinking in the middle period of time, the construction of thinking in the long period of time and the explanation of phenomena in the short period of time. According to the logic of historical evolution, the metaphor of the characteristics of vocational education informatization benchmarking system is embodied in the following three aspects:

First, the benchmarking system of vocational education informatization refers to the excellent level of informatization effect. "Benchmarking" clearly implies an evaluation of past experience, referring to the ability and effectiveness of the previous application of information technology to achieve a pre-eminent position. It is reflected in the degree of perfection and governance effectiveness of the school's governance system through informationization, whether it has promoted the optimization of the operation mechanism of vocational education and established a curriculum system that meets the needs of informationization, and whether it has been implemented through information technology.

Now teaching and learning mode innovation and effectively solve the important problems in vocational education. Most importantly, the school information to realize the change of the concept of school development and value orientation, especially associated with modern vocational education concept of vocational education knowledge, career skill education and vocational education and cultural value, and realized based on the information technology education and the education information of the whole, in the school of the achievements have been made in the all-round improvement of comprehensive strength.

Secondly, the benchmarking system of vocational education informatization refers to the promotion level of informatization ability. The most intuitive manifestation of the development level of vocational college informatization is the degree to which the existing informatization status can promote the rapid development of business. It can be embodied as follows: First, informatization has the advantages of wide field scope, deep level and far influence. Applying informatization to all aspects of education and teaching can produce stable performance, improve the operating efficiency and quality of teaching business related to the school system, and export information technology-related products to the outside. Secondly, the application of informatization innovates the teaching format and management process, improves the teaching process and the supporting situation for teaching, produces different teaching products and service products from ordinary colleges and universities, and affects the innovation of vocational colleges and universities' informatization. Third, the research and management related to the application of information technology can provide continuous support for the development of informatization. Informatization is a complex system project, and the most important factor that determines the effectiveness of informatization is management. The research and management of informatization in the "middle period" of school can promote the development of informatization through management.

The third, the benchmarking system of vocational education informatization refers to the guarantee force facing information informatization in the future. Since information technology is a process of continuous development, past performance and current capability are not indicative of future capability of sustainable development. Vocational education informatization standard system need to support the continuous development of system with the help of "education technology ability training system, research support system and talent training system". That is to say, vocational education informatization benchmarking system contain the guarantee power of "winning both now and in the future". First, the establishment of information sustainable development mechanism, can ensure the personnel, assets and other related resources of the sustained investment and scientific operation; Secondly, through the construction of information management mechanism, the space for the application of information has been expanded to support scientific research personnel and technology Maintain good working condition of personnel and management; Third, it has become a long-term information talent selection and cultivation mechanism, which can carry out research work around the corresponding topics.

3 The Selection Concept and Principle of Vocational School Informatization Benchmarking System

3.1 Selection Concept of Vocational Education Informatization Benchmarking System

On the one hand, vocational college information construction is a school development project under the dual logic of "problem-driven" and "benefit-driven". "Problem-driven" refers to the application of information technology to solve problems faced by vocational education, such as teaching model, teaching content, evaluation model, governance system, etc. The "benefit drive" is reflected in the continuous expansion of learning content of vocational education, especially the new development opportunities brought about by the integration of different fields, which requires learners to acquire more knowledge, and also puts forward the corresponding managers' updating demands from governance concepts to actions. On the other hand, the characteristics of vocational education informatization benchmarking system are also influenced by the dual logic of "problem driven" and "benefit driven". On the problem of vocational education informatization, the orientation of informatization input is not clear, and the phenomenon of attaching importance to "hard" rather than "soft" always exists, which perplexes the education decision-makers' faith in vocational education informatization and causes the imbalance of input in fact. In the benefit, the huge amount of information resources investment did not bring the corresponding significant results. Therefore, in setting up vocational college informatization appraisal standards in the process of benchmarking, the information construction should be fully considered in solving the problem of the education teaching, teaching management, second, we must scientifically evaluate efficiency problem in the process of informatization construction, prison hold good problem solving and continuous influence orientation, overall architecture and use efficiency evaluation.

3.2 Use Problem Solving to Shape the "Good Value" of Technology

Problem solving is the first driving force of vocational college information construction. In the early stage of the development of information technology, it is usually through the introduction of information technology to solve the problems of personalized learning, learning space shaping, teacher learning analysis, teaching process management, school governance system. Only on the basis of solving the problem can we gradually realize the value of information technology in education quality, education equity, education reform and education innovation, and in the view and value of information technology method which takes global benefit and common commitment as the common value goal to achieve a consensus on the value orientation, to support the high-quality development of vocational education, and to create a good environment for its development.

3.3 Expand the Application Space of Information Technology with Continuous Influence

In reality, the contradiction between the rapid expansion of vocational education and the lack of supporting resources, the contradiction between the extensive development of vocational education and the demand for high quality, and the contradiction between the superficial teaching research of vocational education and the demand for large-scale personalized teaching gradually emerged. The existence of these contradictions requires virtual reality technology to expand learning space through the creation of virtual space, big data to form personalized learning content, artificial intelligence to support learners' adaptive learning, and internetworking technology to form "connected learning" (a form of learning that supports learners to teach and educate learners). The final result of informationization is to form an intelligent learning ecology that is "intelligent, integrated, creative, situational and open", realize the integration of information technology with education and teaching, and promote the expansion of information technology application space in the continuous integration with education and teaching.

3.4 Promote a Holistic Approach to the Application of IT

Only by focusing on specific aspects can there be a quick solution to a problem. Due to the diversity of information elements, the in-depth application of information technology cannot be fully explained by relying on technology, nor can it be separated from the discussion of technology between people and business. Instead, the effectiveness of information construction in vocational colleges should be evaluated from the point of view of system integration. Therefore, vocational education informatization benchmarking system selection work need to use the concept of overall architecture, deep understanding of education informatization of education concept, education content, education evaluation and its governance mode change, the informatization infrastructure resources, simulation training space and the influence of the digitalization construction of venues and so on, based on the information of teaching and learning, evaluation and management of the overall effect, promote the information technology application in the field of vocational education the all parties.

3.5 Regulating the Health Application of Information Technology with Benefit Evaluation

The ability of information technology, especially the ability of sustainable development of information technology, determines the benefit of information technology application. At present, the investment benefit of information technology in certain fields and some system is not high, especially under the premise that the resources occupied by vocational education is not enough, it needs to be regulated by benefit evaluation.

Health applications of information technology. The selection of benchmarking system for vocational education informatization needs to introduce the concept of benefit evaluation into vocational education informatization, and explore and form a shared, iterative and modular problem-solving concept in the process of informatization construction, so as to efficiently solve complex and diversified problems by using information technology.

4 Principles for the Selection of Benchmarking System for Vocational Education Informatization

The selection of benchmarking system for vocational education informatization is mainly to establish guiding standards for the construction of vocational education informatization under the support of specific concepts. From the perspective of selection, one needs to consider the measurement capability of the standard, and the other needs to consider the realistic environment of evaluation. Specifically, the selection principles of the following three aspects should be included.

4.1 Combine Science and Comparability

From the selection mechanism for benchmarking system selection is a kind of based on the benchmarking management, is a kind of practical reason, its value is "to change or achievements To point to in the world, and for the related appraisal activities more, make the evaluation objects presents the characteristics of the normative "(3), reflects the transformation of" how to "rational. The value of selection lies in providing reference for the informationization construction of vocational colleges and universities. The criteria of selection are based on the theoretical basis with practical reference, and finally become the "cognitive externalization" of practical rationality. However, not all behaviors can be accurately valued on a comparable scale. If the existing data acquisition environment can't be condensed corresponding standards as a reference for other system, it will lose the value of benchmarking.

4.2 Integrity and Dispersion

Professional education from the perspective of the demand of information technology, information technology by blended learning space make learners with the school teaching and cultural Angle, multi-level, need through the teaching and learning, individualized learning, fine management, and service to solve the deep-seated problems facing the vocational education, to build a new platform and enterprise cooperation, realize social service extension of the scope and level up, these are embodied in the overall architecture of vocational education informatization. However, it is difficult for the overall evaluation to have clear directivity and play the role of benchmarking. It is necessary to put specific contents into the standard system for evaluation, form the interaction between the whole and the parts, and give the whole a specific meaning.

4.3 The Combination of Representativeness and Orientation

Representativeness is usually related to the special color, which refers to the formation of certain characteristics in the whole or a certain aspect of university informatization. In reality, some system have transformed the classroom through the deep integration of information technology and education teaching. Some system have promoted the reform of teaching process based on information environment by enhancing teachers' information-based teaching ability. With the help of data acquisition system, some system have constructed a learner evaluation system involving multiple stakeholders. Some system, with the help of information resource integration technology, have completed the communication and connection of multiple types of data, forming a small "big data" ecology. Representation performance accurately describes the achievements of specific system in the field of informatization, which is an important criterion for selecting the benchmarking system of informatization. However, while considering the representativeness of selection and selection standards, we should also consider the guiding function of standards to accurately grasp the development level of information technology at the present stage.

4.4 The Evaluation Criteria and Content of Vocational Education Informatization Benchmarking System

A number of researches have been carried out on the evaluation of enterprise informatization at home and abroad, among which the most influential ones are Nolan model, SW-CMM model, and technology-information excellence model. At the same time, a lot of informationization technical standards have been introduced at home and abroad, which contains certain implication of price evaluation. In 1996, the United States issued the first National Educational Technology Plan, which required every teacher to have an Internet-connected computer, high-quality learning software and good training. In 2002, Singapore comprehensively reviewed the dynamic ratio, teacher/machine ratio, network transmission technology speed and teachers' requirements for curriculum integration ability. In 2001, China began to release the National Informatization Indicator, taking the lead in putting forward the "National Information Index", which realizes the evaluation of the national informatization degree and covers 20 quantitative indicators. However, in the field of vocational education, there are few diagnostic evaluations on the degree of informationization of specific colleges and universities. According to the existing research, the evaluation demand and application of vocational education informationization have the problem of supply and demand decouple. On the one hand, the rapid development of information technology has led to the systematic reform of vocational education. On the other hand, when the government organizes information construction, it cannot find a reasonable evaluation standard to guide the systematic advancement of information construction. Therefore, it is necessary to design vocational education scientifically according to the goal and stage characteristics of Informationization.

4.5 Evaluation Criteria of Informationization Benchmarking System and the Formation Process of Evaluation Criteria

Open coding based on expert interviews. This study adopts the Delphi method to issue an open questionnaire to 34 experts in the field (including 11 vocational education informatization research experts, 12 university informatization directors, 6 government administrators in charge of information technology, and 5 school leaders in charge of information technology). The first survey centered on the following questions: What do you think about the information system for vocational colleges? In your opinion, what factors can summarize the degree of informationization of a school? What do you think your accredited vocational system do well in informationization? In your opinion, what aspects should be paid attention to in the informationization of vocational education? Through the research, the text material of 230,000 words (recording conversion) was formed. The investigation materials were coded in an open manner, and specific expressions of the application of informatization were extracted, as shown in Table 2 below.

4.6 Information Research Content Analysis Based on Nvivo

CSSCI was obtained by obtaining research data related to informationization from 2015 to 2020, 1390 journal papers were imported by Nvivo to carry out content analysis, and 110 keywords were formed in 7 dimensions, as shown in Table 1.

Table 1. Text analysis results of informationization research based on Nvivo

The serial number	The dimension	Keywords
01	Content	Rural education informatization; National education informatization; Special education informatization; Educational technology; "InternetNet+"; Basic education; Regional planning; Regional education informatization;

(continued)

Table 1. (*continued*)

The serial number	The dimension	Keywords
02	Function	Information leadership; Intelligent education; Big data; Targeted poverty alleviation through education; Smart campus; The beauty of morality, intelligence and physiquelaw; Rural education; Special education; Supply-side reform; Information literacy;
03	System	Evaluation index system; Educational governance; Intelligent education; Educational technology; Basic education; Information-based teaching; Education cloud; Learning society; Digital education resources;
04	Standard	Technical standards; Curriculum standards; Quality standard; Competency standards; Policy orientation; Application; International experience; information. The source construction; Quality management;
05	Value	Educational equity; Informationization of education management; Educational resources

Table 2. Information application and benefit description

The serial number	Keywords	The serial number	Keywords
01	The technical level	151	Information concept
02	Business covers	152	Standard interaction
03	Content to deepen	153	Talent cultivation
04	Strengthen cooperation	154	Policy
05	Students analysis	155	Social influence
…	…	…	…
50	Way to change	194	Information ethics

4.7 Spindle Coding Combining the Two Methods

The research team clustered the above keywords from the perspective of evaluation. Through the open coding structure and research data combing, the relationship among relevant concepts was formed and new concepts were given. On this basis, six core dimensions were preliminarily summarized and formed. There were 28 observation indexes. The dimension of information technology level includes six observation indicators: technical standard, system application technology, data resources, system platform, information network and information security design. The dimensions of information technology application performance include operation efficiency, satisfaction of talent cultivation, organizational growth ability, student service ability, teacher service ability and management. 6 observation indexes of management service ability; The dimension of information management ability includes information management and information group. The four observation indexes are the ability of weaving, the process and system of information construction, and the development of information chemical tools [4]. The continuous development ability of informationization includes four observation indexes: educational technology training ability, reserve talent training ability, educational technology research ability and educational informationization standard construction ability. The dimension of informationization guarantee capability includes four observation indexes: capital input, system norm, technology basis and governance basis.

5 Evaluation Standard Optimization Based on Delphi Method

Summarizing the above research process, experts were consulted on 29 observation indicators in 4 core dimensions [5]. Figure 1 Evaluation dimensions and observation indexes of vocational education informatization benchmarking system.

$$K = (TA - \sum\nolimits_{n=1}^{\infty} EF) + (TU - \sum\nolimits_{n=1}^{\infty} EF) \tag{1}$$

The dimensionindicators. Information business supportInformation technology coverage, information technology application depth, information technology application intensity, information technology business synergy degree. (The formula1).

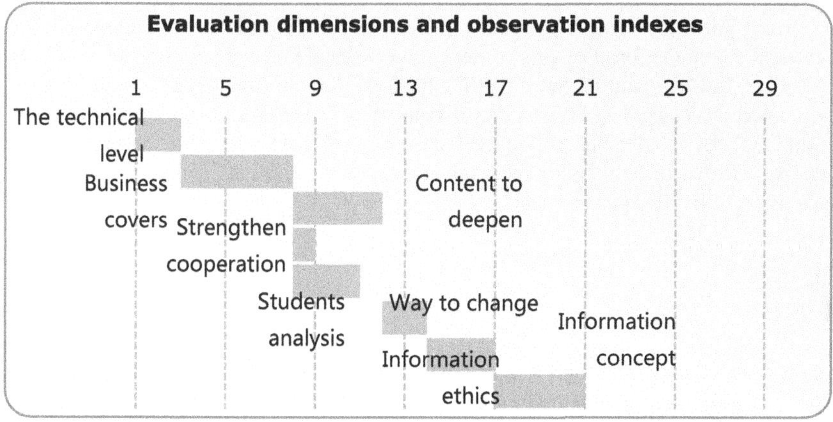

Fig. 1. Evaluation dimensions and observation indexes of vocational education informatization benchmarking system

Total units of protocol (TA) between two users minus the expected frequency of incidental protocols (ΣEF) divided by the total units (TU) in the file minus the expected frequency of incidental protocols (full EF). Information technology level. Technical standards, system application technology, data resources, system platform, information network, information security design. Information technology application performance-Operational efficiency, personnel training satisfaction, organizational growth ability, student service ability, teacher service ability, management service ability. Information management abilityInformation management mode, informationization organization ability, informationization construction process and system, informationization tool development, system norm. Information technology sustainable development ability. Educational technology training ability, reserve talent training ability, educational technology research ability, educational informationization standard construction ability, capital investment. Opponents argue that relevant observations can be grouped into five other core dimensions. On the basis of expert discussion, the research team made an in-depth analysis of the evaluation dimension and observation index of information barrier protection ability, and concluded that it is difficult to select materials for technical basis and governance basis in the actual evaluation of vocational education informatization standard poles schools. Therefore, the six core dimensions were compressed into five, and 29 observation markers were maintained. At the same time, according to the results of data processing, experts were further asked for their opinions, and three options were set, "approve", "basically approve" and "disapprove", so that experts could vote anonymously through "Questionnaire Star". There were 29 votes from1experts, of which the number of approved votes was 21, the basic number of approved votes was 10, and there were no approved votes.

Acknowledgement. This work was supported by grant of No. pdjh2021b0744 from the special fund for science and technology innovation strategy of Guangdong Province in 2021; **and by grant of No. 2019gktscx021 from the** 2019 general university scientific research project of Guangdong Provincial Department of education "Research on helmet wearing behavior based on deep learning under low visibility "; **and by grant of No. 2020zdzx2095 from the** Refe2020 key scientific research project of colleges and universities of Guangdong Provincial Department of Education; **and by grant of No.** (GDPIC)-**2021-zx-18 from the** 2021 school level entrusted special project of Guangdong Polytechnic of Industry & Commerce; **and by grant of No. 1714 from the** 2022 basic and applied basic research project of Guangzhou basic research plan (general project) "Research on bonding mechanism of seawater and sand concrete based on thread characteristics of BFRP reinforcement"。

References

1. Megan, S.B.: Experiences of VA vocational and education training and assistance services: Facilitators and barriers reported by veterans with disabilities. Psychiatr. Rehabil. J. **44**(2), 48–156 (2021)
2. Hou, Z.: Dilemma and breakthrough: research on the developmental evaluation of vocational college students under the new educational concept. J. Educ. Res. Pol. **3**(4), 120–127 (2021)
3. Nouwen, W., Clycq, N., Struyf, A., Donche, V.: The role of work-based learning for student engagement in vocational education and training: an application of the self-system model of motivational development. Eur. J. Psychol. Educ. **2**(1), 1–24 (2021). https://doi.org/10.1007/s10212-021-00561-1
4. Du, J.: Exploration on the Integration Path of Distance and Open Education and Vocational Education under the Background of "Internet+." Open Access Lib. J. **8**(4), 1–15 (2021)
5. The European Parliament and the Council. Recommendation on the Establishment of the European Qualification Framework for Lifelong Learning. Official J. Eur. Union, (6) (2008)

Research on the Application of Virtual Reality in Higher Vocational Education

Ying Mai(✉) and Yan-e Li

Guangzhou City Polytechnic, Guangzhou 510405, China
1368256332@qq.com

Abstract. Virtual reality technology enables learners to master the learning content in a specific virtual environment, and solve the problems of lacking context, interactivity, personalization, and immersion in traditional classrooms. Based on the analysis of the characteristics of virtual reality, this paper proposes that the application of virtual reality in higher vocational education can promote students' autonomous learning and provide corresponding virtual skills training. At last, it puts forward the idea of developing a new virtual reality technology teaching mode and teaching platform design.

Keywords: Virtual reality technology · Higher vocational education · Teaching model

1 Introduction

The wide application of the new generation of information technology represented by big data, virtual reality, and artificial intelligence technology in education has led to changes in educational philosophy, teaching methods, learning methods and other aspects. Among them, virtual reality technology has brought new opportunities for the development of education. It is a kind of high-performance comprehensive computing technology with a powerful three-dimensional display that occurred at the end of the 20th century, giving users a sense of immersion. Virtual reality technology enables learners to master the learning content in a specific virtual environment, and solve the problems of lacking context, interactivity, personalization, and immersion in traditional classrooms [1]. Vocational education is a kind of employability education oriented to professional posts. It pays attention to skill training, and emphasize practicality. In the process of vocational education teaching, the practical teaching effect is not ideal due to the factors such as training site, equipment and facilities, pollution, safety, and non-reappearance. Therefore, the characteristics of virtual reality technology, such as multi perception, existence, interaction, and autonomy, can perfectly meet the demands of simulation teaching resources in higher vocational education, and determine the necessity of its application in vocational and technical education.

Supported by The innovation team project of Guangdong Province universities: Collaborative Innovation Research Team of Guangdong Strategic Emerging Industry Group (2020WCXTD032).

© ICST Institute for Computer Sciences, Social Informatics and Telecommunications Engineering 2022
Published by Springer Nature Switzerland AG 2022. All Rights Reserved
S. Shi et al. (Eds.): 6GN 2021, LNICST 439, pp. 565–572, 2022.
https://doi.org/10.1007/978-3-031-04245-4_49

2 Characteristics and Development of Virtual Reality Technology

Virtual reality is the combination of virtual and reality. Theoretically speaking, virtual reality technology (VR) is a kind of computer simulation system that can create and experience the virtual world. It uses the computer to generate a simulation environment, so that users can immerse themselves in that situation. Combined with a variety of output devices, virtual reality technology uses real-life data and computer technology to generate electronic signals, so that it can be transformed into a phenomenon that people can feel. These phenomena, developed through the three-dimensional model, can be tangible objects in reality or materials that cannot be seen with our naked eye. These phenomena are not what we can see directly but simulated by computer technology, so they are called virtual reality [2].

Users can interact in virtual reality to promote mutual influence. The characteristics of virtual reality are immersive and interactive. At the same time, it will have a more intuitive visual experience [3]. When users use interactive devices and exist in the virtual environment, they will be integrated with the virtual environment to produce a feeling of their spiritual environment. Interactivity mainly refers to the specific operable technology of users to the objects in the simulated environment and the degree of feedback they can get from the environment. Students can interact with the computer keyboard or mouse, and interact with the three-dimensional environment through some corresponding specific helmet, data glove, and other sensing devices, so as to help users obtain not only realistic vision and hearing but also touch and motion when they are in the virtual environment. To make the virtual environment more intuitive and realistic, many concepts have changed in the teaching practice of virtual reality technology.

Starting from the learners, taking the participants in the virtual environment as the unit breaks the restrictions of age, background, class (Group) division, and other factors. From the perspective of teachers, they no longer appear as preachers of knowledge, but more as guides or proponents of projects or tasks. They become collaborators or partners of learners in the cognitive process, helping learners better understand and internalize the knowledge learning process. As for the teaching environment, things in the virtual classroom are visualized according to the practical conditions, and will change according to the development of projects or tasks. In terms of the teaching resources, they have dynamic development in the virtual environment. The teaching resources will dynamically change according to the learning objectives that learners should achieve, so that learners can obtain resources more conveniently and the utilization rate of resources is higher.

3 Characteristics and Development of Virtual Reality Technology

3.1 Promoting Students' Autonomous Learning

In the traditional higher vocational education in China, due to the great differences in students' learning levels, it is difficult for students with insufficient foundation and ability to have a comprehensive and deep understanding of the knowledge imparted by teachers. However, students with higher basic levels will be able to understand quickly, and hope to further improve the teaching progress. The long-term existence of this problem has a certain impact on students' learning enthusiasm [4]. With the help of virtual reality technology, the learning mode is gradually developing towards a vivid and effective direction, and the number of teaching resources and platforms will increase progressively, which brings convenience for the combination and production of teacher's teaching resources. Students can start from their own actual situation, choose different facilities, combine with the virtual teaching resources distributed by teachers, carry out targeted autonomous learning. In this way, it can meet the actual needs of different levels of students, so as to stimulate students' autonomous learning ability and awareness.

3.2 Promoting Students' Autonomous Learning

In the traditional teaching mode, due to the limitation of time, space, funds and other factors, the teaching situation is usually fixed and single, which cannot provide learners with a rich and effective learning situation. The application of virtual reality technology in vocational education teaching can present a variety of teaching methods. Stimulating learners' senses with virtual reality teaching can help them obtain knowledge. Virtual reality teaching creates a virtual situation for learners to observe and experience through each learner's physical and mental immersion. The virtual simulation practice gives learners a sense of being on the scene, constantly internalizes technical knowledge, and further summarizes and discusses from the virtual practice, so that learners can immerse themselves in the process of virtual perception of life and production practice [5]. Taking computer technology major as an example, in some theoretical courses, such as the computer basic course, the teaching method of virtual and real segmentation can be adopted. First, the theory is explained, and then the virtual reality technology is displayed so that learners can intuitively understand the composition and assembly process of components.

In the courses that need to be verified repeatedly, such as the data structure course, teachers can adopt the teaching mode of combining virtual with reality. Since algorithm thinking is abstract, it is usually difficult for learners to understand. Through virtual reality technology, the process of algorithm is shown in an easy-to-understand form [6]. In more comprehensive courses, such as the website development course, we can adopt the teaching mode of virtual reality integration, and then create the teaching environment and equipment conditions needed for teaching.

3.3 Provide Corresponding Virtual Skills Training

Higher vocational education pays attention to the training of corresponding vocational skills. Through the application of virtual reality technology, a virtual training system is born. Compared with the traditional training system, this system has great advantages in stimulating students' interest in learning, improving the teaching environment, and enhancing the safety factor. In this virtual training system, students can complete some activities that cannot be done in a general setting, such as high-risk explosion tests, close observation of planets, and some large-scale instrument operation tests. In the actual teaching process, teachers can gradually guide students to apply what they have learned to practice [7]. At the same time, students can also set up their own virtual training environment and carry out their own knowledge exploration and research with the help of virtual reality technology.

3.4 Provide a Platform for Communication and Dialogue

In virtual teaching mode, cooperation and conversation can promote learners to understand and master knowledge. Virtual reality technology provides learners with two ways of cooperation and conversation, namely human-human interaction, and human-computer interaction. In the interaction between people, in order to meet the speed of responding people's instructions to virtual reality technology, the computer constantly rectifies through the feedback received so as to achieve interactive feedback in particular situations. With modern information technology as a tool, learners can communicate more smoothly in virtual reality technology. The essence of conversation in virtual reality teaching practice is the interactive sharing process of knowledge, experience and wisdom. In human-computer interaction, the presentation of human sensory function is very important. Usually, we will use people's vision, hearing, and touch to design a three-dimensional input and output device, making learners intuitively operate the computer in real-time to complete the interactive task [8].

3.5 Providing Virtual Reality Tasks

Higher vocational skills training is based on the working situation, aiming at solving problems and tasks, and taking "learning by doing" as the starting point of teaching logic. In the traditional computer technology classroom, most teaching methods are cramming; learners passively accept the teacher's teaching content, making it easy to produce negative and stereotyped knowledge content. Virtual reality technology can provide simulation, verification, exploration, and other forms of tasks. For example, with real problems and tasks as the focus, learners solve problems and tasks through empirical research, and teachers guide learners through questioning and setting up situations, and provide new ways for further problem solving [9].

In short, the current application of virtual reality technology in higher vocational education focuses on presenting the practical situations that are "unable to enter, invisible, unable to move and difficult to reproduce" to learners. It will help learners develop their thinking and ability together, promote learner's active learning, and create an ideal environment for learner's autonomous learning. Compared with traditional methods, learners will realize the dream of learning in an ideal environment through the virtual situation platform; improve learning efficiency to obtain more knowledge. At the same time, virtual reality technology provides learners with an immersive multi-perception environment, and promotes learners to continuously explore, analyze, evaluate, optimize and further process knowledge.

4 The Application of Virtual Reality in Higher Vocational Teaching Mode Design

4.1 Design Principles

The first principle is to take the learner as the center, to promote the learner's interest in learning as the main design principle. The multi-level knowledge structure content constantly stimulates the learner's spirit of inquiry so that the whole learning process of learners can be guided, monitored and evaluated. The second principle is to find and solve problems in time through the feedback of learning achievements. The third principle is to give full play to the intermediary function of virtual reality technology, master the correct teaching strategies, combine the relevant teaching resources with learner's interests, and let learners evaluate them, make the design of virtual reality technology teaching mode more perfect, and promote the continuous leading development of education [10].

4.2 Design Content

The purpose of the application of virtual reality technology in teaching is to realize the construction of learners' skills, and the "learner-centered" teaching mode by improving the teaching design. The design of the new learner-centered virtual reality technology teaching mode and teaching platform is carried out from three aspects: one is to support personalized learning. In order to enable each learner to achieve the learning goal, virtual reality technology can effectively solve the problem of learning subject simplification. According to the personality characteristics of each learner, different designs are made to create different scenes, so that learners can better study. The second is to support autonomous learning. For learners, the fun of learning is very important. Virtual reality technology provides learners with a rich learning environment. As the curriculum becomes more diversified, VR will stimulate learner's interest in learning. VR/AR technology supports autonomous learning, which allows learners to control and exercise their problem-solving ability, so as to improve learning efficiency. Third, support online teaching. Due to the more needs of learners, virtual reality technology can provide significant help for learners who cannot attend class in time. MOOC and other distance online education cannot be limited by space and time, and combine VR/AR technology with online courses to improve their technical ability and employment competitiveness (see Fig. 1).

4.3 Design of a New Teaching Platform Supported by Virtual Reality Technology

According to the above teaching mode design principles and elements, combined with practical teaching experience, the design of a new teaching platform supported by virtual reality technology should include the following contents:

One is the analysis of the learner's learning situation. Learning situation refers to the relevant knowledge and intelligence that learners have mastered when learning specific knowledge. The second is the analysis of learner's personality differences. Personality difference refers to the different ways and characteristics of problem-solving in learner's learning activities, which constitutes the psychological differences of individuals in the

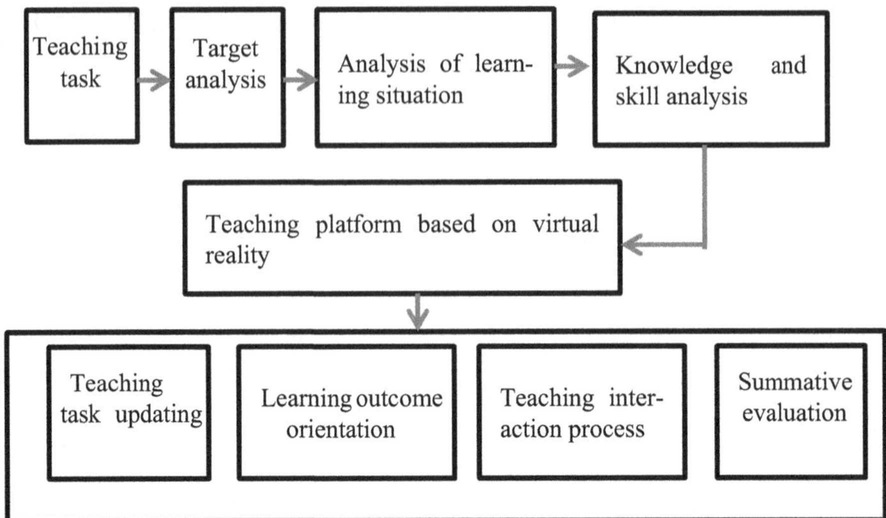

Fig. 1. Higher vocational teaching design process based on virtual reality.

virtual environment. It is characterized by motivation and interest, emotion and will, character and temperament. The third is the analysis of the learner's cognitive style. Cognitive style refers to the way of information processing that the learners like or develop. If we can make clear the difference, we can guide and help the learners.

The new teaching platform can combine virtual reality technology, big data infrastructure, distributed computing and distributed storage methods to build a virtual reality teaching application and resource management intelligent training platform combined with big data intelligent analysis. The new teaching platform includes eight functional applications, and the subsystems include: teaching support management subsystem, training project management subsystem, teaching resource management subsystem, teaching evaluation analysis and guidance subsystem, training experience subsystem, data display subsystem, system management subsystem and innovation incubation subsystem, as shown in Fig. 2.

The research and development of a virtual reality technology teaching platform system, based on the learning theory of modeling, provides important support for student-centered personalized learning and autonomous learning. In the teaching process of higher vocational education, the new virtual reality teaching platform system can improve the traditional mode of learning, innovate teaching methods, and provide professional support for students' education. Therefore, the active use of the teaching platform system can make students more and more interested in learning. At the same time, using the diversity of the new teaching platform, students can choose different courses to make the lessons more flexible, and repeat the learning courses according to their own needs, so as to apply personalized strategies to improve the effect of skill learning.

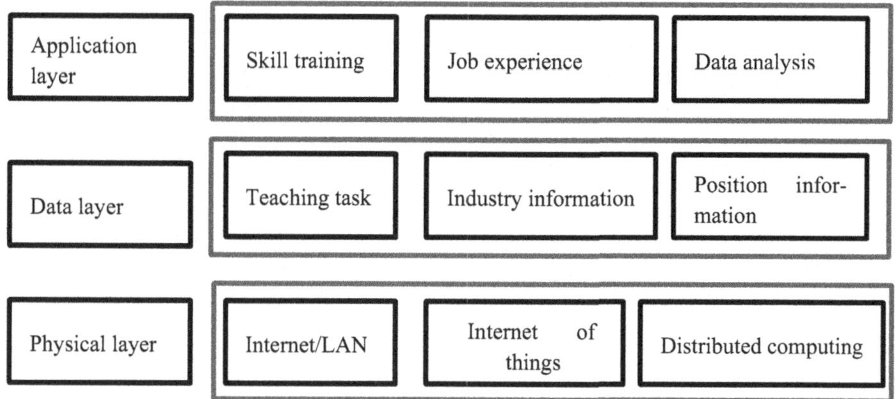

Fig. 2. Construction of teaching platform based on virtual reality.

5 Epilogues

At present, the reform of Higher Vocational Education in China is in full swing. In the process of reforming teaching ideas and methods, with the help of virtual reality technology, we have formed a set of virtual reality training system. By using this system, we provide a more realistic virtual reality environment for students' autonomous learning, as well as the changes of virtual skills training. In this way, we can realize the deep integration of virtual reality technology and higher vocational education by combining practical teaching, continuous improvement of teacher's quality, and reasonable development of the virtual platform.

References

1. Virtual reality industry promotion conference: White paper on industrial virtual (augmented) reality application scenarios, vol. 7. Virtual reality industry promotion conference, Beijing (2019)
2. Hui, B.: Application and development of VR technology in museums, vol. 9. Yunnan University, Kunming (2019)
3. Ministry of industry and information technology: White paper on VR industry development in 2016, vol. 1. China Institute of electronic technology standardization, Beijing (2016)
4. Tao, Y.: Application of virtual reality technology in higher vocational college teaching. Comput. Prod. Circ. **12**, 161 (2019)
5. Jing, F.: Application of virtual reality technology in higher vocational education. Intelligence **23**, 118–119 (2019)
6. Huanhuan, L.: Research on the construction and application of VR training room in higher vocational colleges. J. Nanjing Radio Televis. Univ. **2**, 91–94 (2018)
7. Yuanyuan, M.: Research on curriculum design of university tourism management based on VR technology. Think Tank Era **43**, 286–287 (2019)
8. Xie, J.: Analysis on the application effect of virtual reality technology in teaching practice – review on the application and effect evaluation of virtual reality technology in the field of education. Chin. J. Educ. **8**, 139 (2019)

9. Pan, N.: Research on the application of computer virtual reality technology in college physical education. Contemp. Sports Sci. Technol. **9**(22), 136138 (2019)
10. Lai, J., Wang, K.: The application of virtual reality technology in vocational education teaching—based on the perspective of constructivism. J. Guangdong Ind. Polytechnic **6** (2020)

Acceptance and Use of Mobile-Assisted Language Learning for Vocational College Students

Yunyi Zhang, Ling Zhang(✉), Tinghua Chen, Hai Lin, Shengke Ye, Jun Du, Tao Yu, and Chuqiao Chen

City College of Huizhou, Huizhou 516025, China
68588368@qq.com

Abstract. Few research reports can claim that students have accepted MALL (Mobile-assisted language learning). Exploring the key influencing factors of students 'mobile language learning will promote the ultimate effect of students' language learning. However, there are little researches on MALL of students, especially vocational students. This study aims to explore the factors that influence the acceptance and use of MALL of Chinese vocational college students. UTAUT (Unified Theory of Acceptance and Use of Technology) was used to propose a behavioral model for the acceptance of MALL by vocational students. The questionnaire data were analyzed through SPSS25 and SmartPLS3, and the factors affecting the acceptance of MALL by vocational students were evaluated. The results show that ATT (Attitude towards behavior) and SI (Social influence) were the key influencing factors of BI (Behavior intention) and FC (Facilitating conditions) were the key influencing factors of BI and ATT. Recommendation: The relevant stakeholders of mobile language learning in higher vocational colleges should promote the convenience of MALL, influence higher vocational students, and improve the learning effect of MALL through community influence.

Keywords: MALL · UTAUT · Vocational college students · SmartPLS3 · Influence factor

1 Introduction

Mobile-Assisted Language Learning (MALL) is considered a method of using mobile devices to support and enhance language learning. Mobile devices have created a new research field related to language learning and mobile technology. Learners can independently learn a second language (L2) anytime, anywhere. Mobile learning and MALL have become the focus (Cakmak 2019). These emerging studies have begun to focus on different aspects of language learning, Such as there have been related acceptance (Hoi 2020), reading (Gutiérrez-Colón et al., 2020), vocabulary, listening, and speaking, writing (Al-Shehab 2020), pronunciation, memory (Ozer and Kılıç 2018). Many studies have shown that mobile devices can be ideal language learning tools (Nasr and Abbas

© ICST Institute for Computer Sciences, Social Informatics and Telecommunications Engineering 2022
Published by Springer Nature Switzerland AG 2022. All Rights Reserved
S. Shi et al. (Eds.): 6GN 2021, LNICST 439, pp. 573–589, 2022.
https://doi.org/10.1007/978-3-031-04245-4_50

2018). New technologies such as 5G will continue to enrich the connotation of the education scene, promote the transformation of the education scene, and become the driving force of China's education information innovation. The changes brought about by new technologies such as 5G will also bring new experiences to university education (Baratè et al. 2019; Lee and Kim 2020).

However, few studies report student acceptance of MALL (Azli et al. 2018; Shadiev et al. 2020). Today, the scale of China's higher vocational education ranks first in the world, with more than 1,400 higher vocational schools and more than 15 million students. According to the data currently available to the author, the research on MALL in higher vocational colleges in my country started relatively late, and empirical research accounts for a relatively low proportion. There are relatively few studies on the acceptance and use of MALL by higher vocational students.

The UTAUT model is becoming popular with educational research (Salloum and Shaalan 2018; Kayali and Alaaraj 2020). UTAUT provides a theoretically enhanced research framework, It can study the determinants of technology use and acceptance in different contexts. For example, Botero (2018) Research on the acceptance and use of MALL by higher education students based on the UTAUT model. Morchid (2019) studied the determinants of Morchid students ' use and acceptance of MALL based on the UTAUT model. In addition, many studies in the educational environment incorporate ATT (Attitude towards behavior) into the UTAUT model. Their research found that ATT (Attitude towards behavior) is an important factor affecting acceptance of MALL (Liebenberg et al. 2018). At the same time, in the MALL research, many scholars have adopted the SEM research method (Ozer and Kılıç 2018; Loewen et al. 2019).

City College of Huizhou is the largest vocational school in Huizhou City, with more than 15,000 students. Students in the business and international Department need to study professional English for three years. They all have experience in using mobile terminals to learn English. Construct a behavioral model suitable for Chinese vocational students' acceptance of MALL, and explore the influence that affects vocational students' acceptance of MALL, so that vocational education can make better use of MALL, and MALL can help vocational students to better improve their professional English. We will adopt quantitative analysis methods. Search out the factors that affect the acceptance and use of MALL by vocational college students. Therefore, the main goals of this research are as follows:

(i) Based on the UTAUT model, put forward a model of Chinese higher vocational students accepting MALL, and develop and statistically verify MALL-specific tools.
(ii) Assess the dimensions that affect the behavioral intentions of vocational students and the actual use of MALL.
(iii) Determine the influencing factors of Chinese higher vocational students' acceptance of MALL. Provide reference for developing countries and college students who have never received formal introduction or training from MALL, and provide reference for higher vocational English education in China.

2 Literature Review

2.1 UTAUT

UTAUT was first proposed in 2003 by Venkatesh, Morris, and Davis. UTAUT is a synthesis of eight acceptance models. This model integration can explain behavioral intentions better than any single technology acceptance model (Marchewka et al. 2007). The UTAUT model is a synthesis of eight theories: IDT (Innovation Diffusion Theory) and SCT (Social Cognition Theory), TRA (Rational Action Theory), MPCU (PC Usage Model), TPB (Planned Behavior Theory) and TAM (Technology Acceptance Model), MM (Motivation Model) (Venkatesh et al. 2003). UTAUT provides a theoretically scalable research framework that can examine the determinants of technology use and acceptance in different circumstances. Figure 1 shows the UATUT model.

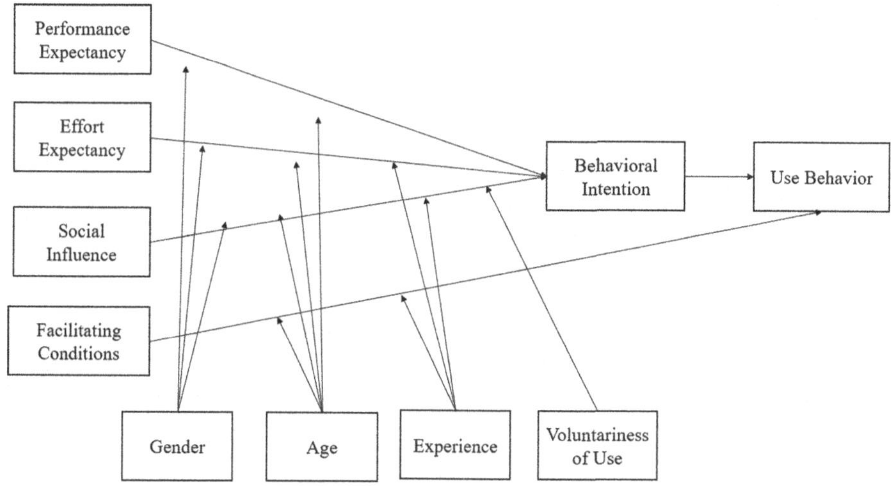

Fig. 1. The UTAUT model (Venkatesh et al. 2003, p. 447)

See Fig. 1, the UTAUT model is configured to supply PE (Performance expectancy), EE (Effort expectancy), SI (Social influence), and the impact on FC (Facilitating conditions) on BI (Behavioral intention) and use behavior. In addition, these connections are also influenced through gender, age, experience, and voluntary use. The basic structure of UTAUT has been verified many times.

The model is suitable for research in multiple scenarios, including mobile payment (Raza et al. 2019; Patil et al. 2020; Al-Saedi et al. 2020), e-learning (Persada et al. 2019). According to research reports on mobile learning, UTAUT has been used to estimate the acceptance of mobile learning in higher education (Aliaño et al. 2019) to investigate the acceptance in developing countries (Dwivedi et al. 2020). UTAUT is becoming more and more popular in the educational environment, but the research on MALL is still limited.

The UTAUT model integrates research on technology use and acceptance, it can measure behavior patterns in different contexts by extending the framework. Since MALL is a branch of mobile learning, this research on MALL can draw on UTAUT's research results in mobile learning and e-learning, including its related research results to analyze the acceptance of developing countries.

In summary, this research on the acceptance and use of MALL by Chinese vocational students chooses UTAUT as the benchmark research model. In addition, based on similar research in mobile learning environments, the model is expanded by adding attitude towards behavior (Liebenberg et al. 2018; Chao 2019; Kayali and Alaaraj 2020).

2.2 Research on Mobile-Assisted Language Learning

Based on different perspectives, scholars have researched the use of MALL. Mooneeb Ali (2020) explored the mentality of private university students to learn English through MALL and found that learning English through MALL also helps them increase their confidence in other fields. Sun (2018) explored the relationship between intrinsic motivation, key variables related to technology adoption, and students' behavioral intentions in MALL. Yang (2020) research in MALL shows that the lack of motivation of unsuccessful learners is the main obstacle to their self-regulated learning. This research attempts to analyze an important part of learners' motivation. The results of Miqawati (2020) in MALL show that MALL is very important and can be used as a choice to promote students' pronunciation learning. (Butarbutar et al. 2020) analysis results show that the use of MALL can effectively stimulate students' motivation, establish self-learning language, help enrich vocabulary, and promote speaking, grammar, and listening skills. Some scholars have explored the characteristics of students' English learning behavior in the mobile technology environment and grasped the students' learning habits and learning path from the behavioral level. There have also been researches aimed at higher vocational students, and investigations have been conducted from the overall current situation, group differences, and influencing factors of the higher vocational student MALL. Gonulal (2019) proved that the MALL application is an effective mobile language learning tool. Cakmak proposed the design principles of MALL in 2019 and proposed the conceptual framework of MALL. Kan (2018) research shows that in the eyes of students, the role of teachers is very limited, and students expect more support from teachers for MALL in extracurricular activities.

According to the literature, the related research on mobile language learning has roughly gone through four stages.

(i) Research on information interaction methods such as the organization of English teaching content and the design of teaching tasks.
(ii) Build an intelligent mobile learning system.
(iii) Study on learning effectiveness and satisfaction.
(iv) The development of mobile language learning theory research.

There are few MALL kinds of research on vocational students. In addition, vocational students have a relatively poor foundation, relatively poor initiative, and relatively poor learning ability. The research content of MALL is relatively inclined to the effectiveness of the MALL system and pays more attention to the research of system-level design and development. Reports on the acceptance of MALL by higher vocational students are still lacking. There is no report claiming to fully reflect the actual situation of higher vocational students' acceptance of MALL.

It is very important to study the acceptance and use of MALL by students. To this end, this article will conduct research on the acceptance of MALL by higher vocational students based on UTUAT theory. For this reason, taking vocational students as the research object, a multi-dimensional questionnaire was designed to extract the current situation of vocational college students' acceptance of MALL learning English, aiming to pick up the important factors that appertain the acceptance and use of MALL by vocational students. Expand UTAUT model research in the field of Chinese higher vocational English education, and provide empirical references for related MALL users.

2.3 Research Model and Hypothesis

UTAUT provides a theoretically scalable research framework that can examine the determinants of technology use and acceptance in different circumstances. Scalability happens to be a key feature of UTAUT. So in this study, the internal structure of the UTAUT model is reconfigured and expanded, ATT (Attitude towards behavior) variables are introduced into the UTAUT model to adapt to the reality of the City College of Huizhou. Figure 1 shows a research model, which will be used to explain the usage of MALL by vocational students and the hypothetical relationship between variables.

Performance Expectancy (PE)
In the UTAUT model, Venkatesh et al. (2003) defined PE as the degree to which the individual feels that using the system can improve work performance. In this study, PE is further defined as the degree to which vocational students subjectively believe that MALL can improve English learning performance. Many reports acknowledge the importance of PE acceptance research in the educational environment (Salloum and Shaalan 2018; Chao 2019).

Effort Expectancy (EE)
Venkatesh et al. (2003) defined EE as the amount of effort an individual must put in to use the system. In this study, EE is defined as the degree to which higher vocational students believe that using MALL to achieve their goals can save effort.

Social Influence (SI)
A program that people who have an important personal impact think that using the system is important. In different acceptance models, it is expressed as a "subject specification."
Venkatesh et al. (2003) distinguished between mandatory and non-mandatory social impacts in the environment because they found it to be meaningful in the former case, but not important in the latter case. Subsequent studies found similar trends (Shukla 2020).

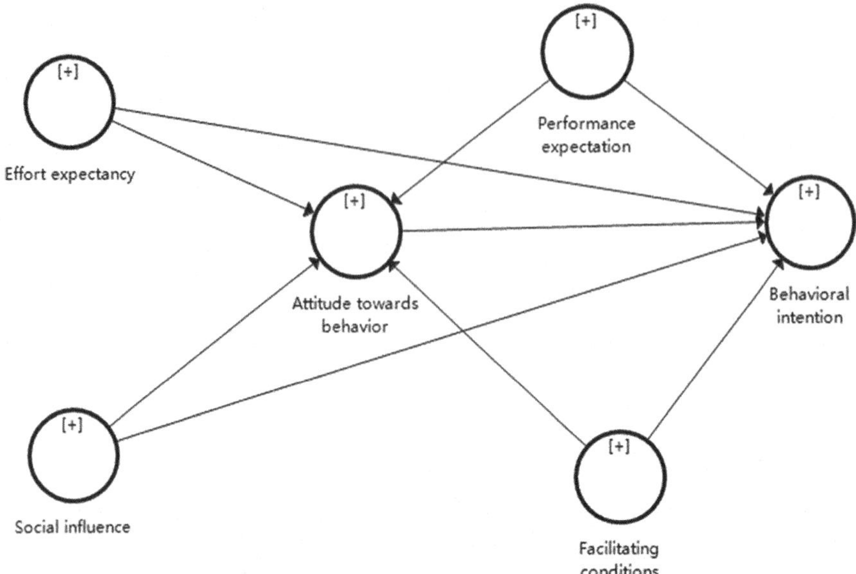

Fig. 2. The research model of accepting and using MALL by Chinese higher vocational students

Facilitating Conditions (FC)

Venkatesh et al. (2003) pointed out that FC has no added value to PE and EE when predicting intent. However, other studies have shown this relationship (Alsswey and Al-Samarraie 2019). FC also has a positive impact on the use of UB (Kemp et al. 2019; Bervell and Arkorful 2020). Here, FC is defined as the degree to which higher vocational students subjectively believe that the currently available software and hardware technologies and equipment support the use of MALL.

Behavioral Intention (BI)

In theory, BI has a significant positive impact on the use of technology. This relationship has been confirmed in many educational technologies research.

Attitude Towards Behavior (ATT)

ATT is an assessment of how much an individual likes or dislikes performing a certain behavior (Fishbein and Ajzen 1975). This study is based on the ATT as the degree of love or dislike of MALL for higher vocational students.

Cumulative studies have shown that many research and education literature has incorporated ATT into the UTAUT model and regarded it as a necessary factor for acceptance. Therefore, the following assumptions are made:

H1: ATT positively affects BI
H2: EE positively affects ATT
H3: EE positively affects BI
H4: FC positively affects ATT
H5: FC positively affects BI

H6: PE and ATT are positively correlated.
H7: PE and BI are positively correlated.
H8: SI and ATT are positively correlated.
H9: SI and BI are positively correlated.
H10: Through ATT, PE has a mediating effect on BI.
H11: Through ATT, EE has a mediating effect on BI.
H12: Through ATT, SI has a mediating effect on BI.
H13: Through ATT, FC has a mediating effect on BI.

3 Methodology

Students from the business and international departments of the school have experience in MALL. The subjects of this survey are students from these two departments. The questionnaire will quote items from MALL-related literature. In the pre-test stage of the questionnaire, use SPSS25 software to inspect the reliability and validity of the questionnaire. After confirming the formal questionnaire, publish it on the Internet, allowing students to fill in the questionnaire via the Internet. The results of the questionnaire will use quantitative analysis methods, mainly using SmartPLS3 for analysis. Measure and evaluate the proposed model. Including reliability and validity measurement, including path analysis, mediation effect test, and hypothesis test.

3.1 Measuring Instrument

Respondents are from City College of Huizhou students in the three grades in 2018, 2019, and 2020, and they are students with a mobile language learning experience. Because in the department of business and international, the English courses of the international department and the business department are corresponding professional courses, and talent training goals are closely related. Therefore, the subject of this survey will be targeted at vocational students in the three grades in the international department and the business department of our school. Respondents were randomly selected from two departments; through the questionnaire, members of this course group produced and designed questionnaires including demographic attributes, ATT, SI, PE, EE, FC, BI, frequency, and experience.

The questionnaire adopted and modified the PE, EE SI, FC, ATT, and BI items of the predecessors. The questionnaire uses a Likert scale. The scale is set from 1–7, from "strongly disagree" to "strongly agree", with 1–7 points in turn.

3.2 Partial Least Square Structural Equation Modeling (PLS-SEM)

PLS is an analysis technology used to detect models. In addition, PLS can also analyze predictive models. PLS is better than general linear structural relationship models (such as LISREL). PLS can handle multiple dependent variables and multiple independent variables, PLS can overcome the problem of multicollinearity, PLS effectively handles interfering data and missing values, PLS input response variables have a large impact on potential variables, and PLS Reflectance and formative indicators can be processed at the same time, especially PLS is suitable for small samples, and PLS is not limited by data distribution.

The SmartPLS software was developed by Ringle, Wende & Will in 2005. This study uses the SmartPLS3 to analyze the data, uses the partial least squares method to estimate the reliability and validity of the measurement model and the path coefficient of the structural model, and uses the bootstrap method to repeatedly sample 5,000 Secondly to verify the significance of all estimated parameters. Since PLS can not only handle multiple dependent variables and multiple independent variables, but also the latent variable estimation of an observed variable, it can also overcome the problem of multivariate collinearity, and it has strong handling of interfering data and missing values. the reactive index variable has a strong ability to predict potential variables, and more importantly, it is not restricted by data allocation (Henseler and Chin 2010; Sarstedt, Wong 2019), so it is suitable for the variable characteristics of this study.

The PLS analysis of this study has two steps: first, test the reliability and validity of the measurement model; second, test the significance and predictive ability of the path coefficient. Structural model (Wong 2019).

3.3 Items Validity and Reliability

At the pre-testing stage of the questionnaire, we collected 100 valid questionnaires. The CR value of all question items passed the test. The VIF values of EE4, EE5, and FC3 are all greater than 5, So EE4, EE4, and FC3 have been deleted. The final formal questionnaire was determined to be 5 questions in the PE dimension, 5 questions in the EE dimension, 4 questions in the SI dimension, 5 questions in the FC dimension, 5 questions in the ATT dimension, and 3 questions in the BI dimension. ATT is the intermediate variable, and BI is the target variable. Use the Likert seven-point scale to obtain data from the target sample, adopt quantitative analysis research methods, and use SPS25 and SmartPLS3.

3.4 Population and Sample

In the formal questionnaire stage, we collected 352 questionnaires, of which 18 questionnaires had a response time lower than the normal range, and 12 questionnaires had repeated options of 70%. After processing, there are 322 valid questionnaires. The effective response rate of the questionnaire was 91%, which met the measurement requirements of SPSS25.0 and SmartPLS3.0.

For the returned questionnaire, SPSS25 was used for preliminary analysis. There are 181 first-year college students, accounting for 56.21%, 102 s-year college students, accounting for 31.69%; 29 third-year college students, accounting for 12.11%; 112 boys, accounting for 34.78%, and 210 girls. Accounted for 65.22%; 100 people aged 18 and below, accounting for 33.06%; 107 people aged 19, accounting for 32.23%; 76 people aged 20, accounting for 23.6%; 27 people aged 21, accounting for 8.39%; 22 years old and 12 people above the age, accounting for 3.73%; among the respondents who use mobile learning English every day, 89 people, accounting for 27.02%, 35 people using it 3 times a week, accounting for 10.87%; those using it twice a week There were 77 people, accounting for 23.91%; 84 people used it once a week, accounting for 26.09%;

39 people used it once every half month, accounting for 12.11%; among the respondents, 110 people had less than 3 months 34.16% of the use experience; 56 people have 3 to 6 months of use experience, accounting for 17.39%; 52 people have 6 months to 1 year of use experience, accounting for 16.15%; 28 people have 1 year to 2 years of experience, accounting for 8.7%; 76 people have more than 2 years of experience, accounting for 23.6%.

4 Findings and Discussion

4.1 Measurement Model Analysis

Measurement model verification includes three aspects: internal consistency, convergence validity and discriminative validity.

J. Nunnally and Bernstein (1994) pointed out that exploratory research can accept a CR (composite reliability) value between 06 and 0.7, and for exploratory research, the CR value greater than 0.7 and less than 0.9 is considered very appropriate. The CR value must be higher than 0.7 to guarantee enough internal consistency (Hair et al. 2016; Gefen, Straub, and Boudreau 2000). An indicator to measure the reliability of structured projects is that the value of Cronbach's Alpha α is greater than 0.7 (Nunnally and Bernstein 1994). The details of CR and Cronbach's Alpha α in this study are shown in Table 1.

See Table 1, CR (ATT = 0.936; BI = 0.951; EE = 0.949; FC = 0.941; PE = 0.947; SI = 0.943), the smallest CR value obtained for each construct is 0.936, and the largest CR value is 0.957. Cronbach's Alpha α (ATT = 0.915; BI = 0.923; EE = 0.933; FC = 0.921; PE = 0.930; SI = 0.918). The smallest Cronbach's Alpha α is 0.915 and the largest is 0.933. CR is greater than 0.7 and Cronbach's Alpha a is greater than 0.7. They are acceptable values. These 6 sub-constructors (ATT, SI, PE, EE, FC, and BI) and formation structures have a high degree of internal consistency and reliability.

Convergence validity is evaluated by three tests: external load, CR, and extracted average variance (AVE). External load value > 0.7, AVE value > 0.5 (Hair et al. 2016).

See Table 1 and Table 3. The AVE values of all structures in this study (ATT = 0.745; BI = 0.866; EE = 0.789; FC = 0.761; PE = 0.781; SI = 0.805) all exceed 0.5 (Bartlett, Kotrlik, and Higgins 2001), their CR values (ATT = 0.936; BI = 0.951; EE = 0.949; FC = 0.941; PE = 0.947; SI = 0.943) all exceed 0.7 (Hair et al. 2016). The external load exceeds 0.7.

Perform discriminant validity analysis to assess how discrepancy the experiment structure is from other structures. This analysis can judge the degree of correlation between one structure and another and how many items can express a single structure (Hair et al. 2016). This study uses cross-loading, Kriteria Fornell & Larcker to estimate discriminant validity.

See Table 2. The value of the square root of AVE is greater than the other structural correlation values, indicating that the measurement model this time has good discriminative validity (Hair et al. 2016).

The measurement has good convergent validity and discriminative validity.

Table 1. Basic results of the measurement model

Construct	Items	Factor loading	Cronbach's Alpha	CR	AVE
ATT	ATT1	0.867	0.915	0.936	0.745
	ATT2	0.874			
	ATT3	0.873			
	ATT4	0.859			
	ATT5	0.844			
BI	BI1	0.943	0.923	0.951	0.866
	BI2	0.934			
	BI3	0.915			
EE	EE1	0.891	0.933	0.949	0.789
	EE2	0.878			
	EE3	0.881			
	EE6	0.907			
	EE7	0.884			
FC	FC1	0.804	0.921	0.941	0.761
	FC2	0.893			
	FC4	0.890			
	FC5	0.906			
	FC6	0.864			
PE	PE1	0.837	0.930	0.947	0.781
	PE2	0.892			
	PE3	0.917			
	PE4	0.888			
	PE5	0.884			
SI	SI1	0.904	0.918	0.943	0.805
	SI2	0.929			
	SI3	0.921			
	SI4	0.831			

Table 2. Fornell & Larcker

	1	2	3	4	5	6
ATT	**0.863**					
BI	0.814	**0.931**				
EE	0.756	0.793	**0.888**			
FC	0.815	0.853	0.821	**0.872**		
PE	0.676	0.72	0.882	0.722	**0.884**	
SI	0.76	0.819	0.877	0.839	0.801	**0.897**

Table 3. The result of cross–loadings

	1	2	3	4	5	6
ATT1	**0.867**	0.65	0.623	0.672	0.569	0.633
ATT2	**0.874**	0.634	0.589	0.62	0.556	0.609
ATT3	**0.873**	0.584	0.609	0.67	0.518	0.594
ATT4	**0.859**	0.849	0.736	0.767	0.647	0.742
ATT5	**0.844**	0.742	0.674	0.757	0.602	0.673
BI1	0.768	**0.943**	0.772	0.824	0.681	0.795
BI2	0.741	**0.934**	0.744	0.76	0.694	0.775
BI3	0.763	**0.915**	0.698	0.796	0.635	0.715
EE1	0.655	0.67	**0.891**	0.685	0.81	0.721
EE2	0.626	0.694	**0.878**	0.662	0.804	0.734
EE3	0.664	0.701	**0.881**	0.728	0.758	0.755
EE6	0.692	0.708	**0.907**	0.781	0.772	0.827
EE7	0.715	0.748	**0.884**	0.783	0.785	0.848
FC1	0.652	0.686	0.643	**0.804**	0.553	0.668
FC2	0.726	0.712	0.753	**0.893**	0.658	0.759
FC4	0.706	0.732	0.736	**0.89**	0.645	0.73
FC5	0.764	0.85	0.778	**0.906**	0.701	0.798
FC6	0.7	0.727	0.661	0.864	**0.582**	0.695
PE1	0.542	0.581	0.72	0.56	**0.837**	0.662
PE2	0.593	0.633	0.777	0.648	**0.892**	0.729
PE3	0.61	0.658	0.803	0.637	**0.917**	0.742
PE4	0.622	0.674	0.797	0.684	**0.888**	0.721
PE5	0.616	0.632	0.806	0.655	**0.884**	0.686

(continued)

Table 3. (*continued*)

	1	2	3	4	5	6
SI1	0.7	0.727	0.86	0.769	0.782	**0.904**
SI2	0.697	0.756	0.807	0.76	0.758	**0.929**
SI3	0.67	0.737	0.799	0.756	0.718	**0.921**
SI4	0.659	0.717	0.675	0.724	0.613	**0.831**

4.2 Structural Model Analysis

In this study, PLS was used for structural model verification, and the bootstrap method was used to repeatedly sample 5,000 times to verify the path coefficient and significance of the structural model.

R^2 value refers to the part that can be explained in the total variance of a variable. If its value is approximately 0.67, it is considered to be large, approximately 0.333 is considered to be moderate, and approximately 0.19 is considered to be weak. Figure 2 shows the analysis result of the structural model. The value in the circle is the R^2 value.

As shown in Fig. 3, it can be seen that the results of this study found that PE, EE, SI, FC explain the variation of ATT to 69.1%, and performance The explanatory power of PE, EE, SI, FC, and ATT to the variation of BI is 79.2%. As far as Chin (1998) and Ringle (2004) are concerned, the explanatory power of the relevant variables of this model can be said to be quite large.

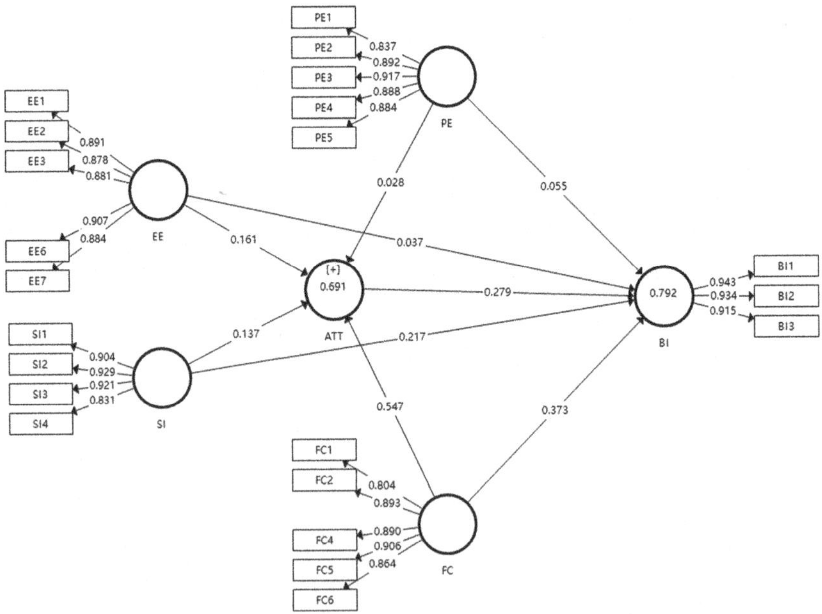

Fig. 3. PLS algorithm results

See Table 4, it can be seen that H1(ATT-> BI) ($\beta = 0.279, T = 4.298, p < 0.01$), so H1 is established, that is, ATT has a significant impact on BI. H2 (EE-> ATT) ($\beta = 0.161, T = 2.185, p < 0.05$), so H2 is established, that is, EE has a significant effect on ATT. H3 (EE-> BI) ($\beta = 0.037, T = 0.524, p > 0.05$), so H3 does not hold, that is, the effect of EE on BI is not significant. H4 (FC-> ATT) ($\beta = 0.547, T = 8.095, p < 0.01$), so H4 is established, that is, FC has a significant effect on ATT. H5 (FC-> BI) ($\beta = 0.373, T = 4.187, p < 0.01$), so H5 is established, that is, FC has a significant effect on BI. H6 (PE-> ATT) ($\beta = 0.028, T = 0.46, p > 0.05$), so H6 is not valid, and PE has no significant effect on ATT. H7 (PE-> BI) ($\beta = 0.055, T = 1.087, p > 0.05$), so H7 does not hold, that is, the effect of PE on BI is not significant. H8 (SI-> ATT) ($\beta = 0.137, T = 2.012, p < 0.05$), so H8 is established, that is, SI has a significant effect on ATT. H9 (SI-> BI) ($\beta = 0.217, T = 2.694, p < 0.05$), so H9 is established, that is, SI has a significant impact on BI.

Table 4. The result of relationship

Hypothesis	Path	β	T	P	Yes/No
H1	ATT -> BI	0.279	4.298	0.000	Yes
H2	EE -> ATT	0.161	2.185	0.029	Yes
H3	EE -> BI	0.037	0.524	0.600	**No**
H4	FC -> ATT	0.547	8.095	0.000	Yes
H5	FC -> BI	0.373	4.187	0.000	Yes
H6	PE -> ATT	0.028	0.460	0.646	**No**
H7	PE -> BI	0.055	1.087	0.277	**No**
H8	SI -> ATT	0.137	2.012	0.044	Yes
H9	SI -> BI	0.217	2.694	0.007	Yes

4.3 Analysis of Intermediary Effect

See Table 5, the mediating effect of EE on BI through ATT, (EE-> ATT-> BI) ($\beta = 0.045, T = 1.86, p > 0.05$), the mediating effect is not significant. FC has a mediating effect on BI through ATT, (FC-> ATT-> BI) ($\beta = 0.153, T = 3.729, p < 0.01$). The mediating effect of PE on BI through ATT, (PE- > ATT-> BI) ($\beta = 0.008, T = 0.426, p > 0.05$), the mediating effect is not significant. SI can mediate BI through ATT, (SI- > ATT-> BI) ($\beta = 0.038, T = 1.711, p > 0.05$), and the mediation effect is not significant.

VAF is further calculated by the relationship between direct effect and indirect effect (explained variation ratio = indirect effect/recombination effect), because VAF > 80% is a complete mediation; VAF between 20% and 80% is a partial mediation; VAF < 20% Means that there is no mediating effect. FC has an intermediary effect on BI through ATT, that is, the VAF of (FC-> ATT-> BI) is 29%, so there is a partial intermediary effect.

Table 5. The result of intermediary effect

Path	β	T	P
EE -> ATT -> BI	0.045	1.860	0.063
FC -> ATT -> BI	0.153	3.729	0.000
PE -> ATT -> BI	0.008	0.426	0.670
SI -> ATT -> BI	0.038	1.711	0.087

5 Conclusions and Recommendations

5.1 Conclusion

This research is based on the UTAUT model and combined with Attitude and Behavior (ATT) to construct a model of influencing factors of mobile language learning (MALL) for vocational students. And taking 3 grade students with mobile language learning experience in City College of Huizhou as a sample, using quantitative analysis methods, analyzing data through structural equation modeling, extracting key influencing factors that affect the use of MALL by vocational students, and exploring its possibilities Existing relationships, including mediation effects, etc. The findings of this discussion:

(i) Attitude towards behavior (ATT) has a significant impact on behavioral intention (BI), ($\beta = 0.279$, $T = 4.298$, $p < 0.01$); effort expectation (EE) has no significant impact on attitude behavior (ATT), ($\beta = 0.161$, $T = 2.185$, $p < 0.05$); Expectation of effort (EE) has no significant impact on behavioral intention (BI), ($\beta = 0.037$, $T = 0.524$, $p > 0.05$); Facilitating conditions (FC) on behavioral attitude. The influence of ATT is significant, ($\beta = 0.547$, $T = 8.095$, $p < 0.01$); Facilitating conditions (FC) have a significant influence on behavior intention (BI), (FC- > BI) ($\beta = 0.373$, $T = 4.187$, $p < 0.01$); the effect of performance expectation (PE) on ATT is not significant, ($\beta = 0.028$, $T = 0.46$, $p > 0.05$); the effect of performance expectation (PE) on BI, The effect is not significant, ($\beta = 0.055$, $T = 1.087$, $p > 0.05$); the influence of Social influence on ATT is significant, ($\beta = 0.137$, $T = 2.012$, $p < 0.05$); Social influence (SI) has a significant impact on BI, (SI- > BI) ($\beta = 0.217$, $T = 2.694$, $p < 0.05$).

(ii) FC's mediating effect on BI through ATT, (FC-> ATT-> BI) ($\beta = 0.153$, $T = 3.729$, $p < 0.01$), The mediating effect of BI is exists, and the VAF of (FC-> AT-> BI) is 29%, so there is a partial mediating effect.

(iii) PE, EE, SI, and FC can explain up to 69.1% of the variation of ATT; PE, EE, SI, FC, and ATT can explain the variation of BI reached 79.2%.

This research shows that FC and SI form the most critical factors in the use of MALL by higher vocational students. ATT and FC are the key factors that determine the continuous use of MALL by vocational students.

5.2 Research Limitations

In terms of research, research always has certain limitations. In this study, this study used subjective measures collected through self-reports, so students' responses may be biased. Moreover, this research is non-experimental, and acceptance is only measured at a certain point in time. However, as individuals gain experience, perceptions will change over time. Repeated research on measures will enable people to better understand and analyze the causality of variables, and at the same time can provide insights into the possible changes in acceptance over time. In addition, the data collected only come from the relevant students of City College of Huizhou International department and Business department. As a regional higher vocational college, City College of Huizhou has certain representativeness. Next, we need to further understand the understanding and acceptance of MALL by vocational students from different regions and vocational students from different majors. Future research should also include other potential and moderating variables, and research related factors from different mobile language learning platforms.

5.3 Recommendations

Higher vocational schools continue to carry out relevant research on mobile language learning, to further grasp the needs of higher vocational for MALL and related promotion of privacy, conduct more objective quantitative research on the goals of MALL, and provide more and more effective empirical evidence, Furthermore, more English teachers are encouraged to recommend MALL to students to improve the effect of mobile language learning for vocational students.

Give full play to the driving force of community influence. Stakeholders of higher vocational education, namely MALL industry and English language teachers should be widely MALL.

Vocational education stakeholders, that is, MALL industry and higher vocational school managers, and related policy makers, need to further improve and optimize the convenience of using MALL in higher vocational schools. As the status of mobile language learning in education continues to improve, and behavior intentions are mainly affected by convenience, community influence, and behavior attitude, vocational students believe that MALL will help them achieve their learning goals.

We suggest: The relevant stakeholders of mobile language learning in higher vocational colleges should promote the convenience of MALL, influence higher vocational students, and improve the learning effect of MALL through community influence.

References

Azli, W.U.A.W., Shah, P.M., Mohamad, M.: Perception on the usage of mobile assisted language learning (MALL) in English as a second language (ESL) learning among vocational college students. Creat. Educ. **9**(01), 84 (2018)

Al-Shehab, M.: The role of Mobile-Assisted Language Learning (MALL) in enhancing the writing skills of intermediate IEP students: expectations vs reality. Lang. Teach. Res. Q. **20**, 1–18 (2020)

Alsswey, A., Al-Samarraie, H.: M-learning adoption in the Arab gulf countries: a systematic review of factors and challenges. Educ. Inf. Technol. **24**(5), 3163–3176 (2019)

Al-Saedi, K., Al-Emran, M., Ramayah, T., Abusham, E.: Developing a general extended UTAUT model for M-payment adoption. Technol. Soc. **62**, 101293 (2020)

Aliaño, Á.M., Hueros, A.D., Franco, M.G., Aguaded, I.: Mobile learning in university contexts based on the unified theory of acceptance and use of technology (UTAUT). J. New Approach. Educ. Res. (NAER J.) **8**(1), 7–17 (2019)

Butarbutar, R., Uspayanti, R., Bawawa, M., Leba, S.M.R.: Mobile assisted language learning. In: 3rd International Conference on Social Sciences (ICSS 2020), pp. 390–392. Atlantis Press, October 2020

Bervell, B., Arkorful, V.: LMS-enabled blended learning utilization in distance tertiary education: establishing the relationships among facilitating conditions, voluntariness of use and use behaviour. Int. J. Educ. Technol. High. Educ. **17**(1), 1–16 (2020). https://doi.org/10.1186/s41239-020-0183-9

Baratè, A., Haus, G., Ludovico, L.A., Pagani, E., Scarabottolo, N.: 5G technology for augmented and virtual reality in education. In: Proceedings of the International Conference on Education and New Developments, vol. 2019, pp. 512–516, June 2019

Chao, C.M.: Factors determining the behavioral intention to use mobile learning: an application and extension of the UTAUT model. Front. Psychol. **10**, 1652 (2019)

Cakmak, F.: Mobile learning and mobile assisted language learning in focus. Lang. Technol. **1**(1), 30–48 (2019)

Dwivedi, Y.K., Rana, N.P., Tamilmani, K., Raman, R.: A meta-analysis based modified unified theory of acceptance and use of technology (meta-UTAUT): a review of emerging literature. Curr. Opin. Psychol. **36**, 13–18 (2020)

Gutiérrez-Colón, M., Frumuselu, A.D., Curell, H.: Mobile-assisted language learning to enhance L2 reading comprehension: a selection of implementation studies between 2012–2017. Interact. Learn. Environ., pp. 1–9 (2020)

Gonulal, T.: The use of Instagram as a mobile-assisted language learning tool. Contemp. Educ. Technol. **10**(3), 309–323 (2019)

Hoi, V.N.: Understanding higher education learners' acceptance and use of mobile devices for language learning: A Rasch-based path modeling approach. Comput. Educ. **146**, 103761 (2020)

Hair Jr, J.F., Sarstedt, M., Matthews, L.M., Ringle, C.M.: Identifying and treating unobserved heterogeneity with FIMIX-PLS: part I–method. European Business Review (2016)

Kayali, M., Alaaraj, S.: Adoption of cloud based E-learning in developing countries: a combination A of DOI, TAM and UTAUT. Int. J. Contemp. Manag. Inf. Technol **1**(1), 1–7 (2020)

Kemp, A., Palmer, E., Strelan, P.: A taxonomy of factors affecting attitudes towards educational technologies for use with technology acceptance models. Br. J. Edu. Technol. **50**(5), 2394–2413 (2019)

Liebenberg, J., Benade, T., Ellis, S.: Acceptance of ICT: applicability of the unified theory of acceptance and use of technology (UTAUT) to South African students. African J. Inf. Syst. **10**(3), 1 (2018)

Loewen, S., et al.: Mobile-assisted language learning: A Duolingo case study. ReCALL **31**(3), 293–311 (2019)

Morchid, N.: The determinants of use and acceptance of Mobile Assisted Language Learning: The case of EFL students in Morocco. Arab World English Journal (AWEJ) Special Issue on CALL (5) (2019)

Miqawati, A.H.: Pronunciation learning, participation, and attitude enhancement through mobile assisted language learning (Mall). English Rev. J. English Educ. **8**(2), 211–218 (2020)

Nasr, H.A., Abbas, A.A.: Impact of mobile assisted language learning on learner autonomy in EFL reading context. J. Lang. Educ. **4**(2 (14)) (2018)

Shadiev, R., Liu, T., Hwang, W.Y.: Review of research on mobile-assisted language learning in familiar, authentic environments. Br. J. Edu. Technol. **51**(3), 709–720 (2020)

Ozer, O., Kılıç, F.: The effect of mobile-assisted language learning environment on EFL students' academic achievement, cognitive load and acceptance of mobile learning tools. EURASIA J. Math. Sci. Technol. Educ. **14**(7), 2915–2928 (2018)

Persada, S.F., Miraja, B.A., Nadlifatin, R.: Understanding the generation Z behavior on D-learning: a unified theory of acceptance and use of technology (UTAUT) approach. Int. J. Emerg. Technol. Learn. **14**(5) (2019)

Patil, P., Tamilmani, K., Rana, N.P., Raghavan, V.: Understanding consumer adoption of mobile payment in India: Extending Meta-UTAUT model with personal innovativeness, anxiety, trust, and grievance redressal. Int. J. Inf. Manage. **54**, 102144 (2020)

Raza, S.A., Shah, N., Ali, M.: Acceptance of mobile banking in Islamic banks: evidence from modified UTAUT model. J. Islamic Mark. (2019)

Salloum, S.A., Shaalan, K.: Factors affecting students' acceptance of e-learning system in higher education using UTAUT and structural equation modeling approaches. In International Conference on Advanced Intelligent Systems and Informatics, pp. 469–480. Springer, Cham, September 2018. https://doi.org/10.1007/978-3-319-99010-1_43

Shukla, S.: M-learning adoption of management students': a case of India. Educ. Inf. Technol. **26**(1), 279–310 (2020). https://doi.org/10.1007/s10639-020-10271-8

Venkatesh, V., Morris, M.G., Davis, G.B., Davis, F.D.: User acceptance of information technology: toward a unified view. MIS quarterly, 425–478 (2003)

Wong, K.K.K.: Mastering partial least squares structural equation modeling (PLS-Sem) with Smartpls in 38 Hours. IUniverse (2019)

Research on Intelligent Management of Engineering Construction Safety Oriented to Internet of Things + BIM

Min Lin[1(✉)], Haiying Wu[2], and Hongtao Zhang[1]

[1] Institute of Surveying, Mapping and Remote Sensing Information, Guangdong Polytechnic of Industry and Commerce, Guangzhou 510510, China
linmin3000@163.com

[2] College of Economics and Trade, Guangdong Polytechnic of Industry and Commerce, Guangzhou 510510, China

Abstract. By integrating advanced information technologies such as BIM, Internet of things, big data and artificial intelligence algorithm, an intelligent management platform for engineering construction safety. Construction safety intelligent early warning system and intelligent management and control methods and builds an intelligent construction safety management system from the three aspects of identification warning and control, then puts forward the construction plan of the construction safety intelligent management platform, in order to provide references for the creation of smart construction site.

Keywords: Internet of Things · BIM · Engineering construction safety

1 Quotation

1.1 Internet of Things + BIM

The emergence of BIM and the rapid development of big data, artificial intelligence, cloud computing, Internet of Things, 5G and other emerging information technologies have brought vitality and vitality to the intelligent management of engineering construction safety. As an important part of the construction industrialization, prefabricated building has been paid more and more attention and become the inevitable trend of the future development of the construction industry. As the construction process of prefabricated building is divided into two parts: the off-site production process of prefabricated components and the on-site assembly construction process, the successful implementation of prefabricated building must fully coordinate the production and distribution of prefabricated components and the on-site construction activity arrangement, which makes the role of project scheduling in the smooth implementation of prefabricated building increasingly apparent, and effective scheduling scheme has become the whole process a necessary condition for the successful completion of a project. However, the process of prefabricated building construction has the characteristics of "multi space", "non

© ICST Institute for Computer Sciences, Social Informatics and Telecommunications Engineering 2022
Published by Springer Nature Switzerland AG 2022. All Rights Reserved
S. Shi et al. (Eds.): 6GN 2021, LNICST 439, pp. 590–596, 2022.
https://doi.org/10.1007/978-3-031-04245-4_51

synchronization", "different region" and "relevance", the traditional project scheduling mode is difficult to realize the real-time interaction between physical construction system and virtual construction system. The lack of effective docking and fusion of the two system space data hinders the timely and effective. Scheduling decision-making. How to achieve intelligent project scheduling with the help of cutting-edge technology has become a major challenge.

Based on the background of the rapid development of prefabricated buildings in China, aiming at the characteristics of prefabricated building scheduling, this paper constructs an intelligent management platform of prefabricated building project scheduling based on BIM + Internet of things, and proposes an intelligent scheduling idea integrating Internet of things, big data, artificial intelligence algorithm and other advanced information technologies under the dynamic interference of multiple uncertain factors it has certain theoretical significance and practical value to improve the autonomy, intelligence and predictability of assembly construction project scheduling.

1.2 Application Status of BIM in Construction Safety

Scholars have done a lot of research on the practical application of BIM in the design, construction, operation and maintenance of prefabricated building projects, but the actual application effect is far from the expected. Because BIM is not designed to process real-time data, it is used for design, construction, maintenance tasks and interoperability in industry. The realization of these functions does not necessarily require real-time capability. Therefore, the relevant work of inputting real-time data (such as through sensors and Internet of things devices) into BIM to supplement and improve the functions of BIM is in-depth study. For example, Li et al. Reduced the schedule risk of prefabrication construction by integrating BIM and RFID technology. Ding et al. Proposed to integrate BIM model with Internet of Things devices to monitor real assets on site. Some scholars have noticed that the parametric modeling and visual simulation functions of BIM Technology are consistent with the requirements of prefabricated construction technology, which is beneficial to solve the problems of prefabricated construction project scheduling and information management. Although it has not been well applied, it has gradually formed a research trend.

2 Intelligent Identification of Construction Safety Risks

One of the important reasons leading to construction safety accidents is that the data collection and transmission of construction safety risk are not timely, and the risk identification is not intelligent enough. It is very important to form the corresponding security intelligent identification technology with the support of emerging information technology and the uniqueness of specific engineering activities.

2.1 Security Identification Technology Based on the Internet of Things

The security identification based on the Internet of Things is to collect and transmit engineering safety related data automatically in real time through the integrated application of various sensors and network facilities (wired or wireless), and carry out real-time analysis and discrimination of safety risks by combining data analysis methods and early warning mechanisms.

This technology involves many kinds of sensors, such as temperature, humidity, pressure, gas body, light, sound, stress, strain, displacement, position, identity identification and other sensors, often used in geological environment, deep foundation pit, main structure, edge hole, dangerous gas monitoring. However, due to the complexity of the engineering environment and the large number of RFID tags identified by personnel, materials and equipment, the intelligent perception technology needs to solve the power supply, electromagnetic shielding, huge amount of communication data and other problems of the sensor. Data transmission and transmission are susceptible to the impact of the field environment, resulting in great fluctuations in its accuracy.

2.2 Security Identification Technology Based on Machine Vision

Machine vision based security identification technology is to use image or video analysis methods or technologies to quickly and automatically process engineering safety-related images or videos and extract safety elements, and then to identify security risks. This kind of technology depends on the project site video acquisition equipment and image processing technology. Often used in worker behavior, dangerous areas, material safety testing, etc. However, this kind of technology is greatly affected by the field light, line of sight, dynamic, etc., and is also limited by the performance of algorithm and computing equipment.

2.3 Mobile Terminal Based Security Identification Technology

The security identification technology based on mobile terminal is to obtain engineering safety related data by manual means, identify and report the hidden security problems existing in the project, and then carry out the comprehensive identification of security risks. This kind of technology benefits from mobile terminal equipment and WeChat or small program. Through scanning QR code on the spot, the information transmission and processing of real data are often used for on-site inspection and identification of potential safety hazards or wind risk factors. This kind of technology is applicable to a wide range of applications, but limited by manual detection and reporting of relevant data, resulting in a narrow or incomplete data coverage.

3 Intelligent Early Warning of Construction Safety Risks

Internet of things technology is a new technology which is developing rapidly. It has great potential in intelligent management and can provide solutions for the physical information fusion of complex dynamic systems. At present, Internet of things has been tried in industry, transportation and other fields. Tao Fei et al. Elaborated the basic theory and key technology of Internet of things Workshop Information Physics fusion from four dimensions of physics, model, data and service, and put forward the criteria and application ideas of Internet of things drive.

In the construction industry, studies have shown that Internet of things is a promising solution to realize intelligent automation in the construction industry. A few scholars have applied Internet of things to the research of construction progress monitoring, construction personnel safety management, building materials monitoring and waste tracking. Due to the characteristics of both manufacturing industry and construction industry, the solution of assembly building project scheduling problem cannot simply refer to the application methods of Internet of things in workshop scheduling and satellite assembly space, but the existing research results can provide a good reference for the application of Internet of things in assembly building project scheduling.

BIM is a rich intelligent digital warehouse, which uses object-oriented method to describe the characteristics of architecture, engineering and architecture, that is, semantics, geometry and relationship. Internet of things visualization of buildings can rely on 3D CAD model extracted from BIM or customized 3D model of buildings. However, the information provided by BIM is usually limited to the level of facilities or buildings, lacking the real-time dynamic data information of personnel, materials and equipment on the project site. In the process of prefabricated building construction, the Internet of things technology can collect and transmit the information of component materials, equipment and personnel in the construction site to the information system background through RFID tag, sensing equipment, two-dimensional code, video monitoring and other sensing technologies, so as to realize the real-time information tracking of the basic information, location information and transportation status of the monitoring object. The Internet of things of buildings can use various sensor networks to create real-time views of buildings. On the basis of real-time data acquisition and monitoring, artificial intelligence algorithm and data mining technology can fuse data and mine relevant scheduling knowledge for scheduling optimization. The BIM based Internet of things prefabricated building model is shown in Fig. 1.

Fig. 1. The BIM based Internet of things prefabricated building model

Aiming at a series of problems in the process of prefabricated building construction, which are caused by the diversity of construction elements, uncertainty of prefabricated component supply and multi-source of disturbance elements, real-time interaction with on-site construction system in virtual space can realize the informatization, convenience, foresight, networking, intelligence and self-management of project scheduling through simulation feedback, disturbance prediction, decision optimization and other means It's dynamic. The Internet of things model based on BIM is integrated with project scheduling. Before the implementation of the scheduling scheme, the Internet of things model of the project can be established through digital technology, and the project scheduling can be realized.

Interface, plus material attributes, boundary conditions and load conditions, can real-time monitor the safety state of personnel and mechanical substances in the construction of the project, simulate the stress and strain state of the engineering structure in the construction, effectively prepare safety management measures, real-time maintenance and correction of safety emergency management plan. BIM technology can be used for dangerous partial projects or complex heterosexual structure installation.

Taking the dynamic database of engineering construction safety risk as the platform connotation, building the intelligent management platform of engineering construction safety based on BIM is the inevitable way to realize the linkage management of "awareness", "police" and "control" of engineering construction safety risk. The platform includes five layers: perception layer, transmission layer, data layer, algorithm layer and functional application layer, as shown in Table 1.

Table 1. Perception layer, transmission layer, data layer, algorithm layer and functional application layer

Management platform	Layer	Construction safety
Intelligent early warning	**Functional application layer**	BIM
contingency management	**Algorithm layer**	Awareness
Assistant decision	**Data layer**	Police
5G technology	**Transport layer**	Control
AI	**Conclusion layer**	Internet of things

Euclidean distance is used in KNN algorithm. The Euclidean distance between two points in two-dimensional space is calculated as follows:

$$\rho = \sqrt{(x_2 - x_1)^2 - (y_2 - y_1)^2} \tag{1}$$

The simplest and rudimentary of KNN algorithm is to calculate the distance between the prediction point and all the points, then save and sort, select the first k values to, When we expand to multi-dimensional space, the formula becomes like this:

$$d(x, y) := \sqrt{(x_1 - y_1)^2 + (x_2 - y_2)^2 + \cdots + (x_n - y_n)^2} = \sqrt{\sum_{i=1}^{n} (x_i - y_i)^2}. \tag{2}$$

Average error of KNN algorithm as shown in Fig. 2.

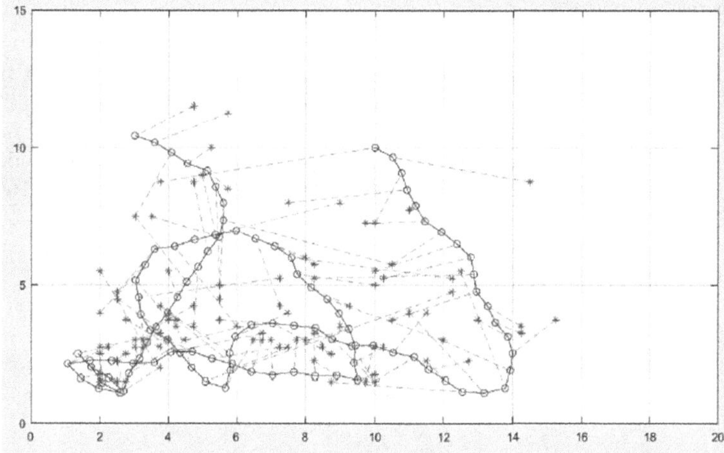

Fig. 2. Average error of KNN algorithm

4 Epilogue

Based on BIM + Internet of things technology, the automatic identification of engineering construction safety risk factors, intelligent early warning of safety accidents, efficient decision-making of safety emergency rescue management, and the establishment of a scientific and perfect engineering construction safety intelligent management system is a scientific and modern solution to the problem of frequent safety accidents. Smart compared with traditional safety management, safety management with the aid of BIM to visualization of dynamic simulation, realtime monitoring of the Internet of things, the depth of the large data analysis and auxiliary decision-making of artificial intelligence, real time control of the construction site can be realized Conditions, the dynamic analysis of safety risk factors, predict the safety trend, accurate formulate safety protection measures, effectively implement the safety management measures.

Acknowledgement. This work was supported by grant of No. pdjh2021b0744 from the special fund for science and technology innovation strategy of Guangdong Province in 2021;**and by grant of No. 2019gktscx021 from the** 2019 general university scientific research project of Guangdong Provincial Department of education "Research on helmet wearing behavior based on deep learning under low visibility"; **and by grant of No. 2020zdzx2095 from the** Refe2020 key scientific research project of colleges and universities of Guangdong Provincial Department of Education; **and by grant of No.** (GDPIC)-**2021-zx-18 from the** 2021 school level entrusted special project of Guangdong Polytechnic of Industry & Commerce; **and by grant of No. 1714 from the** 2022 basic and applied basic research project of Guangzhou basic research plan (general project) "Research on bonding mechanism of seawater and sand concrete based on thread characteristics of BFRP reinforcement".

References

1. He, Y.L., McLaughlin, S.R., Lo, J.S.H., Shi, C., Vincelli, A., et al.: Radio frequency identification based on monitoring construction site and Internet of things **11**, 1629–1639 (2015)
2. Kumar, S.S., Cheng, J.C.P.: A BIM-based automated site layout planning framework for congested construction sites. Autom. Constr. **59**, 24–37 (2015). https://doi.org/10.1016/j.autcon.2015.07.008
3. Liu, X., Zhu, Y., Jin, Y.: Research on automatic identification and pre-warning of safety risks in subway construction under complex environment. Eng. Sci. **12**, 85–93 (2012)
4. Guo, M.: Research on railway engineering safety management system based on building information model. J. Saf. Sci. Technol. **12**, 174–178 (2017)
5. Wang, Z., Ren, G., Hu, Z., Zhang, C., Zhou, K.: Safety monitoring technology for construction of new highway tunnel through existing water supply tunnel. Highway **1**, 303–308 (2020)

Research and Practice of Virtual Reality Technology in Vocational Education

Take Guangdong Innovative Technical College as an Example

Baorong Zhan[1], Xichang Yu[2(✉)], Juan Zhang[1], Pengfei Luo[2], and Dengkui Sun[2]

[1] Guangdong Innovative Technical College, Xuefu Road, Dongguan, Guangdong, China
[2] China Mobile Group Guangdong Co., Ltd., Dongguan Branch, Dongcheng Road 380th, Dongguan, Guangdong, China
yuxichang@gd.chinamobile.com

Abstract. As an emerging information technology, virtual reality technology has advantages of immersion and interactivity, which enable students to simulate the real training in the virtual learning environment and effectively improve students' vocational skills. The issues encountered in traditional skill training field of vocational education are discussed, includes high cost, high risk, low return rate, long training time, low efficiency, environmental pollution, difficult to reproduce and so on. It is explained that how the issues could be solved by integration of vocational education and virtual reality. Five different virtual reality modes are illustrated and demonstrated, which are multi-channel virtual reality technology, networked virtual reality technology, desktop virtual reality technology, panoramic virtual reality technology and wearable virtual reality technology. The application results in college shows that virtual reality technology enables students to explore in an immersive environment, inspire their enthusiasm for learning and innovation, cultivate their practical capability, and improve the average score and pass rate of courses.

Keywords: Virtual reality · Vocational education · Skill training

1 Introduction

Informatization is the requirement of education development and an essential way to realize education modernization. However, in the field of vocational education, there are few breakthroughs in informatization. For this reason, since 2012, the Ministry of Education in China has introduced policies to propose the development of virtual experiment and practical training projects, in order to improve the efficiency and effect of practical skill training in vocational education. With the arrival of the first year of virtual reality in 2016, various hardware platforms and resources related to virtual reality are gradually popularized in the market, bringing changes to the vocational education skill training mode [1].

© ICST Institute for Computer Sciences, Social Informatics and Telecommunications Engineering 2022
Published by Springer Nature Switzerland AG 2022. All Rights Reserved
S. Shi et al. (Eds.): 6GN 2021, LNICST 439, pp. 597–605, 2022.
https://doi.org/10.1007/978-3-031-04245-4_52

Because of its advantages of immersion and interactivity, the virtual reality technology enables students to simulate the training of the real environment in the virtual learning environment and improves the students' professional skills effectively. It also solves the problems of high cost, high risk, environmental pollution, difficult to observe, difficult to check, difficult to operate in traditional vocational education skill training field. So, the integration of theory, practice and virtual reality technology must be the direction of teaching reform and development of vocational education in future [2]. In 2018, an independent computer simulation research and development center was established in Guangdong Innovative Technical College, which was used to develop training software and support new training in virtual reality way. By using the center, the college can develop virtual reality practical training system to fit the relative courses and cultivate talents to meet social requirement.

2 Virtual Reality Solves the Issues in Skill Training Field of Traditional Vocational Education

2.1 Issue1, High Cost, Low Rate of Return on Investment

The real training cost are high for some majors, like petrochemical equipment maintenance, automobile testing and maintenance, building and so on. Take major of automobile testing and maintenance for example, which traditional training require to be practiced in real environment. That means it must purchase cars, automobile spare parts, detect and repair equipment, which cannot be afforded by most of the colleges.

By using virtual simulation environment, the trainer doesn't need to own cars, auto spare parts and other detect equipment. It not only reduces the investment of fixed assets and future maintenance, but also meets the demand of skill cultivation.

2.2 Issue2, Low Learning Efficiency and Long Practical Training Time

Some programs are designed to train students in one special skill, but it requires several other supporting skills. In order to complete this training, both trainer and trainee take a long time to make preparations, which lead to very low efficiency. For example, in program of circuit design practice, it requires to go through all kinds of welding. But due to welding skill levels of most trainees are low, many students have to spend a lot of time on it and just leave little time in circuit design, which leads to low quality in main skill training of the program [3].

By using virtual reality training software, students only need to click the mouse to weld the object to complete the preparations, so they can focus on circuit design, which means greatly improvement in efficiency of main skill training.

2.3 Issue3, Unsafe or Difficult to Reproduce Scenarios in Training

Some skill trainings involve unsafe factors such as explosions and toxic substances, which cannot be executed in training course, but can only be performed in virtual reality way, such as ethylene separation process or catalytic cracking process in petrochemical major.

Some skill trainings need to be carried out under specific conditions, which are difficult to reproduce, such as automobile fault detection and maintenance. In this type of training, it is difficult to set a variety of faults, but it can be solved and reproduced by virtual simulation technology.

Some skill trainings need to be prepared in the early stage and students are not allowed to make mistakes so as not to damage the equipment. However, in real scenario, it is difficult for students to completely ensure that they do not make mistakes due to their inadequate capability. Through virtual simulation training, students can be allowed to make mistakes and simulate the serious consequences of mistakes, so as to cultivate students' awareness of safety and rule.

2.4 Issue4, Environmental Pollution

Some skill trainings will cause environmental pollution. In order to protect the environment and students' health, such vocational training can only be carried out through virtual simulation practice, such as electric welding, arc welding training programs.

2.5 Issue5, Large Space of Occupation

Some skill trainings require large space, either for bulky professional equipment or practical scenario, like logistics warehouse construction, building, etc. Most colleges cannot offer enough room, so it is very difficult for students to get adequate skill training in them.

Virtual reality vocational skill training can simulate the functions of actual equipment and provide a strong sense of immersion to trainees. Students can get sufficient skill training through virtual simulation training before they doing practice on real equipment, which help them to achieve the goal of skill training in an easier way.

2.6 Issue6, The Form Is Monotonous and the Participation Rate Is Low

Because limitation of resource, some traditional skill trainings just provide demo, without interaction and student participation. Virtual reality provides a funny way of interaction, which makes training more interesting. It can also provide enough resource for all participations, and even realize personalized guidance for each student, which means every student can choose relevant learning content according to his/her own interests and needs. By using virtual reality technology, all students can participate the training and conduct self-assessment anytime.

3 The Integration of Virtual Reality Technology and Vocational Skill Training

3.1 Model1, Multi-channel Virtual Reality Technology

It refers to the multi-channel large-screen display technology composed of multiple projectors or LCD screens. Compared with ordinary display systems, the equipment has larger display size, wider field of vision, more display contents, higher display resolution, and more impact and immersive visual effects. The technology can be used in large vocational training programs [4].

Guangdong Innovative Technical College introduced five channels immersive virtual simulation platform, used to carry out automotive machining, disassembly of motorcycle, disassembly and installation of automobile engine, disassembly and installation of automobile gearbox, vehicle dismantling, city planning, etc. In the platform, there are new technologies, e.g. infrared tracking system, data gloves, 3D glasses, which can provide a strong sense of immersion and simulate the real situation. It ensures students can get a good experience and develop their skills (Fig. 1).

Fig. 1. Multi-channel virtual reality system for city planning.

3.2 Mode2, Networked Virtual Reality Technology

It refers to the technology that virtual reality projects are released through the Internet and run directly through the web browser. Virtual reality training is carried out through the network, which is not limited by time and place. Students can attend the training at anytime anywhere.

In Guangdong Innovative Technical College, a variety of web-based virtual reality skill training resources are developed to support vocational education, includes generic cabling, art of catering, campus fire safety training, financial accounting, logistics and express practice and so on (Fig. 2).

Fig. 2. Networked virtual reality for logistics and express.

3.3 Mode3, Desktop Virtual Reality Technology

It is mainly aimed at the training projects that require complicated calculation and high precision. For example, three-dimensional model displaying requires so much calculation and memory that it must be run in the desktop computer or special server.

In Guangdong Innovative Technical College, two simulation software toolkits were developed for numerical control machine major and industrial robot major. Using these toolkits, students can complete pre-programmed debugging in numerical control area and simulate online operation in industrial robot area (Fig. 3).

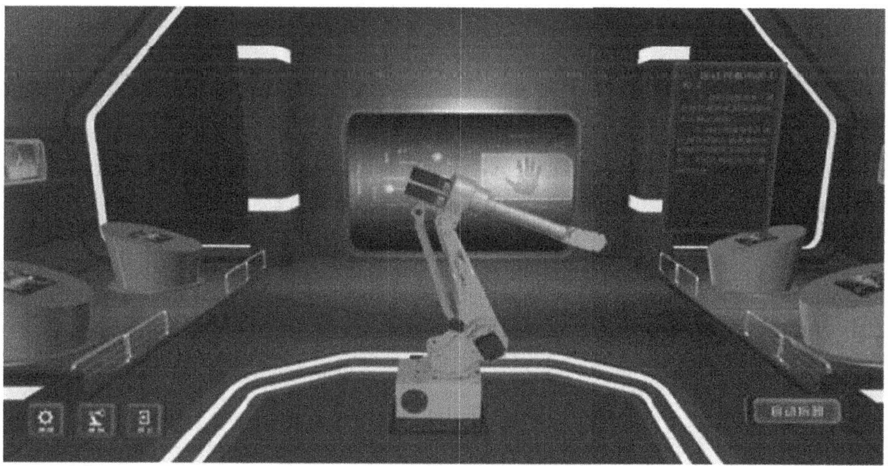

Fig. 3. Desktop virtual reality for industrial robot.

3.4 Mode4, Panoramic Virtual Reality Technology

It displays the real scene in the way of panoramic pictures or videos, which is widely adopted in tourist spot introduction or building introduction.

In Guangdong Innovative Technical College, 360° panoramic education software system was developed based in mobile platform. By using corresponding APP in mobile phone, user can take photos and join them together to create a simulation scene easily. After uploading to online system, everyone can browser and share the scene via Internet (Fig. 4).

Fig. 4. Panoramic virtual reality for tourist spot introduction.

3.5 Mode5, Wearable Virtual Reality Technology

It refers to the virtual reality technology that realizes virtual reality immersive display with headset display device. Because it has better sense of immersion and interactivity, it become a popular manifestation form of virtual reality at present [5].

In Guangdong Innovative Technical College, a virtual reality vocational skill training software based on HTC helmet was introduced. It includes architecture design simulation subsystem, premises distribution subsystem, lighting art and space design simulation subsystem, etc. (Fig. 5).

Fig. 5. Wearable virtual reality for architecture.

4 The Effect After Applying Virtual Reality Technology in Vocational Education

Firstly, virtual reality technology improves the vocational skills of students significantly. On the one hand, Guangdong Innovative Technical College had participated in 21 provincial competitions in 2019–2020, won 11 first prizes, 17 s prizes and 12 third prizes. Compared to 2017–2018, the total number of awards increased by 36%. On the other hand, the satisfaction with graduates feedbacked from employer in 2019–2020 increased 23% compared to 2017–2018, which shown virtual reality technology improves the vocational skills of students and enhances their competitiveness.

Secondly, virtual reality technology also greatly reduces the skill training cost of the school. Table 1 lists the comparison between some traditional skill trainings and virtual skill trainings, from which it can be seen that the cost of virtual skill training is lower than that of traditional skill training in terms of investment, consumable materials, maintenance fees and experimental time consumption.

Table 1. Cost comparison between virtual reality trainings and traditional skill trainings.

Training course	Mode	Investment (CNY)	Consumable materials (CNY)	Maintenance fees (CNY)	Time consumption(HR)
Chemical pump disassembly	Traditional	>200000	>35000	>15000	>4
	Virtual reality	<30000	0	0	<2

(continued)

Table 1. *(continued)*

Training course	Mode	Investment (CNY)	Consumable materials (CNY)	Maintenance fees (CNY)	Time consumption(HR)
Generic cabling	Traditional	>850000	>15000	>15000	>6
	Virtual reality	<35000	0	0	<2
Shadow and space design	Traditional	Infeasible	Infeasible	Infeasible	Infeasible
	Virtual reality	<20000	0	0	<4
Engine disassembly	Traditional	>350000	>30000	>15000	>12
	Virtual reality	<35000	0	0	<6
Catering art table design	Traditional	>600000	>30000	>15000	>8
	Virtual reality	<30000	0	0	<4

Thirdly, after the introduction of virtual reality technology, the students' learning enthusiasm had been inspired, and the quality of teaching had also been greatly improved. As shown in Table 2, compared with traditional vocational education, the evaluation indexes of skill training courses were improved a lot, includes students' interestingness, attendance rate, pass rate and average score.

Table 2. Quality comparison between virtual reality training and traditional skill training.

Training course	Mode	Interestingness	Attendance rate	Pass rate	Average score
Chemical pump disassembly	Traditional	56	71%	68%	67.8
	Virtual reality	72	85%	74%	72.7
Generic cabling	Traditional	61	79%	65%	74.6
	Virtual reality	78	89%	79%	78.9
Shadow and space design	Traditional	75	84%	89%	85.2
	Virtual reality	83	92%	93%	89.3
Engine disassembly	Traditional	73	87%	78%	76.3
	Virtual reality	89	93%	88%	82.7
Catering art table design	Traditional	80	91%	92%	83.5
	Virtual reality	92	98%	95%	88.4

5 Conclusion

The application of virtual reality technology in vocational education has brought great changes in the content and presentation of learning, enabling students to experience an immersive learning environment in the virtual world. By providing new mode and mechanism, it solves the issues of high cost, high risk, low return rate, long training time, low efficiency, environmental pollution, difficult to reproduce in traditional vocational practical training. At the same time, it enables students to explore in an immersive environment, thus cultivating students' practical capability, inspiring their enthusiasm for learning, and improving the level of vocational education. As a new type of teaching media, virtual reality has gradually caught the attention of educators by its advantages and potential. It is expected to play a more important role in vocational education in future.

Acknowledgments. The authors acknowledge the financial support of the Colleges and Universities Young Innovative Talents Project Foundation in Guangdong Province (Grant: 2018GkQNCX056), the University Recognized Scientific Research Foundation in Guangdong Province (Grant: 2019GKTSCX171), and the University Level Scientific Research Project Foundation in Guangdong Innovative Technical College (Grant: 2022TSYB004).

References

1. Shian, W.: Research on new form teaching of virtual reality vocational skills training. J. Southern Vocat. Educ. **8**(3), 72–76 (2018)
2. Jinjin, L., Tiantian, T.: Research on the co-construction and sharing of the information platform of higher vocational education core courses under the background of "internet + education." Farm Prod. Process. **4**, 109–113 (2021)
3. Chunping, D., Xiaoyuan, L.: Construction of practice teaching system of health vocational information technology specialty group. J. Guangzhou Open Univ. **21**(1), 44–47 (2021)
4. Huan, Z., Dequan, Z.: The logical framework of construction of vocational education's smart classroom in the new technological era. China Educ. Technol. **6**, 6–13 (2019)
5. Pengjun, Z.: The logic of practice and construction of wisdom classroom in an information technology era. J. Guangzhou Open Univ. **8**(1), 18–24 (2020)

Intelligent Teaching System of Vocational Education Based on a New Generation of Information Technology

Hai Lin(✉)

Department of Information Science, ZhanJiang Preschool Education College, Guangdong, China
linhai@zhjpec.edu.cn

Abstract. With the increasing demand for technical talents in all walks of life, the status and role of vocational education have become increasingly important. The use of a new generation of information technology to accelerate the reform of the talent training model and build an intelligent teaching system for vocational education has become an urgent problem in the development of vocational education. This study analyzes the teaching and learning needs and teaching management of vocational colleges from five aspects, namely, smart classroom, teaching model innovation, teaching cloud platform, teaching evaluation, and issuance of qualification certificates. Such a teaching system uses artificial intelligence, Internet of Things, big data, and cloud. A new generation of information technology such as computing and blockchain has created an integrated intelligent teaching, management, and service system that closely combines offline physical classroom teaching and online cloud platform teaching. The system is green and energy-saving, reduces the investment in teaching equipment and hardware, and fully covers the "teaching, learning, evaluation, management, and certification" links of the vocational education process. Furthermore, this system promotes the reform of the vocational education teaching system.

Keywords: Vocational education · Artificial intelligence · Information technology

1 Introduction

The "China Education Modernization 2035" issued by the Central Committee of the Communist Party of China and the State Council focuses on the deployment of 10 strategic tasks for educational modernization. The objectives are to implement the spirit of the 19th National Congress of the Communist Party of China

This work was supported by the Guangdong University Scientific Research Characteristic Innovation Project (Natural Science) under Grant 2021KTSCX323 and Zhanjiang Preschool Education College Online Course Construction Project under Grant JPKC20210602.

© ICST Institute for Computer Sciences, Social Informatics and Telecommunications Engineering 2022
Published by Springer Nature Switzerland AG 2022. All Rights Reserved
S. Shi et al. (Eds.): 6GN 2021, LNICST 439, pp. 606–616, 2022.
https://doi.org/10.1007/978-3-031-04245-4_53

and the National Education Conference and accelerate the modernization of education. Moreover, one of the tasks for educational modernization is to accelerate the modernization of education. The educational reform in the information age aims to build an intelligent campus and coordinate the construction of an integrated intelligent teaching, management, and service platform. Modern technology is used to accelerate the reform of the talent training model and realize the organic combination of large-scale education and individualized training. Furthermore, the educational reform aims to innovate educational service formats, establish a mechanism for co-construction and sharing of digital educational resources, and promote precision management and scientific decision-making.

With the rapid development of a new generation of information technology, the increase of applications based on artificial intelligence (AI), Internet of Things, big data, cloud computing, and blockchain technology has accelerated the construction of smart campuses. Examples of blockchain technology include smart classrooms [1], online and offline hybrid teaching [2], educational data co-construction, and sharing [3]. Domestic mainstream enterprises in the education field have also successively launched corresponding smart education and teaching construction programs. For example, the "Intelligent Education Solution" launched by Tencent Cloud implements AI education scenarios in the teaching process of "teaching, testing, management, and marketing," providing AI education products and services, such as classroom quality analysis, intelligent scoring, and homework correction. The Ebbinghaus Smart Education 4.0's new teaching product starts from four systems, that is, student portrait, knowledge map, learning content recommendation, and learning path planning, officially entering the era of intelligent mode. Companies such as Baidu AI, Megvii Technology, EqualOcean, and Aidi Technology have also launched their own smart teaching and smart campus solutions and promoted and built them in key vocational colleges. However, in terms of specific solutions, almost all use "cloud + terminal" as the construction model, with hardware system construction as the main component, and product homogeneity is serious.

The vocational education intelligent teaching system based on the new generation of information technology proposed in this study has completely absorbed the current mainstream enterprises' informatization construction and development experience in the current education field. Moreover, the pain points and difficulties of vocational education, using AI, the Internet of Things, big data, cloud computing, and core key technologies, such as blockchain, have created an integrated intelligent teaching, management, and evaluation system. This system closely combines offline physical classroom teaching and online virtual classroom teaching. The direction of change in the teaching system aims to meet the needs of the current vocational education reform and development, realize the deep integration of teaching and learning, strengthen the integration of industry and education and school–enterprise cooperation, promote the integration of documents under the 1 + X certificate system, and lead vocational education to a certain extent.

2 Current Status of Development of Informatization Teaching System Construction

In recent years, relying on a sound informatization development plan, the informatization development of the teaching system of vocational colleges has been service-oriented, committed to technology and service innovation, and has made considerable progress. The first MOOC jointly developed by MIT and Harvard University in March 2012 overturned the traditional university education model. MOOC was composed of online video lectures, interactive questions, online laboratories, and forums and attracted 150,000 students to register. The course ended in June 2012, and researchers such as BRESLOW [4] began to analyze the rich data sources it generated. We check in chronological order how students use resources and how the interaction of the teaching part facilitates their learning of the course. Chunfeng et al. [5] discussed the feasibility and effect of small-scale restrictive online courses (SPOC) combined with flipped classroom teaching in nurses' professional knowledge and skills training. Experiments prove that using SPOC and flipped classroom methods to train new graduate nurses in general knowledge and skills will help stimulate nurses' interest in learning and improve nurses' technical skills and clinical application capabilities. These new online intelligent education teaching models can provide high-quality teaching resources and education consultations to the public. In addition, vocational colleges pay attention to the application of a new generation of information technology. Cloud computing, AI, and the Internet of Things break the traditional classroom boundaries, turning traditional campuses into scientific research libraries and smart classrooms that can be visited and roamed anytime and anywhere. The smart classroom lighting control system [6] is a design scheme based on machine vision. Smart classrooms based on the Internet of Things and big data [7] have a great role in improving the learning environment of universities and realizing smart teaching and management. The cloud computing-based teaching resource platform [8] can optimize and integrate the introduction of more high-quality teaching resources. This system can also enable the reasonable allocation and sharing of teaching resources and maximize the utilization of school teaching resources. Moreover, the system can meet the needs of teachers and students in teaching and learning. Demands have strengthened the integration of a new generation of information technology and teaching. The smart campus built by Shandong University of Science and Technology based on the big data ecological chain [9] has explored a set of practical and feasible models with a promotion value in the aspects of online learning space, remote teaching platform, media resource platform, and teacher information education guarantee system. The campus has achieved good results in promoting school education and teaching reform. Moreover, the smart campus of the mixed reality holographic learning model [10] builds a "ubiquitous learning system" on the basis of "5G+MR," that is, a holographic school that integrates online and offline (hybrid) time and space learning. The student status management system based on blockchain technology [11] provides a new way of thinking for the improvement of the student status management system.

In summary, the current construction of the vocational education teaching system focuses on the integration of information technology and education and teaching. However, the general lack of a unified layout makes realizing the interconnection of teaching data impossible. The direction of education informatization investment is not always clear, and the emphasis on "hard" rather than "soft" always exists. In terms of efficiency, the large investment in teaching hardware has not brought significant results that match it.

3 Intelligent Teaching System of Vocational Education

3.1 Overall Model Architecture Design

The intelligent teaching system of vocational education proposed in this study is divided into five modules: intelligent classroom, intelligent teaching mode, intelligent cloud platform, digital intelligence evaluation, and intelligent certification. Figure 1 shows that the use of a variety of new-generation information technologies, such as the Internet of Things, AI, big data, cloud computing, and blockchain, comprehensively covers the "teaching, learning, management, evaluation, and certification" links of the teaching process to create A new intelligent teaching system for vocational education. Multi-directional technology radiation to each module through a new generation of information technology can effectively support the transformation of traditional teaching models to MOOC, SPOC, and flipped classrooms, enabling accurate teaching management and scientific decision-making.

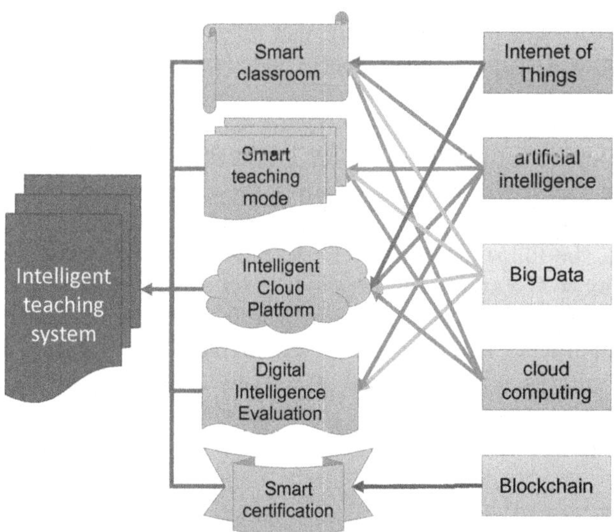

Fig. 1. Intelligent teaching system model

3.2 Smart Classroom Model Design and Application

The functional design of information-based smart classrooms should be able to meet the requirements of intelligent perception and control related hardware equipment, including wallpaper color matching, lighting and temperature control of the entire space of the classroom, and various forms of desks and chairs. This design emphasizes the harmony and unity of people, classrooms, and control systems, which should meet the teaching needs of multiple teaching modes, such as traditional teaching, micro-classes, MOOC, SPOC, and flipped classrooms. This design aims to create a full-time, flexible, and support ubiquitous learning intelligent classroom and achieve the purpose of closely connecting the intelligent cloud platform system online and connecting the actual teaching activities offline.

Figure 2 shows the smart classroom model. The smart classroom has a large LED display or projection screen, an electronic whiteboard, computer teaching aids, human–computer interaction functions, and others to present teaching content in multiple angles and ways. The classroom also has a temperature and humidity sensor and smoke sensor, and classroom temperature intelligent control and fire safety monitoring are realized through the Internet of Things technology. This classroom has a wireless network function, supports the access of various mobile terminal devices, and ensures that multiple terminal devices can access the network anytime and anywhere. Moreover, it has an intelligent sound reinforcement function and supports audio playback and classroom sound collection, teacher pickups, student pickups, speakers, student tracking cameras, teacher tracking cameras, and other equipment that can meet daily teaching, micro-classes, MOOC, SPOC, and flipped classrooms and other teaching needs. Furthermore, this smart classroom has a teaching recording and broadcasting function, provides teaching video playback resources for students' review after class, and supports daily teaching observation class, leadership tour, supervision, and evaluation class.

AI deep learning technology plays an important role in the construction of smart classrooms. Through AI based on YOLO's multi-scale parallel face detection algorithm [12], the distribution data of the class face are obtained using an AI camera, and the AI host can realize intelligent roll-calling. The AI of this classroom has the following characteristics: intelligently control the number of lights according to the number of people to achieve energy saving; detect the situation of listening to the class with faces (the face will be in front of the teacher in class), and upload the data to the cloud platform big data center as the situation of students attending class attentively, which can not only effectively prevent students from playing with their mobile phones in class but can also achieve an intelligent attendance function.

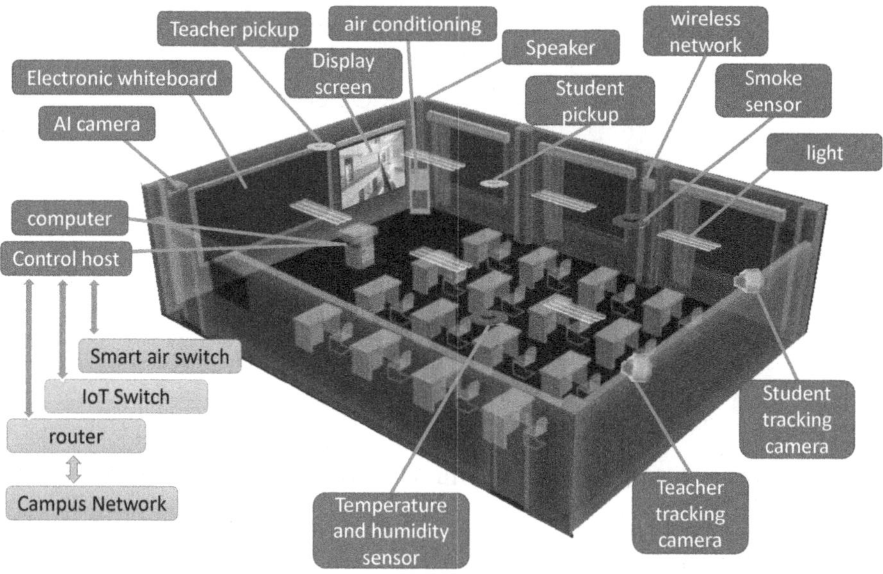

Fig. 2. Smart classroom model

3.3 Application of Smart Teaching Model

The smart teaching model based on the new generation of information technology has completely changed the traditional teaching model and formed a mixed teaching model with traditional models, MOOCs, micro-courses, SPOCs, and flipped classrooms. Figures 3 and 4 show that teachers use the cloud platform to implement intelligent lesson preparation and resource indexing, record micro-classes in the smart classroom before class, and carefully design MOOC online courses. In the course of class, the smart classroom is used to realize smart attendance, in-class evaluation, teaching recording and broadcasting, classroom interaction, and various teaching activities, such as SPOC and flipped classrooms. After class, teachers can implement online homework assignments, launch questionnaire surveys, online voting, online exams, and tutoring and answering questions through the cloud platform. This smart teaching model can help facilitate the development of teachers' teaching work, teach students in accordance with their aptitude, and improve teaching efficiency.

Students can preview online MOOC courses by logging in to the cloud platform before class. During class, students can rely on the intelligent classroom to realize the functions of group collaboration, inquiry and discussion, question raising, and answering on demand. After class, students can also use the student terminal of the teaching cloud platform to perform MOOC learning, online questioning, submission of homework, intelligent missing and filling vacancies, and other learning activities. This function allows achieving the combination of student online independent learning and precise guidance, which will greatly improve students' autonomy and flexibility of learning.

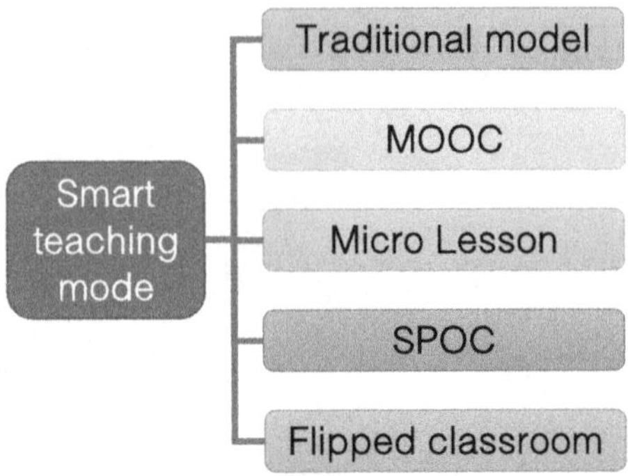

Fig. 3. Smart teaching model

3.4 Design and Application of Smart Cloud Platform Model

The intelligent cloud platform based on AI, big data, cloud computing, and Internet of Things technologies integrates platform, teaching, and management functions to build an integrated information environment and new media teaching methods. Figure 4 shows that the platform can be divided into intelligent classroom end, intelligent management end, teacher end, student end, and enterprise end. Through the application of "cloud + terminal," the seamless connection of students, teachers, schools, and enterprises, including the integration of schools and enterprises, is realized. Teachers log on to the intelligent cloud platform, make MOOCs and online teaching activities, obtain students' learning status data according to the big data analysis provided by the big data center, and provide accurate guidance to poor students. Students log on to the intelligent cloud platform to complete online previews before class and targeted reviews after class to better achieve personalized and differentiated learning. Enterprise engineers log in to the enterprise client to provide real-time guidance on students' internship plans, content, process, and situations. Teaching managers log in to the intelligent management terminal of the cloud platform to monitor the electrical equipment in the smart classrooms of the school, achieve green energy conservation, and effectively manage the teaching and learning situation through the data analysis of the big data center. The intelligent cloud platform also provides cloud storage services for various users, which can realize the storage and sharing of files on the cloud U disk anytime and anywhere in the smart campus. This function not only guarantees the safety of data but also eliminates the trouble of bringing a U disk.

3.5 Functional Design of Digital Intelligence Evaluation Model

Traditional teaching evaluation is manifested by teachers' multiple evaluations of students' knowledge level and learning performance, evaluation of teaching process and teaching effect, and on-site evaluation of experts and peers. The application of a new generation of information technology has promoted the reform

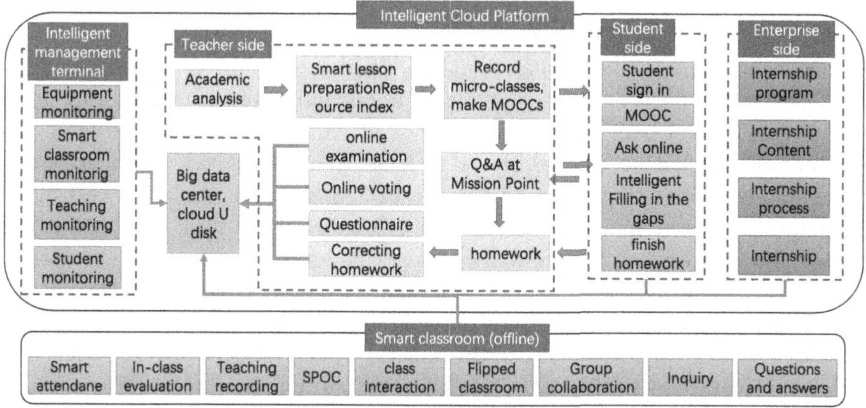

Fig. 4. Smart cloud platform model

of the evaluation subject, content, method, and result of classroom teaching evaluation. Figure 5 shows that the big data center of the intelligent cloud platform measures the learning progress of online knowledge points in the learning process of students, online participation in learning and discussion, offline classroom listening, homework scores, test scores, practical ability, and others. The academic situation data of the aspect are collected. After data analysis and data mining, intelligent analysis and evaluation of students' learning conditions are carried out, and a personalized chemical situation diagnosis for the students is further obtained. AI technology is used to provide learners with accurate learning strategy guidance through the intelligent cloud platform to push the intelligent leakage and filling of learning materials for students' personal academic conditions. The AI technology maximizes the function of stimulus and guidance of digital intelligence evaluation, helps teachers and students to complete the teaching goals, and improves the teaching effect.

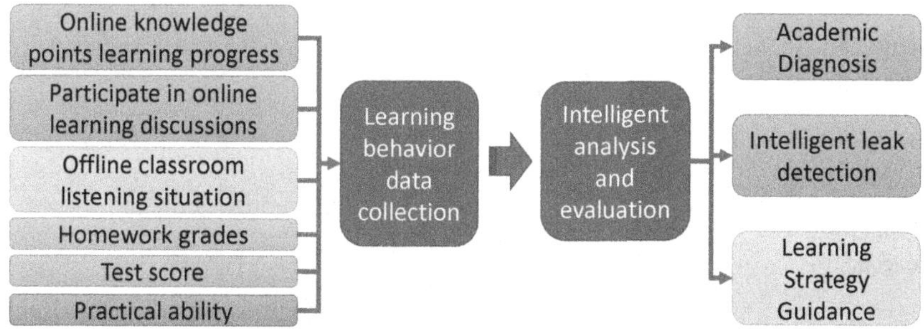

Fig. 5. Digital intelligence evaluation model

3.6 Functional Design and Application of Smart Certification

The smart authentication module is mainly implemented by blockchain technology. The blockchain is composed of multiple mutually distrusting blocks, which are decentralized, open, and transparent and cannot be tampered with. The non-tamperable feature of the blockchain can realize digital certificates, that is, the anti-counterfeiting function. At present, vocational education certificates are generally stored in paper form, and academic education information can be filed and inquired on Xuexin. However, other skills qualification certificates, such as 1+X vocational qualification certificates, may not have query services on related websites. If the blockchain is used to store academic education and training authorization certificates, including the digital signatures on the certificates, then the relevant certificate information can be permanently and safely stored on the blockchain. This case can effectively reduce the loss and damage of the certificates and can also quickly complete the verification of the certificate. Hence, the use of blockchain to save certificates not only solves the efficiency problem of learning achievement verification but also forms traceable records of students' lifelong learning achievements, which can greatly reduce academic fraud, academic qualifications, and inquiries in society. Furthermore, this blockchain can retrace the time-consuming and laborious issues and promote the integration of documentary certificates under the 1 + X certificate system.

We take the 1 + X vocational qualification certificate application for a digital certificate as an example. Figure 6 depicts that, after a student participates in

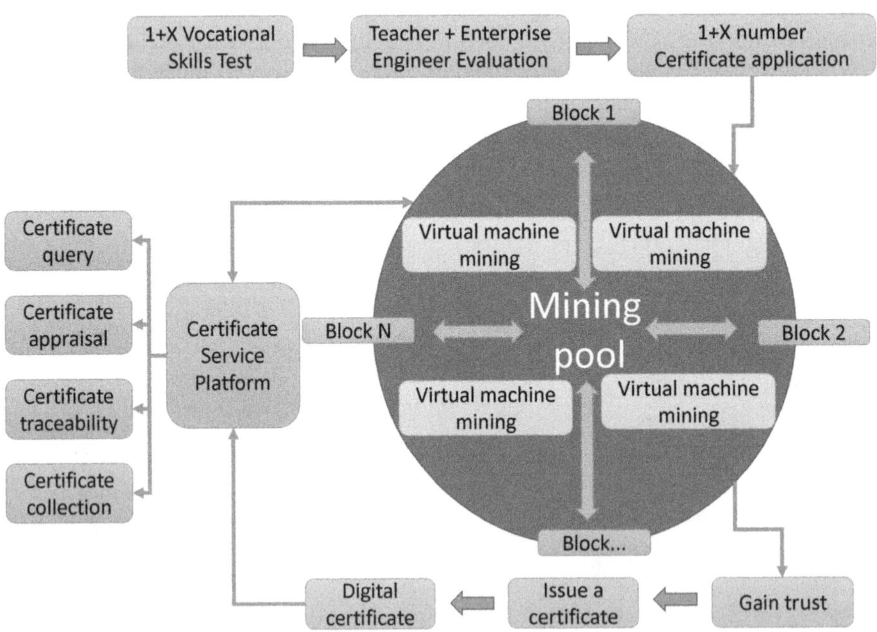

Fig. 6. Blockchain releases the model of 1 + X professional qualification certificate

the 1+X vocational skills test, teachers and enterprise engineers will evaluate the student's skill level. They will generate relevant digital certificates and digital signatures for qualified students and upload the application information to the blockchain. The mining pool and each block in the blockchain can be realized by virtual machine mining, which reduces the input of physical machines and thus reduces equipment costs. The block records information about the entire life cycle of the certificate, such as sample acceptance, testing, verification, approval, modification, and invalidation. Thus, users can query the e-certificate production process. After the key information and digital signature of the digital certificate are trusted through blockchain technology, the digital certificate is issued to the customer. The certificate service platform provides functions, such as certificate inquiry, certificate identification, certificate traceability, and certificate receiving.

4 Conclusion

Through in-depth research on the Internet of Things technology related to space environment management, big data analysis and processing technology, AI detection technology based on deep learning, cloud computing, blockchain, and other technologies, this study proposes intelligent teaching of vocational education based on a new generation of information technology system. The system strengthens the integration of offline and online teaching, with teacher–student interactive teaching as the core, service teaching as the orientation, and integration of the teaching process before, during, and after class. This system can collect teaching data in various aspects and provide multi-dimensional evaluations to realize the ubiquity of classroom learning and extracurricular learning. The system can also form a student-centered teaching environment, improve the intelligence of the intelligent classroom environment control, and realize multi-management and multi-type user terminal equipment access. The introduction of the smart cloud platform has strengthened the integration of industry and education and school–enterprise cooperation and promoted the integration of documents and certificates under the 1 + X certificate system. Therefore, the teaching system fully covers the "teaching, learning, evaluation, management, and certification" links of the teaching process. The smooth implementation of this teaching system provides a reference for the theoretical research and practical application of vocational education intelligent teaching, thereby promoting the reform of the vocational education intelligent teaching system.

References

1. Yan, Liu, Yingsheng, Chen: Evaluation of smart classroom design scheme based on Internet of Things. Mod. Electron. Technol. **43**(570(19)), 171–174 (2020)
2. Zhang, Y., Zhu, L., Zeng, S., Zheng, X.: Practice and thinking of online-online hybrid teaching under the background of the new crown epidemic. China Agric. Educ. **21**(154(02)), 4–48+59 (2020)

3. Yang, X., Cai, T.: Research on the co-construction and sharing of information resources of the university of applied technology in the environment of cloud computing and big data. Educ. Modernization **000**(045), 183–186 (2017)
4. Breslow, L., Pritchard, D.E., Deboer, J., Stump, G.S., Ho, A.D., Seaton, D.T.: Studying learning in the worldwide classroom research into edx's first MOOC. Res. Pract. Assess. **8**, 13–25 (2013)
5. Chunfeng, R., et al.: Application of small private online course combining flipped classroom approach in training of general knowledge and skills for new graduate nurses. J. Nurs. Sci. (2019)
6. Liu, T., Zhao, T., Chen, Q., Feng, Q., Zhang, R.: Smart classroom lighting control system design based on machine vision. Artif. Intell. Rob. Res. **8**(4), 7 (2019)
7. Jiahai, K.E.: Discussion on the construction of smart classrooms in colleges and universities based on the internet of things and big data. Wirel. Internet Technol. **17**(18715), 44–46 (2020)
8. Wu, Y., Mi, J., Sun, Y., Hu, C.: Construction and management of university teaching resource platform under cloud computing. Int. Publ. Rel. (12) (2020)
9. Zhang, B., Li, Y.: Discussion on the construction of smart campus based on big data enginetaking shandong university of science and technology as an example. Shandong Education (Higher Education) (4) (2020)
10. Zeng, X., Ding, L.: Smart campus construction based on "5g+mr" mixed reality holographic learning mode. Educ. Commun. Technol. (4) (2020)
11. Li, Z., Gao, C., Liu, M., Dai, C., Fan, Y.: student status management system based on blockchain technology. J. Sichuan Univ. Nat. Sci. Ed. **3**, 450–456 (2019)
12. He, H., Wang, J., Hui, K., Chen, Q.: Multi-scale parallel face detection algorithm based on yolo. Comput. Eng. Des. **41**(40509), 167–173 (2020)

Research on the Reform of Governance System of Higher Vocational Colleges Under the Background of Modern Information Technology

Pang Li(✉)

Guangzhou Vocational College of Technology and Business, Guangzhou 510091, Guangdong, China
37692345@qq.com

Abstract. Modern information technology promotes the reform of governance mode in higher vocational colleges, promotes the scientificity and accuracy of decision-making, and realizes the reasonable allocation of campus resources. At the same time, promoting management with modern information technology is the need for the development of higher vocational colleges. To promote the informatization of governance in higher vocational colleges, we need to improve the informatization construction mechanism, build a shared informatization system, rationally set up the management process of higher vocational colleges, improve the information skills of faculty and staff, and strengthen online moral education.

Keywords: Modern information technology · Governance of higher vocational colleges · Reform

Today's society has stepped into the information society, human production, life, thinking, learning methods have been greatly affected, the global education development has been deeply marked by information technology, information technology is not only changing the present education, but also shaping the future of education. The governance of future education must be modernized governance relying on information technology. The full use of information technology to strengthen the governance of higher vocational colleges, promote the construction of an intelligent level of governance, and build a smart campus are also important signs of the modernization of vocational education. Applying information technology to assist the administrative management of higher vocational colleges, building an information platform, incorporating the main processes and key links of the school's human, financial, material, and affair management work into the information management system, achieving informatization and intelligent management of school work, and promoting Information transmission is more direct and rapid, ensuring the accuracy and timeliness of information, saving time and cost of doing things, breaking traditional departmental boundaries and geographical restrictions, making hierarchical organizations more flattened, and coordinating management between departments more

© ICST Institute for Computer Sciences, Social Informatics and Telecommunications Engineering 2022
Published by Springer Nature Switzerland AG 2022. All Rights Reserved
S. Shi et al. (Eds.): 6GN 2021, LNICST 439, pp. 617–624, 2022.
https://doi.org/10.1007/978-3-031-04245-4_54

closely Seamless and clearer implementation of responsibilities, thus providing important technical support for the construction of advanced, scientific, and efficient higher vocational college governance [1].

1 The Influence of Modern Information Technology on the Management of Higher Vocational Colleges

1.1 Promote the Reform of Governance in Higher Vocational College

Information technology has entered the management system of higher vocational colleges, which has changed the school's management mode, management thought and management system. Using artificial intelligence technology to change the organizational structure and management system, optimize the operation mechanism and service mode, and realize the campus fine management and personalized service, can comprehensively improve the school governance level. For the problems faced by higher vocational college governance, such as unclear departmental responsibilities, asymmetry of individual rights and responsibilities, unclear resource management background, and unimplemented assessment management system, information construction can provide a solution path with the least resistance. Through data support, development and sharing, resource integration, interconnection and other capabilities, schools are encouraged to establish a shared, open and transparent governance environment. Through modern information technology, the different governance bodies of higher vocational colleges can be clearly defined in the division of responsibilities and powers, and effectively solve the problems of absence and offside in the traditional education administration process. Through the reorganization of the process, the role of each subject can be brought into full play.

1.2 Promote the Scientificity and Accuracy of Decision-Making

With the introduction of information technology, the importance of data in management becomes more prominent. Using data to find, analyze and solve problems, with the help of data reporting, online analysis and processing, benchmark analysis, data mining, etc., is conducive to the scientificity and accuracy of decision-making. With the advent of the information age, the emergence of rich and varied learning platforms, interactive software and other data collection software provides an effective way for higher vocational colleges to make scientific decisions. When making relevant decisions, leaders can analyze the data in the network information system, so as to make more scientific and advanced decisions. Through the deep mining of the massive data produced by higher vocational colleges, the decision-making mode of higher vocational colleges will change from the traditional empirical management to the scientific and precise decision-making mode driven by data [2].

1.3 Realize the Reasonable Allocation of Campus Resources

The traditional mode of management and resource allocation in higher vocational colleges requires a large amount of human resources and takes up much time and energy, which greatly hinders the improvement of the efficiency of education management. Modern network information management technology can change the traditional management mode and resource allocation mode of higher vocational colleges, and can more effectively allocate management resources and human resources in higher vocational colleges. In the management of higher vocational colleges and in the process of implementing network information processing, the internet can quickly and conveniently distribute all its resources rationally, effectively saving the time and manpower wasted in the resource allocation of all departments and levels, and greatly improving the work efficiency [3].

2 Promoting Governance with Modern Information Technology is the Need of Higher Vocational Colleges' Own Development

2.1 The Modernization of National Governance System Requires the Informatization of Governance Means in Higher Vocational Colleges

National policies and systems restrict the development of vocational education. At the same time, the reform of vocational education must adapt to the requirements of the country's major policies. Since the 18th National Congress of the Communist Party of China (CPC), the CPC Central Committee has continuously improved its governance through a series of major institutional arrangements and institutional reform and innovation. T The 19th CPC National Congress once again stressed the need to continuously modernize China's governance system and capacity. In 2016, the "13th Five-Year Plan for Educational Informatization" issued by the Ministry of Education proposed to "enhance the modernization level of education governance system and governance ability, form an education information system that is compatible with the development goal of education modernization, and give full play to the revolutionary impact of information technology on education." "Promote the implementation of the Code for the Construction of Vocational Colleges' Digital Campus, and ensure that schools of all levels and types generally have an information based teaching environment". In 2017, Du Zhanyuan, Vice Minister of Education, pointed out in the first "Education Think Tank and Education Governance Roundtable Forum of 50 People" that education informatization 2.0 under the "Internet+" environment should be promoted to promote the transformation of education informatization from integrated application to innovative development. In 2018, Lei Chaozi, director of the Department of Science and Technology of the Ministry of Education, pointed out the need to explore a new model of education governance in the information age. This series of policies and systems related to governance provide a policy and institutional environment for the informatization governance of higher vocational colleges.

2.2 The Development of the Scale of Higher Vocational Colleges Needs Information Management

With the country's strong support for vocational education, the number of vocational schools and the number of people receiving vocational education has also increased sharply. According to the Statistics Communique on the Development of National Education in 2019, there are 1,265 undergraduate colleges and 1,423 higher vocational colleges (junior colleges). Higher vocational colleges have become an important part of higher education. In 2019, the Government Work Report proposed that higher vocational colleges increase enrollment by 1 million, and in 2020, the Government Work Report further proposed that higher vocational colleges increase enrollment by 2 million. This is a major measure to stabilize employment and promote development. For higher vocational colleges, it is not only an opportunity for development, but also a challenge to governance ability. The expansion of the scale of students in the school, the structure of the source of students presents multi-layered and complicated, the starting level of students' learning is uneven, and the diversification of learning needs, etc., have increased the difficulty of teaching governance. The use of modern information technology can continuously optimize the policy implementation environment, integrate policy implementation resources, form a policy implementation force, and improve policy implementation efficiency.

2.3 The Management of Modern Higher Vocational Colleges Needs Information Support

Under the background of the information age, the teaching and research work of higher vocational colleges cannot be separated from information technology, which has penetrated into all aspects of campus life. Higher vocational colleges with advanced information development concepts, solid information infrastructure support, and strong information technology application capabilities often have core competitiveness in development. Informatization construction has become a strategic measure to promote the modernization of higher vocational colleges and universities, and it is an important driving force for higher vocational colleges to implement the fundamental task of establishing morality and improving the ability of science and technology to create and serve society.

2.4 The Impact of the Epidemic Has Further Promoted the Information Governance of Higher Vocational Colleges

The important role of informatization in university governance has been further highlighted in the COVID-19 outbreak. Many higher vocational colleges have promoted informationization to a strategic, fundamental and leading important supporting position. During the epidemic period, all higher vocational colleges adopted new methods such as online teaching, online office and online academic conference to replace the traditional teaching, scientific research and management. Zheng Qinghua believes that the epidemic has brought three major changes to the informatization construction of colleges and universities. First, online education has changed from the exploration of the past and demonstrated by a few people to the new normal and universal. Second, the information literacy of school administrators and teachers and students has been comprehensively improved; The third is to let people's understanding of education informatization from point to point, teaching becomes the superposition of reality and virtual [4].

3 Difficulties in the Application of Information Technology in the Management of Higher Vocational Colleges

3.1 Weak Awareness of Information Management

Due to the inertia of the traditional school management mode for many years, the staff lacks certain information technology knowledge. Some managers are accustomed to traditional management methods, fail to correctly recognize the positive effects of emerging technologies on the management of higher vocational colleges, do not have a good understanding of informatization, and cannot combine emerging information technologies with the actual situation of higher vocational colleges. It restricts the development of information governance in higher vocational colleges.

3.2 Incomplete Information Construction Facilities

Informatization construction needs to improve the corresponding equipment and facilities, but in reality, many higher vocational colleges are unwilling to spend manpower and financial resources in the informatization construction, resulting in insufficient hardware facilities. Only some simple and basic technical equipment and software are introduced. Although these equipment and software assist the school's administrative management work to a certain extent, they have not exerted the substantive effect of information management. Most of the management work is still continue the traditional model. Insufficient database capacity, inability to process information in a timely and effective manner, and other issues have seriously affected the governance level of higher vocational colleges. The construction of information platform is not comprehensive, and the transmission, processing and communication of information are slow. The traditional bureaucratic management is adopted, administrative instructions are conveyed at one level, and people and paper documents are the main means of information transmission, so the efficiency of governance is relatively low.

3.3 Lack of Unified Planning for Informatization Construction

Each department of higher vocational colleges lacks the corresponding information communication and the relevant data is incoherent, which seriously affects the efficiency of information management in higher vocational colleges. In the early stage of development, the management system has not been able to meet the requirements of social education reform and development in a comprehensive and systematic way, and there are many design defects and deficiencies, which make the whole system unable to be timely updated, resulting in low efficiency of higher vocational education management. At the same time, the compatibility of information system among multiple departments in higher vocational colleges is poor, and there is a lack of effective contact and communication system among departments, which results in low efficiency of information transmission and resource sharing among departments in higher vocational colleges, and poor resource allocation [5].

3.4 Lack of Information Management Talents

Informatization construction requires corresponding talents to manage it. However, as far as the current situation is concerned, there is a serious shortage of informatization construction personnel in higher vocational colleges. Some liberal arts personnel who do not understand technology are placed in management positions in the information technology department. The personnel are not strong in professional ability, and they do not have sufficient mastery of big data and communication technology, and cannot be used in practice. The lack of talents in information construction is a serious obstacle Informatization governance of higher vocational colleges [6].

4 Promoting the Path of Informationization Management in Higher Vocational College

We must focus on promoting the modernization of governance technology, adapt to the requirements of the "Internet+" era, actively use modern advanced information technologies such as big data, cloud technology, Internet of Things, and blockchain, and use the construction of smart campuses as a starting point to promote modern advanced information technology and In-depth integration of the governance of higher vocational colleges, and strive to build a new pattern of governance technology informatization in higher vocational colleges where "networked governance", "big data governance" and "cloud governance" coexist, and promote the governance methods of higher vocational colleges to move from traditional to modern, highlighting the modernization level of governance technology in higher vocational colleges.

4.1 Improve Informatization Construction Mechanism

We should build a large network security informatization work pattern, incorporate the college management information into the overall development plan of the college, and include education informatization funds in the financial budget, establish an informatization leading group, with the school's top leader as the team leader, and the vice president in charge of informatization as the deputy team leader. The informatization construction expert advisory committee and the informatization construction coordination working group are formed to form a unified leadership of the party committee, the division of labor and coordination of the party and government, The overall work pattern in which all departments actively participate provides organizational guarantee for the development of school informatization [7].

4.2 Unified Planning to Build a Shared Information System

We will promote cross-department, cross-level, cross-field process linkage, open up the "last mile" of serving teachers and students, and realize collaborative governance. In the process of development and application of the management system, a platform for mutual communication and sharing has been established with various colleges and departments in the school, and the corresponding ports are connected. As a result, a unified standard of information management can be formed in higher vocational colleges, and the required students, school status, teachers' course information and materials can be unified and standardized input and storage, convenient and timely retrieval and browsing, comprehensive resource sharing, and improve the work efficiency of education management information. Building a shared data center of the school, coordinating business management departments, strengthening data quality management, data sharing, can realize the sharing and interworking of structured data of all departments of the school.

4.3 Intensify Investigation, Set up Reasonable Management Process of Higher Vocational Colleges

The information technology department should strengthen the research and communication of various business demand departments, jointly straighten out the data circulation requirements and the full-cycle management process, and investigate the data needs and data problems of each department. According to the requirements and standards of the superior departments and the construction and development of the school, the information technology department should also reasonably set the management process to ensure that the management process can effectively and accurately realize information integration. Combined with scientific management system, process standard, tool standard, etc., we can minimize the contact frequency between clerks and service objects. After the task is integrated, all work steps, work links, work points, precautions, etc. related to the completion of a specific work can be fully integrated. In turn, we create a comprehensive business process.

4.4 Strengthen Training to Improve the Information Skills of Faculty and Staff

According to the actual situation of campus operations and the actual application requirements of big data technology and information management in teaching and scientific research, effective measures have been taken to strengthen the training of faculty and staff according to local conditions, and all management personnel will be given basic training on information technology-related business knowledge on a regular basis. So that all management personnel can continue to accumulate relevant knowledge on the basis of enhancing the awareness of modern science and technology. It enables them to truly feel the positive changes brought about by modern information technology to their management work, and stimulates their initiative to apply cutting-edge technologies. Through organizing faculty and staff to learn practical skills related to the information management system, regularly carrying out skills training and updates, keeping pace with the development of current information, improving the quality and skills of college education management information personnel and better using the internal software of the system to facilitate, we can realize a modern working mode to improve work efficiency and save related resources.

4.5 Build an Information Culture and Strengthen Online Moral Education

In order to effectively improve the information management capabilities of higher vocational colleges, it is necessary to strengthen the promotion of information culture, raise the awareness of all teachers and students in the era of big data, deeply understand the importance of improving information management capabilities, and form a digital management atmosphere throughout the school. At the same time, because the network, the carrier of information dissemination, is a virtual world, by strengthening the security awareness of campus network center managers, they can uphold a high sense of responsibility and work enthusiasm, and conduct strict supervision and investigation of network security in order to find and prevent the occurrence of network adverse events in time. By strengthening network security publicity on campus, all faculty and students are aware of the harm and consequences of network information leakage.

5 Conclusion

In summary, modernization is inseparable from informatization, and an important symbol of modernization is informatization. In the context of the modernization of the national governance system, the construction of the modernization of the governance of higher vocational colleges is to realize the informatization of governance methods. In a modern society with highly developed network and information technology, The application of information strategy, the construction of information management platform, the maximum integration and use of information data resources, optimize the management process of higher vocational colleges, improve the information management mechanism, improve the level of information management personnel, is an important support for the modernized management of higher vocational colleges.

References

1. Hui, X.: Research on the organizational structure of higher vocational colleges. J. Natl. Acad. Educ. Adm. **2**, 31–39 (2019)
2. Ying, C.: University management innovation in the era of big data. Chin. Pub. Adm. **8**(8), 150–152 (2016)
3. Li, W.: The importance and practice of information technology in the management of higher education. Modernization Educ. (7), 239 (2018)
4. Yilong, Z.: CIO perspective: how informatization supports university governance. China Educ. Netw. **1**, 19–21 (2021)
5. Zhao, C.: The importance and practice of information technology in the management of higher education e. J. Jiamusi Vocational Inst. (1), 52–53 (2020)
6. Zeng, Y.: Research on the application strategy of big data technology in information management system of colleges and universities. Digit. Commun. World (3), 177 (2020)
7. Wei, C.: Promote the modernization of university governance system and governance ability with informatization. Beijing Educ. (Higher Educ.) (4), 12–14 (2021)

Evaluation of Chinese Smart City Implementations: A Case Study of 'Cloud Seeds Plans' in Shenzhen

Aiping Zheng(✉)

Huizhou Engineering Vocational College, Huizhou 516000, China
shc_scut@qq.com

Abstract. In the past decade, smart city has been regarded as being able to promote urban governance and tackle socio-economic issues. Many scholars have argued the definitions, benchmarks and indicators of such topic from various perspectives and dimensions. However, their conceptual approaches pay over attention on the Anglophone world and lack the capability of explaining Chinese scenario. Therefore, after reviewing the critical bibliography, this paper proposes a new benchmark of Chinese smart city according to the specific situations in China and evaluate this framework based on a smart city project, 'Cloud seeds plans' in Shenzhen. The result indicates that the project performs relatively well in creativity and social innovations, but need to be enhanced in open governances. Moreover, the project shows great potentiality in both smart governance as well as smart specialization strategies during the upsurge holdings era of electricity devices in the future. In conclusion, such localization attempts of smart city on one hand is conducive to building up a better sustainable form of urban development, on the other hand, may lead to a deeper discussion on the smart city implementations in third world countries.

Keywords: Smart city benchmarks · Cloud seeds plans · SWOT matrix

1 Background Introduction of Smart Cities

1.1 Original Definitions and History

Nowadays, with the rapid urbanization process, cities have gradually become the basis of human civilization as more than 50% population, 3.3 billion, live in the urban areas [1]. Meanwhile, the increasing population in urban districts causes many ecological and public disorder problems [2, 3], such as traffic congestion [4] and social segregations [5]. To deal with these issues, plenty of new concepts and subjects, such as sustainable urban planning, have been created and utilized during last few decades. As the most famous one among them, smart city was initially put forward by IBM Corporation in 2008, which aims at establishing an "instrumented, interconnected and intelligent city' [6].

© ICST Institute for Computer Sciences, Social Informatics and Telecommunications Engineering 2022
Published by Springer Nature Switzerland AG 2022. All Rights Reserved
S. Shi et al. (Eds.): 6GN 2021, LNICST 439, pp. 625–635, 2022.
https://doi.org/10.1007/978-3-031-04245-4_55

Nevertheless, except for the original definitions of smart city (See Table 1), many scholars put forward quite a few new but different concepts. According to Table 1, it can be concluded that all of these definitions demonstrate smart city from different perspectives and embody various contents, which means that smart city always involves many different fields and the concept itself is continuously evolving. Thus, giving a universal definition for smart city is considerably difficult, but defining it from wider perspectives is to some extent possible. In our paper, we define smart city as a systematically high-tech intensive city that employs information technology to capture, collect, integrate and analyses all types of real-time or historic data for better optimized decision-making and implementation of various organizations, which eventually endeavors to achieve six fundamental goals: better competitive economy, more efficient and public-participating

Table 1. Different definitions of smart city.

Definition	Source
(Smart) cities can be defined as the "instrumented, Interconnected and intelligent cities" Here, "Instrumented" means the capability of capturing and collecting data by some Instruments such as sensors smartphones and other devices; "interconnected" refers to integrate and upload data into an open platform which allows interacting communication across different c/ty services; "intelligent" means a process of better decision-making and Implementation through a series of complicated analysis and simulations [6]	Harrison et al. (Original Definition)
(Smart) cities as territories with high capacity for learning and innovation, which is built-in the creativity of their population, their institutions of knowledge creation and their digital infrastructure for communication and knowledge management [7]	Komninos
Smart city as a high-tech intensive and advanced city that connects people, information and city elements using new technologies in order to create a sustainable, greener city competitive and innovative commerce, and an increased life quality [8]	Bakici et al.
Being a smart city means using all available technology and resources in an intelligent and coordinated manner to develop urban centers that are at once integrated habitable, and sustainable [9]	Barrionuevo et al.
Smart city refers to a local entity-a district city, region or small country which takes a holistic approach to employing information technologies with real-time analysis that encourages sustainable economic development [10]	IDA
…	…

governance, more convenient mobility, more comfortable living conditions, more sustainable environment and more developed social and human capital. More importantly, under different scenarios, the definition, especially the fundamental goals, possibly needs to be 'calibrated' in terms of specific situations. In other words, the definition of smart city in China may different from it in Europe as their citizen's ideal smart cities are totally different.

1.2 Smart City and Its Benchmarks in China

Similar with cities in developed countries, quite a few metropolitans in China have initialized scores of smart city projects aiming for tackling urban issues triggered by rapid urbanization process. These projects include a shared bicycle project called OFO in Beijing, some smart urban planning documents in Shanghai and commercial smart city projects leaded by Huawei in Shenzhen. It can be said that smart city is currently considered as a feasible and attractive direction to better develop or construct urban areas in China, although the evaluation system of their initializations is still under discussion.

From the aforementioned discussion, the evaluation system of Chinese smart city project is to a certain extent academically worthwhile. To approach this, the definition of smart city in China should be initially worked out. Concerning the previous part in the paper, it is cumbersome but necessary to revise the definition of smart city based on the Chinese specific situations. More specifically, the fundamental part of smart city definition for China is almost same as the original one, but the goals part is possibly different, which is demonstrated in Table 2.

Table 2. Definition revision in China.

	Original	Chinese specific
Fundamental part	Smart city is a systematically high-tech intensive city that employs information technology to capture, collect integrate and analyses all types of real-time or historic data for better optimized decision-making and implementation of various organizations	(Same)
Goals part	It endeavors to achieve six fundamental goals: better competitive economy, more efficient and public-participating governance, more convenient mobility, more comfortable living conditions, more sustainable environment and more developed social and human capital	It endeavors to achieve six fundamental goals: better competitive economy, relatively efficient and public-participating governance, more convenient mobility, more comfortable living conditions, (important)more sustainable environment and relatively developed social and human capital

In addition, based on the revised goals in the smart city definition, a benchmarking system (See in appendix) can be established to assess whether a city or a project achieve these aims. In this system, the first relevant group which consists of six basic characteristics are derived from six basic goals. Under the first order group, the second relevant group which are able to reflect the essential aspects of each characteristic in the first group is comprised of 24 indicators (see Fig. 1).

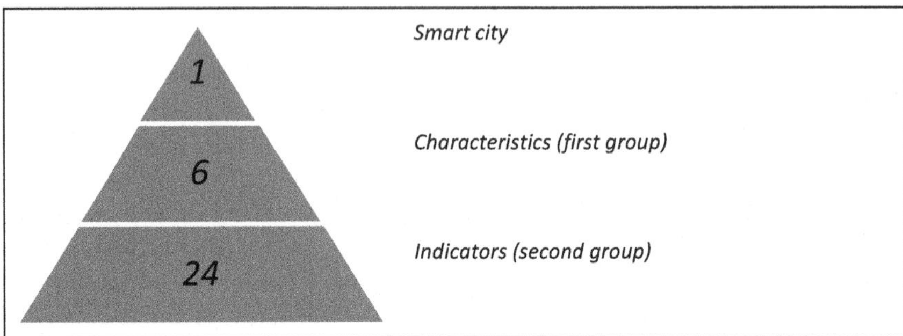

Energy	Sustainable Urban Mobility	Information & Communication Technology	Smart & Open Government	Smart Living	Smart People
Poly-generation and distributed generation	Electrification of transport	Interoperability Platform	Open Government	Healthy environment	Affinity to lifelong learning
Participation in the generation, distribution and marketing of energy	Smart mobility	ICTs infrastructure	Creativity and Social Innovation	Tourism	Social and ethnic plurality
Districts with Nearly Zero Consumption Balance	Smart Transport Infrastructures	Smartization and Connectivity provision of services	Smart Government	Trade	Flexibility
Exemplary and efficiency in municipal facilities		Open Data Platform	Smart Specialization Strategies	Culture	Creativity

Fig. 1. Smart city benchmarking system in China.

2 Introduction of Shenzhen and "Cloud Seeds Plans"

2.1 Introduction of Shenzhen

As one of the fastest-growing metropolitans in the world during past two decades, Shenzhen is both a major city in Guangdong Province and the fourth largest and wealthiest cities of China [11]. About 30 years ago, Shenzhen was merely an ordinary and small Chinese market town of 30,000 people on the route of the Kowloon–Canton Railway, immediately north of Hong Kong. However, the situation was completely reversed in the 1980s when Shenzhen was promoted to city-status and later designated as the China's first Special Economic Zone (SEZ). Since then, Shenzhen has started its rapidly developing era and gradually become the Chinese "Silicon Valley". Nowadays, Shenzhen had not only transformed into a city with a population of 10,778,900 [12] but also become the home to headquarters of numerous high-tech companies and one of the major financial centers in China. However, as one of the Chinese cities experiencing the most rapid urbanization, Shenzhen is facing many urban problems including both typical issues (such as traffic congestion) and unique issues (such as urban village). To handle these problems, Shenzhen attempts to become smarter as well as more efficient and therefore launches many smart city-related projects, which can be either government-driven or business-driven or both. Thus, Shenzhen is selected as the researching target city not only due to its Innovation, creativity and developed economy but also because of its large population scale, typical history and urgent urban problems.

"Cloud seeds plans of Shenzhen", also known as "Urban dream workshop", is a government-driven and business-participated smart city project established in 2015. This project can actually be considered as a hatchery for "incubating" the smart city-related plans put forward by individuals or organizations (entire process in Fig. 2).

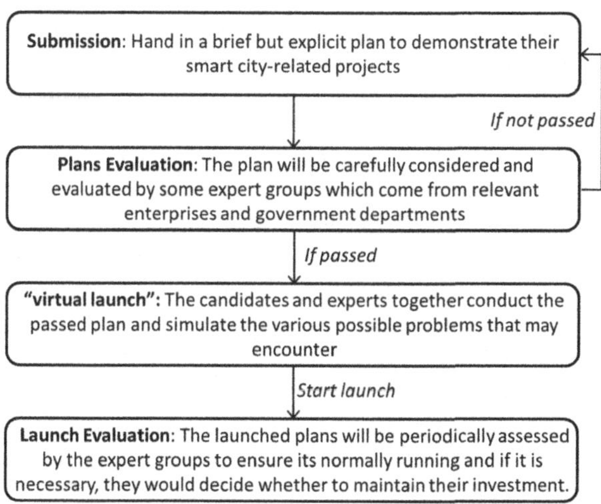

Fig. 2. The structure of 'Cloud seeds plans'.

In the project, government, business and individuals are all involved in this smart city project and play different roles in this initialization, which is one of the reasons why it is selected as the researching target project. Another reason is that this so-called "hatchery" has successfully incubated considerable numbers of smart plans according its website and thereby is regarded as one of the essential smart city projects in Shenzhen since its establishment.

The following essay is a critical assessment, which will employ a built benchmarking system to objectively evaluate the "Cloud seeds plans" in Shenzhen.

3 Evaluation of "Cloud Seeds Plans"

3.1 Evaluative Methodology

A SWOT Matrix, which is widely introduced into various subjects and projects, will be employed to assess the "Cloud seeds plans" (refer as target project in the following part). Here, S, W, O, T stands for strengths, weaknesses, opportunities and threats respectively [13, 14].

3.2 Evaluation

As the main part of the target project is run and managed by the government, the four government indicators under the efficient and public-participating governance characteristic will be considered as the main aspects to assess the target initialization.

Open Government. In the evaluation of this indicator, citizen participation & empowerment and managing transparency will be introduced as two sub-indicators to assess the target project. First of all, similar to the majority of smart initialization in China, the public participation and empowerment of the target initialization is to some extent to exist in name only. More specifically, the government does hold some telematics channels (project official website) and face-to-face channels (some conferences), but these so-called "public engagement channels" never slightly affect the eventual decisions of target initialization. This is possibly caused by two issues that are conducted not well enough. On one hand, suggestions put forward by citizens are always disregard and neglected by government officials, which is mainly because the majority of these suggestions are unreasonable or one-sided although there does contain some incisive, practical and rational suggestions. On the other hand, the government seldom publicizes its channel information, which causes that large numbers of citizens have never realized that they have the opportunity to participate in governance. Thus, due to problems on the suggestions adoption preference and publicity of channels, all the decisions of the target project are made by the government. Such decision-making mechanism may greatly affect the fairness and even damage the interests of some citizens in some scenarios, even if it works relatively efficient. In other words, the target project to some extent shows more weakness than strength from the perspective of citizen participation & empowerment.

Secondly, unlike citizen participation & empowerment, the target project performs relatively acceptable in the transparency, which is to some extent reflected from their official website. On the website, the citizens are empowered to acquire many related information including all the details of each plans (both passed and failed plans), the expert lists and their introductions, etc. Most importantly, for the plans in "virtual launch" process, all the information of them is real-timely refreshed. However, some essential information is still unpublished, for example, the rough funds allocation scheme or the reasons for stopping investment on a specific project. To conclude, the transparency can be considered as strength of the target project.

Nevertheless, there are some opportunities for the government to enhance its public engagement and transparency. Recently, China central government has published a document (Opinions on Strengthening the Construction of the Government, 2010) about government management, which encourages local government to establish a developed public participation system. That means the government may increase public participation in the propaganda meanwhile enhance its suggestions-adoption mechanism, which may create more chances for citizens to engage in decision-making process of each government project. Meanwhile, this document also emphasizes the transparency of governance especially the project involved in public engagement. It means that local governments possibly gradually publicize their work data and processes. However, for both citizen participation & empowerment and transparency sub-indicators, there are some threats may obstruct the promotion of public participation among which consciousness of citizenship is the most significant. In China, due to some cultural and historic reasons, Chinese citizens seldom tend to participate in politics, which is known as the continuation of "peasant consciousness" (Yuan, 2000). In other words, how to change the conservative consciousness of the major Chinese citizens will be a potential problem of future public participation.

Creativity and Social Innovation. For this indicator, the target project performs considerably well that can be reflected in two aspects. First of all, the target project has successfully awakened the enthusiasm of citizens and related institutions to innovate. According to its website, over 3000 smart city related plans are submitted during the first month after the project launched and half of these projects come from students' groups and non-profit oriented business organizations. In other words, considerable numbers of normal young citizens (not in the business field) engage in the target projects and share their innovative ideas. Secondly, the target project attempts to establish an initialized "platform" for supporting the citizen's ideas. As the previous brief introduction of the target projects, the platform can provide candidates sufficient capital and technical supports to ensure that each candidate is able to conduct their plans if they meet all the requirements and conditions of the platform. That means any insight, rational and practical ideas can be realized in the target project. However, such platform also has some shortcomings and the most significant one is about invalid plans. When evaluating the submitted plans, the experts may find that some of them are unreasonable or unpractical, which may inevitably occupy many time resources of the experts and thereby decline the evaluation efficiency. To conclude, it can be said that the target project performs relatively well in the creativity and social innovation part.

Nevertheless, the future of the target project is still uncertain and possibly impacted by some opportunities, or in some sense, threats. Recently, with the popularity of independent entrepreneurships in China, the cooperative development between the large companies and small companies has gradually become the mainstream. It means that there may be more relatively large enterprises tend to participate in the target project for searching the plans that are worthwhile to invest. On one hand, these enterprises can bring sufficient investment to support "incubation" of any plans they are interested in. On the other hand, this trend may lead the target project to an over-commercialization status that only the plans with commercial value or potential commercial value can be supported. This is undoubtedly contrary to the project's original intention and that is the reason why it is considered as both opportunity and threat simultaneously.

Smart Governance. As for this indicator, inner-departmental coordination and inter-departmental coordination will be considered as sub-indicators to assess the target project. It is interesting that the performances of such two sub-indicators are totally different. For the inner-departmental coordination, the target project is quite excellent which can be reflected from its efficiency of handling works. For example, the evaluation of summited plans may be completed and publicized within an average of three days if the plans only involve the planning department (The supervising department of target project). This duration is undoubtedly rapid compared with normal processing duration of other official services. On the contrary, the target project performs relatively inefficient on the inter-departmental coordination part. That reflects in the evaluating duration of plans involving both the planning and other departments, which is possibly a week or more. This phenomenon to some extent is caused by the lack of attention to the request from other departments. To summary, the smart governance performs fairly well in inner-departmental coordination aspect, but the inter-departmental coordination does need to improve.

Fortunately, many local governments have realized the problems on inter-departmental coordination and thereby plan to integrate highly related departments into one in order to replace the inter-departmental coordination by inner-departmental. In addition, some governments also plan to introduce a few documents to attempt to regular the inter-departmental coordination. All of these can be regarded as the opportunities for the target project to enhance its inter-departmental coordination. However, the root of weakness on inter-departmental coordination still exists and quite difficultly eradicates. That is mainly because it to some extent correlated to the Chinese government running mechanism which is always explained as "vertical mechanism" in terminology. It can be simply demonstrated as fact that subordinates only respond to the requests from their superiors and most importantly, it is also considerably difficult to be changed in the future unless the governmental system is totally rebuilt. Thus, the root is still a huge threat for the future of inter-departmental coordination.

Smart Specialization Strategies. In this evaluating aspect, whether the target project launches some policies to support the initialization of selected plans is the specific benchmark. According to information on its website, it can be said that the target project fulfils relatively acceptable in terms of its two facts. Firstly, the target project gives some candidates the rights to reduce their taxes that necessarily need to hand in. This means the candidates could harness their funds more flexible and therefore complete their plans more rapidly. Secondly, the target project establishes a competition aiming at stimulating the candidates to perfectly conduct their plans. For example, in "virtual launch" process, the experts will together select some relatively perfect plans and give them additional financial incentives. However, the competition mechanism still has few weaknesses of which unfairness is one. More specifically, due to the difference of fields that plans involving, the scores is possibly more empirical rather than sufficiently scientific, which eventually may cause an unfair or unpersuasive allocation of awards. All in all, the performance of target project in this aspect needs to maintain.

Similar with other indicators, opportunities and threats in this aspect simultaneously exist. For the opportunities, the target projects especially the involved enterprises, plan to introduce more competitive and cooperative activities to encourage the candidates. In other words, there should be more incentives to earn, which is obviously conducive to the development of all launching plans. Nevertheless, there are some of the threats that may obstruct the improvements of the target project. For example, with the growth of competitions, unfair allocation may appear more frequently and impact the enthusiasm of candidates. In addition, the increasing number of activities inevitably declines the efficiency of "incubation" of the target project.

Other Involved Part. As the passed plans in the target project belong to different fields, they may involve various characteristics and indicators, which means if all the passed plans are assessed, up to 128 indicators need to assess. Thus, it is somewhat tricky to evaluate each passed plans in detail and this can also be regarded as the restriction of the essay.

4 Conclusions

To conclude the paper, it initially defines smart city in general through some literature reviews and subsequently revises its contents as well as benchmarks based on specific environment in China. Secondly, the benchmarks are introduced to carefully evaluate the 'Cloud seeds plans' from the perspective of governance. Finally, a matrix below of entire SWOT evaluation is generated as the final assessment (See Fig. 3).

From the assessment, it can be said that the 'Cloud seeds plans' performs relatively well according to some indicators while there are also many weaknesses needing to overcome. In addition, it also faces many opportunities and threats simultaneously. All in all, although the paper attempts to critically assess the target project and eventually conducts some results, there are still many restrictions on the paper. For example, whether the smart city definition is appropriate and whether it is needed to change its contents are still under discussions. Thus, it is necessary to conduct some further research on this topic.

	Strengths	Weaknesses	Opportunities	Threats
Open governances (public participation and empowerment; Transparency)	1. To few extent highly working efficiency 1. Publication of important details of the target projects	1. Invalidated public participation and empowerment 1. lack of publication on some deeper information	1. A central government document on improving governance	1. The lack of awareness for political participation of Chinese citizens
Creativity and Social Innovation	1. Awakening the enthusiasm of social innovation; 2. Providing a platform for realizing innovative ideas	1. Need to deals with some unreasonable or unpractical plans	1. More business engagement and investment	1. Possibilities of over-commercialization
Smart governances	1. Efficient inner-cooperation	2. Inefficient inter-cooperation	1. Integration of related departments; 2. Introducing documents for regularizing inter-cooperation	1. "Vertical mechanism" of government system
Smart Specialization Strategies	1. Launching some policies and competitions for stimulating candidates	1. Possibilities of Unfair and unpersuasive allocation of awards	1. More competitive and cooperative activities from enterprises	1. More appearance of unfair allocation; 2. Declining the efficiency of "incubation"

Fig. 3. The SWOT matrix of each indicator.

References

1. Albino, V., Berardi, U., Dangelico, R.: Smart cities: definitions, dimensions, performance, and initiatives. J. Urban Technol. **22**(1), 3–21 (2015)
2. Yin, C., Xiong, Z., Chen, H., Wang, J., Cooper, D., David, B.: A literature survey on smart cities. Sci. China Inf. Sci. **58**(10), 1–18 (2015). https://doi.org/10.1007/s11432-015-5397-4
3. Shi, H., Zhao, M., Simth, D.A., Chi, B.: Behind the land use mix: measuring the functional compatibility in urban and sub-urban areas of China. Land **11**(1), 2 (2022)
4. Shi, H., Yue, Y., Zhou, Y.: The comparison between two different algorithms of spatio-temporal forecasting for traffic flow prediction. In: Geertman, S., Zhan, Q., Allan, A., Pettit, C. (eds.) CUPUM 2019. LNGC, pp. 321–345. Springer, Cham (2019). https://doi.org/10.1007/978-3-030-19424-6_18
5. Zhao, M., Wang, Y.: Measuring segregation between rural migrants and local residents in urban China: an integrated spatio-social network analysis of Kecun in Guangzhou. Environ. Plan. B Urban Anal. City Sci. **45**(3), 417–433 (2017)
6. Harrison, C., et al.: Foundations for smarter cities. IBM J. Res. Dev. **54**(4), 1–16 (2010)
7. Komninos, N.: The architecture of intelligent cities: integrating human, collective and artificial intelligence to enhance knowledge and innovation. In: 2nd IET International Conference on Intelligent Environments-IE 2006, IET, vol. 1, pp.13–20 (2006)

8. Bakici, T., Almirall, E., Wareham, J.: A smart city initiative: the case of Barcelona. J. Knowl. Econ. **2**(1), 1–14 (2012)
9. Barrionuevo, J.M., Berrone, P., Ricart, J.E.: Smart cities, sustainable progress. IESE Insight **14**, 50–57 (2012)
10. IDA Singapore. Realizing The iN2015 Vision. https://www.tech.gov.sg/files/media/corporate publications/2015/01/realisingthevisionin2015.pdf. Accessed 25 Aug 2021
11. Shenzhen Government. The Shenzhen statistical yearbooks. http://tjj.sz.gov.cn/zwgk/zfx xgkml/tjsj/tjnj/. Accessed 25 Aug 2021
12. Shenzhen Government. The Shenzhen statistical yearbooks. http://tjj.sz.gov.cn/zwgk/zfx xgkml/tjsj/tjnj/content/post_3085977.html. Accessed 25 Aug 2021
13. Ghazinoory, S., Esmail Zadeh, A., Memariani, A.: Fuzzy SWOT analysis. J. Intell. Fuzzy Syst. **18**(1), 99–108 (2007)
14. Dyson, R.G.: Strategic development and SWOT analysis at the University of Warwick. Eur. J. Oper. Res. **152**(3), 631–640 (2004)

Research on Information Technology of Vocational Education Based on 5G Era

Xinlu Li(✉), Zhenyu Xu, and Canquan Ling

Huizhou Engineering Vocational College, Huizhou 516000, China
49266692@qq.com

Abstract. 5G communication technology has the advantages of Super bandwidth, ultra-low delay and ultra-high transmission rate, which will bring epoch-making changes to the education mode of vocational education. Online teaching will become more popular, and classroom teaching mode will change or flip, Virtual reality technology will be widely used in teaching activities, big data, cloud computing and artificial intelligence will play a greater role in personnel training, cloud training will be more popular. Under the background of 5G era, industry cross-border integration has become an important trend of development. At the same time, the iteration of new and old posts and the cross-border cooperation of professional and technical personnel have become inevitable. The reform of these new formats is the current vocational education. We must accelerate the reform, adapt to the development requirements of the 5G era, vigorously develop vocational education with the help of 5G technology, and actively respond to various challenges in the 5G era. This paper mainly analyzes the changes of new formats in the 5G era, the challenges faced by future vocational education in the 5G era, and the application strategies in vocational education.

Keywords: 5G era · Vocational education · Information technology · Challenge

1 Introduction

Modern vocational education is a type of education that adapts to the new demand of labor force for large-scale machine production [1]. Every technological innovation undoubtedly leads to changes in the production process. In order to play its role, vocational education must cooperate with technological change [2]. On April 20, 2020, the national development and Reform Commission officially defined that 5G construction will be included in the scope of national new infrastructure construction, and the development of 5G technology has entered the "high-speed lane". 5G has become the leader of mobile communication technology in the new era. 5G technology will effectively support the wide application of artificial intelligence, Internet of things, big data and other technologies, and promote the social and economic development to produce revolutionary changes. From the perspective of the development of modern information, 5G technology has built a digital highway for the development of science and technology, become an important information channel for the development of big data, Internet of

© ICST Institute for Computer Sciences, Social Informatics and Telecommunications Engineering 2022
Published by Springer Nature Switzerland AG 2022. All Rights Reserved
S. Shi et al. (Eds.): 6GN 2021, LNICST 439, pp. 636–648, 2022.
https://doi.org/10.1007/978-3-031-04245-4_56

things and artificial intelligence, and have an important impact on the social operation and management mode, business mode and education mode. How to make full use of big data, Internet of things, 5G communication, cloud computing and other modern high-tech means to realize the intelligent release in the field of education, including higher education, is a new topic for education in the current intelligent era.

2 The Influence of 5G Era on the Change of New Business State of Economy

The thrust of China's high-quality economic development is mainly technological progress and industrial structure adjustment. The higher the level of economic development, the greater the contribution of advanced technology and reasonable industrial structure to economic quality development [3]. As a representative of the new generation of communication technology - 5G, the application level is its key value. Through the empowerment of 5G technology, the promotion of emerging technologies can be realized, and the production organization mode of existing industries can be changed. In general, 5G will bring new business forms from the development of industrial system, the structure of job market and the mastery of labor skills.

2.1 The Cross-border Integration of Industries is Gradually Deepened, and the Development Trend is Systematic

All links in the industrial chain will be effectively integrated. The integrity and health of the industrial chain is an important factor to ensure the sustainable development of an industry. Under the development of 5G era, the integration of industrial chain has become an important development trend in the future. Under the development mode of big data technology + platform, great development and change have been made in terms of technology algorithm and computing power, which promotes the convergence of industrial chain, provides accurate basis for information prediction, and realizes the aggregation of production factors. The production mode will change from standard scale production to individual scale production. With the gradual maturity and application of automation technology, machines can replace human resources in more production processes. Standardized and large-scale product production and service greatly improve the production efficiency. However, the bottleneck of technological development also makes it difficult to realize flexible production in the process of machine replacement. Manpower is gradually replaced by automation technology to improve production efficiency [4]. The advent of 5G era improves the reliability and security of the network, realizes the breakthrough in technology, and realizes the intelligent development of production services. Finally, the space expansion is realized in the cross-border industrial cooperation, the technical means in production directly affect the organization mode, the role of workers in production has changed, and the development of cross industry, cross specialty and cross post organization is obvious. The practice around the application level of 5G technology needs to be completed by cross-border teams with different professional and technical backgrounds. For example, the media industry injected with new technologies such as VR and AR needs not only media design talents, but also relevant 5G technology application talents to develop media resources on VR and AR equipment.

2.2 The Iteration Speed of New and Old Jobs is Fast, and the Employment Structure Continues to Be Advanced

The coming of 5G era will inevitably affect the situation of the employment market, which needs to adapt to the development of new industries. 5G era promotes the change of new and old jobs. Through technological innovation driven reform, the development of technology develops to the direction of technology and capital intensive, leading to the disappearance of labor-intensive personnel advantages, and more and more workers are facing job transfer or unemployment. With the destruction of technology to the market, the market will be further compensated. New technology will promote the development of products and promote the rise of new jobs. However, the development of 5G technology will further expand the innovation space and eliminate the adverse effects of the employment market. Therefore, modern vocational education needs to seize the current employment development opportunities and do a good job in personnel training. At the same time, the employment structure of labor force continues to be advanced. With the development of automation technology, machines gradually replace the regular labor activities based on physical strength with the advantages of high efficiency and accuracy. With the effective support of 5G technology for artificial intelligence, big data and other emerging technologies, machines can continuously interact with information and data, flexibly "judge" according to the gap between the goal and the status quo, and independently take corresponding measures, and regular intelligent activities will be gradually replaced. With the development of 5G technology, it plays an effective supporting role in big data, artificial intelligence and other technologies, and needs to make flexible judgment on education in combination with modern information development goals [5]. In addition, the current employment of the labor force presents two choices: on the one hand, the lower compatibility of human capital is relatively strong, and the talent capital is reduced; On the other hand, under the influence of vocational training, talent capital has been effectively improved, and vocational colleges need to transfer to the position of human capital demand to further promote the promotion of human capital value. It can be seen that the huge gap of high-quality labor force and the expansion of industrial demand for high-quality labor force brought by technological development force the labor force to actively improve human capital and gradually squeeze to the middle and high-end labor force, so as to realize the synchronous upgrading of China's labor employment structure and industrial structure.

According to authoritative national statistics, the new generation of information technology industry will face considerable talent demand and the most severe talent shortage in the next few years, requiring a large number of relevant professionals to join. The new generation information technology industry is one of the ten key areas of the made in China 2025 strategy. People.com reported that the talent gap of 5g technology in China will reach 20 million in the future. From 2020 to 2025, the economic output directly and indirectly driven by 5g commerce will exceed 35 trillion yuan. 5g will give birth to new information service posts such as industrial data analysis, intelligent algorithm development and 5g industry application solutions, and cultivate a flexible employment model based on online platform. While 5g is fully commercial, it also creates huge financial and a large number of employment opportunities for the society (see Fig. 1).

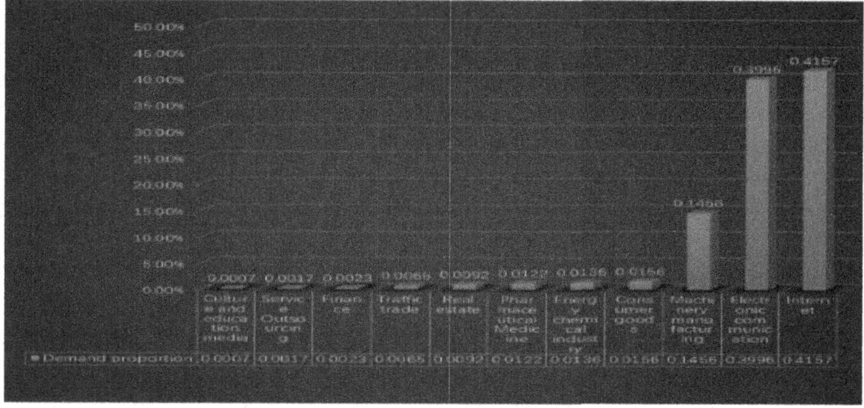

Fig. 1. 5G industry talent demand distribution

2.3 The Boundary of Professional Technology Has Been Strengthened, and Cross Team Cooperation Has Become the Norm

With the improvement of the industrial structure, the employment situation of the labor force is constantly optimized, and the technical level is backward, which leads to the disharmony between the industry and the employment structure. 5G technology as a revolutionary technology, compared with other benign technology, will promote the revolutionary change of economic lifestyle. In order to ensure the scientificity of personnel training, it is necessary to take information technology literacy as an important core literacy according to the future career development of 5G era, and actively respond to the modern revolutionary technological change. Compared with the traditional technology situation, it plays an important role in promoting economic development. 5G technology gradually presents a multi field development mode. On the one hand, talents engaged in 5G technology field must have the ability of network planning, mobile communication, big data and other diversified technology modules. On the other hand, technology needs to be combined with skill driven way to enhance the production value. Industries and posts related to 5G technology need to deeply understand the principle of posts. And use AR, VR and other teaching resources and methods to promote the combination of human and technology. At the same time, strengthen the strengthening of professional technology, promote cross professional exchanges and cooperation, so that the professional cross-border team development. From the perspective of professional technology field, 5G technology industry also needs to strengthen and vertically grasp the boundary of professional technology, emphasizing autonomous learning and professional cooperation.

Based on cross-border exchanges and cooperation, promoting the interaction and penetration of different professional technologies, and forming innovative products and services will be an important feature of future industrial development. On the one hand, 5G technology and its supporting big data, artificial intelligence and other common technologies are interdisciplinary fields. For practitioners in this field, they mainly form support for their own industrial chain from software development, algorithm writing, hardware design and other aspects. On the other hand, the 5G application level often requires cross-border teams to work together to realize the development of application resources. For example, in the field of vocational education, the development of corresponding professional teaching resources for AR and VR equipment requires school teachers to provide the design concept of pedagogy, enterprise personnel to provide the design details of relevant resources, and media designers to carry out the artistic production of resources, 5G resource developers then form resources suitable for corresponding devices. It can be seen that the mastery of labor force's technical skills in the 5G era is to strengthen the vertical and in-depth mastery of professional technical skills, and to emphasize the mastery of soft technical skills such as autonomous learning, knowledge conversion and team cooperation.

3 The Influence and Challenge of 5G Communication Technology on Talent Cultivation in Higher Vocational Colleges

China's 5G communication technology has a broad prospect. According to the relevant data forecast of China information and Communication Research Institute, by 2025, China's 5G users will exceed 800 million, and 30% of the world's connections will be occupied by China, which means that the world's largest 5G market will be China, and China will make a great contribution to global digitization. With the popularity of 5G Internet, online education will enter a new stage of development, and breakthrough reforms will take place in various levels and types of education modes. With the development of 5G technology, the training mode of higher vocational education will also produce unprecedented and epoch-making innovations [6].

With the development of 5G communication technology, education and teaching activities will break the limitation of traditional education area and time. The characteristics of high speed and low delay of 5G communication will determine the interactivity of online live courses, which can approximate the interactive effect of face-to-face teaching, and experience the face-to-face mode of teachers and students, In the course, teachers can observe and supervise the learning process of students, which will bring students a greater sense of achievement, more confidence in active participation, and can maximize the effect of classroom teaching and improve the quality of teaching. The improvement of online teaching effect will change students' and parents' cognition of online class [7]. In the future, there will be more teaching activities moving from ordinary classrooms to cyberspace, and teachers at all levels will face the change of transferring most of the teaching activities to the Internet, which means that new requirements are put forward for teachers, and teachers should make comprehensive changes in teaching mode, teaching methods and means. During the epidemic period, a higher vocational college conducted a survey on the online teaching of 362 teachers. The results showed that 54.6% of the teachers said that the online teaching was carried out for the first time due to the special situation of the epidemic. The survey on 7507 students showed that 83.55% of the students accepted the online teaching mode. Therefore, there is a big gap between teachers' proficiency in online teaching and students' acceptance of online teaching. Teachers need to adapt to the changes of teaching mode in the era of wireless high-speed Internet as soon as possible. According to the survey of the University, 87.7% of the teachers think that they should pay attention to the construction of online classroom and curriculum resources in the future, so as to improve their ability to control the online classroom.

By analyzing the number of popular specialties related to 5g technology in recent three years, it is found that the seven popular specialties have a total of 3124 specialty points in 2020, an increase of 56% compared with 2002 specialty points in 2018. Among them, the number of big data technology and application majors increased from 212 in 2018 to 620 in 2020, an increase of 192%; The artificial intelligence technology service specialty has achieved a leap from zero to 173, which can be seen from the eagerness of industrial demand (see Fig. 2).

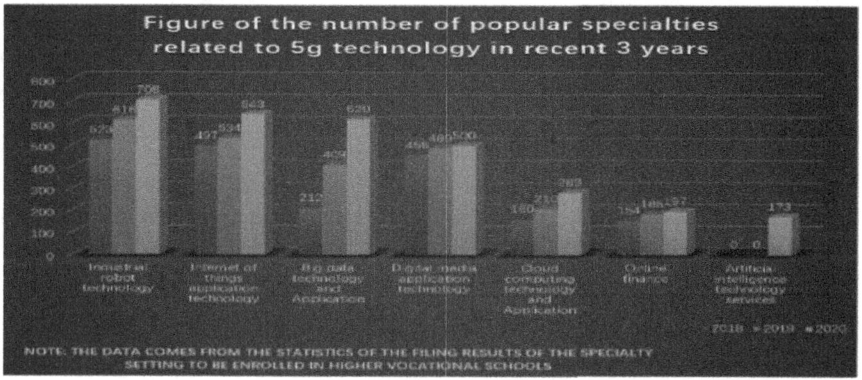

Fig. 2. Figure of the number of popular specialties related to 5G technology in recent 3 years

In addition, with the recognition of online learning by students and their parents, the construction of National Open University and the development of network education in well-known universities, in the 5G era, more and more students will go to universities through the network. The major challenge that colleges and universities are facing is how to attract students to apply for the examination? How to maintain and improve the level of talent training in the competition. A college has done an online questionnaire for the graduated students. The data shows that: as social learners, 42.6% of the respondents are willing to pay for online courses or receive online academic education under the premise of guaranteed quality, which is more obvious in the financial management students, reaching 51.2%. From these data, we can see that education in the future 5G era will be more and more carried out without physical campus.

With the Super bandwidth and ultra-low delay of 5G communication, plus the application of big data, cloud computing and virtual reality technology, panoramic virtual training similar to real scene will challenge the existing training mode and practical teaching mode. In addition, the combination of big data, cloud computing and 5G communication will also have a great impact on the evaluation mode of talent cultivation level in higher vocational colleges. Real time classroom teaching quality analysis and feedback will have a positive impact on teaching diagnosis and improvement as well as college development decisions.

4 The Changing Trend of Talent Training Mode of Higher Vocational Education in 5G Communication Era

4.1 Virtual Reality and Augmented Reality Technology Will Be Widely Used in the Teaching Process

As 5G communication technology is gradually recognized by people, the network communication with ultra-high bandwidth and ultra-low delay makes the interactive virtual training based on virtual reality and augmented reality possible. In the future, virtual simulation technology based on virtual reality and augmented reality technology will be widely used in higher vocational education. Due to the mature technology and preferential price of VR visual equipment, VR glasses are likely to become the standard product of higher vocational training room. Most of the training projects, especially the practical teaching projects with higher requirements for industrial and commercial scenes, the first choice is panoramic virtual training. In the future, with the popularization of 5G communication and the growing maturity of VR technology, ordinary classroom teaching may also use virtual reality technology. Students and teachers can go beyond the physical space limit and complete teaching activities in the virtual classroom through VR technology. The quality of class will be greatly improved compared with the existing live teaching.

4.2 In the Future, Big Data and Artificial Intelligence Technology Will Play an Important Role in Personnel Training

With the wide application of 5G communication technology, the ultra-high bandwidth and ultra-low delay of 5G communication will be solved. In the future, big data and artificial intelligence technology will give vocational education more and more powerful "wisdom" support, and provide more powerful power for the modernization of vocational education. Teachers will be liberated to a greater extent by artificial intelligence technology. The comprehensive use of machine learning, image recognition, language processing and other artificial intelligence technologies to create "smart classroom" can help teachers complete classroom teaching, improve teachers' teaching efficiency, release teachers' time and energy, and improve classroom teaching effect to a certain extent [8].

In the 5G era, through the smooth and interconnected network communication, every student, teacher and even every networking device on campus can become a node and data source in the smart campus. Big data and artificial intelligence technology will significantly improve the scientificity of vocational education management. It provides comprehensive, accurate and effective information support for education management and scientific decision-making. Through the establishment of campus big data center and artificial intelligence management service platform, the analysis, mining and visualization of campus big data can provide data support for the decision-making of vocational college managers and improve the management level of colleges.

4.3 Online Education and Online Learning Will Become an Important Way for Most People to Receive Education

With the advent of 5G era, the network communication with ultra-high bandwidth and ultra-low delay has established the information communication foundation for online education and online learning. The problems of network jam and poor network connection that plagued online education in the past will no longer exist. 5G communication will open up the "last kilometer" of intelligent network education, and real-time two-way audio and video interactive teaching will be realized without jamming. 5G communication can support high-definition multimedia interaction between data and content, realize various forms of student-centered online interactive teaching, better stimulate learning interest and improve the quality of online teaching. Under the background of 5G era, various innovative learning modes based on online education, such as micro class, MOOC and flipped classroom, will move from high-end niche to popularization and popularization [9].

At the beginning of 2020, due to the impact of the epidemic, both primary and secondary schools and colleges and universities are unable to return to school on time, and the vast majority of schools carry out teaching activities through the network platform. After experiencing all kinds of discomfort, from students, parents to teachers, online learning gradually from resistance to acceptance, online education has an explosive growth. After the epidemic, although the number of online education learners will decrease to a certain extent, the whole society's acceptance of online education will increase greatly. In the age of free access to the Internet, whether college students or social learners, there will be a majority of learners learning online through the Internet. The popularization and application of 5G communication technology will break the time and space restrictions of online education, and open up the last bottleneck of online teaching. Online learners only need a smart phone or tablet computer to learn anytime and anywhere, and get rid of the restrictions that they have to rely on the local area network and can learn online in the home and office environment.

4.4 Virtual Cloud Experiment and Cloud Training Will Be Promoted and Applied in the Future

The concept of cloud training is no longer unfamiliar. However, the scene rendering and operation of large-scale virtual training are generally carried out in the cloud. On the one hand, it needs ultra-high hardware configuration host, on the other hand, it needs high bandwidth and low delay network communication, so as to facilitate the data exchange between the cloud and the client. The delay of wireless network greatly affects the effect of cloud training and limits the application of cloud training. The high bandwidth and low delay of 5G wireless communication network are enough to meet the stable transmission of ultra high definition video. The high-performance computing in the cloud supports the rendering of training scenes. The computing and storage are put in the cloud, which reduces the configuration requirements of customer terminals. With about 1000 yuan smart phones and tablet computers, multi person remote collaborative cloud training can be realized. Similarly, the production and programming of high-definition video, which used to be unable to obtain high-quality experience on mobile terminals, need to occupy large memory and powerful computing power, can be completed anytime and anywhere on mobile terminals relying on 5G network to connect to the cloud, greatly improving the convenience [10]. In the future, with the popularization and popularization of online learning, virtual cloud training will be widely used in higher vocational education practice teaching because of its super realistic virtual reality environment, relatively low equipment investment, and collaborative training beyond time and space.

5 Action Route Planning of Future Vocational Education in 5G Era

5.1 Using 5G Concept to Improve Teaching Level

According to the development direction of regional industry, the dynamic adjustment mechanism of professional development direction should be established. In the future development of 5G era, the career development environment faced by vocational college students is more complex, which needs to be combined with the professional connotation and future career development situation, and actively respond to the current career development situation. First, for the emerging industries brought by 5G, according to the regional industrial development planning, we should do a good job in the layout of new majors, and reasonably choose the distribution of colleges and universities, the spatial layout of majors and the scale of enrollment. The second is to promote the construction of professional groups, form the key professional groups and characteristic professional groups closely connected with the regional industrial chain. At the same time, for the weak majors, we should do a good job in the construction demonstration in time, choose to eliminate or integrate into the relevant professional groups based on certain logic. Vocational colleges need to make a comprehensive evaluation of their own teaching characteristics and external influencing factors in teaching. In talent training, they need to transform from traditional single talent training to broader industry and career development, and cultivate diversified technical talents, rather than limited to the linear employment logic in traditional education. The third is to establish the early warning mechanism of the matching degree between the regional professional talent supply and the regional economy. Through the establishment of the matching degree database, with the help of the relevant departments such as the Bureau of statistics and education, the data monitoring platform of the matching degree between the regional vocational college talent supply and the industrial demand is established. Vocational college education is the education situation that is most closely linked with the front-line production and service. In personnel training, we need to firmly grasp the modern education concept, adopt the forward-looking education concept, and better serve the society [11]. In the 5G era, we should emphasize the optimization of talent training standards and evaluation system, adhere to the guidance of new technology for R & D and innovation, and promote the transformation of talents to innovation and wisdom. In the era of 5G technology, higher vocational colleges can no longer use academic and employment information as a single point of application, but also need to pay attention to the cultivation of high-level and comprehensive talents. First time employment and long-term continuous vocational education should be taken as important education contents.

5.2 Deepen the National Education System of Integration of Industry and Education, and Promote the Two-Way Docking of Supply and Demand of Industry and Education

In the 5G era, vocational education should closely follow the development of external formats, deepen the integration of industry and education, open up the talent chain, industry chain and innovation chain, and form a good supply-demand relationship with the industry demand side. In 5G era, professional design and layout should be done well in future vocational education. First of all, we should establish relevant vocational education groups and mixed ownership Vocational Colleges for 5G and other emerging industries, so that enterprises can really participate in the process of industrial talent training, and cooperate with vocational colleges to build teaching resources and training places. From the aspect of specialty setting, we should combine the current situation and strategy of local economic development, and give full play to the advantages of informatization. At the same time, vocational colleges can also get a close understanding of the industrial development trend. Secondly, we should strengthen the applied research in Vocational Colleges and improve the production innovation ability of service enterprises. First, based on the established regular production links of enterprises, it provides services for enterprises from the aspects of technology application talents training and technology application difficulties solving; Second, based on the enterprise's personalized and efficient production reform, it provides technological innovation services for enterprises from the aspects of applied technology research and practice. Through the establishment of a public service platform and think tank for industrial development, we can collect the technical assistance needs of regional enterprise development, and "market-oriented" operation by means of "bidding" and "receiving orders", which will be included in the evaluation index of higher vocational colleges. Adhere to the development of international trade as the basis, the formation of business English, cross-border e-commerce and other diversified professional groups. Driven by the high-level professional group, we should further innovate the high-level professional group of cultural creativity, accounting and information technology, create skilled talents with high quality and high-tech ability, and promote the development of regional economy.

5.3 Combined with 5G Advantages to Build a Modern Teaching System, Improve the National Education Ecosystem of General Vocational Integration

In the 5G era, vocational education is also facing certain reform. Vocational college education needs to combine with the development law of education, fully apply 5G technology to strengthen the reform of teaching. First of all, promote the construction of cultural environment in vocational colleges, and further refine the characteristics of vocational colleges. From the perspective of teachers, the construction of teachers every year needs to invest a lot of financial resources to promote the improvement of teachers, such as carrying out the ten million teacher training project to strengthen the construction of teachers. In the training, the combination of information technology and professional courses is the main method. At the same time, through courseware making competition and information technology competition, we can further strengthen the training of teachers' information technology ability. Build a group of influential and professional network teaching teachers. At the same time, vocational colleges should pay attention to the diversity of vocational education majors and the difference of their closeness to social life, which endows vocational education with multicultural inclusiveness. At the same time, we use 5G technology and smart campus service system to build vocational education mode, break the traditional vocational education restrictions, and enter the era of 5G autonomous learning. Speed up the credit mutual recognition and transformation mechanism between general education and vocational education. The type characteristics between general education and vocational education should be mainly reflected in the differences of knowledge and experience provided in the process of personnel training, which further forms the differences between the two types of education personnel training. Through the update of education concept and 5G vocational education concept, 5G + smart campus and artificial intelligence data center and service platform are constructed. Form a smart campus big data center, combine teaching services with smart management, create a multi integrated smart education environment of smart classrooms, training bases, workshops and various learning venues, and strengthen the in-depth analysis and reform of the teaching system combined with big data technology. The construction of specialty group in teaching can promote the construction of intelligent and digital learning environment and resources of specialty group through the "Cloud Architecture" in campus, and integrate the learning elements of each specialty with big data to form an intelligent teaching mode of closed management and open sharing of resources. Create a fragmented mobile learning mode of learning anytime and anywhere to meet the personalized and mobile learning requirements of education. And the use of information technology to build students' life cycle big data, to describe the students' psychology, behavior and other aspects of the portrait, to form personalized teaching content, and combined with the students' psychological portrait to carry out personalized teaching content and learning situation warning, to promote the development of vocational education. Finally, we should speed up the internal growth channel of vocational education, and further explore the cultivation of master and doctor of vocational education on the basis of undergraduate vocational education, so as to form a talent growth path with the characteristics of vocational education types.

5.4 Strengthen Responsibility and Build a Modern Vocational Education System for All

With the development of 5G era, vocational education institutions in various regions have realized the access and coverage of high-speed Internet. With the support of information technology and equipment, the optimization and sharing of vocational education resources have been realized, and the traditional teaching gap has been narrowed. The vocational enlightenment course is effectively integrated into the primary and secondary school culture class, labor class and other courses. Through professional experience, workplace visit, simulated occupation and other ways, it helps students form multiple professional values, consciously perceive their own learning tendency, and actively choose to study in the appropriate education type system. In the 5G era, the sharing of educational resources in future education is a two-way relationship model of radiation and being radiated, which has asymmetry in information sharing. The application of 5G technology development enlarges the consequences of regional economic imbalance, changes the way of thinking greatly, and there are great differences in the types of employment and conditions, which can not be improved by 5G technology. All regions should do a good job in the overall implementation of career enlightenment, and build public career experience centers with the help of vocational colleges or external social institutions. Under the development background of 5G era, vocational education colleges need to combine the types of specialties and the characteristics of regional economic development, build characteristic colleges and specialties, promote the docking of industry and specialty, and strengthen the adjustment and improvement of specialty construction mechanism. In addition, it emphasizes the optimization of the professional evaluation index and information management system, and further improves the evaluation results and requirements, so as to eliminate the unqualified majors and build the indispensable Vocational Colleges for regional development, so as to help the development of society and regional economy. Using 5G technology combined with targeted poverty alleviation forces to promote the development of education in backward areas and ensure the fairness of education. For migrant workers, veterans, dropout youth and other employment vulnerable groups, "education + skills" compensation training. These groups often become vulnerable groups because of their low skills and education. Through vocational education, on the one hand, this kind of people can have skills to meet the basic ability requirements of post work; on the other hand, through the study of cultural courses, they can get academic certificates to enhance their competitiveness in the job market.

6 Summary

To sum up, under the background of the development of 5G era, vocational education has set off a new scientific and technological change, which promotes the development of the industry and has a certain impact on the field of industrial economy. We should promote economic reform, birth and change, and realize the repetition, reform and improvement of education. The epoch-making 5G communication will have an epoch-making impact on higher vocational education. In the coming 5G era, the talent training mode of higher vocational education will have an epoch-making change. The future talent training mode of vocational education will be a new presentation in the environment of high-speed wireless network communication, big data, cloud computing and virtual reality technology. With the innovation of educational technology and tools in the 5G era, educational resources have gained more convenient access and sharing channels, breaking the time and space constraints of teaching. Vocational colleges need to combine the advantages of 5G technology, create characteristic specialties, scientifically position the talent training objectives, connect with social services, promote the reform and practice of teaching, cultivate more innovative talents for the society, provide favorable conditions of science and technology and industry for the future professional talent training in the 5G era, and actively respond to the future education challenges in the 5G era, Promote the innovation of teaching mode. Higher vocational colleges should take the initiative to adapt to the innovation of technology and mode brought by 5G communication, make full use of the advantages of high-speed interconnection in the era of 5G communication, plan as soon as possible, and carry out beneficial exploration and practice in the construction of teaching resources, teaching mode reform, digital campus, virtual training and cloud training, so as to continuously improve the level of personnel training.

References

1. Jintu, Y.: The rise and fall of vocational education and the replacement of new and old educational ideas – a review of Vocational Education in the past century. Res. Educ. Dev. **2**, 1–4 (2004)
2. Wanhong, L.: Technological development and vocational education. Educ. Res. **11**, 51–55 (2002)
3. Luckin, R., Holmes, W., Griffithsm et al.: Intelligence unleashed: an argument for AI in education (2016). 14,19,21
4. EDSURGE. Decoding Adaptive. Pearson, London (2016). 15
5. Ren, L.: Adaptive Learning, p. 21. Tsinghua University Press, Beijing (2019)
6. Orn, J.E.: The future of Education: educational reform in the age of artificial intelligence. Translated by Li Haiyan and Wang Qinhui. China Machine Press, Beijing (2020). XVI, VII
7. Li, R., et al.: Research on Higher Education Mode in Intelligent Era. Shanghai University Press, Shanghai (2019). 202
8. Xu, Y., Huang, Y.: Research on the relationship between artificial intelligence and higher vocational education. China Vocat. Tech. Educ. (24), 67–72 (2020)
9. Zhao, Z., Duan, X.: The reform of higher education personnel training mode in the era of artificial intelligence: basis, dilemma and path. J. Southwest Univ. Nationalities (Humanit. Soc. Sci. Ed.) (2), 213–219 (2019)
10. Miao, F.: Leading the educational leap in the era of artificial intelligence: a summary of Beijing international conference on artificial intelligence and education in 2019. Res. Audio Vis. Educ. (8), 5–14 (2019)
11. Beijing consensus on artificial intelligence and education. Published by the United Nations Educational, Scientific and Cultural Organization (2019). 3

Information Technology and Its Use in Medical Vocational Education: Present Practice and Future Prospects

Xiao-Ya Yang and Chong Yang(✉)

Guangzhou Health Science College, Guangzhou 510180, China
yangchong@gzws.edu.cn

Abstract. Information technology (IT) is booming in the recent years, which has been changing our world and our lives style broadly. With the development of the new generation of IT and internet, medical education has entered a new era of intelligentization, networking and digitalization. The new-generation IT, including virtual reality (VR), augmented reality (AR), three-dimensional (3D) printing and artificial intelligence (AI), has been applied in medical education and evolved as pedagogical strategies to promote the learner-centered teaching method. In this paper, we review the current applications of VR, AR, 3D printing and AI in the medical education, and further discuss the future prospects of their applications in the medical vocational education.

Keywords: Information technology · Vocational education · Medicine

1 Introduction

Information technology (IT) is booming in the recent years, which has been changing our world and our lives style broadly. Ministry of Education of China has placed great emphasis on vocational education which is in close contact with the social and economic development. A series of policies has proposed that IT application in vocational education, contributing to reform teaching method and talent training mode, should be promoted actively.

With the release of Healthy China 2030, medical vocational education has been placed in a very important position. With the development of the new generation of IT and internet, medical education has entered a new era of intelligentization, networking and digitalization. The new-generation IT, including virtual reality (VR), augmented reality (AR), three-dimensional (3D) printing and artificial intelligence (AI), has been applied in medical education and evolved as pedagogical strategies to promote the learner-centered teaching method [1]. From this perspective, integrating IT with medical vocational education will bring a bright future to the training of health technical personnel.

In this article, we review the current applications of the new-generation IT in medical education and discuss the future perspectives and challenges for the applications in medical vocational education.

© ICST Institute for Computer Sciences, Social Informatics and Telecommunications Engineering 2022
Published by Springer Nature Switzerland AG 2022. All Rights Reserved
S. Shi et al. (Eds.): 6GN 2021, LNICST 439, pp. 649–656, 2022.
https://doi.org/10.1007/978-3-031-04245-4_57

2 Current Applications of IT in Medical Education

A great deal of practice and the following accumulation of experience play a crucial role in medical learning. For centuries, the medical educators have employed simulation training type models, ranging from animals to cadaveric dissections. There is no denying that those models offer realism during the training of operation and provide good practice in managing the mimic complications. However, some limitations of using those models are existed, including consuming large amount of money, having different anatomy from the human body and confronting with the concerns of morality and ethics [2]. With the advances in IT, VR, AR, 3D printing and AI have been used in medical education, which attempts to reappear the real scenarios, situations and procedures with the absence of patients [1]. Those applications could break through the limitations of time and space, compensate for the shortage of experimental resources and avoid dangers in the real scenarios.

2.1 Application of VR/AR in Medical Education

By using immersive, highly visual, 3D characteristics, VR provides opportunities for users to observe, feel and operate in virtual environments resembling real-world objects and events [3]. The immersive simulation is provided by physical or other interfaces such as motion sensors, a head-mounted display, haptic devices, computer keyboard, mouse, voice recognition and speech [4]. Take the head-mounted display for example, users receive sensory input from the displayer instead of the real world [5]. With the immersive simulation, users interact as if they were in the real world, whereas the focus of the interaction is still in the digital environment [4]. Different from VR, AR overlays digital information on objects or places in the real world to make users place themselves in the real world instead of a completely virtual environment [4–6]. Users of AR can interact with virtual objects and the real world simultaneously via employing a head-mounted display, wearable computers, overlays of computer screens or displays projected onto humans and mannequins [4, 5].

With three characteristics of immersion, interaction and imagination, VR/AR is capable of integrating text, images, sound, animation and video into one, and exhibits considerable advantages in medical education. (1) VR/AR is conducive to visualize the abstract theoretical knowledge, bringing a more vivid and flexible teaching way. For example, applying 3D anatomical structure models designed with VR, teachers can zoom into or toggle the anatomical structures to show the relationship between structures in a stereoscopic way, which makes the teaching visualized and improves the teaching effect. (2) VR/AR enables learners to interact with a computer-generated realistic environment, offering a sense of a force feedback by some sensory information like sound and haptics. For example, using the simulator to create the realistic operating environment for learners, they can feel the operation in reality, in addition to theoretical learning, which makes a full combination of the theoretical teaching and practice. (3) By providing objective metrics, VR/AR can assess the performance of the learners with the absence of a teacher, which can even train the learners to make the right decision. For example, in the training program of knot-tying, a basic surgical skill, VR assesses the performance of the knot-tying via the number of hand movements and the time taken when the learners tie a surgical knot. It can further provide information feedback about the security of the surgical knot to improve their performance [2].

Although the above advantages possessed, some limitations are still existing when VR/AR applied in medical education. First, VR still cannot make the virtual environment and real environment indistinguishable. Since the sense of touch, high realism and the opportunity to use real surgical instruments offered by cadavers, they are still considered as the gold standard for stimulation in the medical training, particularly in surgical training. Second, cybersickness, an adverse health effect, has been reported when using VR, which can lead to disorientation, nausea, headache, difficulty concentrating, fatigue and problems with vision [7, 8]. Third, several systematic reviews indicate that the studies of the application of VR/AR in medical education focused primarily on the outcomes of knowledge and skills improvement compared with traditional education. The poor quality and breadth of those studies make the recommendation of the application of VR/AR in medical education unconvincing to some extent [9–11].

2.2 Application of 3D Printing in Medical Education

3D printing, also known as additive manufacturing or rapid prototyping, is defined as the process of making the solid, 3D objects through collecting images in the manner of a digital file [12], printing the objects from flatland to spaceland. 3D printer is the requisite equipment to make the 3D objects. After a 3D model is designed with a computer program, it will be sent to the 3D printer to build the 3D model by depositing layers in a volumetric manner, with employing multiple materials such as plastic, gypsum powder, liquid resin, or even metal melted together with a laser. Current applications of 3D printing in medicine are broad, including developing prostheses, patient-specific implants, and anatomic models for medical education [12]. Among those applications, the most common 3D printing technologies are vat photopolymerization, binder jetting, material jetting, powder bed fusion and material extrusion [13].

Albeit 3D images can be obtained from VR/AR, the visualization of 3D content is limited to using the 2D flat screens, which is insufficient for the understanding of some complex anatomic details [14]. 3D printing performs as a feasible "bridge" to overcome the gap. This is the first advantage of applying 3D printing in medical education. Second, the lack of opportunity to use real surgical instruments in the 3D world results in the lack of tactile feedback and hands-on experience. With the 3D models created by 3D printer, medical learners can operate on them using the real surgical instruments, which can bring a sense of reality during their practice. Last but not the least, the high cost of some simulation models such as VR, AR and AI limits their applications in the teaching. 3D printing can produce low-cost simulation models, playing an integral role in medical education [13].

Several researchers have investigated the effect of applying 3D printing models in medical education [15–18]. In the application in congenital heart disease education, Su *et al.* demonstrated that the students achieved better structural conceptualization when using a 3D printing heart model [16]. Whereas, in a pilot randomized controlled study, Wang *et al.* found that a 3D printing model showed no significant superiority, when compared to a traditional model in hear disease education [15].When using 3D printing models for anatomy teaching, most students preferred the 3D printing models to plastinates, and believed that the color prints improved their learning efficiency [19]. Despite interested in 3D printing models, students expressed that they would not abandon cadaveric specimens [17]. In general, there have been no conclusive results yet and more studies should be carried out to verify the real effect of applying 3D printing models in medical education.

2.3 Application of AI in Medical Education

A working definition of AI, proposed by Ken Masters, is the behaviors designed by computer software to mimic and further extend the rational thinking and actions of human being [20]. There are three main paradigms consisted in AI, including symbolic (logic based and knowledge based), subsymbolic (embodied intelligence and search) and statistical (probabilistic methods and machine learning). Several problem domains, including perception, knowledge, reasoning, planning and communication, are wrestled with those paradigms [21]. The current areas of AI applications are extensive, including finance and economics, automotive, medicine and education [21].

The development of AI in education is rapid and prominent in the twenty-first century. An advanced definition of the role that AI played in education, proposed by Sian Bayne, is a teaching assistant responsible for delivering content, providing feedback and supervising progress [21, 22]. Accordingly, the application of AI in medical education may exert it advancements in curriculum assessment, learning process and learning evaluation [21, 23]. In the curriculum assessment, the application of AI is conductive to solving nonlinear problems and building the relationships between variables. AI can be employed to review the effectiveness of the curriculum and the entire satisfaction with the program of the medical students, as which is critical in training future medical care personnel [21, 23]. In the learning process, the application of AI is conductive to providing learners with personalized educational content. With the feedback from learners, AI can help them to recognize the knowledge gaps [21, 23]. In the learning evaluation, the application of AI is conductive to providing an objective assessment of learners' work and immediate feedback on their assignments, which helps learners to reflect on their work. In addition, AI can make the learning evaluation more cost-effective and time-effective [21, 23].

There are mainly two groups of restrictions of application of AI in medical education, including limitations of AI perceiving the usefulness and the technical problems in the development of AI applications [21]. How to remove those restrictions accurately and effectively may open a new era of future medical education.

3 Future Prospects of Applications of IT in Medical Vocational Education

3.1 Future Prospects of Application of VR/AR in Medical Vocational Education

We have reviewed the advantages and limitations of application of VR/AR in medical education in Sect. 2.1. Where does the future of application of VR/AR in medical vocational education lie?

Before answering this question, we look back at our medical vocational college students. Compared to undergraduate students, students in medical vocational college possess a stronger image thinking rather than abstract thinking. From this perspective, VR/AR facilitates abstract theoretical knowledge visualization, which helps the students to interpret the abstract theoretical knowledge. A combination of learning with working play a crucial role in vocational education. The virtual working scenario like an operating room and clinical laboratories created by VR/AR can make students feel like they are working there. Excitingly, multiplayer VR/AR is becoming available, which allows many learners to see and talk to each other and even interact with the patient in the same scenario [24]. In consequence, VR/AR will be used routinely for medical vocational education in time.

A new concept named "mixed reality (MR)" has emerged recently. MR, combining VR with AR in 3D applications via cutting-edge devices for control, integrates virtual models into the real world and builds interactive feedback loop between the virtual and reality to augment users' sense of reality [6]. MR has been used in anatomy and surgery teaching [10, 25], and may perform as a more pragmatic technology than VR/AR in the future.

3.2 Future Prospects of Application of 3D Printing in Medical Vocational Education

To date, 3D printing has been employed mainly in the teaching of anatomy and surgery, as its advantages described above. Concerning the ability of 3D printing to produce specific and personalized models, 3D printing will be adopted more and more broadly in the future medical vocational education.

In medical field, 3D printing has been widely applied in the dentistry [26]. Little has been reported that the use of 3D printing in the teaching of dentistry yet. Actually, 3D printing is very suitable for applying in the teaching of stomatology technology, since it can produce almost any dental cast you want. In the same vein, 3D printing is also appropriate for the teaching of rehabilitation technology, for the lack of suitable teaching aids on the market. Although 3D printing possesses many advantages, its application in medical vocational education may be limited due to the factors such as production accuracy, preparation time and material cost. For the future application of 3D printing in teaching, it is required to strengthen the school-enterprise cooperation with 3D printing companies.

Nowadays, the novel concept of four-dimensional (4D), integrating a fourth dimension "time" on the basis of 3D printing, has emerged [27]. With the ability to change the configuration (such as shape, property and functionality) with the passage of time, 4D printing is deemed to be a suitable candidate for the use in the pharmacy to produce some personalized "smart drugs" [27]. By the time the technology matures, 4D printing will be used for the teaching of pharmacy and other disciplines in medical vocational colleges.

The concept of five-dimensional (5D) printing has arisen in 2016. Different from 3D printing, 5D printing can produce objects in multiple dimensions with the use of five-axis printing technique [28]. Although it hasn't been applied in medical education, we believe that 5D printing will create disruptive innovation and provide excellent service to medical vocational education in the era of 6G.

3.3 Future Prospects of Application of AI in Medical Vocational Education

There is no doubt that theoretical knowledge and operating skills play a dominant role in medical education. AI possesses a huge advantage in facilitating the medical students with acquiring those knowledge and skills. In the future curriculum reform which integrating AI with, as suggested by Wartman *et al.* [29], the following 4 features we should emphasize: (1) Learning is knowledge capture rather than knowledge retention; (2) We need to collaborate with and manage AI applications; (3) We need to guide our students how to understand better the probabilities provided by AI and apply them accurately in making clinical decisions with patients and families; (4) We need to keep in mind the importance to cultivate the empathy and compassion of our students.

In the future, medical students will not only require to master data science, but also require to train them the nuanced comprehension and awareness of the ethical issues [30]. Accordingly, what we should highlight in the future medical vocational education is health AI ethics, which is defined as the 'application and analysis of ethics to contexts in health in which AI is involved' [30]. Consequently, a new curriculum that illustrates the ethical dimensions of health AI comprehensively will be necessary to be established in the future medical vocational education.

4 Challenges of Applications of IT in Medical Vocational Education

There is no doubt that applications of IT in medical vocational education help students' studies more targeted, more efficient and more convenient. However, there still exist some challenges that require educators to address.

With the booming development of IT, many medical vocational colleges have positioned "future classroom" and "intelligent and wise class" as their future development direction, and have carried out various reforms. The real intelligent and wise class is not to simply apply IT in the traditional teacher-centered teaching, but to conduct the student-centered personalized teaching with the help of IT. Therefore, the first challenge to educators is how to change their teaching concept from the traditional teacher-centered teaching to the student-centered personalized teaching. The second challenge to educators is how to incorporate a variety of IT into curricula, to instruct students to find the most trustworthy and pertinent information. It requires educators not only to have abundant professional knowledge, but also to master those new training techniques. The last but not the least, educators should balance the benefits of applications of IT in teaching with the downside of the social isolation brought by the excessive use of IT [1].

5 Conclusion

No matter what kind of IT applied for the future medical vocational education, what we should emphasize is how and when to use it in the education, but not whether to use it.

During the process of developing the effective application of IT in education, educators and IT developers should discuss and assess the instructional design that integrates IT well. That is to say, we use the advanced IT in medical vocational education only when it is refined.

Acknowledgements. This paper was supported by Guangzhou teaching achievement cultivation project (2020123311).

References

1. Moran, J., Briscoe, G., Peglow, S.: Current technology in advancing medical education: perspectives for learning and providing care. Acad. Psychiatry **42**(6), 796–799 (2018). https://doi.org/10.1007/s40596-018-0946-y
2. Sakakushev, B.E., Marinov, B.I., Stefanova, P.P., Kostianev, S.S., Georgiou, E.K.: Striving for better medical education: the simulation approach. Folia Med (Plovdiv). **59**(2), 123–131 (2017). https://doi.org/10.1515/folmed-2017-0039
3. Weiss, P.L., Tirosh, E., Fehlings, D.: Role of virtual reality for cerebral palsy management. J. Child Neurol. **29**(8), 1119–1124 (2014). https://doi.org/10.1177/0883073814533007
4. McGrath, J.L., et al.: Using virtual reality simulation environments to assess competence for emergency medicine learners. Acad. Emerg. Med. **25**(2), 186–195 (2018). https://doi.org/10.1111/acem.13308
5. Elsayed, M., et al.: Virtual and augmented reality: potential applications in radiology. Acta Radiol. **61**(9), 1258–1265 (2020). https://doi.org/10.1177/0284185119897362
6. Hu, H.-Z., et al.: Application and prospect of mixed reality technology in medical field. Curr. Med. Sci. **39**(1), 1–6 (2019). https://doi.org/10.1007/s11596-019-1992-8
7. Saredakis, D., Szpak, A., Birckhead, B., Keage, H.A.D., Rizzo, A., Loetscher, T.: Factors associated with virtual reality sickness in head-mounted displays: a systematic review and meta-analysis. Front. Hum. Neurosci. **14**, 96 (2020). https://doi.org/10.3389/fnhum.2020.00096
8. Moro, C., Štromberga, Z., Raikos, A., Stirling, A.: The effectiveness of virtual and augmented reality in health sciences and medical anatomy. Anat. Sci. Educ. **10**(6), 549–559 (2017). https://doi.org/10.1002/ase.1696
9. Tang, K.S., Cheng, D.L., Mi, E., Greenberg, P.B.: Augmented reality in medical education: a systematic review. Can. Med. Educ. J. **11**(1), e81–e96 (2020). https://doi.org/10.36834/cmej.61705
10. Gerup, J., Soerensen, C.B., Dieckmann, P.: Augmented reality and mixed reality for healthcare education beyond surgery: an integrative review. Int. J. Med. Educ. **11**, 1–18 (2020). https://doi.org/10.5116/ijme.5e01.eb1a
11. Kyaw, B.M., et al.: Virtual reality for health professions education: systematic review and meta-analysis by the digital health education collaboration. J. Med. Internet Res. **21**(1), e12959 (2019). https://doi.org/10.2196/12959
12. Mishra, S.: Application of 3D printing in medicine. Indian Heart J. **68**(1), 108–109 (2016). https://doi.org/10.1016/j.ihj.2016.01.009
13. Lichtenberger, J.P., Tatum, P.S., Gada, S., Wyn, M., Ho, V.B., Liacouras, P.: Using 3D printing (additive manufacturing) to produce low-cost simulation models for medical training. Mil. Med. **183**(suppl_1), 73–77 (2018). https://doi.org/10.1093/milmed/usx142
14. Deferm, S., Meyns, B., Vlasselaers, D., Budts, W.: 3D-printing in congenital cardiology: from flatland to spaceland. J. Clin. Imaging Sci. **6**(1), 8–11 (2016). https://doi.org/10.4103/2156-7514.179408

15. Wang, Z., Liu, Y., Luo, H., Gao, C., Zhang, J., Dai, Y.: Is a three-dimensional printing model better than a traditional cardiac model for medical education? A pilot randomized controlled study. Acta Cardiol. Sin. **33**(6), 664–669 (2017). https://doi.org/10.6515/acs20170621a
16. Su, W., Xiao, Y., He, S., Huang, P., Deng, X.: Three-dimensional printing models in congenital heart disease education for medical students: a controlled comparative study. BMC Med. Educ. **18**(1), 178 (2018). https://doi.org/10.1186/s12909-018-1293-0
17. Wilk, R., Likus, W., Hudecki, A., Syguła, M., Różycka-Nechoritis, A., Nechoritis, K.: What would you like to print? Students' opinions on the use of 3D printing technology in medicine. PLoS ONE **15**(4), e0230851 (2020). https://doi.org/10.1371/journal.pone.0230851
18. Goudie, C., Kinnin, J., Bartellas, M., Gullipalli, R., Dubrowski, A.: The use of 3D printed vasculature for simulation-based medical education within interventional radiology. Cureus **11**(4), e4381 (2019). https://doi.org/10.7759/cureus.4381
19. Mogali, S.R., et al.: Evaluation by medical students of the educational value of multi-material and multi-colored three-dimensional printed models of the upper limb for anatomical education. Anat. Sci. Educ. **11**(1), 54–64 (2018). https://doi.org/10.1002/ase.1703
20. Masters, K.: Artificial intelligence in medical education. Med. Teach. **41**(9), 976–980 (2019). https://doi.org/10.1080/0142159x.2019.1595557
21. Chan, K.S., Zary, N.: Applications and challenges of implementing artificial intelligence in medical education: integrative review. JMIR Med. Educ. **5**(1), e13930 (2019). https://doi.org/10.2196/13930
22. Bayne, S.: Teacherbot: interventions in automated teaching. Teach. High. Educ. **20**(4), 455–467 (2015). https://doi.org/10.1080/13562517.2015.1020783
23. Garg, T.: Artificial intelligence in medical education. Am. J. Med. **133**(2), e68 (2020). https://doi.org/10.1016/j.amjmed.2019.08.017
24. Pottle, J.: Virtual reality and the transformation of medical education. Future Healthc. J. **6**(3), 181–185 (2019). https://doi.org/10.7861/fhj.2019-0036
25. Chytas, D., Piagkou, M., Salmas, M., Johnson, E.O.: Mixed and augmented reality: distinct terms, different anatomy teaching potential. Anat. Sci. Educ. (2020). https://doi.org/10.1002/ase.2009
26. Kessler, A., Hickel, R., Reymus, M.: 3D printing in dentistry-state of the art. Oper. Dent. **45**(1), 30–40 (2020). https://doi.org/10.2341/18-229-l
27. Trenfield, S.J., et al.: Shaping the future: recent advances of 3D printing in drug delivery and healthcare. Expert Opin. Drug Deliv. **16**(10), 1081–1094 (2019). https://doi.org/10.1080/17425247.2019.1660318
28. Haleem, A., Javaid, M., Vaishya, R.: 5D printing and its expected applications in orthopaedics. J. Clin. Orthop. Trauma **10**(4), 809–810 (2019). https://doi.org/10.1016/j.jcot.2018.11.014
29. Wartman, S.A., Combs, C.D.: Reimagining medical education in the age of AI. AMA J. Ethics **21**(2), E146–152 (2019). https://doi.org/10.1001/amajethics.2019.146
30. Katznelson, G., Gerke, S.: The need for health AI ethics in medical school education. Adv. Health Sci. Educ. **26**(4), 1447–1458 (2021). https://doi.org/10.1007/s10459-021-10040-3

Practice Research on Online and Offline Blended Learning Model Based on Chaoxingerya Platform-Take the Course of "Flower Decoration Technique" as an Example

Lihua Yang(✉), Manling Zeng, and Zhenyu Xu

Huizhou Engineering Vocational College, Huizhou, GuangDong, China
1322950672@qq.com

Abstract. Combining the development of current information technology and the implementation of relevant national teaching reform policies, this article expands exploration and practice of blended learning model for online and offline. "Flower Decoration Technique" is opened online as a high-quality curriculum based on the construction of Chaoxingerya platform, which fully consider the characteristics of online and offline blended learning model, applying information-based teaching design concepts to develop online curriculum teaching resources, and use functional advantages of the platform to design online and offline blended learning organization forms and assessment methods. Through the research and practical analysis of the online and offline hybrid teaching mode, this paper breaks through the traditional teaching mode, and is committed to creating an intelligent flower decoration technology classroom, which overwhelmingly improves the interest and effectiveness of teaching.

Keywords: Chaoxingerya platform · Online and offline · Blended learning model · Practice · Research

1 Research Background Based on the Blended Learning Model of Chaoxingerya Platform

1.1 The Rapid Development of Contemporary Information Technology Promotes the Reformation of Teaching Mode

With modern information technology advances, informatization has become the essential way of the current industrial upgrading and transformation. The traditional teaching model can no longer adapt to the education and teaching activities in the network surrounding. Online teaching has also had a huge impact on the field of education and teaching. It is urgently necessary to solve that utilizing the new pattern of modern information technology to alter the traditional lecturing mode, exploring and constructing a class lessoning model suitable for the network environment in modern vocational education.

© ICST Institute for Computer Sciences, Social Informatics and Telecommunications Engineering 2022
Published by Springer Nature Switzerland AG 2022. All Rights Reserved
S. Shi et al. (Eds.): 6GN 2021, LNICST 439, pp. 657–667, 2022.
https://doi.org/10.1007/978-3-031-04245-4_58

1.2 The Epidemic Has Brought Changes in Teaching Models

Affected by the epidemic, the biggest influences on teachers and students are the changes in teaching mode. According to this problem, our college conducted in-depth research on teaching during the epidemic, which illustrated that the online and offline blended teaching model is a crucial breakthrough in solving the problem.

1.3 Analysis of the Status Quo of the Course "Flower Decoration Technology" in Our College

This course revolves around professional positions such as floral environment designers, and covers several knowledge, including floriculture, western flower arrangement, oriental flower arrangement, modern flower arrangement, flower decoration management, etc. With the development of the times, there are many problems existing in the teaching summary of flower decoration technique. First of all, the teaching content and form are single. In addition, the small amount of lecture information is also a problem. Thirdly, the approaches to learning this course are monotonous. Ultimately, the teacher's demonstration is not clear. This series of problems are the key factors leading to the decline of students' learning enthusiasm and low learning efficiency.

1.4 Features of the Chaoxingerya Platform

Chaoxingerya, known as an intelligent teaching system, is a platform that extending three clients-side which are mobile, teachers and administers. Overall, from teachers' side, they have permission to set lessons, to build classes and to manage classes. What's more, interacting with the classroom, answering questions, activating the classroom via Chaoxingerya platform will enhance teaching results. On the whole, from students and users' side, they can join classes and independent learning. Basically, students can develop their classroom interaction by asking questions, which is convenient for students to learn, improving their learning efficiency.

2 Characteristics of Online and Offline Blended Learning Model

Online and offline blended learning model is a new mode of pedagogy which combines traditional face-to-face teaching with digital learning. In the whole online and offline blended teaching process, the emphasis is "student centered", which enables students to have highly participated and personalized learning experience, and significantly enhance learning effectiveness. Online and offline blended teaching can not only play the leading role of teachers' guidance, inspiration and supervision, but also reflect students' positive and active dominant position in the learning process. Relying on the Chaoxingerya Learning Communication Platform, the online and offline blended teaching mode expands the teaching time and space, which records the student's learning performance throughout the lessons, and personalizes the e-learning file for each student's resume.

3 Teaching Environment Support of the Teaching Model Based on Chaoxingerya Platform

3.1 Construction of Intelligent Class

Intelligent class is a new form of education based on the Internet and Internet of Things technology, which integrates multiple functions, such as smart teaching, teacher-student interaction, cloud storage, video recording and broadcasting, intelligent environment adjustment, self-service attendance and remote interaction, etc. Intelligent class applies modern approaches to cut into the entire teaching process, making the classroom simple, efficient, and intelligent, and help develop students' independent thinking and learning abilities.

3.2 Construction of Chaoxingerya Platform

The learning platform is the condition and guarantee of the online and offline blended teaching mode. Using the mobile terminal to obtain online teaching resources for learning is a convenient and efficient learning mode. Chaoxingerya platform is a professional mobile learning platform for smart phones, tablets, computers, and other mobile terminals. The Chaoxingerya learning platform can perform classroom activities such as sign-in, topic discussions, group coursework, and live broadcasts. By using Chaoxingerya, there is big data technology to monitor the teaching process, fully grasp the learning situation of students, and adjust teaching strategies in time according to the problems found. Relying on the Chaoxingerya learning platform to expand the teaching time and space, and through a variety of teaching methods to solve the problems in the teaching of traditional flower decoration techniques, the teaching key points are emphasized, and the difficulties are broken.

3.3 Construction of "Flower Decoration Technique" Online and Open High-Quality Curriculum

Using Chaoxingerya learning platform to build online courses is relatively complicated and takes a long time. However, once it is completed, it has powerful functions. In addition to more intuitive display of teaching content, it can also carry out teaching interaction before, during and after class, and it can also be used for more off-campus students and social enthusiasts to learn [4]. According to the "Flower Decoration Technology" course standards and teaching objectives, following the rules of vocational education and teaching, combining with the World Skills Competition floristry project skill standards, flower arrangers professional standards, and floral environment designer professional standards, the teaching content is selected, refined, and reconstructed into 5 teaching projects (floriculture, western flower arrangement, oriental flower arrangement, modern flower arrangement, flower decoration management). Each teaching project includes online teaching tasks and offline activities. Each project has multiple learning tasks, and each learning task contains teaching resources such as courseware, explanatory videos, coursework, works pictures, works assessment standards, extended learning, chapter tests, etc. As long as the mobile phone downloads the Chaoxingerya platform, students can access the learning platform anytime and anywhere to achieve autonomous learning and personalized learning. Teachers can monitor student learning through the background and have a fair idea of the learning time and progress of the students (Fig. 1 and Table 1).

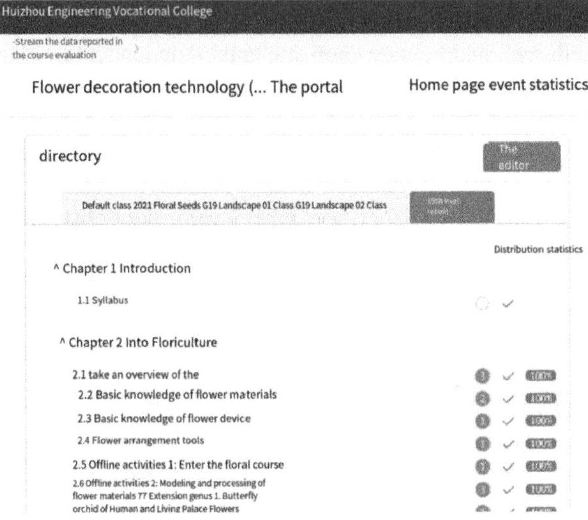

Fig. 1. Application interface

Table 1. Lecture content.

Chapter	Online knowledge	Offline capabilities	Capabilities extension	Apportionment of class hours
Floriculture	1. Overview of floriculture 2. Basic knowledge of flowers 3. Basic knowledge of containers 4. Flower arrangement tools	1. Floriculture lessons 2. Floral styling and processing	1. Popular Lunar New Year Eve Festival-Flower Phalaenopsis 2.Appreciation of Professor Ma's "XiaoSa" Chinese flower arrangement works	4 class hours

(continued)

Table 1. *(continued)*

Chapter	Online knowledge	Offline capabilities	Capabilities extension	Apportionment of class hours
Western flower arrangement	1. Brief history and characteristics of western flower arrangement 2. Hemispherical type, triangular type, vertical type and L-shaped type 3. Inverted T type, horizontal type, fan type, crescent type 4. S type, cone type, waterfall type, parallel design	1. Flower arrangement in the West 2. Production of L-shaped flower works	1. Plant design and production	16 class hours
Oriental flower arrangement	1. Brief History and Characteristics of Oriental Flower Arrangement 2. The basic pattern of oriental flower arrangement 3. Basket flower production 4. Bowl flower production 5. Tube flower production 6. Dish flower production 7. Vase flower production 8. Jar flower production	1. Deeply study Oriental flower arrangement 2. Show the ambition with flowers and walk into the poetry meeting of flowers 3. Basket flower production 4. Bowl flower production 5. Tube flower production 6. Dish flower production 7. Vase flower production 8. Jar flower production	1. China's top ten famous flowers and twelve flower kings 2. Production of floral embossing works	16 class hours
Modern flower arrangement	1. Modern flower arrangement techniques (1). reorganization, folding, folding, cascading, ladder 2. Modern flower arrangement techniques (2): winding, binding, ornamental binding, paved, grouped, piled up 3. Modern flower arrangement techniques (3): cone cup, reel, string hanging, weaving 4. Modern flower arrangement techniques (4): shadow, frame, structure, paste, perspective	1. Design and production of bouquets 2. Flower-cut decoration design and production	1. The production of ribbon flowers 2. Appreciation and analysis of works of the World Cup, China Cup and competition over the years	16 class hours

(continued)

Table 1. (*continued*)

Chapter	Online knowledge	Offline capabilities	Capabilities extension	Apportionment of class hours
Flower decoration management	1. Decoration design of flower shop 2. Flower shop management	1. Research report	1. List of Chinese festivals	2 class hours

3.4 Curriculum Establishment

Teachers can add students from the student library or import students in bulk, or by sending class invitation codes or QR codes to students, who can join the course using a sweep of QR codes or input invitation codes in the upper right corner of the home page of the Chaoxingerya Learning Platform.

4 Pedagogical Design of Online and Offline Blended Teaching Mode Based on Chaoxingerya Platform

Via online and offline blended teaching mode, focusing on the position of floral environment designer, this course covers 5 projects including step into floriculture, western flower arrangement, oriental flower arrangement, modern flower arrangement, flower decoration management. Driven by tasks and based on solving practical problems, this course comprehensively utilizes a variety of teaching methods such as case teaching, heuristic teaching, and on-site teaching. Using the online and offline blended teaching mode, the teacher solves the problems one by one, so that students can master the qualities, knowledge, and abilities needed to complete the project (Fig. 2).

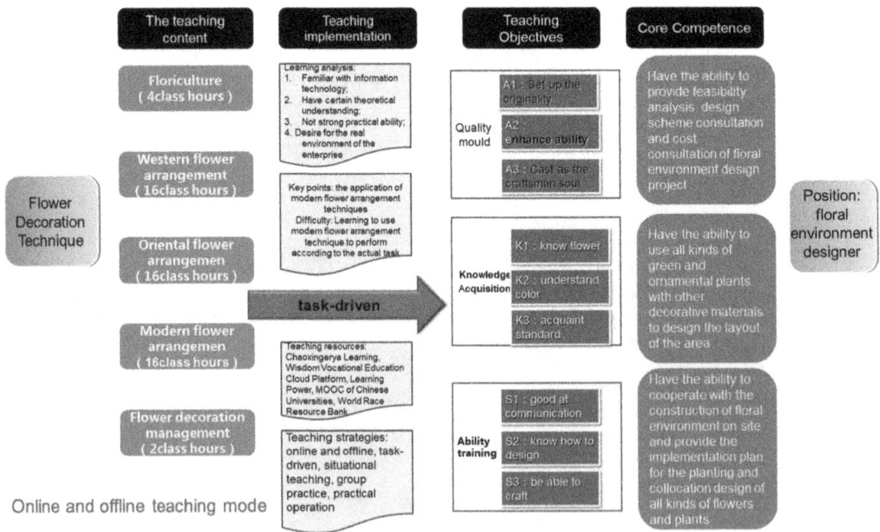

Fig. 2. Online and offline teaching mode

5 Teaching Implementation of Online and Offline Blended Teaching Mode Based on Chaoxingerya Platform

Teachers are task-driven in an information environment, meanwhile, whole teaching process is divided into three parts: pre-class exploration, in-class guidance, and after-class expansion. Students preview before class. The class is driven by real cases of corporate floral projects and is divided into two content: floral performance learning and floral performance production. Furthermore, an "online and offline" blended teaching model is constructed, and the floral performance methods are divided into 6 sub-groups. The tasks are designed to: "remember" reviewing the past and learn the new, "introducing" into the task of professional context, students "analyze" flower art examples, teachers "understand" the performance techniques of flower art based on cases, students and students interact with each other to "make" floral works by using the expression techniques of flower art and multiple "evaluation" of the details of the performance techniques of floral art. Six steps that achieve "learning, teaching, and doing" mutually complement each other, allow students to master the key points of the course and break through the difficulties of the course in an interesting, open and intelligent class. Last but not least, students should expend their capacity and make endeavor for their improvement after class.

5.1 Pre-class Exploration

Before class, teachers upload teaching resources to Chaoxingerya learning platform and release learning tasks. Moreover, lecturers should check the situation of studying, degree of test completion and discussion, which is advantaged to teachers ensuring teaching key and difficult points and adjust the strategies of teaching in time.

5.2 In-Class Guidance

In the class, teachers use the Chaoxingerya learning platform to complete 7 teaching parts, containing sign-in, reviewing the past and learning about the new, introducing professional situations, analyzing tasks, explaining new knowledge, guiding practical training, and evaluating and summarizing. Simultaneously, students use the Chaoxingerya learning platform to complete 7 learning parts, covering sign-in, problem thinking, task analysis, mastering new knowledge, listening, and summarizing, group training, and multiple evaluations.

5.3 After-Class Expansion

After class, teachers use Chaoxingerya learning platform to guide students to study and preview. Subsequently, students use the Chaoxingerya learning platform to consolidate the content of the class and complete the pre-class preview of the next project, forming a good habit of learning at every part (Fig. 3).

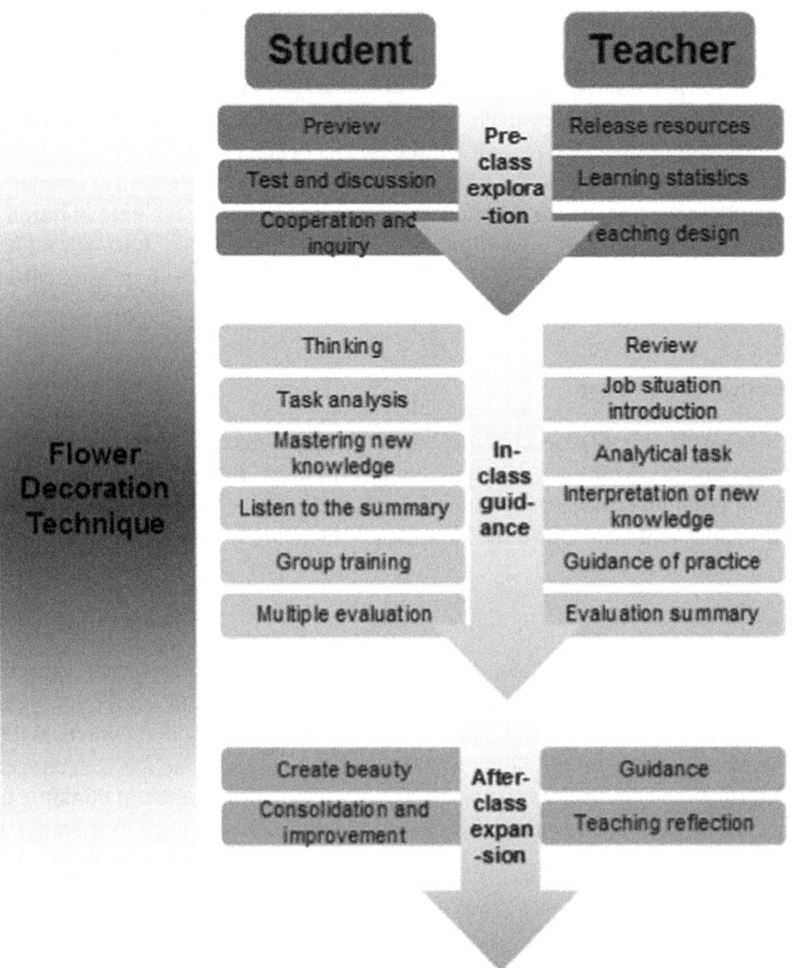

Fig. 3. Teaching process

6 Teaching Evaluations of Online and Offline Blended Teaching Mode Based on Chaoxingerya Platform

6.1 Teacher's Evaluation of Students' Learning

The assessment of online and offline blended teaching mode based on Chaoxingerya platform pay high attention on students' flower decoration design ability, information collection, processing and analysis capabilities, focusing on students' hands-on and language expression skills, divided into three aspects: process evaluation, project outcome evaluation, and comprehensive skill evaluation. The results of the evaluation include survey reports, floral works, to name but a few. The weight of the evaluation is composed of three parts: learning attitude, theoretical knowledge evaluation, and practical ability evaluation (Table 2).

Table 2. Teaching evaluation weight

Evaluation parts	Evaluation content	Weight(%)
Online	Self-learning	20
	Class performance	20
Offline	Evaluation of project outcomes (practical results)	30
	Skills assessment	30
Total	100	

6.2 Students' Reviews of the Online and Offline Blended Teaching Mode Based on the Chaoxingerya Learning Platform

It appears that the background data results from the Chaoxingerya Learning Platform show that the pre-class preview rate of students reaches 100%, indicating that most students have consciously completed the teaching resources uploaded by teachers. By testing the students' pre-class situation through the chapter test, most of the students passed the chapter test and achieved their goals. Definitely, the goal of the course is achieved very good. In terms of student participation, students participate in 100% of classroom interaction, and classroom quality has been significantly improved. By and large, in terms of student satisfaction, student satisfaction with the classroom reached more than 95% (Fig. 4).

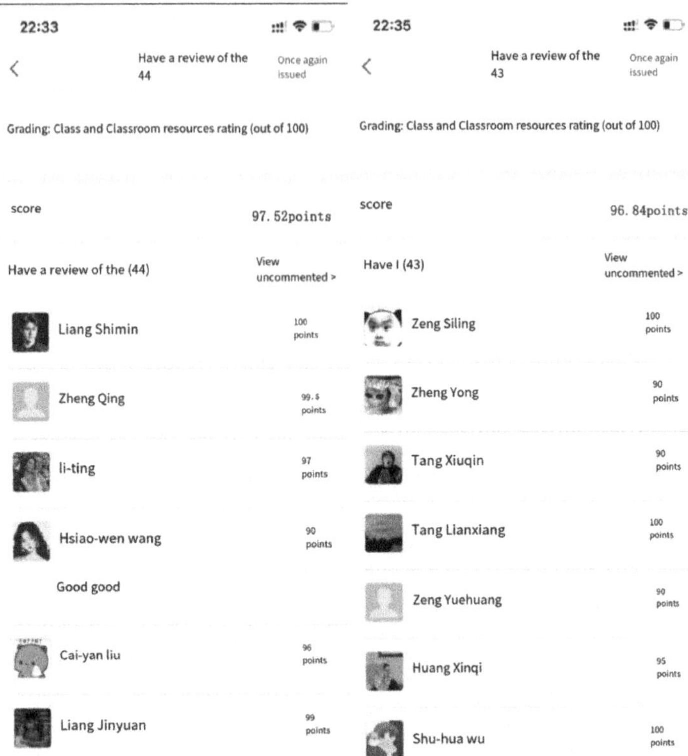

Fig. 4. Students' reviews of the class

7 Reflection and Improvement of the Blended Teaching Mode Based on the Chaoxingerya Learning Platform

7.1 The Adoption of Different Teaching Approaches

Because of the different sources of senior vocational students, even if the teaching content is same, for different learning foundation and learning habits of students, the effect is different. According to the students' personality, we must further explore a variety of teaching methods and use models for students at different levels. Based on their personality and merit, we aim to teach according to their talents, teach by individuals, and teach according to their genre.

7.2 The Necessity of Promotion of Online Teaching

The main target of the project is the students in the general recruitment class. In the face of the new changes in the social recruitment policy situation, not only should we deepen the study of learning background, but also improve the online teaching form and assessment methods.

7.3 Teaching Resources Need to Be Further Supplied

The quantity of teaching resources in the course of "Flower Decoration Technology" is considerable, however, the quality of some teaching resources is not satisfied. More or less, some resources construction is not standardized enough, and the sustainable utilization rate is not enough. At present, the curriculum group has completed the classification and sorting of existing curriculum resources, listing the curriculum resources construction. The group intends to spend about a year to make the course resources construction basically reasonable, sufficient, applicable.

8 Conclusion

The "Flower Decoration Technology" course based on the Chaoxingerya learning platform incorporates information teaching, which increases the effectiveness of the course. The course is accorded to information technology as a platform, applying online and offline blended teaching model, which create an intelligent flower decoration class, breaking through the traditional teaching model, and highly boosting the interest and effectiveness of teaching. Besides, curriculum resources can be stored effectively on the Chaoxingerya learning platform for a long time, and students can also retrieve the content they want to learn at any time to complete online and offline individual learning.

References

1. Liu, D.: Practical research on blended teaching mode based on Chaoxing Fanya platform——taking the course of "electrical engineering and electronic technology" as an example. Theory Pract. Innov. Entrep. **3**(24), 144–145+148 (2020)
2. Song, F.: Online teaching practice and research based on ChaoxingFanya platform——taking the course of "multimedia video production" as an example. Teach. Learn. New Curriculum (e-book) **2021**(01), 148–149 (2021)
3. Cheng, H., Ma, Y., Han, H.: The exploration and practice of online and offline blended teaching model in college teaching——taking our school's modern electrical control technology and PLC courses as examples. China Mod. Educ. Equip. **2021**(09), 55–57+62 (2021)
4. Zhang, L., Zhan, J., Yao, Y.: A comparative study on the application of different online teaching platforms under the background of blended teaching model——taking "Chaoxingerya" and "Yuketang" as an example. Educ. Modernization **7**(43), 26–30 (2020)

Application of Future 5G Technology in the Development of Higher Vocational Education

Bingshuang Han[1], Yinteng Huang[1], Xinlu Li[2], and Fangyang Zhang[1(✉)]

[1] Ctiy College of Huizhou, Huizhou 516025, China
zhangfangyang@tm.hzc.edu.cn
[2] Huizhou Engineering Vocational College, Huizhou 516000, China

Abstract. Industrial convergence will be an inevitable trend in the 5G Era. Crossover cooperation among professional technicians in different trades or posts will be a certainty. These impel higher vocational education to speed up reform, adapt to the requirement of 5G development and meet the challenges positively. This article aims at exploring the challenges the higher vocational colleges meet, and analyzing the application strategies they adopt in 5G new format.

Keywords: 5G era · Vocational education · Challenges · Strategies

1 Introduction

The Ministry of Industry and Information Technology issued commercial licenses for 5G in 2019, meaning China is entering a critically rapid period of 5G development and to be a leaders of new era mobile communication technology. 5G technology has more advantages in terms of operating speed, connection density and capacity, and has built a three-dimensional digital environment for modern industries. It has built a digital highway for the development of science and technology, providing an important information channel for the development of big data, internet of things and artificial intelligence. 5G also has great impact on social operation management mode, business mode and education mode. As a cradle of fostering talents, it is urgent for higher vocational colleges to combine the needs of 5G era, conform to the trend of times and to be ready for 5G vocational education in the future.

2 The Impact of the 5G Era on New Business Formats

2.1 Cross-border Integration

With the incoming of 5G, integration of industrial chain is to be an essential development tendency in the future. Base on the mode of Big Data+Platform, tremendous progress and reform have been achieved in algorithm and computing capacity, which can promote

© ICST Institute for Computer Sciences, Social Informatics and Telecommunications Engineering 2022
Published by Springer Nature Switzerland AG 2022. All Rights Reserved
S. Shi et al. (Eds.): 6GN 2021, LNICST 439, pp. 668–675, 2022.
https://doi.org/10.1007/978-3-031-04245-4_59

connection of industrial chain, provide scientific basis for information forecasting and aggregate productivity factors. From the perspective of mode of production, production efficiency is increasing, standardization is being replaced by individualization, human resource is being replaced by automation technologies. Moreover, with technological breakthrough [1], 5G technology makes the network reliability and security, and makes intelligent production and service possible. At last, with development of crossover cooperation, working space is expanded, the ways of production organization is changed by technical means, rote of labors in production differs from that in the past. Based on Fig. 1, the 5G technology's development has become the leader and mainstream of the industry and higher vocational education also should need to strengthen innovation in combination with social development.

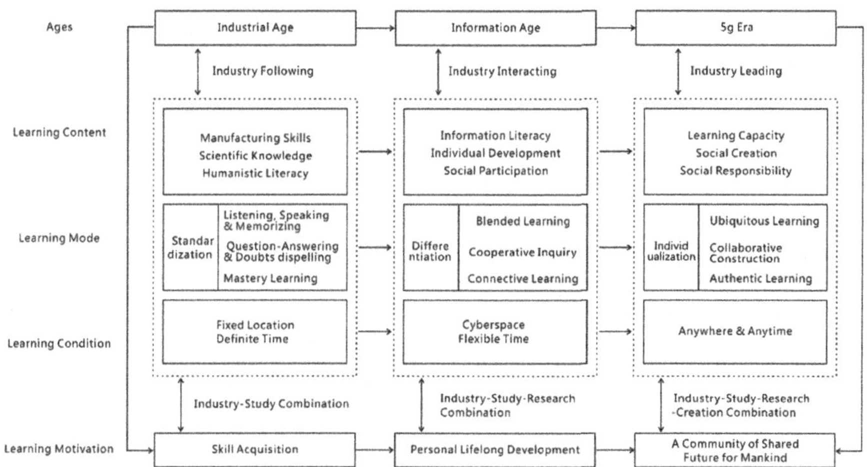

Fig. 1. The development of 5G education in higher vocational college

2.2 Rapid Iteration of New and Old Post

With the arriving of 5G era, the change of the trade will surely influence the employment market, meaning that, the employment market needs to adapt to the new industrial development. Besides, 5G technology prompts a rapid iteration of new and old post, where reform is being driven by technological innovation and technological development is put more on capital-intensive and technology-intensive business. As a result, the advantages of labor resource in labor-intensive business are disappearing, more and more employees are losing their positions, or have to transfer to a new post. The good news is that 5G era is also making compensation, with new technology improving products, bringing more new positions and developing innovative space. Thus, modern higher vocational education should take the opportunity to improve cultivation of talents, training more advanced labor force who can master automation technology accurately and efficiently rather than traditional manual labor force. With 5G technology supporting big data, artificial intelligence and other technologies, flexible judgment is to be made by combining goals of modern information development [2]. Besides, here comes two trends. The general labor force capital is decreasing, for there is higher compatibility of labor force. On the other hand, talent capital is increasing by vocational training. As a consequence, higher vocational colleges should aim at the transition from general labor force post to talent capital post, and heightening employees' capital value.

2.3 Normality of Cross Team Collaboration

When industrial structure is perfected, employment situation is optimized, backward-development technology causes discordance between industry and employment structure. In order to guarantee scientific personnel cultivation, higher vocational college need to take positive response to modern revolutionary technological change and make ICT literacy as the core according to future career development in 5G era. Compared to traditional technology, 5G technology performs an obvious promotion effect on economic development. It gradually presents a multi-field development mode. Further study on industry, post and the principles of the position, engaging in 5G technology should be taken. Training with different kinds of teaching resources, like AR and VR resources, needs adopting to contribute to the combination of human and technology, thus to improve production value by technology together with technique. For the post, the employees engaged in 5G technology are required to grasp the ability of network planning, mobile communication, big data and diversity of technical work. In the meantime, it is essential to strengthen professional technology and to facilitate cross-profession communication and collaboration, on the purpose of developing cross team collaboration among different industries. For the professional technology itself, technology frontier should be reinforced, trends should be grasped longitudinally, and self-learning as well as professional cooperation should be also stressed.

3 Challenges of Future Vocational Education in 5G Era

3.1 Value Diversification of Talent Cultivation

As artificial intelligence and digital economy in 5G era is growing, career boundary has become increasingly blurred, causing obvious tendency among cross-major and cross-post. Great change of labor connotation certainly promotes employment, while it also requests more about labor's sustainable learning ability, information literacy and social emotion. Considering the requirement of talent development in 5G era, Higher vacation college ought to cultivate top-level talents with professionalization and high attainment. As shown in Fig. 2, the number of majors which is related with 5G in Chinese Higher Vocational Colleges is upward from 2019–2021. If deep into the data, most of our higher vocational colleges still adopt single-major teaching philosophy while developing vocational curriculum at present. What's worse, sustainable learning ability, the way of thinking in 5G era and cognitive ability are not brought into vocational curriculum yet. Most colleges are beginning to emphasize information literacy, yet, the teaching content cannot meet the demands of digitization and intellectualization [3]. All of above leads to the situation that professional skills and knowledge are limited in personnel cultivation. Thus, what the students learn cannot meet the demands of development characteristics in the current era.

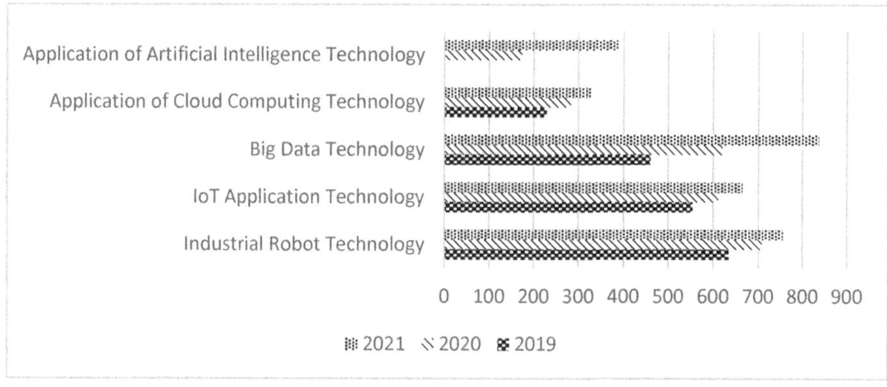

Fig. 2. Number of 5G-related majors established in higher vocational colleges in recent three years

3.2 Intellectualization of Learning Mode

In 5G era, higher vocational college is more than a place where knowledge and skills are taught to students, but an intellectualized educational platform. Intelligent learning is going to be the important content in education. To suit this intellectualization learning mode, higher vocational college should set up teaching management mode for fragmented knowledge and competitive learning, optimize space modality in campus, improve the management system and adopt scientific management, in order to accelerate an intellectualized and open campus. Besides, they should also highlight the conception of students-oriented, establish innovative teaching environment and offer students intellectualized and open circumstance [4]. Yet, under contemporary system, secondary colleges, together with credit system and student- status management, are basic components and still play a pivotal role in higher vocational colleges. Differentiation brought by online teaching among learners is an unfavorable factor to wisdom teaching, that, higher vocational colleges should make reform according to teaching management in industrial stage.

3.3 Influence of Educational Equality

The start of 5G era helps higher vocational college gain more channels, obtain more abundant education resources and achieve teaching optimization. Even those in underdeveloped regions can obtain high-quality teaching resources from outside. For another, teaching or learning resources are no longer limited to schools, students can search related learning resources by themselves on internet, bringing more advantages in theoretical study and skill acquisition. The development of 5G technology helps to contribute favorable conditions for vocational education evolution, employment and poverty alleviation. However, from the actual condition, there still exist some problems in applicating these high-quality teaching resources. For example, systematics measures of college and individual's applicating these resources are to be set up, which makes it difficult for both of them to explore appropriate teaching resources [5]. Even, there are great differences in the economic structure and industrial form of different regions in China, the high-quality resources may not suit the demands in underdeveloped regions. In 5G era, it helps vocational students in underdeveloped regions easier access high-quality resources, they are more likely to get impacted by the content and thoughts within the resources. By comparing these, more talents in underdeveloped regions choose to come into economically developed areas. Consequently, this kind of talent flow is enlarging educational equality.

3.4 Open and Life-Long Education Platform Construction

In traditional vocational education, it aims at promoting one-time employment, while in 5G era, it requests learners to employ persistent and diversified study mode based on their interest, hobbies, career development and even their family background.

Moreover, every individual can share his professional knowledge or skills, search for professional resources or talent, construct information connection channel. And even, they can complete their learning or service in informal ways with the help of 5G. But unfortunately, higher vocational colleges still adopt enclosed classroom teaching mode because of the current educational environment, the influence and limitation of scientific and technological level, management strategies or mentality. Even if colleges develop the teaching mode of school-enterprise cooperation and production-education integration, these are passive adjustment that colleges have to take for their development. The education mode, which can establish open teaching resources, considers further study for continuing learners and realize long-life study, is impossible to achieve yet. It is eager that higher vocational college should reexamine definition and mode of vocational education, to set up an open long-life education mode.

4 Application Strategies for Future Vocational Education in 5G Era

4.1 5G Concept to Improve Teaching

In 5G era, students in vocational college are facing more complicated occupational development environment, meaning they need to respond the current career development situation positively by combining profession connotation and future career development. As for vocational colleges, they ought to comprehensively evaluate their teaching characteristics and external influence factors, set up new personnel training mode on the basis of broader industries and career development rather than the traditional single major training method. They should also break traditional linear employment logic and cultivate pluralization and diverse talented personnel. Higher vocational education needs to grasp the concept of modern education in personnel cultivation, apply prospective educational philosophy, in order to set the closest link to production line and service and to perform much better in serving the society [6]. 5G era lays stress on developing standard of talent cultivation, optimizing assessment system, persevering in new technology research and innovation, thus, encouraging innovative and intelligent professionals. Hereby, higher vocation colleges should concentrate on cultivating high-level and comprehensive talents, and take initial employment together with long-term continuing vocational education as vital educational content, but not focus on academic career and employment in personnel cultivation.

4.2 Reinforcing Coordination to Break the Traditional Professional Layout

Future vocational educational profession design and layout is required to be well programmed in 5G era. Specialty setting ought to suit local present status of economic development and strategy, playing its own value and advantages in informatization; for instant, developing 5G+ Project to evolve digital development projects, expanding digital industry, promoting internet of things, cloud computing and artificial intelligence, etc., and exploring digital finance. In the light of current industry development trends, higher vocational colleges ought to deploy market investigation, construct majors and curriculums, and intensify digital finance majors. Firstly, it is necessary to weed out the majors that cannot fit the market development or are out of date, and to set up the new one based on the demands of the market, such as internet finance, big data technology and artificial intelligence services. In this way, it will be doing a good job in supplying talent force for regional industries and economic development.

What is more, considering the teaching and situation of professional development, higher vocational colleges should regulate the connection between specialty and industry by creating superior specialty and featured majors, developing school-enterprise cooperation, promoting implementation of modern apprenticeship and practicing industrial 1+X certificate system, with the purpose of promoting work in all areas by drawing upon experience gained in the work on key points. Finally, it is helpful to set up "2 with 5" specialty clusters with the demands of big data and inclusive finance. Taking internet finance major as an example, higher vocational colleges can establish a specialty cluster with a core of financial management major, combining 5G technology, digital economy, inclusive finance, international finance and rural finance. As for international trading, a diversified specialty cluster based on international trading, combining business English and Cross-border e-commerce. Driven by high level major clusters, it is easier to cultivate high- competent talents with high-tech capability and entrepreneurial spirit, thus to promote the regional economic development.

4.3 Creating Modern Teaching System with 5G Superiority

5G era also drives vocational education to meet reform. Higher vocational colleges need to analyze the regulation of vocational education development and adopt teaching reform by making good use of 5G technology. There is a necessity that a large number of financial resources are invested in teacher construction and teacher's cultivation, aiming to build a sophisticated teaching group. For instance, the "Hundred-Thousand-Ten Thousand Teacher Project". Cultivation is mainly combined information technology and specialized courses, competition of courseware production and contest of information technology is carried out in order to strengthen their information abilities, therefor, to establish a group of influential and professionalized online teaching masters.

In the meantime, higher vocational college will kick its way to 5G self-regulated learning era by bursting the restraints of traditional education and establishing new vocational education mode with 5G technology and smart campus service system. By renewing education concept and 5G vocational education concept, 5G+ smart campus, artificial intelligence data center and service platform are constructed, forming smart campus data center, making intelligent teaching service, smart classroom, smart training base, smart workshop and kinds of smart learning venues possible, therefor, to fulfill All-in-One intelligent education environment, and to promote teaching system analysis and reform.

When constructing specialty cluster, higher vocational colleges can set up an internal "cloud architecture" to accelerate intellectualization in specialty cluster, digitization in learning environment and resource construction. Intelligent teaching mode, which can be administrated closely with open sharing of resources, will be founded by integrating learning elements of every major and big data. That, students can learn anytime anywhere, or even the way of fragmented, personalized and mobile learning is becoming possible. Furthermore, it can describe students' psychology and behavior, forming their construct life-cycle big data, in this way, offering personalized learning content and learning situation warning, and promoting the development of vocational education.

4.4 Taking Responsibility to Guarantee Education Equity

In 5G era, higher vocational colleges in different regions can access and achieve full coverage of high-speed internet. With the support of information technology and hardware, it is possible to share or optimize vocational education resources, narrowing the traditional gap between teaching and learning. The sharing in 5G future education shall be a two-way relationship mode, including information sending and information receiving, which also entails asymmetry. In another words, the application of 5G technology can amplify the consequence of the imbalanced regional economy development, cause huge change in how people think and bring major difference among types and condition of employment, which cannot be made up by 5G technology.

To ease this consequence, higher vocational colleges should take careful consideration on the type of faculty and features of regional economic development, to construct featured schools and majors, improve docking between industry and specialty and regulate and perfect mechanism of major construction. Moreover, it is necessary to optimize and improve professional evaluation index and information management system, and eliminate unqualified majors, so as to be the college which is indispensable to regional economy development. At last, 5G technology can be used for targeted poverty alleviation, helping to develop the education in undeveloped regions, and guaranteeing education equity.

4.5 Promoting Long-Life Education

Vocational education is becoming a part of long-life education in 5G era. Working force must combine the demands of the society development to form the concept of long-life education and continuing learning with the purpose of improve individual knowledge and skills. Higher vocational colleges can meet this need by using 5G technology to apply credit bank management, control the cost of credit recording, credit converting and certification [7]. In this way, students can fulfill long-life education by accumulating credits. Higher vocational colleges should break framework of thinking restriction and improve employability of vocational education. It is important to improve students' leaning performance by constructing of academic or credit archives, summarizing and storing students' education information, like vocational skill level certificates or online educational outcomes.

5 Conclusion

In summary, in the context of the 5G era, the reform is rising in vocational education, which promotes the development of the industry and influences the Industrial economy. It also gives an impetus to economic change, consummate the education. With the innovation of 5G educating technique and tools, it is more convenient to obtain or share education resources, and it is possible to break the limitation of time and space to make learners to learn anytime anywhere. However, higher vocational colleges should construct featured majors, set the aim of developing talents scientifically, improve the docking between social service and vocational education and promote teaching practice and reform. That, it is positive to cultivate more innovative talents, to supply favorable conditions for 5G future cultivation of modern vocational talents, to positively meet the challenges in 5G era, and to promote innovation in vocational teaching and learning.

References

1. Ye, C.: Exploration of information construction in higher vocational colleges under the background of big data. China Educ. Informatization **17**, 12–14 (2016)
2. Liu, Y.: Optimization measures for information construction in higher vocational colleges under the background of big data. Digit. World **4**, 158–160 (2019)
3. Yonghui, G.: Research and practice of student information management in higher vocational colleges under the background of big data. Educ. Mater. **5**, 121–122 (2017)
4. Yaohong, R., Jie, Y., Dandan, L.: On the development of teaching and management mode of higher vocational education under the background of 5G era. Comput. Knowl. Technol. **17**(8), 135–136 (2021)
5. Wang, G., Du, J., Li, A.: Research on strategies to promote the high-quality development of online education in higher vocational colleges in the 5G era. Digit. Technol. Appl. **38**(10), 203–205 (2020)
6. Xingbo, Y.: Research on the application of "5G+ intelligent education" in online teaching of higher vocational colleges. J. Hubei Vocat. Coll. **34**(7), 133–134 (2021)
7. Yiquan, F., Biyun, H.: Challenges and changes of the development paradigm of higher vocational education in 5G era. Chin. Vocat. Tech. Educ. **28**, 5–8 (2020)

Research on the Construction of Students' Vocational Core Literacy Evaluation System of Big Data Analysis

Baodan Chen and Zhiping Rao(✉)

Huizhou Economic and Polytechnic College, Huizhou, Guangdong, China
hilongok@126.com

Abstract. At present, with the wide application of big data in the field of education, especially through the big data scraping class and individual students' homework, test scores and other learning results for statistical analysis, to gain the conclusion of the whole data can help teachers diagnose teaching effect and improve teaching quality. With the development of post-industrial market economy, the demand for professional talents is not only to stay at the level of academic achievement, but also to consider students' professional accomplishment. It can be predicted that in the future, big data analysis will be more widely used in personnel training, and the core literacy indicators of students will be defined by data. This paper through research and practice, compares and analyzes the definition of professional core literacy by different organizations and scholars, determines the standard of digital core literacy, discusses the construction of digital evaluation system, and explores the application of big data in future education area.

Keywords: Big data · Vocational core literacy · Evaluation system

1 The Definition of Vocational Core Literacy and Lifelong Learning

"Key Competencies" is one of the topics of great concern in the educational field. According to its definition, there are four main representative views:

1.1 Definition for EU

In 2006, the European Union defined the concept of core literacy as: "Is a range of portable, multi-functional knowledge, skills and attitudes, It is necessary for individuals to obtain personal achievement and self-development, integrate into society and be competent for work. It emphasizes that these qualities should be realized in compulsory education as the basis of lifelong education. Thus, the European Union has put forward eight qualities of lifelong learning: mother tongue communication skills, foreign language exchange skills, mathematics literacy, science and technology literacy, learning ability, social citizenship literacy, innovation awareness, cultural awareness and expression.

© ICST Institute for Computer Sciences, Social Informatics and Telecommunications Engineering 2022
Published by Springer Nature Switzerland AG 2022. All Rights Reserved
S. Shi et al. (Eds.): 6GN 2021, LNICST 439, pp. 676–685, 2022.
https://doi.org/10.1007/978-3-031-04245-4_60

1.2 Definition by the Organization for Economic Cooperation and Development

In 1997, the organization stated that core literacy should cover many aspects of life and be a comprehensive reflection of both life and social competence. Through the integration of multiple disciplines, the core literacy of three aspects are: can learn and use tools, can communicate in different situations, can control themselves.

1.3 The "21st Century Literacy" Framework of the United States

It proposes three "R" skills in American schools, namely "Reading, Writing, Arithmetic." Later by extension of the 4 "C," that is, critical thinking and problem solving, Communication and collaboration, creativity and innovation. Until 2007, the framework theory was updated to three core skills: 1, learning skills and innovation skills; Information, media and technical skills; 3. Life and Career Skills.

1.4 Research of Core Literacy in Japan

Japan has built a model of "21st century competence," and put forward curriculum reform around "basic competence" and "thinking ability" to enhance the international competitiveness of talents.

The development process of vocational quality education in China is a process of constantly learning and renewing the concept of "core literacy." As early as in the early 1980s of the 20th worlds, the goal of educational system reform was to improve national quality. In the 1990s, it was emphasized that exam-oriented education should turn to the overall improvement of national quality, and in 1994 the concept of "quality education" was formally used. On the basis of achieving core literacy, and then extended out on the personal "life-long education" new concept, and pay more attention on the basis of knowledge, develop their own skills and attitudes, combine with the needs of society to improve survival ability, practical ability and innovation ability, in order to achieve a healthy state of lifelong learning. Core literacy is the integration of knowledge, skills and attitudes. It is the sustainable development stage of all-round quality education and serves as the educational policy of our country today.

2 The Problems Existing in the Educational Index System of Our Country

With the wide application of big data technology in the field of education, as well as the continuous innovation of educational technology means, the classroom teaching in universities has changed dramatically. The MOOC boom, which began to prevail in China in 2012, is a typical online education model, which uses a lot of information technology to support the realization of online education. Overcome the time and space constraints of learning, let the national and even global quality education resources in a wider space to be shared, so that educational services are reconfigured to maximize the role and value of education.

In 2016, Shanghai Jiao Tong University has opened more than 100 MOOCs and built an online learning platform called "Good University Online," providing a high-quality education platform for universities at home and abroad. The platform expects 24 universities to open courses, and a large number of courses, about 400. More than 400,000 students studied on the platform and more than 40,000 completed MOOCs study. It has created the first cross-university MOOC resource sharing in China and realized the mutual recognition of credits. This exploration of online education has made a major breakthrough. If we want to measure the role and value of such online learning platform, it is obviously biased to use the traditional evaluation index to measure it. Traditional education evaluation tends to consider students' achievements, mostly using a single evaluation index, such as scores, this traditional evaluation index system is difficult to effectively measure students' vocational core literacy. However, the traditional evaluation criteria appear to be vague and unstable. In the evaluation process, more emotional factors are mixed, resulting in inaccurate and unfair evaluation results, making the final educational decision-making biased. The realization of the former needs to rely on a perfect education big data system, including information disclosure between family, school, government and society, that is, data disclosure, data interface should also be made public, to achieve the integration of big data in education.

3 The Establishment of Professional Core Quality Evaluation Indicators

The situation of education has changed greatly. The evaluation standard based on big data will record students' learning behavior more accurately and effectively, collect and accumulate students' activity data, realize data integration and analysis, achieve visual management. This kind of indicator developed through mass data collection is more reliable and objective. Not only the students' curriculum learning information is accurately recorded, but also a collection of school evaluation, social commentary, education environment related factors into the scope of evaluation, so as to obtain scientific and humane educational management decision-making. Therefore, different intelligent terminals should be used in teaching, using real-time face recognition, text recognition, emotion recognition, behavior recognition, speech recognition and other technologies. We will promote data evaluation indicators for monitoring 5G + smart education and establish a sound evaluation index system for vocational education.

3.1 Establish Evaluation Indexes for Online Learning

Online Learning, that means students receive online education through open online resources. The flexible mobile online learning mode, which is called "OL" mode, can be realized without the limitation of time and space. In view of the development of evaluation indicators for this online learning model, this paper argues that the evaluation indicators of big data should be a series of comprehensive quantitative indicators that are digital, measurable and can be used to evaluate students' learning activities and behaviors. Specifically, should include these:

PV (Page Views) means the number of page views, can show students in a learning platform page hit, students visit a website page counts a PV. Through the PV analysis, we can understand all the students for the course preferences and study interest tendency, help to formulate students' personalized needs of the study curriculum and teaching arrangements. This data metric can compare how attractive different courses are to students by how many times they log in on the page.

LT (Learning Time) means time spent studying. Refers to the amount of time students spend on course content, can be specific to the minute, in order to accumulate the student's course study time, the course study length can determine the overall learning attitude of students.

FOL (Feedback Of Learning) means the learning feedback. In this paper refers to students' reaction to the results of learning activities in the course content, such as students' rating of the course, teachers' evaluation, and other meaningful behavioral activities. Through the design of knowledge map of online courses, we can see the number and time of students' interaction and help to judge students' enthusiasm. The database of the learning platform will record these, and further dig out the students' attention to the problem and the type of attention, so as to understand the student's personality characteristics, effectively make a targeted teaching design and curriculum.

The above big data evaluation indicators are mainly for OL learning model, then the offline learning model how to evaluate, the following will be further elaborated.

3.2 The Characteristics and Establishment of Offline Learning Indicators

Online To Offline, this article does not refer to business models here, but refers to online and offline learning models. Offline learning behavior activities mainly refer to students' social behavior performance in daily life, which will also be included in their personal core literacy assessment. It is related to traditional teaching practice evaluation, but it also has some differences.

In the education environment of big data, this offline behavior pattern needs to rely on other nodes outside the school to provide data support, such as community, government, public welfare organizations and so on. When a student participates in volunteer activities in the community, the specific time, place and form of the activity should be provided by his community to prove the reliability of the data generated into the data platform. This offline behavior is more localized, and the accuracy of its description requires the organization or government to produce a unified public official certificate, Therefore, it can be accepted as a kind of reliable data information, as one of the evaluation indicators of family or community learning.

The evaluation index of offline learning revolves around the core qualities of students, including comprehensive education that is not limited to science, technology, engineering, art and mathematics. Around these learning indicators, in order to develop students' core literacy and core ability of comprehensive development. Students' learning process is broken down into specific indicators, such as being able to identify problems, designing solutions, solving problems using knowledge such as science, technology, engineering, mathematics, and the arts, and using rational methods to verify the effectiveness of solutions. The above four indicators give different weights to measure the effectiveness of students' participation in learning activities. Weights are determined using the standard deviation method, as follows:

The original data matrix Xij(i = 1,2,…,n; j = 1,2,…m) is processed without quantity, and the formula of no scale is used by extreme value method:

$$\text{Zij} = (\text{Xij} - \text{Xmin})/(\text{Xmax} - \text{Xmin}) \tag{1}$$

Find the mean of a random variable:

$$\text{Zij} = \frac{1}{n}\sum\nolimits_{i=1}^{n} \text{Zij} \tag{2}$$

Find the mean variance (standard deviation) of the indicator:

$$\delta\text{j} = \sqrt{\sum\nolimits_{i=1}^{n} (\text{Zij} - \text{Zj})^2} \tag{3}$$

Finally, the weights of each indicator are calculated using the mean variance (standard deviation) (Table 1):

$$\text{Wj} = \delta\text{j}/\sum\nolimits_{j=1}^{m} \delta\text{j} \tag{4}$$

Table 1. Weight allocation table.

Evaluation indicators	Be able to identify problems	Design solutions	Use knowledge to solve problems	Verify the effect of the resolution
Weight	0.4	0.3	0.2	0.1
Score	1.6	0.6	0.8	0.3

The results are calculated based on weights and reflect each student's offline learning (see Fig. 1).

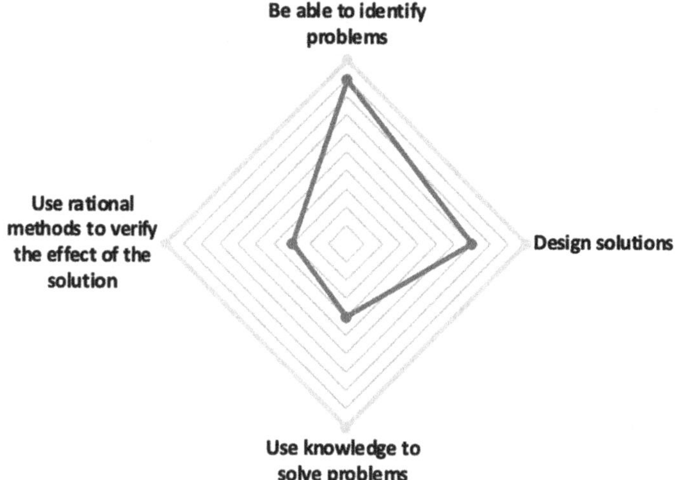

Fig. 1. Each student's offline learning.

At last, the online and offline indicators for weight division, such as the usual study performance accounted for 60%, test scores accounted for 40%, give the relevant weight distribution, make online courses more reasonable and flexible. It can take into account the basic level of most students, and at the same time provide more challenging learning content for more efficient students. This evaluation system will evaluate students' core literacy in the whole learning cycle, help students to realize self-analysis, and provide reliable reference when they choose a school or major. Or employment key links to make a significant role in reference. This kind of educational reform helps society to export more suitable talents and realize the balance of educational resources, which is the value and significance of big data education.

4 The Construction Model of Evaluating Index System of Big Data Information Technology

4.1 Gather Information to Build a "User Portrait" of Students

"User portrait" in the field of data analysis refers to the use of user information in the database records, through this information to enrich and constantly improve the description of users, similar to the process of sketch. In fact, the establishment of "user portrait" of students is to analyze the learning behavior of students, through the database records, tracking and mining students in the course of learning dynamics and course selection tendency. According to the data records of knowledge points, students are classified to understand their mastery degree and behavior personality, so that teachers can adjust teaching methods and progress to achieve the purpose of teaching students in accordance of their aptitude.

4.2 Store Information to Build a Database

All the information that happens around students will become the original data of the big data platform, including students' family background, learning experience, growing up experience, medical records, etc. These original data are not all useful information, and need to be analyzed and filtered to preserve valid data. When this data enters a data center, it can be stored in a low-cost open-source solution such as HDFS or CEPH. Considering the cost, you should choose the right server based on the amount of data.

4.3 Comb Relations to Conduct Data Structural Modeling

How to get useful information from massive data requires technical analysis and screening of data in memory, which is called structural modeling. The logic of the evaluation system of students should be realized by data structuring modeling, eliminating some repetition, error and data, and formatting the original data in a unified way to facilitate inquiry and use. We need computers, RFID and sensor networks, and technical support, including which language to use, such as Python, Java or SQL, and database applications and processing, statistics, mining. Especially data analysis, through keyword modeling, regression analysis and classification, the data will be filtered to get effective data and establish logical relationship.

After the database is established, how to make effective data easy to read? This requires data analysis and mining, with the help of current technology, such as IBM's SPSS and Microsoft's SSRS, of course, are charged. If cost is considered, look for free software such as Spark ML Lib, although they don't work as well. In the presentation way, 3D multimedia information technology and simulation technology can be used to close the distance between virtual and reality. More and more new technical means are used in the design and optimization of platform structure, and educational resources can be fully utilized. The platform, technology, equipment and resources are integrated to realize the evaluation system of data structure, which supports the implementation of big data education platform.

4.4 Establish Quantifiable Data Evaluation Indexes

Formulate unified evaluation indexes according to different online learning models. The menu learning mode, game learning mode and card learning mode should be equipped with uniform evaluation index.

4.4.1 Establish Indicators of Learning Time Dimensions

For example, an online learning platform, the database in the background records and statistics each registered student's total learning time in the platform. Including the time spent on each course and the number of hits on the platform website, each knowledge module and assessment results, the distribution of students' grades, etc. This information is technically processed to become visual indicators of how long a student has spent in a course.

4.4.2 Establish Knowledge Map Progress Indicators

Most of the online learning platforms have been able to design a perfect knowledge map to adapt to the personalized and fragmented learning style. Use knowledge cards or knowledge of the form of small units bearing a knowledge point, as long as the student completed the course content can see their own progress in a course, generally with "%" to show. At the same time, you can see the progress of the student's other elective courses and the percentage of study tasks remaining to be completed.

4.4.3 Establish Student Attitude Indicators

This kind of index corresponds to students' attitude, including study attitude, life attitude and humanistic attitude, which are difficult to quantify. Such indicators must be combined with offline interaction to make a decision, and the main interaction with students can be teachers, parents, classmates or others, their evaluation will be the main reference for such indicators. For example, discussions between students and teachers in class, group work with classmates, participation in competitions or tours, etc. These data records are first completed offline, and then uploaded to the platform by the responsible person to become data retention, to establish students' learning attitude indicators.

4.5 Establish a Transferable Digital Certificate Authentication System

Digital certificate can have several ways, the first, is "credit bank," through the establishment of the "credit banking" system, the accumulation of student learning results, record credits. The second one is to establish the electronic voucher of learning results. The traditional certificates are stored electronically and can be downloaded and passed to prove the learning behavior and results. The above two digital certificates must be established on the basis of educational certification system before they can be circulated. The establishment of the system needs to rely on the strength of many, not a single platform can be achieved. It needs the connection of school, government and society, based on information technology and database construction to support the realization of this authentication mode. This certification system, through the whole process of lifelong learning, retains the process of curriculum learning and comprehensive evaluation results. These digital certificates also have a certain effect if they want to continue to study after they have completed their studies and entered the workplace.

Through the above five technical aspects of the framework, to establish a more objective and scientific core literacy evaluation index system for students, to promote the transformation of classroom teaching and evaluation methods to provide a certain practical significance, promote vocational education high-quality development (see Fig. 2).

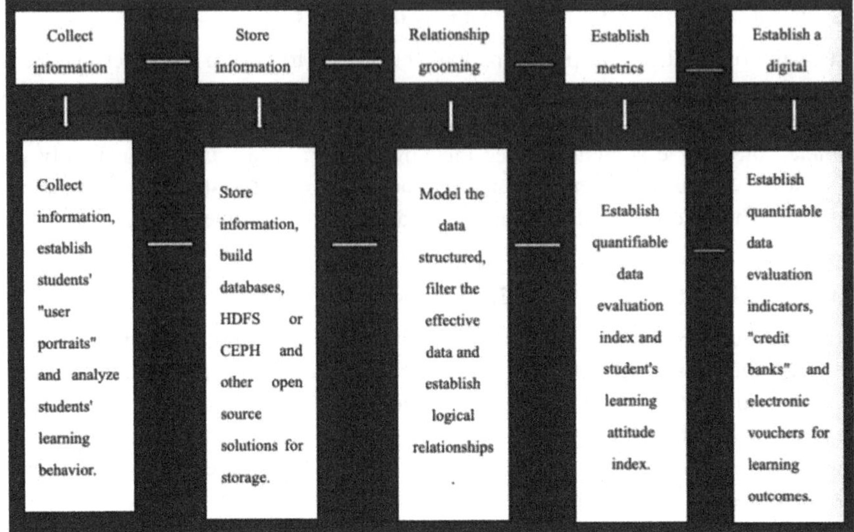

Fig. 2. The construction model of the evaluation index system of big data information technology.

5 The Development Trend of Vocational Education Information

In the future, big data in the field of education scenarios will be more and more popular. The new generation of communications and network technology base, using 5G low delay, high bandwidth, wide connectivity technology, It will promote the deep integration of 5G, Hongmeng, artificial intelligence, big data, cloud computing and education teaching, and promote the co-construction and sharing of quality educational resources. It has become common for students to complete relevant courses at home with the support of information technology platform. For example, in the online live classroom, teachers can choose online live APP to teach, students complete the course independently; Platform curriculum resources can repeatedly learn, and also can accommodate more than 100 people online at the same time, breaking the educational space limitations. Online education platform will become a new way in the field of vocational education in the future, students online learning will also become a normal and traditional teaching methods co-exist, therefore, the implementation of the data-based vocational core literacy evaluation system is an inevitable development trend.

Acknowledgement. This work was supported by grant of No. 2020ZDZX1092 from the Department of Education of Guangdong Province, China.

References

1. Yuan, W., Meng, S.W.: Statistical education in the era of big data. J. Stat. Res. **04** (2015)
2. Qin, Y., Gu, X.P.: Construction of mobile learning model for college students with cloud computing. J. Asia Pacific Educ. **31** (2016)

3. Cai, R.H., Fan, Y.X.: Construction of autonomous learning model based on knowledge map from the perspective of big data. J. Chin. Educ. Technol. Equipment **05** (2017)
4. Chen, B.D.: Research on teaching design and evaluation mechanism of higher vocational curriculum informationization based on results orientation. J. Knowl. Guide **05**(13) (2018)
5. Wang, C.X.: Discussion on the development of online and offline mixed teaching under the background of "Internet + Education". J. Modernization Educ. **44** (2019)
6. Lu, Y.X.: Analysis on the educational model of vocational colleges in the new era of internet. J. Invention Innov. **06** (2021)
7. Yang, Y., Lin, X., Kang, H.: Information technology to help the ecological reconstruction of vocational education: endogenous logic, target direction and development path. J.Theory Pract. Educ. **09** (2019)
8. Huo, J.Y., Si, T.X.: Countermeasure research on the training of professional core competence in logistics management of higher vocational colleges. J. Inner Mongolia Inst. Transp. Vocat. Tech. Coll. **06**(15) (2021)
9. Wang, Q.Y., Sun, J. Deng, B.: Intelligent location system of network abnormal nodes based on big data analysis. J. Modern Electron. **18** (2021)
10. Li, W.: The construction and application of the quality evaluation system of higher vocational education under the "New Normal". J. Tianjin Vocat. Coll. **07** (2015)
11. Sun, L.: Visual analysis of employment data for higher vocational students based on big data. J. Inf. Comput. (Theoret. Edn.) **23** (2020)
12. Tao, X.P.: Dictionary of Educational Evaluation. Monograph of Beijing Normal University Press, Beijing (1998)
13. Zhou, X.: Reflections on the achievements and problems of teaching evaluation reform in the past decade. J. Chin. Educ. **10** (2011)

Multimodal Fusion Blended Teaching Under the New Era of "Internet+" Education

Runfeng Yang(✉)

Dongguan Polytechnic, Dongguan 523808, China
yangrf@dgpt.edu.cn

Abstract. With the rapid development of information and intelligent technology, education informatization is constantly promoted and upgraded, which can open up opportunities for implementing innovative teaching methods for "Internet+" education. Institutions of higher education in China adopt various ways to actively carry out online teaching, and promote the research of online teaching practice. The teaching methods for the courses in intelligent building engineering technology specialty in Dongguan Polytechnic are presented as examples in this paper. Multimodal fusion in blended teaching is practiced and explored in these professional courses, which included Small Private Online Course (SPOC) combing with flipped classroom scheme, integration of course and 1+X certificate of vocational skill level, project site online demonstration and so on. The implementation of online flipped classroom is effectively promoted by the proposed multimodal fusion blended teaching, and more efficient teaching effect is achieved.

Keywords: Education informatization · Blended teaching · Flipped classroom · Vocational skill

1 Introduction

With the rapid development of information technologies such as Artificial Intelligence (AI), 5G technology, big data, and Virtual Reality (VR), the integration of teaching methods into the intelligent environment has become a key measure for the revolutionary impact of "Internet+" education. These information technologies can promote the transformation and upgrading of education informatization, fully stimulate the integration of information technology into education, and accelerate the implementation of educational modernization. In today's "Internet+" education information era, online teaching modes have been known gradually. Online education has been widely used as breaking the spatio-temporal limitations and offering one of the best ways in public education [1]. Blended teaching can offer a continuous and innovative way for classroom teaching reform, gradually merge and replace the traditional teaching approaches [2]. Learning methods such as task-driven, case-based, and problem-oriented are widely applied in blended teaching. It is regarded as students-centered teaching method to carry out online and offline interactive teaching, which has a positive effect on stimulating students' interest in learning and mobilizing students' learning initiative [3].

© ICST Institute for Computer Sciences, Social Informatics and Telecommunications Engineering 2022
Published by Springer Nature Switzerland AG 2022. All Rights Reserved
S. Shi et al. (Eds.): 6GN 2021, LNICST 439, pp. 686–698, 2022.
https://doi.org/10.1007/978-3-031-04245-4_61

Vocational education in engineering is associated with theoretical and practical knowledge, where students are obligated to go beyond the conceptual understanding of theoretical knowledge and to acquire practical skills. Different technical means, incentive measures and comprehensive application methods are flexibly used to realize the optimization of blended teaching for different courses. In this paper, taking the building intelligent engineering technology specialty as an example, multimodal fusion blended teaching and a variety of teaching management mechanisms are implemented in the professional courses. Through the teaching practice and exploration in a "classroom revolution" of online teaching, the teaching experience and achievements are accumulated, which offers a referred scheme for the reform and innovation of blending teaching courses.

2 Teaching Scheme Design

In view of the characteristics of talent training for building intelligent engineering technology professionals, curriculum design ideas in each professional course are adopted by combining theory, experiment and practical training, combining teaching contents with engineering cases, and combining group learning contents with job tasks. Various applications and platforms ranging from online education platforms to additional resource are employed. Multimodal fusion blended teaching for intelligent building engineering technology specialty is designed as a whole from the teaching objectives, content, organization and evaluation, as shown in Fig. 1. The teaching design should be conformed to the characteristics and requirements of online teaching to ensure the feasibility of implementing multimodal fusion blended teaching in the professional courses.

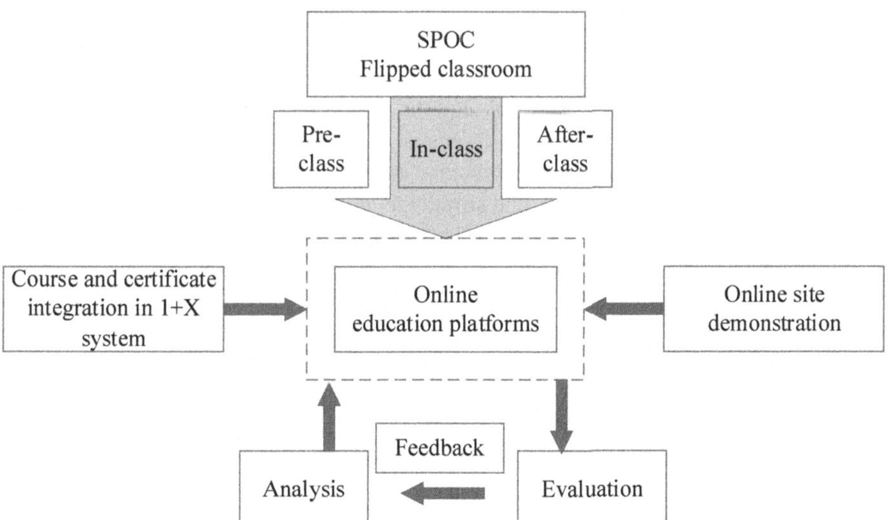

Fig. 1. Multimodal fusion blended learning design system.

2.1 Teaching Objectives

The specialty of building intelligent engineering technology mainly cultivates high-quality technical talents engaged in fire engineering, security engineering, communication and generic cabling engineering, intelligent building equipment monitoring system, building power supply and distribution system design, construction, detection, operation, maintenance, etc. [4]. The teaching of these specialty courses focuses on the cultivation of students' engineering technology practice ability and innovation ability. Through blended teaching, the professional teaching process and teaching quality are guaranteed. It also cultivates students' ability to learn independently and assisted in learning for the information society and the intelligent age, as well as the sense of innovation.

2.2 Teaching Content

The specialty courses mainly include architectural engineering drawing, information system and generic cabling, security system engineering, Building Information Modeling (BIM) Technology and engineering, electrical control and Programming Logic Control (PLC), building electrical equipment monitoring system, comprehensive training, enterprise order-oriented training, apprenticeship class training course, etc., and involve elective courses for teaching different administrative classes and mixed classes. According to the requirements of online and offline courses, the teaching content of related courses are reconstructed, which focuses on the basic knowledge and skills of engineering application, and integrate new technology, new process and new specification into the course or course module. Each professional course carries out task driven teaching around the typical case engineering projects. Learning tasks are range from easy to difficult and simple to complex, so that students can be full of enthusiasm for learning tasks and keep maintaining interest in learning. The theory involved in professional courses should not only be connected with reality, but also emphasize its practicality, set up more enlightening questions, and cultivate students' ability to solve practical problems.

In terms of teaching and learning resources, the curriculum resources of the specialty teaching resource library are fully used, and the digital teaching resources suitable for student's self-learning are reorganized to ensure a clear organizational structure. Each course provides rich and diverse development resources, which enable hierarchical teaching implementations. In addition to the simultaneous use of digital teaching re-sources for each course, the resources need to be updated, enriched, optimized and im-proved continuously. In general, teaching courseware, micro-lecture videos, engineering cases, excellent works, expanding practice and other learning materials are provided in the project as a unit to upload to the online learning platform, which is fragmented learning resources linking up to students' personal learning space and mobile learning terminal. The contents of teaching courseware and the micro-lecture video are synergistic and complementary to each other, covering the knowledge system and skill operation. When using the technology application software platform and virtual reality simulation experiment software platform to carry out teaching tasks, we should pay attention to the operating procedures of the post as the requirements of teaching standards, and guide students to complete each experiment and practical task. Rich and diverse resources for development are provided for each course, which is benefit for teaching students at different levels.

2.3 Teaching Organization

The teaching group is composed of teachers, enterprise tutors and technical support personnel of learning platform to jointly carry out curriculum structure optimization, curriculum content reconstruction, teaching progress management, digital resource construction, curriculum assessment, and learning platform data analysis. The teaching is carried out in accordance with the teaching plan to ensure the teaching order of all courses. Each professional core course combined with the curriculum knowledge structure system and the needs of course teaching is implemented in 4 consecutive sessions as one lesson at one time, which carry out teaching modes such as flipped classrooms, integration of course and 1+X certificate of vocational skill level, and connection engineering on-site "presentation".

Online and offline learning tasks are covered on the pre-class, in-class, and after-class, and guide students to realize the importance of mastering the initiative in learning and realize self-learning throughout the entire learning process. For pre-class, students are motivated by task-driven learning, including video log for learning outcomes, questioning, online seminars, questionnaire surveys, and assessments, so that students would be interested in learning. For in-class, tasks are divided according to job roles, each student is involved in the task, and the learning tasks are completed in groups. In addition, during online live teaching. Various interactive activities such as achievement display, task report, problem discussion and troubleshooting are carried out to promote students' knowledge application and technical skill improvement, so that they can harvest learning achievements. For after-class, through guiding students to complete homework and try to expand the task, strengthen the ability of comprehensive use of knowledge, improve the ability of innovation and practice, let students get the sense of achievement.

2.4 Teaching Evaluation

We realize the importance of online and offline learning through the whole learning process. Hence, assessment criteria must be clear for students. Teaching assessment focuses on the learning process. It is composed of online learning, group work task completion, learning achievement, learning attitude, learning ability, online assessment at the end of the term, which is multi-faceted, multi-angled and diversified assessments. The process assessment of each course accounts for 60% of the total score. Self-evaluation and inter group evaluation are included in the assessment. The proportion of online assessment at the end of the term is 40%. Part of the courses are set up with a comprehensive project of personalized and differentiated assessment content as the final exam content, which is completed and submitted within the time required online or offline. The teaching process can be tracked effectively by using information collection tools such as survey, test and check-in, which can feedback assessment information effectively and continuously improve teaching based on the feedback information.

3 Multimodal Fusion Blended Teaching Practices

3.1 SPOC Combing with Flipped Classroom Scheme

The blended teaching model based on flipped classroom breaks the traditional teaching restrictions, which is no longer subject to the limitations of time and space. Teachers and students can build dynamic classrooms together and change the classroom form [5]. Each professional course group offers Small Private Online Course (SPOC) courses through online platforms such as Chaoxing Learning, Wisdom Vocational Education, Wisdom Tree, etc. It mainly guides students to complete learning tasks through the platform's notification, sign-in, discussion, and supervision functions, and also uses information communication tools such as WeChat and QQ to assist communication, live broadcast and offline learning activities. In order to avoid network congestion, live teaching is carried out according to different teaching time, and different live platforms are used, such as Tencent Classroom, ZOOM, DingTalk, etc. Additionally, teachers use the online platform to manage course progress, classes management, coursework, exams, materials, discussion, Q&A, notification and course statistics. Instructor characteristics and facilitating conditions will positively influence students' perceived accomplishment and enjoyment in the blended class [6]. Implementation diagram of SPOC combing with flipped classroom scheme is shown in Fig. 2.

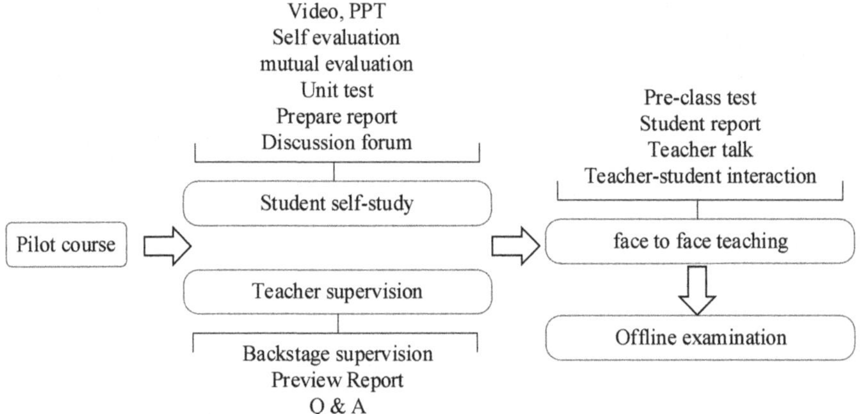

Fig. 2. Implementation diagram of SPOC combing with flipped classroom scheme

Each specialty course group arranges learning tasks in the platform, and issues a notice at least one day before each class, which guides students to study and explore independently, and consult reference books, engineering technical standards and specifications and other materials before the class. Every online classroom is carried out a variety of teaching activities, such as sign-in, voting, discussion, quiz, group confrontation, brain-storming, questionnaire survey, etc. According to the actual teaching situation in the online classroom, the teacher controls and adjusts the teaching progress, and require students following the working list to complete the learning tasks. Live broadcast setting up at each lesson is required more than 1/6 of the total time for the course. Teachers collect students' questions before launching each live class, and assist students to solve the difficulties and problems encountered in self-study before the class. During the live broadcast, the teacher explains the important points and difficulties, and discusses the outstanding issues in the discussion posts. They also analyze some typical problems comprehensively and sort out the knowledge points. In order to strengthen the interaction and communication with students, the teachers demonstrate good preview results for pre-class, excellent projects and creative designs. This helps students to gain the sense of achievement from self-learning. To gain deeper understanding and refine the students' lack of knowledge, the teachers carry out discussion along with the students. The teachers also provide question and answer session to engage the students and solve their learning problems.

Offline communication and discussion are mainly based on the way of creating discussion posts on the online platform, which helps teachers and students to participate and interact together, and also facilitates teachers and students to consult the discussion results at any time. The teachers then give personal feedback on the students' works. The feedback is meant to help the students to progress in their learning personally. Learning outcomes can be evaluated from online study assignments, coursework, extra project task and online test in an all-round way. Students living situation and network condition are also considered, the completion deadline of each online study assignment are allowed to extend for students to complete their learning tasks independently and ensure the quality of learning.

3.2 Integration of Course and 1+X Certificate of Vocational Skill Level

The essential characteristic of vocational education is to train students' professional skill. In the pilot work of implementing the national 1+X certificate of vocational skill level, higher vocational colleges become the main force of pilot work [7, 8]. Intelligent building engineering technology specialty in Dongguan Polytechnic is a pilot specialty of this 1+X certificate system, which is corresponding to the BIM professional skill level certificate. In the pilot work of implementing the 1+X certificate system, we should promote the integration of course and 1+X certificate of vocational skill level vigorously. The knowledge system and teaching content are reconstructed through the teaching reform at intelligent building engineering technology specialty, and the professional knowledge teaching is combined with the training of BIM application ability, as shown in Fig. 3.

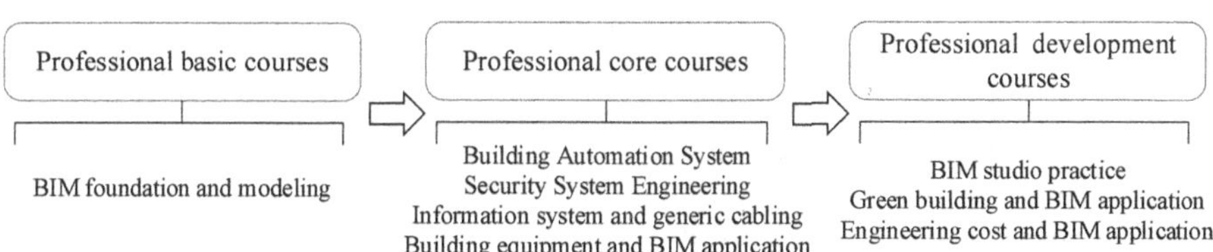

Fig. 3. Integration of course and 1+X certificate of vocational skill level for intelligent building engineering technology specialty

The course of BIM Technology and engineering in the building intelligent engineering technology specialty accurately points to the knowledge goal, ability goal and quality goal of BIM vocational skill level (construction equipment section). Hence, the teaching content of this course is reorganized. Each learning project is connected with the requirements of professional skill levels to ensure that all learning projects cover the advanced and optimized building equipment modeling, systematic analysis, engineering construction simulation, result output, and comprehensive project practice knowledge and skills. The course group refine the BIM learning content and operation process according to job task requirement, and record micro-lecture videos based on each job task assignment. Before each lesson, teachers upload micro-lecture videos and other teaching materials to the online platform, and post the notification of the learning tasks and homework requirements for this lesson. During the live class, teaching activities are mainly carried out around the important and difficult points of the project and the Q&A links. For individual error-prone and difficult-to-understand technical operations, the teacher makes practical demonstrations repeatedly and introduces some error demonstrations to deepen students' understanding. After class, students are required to record the whole process of BIM design platform operation in groups, and describe each operation step for the coursework. These methods improve students' operation proficiency, practice their oral expression skills and improve professionalism.

In addition, the comprehensive practical project of the original teaching plan is based on the real campus scene to restore all the campus building by BIM design. This teaching project can be taken for make the house where student lived as the BIM objects instead, and they need to complete the models of civil engineering, water supply and drainage, electric lighting and other models step by step, so as to "restore" their home.

BIM technology is covered in the teaching of professional core courses with comprehensive BIM application so as to realize integration of course and 1+X certificate of vocational skill level. This technology can be used to create building civil engineering and building equipment models for teaching projects of various core courses. The performance of project details and internal description are realized by BIM, which offers three-dimensional visualization effect. This can help students to increase the authenticity and experience of the overall building electrical equipment, and understand the knowledge and technical application of related courses more easily. The BIM model enables teachers to effectively explain the system structure, equipment principles and construction process of the project in online teaching. For senior students who had learned BIM technology, they are required to have further design of the BIM model using in other courses, or create a new BIM model based on the needs of other teaching project. For example, BIM model for generic cabling is used in building generic cabling teaching project of information system and generic cabling course. BIM model for weak current system is used in security monitoring project of security system engineering course. BIM model for Heating, Ventilation and Air Conditioning (HVAC) is used in central air conditioning teaching project of building equipment monitoring system course. By using the above methods, the application of BIM Technology is fully integrated into the professional core courses, hence consolidating and improving students' application ability of BIM Technology, and promoting their mastery, expansion and deepening of professional knowledge.

3.3 Project Site Online Demonstration

We carry out project site for teaching activities by connecting on-site engineering demonstration. In the live broadcast class, alumni working at the engineering site are invited to introduce the on-site equipment functions, engineering applications, and engineering project conditions, as shown in Fig. 4. Let student to understand different project scenes and the application of system equipment on different projects. They also make a deep impression for the contrast between classroom learning and work practice.

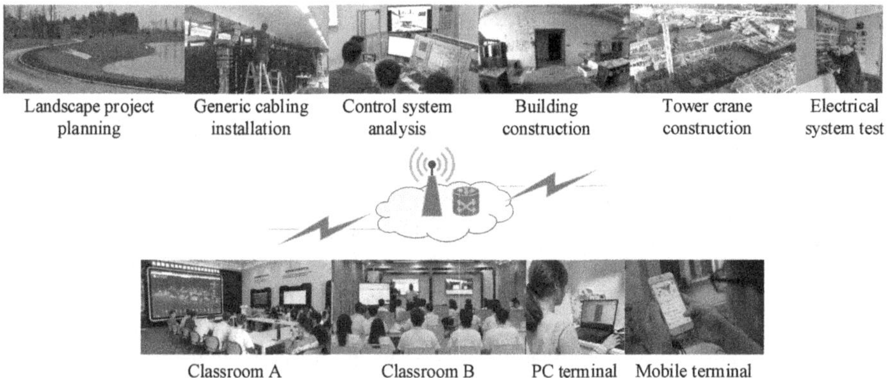

Fig. 4. Project site online demonstration

Due to the needs of epidemic prevention and control, there were a significant increase in engineering projects for installing access control and surveillance cameras with human temperature measurement functions in public places. The alumni at the project site explained the basic functions and principles of these devices to students in the way of mobile phone remote video communication, so that the online learning students could understand the monitoring equipment based on thermal imaging human body temperature screening technology, and make them realized the key role of building intelligent technology in epidemic prevention and control.

Some alumni work in facility operation and maintenance and management positions in residential communities and technology industrial parks. During the epidemic, they stuck to their posts, and returned to project positions on new year holidays, insisted on daily inspections of sites in their jurisdictions, routine inspection and maintenance of intelligent building equipment, such as building power supply and distribution systems, central air conditioning systems, fire linkage system, water supply and drainage control system, video surveillance system, entrance and exit access control system, parking lot system, group control elevator system, etc. Through on-site connection, alumni explained and analyzed the on-site cases including the actual situation encountered problems at work and the corresponding solutions, so that students realized that the knowledge and technology learned from the professional core course were so important to the application of engineering. For example: checking the operation of water pump when the water supply is insufficient in the residential area, checking the circuit and maintenance monitoring when the monitoring is off-line in rainy days, making preparation of the operation for the central air conditioning ventilation system according to the specific guidelines for epidemic prevention, etc. In addition, through the platform, we could share some excellent reports evaluation online from the current and previous internships students, so that they could understand the internship experience and gain from senior students, and learn how to make a correct outlook on career.

4 Teaching Effect and Reflection

4.1 Summy of Successful Experience

Through the teachers' design of online teaching content and interactive links, the traditional teaching methods of teachers and students have been changed, and the enthusiasm of teachers to teach and students to study seriously has been fully aroused by diversified online teaching. We design online teaching content and interactive activities attentively to offer diversified online teaching modes, which fully aroused the enthusiasm of teachers in teaching and students in learning seriously, as shown in Table 1. Each course group focuses on teaching effects and try their best restore online teaching to face-to-face teaching. Through the application of BIM technology, the construction of digital building and equipment models helps students to understand the knowledge that they learn in different scenarios of professional core courses. This method also solves the problem that students could not learn in the working scene and implement integration of course and 1+X certificate of vocational skill level effectively. The teaching method of project site online demonstration provides students with learning cases that are closest to the actual working situation. The above measures effectively promote the implementation of online flipped classroom. On the basis of the investigation and analysis, students' learning willingness and test scores have been greatly improved, and the employment satisfaction of enterprises has been significantly improved after the practice of the proposed multimodal fusion blended teaching, as shown in Fig. 5.

Table 1. Statistics of blended teaching activities in an adamic term

Time	Teacher activities	Student activities	Attendances	Video watch	Discussions	Tools
Pe-class	Course design Platform preparation Task assignment	self-learning self-learning Discussion	100%	66%	29%	[a]MT 23% PC 77%
In-class	Discussion Answer question Demonstration Problem solving Difficulty analysis	Discussion Asking question Virtual labs Task report Online test	100%	5%	41%	MT 2% PC 98%

(*continued*)

Table 1. (*continued*)

Time	Teacher activities	Student activities	Attendances	Video watch	Discussions	Tools
After-class	Survey Evaluation Course analysis	Coursework Extra task Discussion	100%	29%	30%	MT 16% PC 84%

[a]MT-Mobile Terminal, PC- Personal computer

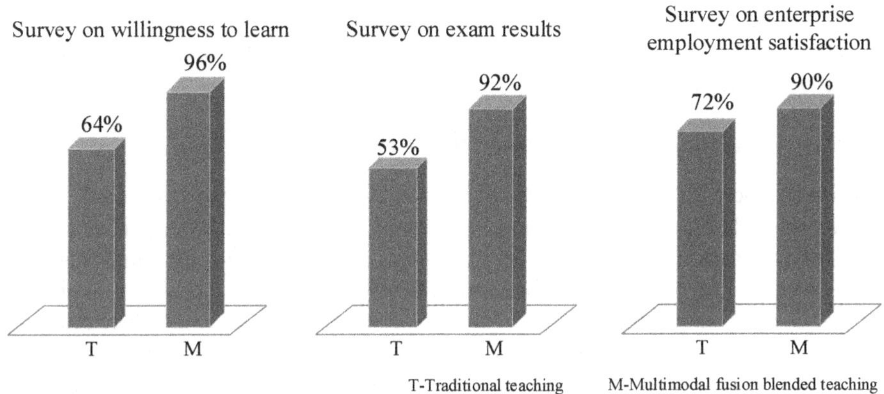

Fig. 5. Surveys of teaching effectiveness for multimodal fusion blended learning

4.2 Analysis of Deficiencies

Although the teaching activities are on the right track by the implementation of online flipped classroom, there are still some problems and deficiencies. At the professional level, the course group needs to strengthen communication, fully exchange their respective teaching experience, comprehensively use various platform tools, and listen to the opinions of teaching supervisors and student feedback. The most difficult problem for online teaching is how to monitor the actual learning effects of students. This needs to strengthen the contact with students, especially for some individual students who have needs or difficulties. Some students find difficulties in having communication and interaction with teachers in online learning environment. Teachers are demanded to provide individual tutoring, so as to customize teaching to deal with students' individual differences. Therefore, we collect feedback information from students in different ways, such as questionnaires, discussions, reports, tests, etc. According to the feedback, we summary learning tasks and sort out their knowledge problems in time, then adjust the online teaching method, live broadcast duration and learning task arrangement appropriately. We realize that it is so important for teachers to have guidance, inspiration and supervision in the online teaching process to encourage students to learn independently and help students solve learning problems by themselves. Some core courses or course modules are subjected to use hardware equipment to carry out practical training, which result in limitations to the teaching content. It is difficult to complete all the courses online.

By summarizing the gains and losses in the process of teaching implementation, we need humanized teaching management and focus on the effectiveness of the teaching process and ensure the participation rate and completion of students' online learning. Course management, communication and interaction are the key factors affecting student study. Teachers are encouraged to have active participation in exploring technology for multimodal fusion blended teaching. The challenges encountered will inspire teachers to be reflective, open, creative, and adaptive to dynamic changes.

5 Thoughts on the Reform of Blended Teaching in Education Information Age

5.1 Complementation of Online and Offline Classroom Teaching

It becomes a new challenge to teach students with low cognition and various learning style in online learning environment. In the era of educational information, facing the changes and demands brought about by the "new normal" of large-scale online teaching, it is necessary to explore new practices of online and offline hybrid teaching and form a new paradigm of online teaching. Through the synergy and complementarity of online and offline teaching, the students who teach the class are reasonably allocated online and offline learning tasks, and students' personal learning space is built. By combining the advantages of face-to-face teaching, online interaction, and digital teaching, we have vigorously promoted the hybrid teaching model in some professional core courses to better improve teaching quality.

5.2 Deep Integration of Information Technology and Education

Information technology has promoted the acceleration of education informatization. It cultivates a new ecology of education and teaching, and poses more challenges to the integration of modern educational technology and educational content. With the development of AI, 5G technology, virtual reality and real-time interactive teaching modes will be rapidly applied [9], and more and more cutting-edge information methods will be used to assist teaching [10]. It is a good time for blended teaching to cultivate students' learning habits in this information era, and comprehensively enhance students' independent learning ability and practical ability for the informatic society. Meanwhile, higher requirements are put forward for teachers' information technology application ability, such as "Internet+" teaching skills, "AI+" teaching mode [11]. Through demonstrations, competitions, training and other practical methods, teachers will comprehensively be improved their ability to control blended teaching design and teaching process, so that the innovative application of teachers in informatization teaching will become an inexhaustible driving force for teaching reform. In addition, we should continue to develop and apply high-quality digital teaching resources, deeply integrate modern information technology into the whole process of education and teaching, couple with a long-term teaching information management mechanism, and promote the healthy development of education informatization.

5.3 Integration of Ideological and Political Theories Teaching and Blended Teaching

The ideological and political education of curriculum is new requirement of strengthening the ideological and political work for higher education in China in the new era [12]. Integrating the ideological and political education into all courses can effectively stimulate students' learning motivation and promote the generation of learning objectives. Ideological and political theories teaching in all courses is systematic project [13]. For the ideological and political education of professional courses, we need to maintain the content and characteristics of professional courses, and implement the professionalism, craftsmanship and professional spirit into the classroom. The ideological and political elements in professional courses already exist, and they need to be further explored, sorted, brought into play, and integrated into all aspects of teaching class. Teachers of professional courses need to deepen the logic and methods of ideological and political practice in professional courses. In the above-mentioned blended teaching of building intelligent engineering technology professional courses, the engineering technology case set of project site online demonstration can be reconstructed into the ideological and political elements of professional courses. The cases of body temperature monitoring, access control and camera technology application during the epidemic period are good examples to cultivate students' scientific outlook and make them feel the significance of actively participating in science and technology. The alumni persisting in their posts in facility operation and management is one of the anti-epidemic cases, which can tell students their professional performance in sticking to ordinary jobs, and take their responsibilities to deliver positive energy. The whole set of special teaching cases during the epidemic period can be formed into a set of ideological and political cases, and the professional knowledge and the relevant stories are combined to ignite the students' patriotic enthusiasm and struggle spirit. In the specialty courses, we guide students to perceive these stories systematically, and encourage the students to learn the internal motivation, and make the specialty courses truly achieve the effect of education.

6 Conclusions

Multimodal fusion blended teaching is introduced in this study. In the proposed teaching activities, the interaction for teacher-student and student-student are increased significantly. Students, alumni and teachers participated in the discussion, which stimulates students' great learning enthusiasm and achieved good learning effect. The comprehensive implementation of blended teaching in colleges and universities across the country provides practical confidence in the reform of education informatization, which provides an opportunity for exploration of blended teaching reform and innovation and integration. Facing the new ecology of "Internet+" education and teaching in the era of education informatization, higher education needs to be bold in trying to innovate, promote the reform of learning methods, and create a new hybrid teaching model. Continuously explore and advance in the direction of reform and innovation of the in-depth integration of information technology and education and teaching, implement information technology to the entire process of teaching and educating, comprehensively improve the quality of training technical skills, and provide a strong driving force for the innovation and development of higher education.

Acknowledgement. This research was supported by Educational Research Project from Guangdong Academy of Education in 2019: Exploration and research on the implementation and promotion of 1+X certificate system in vocational colleges (grant No: GDJY-2019-B-X01), the key project of education and teaching reform from Dongguan Polytechnic in 2020: Research on the implementation path of course certificate integration of professional groups under the 1+X certificate system (grant No: JGZD202009) and the project curriculum demonstration course from Dongguan Polytechnic in 2020: BIM Technology and Engineering (grant No: XMKC202014).

References

1. Wong, M., Billy, T.: Pedagogic orientations of MOOC platforms: influence on course delivery. Asian Assoc. Open Univ. J. **10**(2), 49–66 (2015)
2. Saichaie, K.: Blending, flipped and hybrid learning: definitions, developments, and directions. New Dir. Teach. Learn. **164**, 95–104 (2020)
3. Chung, C.-C., Cheng, Y.-M., Shih, R.-C., Lou, S.-J.: Research on the learning effect of the positive emotions of "ship fuel-saving project" APP for engineering students. Sustainability **11**(4), 1136 (2019)
4. Yang, R., Wang, Q., Chen, X.: Research on the planning and arrangement of the intramural practice base in the construction intelligent engineering technology major based on constructivism. Int. J. Simul. Syst. Sci. Technol. **16**(3A), 15.1–15.6 (2015)
5. Ding, C.: Research on the multi-dimensional and interactive SPOC blending teaching model. Mod. Educ. Technol. **27**, 102–108 (2017)
6. Dang, Y., Zhang, Y.: Examining student satisfaction and gender differences in technology-supported, blending learning. J. Inf. Syst. Educ. **27**(2), 119–130 (2016)
7. Li, Z.: Vocational education "1+X" certificate system: background, positioning and pilot strategy – interpretation of implementation plan of national vocational education reform. Commun. Vocat. Educ. **03**, 30–35 (2019)
8. Xu, G., Fu. M.: "1+X" is an important innovation of talent training mode of vocational education in the era of intellectualization. Res. Educ. Dev. **07**, 21–26 (2019)
9. Ali, A.: Performance impact of simulation-based virtual laboratory on engineering students: a case study of Australia virtual system. IEEE Access **07**, 177387–177396 (2019)
10. Kimberley, F.: Massive Open Online Courses (MOOC) evaluation methods: protocol for a systematic review. JMIR Res. Protoc. **8**, e12087(2019)
11. Magnisalis, I., Demetriadis, S., Karakostas, A.: Adaptive and intelligent systems for collaborative learning support: a review of the field. IEEE Trans. Learn. Technol. **04**(01), 5–20 (2011)
12. Cheng, G.: Three key points in promoting the teaching reform of ideological and political education through curriculum. Leading J. Ideol. Theoret. Educ. **09**, 64–67 (2018)
13. He, Y.: College specialized faculty's abilities in curricular ideological and political education and its cultivation paths. Lead. J. Ideol. Theoret. Educ. **11**, 80–84 (2019)

Optimization of Talent Training Management System in Huizhou Engineering Vocational College

LiNa Yan(✉), BaoHua Zhong, and ZhenYu Xu

Huizhou Vocational College of Engineering, Huizhou 516023, Guangdong, China
hitusa@126.com

Abstract. Based on the object-oriented method, the training management information system of higher vocational colleges is studied and analyzed. This paper puts forward the main problems existing at present. Firstly, the original business process is analyzed, and the optimized business process is given. The actual needs of the training management system are divided into training trainees basic information management module, training enterprise information management module, trainee training arrangement management module, trainee training process management module, trainee training safety management module, evaluation management module and system management module. The overall function and seven sub-functions of the system are analyzed, and the existing problems are pointed out. Finally, according to the existing problems, the original business process is optimized, and the optimized business process is given.

Keywords: Students produce training · Management system

1 Introduction

1.1 Background

Vocational education has always attached great importance to improving students' training skills. As an important part of the teaching tasks of vocational colleges, at least 60% of the training time must be arranged for each professional course. The academic affairs department must organize a week-long comprehensive practice every semester. Training; from the fifth semester, the internship and employment department organizes students to do dual internships, and the sixth semester organizes students to take on-the-job internships. It can be seen that organizing students' training is a demanding, difficult, and tedious job. In order to facilitate college management, Huizhou Vocational College of Engineering has developed a set of practical training management system. The system includes the training student basic information management submodule, the training enterprise information management submodule, the student training arrangement management submodule, the student training process management submodule, the student training safety management submodule, and the student training evaluation management

© ICST Institute for Computer Sciences, Social Informatics and Telecommunications Engineering 2022
Published by Springer Nature Switzerland AG 2022. All Rights Reserved
S. Shi et al. (Eds.): 6GN 2021, LNICST 439, pp. 699–712, 2022.
https://doi.org/10.1007/978-3-031-04245-4_62

submodule. Study how to combine the technology of information engineering to establish an information system specifically for student training management, study how to effectively arrange the work of training, study how to improve the business level of training process management, and study how to effectively improve the efficiency of training evaluation, Studying how to effectively carry out training and safety management is a problem currently faced by every vocational college [1].

At present, Huizhou Vocational College of Engineering has opened its own portal website and deployed some teaching-related information management systems, but these systems focus on course examinations, student status, student behavior management, etc., and basically do not involve student training management; However, for a vocational college, the training of students' practical skills is the focus of the school's attention; in professional courses involving student training, teachers and students also strongly urge the development of student training management information systems to make students practical Training management is informatized and efficient; therefore, in order to improve the science and standardization of student training management in our college, Huizhou Vocational College of Engineering needs a set of information system specifically for student training management [2].

1.2 Current Status of Research and Application

The degree of informatization in most domestic enterprises in the production process is still in its infancy. In order to improve the competitiveness of students' practical training, many enterprises have conducted extensive and in-depth research on the informatization of production management. For example, the School of Information, Dalian University of Technology, based on the status quo of informatization development, combined with in-depth analysis of student training, proposed an information integration system structure for student training, and carried out experimental applications in local student training; Huazhong In order to solve the dynamic management of student training, the University of Science and Technology has put forward a corresponding dynamic alliance management model after years of research. At present, this technology is in the stage of application and improvement; Shenzhen Weibosi company has developed a management system for student training, this system With the functions of cost management, schedule management and capacity management, it basically covers all aspects of production management [3].

The informatization of foreign student training started earlier, and the degree of informatization is also very high. The university has invested a lot of manpower and material resources in student training and production management technology to conduct extensive research, and has also achieved good results. For example, offer company in the United States has developed a set of student training management system. This system realizes the intelligentization of production management by collecting data from the existing production process and integrating student training experience. This system mainly includes two parts: planning and production monitoring. Planning is mainly responsible for making detailed production plans. Production monitoring is to monitor the execution of the production plan and provide feedback to users. Researchers at the University of Birmingham in the United Kingdom use the principles of the knowledge base management system. A set of student training system is designed to provide the school training with production technology, production experience and help in handling problems [4].

The current student training system is difficult to fully meet the actual situation of our school, and it is not a good way to cut into the management of our school's training. Mainly manifested in the following aspects: First, the business cannot be well connected. Each school's student training has its own characteristics, the management departments are different, and the forms and requirements of the training are very different. Second, among similar software, some are more concerned about daily registration, daily attendance registration, focus on data collection, and lack the management function of indicators. The third is that each school has a difference in the division of roles of personnel for training. Some schools have departments dedicated to training, and some schools are still in charge of the educational administration department. The personnel involved and the approval process are also different. Currently, there is no system software that meets our school's student training management business. Fourth, some software mainly reflects the function of on-the-job internship, but does not reflect the function of teaching, and does not reflect the function of tutors participating in evaluation and attendance management in the process of enterprise internship. Fifth, the index system does not have a unified standard for the evaluation or evaluation function of similar software; each school has its own evaluation index. Sixth, similar software lacks the function of safety management. Internship training companies are generally far away from the school. The management process of the company for practical training cannot meet the needs of our school's safety management [5].

2 Business Analysis

2.1 Business Description

Huizhou Vocational College of Engineering's student training management work mainly involves the basic information management sub-module of training students, the training enterprise information management sub-module, the student training arrangement management sub-module, the student training process management sub-module, and the student training Security management sub-module, student training evaluation management sub-module and other services; the main personnel involved in student training management business are composed of students, instructors, corporate tutors, employment office administrators and school leaders; the main business includes collecting training students Information, selection of training companies, development of training plans, determination of instructors, determination of training classes, collection of training information, collection of attendance information, training safety management and student training evaluation [6].

(1) The students who choose to participate in the training are generally based on the class. At this time, the student must submit an application for training, provide basic personal information, including ID card information and parent information,

and the employment office administrator must purchase corresponding insurance for the student.

(2) To review the qualifications of the enterprises for training, the Employment Office shall organize personnel to conduct on-site inspections and analysis, and sign long-term cooperation agreements with the enterprises. At the same time, it is necessary to carefully analyze whether the positions provided by the company meet the requirements of student training.
(3) The school shall formulate an arrangement plan for student training, including the selection of enterprises, the selection of instructors, and the selection of classes.
(4) In the process of student training, the instructor should go to the site to conduct inspections and participate in the guidance of the training. Students should record the completion of each training task, and the company instructor should provide students with attendance data for participating in the training..
(5) Leading teachers should do a good job in safety inspections and report safety inspection logs to the school every day.
(6) The instructor of the enterprise should evaluate the performance of each student's training, and the leading teacher should collect and summarize the evaluation data of each student's training. After returning to the school, the employment office administrator should organize the staff to select the outstanding performance Students are commended [7].

2.2 Business Needs

In order to provide the level of practical training management and improve the processing efficiency of related businesses; the use of computer systems and software engineering technology to establish a practical training management information system for Huizhou Vocational College of Engineering is of great significance. System business requirements include [8]:

(1) Students can maintain their own information online and apply for online training. The employment office administrator can maintain the relevant information of the training students through the computer.
(2) Companies can maintain corporate information online, employment office administrators can review the company's qualifications online, and school leaders can review corporate information online. Enterprise qualification materials can be well archived.
(3) The employment office administrator can implement online training tasks distribution, set up training units through the computer system, set up classes for work-combined tasks, and set up instructors; and can submit data to school leaders for approval; School leaders can use the computer system to review and approve the training arrangements, approve those who meet the conditions, and give approval opinions for those who do not meet the conditions, so that the Employment Office can continue to improve the plan.

(4) The employment office management can use the computer system to set up the function of training process management online; school leaders can set up the training task registration of the approval training process management online. After the approval is passed, the employment office management can release it. If the approval fails, continue to improve the relevant data; instructors can use the computer system to select the templates they need to fill in online to fill in the information for the team [9].
(5) Employment office administrators can formulate training evaluation indicators online; school leaders can use the computer system to review and approve evaluation tasks. If the conditions are met, the implementation will be approved; if the conditions are not met, comments will be given online; the employment office management can be based on actual conditions Publish evaluation tasks online; training units can process student training evaluations based on their specific performance in student training.
(6) The employment office administrator can formulate indicators and parameters of safety management online according to the actual situation; school leaders can approve the setting of indicators and parameters, if the conditions are met, the implementation will be approved, and if the conditions are not met, the comments will be given online; the instructor will be based on the students The actual situation of training safety management is processed for safety log information.
(7) The system administrator can use the computer system to maintain school staff information, corporate mentor information, post information, department information, authority information, etc., and effectively manage users and assign authority.

2.3 Analysis of Organizational Functions

As shown in Fig. 1, the leadership office, the educational affairs department, the training center, the security department, the training center, the general affairs and property management department, the teacher's office, each class, the student department, and the employment department are composed.

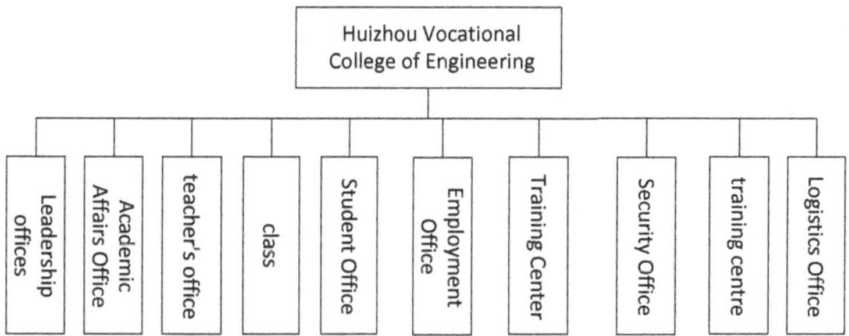

Fig. 1. Organizational structure of Huizhou vocational college of engineering

The Employment Office is the main responsibility department for student training in our school. It is responsible for the basic information management of training students, the management of corporate information for training, the management of student training arrangements, the management of student training process, the management of student training safety, and the management of students. Training evaluation management, etc.; the specific division of labor is as follows: the leadership office is responsible for the policy formulation of the entire Huizhou Engineering Vocational College student training and the approval of student training related businesses; the Office of Academic Affairs shall provide information based on the actual situation of the training classes involved in our school The training time is recommended, according to the arrangement of the training of the employment office, the corresponding course is allocated; the teacher office should select excellent teachers as instructors to participate in the whole process of student training; in each class, it should be arranged according to the teaching progress, According to the actual situation of the company, provide a list of students participating in student training. The students involved should participate in the training of student training; the student office should cooperate with the employment office to formulate student training-related management plans; the employment office should provide basic training for students To process information, it is necessary to process the basic information involved in the training company, to arrange and organize the personnel of the company to cooperate with the instructor to participate in the management of the student training, and to arrange and organize the company's personnel to manage and organize the process of student training. Processing of relevant materials; the training center should be mainly responsible for the examination room and support work of the training venue; the security department should cooperate with the employment office to formulate a safety management plan during the student training process; the training center should cooperate according to the actual needs of student training management The Employment Office and the enterprises involved carry out the training of student training; the Logistics Office shall be responsible for arranging the vehicles for the students, instructors and other personnel participating in the training [10].

2.4 Analysis of Business Personnel

(1) Students: In the original business process analysis, students need to provide personal information paper materials, provide training application paper materials, students fill in paper training materials, and provide paper generation training materials for guidance teacher. Need to participate in pre-job training, need to participate in training, and need to understand the evaluation information of the training.
(2) Instructor: In the original business process analysis, the instructor needs to fill in a large number of training guidance information materials, students need to fill in the attendance status of students, need to summarize the evaluation data of students' training, and need to fill in the paper safety log data. Understand the distribution information of the training.
(3) Employment office administrator: In the original business process analysis, the employment office administrator needs to review the personal information of students and the training application materials, and the employment office administrator needs to fill in the paper training distribution materials, which involve instructors

and classes, Business and other information. A large number of processes and registration materials need to be printed and distributed. Need to collect daily management materials submitted by instructors, need to collect student training materials, need to collect evaluation materials, need to collect safety log materials, etc.

(4) School leaders: In the original business process analysis, school leaders need to review a large number of paper materials, and they cannot understand the information of the training management process in time, and are in a waiting state. The approval efficiency is relatively low.

(5) Corporate mentors: In the original business process, corporate mentors should provide information such as corporate information and job information, attendance information for student training, and evaluation information during each student's training process. Use a lot of paper materials, the efficiency is relatively low, and easy to make mistakes.

3 Process Optimization

3.1 Optimization of Student Basic Information Maintenance Business Process

Compared with the original basic information management process of training students, the business process of information approval has been optimized, and the business process of querying the situation of training students has been added; relevant students involved in training can be allowed to maintain their personal information online; The administrator obtains the student information related to the training through the system, and uses the functions provided by the computer system for information approval work; the employment office administrators, students, and enterprises can query the details of the training students through the functions provided by the computer [11] (Fig. 2).

After business optimization, students do not need to fill in paper materials, and can fill in basic personal information and apply for practical training online through the computer system. The basic information of the students is kept in the computer system and can be reused to realize rapid updates; the administrator of the Employment Office can review the basic information and practical training applications of the students online, and can give the review opinions in time [12] (Fig. 3).

3.2 Optimization of the Business Process for Querying the Situation of the Training Students

After the business is optimized, authorized users can retrieve the specific information of the students participating in the student training at any time. There is no need to call for consultation and check the paper-based registration materials, which is easy to operate.

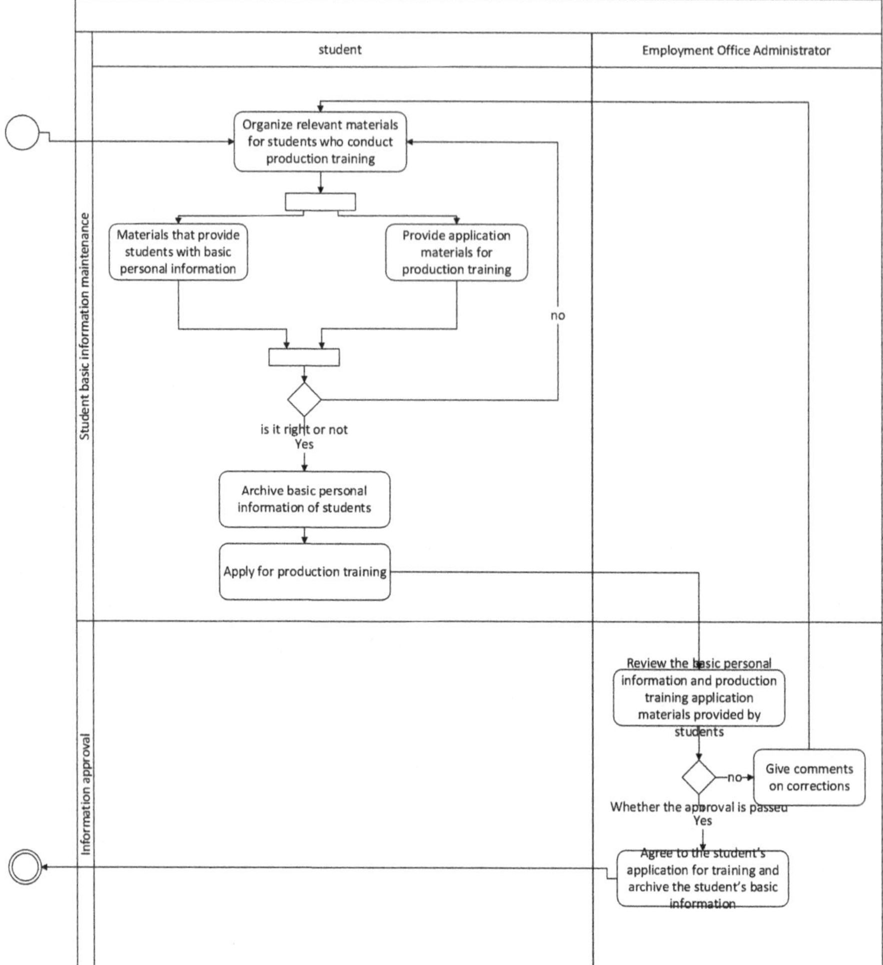

Fig. 2. Flow chart of optimization of student's basic information maintenance business

3.3 Optimize the Business Process of Training Enterprise Information Management

Compared with the original training enterprise information management process, the business process of training enterprise information approval has been optimized, and the business process of training enterprise information review has been added; relevant companies involved in training can be allowed to maintain their own corporate information online; Let the employment office administrator obtain the enterprise information related to the training through the system, and use the functions provided by the computer system to conduct information approval work; school leaders can obtain the employment office management through the system to manage the enterprise information involved

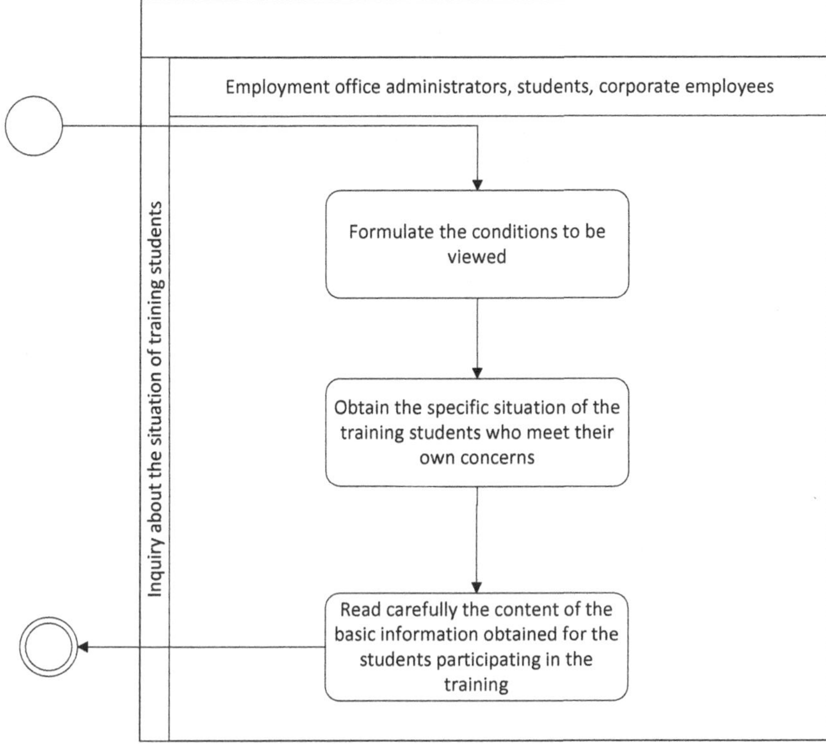

Fig. 3. Business optimization flowchart for querying the situation of training students

in the preliminary training, and use the computer system The function provided is to review the information related to the training company [13] (Fig. 4).

After business optimization, corporate mentors can maintain corporate information online, and can maintain post-related information online. There is no need to fill in paper materials. Many corporate information and post information can be reused; employment office administrators can obtain practical training involving students at any time The information of relevant companies is reviewed and processed; school leaders can give online review opinions specifically for companies involved in student training. There is no need to face paper materials or give written opinions [14].

3.4 Student Training Arrangement Management Business Process Optimization

Compared with the original student training arrangement management business process, the computer system has been used to optimize the business process related to training arrangement maintenance, increase the business process of training release, and increase the business process of querying training arrangements; employment office administrator The functions provided by the computer system can be used to quickly formulate the data of student training arrangements; school leaders can use the computer system to extract the data of student training arrangements, and conduct corresponding approval

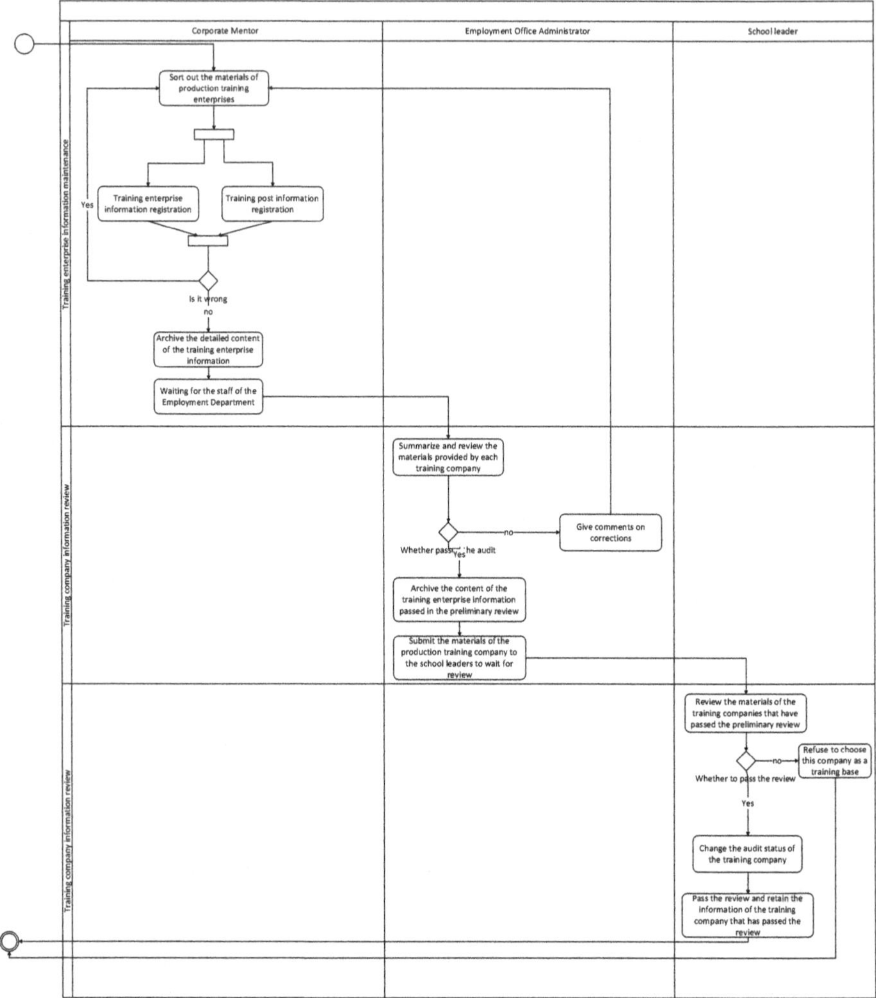

Fig. 4. Flow chart of optimization of training enterprise information management business

processing according to the actual situation; the employment office administrator can use the computer system to transfer the school The training arrangement data approved by the leaders is released, so that students, instructors and corporate tutors can quickly grasp the specific content of our school's student training arrangements.

After business optimization, the employment office administrator can extract the training unit information, class information and instructor information stored in the system data through the computer system settings. Quickly set the training schedule information through the interface provided by the system. School leaders can extract the training arrangements waiting for review through the computer system online, and those who meet the conditions will be approved for review and approved for implementation. For those who do not meet the conditions, the approval comments will be given online, so that the employment office administrator can continue to improve the plan. The data of the training arrangement is stored in the system database, and the operation is simple and convenient.

After the business is optimized, the employment office administrator can obtain the approved training arrangement information through the computer; and can publish the information about the student training according to the actual situation of the student training arrangement of our school.

After business optimization, instructors, students, and corporate tutors can obtain detailed information about training arrangements online at any time, which is simple and convenient to operate, and can set query conditions to obtain training arrangements that they care about.

Compared with the original student training process management business process, the business process of training task registration is optimized, and the business process of leading information registration is optimized; the business process of training information registration is optimized; the process of attendance management business is optimized; The business process of the student training situation; the training tasks, team information, attendance information, and training information registration involved in the student training process can be saved and related summary processing by using the functions provided by the computer system; authorized Users can use the functions provided by the computer system to obtain and consult detailed materials during student training at any time.

After business optimization, the employment office administrator can obtain training arrangement information related to production tasks online through the computer system, including obtaining training unit information, instructor information, class information, etc.; school leaders can conduct online training tasks registration templates Approval. For those who meet the conditions, they will be approved. For those who do not meet the requirements, the employment office administrators are required to complete; after the approval, students, instructors, employment office administrators, corporate mentors, school leaders and other users can query the actual situation online. Relevant information about training tasks; real-time tracking and filling in the training business related to them; students can fill in the process materials of their own training within the specified time, and can enter them through the network login system at any time; instructors can also You can fill in your own information and materials related to the team leader process online at any time within the specified time; corporate instructors can log in to the system online at any time to maintain the attendance of students during the training process; paper materials are not required, and they can be well grasped in time The data materials in the training process help users to fully understand the training information and collect relevant materials in time, which is simple and convenient.

After the business is optimized, the instructor can maintain the information in the training process of their students online. The operation is simple and convenient. You can choose the template for the training task registration, fill in the content related to yourself, and save the data in the system database. Accurate collection of data and future extraction and use.

After business optimization, students can maintain the training information during their training process online. The operation is simple and convenient. They can select the template for training task registration, fill in the content related to them, and save the data in the system database. Accurate collection of data and future extraction and use.

3.5 Attendance Management Business Process Optimization

After business optimization, the corporate instructor can record the attendance status in the computer system according to the attendance status of the student training, and can obtain the registration template of each generated training task through the computer, and accurately record the attendance status of each student during the training.. The student's attendance status is stored in the system's database, which provides convenience for future extraction and use.

After business optimization, employment office administrators, corporate mentors, instructors, students, and school leaders can query relevant information about training tasks online. You can set relevant query conditions, perform queries under your permission, and get the data you care about. Can fully grasp the information on the management of the training process.

Compare the original business process of student training safety management; add the function of setting safety indicators specifically for student training safety management; increase the approval processing specifically for student training safety management related information; optimize the security log registration business The process; authorized users can use the functions provided by the computer system to adjust and set the safety indicators involved in student training according to the needs of student training safety management; they can use the functions provided by the computer system to perform the safety indicators involved Approval; the functions provided by the computing system can be used for effective archiving of security logs.

After business optimization, the employment office administrator can set security indicators online through the system, and adjust the indicator system according to actual requirements. The data of the safety index settings involved in the student training is stored in the computer system database; the school leaders conduct online auditing and processing of the indicators involving the safety management of the student training.

After business optimization, the instructor can compile the security log online, submit the security log at the specified time every day, and record the specific situation of the security management in the training in time, and all the data is stored in the system database. The operation is simple and convenient.

Compared with the original business process of training evaluation management, the business optimization of evaluation index management involved in student training has been added; the business process of evaluation information registration has been optimized; the business process of query and evaluation has been added; authorized users can use The function provided by the computer system adjusts and updates the indicators involved in the evaluation of student training; the computer system can be used to archive the information of the evaluation of student training; the function provided by the computer system can be used to evaluate the results of student training. Check it out.

After business optimization, the employment office administrator can set up the evaluation index involving student training through the system online, and adjust the index system according to the actual requirements of student training.

After business optimization, corporate instructors can evaluate the students' training activities based on the students' performance during the training period and the evaluation indicators prompted by the system. The evaluation information is stored in the system database. The system will automatically generate evaluation results based on the collected evaluation information.

After business optimization, employment office administrators, school leaders, instructors, and students can query the evaluation results of their concerns online. Authorized users can set query conditions to fully understand the performance of students in the training process. Because the data comes from the usual collection, the evaluation results produced in this way are relatively objective and have good reference value.

4 Conclusion

This article adopts an object-oriented method, consults and learns a large amount of literature and materials about the training management system; launched a survey of the business content involved in the student training management of vocational colleges, especially similar vocational colleges in Huizhou area And analysis; expounds the background of the research on the student training management system of vocational colleges, studies the original business processes of students, training units, leading teachers, and employment departments. At the same time, it analyzes the original business processes and proposes the existence The problem. In view of the existing problems, the original business process is optimized, and the optimized business process is given.

References

1. Fangzhou, S.: Investigation and research on the current situation and influencing factors of basketball students' endurance quality training – taking Olympic College of Nanjing Institute of physical education as an example. J. Jiangsu Second Normal Univ. **33**(12), 39–41 (2017)
2. Hui, L.: Preliminary study on the selection of female javelin athletes in China's Olympic training camp. Youth Sports **06**, 43–44 (2016)
3. Binyu, Z.: Feasibility analysis and Countermeasures of introducing outward bound teaching into university public sports teaching – taking Olympic College of Nanjing Institute of physical education as an example. Contemp. Sports Sci. Technol. **5**(35), 34–35 (2015)
4. Youyang, S.: Research on design and construction technology of steel grid structure for training building of Nanjing Olympic training base. Southeast University (2016)
5. Aimin, C.: 2015 national high level reserve training camp for middle and long distance running and women's throwing Olympics was successfully closed in Rugao juvenile sports school. Youth sports **08**, 139–140 (2015)
6. Panjun, J.: Research on the management of track and field single Olympic high level reserve talent training base. Beijing Sport University (2015)
7. Meng, Z.: Research on the training situation of Olympic high level reserve talent base for National Women's shot put. Capital Institute of Physical Education (2015)
8. Xiaojie, S.: Research on the management and operation mechanism of the training camp for high level reserve talents of track and field. Beijing Sport University (2015)
9. Meng, Z., Jianchen, L.: Research on the training situation of national track and field single Olympic high level reserve talent base in Hebei Province. Youth Sports **11**, 62–64 (2014)

10. Chi, M., Jie, Y.: Scientific Exploration of Modern Basketball and Volleyball. Xinhua Press, Beijing 09.165 (2014)
11. The Fifth National Hockey Olympic reserve training camp and 2013 national youth hockey championship. Youth Sports (06), 19–20 (2013)
12. Youqun, L.: Research on training mode of high level reserve talents in national track and field Olympic training base of Wuhan Institute of Physical Education. Central China Normal University (2013)
13. Long, S.: Enlightenment and thinking of German sports (1). Sports (07), 154–156 (2013)
14. Rui, M., He, S., Chunhua, L.: Research on physical training of curling athletes–based on the analysis of physical training plan of Canadian Olympic curling team. J. Harbin Instit. Phys. Educ. **30**(04), 14–18 (2012)

The Construction of Modern Horticulture Training Room and Its Application on the Internet of Things

Xiulian Lin, Junhong Zhong, and Zhenyu Xu(✉)

Huizhou Engineering Vocational College, Huizhou 516023, Guangdong, China
hitusa@126.com

Abstract. With the rapid development of the new generation of information technology, the Internet of Things, big data and artificial intelligence are also expanding in the field of facility gardening. However, in terms of the current situation, modern horticulture teaching in secondary vocational schools has been lagging behind, especially in the training of talents in emerging industries, and the lack of rural scientific and technological team ability and other factors, these factors have seriously restricted the development of the whole planting industry. In this paper, intelligent horticulture technology is adopted to solve the difficult problems in modern horticulture technology teaching. By building an intelligent horticulture Internet of Things platform, the integrated horticulture training system can quickly and accurately feedback environmental factors, and provide training guarantee for training modern horticulture technology talents.

Keywords: Modern gardening technology · Integrated gardening training room

1 Background

1.1 Introduction

The national "14th Five-Year Plan" proposes to "accelerate the development of smart agriculture", and smart gardening is an important part of smart agriculture and one of the important ways to realize rural revitalization. For a long time, the modern horticultural technology major of secondary vocational schools has actively adapted to the needs of reform and economic construction, and has achieved considerable development. It has trained a large number of professional and technical personnel for the planting industry in my country, especially in rural areas. The modern horticultural technology major of our school has played a pivotal role in cultivating professional and technical talents in Guangdong's planting industry.

With the popularization of modern information technology applications and the continuous deepening of education mechanisms and teaching reforms in my country, the teaching modes and teaching methods of secondary vocational schools increasingly rely on modern education technology with network technology and multimedia technology

© ICST Institute for Computer Sciences, Social Informatics and Telecommunications Engineering 2022
Published by Springer Nature Switzerland AG 2022. All Rights Reserved
S. Shi et al. (Eds.): 6GN 2021, LNICST 439, pp. 713–728, 2022.
https://doi.org/10.1007/978-3-031-04245-4_63

as the core [1]. Modern educational technology is also regarded by more and more schools as an important way to carry out teaching reform and improve teaching quality [2].

In recent years, our people's living standards have been continuously improved, and people's requirements for the quality of horticultural products have also been continuously improved. With the continuous progress of agricultural science and technology and the continuous adjustment of the layout of the agricultural industry, the quality of modern horticultural technical personnel training is particularly important.

Modern gardening technology is a major with strong practicality [3]. Due to factors such as limited equipment, it has brought many difficulties to the teaching of this major in schools. Only by using information technology and teaching resources, can we keep up with technological updates without increasing the investment in hardware equipment, ensure the training of students' learning skills and operation, and ensure the quality of teaching.

1.2 Integrated Gardening Training Room

In recent years, the rapid development of new generation information technology, the continuous expansion of the Internet of Things, big data, and artificial intelligence in the field of facility gardening has opened up a broad space for the high-quality development of smart gardening. Based on the integration of emerging mobile Internet, Internet of Things, cloud computing and other technologies, Smart Horticulture realizes the intelligent perception of the horticultural production environment by deploying various types of sensor nodes and wireless communication networks in different locations in the park. Intelligent early warning, intelligent decision-making, intelligent analysis, expert online guidance and other functions realize the visual management, precise planting, and intelligent decision-making functions of horticultural production. The user login interface is as follows (Fig. 1):

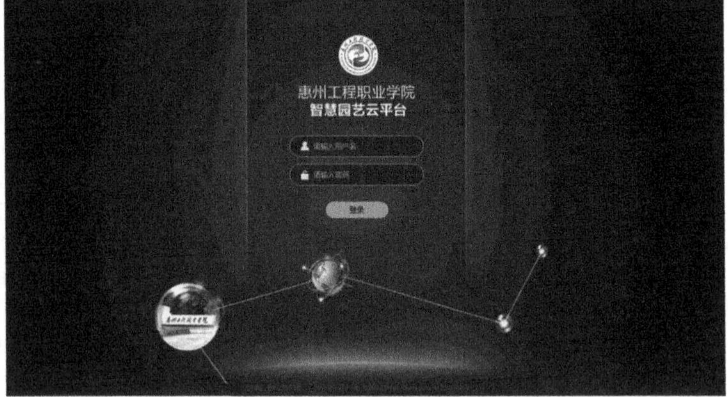

Fig. 1. User login page

The construction of our school's integrated horticulture training room includes an edible fungus cultivation base (including independent seed production room, sterilization room, processing room, cultivation room on the first floor, a total of 600 m^2, with seed production, processing and other related equipment.), Greenhouse (including 700 m^2 of flower cultivation greenhouse, 700 m^2 of vegetable cultivation greenhouse), 300 m^2 of horticultural student entrepreneurship and insect specimen exhibition center, the training room through the Huizhou Vocational College of Engineering Smart Horticulture Cloud Platform, the whole process of monitoring edible fungi, Flowers, vegetables and other production processes.

The platform can grasp the information of horticultural crop seedlings in real time through the remote monitoring system of the Internet of Things, and can realize functions such as data acquisition, data storage, data resource management, data mining, data calculation, and data visualization. The platform can not only regulate and control horticultural production, but also record and analyze the dynamic changes of horticultural planting, breeding process and circulation process, and through data analysis, formulate a series of regulation and management measures to promote the orderly and efficient development of horticulture and improve Horticultural production efficiency and product quality.

Relying on the smart gardening cloud platform, it provides data support and decision-making services for the whole process of gardening production. Before horticultural production, the historical data collected by the horticultural information perception system based on the Internet of Things is used to predict and apply to scientific production; in horticultural production, video and image-based pest monitoring systems and intelligent control of horticultural greenhouses can be used The system realizes real-time monitoring of horticultural products, achieves scientific planting, improves production efficiency and product quality; after horticultural production, through the production process traceability function in the horticulture cloud platform, the entire production process of horticultural products can be traced to facilitate management People and consumers understand and track production information.

Fig. 2. Real view of the base

The system includes 6 modules, namely the base reality, IoT monitoring, historical data, water and fertilizer system, alarm management and traceability system. They are briefly described as follows (Fig. 2):

Base Reality Module
Add the real map of the base and the name of the area through the background, and the user can log in through the platform account to view their own real map and the location of the area. You can drag the sign of the area with the mouse, and click the icon to enter the IOT monitoring interface of the area.

IoT Monitoring Module
The IoT monitoring module has 5 secondary menus on the left, which are data center, control center, parameter setting, video center and picture center. Click this module to enter the data center by default. There is a choice of production area at the bottom of the first-level menu, and you can choose to view the data, video, control equipment, etc. of the corresponding area (Fig. 3).

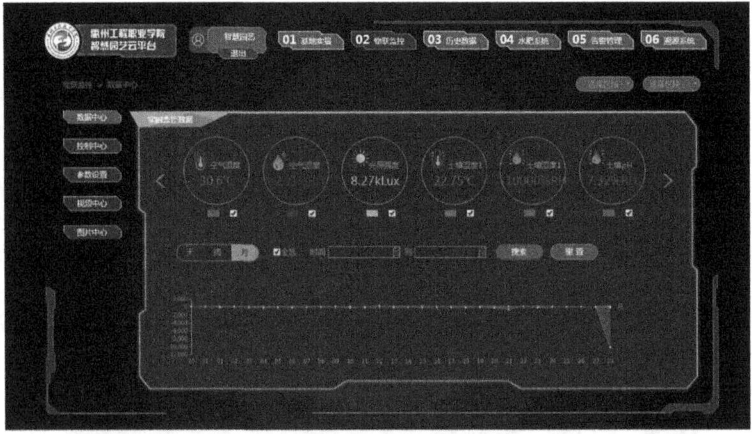

Fig. 3. IOT monitoring page diagram

The secondary menu includes: data center, control center, parameter setting, video center, and picture center (Fig. 4).

In the data center, select the production area and block to view the real-time sensor data of the current block and the most recent day, week, and month data curve, and can export the data to a table.

Control center, display all the controlled equipment information of the selected block. The device can be remotely controlled by clicking the device switch on the page, and the real-time data of the sensor in the corresponding area can be seen at the top (Fig. 5).

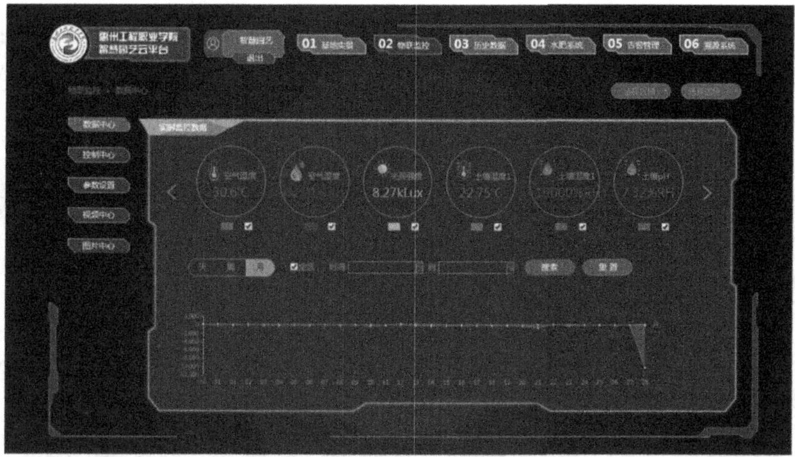

Fig. 4. IoT monitoring-data center diagram

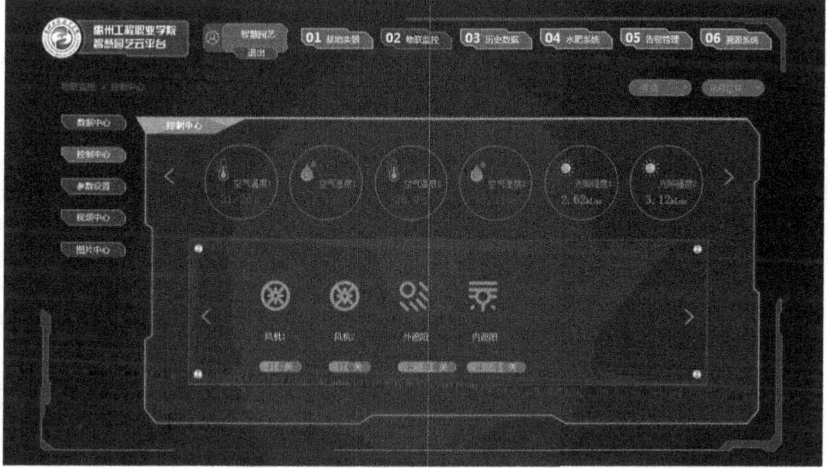

Fig. 5. IoT monitoring-control center

Parameter settings are mainly used to remotely configure the parameters of automatic operation on the local intelligent control cabinet. For example, if you configure the start value of fan 1 in the landscape area, click Save after modification, then the start value is saved successfully; click start, it means fan 1 Enter the automatic operation mode, when the field value reaches the start value, the fan 1 will be automatically started (Fig. 6).

Video center, used to display video information in the greenhouse. The video can be viewed in 1 split screen, 4 split screen, 9 split screen, 16 split screen, 36 split screen, full screen, etc., to view video information.The dome equipment can be controlled by PTZ. Areas that can be controlled by PTZ: landscape area one and two, soil planting

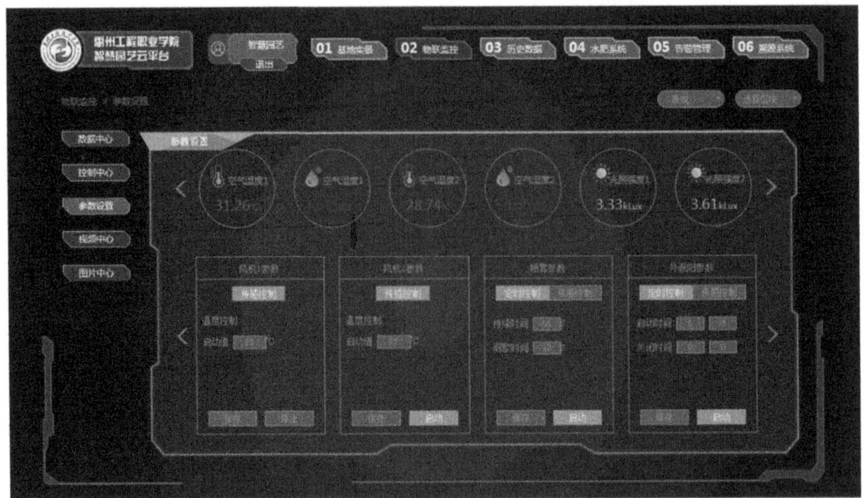

Fig. 6. IoT monitoring-parameter setting

area left and right, substrate cultivation area one and three, water and ertilizer control area (Fig. 7).

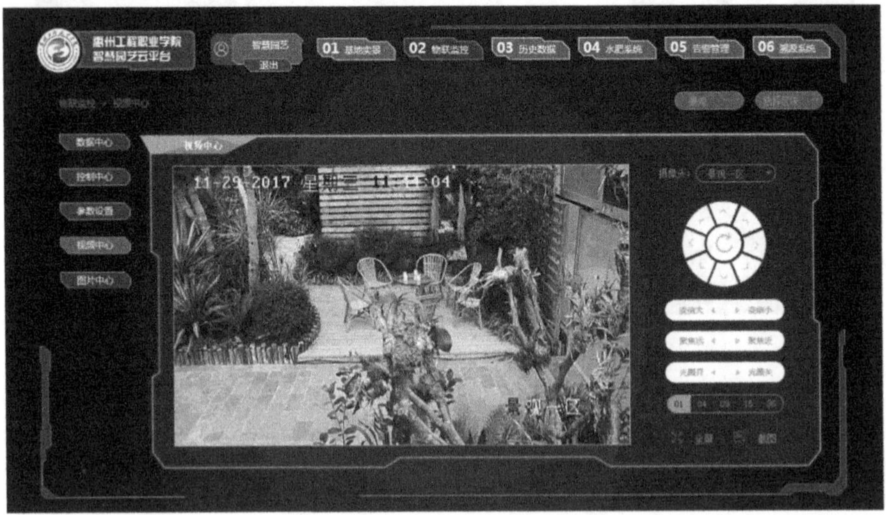

Fig. 7. IOT monitoring-video center

Picture Center, used to view the picture information captured by the video. It can be viewed according to block and time (Fig. 8).

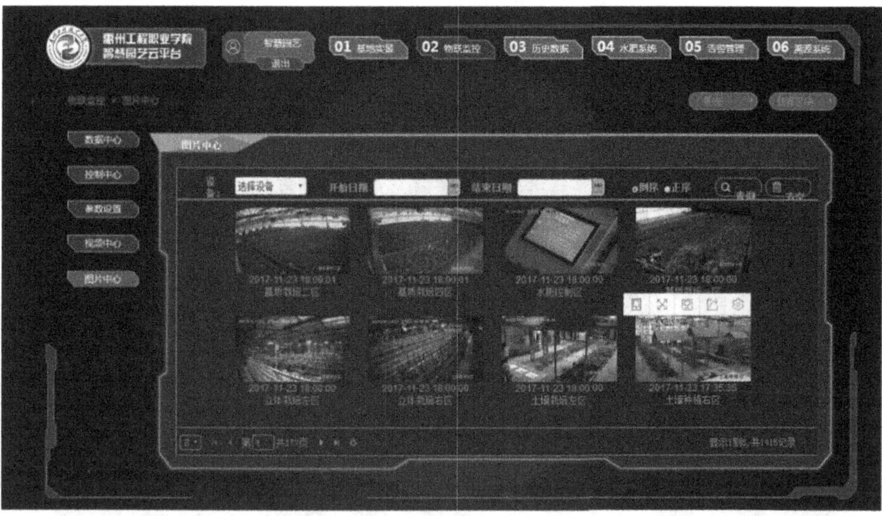

Fig. 8. IOT monitoring-picture center

Historical Data Module

According to their needs, users can view the historical data of the sensors they want to view according to the day, week, and month (Fig. 9).

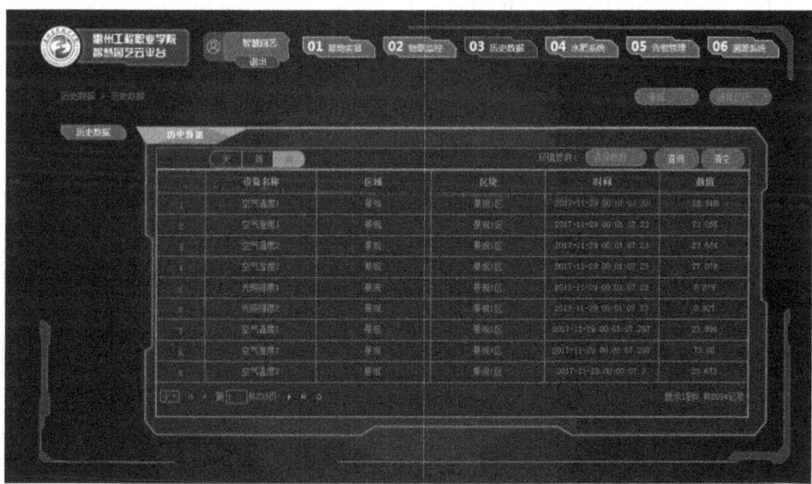

Fig. 9. Historical data

Water and Fertilizer System Module

The interface of the water and fertilizer system is used to remotely configure the operating parameters of the local water and fertilizer machine, such as viewing the operating status, manual automatic switching, remote configuration of automatic irrigation parameters, and automatic sequence parameters (Fig. 10).

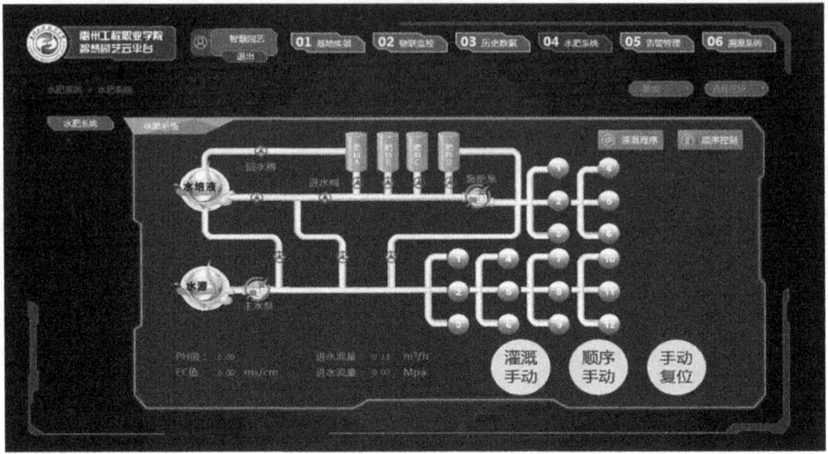

Fig. 10. Main interface of water and fertilizer system

Alarm Management Module

Add the real map of the base and the name of the area through the background, and the user can log in through the platform account to view their.

The alarm management module is used to view the alarm information when the sensor data exceeds the upper and lower limit values (Fig. 11).

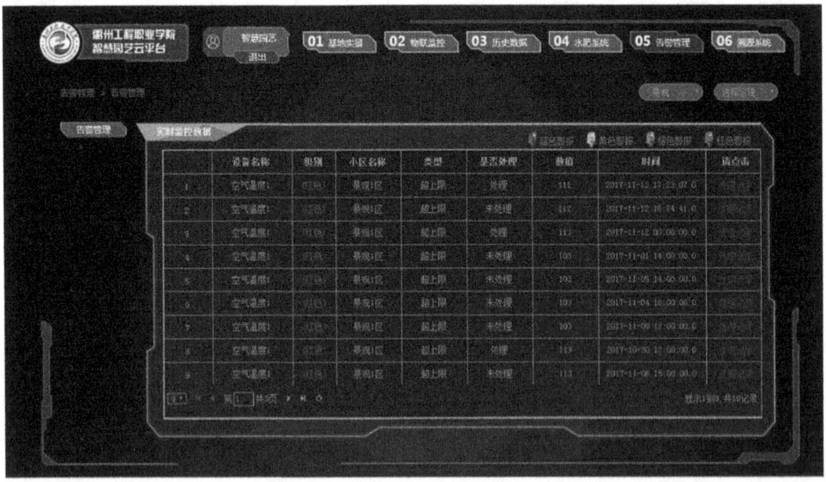

Fig. 11. Alarm management

Traceability System Module

Click the first-level menu, the triangle icon on the far right side, you can directly enter the traceability management system. There are two traceability methods for horticultural species: two-dimensional code scanning and RFID reading, which can be used by users (Fig. 12).

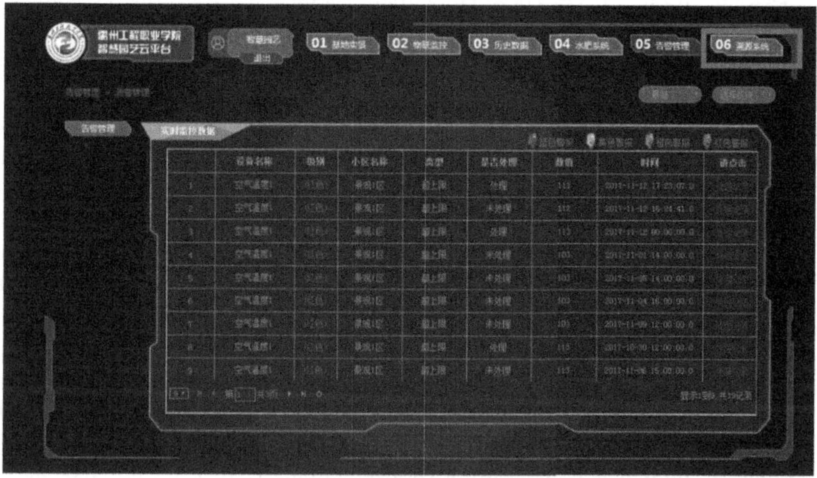

Fig. 12. Traceability system

The above is the basic interface display of the integrated gardening training room of Huizhou Vocational College of Engineering. The platform is essentially an integrated gardening training monitoring and control system. The following article will systematically discuss the construction of the integrated gardening training room.

2 Gardening Information Perception Based on the Internet of Things

2.1 Data Collection and Transmission of Smart Gardening Platform

In the smart gardening cloud platform, the Internet of Things technology is mainly used in the collection and transmission of data information. According to the needs of the horticulture training business, the data information in each greenhouse control device is collected and transmitted to the network cloud platform. This is the entire The data source of the information platform. Smart horticulture management data collection is achieved by arranging various sensor nodes in a large-scale, multi-regional orchard. These front-end collection devices together form the entire local area network, and the network composed of wireless sensors is the wireless sensor network WSN. A large number of sensors together form a network to realize rapid monitoring and alarming of information inside the observation area.

In smart gardening management, there are many types of sensors that can be applied, including temperature and humidity sensors, photosensitive sensors, infrared sensors, and smoke sensors. The system transmits various data information to the cloud platform in real time through sensors. The cloud platform realizes remote control of the automatic control device through processing algorithms. If the automatic control device fails, the cloud platform will remotely send the corresponding failure information to the maintenance personnel for reference. The smart gardening cloud platform collects, counts, and analyzes the data information of each Internet of Things terminal in time, controls the automatic control device according to the plan formulated in advance, records the user's usage, maintenance and other data, and provides usage suggestions.

The data information generated by the sensor must be transmitted to the data center through wireless communication technology. At present, the more wireless communication technologies used in the field of smart gardening management mainly include Wi-Fi, Bluetooth, and ZigBee. Wi-Fi is a wireless expansion technology based on Ethernet, which solves the 100-m network communication problem. It has a wide range of applications but high power consumption. Bluetooth technology is a communication technology of 2.4G short-distance communication, and the communication distance is within 10 m. With the characteristics of low power consumption, it is generally suitable for scenarios such as mobile medical equipment and wearable devices. The disadvantage of Bluetooth technology is that the chip is expensive, easy to be interfered by other electronic devices, and the transmission distance is short, so the application in the field of smart gardening management has not yet been popularized. The ZigBee technology protocol is mainly used for low-speed and short-distance signal transmission, which can connect tens of thousands of wireless devices. This technology has stable signal transmission, low cost and simple operation, and is suitable for use in smart gardening scenarios. However, with the rapid development of information technology, people's communication needs have risen sharply, so low-power, wide-range, and long-distance IoT communication connections have become a development trend. The Internet of Things technology can be developed based on the mobile cellular networks that telecom operators have built on a global scale, but the development of Internet of Things equipment based on cellular mobile communication technology has the disadvantages of high cost and high power consumption, so the main application scenarios of its communication network It is still communication between people. Therefore, in order to meet the needs of more and more long-distance IoT communication connections, we have introduced LPWAN (low-power Wide-Area Network, low-power wide-area network) technology.

2.2 Overview of LPWAN

LPWAN has the characteristics of low bandwidth, long distance, low power consumption, and a large number of connections. The applied communication technology can be divided into two according to the different working frequency bands: One is LoRa, SigFox and other technologies that work in unlicensed spectrum, and the other is LPWAN that is supported by the 3GPP protocol and works on the spectrum authorized by operators. Communication technologies such as EC-GSM, NB-IoT and other technologies should be developed based on 2/3/4G cellular communication networks [4].

GSMA has made data estimates in recent years that by 2025, the number of connections for LPWAN applications will account for 60% of the total number of connections in the entire Internet of Things industry, which will directly accelerate the development of the Internet of Things industry, and the prospects are very promising. LPWAN technology and industry began to develop rapidly in 2015. The domestic market LPWAN industry scale reached 550 million yuan. By the end of 2020, the number of LPWAN networking equipment reached 231 million units, an increase of 110% compared with 2019. According to statistics in 2020, the total number of equipment developed for domestic LPWAN networks will reach 190 million, more than three times that of 2015, and the LPWAN market will reach 3.01 billion yuan, which is nearly six times that of 2015. In addition, not only has the potential for development in the industrial market scale is huge, but the LPWAN industry chain is also rapidly being completed. Chip technology, technical standardization, and market application pilots are all making good progress. Operators all play an important role in the process of completing the industrial chain [5].

2.3 LoRa Overview

LoRa (LongRange) is an ultra-long-distance wireless transmission scheme based on spread spectrum technology adopted and promoted by Semtech in the United States.

In terms of global LoRa IoT technology development, the LoRa Alliance was initiated by Semtech in the United States in March 2015. It is an open, non-profit organization. Since its establishment, there have been more than 500 members, and it has become one of the largest and fastest-growing alliances in the technical field. Members come from all over the world, including multinational communications companies, equipment manufacturers, system integrators, sensor manufacturers, startups, and semiconductor companies, etc., to promote LoRaWAN as a leading open global standard and realize a secure, carrier-class Internet of Things LPWAN connection. On January 28, 2016, ZTE and Semtech signed a strategic cooperation agreement at the Shenzhen headquarters, and jointly initiated the establishment of the China LoRa Application Alliance (CLAA) with nearly 20 partner manufacturers. In July 2018, Tencent joined the LoRa Alliance and announced plans to establish a LoRaWAN network with local partners in Shenzhen to provide LoRaWAN integrated solutions for various IoT applications and end users; in September 2018, Semtech and Alibaba Cloud IoT officially signed a licensing agreement to obtain the authorization of LoRa IP, and released the first LoRa system chip ASR6501, which comprehensively promoted the development of LoRa IoT technology [6].

LoRa uses linear spread spectrum modulation technology, which maintains low power consumption characteristics and significantly increases the communication distance. Terminals with different spread spectrum sequences will not interfere with each other even if they use the same frequency to transmit at the same time. Therefore, the equipment developed on this basis It can receive and process data from multiple nodes in parallel, greatly expanding the system capacity. The LoRa gateway can provide more than 20,000 terminal connections; the coverage distance of a single LoRa gateway is usually in the range of 3–5 km, in a complex urban environment It can surpass the traditional cellular network, and the open area is even as high as 15 km or more, and the distance of 100 km can also be successful under certain conditions. LoRa transmission is based on the asynchronous ALOHA protocol, and nodes can sleep long or short according to specific application scenarios. In the working mode, LoRa has low requirements on the signal-to-noise ratio, and the signal power is therefore very low. Battery power can last for several years to more than ten years. The overall cost of the LoRaWAN module is around US$8–10, which is about half of the price of cellular LTE modules such as NB-IoT. The higher the complexity of the NB-IoT network, the higher the costs related to intellectual property rights (in terms of authorized frequency bands), which increases the total cost of NB-IoT. The upgrade of NB-IoT to advanced 4G/LTE base stations is more expensive than LoRa deployment through industrial gateways or tower-top gateways. As the market becomes more mature, the cost of LoRa technology is expected to drop further. The threshold of LoRa can be self-organized network is slightly higher. From the bottom terminal to the gateway to the server to the application server, it must be developed by itself, and the gateway must be set up by itself. If the amount of terminal equipment in the area is large, you can choose LoRa to deploy the network. Controllable, safe and controllable, without third-party routing and forwarding.

LoRa has three working modes: ClassA, ClassB, and ClassC.

(1) Class A: The terminal sends first, and a receiving window is opened for a period of time after sending. The terminal can receive only after sending. That is to say, there is no restriction on the uplink, and the downlink data can only be received by the terminal when the uplink packet is sent up. (Lowest power consumption)
(2) Class B: The terminal and the server negotiate the opening time and when the receiving window will be opened, and then receive at the agreed time. Multiple packets can be received at one time. (The second lowest power consumption)
(3) Class C: The terminal opens the receiving window at any time other than sending. It consumes more energy, but the communication delay is the lowest. (Highest power consumption)

2.4 Smart Gardening Information Collection

LoRa (LongRange) is an ultra-long-distance wireless transmission scheme based on spread spectrum technology adopted and promoted by Semtech in the United States.

The hardware construction of smart gardening IoT devices includes multiple modules. The core data information collection is mainly through various sensors, including soil moisture sensors, temperature and humidity sensors, etc. These IoT devices sense all kinds of real-time data information in time, and then transmit them after collection. Mainly through the LoRa module, its data transmission protocol has the characteristics of low use cost, low power consumption, and long transmission distance, making it widely used. The power supply of the smart gardening equipment is mainly supplied by the power board, including wireless nodes and sensor control modules; the core control module of the smart gardening equipment is the MCU, and each sensor sends the collected data back to the control center through the communication module, and at the same time, the smart gardening management The staff of the system can remotely control these IoT devices through various sensor networks.

Sensor nodes are sub-nodes in the entire network. During network deployment, these IoT devices are mainly operated through the network, including device sleep, sensor node wake-up, and data information sending operations; sensor nodes complete the association and measurement of measurement targets through the network. Measurement of parameter information. Generally speaking, these IoT devices are in sleep mode at the beginning of their work. When the system is turned on for debugging or enabled, the system platform can remotely wake up these sensor nodes. The first operation of the wake-up operation is to initialize the sensor nodes. After the operation, follow the requirements to find the relevant protocol stack and join the network. The system judges whether these devices have successfully joined the network. If it is unsuccessful, the system management will give a corresponding prompt. If the sensor node can successfully join the network, it can complete the collection of temperature, humidity, smoke and other data information in different areas of the agricultural park. When a sensor node is working in a normal state, the phase status needs to be fed back to the gateway node of the sensor node's network. The gateway node is responsible for the management and supervision of the entire sensor network. According to the settings of the system administrator, the different sensor nodes in the network are monitored. Allow or deny the operation, and finally transmit the data information gathered by the sensor node to the background server.

3 Smart Gardening Information System

3.1 System Construction

The basic network facilities of the smart gardening cloud platform are the basis for implementing the application of the smart gardening cloud platform, including infrastructure, support platforms, application systems and other parts. The basic network facilities of the smart gardening cloud platform mainly include the following three construction contents: First, basic software and hardware facilities. It mainly includes data cloud storage, cloud computing and exchange physical equipment and cloud environment, as well as wired and wireless network infrastructure; the second is the support platform. Built on basic hardware and software facilities, it mainly provides database systems, data exchange platforms, and geographic information systems and video systems that support special application functions. The third is application cloud platform. Including specific business systems such as cloud platforms, cloud data centers, and cloud applications, it is the core layer for the realization of the entire smart gardening system business. All business systems are uniformly deployed in the form of software applications, and users can access at any time through computers, tablets, mobile phones and other networked devices.

The smart gardening training system adopts a combination of technologically advanced wireless sensor network technology, ARM embedded technology and wireless sensor technology. Through the data collection of the intelligent agricultural remote monitoring system, it can accurately grasp the indicators of the internal environment of the greenhouse. To control the corresponding system control devices (fans, humidifiers, heaters) to smoothly control the changes in the internal environment of the greenhouse, maintain it in a relatively stable and suitable environment, and provide a suitable growth environment for horticultural crops. The front-end sensor control system will self-adaptively complete the adjustment of the greenhouse's internal environment according to the pre-set program flow, without human control.

In the technical realization of the collection and transmission of the smart gardening system, the gateway node needs to initialize the entire system in the early stage of work, and then needs to complete the information scanning and the establishment of a new network, and is responsible for the management and operation of the sensor nodes in the entire network. The sensor node sends a request to the gateway node according to the business needs. The gateway node needs to judge the addition of the sensor node based on the resource configuration and business needs. If it is not required, it will reject it. If it is allowed, it needs to set the corresponding sensor node. Network address, and receive the data information sent by this sensor node, gather the data of different sensor nodes in the network and send it to the back-end smart gardening management system.

The horticultural greenhouse intelligent control system extends the network from the desktop to the field, makes the intelligent greenhouse online in real time, and realizes the integration of the greenhouse and the data world. Combining real-time sensor data and traditional planting experience, so that horticultural experts can remotely view various data in the field (temperature, humidity, light, precipitation, crop growth video recording) at any time to determine whether the optimal crop growth conditions have been reached, You can also use the remote video screen system to set up a fixed-point timing camera function on the cloud platform to take multiple photos of the seedling process, fruit tree and fruit growth process at the same angle every day. In the process of long-term accumulation, the photos of the same latitude are passed through time and space. The evolving form is automatically generated on the platform through the model, and by clicking to play, you can understand the growth characteristics of the seedling process, the fruit tree and the fruit growth process, and provide favorable data support for scientific research. Smart horticulture is a modern horticultural production method that can fully improve horticultural production efficiency and reduce waste of horticultural resources and farmland pollution.

The data center of the smart cloud platform establishes a complete information system for the growth process of horticultural crops. Through this information system, the planting process is made more scientific, intelligent and refined. Enable managers to access the cloud platform data center through PC or mobile terminals, easily obtain the real-time growth environment of crops, and make intelligent management decisions on the crop growth process through the acquired data. The construction of the cloud platform data center is mainly based on the basic big data of four application modules: one is based on the training room real scene fixed point to capture the record of the crop growth process; the second is the environmental big data based on the cloud platform; the third is the operation process of the crop growth process The traceability basic data; the fourth is the big data of the insect situation based on the cloud platform.

3.2 System Application

The smart gardening system obtains network map data (map data is optional) and combines panoramic map technology to display the real gardening scene in the park on the cloud platform. The user can click on the real-time real-time map of any gardening planting area through the map navigation function., Combined with the cloud real scene online system, mark the cloud real scene camera point on the panoramic map real spot location, and you can view the real-time picture in the area in real time.

The smart horticulture system connects the environmental monitoring data obtained by the sensors to the cloud platform in real time through a large number of environmental monitoring sensors arranged in orchards and seedling greenhouses. Through long-term and multi-dimensional data accumulation, the data chart is visually displayed while building the future The trend prediction model for the possible development of the environment, combined with the pest database and the changes in the data structure during the pest occurrence process, predicts the occurrence of pests and diseases. Users can view the status information of various smart gardening equipment through the Internet through the computer and mobile terminals, and can remotely control and monitor the relevant automatic control facilities in the smart gardening training room in real time, and process and analyze the gardening business.

The smart horticulture system adopts a cloud platform-based environmental data collection, transmission and storage construction plan. By arranging a large number of soil moisture, soil conductivity, soil PH and other sensors in the park, it is used to observe the park air temperature and humidity, wind speed and direction, carbon dioxide, and rainfall., Light radiation and other data parameters that have an impact on crop growth, are transmitted to the cloud server through the network and the data is stored and processed. The horticultural information perception module completes the function of querying and visualizing horticultural environmental data. Horticultural experts can view the data change curve of weather or soil moisture by selecting different park monitoring points, and input the specific time interval that they want to view, so as to facilitate querying different monitoring points The historical data and historical data trend chart of the data, the data is automatically uploaded every one minute by the system, and the historical data automatically generates the historical data trend chart in units of days.

The alarm setting in the gardening information perception system is mainly to set the alarm range of the system. By selecting different monitoring points and different sensors, you can set different threshold ranges for different monitoring points. There is no need to alarm within the effective range. When the sensor detects When the relevant index exceeds the threshold range, the system will send out an alarm system on the main interface to notify the relevant personnel of the park to deal with it in time.

4 Conclusion

In today's society, the labor force is in a downward trend, and people's demand for various intelligent systems and services is increasing. This has led to an increase in the types and functions of system data, and the need for more staff behind it. Many, traditional manpower is gradually unable to meet such a large amount of demand. However, due to the rapid development of intelligent technology, people's pursuit of automation becomes possible. This article breaks the limitations of traditional automation equipment using smart gateways as the system, combined with the extensive application of the Internet of Things and big data analysis technologies in its fields, and has made an IoT smart cloud platform for gardening management, which has changed the traditional gardening affairs management. The composition structure of the smart gardening cloud platform has been constructed to achieve efficient management and operation. Use data mining related algorithms to mine and analyze various data information collected by front-end Internet of Things equipment, complete the analysis of crop growth trends, smart agriculture-related equipment failure rates, etc., and enhance the value of existing data information. Through the study of the system, students can truly "learn by doing, doing while learning, and learning by doing", organically integrate theoretical teaching and practical teaching from space, system, and information, and complete the combination of professional theory Expansion of practical knowledge. Through this system, innovating the teaching management model, greatly improving teachers' application of information technology and network means to solve teaching problems, is conducive to stimulating and cultivating students' potential and creativity in the information environment, and promoting their professional and vocational skills.

References

1. Dorais, M.: Recent advances in organic horticulture technology and management. Scientia Horticulturae **100**(208), 1–2 (2016)
2. Kitinoja, L., Barrett, D.: Extension of small-scale postharvest horticulture technologies—a model training and services center. Agriculture **5**(3), 441–455 (2015)
3. Hall, A., Clark, N., Taylor, S., Sulaiman, V.R.: Institutional learning in technical projects: horticulture technology R&D systems in India. Int. J. Technol. Manage. Sustain. Dev. **1**(1), 21–39 (2002)
4. Zhiwei, X., Jie, N.: A study on key LPWAN technologies. J. Phys. Conf. Ser. **1871**(1), 012011 (2021)
5. Nuttawat, P., Marut, M., Parinya, A., Sanga, S., Krongboon, S.: Long range UAS mission by LPWAN communication. IOP Conf. Ser. Mater. Sci. Eng. **965**(1), 012039 (2020)
6. Yang, Z., Yang, D., Zhang, H., Liu, K.: Lora wireless sensor network research. Int. Core J. Eng. **7**(6), 37–42 (2021)

Author Index

Printed in the United States
by Baker & Taylor Publisher Services